MOTIF TOOLS

Streamlined GUI Design and Programming with the Xmt Library

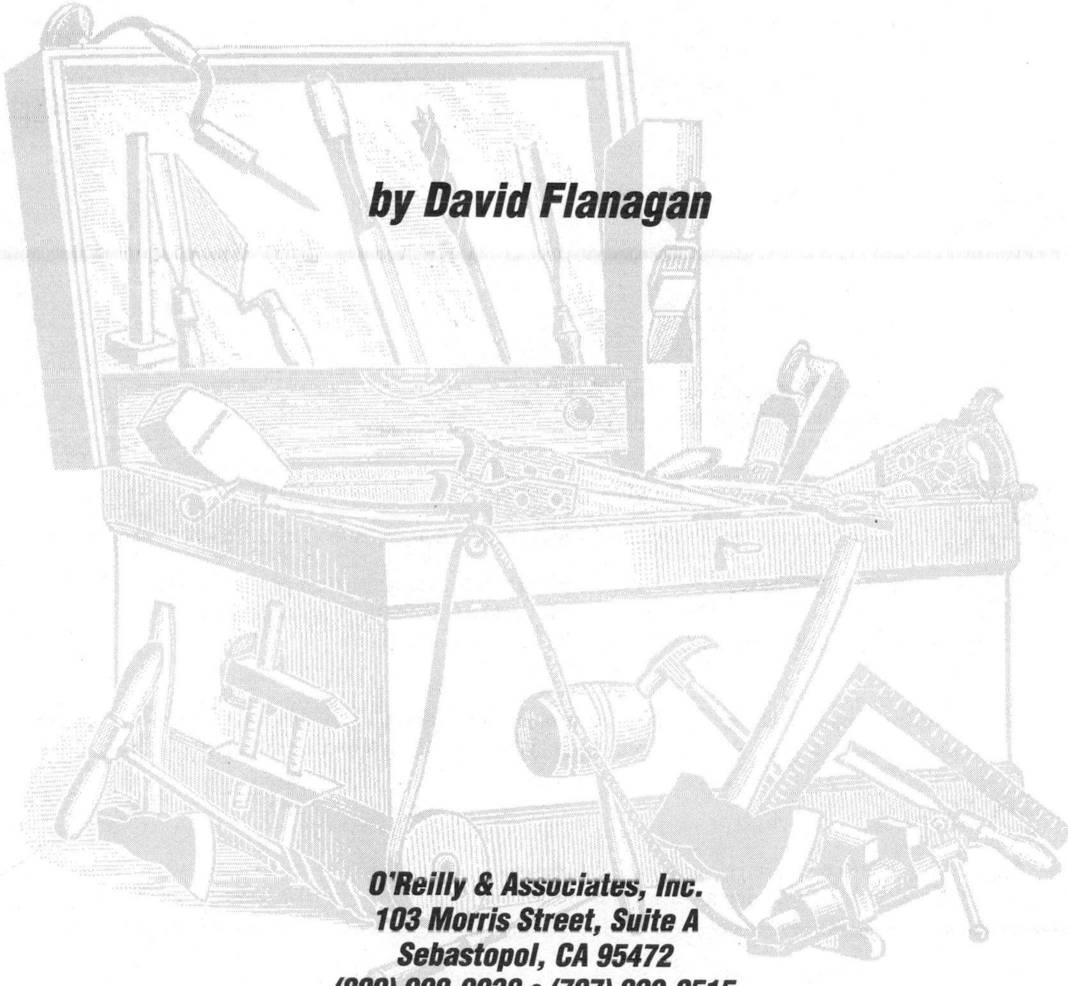

by David Flanagan

O'Reilly & Associates, Inc.
103 Morris Street, Suite A
Sebastopol, CA 95472
(800) 998-9938 • (707) 829-0515

Motif Tools: Streamlined GUI Design and Programming with the Xmt Library
by David Flanagan

Printed in the United States of America.

Editor: Tim O'Reilly

Production Editor: Kismet McDonough

Printing History:

August 1994: First Edition.

This book is printed on acid-free paper with 50% recycled content, 10-15% post-consumer waste. O'Reilly & Associates is committed to using paper with the highest recycled content available consistent with high quality.

ISBN 1-56592-044-9

Table of Contents

Part Seven: Reference Manual

Figures

Examples

Tables

Preface

How to Use the Software

The Motif Tools library that accompanies this book will simplify your job as a Motif programmer. This library, usually known as "the Xmt library," or just "Xmt," contains widgets and utility routines designed to dramatically simplify the common tasks of Motif programming: interface prototyping, building menu systems, creating dialog boxes, providing online help, and so on.

Legal Issues

The Xmt library is not free software. The purchase price of this book entitles one programmer to use the library on one CPU. If other programmers in your organization will be using the software, or if you will be using it on multiple platforms, you may purchase additional licenses (at a very reasonable price) by calling O'Reilly & Associates.

The Xmt license gives you broad rights to use and modify the Xmt library in your software, and to distribute that software without any kind of runtime fee. It does not give you the right, however, to resell or to distribute the Xmt library or any of the tools contained in the library. See Appendix B for the legal details, and Appendix C for information about how to purchase additional licenses.

Also note that there is no warranty of any kind associated with the Xmt library. Again, you should read Appendix B for the details.

Source Code

The Xmt library is provided in source code form—you will have to compile it for your particular platform or platforms, and for whatever version of Motif and X that you are running. (You'll need a version of Motif 1.1 or 1.2 in order to use Xmt—it will not work with Motif 1.0.) Compiling and installing Xmt is easy to do; the process is explained in Appendix A.

Everything for Everyone?

With the legal issues of licensing the software and the mechanical issues of compiling and installing the software out of the way, we can now discuss the real point of this section—what is the best way to make use of this software in your programs?

Xmt is a library of coherent tools that are, in some cases, closely integrated with one another. So the most obvious approach to using it is to install it in */usr/lib/*, */usr/local/lib*, or some other standard place, and to use it unmodified, just as you use the Motif, Xt, and Xlib libraries.

On the other hand, no library or toolkit can be "everything for everyone." Motif and Xt became standards because they try to satisfy everyone—this means, however, that they can only provide that base functionality that everyone agrees on. Xmt obviously can't provide "everything" either, but it leans much more to the "everything" side than to the "everyone" side. There are a lot of useful tools in this library, and while they are designed to solve common problems, they will not be appropriate for all developers in all circumstances.

Part of my motivation for the Xmt library was to empower individual Motif programmers, to free them from the tyranny of fixed, inflexible, and non-negotiable standards like the Xt and Xm APIs. In order to do this, it is obviously no good to simply layer another fixed API on top of those libraries. This flexibility is the beauty of source-code distributions—when you find that some feature of Xmt is not quite right for your needs, I encourage you to get out the source code and make it work the way you want. Don't change any of the Xmt functions or widgets themselves, though—instead, make a copy of the functions or widgets that you want to modify, give them new names, and modify them to your heart's content. Then you can take your modified source code and include it directly in your application source code, or you can compile it and create your own library of personal extensions (or your company's or group's extensions) to the standard Xmt functions.

How to Read This Book

This book is the official programmer's guide and reference manual for the Xmt library. But it is more than just a software manual. I've tried hard to keep it lively and readable, and my hope is that you will find it worth reading even if you never use the Xmt library. The book advocates a holistic approach to application design and development; you'll find tips on programming, user-centered application design, and good graphic design throughout. Also scattered throughout the book are programming tips and techniques I've solicited from programmers on the network. These "programming pearls" show just how many good ideas are out there, and how many ways you can use Xt, Motif, and Xmt. Even if you don't use the techniques directly, I hope they will inspire you to develop your own favorite techniques.

You can read this book in just about whatever order you want. Everyone (or at least everyone who bothers to read this Preface :-) should read the introduction (Chapter 1) first. This chapter provides an overview of the Xmt library and of the contents of this book. Once you've read the introduction, you'll know what features Xmt has and where to find documentation on them. If you are in a hurry, you can turn to the appropriate chapters and the appropriate reference pages (at the back of the book) and start programming with Xmt right away.

Later, when you are in less of a hurry, please consider re-reading this book in the order I've arranged it. The chapters are organized to present a more-or-less top-down approach to the tasks of GUI design and development. There are eight parts to this book, followed by the reference pages for the Xmt functions and widgets, and the appendices. The parts each describe one broad area of application design and development. They are the following:

Part One, *Application Design and Development with Motif*, contains the introduction to and overview of the Xmt library, and two chapters about the very high-level processes of application design. In these chapters I advocate an approach to application design that considers the users of the application and pays attention to the tasks that they are trying to accomplish.

Part Two, *Programming Preliminaries*, contains chapters about a number of the utilities for handling XmStrings, colors, icons, auxiliary files, and application resources that are used throughout the Xmt library. These are tools that you may use throughout your application.

Part Three, *Programming with Resources*, documents tools that allow you to specify much of your user interface through X resource files. These tools are particularly useful when prototyping applications, and are used in code examples throughout the book.

Part Four, *Patterns and Tools for the Desktop*, returns to the top-down approach to application design and development, and contains chapters about how an application and its windows fit on the user's "desktop." These chapters discuss interactions with the window manager, the session manager, and with other clients on the desktop.

Part Five, *Patterns and Tools for the Main Window*, narrows the design focus further, and (finally!) considers the design and implementation of an application's main window. The chapters in this longest part of the book document some of the most important and useful widgets in the Xmt library—a flexible manager widget for layout, a widget for automatically creating pulldown menu systems, widgets for implementng message lines and command-line interfaces, and so on.

Part Six, *Patterns and Tools for Dialogs*, concludes the book by considering the design and implementation of dialog boxes. The chapters in this part document widgets that are particularly useful in dialog boxes, and also describe tools for automatically creating and managing message dialogs, simple input dialogs, and even complex custom dialogs. This part also contains chapters on implementing online help with dialog boxes and on handling application-busy states with "please wait" dialogs and other feedback.

Part Seven, *Manual*, is the reference section of the book. It documents each function in the Xmt library using UNIX "man page" format.

Part Eight, *Appendices*, contains the appendices for the book. These explain (among other things) how to compile the Xmt library, how to obtain additional licenses for it, and how to report bugs.

Good Ideas

Scattered throughout the book, you'll find icon-flagged sections like this one. The "light bulb" icon indicates that this is a good idea that you might want to use in your programs. Some of these programming tips were submitted by Motif programmers from around the world. Others are my own.

The last line or lines of each of these sections indicates who wrote it. The ones I've written are signed with my initials—*djf.*

—*djf*

Important Information

Another kind of section that you'll see in this book has this "information" icon in it. These sections often contain related information that may be of interest. Or they may contain review information which will be useful to beginning X programmers and may be skipped or skimmed by experienced programmers.

There is another kind of icon as well. When you see a CD icon like this one, it directs you to some file within the Xmt distribution. These icons are used whenever a new function is introduced, to point you to the source-code that implements the function. For example, the icon below refers you to the file *Xmt/Color.c*.

These icons are also used for some examples and screendumps to show you where you can find the example code or the code that produced the screendump. Some sections will also refer you to contributed code in this way.

—*djf*

A Note on the Examples

Many of the examples shown in this book are also available on the CD-ROM, often as part of larger, working programs. Marginal icons often direct you to the location of the example code in the Xmt distribution. This one, for example, directs you to the file *examples/19/hello*.

Most of the examples are written in ANSI-C, because of its useful, elegant, and compact function declaration syntax. Some examples also rely on the ANSI-C string concatenation feature; two adjacent strings, with no commas or operators between them, are concatenated into one. When this feature is used in function calls, you'll need to pay attention to determine when multiple strings are being passed and when one long string is being passed. The advantage to using this syntax is that long strings can be nicely formatted without being awkwardly wrapped onto subsequent lines.

Assumptions and Related Reading

This book is about advanced Motif programming tools, but it does not assume that you are already a Motif expert. It does assume that you are comfortable with the C programming language and have a basic familiarity with the concepts of Xt and Motif—widgets, callbacks, the event-driven programming model, and so on. If you are a beginner in the X world, you will find references to other concepts, functions, and widgets from Xlib, Xt, and Motif that you will want to look up and learn about as you go. Even experienced Motif programmers may occasionally want to refer to an Xt or Motif manual for a refresher on various topics. In some places in the book, you'll find quick summaries of X, Xt, and Motif topics. Experienced programmers may find these to be useful refreshers and new programmers can use them as pointers for further learning.

To do any serious Motif programming, you'll need Xt and Motif reference manuals for day-to-day use. I recommend Volume 5, *X Toolkit Intrinsics Reference Manual*,* and Volume 6B, *Motif Reference Manual*, both part of the X Window System series from O'Reilly & Associates.

If you are new to Xt and Motif, then you will also want a "programmer's guide" that will teach concepts and provide the kind of detailed explanations that reference manuals cannot. Volume 4, *X Toolkit Intrinsics Programming Manual*, and Volume 6A, *Motif Programming Manual*, again from O'Reilly & Associates, are good choices—they go into much greater detail than some of the introductory manuals on the market that only survey selected topics in Xt and Motif programming.

Finally, while Xt and Motif hide most of the Xlib from the application programmer, some applications will still require Xlib programming. If this is the case for you, Volumes 1 and 2 from O'Reilly & Associates are a good Xlib programmer's manual and reference manual.

Font and Character Conventions

The following typographic conventions are used in this book:

Italics are used for:

- new terms where they are defined
- file and directory names
- command names
- annotations in some code examples

*I am the editor of this book, but even I keep it next to my keyboard for frequent reference when programming.

`Courier` is used for C and resource-file code examples, and also for just about anything that you'd type verbatim while programming, including:

- resource names
- function names
- widget instance names
- environment variables
- data types

Long strings or messages (such as "Type any key to continue") that might be used verbatim in your programs are enclosed in quotes for legibility instead of being set in Courier.

`Courier Italic` is used for function argument names in function signatures and in the body of the text, and is also used in any similar circumstances when the text should not appear verbatim but requires some context-dependent substitution. For example, `mockup` *`filename`* means to type the *mockup* command, using an appropriate file name.

`Courier Bold` is occasionally used to show command lines that should be typed verbatim to a shell.

Bold is used for text that appears directly in a user interface or widget; it is a way of referring to a particular widget or user-interface component. For example, **Help** refers to the button or menu labeled "Help", not to the string "Help" itself.

Request for Comments

Please tell us about any errors you find in this book or ways you think it could be improved. You can send electronic mail to:

bookquestions@ora.com

Or, you can call us:

U.S. and Canada: 1-800-998-9938
International: +1-707-829-0515
FAX: 1-707-829-0104

Or, you can write to our postal address:

O'Reilly & Associates, Inc.
103 Morris Street, Suite A
Sebastopol, CA 95472
U.S.A.

If you find bugs in the Xmt library that accompanies this book, please report them as described in Appendix D, *Reporting Bugs in Xmt.*

Acknowledgments

This book-plus-software project has been an unusual, time-consuming, and rewarding one. One of the pleasures of working with O'Reilly & Associates is the corporate culture that encourages this kind of innovation and experimentation, and the ideal that we should all be able to pursue our ambitions. I'd like to thank my editor and the president of O'Reilly & Associates, Tim O'Reilly, for encouraging me to take on this project, for forgiving me for finishing it a year-and-a-half late, and for his generous support for my ideas and dreams.

I am also indebted to Alvin Wen, my business partner at Dovetail Systems, for reviewing early drafts of this book, for his many suggestions that helped to improve the Xmt library, and, most especially, for handling the vast majority of our consulting work while I was tied up with the book.

Contributors

Many of the "programming pearls" found in this book were submitted by Motif programmers scattered across the net. They are George Ferguson of the University of Rochester, Scott Gregory of the Canadian Imperial Bank of Commerce, Greg Janee of General Research Corporation, Scott Johnson of NORAN, Inc., Bill Kayser of Schlumberger Geco-Prakla, Joe Kraska of BBN Systems and Technologies, David B. Lewis, Mike McGary then of AutoTester, Inc., Terry Poot of The McCall Pattern Company, Jonathon Ross of BBN Systems and Technologies, Greg Ullman of Unique Systems Design, and Alvin Wen, my business partner at Dovetail Systems.

Steve Anderson of Hewlett Packard kindly gave me permission to excerpt portions of his paper *Tools and Tips for Icon Design.* Arnaud Le Hors of Groupe Bull allowed me to reprint the first chapter of his *XPM Manual,* which is copyright 1990-1993 by Groupe Bull (see the file *COPYRIGHT* in the Xmt distribution for the complete Groupe Bull copyright). I have also borrowed, with permission, relevant pieces from other O'Reilly & Associates books by Adrian Nye, Tim O'Reilly, and Jerry Peek. Adrian Nye also gave me permission to reprint much of an article I wrote for *The X Resource.*

Kevin W. Hammond, Donna Converse, Miles O'Neil, Zack Evans, Frank Sheeran and Rick Richardson let me use their email and news postings on the subject of app-defaults files and fallback resources.

I'd like to thank all of these people. Their contributions give the book a wider scope and more "real-world" flavor than I could have done on my own.

Early Xmt Users

I'd like to thank all of the early users of the Xmt library (especially those who took the time to get their company to actually pay the license fee!) for making do with the inadequate documentation, for waiting patiently (more-or-less) for the release of this book, and mostly, for their bug reports, enhancement requests, and their encouragement. Without this community of users, the Xmt library could not be as robust or as useful as it is.

While I cannot thank all Xmt users individually, there are some that I would like to single out for their exceptional contributions: Terry Poot of The McCall Pattern Company ported Xmt to VMS. Terry was one of the earliest and most active Xmt users and one of the most enthusiastic Xmt supporters. His many thoughtful suggestions for the improvement of Xmt are appreciated (and some of them are even implemented!). Karsten Spang of Kampsax Data in Denmark contributed UIL integration files for some of the Xmt widgets, and had scores of other comments and bug reports. Scott Grosch from the University of Michigan was probably my most prolific reporter of bugs. He was always willing to take the time to clarify them and provide extra information to help me track them down. Ulrich Ring of Daveg GmbH in Germany reported many bugs, performed some mind-bending experiments with the Xmt callback converter, and came up with a novel way to pay the Xmt license fee from Europe. Scott Johnson and Chris Wilbricht at NORAN Instruments were a team of early Xmt users. They gave the library a real run for its money and helped with mysterious bugs on SGI platforms. Peter Klingebiel at the University of Paderborn in Germany took the time to track down and solve a nasty bug on the IBM RS/6000. Finally, Dan Connolly, David Favor, Scott Gregory, Armin Kuepfer, Mike McGary, Rick Richardson, David Vollandt, and Piotr Wypych have all been active users with valuable comments, suggestions, and bug reports.

Technical Reviewers

As important as those who commented on the library are those who took the time to be technical reviewers for the book. They caught bugs in the text, and made important suggestions for improving the technical organization and content of the chapters. The reviewers were: Stephane Aubry, *et al.* at Algorithmics, Inc, Scott Johnson and Chris Wilbricht at NORAN Instruments, the irrepressible David B. Lewis, Mike McGary of AutoTester, Inc., Jane Merrow of Mentor Graphics, Terry Poot of The McCall Pattern Company, and Ulrich Ring of Daveg GmbH. Thanks go to them all.

Technical Influences

No project as large as Xmt could spring fully-formed from one mind. I owe a large intellectual debt to David Smythe and Martin Brunecky who developed the Widget Creation Library (Wcl)—the widget converter, callback converter, and automatic widget creation facilities of Xmt are all strongly influenced by Wcl.

Marc Horowitz, then a colleague at MIT's Project Athena, was the first person I heard mention the idea of a manager widget based on the layout scheme of the TeX text formatter. The XmtLayout widget grew from the seed he planted in my head. My work at Project Athena under Naomi Schmidt gave me the opportunity to develop prototypes of many of the widgets and convenience functions that now appear in the Xmt library.

David Vollandt suggested the idea of font list indirection using symbolic font list names. Much of the XPM code in Xmt is derived from Arnaud Le Hors's XPM library. The multi-color window manager icon code is derived from Dan Heller's code in *Volume 6A: Motif Programming Manual.* The function `XmtSetInitialFocus()` is based on Kee Hinckley's code in the Motif FAQ list, and `XmtWaitUntilMapped()` is simply a re-named version of David Brook's code, also from the FAQ list.

This list is only the very beginning, of course. Other influences have come, consciously or unconsciously, from many other people. My apologies to those I've omitted.

Design and Production

Finally, I want to give my sincere thanks to the design and production departments at O'Reilly & Associates for their wonderful job of transforming my ungainly manuscript into the elegant final form you see here. Edie Freedman designed the cover. Jennifer Niederst designed the interior layout, which was then implemented in *troff* by Lenny Muellner (I'd also like to thank Lenny for always allowing me to pester him, and for answering all of my many text formatting questions cheerfully.) Chris Reilley drew the figures and worked his magic with the megabytes of screendumps I handed off to him.

Kismet McDonough copyedited and proofread the entire book, and put it into its final form. She had proofing and formatting help from Nicole Gipson, Jessica Hekman, and Clairemarie Fisher O'Leary. Seth Maislin and Jessica Hekman wrote the index entries, while Chris Tong oversaw the indexing process and produced the final index. Sue Willing, Tanya Herlick, and Norman Walsh all helped getting the CD-ROM mastered, tested, and duplicated. Sheryl Avruch oversaw the whole production process.

Despite all the help I have received, the errors that remain are, of course, my own.

—djf
Boston, Massachusetts
July, 1994

Part One

Application Design and Development with Motif

This first part of the book puts the rest in perspective.

The first chapter introduces the various components of the Xmt library and gives you an overview of the tools that will be described in later parts of the book. It also describes the strategies that Xmt uses to make Motif programming easier.

The second chapter presents a holistic, user-centered approach to the design of computer applications. It asks you to consider the *why* of application design and not just the *how* of Motif programming.

You'll find that the themes of these first two chapters are echoed throughout the book.

1

Introduction: GUI Development with Motif and Xmt

This book is about designing and developing good graphical user interfaces with the X Toolkit, the Motif widget set, and the "Motif Tools Library," Xmt, that accompanies the book. The overriding goal of the Xmt library is to simplify the tasks that Motif programmers do over and over again—prototyping interfaces, creating menu systems, getting user input through dialog boxes, and so forth.

This introductory chapter starts with an analysis of why Motif programming is difficult, and then discusses theoretical approaches to simplifying it. The chapter concludes with an extended overview of the widgets and other components of the Xmt library and shows concretely how these tools can simplify your job as a Motif programmer.

1.1 Why Motif Is Difficult

Anyone who has programmed with the X Toolkit and the Motif widgets certainly knows that the process can be annoying, tedious, and frustrating. There are the inevitable problems with bugs, of course, but these are gradually being fixed. The X Toolkit in X11R4 and X11R5 has become very stable and robust, and the Motif widgets in releases 1.1 and 1.2 are vastly improved over the bad old days of 1.0.

So if the bugs are getting fixed, why is Motif programming still hard? Before judging Motif too harshly, it is important to realize that ease of use and programmer convenience simply were not design criteria for the X Toolkit or the Motif library. Xt was designed around the X Consortium motto of "mechanism, not policy" to be a standard UI architecture that would be acceptable as an industry standard, and Motif was designed to provide only a base level of UI functionality, such as buttons, lists, and scrollbars that could also be adopted as a standard.

For example, almost every application has a menubar and pulldown menus, but Motif doesn't provide a convenient Menu widget. Instead, programmers must create menus from scratch out of tens (or hundreds) of individual buttons. Similarly, every non-trivial application ought to have online help, but there is no Motif Help widget. This is the first major frustration with Motif—that a lot of useful widgets are not part of the library. No widget set can anticipate the needs of every application, of course, but the Motif widget set deliberately stays away from all but the simplest UI building blocks.

If the lack of widgets is the first major frustration with Motif programming, then the awkwardness of the Motif API is the second. Again, the goal was to develop an API that could be adopted as a standard, not one that was necessarily easy to use. So, for example, we are stuck with the `XmString` data type, even though it is tremendously awkward and provides no real advantage over a traditional array-of-char string (and it has become clear with the release of Motif 1.2 that the `XmString` is not even of any use in internationalization). The `XmString` is particularly annoying in the XmList widget, for example, because a selected item returned as an `XmString` is of little use to the programmer, who cannot do anything with an `XmString`. Another awkward Motif API is that of the XmForm widget. The XmForm's constraint-based layout method provides a fully general way to lay out child widgets in any arrangement, but it is a constant source of confusion for beginning programmers, and its reliance on constraints for every child widget makes setting up layouts tedious.

Motif cannot be blamed for all the inconveniences of user interface development; the X Toolkit architecture deserves to be indicted as well. Initializing argument lists, either statically or via repeated calls to `XtSetArg()`, is perhaps one of the most frustrating things about programming with the X Toolkit. `XtVaCreateWidget()` and the other variable-length argument list routines introduced in X11R4 do address this problem, but there is still the fundamental problem that the *descriptive* task of building a graphical user interface is not well suited to a *procedural* language like C.

Finally, I'm convinced that UI development is still harder than it ought to be because it is still a relatively new field. In the days of terminal-based programs, you could simply use `printf()` to display a message to the user. Today you must create a dialog box, place the message in it, and pop up the dialog box. We need to evolve new standard ways of handling common tasks like this.

It is clear that the problem of displaying messages in a dialog box can easily be simplified with a convenience routine just as straightforward as `printf()`. It is easy to do, and it has probably been done many times—every company I have visited that is doing serious UI development work has their own internal toolkit of convenience routines, and if you have been programming with Motif for a while, you are probably beginning to accumulate your own personal library of useful functions. The need for such a convenience toolkit is something that not enough programmers and managers understand; Motif is too often viewed as a complete UI development package, when in reality it only provides a very basic (but standardized) level of functionality.

This is where the Xmt library comes in; it provides many of the widgets and functions that are implemented over and over again by developers. It cannot, of course, provide everything to everyone, but my hope is that it will raise that base level of functionality to the point where developers can start creating serious applications without first writing a library, or can start adding really innovative features to their libraries, rather than getting bogged down with the basics.

The following sections discuss the general strategies taken by the Xmt library to simplify UI programming, and also provide an overview of the specific tools included in the library.

1.2 Strategies for Simplifying Motif Development

There are a number of approaches that can be taken to simplify the process of user interface development, some more successful than others. I describe some of the common approaches below, and also the approaches taken by the Xmt library.

1.2.1 Use an Interface Builder

One indication of how difficult Motif programming can be is the proliferation of "interface builder" applications on the market. These are applications that allow a developer to visually create an interface, usually by selecting widgets from a palette and then placing them at the desired location in a window. This is one legitimate strategy for simplifying the programmer's job, but I believe that most interface builders really don't address the core problems. Many builders are simply "interface painting" programs that still rely entirely on the base functionality provided by Motif. Thus to build a pulldown menu system, the programmer no longer has to write tedious C code, but he still has to drag buttons one-by-one into the menus, and specify the text to appear in each button by filling out dialog box after dialog box. Many builders have the additional shortcoming that they don't allow child widgets to be positioned by using the constraint-based scheme of the XmForm widget, for example, and therefore interfaces generated by these builders do not handle resize events gracefully. Also, interface builders (like all code generators) often produce code that is unwieldy, hard to read, and hard to maintain without access to the original builder tool.

While interface builders may be useful to allow non-programmers to prototype user interfaces, they don't actually make UI development any easier for experienced programmers: they are no quicker than the programming techniques presented in this book, and, by hiding the details of what is going on, they tend to disempower the programmer. I don't want to suggest that interface builders are never useful, and I am forced to admit that over the last few years some very sophisticated builders have appeared on the market. Still, I think that builders are not a complete solution to the problem of UI development. I believe that the widgets and programming techniques described in this book and implemented in the Xmt library will prove as convenient as or more convenient than any builder application on the market. Though the Xmt library was not designed for use with a builder, those programmers who have builder applications flexible enough to use new widgets may find the combination of their builders and this library particularly useful.

1.2.2 Use C++

There is growing interest in C++, and particularly in the combination of the Motif library and C++. Unfortunately, the X Toolkit architecture is based on C and there are some difficult problems in adapting it to work with C++. While both Xt and C++ are "object-oriented," they are object-oriented in different ways, and their hierarchy of objects will not necessarily fit together well. With some work, it is possible to achieve a synergy between the features of C++ and Motif, but this does not come automatically, and what it really requires is the development of a toolkit of C++-based Motif tools.

There are lots of good reasons to program in C++, but the choice of language does not actually have much bearing on the difficulty of programming with Motif. Use C++ if you have reason to, but be aware that it will not automatically solve your UI development problems. You can certainly use the Xmt library with C++, but note that it was not designed to take advantage of the special capabilities of that language.

1.2.3 Use Components at the Right Level of Abstraction

When a designer thinks about a GUI, she thinks in terms of the high-level components of the interface: she might place a menubar at the top of the window, a message line at the bottom, and a palette of tools along the left edge. This high-level approach is a natural way to approach application design. Unfortunately, when the designer begins to implement the design with the Motif widgets, she will find that she has to individually create each item in the menu and each button in the palette as separate widgets, and she will also have to work to adapt the XmLabel or XmText widget to serve as a message line.

Motif provides the "building blocks" for user interfaces, but it takes a lot of these blocks to put together a complete application. What an application programmer really wants is higher-level, prefabricated interface components that can be used directly in applications.

This is one of the important philosophies behind the Xmt library: the programmer should have tools available that are at the same level of abstraction as those used by the designer. If the available interface components are at the right level of abstraction, then developing applications becomes much easier. Many of the tools in the Xmt library were inspired by this philosophy. The XmtMenu widget, for example, is a single widget that can create an entire pulldown menu system based on a menu description passed to it. The XmtChooser is a single widget, with a single state variable, that makes it easy to present choices to the user. These choices can appear in a palette, or in a radio box, check box, list widget, or option menu. And because a message line is an important component for many applications, the XmtMsgLine widget is a subclass of the XmText widget that has been adapted specifically for this use.

1.2.4 "Program" with Resources

Creating a GUI is largely a task of describing where every interface component should appear on the screen, how it should appear, and what should happen when the user interacts with it. One of the reasons that the Motif and Xt API seems so cumbersome in places is because a *procedural* language like C is not necessarily well suited to this fundamentally *descriptive* task of building interfaces.

This, then, is the reason that resource files are easy to work with: they have a purely descriptive syntax, ideal for the task of describing an interface. Resource files are often used to specify simple resources, like fonts and colors, that the end user should be able to customize. Strings and labels are also often placed in a resource file, so that an application can more easily be customized or internationalized. These resources describe, more or less, the appearance of the individual widgets in an interface, but it is possible to go further.

One of the most important features of the X Toolkit is the ability to register new "resource converters." These conversion procedures convert strings that appear in a resource file to a given type. By registering certain useful resource converters, we can make resource files function even more powerfully. A string-to-widget converter takes a widget name as a string, then looks up and returns a widget with that name. Once a string-to-widget converter is registered it is then possible to specify XmForm widget attachments from a resource file, for example. This means that not only can the appearance of the widgets in an interface be described from a resource file, but the layout of those widgets in relation to one another can also be described.

But we can go a step further. If the application programmer registers a name for the important callback procedures that the interface must call (in much the same way that the programmer specifies a name for any action procedures he registers), then it is possible to write a string-to-callback resource converter that looks up the specified callback procedure (or procedures) by name. With this converter registered, the appearance, layout, *and* behavior of the widgets can be specified.

It is even possible to take one final step with resource files. If widget appearance, layout, and behavior can be specified, why not the widgets themselves? We are accustomed to creating widgets by calling a widget creation procedure, but specifying which widgets are to appear in an interface is, again, really a descriptive rather than a procedural task. A resource file contains many widget resource specifications, but it may also contain specifications for resources that are not read directly by the widgets. It is possible, for example, to associate a "pseudo-resource" with any widget in a resource file that describes each of the widget children that the widget should have. If the programmer has registered a name for each of the widget types that the application uses, then it is possible to write a program that reads this pseudo-resource, parses it into a list of widget names and types, and creates the described children.

In practice, using these interface description techniques in resource files really does seem to speed interface development, and especially interface prototyping. Adding a line to a resource file is quicker than adding a procedure call to an application, and once done, the change can be tested immediately, since it does not require recompiling and relinking the application. Because resources can be so convenient, "programming with resources" is another of the philosophies behind the Xmt library. Xmt contains the widget and callback resource converters described above, and also supports a system for automatically creating a widget hierarchy described in a resource file. Also, many of the widgets in the library take advantage of the power of resource files. For example:

- The XmtMenu widget registers a converter that allows the programmer to completely describe the menu system from a resource file.
- The XmtChooser widget has a "string list converter" and a "pixmap list converter" so that with a single resource you can specify the text or graphics for all of the choices in a radio box, check box, tool palette, option menu, or list widget.
- The XmtLayout manager widget parses a special grammar that describes the layout of each of its children.

1.2.5 Separate Interface from Application

The GUI is the part of the application that the user sees. It must work smoothly and look polished, but it is usually not really the important piece of the application. The crucial pieces of an application are the modules that perform the computations, manipulate the data, or otherwise do whatever it is that the user wants done. The GUI is really just a front end to these underlying "guts" of the application.

Separating the user interface from the rest of the application is common-sense modular design. If the UI is separate from the back end of the application, then the two pieces can be changed independently: while the graphic design department is touching up the interface, the systems programmers can be working on the low-level code behind that interface. If the UI is separate, then it can more easily be customized, without changing the back end, by end users, by application resellers, or for internationalization.

Unfortunately, keeping the interface separate from the rest of the application can be trickier than it seems. Because the interface drives and controls the back end of an application, it must call procedures in the back end. This is the first place where the application and the UI meet; the interface between the two generally takes the form of callback procedures defined in the back end and registered on widgets in the UI.

Sharing procedures between back end and interface by registering them on callback lists is a fairly clean way to do things. But applications must also share data between these modules: when the user selects a toggle button in a menu or a dialog box, for example, it must affect the behavior of the rest of the application. And when the back end enters a new mode, or determines a result, or encounters an error, it must communicate this information to the user by displaying it through the UI. Data is generally shared between the GUI and the back end with widget resources, and unfortunately this technique is not nearly so clean as the callback list mechanism is. Once a callback procedure is registered, the rest is automatic. The same is not true for resources, however, and an application must set and query resource values over and over.

Many applications make little attempt to keep UI and application code separate. It is not uncommon to see programs that read resources from widgets deep in the guts of the back end and that use internal state variables in code that should be purely user interface. The UI and the back end of an application will always overlap to some degree, but an important goal of good UI programming should be to keep this layer of overlap as small as possible. While this may sometimes seem like extra work, it results in better code, a better interface, and an application that is more customizable, portable, and maintainable.

Separation of UI from back end is another of the philosophies behind the Xmt library; Xmt provides some tools that help with this approach. Describing the UI in a resource file is a good first step, if for no other reason than that it strongly emphasizes that the UI is a separate module from the rest of the application. If a callback converter is used so that callbacks can be directly specified in the resource file, this also aids in the separation, because it forces the programmer to explicitly register a name for each procedure that is shared between UI and back end. This explicit enumeration of shared procedures is a good discipline and makes clear exactly what is being shared. The separation is also a very clean one: the back end registers names for the procedures it exports and the UI uses those procedures by name from a resource file. The actual sharing between front end and back end is hidden within the Xmt library, as illustrated in Figure 1-1.

If procedures can be shared this way, so can data values, and the Xmt library supports a system of registering names for particular state variables of the application. This system works in much the same way as callback registration: the programmer enumerates each of the variables that must be shared between interface and application and associates a name with the address (and the type and size) of each of those variables. Then in the interface, the values of these variables can be set and queried by name. Once again, the area of overlap—the actual sharing of the data—is hidden by the Xmt library. A number of the Xmt widgets are designed to make use of this scheme. The XmtChooser widget, for example, takes the registered name of a variable as a resource, and will automatically update the named variable when the widget's state changes (i.e., when the user makes a choice in the widget). With this scheme, the application code no longer has to maintain a pointer to the widget to be able to read the widget's state. Instead, it can use the state variable directly, with the knowledge that it always reflects the current state of the widget.

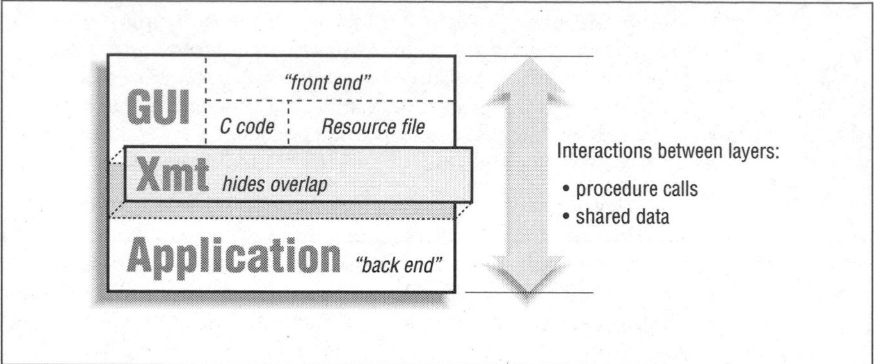

Figure 1-1. Xmt helps separate UI from application back end

Data sharing issues are at their worst in the case of dialog boxes. The purpose of most dialog boxes is to get the user to input a number of values. A typical usage of a dialog box is a multi-step process. First, the application stores default values for each of the data fields into the widgets of the dialog box. Second, the application pops up the dialog box and allows the user to interact with it. Third, when the user is done with the dialog, the application reads the values out of the widgets of the dialog and stores them into a data structure. Finally, the application can take that data and operate on it. This is a cumbersome process, generally requiring a couple of custom procedures to be written for each dialog box. Xmt provides a way to automate this process—it gives names to each of the data fields to be input into a structure, and associates those names with particular widgets in a dialog box. With this mapping of a field in a structure to a name and the name to a widget, Xmt can automatically transfer data in either direction between the data structure and the dialog box. Once again, the overlap between interface and back end is hidden by the Xmt library.

1.3 Programming Preliminaries

The Xmt library contains eight custom widgets and over 250 functions. The remainder of this chapter is an overview of the library and highlights some of its most exciting and useful features. The overview follows the same overall outline as the book itself. It begins with a discussion of Xmt "preliminaries"—the convenience functions that are used throughout the library. Then it describes the suite of tools that support the "programming with resources" philosophy of the library. After discussing these fundamentals, the book (and this overview) proceeds with the same top-down approach you might take while designing an application. First of all, it describes tools and techniques that control your application's behavior on the desktop. Next, it describes Xmt tools (widgets, mostly) that are useful in the main window of your application. And finally it describes the Xmt tools (widgets and convenience procedures) that support dialog boxes in all of their forms.

The subsections below describe some fundamental Xmt utilities. They are documented first, not because they are the most interesting features of the library, but because other tools in the library rely on them, or assume that you are familiar with them. These utilities are documented in detail in the chapters of Part Two of the book.

1.3.1 Using XmStrings

One of the annoying features of Motif has always been the requirement to convert strings into XmStrings before they can be displayed in labels, buttons, or lists. The XmString was designed to support the display of strings in languages like Japanese that require characters from multiple fonts. (Japanese requires a Latin alphabet font, a *kanji* font, and a *kana* font, for example.) In X11R5, this problem is solved at the Xlib level with the introduction of the `XFontSet` abstraction, and so XmStrings really have very little to do with internationalization any more.

One thing that XmStrings are good for, however is the display of strings that contain multiple typefaces (plain, bold, and italic, for example), regardless of language. Motif has always supported multi-font XmStrings, but the API for creating these strings is so awkward that very few applications take advantage of this feature. The Xmt library provides a new function for converting strings to XmStrings, and a new resource converter for doing the same conversion from resource files. This function and resource converter understand special escape sequences for font changes, so you can specify multi font XmStrings in resource files with lines like the following:

```
*about_dialog.messageString: \
@f[Big]About XWriter@f[Plain]\n\n\
@f[Italic]XWriter@f[Plain] was written by Ben Bitdiddle.\n\
Copyright (c) 1993 by BenCo.\n\
\n\
Click @f[Helv]Ok@f[Plain] to continue.
```

To make this work, of course, the named fonts must be specified in a corresponding `XmFontList` resource.

Figure 1-2 shows a dialog box that displays a more extravagant version of this multi-font message string. The text pictured is displayed by a single XmLabel widget using a single XmString.

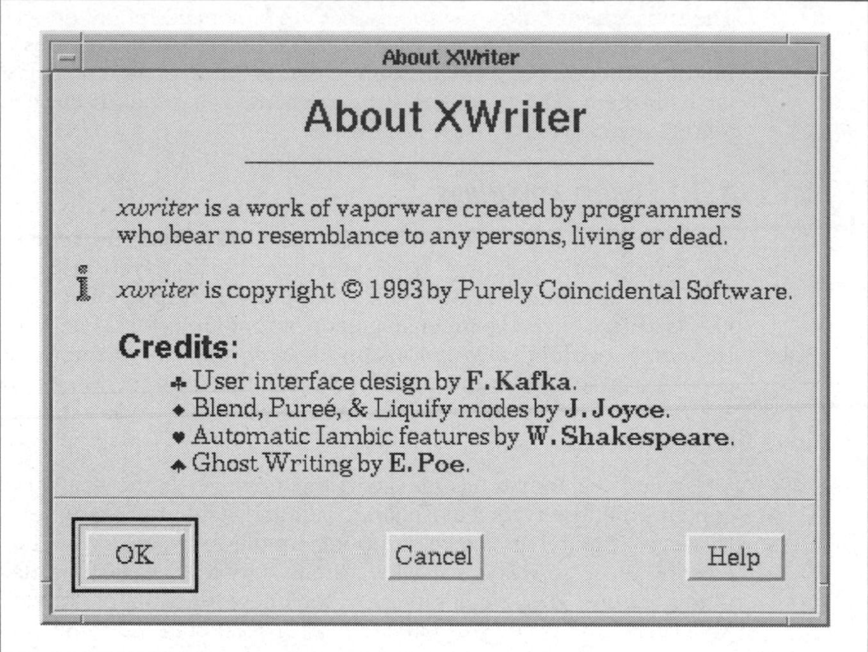

Figure 1-2. A multi-font XmString

1.3.2 Pixmaps, Bitmaps, and Colors

If you compare a typical free X application, like *xmh*, with a commercial application for X, or for the Macintosh, say, you'll probably notice that the commercial application looks a lot nicer. You'll probably also decide that an important reason for this is that it uses more icons in its interface. Icons, and particularly multi-color icons on color displays, can make a huge difference in the appearance of an application. The reason that more applications do not use them is that they are hard to work with. To place a textual label in a button, you only have to place that text between quotes in your C code. To place a monochrome bitmap in the button, you need to create the bitmap file with an editor, arrange to read in the bitmap data, and create the bitmap on the server. Motif provides some functions that make this process a little easier. There is no easy way, however, to display a multi-color pixmap in a Motif application: there is not a standard pixmap file format and there are no tools for creating and manipulating multi-color pixmaps in an application.

The Xmt library addresses this problem. It adopts the XPM pixmap format, which is an emerging standard, and provides tools and resource converters for creating, caching, and using multi-color pixmaps from XPM data. One of the most important features of the XPM format is that it allows symbolic names to be defined for each of the colors in a pixmap and allows actual colors to be substituted for those symbolic color names at runtime. You can therefore create pixmaps and change their colors later, based on the user's runtime choice for the application's foreground and background colors. Xmt helps with the selection of colors as well—it supports an extended syntax for naming colors and defines a "color table" abstraction that maps symbolic color names to actual color names.

Figure 1-3 shows a simple dialog box which uses a custom multi-color icon. Compare it to the standard monochrome icon used in Figure 1-2.

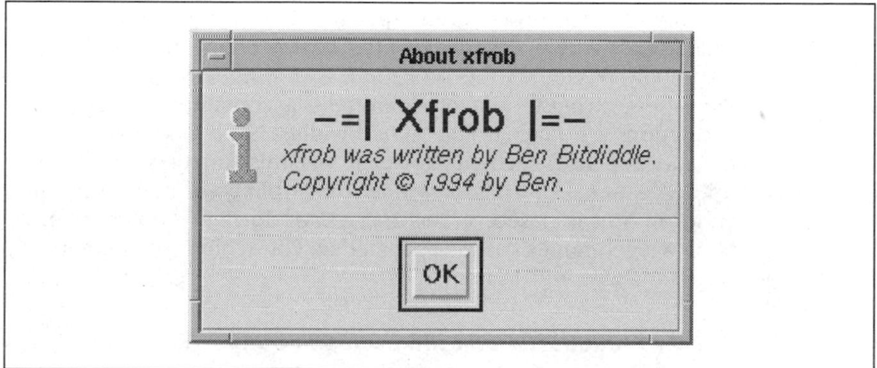

Figure 1-3. A dialog with a multi-color icon

1.3.3 Utility Routines

Xmt also provides a number of utility routines. `XmtFindFile()` is an extension to `XtResolvePathname()` that provides a very flexible way for an application to look up any auxiliary files it requires (online help, pixmap data, and configuration files, for example) without hard-coding the pathnames of those files in the executable.

`XmtWarningMsg()` is an interface to `XtWarningMsg()` that takes a variable-length list of arguments, rather than an array of arguments.

`XmtSetInitialFocus()` makes it easy to specify a widget other than the default **OK** or **Cancel** button that should receive the initial keyboard focus when a dialog widget pops up. This is a very difficult task to accomplish in Motif 1.1. While it has been made simple in Motif 1.2, the Xmt function can be used portably in either case.

`XmtWaitUntilMapped()` can be called after a dialog box has been popped up, and blocks until the dialog has actually appeared on the screen and has processed its first expose events to draw itself. You can use this function to ensure that a message dialog has become visible before executing some time-consuming process. Similarly, `XmtDiscardKeyPressEvents()` and `XmtDiscardButtonEvents()` can be used after performing some time-consuming process to disable type-ahead and click-ahead.

1.4 Programming with Resources

As discussed above, one of the important approaches to UI prototyping and development supported by the Xmt library is programming with resources. The Xmt features that support this kind of programming are summarized in the sections that follow and are documented in detail in the chapters of Part Three, *Programming with Resources.*

1.4.1 The Widget Converter

When a callback procedure is specified in a resource (which is allowed by the callback converter, described in the next section), one of the arguments that is commonly passed to the procedure is a widget. To make this possible, there must be a string-to-widget converter—a converter that takes a widget name and returns a pointer to the named widget. Such a converter could be based on the function `XtNameToWidget()`, but this function only allows you to look up descendants of a given widget, not siblings or ancestors. Instead, the converter in Xmt is based on `XmtNameToWidget()`, which extends the Xt function. Widget names can be specified as you would in a resource file, with wildcards, and also with class names.

1.4.2 Procedures and the Callback Converter

Xmt provides a string-to-callback converter that allows callbacks to be specified from a resource file. To make it work, names must be specified for the procedures that are to be called. Once the callback converter is registered, and procedure names are specified, you can use lines like the following in your resource files:

```
*menubar*help*about.activateCallback: \
    XtSetSensitive(*menubar*help*about, False);\
    XtManageChild(*about_dialog);
```

Note that this example uses procedures that require widget arguments. To invoke these callbacks, Xmt will use the string-to-widget converter described above.

Callback procedures registered with `XtAddCallback()` always expect three arguments of fixed types. The procedures registered for the string-to-callback converter do not have this restriction—they can have up to eight arguments of arbitrary types. And, as shown above, a single resource specification can contain multiple procedures calls.

While writing the back end of an application, it is useful to register important procedures so that they can be easily called from the front end. Then, when the front end is being prototyped, those procedures can easily be called from menus, buttons, or anywhere else in the interface. And while developing an interface, there are a number of functions, like `XtManageChild()`, `XtSetSensitive()`, and `XmtDisplayWarning()`, that affect only the interface and are conveniently called from a resource file.

1.4.3 Automatic Widget Creation

With the definition of appropriate resource converters, almost any resource can be specified from a resource file, as we've seen with the widget and callback converters described above. Resources describe the appearance and behavior of the widgets in an interface; the next step is to use the resource file to describe the widget hierarchy itself.

The Xmt library supports automatic widget creation with `XmtCreateChildren()` and a number of related functions. These functions read the `xmtChildren` resource for a given widget and create any children it specifies. If any of these children widgets themselves specify the `xmtChildren` resource, the functions next create the children of those widgets. Example 1-1 shows how you might specify the widget hierarchy for a dialog box with the `xmtChildren` resource.

Example 1-1. Specifying a Widget Hierarchy in a Resource File

```
*about_shell.xmtChildren: XmForm about_dialog;
*about_dialog.xmtChildren: \
        XmLabel title, icon; \
        XmSeparator sep; \
        XmScrolledWindow sw; \
        XmPushButton okay;
*about_dialog.sw.xmtChildren: XmLabel message;
```

Describing a widget hierarchy in this way can really speed up interface development, particularly during the prototyping phase. Because the interface can be easily changed in a resource file, there is no need to recompile and relink the application in order to try out each change.

1.4.4 Symbols

Just as registering a name for a procedure in the back end of an application allows the interface to call that procedure from a resource file, registering a name for a variable used by the application allows the interface to easily read and set the value of that variable. Xmt allows variables to be registered through an abstraction known as the `XmtSymbol`. Variables are registered with `XmtVaRegisterSymbols()` by specifying their names, types, sizes, and addresses.

Once a symbol is registered, there are a number of places it can be used. The Xmt callback converter understands symbols, for example: symbol values may be passed as callback arguments by prefixing the symbol name with a dollar sign (`$`). Several Xmt widgets understand symbols as well. The XmtMenu widget, for example, accepts a symbol name to be associated with any toggle button it creates. When the state of a toggle button changes, the XmtMenu automatically changes the value of the named variable to reflect the new state of the toggle button. This means that the application never needs to query the toggle button to get its state, and it doesn't even need to register a callback to find out when the state has changed. Instead, it can simply read the variable it registered, knowing that the value of that variable will always reflect the state of the interface. If the application needs to be notified when the value changes (instead of just using the value when needed), it can register a callback on the symbol itself, rather than on the toggle button. Again, this means that the back end of the application need not know about the details of the interface, which makes the application more modular.

1.4.5 The mockup and checkres Clients

As we've seen above, Xmt allows an interface to be almost completely described from a resource file. This feature can be very useful while prototyping an interface, because it allows experimentation and rapid changes without the need to recompile your application. The *mockup* client that accompanies the Xmt library makes the prototyping process even easier. It reads a resource file and displays a mockup of the interface described there—there is no need to write even a single line of C code.

The *checkres* client is also quite useful when programming with resources. It performs syntactic checks on a resource file and flags common errors, such as forgetting to escape the newlines in multi-line resources with a backslash (\).

1.5 The Desktop

Part Four of this book, *Patterns and Tools for the Desktop*, is about designing applications that are well-behaved, fit well on the user's "desktop," and can interact with the window manager, the session manager, and other clients. The chapters in this section explain some of the murkier areas of Xt and Motif programming, and document Xmt functions for providing window-management capabilities (iconifying and deiconifying, raising and lowering windows, specifying colored, non-rectangular icons, etc.) within your applications. Session management and interclient communication on the desktop are aspects of GUI programming that we will be hearing more and more about in the future. This part of the book also explores some of the emerging technologies involved in these areas.

1.6 The Main Window

Part Five, *Patterns and Tools for the Main Window*, is about designing and implementing the main windows of your application. Xmt provides a number of widgets to implement menus, message lines, command-line interfaces, and other common components of an application's main window. Xmt also provides a very flexible and easy to use manager widget for laying out your main window and dialog boxes. These tools are higher-level than most of the standard Motif widgets; they help you to implement an interface at the same level of abstraction that you design it.

1.6.1 The XmtLayout Widget

The XmtLayout is a manager widget that allows the very flexible layout of its children into nested rows and columns, using a layout scheme derived from the TeX text formatting program. Layout can be dynamically controlled by constraint resources on the children widgets, or the layout of all children can be statically specified with a single string resource when the XmtLayout widget is created. Example 1-2 shows the layout string resource that might be used to arrange the children of a dialog box, and Figure 1-4 shows the resulting dialog box.

Example 1-2. The XmtLayout Widget's Layout Grammar

```
*dialog.layout: \
    Line Bottom 0 4 Fixed LREvenSpaced Row { \
            Bitmap "phone"\
            FlushBottom "@f[HUGE]Rolodex Search"\
    }\
    Row {\
            Col {\
                1.5 in FlushRight Caption "@fIFirst name:" fname \
                1.5 in FlushRight Caption "@fILast name:" lname \
                1.5 in FlushRight Caption "@fIPhone number:" phone\
            }\
            Etched Through 6 4 Caption tll "@fB Search " chooser\
    }\
    ##\
    Fixed Etched Top Equal Even Row { \
            XmPushButton okay\
            XmPushButton cancel\
            XmPushButton help\
    }
```

Besides laying out children, the XmtLayout widget can also handle some display tasks on its own, saving you the need to create a number of expensive output-only widgets. Constraint resources allow you to specify that the XmtLayout should draw a frame around any of its children, or that it should label them with a caption. Also, the XmtLayout widget supports some special RectObj "gadget" children (which are cheaper than the relatively "heavyweight" Motif XmGadgets) that will display text and pixmap labels.

The XmtLayout widget is a very flexible general-purpose manager widget. It is as powerful as the XmForm widget, but makes it easier to create static layouts and easier to change those layouts dynamically.

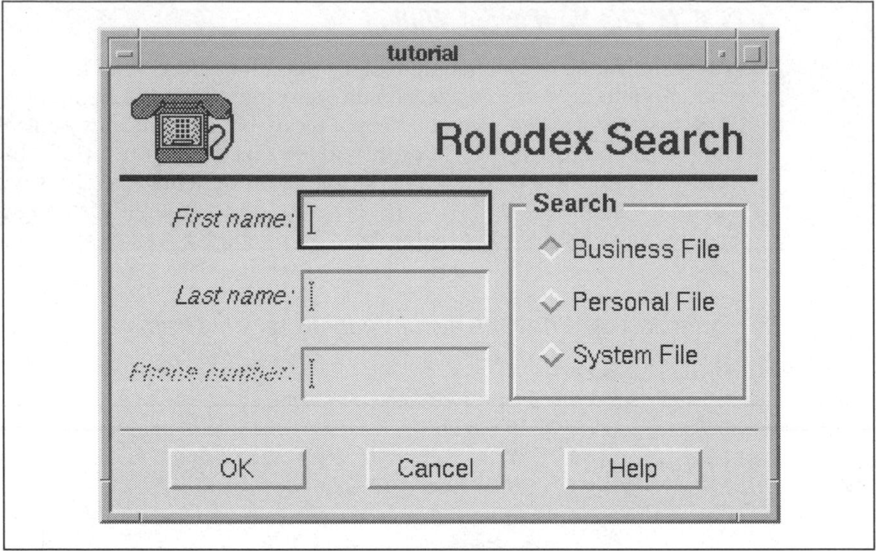

Figure 1-4. A dialog box laid out with the XmtLayout widget

1.6.2 The XmtMenu Widget

One of the most tedious parts of developing a Motif application can be creating the pulldown menu system. Each push button, toggle button, and separator in the menu must be individually created as a child of a menu pane and each menu pane must be hooked up to its cascade button. A medium-sized application can easily require 50 separate widgets for the pulldown menu system. Creating each of those widgets explicitly requires a lot of C code.

In my experience, menu creation is one of the first things that Motif developers automate. It is straightforward to describe the contents of a menu in a statically initialized array of structures and to pass those structures to a menu creation routine that loops through the array and creates the described items. The Xmt library provides similar automatic menu creation routines, but builds them into a special widget. The XmtMenu widget takes an array of `XmtMenuItem` structures as a resource and creates the items described by those structures. An `XmtMenuItem` can point to another array of structures which describe the contents of a submenu; an XmtMenu widget will be automatically created for that submenu.

One of the most useful features of the XmtMenu widget is that it supports a resource converter for the menu description resource, so menus can be completely described from a resource file. Example 1-3 shows a simple menu description in a resource file.

Example 1-3. Describing a Menu from a Resource File

```
*menubar.items: \
        "_File" -> file ;\
        "_View" -> view ;\
Help    "_Help" -> help ;

*file.items: \
        "_New"      [Meta+N]    NewFile();\
        "_Open..."  [Meta-O]    OpenFile();\
        "_Save"     [Meta+S]    Save();\
        "Save _As"  [Meta+A]    SaveAs();\
        ----------; \
        "_Quit"     [Ctrl-C]    exit(0);
```

1.6.3 The XmtMsgLine Widget

The XmtMsgLine widget displays a message line, which is an important component of many interfaces. It can be used to display simple messages and provide important feedback to the user. While your application is saving a file, for example, you might use an XmtMsgLine to display the message "Saving . . . ", which tells the user that the application is busy and that he should wait. When the save is complete, you might append the string "done." to the message line, to inform the user that the save was successful, and that he can now resume working. Note that dialog boxes are not appropriate for this sort of very simple, non-intrusive feedback. Figure 1-5 shows a message line being used in an application.

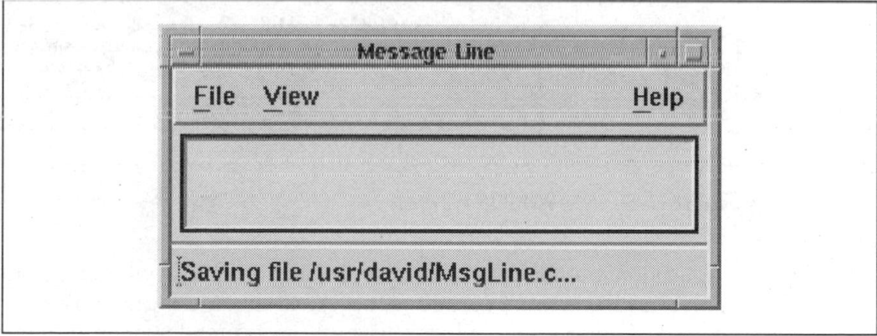

Figure 1-5. The XmtMsgLine widget

The XmtMsgLine widget can also be used to get modal, synchronous input of strings, numbers, or single characters. ("Synchronous" input functions are like `scanf()`—they get the user's input string or number or filename or whatever, and return it directly to the application, without the need for the application to use callbacks or other indirect, asynchronous methods.) Advanced users who use keyboard shortcuts in the application, and rarely touch the mouse, will likely prefer to enter input on a message line rather than having a dialog box pop up to prompt for the input. Once a user is accustomed to typing input on the message line, using a message line can improve the flow of an application and let the user work faster, where a dialog might transform a simple operation into a choppy, complicated one.

1.6.4 The XmtCli Widget

The XmtCli widget provides a command-line interface. It is a subclass of the XmText widget with features added to make it behave more like an *xterm*, or a shell-style interface. Command-based interfaces are not often used in the point-and-click world because there aren't good tools that support them, and because command-line interactions are automatically judged "user-unfriendly." In fact, if you are developing a complicated application with a rich set of commands or features, a command-based interface can work very well in conjunction with a pulldown menu system. The XmtCli widget is also useful when porting terminal-based applications to X. The XmtCli widget makes it easy to make an application run in its own window (rather than through an *xterm*). Figure 1-6 shows the XmtCli widget.

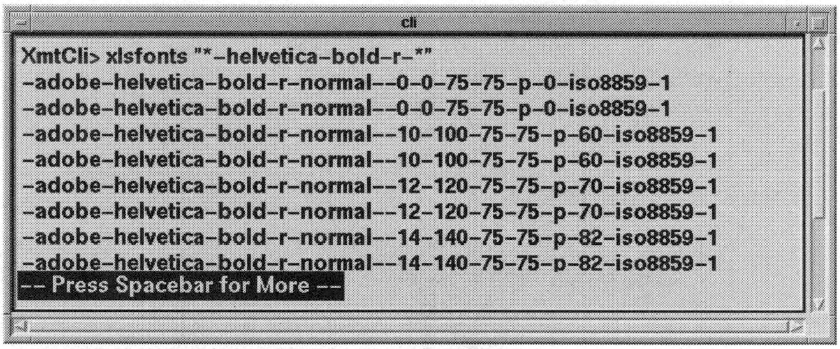

```
cli
XmtCli> xlsfonts "*-helvetica-bold-r-*"
-adobe-helvetica-bold-r-normal--0-0-75-75-p-0-iso8859-1
-adobe-helvetica-bold-r-normal--0-0-75-75-p-0-iso8859-1
-adobe-helvetica-bold-r-normal--10-100-75-75-p-60-iso8859-1
-adobe-helvetica-bold-r-normal--10-100-75-75-p-60-iso8859-1
-adobe-helvetica-bold-r-normal--12-120-75-75-p-70-iso8859-1
-adobe-helvetica-bold-r-normal--12-120-75-75-p-70-iso8859-1
-adobe-helvetica-bold-r-normal--14-140-75-75-p-82-iso8859-1
-adobe-helvetica-bold-r-normal--14-140-75-75-p-82-iso8859-1
-- Press Spacebar for More --
```

Figure 1-6. The XmtCli widget

Application output can be displayed in an XmtCli widget through functions analogous to `printf()` and `puts()`. Command input can be obtained asynchronously through a callback list, or can be read synchronously with a function analogous to `gets()`. The XmtCli widget provides command-line history, in the way some advanced shells do: by typing the up and down arrows, the user can scan through the list of previously-typed commands to select one to edit and enter again. The XmtCli widget will automatically display a prompt before user input, if a prompt is specified, and it will also optionally page long output, allowing the user to view the output a page at a time.

1.7 Dialog Boxes

Part Six of this book, *Patterns and Tools for Dialogs*, leaves the main window behind and moves on to consider the design and implementation of dialog boxes. Implementing dialog boxes is one of the most time-consuming tasks of application development, and Xmt provides a lot of tools to simplify the implementation of various types of dialogs.

1.7.1 Simple Message Dialogs

A terminal-based application can display a message to the user by calling `printf()`, but to display the same message in a dialog box, you must create a dialog box, set the message as a resource, pop up the dialog box, register a callback to detect when the user clicks **OK**, lowcring windows, specifying colored, non-rectangular icons, and, from within that callback, pop down the dialog box and destroy it. This process is obviously too cumbersome for this simple case of displaying a message.

Because displaying information, warnings, or error messages in dialog boxes is such a common thing to do, the Xmt library provides convenience routines that are as simple to use as `printf()`. `XmtDisplayInformation()`, `XmtDisplayWarning()`, `XmtDisplayError()`, and related functions automatically create, cache for reuse, and manage XmMessageBox dialogs—the application can call these functions and need never know about the dialog box widgets themselves. These functions also provide support for easy internationalization of your messages. Figure 1-7 shows a dialog created by one of these simple message dialog functions.

Figure 1-7. An automatically created and managed message dialog

1.7.2 Simple Input Dialogs

Getting user input with a dialog box is even more complicated than displaying a message in a dialog box. A terminal-based application can get an input string or value by calling `scanf()`. When the call to `scanf()` returns, the application can proceed to operate on the input value. With dialog box input, however, an application must pop up the dialog box in one procedure, and then extract the input and act on it in some other procedure invoked when the user clicks the **OK** button. This split is required by the "event driven" model upon which the X Toolkit is based, but again this model is more cumbersome than is justified for this task of simple input. To address this problem, the Xmt library has a set of functions that perform "synchronous" input using modal dialog boxes. These functions enter an internal event loop until the user clicks **OK** or **Cancel**, and so they appear to block (like `scanf()`) while waiting for input. This means that an application can call these functions to obtain input from the user in a single step.

Xmt provides functions to automatically create, cache, and manage dialog boxes for getting user input of strings, integers, floating-point numbers, and Boolean values. There are also functions for getting filename input and for prompting the user to choose an item from a list of items. Figure 1-8 shows a dialog box created and managed by the simple input dialog function `XmtAskForItem()`.

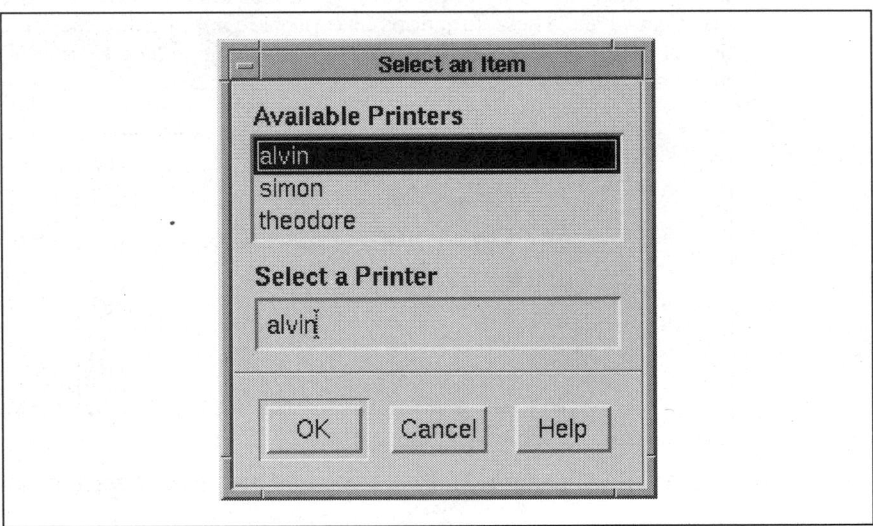

Figure 1-8. A simple input dialog

1.7.3 Presenting Choices

Applications often use dialog boxes to present choices to the user. Motif provides primitive widgets that allow you to present these choices in a number of ways:

- Using toggle buttons in a "radio box" or a "check box"
- Using toggle buttons displaying icons in a "palette"
- With the XmList widget, in single-select or multi-select mode
- In an option menu

One problem with creating radio boxes, check boxes, palettes, and option menus is much like the problem of creating pulldown menu systems—there is no reason that you should have to create each of the items explicitly. A more serious problem, however, is that when you present a choice to the user, you'd like a single state variable to hold the user's choice. When you create a radio box by placing toggle buttons in a row column widget, however, there is no single state variable to read, and you have to register a callback on each toggle button and maintain that state variable yourself. The XmList widget addresses some of these issues, but an XmList widget is not always a good substitute for toggle buttons and the XmList API is still quite awkward.

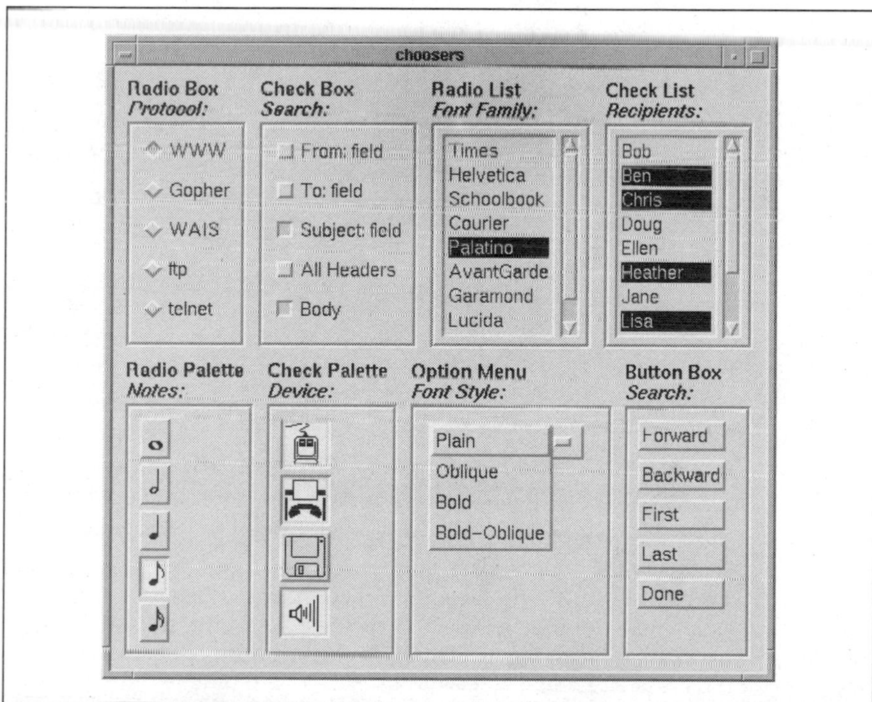

Figure 1-9. Presenting choices with the XmtChooser widget

The XmtChooser widget addresses these issues and provides a single, consistent API for all of these methods of presenting choices. It takes an array of strings or icons as a single resource; these are the choices to be displayed to the user. Another resource specifies the format that the choices should be presented in (radio box, palette, option menu, etc.). The XmtChooser also maintains a single state variable that can be set and queried and a single callback list that will be invoked when the user makes a choice. The XmtChooser widget can also maintain an array of values associated with each item. The widget does not interpret these values in any way, but this feature provides a convenient way to map between the index of a selected item and some value or object (an `XmFontList`, perhaps) associated with that item. The choices displayed in Figure 1-10 were all implemented using the XmtChooser widget.

1.7.4 The XmtInputField Widget

Just as common as asking the user to choose from a list of items is asking the user to enter simple input—a short string or a number, for example—into a single line text widget. Both the Motif XmText and the XmTextField widgets can be used for this purpose, but these widgets are missing a number of subtle features that are important for this sort of input. The XmtInputField widget (shown in Figure 1-10) is a subclass of the XmText widget which provides these missing features.

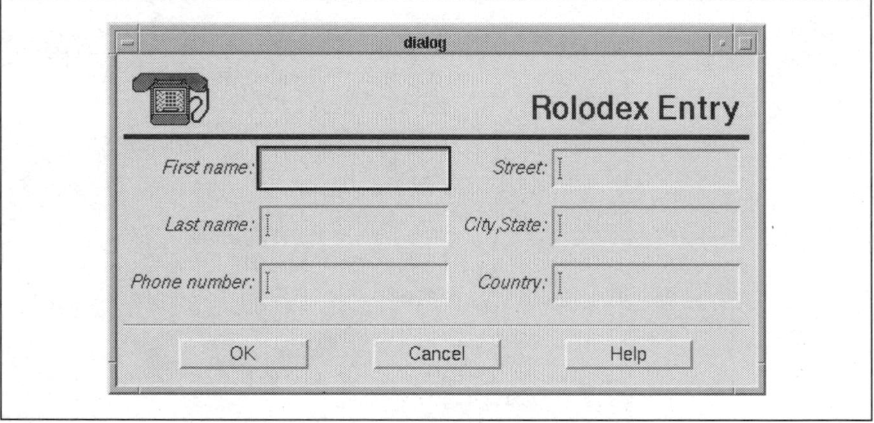

Figure 1-10. Getting input with the XmtInputField widget

The primary difference between the XmtInputField and the XmText widgets is shown when they update their values. The XmText widget updates its stored value (the `XmNvalue` resource) and calls its `XmNvalueChangedCallback` every time the user types a character. The XmtInputField widget, on the other hand, only updates its value (its `XmtNinput` resource) and calls its `XmtNinputCallback` when the user is done typing and indicates this by striking the **Return** key, or by moving input focus out of the XmtInputField widget.

Although the difference between the XmtInputField and XmText approaches may seem cosmetic, there are some important advantages to the XmtInputField widget. Since the `XmtNinput` resource is only updated when the user finishes the input, you can be sure that this resource always contains a complete value. If you need to perform verification on user input, the `XmtNverifyCallback` can be used to reject invalid input values. When an invalid value is rejected in this way, the XmtInputField can automatically restore its last legal input value, since it has not yet updated its `XmtNinput` resource. (The XmtInputField can also handle invalid input by beeping, by changing colors, or by displaying a special string.)

You can use the XmtInputField `XmtNpattern` resource to restrict input to a particular type or sequence of characters. When requesting a zip code, for example, you could use this resource to require that exactly five digits are entered. You could also use this resource to require that phone numbers contain exactly 10 digits, and have the widget automatically insert appropriate punctuation characters in the phone number.

1.7.5 Automatic Dialog Management

The purpose of any dialog is to get input from the user or to display data to the user. The difficult part of implementing dialogs is transferring the data between the application and the widgets in the dialog box. Typically you write two custom procedures: one that takes application data and displays it in the dialog widgets and one that queries the dialog widget for the user's input values and stores those values into the appropriate application data structures.

Xmt provides a mechanism for substantially automating this process. When widgets are created with `XmtCreateChildren()` (as described above), each widget in a dialog can have a resource name associated with it. This creates a mapping between the widgets of a dialog box and resource names. By defining an `XtResourceList`, these resource names can be mapped to the fields of a data structure. These two mappings are sufficient to allow automatic transfers of data between the widgets of the interface and the fields of the internal data structures. Because each widget type stores its data differently, however, custom procedures are required to actually transfer the data for each widget type. These procedures are registered with the widget type with `XmtRegisterWidgetTypes()`.

Once the mappings are defined and the transfer procedures are registered, data can be automatically transferred to and from a dialog with `XmtDialogSetDialogValues()` and `XmtDialogGetDialogValues()`. In addition, there are higher-level convenience functions like `XmtDialogDo()` and `XmtDialogOkayCallback()` that automatically transfer data to the dialog and pop it up, and automatically transfer data from the dialog and pop it down.

1.7.6 Busy Cursors and the XmtWorkingBox Widget

When an application will be busy for any noticeable length of time and will not be responding to user events during that time, it should always provide some kind of feedback to the user that it is in a busy state. One simple way to do this is to change the pointer cursor to display a wristwatch, an hourglass, or some similar icon. Xmt provides the function `XmtDisplayBusyCursor()` for this purpose. As described above, an application can also use an XmtMsgLine widget to display a simple message that explains what the application is doing, and to display a further message when it is done.

When an application will be busy for more than a few seconds, it is a good idea to actually pop up a dialog box to display this feedback to the user. The XmtWorkingBox widget is designed for this purpose, and `XmtDisplayWorkingDialog()` is a convenience function that automatically creates, caches, and manages an XmtWorkingBox widget in a dialog shell. The XmtWorkingBox widget displays a message and an icon (a clock face by default), as shown in Figure 1-10. Optionally, it displays an XmScale widget that can be used to provide an indication of how much longer the application will be busy. It also optionally displays a **Stop** button that can be used to allow the user to cancel whatever operation is in progress.

Figure 1-11. The XmtWorkingBox widget

1.7.7 Online Help

Online help is an important part of any non-trivial application. The simplest style of online help is to pop up a message in a dialog box when the user clicks on a **Help** button. The Motif XmMessageBox widget can be used for this purpose, but because that dialog displays unscrolled text, it is limited to help messages of about 10 lines or so. As an alternative, Xmt provides the XmtHelpBox widget which displays an icon, a title, and a scrolled XmLabel widget, which can display multi-font text with an XmString. Figure 1-12 shows an XmtHelpBox widget displaying a help message.

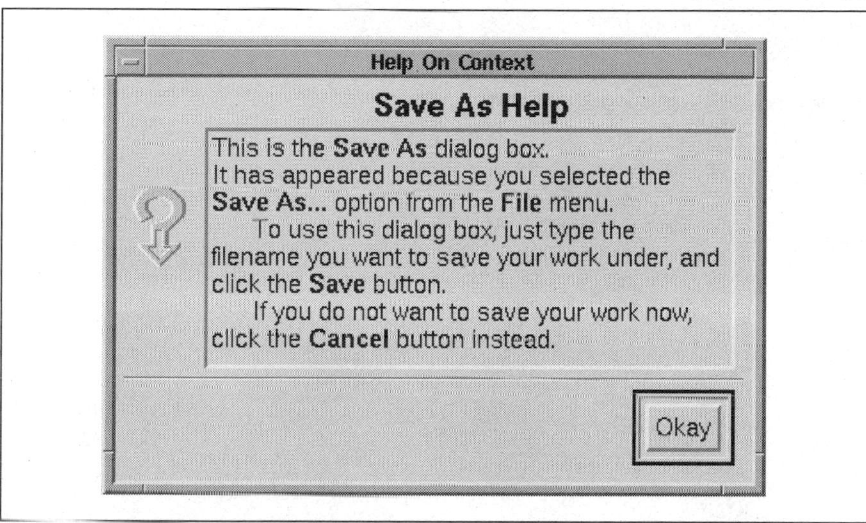

Figure 1-12. The XmtHelpBox widget

Context-sensitive help is a second kind of online help. In a pure sense, the term "context help" means that the help that is offered to the user should be relevant to whatever the user is doing (what context she is in). In practice, for Motif applications, context help means help that is provided on any particular widget when that widget is selected by the user. To implement this kind of context help, there must be a way of associating arbitrary help text with specific widgets, or specific subtrees of widgets. Xmt uses the X resource database as a natural way to make this association. When the user requests help on a particular widget, Xmt searches a special resource database for help on that widget, and if it finds any, it will display it in an XmtHelpBox dialog.

1.8 Moving On: The Rest of the Book

If you've made it to this point in the chapter, you now have a good idea about what kind of features are available in the Xmt library. If something in particular has caught your interest, feel free to jump right to the appropriate chapter. Bear in mind, though, that you might need some of the preliminary material in Part Two, *Programming Preliminaries*, and Part Three, *Programming with Resources*, to make complete sense of the rest of the book.

Or, if you're the more patient sort, you might consider reading this book as it is organized. This chapter was an introduction to the application development tools in the Xmt library. The next chapter is an introduction to the "holistic" application design philosophies that motivated the development of Xmt and that permeate this book. It discusses a number of high-level design issues that you should think about before you start writing code for an application.

2

High-Level Application Design

This is a book about tools and techniques for developing graphical user interfaces. But it is also about the design of those interfaces. It is about designing computer applications that are intuitive, not difficult to figure out; that are easy to use, not awkward; that empower users, not frustrate them; that address the user's task head-on, not in a roundabout way; that are stylish and professional looking, not cobbled together and shoddy. Application design and development go hand in hand, and you'll find them intertwined throughout the book.

This introductory chapter is an extended survey of high-level issues in application design. You'll find it significantly different from the more technical chapters that follow, but it is worth reading, since these design issues permeate the book, and because this introduction helps to put the remaining chapters in context. The first sections describe some philosophies about application design, and later sections describe a "holistic" application design methodology that considers the audience for the application and the task they are trying to accomplish.

2.1 Application Design Follows Patterns

Think for a moment about how people use computers. Most computer users have a computer at their desk and use it continuously or periodically throughout the day. We have a small set of applications that are the primary tools of our trades and a large number of secondary applications that we will use as the need arises. (As a programmer and writer, my primary application is *emacs*—at least 90% of my time at the computer is spent interacting with this text editor.)

And think about what happens when you are using your primary applications. If a program is well designed, and if you've become sufficiently experienced with it, then the user interface fades into the background and the task you and the computer are working to solve comes into the foreground. As you master the keyboard commands of a program, for example, your fingers learn to fly to the correct keys, without interrupting your concentration on your task. When the human-computer interaction begins to flow like this, it is possible to lose yourself in the task. In some important sense, you enter the computer; you spend your day "inside" your primary applications, using them to manipulate your abstract and intangible electronic data.

Perhaps it is because we get inside our applications in this way that we talk about them as if they were places. We say things like "get into your word processor," or "go to the File menu," and we speak of "exiting" applications. This place-nature of applications is heavily emphasized when we give those applications graphical user interfaces and display them as windows on a "desktop" of windows. Applications are our tools, but also our work spaces.

Imagine what a computer would be without applications. We'd be up against megabytes of core memory and gigabytes of data on disk. Faced with this datascape, this sea of bits, what could we do but drown in it? Our applications are the tools that allow us to understand our data: to read or visualize it, to filter it, search it, and interpret it. Applications give shape to our data. These factors take this place/form metaphor one step further. It is useful, I think, to regard applications as the built-form of cyberspace, the buildings and structures on the electronic datascape. It follows that application designers and programmers are the architects and carpenters of cyberspace (Figure 2-1).

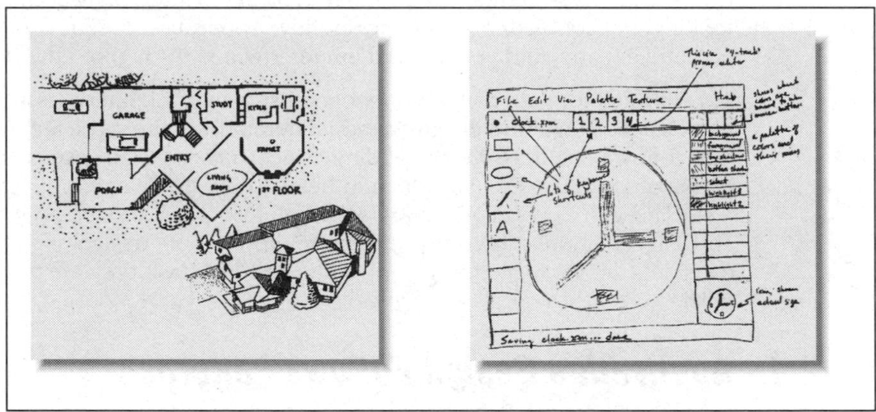

Figure 2-1. Application design in architecture

This insight leads to observations like the following: a person's primary applications are his "home," the "place" where he spends most of his day. Above all, these applications must be a personal, customizable space that is comfortable to spend time within. On the other hand, auxiliary applications that a person uses only now and then are more like public buildings where he goes to run errands. These applications should have well-marked signs and an easy-to-understand process, so the visiting user doesn't get confused.

We could take this metaphor further along these lines, drawing an analogy between applications and buildings, but we would probably quickly stretch the metaphor to its limits. The more interesting analogy is between the *process* of application design and architectural design. I was inspired to this conclusion by a remarkable book called *A Pattern Language* by Christopher Alexander et al. of the Center for Environmental Structure in Berkeley, California.* It is a book about architecture, not about computers, but it is valuable because it is fundamentally about the interactions among people and their structures. And it is a quietly revolutionary book, calling for profound changes in the way architecture is practiced, and in the ways we structure our cities, our buildings, and our lives. The premise of the book is that there is a language of architectural patterns in our common heritage. If we can relearn and reclaim that language, we can begin to put the patterns together into our own designs and can take architecture out of the hands of the architectural elite and rediscover "the timeless way of building."

The Timeless Way of Building is the name of the accompanying theoretical volume. *A Pattern Language,* however, is a thoroughly practical book; it is an 1150-page exploration and illustration of 253 patterns in the design of towns, the design of buildings, and the construction of buildings. I recommend this book to anyone who is interested in any kind of design: architectural, graphic, computer, mechanical, or whatever. It is a book that challenges the reader to think in new ways.

Computers and computer applications have not been around long enough for us to talk about a "timeless way" of designing them. But there are certainly patterns that appear again and again in their design. A goal of this book is to explore as many of these patterns as possible. They are the alphabet of application design and a programmer who is familiar and comfortable with them will be able to combine them into applications that are, if not "timeless," then at least well designed, useful, easy to use, pleasant to look at, and so forth.

What are these patterns in application design? The following sections survey some of the highest-level patterns, and you'll find others explored throughout the book. Some chapters deal mostly with the patterns. This is primarily a practical book, however, and most chapters briefly describe an important pattern, and then devote their remaining pages to documenting tools for implementing the pattern.

2.1.1 The Audience and the Task

The first patterns to consider when designing an application concern the audience for the application and the nature of the task they are trying to accomplish. "Consider the user" and "Know your audience" are the first commandments of good design. Will your users be computer experts or novices? Will they be using your application continuously, frequently, or only occasionally? What other applications do they use? What styles of computer interaction are they accustomed to?

*The book was published by Oxford University Press in 1977, and should be available in any good bookstore with an architecture department.

In order to design an application for this audience, you must understand the task they want to accomplish with the application. Think about the nature of the task. How do your potential users accomplish it now? What are the bottlenecks? How can a computer help, in a fundamental way, to make this task easier?

To design a useful application, you must think deeply about the *nature* of the task. What is it that makes it difficult? If you understand the sort of complexity that you are up against, you can design the structure of the application to match the structure of the problem. There are patterns for a number of categories of tasks: display of data, browsing of data, communication, training, entertainment, and so on.

It is also important to think about the *scope* of the application. There are patterns here as well: there are desktop utilities that are small and self-contained. There are transient applications that are invoked, worked with, and dismissed. There are applications that are a complete environment that envelops the user. Different scopes are appropriate in different circumstances. This kind of audience and task analysis is considered in detail later in this chapter, as part of a methodology of application design.

2.1.2 The Desktop

Once you understand the nature of the task and have thought about the scope of the application, you should think about the application's appearance and interactions on the desktop; this is where the user will confront it first. There are patterns here as well: some applications have small, unobtrusive windows. Others open large windows that occupy most of the screen. Others open a whole suite of windows that the user can move around independently. Other desktop patterns concern window manager titles and icons, and communication with the window manager, the session manager, and other clients. Chapter 14, *Windows on the Desktop*, explores these patterns and their implementations.

2.1.3 The Main Window

If an application is a building, then its windows are its rooms, and the main window must be the living room.* This is the "space" where the user will spend most of her time. There are patterns that involve the various components (menubar, palette, message line, mode line, and so on) of the main window, and their layout in that window. There are important considerations about the "flow" of user-computer interactions in the main window. These issues are explored in Part Five, *Patterns and Tools for the Main Window,* and the patterns for menus, message lines, and other main window components are explored in their own individual chapters throughout the book.

*For some applications, the first window you see is just an entry hallway and all the work is done in auxiliary main windows—the kitchen and the study, perhaps.

2.1.4 Dialog Boxes

Just as there are different types of main window patterns suitable for different tasks, there are different patterns of dialogs suitable on different occasions: some dialog boxes display simple messages, some request simple input (a filename, an item chosen from a list). Some dialogs are designed to display online help, other dialog boxes have data input as their primary purpose, and still others are designed to allow the user to configure the application's behavior at runtime. There are patterns for modal dialog boxes and patterns for modeless dialogs. There are patterns that describe the ideal layout of components within a dialog box.

Dialog boxes are a major component of just about every application. Chapter 25, *Message Dialogs*, and Chapter 26, *Simple Input Dialogs*, discuss two kinds of simple dialog boxes that Xmt will create and manage for you automatically. Chapter 30, *Context Help*, describes tools for implementing context help for your application through dialog boxes. Chapter 29, *Custom Dialogs and Automatic Dialog Management*, describes the patterns that apply to more complicated dialogs and presents tools in the Xmt library that make it easier to implement these complex dialogs.

2.1.5 User-Computer Interaction

It is only when the interaction between a user and an application flows smoothly back and forth without jarring or annoying interruptions that the user can really concentrate on the task at hand and, as described earlier, get "inside" the application. Just as there are patterns in the layout of components within main windows and dialog boxes, so there are patterns of human-computer interactions that occur when using those components. Consider the ways a user might issue a command within an application, for example: by clicking a button in a button box, by selecting an item from a pulldown menu, by selecting an item from a popup menu, by invoking a keyboard shortcut, by invoking a mouse shortcut, such as a double-click in some special region, or by typing a command at a command-line interface. Each of these interaction styles has pros and cons, and once you really understand each of the patterns you'll be able to choose which is most appropriate in any given circumstance.

Other patterns of computer-human interactions are *cues*—text, icons, cursors, animated graphics displayed by the application, or sounds emitted by the application that gently and unobtrusively remind the user what her options are in a given window, point out to her when the application has entered a new mode, and so forth. Still another kind of interaction pattern is *feedback*. Feedback is how an application acknowledges that it has received and is acting upon user commands—by displaying a wristwatch cursor when the application is temporarily busy, for example.

Another, somewhat different, kind of human-computer interaction is user customization of fonts, colors, keyboard commands, and the like. If we can say that applications are buildings and that windows are the rooms, then perhaps we can stretch the metaphor to say that customizing an application is like moving the furniture around. More dynamic types of customization are important too—selecting a larger font at runtime when your eyes are sore is perhaps like turning up the thermostat when a room is too cold. Applications must allow some degree of customization if users are ever to begin to feel "at home" with them.

These patterns of human-computer interaction do not have a chapter of their own devoted to them, but you will find interaction considerations brought up in most of the chapters.

2.1.6 Finishing Touches and Style

A myriad little details make the difference between an application that looks sharp and one that just looks ordinary, or the difference between one that is a pleasure to use and one that is just usable. Once you have put together your main windows and their subcomponents and considered the desktop and user-computer interaction, it is time to add these details: to adjust margins so that the widget layout looks balanced, for example, to use a secondary background color to add some visual interest to your windows, to rearrange the order of items in menus so that the most frequently used are conveniently near the top, to proofread the messages, labels, and prompts displayed by the application to ensure that they are to the point and free of jargon.

These details are not patterns themselves; instead they are the various corollaries of the larger patterns that define good design. You'll find suggestions about these little stylistic details in the "Style" section of many chapters in this book.

2.2 Application Design and Development Are Intertwined

After some preliminary chapters on fundamental development tools, this book proceeds, more or less, from high-level design patterns to lower-level patterns, on to chapters about specific tools for application development, and then to a section of reference material documenting specific C functions and widgets in detail.

Application design and development also proceed in an approximation of the top-down model. When making a rough first pass at the design of an application, it is a useful practice to consider the patterns that make up your design in the order that they are presented here. In practice, however, design and development are part of the same iterative cycle, in the same way that programming is a cycle of editing, compiling, and testing, over and over. A sketchy design must be in place before development can begin, but at the same time it is difficult or impossible (or if not strictly impossible, then at least not cost-effective) to anticipate every detail and flesh out the design completely in the absence of any development. As development proceeds and a prototype of the application becomes available, that prototype will allow the designer to better visualize the details of the application, and to experiment with layouts, keyboard shortcuts, and so on. This process continues until the design is fully refined and development is completed.

Since they are part of the same iterative cycle, design and development are intertwined processes. This means, primarily, that the designer and developer must work closely together, must communicate well, and must respect one another's ideas. (This is true even when the designer and developer are the same person—that person must be able to switch roles frequently and to value the insights gained in both roles.)

As a designer, the worst thing you can do is to impose a fully detailed design on a programmer or programming team and require them to code it strictly to the specification. Coding to a spec is a job for a machine, and, for better or worse, the state of the art in automatic code generation software is not yet up to the task of developing real applications. Programmers can code to someone else's specifications if you make them, but there is no better way to destroy morale than to make someone do mindless work. And a disgruntled programmer forced to conform to the letter of the specification may well ignore (intentionally or not) the spirit of the design.

Programmers are far more closely involved with the details of an application, and this enables them to gain insights about an application that are not available from the more aloof perspective of the designer. For example, a designer might specify that an application should pop up a dialog box when it is busy performing some difficult computation. The programmer, however, might discover that this calculation typically takes only a second to complete, and that a simple "please wait" message or cursor, without a dialog, would be more appropriate for this shorter-than-expected busy period.

Also, remember that programmers are intimately familiar with the possibilities and limits of the available technologies, and you must be willing to alter your design to the demands of development expediency. If programmers say that some aspect of your design is too hard or "impossible," take them seriously, and abandon it, or alter it so that it can be implemented reasonably. Otherwise, the programmers may be forced to spend a lot of time writing code that is non-portable, difficult to maintain, or otherwise a liability to the future of your application. On the other hand, your programmers may point out to you useful features of the available technology that you can incorporate into your design—for example, that a particular widget has a double-click callback and that you could add a double-click shortcut to the design where you hadn't had one before.

And if you are a programmer, the worst thing you can do is to program strictly to the specifications, without understanding the design as a whole, and without considering design issues as you go. Realistically, no designer can adequately flesh out all the details of a design, and you will be making "design decisions" all the time while you code. If you understand the task the users are trying to accomplish, the overall structure of the design, and the "patterns" that make up the design, you will be able to make the right choices when confronted with these decisions. The alternative is to be simply a programming unit, little better than a machine. There is no such thing as "just a programmer"; we are all doing design all the time.

The design-development cycle is not complete by itself. Documentation and user testing are also important and integral parts of it. While working on the widgets described in this book, I several times had great design insights while writing the documentation for a widget, and went back to re-code and re-document portions of those widgets. Similarly, while consulting recently with a group to design and develop a large application, I found that it was often the technical writer of the group who found bugs to be fixed by the programmers and also found inconsistencies or flaws in the design. The technical writer's task is fundamentally unlike that of the designer or the developer, and because of the unique nature of this task it is bound to yield new insights. The process of documenting an application is also unique in its scope and level of detail. The person writing the documentation for a product is often the only one who is familiar with all of its parts in some detail—the designer's view is too abstract, and the programmer's views are too narrow and specialized. The lesson here is that documentation should be an integral part of the design and development task, and that both designers and programmers should be responsive to the suggestions of the technical writer.

Similarly, you should never neglect the opinions of the end user. It is the users who will ultimately accept or reject the application (or if they have no choice in the matter will simply be happy or unhappy with it). Just as the programmers are most familiar with the available technology for implementing a design, the users are the ones who most intimately understand the problem the application is designed to solve. Some of the best-designed applications, it seems to me, are those written for programmers, because the programmers who write them really understand the need they are trying to fill. Ask the users how they think the applications should work, ask for their feedback on the preliminary design, let them see and try out early versions of the application, and plan time for this trial and feedback cycle into your development schedule. Users may offer valuable and useful design suggestions (undoubtedly, along with many unworkable suggestions) or at the very least serve to judge, approve, or veto your various design components.

The Motif widget set, incidentally, is a good example of what can happen when design, development, documentation, and user testing are not part of an integrated process. The designers and developers of Motif were at different sites in different companies. The API design was handed down from on high—the developers were more or less obliged to copy the API of the DECWindows toolkit, even though that API was designed before X Toolkit technology had matured or was even thoroughly understood. That design has remained frozen through several versions of Motif, and there has been no opportunity for suggestions from users. The result? The incredible inconvenience of the `XmString` abstraction, the impossibly frustrating XmList widget, and a relatively simple manager widget, the XmRowColumn, whose implementation requires 11,600 lines of code, much of which is unrelated code dedicated to pulldown and popup menus.

To be fair to its designers and developers, Motif was a large undertaking, and the design and development difficulty of a project grows exponentially with its size, because the amount of communication required between the various teams and individuals grows exponentially. In this discussion I've talked about designers, developers, and writers as if they were separate individuals or even separate teams. In some smaller and medium-sized projects, though, you'll take on all three of these roles yourself, and, if you are given the time to do the job right, I believe that these projects will be the ones with the best designs.

2.3 Application Design Is Influenced by Development Tools

At the highest levels, application design can be (and should be) a fairly abstract undertaking. At these highest levels an application design might look the same whether it is implemented on a UNIX workstation, a Macintosh, or a PC running Windows or DOS. Once the design becomes somewhat fleshed out, however, it inevitably is (and should be) influenced by the particular technologies available on each of those platforms.

It is important for you as a designer to be familiar with the tools (widgets, in the case of Xt and Motif) that are available for the implementation of your design. These tools enable the patterns that make up your design. If you don't understand the nuances of the technology, you won't be able to make the subtle design decisions: when should you use a list widget, and when a radio box of toggle buttons, for example?

The tools available to you will always impose constraints upon your design, but you must be careful not to let them cripple your design. Back in the days of X10, before the X Toolkit and widgets, one of the few widely available user interface tools was a package for implementing popup menus that were stacked like index cards. Applications were written using this package in which every user action entailed popping up a stack of menus, choosing the correct menu, and then choosing an item from the menu. It was a hideous user interface; it was simply not possible to implement a good design with this tool.

The situation is a lot better now. But the existing widget sets can only cover the most commonly needed user interface tools, and sometimes you will have to buy or develop custom tools. For example, the Motif widgets don't include a multi-column list. I've seen applications that simulate one either by placing multiple single-column XmList widgets side-by-side, or by carefully arranging text into columns in an XmText widget. Both solutions are hacks, and both are awkward for the user. It would be better to just write a simple multi-column list widget for this purpose. Accept and work within the design constraints imposed by your implementation tools, but if you find that those constraints turn a good design into a bad one, then come up with a new tool.

Just as you should not let lack of widgets cripple your design, you should not let yourself be awed by "cool" or complex widgets when simpler ones would work as well. I consulted with a designer/developer once who had just started playing with a nifty commercial table widget. This tool displayed data in columns and rows, allowed user input into any cell, and even allowed the user to rearrange columns through a drag-and-drop interface. This was an ideal tool for one part of the application: the display of reports extracted from a database.

The designer liked this widget so much, however, that he wanted to use it for the input of data as well—each row would represent one record of data and each column, one field. Since the user would no longer be constrained to enter all the fields of a record before starting the next record, the designer had to add some strange and artificial constraints to the design to support validity checking of the input data. After getting thoroughly bogged down in these awkward details we realized that although the tool was very flexible and fun to program with, it was not the right tool. The established metaphor for database input is through form input dialogs, which solve the problem of input verification, allow better prompting, and create a more smoothly flowing user-computer interaction.

Start your design with an open mind, unconstrained by thoughts of implementation. But at the same time know both the strengths and limitations of your tools so that when you begin to refine your design you can choose tools that fit. When you need to, don't shy away from purchasing or developing custom tools and widgets.

2.4 Application Design Carries Social Responsibility

Application design and development do not occur in a vacuum. Every design decision you make will affect the people who use your application in one way or another, and you should carry this always in mind.

As programmers, we deal with abstractions all day long, and even when we are working as application designers, we refer to the people who will be working with our applications as "users"—an abstract and inhuman term that we've all grown accustomed to. We must keep in mind that these "users" are in fact human beings. And we must remember that if our applications are successful there will be thousands or, in the mass market, millions of people using them. If we design our applications well, these people will accomplish the tasks they need to accomplish more easily. If we design them poorly we will increase the frustration and stress levels of these people.

And not only must we remember that these "users" are real people, we must remember that they do not behave like the machines we work with all day. Computers are good at repetitive tasks and at the manipulation of abstract data. Humans are good at directing tasks and organizing subtasks at a higher level. Computers should be tools that people can direct to accomplish their work more easily. But unlike mechanical tools, our new electronic tools can "talk back" and make demands on the user. The ideal model of human-computer interaction is a "dialog" in which the human and the application cooperate to accomplish the task at hand. In poorly designed applications, this interaction can become reversed, with the computer directing the overall task and making demands for mechanical, repetitive input from the user. When this is taken to an extreme we get the data-entry sweatshops that have sprung up in the computer age—inhuman offices where people serve computers, and computers act as human performance monitors and taskmasters.

If it is hard to remember that "users" are not abstract entities, but real human beings, it is even harder to remember that our applications for manipulating abstract data can affect the *physical* well being of those people. If a poorly written application causes increased stress to its users, that stress is not "all in their heads"; work-related stress affects health in any number of ways. Remember too that people may be sitting in front of a computer using your application for hours at a stretch. If the font you use is too small, or if the color scheme you choose as a default is not legible to your users, your application may cause eyestrain and headaches. If your application has a poorly designed keyboard command structure that requires a lot of stretching for awkward key combinations, or if your application requires a lot of mousing back and forth across the screen, then it may cause wrist pain for your users, or even contribute to problems like carpal-tunnel syndrome, which can be crippling and career-ending.

The promise of computers is that they will empower us to perform more quickly and effortlessly the abstract tasks of the electronic age we've entered. The menace they present is that they can just as easily become tools for tyranny. As application designers and developers we share responsibility for the way our applications are used.

2.5 Consider the Audience

The previous sections of this chapter have described *philosophies* about application design. The rest of the chapter describes a *process* of application design:

1. Think about the people who will be working with your application.
2. Think about the task those people are working on.
3. Think about how your design solution will help to accomplish that task.

Steps 2 and 3 will be taken up in detail in later sections of the chapter. For now, ask yourself the following questions about the "audience" for your application:

How much computer expertise do they have?
A program designed for a computer programmer can obviously make a number of assumptions about its users that applications designed for novice computer users cannot. Applications aimed at novices will generally have to provide more online help, and should perhaps include a built-in tutorial, for example. And if you are writing a program aimed at programmers, you can freely use words like "source code," "link," "runtime" and so forth in your documentation and online messages without worrying that you will be confronting your users with unfamiliar jargon.

What training will they receive?
If you are designing a complex piece of software that your audience will use as the primary tool for their job (say an airline reservation system) then it is safe to assume that each of your users will receive hands-on training with the software. For other applications, you can assume that your users will be able to read the UNIX man page before attempting to use the software. For many applications, though, you must assume that some of your users will start working with the

application without training or instruction at all. Each of these different cases has implications for the amount of online help to provide and the trade-off between powerful features and an intuitive interface.

How often do they use computers?
Some users let their keyboard get covered with piles of paper, and then dig it out every few days to use the computer. If you have infrequent users like these, then you should not expect them ever to become familiar enough with the application to master the keyboard shortcuts, for example. On the other hand, your audience may be "power users" who spend all day using a computer and who want powerful features, and are willing to read a manual to find out how to use them. This frequency-of-use factor influences many of the same design decisions that the expertise and training factors influence.

What is their workplace and work-style like?
Take a look at the environment that the application will be used in. If it is intended for use on a factory floor, or a trading floor on Wall Street, for example, then the noise level may drown out any aural feedback the computer makes. On the other hand, an application designed for use in a library should perhaps avoid beeping or making other noises. If the application will be used by a sales team for whom the telephone is a more important business tool than the computer then perhaps the keyboard commands should be designed for one-handed use, while the other hand holds the phone (or a coffee mug, depending on how slow business is). If your users are under time pressure (a stock broker or travel agent on the phone with a customer, for example) then perhaps your application should allow macros or "hot keys" that let the user call up frequently needed information or reports.

What other software do they use?
If your users are already comfortable with other software packages, then any commands you can duplicate from those packages will automatically be familiar to them. Similarly, if you can mimic the underlying metaphor of those other applications (command-line interface, forms input, direct manipulation of iconic objects, or whatever) then users will be able to more easily learn your new application, and will be able to make a smoother transition back and forth between the two software packages. Also, if you can design your application for interoperability with these other applications (through drag-and-drop, for example) then you will obtain a synergy between the applications that makes the suite more useful than the applications considered individually. Similar arguments apply to hardware systems. If your users have only used Macintoshes before, then you should probably not design a suite of UNIX-style command-line applications without also providing a graphical front end for it. And if your users are used to using IBM 3270 terminals, then perhaps the input field widgets in your form input dialogs should default to being in overstrike mode.

Do they have any handicaps?
Don't rely on aural cues if your application will have many deaf users. Be sure the application has the capability to display using large fonts if there will be elderly users with weak eyesight. If your users suffer from wrist problems or partial paralysis, you may want a one-handed interface to common commands, and may also need to provide somehow for locking modifier keys. Also,

remember that about one in ten males suffer from a mild form of red-green color blindness. There is a growing field of "equal access" computing technologies, which are beyond the scope of this book, but these are also questions that you should consider.

2.6 Consider the Task

After studying the audience for your application, the second, most detailed and important step in our design methodology is to think deeply about what they are trying to accomplish—that is, to be sure you understand the purpose of your application. While this may seem self-evident, there are a surprising number of factors to consider, and once you have thought them through, you may find yourself with a very different set of design goals than when you started.

2.6.1 What Does Your Audience Want to Do? (And Why?)

Once you have studied the audience for the application, think about what it is they are doing, the task they are trying to accomplish. A good way to do this is to "walk a mile in their shoes." Spend a day in the office watching the work that goes on, or, even better, doing the same work that your users do. This will help to give you the requisite understanding of the task. Then ask yourself questions like the following:

Why is the task worth doing?
I have a friend who, as a student, spent one summer writing a database program to help the U.S. Navy keep track of when each of its jeeps had last been washed. She didn't have much say in the matter, and went along with this absurd task. You probably won't have much say either about the ultimate value of the task that your audience wants to get accomplished; that the task is important has probably already been decided by the powers that be. It is a question that is worth asking, however, because it can yield insights that will help you design a better application. (And because it can help you keep your cosmic perspective on things and maintain your sense of humor.) On the other hand, you may also find that no one has really asked the question before; perhaps your analysis will convince your audience that they don't actually need to work at this particular task, or that it can be more efficiently accomplished when merged with some other task.

How is the task accomplished now?
Think about how your users are getting their work done now. What are the strengths and weaknesses of the current approach? If the current method works well enough, ask whether there is actually any need for the application you are writing. Before the Navy had their spiffy jeep database, for example, perhaps they kept track of the cleanliness of their jeeps on index cards. This would have been an arduous task, well suited to computerization. On the other hand, perhaps they just looked at the jeeps and washed them when they needed it. This seems like an elegant solution, with no obvious flaws, and is difficult to

improve upon with a computer application. "If it ain't broke," as they say, "don't fix it."

Study the good points of the current methods. If your audience is currently using a computer application, then you may be able to duplicate the good points of the old application, making the adjustment to the new system easier. If you are computerizing a non-computerized task, pay attention to how it is currently done. There may be useful metaphors from the current technique that you can borrow for your computerized version. Also, if it is a task that people have been performing for a number of years, you can be fairly sure that they have evolved a fairly efficient way to accomplish it. Their techniques and algorithms may be worth studying. If the task involves paperwork and forms to fill out, pay attention to how those forms are laid out on paper, and consider duplicating that layout in your electronic version of those forms. This may be the most convenient layout, and it is certainly the most familiar layout to your audience.

Also study the failings of the current methods of performing the task. This will show you where you need to concentrate your efforts and do your most serious design work. If you will be writing a replacement application for software that everyone hates, be sure to ask why they hate it, so you don't end up making the same odious design decisions.

Is the task specified correctly?
Your audience will be intimately familiar with the work they do and the tasks they are trying to accomplish, and you must take them seriously when they tell you how they want your application to perform. But just because they understand the task doesn't mean that they are qualified to design software—they may not be aware of all the options that are open to them. You should use your knowledge of software technology to make them aware of the various possible technical approaches to a problem, and you should also use your design and analysis expertise to look at the larger picture and see if they are asking the right questions.

I spent about half an hour in a travel agent's office once, while the agent struggled to reroute a ticket for me. She had had years of working with various airline reservations systems, but this was a new software package her current airline was using, and the commands were still in flux. It took her three telephone calls before she was able to determine the right "form" she needed to accomplish her task. To perform an operation like booking excess baggage, for example, she had to type a very specific sequence of characters and punctuation that identified the excess baggage command, and also encoded the number of pieces of baggage and their dimensions. She was exasperated because the command format had changed, but not because it was a terrible interface (memorizing arbitrary command sequences is a good job for computers, not for travel agents). When I suggested that she ought to have a function key labeled "Excess Baggage," and that the computer ought to prompt her for the number of pieces and their dimensions, and that she shouldn't have to look up the correct "form" for this command, she was elated—it had never occurred to her that it could be done this way. In this case, my knowledge of computer technology enabled me to propose a better design than the one the users would have asked for. Having proposed this new design, however, I would still need to consult with the users when filling in all the details of the application—it is travel agents, after all, who are the experts on travel reservation software.

Just as you can use your technical knowledge of user-interface techniques to help users think about the kind of application they want, you may be able to use your design experience to look at the task from a more aloof point-of-view and help ensure that they are actually asking the right questions. This is where analysis skills are important, and where it is useful to look at the task as just one component of a larger system. To return to our almost-farcical Navy database example, a designer might try to point out that instead of asking "how can we simplify our index-card database of jeeps by computerizing it?" they should be asking "how can we ensure that our jeeps are washed when they need it?" The first question has a simple answer—hire a contractor to write a database program—but misses the fundamental problem. The second question is a much more difficult, and rewarding, one—it might yield insights about the training or morale levels of workers in the motor pool, for example.

Will computerization make the task any easier?

Computers are useful for many things. But don't fall into the assumption (as many people do) that computerizing a task will automatically make it easier. The failure of the "home computer" market to catch on, I believe, is a lack of interesting things for computers to do around the home. The major difficulty of balancing a checkbook, for example, isn't the arithmetic, but the data entry. People keep track of the checks they write in their checkbooks. To ask them to re-enter all these numbers into a special "checkbook balancing" program means that they have to enter the data twice. Arguably, this makes the task harder, rather than easier. (A time may come, however, when our checkbooks all contain computers that can read our handwriting and keep our accounts balanced automatically. Then computers will have succeeded at making the job easier.)

Similarly, the easiest way I know of to record my appointments is to scrawl them down in a physical appointment book. Every electronic calendar program I've seen is burdened with an overly complex interface for handling daily, weekly, monthly, and yearly displays, for adjusting the granularity of the daily schedule display, for scheduling repeating meetings on the third Friday of each month, and so forth. Using a program like this just to record appointments is far slower than jotting them down on paper. On the other hand, electronic calendar programs offer the feature of automatic reminders, and some "distributed calendar" programs allow users to scan the calendars of other users, automatically schedule meetings at mutually available times, and reserve conference rooms. So even though computerized calendars do not make it any easier to record appointments, the technology offers other benefits (at least to forgetful people and those who work in groups) that may make the applications worth using anyway.

Once you have decided that a task will be made easier by computerizing it, don't jump to the conclusion that you will automatically require a GUI for the application. Depending on your audience, of course, and other design factors, there may be better solutions that use a command-line or tty-based interface. As a computer expert, for example, my favorite electronic calendar is the ancient UNIX *calendar* program that reads appointments from a simple text file, and prints the day's appointments to the terminal. And similarly, few graphical email programs offer much that *emacs* RMAIL mode doesn't also provide.

Is the task done individually or in groups?
While studying your audience and the work they do, look at how the work gets done. Do individuals each take a task and see it through from start to finish? Do different people work on the same task at different phases of its completion? Or do people work on the task as a free-form group, each contributing as needed or as they are able? The term "groupware" has become a buzzword without much specific content. The concept, however, is an important one: now that computers are networked, applications can enable users to cooperate more effectively to get their tasks accomplished. If you notice, for example, that your users are frequently calling one another with simple messages, you might want to build an electronic message facility into your application. The form that this computerized cooperation takes will depend on the task at hand, of course, but you should study the kind of cooperation that goes on currently and try to incorporate that into your design.

2.6.2 What Kind of Task Is It?

Once you have considered the audience and studied the work they do, the next phase of your design should be to spend some time analyzing the task, thinking about the various subtasks that comprise it, and thinking about how you are going to translate those subtasks into a computer application. The basic types of tasks form some fundamental patterns. If you can fit your task and its subtasks into these basic categories, then there are existing applications that you can model yours after, and existing implementation patterns that you can use.

As you think about the nature of each of the subtasks for your application, you should also try to identify which one or two are the most central and important ones—these task patterns will be a central theme in your design, and will determine the overall shape of your application.

If you plunge right into design and development without taking the time to think about what you are really trying to accomplish, then you may find yourself floundering about without a clear direction. You may find yourself implementing patterns that don't really fit, and then having to backtrack and redo them. The application will grow by accretion of features, but will not have a focused design or purpose.

The following paragraphs describe some of the common task patterns. Figures 2-2 through 2-9 show applications that satisfy those tasks, and illustrate some of the implementation patterns you might choose in your design.

Displaying Text. Almost every conceivable application will display text in some form. In some cases, this is simply incidental, but in others it is central to the purpose of the application. Notice that text display does not strictly require a graphical interface.

Visualizing Data. One of the most important things that computers can do for us is to help us understand data. One common way of doing this is by displaying it graphically in some way that makes it easier to grasp.

Organizing Information. Another way that applications can help us to understand our data is by organizing and structuring it. It might do this by structuring it in tree or tabular form, for example.

Monitoring Data. Any application that will be manipulating "real time" or "real world" data may have a monitoring role to play. Applications can simulate gauges, warning lights, strip charts, tickertape, and so forth.

Presentation of Data. Some applications not only need to display information to make it understandable, but also need to make it look good, because information that is well presented is more accessible and useful. (Or sometimes, because information that is well presented is more impressive, flattering, intimidating, or even misleading.)

Entering Data. Data input is almost as ubiquitous as data display—just about every application will get some sort of input from the user. In some cases it is incidental, and in some cases central to the application's main task. When an application is designed mainly for data input, the key is to do all you can to make the input process simple and flexible.

Browsing Data. Another way that computers can make data understandable (once that data has been entered, of course) is selective display of the data—i.e., searching for and displaying only the particular information the user has requested.

Editing Data. Editing data is just about as fundamental a task for computers as is displaying data. Almost every application performs some sort of editing. Some applications, though, have editing as their primary purpose and are specifically designed as editors—text editors, bitmap editors, music editors, and so on.

Manipulating Complex Data. All data manipulation is a kind of editing, of course, but when the data involved is particularly complex, an application will require specialized interfaces for viewing and working with the data. If the complex data is displayed graphically, for example, then perhaps the application will allow the user to manipulate the data by interacting with it graphically as well.

Communication. Communication is a common high-level task with its own particular set of patterns and metaphors to adopt. We see these patterns in electronic mail and news-readers, of course, but also see them in bug-tracking and version-control software, when individuals in a group need to leave messages for each other.

Instruction. Some applications are intended to teach the user. Teaching may be as simple as providing online help in an application. It can also take the form of a more orchestrated presentation of information, as in a product tutorial or demo.

Design. Another major category of applications is for design: pictures, user interfaces, integrated circuits, buildings, airfoils, chemical plants, or whatever. These are usually programs that display the design graphically and allow the user to interact with it graphically.

Modeling. A category related to design applications is that for modeling systems—such as the long range climate patterns due to the greenhouse effect, the frequency response of a specified filter circuit, or the future of the foreign currency options market. These applications allow the user to vary the input parameters, usually perform complex computations based on those parameters, and then show the variation in output.

Cooperation. "Groupware" is a hot buzzword these days. More and more of these applications that help people to work more effectively together are appearing. The patterns and metaphors for this sort of application are still evolving, but they are definitely patterns that are worth considering for your own applications.

Multimedia and Hypertext. "Multimedia" and "hypertext" (and more generally, "hypermedia") are other hot buzzwords today. Software in these evolving areas is interesting not because of its capabilities, but because of the information it presents. The developer of a hypermedia "application" is doing less traditional computer programming than graphic design, sound and video editing, and so forth. As the information age proceeds, the term "software" may well come to refer to this sort of multimedia information presentation, instead of the actual computer programs that underlie it.

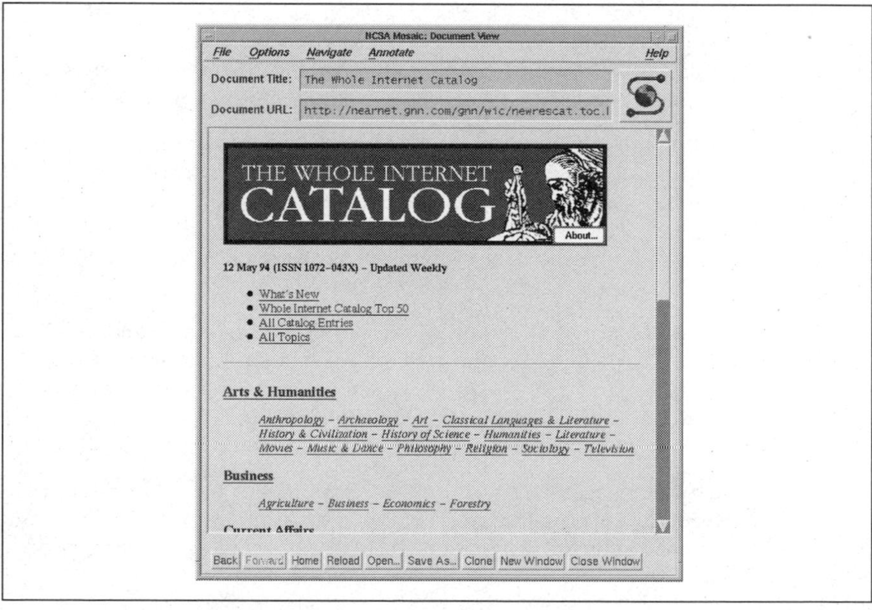

Figure 2-2. Applications that are media

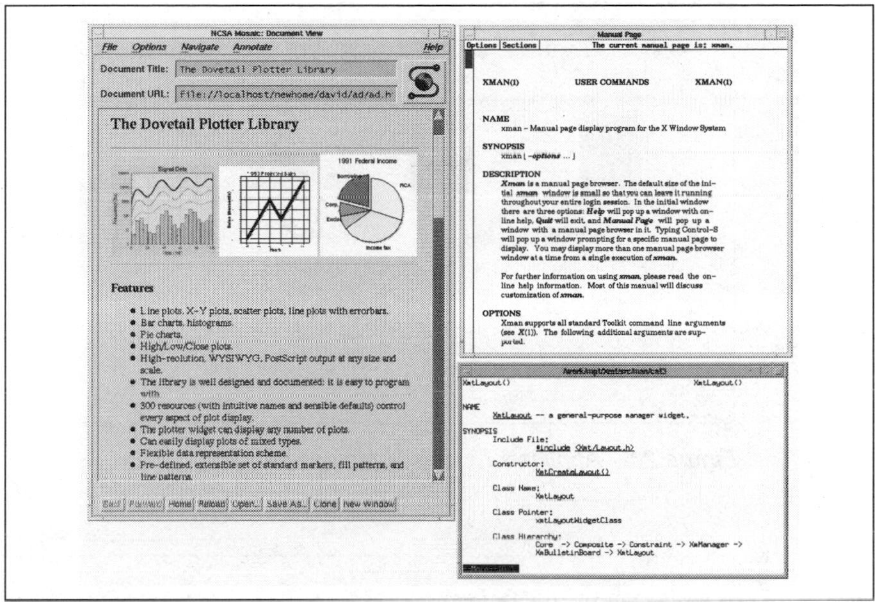

Figure 2-3. Applications for displaying text

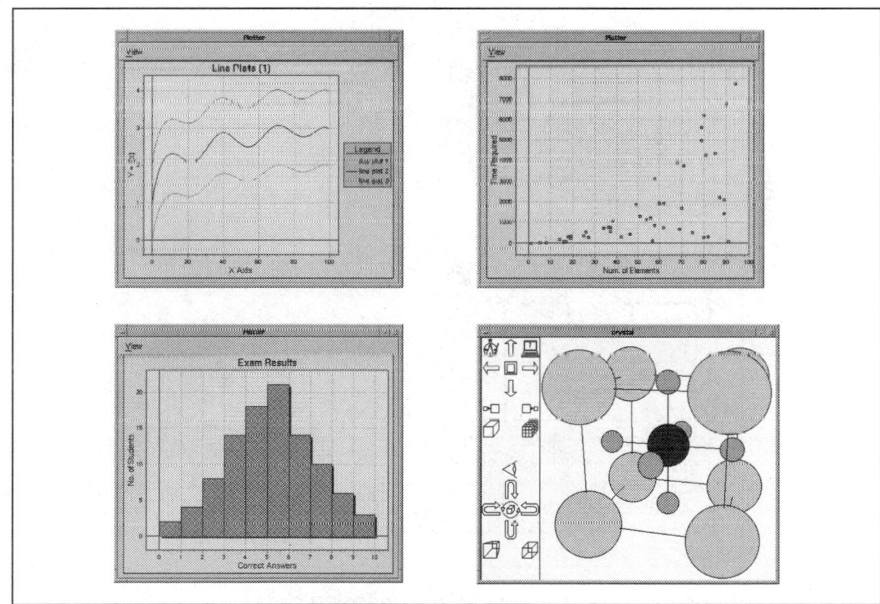

Figure 2-4. Applications for data visualization

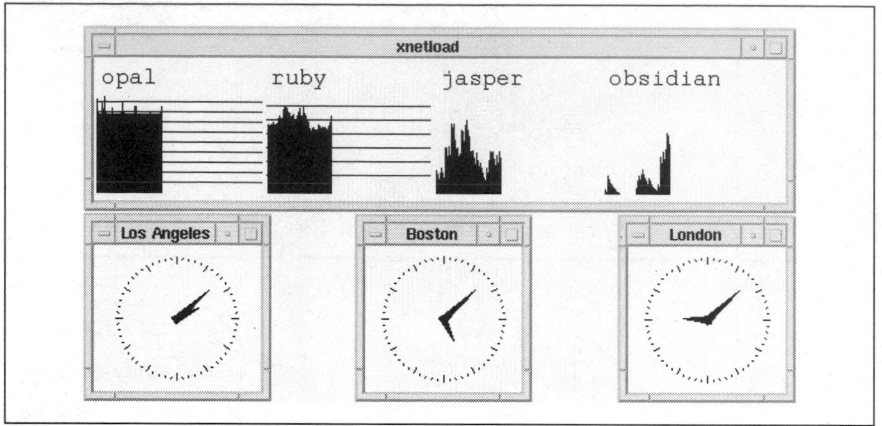

Figure 2-5. Applications that organize information

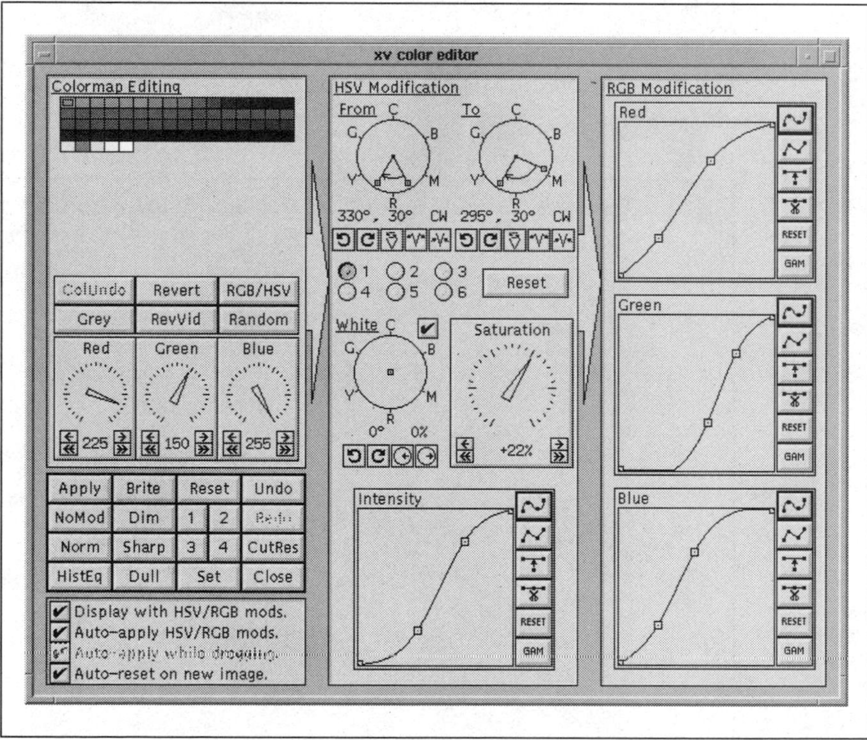

Figure 2-6. Applications for monitoring data

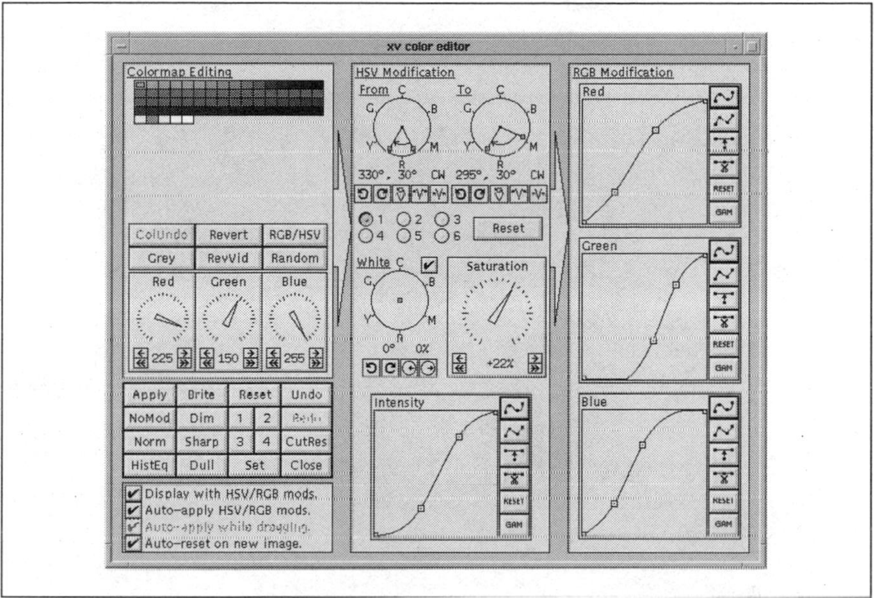

Figure 2-7. Applications for manipulating complex data

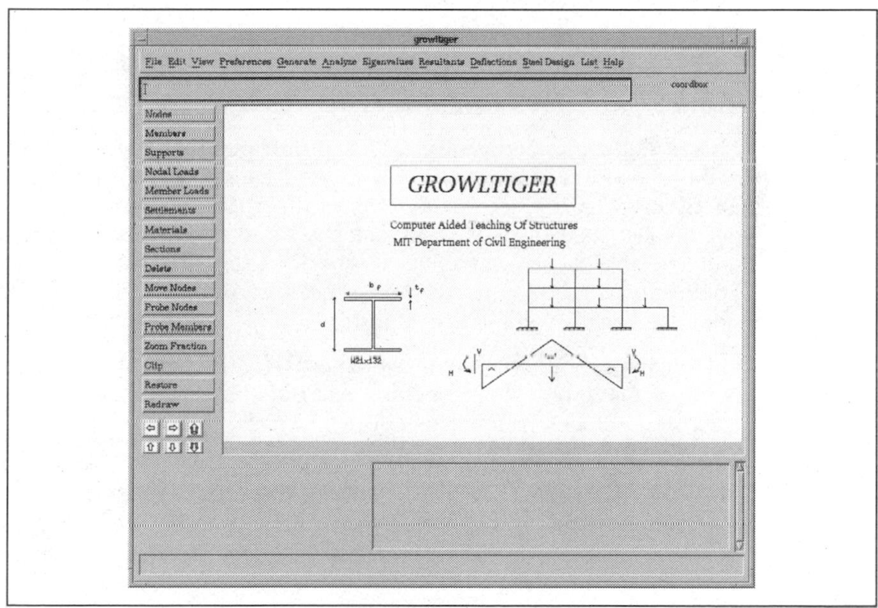

Figure 2-8. Applications that teach

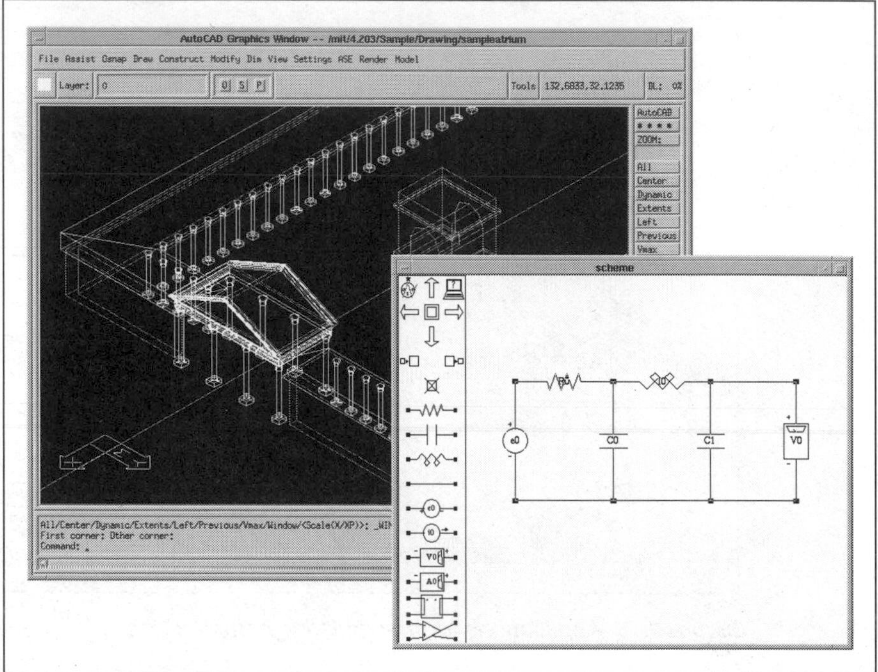

Figure 2-9. Applications for design

2.6.3 What Is the Frequency of the Task?

This is not a comprehensive list of all the possible types of tasks you might want to perform in your application, but it is a good starting point for thinking about just what the important parts of the application are. Don't think of your task as just "text display" if, in fact, the more salient features are its searching and selective display capabilities. And don't start designing a data visualization application if the systems modeling metaphors come closer to describing what your users really want to accomplish.

Once you've thought about these patterns, try to come up with a succinct statement of the problem, mentioning each of the salient task patterns. This will force you to focus your design effort.

If you can come up with such a problem statement, then you can begin thinking about existing applications that you can use as models, or even find commercially available widgets that you can build upon. Sometimes, though, you may not be able to come up with a satisfactory statement of the problem. The electronic manipulation of information is a new field, and some tasks are unfamiliar and not well understood even by the users yet. In cases like this you think most deeply; here you might have to invent and experiment with your own metaphors, come up with innovative designs, develop custom widgets, and so forth.

Thinking carefully about how often the task is performed by your users will give you important information about the usage patterns you can expect for the application, which will affect all aspects of your design. I think it is useful to distinguish four different frequency levels of interaction.

Continuous Tasks
These are tasks that the user will be doing all day. Order-entry systems and airline travel reservation systems are examples. You can expect users to learn the application's features inside and out and you can expect their employers to be willing to take the time to train them well. It is these applications where you must be most careful about user-friendly design, however. You may want to do things like analyze your keyboard-command structure for its keystroke efficiency, for example.

Frequent Tasks
These are tasks that the user will perform often, like reading electronic mail, or composing a letter, perhaps. Your application must be efficient enough and pleasant enough for frequent use, but you cannot assume that all your users will be experts—you must take care to provide options (online help, pulldown menus for browsing) for novices.

Occasional Tasks
These are tasks that the user may only have to do once a week or so. An example, in a small organization, might be the process of adding a new user to the system. Here you can assume that all your users will be novices, and your purpose is not to help the users accomplish their task quickly, but to enable them to accomplish it easily. Keyboard shortcuts and power features may be sacrificed in favor of a more intuitive, self-documenting interface.

Background Tasks
Some tasks, finally, never really occupy the foreground of the user's attention. One of a user's background "tasks" might be to monitor the passage of time. A clock program fulfills this task; it runs continuously, but never requires any interaction with the user. A window manager is another kind of background application. It does require the user to interact with it occasionally, but should never distract the user, or require his full attention—moving windows around must be simple enough that it is thoroughly transparent, something the user can do with only a "background" awareness.

Deciding the frequency of the task and following through its implications is one of the basic steps towards designing an application that will address the user's needs. Take the time to think about this issue, and then take the time to write down the design decisions that result from your analysis.

2.6.4 What Kind of Interaction Is Required

Another related question concerns the nature of the interaction between human and computer that is required by the task. In the previous section, we've considered whether the user will be interacting with your application continuously, frequently, occasionally, or only in the background. It is also important to think about the *style* of that interaction:

Who's in control?
In some applications, the user asks the application for information and gets it. A database query application works this way, for example. In others, the user asks the application to do something, and then must provide input to the application so that it can do it. A tool that helped a system administrator create new user accounts on a system, for example, can do the necessary file manipulations easily, but first the system administrator must answer a lot of questions about the user's name, preferred shell, and so forth. A third style of interaction puts the computer firmly in control—it is not only asking the questions, but also deciding what questions are going to be asked. This is obviously an interaction style to avoid if you want the user to feel involved in the process.

Is the task a single repetitive one?
Some applications do the same thing over and over again. Computers are good at this. But for an application with a graphical user interface, this means that the applications will have to perform the same interaction with the user over and over again. Usually, for this type of application, this will mean prompting the user for input, as with an order-entry system. For a task like this, you'll want to focus some design effort on things like keyboard shortcuts, macro facilities, or anything else that might optimize the interactions—even small speedups will become large when repeated many times a day.

On the other hand, some tasks—the more interesting ones—are not so repetitive. In this case, the user/computer interaction is more varied, as the user moves from subtask to subtask. During some phases of the process, the user may be issuing commands to the application, and during other phases, the application may be in control, prompting the user for input. When a task is composed of a number of non-repetitive subtasks like this, we must ask other questions:

What are the dependencies between subtasks?
If a given task requires the completion of subtasks A, B, and C, think about the order these must be accomplished in. Sometimes, the application will have to enforce a particular order, guiding the user from one subtask to the next. In other cases, the order that the subtasks are performed in may not matter so much, and the application may give the user the freedom to work on the subtasks in whatever order he chooses (because of personal preference, or whim, or because the information he currently has available only allows him to work on portions of the task). An application like this will allow a more flexible style of work.

Can tasks be performed in parallel?
Some applications will not only allow users to work on subtasks in any order, but they may allow them to work on several subtasks at once (through multiple

dialog boxes, popped up at the same time, for example) or they may even allow the users to work on multiple instances of the same basic task. Our hypothetical order-entry application, for example, might allow users to have multiple pending orders in separate windows. Adding parallel-task capability is another step that will make an application more flexible and easier to work with.

Does the task proceed by incremental refinement?
Not all tasks are either repetitive or sequential, or performed in series or parallel. Some (like this process of application design) proceed by incremental refinement—rather than completing a task by proceeding through a straight line of subtasks, the user completes the task by spiraling around it, adjusting and adding more and more details with each cycle. Tasks like circuit design can proceed this way. A word processor with a built-in outline editor might encourage a user to write technical papers in this style.

2.6.5 Is the Task Ethical?

We live in a complex world, and, as with so many undertakings, there are ethical issues to consider in application design. For example, one of the big ethical issues confronting computer engineers has always been that much of the work in the computer field is directly or indirectly done for the military. We've had to ask whether it is right, as engineers, to lend our specialized skills and devote our creative energies to the military's destructive ends. This is less of an issue in the 1990's than it was in the 60's and 70's, since computers are now ubiquitous in all industries, and are no longer almost exclusively the domain of the military. But one does not have to look hard to find destructive ends in other industries and if anything, the ethical question has only become a subtler, more complicated one.

Another big issue in past decades was the fear that computers would replace workers. Though less emphasized now, it is still worth thinking about whether your applications will put people out of work. When people are doing meaningful, interesting work, no computer will be able to replace them. The best applications aren't designed to replace people anyway; they are designed to work with people, to augment their capabilities, and you should strive to design applications like this.

You can make a good argument that any job that can be filled by a computer involves menial work that is beneath the dignity of human workers. You can also argue that computerization is an inevitable consequence of the drive towards efficiency and "competitiveness," that job loss is the price we pay for progress. Be that as it may, there are people in our current economy whose livelihood depends on these menial jobs. If your application automates a task that had been performed manually, and is not part of a larger plan of worker empowerment or job retraining, then it may well put one or more people out of a job.

These are two of the ethical issues in our field that we must each resolve on our own. I don't mean to take a personal stand on those issues here, but what I do mean to suggest is that application design should not occur in the vacuum of technical sterility. When you design an application, the most difficult questions you should ask may not be the technical ones.*

2.7 Consider the Solution

Once you've thought about your audience and the tasks they do, it is time to start designing a solution. Before you start sketching window layouts on paper, however, there are still some fundamental issues to consider that will help to target your solution accurately at the problem.

2.7.1 What Is the Scope of the Solution?

Consider the whole system of tasks that your users perform in their daily work. Even if you are only working on an application for one of those tasks, consider how your solution will fit in with the whole flow of their work. Will your application be a simple, autonomous solution that can stand alone? Will it be a larger, more complicated solution that must interact and interoperate with other applications? Will it be a basic tool, that your users will use throughout their day for many different purposes, or a more specialized tool that addresses one particular need?

There are a number of common "scope patterns" that you can consider for your application; they are described in the following paragraphs. The "scope" of an application is usually defined by three variables. The first is simply size—will the application be a small, simple one, or a large, complex one? The second is specificity—is the application a general-purpose tool or a single solution to one particular problem? The third variable is autonomy—is the user free to apply her intelligence to the problem, and use the application as a tool to enhance her intelligence, or does the application constrain this autonomy and limit the ways in which it can be used?

Tools

The "UNIX Philosophy" is an often-praised one. It holds that applications should be simple, general-purpose tools that can be used in a variety of circumstances to a variety of ends. For the experienced UNIX user, this philosophy works superbly in practice. By combining commands like *grep*, *sed*, *sort*, *uniq*,

---

*I am taking a personal stand, of course, by even raising the issues. Ethics is not a field to be confined to the classroom (on the rare occasions that it is studied there), and shunned in the workplace—I feel that it is *appropriate* and *important* to bring ethical questions into our everyday work and professional discourse and I have tried to do so in this book.

One reviewer of this book pointed out that this ethical phase of task analysis that I propose has little to do with application design and "has more to do with choice of employers." He is right. Another reviewer wrote, "Get serious.... usually the moral dimension... is moot unless you're self-employed." I don't think that this reviewer is correct—ethical concerns are never moot, and are too often inappropriately overshadowed by economic concerns. It takes courage to follow one's conscience in spite of the economic consequences that may result, but it can be done.

This book is, in large part, about the empowerment of programmers. I hope that part of that empowerment will be to help readers understand that there need not be a barrier between our professional and personal lives; that we *can* think about, and speak out about, and act upon the issues that matter to us.

and *pr*, you can perform an unlimited number of useful manipulations on text files, for example. The UNIX philosophy is a valuable one even for windowed applications. We see this kind of "tool" application in the form of "desktop accessories"—clocks, calculators, notepads, and so on.

Power Tools

The fact that there aren't more UNIX-style tools developed with graphical interfaces is because those simple tools don't need graphical interfaces. If you've already chosen a graphical interface for your application, it probably means that you have a somewhat more complicated task in mind, and a solution that is not entirely general purpose. It is still possible to take guidance from the UNIX philosophy, however. A "power tool" (to choose a term that is in vogue) is an application that, instead of performing one simple task well, performs one more complex task (or a number of related subtasks) well. *grep* searches files; it is merely a tool. *xmh* allows you to read, file, and reply to your electronic mail; it is a power tool. Power tools know their limits; they admit the existence of other applications that perform other tasks, and they have mechanisms (cut-and-paste, portable file formats) for interacting with other applications.

Monoliths

A monolithic application envelops the user and doesn't want to let him out. It assumes it is the most important (or only important) application the user is running, tries to serve as a complete work environment for the user, and sometimes takes up the user's entire screen. Since a monolithic application does not admit the possibility that a user could find other applications useful, it generally will not interact or communicate with other applications well. Monolithic applications are often leftovers from the days before windowing systems, when a user could only effectively have one application active at a time. The application RS/1 is (or was; if it is gone now, may it rest in peace) a monolith—it was a package for entering, analyzing, and graphing experimental data. It saved the numbers you entered in a proprietary format so you couldn't use them with any other plotting system, and it even implemented its own filesystem: it offered hierarchical directory names and filenames to the user, but somehow mapped all these into a single, flat directory full of files in proprietary formats and numbers instead of names.

Monolithic applications are usually, but not always, a bad choice. When you are designing an application that will serve a continuous task (as discussed in the previous section) such as order entry or airline cockpit simulation, it is legitimate to assume that your application *will* be the most important one running. Keep in mind, though, that monolithic applications must not just do one thing or a small set of related things well; they must do *all* things well. Designing and developing a good monolithic application will be much, much harder than designing and developing a "power tool" application.

Suites of Tools

The UNIX operating system has a scope at least as large as any monolithic application. What keeps it from being a monolith itself is the large number of individual tools that can be used and combined in so many ways. UNIX and the UNIX philosophy are not successful because of the individual tools that comprise it, but because together they form a comprehensive suite of tools.

The "suite of tools" pattern can often be a useful alternative to the monolithic application. I used *xmh*, with its graphical user interface, as an example of a "power tool" application. With its underlying ability to read, send, file, sort, and search mail, however, one could argue that *xmh* is a monolithic application that tries to do everything. But the underlying *MH* mail handling system is in fact implemented as a suite of separate tools—*inc* for getting new mail, *scan* for scanning the subject lines of messages, and *show* for reading individual messages, for example.

As another example, I once designed (though never built) a system for doing dual-entry bookkeeping for a small organization. Instead of designing a single application with pulldown menus and a graphical balance sheet widget, I chose a simple suite of shell scripts. They would all act on a common set of text files, each script performing a single bookkeeping function. When the bookkeeper wrote a check, for example, the shell would prompt for the check number and the amount, and record those in the checking account balance sheet, and it would also ask which budgeted account the check should be charged against—office supplies, maintenance, utilities, and so on. Another script would handle the various entries required when payment was received from a client, and another would handle making charges to a client. Other scripts would print balance summaries for all accounts and would run the balance sheets through *tbl* and *troff* to produce nicely formatted output for printing. By being able to rely on a simple file format and powerful UNIX tools like *awk* for adding columns of numbers and *tbl* for formatting those numbers nicely I would have saved myself lots of implementation effort.

Environments

Any suite of tools must run in an environment that allows them to communicate and interact with each other. In the case of UNIX tools, this environment is the shell, with its facilities for defining scripts and its handling of pipes and file redirection. In the case of my bookkeeping scripts, the environment would be this same UNIX shell, plus the file formats and directory structure that I had settled upon. For a windowed application, the environment is, loosely, the "desktop," and interclient communication facilities (like cut-and-paste and drag-and-drop) are provided on the desktop. (The "desktop" is still an evolving concept; we'll have a lot more to say about it in Part Four, *Patterns and Tools for the Desktop*.)

Because environments are themselves applications, they form another pattern, a very broad kind of application scope. You probably will not find yourself writing another UNIX shell, a window manager, or a session manager, but you may still end up using some aspects of this pattern. If you choose the "suite of tools" pattern and develop a package of interacting windowed applications, you may well also want to develop some kind of "manager" application that goes with them. This will form the "main window" or "home base" for users. It may be the application to which they return to launch other applications in the suite, or to see summaries of their work. This may not be as grand an environment as a shell or a desktop, but it does provide an environment for the user.

Also, if your suite of interacting applications handles special data types, it may need to define custom file formats or custom data-transfer formats for cut-and-paste. You would likely implement these with library routines that you would then link into each of the applications in the suite. While these implementation details are not visible to the user, the ability to share files and perform cut-and-paste is visible, and is part of the environment.

When you've thought about the scope for your application, and how it will fit in the larger context of your audience's work, make a note of your thoughts. Add these notes on application scope to the design document that you are now beginning to evolve.

2.7.2 How Will Users Relate to the Application?

The users of an application will develop a relationship with that application. As with relationships between people, this relationship will have a lot to do with trust, fidelity, and dependency. Most importantly, though, the relationship will depend on how power is shared between the user and the application, and the degree of autonomy the user is granted over his actions. The anthropomorphically named patterns below describe some of the possible "personalities" your applications can take on. Take some time to think about the personality you'd like for your application.

Assistant. Computers are good at many mechanical tasks. In any interesting (i.e., not purely mechanical) application, however, a computer cannot substitute for the analytical skills of the user. This suggests that the application should serve as an assistant, doing what it does well, under the direction of the user, and allowing the user to do the thinking. In this way, the application and the user cooperate towards the completion of their task.* The application might serve to augment the user's powers, by providing a visual representation of data, for example, but it would not attempt to perform any analysis based on that representation. Or it might analyze a set of data to compute a standard deviation, for example, but it would not then draw any conclusions based on that calculation. An "assistant" application acts as an extension of the user's senses, not as an alternative to his brain.

Sidekick. A "sidekick" is an important special case of an "assistant" application, which I've named after the Sidekick PC software from Borland that was so popular in the 1980's. At the touch of a hotkey, this package would pop up a notepad, a calculator, an address book, and other simple "accessories." This was on an operating system that did not provide windowing or multi-tasking, so this was an impressive piece of software that many people learned to love. A

*Or, in some cases, like chess-playing programs, the user and the application compete at the same task!

"sidekick" is always ready to serve—it might open itself up as an icon on the desktop, for example, or bind itself to a hotkey.

Tutor. Another kind of application is the tutor—an application that guides the user step-by-step through some process. You see this personality pattern in tutorials for word processors, for example, in tax preparation programs, and also in much educational software. This is an extremely specialized kind of software, often designed to be run once by a user, and then never used again. This pattern is useful in some very specialized circumstances—as when training novice users in the basic skills of using a mouse or a word processor.

There are some things to watch out for if you adopt this pattern, however. First, notice that it puts most of the control in the hands of the application. The only autonomous choice the user is left with, often, is to continue with the tutorial or to get up and walk away. This uneven division of autonomy between application and user can result in some pretty overbearing tutorials. One educational program I worked on had the following messages in it. I've simplified the code for clarity; the messages, unfortunately, are all for real:

```
if (get_answer() == DONE) {
    if (really_finished()) {
        printf("I don't believe it! You finally finished!\n");
    }
    else {
        printf("You're not finished yet...\n");
        printf("Do you want to be called a quitter? [y/n] ");
        if (get_answer() == YES) {
            printf("QUITTER! ...\n");
            exit(0);
        }
    }
}
```

Mercifully, the module that contained this code had been commented out and went unused. One thing that can be said for this tutorial was that it did ask the student to use his brain and solve problems, not to simply sit back and take a passive role. Only when he was done with the problems did he have to surrender his autonomy back to the application to be insulted and then perhaps guided on to the next stage of the tutorial.

Slavedriver. This is the kind of application that grants the user no autonomy whatsoever, and uses her like a machine. There are data-entry systems, for example, that will chastise a user for logging in a few minutes after the start of work, and then will monitor her typing speed all day to make sure she reaches her quota. There is really only one thing to say about systems like this: don't design them.

2.7.3 What Are the Sources of Complexity?

While thinking through the basic nature of the task, you may well have found enough similarities to existing applications that you will know right away how you want to present the task to the user—i.e., what metaphor you will choose for your application. On the other hand, you may have found that the task (or at least parts of it) is new or poorly understood, and that there are not good metaphors that are immediately obvious. In this case, you'll have to come up with one of your own.

Using a metaphor in a graphical user interface has a twofold purpose. First, it presents the task to the user in familiar terms, making the software easier to learn, and easier to use. The Macintosh, for example, was such an innovation because it did things like draw black characters on a white background so that windows looked like sheets of paper—until then computers had generally drawn white (or green or amber) characters on a black background.

The second purpose of selecting the right metaphor is a more subtle and more important one. A good metaphor will be a solution that matches the complexities of the task. For example, if the task is a difficult one because it requires the user to analyze and draw conclusions about volumes of three-dimensional data points, then probably a metaphor that allows 3D visualization of that data will be a good one.

So, as you begin to develop your design, think deeply (once again) about the user's task. Why is it a hard one? What are the sources of complexity? How can you structure your solution to attack each of those sources of complexity? Attack the complexity head-on. If you shy away from it, you can be certain that you won't actually end up simplifying anything—the complexity will slip by, and you'll be left with an application that doesn't really accomplish anything.

As technology evolves, you may come across new and difficult problems that don't have immediate solutions. What is often required in these cases are new and innovative solutions. This book cannot supply those solutions for you, but the paragraphs that follow list some common sources of complexity you might want to think about, and also some approaches you might take to attack those complexities.

As I mentioned, if the complexity of a task comes from the sheer volumes of data involved, then visualization and image processing techniques may be a good way to approach it. Selective display of data by searches or other user-defined filters may be useful, as may statistical summaries of the data.

If the problem isn't so much the quantity of the data as its abstractness (maybe it represents the design of a bridge or the names of computers on a network), then it may be useful to draw a picture of the data. If the user has to be able to manipulate this abstract data, then it would be natural to allow the user to interact with the representation of the data you've drawn.

Perhaps the data is of some type for which there is no conventional representation you can draw. Then your best approach may be to design a new representation using whatever new symbols and notation are required to capture the essential features of the data succinctly.

Sometimes the complexity is in the manipulations that the user must perform on the data. In this case you may be able to encapsulate some of this complexity by defining common high-level operations on the data, and providing these operations to the user.

Sometimes a task is difficult because there are an overwhelming number of commands, options, modes, parameters, and so on, to present to the user. If you present all of these commands and options in a graphical interface, then you will simply end up with an overwhelming interface. Instead, you should probably try to structure the options into related groups that can be handled separately. And you should probably also consider supporting a configuration file for setting options and a command-line interface for issuing commands.

If the scope of the task is broad, or if the definition of the task is open ended, then consider adding a programming language to your application. Then the user can, in effect, extend your application to suit her particular needs at the time.

If the problem isn't so much the breadth of scope, as simply the overwhelming *size* of the task, then consider designing the solution as a suite of cooperating applications. Or at least consider designing an interface that occupies many different windows, each used for a different facet of the task.

If none of these approaches is right for your application, you do still have some options. You can go back to the beginning of this chapter and start the process of analysis over again; perhaps something new will occur to you a second time through. You may want to study existing solutions, or solutions to similar problems, whether they are computerized or not. If the task is not one that is completely new with the information age, you may want to study historical approaches and solutions to it to see if there are useful techniques you can use.

If you are at a loss for a way to tackle a problem, perhaps what you need to do is switch frames of reference somehow, to find a new way of looking at it. The mathematics of orbital mechanics was very complex, for example, when everyone thought that the sun and planets revolved around the earth. By shifting frames of reference from a geocentric model to a heliocentric model, however, the mathematics was dramatically simplified.

And, if your search for a revolutionary new paradigm fails, if you are up against a problem that simply will not yield to your design efforts, then you may just have to simplify the task and reduce the scope of the solution until you have at least some part of it that you can handle.

2.7.4 What Are the Constraints on the Solution?

In the first stages of design, you should proceed with an open mind, brainstorming for ideas without limiting yourself by worrying about the constraints that will affect your design. Before you get too far down the road, however, you will have to begin to consider those constraints. This section mentions some of the common ones.

Development Time

No matter how much we'd like to be perfectionists, there are, in fact, times when a "quick hack" is the right solution to a problem. Don't spend more time on a program than will be saved by its use. And if you know that your development time will be limited, don't design in features that you won't be able to implement. Remember the saying: "You can have it good, cheap, or fast. Pick two."

Software Technologies

Your design will necessarily be limited by the libraries, widgets, and so forth that you have at your disposal. You won't be able to use tearoff menus, for example, if you are still using Motif 1.1. And if you don't have a widget for displaying pie charts and don't have the budget to buy one, then you may not want to design one into your application. (Unless, of course, you have the time to implement one yourself.)

Hardware Technologies

The hardware you are developing for will affect your design as well. Your workstation may support the X11R5 PEX server extension, and a commercial Display PostScript extension, but if your application will be deployed widely on X terminals (many of which run X11R4), then you won't want to rely on these extensions. Or if your site still has a number of ASCII terminals, then your application may have to have both X and *curses* modes of operation.

Compatibility and Portability

You may be constrained to be compatible (in look-and-feel, file formats, or otherwise) with other applications, or portable to other architectures. If your application must run under X, MS Windows, and on the Macintosh, then you will want to use only GUI components that are available on all three platforms, for example.

Stubborn Boss

And finally, you may be constrained by the opinions of those who pay you. Examine your superiors' opinions carefully before you criticize them some times they know what they're talking about. But when they don't, and when your attempts at persuasion fail to make them see the light, try to suffer them, if not gladly, then at least as gracefully as you can.

2.8 Summary: Write Your Answers Down

Application design is not a purely technical problem, but involves all sorts of issues that lie at the junction between technology and society. Many of the sections about application design in this chapter have been formulated as lists of questions to spur your thinking about these issues. I recommend that you write down your answers to these questions as an integral part of the design process.

Your writeup can be formal or informal. You might impress your colleagues with a carefully written and thoughtfully organized design document, but even if you never have to present your design to anyone, writing it down will help you organize your thoughts. I find that my clearest and most innovative thinking occurs when I'm scrawling on scratch paper—then I can draw sketches, make lists, scratch things out, make new sketches, and so on. What I end up with is still just scrawled on scratch paper, but is a valuable document of my ideas, and gets filed away in a binder I keep for this purpose.

You'll notice that nowhere in this chapter about application design did we talk about windows within an application or widgets within a window. Those design topics will come in later parts of the book, when we discuss the desktop, the main window, and dialog boxes. First, though, are a number of chapters about application *development* using the Xmt library.

Part Two

Programming Preliminaries

This part of the book introduces the various utilities and Xmt programming techniques that will be used throughout the rest of the book.

3

Displaying Text

After integers, strings are the most fundamental data type in computer applications. And in user interfaces, strings are the primary means of communicating with users: text appears in buttons and in menus; it is used to prompt, cue, and provide feedback to the user; it is used for online help and for warning messages. And for applications like word-processors, and email readers and data entry systems, text doesn't just appear in the user interface; it is also the fundamental data type manipulated by the program.

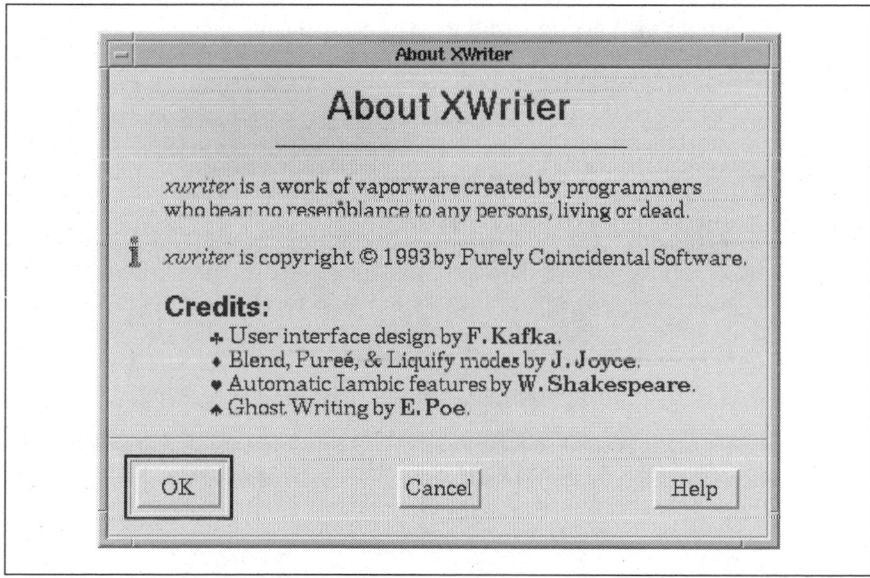

Figure 3-1. Displaying information with text

Because text display is such a fundamental part of user interfaces, Xmt has a number of utilities that can help with it. This chapter begins with a long section about the Motif `XmString` type—Xmt provides a function and resource converter that make XmStrings far less awkward to use, and that also make it very easy to display multi-font, multi-line text. (Figure 3-1 shows text displayed with a single XmString, specified using the `Xmt String-to-XmString` resource converter.)

The next section describes the Xmt `XmFontList` resource converter, and the indirect font list specifications that it allows. And the following section discusses techniques and some special Xmt functions for localizing the strings in your applications—i.e., for displaying different strings depending on the language of the user.

3.1 Simplified Strings

One of the annoying things about using XmStrings is the awkwardness of the XmString API. While `XmStringCreateLocalized()` and its Motif 1.1 equivalent, `XmStringCreateSimple()`, are very simple functions, neither can handle the multi-line strings that are necessary in message dialogs and other places. `XmStringCreateLtoR()` can handle multi-line strings, but it requires you to specify an extra argument—usually something difficult to type like `XmFONTLIST_DEFAULT_TAG`.

Furthermore, none of these functions let you create multi-font strings, which is the one really powerful feature that makes XmStrings worthwhile. To create a multi-font XmString with the Motif functions, you have to create each "component" of the string separately and concatenate them together. This is so awkward that it is rarely done in practice. The Motif XmString resource converter doesn't let you specify multi-font strings either, and this is particularly problematical because the first tenet of writing customizable and internationalizable applications is to place all strings in resource files.

Xmt addresses these problems with a function, `XmtCreateXmString()`, and a resource converter based on that function, which understand special escape sequences within the string as commands to switch fonts. The following subsections explain how this function and resource converter can make XmStrings far easier to work with.

3.1.1 Creating Multi-Line, Multi-Font XmStrings

`XmtCreateXmString()` has the same, simple signature that `XmStringCreateLocalized()` and `XmStringCreateSimple()` do:

Xmt/

XmStringCvt.c

```
#include <Xmt/Xmt.h>
XmString XmtCreateXmString(char *string)
```

XmtCreateXmString() is much more powerful than those Motif functions, however:

- Like XmStringCreateLtoR(), it recognizes the newline character (\n) in the input string and allows the creation of multi-line XmStrings. It has a simpler interface than XmStringCreateLtoR(), however.
- Unlike any of the Motif XmString functions, it allows font changes to be embedded directly in the input string, using special escape sequences. The grammar for these font-shift sequences is described below. The only way to create multi-font strings with Motif is to build them segment-by-segment, which is quite tedious.

Using XmtCreateXmString() will simplify your code, but you can simplify your applications even further by placing your strings in a resource file, wherever possible. Strings in a resource file will be automatically converted to XmStrings, and you will need never create them explicitly. The default XmString converter does not allow multi-font strings, but if you call **XmtRegisterXmStringConverter()**, you'll be able to use the Xmt XmString resource converter, which uses XmtCreateXmString() and supports the same font-shift escape sequences as that function does.

Xmt/

XmStringCvt.c

```
#include <Xmt/Converters.h>
void XmtRegisterXmStringConverter(void)
```

Fonts are specified for an XmString with font "tags"—these are short names that will be associated with an actual font in an XmFontList. Sometimes these font tags are called "charsets," because their original purpose was for internationalization—to specify the encoding of the text they were associated with. But font tags need not be limited to charsets like "ISO8859-2" and "JISX-201.1976-0"; tags like "BOLD", "ITALIC", and "BIG" are generally far more useful in most applications.

XmtCreateXmString() uses @ as its escape character.* When it sees a character sequence of the form @f[*font tag*], it will start a new component of the XmString it is building which uses the typeface specified by the tag. Thus the call:

```
message = XmtCreateXmString("This word is in @f[BOLD]boldface");
```

will create an XmString with two components, the second of which has the "charset tag" BOLD. If this XmString is drawn using an XmFontList which defines this tag to be a boldface font, then the string will indeed be displayed with one word in boldface text.

*Even though I call these embedded font-changing commands "escape sequences," they do not use the ASCII "Escape" character \033. The @ is a lot easier because it is otherwise infrequently used, and is legal in resource files.

XmtCreateXmString() also supports two alternate forms for specifying a fontface. If the name of the fontface is only one character long, you can omit the square brackets: @fB or @fI, for example. If the name of the fontface is two characters long, you can omit the closing square bracket and replace the opening bracket with an open parenthesis: @f(HB, or @f(CW, for example.* If you call XmtRegisterXmStringConverter(), then you can use this font-specification grammar in your resource files as well:

```
*dialog1.message: This word is in a @fBboldface@fR font.
*dialog2.message: This is a\n@f(HBmultiple-line@fR\nmessage.
```

This example assumes, of course, that there is an applicable XmFontList that defines the B, R, and HB font tags (it would probably define them to be bold, roman, and Helvetica bold fonts). Notice that you can create multi-line XmStrings simply by including the \n newline character in the string. Also, note that the @ character, as with most escape characters, can be inserted literally into a string by doubling it. That is, if you want an @ character to actually appear in an XmString created by XmtCreateXmString(), you should type @@.

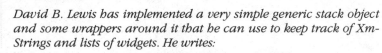

Managing XmStrings

David B. Lewis has implemented a very simple generic stack object and some wrappers around it that he can use to keep track of XmStrings and lists of widgets. He writes:

Motif code that creates an XmLabel, XmPushButton, XmMessageBox, or other objects that use XmStrings typically declares several XmString variables, assigns those variables from converted text strings, and uses them in set-values requests; the application programmer typically declares as few as possible and then is very careful about freeing each after usage, often leading to incorrect sequencing or leaks. You can alternatively create a small local stack, create the strings in-line, and then free them in a single batch. You can also use a stack to keep track of sibling widgets so that they can be managed in a single batch. You trade off time and memory usage for readability and maintenance.

This excerpt from the *Stack.h* header file shows how these stacks work:

```
extern Stack *InitStack(void);
extern void FreeStack (Stack *stack);
extern XtArgVal PushStack (Stack *stack,XtArgVal value);

#define PopStack(stack)          ((stack)->data[--((stack)->top)])
#define StackIsEmpty(stack)      (0==(stack)->top)
#define StackSize(stack)         ((stack)->top)
```

*Those who have used the *troff* text formatter will recognize these escape sequences as a variation on the *troff* font-changing escape sequences. *troff* uses the backslash as its escape character, and this would have been a natural choice for XmtCreateXmString(), except that the backslash is already used as an escape character in C and in resource files, so it would have been necessary for programmers to type a double backslash. The @ character is another somewhat common escape character, and avoids the confusion of the backslash.

Managing XmStrings (continued)

```
#define StackArray(stack)         ((stack)->data)

/* Here are some macros that use these generic functions for
 * specific purposes. */
#define PushXmString(stack, string) \
    (XmString) PushStack((stack), (XtArgVal)(string))
#define FreeXmStrings(stack)\
    while (!StackIsEmpty((stack)))
        XmStringFree((XmString)PopStack((stack)))

#define PushChild(stack, w) \
    (Widget) PushStack((stack), (XtArgVal)(w))
#define ManageChildren(stack) \
    XtManageChildren(StackArray(stack), StackSize(stack))
```

Using these functions and macros results in code like this:

```
Stack *strStack = InitStack();
Stack *kidStack = InitStack();

for(i = 0; i < XtNumber(msgs); i++) {
    XtSetArg(args[0], XmNlabelString,
             PushXmString(strStack, XmtCreateXmString(msgs[i])));
    PushChild(kidStack, XmCreatePushButton(rowcol, "", args, 1));
}

FreeXmStrings(strStack);
ManageChildren(kidStack);
FreeStack(strStack);
FreeStack(kidStack);
```

—*David B. Lewis*

3.1.2 Specifying XmFontLists with Multiple Typefaces

Any font tag used in an XmString must be mapped to an actual font in an XmFontList in order for the string to be drawn. It is possible to create an XmFontList in C code and add fonts to it, but this is rarely done—to allow customization, fonts and font lists are almost always specified in resource files.

The default Motif String-to-XmFontList converter parses a comma-separated list of *font-name=font-tag* definitions. If you plan to use bold and italic typefaces throughout your interface, you might define a default font list as shown in Example 3-1.

Example 3-1. A Default XmFontList with Bold and Italic Typefaces

```
*FontList: -*-helvetica-medium-r-*-*-*-140-*-*-*-*-*-*=R,\
           -*-helvetica-bold-r-*-*-*-140-*-*-*-*-*-*=B,\
           -*-helvetica-medium-i-*-*-*-140-*-*-*-*-*-*=I
```

It is often convenient to have all the fonts you'll need for an application collected into a single, "global" font list, and I recommend this kind of "fully loaded" font list for most applications. The resource conversion cache makes it efficient to specify this kind of resource globally—the long font list specification will only have to be converted to an XmFontList once; all other widgets will obtain the cached value of this first conversion.

Note that the first font in the font list of Example 3-1 is given the tag R. This is the roman typeface—neither bold nor italic. Since it is the first font in the list, it is also the default font, and will be used in the XmString whenever no font tag is explicitly specified, or when an undefined tag is specified.

Note: Some versions of Motif 1.2.3 were shipped with a serious bug in the XmFontList converter. What this bug does is issue a spurious warning about a missing quotation mark if any space or tab characters appear in your font list definitions. On some platforms, it will dump core instead of issuing this warning. The bug is usually not a problem when using a single font, because there is usually not any extra whitespace in single-font font list definitions. When defining multiple font tags in a font list, however, it often appears. (This bug is the result of a patch for a different bug, applied in the wrong place in the source code.)

One workaround is to remove all whitespace from your font list definitions. Another workaround is to use the Xmt extended XmFontList converter that is described later in this chapter.

3.1.3 Tricks with Multi-Font Strings

Example 3-2 shows the XmString and XmFontList that were used to create the dialog box shown at the beginning of this chapter.

Example 3-2. A Fully Loaded XmFontList and XmString

```
*FontList:\
    -*-new century schoolbook-medium-r-*-*-*-140-*-*-*-*-*-*=R,\
    -*-new century schoolbook-bold-r-*-*-*-140-*-*-*-*-*-*=B,\
    -*-new century schoolbook-medium-i-*-*-*-140-*-*-*-*-*-*=I,\
    -*-new century schoolbook-bold-r-*-*-*-180-*-*-*-*-*-*=BIG,\
    -*-new century schoolbook-medium-r-*-*-*-120-*-*-*-*-*-*=SMALL,\
    -*-new century schoolbook-medium-r-*-*-*-80-*-*-*-*-*-*=TINY,\
    -*-helvetica-bold-r-*-*-*-240-*-*-*-*-*-*=TITLE,\
    -*-helvetica-bold-r-*-*-*-180-*-*-*-*-*-*=SUBTITLE,\
    -*-symbol-medium-r-*-*-*-140-*-*-*-*-adobe-fontspecific=SY

*about.messageString: \
@f[TITLE]                     About XWriter@fR\n\
@f[TINY]                                        \
______________________________________________________________@fR\n\
\n\
@fIxwriter@fR is a work of vaporware created by programmers\n\
who bear no resemblance to any persons, living or dead.\n\
\n\
```

Example 3-2. A Fully Loaded XmFontList and XmString (continued)

```
@fIxwriter@fR is copyright \251 1993 by Purely Coincidental Software.\n\
\n\
@f[SUBTITLE]Credits:@fR\n\
         @f(SY\247@fR User interface design by @fBF. Kafka@fR.\n\
         @f(SY\250@fR Blend, Pure\351, & Liquify modes by @fBJ. Joyce@fR.\n\
         @f(SY\251@fR Automatic Iambic features by @fBW. Shakespeare@fR.\n\
         @f(SY\252@fR Ghost Writing by @fBE. Poe@fR.
```

There are a number of points to notice about the XmFontList and the XmString in this example, and there are some useful tricks here that you might want to use in your own XmStrings.

- The font list is specified with a global resource, `*FontList:`, which means that it will apply to just about every widget in the application. Also, it is a "fully loaded" font list, with every possible font face and size that the application is likely to need.
- Both the font list and the XmString are multi-line resources, and so we use the `\` character to escape the newline character at the end of each line. In the XmString, we also use the `\n` escape sequence to embed a newline character in the string. As we've seen above, this will result in line breaks in the XmString.
- The XmString uses a large Helvetica font for the title of the dialog, and another large Helvetica font for the `Credits:` subtitle. Helvetica is a sans-serif font, and works well in titles like these as a contrast to the serifs of New Century Schoolbook.
- The title of the dialog is centered simply by preceding it with spaces. The required number of spaces is determined simply by trial and error. Remember, though, that most fonts are proportionally spaced, and the space character is relatively narrow.
- Similarly, the indentation for the lines following the `Credits:` subtitle is implemented with spaces. There must be the same number of spaces, in the same font, on each line in order for them to line up on the left. Note that TAB characters will not work for centering or indentation; the Motif XmString drawing mechanisms do not interpret tabs in any special way.
- The line drawn beneath the title is implemented with a string of underscore characters, and centered, again with spaces.
- To minimize the vertical space occupied by this line, and to keep the underscores reasonably close to the title, we draw them in an 8-point font with the tag TINY. Since we do this, however, we need quite a few space characters to produce the appropriate indentation. Notice that the line of spaces in the resource file is terminated with `\`, and not with `\n\`—this simply allows us to wrap a longer line, and does not create two separate lines in the resulting string.
- The `\251` escape sequence in the string specifies the copyright symbol (©) that appears in the resulting dialog. X resource files interpret the same escape sequences that C strings do, so `\251` specifies a byte value of 251

octal. If you use the *xfd* client to view a font with the ISO8859-1 encoding, you'll see that 0251 octal corresponds to the copyright character. Similarly, the `\351` elsewhere in the string indicates the accented e that appears in the dialog.

- There are some other special characters in the "symbol" font that comes with the X distribution. We've given this font the SY tag in the font list, and the playing card symbols used in the `Credits:` section of the dialog are implemented using characters (indicated by escape sequences) from this font. Note that we explicitly specify the charset `adobe-fontspecific` for this font, instead of wildcarding it. Since there are no standards for the encodings of symbol fonts, this is so that we don't inadvertently get some other font named "symbol" with some other encoding.
- Finally, note that if you use as many fonts and special characters as we have in this example, you may end up with a dialog box just as gaudy as this one.

3.1.4 Displaying Paragraphs with XmStrings

Some programmers would find it surprising that the text in the dialog box of Example 3-2 is implemented as a single XmString. Because XmStrings are so often used in XmPushButton widgets, many programmers tend to think of XmStrings as suitable only for a single word of text in a button, or maybe a single sentence of text in a warning dialog box. When an application must display a paragraph or two of text, that text is often displayed using an XmText widget with the `XmNeditable` resource set to `False`.

In fact, however, both XmStrings and the XmLabel widget are designed to handle multi-line text, and both do so with reasonable efficiency. The XmString format is fairly compact, given the multi-font features it must support, so you can use XmStrings without worrying about wasting memory. While you obviously don't want to use an XmString to display the entire contents of a text file, for example, it is perfectly reasonable to use XmStrings of 20 lines or so. In fact, it is even possible to place a multi-line XmLabel widget within an XmScrolledWindow widget (with `XmNscrollingPolicy` set to `XmAUTOMATIC`) and have scrolled, multi-font text.

If you find that you want to display more than a few lines of text to the user, first ask yourself whether the user really wants (and needs) to read that much text in order to use the application. Then if you decide the text *is* actually important, consider using a single XmString in a single XmLabel widget to display it. The ability to use multiple fonts will make the text look much nicer than it would if displayed in an XmText widget.

3.1.5 XmStrings and Internationalization

The original design purpose of XmStrings was for internationalization—they allowed the display of strings in languages that required the use of multiple fonts. Although they are no longer necessary for this purpose, it is still valuable to understand a bit about internationalization.

A basic term in any discussion of internationalization is the *charset*. A charset is a set of characters with a standardized encoding. ISO8859-1, commonly called Latin-1, is a charset that contains all the characters used in English and most Western European languages, with an encoding that is an extension to ASCII. Some languages, notably Japanese, require characters from multiple charsets. Japanese text, for example, mixes Latin characters with characters from two different phonetic alphabets, *Katakana* and *Hiragana*, and with ideographic *Kanji* characters. Each of these types of characters has its own encoding and own charset.

In X, fonts define characters from a single charset only. If you look at the full name of a font using *xlsfonts*, you'll notice that the last two fields of the font name are the official name of the charset of the font. For most fonts in the X distribution, this charset is ISO8859-1, but there are some others, like the *Kanji* charset jisx0208.1983-0. Since a font only contains characters from a single charset, it is not possible to display Japanese text with a single font, and this is where XmStrings come in—they provide a primitive (and laborious) way to represent a string as a set of components, each component to be drawn using a different font.

The ability to display Japanese text is obviously a crucial feature for applications written in Japan, but for those applications that are not, the mechanism is simply a nuisance. It is annoying to have to convert normal (single-font) C character strings to XmStrings before displaying them in a Motif widget. I've always felt that the XmString datatype should have been designed so that a null-terminated array of characters was a legal, degenerate, case of an XmString, so that the conversion step was not required except when representing Japanese, or other languages that required more than one font.

Unfortunately, that is not the case, and we are stuck with XmStrings as they are. Interestingly, as of X11R5 and Motif 1.2, XmStrings are no longer needed for internationalization. X11R5 provides full-featured support for internationalized text display. It addresses the problem of needing multiple fonts for Japanese text by defining a new datatype, the `XFontSet`, and new text drawing routines that use the fonts contained within an `XFontSet`. Japanese text can now be represented in its natural form (the way it has always been represented in Japanese computer systems) as an array of characters, with embedded escape sequences used to indicate which charset each character comes from.

The X11R5 solution is much more general than the Motif XmString solution, and in Motif 1.2, XmStrings incorporates the X11R5 functionality: only a single "component" is now needed in an XmString to represent a Japanese string, rather than a single component for each font shift within the string. As evidence that XmStrings are no longer necessary for internationalization, consider the

Motif 1.2 XmText widget: it is now internationalized, and can display Japanese text, but does not use XmStrings.

XmString and XmFontList Changes Between Motif 1.1 and 1.2

There are a couple of fairly minor changes to the way XmStrings are handled in Motif 1.2: `XmStringCreateSimple()` has been superseded by `XmStringCreateLocalized()`, and the constant `XmSTRING_DEFAULT_CHARSET`, which was used in calls to `XmStringCreate()` and related functions, has been superseded by `XmFONTLIST_DEFAULT_TAG`.

The reasons for these changes are very subtle and are lost in the complexities of internationalization. Since XmStrings are no longer required for internationalization, however, the changes are fairly gratuitous. If you use `XmtCreateXmString()` and the Xmt resource converter, then you will not have to worry about it. Alternatively, you can write all your code using the Motif 1.2 API, and retain backward compatibility with code like this:

```
#if XmVersion <= 1001
#  define XmStringCreateLocalized XmStringCreateSimple
#  define XmFONTLIST_DEFAULT_TAG XmSTRING_DEFAULT_CHARSET
#endif
```

The Motif 1.1 function and constant continue to be defined in Motif 1.2, so your existing code should continue to work even if you take no action.

There is a new set of functions for creating XmFontLists in Motif 1.2 as well. The old API continues to be supported for backward compatibility. The new API is a cleaner one, and adds support for including the X11R5 `XFontSet` into an `XmFontList`. In practice, you will probably define all your font lists in resource files, for customizability, so these API changes will not affect you.

—*djf*

3.2 Flexible Font Lists

The X Toolkit will automatically parse the `-font` or `-fn` command-line argument, and use the value of this argument to set the `*font` resource in the resource database. This means that in applications like *xterm* and *emacs*, the user can use a single command-line argument to conveniently specify a font. This won't work with Motif applications for the obvious reason that none of the Motif font resources are named `font`. More fundamentally, however, it is rare to have an application that uses only a single font—at the very least you'll want to use different fonts to distinguish your buttons, menus, and other controls from the text in the actual work area of the application.

Still, however, it can be a tremendous convenience for the user to be able to easily specify the fonts to be used in an application. A user concerned about eyestrain might want to specify a large font, for example, and a user with a loathing for sans-serif fonts might want to override your Helvetica defaults with New Century Schoolbook. The approach to multi-font text display with XmStrings described above advocates "fully loaded" font lists, and it is really not reasonable to ask users to type such long font lists on the command line or in their personal *.Xresources* files. Instead, we'd like them to be able to use a simple command-line argument like `-fontFamily big` or a one-line resource like:

```
xwriter.fontFamily: schoolbook
```

The following sections show how you can provide this flexibility with Xmt.

3.2.1 The Xmt FontList Converter

Xmt provides its own String-to-XmFontList converter, which you can register with `XmtRegisterXmFontListConverter()`:

Xmt/

FontListCvt.c

```
#include <Xmt/Converters.h.h>
void XmtRegisterXmFontListConverter(void);
```

This converter works around the Motif 1.2.3 bug mentioned earlier, and parses the same basic XmFontList grammar that the Motif converter parses, and that we've used in the font list examples elsewhere in the chapter. For simplicity, the Xmt converter does not handle `XFontSet` elements (an internationalization feature of X11R5), so if you are using multi-charset Asian languages, you'll want to use the standard Motif 1.2 converter instead. Also, the Xmt converter doesn't allow double-quotes, as the Motif converter does, but since this feature of the Motif converter seems to be undocumented, this incompatibility should not be a serious problem.

What the new Xmt font list converter does is to handle symbolic font list names and allow the kind of font list indirection we described above. The next sections show how.

3.2.2 Symbolic Names for Font Lists

If you call `XmtRegisterXmFontListConverter()`, then you can use regular font list specifications in your resource file, or you can specify a font list with a symbolic name. A font list symbol begins with a `$` character. You might use a symbolic name like this:

```
*menubar*fontList: $menu
```

When you do this, the Xmt converter will look for a definition of the font list named "menu" in a special place in the resource file. You could define this font list with a line like the following:

```
_FontLists_*menu: *-helvetica-bold-r-*-*-*-140-*
```

All symbolic font list names are defined under this special `_FontLists_` "branch" of the resource file. This prevents the definitions from conflicting with any actual widget resources. (Unless you perversely choose to name your application *_FontLists_*, of course.)

One reason to use symbolic font names is to save yourself typing. For example, with a specification like this:

```
*menubar*fontList: $bold
*warning_dialog.fontList: $bold
```

The definition of the "bold" font list would only have to appear once in your resource file, rather than being given explicitly in specification.

The next section shows a more important reason to use symbolic names, however.

3.2.3 Font List Indirection

Notice that we defined the font list named "menu" above with a wildcard in the resource specification: `_FontLists_*menu`. A tight binding (`_FontLists_.menu`) would have worked in some circumstances, but not always. This is because the Xmt font list converter doesn't looks up symbolic names directly beneath `_FontLists_`. Instead it looks them up as:

FontLists.*family*.*language*.*territory*.*codeset*.*name*:

The components of this resource specification are as follows:

family	The value of the `fontFamily` application resource
language	The "language part" of the language string
territory	The "territory part" of the language string
codeset	The "codeset part" of the language string
name	The symbolic name of the font list. It would be "menu" in our example.

If any of the *family*, *language*, *territory*, and *codeset* components are undefined, then they are not used in the font family look up. Thus, by default, the converter will simply look for our "menu" font list as:

```
_FontLists_.menu:
```

But, if the user ran the application with the command-line argument `-xrm "*fontFamily: big"`, then the converter would look for its definition as follows:

```
_FontLists_.big.menu:
```

And if the user had first done:

```
setenv LANG French
```

then, the converter would look up the font list as:

```
_FontLists_.big.French.menu:
```

And, finally, if the user had specified a language string with a territory and codeset specification,* such as `ja_JP.pjis`, then the converter would look for:

```
_FontLists_.big.ja.JP.pjis.menu:
```

In any of these cases, our original font list definition would match:

```
_FontLists_*menu: *-helvetica-bold-r-*-*-*-140-*
```

What this extra level of indirection gives us, however, is the ability to specify font lists that depend on the setting of the `fontFamily` resource and on the user's language. For example, we might specify a default font list, and also a larger alternative that the user could select.

```
_FontLists_*menu: *-helvetica-bold-r-*-*-*-140-*
_FontLists_*big*menu: *-helvetica-bold-r-*-*-*-180-*
```

Similarly, we could specify different font lists to be used for different settings of the language string. This method is unusual: the standard approach to internationalization is to produce an entirely different resource file for each language. This technique allows us to simply provide different font lists for each language. Example 3-3 shows a more complete example of font list indirection. It shows font list specifications and definitions for an application that uses two different font lists, one symbolically named `interface` and used for buttons, menus, dialogs, and other parts of the user interface, and one named `body` and used for the main text area, the "body" of the application. The example provides default definitions of each font list, but also provides alternative definitions that the user can select by setting the `fontFamily` resource to `small` or `large`.

---

*If you don't really understand the "language string," and its language, territory and codeset parts, then you probably aren't doing internationalization, and can ignore them. For the curious, however, a language string like "en_GB.iso8859-1" might mean the language English, as spoken in the territory of Great Britain, and encoded in the ISO8859-1 codeset (a.k.a. Latin-1, a superset of ASCII). Language strings are system-dependent, so you should see your vendor's documentation on internationalization for more information.

Example 3-3. Indirectly Specified Font Lists

```
!! This application uses one font list for the UI:
*FontList: $interface

!! And a different one for its main text area:
*main_text.fontList: $body

!! Here are the default definitions of these font lists:
_FontLists_*interface: \
        *-helvetica-medium-r-*-*-*-140-*=R,\
        *-helvetica-medium-i-*-*-*-140-*=I,\
        *-helvetica-bold-r-*-*-*-140-*=B

_FontLists_*body: *-times-medium-r-*-*-*-140-*

!! and here are definitions for small and large versions
_FontLists_*small*interface: \
        *-helvetica-medium-r-*-*-*-120-*=R,\
        *-helvetica-medium-i-*-*-*-120-*=I,\
        *-helvetica-bold-r-*-*-*-120-*=B

_FontLists_*small*body: *-times-medium-r-*-*-*-120-*

_FontLists_*large*interface: \
        *-helvetica-medium-r-*-*-*-180-*=R,\
        *-helvetica-medium-i-*-*-*-180-*=I,\
        *-helvetica-bold-r-*-*-*-180-*=B

_FontLists_*large*body: *-times-medium-r-*-*-*-180-*
```

Our examples look up a font list based, in part, on the `fontFamily` resource, which the user can specify in a personal *.Xresources* file, or can specify with an *-xrm* command-line argument. If you call `XmtParseCommandLine()`, as described in Chapter 7, *Application Resources and Command-Line Arguments*, however, then the user will also be able to specify this resource with the `-fontFamily` command-line argument.

We've accomplished what we set out to. Just as a user can easily specify a font for *xterm* with the `-font` argument, she can easily specify a set of fonts for a more complicated application with the `-fontFamily` argument:

```
xmail -fontFamily large
```

Font List Resources and Inheritance

In this chapter we've recommended using a single "fully loaded" font list everywhere in your interface. You can specify such a font list with a wildcarded resource specification of the form `*FontList: $loaded`. This is an easy approach, but in practice, you may need to use more than a single font list specification, and there are also subtler ways to specify font lists that you should be aware of.

When a font list resource is not specified for a Motif widget, its value is inherited from an ancestor. If a Motif label, button (push button, toggle button, or cascade button), or text widget does not have its `XmNfontList` resource set,

Font List Resources and Inheritance (continued)

the value for that resource will be inherited from its nearest XmBulletinBoard, Motif VendorShell, or XmMenuShell ancestor. The XmBulletinBoard supports three default font lists for different kinds of children: `XmNbuttonFontList`, `XmNlabelFontList`, and `XmNtextFontList`. In Motif 1.1, the VendorShell and XmMenuShell have an `XmNdefaultFontList` resource that is used for all font list inheritance. In Motif 1.2, these shells also have `XmNbuttonFontList`, and `XmNlabelFontList` resources that will be used in place of the `XmNdefaultFontList` resource, if they are set. In Motif 1.2, the VendorShell widget also has an `XmNtextFontList` resource; the MenuShell widget doesn't have this resource, since menus never have text widget children.

Note that if these XmBulletinBoard, VendorShell, and XmMenuShell font list resources are not set, then they themselves will be inherited from the nearest bulletin board or shell ancestor. What this confusing web of inheritance relationships comes down to is that you can replace a specification like:

```
*FontList: $loaded
```

and achieve the same effect with:

```
xwriter.defaultFontList: $loaded
```

The latter specification is a little more elegant to use in a resource file, and probably a little more efficient. (It would be a lot more efficient, if Xt wasn't so good at caching converted resource values.) Although they are only a little more elegant and efficient, what is really valuable about these default font list resources is that they are not so "heavy-handed" as global wildcards are, and let you easily specify different font lists for different types of widgets. Consider the following:

```
xwriter.defaultFontList: \
        *-helvetica-medium-r-*-*-*-140-*=R,\
        *-helvetica-medium-i-*-*-*-140-*=I,\
        *-helvetica-bold-r-*-*-*-140-*=B
xwriter.textFontList: *-times-medium-r-*-*-*-140-*
xwriter.buttonFontList: *-helvetica-bold-r-*-*-*-140-*
```

This example supplies a "loaded" default font list, which will be useful for multi-font messages in dialog boxes, for example. But it overrides the default in a couple of cases. First, since XmText widgets can only display a single font, there is no point in specifying a complex for list for that widget. And second, suppose we want to use a bold font for all the buttons in an interface. Since the default font in the default font list is not bold, it is easier and more efficient to specify the `XmNbuttonFontList` resource than it is to add the `@fB` escape sequence to every button label you want to display.

Note that these default font list resources *are* only defaults, and will be ignored if a font list resource is give for a widget with a direct specification, or with a

Font List Resources and Inheritance (continued)

wildcard. Thus, if you wanted to use a smaller font for buttons in dialog boxes, you could specify:

```
*XmDialogShell*XmPushButton.fontList: *-helvetica-bold-r-*-*-*-120-*
```

Though of course, you could just use the default button font list for all dialogs like this:

```
!! Motif 1.2 only -- use the vendor shell resource
XmDialogShell.buttonFontList: *-helvetica-bold-r-*-*-*-120-*
!! Alternative for Motif 1.1 -- set the BulletinBoard resource
XmDialogShell*buttonFontList: *-helvetica-bold-r-*-*-*-120-*
```

—*djf*

3.3 Localized Language

If you want your program to be used in other countries, you must make provisions to allow the strings it displays to be translated into other languages. Writing your program so that it has this capability is called *internationalization*. The process of looking up the correct strings to display at runtime is called *localization*.* If strings are to be localized at runtime, they obviously cannot be hard-coded into your application executable. One approach is to use an external database of strings known as a *message catalog*. Many systems support message catalogs with the function `catgets()`, which retrieves a numbered message from a numbered *message set* in a message catalog opened by the application. A useful feature of `catgets()` is that it allows you to specify a default message to use if no message is found in the catalog. This means that your application can run in its default language without a message catalog, but running it in another language is simply a matter of translating the message catalog.

Message catalogs and `catgets()` are not commonly used in X applications, because they have convenient access to a database of another kind—the X resource database. In X, you can internationalize your application by specifying all user-visible strings (generally the `XmNlabelString` resource for all Motif buttons and labels) in the application's app-defaults file. Then localization becomes a matter of translating the strings in a resource file. Xt has a mechanism for looking up an application's resource file depending on the requested language, so you can just install one app-defaults file for each language you

*Localization of strings is only one part of the full process of internationalization. Icons may also need to be localized, as well as such things as the format for displaying dates, times, numbers, and currency. String localization is the most important and user-visible difficult aspect, however, and the one we'll consider here. A full discussion of internationalization is beyond the scope of this book.

want your application to run in. (Chapter 6, *Managing Auxiliary Files*, will explain this in a little more detail.)

In practice, this resource database approach is not so simple as it sounds. For example, not all strings are displayed statically in a widget—you might use one XmMessageBox widget to display many different warning messages. Also, the resource database approach does not allow you to specify a default string, which is one of the most convenient features of the `catgets()` approach.

Xmt also provides facilities for the localization of strings. One kind of localization works with the Xmt simplified dialog functions that will be presented in Chapter 25, *Message Dialogs*, and Chapter 26, *Simple Input Dialogs*. These functions allow you to specify a default message to appear in the dialog box, but will also look in the resource database for a message to override it with. This is a specialized kind of localization, however. Xmt also provides a general facility for the localization of strings; it is described in the following sections.

3.3.1 Internationalizing Strings with Xmt

Xmt combines the best features of the `catgets()` and resource file approaches to internationalization in functions that allow hard-coded default values, but use the existing resource database instead of an awkward message catalog:

Xmt/

Localize.c

```
#include <Xmt/Xmt.h>
String XmtLocalize(Widget w, String default_string, String tag)
String XmtLocalize2(Widget w, String default_string,
                    String category, String tag)
```

These functions look up a localized version of the specified *`default_string`* by name, rather than by number as `catgets()` does. `XmtLocalize()` uses a single name, *`tag`*, and `XmtLocalize2()` uses an additional name, *`category`*, as well. Using this extra *`category`* name allows separate modules of an application to localize their strings without fear of name conflicts. The functions return the localized string found in the resource database, or the default string, if no localized string is found. In either case, the returned string should *not* be freed after use.

Example 3-4 shows how you might use `XmtLocalize2()`.

Example 3-4. Using XmtLocalize2()

```
XmString label;

label = XmtCreateXmString(XmtLocalize2(dialog, "Hello World!",
                                       "global_dialog", "greeting"));
```

Example 3-4. Using XmtLocalize2() (continued)

```
XtVaSetValues(dialog, XmNmessageString, label, NULL);
XmStringFree(label);
XtManageChild(dialog);
```

3.3.2 Localizing Strings with Xmt

The previous section showed how you can internationalize the strings in your application by calling `XmtLocalize()` and `XmtLocalize2()`. To make this work, of course, you must also localize your application by defining the strings named by your *`category`* and *`tag`* arguments.

Localization is done in the resource database. Defining a named localized string in the resource database is very similar to defining a symbolically named font list. `XmtLocalize()` looks up a named string by checking for this resource:

```
_Messages_.language.territory.codeset.tag
```

And `XmtLocalize2()` adds the *`category`* argument as well:

```
_Messages_.language.territory.codeset.category.tag
```

As we saw for symbolic font lists, the *`language`*, *`territory`*, and *`codeset`* components of this resource specification are the language, territory, and codeset parts of the language string, and are used only if they are defined. Thus, if no language string is set, then the call to `XmtLocalize2()` in Example 3-4 would search for a resource like this:

```
_Messages_.global_dialog.greeting: Yo, Brother!
```

And if the language string were set to "French" or "en_GB.8859-1", then `Xmt-Localize2()` would look for resources like these:

```
_Messages_.French.global_dialog.greeting: Bonjour, Tout le Monde!
_Messages_.en.GB.8859-1.global_dialog.greeting: Cheers, Everyone!
```

Xmt defines some high-level functions that do things like display dialog boxes. These functions display strings to the user, and so must be internationalized. Almost all of the strings that Xmt displays in this way can be overridden with widget resources in the resource database. For further convenience, however, Xmt also uses `XmtLocalize2()` to look up the default values of each of these strings. Table 3-1 lists the category, tag, and default string for each of these localizations. Notice how the category name is used to identify the module in which the localization occurs.

Table 3-1. String Localizations in Xmt

Category	Tag	Default String
XmtAskForBoolean	cancel	Cancel
XmtAskForBoolean	help	Help
XmtAskForBoolean	no	No
XmtAskForBoolean	title	Question
XmtAskForBoolean	yes	Yes
XmtAskForDouble	badInput	Please enter a number.
aXmtAskForDouble	title	Enter a Number
XmtAskForFile	prompt	Selection
XmtAskForFile	title	Select a File
XmtAskForInteger	badInput	Please enter an integer.
XmtAskForInteger	title	Enter an Integer
XmtAskForInteger	tooBig	Please enter a smaller number.
XmtAskForInteger	tooSmall	Please enter a larger number.
XmtAskForItem	noMatch	Please select an item that appears \non the list.
XmtAskForItem	title	Select an Item
XmtAskForString	title	Enter a String
XmtCli	pageString	-- Press Space-bar for More --
XmtDisplayMessage	errorTitle	Error
XmtDisplayMessage	helpTitle	Help

Table 3-1. String Localizations in Xmt (continued)

Category	Tag	Default String
XmtDisplayMessage	messageTitle	Message
XmtDisplayMessage	warningTitle	Warning
XmtDisplayWorkingDialog	scaleLabel	% Complete:
XmtDisplayWorkingDialog	stop	Stop
XmtDisplayWorkingDialog	title	Working
XmtHelpBox	ok	Okay
XmtHelpDisplayContextHelp	dialogTitle	Help On Context
XmtHelpDisplayContextHelp	helpTitle	Context Help
XmtHelpDisplayContextHelp	noHelp	There is no help available there.
XmtWorkingBox	scaleLabel	% Complete:
XmtWorkingBox	stop	Stop

3.3.3 Localizing an Xmt Application

If you want to localize an Xmt application to display strings in a different language, your first step will probably be to translate some of the default strings shown in Table 3-1 and defined localized versions of them.

If the application was written by someone else, then you can look through the source code or the documentation to find out what other strings you can localize in this way. Or, if you can't find this information that way, then you can set the `XMTDEBUGLOOKUP` environment variable and run the application again. Unless you are using a version of the Xmt library compiled with the `-DNDEBUG` flag, setting this environment variable makes Xmt print a message each time `XmtLocalize()` or `XmtLocalize2()` looks in the database to find a localized version of a string. The output you see might look something like this:

```
harmony:107> setenv XMTDEBUGLOOKUP
harmony:108> mockup demo
Looking for: _Messages_.XmtWorkingBox.scaleLabel
Looking for: _Messages_.XmtWorkingBox.stop
Looking for: _Messages_.XmtCli.pageString
```

You can use this output to help you define localized versions of the strings. Note that the XMTDEBUGLOOKUP environment variable will also cause messages to be printed when the application looks up named font lists and also, as we'll see in later chapters, when it looks up named color tables, bitmaps, and pixmaps.

3.3.4 Localized Strings with the XmString Converter

Finally, there is one further feature of the Xmt XmString converter that we can now describe. As explained above, the XmString converter is based on XmtCreateXmString(). What was not mentioned earlier is that it can also use XmtLocalize() and XmtLocalize2().

If the first two characters of a string passed to the Xmt XmString converter are @[(note, not @f[as would be used for a font-changing sequence), then the converter uses the string in square brackets as the tag or as the category and tag in a localization call, and uses everything after the square brackets as the default string. For example, specifying this resource:

```
dialog.messageString: @[greeting]Hello, World!
```

is like using XmtLocalize() and XmtCreateXmString():

```
message = XmtCreateXmString(XmtLocalize(dialog, "Hello, World!",
                                        "greeting"));
```

Further, specifying this resource:

```
dialog.messageString: @[global.greeting]Hello, World!
```

is like using XmtLocalize2() and XmtCreateXmString():

```
message = XmtCreateXmString(XmtLocalize2(dialog, "Hello, World!",
                                         "global", "greeting"));
```

This feature of the XmString converter is valuable because it means that you can localize *all* of the strings in your interface, not just those coded in C. It also means that you don't have to localize strings by replacing widget resources scattered throughout the resource file. Instead, you can simply override the strings in those resources with a list of translated strings neatly grouped under the _Messages_ "branch" of the database.

Note that XmtLocalize(), XmtLocalize2(), and the localization capability of the XmString converter allow you to define localized strings for any number of languages in the same resource file. There is no need to install a separate resource file for each desired language. However, if the application uses a lot of strings, then it may in fact be more efficient to use separate files for each language.

3.4 Style

Just because it is easy to use multiple typefaces in an interface doesn't mean it is always a good idea. The advent of bit-mapped graphics and laser printers has led to a lot of abuses of multi-font text and has resulted in documents and user interfaces that look confusing and have no unity. As mentioned above, you'll want to allow your application's fonts to be customizable through the app-defaults file. This does not mean, however, that you should ignore the choice of fonts and leave them entirely to the user—you are still responsible for the typographic design of your application and a good set of default fonts. Typography is a whole field of study in its own right, but here are a few basic rules of thumb that will keep your applications looking good.

- Choose a font family and use it throughout your interface. This will give an important sense of uniformity to the application. Alternatively, choose one font family for use in all buttons, menus, captions, and so forth, and choose a different font family for text that appears in the main work area of the window. This distinguishes text that is part of the interface from text that is part of the user's data. New Century Schoolbook is a clean font, and is easy to read, even at the resolution of computer monitors. Helvetica is another good choice; it is not nearly so wide as Schoolbook, so you can fit more text horizontally, into buttons, etc.
- Use a large default font. Many programmers like to cram lots of windows onto their screens by using tiny fonts, but users often prefer not to have to squint. I recommend a 14-point font as the default for most applications. If the user wants something smaller or larger, it is easy enough to change through a resource file.
- Be sparing in your use of different typefaces and font families; they are good for emphasizing individual words or short phrases, but overused, they just make an interface look cluttered. Use bold and italic for emphasis in multi-line text, such as a paragraph of explanation in a help dialog, for example, but don't use them in short pieces of text, such as would appear in buttons. Bear in mind that italic text can be difficult to read at typical computer monitor resolutions.
- A sans-serif font like Helvetica contrasts nicely with serif fonts like Times and New Century Schoolbook, and can be used with good effect in titles, and to highlight certain types of words. In an online help system, for example, you might use Helvetica to refer to pieces of the interface itself ("Pull down the File menu and select the Save As item."). This choice makes particular sense if you've chosen the Helvetica family for all the labels and buttons in the interface. Mixing font families in this way is reasonable, if done in moderation.

3.5 Summary

This chapter has explained how you can use multi-font XmStrings more easily, how you can allow easy user customization of font lists, and how you can allow the strings in your application to be localized:

- `XmtCreateXmString()` makes it quite easy to create multi-font XmStrings—simply embed escape sequences like `@fB`, `@f(HB`, and `@f[BIG]` into your strings.
- By calling `XmtRegisterXmStringConverter()` you can register a resource converter for XmStrings that allows you to use these font-changing escape sequences in resource files.
- Associate the font tags specified in these escape sequences with actual fonts through an XmFontList. Try to use one or a just few "fully loaded" global font lists, instead of specifying a font list for each widget.
- XmStrings and the XmLabel widget are suitable for paragraph-length text, and the multi-font capability makes a paragraph of text in an XmLabel widget more attractive than the same text in an XmText widget.
- Motif XmStrings have very little to do with internationalization. They are good for incorporating text with multiple typefaces into an application.
- The XmString API changed between Motif 1.1 and Motif 1.2, but the changes are easy to work around.
- Use multiple fonts for emphasis, particularly in long strings of text, but don't overuse them.
- Call `XmtRegisterXmFontListConverter()` to register the Xmt font list converter, which supports symbolic font names, defined under the `_FontLists_` "branch" of the resource database.
- If you use symbolic font names, and provide appropriate definitions for them, you can allow the user to choose a base font size or family for your application with the `-fontFamily` resource.
- `XmtLocalize()` and `XmtLocalize2()` allow you to look up localized versions of strings by name, under the `_Messages_` branch of the resource database.
- If a string begins with `@[`, the Xmt XmString converter will attempt to localize it before converting it.

4

Using Color

Adding color to your applications is an important way to add visual interest to the user interface. Color can also make it easier for the user to interpret the data your application displays. This chapter describes both these decorative and data-display uses of color. It begins with a description of the simplified color-handling facilities provided by Xmt. This first section is followed by a discussion of specific techniques for use with decorative and data display colors. The chapter concludes with some important style tips—how to choose colors that enhance your application and do not simply distract the user.

Color in X

A color in X is often referred to as a *pixel*. In this usage the term does not mean "a dot on the screen," as it usually does, but instead, "the bit pattern stored in screen memory in order to specify the color of a particular dot on the screen."

A pixel is a 32-bit quantity—`unsigned long` in Xlib, or type `Pixel` in Xt. The *depth* of a screen indicates how many of those bits are actually significant. A monochrome screen has a depth of one bit, for example, and only one bit in each pixel value is significant—there are two possible colors, which have pixel values 0 and 1. Many color displays are eight bit planes deep, which means that they can display 256 colors at a time.

The interpretation of a particular pixel value depends on the *visual* of the window that is drawn into. In a `TrueColor` visual, for example, the pixel value directly specifies the red, green, and blue components of the desired color, and in a `StaticGray` visual, the pixel value directly specifies which of a number of fixed levels of gray to display. (Monochrome screens are a type of `StaticGray` visual.)

More commonly, though, the interpretation of a pixel value will also depend on entries in a *colormap*. The most commonly used visual type is probably `PseudoColor`. In this visual, a pixel value refers to a "color cell" in a colormap.

Color in X (continued)

The colormap entry defines the actual color to appear on the screen, and the programmer is able to modify the red, green, and blue levels specified in the colormap. In a `PseudoColor` visual with a depth of eight bits, there are 256 entries in a colormap.

Different hardware will support different types of visuals. Xlib does an effective job of hiding the differences between the color models in the way it makes you allocate colors. If the visual type allows the colormap to be modified, then `XAllocColor()` and related color allocation functions will allocate one color cell in the colormap and set your requested color values in it. If the visual type does not allow modifications to the colormap, then these functions will return the pixel value that produces the color closest to the one you requested.

Colors can be specified at the Xlib level in an `XColor` structure, and allocated with `XAllocColor()`, or can be specified by name and allocated with `XAllocNamedColor()`. In X11R5, the new Xcms functions allow the allocation of colors specified through device-independent color spaces. At the Xt level, it is easiest to specify colors by name in a resource file and have resource converters handle the allocation. To convert a color explicitly, though, you might invoke a resource converter with `XtConvertAndStore()`, or force a conversion in a call to `XtVaSetValues()` by using an `XtVaTypedArg` resource specification.

Pixels allocated by any of these techniques are read-only—once allocated you are not allowed to change the red, green, and blue values they represent. Since most color displays only support 256 colors, read-only colors are important so that multiple applications can share the same colors. For visual types that allow changes to the colormap, however, it is also possible to allocate private color cells in the colormap, and the colors associated with these private pixel values can be changed at any time.

Color in X is a tricky topic. For a detailed explanation, see Volume One, *Xlib Programming Manual*, from O'Reilly & Associates.

—djf

4.1 The Xmt Color Converter

The Xlib functions `XAllocNamedColor()` and `XParseColor()`, and the standard Xt String-to-Pixel resource converter can parse a few standard forms of color specifications:

- Color names known to the X server. These names are often listed in */usr/lib/X11/rgb.txt*, and include standard colors like "red" and "navy" and also unusual ones like "papaya whip."

- Hexadecimal color specifications, which begin with the character #, and are followed by 3, 6, 9, or 12 hexadecimal digits, which are 1, 2, 3, or 4 digits of red, green, and blue, respectively. If the red, green, and blue values don't have the full four hexadecimal digits, then zeroes are added on the end. Thus the color `#abcdef` is the same as `#ab00cd00ef00`. This is a red component of 0xab00, a blue component of 0xcd00, and a green component of 0xef00. The maximum value for each component is 0xffff, of course.
- Xcms color specifications, in X11R5 and later. These are names like `Tek-HVC:50/60/70` which specify a color space, and then the coordinates of a color in that space. Most of the color spaces supported by Xcms are device-independent (i.e., they should look the same on different monitors), which is important for some applications. The computational overhead associated with Xcms often makes it undesirable to use this form of color specification, however.

Xmt provides its own color allocation functions and String-to-Pixel converter which support each of these standard color specification types, and also provide some additional features. You can register the Xmt converter by calling `XmtRegisterPixelConverter()`:

Xmt/

PixelCvt.c

```
#include <Xmt/Converters.h>
void XmtRegisterPixelConverter(void);
```

The sections below describe the new features of this converter, and also describe the Xmt functions you can use to allocate colors directly in your C code.

4.1.1 Color-to-Monochrome Portability

One of the difficulties of using colors in X applications is ensuring that the application will still run on monochrome systems. You won't get an error if you try to allocate the color "red" on a monochrome system—you'll just get black instead. If you try to allocate "pink," however, you'll probably get white, because pink is closer to white than it is to black. If you choose your colors carefully you can end up with a scheme that works well both in color or in monochrome. Providing a portable application does restrict your flexibility in choice of colors, however.

The standard solution to the portability problem is to provide two different app-defaults files for your application, one for use with color and one with monochrome systems. In X11R5, the `customization` application resource makes this solution more feasible, but handling two app-defaults files is a configuration headache for a system administrator.

Xmt's solution is to make the String-to-Pixel converter aware of monochrome systems, and to extend the color specification syntax to distinguish background colors from foreground colors. If a color name begins with a `-`, this tells the converter that it is intended as a background color. If it begins with a `+`, then it is a foreground color. On color and grayscale systems, these characters are simply discarded, and the rest of the color specification is parsed as normal. On monochrome systems, however, the converter discards the rest of the color specification and simply returns the background or the foreground color. If a color specification does not begin with a `-` or a `+`, then it will be allocated on a monochrome system just as it would be allocated on a color system, and the result will depend on the lightness or the darkness of the color.

Motif's monochrome default colors are a black foreground on a white background. You can override these by setting the Xmt `foreground` and `background` application resources, and you can swap the values by setting the `reverseVideo` application resource, or by using the `-rv` command-line argument.

These foreground and background "fallbacks" will not solve all your monochrome portability problems—in some places you may want to use stipples to simulate shades of gray, for example—but it is still a good idea to get in the habit of using them. Then you know that the color `+red` will be treated as a foreground color on a monochrome system, even if the user is using white on black instead of black on white.

4.1.2 HSL Color Specifications

The # hexadecimal color specifications we saw earlier provide a way to directly specify the red, green, and blue values of the color you want. In general, though, the RGB (red, green, blue) color space is not an intuitive or useful one. If you know the color you want, trying to figure out how to match it in RGB coordinates is basically a matter of trial and error. If you want to take an RGB color and make it darker, you'll have to reduce each of the red, green, and blue components, but not all by the same amount. And if you have one color, and want to compute its complementary color (green is the complement of red, for example, and orange is the complement of blue) there is no easy way to do this in the RGB color space.

In X11R5, Xcms provides alternatives to the RGB color space, but as we've noted earlier, they can be computationally expensive. Xmt supports a simpler alternative, the HSL (hue, saturation, lightness) color space. HSL is an easier color space to use, because it describes colors in the same way that we tend to think about them. *Hue* is the basic family of the color—there are many different shades of red, for example, but they all have the same basic hue. *Saturation* measures the purity of a color—a fully saturated red, for example, is pure red. A less saturated red will have amounts of blue and green mixed in. The grays have equal amounts of each of red, green, and blue, and are not saturated at all. "Chroma" is sometimes used to mean the same basic thing as saturation. Other words used to describe the saturation of a color are vibrancy and intensity. Finally, *lightness* describes how much white or black is mixed in with a color. As you can see, describing colors in this HSL color space makes it easier to manipulate them—to make a color lighter, increase its lightness; to make it grayer, decrease its saturation.

The RGB color space in X is measured in standard three-dimensional coordinates, with each of the R, G, and B axes running from 0 to 65,535 (though most hardware does not actually support this many distinct levels of each color component); it is a cube. The HSL space supported by Xmt differs significantly—it is measured in cylindrical coordinates, and looks like two cones, placed base to base. Hue is the angular coordinate; its value varies from 0 to 359 (HSL is implemented with integers only in Xmt), and a Hue of 360 is equivalent to a Hue of 0. Complementary colors are separated from each other by 180 degrees. Lightness is the coordinate in the Z dimension, and varies between 0 and 100. At a Lightness of zero, there is only one color: black. At a Lightness of 100, the only color is white. These two points are the tips of the two cones that make up the color space. Saturation is the radial coordinate—it also varies between 0 and 100. Any color with a Saturation of 0 is a shade of gray (the shade depends on the Lightness, and Hue is irrelevant). A color with a Saturation of 100 is a pure color. Note that a color with a Saturation of 100 must have a Lightness of 50—if you think about the double-cone geometry it becomes clear why this must be. See Figure 4-1 for a clearer view of the space.

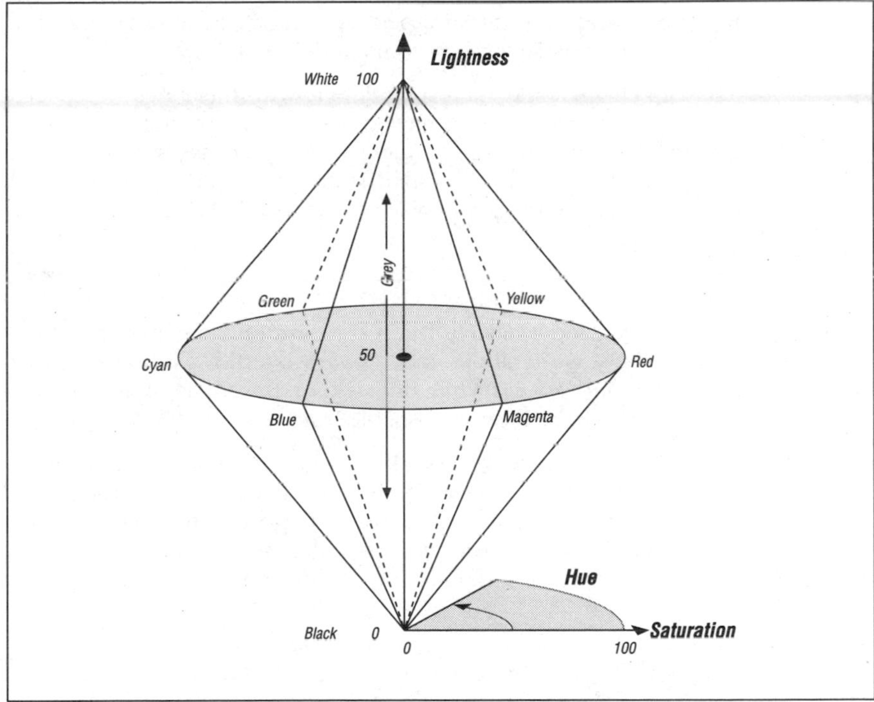

Figure 4-1. The HSL color space

4.1.2.1 HSL Color Specification Syntax

The Xmt Pixel converter and color allocation functions recognize a color specification beginning with `%` as an HSL color. (If you use the foreground and background fallbacks described above, then an HSL color will begin `+%` or `-%`, of course.) The rest of the string is composed of the Hue, Saturation, and Lightness, expressed as decimal integers, and separated by a `/`. Here are some valid specifications:

`%30/60/40`	*A dark shade of orange*
`-%30/60/60`	*A lighter, background, shade of the same basic color*
`+%210/60/40`	*A complementary, foreground color*

4.1.2.2 Relative HSL Color Specifications

There's another twist to Xmt HSL color specification—colors may be relative as well as absolute. If any of the Hue, Saturation, or Lightness values are preceded by a `+` or a `-`, then those values are relative amounts to be added or subtracted from a base color. If the color specification begins with a `%` or a `-%`, then these relative specifications are added to those of the application's background color. If the color specification begins with `+%`, then they are added to the application's foreground color. Recall that the application's foreground and background colors are specified with the `foreground` and `background` application resources, and may be swapped by setting the `reverseVideo` application resource or by using the `-rv` command-line option.

You can create some interesting effects with these relative specifications. Suppose, for example, that you have one basic foreground color, but need two others for highlighting here and there. You could use specifications like these to automatically select two colors that are maximally separated in Hue from one another, but have the same basic Saturation and Lightness:

```
+%+120/+0/+0
+%-120/+0/+0
```

When computing a relative Hue value, arithmetic is performed modulo 360, so you need not worry about underflow or overflow. In this example, note that if the foreground color is white or black, or any shade of gray, then these two relative colors will be indistinguishable from it.

Another good use of relative HSL specifications is to produce variations on a background color. Using a different background color for your dialog boxes makes them stand out well, but it is important to keep the dialog box color clearly related to the main window color, so that the user knows that they are part of the same application. You can do this by varying the Saturation and/or the Lightness:

`-%+0/-20/+10`	*Produces a lighter tint of background*
`-%+0/+10/-5`	*Produces a darker shade of background*

When computing a relative Saturation or Lightness, resulting values less than 0 are rounded up to 0, and resulting values greater than 100 are rounded down to 100. Note that if the background color is white, it is not possible to produce a lighter tint. And darkening a white background like this will probably produce a reddish color, since the undefined Hue of white will generally be represented as a value of zero (but this is obviously implementation dependent).

4.1.2.3 HSL <—> RGB Conversions

If you want to manipulate and allocate HSL colors on your own in your applications, you can use these conversion routines provided by Xmt:

Xmt/

HSLtoRGB.c
RGBtoHSL.c

```
#include <Xmt/Color.h>
void
XmtHSLToRGB(unsigned h, unsigned s, unsigned l,
                    unsigned *r, unsigned *g, unsigned *b);
void XmtRGBToHSL(unsigned r, unsigned g, unsigned b,
                    unsigned *h, unsigned *s, unsigned *l);
```

4.1.3 Symbolic Color Names

The final important difference between the Xt and Xmt Pixel converters (and color allocation functions) is that the Xmt converter and functions support *symbolic colors.* Any color name that begins with a `$` (or, if you are using foreground/background fallbacks, any name beginning with `+$` or `-$`) will be looked up in a special *color table* which maps symbolic color names to actual color names or color specifications.

Color tables are implemented with the `XmtColorTable` data type. Xmt includes functions for creating color tables, registering colors in them, and then looking up colors by their symbolic names. Most commonly, though, you will specify color tables in a resource file (using the Xmt String-to-XmtColorTable resource converter).

When the Xmt String-to-Pixel converter needs to look up a symbolic color, it uses the color table specified on the `colorTable` application resource. Example 4-1 shows how you can specify a color table on this resource, and also shows how you can specify symbolic colors that refer to that color table.

Example 4-1. Specifying a Color Table and Symbolic Colors

```
!!
!! Define three application resources: the foreground and background colors
!! used for relative HSL color specifications, and the application color table.
!! The foreground and background colors will automatically be inserted
!! in the color table, so they can be referenced as symbolic colors as well.
!! Note the X11R5 '?' wildcard that allows these to be easily overridden from
!! the command line.
!!
?.background: gray
?.foreground: maroon
?.colorTable: \
```

Example 4-1. Specifying a Color Table and Symbolic Colors (continued)

```
        menu_bg   = "-%+0/+0/-10",   \
        menu_fg   = "$foreground", \
        dialog_bg = "$menu_bg",    \
        highlight = "+%+180/+0/+0"

!!
!! Now set the colors of all descendants of the menu bar, and
!! all descendants of any dialog shell.  Also, give all Help buttons
!! (by convention they are all named 'help') the highlight foreground
!! color to make them stand out.
!!
*menubar*Background: $menu_bg
*menubar*Foreground: $menu_fg
*XmDialogShell*Background: $dialog_bg
*help.foreground: $highlight
```

The advantage to defining symbolic colors in a color table as shown in the example is that it gives you (or your users) a single resource to edit in order to change the color scheme used by an application. It allows you to define a palette of colors that the application will use, and groups the colors in a single place so that they are easy to modify.

We'll discuss color tables and palettes in the next section.

4.2 Color Tables and Palettes

Color tables are a convenience that allows the use of symbolic color names in your interface descriptions. And as we'll see in Chapter 5, *Using Icons*, they also provide a way to specify the colors for icons with the Xmt pixmap and bitmap converters. But most importantly, color tables define a palette of colors for your application. By placing an application's colors into a single color table, you provide an easy way to manipulate and customize those colors. The following subsections discuss color tables and palettes in detail.

4.2.1 The ColorTable Converter

Example 4-1 showed how you can specify a color table in a resource file. The color table syntax is simply a comma-separated list of specifications of the form:

```
symbolic_name = "color_name"
```

The `symbolic_name` can be any legal C identifier. It should *not* begin with `$`. The `color_name` should be enclosed in double quotes, and can be any legal Xmt color specification, including portable colors beginning with `+` or `-`, HSL colors beginning with `%`, and symbolic colors beginning with `$`. If you specify a symbolic color in a color table, the Xmt Pixel converter will look up that symbolic color recursively. You must be careful to avoid symbolic colors that refer to themselves, since this will cause an infinite loop.

To specify color tables in a resource file you must register the String-to-Xmt-ColorTable converter by calling `XmtRegisterColorTableConverter()`:

Xmt/

ColorTblCvt.c

```
#include <Xmt/Converters.h>
void XmtRegisterColorTableConverter(void);
```

4.2.2 The Default Palette

As mentioned above, the Xmt String-to-Pixel converter looks up symbolic colors in the color table specified by the `colorTable` application resource. If you do not specify this resource, then a default color table will be used. Table 4-1 lists the symbolic colors that are available in this default color table.

Table 4-1. The Default Symbolic Colors

Symbolic Color	Description
`background`	The value of the `background` application resource, or the Motif default background if this is not specified.
`foreground`	The value of the `foreground` application resource, or the Motif default foreground (which is based on the background) if this resource is not specified.
`top_shadow`	A lighter version of the background color—this is the top shadow color used by buttons and other Motif widgets.
`bottom_shadow`	A darker version of the background color—this is the bottom shadow color used by buttons and other Motif widgets.
`select`	Another dark version of the background color—this is the select color used by push buttons when they are armed, and in a few other circumstances as well.

The `$top_shadow`, `$bottom_shadow`, and `$select` symbolic colors are computed by Xmt by calling `XmGetColors()`, which is the same function Motif widgets use to determine their default colors.

A feature of the `XmtColorTable` data type is that it has a parent, which points to another `XmtColorTable`, and this feature can be used to produce a chain of color tables. When a specified symbolic color is not found in a color table, the search continues on to the parent of the color table, and on to the parent's parent, and so on up the color table chain until a definition of symbolic color is found or until a color table with no parent is reached. (This is something like the scoping of variable names in the symbol tables of some programming languages.)

Table 4-1 lists the symbolic colors defined in the default Xmt color table. If you do not specify a color table on the `colorTable` application resource, then this default color table is used. But if you do specify a color table on that resource, then this default color table will be used as its parent. What this means is that those default symbolic colors are always available for use with the Xmt Pixel converter. They comprise a default palette for all Xmt applications. You can augment this palette with your own specifications, and you can even override the definitions of the standard colors.

4.2.3 Specifying Relative and Hard-coded Palettes

Take a look at the palette shown in Example 4-2.

Example 4-2. A Palette of Relative Colors

```
*Background: gray
*Foreground: maroon
*colorTable: \
        menu_bg   = "-%+0/+0/-10",  \ A darker shade of background
        dialog_bg = "-%+20/+0/-10", \ A darker, related color
        menu_fg   = "$foreground",  \ Same as the foreground color
        highlight = "+%+180/+0/+0"    The complement of foreground
```

In this palette, all of the symbolic colors are defined either in terms of other symbolic colors, or are relative HSL colors based on the foreground or background colors. Therefore, this basic color scheme will work no matter what basic foreground and background colors the user chooses in her *.Xresources* file, or specifies with the `-fg` and `-bg` command-line arguments.

For most applications, this is a safe, useful technique that allows user customization, and almost always results in a reasonable color scheme. If you were to hard-code the menu background color, instead of using a relative specification, you could end up with colors that clashed badly when the user set the `-bg` argument. If you do want to use hard-coded colors in a palette, you should be sure to set up your resources so that the `-fg` and `-bg` resources have no effect. Example 4-3 shows how you might do this.

Example 4-3. A Palette with Hard-Coded Colors

```
!! the color table has hard-coded colors; a "hand-tuned" palette.
*colorTable: \
        main_bg   = "wheat",     \
        menu_bg   = "tan",       \
        dialog_bg = "$menu_bg",  \
        main_fg   = "navy",      \
        menu_fg   = "$main_fg",  \
        dialog_fg = "$main_fg",  \
        highlight = "maroon"

!!
!! We specify colors explicitly so that our specifications take
!! precedence over the -fg and -bg command line resources, and over
!! the *foreground and *background resources that they set.
!!
*main_window*Background: $main_bg
*main_window*Foreground: $main_fg
```

Example 4-3. A Palette with Hard-Coded Colors (continued)

```
*menubar*Background: $menu_bg
*menubar*Foreground: $menu_fg
*XmDialogShell*Background: $dialog_bg
*help.foreground: $highlight
```

4.2.4 Symbolic Color Table Names

The Xmt color table resource converter has a feature we haven't discussed yet—it can convert color tables which themselves have a symbolic name. While it may seem like we're going overboard to allow symbolic colors to be looked up in symbolic color tables, this is actually just like the situation we saw in Chapter 3, *Displaying Text*: XmStrings look up fonts by name in a font list that can itself be specified by a symbolic name. And, as we'll see, symbolic color tables are useful for some of the same reasons that symbolic font lists are.

As with symbolic font lists, symbolic color tables begin with the $ character. When the color table converter sees this character at the beginning of a color table specification, it interprets the rest of the string as the name of a color table to be looked up.

And just as font lists were looked up beneath the `_FontLists_` "branch" of the resource database, color tables are looked up beneath the `_ColorTables_` branch. Example 4-4 shows how you can define symbolic color tables and then refer to them by name.

Example 4-4. Defining and Using a Symbolic Color Table

```
!!
!! Here we define two symbolic color tables.
!!
_ColorTables_*default_table: \
        main_bg    = "wheat",     \
        menu_bg    = "tan",       \
        dialog_bg = "$menu_bg"

_ColorTables_*select_table: background = "$select"

!! And here we use one as the default color table for the application
*colorTable: $default_table

!!
!! Color tables are also useful to specify the colors to be used
!! in pixmaps.  Here we specify the same image for use with the default
!! color scheme, and with a modified scheme that gives it a darker background.
!!
mailbutton.labelPixmap: envelope
mailbutton.armPixmap: envelope : $select_table
```

The example shows one good use for symbolic color tables—the Xmt Pixmap converter, introduced in Chapter 5, uses color tables to supply symbolic color definitions for pixmaps. If you will be using the same color table for pixmaps throughout your interface, then giving that color table a symbolic name will save you typing, and make the color table easier to modify.

There is an even more important reason to use symbolic color tables, however. It is explained in the next section.

4.2.5 Letting the User Choose a Palette

We saw in Chapter 3 that the font list converter does not look up symbolic font lists directly beneath the `_FontLists_` branch of the resource database. Instead, it looks them up depending on the setting of the `fontFamily` application resource and upon the "language string." This allows you to provide different font lists for use with different languages, and also lets you give the user an easy way to select a font list.

Symbolic color tables work in a similar way. They don't need to be customized depending on the language, but they may need to be customized depending on the type of screen (color, grayscale, or monochrome) the application is being displayed on, and also depending on the number of colors available on that screen. Also, it is valuable to give the user a simple way to select color tables for an application by name. To accomplish this, the color table converter looks for symbolic color tables that most closely match a specification of this form:

`_ColorTables_.`*`visual.depth.palette.name`*

The components of this resource are the following:

`visual` — The default visual type of the screen. This will be one of the strings "color," "gray," or "monochrome."

`depth` — The default depth, in bitplanes, of the screen. This will be an integer. Typical values are 1 and 8.

`palette` — The setting of the `palette` application resource. This gives the user an easy way to choose among various color tables that you provide. If your application calls `XmtParseCommandLine()` (see Chapter 7, *Application Resources and Command-Line Arguments*), then the user can also set this resource with the *-palette* command-line argument.

`name` — The symbolic name of the desired colormap.

Example 4-5 shows how to use the various components when specifying user-selectable and screen-dependent color tables. For simplicity, the actual color table data has been omitted in this example. Notice how many of the palettes in this example can be selected by the user with the `palette` application resource of the *-palette* command-line argument.

Example 4-5. Specifying Customized Color Tables

```
!! The application's palette has the symbolic name "main".  It might also
!! use other color tables for pixmaps, but they won't be considered here.
!!
```

Example 4-5. Specifying Customized Color Tables (continued)

```
*colorTable: $main

!! This is the default value of the color table named 'main'
_ColorTables_*main:

!!
!! Here we provide some alternate versions of the color table that
!! give the application hard-coded tan, mauve, and blue color schemes.
!! The user can select these palettes with "-palette tan", "-palette mauve"
!! and so on.
!!
_ColorTables_*tan*main:
_ColorTables_*mauve*main:
_ColorTables_*blue*main:

!!
!! Rather than specifying specific, hard-coded colors, these palettes
!! could use relative HSL specifications so that they are based on the
!! foreground and background colors.  Instead of being named for the colors
!! in the palette, they are named for the way the colors are generated.
!!
_ColorTables_*shades*main:
_ColorTables_*complements*main:

!!
!! We can also specify special palettes for use on monochrome systems,
!! grayscale systems, and 4-level grayscale systems.  Note that the
!! monochrome and gray palettes can also be selected on color systems
!! with "-palette monochrome" and "-palette: gray"
!!
_ColorTables_*monochrome*main:
_ColorTables_*gray*main:
_ColorTables_.gray.2*main:

!!
!! Finally, we might defined a simplified version of the color palette
!! automatically selected on color systems with only 16 colors, and also
!! selectable by name (-palette simple) for people who like simple colors.
!!
_ColorTables_.color.4*main:
_ColorTables_*simple*main:
```

4.2.6 Palette Design

As we mentioned above, a good reason to use the `colorTable` application resource to define a palette for your application is that it will encourage you to keep all your color specifications in the same place, which will make customization much easier. The first step is to decide what parts of your interface will require special colors, and to assign those colors using symbolic names:

```
*XmDialogShell*background: $dialog_bg
*menubar*background: $menu_bg
*popup_menu*background: $menu_bg
```

A fairly simple, conservative approach like the one above is usually fine, but you could go even further and define symbolic colors for each different kind of widget in your interface, and even define colors for widget shadows:

```
*XmPushButton.background: pushbutton_bg
*XmPushButton.foreground: pushbutton_fg
*XmPushButton.topShadowColor: pushbutton_ts
*XmPushButton.bottomShadowColor: pushbutton_bs
```

Another approach, not quite so mechanical as the last, is to assign colors in the interface based not on widget class, but on widget function. For example, you might use special colors to indicate buttons that supply help, or widgets that you should type into.

```
*help.foreground: help_fg
*XmtInputField.background: input_color
*XmTextField.background: input_color
```

The second step in designing a palette for your application is to map this list of symbolic colors to actual colors through the `colorTable` resource. Note that many of the symbolic colors you define might map to the same actual color in this palette.

```
*colorTable: \
        dialog_bg     = "-%+0/+0/-10",      \
        menu_bg       = "$dialog_bg",       \
        pushbutton_fg = "navy",             \
        pushbutton_bg = "gray",             \
        pushbutton_ts = "$top_shadow",      \
        pushbutton_bs = "$bottom_shadow",   \
                .
                .
                .
```

Setting the `colorTable` resource is merely the mechanical part of palette design. The hard part is choosing a set of colors that work harmoniously with one another. Deciding on the colors to use for an interface can be a lot like choosing colors to paint a house with—you'll want one main "body" color supplemented by one to three "trim" or accent colors for highlighting details or important parts. A conservative approach is to choose a monochromatic palette, in which the accent colors are simply lighter or darker versions of the body color. Shades of gray and other low-saturation neutral colors are useful because they blend nicely with just about any color. Other color schemes might use accent colors with hues near that of the main color, or might use a complementary hue.

As described in previous sections, you might define your palette using relative color specifications, so that the user can customize the color scheme with the standard Xt `-fg` and `-bg` arguments. Or, you might a define a number of different hard-coded color schemes and allow the user to choose among them with the `palette` application resource.

Changing Colors at Runtime

In some applications you may want to allow the user to change colors (or entire palettes) at runtime. Doing this can be a little tricky, though—while it is easy to specify colors for an entire interface using wildcards in a resource file, changing colors at runtime requires you to explicitly allocate the colors you need and to set them as resources on *every* widget in your interface.

There is a further difficulty with Motif widgets. When you create a widget, its `XmNtopShadowColor` and `XmNbottomShadowColor` resources are automatically set based on the `XmNbackground` color you specify. When you set the `XmNbackground` color after creation, however, these shadow colors are not updated. So, when you specify new colors for your widgets, you should set these shadow resources as well. You can compute appropriate shadow colors (as well as foreground and select colors) with the function `XmGetColors()`. The select color is a special case—you should use it for the `XmNarmColor` of XmPushButton widgets, for the `XmNselectColor` or XmToggleButton widgets, and for the `XmNtroughColor` of XmScrollBar widgets.

In Motif 1.2 you can also use `XmChangeColor()` to set the background color for a widget, and to update the foreground color, shadow colors, and select color appropriately. The only trouble with this function is that it computes the colors each time you call it, and if you will be changing the colors of every widget in your interface, this becomes wasteful.

—djf

4.2.7 Creating and Manipulating Color Tables

Many applications will never need to use color tables except through the String-to-ColorTable resource converter. Occasionally, though, you may want to explicitly create and manipulate a color table. You can create an `XmtColorTable` with `XmtCreateColorTable()`, and destroy it with `XmtDestroyColorTable()`. You can register symbolic colors in a color table with `XmtRegisterColor()`, `XmtRegisterColors()`, or `XmtVaRegisterColors()`. You can look up a symbolic color in a color table with `XmtLookupColorName()`. This function returns a color specification (a string) that you can allocate with `XmtAllocColor()` (which is introduced later in this chapter). See the reference pages for more information on these functions.

The most common reason to create and manipulate color tables in your C code is to set the `colorTable` resource explicitly. You can override any color table specified in the resource database when you call `XmtInitializeApplicationShell()` or by calling `XmtSetApplicationValues()`. (See Chapter 7, *Application Resources and Command-Line Arguments*, for more information.) There is a less heavy-handed possibility, however. Color tables can be "chained"—you can specify a parent table that will be searched if a desired symbolic color isn't found. You specify this color table parent when you create the table, or with the function `XmtColorTableSetParent()`.

So, for example, if you want to specify some default symbolic color values in your C code, but still allow the user to override them from the resource database, you might create your own color table, then use `XmtGetApplicationValues()` (see Chapter 7) to query the `colorTable` application resource. If you insert your new color table between this color table and its parent, then any colors not found in the user's color table will be looked up in your application's default table. Example 4-6 shows how you can do this.

Example 4-6. Defining Symbolic Colors Without Overriding

```
/*
 * insert my_table between the user's colorTable and its parent
 */
void insert_color_table(XmtColorTable my_table)
{
    XmtColorTable user_table;
    XmtColorTable parent_table;
    Arg args[1];

    XtSetArg(args[0], "colorTable", &user_table);
    XmtGetApplicationValues(toplevel, args, 1);

    parent_table = XmtColorTableGetParent(user_table);
    if (parent_table) XmtColorTableSetParent(my_table, parent_table);
    XmtColorTableSetParent(user_table, my_table);
}
```

Similarly, suppose you want to override some of the user's color selections with a few explicitly specified colors of your own. You would query the `colorTable` resource, create your own color table with this default color table as its parent, register your colors in this new color table, and then set the table as the new value of the `colorTable` resource. You must do this before you create any widgets, of course, or they will look up their colors in the default color table, and never find your overriding color specifications.

Color as Cue

Bill Kayser suggests an elegant use of color here— as a way to distinguish read-only text widgets from regular, editable text widgets. This provides an important cue to users, and helps to prevent them from becoming confused.

Q: What's the best way to specify a background color for read-only text widgets to distinguish them from editable text widgets?

A: One nice solution is to name all read-only text widgets "readonly_text" when you create the widget. Then you can put something like this in the resource file:

Color as Cue (continued)

```
*readonly_text.background:      gray
*readonly_text.editable:        false
*readonly_text.cursorVisible:   false
```

—*Bill Kayser*

Notice that you could use the symbolic color facilities documented in this chapter to specify the background color as `$readonly_color`. You could make this color a darker shade of the regular background color with a relative HSL specification like this: `-%+0/+0/-10`.

Xmt provides another way of implementing the same idea: Chapter 11, *Automatic Widget Creation* shows how you could define a "style" (a named collection of resources) that you could apply to any read-only text widgets you create. This allows the widgets to have different names.

4.3 Allocating Colors in C

Using the Xmt String-to-Pixel converter is usually the easiest way to specify colors for your application. Sometimes you will want to allocate colors explicitly, however, and Xmt provides functions to support this. The Xmt Pixel converter is based on the function `XmtAllocColor()`, which you can call directly:

Xmt/

Color.c

```
#include <Xmt/Color.h>
int XmtAllocColor(Widget w, Visual *visual, XmtColorTable colortable,
                  StringConst color_name, Pixel *pixel_return);
int XmtAllocWidgetColor(Widget w, StringConst color_name, Pixel *pixel_return);
```

Both functions allocate the color named by *`color_name`* for the display and colormap of the widget *w*, and return the resulting pixel at the address specified by *`pixel_return`*. `XmtAllocColor()` also takes a `Visual *` argument, which allows it to determine whether it is running in monochrome and thereby handle foreground/background fallbacks in color specifications, and an `XmtColorTable` argument which it uses to look up symbolic colors. Usually, you will be able to use the simpler `XmtAllocWidgetColor()` function, which uses the visual of the shell widget of *w* and uses the `colorTable` application resource instead of an explicitly specified color table.

Both functions return 0 if they successfully allocate the color, and return a non-zero code if an error occurs. See the reference section for more details.

Usually you allocate colors that will be used for the lifetime of an application—in this case the colors never need to be deallocated. If, however, you know that a color that you have allocated will never be used by your application again, then you should deallocate it with `XmtFreeColor()` or `XmtFreeWidgetColor()`:

Xmt/

Color.c

```
#include <Xmt/Color.h>
void XmtFreeColor(Widget w, Visual *visual, XmtColorTable colortable,
                  StringConst color_name, Pixel pixel);
void XmtFreeWidgetColor(Widget w, StringConst color_name, Pixel pixel);
```

The arguments to these functions are the same as the arguments to the corresponding allocation functions, except that the last *`pixel`* argument is the pixel value to be freed, not the address at which the pixel value is to be stored. Note that these functions require you to pass the name with which the color was allocated. This is so that symbolic colors can be correctly freed from the internal `XmtColorTable` cache.

Finally, it is also possible to use the Xmt color specification syntax with read/write color cells. Once you have allocated a read/write color cell with `XAllocColorCells()`, the usual technique is to store a color into that cell with `XStoreColor()` or `XStoreNamedColor()`. Xmt provides `XmtStoreColor()` and `XmtStoreWidgetColor()`, which do the same thing, but allow colors to be specified with the extended Xmt syntax.

Xmt/

Color.c

```
#include <Xmt/Color.h>
int XmtStoreColor(Widget w, Visual *visual, XmtColorTable colortable,
                  StringConst color_name, Pixel color_cell);
int XmtStoreWidgetColor(Widget w, StringConst color_name, Pixel color_cell);
```

`XmtStoreColor()` and `XmtStoreWidgetColor()` are analogous to `XmtAllocColor()` and `XmtAllocWidgetColor()`. The only difference in their arguments is the last, `Pixel` argument. Where `XmtAllocColor()` takes an address at which to store the allocated pixel, `XmtStoreColor()` takes a `Pixel` value directly—this is the color cell (allocated elsewhere) into which the color will be stored.

Another difference between the color allocation and color storing functions is that since monochrome screens never support read/write color cells, these color storing functions will always ignore a foreground/background fallback specification in color names. These functions also have an important advantage over `XStoreNamedColor()`—if you pass a bad color name to `XStoreNamedColor()` it will cause an X error which will probably cause your application to exit. `XmtStoreColor()` and `XmtStoreWidgetColor()` check the color name first to ensure that no X error will occur. This requires additional X protocol traffic between the client and server, but the added robustness generally makes this precaution worthwhile.

4.4 Colors for Data Display

When you use colors in your user interface, it is generally for decorative purposes—to make your interface look nice. Sometimes, though, you will use colors for data display—to enable the application to present information more clearly. Different applications may have very different needs in their usage of color for data display. A program for manipulating photo-realistic color images, for example, will have to allocate many very precise colors, while applications that display scientific or medical images may instead use false colors to enhance certain details of the image. And an application that displays demographic data on a map, for example, may need to allocate a number of shades of the same color (or of related colors) to suggest a scale of intensity.

An application that graphs several line plots within one set of X and Y axes may want to choose a set of colors that are all distinct from each other and have high contrast with the background color of the application. Similarly, a geographical information system that can display many layers of data (contours, rivers, roads, railroads, and so on) may also want to choose a set of distinct colors to keep the layers of information separate and to maximize the amount of information that can be clearly presented in a single display.

In some of the cases above, the Xmt HSL color allocation facilities will work well for allocating the necessary groups of related colors. Some programs have even stricter color needs, however: applications used by graphic designers may need to be able to allocate "device independent" colors that can be accurately reproduced on other computer monitors (or on printing presses, textiles, or automobile paint, for example). And some visualization applications may want to be very careful to choose colors that are spaced at "perceptually uniform" intervals. In cases like this, you should consider using the X Color Management System, introduced into Xlib in X11R5. The `Xcms` Xlib functions provide support for a number of common device-independent color spaces. The `TekHVC` color space is particularly worthy of note—it is an irregularly shaped color space, designed with built-in corrections for the non-linear nature of human color perception. Modifying the Hue, Value, or Chroma of a `TekHVC` color by equal intervals will result in colors that are spaced at perceptually uniform intervals.

A full discussion of computer color usage could fill a book of its own. The following subsections discuss a couple of common situations that arise when using colors for data display.

4.4.1 Handling Full Colormaps

Any application that allocates colors must be prepared to cope with failures in color allocation. Even if color names are always specified correctly, the application may fail to allocate colors if the default colormap is full or nearly full. When colors are specified through application or widget resources, and allocated by the String-to-Pixel converter, then an allocation failure will simply mean that the default color will be used. (Xt defines strings with the symbolic values `XtDefaultForeground` and `XtDefaultBackground`. Both the Xt and Xmt color converters guarantee that color conversion will succeed for these values—for this reason you should use them as defaults for all your `XtRPixel` resources.)

One way to handle color allocation for data display is to make each of the required colors an application resource—then each will have a default fallback value, and the user will see a reasonable warning message when allocation fails. Often, though, you'll allocate data display colors "by hand," using `XmtAllocWidgetColor()` or some related function. In this case, you should pay attention to the return code to be sure that the returned `Pixel` is a valid one; otherwise you may end up using a garbage `Pixel` value which could cause an Xlib error.

If color allocation does fail, one straightforward way to handle it is to print an informative error message and exit. The user will simply have to stop using whatever application or applications are filling up the colormap before she can run your application. For many applications, this problem occurs infrequently enough that it is not worth worrying about.

Another approach is to have default colors to fall back on when allocation fails. You can use the `WhitePixel()` and `BlackPixel()` macros, for example to get pixel values that are guaranteed to be legal and are guaranteed to be distinct from each other. For some applications this approach will simply not work. For visualization and imaging applications, for example, colors are required for accurate display of the data and the application is useless without them—imagine a medical CAT scan for which color allocation has failed and all data is displayed in black.

Applications that require a fair number of colors (more than 16, say) are obviously more likely to have problems with full colormaps. For these applications it is less acceptable to simply print an error and exit. When the default colormap of the screen is too full for an application to run, one possible approach is to run the application with its own custom colormap.

One way to do this is with `XCopyColormapAndFree()`. When color allocation fails in the default colormap, you can call this Xlib function to create a new colormap, copy all the colors your application has allocated into that colormap, and then free those colors from the default colormap. If you want to use this approach, it means that you'll have to initialize your application in several steps. Instead of calling `XtAppInitialize()`, you'll first call `XtToolkitInitialize()`, `XtCreateApplicationContext()`, `XtAppSetFallbackResources()`, and `XtOpenDisplay()`. Then, with the connection to the X server established, you will go ahead and allocate the colors you want. If the colormap overflows, you'll use `XCopyColormapAndFree()` to create a new colormap, and proceed with color allocation in that new colormap. Once the colors you need are successfully allocated, you can go ahead and create the toplevel shell for your application with `XtAppCreateShell()`, specifying the custom colormap, if any, on the `XtNcolormap` resource. The description under the "Using Non-Default Visuals" light bulb shows this style of application initialization.

If your data display colors will all be used in a single window, another approach is to initialize the application and create the widgets normally, using the default colormap for all the decorative colors in your application. Then, when it comes time to allocate your data display colors, you can create a new colormap if you need to and set it on the one widget that will be used to display those colors. Note that in this case you won't want to use `XCopyColormapAndFree()`, because you don't want to deallocate the decorative colors used in the default colormap. In this case, you'll also want to call `XtSetWMColormapWindows()` so that the window manager can correctly install the custom colormap.

The main problem with using a custom colormap is that, on most hardware, it causes "color flashing"—when the mouse pointer enters a window with a custom colormap, all the colors outside of that window are interpreted relative to the wrong colormap and "go technicolor." One way to work partially around this problem is to allocate all the color cells in your custom colormap and to duplicate most of the entries in the default colormap. You'll definitely want to duplicate any decorative colors your application uses in the default colormap and will also want to duplicate the low-end of the colormap, which will generally contain important colors like those used by the window manager.

4.4.2 Interpolating Colors in HSL and RGB

Something you'll sometimes want to do with data display colors is to allocate a set of colors between two known colors by interpolation. Since the HSL color spaces use cylindrical coordinates and RGB uses cartesian coordinates, interpolating between the same two colors will yield different results in the two spaces.

If you want to produce a fairly smooth fade from one arbitrary color to another, you'll usually get better results with RGB. If you use HSL for this kind of interpolation, you'll have to go through the colors of the spectrum to get from one hue to another, and the transition may not appear as smooth as you want.

On the other hand, if your colors are not arbitrary and you want to interpolate along one dimension at a time, then HSL is better. To produce a series of colors of the same Hue and Saturation but varying Lightness, for example, you hold H and S constant and vary L over the desired range. You can similarly hold H and L constant and vary S as desired. Or, if you want to produce a series of colors that all have distinct Hues, you might vary H while holding S and L constant. When interpolating by Hue, note that there are two directions you can go in—by increasing H around the circle, or by decreasing it around the circle. You'll want to do your arithmetic modulo 360.

Using Non-Default Visuals

A common problem in image processing is too few available colors. The colors may have been previously allocated by other applications, or the default visual may simply provide too small of a colormap to be useful for displaying the data.

The simple solution, if it's available, is to use a visual which expands the number of available colors, or to use a colormap which other applications do not have access to. Unless the platform on which the X server is running provides multiple hardware colormaps, either approach may be problematic because of colormap flashing. If the default visual for the server provides enough colors for the application, no special action need be taken. However, if, for example, a 24-bit TrueColor visual is required for drawing, and the default visual for the server is 8-bit PseudoColor, there is a little more work to do.

To use a non-default visual in Xt, you must set the `XtNvisual` resources of your application shell. You'll have to create a colormap that uses the visual, and set it on the `XtNcolormap` resource. If the depth of the visual is different from the default depth of the screen, you'll also have to set the `XtNdepth` resource. All widget children of the application shell will inherit the visual, colormap, and depth you specified for the shell.

The main thing to remember is that everything has to match. All pixmaps must be of the same depth as the visual, and all colors used in the creation of windows or widgets must be allocated from the colormap the application creates. The same goes for any drawing the application has to perform.

You need the visual and colormap before you create your applications shell, but you need a display pointer in order to obtain the visual and colormap. This means that the application cannot use `XtAppInitialize()`, and must initialize itself in five separate steps, as shown in Example 4-7.

Example 4-7. Using a Non-Default Visual

```
#define VISUAL_DEPTH 24
#define VISUAL_CLASS TrueColor
extern String *fallbacks; /* array of fallback resources; defined elsewhere */

main(int argc, char **argv)
{
    XtAppContext context;
    Display      *display;
    XVisualInfo  vinfo;
    Colormap     colormap;
    Widget       appShell;
    Arg          args[4];
    Cardinal     argcnt;

    XmtPatchVisualInheritance();
```

Using Non-Default Visuals (continued)

Example 4-7. Using a Non-Default Visual (continued)

```
    /* first four initialization steps */
    XtToolkitInitialize();
    context = XtCreateApplicationContext();
    XtAppSetFallbackResources(context, fallbacks);
    display = XtOpenDisplay(context, 0, NULL, "Visual", 0, 0, &argc, argv);
    if (display == NULL) XtError("cannot open display");

    /* Now see if the desired visual can be found. */
    argcnt = 0;
    if (XMatchVisualInfo(display, DefaultScreen(display),
                        VISUAL_DEPTH, VISUAL_CLASS, &vinfo))
    {
        if ((colormap=XCreateColormap(display, DefaultRootWindow(display),
                                      vinfo.visual, AllocNone)))
        {
            XtSetArg(args[argcnt], XmNvisual, vinfo.visual); argcnt++;
            XtSetArg(args[argcnt], XmNdepth, VISUAL_DEPTH); argcnt++;
            XtSetArg(args[argcnt], XmNcolormap, colormap); argcnt++;
        }
        else
            XtError("Failed Colormap create");
    }
    else
        XtError("Failed to find an appropriate visual");

    /*
     * the fifth initialization step:  create the initial shell
     * with the visual, depth, and colormap resources.
     */
    appShell=XtAppCreateShell("visual", "Visual",
                              applicationShellWidgetClass, display,
                              args, argcnt);
        .
        .       /* create the rest of the interface */
        .
    XtRealizeWidget(appShell);
    XtAppMainLoop(context);
}
```

One last problem must be overcome if your application creates any other shell widgets (such as pulldown menus or dialog boxes). The `XtNcolormap` and `XtNdepth` resources are Core widget resources, and any widget inherits these values from its parent widget. The `XtNvisual` resource is a Shell widget resource, and it is inherited from the shell's parent window—this is always the root window. So unless you explicitly set a visual, shell widgets always have the default visual of the screen, which will probably not match the non-default colormap inherited for the `XtNcolormap` resource. To work around this, you must either set your non-default visual on the `XtNvisual` resource of each shell you create, or you must reset the `XtNcolormap` and `XtNdepth` resources for each shell back to the default values for the screen.

Using Non-Default Visuals (continued)

One way to set the visual for all shell widgets is to use the Xt String-to-Visual converter with a resource file line like the following:

```
*.visual: TrueColor
```

This approach may not work if there is more than one visual of a given class available. Another approach, used in the example above, is to call `XmtPatchVisualInheritance()`. This function tweaks the Shell widget class so that the default value of the `XtNvisual` resource is copied from the widget's shell ancestor, rather than from its parent window. This means that the visual resource is handled just like the colormap and depth, and you no longer have to worry about it.

One more point is worth noting: In Motif, the `XmGetPixmap()` function returns pixmaps of the default depth, which is a problem if you are using a visual with some non-default depth. In Motif 1.2, you can solve this problem with `XmGetPixmapByDepth()`, which returns a pixmap of a specified depth.

—Scott Johnson
(with contributions by djf)

4.5 Style

Color is a surprisingly complex topic. Texts on colorimetry are dense and stuffed with equations. And even the more subjective matters of using color effectively are remarkably complex—art students can spend semesters studying color. This book cannot hope to be a complete introduction to the field—your best bet is to work with a graphic designer to come up with a color scheme for your application. Failing that, however, this section presents a few stylistic points that are worth thinking about.

The most important rule about using colors in your applications is to be conservative about it—the temptation to overuse color is strong (as it is with fonts) and it is far too easy to overdo it and end up with a garish result. There is no need to be as conservative as the Motif default colors are, however—the uniform light blue color of so many Motif applications is enough to put users to sleep.

Whatever you do, don't choose colors at random—you're very likely to end up with something ugly that way. Using the HSL color space is a good way to help rationalize your color choices, since you can reasonably predict the effect of varying any component of the color. Also, since there is no accounting for taste, do allow your users to override your choices. If *they* end up choosing colors at random, well, then it is no longer your problem.

If you will be using foreground colors of a number of different Hues, then a neutral background is a good choice because it will harmonize with the foreground colors. Neutral colors are the grays, and other colors with a low Saturation—beige, tan, and so forth. If you are using a single primary foreground color, then consider using a shade of its complement as the background—complementary colors (which differ by 180 degrees in Hue) also harmonize well.

Choosing different Hues and Saturations for foreground and background colors is not sufficient for things like text and line drawings. For small features like these to be easily visible, they must have a high contrast in Lightness as well. Larger, filled areas of color are visible even without the contrast in Lightness, but avoid large areas of saturated color—they are bright and distracting, and cause afterimages on the user's retina.

While the HSL color space simplifies things, remember that it is not perceptually uniform, and colors with the same mathematical lightness may have very different perceived lightnesses. The yellows, for example, are very light, while the blues are quite dark. For this reason a yellow foreground on a white background is a bad choice, as is a blue foreground on a black background. On the other hand, if you displayed black text on a white background, you could very effectively display selected text by highlighting the background with yellow.

Warm colors like red and orange tend to "advance" (appear in the foreground) while the cool colors (like blue) at the other end of the spectrum "recede." If you draw intersecting red and blue lines, for example, with the blue line drawn over the red, the red will look like it is struggling to come forward, trapped behind the blue line. If the red line overlaps the blue, the result will be less distracting.

Be aware of the cultural connotations of the colors you choose. In the US, for example, you wouldn't want to use red to chart financial statistics for a company, because it could imply that the company was "in the red" (i.e., losing money). Similarly, don't use the same color for decoration of your interface and for data display, unless you actually want to imply a connection. If certain menu items are only applicable to certain objects drawn in the application, for example, then you might display the menu items and the objects in the same color.

Finally, when choosing colors, remember that red/green color blindness is fairly common. If you use these colors, give them a different Saturation or Lightness, so they can be distinguished on some basis other than their Hue.

4.6 Summary

This chapter has explained the Xmt extended color specification syntax.

- Call `XmtRegisterPixelConverter()` to register the Xmt color converter.

- In addition to the standard color names and hexadecimal color specification recognized by the default converter, the Xmt color converter recognizes HSL colors beginning with a `%` and symbolic colors beginning with a `$`.
- Precede any Xmt color specification with a `-` or a `+` to indicate whether it should be treated as a background or a foreground color on monochrome systems.
- The H, S, and L coordinates of an HSL color may be specified as relative rather than absolute values—the resulting color will be computed relative to the foreground or background colors (specified by the `foreground` and `background` application resources).
- Symbolic colors are looked up in the `XmtColorTable` specified by the `colorTable` application resource.
- You can use the `colorTable` resource (perhaps with relative HSL specifications) to define a palette of colors for use by the various parts of your interface. When choosing colors, the most important rule is to be conservative.

5

Using Icons

Compare a typical free X application with a commercial application for X (or for the Macintosh, for example) and one of the big differences you'll probably notice is that commercial applications make more frequent use of icons. Using iconic graphical symbols in your applications is a good way to provide easily recognizable cues for your users, to build up a product identity for your application, and to provide the user-friendly look that has become as important as actual user-friendliness.

The reason icons are not more heavily used in X applications is that there are few good tools for doing so, and this is particularly true for multi-color pixmaps. This chapter presents the Xmt facilities for handling bitmaps and pixmaps. It starts with a review of X concepts related to icons and an introduction to the XPM file format. Then it explains the features of the Xmt String-to-Pixmap and String-to-Bitmap resource converters and briefly documents how you can access these same features directly in your C code. It concludes with some stylistic comments about using icons in your application.

Icons in X

In GUI terminology, an *icon* is a small graphical image that cues the user. As with highway signs, icons in an application do not attempt realism in their representations, but instead attempt to communicate a simple concept with an easily recognizable graphical symbol.

You can draw graphical symbols with Xlib drawing functions, of course, but most of the time you implement icons with a `Pixmap` instead. The `Pixmap` is an Xlib data type that refers to a rectangular array of pixels stored in the X server. Because pixmaps are rectangular, they can easily be drawn into windows with an efficient block copy operation. Because they are stored in the server, they can be reused, and copies can be made without sending all the pixels of the

Icons in X (continued)

icon "over the wire" between the client and server. And, finally, because pixmaps are stored in the server, they consume server memory, which is a shared, limited resource (particularly on X terminals) and so they should not be used for large images, except in special cases.

pixmap is a generic term for a rectangular array of pixels, but the term *bitmap* is often used when the array is only one bit-plane deep (i.e., for monochrome images, where each pixel is either on or off, with no color information). A bitmap is simply a degenerate case of a pixmap, and the Xlib `Pixmap` type is used for both.

On monochrome systems, both pixmaps and bitmaps are one plane deep, and can be treated the same. On color systems, however, there are some important differences. A pixmap is copied into a window with the function `XCopyArea()`, which requires that the pixmap and the destination window have the same depth. Since each pixel of a pixmap has as many bits as the window does, a pixmap has its own color information encoded into it. (And, obviously, you should define a pixmap in terms of the same colormap as the windows you will be displaying it in. See Chapter 4, *Using Color*, for a review of color-related concepts such as "depth" and "colormaps".)

Bitmaps are handled differently. Since a bitmap is only a single plane deep, it is copied into a window using the function `XCopyPlane()`, which takes each single "on" or "off" bit in the bitmap and converts it into a foreground or background color of the appropriate depth for the destination window. To do this, it uses the foreground and background attributes of the GC (graphics context) that is passed to it. So, while bitmaps can only have two colors, they can be easily drawn with any pair or colors you choose. Pixmaps can have multiple colors, but once a pixmap is created, those colors are fixed. Since bitmaps only have one bit plane (as opposed to eight, on a typical color system), they are significantly cheaper to use in terms of X server resources consumed.

Unfortunately, the Motif XmLabel widget and its button subclasses do not support bitmaps. Even when you want to display a monochrome icon, they require you to use a pixmap. Pixmaps take up more memory usage in the server and make it impossible to change the colors of the icon displayed by a Motif widget without actually changing the icon. The XmLabel's lack of bitmap support is a serious oversight in Motif, because, as we'll see, Motif provides no support for icon file or data formats other than the XBM bitmap format. The XmtLayoutPixmap gadget, designed for use with the XmtLayout widget (see Chapter 19, *The Layout Widget: The Details*), supports both bitmaps and pixmaps.

Sometimes you want to display an icon that is non-rectangular. You can do this with the use of a *bitmask*. A bitmask is a bitmap that defines what bits of a

Icons in X (continued)

rectangular region are part of an icon, and which bits are outside of the icon. By using this bitmask as a clipping region (specified in the GC) you can copy a rectangular icon (bitmap or pixmap) and only set the pixels specified in the bitmask, leaving the others undisturbed.

—*djf*

5.1 The Xmt Pixmap and Bitmap Converters

One reason that text is used in GUIs far more frequently than icons is that strings are a simple type that can be easily specified in your C code or resource file. Icons, on the other hand, are more complex objects that must be created and manipulated in your code. Xmt's approach to simplifying the use of icons is to make them easier to name—the Xmt String-to-Pixmap and String-to-Bitmap converters allow you to specify icons by name in a resource file without ever having to manipulate them directly. (Another difference between the text and icons is that you can just type text at the keyboard. Icons need to be edited with some kind of pixmap editor, and for commercial applications, they also need to be specially designed by a computer artist. Xmt can't help with this problem.)

You can register the pixmap and bitmap converters with these functions:

```
#include <Xmt/Converters.h>
void XmtRegisterPixmapConverter(void);
void XmtRegisterBitmapConverter(void);
```

With these converters registered, you can specify icons with resources like the following:

```
*organizer.mail.labelPixmap: envelope
*organizer.todo.labelPixmap: list
*organizer.appt.labelPixmap: calendar
```

In order for these converters to work, you must of course provide a definition of the icons named `envelope`, `list`, and `calendar`. The sections that follow show how you can do this in C code, in resource files, and in auxiliary files read in at runtime. A later section explains how you can use Xmt functions to look up and manipulate pixmaps and bitmaps directly in your C code, without using the resource converters.

The XPM File Format

The X Consortium defines a standard format for bitmap data—the XBM format, which is output by the bitmap client. There is no corresponding official standard for pixmap data, but the XPM format appears to have become a de facto *industry standard—it is used by a number of major commercial products, by the CDE desktop, and by Xmt. The XPM file format (and an accompanying library for manipulating XPM data) was developed by Arnaud Le Hors at Bull Research in France. The following excerpt from his* XPM Manual *explains the motivations behind XPM and documents the format itself. I've added notes where the Xmt handling of XPM files differs from the general case.*

Why another image format? We (Koala team at Bull Research, France) felt that most images bundled with X applications will be small icons that must be color-customizable. Existing image formats such as GIF, TIFF, etc. are intended for big images with well-defined colors and so aren't adapted to the task. XPM was designed with these goals in mind:

- It should be editable with a text editor on a monochrome system.
- It should be includable in C code. It is unreasonable to load 1000 pixmap files on each start of an application.
- It should be a portable, mailable ASCII format.
- It should provide default colors for monochrome, color, and grayscale renderings.
- It should allow overriding of default colors. This way, if the user wants your application to be bluish instead of greenish, you can use the SAME icon files.
- It should allow comments to be included in the file.

An XPM file is formatted as an array of strings in C syntax—this provides the ability to include XPM files in C and C++ programs. The basic structure of an XPM file looks like this

```
/* XPM */
static char * icon_name[] = {
Values
Colors
Pixels
Extensions
};
```

Example 5-1 shows a complete example of an XPM file—you may want to refer to it in the following description of the XPM file format.

The leading `/* XPM */` comment is required to identify the format of the file. The second line is a C declaration and provides a name, *`icon_name`*, for the XPM data when the XPM file is included into C code. Tokens in an XPM file are

The XPM File Format (continued)

separated by whitespace, which can be composed of spaces and TAB characters. The following four sections, `Values`, `Colors`, `Pixels`, and `Extensions`, are comma-separated strings, one to a line. Each section may be preceded by a comment, using the C syntax. [*The* `Extensions` *section is never used in the Xmt library, and its format will not be described here.*]

The `Values` section is a string containing four or six integers in base 10 that specify:

1. The pixmap width
2. The pixmap height
3. The number of colors used in the pixmap
4. The number of characters used for each "color tag" in the data that follows
5. (Optionally) the X coordinate of the hotspot
6. The Y coordinate of the hotspot

This section is a string with this syntax:

```
width height ncolors cpp [ x_hotspot y_hotspot ]
```

[*The Xmt parser for XPM files requires that* `cpp` *("characters-per-pixel") be 1 or 2. The Xmt internal storage format for XPM files limits them to 256 distinct colors—this should be sufficient for any icon.*]

The `Colors` section contains as many strings as there are colors, and each string is as follows:

```
chars { key color }+
```

where `chars` is the `cpp` length string [*one or two characters in Xmt*] that will represent the color in the data below. There should be no leading whitespace before `chars`, or they will be interpreted as color characters. `chars` is followed by one or more `key`/`color` pairs, where `color` is a color specification, and `key` is a keyword describing in which context this color should be used. The legal keywords and their meanings are listed below:

Key	Meaning
m	Use this color on monochrome screens.
g4	Use this color on 4-level grayscale screens.
g	Use this color on grayscale screens.
c	Use this color on color screens.
s	Use this symbolic name to override color defaults

Colors can be specified by giving the color name, or a # followed by the RGB code in hexadecimal. The symbolic name provides the ability to specify colors

The XPM File Format (continued)

at load time and not to hard-code them in the file. [*In Xmt, an* `XmtColorTable` *is used to look up symbolic colors.*]

The color name "None" is treated specially in XPM files—it is taken to mean "transparent." Transparency is handled by providing a bitmask in addition to the pixmap.

Finally, the *`Pixels`* section is composed of *`height`* strings, each composed of *`width`* color tags. Each color tag is *`cpp`* characters long, and must be one of the *`chars`* strings previously defined in the *`Colors`* section. The last string in the file is followed by a closing brace and a semicolon, which is required by the C syntax of the file.

Example 5-1 shows an XPM file that defines a plaid pixmap. It is a 22x22 pixmap, with four colors and color tags that use two characters per pixel. The hotspot coordinates are (0, 0). There are default colors for color and monochrome visuals, and symbolic color names that allow these to be overridden. Note that one of the colors is represented with spaces—this is often useful for background colors.

Example 5-1. An XPM File

```
/* XPM */
static char * plaid[] = {
/* plaid pixmap
 * width height ncolors chars_per_pixel hotspot_x hotspot_y */
"22 22 4 2 0 0",
/* colors */
"   c red       m white  s light_color ",
"Y  c green     m black  s lines_in_mix ",
"+  c yellow    m white  s lines_in_dark ",
"x              m black  s dark_color ",
/* pixels */
"x   x   x x x   x   x x x x x x + x x x x x ",
"  x   x   x   x   x   x x x x x x x x x x x ",
"x   x   x x x   x   x x x x x x + x x x x x ",
"  x   x   x   x   x   x x x x x x x x x x x ",
"x   x   x x x   x   x x x x x x + x x x x x ",
"Y Y Y Y Y x Y Y Y Y Y + x + x + x + x + x + ",
"x   x   x x x   x   x x x x x x + x x x x x ",
"  x   x   x   x   x   x x x x x x x x x x x ",
"x   x   x x x   x   x x x x x x + x x x x x ",
"  x   x   x   x   x   x x x x x x x x x x x ",
"x   x   x x x   x   x x x x x x + x x x x x ",
"          x           x   x   x Y x   x   x ",
"          x             x   x   Y   x   x   ",
"          x           x   x   x Y x   x   x ",
"          x             x   x   Y   x   x   ",
"          x           x   x   x Y x   x   x ",
"x x x x x x x x x x x x x x x x x x x x x x ",
"          x           x   x   x Y x   x   x ",
```

The XPM File Format (continued)

Example 5-1. An XPM File (continued)

```
"          x             x   x   Y   x   x   ",
"          x           x   x   x Y x   x   x ",
"          x             x   x   Y   x   x   ",
"          x           x   x   x Y x   x   x "
};
```

—Arnaud Le Hors
(modified by djf from the XPM Manual)

5.2 Specifying Icons in C

The Xmt pixmap and bitmap converters and related routines maintain a cache of named icon data. The first time a named icon is requested (for a particular screen and colormap) Xmt creates a `Pixmap` object with the named data. If the icon is requested again (for the same screen and colormap) then the `Pixmap` object is reused. (This is the way the Motif functions `XmGetPixmap()`, `XmGetPixmapByDepth()`, and `XmInstallImage()` work too, but the Xmt caching scheme is easier to use and supports XPM pixmap data.)

5.2.1 Registering Bitmaps

You can register named bitmap data in the cache with `XmtRegisterXbmData()`:

Xmt/

Pixmap.c

```
#include <Xmt/Pixmap.h>
void XmtRegisterXbmData(String name, char *imagedata, char *maskdata,
                        int width, int height, int hotspot_x, int hotspot_y)
```

The *`name`* argument specifies a name for this data—this is the name you would provide in a resource file when using the converter. *`imagedata`* is the bits of the bitmap, and *`maskdata`* is an optional bitmask that specifies the shape of the icon—you can specify `NULL` if the icon is rectangular. The *`width`* and *`height`* arguments are defined in the XBM file with the data, and *`hotspot_x`* and *`hotspot_y`* are the optional coordinates of a cursor hotspot. Example 5-2 shows an example XBM file listing, and then shows how you might include this file in your code and register it with `XmtRegisterXbmData()`.

Example 5-2. Registering XBM Data

```
/* Here are the contents of the XBM file 'pin.xbm'--a pushpin icon */

#define pin_width 32
#define pin_height 16
static char pin_bits[] = {
 0x00,0x00,0x07,0x00,0x00,0x00,0x09,0x70,0x00,0x00,0x11,0x88,0x00,0x00,0xf1,
 0x8f,0x00,0x00,0x01,0x88,0x00,0x00,0x01,0x80,0x00,0x00,0x01,0x80,0x80,0xff,
 0x01,0x80,0x00,0xff,0x01,0x80,0x00,0x00,0x01,0x88,0x18,0x00,0xf1,0x8f,0x24,
 0x00,0x11,0x88,0x24,0x00,0x09,0x70,0x18,0x00,0x07,0x00,0x00,0x00,0x00,0x00,
 0x00,0x00,0x00,0x00};

/* Here is some code that uses that file */

#include "bitmaps/pin.xbm"
        .
        .
        .
XmtRegisterXbmData("pin", pin_bits, NULL, pin_width, pin_height, 0, 0);
```

5.2.2 Registering Pixmaps

Registering XPM pixmap data is one step more complicated than registering XBM data. Because the XPM format is designed to be human-readable and editable with a text editor, it is not particularly efficient to parse into an actual pixmap. So before you can register XPM data for use over and over again in the cache, you must convert it to an internal compiled form known as an XmtImage.

You can convert an XPM file to an XmtImage with XmtParseXpmFile(), or if you have included the XPM file directly into your C code, you can convert the resulting array of strings to an XmtImage with XmtParseXpmData():

Xmt/

XpmParse.c

```
#include <Xmt/Xpm.h>
XmtImage *XmtParseXpmFile(String filename)
XmtImage *XmtParseXpmData(String *data)
```

Once you have the XmtImage returned by one of these XPM parsing functions, you can register it with the Xmt icon cache with XmtRegisterImage():

Xmt/

Pixmap.c

```
#include <Xmt/Pixmap.h>
void XmtRegisterImage(String name, XmtImage *data)
```

Note that the size of the pixmap and its hotspot coordinates, if any, are encoded into the XmtImage, so you do not need to pass these to XmtRegisterImage as you do to XmtRegisterXbmData(). Also, recall that the XPM format supports the special "transparent" color named "None." If there are any transparent bits in the pixmap, then the Xmt icon caching mechanism will automatically generate a bitmask for the icon; thus there is no need to explicitly specify a bitmask.

Example 5-3 shows how you can register XPM pixmap data with these functions.

Example 5-3. Registering XPM Data

```
#include "pixmaps/bell.xpm"  /* defines char *bell[] array of strings */

XmtImage *bell_image;
        .
        .
        .
bell_image = XmtParseXpmData(bell);     /* parse the raw data */
XmtRegisterImage("bell", bell_image); /* register the parsed form */
```

There is one more point to note. The Xmt bitmap converter will obviously only look for named XBM data in the cache. But it is possible to create a pixmap from either XPM data or XBM data, so the Xmt pixmap converter first checks for XPM data with the specified name, and if it doesn't find any, it then looks for XBM data.

5.3 Specifying Icons in a Resource File

The Xmt pixmap and bitmap converters look first for icon data in the icon cache described above. If the named icon is not found in the cache, they next look in the resource database. Xmt reserves two special resource branches for pixmap and bitmap data: `_Pixmaps_` and `_Bitmaps_`. These are a lot like the `_FontLists_` and `_Messages_` branches we saw in Chapter 3, *Displaying Text*, and the `_ColorTables_` branch we saw in Chapter 4, *Using Color*.

Thus, if you wanted to specify XBM data for the icon named `envelope`, you could specify it as the resource `_Bitmaps_*envelope`. Example 5-4 shows how you could specify a bitmap and a pixmap in a resource file.

Example 5-4. Icons in a Resource File

```
_Bitmaps_*pin_in: \
#define pin_in_width 32\n\
#define pin_in_height 16\n\
static char pin_in_bits[] = {\n\
 0x00,0xc0,0x07,0x00,0x00,0x38,0x08,0x00,0x00,0x16,0x10,0x00,0x00,0x09,0x20,\n\
 0x00,0x80,0x08,0x20,0x00,0x80,0x08,0x20,0x00,0x40,0x08,0x20,0x00,0x40,0x08,\n\
 0x20,0x00,0x40,0x18,0x10,0x00,0x40,0x30,0x18,0x00,0x40,0xe0,0x17,0x00,0xc0,\n\
 0xc0,0x0b,0x00,0x80,0x01,0x08,0x00,0xc0,0x03,0x04,0x00,0x60,0x0f,0x03,0x00,\n\
 0x30,0xfc,0x00,0x00};

_Pixmaps_*hourglass: \
32 32 4 1\n\
        s None              m white        g white\n\
o       s select            m black        g #888\n\
x       s bottom_shadow     m black        g #555\n\
```

Example 5-4. Icons in a Resource File (continued)

```
~       s top_shadow          m black          g #aaa\n\
~~~~~~~~~~~~~~~~~~~~~~~~~~~~~~~~\n\
oooooooooooooooooooooooooooooooo\n\
oooooooooooooooooooooooooooooooo\n\
################################\n\
  ~o#   ~~oooooooooooo##   ~o#  \n\
  ~o#   ~~oooooooooooo##   ~o#  \n\
  ~o#   ~~oooooooooooo##   ~o#  \n\
  ~o#   ~~oooooooooooo##   ~o#  \n\
  ~o#    ~~oooooooooo##    ~o#  \n\
  ~o#    ~~oooooooooo##    ~o#  \n\
  ~o#    ~~oooooooooo##    ~o#  \n\
  ~o#     ~~oooooooo##     ~o#  \n\
  ~o#     ~~oooooooo##     ~o#  \n\
  ~o#     ~~oooooooo##     ~o#  \n\
  ~o#      ~~oooooo##      ~o#  \n\
  ~o#       ~~oooo##       ~o#  \n\
  ~o#       ~~oooo##       ~o#  \n\
  ~o#      ~~oooooo##      ~o#  \n\
  ~o#     ~~oooooooo##     ~o#  \n\
  ~o#     ~~oooooooo##     ~o#  \n\
  ~o#     ~~oooooooo##     ~o#  \n\
  ~o#    ~~oooooooooo##    ~o#  \n\
  ~o#    ~~oooooooooo##    ~o#  \n\
  ~o#    ~~oooooooooo##    ~o#  \n\
  ~o#   ~~oooooooooooo##   ~o#  \n\
  ~o#   ~~oooooooooooo##   ~o#  \n\
  ~o#   ~~oooooooooooo##   ~o#  \n\
  ~o#   ~~oooooooooooo##   ~o#  \n\
~~~~~~~~~~~~~~~~~~~~~~~~~~~~~~~~\n\
oooooooooooooooooooooooooooooooo\n\
oooooooooooooooooooooooooooooooo\n\
################################
```

To specify a bitmap, you simply place the contents of an XBM file in your resource file, and terminate each line, except the last, with `\n\`. Specifying an XPM file requires a little more manipulation—you want only the strings themselves, not the quotation marks, commas, and other C syntax. And as with XBM files, you must end every line but the last with `\n\`. The **`xbm2res`** and **`xpm2res`** scripts make this conversion easy.

Once you have specified bitmap or pixmap data under `_Bitmaps_` or `_Pixmaps_`, you need do nothing more—the Xmt converters will read the data when it is requested by name. When named icon data is read (and parsed) from the resource database, it is automatically stored in the icon cache, just as if you had registered it in your C code. This makes it more quickly available the next time it is requested.

As noted above, the bitmap converter requires XBM data, but the pixmap converter can use either XPM or XBM data. So when looking for an icon named `envelope`, for example, the pixmap converter will first check the `_Pixmaps_*envelope` resource, and if no data is found there, it will check the `_Bitmaps_*envelope` resource.

5.3.1 Customized Icons

As we saw in Chapter 3, *Displaying Text*, the Xmt XmFontList converter does not look up symbolic font list names directly under the `_FontLists_` branch of the resource database; instead it allows different font lists to be specified depending on the language string. And in Chapter 4, *Using Color*, we saw that different named color tables can be specified under the `_ColorTables_` branch, depending on the visual type and depth of the screen.

Pixmaps may require both of these kinds of customization. Because icons communicate with simple images that are often part of the cultural base of a certain country, they often need to be "translated," just like text, before they will work effectively in other countries. Also, because pixmaps contain colors, they may need to be customized based on the type of the screen (color, grayscale, or monochrome) and upon the depth of the screen (i.e., the number of colors or shades of gray that are available).

The previous examples have shown pixmap and bitmap data being specified in a resource file with a wildcard: `_Pixmaps_*hourglass:`, and `_Bitmaps_*envelope`, for example. These are legal specifications, and you may often specify default icons in this way. The pixmap and bitmap converters actually look for the specification that most closely matches the following resources:

```
_Pixmaps_.visual.depth.size.language.territory.codeset.name
_Bitmaps_.size.language.territory.codeset.name
```

The components of these searches are the following:

visual — The default visual type of the screen. This will be one of the strings "color," "gray," or "monochrome."

depth — The default depth, in bitplanes, of the screen. This will be an integer. Typical values are 1 and 8.

size — The size or "resolution" of the screen, as determined by the number of pixels. This will be one of the strings "small" (screen is less than 750 pixels wide), "medium," or "large" (screen is more than 1150 pixels wide).

language — The "language part" of the language string.*

territory — The "territory part" of the language string.

codeset — The "codeset part" of the language string.

name — The name of the desired icon. In our examples, this has been "envelope," "hourglass," and so forth.

Note that the bitmap converter does not use the visual type or depth in its search—bitmaps do not include color data, and so this kind of customization is not required.

*If you will not be doing internationalization, then you do not need to understand the language string or its various parts.

Example 5-5 shows some resource specifications you might use for customized icons. For simplicity, the actual icon data has been omitted from this example.

Example 5-5. Specifying Customized Icons

```
!! This is the default specification for our stop sign icon.
!! For brevity, we omit the actual pixmap data in this example.
_Pixmaps_*stop:

!! But we also provide versions for use on grayscale and monochrome monitors.
!! Note that we could achieve the a similar kind of portability with careful
!! use of symbolic colors and colortables.
_Pixmaps_*gray*stop:
_Pixmaps_*monochrome*stop:

!! If the application is to used on old-style NeXT machines that support four
!! shades of gray (2 planes), we might provide a special icon for this case.
_Pixmaps_*gray*2*stop:

!! For small monitors, we provide a smaller version of the icon that won't
!! take up so much of the limited screen space.  For large or "high-resolution"
!! monitors, we provide a bigger version of the icon, so that the icon
!! won't appear too small on the screen.
_Pixmaps_*small*stop:
_Pixmaps_*large*stop:

!! Our default icon is based on the American traffic sign.  For other
!! countries, like France, we need to provide a different symbol.
_Pixmaps_*Fr*stop:

!! There are lots of other possible combinations we can provide as well.
!! Suppose there are a lot of small 16-color (4 planes) monitors in France:
_Pixmaps_.color.4.small.Fr*stop:
```

The xbm2res and xpm2res Scripts

xbm2res and *xpm2res* are simple UNIX shell scripts that use *sed* to convert XBM and XPM files, respectively, to the format required for inclusion in resource files. They read the file or files specified on the command line (or read the standard input, if no files are specified) and write their output to the standard output. Both XBM and XPM files have the icon name encoded into them, and these scripts use that name as the resource name under `_Bitmaps_` or `_Pixmaps_`.

Suppose you had the following line in your application's app-defaults file:

```
myapp.xmtRequires: "icons.ad"
```

(The `xmtRequires` "pseudo-resource" causes a named resource file to be read in to the resource database at runtime. It will be introduced in Chapter 11, *Automatic Widget Creation*.) Then you might automatically generate the *icons.ad* file with lines like these in a Makefile:

```
BITMAPS = bitmaps/warning.xbm bitmaps/error.xbm bitmaps/help.xbm
PIXMAPS = pixmaps/envelope.xpm pixmaps/clock.xpm pixmaps/calendar.xpm
```

The xbm2res and xpm2res Scripts (continued)

```
icons.ad: $(BITMAPS) $(PIXMAPS)
        xbm2res $(BITMAPS) > icons.ad
        xpm2res $(PIXMAPS) >> icons.ad
```

—*djf*

5.4 Specifying Icons in Auxiliary Files

If the pixmap and bitmap converters cannot find XPM or XBM data with the specified name in the icon cache or in the resource database, then they assume that the icon name must specify the name of an auxiliary file. As usual, the bitmap converter only looks for an XBM file, while the pixmap converter first looks for an XPM file with the specified name, and then looks for an XBM file by that name if no pixmap file is found. When icon data is found in an auxiliary file, it is read in, parsed, and then stored in the icon cache for rapid lookup the next time it is needed.

The pixmap and bitmap converters use `XmtFindFile()` to search for named pixmap and/or bitmap files. `XmtFindFile()` is an enhanced version of `XtResolvePathname()`. It is used in several places in the Xmt library and is explained in Chapter 6, *Managing Auxiliary Files.* You'll need to understand how `XmtFindFile()` works in order to fully understand how the pixmap and bitmap converters find their files, but this section provides a simple overview that is sufficient for now. You may want to come back to this section once you've read Chapter 6.

You will generally install your auxiliary XPM and XBM files beneath the directory specified by the `configDir` application resource. The `configPath` application resource tells `XmtFindFile()` how to locate files beneath that directory. `configPath` specifies a colon-separated list of filenames in which substitution variables replace things like the root directory, the application name, the base name of the file being looked for, and the type and suffix of that file. `XmtFindFile()` works by performing the specified substitutions, and then returning the first file in the list that exists.

Example 5-6 shows how you might set `configPath` and `configDir`, and how you can specify the base filename of an auxiliary pixmap or bitmap file to be looked up. It also shows the files that will be checked during this search. Note that the pixmap converter uses `pixmaps` and `.xpm` for the file type and suffix substitutions (`%T` and `%S`), and the bitmap converter uses `bitmaps` and `.xbm`.

Example 5-6. Looking Up Auxiliary Pixmap and Bitmap Files

```
!!
!! The configPath resource specifies where XmtFindFile() should
!! look for auxiliary files.  This setting specifies two files to check
!!    root-directory/app-name/file-type/base-file-name
!!    root-directory/app-name/base-file-name+file-suffix
myapp.configPath: %R/%a/%T/%N:%R/%a/%N%S

!! The root directory, %R in the above path, is specified by configDir
myapp.configDir: /usr/local/lib

!! Now to specify a pixmap, we just give the base-file-name
!! The root directory is specified by configDir, the app-name
!! is implicit, and the file type and suffix are supplied by
!! the pixmap converter.
*mailtool.labelPixmap: envelope

!! This specification will make XmtFindFile() look in two different places.
!! The Xmt pixmap converter calls XmtFindFile() twice; once to look for
!! a pixmap, and once to look for a bitmap.  In all, it will check for
!! the following four files, in this order, and use the first it finds:
!!       /usr/local/lib/myapp/pixmaps/envelope
!!       /usr/local/lib/myapp/envelope.xpm
!!       /usr/local/lib/myapp/bitmaps/envelope
!!       /usr/local/lib/myapp/envelope.xbm
```

When prototyping an application, you might choose to simply specify the full filename in your icon specifications. For example, you might use resources like these:

```
*mailtool.labelPixmap: /home/david/myapp/pixmaps/envelope.xpm
*todotool.labelPixmap: ./bitmaps/clock.xbm
```

If an icon name begins with `/`, `./`, or `../`, then it is taken to be an absolute or a relative filename, and is read directly, without ever calling `XmtFindFile()`.

5.4.1 The Full Story

Example 5-6 and the preceding paragraphs have only explained what you will *typically* do to install and look up icons in auxiliary files. In fact, the pixmap and bitmap converters look for auxiliary files in a number of other places as well. You may never choose to take advantage of these other places, but they do provide a lot of flexibility that allows users and system administrators to override your icon files with their own. The following list shows the places the pixmap converter searches, and the order it searches in. The bitmap converter behaves similarly, but since it cannot use XPM data it only does the XBM searches that are listed. You should read Chapter 6 before trying to fully understand this section.

1. If the name begins with `/`, `./`, or `../`, then it is assumed to be an absolute or relative filename, and no search is required; it is just read directly.
2. If the `XPMLANGPATH` environment variable is set, then `XmtFindFile()` is used to search this path for an XPM file with the specified name. `XPMLANGPATH` is an Xmt environment variable that is analogous to the `XBMLANGPATH` variable that is searched by the Motif function `XmGetPixmap()`.
3. If the `XBMLANGPATH` environment variable is defined, then `XmtFindFile()` is used to search that path for an XBM file. This is done for compatibility with the search done by `XmGetPixmap()`.
4. Next, `XmtFindFile()` is called again to search for an XPM file in four more places:
    a. The user path specified by the `userConfigPath` resource and the `XUSERFILESEARCHPATH` and `XAPPLRESDIR` resources (see Chapter 6 for details).
    b. The path, if any, specified by the `pixmapFilePath` application resource. The default for this resource is `NULL`, so this search is not usually performed.
    c. The path specified by the `configPath` application resource.
    d. The standard system path (see Chapter 6 for details).
5. Finally, `XmtFindFile()` is called again, to look for an XBM file in four analogous places:
    a. The user path.
    b. The path, if any, specified by the `bitmapFilePath` application resource.
    c. The path specified by `configPath`.
    d. The system path.

5.5 Specifying Pixmap Colors

As we've noted, the XPM pixmap format allows you to specify symbolic names for the colors used in the icon. The Xmt pixmap converter will use the `XmtColorTable` specified by the `colorTable` application resource (see Chapter 4, *Using Color*) to look up these symbolic names. The pixmap converter even uses this color table when converting XBM data—it looks up the symbolic names "foreground" and "background" and uses those as the foreground and background colors in its call to `XCreatePixmapFromBitmapData()`. (The String-to-Bitmap converter does not use symbolic colors, of course—it returns a pixmap that is one bit deep, and contains zeros and ones, exactly as specified in the registered XBM data.)

But the Xmt pixmap converter is not limited to using the application-wide color table specified by the `colorTable` application resource—you can specify a color table for the conversion by following the icon name with a colon and a color table specification. (Again, see Chapter 4 for a description of resource file syntax for color tables.) Example 5-7 shows how you might take advantage of this capability.

Example 5-7. Specifying Pixmap Colors

```
!!
!! Motif push buttons get darker when clicked on, to indicate
!! that they are "armed".  This is automatic with text
!! labels, but not with pixmap labels, because colors are
!! hard-coded into pixmaps.  So, what we've got to do is
!! provide two different pixmaps, one for the button's normal
!! state, and one for its "armed" state.
!!
myapp.colorTable: foreground=navy, background=gray, arm_color=gray60

*mailtool.labelType: XmPIXMAP
*mailtool.labelPixmap: envelope
*mailtool.armPixmap: envelope : background=$arm_color
```

Note that the color table used with the `XmNarmPixmap` resource in the example only defines the background color for the icon. Color tables created by the pixmap converter have their parent set to the color table defined by the `colorTable` application resource. So any colors that are not found in the specified color table will be looked up in the application-wide table.

5.6 Looking Up Icons in C

The sections above have explained how the Xmt pixmap and bitmap converters work—how they look for XPM and/or XBM data defined in the icon cache, in special branches of the resource database, and finally in auxiliary files. These converters are implemented simply as calls to the functions `XmtGetPixmap()` and `XmtGetBitmap()`. You can perform the equivalent searches and conversions by calling these functions directly in your C code:

Xmt/

GetPixmap.c

```
#include <Xmt/Pixmap.h>
Pixmap XmtGetPixmap(Widget object, XmtColorTable table, String name)
Pixmap XmtGetBitmap(Widget object, String name)
```

These functions even allow you to specify a color table following a `:` in the icon name, just as you can do in a resource file. The only difference between these functions and the pixmap and bitmap converters is that `XmtGetPixmap()` takes an explicit color table argument. If you specify `NULL`, as the pixmap converter does, then the `colorTable` application resource will be used. Otherwise, this argument specifies the color table that will be used to look up pixmap colors, or that will be used as the parent of any color table specified with the pixmap name.

Keep in mind that the pixmaps and bitmaps returned by these functions are cached for reuse. Since they are shared for use by different parts of the application, they should be treated as read-only (unless you are very sure you know what you are doing). Drawing into a pixmap may change it everywhere it appears in the application (though the change will only take effect the next time the icons are redrawn).

When you allocate a pixmap or a bitmap with one of these functions, you'll often use the resulting `Pixmap` throughout the lifetime of your application, and it will automatically be deallocated when the application exits. If, on the other hand, you can know for certain when a `Pixmap` is no longer in use, you can explicitly free it by calling `XmtReleasePixmap()`:

Xmt/

Pixmap.c

```
#include <Xmt/Pixmap.h>
void XmtReleasePixmap(Pixmap icon)
```

You only have to worry about freeing pixmaps if you call `XmtGetPixmap()` or `XmtGetBitmap()`—the Xt resource converter mechanism will automatically call `XmtReleasePixmap()` on pixmaps and bitmaps created by the resource converters when the widgets that are using those icons are destroyed.

`XmtGetPixmap()` and `XmtGetBitmap()` are a high-level interface to the Xmt icon-handling facilities, and look for icons in a number of places, as we've described. At times, you may prefer to use the lower-level interface which looks only in the icon cache, for XPM or XBM data registered with `XmtRegisterImage()` and `XmtRegisterXbmData()`. The functions `XmtLookupPixmap()`, `XmtLookupBitmap()`, and `XmtLookupBitmask()` provide this lower-level interface. There are also two simplified versions of `XmtLookupPixmap()`: `XmtLookupSimplePixmap()` and `XmtLookupWidgetPixmap()`, which use the Visual, Colormap, and depth of the specified screen or widget. See the reference section for details on these functions.

There is an even lower-level interface that can be useful as well. Recall that in order to register XPM data you first had to parse it to an `XmtImage` with `XmtParseXpmFile()` or `XmtParseXpmData()`. Once you have this compiled form of the XPM data, you can manipulate it directly instead of storing it in the icon cache. See `XmtCreatePixmapFromXmtImage()`, `XmtCreateXImageFromXmtImage()`, and `XmtFreeXmtImage()` in the reference section for more information.

Style: Tips for Icon Design

Steve Anderson is a designer with Hewlett-Packard. The paragraphs below about icon design are excerpted from a paper Steve presented at a developer's conference for the COSE CDE (Common Desktop Environment). Some of his comments are specific to the CDE desktop, but valuable nonetheless:

The Front Panel, being ever-present, is the center stage position in CDE. It presents to the user the "Top Ten" icons. Imagine your application icon being on everyone's Front Panel. Surely your company is successful then, the stock options will be plentiful, and the next-generation enhancements will be pondered from a hot tub! . . .

. . . our first recommendation is to do the basics of icon design on paper. Arriving at the correct graphic symbol is definitely an iterative process, subject to much user testing, and the tools available on the computer are not as efficient at that as simple pencil and paper. The temptation in the paper realm, however is to make them complex. Somehow you have to restrain yourself, because when they are reduced down . . . the basic design must be very simple.

The "color philosophy" used in the design of CDE icons is to keep them crisp, using mostly grays, with colors used as accents . . . This gives icons a design that blends gracefully with the already colorful CDE environment. The grays also allow for reasonable "anti-aliasing."

Of the . . . icons you need to design, the Application Icon is the most important to you, as this is the place for your visual signature. This is what the user double-clicks on to bring up your application, so it should carry the most weight in terms of your company or product identity.

Icons run a complete gamut of graphical styles. From the earliest GUI days the favorite has been a simple black outline style, and as color has been added, it has been like in coloring books, filling color within the black lines. Many icons seek to be pictographic, while others are very abstract. All styles have their place. With the availability of color and medium value backgrounds, the CDE style uses both lighter and darker shades to create fairly realistic images, and we generally avoid the black outline approach. . . . We encourage you to explore this "rendered" style, but the outline style will continue to have a place in the scheme of things as well, especially because of the ease of its transition to monochrome. . . . We favor a more-or-less head-on view, usually from slightly above, if the object in question is a 3-dimensional one . . . an appropriate approach would be to make them look like small, slightly 3-dimensional pins, ones you might pin to a cap or shirt.

Good icon design does not insure good usability. Good metaphors, good panel layout [and] good menu structure . . . are all important. Just in the area of panel layout, for example, I know from first-hand experience how awkward and complex it can be in Motif to get things right: to get the fonts to match, the panel elements to line up, to keep the layout intact as the windows are resized.

Style: Tips for Icon Design (continued)

Unless your application does something that everyone needs done in a truly unique way, you will have some formidable competition out there. It is never too early to get some "visualizers" involved in your product. Their early prototyping work can serve as a guiding beacon for the final product. Instead, the norm is to call the "artists" in at the last minute to fix it with some snappy icons. Unless you have a truly compelling application, the artistic band-aids will not get you in the "Top Ten," which we hope will be a true measure of success for your product.

—*Steve Anderson*
from the paper Tools and Tips for Icon Design

5.7 Summary

This chapter has described how you can look up icons by name in resource files or C code, and how you can specify icon data in C, in resource files, and in auxiliary files read in at runtime.

- Register the Xmt pixmap and bitmap converters with `XmtRegisterPixmapConverter()` and `XmtRegisterBitmapConverter()`.
- These converters look for XPM and/or XBM data in the icon cache, in the resource database, and in auxiliary files.
- You can register XBM data in the icon cache by including the XBM file into your C code and calling `XmtRegisterXbmData()`.
- You can read and parse an XPM file with `XmtParseXpmFile()` or parse an included XPM file with `XmtParseXpmData()`. An `XmtImage` is a parsed XPM file, and can be registered in the icon cache with `XmtRegisterImage()`.
- You can register XBM data in a resource file under the name `_Bitmaps_`, and you can register XPM data under `_Pixmaps_`. Use the *xbm2res* and *xpm2res* scripts to convert XBM and XPM files to the appropriate form.
- The pixmap converters uses `XmtFindFile()` to look for XPM files using the type `pixmaps` and the suffix `.xpm`. The pixmap and bitmap converters look for XBM files using the type `bitmaps` and the suffix `.xbm`. They look relative to `configDir` using `configPath`, and search a number of other locations as well.
- You can also use `XmtGetPixmap()` and `XmtGetBitmap()` to find named pixmaps and bitmaps explicitly in your C code, and can use a number of lower-level functions to avoid the searching and caching performed by those high-level functions.

6

Managing Auxiliary Files

When you write an application, the main file of interest is of course the program executable. But almost all non-trivial applications will have to read in other, auxiliary files at runtime. The most obvious auxiliary file for an Xt application is its app-defaults file. Other auxiliary files might be bitmaps or pixmaps to be displayed in the application, online help text, or even other resource files. Applications also often have their own specific types of auxiliary files, often stored as dot files: saved user preferences, configuration information, or a startup script to be run automatically for the user.

Auxiliary files present a few challenging problems:

- They have to be installed somewhere, and the application must know where they are installed. But different sites will have different conventions about where these sorts of files may be installed, so your program must be adaptable enough to be able to find the files wherever they end up. Also, different operating systems may have very different ways of naming files.
- For internationalization, you may want to read different auxiliary files depending on the setting of the locale. Similarly, in X11R5 and later, you may want to read files depending upon the user's setting of the standard Xt `customization` resource.
- Each auxiliary file that your application requires is one more opportunity for something to go wrong, an extra burden of responsibility placed on the person installing your software. Thus, it is important that there are uniform and logical conventions that control how auxiliary files are named and where they are installed.

This chapter describes tools and techniques for dealing with auxiliary files in your application. It starts with the app-defaults file, and a review of the function, `XtResolvePathname()`, that Xt uses to read in that file. It then describes the function `XmtFindFile()`, which Xmt uses to read in its auxiliary files, and describes why you should use this function instead of `XtResolvePathname()`. Another section summarizes the methods Xmt uses to handle some specific types of auxiliary files, and a final summary includes recommendations about where and how you should store your application's files.

If the idea that auxiliary files deserve an entire chapter in this book seems unlikely (or boring) to you, read on. There are a lot of important points here that help make the difference between a hacked-together program, and a finished, professional application.*

Why Use Auxiliary Files At All?

I've often heard advice that applications should not have any auxiliary files, because you can never really rely on the person installing the application to get everything installed correctly. There is something to this argument, of course, but remember the following points:

- Auxiliary files add customizability—the system administrator can customize the application to a particular site, and users can customize it to their individual preferences.
- Putting information in an auxiliary file reduces the size of the executable. If your application has 100K of online help, for example, you probably don't want this to be hard-coded into the executable—you want to store it in smaller individual files, and read in the individual pieces as the user requests them.
- Some auxiliary files are simply unavoidable—you may have to read a configuration "dot file" from the user's home directory, for example.
- Even if your final, released product will not rely on external resource files, bitmap files, and so forth, it is easier to prototype and begin development of the application with auxiliary files.

So perhaps the problem is not the very existence of auxiliary files, but the fact that there aren't good tools for handling auxiliary files in a program that also give the system administrator the flexibility she needs when installing those files.

—*djf*

*Much of this chapter originally appeared as an article in *The X Resource*, a quarterly journal published by O'Reilly & Associates. Much of this chapter is also UNIX-specific. The `XmtFindFile()` function described here has been ported to VMS and works in a similar way for that operating system.

6.1 Managing the app-defaults File

An application's app-defaults file is generally its most important auxiliary file. This first section is about techniques for managing this file (or getting rid of it altogether). It starts with a review of that mysterious and poorly understood Xt function, `XtResolvePathname()`.

6.1.1 XtResolvePathname()

`XtResolvePathname()` has the signature shown below.

```
String XtResolvePathname(Display *display,
                         String filetype, String filename, String filesuffix,
                         String path,
                         Substitution subs, Cardinal num_subs,
                         XtFilePredicate predicate)
```

The most important of these arguments are the strings: the file type ("app-defaults," or "bitmaps," for example), the filename, the file suffix, and the path that the function should search. To understand `XtResolvePathname()`, it is important to realize that the path is not (as is typical in UNIX) a list of directories to search, but a list of specific files to check for. The path may contain substitution characters following a % character. These are replaced via a number of standard substitutions—`%T` is replaced with the file type, for example—and also via any non-standard substitutions specified in the *`subs`* argument.

Once the substitutions have been performed on the path, each filename in the path is passed to the specified *`predicate`* function. `XtResolvePathname()` returns a copy of the first filename for which the predicate returns `True`. If no predicate is specified (this is the usual case), a default predicate is used which checks that the named file exists and is readable.

If no path is specified, then the contents of the `XFILESEARCHPATH` environment variable are used, or if this variable is not defined, then a default path is used. The default path used by the MIT implementation of Xt is shown below. We'll use this path as an example to demonstrate just how `XtResolvePathname()` works. While examining this path, refer to Table 6-1, which lists the standard substitutions that are performed on it.

```
/usr/lib/X11/%L/%T/%N%C%S:\
/usr/lib/X11/%l/%T/%N%C%S:\
/usr/lib/X11/%T/%N%C%S:\
/usr/lib/X11/%L/%T/%N%S:\
/usr/lib/X11/%l/%T/%N%S:\
/usr/lib/X11/%T/%N%S\
```

Table 6-1. Substitutions Performed by XtResolvePathname()

String	Substitutions
%T	The file type argument.
%N	The filename argument, or the application class, if no name is specified.
%S	The file suffix argument.
%L	The "language string"—generally the value of the `xnlLanguage` resource, or the `LANG` environment variable.
%l	The "language part" of the language string.
%t	The "territory part" of the language string.
%c	The "codeset part" of the language string.
%C	The value of the `customization` application resource. (Only available in X11R5 and later.)
%D	The default Xt search path, so that elements can be appended or prepended to it. (Only available in X11R6 and later.)

XtResolvePathname() Example

Now consider the case of an application "xmail" that wants to find an app-defaults file named `XMail` (the same as the application's class name) with a suffix `.ad`. (App-defaults files are customarily not installed with extensions, but we use one in this example for clarity.) This can be done with a call like the following:

```
filename = XtResolvePathname(dpy, "app-defaults", NULL, ".ad",
                             NULL, NULL, 0, NULL);
```

Since the name isn't specified, `XtResolvePathname()` will use the application's class name (`XMail`). Since the path isn't specified, it will use `XFILESEARCHPATH` or the implementation's default path.

Now suppose that a Japanese user is using this application, running it in the locale "ja_JP.pjis" (the language Japanese, as spoken in the territory Japan, and represented with the pjis encoding). Also suppose that this user has a color display, is running X11R5, and has placed the following line in her *.Xresources* file to request color customizations where available:

```
*customization: -color
```

Finally, assume that `XFILESEARCHPATH` is not set, so that the default path shown above is used. In these circumstances, `XtResolvePathname()` will check for the following files, and will return the first one that is readable:

```
/usr/lib/X11/ja_JP.pjis/app-defaults/XMail-color.ad
/usr/lib/X11/ja/app-defaults/XMail-color.ad
/usr/lib/X11/app-defaults/XMail-color.ad
/usr/lib/X11/ja_JP.pjis/app-defaults/XMail.ad
/usr/lib/X11/ja/app-defaults/XMail.ad
/usr/lib/X11/app-defaults/XMail.ad
```

Now instead, suppose that an American user is running *xmail* with no language string set. In this case the `%L` substitution will be replaced with the empty string, and any adjacent / characters in the path will be collapsed into a single separator. If everything else is the same, `XtResolvePathname()` will have to check only two different files:

```
/usr/lib/X11/app-defaults/XMail-color.ad
/usr/lib/X11/app-defaults/XMail.ad
```

Finally, of course, if there is no customization resource or language string set, then `XtResolvePathname()` (with the default path) would have to search for only a single untranslated, uncustomized file.

Note that `XtResolvePathname()` does the right thing for any language or customization. It also allows system administrators to install files in locations other than */usr/lib/X11* as long as their users always set `XFILESEARCHPATH`.

6.1.2 The Difference Between app-defaults Files and Resource Files

This book emphasizes "programming with resources." Since building a user interface is primarily a descriptive rather than a procedural task, setting resources in a file is better suited to the job than calling functions in a C program is. In the next part of the book, we'll see many resource programming techniques that are available with the Xmt library.

If you do adopt the programming with resources style, you may end up with a *lot* of resources. Bear in mind that there is no inherent reason that these resources must be in the app-defaults file. Remember: the app-defaults file is a resource file, but not all resource files are app-defaults files. An app-defaults file is a special file that is read into an application's resource database during the Xt initialization process. The resources in this file may be overridden by resources from a variety of other sources. (See documentation for `XtAppInitialize()` or `XtDisplayInitialize()` for a detailed description of the process of building the initial resource database.)

The name *app-defaults* tells us something—this file is meant to contain default values for the application. But not all resource files have to contain overridable defaults—there is no reason you can't read other resource files into the resource database after the Xt initialization is done, and after all the user's resource settings have been read in. A resource file read in this way would not be a "defaults" file, because it would not be overwritten by user defaults. We'll see in Chapter 11, *Automatic Widget Creation*, for example, that you can describe the entire widget hierarchy of an application with resources. If you did this, then you would probably not want those resources to be stored in the app-defaults file where they could be modified by user resources.* You can read a resource file in at runtime with the function `XmtLoadResourceFile()`:

*This is a subtle point. If you read in a resource file after Xt initialization, then you can be sure that no user resources will be read in after that point. If you want to be sure that no user resources override your application's private resources, however, you'll want to specify the full widget name for each resource—otherwise, if the user specifies a resource in a more specific way than you do, his specification will take precedence over yours.

Xmt/

Include.c

```
#include <Xmt/Include.h>
Boolean XmtLoadResourceFile(Widget w, String filename,
                            Boolean user, Boolean override);
```

The `filename` argument specifies the file to read; if it is an absolute filename beginning with `/`, or a relative name, beginning with `./` or `../`, then the file is simply read. Otherwise, the file is searched for with a technique that is similar to the app-defaults search performed by `XtResolvePathname()`. This search will be described later in the chapter.

If the `user` argument is `True`, then the function will also look for a user-specific version of the resource file. You will not want to set this argument if you are trying to keep users from modifying application-private resources.

If the `override` argument is `True`, then the resources in the specified file will override resources with the same specification in the database. If `False`, then these new resources will augment those already in the database, but will not override them when conflicts occur.

We'll return to `XmtLoadResourceFile()` in Chapter 11, *Automatic Widget Creation*, when we discuss automatic loading of resource files with the `xmtRequires` pseudo-resource.

6.1.3 Coding Resources into Your Application

Sometimes you will want to deliver a finished application to your users without any app-defaults file at all, perhaps because your users don't have access to */usr/lib/X11* to install the file, or simply for the convenience of the system administrator. One approach is to hard-code all widget resources with `XtSetValues()` so that the application does not rely on any resource file at all. But there is no need to go to this extreme—describing an interface with resources is still far easier than creating it with function calls.

Instead, what you can do is to go ahead and prototype your interface using a resource file. Then, when it comes time to produce a production version of the file, take the resource file, and using a macro in your editor or an *awk* script, for example, convert it to a static array of strings in your application. One approach that some programmers take at this point is to `NULL`-terminate this array of strings and specify it as "fallback resources" in their call to `XtAppInitialize()`. This is a bad idea though—these fallback resources will only be used if no app-defaults file can be found, so if a system administrator goes ahead and creates an app-defaults file for your application in order to specify some site-specific fonts, perhaps, then your application will get none of its resources and will almost certainly break.

What you probably want to do instead is set those resources in the database after initialization is done. You can do this by first calling `XtDatabase()` or `XtScreenDatabase()` to obtain the resource database, and then by inserting your resources into it, one after another, with `XrmPutLineResource()`.

Note, though, that since these resources are inserted into the database after initialization is done, it can be difficult or impossible for the user to override them with resource specifications of his own. Depending on your application, this may be a good or a bad feature. What you may want to actually do is to divide your resources into two arrays and specify those that should be overridable (probably the smaller set of resources) as fallback resources. Then what you need to do is to document these resources, so that a system administrator who wants to create an app-defaults file can duplicate these resources in that file. One approach is to have a special command-line argument that will cause your application to print its fallback resources to the standard output stream—then the system administrator can easily get a list of defaults that he can modify.

Chapter 13, *Resource File Utilities: mockup, checkres, and ad2c*, covers these issues in more detail, and presents a script, *ad2c*, that will convert a resource file into an array of strings for use in C code.

6.2 Where Should Auxiliary Files Be Installed?

If you use an app-defaults file for your application, there is a standard directory it needs to be installed in (*/usr/lib/X11/app-defaults* on most systems*), and a standard name it must have—the application class name. For any other auxiliary file your application will read, you'll have to decide its name and location, and unfortunately, there are no standards to guide your decision.

Your application usually needs a private directory of its own that it can store its files in. The standard X11 clients *xdm*, *twm*, and *fs* install their files in subdirectories of */usr/lib/X11*: */usr/lib/X11/xdm*, */usr/lib/X11/twm*, and so on. Some other common X clients do the same: I have the directory */usr/lib/X11/xfig* on my machine, for example. This is a reasonable enough convention, but it is not one I recommend. There is not anything particularly special about X applications that separates them from other applications—I recommend that you install your application's auxiliary files in under */usr/local/lib* (or the equivalent standard location on your system) along with the auxiliary files of all your non-X applications. If I were the author of *xfig*, that is, I would have placed its auxiliary files in */usr/local/lib/xfig*, rather than */usr/lib/X11*. One important reason for this is that when your users do not have superuser access to their machines, it may be much easier for them to obtain permission to create a directory and install files under the "site directory" */usr/local* than under the "system directory" */usr/lib*.

Whether you choose */usr/local/lib* or */usr/lib/X11*, or some other location, we'll call this directory the "root directory", and all of your application's auxiliary files will be installed somewhere under this root. We'll see later that Xmt provides tools that let the system administrator set application resource that specify the location of this root directory, and in this way allow your application to be free of hard-coded paths.

*This directory depends on the setting of the $PROJECTROOT *imake* variable when your X distribution was built.

Once you've decided on a root directory (that the sysadmin can perhaps override) for your files, you need to decide how the files will be installed beneath that directory. Table 6-2 shows some possible schemes.

Table 6-2. Some Schemes for Installing Files

No.	Installation Scheme	Example File
1	%R/%T/%N%S	*/usr/lib/X11/app-defaults/XMail*
2	%R/%T/%N	*/usr/lib/X11/app-defaults/XMail*
3	%R/%a/%N%S	*/usr/local/lib/xmail/uparrow.xbm*
4	%R/%a/%T/%N	*/usr/local/lib/xmail/bitmaps/uparrow*
5	%R/%T/%a/%N	*/home/david/bitmaps/xmail/uparrow*

The table uses the `XtResolvePathname()` substitutions to describe the installation schemes, with the addition of `%a` to represent the application name and `%R` to represent a "root directory". If your application will be internationalized, you may also want to use separate directories for different languages, but, for simplicity, we've omitted the `%L` substitution (and also the `%C` substitution).

The first scheme shown in Table 6-2 is the one used by the `XtResolvePathname()` default path. Files are installed, with suffixes, in subdirectories by type, but these subdirectories are public, rather than private to a specific application. With this scheme, it is traditional to omit the suffix, as shown in the example. The second scheme is the same one, with the superfluous suffix substitution removed.

Under the third scheme, each application installs its files in a subdirectory of the root directory. This subdirectory has the same name as the application executable, which prevents name conflicts. Since the files are not placed in separate directories according to their types, they are installed with suffixes. This is a good scheme for medium-sized applications with a relatively small number of auxiliary files. Having only a single directory makes installation scripts simpler and makes installing files by hand much easier.

The fourth scheme is similar to the third, but it does segregate auxiliary files into separate subdirectories of the application directory depending on their type. Since these files are separated by type, they are installed without suffixes. This is a good scheme for applications that have a large number of auxiliary files, because it breaks them into more manageable groups.

The fifth scheme places per-application directories within type subdirectories of the root directory. This organization means that an application will have to install files under a number of distinct directories, but also means that the root directory will have only a small number of directories—one for each type—rather than becoming cluttered with one directory for each application. As shown in the example for this scheme, installing files in this way might be particularly desirable when the root directory is a user's home directory.

Xmt uses the third scheme by default, but, as we'll see below, you or the system administrator can override this by setting an application resource. You can also specify other schemes for particular cases—you might use the fifth scheme, for example, when searching for a user-specified pixmap.

6.3 Using XtResolvePathname() with Other File Types

`XtResolvePathname()`, used in conjunction with the default path, makes it very simple to find app-defaults files. When used in other situations, however, it no longer works so well. In this section we examine the main problems with `XtResolvePathname()`, and in the next we'll document the function `XmtFindFile()`, which addresses those problems.

Searching for app-defaults files is not a particularly good example of using `XtResolvePathname()`, because this is automatically handled by the Intrinsics, and application programmers should never have to do it. A more reasonable example would be searching for a bitmap file, or a file of online help text. If our *xmail* application wanted to find a bitmap file which contained an envelope icon, it might call `XtResolvePathname()` like this:

```
filename = XtResolvePathname(dpy, "bitmaps", "envelope", ".xbm",
                             NULL, NULL, 0, NULL);
```

And if it wanted to find its online help file, it might use:

```
filename = XtResolvePathname(dpy, "help", NULL, ".hlp",
                             NULL, NULL, 0, NULL);
```

These calls (assuming no language string or customization, for simplicity) would look for files like:

```
/usr/lib/X11/bitmaps/envelope.xbm
/usr/lib/X11/help/XMail.hlp
```

The problem with this bitmap file is that it is in what amounts to a public directory. Unless the contents of */usr/lib/X11/bitmaps* were to be standardized by the X Consortium, say, *xmail* cannot safely install bitmaps here—another application *ymail* might install a different bitmap by the same name in the same directory.

The help file, on the other hand, is clearly private to *xmail*, because it uses the application class name as its filename. The problem, though, is that this scheme only allows each application to have a single help file. Many applications might want to have several or many files to document different topics.

One way around these problems would be to pass the application name in the *type* argument to `XtResolvePathname()`. If we do this in the above examples, then we might end up searching for files like these:

```
/usr/lib/X11/xmail/envelope.xbm
/usr/lib/X11/xmail/sending_mail.hlp
```

This seems like a reasonable scheme for installing the files, but searching for them this way is a hack—it depends on the fact that the default path uses the %T substitution in an appropriate place.

The fundamental problem here is that we cannot specify both an application name and a base filename for a file we want to look up. This is a problem with the default path, and with the standard substitutions performed by `XtResolvePathname()`.

Other problems with the `XtResolvePathname()` default path include the use of the superfluous %S suffix substitution, which discourages programmers from specifying the *suffix* argument to the function. Also, the way the default path is defined in X11R5, if a user requests both a language and a customization, and no customized, translated resource file is installed, `XtResolvePathname()` will find a customized, but untranslated file before it finds the more appropriate uncustomized, translated file.

Finally, there are a couple of very useful features that are lacking from `XtResolvePathname()`. First, as we hinted above, it is very useful to decouple the root directory from the path. Then by specifying the root directory in the app-defaults file, the system administrator can specify where all the other auxiliary files will be installed. With `XtResolvePathname()`, however, you either accept the */usr/lib/X11* root directory of the default path, or you hard-code some other root directly into an explicitly specified path. Second, the Intrinsics also search for user-specific application resources by searching relative to the user's home directory or the XAPPLRESDIR environment variable, if it is specified. This would be a useful search to be able to duplicate in many applications, but `XtResolvePathname()` does not provide any easy way to do so.

6.4 XmtFindFile()

`XmtFindFile()` addresses the shortcomings of `XtResolvePathname()` described above. It is a lot like `XtResolvePathname()`, but has a couple of new arguments, supports some new substitutions, and has a new default path:

Xmt/

FindFile.c

```
#include <Xmt/Xmt.h>
String XmtFindFile(Widget w, String type, String objname, String suffix,
                   String rootdir, String path, int where)
```

The widget argument *w* replaces the Display pointer argument to `XtResolvePathname()`. The *type* and *suffix* arguments are the same as for `XtResolvePathname()`. The *objname* argument is the base name of the file to be found. Unlike the `XtResolvePathname()` argument *filename*, however, this argument may not be omitted. If *objname* begins with /, ./, or ../, then it is assumed to be an absolute or relative filename, and is simply returned without a search. The *path* argument is like the corresponding `XtResolvePathname()` argument, but note that a root directory for the path may now be specified with the *rootdir* argument. The value of the `rootdir` argument will be substituted into the path using the new `%R` substitution.

Both `rootdir` and `path` may be omitted. If `rootdir` is omitted, the value of the `configDir` application resource will be used instead. The default value for this resource is */usr/lib/X11*, which makes this the default root directory. (Even though I recommend against its use above, this is still the most logical default value.)

`path` may also be omitted—the final `where` argument can be used to specify alternative locations and paths that `XmtFindFile()` should search. If you supply a path, `XmtFindFile()` will always search there. But using the `where` argument, you can also request it to search user-specific directories, the default path, and the */usr/local/lib* "system" directories. This argument will be explained in more detail in a later section.

6.4.1 New Substitutions

We've already mentioned the new `%R` substitution that `XmtFindFile()` recognizes. Table 6-3 lists this and six other new substitutions.

Table 6-3. New XmtFindFile() Substitutions

String	Substitution
%R	The specified root directory, or the `configDir` resource.
%H	The user's home directory.
%a	The application name.
%A	The application class name.
%v	The visual type. One of: "color," "gray," "monochrome."
%z	The approximate screen size. One of: "small," "medium," "large."
%d	The screen depth in bitplanes.

An application named "xmail," for example, might use `XmtFindFile()` as follows to find either the user's *xmail* configuration file:

```
file = XmtFindFile(toplevel,              /* any widget */
                   NULL,                  /* no type for %T */
                   "config",              /* the base filename for %N */
                   NULL,                  /* no suffix for %S */
                   NULL,                  /* use default root directory */
                   "%H/.%a:%R/%a/%N",     /* search this custom path */
                   XmtSearchPathOnly);    /* and don't search anywhere else */
```

Since the hard-coded path does not contain a `%T` or a `%S` substitution in this example, we don't have to specify either the `type` or `suffix` arguments. The `where` argument `XmtSearchPathOnly` specifies that `XmtFindFile()` is to search only the specified path, and not any special user, application, or system paths. If the user's home directory is */home/david*, and the application's `configDir` resource has been specified as */usr/local/lib*, then we can expand this specified path and see that this call would check for two files:

```
/home/david/.xmail
/usr/local/lib/xmail/config
```

Note that it is never useful to specify both %R and %H in the same element of a path—both are replaced by fully-specified directory names.

The %v, %z, and %d substitutions can be useful when using XmtFindFile() to look for things like pixmap files. You might use different pixmaps on color, grayscale, and monochrome screens, for example, or you might use a different size pixmap on a small screen than you would on a medium or large one, for example. And, if you expected your application to be used on color hardware that only supported four bitplanes (16 colors) instead of the more common eight (256 colors) you might define a color pixmap that used only a few colors, so as not to overflow the colormap. Note that the values for the %z substitution are not based on the screen's physical size in inches or centimeters, nor on the screen's resolution in dpi (dots-per-inch), but instead on the absolute number of pixels available (which is often referred to as its resolution). The "small" value for this substitution usually occurs for users running X on a PC screen that is 640 pixels wide. The "medium" value is the most common, although some workstations have "large" screens.

6.4.2 Searching the Default Path

If we omit the *path* argument, and specify *where* to be XmtSearchAppPath, then XmtFindFile() will search the application path (as opposed to the user path or system path described below). The application path is specified by the value of the configPath application resource, which has the following default value:

```
%R/%L/%a/%N%C%S:
%R/%L/%a/%N%S:
%R/%l/%a/%N%C%S:
%R/%l/%a/%N%S:
%R/%a/%N%C%S:
%R/%a/%N%S:
%R/%N%C%S:
%R/%N%S
```

If we remove the language and customization substitutions for simplicity, this path collapses into two distinct elements:

```
%R/%a/%N%S:
%R/%N%S
```

The first element of this path is "installation scheme #3" from Table 6-2. The second element, %R/%N%S, is a variation intended as a safeguard in case a programmer or system administrator makes the mistake of setting the configDir resource to something like */usr/local/lib/xmail* instead of simply */usr/local/lib*.

Let's revisit the *envelope.xbm* example, using XmtFindFile() this time, instead of XtResolvePathname(). We can have XmtFindFile() search the default path with a call like the following:

```
filename = XmtFindFile(toplevel, "bitmaps", "envelope", ".xbm",
                       NULL, NULL, XmtSearchAppPath);
```

If `configDir` is set to */usr/local/lib*, if the application name is *xmail*, and if there is no language or customization set, then this call will look for the files:

```
/usr/local/lib/xmail/envelope.xbm
/usr/local/lib/envelope.xbm
```

Note that we specified the *type* argument, "`bitmaps`", even though we know that the default path does not contain the `%T` substitution. It is important to do this, so that you or a system administrator can modify the default path with the `configPath` resource.

Suppose *xmail* is a large application, with maybe 50 auxiliary files of various types. In this case it might be convenient to install those files in directories by type. To do this, you might set `configPath` in a resource file as follows:

```
*configPath:\
%R/%a/%T/%L/%N%C:\
%R/%a/%T/%L/%N:\
%R/%a/%T/%N%C:\
%R/%a/%T/%N
```

This is the fourth installation scheme listed in Table 6-2, with `%L` and `%C` substitutions added in four possible permutations. Notice that we don't use the `%S` substitution since we do use the `%T` substitution here. We removed the `%l` substitution for brevity, and placed the `%L` at a different place in these path elements than it is in the default path. With this setting of `configPath`, and with the language `ja_JP.pjis` and the customization `-color`, this same `XmtFindFile()` call would check for these four files:

```
/usr/local/lib/xmail/bitmaps/ja_JP.pjis/envelope-color
/usr/local/lib/xmail/bitmaps/ja_JP.pjis/envelope
/usr/local/lib/xmail/bitmaps/envelope-color
/usr/local/lib/xmail/bitmaps/envelope
```

Debugging with XmtFindFile

It can become pretty confusing to figure out where `XmtFindFile()` is looking for your files, especially when you've modified the default `configPath` resource or environment variables like LANG, `XAPPLERESDIR`, and `XFILESEARCHPATH` are set.

If `XmtFindFile()` isn't finding a file that you think it should be, set the `XMTDEBUGFINDFILE` environment variable, and run your program again. With this variable set, `XmtFindFile()` will tell you what it is looking for, and where it is looking. You should see output like this:

```
ozone:34> setenv XMTDEBUGFINDFILE
ozone:35> mockup telecomm
XmtFindFile: looking for object 'phone' of type 'pixmaps'...
        /usr/david/telecomm/phone.xpm
```

Debugging with XmtFindFile (continued)

```
        /usr/david/phone.xpm
        /usr/david/Xmt/src/pixmaps/phone.xpm
        /usr/lib/X11/pixmaps/phone.xpm
        /usr/lib/X11/pixmaps/phone
XmtFileFile: no file found.
XmtFindFile: looking for object 'phone' of type 'bitmaps'...
        /usr/david/telecomm/phone.xbm
        /usr/david/phone.xbm
        /usr/david/Xmt/src/bitmaps/phone.xbm
XmtFindFile: found '/usr/david/Xmt/src/bitmaps/phone.xbm'.
```

If you want to remove this debugging facility from production versions of your application, recompile the Xmt library with the `-DNDEBUG` flag.

—*djf*

6.4.3 Searching the User Path

Sometimes you want to read a file out of the user's home directory, as we did with the `%H/.%a` path earlier in this section. Other times you want the user to be able to optionally override your application's auxiliary files by specifying her own files in some private location—so that the user's auxiliary file will be found before the application's, and be used in place of them. You can arrange for this to happen by having `XmtFindFile()` search the user path.

If the `XUSERFILESEARCHPATH` environment variable is specified, then, for compatibility with the Intrinsics, this is taken as the user path. If this variable is not set (and it usually is not) then the `userConfigPath` application resource specifies the user path. The default value for this resource is the same default path, shown above, used by the `configPath` resource. An important difference between searching the application path and the user path is in the interpretation of the `%R` substitution. When searching the user path, `%R` is replaced with the user's home directory, or if the `XAPPLRESDIR` environment variable is set, with the value of that variable (again, this is for compatibility with the way the Xt Intrinsics search for user app-defaults files).

Generally, you do not want to search only the user path, because you do not want to require the user to have files installed in her home directory. Instead, you search it as the first step, to allow user customizations, before searching the main directory where the application's auxiliary files are installed. If you specify the *`where`* argument to `XmtFindFile()` as `XmtSearchUserPath`, then it will do just this—search the user path and then search whatever path is specified on the *`path`* argument. The values to the *`where`* argument may be OR'ed or added together, so if you wanted to search the user path, and then the "default" or "application" path as we did above, you might specify *`where`* to be:

```
XmtSearchUserPath | XmtSearchAppPath
```

This combination will make `XmtFindFile()` search the user path, the path, if any, specified by the *`path`* argument (you probably won't specify one) and then finally the application path specified by the `configPath` resource. If a file is found in the user path, then `XmtFindFile()` will return it without checking the remaining paths.

So, to return once more to our *envelope.xbm* example, if the *xmail* application wanted to allow the user to override its icons, it might search for them with a call like the following:

```
filename = XmtFindFile(toplevel, "bitmaps", "envelope", ".xbm",
                       NULL, NULL, XmtSearchUserPath | XmtSearchAppPath);
```

Using the default paths, with a root directory of */usr/local/lib*, with no language or customization specified, with `XAPPLRESDIR` unset, and for a user with home directory */home/david*, this call would check for the following files:

```
/home/david/xmail/envelope.xbm
/home/david/envelope.xbm
/usr/local/lib/xmail/envelope.xbm
/usr/local/lib/envelope.xbm
```

If one of these first two files existed in the user's home directory (perhaps it would be an icon of a postcard instead of an envelope) then it would be used instead of the application's standard bitmap.

Note that the default `XmtFindFile()` path is not particularly appropriate for use with the user's home directory as the root—it clutters up that directory with one directory for each application to be customized. To remedy this, the user might set his `XAPPLRESDIR` environment variable to something like */home/david/lib*, which is a directory that it is okay to clutter up.

Or, instead, you (or the system administrator, or the user himself) might set the `userConfigPath` application resource to something different:

```
%R/%T/%a/%N%C:
%R/%T/%a/%N
```

This is the fifth file installation scheme proposed in Table 6-2. Note that we use the `%C` substitution, because the user might sometimes work on a color display and sometimes on a monochrome display, and may want to provide different values for these two cases. But we do not use the `%L` or `%l` substitutions—we assume that the user always uses and writes customized files in the same language. With this new value for the `userConfigPath` resource, and without the `XAPPLRESDIR` setting described above, our most recent call to `XmtFindFile()` would search for the following files:

```
/home/david/bitmaps/xmail/envelope
/usr/local/lib/xmail/envelope.xbm
/usr/local/lib/envelope.xbm
```

6.4.4 Searching the System Path

Besides the user path and the application path, `XmtFindFile()` can also search the system path. If you add the value `XmtSearchSysPath` to the *where* argument, `XmtFindFile()` will perform a search that duplicates the default search performed by `XtResolvePathname()`. That is, it will search the path specified by the `XFILESEARCHPATH` environment variable, or if that is not specified, it will search the default Xt path shown earlier in this chapter (remember that it is different from the `XmtFindFile()` default path). Furthermore, since `XtResolvePathname()` is often called without a *suffix* argument, and `XmtFindFile()` is designed to always have one, `XmtFindFile()` will search the system path twice, if necessary: the first time using the specified suffix, and the second time omitting it.

You will probably not need to search the system path often—it was designed for finding system-wide auxiliary files, but there are no standards in this area. Suppose, however, that in a future release of Motif, the OSF placed a small, standard library of commonly used bitmaps in */usr/lib/X11/motif-bitmaps* (and also under */usr/lib/X11/ja_JP.pjis/motif-bitmaps* and other internationalized directories in the cases for which the icons had to be adjusted to work with different cultures). Then an application that wanted to find the standard envelope icon might use `XmtFindFile()` like this:

```
filename = XmtFindFile(toplevel, "motif-bitmaps", "envelope", ".xbm",
                       NULL, NULL, XmtSearchSysPath);
```

We omit the *path* argument because we only want to search the system path, and we omit the *rootdir* argument, because it is unused in the `XtResolvePathname()` default path that will be searched—the "system path" has a hard-coded root at */usr/lib/X11*.

We could perform the same search of the system path using `XtResolvePathname()`. If, however, we wanted to allow the user the opportunity to provide an alternative envelope icon in her home directory, and allow the system administrator the opportunity to provide an alternative icon in the application configuration directory, we could use `XmtFindFile()` like this:

```
filename = XmtFindFile(toplevel, "motif-bitmaps", "envelope", ".xbm",
                       NULL, NULL, XmtSearchEverywhere);
```

The value `XmtSearchEverywhere` is shorthand for:

```
XmtSearchUserPath | XmtSearchAppPath | XmtSearchSysPath
```

We've seen that `XmtFindFile()` can search four separate paths. These searches are always performed in a fixed order, under specific conditions. They are summarized below.

1. If `XmtSearchUserPath` is specified, the user path is searched. The user path is `XUSERFILESEARCHPATH` or the `userConfigPath` resource. The root directory for this path is taken to be `XAPPLRESDIR` or the user's home directory.

2. Then, if the *path* argument is specified, that path is searched, using the specified *rootdir* or the `configDir` resource.
3. Then, if `XmtSearchAppPath` is specified, the application path is searched. The application path is specified by the `configPath` resource, and uses the root directory specified by the *rootdir* argument or the `configDir` resource.
4. Finally, if `XmtSearchSysPath` is specified, the system path is searched. The system path is `XFILESEARCHPATH` or the Xt default path. The root directory and other special `XmtFindFile()` substitutions are unused for this search.

An Alternative to configDir

The point of the `configDir` application resource is to allow flexibility in the installation of an application's auxiliary files—the system administrator can just set the `configDir` resource in the application's app-defaults file to point to the rest of the application's files.

A common model for many UNIX applications, however, is to use an environment variable to point to the configuration directory instead. If you like this model, or if you are hard-coding all resources into your application so that there is no app-defaults file to be modified, recall that you can set the `configDir` application resource directly when you call `XmtInitializeApplicationShell()`.

You might use code like the following. In this example, the application is named "xwriter," and it reads its configuration directory from the `XWRITER` environment variable.

```
#include <Xmt/Xmt.h>
#include <Xmt/AppRes.h>

Widget toplevel;
char *config;
Arg arglist[10];
int n = 0;

toplevel = XtAppInitialize(...);

config = getenv("XWRITER");
if (config) {
    XtSetArg(XmtNconfigDir, config);
    n++
}

XmtInitializeApplicationShell(toplevel, arglist, n);
```

—djf
Thanks to Scott Johnson

6.5 Special Auxiliary File Types in Xmt

Throughout this chapter we've been using `XmtFindFile()` to look up bitmap files. As we'll see in Chapter 5, *Using Icons*, however, the Xmt library contains pixmap and bitmap caching functions and resource converters that use `XmtFindFile()` internally, so you may never need to use `XmtFindFile()` in this way.

Similarly, the `XmtLoadResourceFile()` function described at the beginning of the chapter (and also in Chapter 11, *Automatic Widget Creation*) also makes use of `XmtFindFile()` internally, so that you will probably never need to use it explicitly when loading auxiliary resource files. And finally, the Xmt online help facilities (see Chapter 30, *Context Help*) also use `XmtFindFile()`.

If you'll be using other types of auxiliary files, `XmtFindFile()` may be extremely useful to you. Even if you never need to use it explicitly, it is still important to understand—if you don't understand `XmtFindFile()`, then you won't be able to understand how the Xmt bitmap converter looks up bitmaps by name, for example.

6.6 Summary

In this final section, I offer some simple recommendations on how and where you should install your application's auxiliary files:

- An application's auxiliary files (except its app-defaults file) should not be installed under */usr/lib/X11*, unless the application is part of the X distribution. Instead, they should be installed wherever auxiliary files are traditionally installed on the system, */usr/local/lib*, for example.
- The files (except the app-defaults file) should be installed in (or under) a directory that has the same name as the application's executable—*/usr/local/lib/xmail*, for example.
- The files may be installed directly within the application subdirectory, with a suffix that identifies their type, or they may be installed in subdirectories of the application directory. In this case, the subdirectory names identify the file types, and the files should be installed without suffixes.
- If you will be allowing the user to provide alternative version of auxiliary files, look for them in the user's home directory, in subdirectories named by type and then by application, */home/david/bitmaps/xmail*, for example.
- If you are installing "system files" that may be used by many X applications, place them in a directory under */usr/lib/X11* .
- Don't hard-code the location of any of an application's auxiliary files except for the app-defaults file; always allow the system administrator to install the files where she chooses. Use the `configDir` application resource to allow the system administrator to specify an alternative root directory, and optionally use the `configPath` resource to allow the administrator to specify an alternative installation location and scheme.

7

Application Resources and Command-Line Arguments

One of the powerful features of Xlib is the X Resource Manager, which allows application customization through a resource database. The X Toolkit builds upon these Xlib `Xrm` functions to make all widget resources customizable. But resources needn't all be at the widget level—Xt also supports *application resources* that allow customization of application variables that are not specific to one particular widget. Another useful feature of the X Resource Manager is its ability to automatically convert command-line options passed to an application into resources in the database. This can be used in conjunction with application (and widget) resources to allow the user to customize your application without having to edit her personal *.Xresources* file.

Application resources and automatic parsing of command-line arguments are both powerful features of X and Xt, but are underutilized by many programmers. Although they are not Xmt-specific features, this chapter explains how you can take advantage of them in your applications. The Xmt library itself uses application resources and command-line arguments, and the chapter begins by explaining these.

7.1 Standard Xmt Resources and Arguments

Table 7-1 lists the application resources that are read by the Xmt library, and the paragraphs below explain each of the resources.

`bitmapFilePath`
: If this resource is defined, it is used instead of `configPath` when the Xmt library looks for bitmap files. See Chapter 6, *Managing Auxiliary Files*, for information on auxiliary application files, and Chapter 5, *Using Icons*, for specific information on looking up bitmap files.

Table 7-1. Xmt Application Resources and Command-Line Arguments

Resource Name	Command Line	Type	Default Value
bitmapFilePath	-bitmapFilePath	String	NULL
busyCursor	-busyCursor	Cursor	watch
busyCursorBackground	-busyCursorBackground	Pixel	white
busyCursorForeground	-busyCursorForeground	Pixel	black
colorTable	-colorTable	XmtColorTable	NULL
configDir	-configDir	String	/usr/lib/X11
configPath	-configPath	String	*see below*
contextHelpFile	-contextHelpFile	String	NULL
contextHelpPixmap	-contextHelpPixmap	Pixmap	*see below*
cursor	-cursor	Cursor	None
cursorBackground	-cursorBackground	Pixel	white
cursorForeground	-cursorForeground	Pixel	black
focusStyle	-focusStyle	XmtFocusStyle	*dynamic*
fontFamily	-fontFamily	String	NULL
helpCursor	-helpCursor	Cursor	"question_arrow"
helpCursorBackground	-helpCursorBackground	Pixel	white
helpCursorForeground	-helpCursorForeground	Pixel	black
helpFilePath	-helpFilePath	String	NULL
palette	-palette	String	NULL
pixmapFilePath	-pixmapFilePath	String	NULL
resourceFilePath	-resourceFilePath	String	NULL
userConfigPath	-userConfigPath	String	*see below*

`busyCursor`
: The cursor to display when `XmtDisplayBusyCursor()` is called. The default is the "watch" cursor in the standard X cursor font. See Chapter 31 for more information on the busy cursor.

`busyCursorBackground`, `busyCursorForeground`
: The foreground and background colors for the busy cursor.

`colorTable`
: A table of symbolic color names to be used by the application. See Chapter 4 for an explanation of color tables and a description of how you can specify them in resource files. Use `XmtRegisterColorTableConverter()` to register a resource converter for this resource.

`configDir`
: The base directory beneath which the application's auxiliary files are installed and looked up. This directory is used by `XmtFindFile()` as the value of the `%R` substitution. On UNIX systems, the default directory is */usr/lib/X11*. See Chapter 6 for more information.

`configPath`
: The default path used by `XmtFindFile()`, and the default path searched by Xmt when looking for auxiliary files for an application. On UNIX systems, the default path is:

```
%R/%L/%a/%N%C%S:
%R/%L/%a/%N%S:
%R/%l/%a/%N%C%S:
%R/%l/%a/%N%S:
%R/%a/%N%C%S:
%R/%a/%N%S:
%R/%N%C%S:
%R/%N%S
```

See Chapter 6 for more information.

`contextHelpFile`
: The name of a resource file containing context help information. If specified, this file is looked up and read in the first time that context help is actually requested. If no file is specified, context help is looked up in the default resource database. See Chapter 30, *Context Help*.

`contextHelpPixmap`
: The icon to display in the upper-left corner of the XmtHelpBox widget used for context help. The default icon is an enlarged version of the "question_arrow" cursor used as the default `contextHelpCursor`. See Chapter 30.

`cursor`
: The "default" cursor for the application. This cursor is not actually displayed by default; you must call `XmtDisplayDefaultCursor()` to have it set on your shell widgets. If this resource is not set, then the application's cursor will depend on the window manager that is in use. See Chapter 31, *Busy States and Background Work*, for more information.

`cursorBackground`, `cursorForeground`
: The foreground and background colors for the cursor specified by the `cursor` resource.

`focusStyle`
: Specifies how the function `XmtFocusShell()` should behave. If this resource is unset, then the default value depends on whether or not the *mwm* window manager is running. See Chapter 15, *Working with the Window Manager*.

`fontFamily`
: A string that controls how the Xmt XmFontList resource converter looks up symbolically named font lists. If an application's resource file is properly set up, the user can use this resource to select a family of fonts to be used. See Chapter 3, *Displaying Text*.

`helpCursor`
: The cursor displayed by `XmtHelpDoContextHelp()` to prompt the user to click on the widget for which help is desired. The default is the "question_arrow" cursor from the standard cursor font. See Chapter 30, *Context Help*, for more information.

`helpCursorBackground`, `helpCursorForeground`
: The foreground and background colors for the help cursor.

`helpFilePath`
If this resource is defined, it is used instead of `configPath` when the Xmt library looks for context help files. See Chapter 6, *Managing Auxiliary Files*, for information on auxiliary application files, and Chapter 30 for specific information on looking up help files.

`palette`
A string that controls how the color table resource converter looks up symbolically named color tables. If the application's resource file is properly set up, the user can use this resource to select a palette of colors for the application. See Chapter 4, *Using Color*.

`pixmapFilePath`
If this resource is defined, it is used instead of `configPath` when the Xmt library looks for pixmap files. See Chapter 6 for information on auxiliary application files, and Chapter 5, *Using Icons*, for specific information on looking up pixmap files.

`resourceFilePath`
If this resource is defined, it is used instead of `configPath` when the Xmt library looks for auxiliary resource files. See Chapter 6 for information on auxiliary application files, and Chapter 11, *Automatic Widget Creation* for specific information on looking up resource files.

`userConfigPath`
The path used by `XmtFindFile()` when searching for auxiliary application files in the user's home directory, or relative to the user's `XAPPLRESDIR` directory. The default is the same as for the `configPath` resource. See Chapter 6.

7.1.1 Reading the Standard Resources

The application resources listed in Table 7-1 are automatically read the first time that any one of them is needed. You can also force them to be read during your application's initialization by calling the function `XmtInitializeApplicationShell()`:

Xmt/

AppRes.c

```
#include <Xmt/AppRes.h>
void XmtInitializeApplicationShell(Widget w,
                                    ArgList args, Cardinal num_args)
```

You are not required to call this function when you use the Xmt library, but it does serve a couple of important functions. First, it allows you to specify a `XtSetValues()`-style resource argument list that will be used to set application resources—this gives you a way to hard-code application resources that you do not want to specify in an app-defaults file or that you do not want users to be able to override. And second, `XmtInitializeApplicationShell()` registers the name of your root application shell for use by the Xmt String-to-Widget resource converter, which will be described in Chapter 9, *Looking Up Widgets by Name*. When you are writing an application with multiple root shells (an uncommon thing to do), it is a good idea to call this function for each application shell you create.

Before you call `XmtInitializeApplicationShell()`, you may want to register resource converters for some of the application resource types. For example, Xmt looks for a `colorTable` application resource, but will not be able to parse this resource unless you have also called `XmtRegisterColorTableConverter()`.

Note that application resources must be set in your application's app-defaults file. If you specify application resources in an auxiliary resource file read in with `XmtLoadResourceFile()` (see Chapter 6, *Managing Auxiliary Files*) or included with the `xmtRequires` pseudo-resource (introduced in Chapter 11, *Automatic Widget Creation*) those resources will have no effect. This is because `XmtLoadResourceFile()` (and the `xmtRequires` resource which uses that function) reads in the application resources as part of its process of loading the specified file. Application resources are read from the database once, and then never updated, so only those specified in the initial resource file will have any effect.

Often, your only involvement with these application resources will be to specify them in the app-defaults files of your applications, or perhaps to hard-code some of them in a call to `XmtInitializeApplicationShell()`. But, like widget resources, you can also set and query them at runtime:

Xmt/

AppRes.c

```
#include <Xmt/AppRes.h>
void XmtSetApplicationValues(Widget w, ArgList args, Cardinal num_args)
void XmtGetApplicationValues(Widget w, ArgList args, Cardinal num_args)
```

These functions behave just like `XtSetValues()` and `XtGetValues()` do, except that they look up application resources for an application shell widget, rather than widget resources. The argument *w* may be any descendant of the toplevel application shell.

7.1.2 Parsing Standard Arguments on the Command Line

Table 7-1 also lists arguments that Xmt will parse from the application's command line. You can get Xmt to do this by calling the function `XmtParseCommandLine()`:

Xmt/

AppRes.c

```
#include <Xmt/AppRes.h>
void XmtParseCommandLine(Widget w, int *argc, char **argv)
```

This function scans the application's command line, looking for any of the strings that are listed in the table. If it finds one, then it sets the corresponding application resource to the value of the next argument on the command line. For example, suppose you invoke an application with arguments like these:

```
xapp -busyCursor circle -contextHelpFile expert_help
```

`XmtParseCommandLine()` will convert these four command-line arguments into two application resource specifications in the resource database:

```
xapp.busyCursor: circle
xapp.contextHelpFile: expert_help
```

When `XmtParseCommandLine()` recognizes and handles arguments, it removes them from the argument array *argv* and decrements *argc* appropriately. (Note that the *argc* argument is the address of the argument count, not the argument count itself.)

Since `XmtParseCommandLine()` converts command-line arguments into application resource specifications, you must obviously call it before you call `XmtInitializeApplicationShell()`. The next section shows an example initialization sequence you might use in your Xmt applications.

7.2 Initializing Your Application

The previous section made a number of points about how you should initialize your Xmt application:

- After you call `XmtAppInitialize()`, it is a good idea (but not required) to call `XmtInitializeApplicationShell()`.
- Since `XmtInitializeApplicationShell()` reads the application resources, you also need to register any special resource converters before calling this function.
- You should call `XmtParseCommandLine()` to give the user an easy way to set the standard Xmt application resources on the application command line. But you have to call it before calling XmtInitializeApplicationShell.

These points are confusing. Example 7-1 shows an initialization sequence that should clarify them.

Example 7-1. Initializing an Xmt Application

```
Widget XmtInitialize(XtAppContext *app_context_return,
                     String application_class,
                     XrmOptionDescList options, Cardinal num_options,
                     int *argc_in_out, String *argv_in_out,
                     String *fallback_resources,
                     ArgList args, Cardinal num_args)
{
    Widget root;

    /*
     * Initialize Xt and create the root shell widget.
     */
```

Example 7-1. Initializing an Xmt Application (continued)

```
    root = XtAppInitialize(app_context_return,
                           application_class,
                           options, num_options,
                           argc_in_out, argv_in_out,
                           fallback_resources,
                           args, num_args);

    /*
     * parse Xmt-specific command-line options
     */
    XmtParseCommandLine(root, argc_in_out, argv_in_out);

    /*
     * register some type converters.
     * We do this now so we can convert
     * Xmt application resources read below.
     */
    XmtRegisterPixelConverter();
    XmtRegisterBitmapConverter();
    XmtRegisterBitmaskConverter();
    XmtRegisterPixmapConverter();
    XmtRegisterColorTableConverter();
    XmtRegisterWidgetConverter();
    XmtRegisterCallbackConverter();
    XmtRegisterXmStringConverter();
    XmtRegisterXmFontListConverter();
    XmtRegisterStringListConverter();
    XmtRegisterMenuItemsConverter();
    XmtRegisterPixmapListConverter();

    /*
     * These aren't strictly type converters, but
     * the idea is the same.
     */
    XmtRegisterLayoutParser();
    XmtRegisterLayoutCreateMethod();

    /*
     * Now register the shell, and look up the app-resources
     * (and do app-resource-related initialization.)
     */
    XmtInitializeApplicationShell(root, args, num_args);

    return(root);
}
```

Example 7-1 shows the definition of `XmtInitialize()`. You can copy the initialization sequence it shows in your own applications, or you can call the function directly—`XmtInitialize()` is an actual convenience function defined by Xmt. You can use it in place of XmtAppInitialize(); it takes identical arguments:

Xmt/

Initialize.c

```
#include <Xmt/Xmt.h>
Widget XmtInitialize(XtAppContext *app_context_return,
                     String application_class,
                     XrmOptionDescList options, Cardinal num_options,
                     int *argc_in_out, String *argv_in_out,
                     String *fallback_resources,
                     ArgList args, Cardinal num_args)
```

See your Xt documentation for XtAppInitialize() for an explanation of these arguments.

Note that XmtInitialize() registers a large number of resource converters (some of which we haven't introduced to you yet). If you will not be using all of these converters, then for the sake of efficiency you may want to write your own version of this initialization function that does not register them all. If you are not using the XmtMenu widget, for example, then you do not need the XmtMenuItems resource converter. (See Chapter 20, *Easy Menu Creation.*)

Calling XmtInitialize() will only be a part of your initialization sequence, of course. Example 7-2 shows the main() procedure for a typical Xmt application. Note that it uses some of the "programming with resources" features that are introduced in Part Three, *Programming with Resources*, of this book. It calls another Xmt convenience procedure, XmtRegisterAll(), which registers standard callback procedures for use with the Xmt callback converter (see Chapter 10, *Callbacks in Resource Files*) and also registers the standard Motif and Xmt widget classes for use with the Xmt automatic widget creation facilities. The example also calls XmtCreateChildren() to perform automatic widget creation (see Chapter 11, *Automatic Widget Creation*), calls XmtRegisterImprovedIcons() to make message dialog boxes look better (see Chapter 25, *Message Dialogs*), and calls XmtDisplayDefaultCursor() to make the cursor application resource cursor take effect over the toplevel shell.

Example 7-2. A Typical Xmt Application

```
main(int argc, char *argv[])
{
    XtAppContext app;
    Widget toplevel;

    /* Initialize Xt and Xmt all at once */
    toplevel = XmtInitialize (&app, app_class_name, NULL, 0,
                              &argc, argv, NULL, NULL, 0);

    /* Register all known Motif and Xmt widgets and procedures */
    XmtRegisterAll();
```

Example 7-2. A Typical Xmt Application (continued)

```
    /* Give message dialogs bigger, nicer icons */
    XmtRegisterImprovedIcons(toplevel, NULL);

    /* Create the widget hierarchy described in resources */
    XmtCreateChildren(toplevel);

    /* Create windows for all the widgets */
    XtRealizeWidget(toplevel);

    /* Make the cursor application resource take effect */
    XmtDisplayDefaultCursor(toplevel);

    /* Enter the standard event loop */
    XtAppMainLoop(app);
}
```

7.3 Implementing Application Resources

The standard Xmt application resources described previously serve Xmt-specific purposes. Every application will have its own customization needs, and should have its own set of application resources. Using application resources is an ideal way to handle customization, for a few important reasons:

- Application resources can easily be set from the command line, with the `-xrm` argument, or through automatically-parsed custom command-line arguments, as we'll see below.
- Application resources are more useful than command-line arguments, however, because once the user has decided on the options he likes, he can place them permanently in his *.Xresources* file. Command-line arguments must be typed explicitly each time the application is started.
- Resource files have a standard, well-known syntax among users of X applications. It is easier for a user to customize resources in his *.Xresources* file than it is for him to learn the syntax of a custom configuration file format that you would otherwise define for your application.

Defining your own application resources is not difficult to do. First, you define a data structure to hold each of the variables that you want to allow the user to customize. Second, you statically initialize an `XtResourceList`—an array of `XtResource` structures (see the information icon, "The XtResource Structure")—that describe the fields in your application resource data structure and give those fields names and default values. Third, you declare an instance of your data structure type, to actually hold the resource values—this will usually be a global variable, accessible throughout your application. And finally, you call `XtGetApplicationResources()`:

```
void XtGetApplicationResources(Widget object, XtPointer base,
                               XtResourceList resources, Cardinal num_res,
                               ArgList args, Cardinal num_args)
```

The arguments you pass to `XtGetApplicationResources()` are your toplevel widget, the address of your global data structure, and the list of `XtResource` structures. You can also pass an `XtSetValues()`-style argument list that is used to override resource settings from the database. If you are going to hard-code values for your application resources, though, it doesn't make much sense to make them resources in the first place, so you will usually pass `NULL` for the *`args`* argument.

Example 7-3 shows how you might use `XtGetApplicationResources()` in your application.

The XtResource Structure

The `XtResource` structure describes a single field in an application data structure. Elements of the `XtResource` structure specify the size of the field and its position in the application data structure. Other elements in the `XtResource` structure specify a name, a class, and a type for the field, allowing us to refer to the field by name, and to perform automatic type conversions on values for the field. Finally, two other elements of the `XtResource` provide a default value for the field.

The `XtResource` structure is defined as follows. The meaning and usage of each of its elements is described in the paragraphs below.

```
typedef struct _XtResource {
   String    resource_name;   /* Resource name */
   String    resource_class;  /* Resource class */
   String    resource_type;   /* Representation type desired */
   Cardinal  resource_size;   /* Size in bytes of representation */
   Cardinal  resource_offset;/* Offset from base to put resource value */
   String    default_type;    /* Representation type of specified default */
   XtPointer default_addr;    /* Address of resource default value */
} XtResource, *XtResourceList;
```

`resource_name`

This element specifies the name of the resource, i.e., the name that must appear in a resource file to set this resource. By convention, the first letter of a resource name is lowercase, and any subsequent words are capitalized and concatenated without a hyphen or underscore—"background" and "backgroundPixmap", for example. If you define a symbolic constant for the resource name, it should be the same as the resource name, with a prefix, which should end with an N—`XtNbackground` or `XmNbackgroundPixmap`, for example. It is also convention that the field in which this resource's value will be stored has the same name as the resource, using all lowercase letters, and using underscores to separate the words—`background` and `background_pixmap`, for example. Resource names beginning with "xt" are reserved by the Intrinsics. (Note: this is an "xt" in the resource name itself, not an "Xt" in `XtNbackground`, for example.)

The XtResource Structure (continued)

`resource_class`

This element specifies the class name of the resource. If a number of resources have the same class, you can specify a value for all those resources with a single line in a resource file. The "normalFont" and "bold-Font" resources might both be of class "Font", for example. Class names conventionally begin with capital letters, and, as with resource names, subsequent words are capitalized and underscores are not used. Symbolic names for class names are conventionally spelled the same way as the class name with a prefix which ends with C—`XtCFont`, for example. If there is no general category to use for a resource's class, the class should be the same as the resource name, but capitalized. Class names beginning with "Xt" are reserved by the Intrinsics.

`resource_type`

This element is a string that identifies the type of the resource. By convention, it is spelled the same way as the type of the field that this resource will set, but begins with a capital letter. Symbolic names for resource types are spelled the same as the type name, but begin with a prefix which end with R—`XtRInt` and `XmRFontList`, for example. Type names are used to identify which resource converter should be used to convert a string value from the resource database into the appropriate type. If one of your fields is not one of the standard types listed below, use a type of your own, but be aware that you will have to write and register a converter procedure if you want to get values for that field from the resource database.

`resource_size`

This element specifies the size in bytes of the field in your structure that this resource will set. Use the `sizeof()` operator to compute this value.

`resource_offset`

This element specifies the offset of this resource's field from the beginning of the structure. This value is added to the ***base*** argument passed to `XtGetApplicationResources()` in order to determine where the resource value is to be stored. This field plus the `resource_size` field provide enough information to correctly store the resource value. Use the `XtOffsetOf()` macro to determine the offset of a field in a structure.

`default_type`

This is a string which specifies the type of the default value in the `default_addr` field. `default_type` is a representation type, like the `resource_type` field explained above. The representation type of the default does not have to be the same as the type of resource. If they do not match, an appropriate resource converter will be invoked to convert the default value when it is required.

There are two special values that can be specified for this element. If `default_type` is `XtRImmediate`, then `default_addr` is interpreted

The XtResource Structure (continued)

as the resource value itself, rather than a pointer to the value. This is useful for resources that are integers, Booleans, or other scalar types. If `default_type` is `XtRCallProc`, then `default_addr` is a pointer to a procedure of type `XtResourceDefaultProc`, which is responsible for storing the default value in the correct location. See `XtResource-DefaultProc` in your reference manual for details on the responsibilities of such a procedure.

`default_addr`

This element specifies a pointer to the default value of the resource, which must be of the type identified by `default_type`. This field is interpreted differently for types `XtRImmediate` and `XtRCallProc`, as explained above. Also, if `default_type` is `XtRString`, then `default_type` is the string itself (a `char *`), not the address of the string (a `char **`).

—*djf*
from Volume Five, X Toolkit Intrinsics Reference Manual

Example 7-3. Handling Custom Application Resources

```
/*
 * First: define a data type.
 */
typedef struct {
    XFontStruct *bold_font;
    Boolean palette_on_left;
    Pixel highlight_color;
} application_resource_t;

/*
 * Second: describe each of the resources in an XtResourceList.
 * First, though we set up some stuff for handling default values--
 * notice the three different ways we handle defaults below.
 */

/*
 * A Motif internal procedure to obtain default Motif foreground.
 * This function should be made public, under a different name,
 * in Motif 2.0.
 */
extern void _XmForegroundColorDefault(Widget, int, XrmValue *);

/*
 * A default font name that we'll use below.  The default string will
 * be automatically converted to a font if it is needed.
 * We define it within #ifndef so it can be overridden when compiled.
 */
#ifndef DEFAULT_BOLD_FONT
#define DEFAULT_BOLD_FONT "*-helvetica-bold-r-*-*-*-140-*"
```

Example 7-3. Handling Custom Application Resources (continued)

```
#endif

/*
 * Here's the resource list itself.
 * Note the use of sizeof(), and XtOffsetOf().  Also, note the
 * use of some standard class names, and basic representation types.
 */
static XtResource resources[] = {
    {"boldFont", XtCFont, XtRFontStruct, sizeof(XFontStruct *),
        XtOffsetOf(application_resource_t, bold_font),
        XtRString, (XtPointer) DEFAULT_BOLD_FONT},
    {"paletteOnLeft", "PaletteOnLeft", XtRBoolean, sizeof(Boolean),
        XtOffsetOf(application_resource_t, palette_on_left),
        XtRImmediate, (XtPointer) True}
    {"highlightColor", XtCForeground, XtRPixel, sizeof(Pixel),
        XtOffsetOf(application_resource_t, highlight_color),
        XtRCallProc, (XtPointer)_XmForegroundColorDefault},
};

/*
 * Third: declare a global structure to hold the application resources
 */
application_resource_t app_resources;

main(int argc, char **argv)
{
    XtAppContext app_context;
    Widget toplevel;

    /* initialize Xt, create the toplevel widget */
    toplevel = XtAppInitialize(&app_context, "XDraw", NULL, 0, &argc, argv,
                               NULL, NULL, 0);

    /*
     * Fourth: call XtGetApplicationResources()
     * If the app is named 'xdraw', it will look for resources like these:
     *      xdraw.boldFont: *-times-bold-r-*-*-*-180-*
     *      xdraw.paletteOnLeft: False
     *      xdraw.highlightColor: blue
     */
    XtGetApplicationResources(toplevel,              /* app. shell widget */
                              (XtPointer)&app_resources,  /* base address */
                              resources,        /* description of resources */
                              XtNumber(resources),    /* how many resources */
                              NULL, 0);                /* an empty ArgList */
        .
        .
        .
}
```

7.3.1 Using Application Resources

Once you've defined your resource list and queried the application resources from the resource database, you can simply go ahead and use them however you want, with no further worries. `XtGetApplicationResources()` guarantees that each of the fields described in your resource list will be filled in with a value (converted as necessary) from the resource database, or with the default value you specified.

It is worth emphasizing just how easy it can be to make use of application resources, so that you will not be reluctant to add them liberally to your applications. Suppose, for example, that your application beeps in various places to indicate errors. You could make it do this by calling:

```
XBell(XtDisplay(toplevel), 0);
```

Or, if you weren't sure what volume would be appropriate for the beeps, and wanted to be able to specify it at compile time, you might have used code like this:

```
#ifndef BELL_VOLUME
#define BELL_VOLUME 0
#endif
XBell(XtDisplay(toplevel), BELL_VOLUME);
```

Then, when you had finished a prototype of your application, you might revisit this code and realize that the bell volume is really one of those things that the user should be in control of. You could do this by adding a `bell_volume` field to your `app_resources` data structure, adding one more `XtResource` structure to your resource list, and making a single further change to your code:

```
        .
        .
        .
{"bellVolume", "BellVolume", XtRInt, sizeof(int),
    XtOffsetOf(application_resource_t, bell_volume),
    XtRImmediate, (XtPointer) 0},
        .
        .
        .
#ifndef BELL_VOLUME
#define BELL_VOLUME app_resources.bell_volume
#endif
```

The flexibility this gives the user is well worth the five or ten minutes it takes to implement in your code. In fact, the only serious work involved is the documentation you'll have to write so the users know that this application resource is available to them.

The moral to this example is that implementing application resources is easy and that you should use them freely whenever you find yourself making any arbitrary choice about fonts, colors, sounds, icons, or whatever.

Floating-Point Numbers as Resources

Some applications (and some widgets) will require floating-point numbers as resources. Alvin Wen explains the difficulties of using resources of type `float`*, and instead recommends using* `double` *for any floating-point resources you require.*

From time to time you may need to set the value of a resource of type `XtRFloat`, corresponding to the C `float` base type. Such a resource could contain an endpoint of an axis of a plotter widget, for example. Unfortunately, both of the following approaches will fail:

```
/* approach #1: doesn't work */
int i=0;
Arg args[10];
float max = 5.4;                          /* set the origin to 5.4 */
XtSetArg(args[i], XtNxMax, max); i++; /* max is cast to an integer */
XtSetValues(widget, args, i);

/* approach #2: doesn't work either */
XtVaSetValues(widget,
              XtNxMax, max,             /* max is promoted to a double */
              NULL);
```

The `XtSetArg()` macro fails because it casts the resource value you provide to an `XtArgVal`, which is usually defined as `long`. When you pass a `float` value like 5.4 (which has an internal bitwise representation involving bases and exponents) to `XtSetArg()`, it is converted to the long integer 5 (which has a completely different internal representation). The subsequent call to `XtSetValues()` copies this now integral value into a place reserved for a `float`, and the results are unpredictable.

The call to `XtVaSetValues()` fails for a somewhat different reason. Since `XtVaSetValues()` takes a variable-length argument list, C compilers apply their default parameter passing rules to its arguments; in this case, arguments of type `float` are promoted to type `double`. Unfortunately, the Intrinsics are not aware of this promotion, and when they extract resource values from this argument list, havoc results.

There are two ways around this problem. The first avoids implicit type conversions by casting the float value explicitly:

```
XtArgVal my_val;
float max = 5.4;

my_val = *(XtArgVal *)&max;
XtSetArg(args[i], XtNxMax, my_val); i++; /* this works */
XtSetValues(widget, args, i);
/* or */
XtVaSetValues(widget,
              XtNxMax, my_val,            /* so does this */
              NULL);
```

Floating-Point Numbers as Resources (continued)

An easier (if somewhat less efficient) method makes use of the special XtVaTypedArg argument to XtVaSetValues() to force a resource conversion:

```
XtVaSetValues(widget,                  /* take advantage of Xt's */
              XtVaTypedArg, XtNxMax,   /* String-To-Float type converter */
              XtRString, "5.4", 4,     /* 4 is length of string "5.4", */
              NULL);                   /* including NUL terminator */
```

Note that you should never have any trouble querying the value of an XtRFloat resource; in this case, both XtSetArg() and XtVaGetValues() are passed pointers to floats, which avoids the typecasting problems we saw above.

Because XtRFloat resources can be so tricky to use you should avoid this type in your own application resources or widgets. One solution is to instead use the C double type, which is usually larger than an XtArgVal. Resources larger than XtArgVal are passed to XtSetArg() and XtVaSetValues() by reference, bypassing thorny type conversion issues. (Note, though, that there is no default Xt resource converter for double values, and no predefined XtRDouble type.)

—Alvin Wen

7.3.2 Other Application Resource Techniques

There are a few other application resource techniques that are worth mentioning. Querying the resource database is a fairly efficient thing to do. At times, though, you may want to defer queries until the resource values are actually needed. So if you have application resources that affect only the appearance of a special dialog box, then you might want to describe those resources in a separate XtResourceList and not query them until the first time the dialog is popped up. Another reason you might want to defer queries is for modularity and data hiding—application resources that affect only a dialog box can be kept in a static structure visible only in the dialog box module. In practice, it is often easiest to query all your resources at once, but be aware that you can call XtGetApplicationResources() whenever you want, not just in your initialization code in main().

Application resources are usually most conveniently stored as fields in a single data structure, but you don't have to do it this way. If you pass NULL as the *base* address to XtGetApplicationResources(), then you can just use the address of variables directly in the resource_offset fields of your XtResourceList, instead of using XtOffsetOf() to compute their offset from the start of a structure. This gives you more flexibility when you want to store your application resource values in a variety of global variables or global structures.*

An important advantage, though, to collecting all your application resources into a single structure is that you can then call `XtGetApplicationResources()` multiple times with the same resource list but with different copies of your data structure. If your application opens root windows on two different screens, for example, then it might query the application resources twice, since each screen (in X11R5 and later) has a separate resource database.

Finally, note that you can pass any widget to `XtGetApplicationResources()`, not just your root application shell. If you do this, it will look for resources that appear to be resources of the widget you specify, rather than resources that apply to the application as a whole. The Xmt library looks up this kind of "pseudo-resource" in a number of places—it implements context help for a given widget, for example, by looking for a special **`xmtHelp`** resource specified for that widget. `XtGetSubresources()` is similar to this usage of `XtGetApplicationResources()`, but queries "subpart" resources instead. A widget that displays data plots, for example, might use `XtGetSubresources()` to query defaults for its X axis and its Y axis—a plotter resource might look like **`plotter.title`**, while a "subpart resource" might look like **`plotter.xaxis.max`**, even if there is no widget named **`xaxis`**.

7.4 Implementing Command-Line Arguments

As noted in the previous section, application resources are often more useful than command-line arguments, because they can be set permanently in a user's *.Xresources* file, rather than having to be typed each time the application is started. The flip side to this argument, of course, is that if the resource is just to be set once, then typing an argument on the command line is easier than editing a resource file. Fortunately, the X Resource Manager has a facility that will automatically parse command-line arguments and convert them to resource specifications in the resource database, where they can then be read in as application resources.

Thus, if you've taken the fairly simple steps required to implement application resources for your program, then it is worth taking one further simple step to make these resources available as command-line arguments. Just as you must describe each application resource with an `XtResource` structure, you must first describe each command-line argument with an `XrmOptionDescRec` structure (see the icon "Describing Command-Line Arguments"). Then, all you need to do is pass this array of structures as the *`options`* argument to `XtAppInitialize()` (or to `XmtInitialize()`, of course), and pass the number of elements in the array as the *`num_options`* argument. You must also pass *`argv`* and the address of *`argc`* to `XtAppInitialize()`, of course, so that the function can actually read the command line.

---

*But note that this technique might not be portable to architectures for which `sizeof(Cardinal)` differs from `sizeof(XtPointer)`. I don't know of any such architectures.

As `XtAppInitialize()` parses the command line, it removes arguments that it recognizes from *argv* and decrements *argc* appropriately. As described earlier in this chapter, you may pass any arguments remaining in *argv* to `XmtParseCommandLine()` in order to parse the standard Xmt command-line arguments listed in Table 7-1 After calling `XtAppInitialize()` and `XmtParseCommandLine()`, any arguments remaining in *argv* are either errors (and you should probably print a warning message) or are arguments that your application will parse "by hand."

Example 7-4 shows how you can declare an `XrmOptionDescList` that corresponds to the `XtResourceList` shown in Example 7-3. Note that two of the arguments take the next argument in *argv* as the resource value, and that the other two (`-left` and `-right`) have their resource value encoded directly into the `XrmOptionDescRec`.

Example 7-4. Describing Command-Line Arguments for Application Resources

```
static XrmOptionDescRec options[] = {
    {"-boldFont",    ".boldFont",       XrmoptionSepArg},
    {"-right",       ".paletteOnLeft",  XrmoptionNoArg, (XPointer)False},
    {"-left",        ".paletteOnLeft",  XrmoptionNoArg, (XPointer)True},
    {"-highlight",   ".highlightColor", XrmoptionSepArg },
};
```

Describing Command-Line Arguments

In order to have the X Resource Manager automatically parse command-line arguments for you, you must describe the arguments that your application understands and also describe how they should be handled. You do this by initializing an array of `XrmOptionDescRec` structures, one for each command-line argument. This structure, and an associated enumerated type, look like this:

```
typedef struct {
    char *option;           /* Option specification string in argv */
    char *specifier;        /* Resource name and binding (w/o app name) */
    XrmOptionKind argKind;  /* Which style of option it is */
    XPointer value;         /* Value to provide if XrmoptionNoArg */
} XrmOptionDescRec, *XrmOptionDescList;

typedef enum {
    XrmoptionNoArg,      /* Value is specified in XrmOptionDescRec.value */
    XrmoptionIsArg,      /* Value is the option string itself */
    XrmoptionStickyArg,  /* Value is chars immediately following option */
    XrmoptionSepArg,     /* Value is next argument in argv */
    XrmoptionResArg,     /* Resource and value in next argument in argv */
    XrmoptionSkipArg,    /* Ignore this option and next argument in argv */
    XrmoptionSkipLine    /* Ignore this option and the rest of argv */
    XrmoptionSkipNArgs   /* Ignore this option and the next
                            XrmOptionDescRec.value arguments in argv */
} XrmOptionKind;
```

Describing Command-Line Arguments (continued)

The `option` field of the `XrmOptionDescRec` structure is the string that is to be searched for on the command line—something like "-busyCursor". The `specifier` field is the left-hand side of the resource specification that should be inserted into the database if the specified argument is found—something like ".busyCursor", "*FontList", or "*work_area.background". Note that these specifications do not include the application name, nor a colon. The `argKind` field specifies how the value of the resource—the right-hand side of the resource specification—should be obtained. The `value` field is used for some values of `argKind`, as described in the paragraphs below.

The `XrmOptionKind` enumerated type describes eight different ways that an argument can be handled. The meanings of these eight values are described below. Note the lowercase letter `o` in these enumerated types—they are an exception to the standard Xlib and Xt capitalization conventions.

`XrmoptionNoArg`
: The value of the resource is specified (as a String) in the `value` field of the `XrmOptionDescRec` structure. This can be useful for Boolean resources, where the presence of an argument is sufficient to specify its value.

`XrmoptionIsArg`
: The value of the resource is the argument string itself. This argument kind is not often useful, because arguments strings usually begin with a - or +, while resource values usually do not.

`XrmoptionStickyArg`
: The value is the characters immediately following the option with no whitespace intervening. This is useful for options like *-I/usr/local/include*.

`XrmoptionSepArg`
: The value of the resource is the next argument on the command line. This is generally the most common type of argument—e.g. *-fg blue*.

`XrmoptionResArg`
: The resource name and its value are the next argument on the command line. This is how the standard *xrm* argument is implemented, and is not really useful for anything else.

`XrmoptionSkipArg`
: Ignore this option and the next argument in `argv`. When you will be parsing some arguments yourself, you may want to specify them to be skipped, so that they are not mistakenly parsed.

`XrmoptionSkipLine`
: Ignore this option and the rest of `argv`.

Describing Command-Line Arguments (continued)

`XrmoptionSkipNArgs`
: Ignore this option, and also skip the number of arguments specified in the `value` field of the `XrmOptionDescRec` structure.

—*djf*
Based on Volume One, Xlib Programming Manual, by Adrian Nye

7.4.1 Command-Line Arguments for Widget Resources

The command-line arguments we've seen so far in this chapter need not be used only to set application resources. In many cases, it can be useful to provide command-line arguments that are shortcuts for setting widget resources. In an application that uses a text widget as its main work area, for example, you might want to provide ways of separately specifying the color and font of the work area:

```
static XrmOptionDescRec options[] = {
    {"-font",     "*FontList",               XrmoptionSepArg},
    {"-textFont", "*main_text.fontList",     XrmoptionSepArg},
    {"-textBg",   "*main_text.background",   XrmoptionSepArg},
};
```

Given the minimal extra effort it takes to add command-line options, it is worth your time to think about the important widgets in your application and the resources that your users might commonly like to set on them.

7.4.2 Modular Parsing of the Command Line

Sometimes you will find that you have a set of command-line arguments that you want to describe in an `XrmOptionDescList` that is separate from the main application options array that is passed to `XtAppInitialize()`. This might be because they are all options related to a particular module of your application, and you do not want to declare them globally, for example.

Passing a list of command-line arguments to `XtAppInitialize()` is quite convenient, but it is not the only way to parse them. `XmtParseCommandLine()`, for example, can be called any time you want. The one restriction, of course, is that it doesn't make sense to parse the command line and set resources in the resource database after you have read the corresponding application resources or created widgets that will use those resources.

To parse the command-line arguments after you have called `XtAppInitialize()`, call `XrmParseCommand()` (an Xlib function, not an Xt function):

```
void XrmParseCommand(XrmDatabase *database,
                     XrmOptionDescList options, int num_options,
                     char *app_name, int *argc, char **argv)
```

The first argument to this function is the resource database, which you can obtain with `XtDatabase()` or, in X11R5 and later, with `XtScreenDatabase()`. *options* and *num_options* are the array of `XrmOptionDescRec` structures and the number of elements in the array. *app_name* is the application name, used when inserting resources into the database. You can hard-code this name, but the most flexible way to obtain it is by calling `XtName()` on the widget returned by `XtAppInitialize()`. This will be the final component of `argv[0]` or the value of the `-name` command-line argument. `XrmParseCommand()` takes the address of *argc* and *argv*, just as `XtAppInitialize()` and `XmtParseCommandLine()` do, and removes any arguments it parses from the *argv* array and decrements *argc* appropriately.

7.5 Summary

This chapter has listed the standard Xmt application resources with their corresponding command-line arguments and has summarized their purposes. It has shown how you can initialize your Xmt application in order to parse the Xmt command-line arguments and read the Xmt application resources. It has also shown how you can implement your own application resource and command-line arguments:

- Call `XmtParseCommandLine()` to parse the standard Xmt command-line arguments from your `argv[]` command line.
- Call `XmtInitializeApplicationShell()` to read the standard Xmt application resources and do other Xmt initialization based on those resources.
- Call `XmtInitialize()` to initialize Xt and call the above two functions.
- Implement your own application resources, describe the resources in a statically-initialized array of `XtResource` structures, and call `XtGetApplicationResources()`.
- Implement command-line arguments that correspond to your custom application resources, or to widget resources, describe the arguments in a statically-initialized array of `XrmOptionDescRec` structures, and pass the array in your call to `XtAppInitialize()` or `XmtInitialize()`, or parse the arguments by calling `XrmParseCommand()` directly.

8

Utility Functions

Most of the chapters of this book treat a single major topic at a time, and document the Xmt functions related to that topic. This chapter documents the remainders. These are miscellaneous utility functions that do not warrant a chapter of their own, but which are certainly useful anyway.

It is worth at least skimming each of the sections in this chapter. Then, if you find you need one of the utility functions described, you will know where to find out about it.

8.1 Setting Initial Focus in Dialogs

When a Motif dialog box pops up, the keyboard focus is initially on the default button. For simple warning and error messages, this is great—the user can simply hit the **Return** key to dismiss the dialog box. But for any dialog that requests input from the user, the keyboard focus ought to be on the widget that needs the input; that way, the user can simply start typing into an XmText widget, or use the arrow keys to scroll through an XmList widget, for example. Unfortunately, Motif leaves the focus on the default button, so the user must either take his hands off the keyboard to use the mouse, or must use the Tab key to move focus to the widget that requires input.

In Motif 1.2, there is a simple way to fix this problem: set the `XmNinitialFocus` resource of the XmManager widget to the descendant widget that should get input focus when a dialog first pops up. This resource was only added in Motif 1.2, however. Setting initial focus in Motif 1.1 is much more complicated: you can use `XmProcessTraversal()` to change the keyboard focus, but you can't do this until the dialog box itself is first given focus, which is not until some unknown time after you manage it. You can use the `XmNfocusCallback` to determine when the dialog gets focus, but Motif traversal is not completely initialized when this callback is invoked, so calling `XmProcessTraversal()` from the callback may not always work either. What you are forced to do is register a procedure on the focus callback list, and set a zero-length timer when this callback procedure is invoked. This timer will expire the next time control returns to the event loop, and in the timer callback, you can finally call `XmProcessTraversal()`.

This is exactly the sort of situation that demands a convenience routine, and Xmt provides one:

Xmt/

InitFocus.c

```
#include <Xmt/Xmt.h>
void XmtSetInitialFocus(Widget dialog, Widget initial)
```

`XmtSetInitialFocus()` is a portable way to set the initial focus of a dialog. It takes two `Widget` arguments: the dialog (the child of the shell, not the shell widget itself) and the descendant of that widget, which is to receive the initial keyboard focus when the dialog pops up. In Motif 1.2, this function simply sets the `XmNinitialFocus` resource, and in Motif 1.1, this function jumps through all the hoops described above to achieve the same effect. The dialog boxes created and managed by `XmtAskForString()` and the other `XmtAskFor` functions (see Chapter 26, *Simple Input Dialogs*) use `XmtSetInitialFocus()` to ensure that focus is initially set to the widget that the user is most likely to interact with first.

8.2 Issuing Warning and Error Messages

When your application has to issue a warning message or display an error message to the user, you will often use one of the Xmt simple message dialog functions, like `XmtDisplayWarning()` to display the warning in a dialog box. Sometimes, though, you will want to issue a warning or error message intended not for the user, but for a programmer or a system administrator. These are text messages that you want to go to the terminal from which the application was started. You often see messages like this generated by widgets. A common one that you've probably run across in your own programming is:

```
Error: shell widget has zero width or height.
```

Though applications will usually display messages in dialogs, there are times when a text-only error or warning of this form is useful. An application might display a message like this at startup when it is incorrectly installed, for example:

```
Warning: cannot find app-defaults file; continuing with fallback resources
```

Xt provides the functions `XtAppWarning()` and `XtAppError()` to display error and warning messages like this. These are simple functions; they take a string argument and display it. `XtAppError()` exits and `XtAppWarning()` returns.

The major shortcoming of these functions is that they require you to hard code strings into your application; this makes it difficult to customize the messages, for example, when you want to internationalize the application. For this reason, the recommended way to display warning and error messages to the terminal is with the functions `XtAppWarningMsg()` and `XtAppErrorMsg()`. These functions also take the message to display, but the message is allowed to contain `printf()`-style substitutions. They take an array of arguments to substitute into the message. More importantly for customization, however, these functions take three string arguments that specify a name, type, and class for each message. The message text you specify is simply the default message to be printed—when you call `XtAppWarningMsg()` or `XtAppErrorMsg()` they first check a special error resource database to look up a message of the specified name, class, and type.

The problem with these more sophisticated warning and error functions is that they are too complicated. In particular, it is quite annoying to fill an array with the arguments to be substituted into the message and then pass the array to these functions. A variable-length argument list, like that used by `printf()` would be much more convenient. Xmt does just this with the functions `XmtErrorMsg()` and `XmtWarningMsg()`:

Xmt/

Warning.c

```
#include <Xmt/Xmt.h>
void XmtErrorMsg(String name, String type, String default_msg, ...)
void XmtWarningMsg(String name, String type, String default_msg, ...)
```

These functions take three string arguments: a message name, message type, and the default message to display, followed by a `printf()`-style variable length argument list. In addition, they automatically prepend the message name onto the message.

So, for example, the XmtChooser widget uses `XmtWarningMsg()` internally as follows:

```
XmtWarningMsg("XmtChooser", "bounds",
              "Widget '%s' has %d items.  Item %d requested.",
              XtName((Widget) cw), cw->chooser.num_items, n);
```

When invoked, this function might print the following message:

```
Warning: XmtChooser: Widget 'choice1' has 4 items.  Item 6 requested.
```

`XmtErrorMsg()` operates in the same way, but exits once it has displayed its message.

Changing Warning and Error Handlers

You can use the functions `XtAppSetWarningHandler()` and `XtAppSetErrorHandler()` to provide an alternative routine for displaying error messages. You might use these functions if you want to display any output messages and also log them to a file. Or you could use these functions as a last resort to filter out spurious (or benign) messages that your widgets are outputting.

Changing Warning and Error Handlers (continued)

You could also use XtAppSetWarningHandler() to register a warning handler function that uses XmtDisplayWarning() to display the message in a dialog. Unless you are writing an interface builder application, however, these messages are probably not intended to be displayed to the end user.

XtAppSetWarningHandler() and XtAppSetErrorHandler() change the "low-level" handlers that are simply responsible for displaying a string. You can also replace the "high-level" handlers that are responsible for looking up the warning or error message (based on its name, class, and type) with XtAppSetWarningMsgHandler() and XtAppSetErrorMsgHandler().

See your Xt documentation for an explanation of all these functions.

—djf

8.3 Finding Shell Widgets

Now and then while programming with Motif and Xt, you will find that you need a handle for the shell widget of a given widget. It is not hard to find this shell by traversing up the widget hierarchy in a loop using XtParent() and XtIsShell(), but this is a common enough operation that Xmt provides convenience routines:

Xmt/

ShellUtil.c

```
#include <Xmt/Xmt.h>
Widget XmtGetShell(Widget w)
Widget XmtGetTopLevelShell(Widget w)
Widget XmtGetApplicationShell(Widget w)
```

XmtGetShell() takes a widget argument and returns the closest ancestor widget that is a shell.

XmtGetTopLevelShell() takes a single widget argument and returns the closest ancestor widget that is an Xt TopLevel shell widget. It will not return an XmDialogShell widget.

XmtGetApplicationShell() takes a single widget argument and returns the shell widget that is at the root of that widget's hierarchy. This is the widget that has no parent widget; it is an ApplicationShell widget created with XtAppInitialize() or XtAppCreateShell().

8.4 Getting the User's Home Directory

Applications that save their state or save user customizations often do so in a file or subdirectory in the user's home directory. If you are writing an application like this, you can use `XmtGetHomeDir()` to get the name of the user's home directory:

Xmt/

FindFile.c

```
#include <Xmt/Xmt.h>
String XmtGetHomeDir(void)
```

This function takes no arguments and returns a string that you must not modify or free. `XmtGetHomeDir()` caches its result so multiple calls are efficient. Calling this function is probably more portable than trying to look up the user's home directory yourself.

If your application reads configuration files of any sort, you may want to use `XmtFindFile()` to get the name of those files, as described in Chapter 6, *Managing Auxiliary Files*. In this case, you should not have to use `XmtGetHomeDir()`.

8.5 Converting Enumerated Types

Whenever you define a resource that has an enumerated type, it is a good idea to register a type converter for that enumerated type, so that the resource can be set from a resource file. If you are a widget writer, then you may find yourself in this situation frequently, but even if you have never written a widget, you have probably defined new application resources for your programs (See `XtGetApplicationResources()`).

Writing resource converters for your application resources is not particularly hard. (See the documentation for the `XtTypeConverter` type and the `XtSetTypeConverter()` function.) If you have written more than one resource converter for an enumerated type, you'll begin to notice a pattern: these resource converters always seem to be a repeated series of `strcmp()` calls testing the input string against a fixed set of possible values for the enumerated type. Xmt provides a simpler way to do this:

Xmt/

EnumCvt.c

```
#include <Xmt/Converters.h>
void XmtRegisterEnumConverter(String type, String *names, int *values,
                              int num, String *prefixes)
```

`XmtRegisterEnumConverter()` takes an array of strings and an array of integers as arguments, and registers a resource converter that will convert from each string in the array to the corresponding integer in the array. This function also takes a NULL-terminated array of optional prefixes that will be stripped off the input string before conversion. This function is used throughout Xmt to register converters for enumerated types. The XmtLayout widget, for example, has constraint resources that specify which edge of a child its caption is to be drawn against. It uses the following code to register a converter for that enumerated type:

```
typedef enum {
    XmtLayoutTop,
    XmtLayoutBottom,
    XmtLayoutLeft,
    XmtLayoutRight
} XmtLayoutEdge;

static String edge_names[] = {
    "Bottom", "Left", "Right", "Top"};
static int edge_values[] = {
    XmtLayoutBottom, XmtLayoutLeft, XmtLayoutRight, XmtLayoutTop
};
static String edge_prefixes[] = {"Xmt", "Layout", NULL};
XmtRegisterEnumConverter(XmtRXmtLayoutEdge,
                         edge_names, edge_values,
                         XtNumber(edge_names),
                         edge_prefixes);
```

Since this converter provides a list of prefixes, it will recognize strings like `Bottom`, `LayoutBottom`, and `XmtLayoutBottom`. Note that the converter *is* case-sensitive—it will not recognize `bottom`.

See the reference page for more information on `XmtRegisterEnumConverter()`.

8.6 Associating Values in Hash Tables

At times, while programming with Xt, you will find that you want to associate some additional information with a widget. With Motif widgets, you can store this additional data on the `XmNuserData` resource. But setting and querying this resource is not particularly efficient, and when you have more than one piece of information to store, it can be awkward to put them together into a single structure to hang off that resource.

The solution is to use an associative array or hash table.* Xmt uses a hash table, for example, to implement its simple dialog cache. Each shell widget has an entry in a special hash table that points to its cached dialog widgets.

Xlib provides a simple hash table scheme, in the functions `XSaveContext()` and `XFindContext()`. Though these can be used to associate data with widgets or other arbitrary keys, they were designed to associate data with Window IDs. They also require you to specify a `Display` pointer.

*A hash table is a data structure for associating an arbitrary data value with an arbitrary key. Storing and looking up values in a hash table is quite efficient, and they do not use much memory either. If you are not familiar with hash tables, you can read about them in any good book on data structures.

Xmt provides another hash table system: you can create a new hash table with `XmtHashTableCreate()`, associate a value with a key in the table with `XmtHashTableStore()`, look up the value associated with a key with `XmtHashTableLookup()`, remove an association from a table with `XmtHashTableDelete()`, enumerate the entries in a table with `XmtHashTableForEach()`, and destroy a hash table with `XmtHashTableDestroy()`. These functions are all documented in the reference section.

The Xmt hash table functions are not limited to associating data with widgets. You can use them to associate arbitrary data with arbitrary keys. If you want to associate data with a string value, then you should first convert the string to a quark with `XrmStringToQuark()` or `XrmPermStringToQuark()` (these are Xlib functions). A *quark* is an integer that uniquely identifies the contents of a string—if two copies of the same string are "quarkified," they will result in the same quark.

8.7 Checking Widget Classes

When writing an application or developing your own custom utility routines, you will sometimes write functions that take a `Widget` argument but expect only a specific class of widget. In this case, you may want to do error checking on entry to the function to see that the function is being called with the correct type of widget. You can do this with `XmtAssertWidgetClass()`:

Xmt/

AssertClass.c

```
#include <Xmt/Xmt.h>
void XmtAssertWidgetClass(Widget w, WidgetClass c, String procname)
```

`XmtAssertWidgetClass()` is a function that takes a widget, a `WidgetClass`, and the name of the procedure that it is called from. If the specified widget is not of the specified class and is not a subclass of it, `XmtAssertWidgetClass()` prints an error message containing the name of the procedure and calls `abort()` to exit the application and generate a core dump.

This may seem like a drastic action to take, but when developing and debugging an application, this kind of controlled core dump can be more useful than the uncontrolled kind that can result from passing an XmList widget to a function that expects an XmtChooser widget, for example. Like the `assert()` macro defined in *<assert.h>*, `XmtAssertWidgetClass()` is defined out of existence if the `NDEBUG` symbol is set when compiling. Thus you can use `XmtAssertWidgetClass()` liberally when developing an application, and when it is stable, you can compile it with the `-DNDEBUG` flag to avoid the overhead of the widget class checking.

8.8 Implementing Synchronous Behavior

Xmt provides a number of functions with "synchronous" behavior—functions that appear to block until the user completes some action (such as entering a string into a dialog) and then return with the results of the user's action. These functions are all implemented with an internal event loop so that events are always obtained and dispatched through the normal Xt mechanisms.

These internal event loops are themselves implemented with `XmtBlock()`:

Xmt/

Block.c

```
#include <Xmt/Xmt.h>
void XmtBlock(Widget w, Boolean *block)
```

This function takes the address of a Boolean as its single argument. It enters a loop, obtaining and dispatching events until the value stored at the specified address becomes `False`. This variable must change state as the result of some user action—in a synchronous dialog box, for example, the callbacks attached to the **Ok** and **Cancel** buttons would change the state of the variable in order to terminate the internal event loop. Note that the `XmtBlock()` event loop is a normal Xt event loop, and handles timers, work procedures, and external event sources (see `XtAppAddTimer()`, etc.) just as `XtAppMainLoop()` does.

You can use `XmtBlock()` to implement your own synchronous utility functions. You might use it, for example, to write a function that waits until the user clicks the mouse to select a point in an XmDrawingArea widget, and then returns the coordinates of the mouse click. If you do this, be sure you understand how the internal loop will be terminated, and also be sure that the user is made aware that the application has entered a special mode and that some specific action is required. In the XmDrawingArea example above, you might display a prompt in the message line and change the cursor to a crosshair.

See the reference section for full information on `XmtBlock()`.

9

Looking Up Widgets by Name

This chapter documents the function `XmtNameToWidget()` and, more importantly, the resource converter that is based upon it. `XmtNameToWidget()` takes a base or reference widget and a widget name, and looks for the named widget relative to the reference widget. This is the same basic function as that provided by the Intrinsics function `XtNameToWidget()`, except that the Xmt version is far more flexible—it can find ancestors of the reference widget, for example, instead of just descendants, and it can handle widget class names.

As an example, the XmtMenu widget (see Chapter 20, *Easy Menu Creation*) automatically creates all the push buttons and other widgets necessary to create a pulldown menu system. The XmtMenu widget does not provide access to the individual widgets it creates, and usually your applications will not need them. But some applications may occasionally need one of these widget handles (to highlight a menu item with a new color, perhaps). If you have specified the name open_button, for example, for a menu item, then you might look up the widget pointer for that item with the following call:

```
item = XmtNameToWidget(toplevel, "*menubar*open_button");
```

It is not uncommon to use `XmtNameToWidget()` in your C code, but what is far more common is to make use of the Xmt String-to-Widget converter in your resource files. This resource converter allows you to do things like specify an XmForm widget layout from a resource file, because it provides a way to specify resources like `XmNleftWidget` that would otherwise have to be specified from C code. Suppose, for example, that you have a **Cancel** button in an XmForm widget attached on the left to the **Okay** button. Assuming that the "okay" widget was created before the "cancel" widget, you could describe this attachment with resources like the following:

```
form.cancel.leftAttachment: XmATTACH_WIDGET
form.cancel.leftWidget: okay
```

An even more common use for this widget converter, as we'll see in the next chapter, however, is in conjunction with the String-to-Callback converter to pass widget arguments to the procedures you specify on callback lists. Together, the widget and callback converters enable you to specify a lot of useful dynamic behavior in a resource file. For example, you might specify procedures like the following to pop up and pop down a dialog box:

```
*menubar*help.activateCallback: \
        XtSetSensitive(self, False); \
        XtManageChild(*help_dialog);
*help_dialog.okay.activateCallback:
        XtUnmanageChild(^); \
        XtSetSensitive(*menubar*help, True);
```

The callback syntax will be explained in Chapter 10, *Callbacks in Resource Files.* For the purposes of this chapter, though, notice how widgets are specified relative to the button which invokes the callback. The widget name "self" is a special case that refers to the invoking widget, and the name ^ refers to the parent of the invoking widget. The other two widget names, "*help_dialog" and "*menubar*help," are global and refer to widgets in the same way that they do when they are used in resource specifications.

The first section of this chapter explains in detail the function `XmtNameToWidget()` and the widget name grammar it understands. The second section explains how you can register and use the Xmt String-to-Callback converter which is based on `XmtNameToWidget()` and which uses exactly the same widget specification grammar.

9.1 XmtNameToWidget()

As mentioned above, the function `XmtNameToWidget()` is similar to `XtNameToWidget()`:

Xmt/

NameToWidget.c

```
#include <Xmt/Xmt.h>
Widget XmtNameToWidget(Widget reference, String name);
```

`XmtNameToWidget()` has the same signature as `XtNameToWidget()`. The first argument is a reference widget, and the second argument is a widget name that describes how to find the target widget by searching from the reference. For `XtNameToWidget()`, *name* is a list of widget names, separated by tight or loose bindings (`.` or `*`). This name looks a lot like a widget name specified on the left-hand side of a resource specification in a resource file. A limitation to `XtNameToWidget()` is that its widget-naming syntax only allows *name* to describe widgets that are descendants of *reference*.

`XmtNameToWidget()` is more flexible than this. It understands *name* arguments that contain modifiers that allow you to move from the *reference* widget up the widget hierarchy to an ancestor widget before beginning the downwards search through the descendants of that ancestor.* Besides allowing ancestors of *reference* to be described, `XmtNameToWidget()` also allows descendants to be described more flexibly: it understands widget class names, and the X11R5 `?` wildcard. The following subsections explain `XmtNameToWidget()` modifiers first. Once they've described how the first part of *name* can specify an ancestor of *reference*, they explain how the remaining part of *name* specifies a descendant of that modified reference widget.

9.1.1 Modifiers

The modifiers supported by `XmtNameToWidget()` are specified at the beginning of a widget name, and act as unary operators, operating on the reference widget from which the search is conducted. Multiple modifiers are allowed; like most unary operators, they are evaluated from right-to-left. The supported modifiers are the following:

`^`
: This operator changes the reference widget to the parent of the current reference widget. It is like a `../` in a UNIX directory name. Thus the widget name "^okay" means, "go up to my parent, and then look for a widget named 'okay.'" This name specifies a sibling widget of the original reference widget.

`~`
: This operator changes the reference widget to the nearest shell ancestor of the reference widget. Thus, the widget name `~*okay` means "go up to the shell widget, and then look for any descendant of it named 'okay.'" It is a way of finding a widget in the same shell as the reference widget.

`^{`*name*`}`
: This operator changes the reference widget to the nearest ancestor widget with the instance name *name*, or if no such ancestor is found, the nearest ancestor with a class or superclass name *name*. For example, the widget specification `^{XmDialogShell}*okay` is quite similar (though a little more specific about shell type) than the previous example `~*okay`.

`self`
: The `self` keyword is a modifier that explicitly performs no modification; it specifies that the reference widget should be used unmodified as the base widget in the search. This is useful in resource files to allow widgets to refer to themselves. As we'll see below, the `self` keyword is also useful to prevent some of the implicit modifications that `XmtNameToWidget()` can make to the reference widget. Note that, unlike the other modifiers listed here, `self` must be used alone, and cannot be combined as a unary operator, as the other modifiers can.

*Wcl users will notice that the modifiers used by the Xmt String-to-Widget converter are derived from the modifiers of the corresponding Wcl converter. The Xmt converter has some useful new features, however, and one important difference: modifiers are interpreted right-to-left, as unary operators in Xmt, while they are interpreted left-to-right in Wcl.

Most of these modifiers provide a way to move up the widget hierarchy, to refer to the ancestors of a given reference widget instead of only its descendants. This is a feature that is simply not available with the Intrinsics `XtNameToWidget()`.

9.1.2 Implicit Modifiers

If there are modifiers at the beginning of the specified name, those modifiers explicitly specify which widget is to be used as the reference, and the search begins from that widget. If there are no modifiers, however, then the reference widget may be implicitly modified by one of the following rules. These rules may make the function seem complicated. In practice, however, they are fairly intuitive.

1. If there are no modifiers, and the name begins with a `*` wildcard, then the reference widget is not used, and the search is performed relative to the root application shell widget of the specified widget. This provides the same semantics in a resource file as resource specifications that begin with `*`. Thus, the specification **`*target`** would find a widget named "target" anywhere in the widget hierarchy. Note that the search is only performed from the root widget when the name *begins* with the `*` wildcard. If you want to perform a wildcard search starting from the specified reference widget, use the special `self` modifier in the widget name: `self*target`, instead of `*target`.

If the name does not begin with a modifier or the `*` wildcard, then it must begin with a widget component name. (If the name begins with a `.`, that first character is ignored.) Thus the remaining rules all describe ways of finding a widget that matches this name.

2. If the first component of the name is the name of a sibling of the reference widget, then the reference widget is implicitly changed to the parent of the reference widget so that this matching sibling will be found. This is a counterintuitive behavior when calling `XmtNameToWidget()` explicitly, but makes sense when using the String-to-Widget converter based on that function—when using the XmForm or XmtLayout widgets, for example, it is common to specify sibling widgets as resource values. If you want to explicitly specify that the search is to find a child widget and not a sibling widget, use the `self` keyword: `self.box*target`, not just `box*target`.

3. If the first component of the name is not a sibling widget, then `XmtNameToWidget()` next checks to see if it names a child of the reference widget. If so, then the search proceeds from the specified reference widget without any implicit modification. This rule and the previous one mean that when `XmtNameToWidget()` is passed a widget name without modifiers, it will first attempt the search from the parent of the reference, and then from the reference itself. As noted above, you can use the `self` modifier to force the search to be performed from the specified reference widget. To force the search to be performed from the parent widget, use the `^` modifier: **`^box*target`** rather than simply `box*target`.

4. If the first component of the name does not match a sibling or a child of the specified reference widget, then `XmtNameToWidget()` checks to see if it matches the name of any of the root application shells that have been registered with `XmtInitializeApplicationShell()`. If so, it uses that shell as the root of the search. This rule is only useful for applications that create multiple root shells. Since each root shell has an independent widget hierarchy, this rule provides a way to refer to widgets in separate hierarchies.

5. Finally, if there were no modifiers, and if none of the above rules applies, then the widget name is invalid, and `XmtNameToWidget()` returns `NULL`.

Once the final reference widget has been determined, either through the explicit modifiers listed in the previous section, or through the implicit modification rules listed here, then the search for the named widget can actually begin, using the reference widget as a starting point.

9.1.3 The Widget Name and Wildcards

`XmtNameToWidget()` allows you to specify widget names using the same syntax and wildcards that you use in a resource file to specify widget resources. The difference is that the resource file syntax requires you to always specify the widget name relative to the root widget of the hierarchy, while the `XmtNameToWidget()` syntax allows you to use shorter names, relative to other widgets in the hierarchy. Widget names are specified using the following rules:

- A widget name consists of one or more component names. Each component name may be a widget instance name or a widget class name.
- A `.` between two components is a "tight binding" and indicates that the second component names a direct child of the first. In the name `foo.bar`, the widget "bar" is a direct child of the widget "foo."
- A `*` between two components is a "loose binding" and indicates that the second component names any descendant of the first, with zero or more intervening "generations" of widgets. In the name `foo*bar`, "bar" is a descendant of "foo". It might be a direct child, or it could be removed by any number of "generations."
- A `?` in place of a component name is a wildcard that matches any single widget, but does not elide any number of generations as the `*` modifier does. In the name `foo.?.bar`, "bar" is a grandchild of "foo," and `foo.?*bar` is like `foo*bar` except that it specifies that "bar" is *not* a direct child of "foo." Note that the `?` wildcard replaces a component name, and must be connected to other components with a `.` or a `*`.

If the widget name is fully specified—i.e., if each component names a widget instance, and there are no wildcards—then finding the named widget is simply a matter of finding each of the named components and proceeding down the tree to the eventual target widget. If there are wildcards or class names in the specification, however, then `XmtNameToWidget()` must perform an actual search of the widget tree, looking for a widget with a name that matches the partially specified name. `XmtNameToWidget()` conducts this search in a breadth-first fashion, so that if there is more than one widget that matches the target name, it will return the one that is "closest" to the reference widget. If more than one widget in the same "generation" matches the target, then it is unspecified which will be returned.

There is one special case to this search. If you specify a widget name that consists solely of modifiers, like `^^` or `self`, then `XmtNameToWidget()` need not perform any search; it just returns the modified reference widget. So the name `^^`, for example, will return the grandparent of the specified reference widget.

9.1.4 Examples

All the rules listed in the above sections make `XmtNameToWidget()` seem like a tremendously complicated function. In practice, however, it is not difficult to use, and you will quickly learn some of the common "idioms" of the widget specification grammar. Table 9-1 shows some examples of common widget specifications you might use with `XmtNameToWidget()` or with the resource converter based on it.

Table 9-1. Example Widget Specifications

Name	Meaning
^	The parent of the reference widget.
^^	The grandparent of the reference widget.
~	The shell that contains the widget.
^^~	The grandparent of the shell.
~^	The shell that contains the parent.
^{WMShell}	The nearest ancestor that is a subclass of WMShell, i.e., a dialog shell or toplevel shell, but not a menu shell.
^{rowcol}	The nearest ancestor named "rowcol."
self	The reference widget.
okay	A sibling of the reference widget named "okay," or if no such sibling exists, a child named "okay," or if no such child exists, a root shell named "okay."
^okay	A sibling (a child of the parent) named "okay."
self.okay	A child named "okay."
*okay	Any widget in the hierarchy named "okay." If there are several children with this name, the one closest to the root widget will be returned.

Table 9-1. Example Widget Specifications (continued)

Name	Meaning
*XmRowColumn.okay	A widget named "okay" that is a child of an XmRowColumn widget anywhere in the widget hierarchy.
*XmDialogShell*okay	A widget named "okay" that is a descendant (of any number of generations) of an XmDialogShell widget.
~*okay	A widget named "okay" that is in the same shell as the reference widget.
~?.okay	A widget named "okay" that is a grandchild of the shell of the reference widget.

9.2 Using the String-to-Widget Converter

The most common use of `XmtNameToWidget()` is in a resource converter so that you can specify widget resources from a resource file (and also so you can pass widget arguments to callback procedures, as explained in Chapter 10, *Callbacks in Resource Files.*) You can use `XmtNameToWidget()` freely in your C code, but to make the String-to-Widget converter work in a resource file, you must register the converter by calling `XmtRegisterWidget-Converter()`, usually as part of your application's initialization code.

```
#include <Xmt/Converters.h>
void XmtRegisterWidgetConverter(void)
```

Consider again the example presented at the beginning of this chapter:

```
form.cancel.leftAttachment: XmATTACH_WIDGET
form.cancel.leftWidget: okay
```

The widget that invokes the resource converter is used as the reference widget, so this conversion is equivalent to calling `XmtNameToWidget()` as follows:

```
okay_button = XmtNameToWidget(cancel_button, "okay");
```

The String-to-Widget converter is commonly used to look up siblings of widgets, and so, as described in the previous section, `XmtNameToWidget()` makes a special case for them. We could also have used the name `^okay` in this example to be more explicit that we were looking for a sibling of the **Cancel** button.

9.3 Summary

`XmtNameToWidget()` searches for a named widget relative to a specified reference widget. `XmtRegisterWidgetConverter()` registers a resource converter so that you can do the same in your resource files. In this case, the widget that invokes the conversion is the reference widget.

`XmtNameToWidget()` understands widget names and classes, and the `*` and `?` wildcards, as used in resource file resource specifications. It also understands the following modifiers, which allow it to refer to ancestors of the reference widget:

- `^` refers to the parent of a widget.
- `~` refers to the shell of a widget.
- The syntax `^{`*`ancestor`*`}` refers to the nearest ancestor of a widget with the specified name or class.

Part Three

Programming with Resources

This part of the book documents tools in Xmt that allow a programmer to describe a user interface almost entirely with resources in a resource file. Programming with resources in this way is quick and efficient, and is particularly useful when prototyping an interface.

The tools and interface description techniques presented in this part will be used in many of the examples throughout the rest of the book.

10

Callbacks in Resource Files

Resource files typically allow us to define the static parts of an application—colors, fonts, strings, and so forth. In the previous chapter we saw that the Xmt String-to-Widget converter allows us to specify widget values as resources, and in a later chapter, we'll see that we can use the resource file to actually describe a widget hierarchy that will be automatically created by Xmt. But even this automatically created widget hierarchy is one of the static parts of an application.

In contrast, the dynamic behavior of an application is the way it responds to user events, and this is generally controlled by the callback procedures registered on the various widgets. This chapter presents a method of assigning names to procedures, and a String-to-Callback converter that allows you to specify these named procedures as callbacks in a resource file. What this means is that you *can* affect the dynamic behavior of your application through a resource file.

Every application has some simple dynamic behaviors—pushing the **About** button pops up the About dialog, for example—and it is these simple things that really ought to be part of the static interface description in a resource file. To set up this behavior in C, for example, you'd write a special callback procedure `PopupAboutDialog()` that would call `XtManageChild()` to pop up the dialog box. Then you'd call `XtAddCallback()` to register this custom callback procedure on the **About** button.

Managing a dialog box in response to a user action is a simple and common behavior, however, and should not take this much effort. Furthermore, this kind of behavior is arguably part of the interface definition, and should not require the active intervention of application back end through custom C procedures. The alternative provided by Xmt is to use the String-to-Callback converter to specify a callback in a resource file like this:

```
*menubar*about.activateCallback: XtManageChild(*about_dialog);
```

There is at least one interface builder application on the market that includes a "callback converter" that happens to be a full-featured C interpreter—so you can write arbitrary C code in your resource files and perform any kind of dynamic behavior you want in a resource file. The Xmt callback converter uses a C-like syntax for procedure calls, but does not support other features of a real programming language, such as expression evaluation and variable assignment. Even though limited strictly to procedure calls, this converter can be tremendously convenient. Other examples of its use are shown in Example 10-1.

Example 10-1. Using the Xmt String-to-Callback Converter

```
!! Call the application's LoadFile() procedure when
!! the Load button is clicked.
*menubar*file*load.activateCallback: LoadFile();

!! Display a warning dialog when Save is selected.
!! XmtDisplayWarning is a standard Xmt procedure.
*menubar*file*save.activateCallback: \
        XmtDisplayWarning(NYI, This feature is not yet implemented);

!! Exit normally when the user clicks the Quit button.
*quit.activateCallback: exit(0);
```

This chapter explains how the Xmt String-to-Callback converter works, how you can register your own procedures for use with the converter, and how you can easily register common procedures like `XtManageChild()` for use with the converter.

10.1 Registering and Invoking Callback Procedures

Before you can specify a callback procedure to be called in a resource file, you must, of course, specify a name for the procedure. This allows Xmt to read the name from a resource file and look up the procedure it refers to. If you have ever used `XtAppAddActions()` to register your own custom action procedures for use in translation tables, then you will recognize this as exactly the same case.

You can register a callback procedure (with the standard `XtCallbackProc` signature) with the function `XmtRegisterCallbackProcedure()`, and you can register multiple procedures with `XmtVaRegisterCallbackProcedures()`.

Xmt/

Procedures.c

```
#include <Xmt/Procedures.h>
void XmtRegisterCallbackProcedure(String name, XtCallbackProc procedure,
                                  String type);
void XmtVaRegisterCallbackProcedures(String name, XtCallbackProc procedure,
                                     String type, ...);
```

You register a callback procedure by specifying a name, the procedure pointer, and the type of data the procedure expects as its *client_data* (its second argument) value. The second argument of an XtCallbackProc is an XtPointer, but in fact, you always cast that argument to some other type before using it. This argument is the data that is specified when the callback is registered. If you'll be registering an integer value, then the *type* argument to XmtRegisterCallbackProcedure() should be XtRInt. If you'll be passing a widget, the *type* argument should be XtRWidget. (Read about resource converters in a book on Xt for more information on the XtR, XmR, and XmtR "representation types".)

XmtVaRegisterCallbackProcedures() is just like XmtRegisterCallbackProcedure(), except that instead of taking a single triple of (name, procedure, type) arguments, it takes a NULL-terminated list of these triples. Example 10-2 shows a callback procedure and how you would register it.

Example 10-2. Registering a Callback Procedure

```
/*
 * This procedure pops up the dialog box that is registered
 * and passed as its client_data argument.  Note that it does
 * not use its first argument--the widget that actually invokes it.
 */
static void PopupDialog(Widget w, XtPointer client_data, XtPointer call_data)
{
    XtManageChild((Widget)client_data);
}
     .
     .
     .
XmtRegisterCallbackProcedure("PopupDialog", PopupDialog, XtRWidget);
XmtRegisterCallbackConverter();
XmtRegisterWidgetConverter();
```

Notice that we also call XmtRegisterCallbackConverter() in this example.

Xmt/

CallbackCvt.c

```
#include <Xmt/Converters.h>
void XmtRegisterCallbackConverter(void);
```

This is the procedure that registers the Xmt callback converter with the Intrinsics resource conversion mechanism. If it is not called during your application's initialization, then the converter will not work. The same applies for the XmtRegisterWidgetConverter() function introduced in Chapter 9, *Looking Up Widgets by Name.*

Once we've registered our PopupDialog() procedure like this, it can be used in a resource file. You might use it in a specification like the following:

```
*menubar*about.activateCallback: PopupDialog(*about_dialog);
```

This specification arranges to pop up a dialog box when the user selects the **About** button in a pulldown menu. In effect, what it does is register the procedure `PopupDialog()` as a callback on the `XmNactivateCallback` callback list of the **About** push button. (This is "in effect" what it does, but, as we'll see in the next section, the implementation is a little more complex than this.) The string `*about_dialog` within parentheses is the *`client_data`* for this callback specification. Since the procedure `PopupDialog()` was registered as expecting *`client_data`* of type `XtRWidget`, Xmt automatically invokes the String-to-Widget converter (which invokes `XmtNameToWidget()`) to convert this string into the named widget. When the procedure is called, it is passed the actual widget as its second argument, not the string that names the widget.

10.2 Registering and Invoking Arbitrary Procedures

The `PopupDialog()` procedure used as an example in the previous section is simply a wrapper procedure—it passes its *`client_data`* argument to `XtManageChild()` and ignores its other two arguments. It is annoying to write wrapper procedures like this; instead, it would be nice if we could just register `XtManageChild()` on a callback list directly.

In fact, Xmt *does* allow this. Before explaining how this can be done, however, you must understand something about the underlying mechanism of the Xmt callback converter.

10.2.1 How the Callback Converter Works

All callback resources are of type `XtCallbackList`, which is a `NULL`-terminated array of procedure/data pairs. The Xmt callback converter, then, is actually a String-to-XtCallbackList converter—it parses the string and returns an `XtCallbackList`. When the converter parses a string like `PopupDialog(*about_dialog)`, it does not actually return an `XtCallbackList` containing the procedure `PopupDialog()` with the widget named `about_dialog` as its client data. Instead, the `XtCallbackList` contains the internal procedure `XmtCallCallback()` and a parsed representation of the callback string. When `XmtCallCallback()` is invoked by whatever widget it is registered on, it is called with a *`client_data`* argument that contains a description of the procedure (or procedures—see the sections that follow) to be called and the arguments to be passed to it.

Since the procedures converted by the Xmt callback converter are not being directly invoked by the Intrinsics, but instead indirectly invoked by Xmt, these procedures need not actually be of type `XtCallbackProc`. They can have any signature you want—you just have to say what type each argument is when you register the procedure. The next section explains how you can register these arbitrary procedures for use with the callback converter.

10.2.2 Registering Arbitrary Procedures

The most flexible way to register procedures for use with the callback converter is with the function `XmtRegisterProcedures()`:

Xmt/

Procedures.c

```
#include <Xmt/Procedures.h>
void XmtRegisterProcedures(XmtProcedureInfo *procs, Cardinal num_procs);
```

`XmtRegisterProcedures()` takes a counted array of `XmtProcedureInfo` structures. This structure (with some trailing private fields omitted) looks like this:

```
typedef struct {
    /* Only the first 2 are always required */
    String name;
    XmtProcedure function;
    String argument_types[XmtMAX_PROCEDURE_ARGS];
        .
        .    /* private, internal fields omitted */
        .
} XmtProcedureInfo;
```

The constant `XmtMAX_PROCEDURE_ARGS` is defined to be eight, which means that you can only register procedures that expect eight or fewer arguments. The `XmtProcedure` type used in this structure defines a prototype procedure that takes eight `XtPointer` arguments. You'll have to cast your actual procedure pointers to this type. When Xmt calls the procedure you register, it will pass between zero and eight arguments, and each of these arguments will be the same size as an `XtPointer`. This means that you cannot register functions that take `double` arguments, since a `double` is larger than an `XtPointer` on most architectures. This also means that you cannot register functions that expect `char`, `Boolean`, `short`, `Dimension`, `Position`, or other "narrow" arguments that are smaller than an `XtPointer`, unless you are using a K&R-style C compiler that automatically "widens" these arguments.* Typically, you'll register procedures during application initialization using an `XmtProcedureInfo` array that has been statically initialized in your C code. Example 10-3 shows how you might do this for some common Intrinsics functions (including `XtManageChild()` as discussed previously).

*These "narrow" function arguments are best avoided in any case, since they cause problems if the function is compiled with an ANSI-C compiler and invoked from code compiled with a K&R compiler. Because of this incompatibility, by default, the X, Xt, Xm, and Xmt libraries declare all their functions with wide arguments, even when the documentation says they take narrow arguments. For example, a function that takes a `Boolean` argument would actually be declared to take an integer. If you actually do want these libraries to use narrow arguments, compile with the flag `-DNARROWPROTO`.

Example 10-3. Registering Arbitrary Procedures for the Callback Converter

```
static XmtProcedureInfo xt_procedures[] = {
{"XtManageChild", (XmtProcedure) XtManageChild, {XtRWidget}},
{"XtUnmanageChild", (XmtProcedure) XtUnmanageChild, {XtRWidget}},
{"XtDestroyWidget", (XmtProcedure) XtDestroyWidget, {XtRWidget}},
{"XtSetSensitive", (XmtProcedure) XtSetSensitive, {XtRWidget, XtRBoolean}},
{"XtOverrideTranslations", (XmtProcedure)XtOverrideTranslations,
    {XtRWidget, XtRTranslationTable}},
{"XtAddCallbacks", (XmtProcedure)XtAddCallbacks,
     {XtRWidget, XtRString, XtRCallback}},
};

     .
     .
     .

XmtRegisterProcedures(xt_procedures, XtNumber(xt_procedures));
```

Notice, in this example, that `XtManageChild()`, `XtUnmanageChild()`, and `XtDestroyWidget()` are quite straightforward—they each take a single widget argument. `XtSetSensitive()` takes a widget and a Boolean argument, and `XtOverrideTranslations()` takes a widget and a translation table argument. `XtAddCallbacks()` is an interesting case—it takes a widget, the name of a callback list (a string; no conversion required), and an `XtCallbackList`. The callback converter will have to be invoked again to convert this third argument.

Also notice that the arrays are statically initialized—`XmtRegisterProcedures()` does not copy the `XmtProcedureInfo` structures you cast, so they should be static, or at least permanently allocated. Each of the procedures is cast to the `XmtProcedure` type, and the argument type array is initialized within nested curly braces. Unused arguments are omitted, and those fields of the array will be left uninitialized as `NULL`.

10.2.3 Invoking Multiple Arbitrary Procedures

Example 10-4 shows how you might use some of the procedures registered in the previous section in a resource file.

Example 10-4. Specifying Procedures on Callback Lists

```
!! When the user clicks the about button, first make that
!! button insensitive (so it can't be selected twice) and
!! then pop up the About dialog.
*menubar*about.activateCallback:\
                                XtSetSensitive(self, False);\
                                XtManageChild(*about_dialog);

!! When the user clicks the Dismiss button in the about
!! dialog, first pop down that dialog, and then make the
!! About button sensitive again.
*about_dialog.dismiss.activateCallback:\
                                XtUnmanageChild(^);\
                                XtSetSensitive(*menubar*about, True);
```

There are a number of points to notice about this example.

- When a procedure takes more than one argument, those arguments are separated by commas, just as they are in C. Arguments, even those with `XtRString` type, are never placed within double quotes.
- It is perfectly legal to register multiple procedures to be called on a callback list. Each procedure must end with a semicolon, as in C code. You may format a callback resource on several lines, as you can with any resource—just be sure to escape the newlines by using a backslash as the last character on each line. When multiple procedures are registered, the callback converter does not actually register multiple callbacks on the callback list—all the procedures are invoked through a single call to the internal `XmtCallCallback()` function. Thus Xmt can guarantee that procedures will be called in the order they appear in, which is not the case when multiple callback procedures are registered with `XtAddCallback()`.
- Note the use of the Xmt String-to-Widget converter in this example. As mentioned in Chapter 9, *Looking Up Widgets by Name*, you'll probably use the widget converter in conjunction with the callback converter far more often than you use it to actually set widget resources. Notice also the use of the `self` and ^ widget name modifiers in the example.
- This example shows `XtManageChild()` being invoked directly on a callback list, just as we said we'd do at the beginning of this section!

10.2.4 Special Argument Types

The alert reader may have noticed a peculiar difference between our `PopupDialog()` callback procedure registered with `XmtRegisterCallbackProcedure()` and the `XtManageChild()` registered with the more general `XmtRegisterProcedures()`. When specified in a resource file, both procedures are given a single widget argument. `XtManageChild()` actually expects a single widget argument, but `PopupDialog()` was written to expect three arguments, and the argument specified in the resource file is passed as its second argument!

`XmtRegisterCallbackProcedure()` is a convenience function, and in fact what it does is to register the specified procedure as taking three arguments. Two of these arguments are of special types that indicate that Xmt should pass the *`widget`* and *`call_data`* arguments of a standard callback procedure. Registering `PopupDialog()` with `XmtRegisterCallbackProcedure()`, as we did above, is equivalent to the following code:

```
static XmtProcedureInfo proc =
    {"PopupDialog", (XmtProcedure)PopupDialog,
     {XmtRCallbackWidget, XtRWidget, XmtRCallbackData}};
XmtRegisterProcedures(&proc, 1);
```

This means that `PopupDialog()` should be called with three arguments. The first argument should be the standard widget argument that is passed to callbacks—this is the widget that invoked the callback. The second argument will be specified as a string in the resource file; it should be converted to type `XtRWidget` before being passed. The third argument is the *`call_data`* argument passed to all callback procedures—this is whatever data the widget that invoked the callback thinks is relevant to the callback processing. In fact, the `PopupDialog()` procedure we wrote ignores its first and third arguments, so we could have omitted them. Or, if we had used only one, we could have omitted the other. There is no requirement that these be used as the first and third arguments either; Xmt can pass them at any position in the argument list.

There are a few other special argument types supported by the callback converter. They are listed, with their meanings, in Table 10-1.

Table 10-1. Special Argument Types for the Callback Converter

Type	***Meaning***
XmtRCallbackWidget	Pass the widget that invoked the callback.
XmtRCallbackData	Pass the *call_data* argument.
XmtRCallbackAppContext	Pass the application context of the widget.
XmtRCallbackWindow	Pass the window ID of the invoking widget.
XmtRCallbackDisplay	Pass the display pointer of the invoking widget.
XmtRCallbackUnused	Pass NULL; good for unused arguments.

10.2.5 Argument Evaluation and Caching

There are two more important points to understand about how the Xmt callback converter works. Consider the example we've been using above:

```
*menubar*about.activateCallback: XtManageChild(*about_dialog);
```

The callback converter will parse this callback specification when the **About** button in the menu bar is created. But, depending on how the widget hierarchy is arranged, the `about_dialog` widget may not have been created at this point. If the callback converter tried to convert the string `*about_dialog` to a widget when it converted the whole string to a callback list, the conversion might fail, simply because the target widget did not yet exist.

What the callback converter does instead is to parse the comma-separated argument list into individual arguments, which are stored as strings, and passed as *`client_data`* to the internal function `XmtCallCallback()`. When the callback is actually triggered, `XmtCallCallback()` is invoked, and it does the necessary conversion of argument strings to argument values.

So the first important point about callback arguments is that their evaluation is delayed until the callback is actually invoked. The second important point is that once the argument string is converted, the resulting converted value is cached for reuse in subsequent invocations of the callback—this caching dramatically improves the performance of these "interpreted callbacks".*

10.2.6 Passing Symbols as Arguments

The preceding sections have shown that you can register names for application procedures and thereby use those procedures from resource files. Xmt also allows you to register names for application variables and then refer to these variables from resource files. These symbolic names for variables are known as "Symbols" in the Xmt library, and Chapter 12, *Symbols*, explains how you can register and use them.

The Xmt callback converter allows you to specify symbol names as arguments. When you do this, the value of the symbol will be looked up and passed each time the callback is invoked. To pass a symbol, simply precede its name with a $ in the argument list. For example, suppose the symbol "selection" names a Boolean variable that specifies whether there is currently a selected region in the main text window for an application. Then you might use a specification like the following to make the **Cut** button in the **Edit** menu sensitive or insensitive:

```
*menubar*edit.mapCallback: XtSetSensitive(*menubar*cut, $selection);
```

10.2.7 Quoting Conventions in Callback Arguments

It is not necessary (nor is it allowed) to put the individual comma-separated arguments of a callback specification within double quotes. Therefore, if a comma is to appear literally in one of the arguments, then it must be quoted somehow, so that it does not signal the end of the argument. Similarly, if a close parenthesis is to appear in an argument it must be quoted so that it does not signal the end of the argument list.

There is an exception to this quoting rule that involves parentheses. A close parenthesis does not have to be quoted if there is a matching, unquoted open parenthesis in the same argument. Similarly, any commas within a matching pair of unquoted parentheses do not need to be quoted. This means that while there is an open parenthesis outstanding, commas and close parentheses will never be interpreted as signaling the end of an argument or the end of the argument list. A corollary to this rule is that if an argument is to include an unmatched open parenthesis, that parenthesis must be quoted.

Commas and parentheses may be quoted by preceding them with the \ escape character. Since the resource file interprets these escape characters itself, you must actually use a double backslash: \\.

*This caching is appropriate in almost all circumstances. If you have an argument string that may result in different argument values depending on when it is converted, then you may want to pass that argument as an unconverted string, and perform the argument conversion explicitly in your callback procedure. For example, if you need to refer to a widget that is frequently destroyed and recreated, then a cached value will not be useful—you'll have to look up the widget each time your procedure is called.

Finally, note that Xmt discards any whitespace at the beginning or end of each argument. If you want whitespace to be a literal part of the argument, you can escape the first character of leading whitespace, or the last character of trailing whitespace, again by using a double backslash: \\.

These quoting rules may seem overly complicated. The Xmt argument-list parser was designed, however, so that quoting is almost never necessary in your argument lists. On those rare occasions that you do need to use it, remember that you can turn back to this page to refresh yourself on the details of the rules.

10.3 Registering Common Functions

The Xmt library provides three convenience routines that are useful for registering commonly used Xt, Xmt, and UNIX procedures. These convenience routines are particularly useful when prototyping an interface. Remember, though, that your application will be linked with any procedure you register, regardless of whether or not you ever call the procedure. So once your application design has stabilized, you may want to explicitly register all the procedures you use, and only those procedures.

10.3.1 Xt Procedures

`XmtRegisterXtProcedures()` registers the Xt procedures shown in Example 10-5. The arguments shown in this example are the representation types of the arguments registered for the procedures.

Example 10-5. Procedures Registered by XmtRegisterXtProcedures()

```
XtAddCallbacks(XtRWidget, XtRString, XtRCallback)
XtAugmentTranslations(XtRWidget, XtRTranslationTable)
XtDestroyWidget(XtRWidget)
XtError(XtRString)
XtInstallAccelerators(XtRWidget, XtRWidget)
XtInstallAllAccelerators(XtRWidget, XtRWidget)
XtManageChild(XtRWidget)
XtOverrideTranslations(XtRWidget, XtRTranslationTable)
XtPopdown(XtRWidget)
XtPopupExclusive(XmtRCallbackWidget, XtRWidget)
XtPopupNone(XmtRCallbackWidget, XtRWidget)
XtPopupNonexclusive(XmtRCallbackWidget, XtRWidget)
XtPopupSpringLoaded(XtRWidget)
XtRealizeWidget(XtRWidget)
XtSetKeyboardFocus(XtRWidget, XtRWidget)
XtSetMappedWhenManaged(XtRWidget, XtRBoolean)
XtSetSensitive(XtRWidget, XtRBoolean)
XtUnmanageChild(XtRWidget)
XtWarning(XtRString)
```

You can use most of the procedures registered by `XmtRegisterXt-Procedures()` exactly as you would use them in your C code. Again, one important difference is that arguments of type `String` are not quoted when used with the callback converter. You can find out more about these functions in your Xt reference manual. Also, note the following points:

- `XtAddCallbacks()` takes an `XtCallbackList` as its third argument. When the `XtAddCallbacks()` call is originally parsed by the callback converter, this third argument will simply be treated as an ordinary string. When the callback is actually invoked, the callback converter will be called again to convert this string to the callback list to be registered. Notice that `XtRemoveCallbacks()` is not one of the functions registered here. It is impossible to make `XtRemoveCallbacks()` work from a resource file because that function requires the *`client_data`* in the callback list to match what was originally registered. Since the callback converter allocated the *`client_data`* dynamically, it would never match.
- `XtAugmentTranslations()` and `XtOverrideTranslations()` take a translation table (type `XtTranslations`) as their second argument. The Intrinsics automatically register a resource converter for this type, so you simply need to specify the table as you normally would. If the translation table takes multiple lines, remember to escape the newlines with the backslash, and if the table contains commas, you will have to escape those with a double-backslash.
- `XtPopupExclusive()`, `XtPopupNone()`, and `XtPopupNonexclusive()` are the Xmt synonyms for `XtCallbackExclusive()`, `XtCallbackNone()`, and `XtCallbackNonexclusive()`. These callback procedures are Xt convenience functions for popping up dialogs—they call `XtPopup()` on the widget specified as their argument with the *grab_mode* argument set to `XtGrabExclusive`, `XtGrabNone`, or `XtGrabNonexclusive`. They also call `XtSetSensitive()` on the widget that invoked the callback to make that button insensitive. If you are using a Motif dialog box, these procedures are not useful—Xt and Motif have incompatible methods of popping up and popping down dialog boxes.

An important way to affect the dynamic behavior of a GUI is to set resources dynamically on the widgets. But notice that `XmtRegisterXtProcedures()` does not register `XtSetValues()`, which would make this dynamic resource setting possible. This is because there is no String-to-ArgList converter registered by the Intrinsics or by Xmt. Instead, Xmt provides the function `XmtSetValue()` which sets a single resource—this function is registered by `XmtRegisterXmtProcedures()` described in the next section.

10.3.2 Xmt Procedures

`XmtRegisterXmtProcedures()` registers the Xmt procedures shown in Example 10-6. For each procedure, this example shows the representation types of the arguments registered. Note that a number of these functions use the special `XmtRCallbackWidget` type to automatically pass a widget argument, and thus have different signatures when invoked from a resource file than they do when called from C. Also, some of the functions use `XmtRCallbackUnused` to automatically pass `NULL` for certain arguments.

Example 10-6. Procedures Registered by XmtRegisterXmtProcedures()

```
/* special resource-setting functions */
XmtSetValue(XtRWidget, XtRString, XtRString)
XmtSetTypedValue(XtRWidget, XtRString, XtRString, XtRString)

/* simple message dialog functions */
XmtDisplayError(XmtRCallbackWidget, XtRString, XtRString)
XmtDisplayWarning(XmtRCallbackWidget, XtRString, XtRString)
XmtDisplayInformation(XmtRCallbackWidget, XtRString, XtRString, XtRString)
XmtDisplayWarningMsg(XmtRCallbackWidget, XtRString, XtRString,
                     XtRString, XtRString)
XmtDisplayErrorMsg(XmtRCallbackWidget, XtRString, XtRString,
                   XtRString, XtRString)
XmtDisplayInformationMsg(XmtRCallbackWidget, XtRString, XtRString,
                         XtRString, XtRString)
XmtDisplayWarningMsgAndWait(XmtRCallbackWidget, XtRString, XtRString,
                            XtRString, XtRString)
XmtDisplayErrorMsgAndWait(XmtRCallbackWidget, XtRString, XtRString,
                          XtRString, XtRString)

/* cursor, event, shell and miscellaneous utilities */
XmtAddDeleteCallback(XtRWidget, XmRDeleteResponse, XtRCallback)
XmtAddSaveYourselfCallback(XtRWidget, XtRCallback)
XmtDeiconifyShell(XtRWidget)
XmtDialogPosition(XtRWidget, XtRWidget)
XmtDiscardButtonEvents(XtRWidget)
XmtDiscardKeyPressEvents(XtRWidget)
XmtDisplayBusyCursor(XtRWidget)
XmtDisplayCursor(XtRWidget, XtRCursor)
XmtDisplayDefaultCursor(XtRWidget)
XmtFocusShell(XtRWidget)
XmtIconifyShell(XtRWidget)
XmtLowerShell(XtRWidget)
XmtMoveShellToPointer(XtRWidget)
XmtRaiseShell(XtRWidget)
XmtRegisterImprovedIcons(XtRWidget, XmtRXmtColorTable)
XmtSetFocusToShell(XtRWidget)
XmtSetInitialFocus(XtRWidget,XtRWidget)
XmtWaitUntilMapped(XtRWidget)
XmtWarpToShell(XtRWidget)

/* widget and dialog creation functions */
XmtCreateChildren(XtRWidget)
XmtCreateChild(XtRWidget,XtRString)
XmtBuildDialog(XtRWidget, XtRString, XmtRCallbackUnused, XmtRCallbackUnused)
XmtBuildToplevel(XtRWidget, XtRString)
XmtBuildApplication(XtRString, XtRString, XmtRCallbackDisplay,
                    XmtRCallbackUnused, XmtRCallbackUnused)

/* context help functions */
XmtHelpDisplayContextHelp(XtRWidget)
XmtHelpDoContextHelp(XmtRCallbackWidget)
XmtHelpContextHelpCallback(XmtRCallbackWidget,
                           XmtRCallbackUnused, XmtRCallbackUnused)

/* XmtMsgLine widget functions */
XmtMsgLineClear(XtRWidget, XtRInt)
```

Example 10-6. Procedures Registered by XmtRegisterXmtProcedures() (continued)

```
XmtMsgLineSet(XtRWidget, XtRString)
XmtMsgLineAppend(XtRWidget, XtRString)
XmtMsgLinePrintf(XtRWidget, XtRString, XmtRCallbackUnused)
XmtMsgLinePush(XtRWidget)
XmtMsgLinePop(XtRWidget, XtRInt)

/* XmtCli widget functions */
XmtCliPuts(XtRString, XtRWidget)
XmtCliPrintf(XtRWidget, XtRString, XmtRCallbackUnused)
XmtCliClear(XtRWidget)

/* XmtChooser widget functions */
XmtChooserSetState(XtRWidget, XtRInt, XtRBoolean)
XmtChooserSetSensitive(XtRWidget, XtRInt, XtRBoolean)

/* XmtInputField widget functions */
XmtInputFieldSetString(XtRWidget, XtRString)

/* XmtLayout widget functions */
XmtLayoutDisableLayout(XtRWidget)
XmtLayoutEnableLayout(XtRWidget)

/* automatic dialog callback functions */
XmtDialogOkayCallback(XmtRCallbackWidget)
XmtDialogCancelCallback(XmtRCallbackWidget)
XmtDialogApplyCallback(XmtRCallbackWidget)
XmtDialogDoneCallback(XmtRCallbackWidget)
XmtDialogResetCallback(XmtRCallbackWidget)
```

You can read about most of these Xmt functions elsewhere in this book, but `XmtSetValue()` and `XmtSetTypedValue()` are special functions designed specifically as the resource-file replacement for `XtSetValues()`:

Xmt/

SetValue.c

```
#include <Xmt/SetValue.h>
void XmtSetValue(Widget w, StringConst resource, StringConst value)
void XmtSetTypedValue(Widget w, StringConst resource,
                      StringConst type, StringConst value)
```

`XmtSetValue()` takes a widget, the name of a resource, and the value of the resource, expressed as a string. It queries the widget to determine the type of the named resource, converts the specified string value to that type, and then calls `XtSetValues()` to set the resource on the widget. `XmtSetTypedValue()` is a similar function, except that it takes a widget, resource name, resource type, and then the resource value expressed as a string. This version of the function is necessary for those resources, such as the `XmNvalue` resource of the XmText widget (in Motif 1.1), that are implemented within subparts of the widget, rather than as part of the main resource list for the widget. For these resources, the type must be specified explicitly because Xmt cannot determine the resource type by examining the widget's internal resource list. The resource type is a "representation type" such as `XtRString` or `XtRInt`. The values of these symbolic constants are the strings "String" and "Int". There is no good way to know when you need to use XmtSetTypedValue() instead of XmtSetValue(). However, your widget documentation might sometimes tell you, or you might see a warning message when you call XmtSetValue(). XmtSetValue() and XmtSetTypedValue() are commonly used and important functions in resource files. Example 10-7 shows how you might use them. (Note that in Motif 1.2, XmtSetTypedValue() is no longer necessary for the XmNvalue resource of the XmText widget.)

Example 10-7. Using XmtSetValue() and XmtSetTypedValue() in a Resource File

```
*red.activateCallback: \
        XmtSetValue(*alert_text, background, red);
        XmtSetTypedValue(*alert_text, value, String, Red Alert!);
*yellow.activateCallback: \
        XmtSetValue(*alert_text, background, yellow);
        XmtSetTypedValue(*alert_text, value, String, Yellow Alert!);
```

You can also call these functions from your C code, but usually the standard procedures XtSetValues() and XtVaSetValues() will be more convenient in C.

10.3.3 UNIX Procedures

XmtRegisterUnixProcedures() registers the functions exit(XtRInt), puts(XtRString), and system(XtRString), which can be useful when prototyping an interface.

See your UNIX man pages if you are not familiar with these functions. You can use these functions in a resource file exactly as you would in your C code, except that the string passed to puts() and system() should not be in quotes.

10.3.4 Registering Everything

You can also register all of these Xt, Xmt, and UNIX procedures by calling the convenience procedure XmtRegisterAll():

Xmt/

All.c

```
#include <Xmt/Xmt.h>
void XmtRegisterAll(void)
```

This function calls XmtRegisterXtProcedures(), XmtRegisterXmtProcedures(), and XmtRegisterUnixProcedures(). It also registers all of the Xmt and Motif widget classes for use with the automatic widget creation facilities described in Chapter 11, *Automatic Widget Creation*, and registers all of the Xmt type converters.

10.4 Style: Procedure Registration as Modular Design

Programming with resources allows you to put most of the interface specification for your applications into a resource file. Separating the interface from the back end of the application is a valuable technique because it keeps these distinct parts of the application in very distinct modules.

Resource files are best suited for the static description of an interface, but with the callback converter presented here, they can also be used to describe the dynamic behavior of an interface. The most complex dynamic behavior of an application—looking up information from a database, for example—clearly belongs as part of the application back end. Other, simpler behaviors, however—popping up help dialogs, and setting the sensitivity of buttons for example—clearly constitute part of the user interface. Using the callback converter allows you to describe these simple behaviors in the same module with the rest of the interface description.

In just about any real application, there will also be dynamic behavior to implement that falls in between these two extremes and cannot be separated into purely back end or purely interface parts—some behaviors simply have to be implemented through a cooperation between interface and back end. Defining custom procedures in your application and registering them so that they can be invoked as callbacks specified in a resource file is a useful technique for design reasons: registering procedures like this forces you to come up with a list of all the back-end procedures that need to be shared with the front end. The array of `XmtProcedureInfo` that you initialize to describe these procedures serves as a fairly formal specification for the interface (programming interface, not user-interface) between the front end and the back end of the application. Forcing yourself to define this interface should help you think clearly about communication between the front and back ends of the application, and even for that reason alone is worth doing.

Registering important back-end procedures is also useful because it creates flexibility for the front end. If these procedures are all available for use in a resource file, then it is easy to experiment with alternative bindings for them—to add popup menu bindings, register them as the double-click shortcuts on list widgets, and so on. Having this flexibility available while prototyping an application will allow you the latitude to easily experiment with different designs, and may help to spark new ideas.

10.5 Summary

If you call the function `XmtRegisterCallbackConverter()`, then you can specify callbacks, in a C-style syntax, in your resource files. In order to do this, you must also register named procedures, and specify the type of arguments each procedure expects:

- You can register standard Xt callback procedures with the functions `XmtRegisterCallbackProcedure()` and `XmtVaRegisterCallbackProcedures()`.

- You can register arbitrary procedures with zero to eight arguments by initializing an array of `XmtProcedureInfo` structures and passing this array to `XmtRegisterProcedures()`.
- You can register the commonly used Xt, Xmt, and UNIX procedures with several convenience functions, `XmtRegisterXtProcedures()`, `XmtRegisterXmtProcedures()`, and `XmtRegisterUnixProcedures()`, or with `XmtRegisterAll()`.

11

Automatic Widget Creation

As we've seen in the preceding few chapters of this section, it is possible to set just about any widget resource, including callback lists, from a resource file. Since it is possible to specify all these widget resources externally to an application executable, the natural next question to ask is whether the widgets themselves could be specified externally to the application.

This is not a new idea. In 1988, while at MIT, I prototyped an Interface Description Language (IDL) interpreter which parsed a simple file format and created the widgets described. (The acronym IDL is also used for RPC stub compilers and elsewhere.) At about the same time, the User Interface Language, UIL, was being developed as part of DECWindows. The UIL compiler, which later became part of Motif, is a far more thorough implementation of the same basic idea.

UIL suffers from some important flaws: because applications that use UIL still almost always need an app-defaults file, programmers have to know C, UIL, and X resource file syntax and system administrators have one more file (the compiled UID file) to correctly install before the application will run. Furthermore, the compiled UID format is not portable across machine architectures, which means that multiple versions must be installed in heterogeneous network environments. And finally, while the UIL syntax is simple, it is not particularly elegant or compact.*

The Widget Creation Library, Wcl, originated by Martin Brunecky and greatly enhanced (and currently maintained) by David Smyth, was the next step. It addresses the shortcomings of UIL by allowing the specification of a widget hierarchy directly in a resource file.

The widget and callback converters described in the previous two chapters and the automatic widget creation facilities described in this one were inspired by Wcl, but are not compatible with Wcl. In particular, the Xmt grammar for

*An early user of Xmt with extensive experience with UIL reports that a UIL interface description takes five to ten times as many lines of code as the same interface described in an Xmt resource file.

describing a widget hierarchy is substantially different from the Wcl grammar, and is more elegant.* Examples throughout this book use the Xmt widget creation scheme, and the book does not document Wcl or UIL. Programmers who are already comfortable with Wcl or UIL, or who have a base of applications already implemented with these tools, can continue to use them—the Xmt widgets will work with Wcl and UIL, and most of the other features of the library are independent of the widget creation scheme.

11.1 Overview: Specifying a Widget Hierarchy with Resources

To create a widget in an application with `XtCreateWidget()`, we specify the widget's name, type, parent, and resources. When creating a widget from a resource file, we must specify the same things. The widget resources can all be specified as normal for a resource file; that much, at least, is obvious. A widget name is just a string, so we'll clearly be able to specify it from a file as well. Specifying the widget class (type) is trickier—we'll need some sort of string-to-widget class converter, which means that the application will have to be able to map from widget class name to the widget class itself, or to a widget creation procedure. We'll go into more detail on this point in the next section, but for now note that the programmer will have to register any widget classes or widget constructor procedures that the application will use and provide names for each of those widget types. If a widget type is not registered, then widgets of that type cannot be created from a resource file.

The only argument we still need to specify in order to create a widget from a resource file is the parent of the widget, and this one is a little tricky. What we do is to turn the problem around, and realize that in order to create a whole tree of widgets from a resource file, we need to be able to specify all the children of a widget. If a widget is specified as the child of another widget in the interface, then the parent of the child is implicit in that specification.

So how do we specify the children of a widget? Composite widgets (i.e., manager widgets that are allowed to have children) all have an `XtNchildren` resource, so if we could write a converter for this resource, we'd be all set. Unfortunately, `XtNchildren` is a read-only resource (i.e., it can be queried but not set) and setting it to a converted value has no effect. Instead, we'll specify children with the `xmtChildren` pseudo-resource. "Pseudo-resource" is my term for a resource which is set in a resource file, but which has no corresponding widget resource. When a widget is created, the Intrinsics automatically search the resource database for that widget's resources. Since no widget has a resource named `xmtChildren`, this resource is never automatically read. Instead, our automatic widget creation routines explicitly search the database themselves to obtain the value of this resource for a given widget. Note that since the `xmtChildren` resource isn't handled by the Intrinsics, and doesn't

*Another early Xmt user reports that he ported his Wcl interfaces to Xmt because of the elegance of the Xmt grammar.

represent an actual resource stored by a widget, it can't be set with a call to `XtSetValues()`.

With each of these pieces in place, we can see the big picture of the Xmt automatic widget creation scheme. First, an application calls `XtAppInitialize()` to initialize the Intrinsics and create a toplevel shell widget. Then it registers names for all the widget classes and constructors it will need to create its interface. Then the application calls `XmtCreateChildren()`, passing the toplevel shell widget. `XmtCreateChildren()` searches the resource database for the `xmtChildren` resource of this toplevel widget. If `XmtCreateChildren()` finds this resource, it parses this string into a list of widget children, each with a name and class. Then the function uses the class name to look up the actual widget class or widget constructor procedure and, armed with that information, creates the child widget. For each child widget created in this way, `XmtCreateChildren()` calls itself recursively, searches for the `xmtChildren` resource of the child, and creates any children of that widget.

Example 11-1 shows the C code involved in a simple application that uses `XmtCreateChildren()`, and Example 11-2 shows a resource file that describes a simple widget hierarchy with the `xmtChildren` resource.

Example 11-1. A Simple Application Using XmtCreateChildren()

```
int main(int argc, char **argv)
{
        XtAppContext app;
        Widget toplevel;

        toplevel = XtAppInitialize(&app, ...);

        XmtRegisterMotifWidgets();
        XmtRegisterXmtWidgets();

        XmtCreateChildren(toplevel);

        XtRealizeWidget(toplevel);
        XtAppMainLoop(app);
}
```

Example 11-2. A Resource File for Use with XmtCreateChildren()

```
!!
!! The child of the toplevel shell widget, alert, is an
!! XmRowColumn widget named 'box' with four children:
!! one XmText widget named 'alert_text' and three
!! XmPushButtons named 'red', 'yellow', and 'cancel'.
!!
alert.xmtChildren: XmRowColumn box;
*box.xmtChildren: \
            XmText alert_text;\
            XmPushButton red, yellow, cancel;
```

These examples are only intended to provide an overview of the Xmt automatic widget creation features. The following sections will go into much more detail about the syntax of the `xmtChildren` resource, the functions used to register widget classes and constructors, and the functions used to create widgets described in a resource file. The following sections also describe some advanced features of this widget creation system: creation callback functions, file inclusion, and widget templating. Still other features of the automatic widget creation system are used when creating dialog boxes that must collect data from the user and return it to the programmer. These last features will be described in Chapter 29, *Custom Dialogs and Automatic Dialog Management.*

Understanding Pseudo-Resources

The X resource database mechanism is implemented as part of Xlib, and the resources it contains are not the same as the widget resources used in Xt. In practice, the hierarchical nature of the resource database is ideally suited to the task of describing widget resources for a hierarchical tree of widgets, and this is how resource databases are usually used in Xt applications.

But not all resources in a database must be widget resources. We saw in Chapter 5, *Using Icons*, for example, how Xmt allows you to include named bitmap and pixmap data in a resource database. These bitmap and pixmap resources are stored in a special "branch" of the database, and are not associated with any widgets. (The term "branch" is my own invention; the words "fork" or "subtree" might do as well. The reason for using special branches is so that bitmap and pixmap specifications will never conflict with actual widget resource specification—unless, of course, someone creates a root shell named `_Bitmaps_` or `_Pixmaps_`.)

Bitmap and pixmap resources are stored in a special branch of the database and are not associated with any widgets. The `xmtChildren` resource, on the other hand, does not correspond to any existing widget resource, but it is associated with a particular widget in the database, and Xmt uses it to create the children of that widget. This is what I mean by a "pseudo-resource"—a resource specification that is not a widget resource, but looks like it is.

Xmt reads pseudo-resources with the function `XtGetApplicationResources()`—despite what its name says, this function will read resource specifications associated with any widget, not just the application resources associated with the toplevel shell. Since pixmap and bitmap data is stored in a special branch and is not associated with any widget, however, these resources cannot be read with this Xt convenience function; instead, Xmt has to use much lower-level Xrm functions in Xlib.

You can create your own pseudo-resources to associate data with your widgets through the resource database. To read the data, use `XtGetApplicationResources()` as described in Chapter 7, *Application Resources and Com-*

Understanding Pseudo-Resources (continued)

mand-Line Arguments, and specify the widget for which you want to read the resource as the first argument to this function. Be sure to name your pseudo-resource so that it does not conflict with any existing widget resource.

—djf

11.2 The xmtChildren Syntax

As should be obvious from the example above, specifying widgets with the `xmtChildren` resource is a lot like declaring variables in C. The resource is a list of semicolon-separated declarations, each declaration a list of attributes, followed by a widget type and a list of names of the children of that type to be created. The BNF grammar for this resource is shown in Example 11-3.

Example 11-3. The BNF Grammar of the xmtChildren Resource

```
children::  {declaration}
declaration::  {modifier} type child {`,' child} `;'
modifier::  "managed" | "unmanaged" | registered style name
type::   registered widget type | registered template name
child::  name of child to be created
```

Just as C datatypes can have attributes like `const` and `unsigned`, widget types in the `xmtChildren` resource can have modifiers. The two standard modifiers are `managed` and `unmanaged`. A widget with the `unmanaged` modifier will be created, but will not be automatically managed. Since widgets are automatically managed by default, the `managed` modifier is never actually necessary, but is supported for symmetry. Notice from the grammar that "registered style names" are also legal modifiers for widget types. A style is a set of frequently used resources registered under a single name for convenience. Styles are related to templates which are named groups of widgets and their resources that can be reused in various parts of the interface. Both styles and templates will be described later in this chapter.

An important point to note about the `xmtChildren` resource itself is that you should always specify it with a "tight binding" rather than a "loose binding"—i.e., use `.xmtChildren` instead of `*xmtChildren`. If you use the `*` wildcard like this:

```
*main_window*xmtChildren: XmDrawingArea workarea;
```

you will set up an infinite loop: the `xmtChildren` resource will create an XmDrawingArea widget, and then the `xmtChildren` resource will also apply to the newly created widget, so another XmDrawingArea will be created, and then another, and so on until program memory or stack space is exhausted.

11.3 Registering Widget Classes and Constructors

Before you can use Xmt to create a widget hierarchy described in a resource file, you must first register names for each of the widget types that you plan to use. In C, there are two standard ways to create widgets: by using both `XtCreateWidget()` and the widget class pointer, or by calling a special convenience function, a "widget constructor" like `XmCreateLabel()`. Correspondingly, Xmt allows you to register widgets either by class or constructor:

Xmt/

WidgetType.c

```
#include <Xmt/WidgetType.h>
void XmtRegisterWidgetClass(String name, WidgetClass class);
void XmtRegisterWidgetConstructor(String name, XmtWidgetConstructor constructor);
```

The `XmtWidgetConstructor` type is a procedure with the signature of a standard "Motif-style" constructor:

```
#include <Xmt/WidgetType.h>
typedef Widget (*XmtWidgetConstructor)(Widget, String, ArgList, Cardinal);
```

When you will be registering a number of widget classes or constructors, there are variants on the above two functions that take a NULL-terminated, variable-length argument list of names and classes or names and constructors:

Xmt/

WidgetType.c

```
#include <Xmt/WidgetType.h>
void XmtVaRegisterWidgetClasses(String name, WidgetClass class, ..., NULL);
void XmtVaRegisterWidgetConstructors(String name,
                                     XmtWidgetConstructor constructor,
                                     ..., NULL);
```

The functions listed above should only be used to register widgets that are not popups. If you are registering a widget class, that class should not be a subclass of Shell. If you are registering a constructor, that constructor should not create a shell widget. To register classes and constructors that create popup widgets, use the following functions:

Xmt/

WidgetType.c

```
#include <Xmt/WidgetType.h>
void XmtRegisterPopupClass(String name, WidgetClass class);
void XmtRegisterPopupConstructor(String name, XmtWidgetConstructor constructor);
```

The primary difference between widgets registered with one of the `RegisterWidget` functions and those registered with a `RegisterPopup` function is that Xmt will allow popup widgets to be created as children of a non-composite widget. Thus you could have an XmMessageDialog created as the child of a push button, but could not create an XmText widget as the child of a button. Another important difference is that a widget class registered with `XmtRegisterPopupClass()` will be used with the function `XtCreate-PopupShell()` instead of `XtCreateWidget()`, as required by Xt. Note that there are not `XtVa` varargs versions of these two popup widget registration functions.

When you are registering a large number of widget classes or constructors, as you often will at the beginning of an application, you may find it easiest to use `XmtRegisterWidgetTypes()`, a generalized version of all of the above functions:

Xmt/

WidgetType.c

```
#include <Xmt/WidgetType.h>
void XmtRegisterWidgetTypes(XmtWidgetType *types, Cardinal num_types);
```

`XmtRegisterWidgetTypes()` takes an array of `XmtWidgetType` structures, which you will usually initialize statically in your application. The definition of this structure is shown in Example 11-4, along with an example call to `XmtRegisterWidgetTypes()`. The fields of the `XmtWidgetType` structure allow you to specify a name for the widget type, and a widget class or constructor. There is also a flag you can set to indicate that the widget is a popup. The structure also optionally allows you specify two functions for setting and querying the value of the widget—these functions are used with the automatic dialog management routines and will be described in detail in Chapter 29.

Example 11-4. Using XmtRegisterWidgetTypes( ) and the XmtWidgetType Structure

```
typedef struct {
        String name;
        WidgetClass class;
        XmtWidgetConstructor constructor;
        XmtSetValueProc set_value_proc;
        XmtGetValueProc get_value_proc;
        int popup;
} XmtWidgetType;

static XmtWidgetType widgets[] = {
{"XmArrowButton", xmArrowButtonWidgetClass},
{"XmBulletinBoard", NULL, XmCreateBulletinBoard},
{"XmBulletinBoardDialog", NULL, XmCreateBulletinBoardDialog, NULL, NULL, True},
{"XmDialogShell", NULL, XmCreateDialogShell, NULL, NULL, True},
{"XmDrawingArea", NULL, XmCreateDrawingArea},
{"XmErrorDialog", NULL, XmCreateErrorDialog, NULL, NULL, True},
};
XmtRegisterWidgetTypes(widgets, XtNumber(widgets));
```

There are also some predefined widget registration functions. `XmtRegisterMotifWidgets()` registers the standard names for each of the widgets and constructors in the Motif library, and `XmtRegisterXmtWidgets()` registers the standard names for each of the widgets in the Xmt library. These widget names are shown in Table 11-1. Note that some of these names refer to ordinary widgets (such as XmPushButton), while others refer to "convenience" widgets, created with special constructor procedures (such as XmInformationDialog).

Xmt/

{Motif,Xmt}Widget.c

```
#include <Xmt/WidgetType.h>
void XmtRegisterMotifWidgets(void);
void XmtRegisterXmtWidgets(void);
```

You can use these functions as conveniences while prototyping an application, but once you have decided on a final list of widgets that your application will use, you should register those widgets explicitly. The application must link with each widget you register, even if you never create a widget of that type, so if you register unused widgets it will make statically linked applications larger, and can cause dynamically linked applications to take longer to start up. (See the files *MotifWidgets.c* and *XmtWidgets.c* in the Xmt source code—you can use them to cut-and-paste `XmtWidgetType` structures for most of the standard widgets.)

Note that you can also call `XmtRegisterAll()` to register all Motif and Xmt widgets, and all the standard callback procedures and resource converters. Again, this convenience function is useful when prototyping, but a production application would probably be a little more discriminate in what widgets, functions, and converters it registers.

Table 11-1. Widget Types Registered by Xmt Convenience Functions

Registered by XmtRegisterMotifWidgets( )		
XmArrowButton	XmMainWindow	XmScrolledText
XmBulletinBoard	XmMenuBar	XmScrolledWindow
XmBulletinBoardDialog	XmMenuShell	XmSelectionBox
XmCascadeButton	XmMessageBox	XmSelectionDialog
XmCommand	XmMessageDialog	XmSeparator
XmDialogShell	XmOptionMenu	XmSimpleCheckBox
XmDrawingArea	XmPanedWindow	XmSimpleMenuBar
XmDrawnButton	XmPopupMenu	XmSimpleOptionMenu
XmErrorDialog	XmPromptDialog	XmSimplePopupMenu
XmFileSelectionBox	XmPulldownMenu	XmSimplePulldownMenu
XmFileSelectionDialog	XmPushButton	XmSimpleRadioBox
XmForm	XmQuestionDialog	XmText
XmFormDialog	XmRadioBox	XmTextField
XmFrame	XmRowColumn	XmToggleButton
XmInformationDialog	XmScale	XmWarningDialog
XmLabel	XmScrollBar	XmWorkArea

Table 11-1. Widget Types Registered by Xmt Convenience Functions (continued)

Registered by XmtRegisterMotifWidgets( )		
XmList	XmScrolledList	
ApplicationShell	XmtLayout	XmtMenu
OverrideShell	XmtLayoutBox	XmtMenuPane
TopLevelShell	XmtLayoutCol	XmtMenubar
TransientShell	XmtLayoutDialog	XmtMsgLine
XmtChooser	XmtLayoutPixmap	XmtOptionMenu
XmtCli	XmtLayoutRow	XmtPopupMenu
XmtHelpBox	XmtLayoutSeparator	XmtScrolledCli
XmtHelpDialog	XmtLayoutSpace	XmtWorkingBox
XmtInputField	XmtLayoutString	XmtWorkingDialog

Finally, there are also convenience routines for registering some of the Motif and Xmt widgets individually. These convenience routines are simple wrappers around calls to `XmtRegisterWidgetTypes()`.

```
#include <Xmt/Chooser.h>
void XmtRegisterChooser(void);

#include <Xmt/InputField.h>
void XmtRegisterInputField(void);

#include <Xmt/WidgetType.h>
void XmtRegisterXmScale(void);
void XmtRegisterXmScrolledText(void);
void XmtRegisterXmText(void);
void XmtRegisterXmTextField(void);
void XmtRegisterXmToggleButton(void);
```

You can register each of these widgets yourself, of course, but these convenience functions also register the special procedures, mentioned above, for setting and querying the value of the widget, which makes them useful with the automatic dialog management routines of Chapter 29, *Custom Dialogs and Automatic Dialog Management*. Note that if you call `XmtRegisterMotifWidgets()` or `XmtRegisterXmtWidgets()` you don't have to register these individual registration functions.

11.3.1 Registering Custom Constructors

Note that you need not restrict yourself to the standard widgets and their standard names. If there are certain widgets that you commonly use with a particular set of resources, you may want to write a special constructor function that creates the widget with those resources hard-coded. The XmText widget, for example, defaults to single-line editing mode. Example 11-5 shows you how to write a custom widget constructor function `CreateMultiLineText()`, which creates an XmText widget in multi-line editing mode, and then to register it with the name "XmMultiLineText". In your resource files, you could then use the widget type "XmMultiLineText" anywhere you would use the type "XmText".

Example 11-5. Registering a Custom Widget Constructor

```
Widget CreateMultiLineText(Widget parent, String name,
                            ArgList args, Cardinal num_args)
{
        Widget w = XmCreateText(parent, name, args, num_args);
        XtVaSetValues(w, XmNeditMode, XmMULTI_LINE_EDIT, NULL);
        return w;
}

XmtRegisterWidgetConstructor("XmMultiLineText", CreateMultiLineText);
```

Note that you can also achieve the same effect by defining a template or a style, as described later in this chapter.

11.4 Widget Creation Functions

Once you have registered widget types from your C code, you can call an automatic widget creation routine to create the widget hierarchy described in your resource file. The basic widget creation function is `XmtCreateChildren()`:

Xmt/

Create.c

```
#include <Xmt/Create.h>
void XmtCreateChildren(Widget w);
```

This function looks up the `xmtChildren` resource of the specified widget (usually the toplevel shell returned by `XtAppInitialize()`), creates each of the children described by that resource, and then recurses to perform the same function for each of the newly created children.

Many widgets in an interface, like push buttons, for example, can be created, have a callback registered on them, and then forgotten—there is no need to retain a pointer to them. There are other widgets, however, like multi-line text widgets, or drawing areas that will be manipulated dynamically by the application. If these widgets are automatically created by `XmtCreateChildren()`, it is possible to obtain the necessary pointers to them by looking them up with `XmtNameToWidget()`. But it is often easier to use `XmtCreateQueryChildren()`:

Xmt/

Create.c

```
#include <Xmt/Create.h>
void XmtCreateQueryChildren(Widget w, ..., NULL);
```

This function behaves like `XmtCreateChildren()` but takes an additional NULL-terminated, variable-length argument list of pairs of names and addresses of `Widget` variables. When the function creates a widget with a name specified in this argument list, it will store the widget pointer at the corresponding address specified on the list. Note that the widget names are single widget names like `menubar`, not hierarchical or patterned names like `toplevel.menubar` or `dialog*XmPushButton`. Single-name widgets require the widgets you want to look up to have unique names. If more than one widget has a name that appears in the argument list, it is unspecified which will be returned. Example 11-6 shows how you might use `XmtCreateQueryChildren()`.

Example 11-6. Using XmtCreateQueryChildren()

```
Widget toplevel, menubar, msgline, text;

toplevel = XtAppInitialize(...);
XmtCreateQueryChildren(toplevel,
                       "menubar", &menubar,
                       "msgline", &msgline,
                       "text", &text,
                       NULL);
```

11.4.1 Deferred Widget Creation

With a single call to `XmtCreateChildren()` you can create the entire widget hierarchy for an application, assuming that you specify the entire widget tree through the `xmtChildren` resources of the various widgets. You will not always want to create the entire tree in one fell swoop, however—to speed application startup, you may want to defer the creation of dialogs or other parts of the widget hierarchy until they are needed.

To defer creation of a dialog box, simply omit the dialog widget (or the root of whatever subtree you want to defer) from the `xmtChildren` resource of its parent. When the time comes to actually create the widget, you can create the dialog shell (or whatever) explicitly with a call to `XmCreateDialogShell()`, and then create all of its children, grandchildren, and so on, by calling `XmtCreateChildren()` on this newly created dialog shell.

Rather than creating this dialog shell by hand, however, you can also use `XmtCreateChild()`:

Xmt/

Create.c

```
#include <Xmt/Create.h>
Widget XmtCreateChild(Widget parent, String name);
```

This function creates the named child of the specified parent widget, and then proceeds to create all the descendants of that child, as if `XmtCreateChildren()` had been called on it. Note that the arguments to `XmtCreateChild()` specify the name of the child to create, but do not specify the type of that child. Instead, the type is specified on the `xmtType` pseudo-resource of the widget. Example 11-7 shows how you might use `XmtCreateChild()` in C code, and how you would use the `xmtType` resource in the corresponding resource file.

Example 11-7. Using XmtCreateChild()

```
/* The C code */
Widget toplevel;

static void SaveAsCallback(Widget w, XtPointer tag, XtPointer data)
{
        static Widget shell = NULL;

        if (shell == NULL) {  /* do this the first time we're called */
                shell = XmtCreateChild(toplevel, "saveas_shell");
        }

        /*
         * Pop up the dialog, etc.
         * Note that we use a TransientShell, not an XmDialogShell,
         * so we use XtPopup() rather than XtManageChild().
         */
        XtPopup(shell, XtGrabNone);
                .
                .
                .
}
!! The corresponding resource file.
*saveas_shell.xmtType: TransientShell
*saveas_shell.xmtChildren: XmtLayout saveas;
*saveas.xmtChildren: XmText input; XmPushButton ok, cancel, help;
```

Note that in the previous example the `saveas_shell` widget has both an `xmtType` resource to specify its own type and an `xmtChildren` resource to specify the names and types of its children. Also, notice that the `xmtType` pseudo-resource is a strange one, because it must be read before the widget it describes has been created. (It is read with `XtGetSubresources()`.) Finally, notice that `XmtCreateChild()` returns the widget that was created at the top of the deferred sub-tree. This is unlike `XmtCreateChildren()`, which returns no value.

XmtCreateChild() recursively creates all the descendants of the named child, and, as with XmtCreateChildren(), there are times when you need to retain pointers to some of those descendants. In this case, you can use Xmt-CreateQueryChild():

Xmt/

Create.c

```
#include <Xmt/Create.h>
Widget XmtCreateQueryChild(Widget parent, String name, ..., NULL);
```

This function takes the same NULL-terminated, variable-length argument list of pairs of widget names and addresses of widget variables that XmtCreate-QueryChildren() takes.

11.4.2 Creating New Windows and Dialogs

The example given above of deferring the creation of a dialog box until it is needed occurs often enough that Xmt provides special functions to handle it:

Xmt/

Create.c

```
#include <Xmt/Create.h>
Widget XmtBuildDialog(Widget parent, String name,
                         XtResourceList resources, Cardinal num_resources);
Widget XmtBuildQueryDialog(Widget parent, String name,
                              XtResourceList resources, Cardinal num_resources,
                              ..., NULL);
```

XmtBuildDialog() and XmtBuildQueryDialog() create an XmDialog-Shell named *name* as a child of *parent*, and then they proceed as if Xmt-CreateChildren() or XmtCreateQueryChildren() had been called on this shell widget. Both functions return the child of this shell (recall that shell widgets can only have a single child) and because the shell is an XmDialog-Shell, you can pop up and pop down the dialog by managing and unmanaging this child. Remember that you generally do not want dialog boxes to automatically pop up when they are first created; this means that you will have to specify the "unmanaged" modifier for the child of the shell.

The *resources* and *num_resources* arguments are optional and are used with the automatic dialog management functions as described in Chapter 29, *Custom Dialogs and Automatic Dialog Management*. For simple automatic creation of dialogs, you can simply pass NULL and 0 for these arguments.

Example 11-8 shows how XmtBuildQueryDialog() could be used to create a dialog similar to that created in Example 11-7.

Example 11-8. Using XmtBuildQueryDialog()

```
/* The C code */
Widget toplevel;
```

Example 11-8. Using XmtBuildQueryDialog() (continued)

```
static void SaveAsCallback(Widget w, XtPointer tag, XtPointer data)
{
        static Widget dialog = NULL;
        static Widget inputfield;
        static char filename_buffer[100];

        if (dialog == NULL) {  /* do this the first time we're called */
              dialog = XmtBuildQueryDialog(toplevel, "saveas_shell",
                                           NULL, 0,
                                           "input", &inputfield,
                                           NULL);
        }

        /*
         * Set default filename in text widget and pop up the dialog.
         * This is a Motif-style dialog, so we use XtManageChild().
         */
        XtVaSetValues(inputfield, XmNvalue,  filename_buffer, NULL);
        XtManageChild(dialog);
                .
                .
                .
}

!!
!! The corresponding resource file.
!! Note we don't need Type resource here since we're using
!! XmtBuildQueryDialog() instead of XmtCreateChild().
!!
*saveas_shell.xmtChildren: XmtLayout saveas;
*saveas.xmtChildren: XmText input; XmPushButton ok, cancel, help;
```

Xmt also provides two functions similar to `XmtBuildQueryDialog()` for the creation of widget hierarchies within shell widgets, tasks which are often deferred until just before the shell is popped up.

Xmt/

Create.c

```
#include <Xmt/Create.h>
Widget XmtBuildQueryToplevel(Widget parent, String name, ..., NULL);
Widget XmtBuildQueryApplication(String name, String class, Display *display,
                                ArgList args, Cardinal num_args, ..., NULL);
```

`XmtBuildQueryToplevel()` creates a TopLevelShell widget with the specified name and parent, and then proceeds as if `XmtCreateQueryChildren()` had been called on that shell. It returns the TopLevelShell widget.

`XmtBuildQueryApplication()` creates an ApplicationShell widget by calling `XtAppCreateShell()` with the specified arguments, and then proceeds as if `XmtCreateQueryChildren()` had been called on that shell. It returns the ApplicationShell widget. Note that the returned shell is at the root of a widget tree—it has no parent. This widget also forms the root of a widget hierarchy, and resources are set on it in a resource file as if it were a separate application.

Both of these functions take a variable-length argument list of the type described for `XmtCreateQueryChildren()`. There are also non-query versions of these functions:

Xmt/

Create.c

```
#include <Xmt/Create.h>
Widget XmtBuildToplevel(Widget parent, String name)
Widget XmtBuildApplication(String name, String class, Display *display,
                            ArgList args, Cardinal num_args)
```

Note that all of these functions return the shell widgets they create, while `XmtBuildDialog()` and `XmtBuildQueryDialog()` both return the child of the dialog shell. This is because TopLevelShell and ApplicationShell widgets must be manipulated directly with `XtPopup()` and `XtPopdown()`, rather than being controlled through their children.

11.5 Creation Callbacks

Sometimes building a widget hierarchy involves more than simply creating each of the widgets in the tree. For example, you might create a cascade button in one menu pane, then create a second submenu pane, which needs to be "attached" to the cascade button by setting the `XmNsubMenuId` resource of the button. This is a resource on the cascade button, but it cannot be set when the button is created, because the menu pane that will be attached does not exist yet. Xmt provides "creation callbacks" that can be used to perform arbitrary functions at specific points in the creation of the widget tree.

These creation callbacks are specified as pseudo-resources of each automatically created widget, and can be set exactly as you would set any other callback from a resource file. The procedures that you specify for these callbacks will be invoked exactly once when the widget is created. If you register procedures with a traditional `XtCallbackProc` signature, then they will be called with the newly created widget as their first argument, the value you specify as *`client_data`* (second argument), and `NULL` as their *`call_data`* (third argument). There are three of these "pseudo-callbacks" invoked during the creation of any widget. Table 11-2 lists them and explains when each is invoked.

Table 11-2. The Xmt Creation Callbacks

Callback	**When Invoked**
`xmtCreationCallback`	After the widget is created; before its children are created
`xmtChildrenCreationCallback`	After the widget and its children are created; before it is managed
`xmtManagedCreationCallback`	After the widget and its children are created, and after it has been managed

Example 11-9 shows how you could use the `xmtCreationCallback` to connect a menu pane to its cascade button, as described at the beginning of this section.

Example 11-9. Using the xmtCreationCallback

```
toplevel.xmtChildren: XmMenuBar menubar;

!! The menu bar has a cascade button and a menu pane as children
*menubar.xmtChildren: XmCascadeButton file;
                      unmanaged XmPulldownMenu file_pane;

!! Once the menu pane is created, we set it as the value of
!! the cascade button XmNsubMenuId resource.
*file_pane.xmtChildren: XmPushButton item1, item2, item3;
*file_pane.xmtCreationCallback: XmtSetValue(*file, subMenuId, *file_pane);
```

This example is actually somewhat contrived—the button and menu pane are siblings, so we could just have switched the order of the children in the menu bar `xmtChildren` resource, and then set the `subMenuId` resource of the cascade button statically. There are cases, however, when menu panes and cascade buttons are not siblings, and a callback like the one shown here is necessary. (Note, though, that if you use the XmtMenu widget, you'll probably never have this problem.)

Creation callbacks also serve as a method for widget registration. Instead of querying the widgets by name after they are created, or using `XmtCreateQueryChildren()`, you can call a callback procedure that will save away a pointer to the newly created widget for future use. In general, creation callbacks serve as hooks for performing any necessary additional processing during the widget creation process. You may encounter custom widgets, for example, that force you to set some of their attributes by calling functions rather than setting resources. You could use a creation callback to set these non-resource attributes.

11.6 Resource File Inclusion

Before it reads the `xmtChildren` resource, `XmtCreateChildren()` reads the `xmtRequires` resource for the specified widget. This resource specifies a list of filenames to be read and merged into the resource database. In addition, before creating any child specified on an `xmtChildren` resource, `XmtCreateChildren()` reads the `xmtRequires` resource of the child and merges in any specified files. This file inclusion functionality allows pieces of an application interface to be broken into modules which are easier to maintain separately, and which can sometimes even be reused in other applications. Individual dialog boxes, for example, can be specified in separate files, which can be a real organizational convenience while developing an application.

The `xmtRequires` resource is a list of filenames in quotes or in angle brackets, separated by white space. If the filename is an absolute filename (i.e., if it begins with a `/` or a `.`), it is simply read in; otherwise, it is looked up with

XmtFindFile(). Files in angle brackets are searched for in the application directories (relative to the directory specified by the configDir application resource) and in the system directory. Files in quotes are also searched for in the user directory; if a file is found in the user directory, it is merged in as well, and resources in it override any matching specifications in the previously found application resource file. See Chapter 6, *Managing Auxiliary Files*, for more information on how XmtFindFile() looks up auxiliary files like these.

The list of filenames may be interspersed with #override and #augment directives, which specify whether files following the directive should override or augment resources already in the resource database. By default, included files override existing resources. The #augment directive will not work (and will produce a warning message) if you use it with X11R4; the underlying technology for augmenting one resource database with another was not available until X11R5.

The xmtRequires resource can be particularly useful in conjunction with functions like XmtBuildDialog(). Your main resource file might contain a line like the following:

```
*preferences.xmtRequires: <dialogs/preferences>
```

Then, in your C code, when you call XmtBuildDialog() with the name "preferences", it will create a dialog shell with the given name, read the xmtRequires resource, read in the specified resource file, and then read the xmtChildren resource, which would presumably be one of the resources in the newly merged file. In this way, the entire specification for the dialog box can be moved to a separate resource file.

Note that the Xmt library remembers which resource files have already been loaded, and will not read the same file twice.* You can also include resource files explicitly from your C code with the functions XmtLoadResourceFile() and XmtLoadResourceFileList(). The documentation for these functions provides a more formal specification of the grammar for the xmtRequires resource.

11.7 Creating Widgets with Styles and Templates

The xmtChildren and the xmtType resource grammars support the unmanaged modifier, but also allow a style name to be used as a widget modifier. Also, they allow a template name to be used in place of a widget type. This section explains what styles and templates are, and how you can use them in your programs.

*More precisely, it won't read a file with the same name twice—it will not detect whether a file has been changed since last read, nor does it check whether two distinct filenames refer to the same actual file.

11.7.1 Styles

A *style* is a collection of resource settings that are commonly used together. You could, for example, define a style named `bold` which specifies a bold font and a special foreground color that highlights the widget it is applied to. Then you could use this style in an `xmtChildren` resource in a line like the following:

```
dialog.xmtChildren: bold XmLabel prompt;
```

A style is specified as a string. Each line of this string specifies a resource that will be applied to a widget. When a style is specified for a widget that is to be created, that style is instantiated on the widget by prepending the full, tightly-bound, hierarchical name of the widget to each line of the style and inserting the resulting line into the resource database. The resource database now contains each of the resources of the style specifically modified for the widget that is to be created. When the widget is created, the Intrinsics reads these resources from the database and sets them on the widget.

Styles can be registered with the function `XmtRegisterStyle()`:

Xmt/

Template.c

```
#include <Xmt/Template.h>
void XmtRegisterStyle(Widget w, StringConst name, StringConst style);
```

Since styles are defined simply as strings, they can also be easily defined in a resource file. Styles defined in resource files are stored in a special branch of the resource database, under the reserved name `_Styles_`. Example 11-10 shows how you could use both techniques to define the `bold` style discussed above.

Example 11-10. Registering a style in C and in a Resource File

```
/*
 * A style can be registered in C...
 */
static String bold_style =    /* note Ansi-C string concatenation */
       ".Foreground: red\n"
       ".FontList: *-helvetica-bold-r-*-*-*-140-*"

/* the first argument can be any widget in the application */
XmtRegisterStyle(toplevel, "bold", bold_style);

!!
!! ...or in a resource file
!!
_Styles_.bold: \
       .Foreground: red\n\
       .FontList: *-helvetica-bold-r-*-*-*-140-*
```

The first thing to notice about this style specification is that each of the resources it describes is simply a resource name, without any leading widget names. The widget names will be added when the style is instantiated on a widget. Each resource name should be preceded by a . or a *; when a widget name is prepended, this will result in either a tight or a loose binding.

Like any multi-line resource, the lines in a style must end with \ to escape the newline character at the end of the line. Note, however, that a style is a resource that describes resources, and these resources must themselves be separated by newlines. Therefore a multi-resource style will include explicit \n newline escape sequences to separate the resources. As a further twist, note that some resources within a style specification may themselves be formatted on multiple lines. When these multiple lines are used simply for readability, they will not be separated by the \n escape.

To return to our example, specifying the style bold for a button named **demo.dialog.cancel** is equivalent to specifying the following resources:

```
demo.dialog.cancel.Foreground: red
demo.dialog.cancel.FontList: *-helvetica-bold-r-*-*-*-140-*
```

Note that we use the class names Foreground and FontList in the style definition, rather than the resource names foreground and fontList. Using the class name makes it possible to override the resources specified by the style by providing a more specific specification. Since styles are instantiated using a fully-specified widget name, however, it takes a very explicit resource specification, without any wildcards, to override the style:

```
demo.dialog.cancel.foreground: orange
```

11.7.2 Templates

A *template* is very similar to a style: it is a string which defines a set of resources, and is instantiated into the resource database in the same way that a style is. There is one major difference between styles and templates, however. A style is used as a modifier to a widget type. A template, on the other hand, is used in lieu of a widget type; thus a template must define a type for the widget that is to be created. It does this by defining the xmtType resource (the same resource read by the function XmtCreateChild()).

Since a template can specify its own type, it can also specify its own children, simply by defining an xmtChildren resource for whatever widget it is instantiated on. Thus, you could define a template named "ButtonBox" that created an XmRowColumn with **Ok**, **Cancel**, and **Help** buttons within it. Example 11-11 shows how you could define such a template.

Example 11-11. Defining a Simple Template

```
_Templates_.ButtonBox: \
        .xmtType: XmRowColumn\n\
        .xmtChildren: XmPushButton Ok, Cancel, Help;\n\
        .orientation: XmHORIZONTAL\n\
        .packing: XmPACK_COLUMN\n\
        .entryAlignment: XmALIGNMENT_CENTER
```

The template defined in this example is specified under the special "branch" of the resource database with the reserved name `_Templates_`. We could also have defined it by passing the template string to the function `XmtRegisterTemplate()`, which is analogous to `XmtRegisterStyle()`.

11.7.3 Template and Style Arguments

There is another feature of styles and templates that has been left out of the above discussion for simplicity: when a style or a template is instantiated, macro-style argument substitution is performed on the string. When a percent sign followed by a digit occurs in a style or template string, that sequence is replaced with the corresponding macro argument, which is specified in the `xmtChildren` resource within parentheses following the style or template name. A flexible dialog box template, for example, could be defined using argument substitution as shown in Example 11-12.

Example 11-12. A Template That Uses Argument Substitution

```
! A dialog box template.  Arguments are as follows:
! %0: the text to appear in the window manager title bar
! %1: the title to appear in a large font at the top of the dialog
! %2: the type of the main body of the dialog
! %3, %4, %5: names (and labels) of buttons to appear
!      at the bottom of the dialog.
_Templates_.XmtDialog:\
.xmtType: XmDialogShell\n\
.xmtChildren: XmtLayout dialog;\n\
.dialog.dialogTitle: %0\n\
.dialog.xmtChildren: %2 body; XmPushButton %3, %4, %5;\n\
.dialog.layout: Fixed FlushLeft "@f[BIG]%1"\
                              =\
                              body \
                              Fixed Equal Even Etched Top Row { %3 %4 %5 }
```

To instantiate a template (or a style) that takes arguments, simply specify values for the arguments, separated by commas, in parentheses following the template name. You needn't specify all the arguments; the Xmt library will issue a warning if too many arguments are specified, but not if too few are specified. Given the template definition from Example 11-12, you could create a dialog box that contained an XmText widget by instantiating the dialog as shown in Example 11-13. Note that we know that the template will create our XmText widget with the name "`body`", and we take advantage of this to explicitly specify resources for this text widget.

Example 11-13. Using a Template with Arguments

```
*main.xmtChildren: XmtDialog(Instructions, XApp Instructions, XmText,
                             Okay, Cancel, Help) instructions;
*instructions*body.rows: 24
*instructions*body.columns: 80
*instructions*editMode: XmMULTI_LINE_EDIT
*instructions*body.fontList: *-courier-medium-r-*-*-*-140-*
```

11.8 Other Techniques for Creating Widgets

The xmtChildren resource and the grammar it supports is a fairly elegant way to describe a widget hierarchy in a resource file. When using the XmtNlayout resource of an XmtLayout widget, however, (see Chapter 19, *The Layout Widget: The Details*) it can be convenient to specify widget types at the same time that you specify widget layout. Therefore, the Layout widget will perform some automatic widget creation of its own. It does this by using the function XmtLookupWidgetType() to convert the name of a type into a pointer to an XmtWidgetType structure, and then passing this pointer to XmtCreateWidgetType() to actually create the widget. (See the reference section for information on these functions.)

If you find that you have some non-standard syntax for describing a widget hierarchy (such as the Wcl or UIL syntax, or perhaps the widget tree file format output by *editres*), you can write your own parser for it, and use these functions to create the widgets it describes. All the widget type registration and lookup code remains the same; only the grammar parsing must change.

Similarly, you can look up registered styles and templates with XmtLookupStyle() and XmtLookupTemplate() and instantiate them into the resource database with XmtTemplateInstantiate().

11.9 Summary

Table 11-3 summarizes the resources, and the registration and creation functions introduced in this chapter.

Table 11-3. Automatic Widget Creation Summary

Pseudo-Resources for Specifying a Widget Hierarchy	
Resource	**Purpose**
xmtChildren	Specifies a widget's children
xmtType	Specifies a widget's type for XmtCreateChild()
xmtCreationCallback	Invoked after the widget is created
xmtChildrenCreationCallback	Invoked after the widget's children are created
xmtManagedCreationCallback	Invoked after the widget's children are managed
xmtRequires	Specifies other resource files to include
Styles	Branch of the resource database for style definitions
Templates	Branch of the resource database for template definitions

Widget Creation Functions	
XmtCreateChildren()	XmtCreateQueryChildren()
XmtCreateChild()	XmtCreateQueryChild()
XmtBuildDialog()	XmtBuildQueryDialog()
	XmtBuildQueryToplevel()
	XmtBuildQueryApplication()

Widget Registration Functions	
XmtRegisterWidgetClass()	XmtRegisterWidgetConstructor()
XmtRegisterPopupClass()	XmtRegisterPopupConstructor()
XmtVaRegisterWidgetClasses()	XmtVaRegisterWidgetConstructors()
XmtRegisterMotifWidgets()	XmtRegisterXmtWidgets()
XmtRegisterWidgetTypes()	

12

Symbols

As we saw in Chapter 10, *Callbacks in Resource Files*, Xmt allows you to associate symbolic names with C procedures, so that you can refer to those procedures from resource files. If you can refer to procedures by name in resource files, it would seem reasonable to do the same for variables. So Xmt also allows you to register symbolic names for your application variables, and you can use those names in a number of contexts in your resource files (and also sometimes in your C code.) Using these symbolic names can help you to keep your user interface separate from the underlying back end of the application.

In Xmt lingo, such a symbolic name for an application variable is known as a "Symbol", and these Symbols are encapsulated in the `XmtSymbol` abstraction. This chapter shows how you can register and look up Symbols by name, how you can set and query the value of a Symbol, and how you can get callback-style notification when the value of a Symbol changes. The chapter also provides an overview of how Symbols are used in the Xmt library to enhance the modularity of applications.

12.1 Registering Symbols

You can register symbolic names for application variables with the function `XmtVaRegisterSymbols()`:

Xmt/
Symbols.c

```
#include <Xmt/Symbols.h>
void XmtVaRegisterSymbols(String name, String type, int size,
                          XtPointer address, ..., NULL);
```

This function takes a `NULL`-terminated list of (*`name`*, *`type`*, *`size`*, *`address`*) quadruples. For each set of values, it registers *`name`* as the symbolic name for the variable at *`address`* with size *`size`* and type *`type`*. The *`type`* argument is a standard Xt representation type, like `XtRInt` or `XtRDimension`, for example. Both of the `String` arguments *name* and *type* must be constant strings, or at least permanently allocated strings—the Symbol registration function does not make copies of these strings, so they must not be in memory that will be freed, or in memory on the stack. Similarly, of course, you will want the *address* argument to be the address of a static or global variable, or at least the address of memory that has been allocated and will never be freed.

Example 12-1 shows how you might register three types of symbols in a program.

Example 12-1. Registering Symbols

```
static Boolean show_icons;
static int font_size;
static char filename[100];

XmtVaRegisterSymbols("show_icons", XtRBoolean, sizeof(Boolean), &show_icons,
                     "font_size", XtRInt, sizeof(int), &font_size,
                     "filename", XmtRBuffer, sizeof(filename), filename,
                     NULL);
```

Take a look at the Symbol named "filename" in Example 12-1. The `filename` variable is a character buffer, and we specify a *type* of `XmtRBuffer` for this symbol, and pass the length of the buffer as the *size* argument. Notice that we do not use `XtRString` and `sizeof(String)`. `XmtRBuffer` is a special representation type defined by Xmt—it means that the value of interest is not the four-byte address of a character string, but the actual string itself. The Xmt Symbol functions contain special case code for the `XmtRBuffer` type so that NULL-terminated strings can be copied into the specified buffers without overflowing them.

12.2 Using Symbols

Often, registering Symbols as we did above is the only step you'll need to take in your applications—as we see in the next section, several of the Xmt widgets can take Symbol names as resources. If you ever want to operate on a Symbol directly, however, you'll need to obtain an `XmtSymbol` pointer. You can look up the `XmtSymbol` associated with a symbol name with the function `XmtLookupSymbol()`:

Xmt/

Symbols.c

```
#include <Xmt/Symbols.h>
XmtSymbol XmtLookupSymbol(String name);
```

Once you have the `XmtSymbol` pointer, you can use it to set or query the Symbol value, or to get notification when the value changes. The following subsections show how.

12.2.1 Setting the Symbol Value

You can set the value of a Symbol with XmtSymbolSetValue():

Xmt/

Symbols.c

```
#include <Xmt/Symbols.h>
void XmtSymbolSetValue(XmtSymbol s, XtArgVal value);
```

Recall that an XtArgVal is the type used by Xt for untyped values passed to XtSetArg(). As when you are setting resources, you should pass the value itself, if it will fit within an XtArgVal, and otherwise, you should pass the address of the value (you rarely have to do this, however, except when you are using a double value). Also, notice that XmtRBuffer is a special case here—you always pass the address of the buffer, no matter its size. Example 12-2 shows how you might use this function to set a Symbol when the state of a toggle button changes.

Example 12-2. Using XmtSymbolSetValue()

```
/* a callback registered on an XmToggleButton */
static void ToggleCallback(Widget w, XtPointer tag, XtPointer data)
{
    XmToggleButtonCallbackStruct *tbcs = (XmToggleButtonCallbackStruct *)data;
    static XmtSymbol symbol;

    /* one-time initialization */
    if (!symbol) symbol = XmtLookupSymbol("show_icons");

    XmtSymbolSetValue(symbol, (XtArgVal)tbcs->set);
}
```

If the back end of your application registers a Symbol, you can look it up by name in the front end, and set it using this function, without ever having to know the address of that variable (perhaps it is declared static within a back-end module.) If you wanted to set the Symbol value in the back end itself, you could just set the variable directly, without going through the XmtSymbol interface. If you do this, however, no notification is possible of changes to the Symbol, so if you have made a variable public by registering a Symbol for it, you should set the value of that Symbol with XmtSymbolSetValue().

12.2.2 Querying the Symbol Value

You can query the value of a Symbol with XmtSymbolGetValue():

Xmt/

Symbols.c

```
#include <Xmt/Symbols.h>
void XmtSymbolGetValue(Symbol s, XtArgVal *valuep);
```

The *valuep* argument to this function is the address at which the value is to be stored. Note that it need not actually be the address of an `XtArgVal` variable, but must be large enough to store the value of the Symbol.

Example 12-3 is an extension to Example 12-2. It shows how you can use `XmtSymbolGetValue()` to set the initial state of a toggle button depending on the initial state of a Symbol. Note that we must cast our `Boolean *` to an `XtArgVal *`.

Example 12-3. Using XmtSymbolGetValue()

```
Widget CreateToggle(Widget parent)
{
    Boolean state;

    XmtSymbolGetValue(XmtLookupSymbol("show_icons", (XtArgVal *)&state);
    return XtVaCreateManagedWidget("toggle", xmToggleButtonWidgetClass,
                                   parent, XmNset, state, NULL);
}
```

Note that the module that registers a Symbol can obtain that Symbol's value by reading it directly from the address registered with the Symbol—there is no need to read it indirectly with `XmtSymbolGetValue()`.

12.2.3 Callback Notification for Symbols

We saw above that one way to get the value of a Symbol is to use `XmtSymbolGetValue()` to query it whenever you need the value. Another technique, however, is to request notification whenever the value of the Symbol changes. You can do this with `XmtSymbolAddCallback()`, and you can stop receiving notification by calling `XmtSymbolRemoveCallback()`:

Xmt/

Symbols.c

```
#include <Xmt/Symbols.h>
void XmtSymbolAddCallback(XmtSymbol s, XmtSymbolCallbackProc proc,
                          XtPointer client_data);
void XmtSymbolRemoveCallback(XmtSymbol s, XmtSymbolCallbackProc proc,
                             XtPointer client_data);
```

Registering a callback for a Symbol is much like registering a callback for a widget. The important difference is in the type of the procedure that you register. An `XmtSymbolCallbackProc` has the following signature:

```
#include <Xmt/Symbols.h>
typedef void (*XmtSymbolCallbackProc)(XmtSymbol s,
                                      XtPointer client_data,
                                      XtArgVal value);
```

The first argument to a Symbol callback is the `XmtSymbol` that has had its value changed. The second argument is whatever untyped *`client_data`* was registered with the callback procedure, and the third argument, *`value`*, is the new value of the Symbol. This is either the value itself, or, if the value is too large to fit in an `XtArgVal` (or if it is of type `XmtRBuffer`), it is a pointer to the value.

Example 12-4 shows how you might use a Symbol callback to update the state of a toggle button in the front end of an application when the value of a Symbol defined in the back end changes.

Example 12-4. A Symbol Callback

```
static void UpdateToggle(XmtSymbol s, XtPointer data, XtArgVal value)
{
    Widget toggle = (Widget) data;
    Boolean state = (Boolean) value;

    XmToggleButtonSetState(toggle, state, False);
}
        .
        .
        .
Widget toggle_w;  /* an XmToggleButton, created elsewhere */

XmtSymbolAddCallback(XmtLookupSymbol("show_icons"),  /* registered elsewhere */
                     UpdateToggle, toggle_w);
```

12.3 Using Symbols in Xmt

This chapter is part of the "Programming with Resources" part of this book, but so far, all of our examples have been in C. By providing names for variables, Symbols do raise the possibility of referring to those variables from a resource file. In Chapter 10, *Callbacks in Resource Files*, for example, we saw that you can pass the value of a Symbol as an argument to a callback procedure from a resource file, simply by preceding the name of the Symbol with the `$` character. In addition, three of the Xmt widgets support the use of Symbol names to tell them where to store their values. We'll summarize those uses here; you can find full details in the chapters devoted to each of these widgets.

The XmtMenu widget is one that parses a special menu-description grammar from a resource file and creates the pulldown or popup menus the grammar describes. When you specify a toggle button in a menu, this grammar allows you to also specify a Symbol name (again, preceded by a `$` character). When the user toggles the button, the state of the named Symbol will be updated. And similarly, if the state of the Symbol is set with `XmtSymbolSetValue()` (or perhaps by some other menu widget) then the state of the toggle button in the menu will be updated correspondingly.

The XmtChooser widget presents a choice to the user, using a radio box, a check box, a list widget, a palette, or other display formats. It is simpler than using individual widgets in large part because it has a single state variable that specifies what the user's choice is. It also has an `XmtNsymbolName` resource. If you specify the name of an integer Symbol on this resource (from C or a resource file), then the initial state of the Symbol will be used as the initial selection state of the Chooser widget. When the user makes a choice, the value of the named Symbol will be updated, and if the state of the Symbol is set using `XmtSymbolSetValue()`, then the selection state of the Chooser will be updated to match.

The XmtInputField widget is an extension to the XmText widget with a lot of convenient features for getting text input in dialog boxes. Two of these features are the `XmtNbufferSymbolName` resource and the `XmtNtargetSymbolName` resource. If you specify the name of an `XmtRBuffer` Symbol on the `XmtNbufferSymbolName` resource, then the InputField widget will use that Symbol to get the widget's initial value, will update that Symbol when the input value changes, and will update the widget display if the Symbol value is changed with `XmtSymbolSetValue()`. If you specify the name of a Symbol on the `XmtNtargetSymbolName` resource, then the InputField will attempt to convert any input value to the type of the Symbol (by invoking a resource converter) and will then update the Symbol's value to this newly input and converted value. You can use this feature to convert a numeric input string to an integer, for example, or an input color name to a `Pixel` value.

12.4 Symbol Registration as Modular Design

The previous section explained how Symbols are used in a number of Xmt widgets. We'll return to these uses in the chapters about the individual widgets. For now, what is important to notice is the effect that Symbol registration has on the back end of an application. If one module of an application registers the public name "show_icons" for its internal static variable `show_icons`, then another module, the user interface, might use that Symbol name with a **Show Icons** toggle button in the **View** menu of the application. When the user toggles that button, the `show_icons` variable of the first module will automatically be updated. When that module needs to decide whether or not to draw icons in the application window (our hypothetical example is a graphical file browser, perhaps) it can simply read the `show_icons` variable directly, and need know nothing about the widgets in the user interface. At the same time, the `show_icons` variable can be made static, rather than global, which avoids clutter between the modules.

Registering names for application variables can be good modular design, just as registering names for procedures can be. The use of the "show_icons" Symbol above, for example, makes the modules independent of one another—the menu bar could be completely rearranged, or the **Show Icons** button removed altogether, without any modifications to the other, icon-drawing module.

As with procedures, registering Symbols can force you to think carefully about the interfaces between the modules of your application. Defining a list of all the variables that must be shared can be a useful exercise that may help to improve the design of your modules.

On the other hand, there are times when too much modularity is counterproductive. If you are writing a short application, especially one that will fit in a single file, you may not want to use Symbols and the extra layer of abstraction they introduce. The appropriate choice will vary between applications.

12.5 Summary

You can register symbolic names for application variables with `XmtVaRegisterSymbols()`.

Once Symbols are registered in this way, you can use Symbol names in callback specifications, or with the XmtMenu, XmtChooser, and XmtInputField widgets.

If you want to manipulate a Symbol directly in your C code, use `XmtLookupSymbol()` to look up the `XmtSymbol` pointer for a named Symbol.

Once you have an `XmtSymbol`, you can set the value of the corresponding Symbol with `XmtSymbolSetValue()`, and can query its value with `XmtSymbolGetValue()`.

If you want to be notified when the value of a Symbol has been changed with `XmtSymbolSetValue()` (widgets set Symbol values this way, for example) you can register a Symbol "callback" with `XmtSymbolAddCallback()`. You can remove a callback with `XmtSymbolRemoveCallback()`.

13

Resource File Utilities: mockup, checkres, and ad2c

The chapters in this second part of the book have all presented techniques that allow you to program with resources. This culminating chapter presents three utility programs, *mockup*, *checkres*, and *ad2c*, that make programming with resources even easier.

mockup is a simple client that reads a specified resource file and builds the interface described in it. This client allows you to prototype (or "mock up") interfaces without writing a single line of C code. While designing and experimenting with your interface, you can rapidly make changes to your resource file and see their effects simply by running *mockup*—there is no need to recompile anything.

checkres is a script that performs some simple syntactic checks on a resource file, and detects common errors such as missing backslashes at the end of multiline resources.

ad2c is another script that takes a resource file or files as input and outputs a comma-separated list of C strings. This is useful when, after prototyping an application with resources, you want to hard-code those resources into the executable.

The sections below explain these three clients.

13.1 mockup

The *mockup* client has the following command-line syntax:

Xmt/

clients/mockup.c

```
mockup appname [filename] [options]
```

The first thing *mockup* does is to read in the resource file specified by the `filename` argument. Then it creates a toplevel ApplicationShell with the name specified by `appname`, and calls `XmtCreateChildren()` on that toplevel widget. Thus, the basic requirement for a resource file that is to be used with *mockup* is that it contain an `xmtChildren` resource specification for the toplevel shell widget named by `appname`.

Consider the resource file *simple.ad* shown in Example 13-1.

Example 13-1. A Resource File for Use with mockup

examples/

13/simple.ad

```
*FontList: *-helvetica-bold-r-*-*-*-140-*
simple.xmtChildren: XmRowColumn box;

*box.xmtChildren: XmPushButton push, exit;

*push.labelString: Love, Peace & Harmony
*push.activateCallback: \
        XmtDisplayInformation(msg1, \
                              Sorry, this feature is not yet implemented.,\
                              Love\\, Peace & Harmony)

*exit.labelString: Quit
*exit.activateCallback: exit(0);
```

You could run *mockup* on this file with a command like the following:

```
mockup simple simple.ad
```

producing the very simple interface shown in Figure 13-1.

The most important thing to note about this example is that the `appname` argument to *mockup* is "`simple`", and the resource file contains the necessary `simple.xmtChildren` resource specification. When *mockup* calls `XmtCreateChildren()` for the toplevel shell, it reads this `xmtChildren` resource, creates the XmRowColumn widget it specifies, and then recurses to create all the remaining children in the interface. *mockup* registers all of the Motif and Xmt widgets before calling `XmtCreateChildren()`, so resource files to be run through *mockup* can use any of these widget types. As the children are created, their resources are read from the resource database. Notice that *mockup* registers the Xmt callback converter, and also registers some basic Xt, Xmt, and UNIX functions, so that resource files can contain callback specifications, as they do in the example. *mockup* also registers all the other important Xmt resource converters—we'll list everything it registers later in this chapter.

Figure 13-1. A simple mocked-up client

The *mockup* syntax also allows you to specify any of the standard Xt or Xmt command-line arguments. (See `XmtParseCommandLine()` for information on the Xmt-specific command-line arguments.) This means that you might invoke *mockup* like this:

```
mockup simple simple.ad -bg gray -xrm "*FontList: variable"
```

A final note about specifying options for a mocked-up interface: *mockup* tells the Intrinsics to read the resource file you specify by setting its internal copy of the `XENVIRONMENT` environment variable. Thus, any file you specify with this variable will be ignored by *mockup*. While this may seem like an inconvenience, it is probably for the best: the `XENVIRONMENT` variable is intended to let you specify a set of personal customizations for your applications. While designing interfaces with *mockup*, you probably want to design them independently of your own customizations. (*mockup* still reads any personal resources you've passed to *xrdb*, however, and it may also read your *.Xdefaults* file.)

13.1.1 Shortcut Syntax

You'll notice in the syntax we gave for *mockup* that the *`filename`* argument is optional. If *mockup* is invoked with only the *`appname`* argument, it will search for a suitable resource file to read. So, the example *simple.ad* resource file we used in the previous section could actually be mocked up with a simpler syntax:

```
mockup simple
```

When given only an application name, *mockup* looks for a resource file with that application's name and class. It derives the class name by capitalizing the first letter of the application name, or, if the application name begins with the letter `x`, by capitalizing the first two letters. Thus the class name for the application `simple` is "Simple", and the class name for `xsimple` is "XSimple". Once it has the application name and class names, *mockup* looks for a resource file in six different places relative to the current working directory. With name "simple" and class "Simple", for example, it would look for the following files:

```
simple
simple.ad
Simple
Simple.ad
app-defaults/Simple
app-defaults/simple
```

It uses the first file in this list that exists and is readable.

13.1.2 Procedure, Widget, and Converter Registration

As we've seen in previous chapters, it is necessary to register procedures for the callback converter to work, and it is necessary to register widget types so that `XmtCreateChildren()` can create an interface, and, of course, it is necessary to register any non-standard resource converters that will be used. In a production application, you will only register the procedures, widgets, and converters that you actually use, so that your application doesn't link with unused code. But since the *mockup* client should be flexible enough to handle arbitrary resource files, it goes ahead and registers all the widgets, procedures, and converters that it knows about.

Example 13-2 shows the registration code from *mockup.c* in the Xmt distribution. Most of the functions are self-explanatory, but you can look them up in the reference section to find out the details of their behavior. Incidentally, when writing your own C applications that build their interfaces from resource files, it is often convenient to copy this registration code from the *mockup* client, and then remove the unnecessary lines.

Example 13-2. Registration Code from the mockup Client

```
/* procedures */
XmtRegisterXmtProcedures();
XmtRegisterXtProcedures();
XmtRegisterUnixProcedures();

/* widgets */
XmtRegisterMotifWidgets();
XmtRegisterXmtWidgets();

/* converters */
XmtRegisterBitmapConverter();
XmtRegisterPixmapConverter();
XmtRegisterColorTableConverter();
XmtRegisterWidgetConverter();
XmtRegisterCallbackConverter();
XmtRegisterXmStringConverter();
XmtRegisterStringListConverter();
XmtRegisterMenuItemsConverter();
XmtRegisterPixmapListConverter();
XmtRegisterPixelConverter();

/* converter-like functions */
```

Example 13-2. Registration Code from the mockup Client (continued)

```
XmtRegisterLayoutParser();
XmtRegisterLayoutCreateMethod();
```

13.1.3 mockup and editres

The *editres* client is new in X11R5. It is an application that uses a special protocol to query the widget tree of other Xt clients and allows the user to dynamically set resources on widgets in those clients. Clients that use the Athena widget set automatically respond to the *editres* protocol. Motif clients can be made to "speak" this protocol by registering the `_XEditResCheckMessages()` event handler from the X11R5 Xmu library. If compiled with X11R5, *mockup* will register this event handler, which means that you can use *editres* as an additional tool for application design—it allows you to dynamically set resources on widgets and experiment with colors, fonts, and other simple attributes of the interface.

Using editres and setres

contrib/

setres/

In X11R5, mockup *supports the Editres protocol, which allows you to set resources on your widgets while your application is running. This capability can be quite useful while prototyping and testing. Alvin Wen describes how you can make your own applications understand the Editres protocol, and then explains a more useful alternative to* editres. *(Alvin is a widget writer, and his description talks about testing custom widgets. His* SetRes *tool can be just as useful for prototyping and testing applications, however.)*

When testing widgets in an application, and especially when testing the SetValues method of custom-written widgets, I found the Editres protocol and client particularly useful. The Editres protocol, which is a standard part of the Xmu library as of X11 Release 5, allows you to set arbitrary widget resources on-the-fly through the *editres* client. The *editres* client also displays the widget hierarchy of an application and allows you to view the names of the resources supported by a widget. In order to use Editres, you should include the following two lines in your application and link with the Xmu library (`-lXmu`):

```
#include <X11/Xmu/Editres.h>
XtAddEventHandler(toplevel, 0, True, _XEditResCheckMessages, NULL);
```

(In the above example, `toplevel` is the shell widget returned by a call to `XtAppInitialize()`.)

editres has one or two problems which prompted me to write *SetRes,* a general-purpose widget resource exerciser. First of all, the Editres protocol does not support the setting of resources that are more than four bytes in size. This is particularly troublesome if you are testing a widget that supports `double` floating-point numbers. And second, I found that I was using the *editres* client almost exclusively to set widget resources; for me, the additional *editres* sup-

Using editres and setres (continued)

port for the display of complete widget hierarchies and resource lists results in a client that is too unwieldy for frequent use.

SetRes addresses both of these problems, and supports a few new features of its own. To use *SetRes*, add the following lines to your program and link it with *SetRes.o*:

```
#include "SetRes.h"
SetRes(widget);
```

The `widget` argument to the `SetRes()` function can be any widget in your application. This call will pop up a small dialog box that has two text fields; the first field accepts a widget name and the second field accepts a `resource_name:resource_value` pair. When the **Apply** button is activated, *SetRes* sets the resource named to the specified value. You can name a widget using the full syntax supported by `XtNameToWidget()`, including `*` and `.` characters. (In fact, you will always need to precede widget names with a `*`.)

SetRes supports resources greater than four bytes in size. You can also enter `manage`, `unmanage`, and `destroy` in the resource field to apply the corresponding action to the specified widget. Furthermore, you can specify a resource value in the form `!nnn`, where `nnn` is some integer, to explicitly set the value of a resource that is not more than four bytes long. This is particularly useful for setting the value of enumerated resource types for which a type converter has not been provided.

—*Alvin Wen*

13.2 checkres

One of the difficult things about programming with resources is that a resource file has a line-oriented syntax, but many of the most interesting resources (lists of widgets to create, lists of procedures to call) require multiple lines. When programming with resources, you'll often end up with lines with trailing backslashes used to escape the newline and force a multi-line resource to be treated as a single line. If you omit any of these backslashes, your interface description may fail in confusing ways, and because the X Resource Manager silently ignores malformed lines in resource files, it can be difficult to locate the source of the error.

checkres is a shell script that uses *awk* to scan a resource file and check its syntax. It issues an error message for any line in a resource file that does not follow the X resource syntax. Because the continuation lines of a multi-line resource are generally never valid resource specifications themselves, these error messages allow you to pinpoint the location of missing backslashes.

checkres also issues warning messages for conditions that are not necessarily errors, but which most likely are. If a backslash followed by whitespace appears at the end of a line, for example, *checkres* will issue a warning, because the programmer is most likely not aware that the whitespace is there and thinks that the backslash is serving to escape the newline, when it is not. Similarly, *checkres* warns when whitespace terminates any line—this whitespace is included in the value of the resource, when it is often not intended, and, in a `labelString` resource, for example, can make a push button come out too wide.

Example 13-3 shows the *simple.ad* resource file we used earlier in this chapter, with some errors introduced into it. For clarity, the listing is shown with line numbers added and the end of each line marked with a `$`. Below the file listing is the output of *checkres* when it is run on this file.

Example 13-3. A Buggy Resource File and the Output of checkres

examples/

13/errors.ad

```
anathema% cat -n -e errors.ad
 1  # this comment begins with the wrong comment character (Use `!', not `#')$
 2  simple.xmtChildren: XmRowColumn box;$
 3  $
 4  *box.xmtChildren: XmPushButton push, exit;$
 5  $
 6  *push.labelString: Push Me        $
 7  *push.activateCallback:$
 8          XmtDisplayWarning(msg1, This feature is not yet implemented.)$
 9  $
10  *exit .labelString: Quit$
11  *exit.activateCallback: exit(0);$

anathema% checkres errors.ad
errors.ad: 1: colon expected.
errors.ad: 6: warning: trailing whitespace included in resource value.
errors.ad: 7: warning: no resource value follows colon.
errors.ad: 8: colon expected.  Missing \ on previous line?
errors.ad: 10: malformed name before colon.
```

13.2.1 Other Resource Debugging Hints

Even when your resource files are free of syntax errors, you can still sometimes have difficulty figuring out just which resources are being set on which widgets. The *appres* client, which is one of the standard X clients in */usr/bin/X11*, is a good one to know about. You invoke it with an application name as its single argument. It will pretend that its own name is the name you specified, and read all the resources that pertain to that application. Then *appres* prints out all the resources. This lets you figure out just what resources are being loaded into the application's resource database when it starts up, and can help you diagnose problems caused when a resource file is installed in the wrong place, for example, or even when personal resources in an *.Xresources* file are conflicting with specific application resources. If you include auxiliary resource files into your main resource file with the X11R5 `#include` directive, then *appres* will find these auxiliary resources. If you use the `xmtRequires` resource, however, those auxiliary files will not be read until the widgets are created, and since *appres* never calls `XmtCreateChildren()`, these files will not be included in the listings.

Be careful when creating widgets with convenience routines like `XmCreateScrolledText()` and `XmCreateInformationDialog()`—these functions both create a "hidden" parent widget (an XmScrolledWindow and an XmDialogShell widget, respectively) and create and return a child of that parent. So if you use `XmCreateScrolledText()` to create a widget named `text` and specify a widget named `box` as the parent, the returned widget is *not* `box.text`—the text widget is not a direct child of the specified parent. In a resource file, you should specify this widget as `*box.?.text` or `box*text`, for example. (Remember, though, that the `?` wildcard is only available in X11R5.) These cautions apply even when you are creating widgets automatically with the `xmtChildren` resource. The *mockup* client, for example, registers (by calling `XmtRegisterMotifWidgets()`) the names "XmScrolledText" and "XmInformationDialog" for the convenience routines described above.

When using the `xmtChildren` resource, *never* precede it with a `*` wildcard. This was mentioned in Chapter 11, *Automatic Widget Creation*, but it bears repeating, and the problem can be subtler than was presented there. For example, the specification:

```
*main*xmtChildren: XmText text; XmRowColumn rowcol;
*rowcol.xmtChildren: XmPushButton okay, cancel, help;
```

will cause an infinite loop. The first line creates an XmText and an XmRowColumn widget as a child of the widget `main`. But then when querying the `xmtChildren` resource for this new row column widget, the first line will take priority over the second (resource precedences are explained in the next few paragraphs), and another XmText and XmRowColumn widget will be created, this time as children of the first XmRowColumn widget. This recursive widget creation process will continue until the application runs out of memory and crashes.

Finally, remember the rules of precedence for figuring out which resource specifications apply to a widget. If more than one specification in a resource file might apply to a given widget and a given resource, then the "more specific" specification is used. A specification that uses a widget or resource instance name is more specific than one that uses a class name, for example, and one that uses a "tight binding" without wildcards is more specific than one that uses the `*` wildcard to create a "loose binding." These are fairly intuitive rules:

```
*box.foreground
```

is more specific than

```
*XmRowColumn*Foreground
```

What is less intuitive, but more important, is that a specification with an explicit component name or class earlier in its name will take precedence over a specification with later components specified. Thus:

```
*box.Foreground
```

takes precedence over

```
*foreground
```

even though the first uses a resource class and the second uses a resource name. Even more confusing, though, is the fact that this specification:

```
XApp*Foreground
```

is more specific than

```
*main_window.button_box.okay.foreground
```

Even though the first specification uses class names, and uses a wildcard to omit a number of generations of widgets, it takes precedence over the second specification because the "first match" occurs earlier in the name.

This last is a pretty subtle point, and can be a tricky bug when it bites. It means that you should almost never begin your resource specifications with the application name or class, unless you don't want the user to be able to override them. Instead, begin all resource specifications with a *.

13.3 ad2c

Xmt encourages the heavy use of resources during application prototyping and development. In many "in-house" environments, it will be acceptable to deliver applications along with the suite of external resource files they require. For commercial applications, or in situations where you suspect that there may be difficulties getting resource files properly installed, you may want to hard-code some or all of the resources into the application itself. The first step in doing this is to convert resource specifications in a file into an array of strings that you can use in your C code. The *ad2c* script is designed to do just this—it reads the resource file or files specified on the command line (or reads the standard input), processes them with *sed* to escape backslashes and quotes, and then writes the equivalent C strings to the standard output.

Using ad2c

George Ferguson is the author of ad2c, *and in this excerpt from the* ad2c *man page, he shows how you can use that script in your application build process, and how you might use the resulting file of C strings.*

Using ad2c (continued)

The following example shows a typical use of *ad2c* to ensure that an application always has the latest version of its resources compiled into the executable. Suppose the application defaults file is named *Foobar.ad*, for application *foobar*. Then the following lines in a *Makefile* or *Imakefile* will indicate how and when to run *ad2c*:

```
Foobar.ad.h: Foobar.ad
        ad2c Foobar.ad > Foobar.ad.h
```

The resulting C strings should be included (in *foobar.c*, perhaps):

```
static char fallback_resources[] = {
#   include "Foobar.ad.h"
    NULL
};
```

This array of strings can then be used as fallback resources in a call to `XtAppInitialize()` or otherwise used to initialize the application's resources. Running *makedepend* or adding the line:

```
foobar.c: Foobar.ad.h
```

to the *Makefile* or *Imakefile* will ensure that *foobar.c* is recompiled when necessary (i.e., whenever *Foobar.ad* changes).

—George Ferguson
From the ad2c man page

Using *ad2c* is simple. Deciding when to use it, which resources to use it on, and how to make use of the resources once they are converted to C form is more complex. Xt provides a lot of different ways for an application to establish its resource database, and this flexibility leads to a diversity of opinion about which approach is the best. The main issue in this never-ending debate is usually the choice between the flexibility of an app-defaults file and the reliability of fallback resources. The following subsections present some good arguments and ideas about both sides of the issue—most of these were part of a thread that appeared in the *comp.windows.x.intrinsics* newsgroup.

13.3.1 App-defaults or Fallbacks?

Kevin Hammond poses some of the fundamental questions about app-defaults files and fallbacks. Notice the problems that he points out with fallbacks—they will be entirely ignored if any app-defaults file exists.

From: *hammond@ctt.com* (Kevin W. Hammond)
Subject: *[Q] Which is preferred: app-defaults or fallbacks?*

I (finally) figured out why my application fallback resources were not being honored on some workstations. The workstations that showed the problem had an old application default file in */usr/lib/X11/app-defaults*.

After reading the man page for `XtAppSetFallbackResources()`, I understood that the presence of an application default file will override the application's own internal fallback resources.

My question is this: what is the preferred method for setting the application resources? Fallbacks or an application default file? What are the advantages/disadvantages of each? I read where fallback resources should be a minimum to get the application running or to display an error if the application defaults cannot be loaded. Any idea what a "minimum" is :-) ?

—*Kevin W. Hammond*

13.3.2 Use an app-defaults File

Donna Converse, Xt guru of the X Consortium, replies here to Kevin Hammond's queries at length, with some very important arguments in favor of app-defaults files. Some of her points apply most strongly to applications that are distributed in source code form, however. If you sell a product in binary form, or must provide technical support for an application, then you may not be so swayed by her arguments for flexibility and user customizability.

From: *converse@x.org* (Donna Converse)
Subject: *Re: [Q] Which is preferred: app-defaults or fallbacks?*

> My question is this: what is the preferred method for setting the
> application resources? Fallbacks or an application default file?

I advise using a site-wide application default file.

> What are the advantages/disadvantages of each?

Advantages of using an application default file:

- The site administrator can customize your application for all users at the site.
- You can indicate in the application-defaults file which resources may be changed and the effect of changing them by commenting.
- It's an additional form of documentation for power users of your app. Many users create an application-specific defaults file of their own. Those who do usually read the site-wide application defaults file in order to see what's going on. To allow user-specified defaults to take precedence over site-wide defaults, application developers should always give the loosest resource binding and use class names rather than instance names where possible, in the site-wide defaults file.

- You can supply multiple versions, each implementing different styles, languages, presentation arrangements, options, colors, demonstrating the coherence and adaptability of your application by having the user changing the value of their customization resource for your application. Application default files may include other application default files, making it possible to separate color customization from language customization, from functional customization, for example.

Disadvantages of using fallback resources for the default resources of the application:

- Fallback resources were not designed with this purpose in mind.
- Code bloat.
- Users and site administrators will be tempted to edit your source in order to figure out what resources you have set and to make their own changes, making things messy and difficult for them when it comes time to update their sources.
- Anyone can override all of your default resources by supplying their own application default file, often inexplicably breaking your app.
- You're not taking advantage of one of the most powerful features of the X toolkit—its provision for end-users to customize applications.

> I read where fallback resources should be a minimum to get the
> application running or to display an error if the application
> defaults cannot be loaded. Any idea what a "minimum" is :-) ?

The X Consortium's mail application, *xmh*, has an application defaults file aptly named *Xmh*. If you remove this file, its fallback resources are used. In that case it pops up a dialog box warning you that the application functionality will probably not work because the application defaults file is missing. This same design can be used as a versioning check on the application defaults file, when one is used, and *xmh* implements that as well—so you can update your application and the app-defaults file and implement a versioning check, and report it when the site administrator failed to install your application correctly.

Now, try using the X Consortium's calculator application, *xcalc*, without its application defaults file. Nothing works at all, and, it doesn't say why, so the application is worthless and uncommunicative without its application defaults file.

So a minimum is to report that the application defaults file is missing, or, if you have a simple application, to have the minimum functionality in place with no decorative resources set.

—Donna Converse
X Consortium

Miles O'Neil concurs with Donna and goes into more detail about what comprises a "minimum" set of fallback resources:

From: *meo@pencom.com* (Miles O'Neal)
Subject: Re: *[Q] Which is preferred: app-defaults or fallbacks?*

> So a minimum is to report that the application defaults file is missing,
> or, if you have a simple application, to have the minimum functionality
> in place with no decorative resources set.

I recommend using fallbacks to make sure that the program is usable. No colors (unless it's something that *has* to have color), basic fonts (eg, fixed), usable geometry.

Then do all the really cool stuff via app-defaults files.

There's nothing more frustrating than to get an app and have it be totally useless because of a missing file. For people not very familiar with X, it makes that app *useless.*

—Miles

13.3.3 Use Fallbacks

Kevin Hammond is convinced:

From: *hammond@ctt.com* (Kevin W. Hammond)
Subject: *Re: [Q] Which is preferred: app-defaults or fallbacks?*

Thank you for the very good information, Donna. I will take it to heart and make it a part of my life from now on!! :-)

—Kevin

But Zack Evans is not. Note that he advocates *ad2c*:

From: *zevans@nyx10.cs.du.edu* (Zack Evans)
Subject: *Re: [Q] Which is preferred: app-defaults or fallbacks?*

> I advise using a site-wide application default file.

Ah yes, but you can't always rely on that . . . it means that your code is impossible to install properly unless you have write access to */usr/lib/X11*. . . . You may think that if that is the case you can just mess about with your own app-defaults search path, but what about if you are a non-privileged user installing an app that you intend anyone to be able to use? For instance, on the machine that I use there is a *homegrown/* directory where you can install applications for anyone to use. I have put a number of apps in there and generally end up using *ad2c* to hack in fallback resources if they aren't there already—otherwise I would have to write a shell script as a front end to the binary to ensure that resources got loaded first.

For that reason I think you should ALWAYS include fallback resources that will allow you to use the app. at a fully functional level, but I think you should also provide an identical *.ad* file. That way nobody loses out. Of course both sets of resources should be written as unspecifically as possible so that it is easily possible to override them.

> Code bloat.

Look, if you are going to run an X11 app, code bloat is hardly an issue :)

—Zack "I'm gonna regret arguing with a member of the X consortium" Evans

13.3.4 Use Both

Frank Sheeran proposes that applications should have a set of fallback resources that are identical to its app-defaults file, and proposes a way to make this part of your regular application build process. This is just what we saw in the *ad2c* example above.

From: *sheeran@ndg.co.jp* (Frank Sheeran)
Subject: *Re: [Q] Which is preferred: app-defaults or fallbacks?*

I think the current "best" solution is to write a script in *perl* or *awk* that is run by your makefile when the master app-defaults file is edited, that reads it in and outputs a C code file that makes the same data available as fallback resources. The result being that, run resourcelessly, the behavior is "traditional."

You might design your script to include a "secret" resource flag indicating that fallbacks are being used (e.g., `*usingFallbacks: true`) so that your app can warn that the site resources were not found. Don't make the warning too obnoxious however. Some users wouldn't mind using software on fallbacks every day if they lacked the permission or savvy to install their own.

> This same design can be used as a versioning
> check on the application defaults file

You can also change the application class name to Myapp2, Myapp3, etc., for revisions. This will eliminate the kind of error arising from old defaults being used against a new app. You can leave the executable name as myapp, of course, so users can version-up a bit more painlessly.

—Frank Sheeran

Rick Richardson uses the same approach, but with a twist. He describes it in the following message (which was not part of the same thread as the above):

> **From:** *rick@digibd.com (Rick Richardson)*
> **Subject:** *Re: Fallback resources*
>
> I have all of the resources compiled into fallback resources, but provide a command line option (`-resources`) which will write those resources to a conventional resource file, in case the system administrator wants to hack them.
>
> I actually keep the resources in several arrays, one for each dialog box, so the resources are kept in the same C source file which uses them. They all get massaged into the resource manager at init time (or printed to a file, if requested).
>
> I find this to be most convenient for programming, while still giving the user the option to get all of the resources dumped out into a single file (which is the most convenient form for them to hack on).
>
> —*Rick Richardson*

13.3.5 Resources in Xmt

The chapters in this part of the book have advocated "programming with resources." They have demonstrated a number of tools that make this possible, and we'll see other Xmt features that make heavy use of resources as well. Because Xmt uses resources (or at least can use resources) so heavily, this question of app-defaults files versus fallback resources is a particularly important one.

There is no doubt that using resource files is the easiest approach when prototyping an application, especially in conjunction with tools like *mockup*. When it is time to distribute a completed application, however, you may not want to require users or system administrators to correctly install your resource files. The discussion above notes this problem and proposes several good solutions.

The discussion above limits itself, however, to a discussion of app-defaults, and whether they should be stored in a file or compiled into the application as fallbacks. A medium sized application developed with the Xmt "programming with resources" facilities can have a very large number of resources—certainly more than you would want to casually compile into an application. And even more to the point, not all resource files are app-defaults files, and not all resources should be customizable by the user. Unless your audience consists of sophisticated programmers, for example, you will probably never want to allow a user to customize an `xmtChildren` resource. Later in the book we'll see ways of specifying a pulldown menu system from the resource file, and ways of specifying the complete layout of widgets in a window from the resource file. Again, these are not the sorts of things that you want users to be able to customize.

An application's app-defaults file always *should* contain user "preferences" resources—things like colors and fonts, that a user may want to override. It should also often contain the text that appears in buttons and other widgets, so that sites in other countries can translate the text to another language. It should also contain configuration options, like settings for the `configDir` and `configPath` application resources. But other resources—those that affect the "content" of the interface (its widgets and their layout and behavior), rather than just its appearance do not belong in an app-defaults file. By restricting the contents of the app-defaults file in this way, it does become reasonable to provide a complete working set of app-defaults as fallbacks, as advocated by some of the participants in the foregoing debate.

If the app-defaults file (or fallback resources) contain an `xmtRequires` resource (see Chapter 11, *Automatic Widget Creation*) then Xmt will automatically read in the specified resource files, which may contain all the resources that are not app-defaults. You can achieve the same effect by calling `XmtLoadResourceFile()` or `XmtLoadResourceFileList()`.

This works fine if you are willing to distribute your application with external resource files—the app-defaults file or the fallback resources will tell the application where it should look to find those extra resource files. But if you want to develop a completely self-contained application, then you'll still have to hard-code all those resources into the executable. As noted above, fallback resources are not adequate for this purpose, because they will be ignored if any app-defaults file is found. But fallback resources are not the only way to place hard-coded resource specifications into an application's resource database. You can also do this with the lower-level Xlib function `XrmPutLineResource()`—just iterate through your array of resource specifications and call this function for each string, as described in Chapter 6, *Managing Auxiliary Files.*

As author of this book, I'm entitled to give myself the last word on the resource-handling debate:

> **From:** *david@ora.com*
> **Subject:** *Fallback Resources*
>
> What I recommend instead is developing your app with a regular resource file. Then, if you eventually want to hard-code those resources into your application, write a script that will convert them to an array of constant C strings. In `main()`, after `XtAppInitialize()` (when the app-defaults file, if any, is read), loop through these strings, using `XrmPutLineResource()` to add your resources to the database. (Use `XtDatabase()` or `XtScreenDatabase()` to get the `XrmDatabase` associated with your toplevel shell widget.)
>
> *—djf*

Part Four

Patterns and Tools for the Desktop

Applications do not run in isolation.

One of the first steps in application design should be to consider how an application will appear and interact on the desktop. The *desktop* is the user's screen, and, more importantly, the applications that are displayed on that screen and the interactions between those applications.

When designing an application, you should consider its layout on the desktop, the amount of desktop space it occupies, and the number of windows its places on the desktop. When implementing the application, you should make provisions for communication with the window manager, the session manager, and with other clients.

The chapters in this part of the book explain how you can design and implement applications that work well with other applications.

14

Windows on the Desktop

The last two parts of this book have focused on various Xmt tools for application development. In this chapter, we return to design issues. In Chapter 2, *High-Level Application Design*, we considered very high-level design issues such as the choice of an appropriate metaphor and scope for the application. In this chapter we begin to further refine that design by considering the number and kind of windows an application creates on the desktop, as well as their sizes, positions, and relationships to one another. We do not go so far here as to discuss the *contents* of the windows and dialog boxes on the desktop—those design issues will be taken up in subsequent parts of the book.

14.1 Desktop Window Patterns

As we've seen earlier in this book, there are various common patterns to the tasks a user wants to accomplish, and there are common patterns to the scope of the application that addresses those tasks. Similarly, there are patterns that control the number, size, and placement of windows on the desktop. This section describes and analyzes some of these patterns. By becoming familiar with them, and with their strong and weak points, you will be better able to choose an appropriate window design for your application.

14.1.1 A Single Window

This is the simplest possible pattern, feasible only for those applications that are output-only, or for some other reason do not require any kind of dialog box.

This is a good pattern for "desktop accessory" type applications—any extra windows would make these applications more complicated than their tasks require.

14.1.2 A Window with Dialogs

Applications that are more complex will generally have dialog boxes to accompany their main window (Figure 14-1).

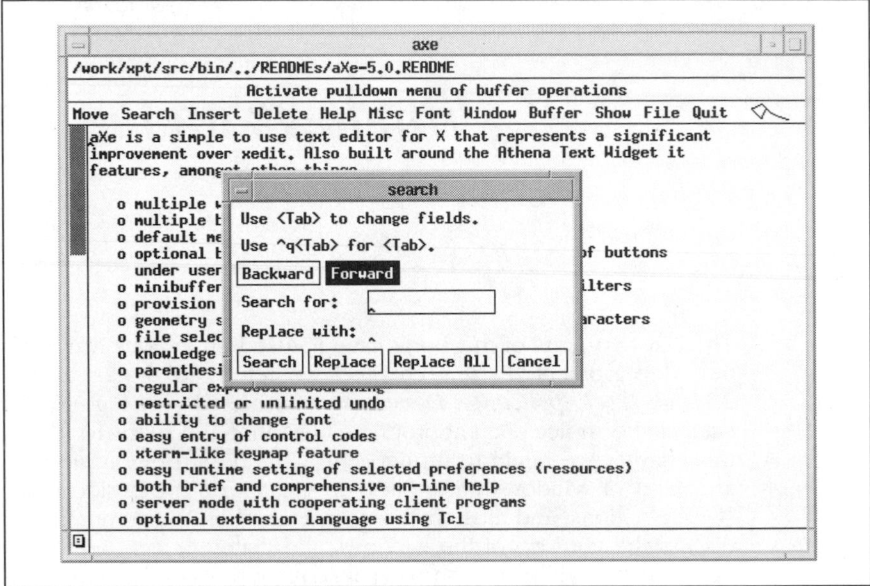

Figure 14-1. A single windowed application with dialogs

Dialog boxes are transient windows that perform specialized tasks that are beyond the scope of the main window. Dialog boxes provide temporary screen-space to this specialized, infrequent subtask, and also keep the complexity of that task hidden from view during the normal operation of the application.

Dialog boxes are most often used for simple message display and for data input. They are often "modal," which means that the main application window cannot be used until the dialog is dismissed. One of the most important defining characteristics of a dialog box is that it is iconified along with its main window, and cannot be individually iconified. (If you use Xt and a window manager that conforms to the ICCCM, this will happen automatically in your applications.) This means that a dialog box is never appropriate for a task that the user could conceivably want to work on while the main window was hidden.

14.1.3 A Main Window with Auxiliary Windows

If an application has auxiliary windows that can be used independently of the main window, then these are something distinct from dialog boxes (Figure 14-2).

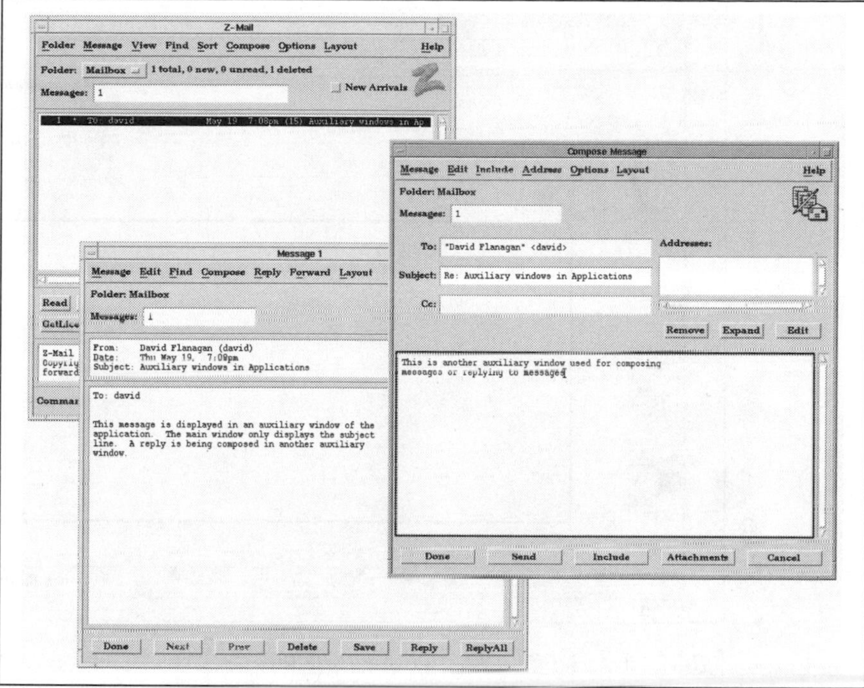

Figure 14-2. A main window and auxiliary windows

When an application is designed to solve related, but distinct problems—reading email and composing email, for example—it often makes sense to implement the solutions to each of the problems in separate windows. This keeps them visually distinct, and gives the user different graphical contexts or "places" to work on the distinct tasks.

If the tasks are entirely unrelated, then they are probably best implemented as entirely separate applications, of course. If they are related, however, then there is probably one task that is more central, more frequent, or more complex than the others. This task will usually become the focus of the main window, with the others implemented in auxiliary windows. Graphical email applications, for example, generally start up with a mail reader as the main window, so that the user can read her mail, and then offer an auxiliary window that allows the user to forward or reply to her mail, or to compose new mail.

14.1.4 One Large Window

Some applications have a lot of features that they fit into a single large window (which may also have dialog boxes) or perhaps need a large work area to draw figures in (Figure 14-3).

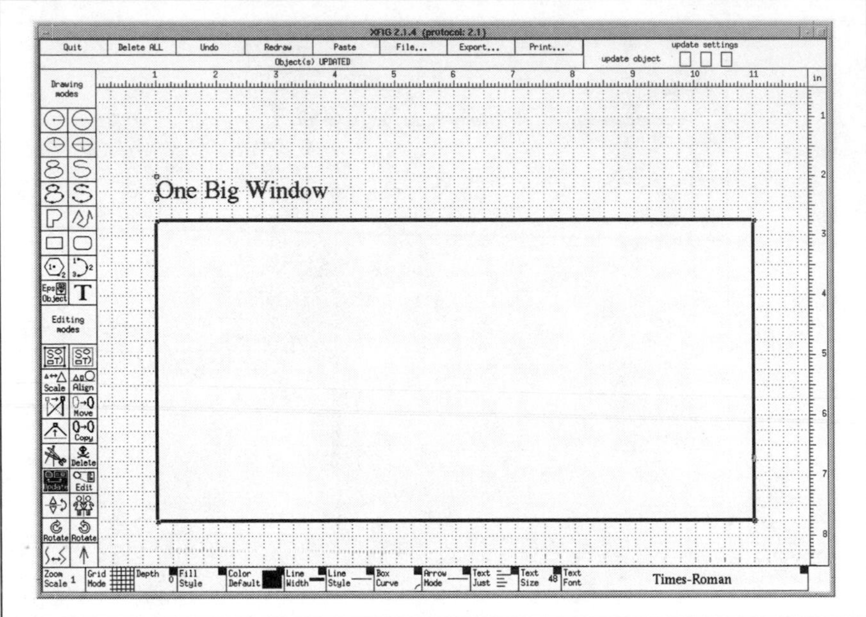

Figure 14-3. One large application window

For complicated tasks, this "one large window" model has some advantages: the various pieces of the application are all always visible to the user, and are in a fixed place that the user can soon become accustomed to. On the other hand, large windows can take over most of the available screen space, or at least take up so much of it that other windows cannot usefully be placed above, below, or to the side of it. Screen space is a very limited resource, and applications should take care not to take more of it than they actually need.

There are some circumstances in which a single large window is appropriate. An arcade-style game, for example, can make a reasonable claim to occupy all of the user's attention while it is running, and so can justifiably take over the screen. An application that serves a "continuous task" such as telephone order entry also has justification to occupy most of the screen. And some times, there is simply no way around it—a page previewer application will require most of the screen (or even more) to display a window the size of a standard sheet of paper, for example. And my *emacs* window takes up much of my screen, for example, because I've configured it to be 50 lines high and to use an 18 point font (since I use *emacs* all day every day, avoiding strain on my eyes is more important than conserving screen space).

Often, though, a single large window can be a sign of an emerging "monolithic" application, or a sign of failure of imagination on the part of the programmer. Most tasks do have some sort of modular structure that could well be reflected in a multiple-window arrangement. When the structure of an application matches the structure of the task, it will be easier for the user to understand and use the application.

14.1.5 A Profusion of Windows

Instead of packing features into a single window, when confronted with a single task, another approach is to pack the desktop with different windows for each of the various subtasks (Figure 14-4).

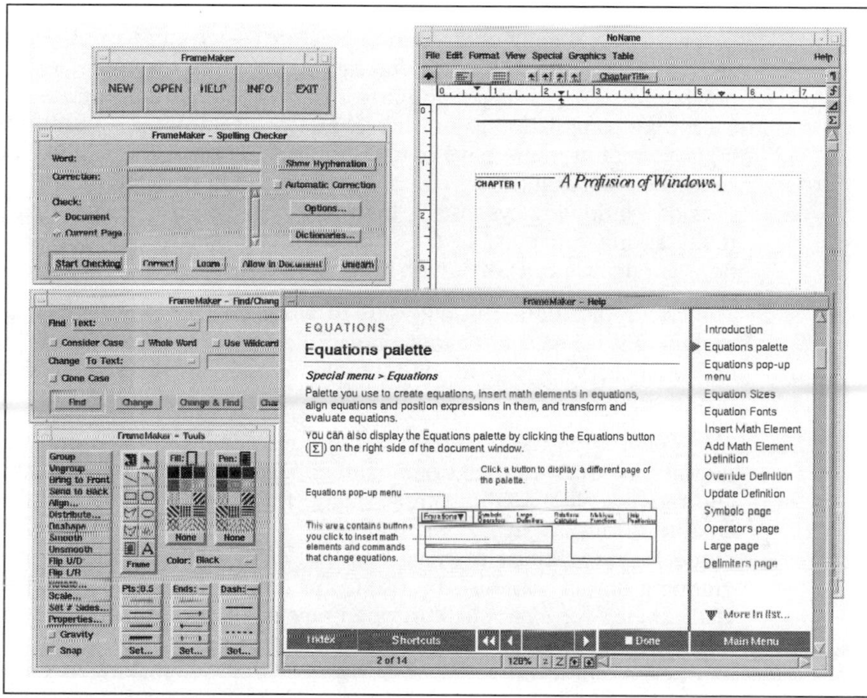

Figure 14-4. A profusion of windows

If this division of one task into multiple windows is done well, the application will become easier to use. Other advantages are that the user can arrange the windows to his liking, and can individually iconify or dismiss those that he is not currently using. If a drawing editor provides a palette of tools in a detached window, for example, then the user can drag those tools close to the portion of the drawing that he is currently working on, and thereby save himself from moving the mouse back and forth across the work area as he would have to if the palette were fixed to one side of the window.

This pattern differs from the "main window with auxiliary windows" pattern mainly in that there may be a larger number of windows, and that these windows do not perform entirely distinct tasks, but rather serve specific sub-tasks that contribute to the whole. In our hypothetical multi-window drawing editor, for example, there might be one window for a palette of tools, one for a palette of graphical attributes, one for mixing colors, and one for designing stipple patterns for backgrounds. The color mixer and stipple editor arguably fall into the "auxiliary windows" pattern, because they can be useful even if the main work area window is iconified. The palette windows, however do not meet this test. Neither are these palettes dialog boxes, however, because the application will let them be individually iconified when not in use.

14.1.6 Multiple Work Windows

Humans are naturally multi-tasking creatures—we can work on several projects at once. (Drinking coffee while reading email for example, or browsing netnews and cutting and pasting articles to forward to colleagues, while waiting for a long compilation to finish.) UNIX (for example) is a multi-tasking operating system, but in the days of text-terminals, it was generally used to run applications one after another, in series, rather than in parallel. One of the main benefits of windowing systems is that they provide an interface that matches our multi-tasking capability to the computer's—when we can see several applications at once we can work with them in parallel.

Multiple applications can allow us to work on multiple distinct tasks at once, and there is no reason that a single application should not "clone" its main window and allow us to work on multiple instances of the same task at once (Figure 14-5).

The *xman* application, shown in the figure, is designed around a widget that displays the multi-font text of a manual page. Since this widget is self-contained and reusable, it is a fairly simple matter for a single instance of the *xman* executable to display many "manual page" windows. This is a very useful technique for most kinds of "data display" tasks—like displaying man pages, or graphing data. It can also be useful for editing tasks—the newest versions of GNU *emacs*, for example, can open any number of X windows to display and edit any number of files. Similarly, a good drawing editor might allow the user to open multiple drawings in separate windows, making it easy to cut-and-paste pieces between figures.

This pattern of multiple work windows complements the other patterns presented above—each window may have its own dialog boxes, for example, or perhaps the cloned windows will all share the same "profusion" of secondary windows. When using this pattern, it is important to make the windows distinguishable—they might display the name of the file being displayed or edited in a prominent modeline, for example. They should also have distinct icons.

Allowing windows to be "cloned" in an application is not particularly difficult. The main implication for the application is that the state variables for the work area must not be global—they must be fields of a structure, so that a new set of them may be allocated when a new window is opened.

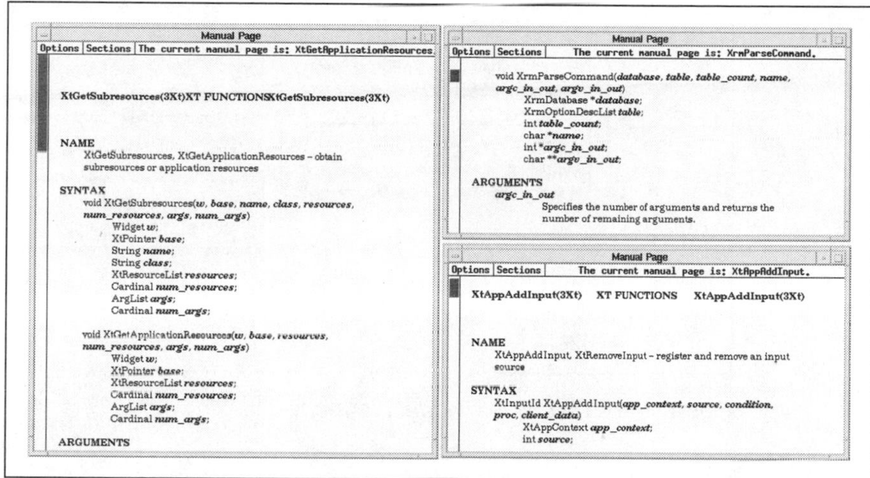

Figure 14-5. A single application with multiple work windows

14.2 Implementing the Patterns: Putting Windows on the Desktop

When programming with the X Toolkit, you place windows on the desktop with shell widgets. There are a number of different kinds of shells, used for main windows, auxiliary windows, and dialogs. This section begins with an overview of the various shell widget classes, and then a description of how you can use shell widgets to implement the window patterns discussed above.

Note that this section is primarily about choosing an appropriate shell widget. We'll have more to say about setting resources on shells and manipulating windows on the desktop in Chapter 15, *Working with the Window Manager.*

14.2.1 The Taxonomy of the Shell

There are ten different kinds of shell widgets in Xt and Motif, and using shells is one of the obscure facets of Xt programming, so we'll begin with a review of shell widget taxonomy. Figure 14-6 shows the shell widget class hierarchy, and the sections below summarize each of the classes.

14.2.1.1 The Shell Widget

This is the meta-class for all shell widget types. It knows how to create a top-level window on a screen, and, like all shell widget types, it accepts a single child widget. It is not intended to be instantiated.

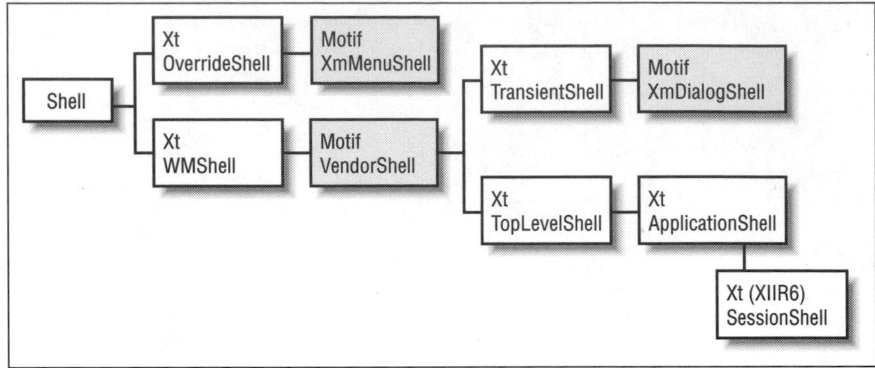

Figure 14-6. The Shell widget hierarchy

14.2.1.2 The OverrideShell Widget

This widget class is used for popup and pulldown menus, and any other window that is to appear only briefly on the screen, without interacting with the window manager. By setting its `XtNsaveUnder` resource, you can request that the X server save the contents of the window or windows that it obscures, so that those windows can be restored without being redrawn when the window pops down.

14.2.1.3 The XmMenuShell Widget

This is a Motif specialization of the OverrideShell, for use with Motif menu panes. You should rarely need to use this widget class explicitly—it is usually created for you by convenience routines. Also, since there are generally far more menus in an application than will ever be visible at one time, the Motif library attempts to minimize the number of XmMenuShell widgets it creates—wherever possible, it will share one shell widget among multiple menu panes.

14.2.1.4 The WMShell Widget

This is another meta-class that provides the functionality for a shell that will interact with the window manager. This class defines lots of new resources for such things as window position and resizing hints, and the window title. It is not intended to be directly instantiated, however.

14.2.1.5 The VendorShell Widget

This meta-class is simply a place-holder in the Xt widget hierarchy. The Xt VendorShell widget defines no new resources or behavior. The Motif library, however, provides its own definition of the VendorShell class and defines custom resources that allow a window to interact with *mwm*-specific features. This redefinition of the VendorShell widget is one reason that you should always link with the Motif library before you link with the X toolkit. Also, bear in mind that you'll find different documentation for this widget in an X Toolkit reference and in a Motif reference.

14.2.1.6 The TransientShell Widget

This is the shell widget class intended for X Toolkit dialog boxes, or other windows that should interact with the window manager but that are "transient" on the desktop. If an ICCCM-compliant window manager is running, a TransientShell widget will be automatically iconified when its main window is iconified. TransientShell widgets are popped up and popped down with `XtPopup()` and `XtPopdown()`.

14.2.1.7 The XmDialogShell Widget

This is the Motif widget class to be used for dialog boxes. It does not have any new resources, but has a number of special features for interaction with XmBulletinBoard children. Motif dialogs are popped up and down following a different model than the underlying Xt scheme: instead of calling `XtPopup()` or `XtPopdown()` on the dialog shell widget, you simply manage or unmanage the child of the dialog shell. This is more consistent with the behavior of other non-popup widgets, but can be confusing for Xt programmers who are switching to Motif.

14.2.1.8 The TopLevelShell Widget

This class, in another fork of the shell widget hierarchy, is intended for windows that do interact with the window manager, and are not transient—that is, the main application window and its non-transient auxiliary windows. This is the first shell widget class we've described that is intended to be independently iconified. It defines resources that specify the icon name, and also an `XtNiconic` resource that specifies whether or not the window is currently iconified.

14.2.1.9 The ApplicationShell Widget

This is the widget class used for an application's *root shell*, the widget that is returned by the call to `XtAppInitialize()`. This is the widget at the root of the widget hierarchy, which has no parent widget. Almost all applications will have only a single ApplicationShell widget. This widget class defines `XtNargc` and `XtNargv` resources so that it can export the command line used to invoke the application, for use by session managers.

14.2.1.10 The SessionShell Widget

This widget class is new in X11R6, and, as its name indicates, it provides a number of new resources for communication with a session manager. In X11R6 and later, you should use this widget class instead of ApplicationShell for your initial root shell. You can initialize Xt and create a SessionShell widget by calling the function `XtOpenApplication()`, which is also new in X11R6. X11R6 session management will be discussed in more detail in Chapter 16, *Working with the Session Manager.*

14.2.2 Implementing Dialog Windows

Dialog box windows are quite straightforward. The XmDialogShell widget is appropriate for most uses. Any child of an XmDialogShell must be a Motif XmBulletinBoard widget, or some subclass of that widget, such as an XmForm or XmtLayout widget. In particular, you should not use an XmRowColumn widget as the child.

The XmDialogShell and the XmBulletinBoard classes are designed to work together, and some attributes of dialog boxes, such as their title and modality, can actually be specified by setting XmBulletinBoard resources. Also, and most importantly, a window implemented with an XmDialogShell widget should be popped up by calling `XtManageChild()` or its XmBulletinBoard (or subclass) child, and should be popped down by calling `XtUnmanageChild()` on that child. This is a nice parallel to non-dialog widgets, which can be made to appear and disappear by managing and unmanaging them.

If you are an Xt purist, or are uncomfortable with the mysterious interactions between the XmDialogShell and the XmBulletinBoard you might want to implement your dialogs with the TransientShell widget instead. You don't lose much by doing this, but you have to use `XtPopup()` and `XtPopdown()` to pop the widget up and down. If you want to use an XmRowColumn, or some custom manager widget that is not a subclass of XmBulletinBoard, you would probably want to use this technique as well.

Recall from Chapter 11, *Automatic Widget Creation*, that `XmtBuildDialog()` and `XmtBuildQueryDialog()` will create an `XmDialogShell` widget for you, and then use the `xmtChildren` resource of that widget to recursively create all of its descendants.

14.2.3 Implementing Auxiliary Windows

An application's main or root window is automatically created when the X Toolkit is initialized. As we saw in some of the window patterns above, however, you may often want to create "clones" of the main window, or other kinds of "auxiliary windows." These are toplevel windows in their own right, not subordinate to any other window, and the user should be able to iconify them independently of other windows. Thus, they are not dialog boxes, and should not be created with the XmDialogShell or the TransientShell widgets.

To create auxiliary toplevel windows, use the TopLevelShell widget. Apparently, the designers of Motif thought that all of an application's auxiliary windows would be dialog boxes, and would use the XmDialogShell widget: Motif does not provide its own subclass of the TopLevelShell nor does it provide any convenience functions for creating and managing auxiliary windows.

So although it feels strange to use these "low-level" Xt functions in a Motif application, you'll have to use `XtCreatePopupShell()` or `XtVaCreatePopupShell()` to create a TopLevelShell widget, and you'll have to use `XtPopup()` and `XtPopdown()` to pop these windows up and down. Note that when you use `XtPopup()` and `XtPopdown()` you pass the shell widget itself, not the child of the shell. Since the XmDialogShell is not used here, managing and unmanaging the child of the shell will have no effect on whether the shell window itself is visible.

At a higher level, you can use `XmtBuildToplevel()` and `XmtBuildQueryToplevel()`, introduced in Chapter 11, to create a TopLevelShell widget for you with `XtCreatePopupShell()`, and then to recursively create all descendants of that widgets, as specified by the **xmtChidren** pseudo-resource. Note that if you are implementng the "multiple work windows" pattern, which allows a number of identical "cloned" windows, you can call `XmtBuildToplevel()` multiple times to build multiple copies of the same widget hierarchy—you only have to describe this hierarchy once in your resource file.

XtPopup() or XtManageChild()?

Terry Poot uses the following routines whenever he wants to pop up or pop down a dialog box or auxiliary window. The routines hide the difference between the two shell types, and they use `XtPopup()`, `XtPopdown()`, `XtManageChild()` *or* `XtUnmanageChild()` *as appropriate.*

```
#include <X11/Xlib.h>
#include <Xmt/Xmt.h>

/*
**      xmui_manage manages a widget. If the widget is the child of a top level
**      shell, the shell is popped up, otherwise, we manage the child (assuming
**      it is the child of a dialog shell). In case it was already up, we raise
**      it to the top of the window stack.
*/
void xmui_manage(Widget id)
{
    Widget                  shell;

    /*
    ** If the shell is top level, pop it up, otherwise manage the child.
    **
    ** If the shell isn't top level, we assume its a Motif dialog shell,
    ** which will pop itself up and down as its child is managed and
    ** unmanaged.
    */
    shell = XtParent(id);
    if(XtIsTopLevelShell(shell))XtPopup(shell, XtGrabNone);
    else XtManageChild(id);

    /*
    ** Raise the window in case it was already up but has been obscured.
    */
    XRaiseWindow(XtDisplay(shell), XtWindow(shell));
}
```

XtPopup() or XtManageChild()? (continued)

```
/*
**      xmui_unmanage unmanages a widget. If it is a top level widget, (see
**      xmui_manage) it is popped down instead.
*/
void xmui_unmanage(Widget id)
{
    Widget          shell;

    /*
    ** If the shell is top level, pop it down, otherwise unmanage the child.
    **
    ** If the shell isn't top level, we assume it's a Motif dialog shell,
    ** which will pop itself up and down as its child is managed and
    ** unmanaged.
    */
    shell = XtParent(id);
    if(XtIsTopLevelShell(shell))XtPopdown(shell);
    else XtUnmanageChild(id);
}
```

—Terry Poot

14.2.4 Implementing Root Windows

A *root shell* is one that has no parent. It is at the root of a widget hierarchy and usually has the same name as the application does. Most applications have only a single root shell—the one returned by the initial call to `XtAppInitialize()`. Some specialized applications may want more than one root shell, however. For example, an integrated "desktop utilities" application might use separate root shells for its "clock", "load", and "calculator" windows, simply so that the user could set resources for these windows *as if* they were actually separate applications. That is, with multiple root shells, a user might specify the resource `clock.background`, rather than the more awkward `utilities.clock.background`.

It is not a special widget class that makes a shell a root shell, but the way the shell is created. The initial root shell is returned by `XtAppInitialize()`, and additional root shells can be created with `XtAppCreateShell()` or `XtVaAppCreateShell()`. These functions allow you to specify the widget class for the root shell you are creating—you can use either a TopLevelShell or an ApplicationShell (or, in X11R6, a SessionShell). Only one shell per application should communicate with the session manager, however, so if you use an ApplicationShell for additional root shells in your application, be sure not to set the `XtNargv` and `XtNargc` resources for that shell. If you created your initial root shell with `XtAppInitialize()`, then those resources will be automatically set for you.

With Xmt, you can also create a root shell with `XmtBuildApplication()` or `XmtBuildQueryApplication()`, which use `XtAppCreateShell()` to create an ApplicationShell widget, and then recursively create the descendants of that shell, as `XmtCreateChildren()` does. When you create a new root shell in an Xmt application, you should call `XmtInitializeApplicationShell()` for it. (See Chapter 7, *Application Resources and Command-Line Arguments.*) This function looks up application resources for the shell—since each root shell has a separate resource hierarchy, each has its own set of application resources. This function also registers the name of the root shell with the Xmt String-to-Widget converter—since each root shell is the root of an independent widget hierarchy, there is no way to look up a widget in one hierarchy from another unless the names of all the root shells are registered.

14.2.5 Using Multiple Screens, Displays, and Application Contexts

An application that opens up a number of auxiliary windows might want to take advantage of multiple screens when they are available. To create a shell widget on a screen other than the default, set its `XtNscreen` resource to the `Screen *` pointer for that screen. In most cases, you will also have to set the `XtNdepth` resource appropriately for the screen, and set the `XtNcolormap` resource to the default colormap of the screen, or to a colormap you have created for the screen. Also, remember that pixmaps created for one screen are not valid on a different screen.

Less commonly, an application might want to open windows on entirely separate displays. This situation might arise in "groupware" applications, for example, that allow a number of users to work together. You can open additional displays by calling `XtOpenDisplay()`, and you can create a root shell on a specified display with `XtAppCreateShell()`. When your application connects to multiple displays, you will usually want to add all the displays to a single application context. If you do this, then your single call to `XtAppMainLoop()` will handle and dispatch all events for all displays.

Usually the only time you will use more than one application context in an application is when you are using multiple threads (as is possible in X11R6). In this case, you can have multiple threads running independent event loops, handling connections to various displays independently of each other.

14.3 Style: Designing the Desktop

The preceding section explained some common patterns for windows on the desktop. This section raises some further stylistic issues that you should consider in your design.

If an application creates multiple windows on the desktop, give the user some way to distinguish the windows from one another. With the "window with dialogs" pattern, for example, you might place a distinguishing icon in the upper left of each dialog box, to give the user a quick way to identify the purpose of a dialog that has popped up. If you have a "main window with auxiliary windows," you might use different background colors for each of the windows to help the user keep the different contexts separate in his mind. If your application creates a "profusion of windows," then using different background colors can also be important. In this case, window shape may also help users to distinguish the purpose of windows—a tall narrow window would be easy to identify as the tool palette in a drawing application, for example. And finally, if your application can "clone" its windows to produce multiple identical windows on the desktop, then it is important to give each window a distinct title (perhaps involving the filename of a document being viewed or edited) and icon name.

While it is important to be able to distinguish the windows of an application from one another, it is also important to indicate to the user that the windows *are* part of the same application, that they work together and function as a suite. You should generally use the same font family (or families) throughout the application, for example. If you use icons to identify different windows, then use them for all your windows (or at least all the dialogs) and draw them in a similar style—with the same palette of colors, the same line weight, and so forth. Use the same style for window manager icons, so that iconified windows are clearly part of the suite. If you use different colors for your windows, use a unifying color scheme—make the windows different shades of the same basic hue, for example. And if you give your windows a default initial position, (rather than requiring the user to position them with the window manager) arrange them so that they form an obvious group.

In an application with more than one window, it is often a good idea to have one window that is clearly the main window, making all others secondary to it. This is a "home base" for the user. It is where the user can go to quit the application (the other windows will have **Close** options, but not **Quit** options). This home base will often be where the user goes to call up the secondary windows, and it may have an option for hiding the secondary windows (when the main window is iconified, for example.)

With the "profusion of windows" pattern, this main "home base" window should often have a **Windows** menu that allows the user to create (or deiconify or raise) any of the application's secondary windows. In simpler applications that only have two or three windows, you may want to implement some kind of keyboard shortcut that will allow the user to quickly jump from one window to the next. (We'll talk about this in more detail in Chapter 15, *Working with the Window Manager.*)

Consider the amount of space your application requires on the desktop. Like memory and cpu cycles, "real estate" on the screen is a limited resource that must be shared by all the windows running. You don't allocate more memory than you need, or busy-wait in your applications, and by the same account, you shouldn't flagrantly take up more space on the screen than you need.

This is not to say that you should design all your applications with tiny fonts and squeeze out all your margins. Considerations of readability and good graphic design should take priority over considerations of window size. Running out of screen space is not like running out of swap space or file descriptors—windows can be stacked and iconified, and users are good at using the window manager to accomplish this.

But there are some options you might consider: If you have one large window in your application, you might find that it can be nicely broken into two or more windows that can be manipulated and positioned independently. If your application opens multiple windows, you might choose to have some of those windows start up in iconic mode, so that they are visible and quickly available when the user wants them, but so that they do not clutter up the desktop before then. You might also consider the shape of your window: some applications, for example, can work well in tall and narrow windows or in short and squat windows—these are shapes that are easier for a user to fit in around the edges of the desktop. You can also consider giving your application a "reduced size" mode that is smaller than its normal size, but is something other than an iconic state. The X11R5 *xterm* fonts menu, for example, allows you to specify an "unreadable" font. Selecting this option produces a working *xterm* with a 2 pixel high font—it is not much bigger than an icon, and you can't read the text, but you can type occasional commands into it, and you can notice when there is activity or new text being printed in that window.

Colors in the colormap are another shared and, on most hardware, limited, resource. Because applications must share colors, the use of color becomes an issue for the desktop, where applications must interact. If your application uses color for anything more than simple interface decoration purposes (for example, if it uses it for data display) then it should be prepared to cope if it cannot allocate the colors it needs. One way to handle this case is to make do with fewer colors (as would be required on monochrome systems, anyway). Another approach is to create a new virtual colormap and allocate its own colors in that one. This approach gets an application the colors it needs, but leads to the "technicolor" problem—windows that are displayed when a colormap other than their own is in effect will appear with the wrong colors, and colors will "flash" when the colormap is changed.

Keyboard keys and mouse buttons are another limited resource. Some applications may want to implement popup menus on the root window. Others may want to define "hot keys"—certain keystrokes that will always be delivered to the application, even when they occur outside of the application's windows. These are resources that can't be shared—two applications cannot use the same hot key. So it is important that any application that makes key or button grabs, or defines root window actions be configurable so that the user can change the key and button bindings. Also, it is valuable if the application provides some way to temporarily relinquish its control of any keys or buttons it has grabbed.

In this chapter we've been talking about the desktop primarily as the visual environment in which the user interacts with her applications. In the following chapters, we'll think about the desktop as the suite of protocols and conventions through which applications communicate with the window manager, the session manager, and other clients. In the most general sense, however, "the desktop" is just another term for an application's complete environment, and it is important to remember that there are other, non-graphical, components of the application environment. A user can interact with applications through X resources, through command-line arguments, and through environment variables. These are tried-and-true facilities, and it is worth taking the time to consider how you might make use of them in your design.

This chapter does not cover all that can be said about stylistic issues on the desktop, of course. You'll find a lot of other stylistic points (mixed with implementation issues) in the following three chapters, which discuss communication with the window manager, with the session manager, and with other clients.

15

Working with the Window Manager

A window manager is the one client that will be running on every user's desktop. This is the X client that allows the user to move, resize, iconify, deiconify, raise, and lower windows on the desktop. The window manager is a privileged client, in that it uses special Xlib calls which, by convention, ordinary clients do not ever call.

In order to properly manage the windows of various clients on the desktop, the window manager (WM) must obtain information about those clients. This information is communicated to the WM by storing it in properties on the client's windows. The names and data formats of these properties are standardized by, and documented in, the *Inter-Client Communications Conventions Manual*. This manual is part of the X distribution, and is reprinted, for convenience, as an appendix to Volume Zero, *X Protocol Reference Manual* of the O'Reilly & Associates X Window System series.

Applications usually do not have to set these special WM properties directly. Xlib supports a number of standard functions that will do this, and the X Toolkit Shell widget automatically sets all these properties to reasonable values. There are times, however, when you will want to do some explicit communication with the window manager in your applications. This chapter explains how you can do this.

15.1 The Title Bar

All modern window managers add a title bar to each window they manage, or at least to the main windows of each application (see Figure 15-1).

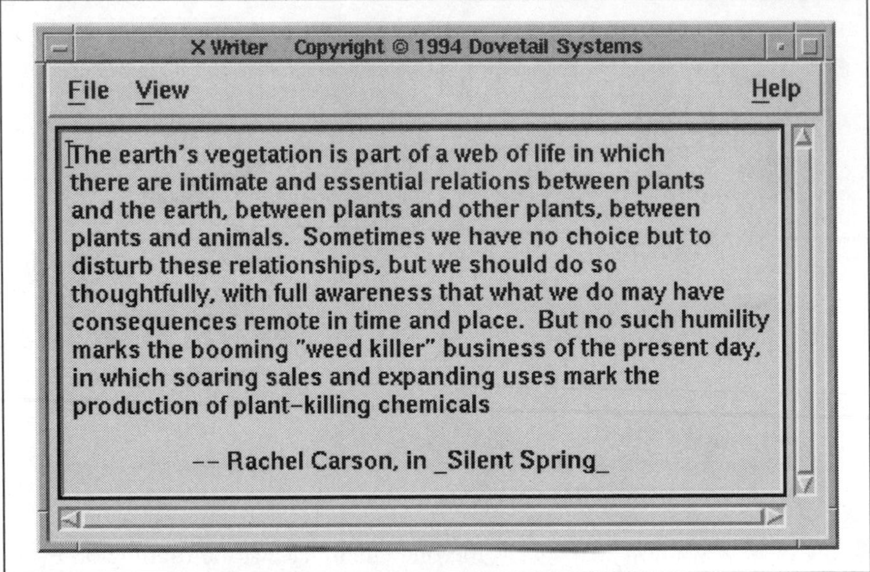

X Writer Copyright © 1994 Dovetail Systems
File View Help
The earth's vegetation is part of a web of life in which there are intimate and essential relations between plants and the earth, between plants and other plants, between plants and animals. Sometimes we have no choice but to disturb these relationships, but we should do so thoughtfully, with full awareness that what we do may have consequences remote in time and place. But no such humility marks the booming "weed killer" business of the present day, in which soaring sales and expanding uses mark the production of plant-killing chemicals
-- Rachel Carson, in _Silent Spring_

Figure 15-1. A window manager title bar

By default, an Xt client will display its executable name in the title bar. This is not always the appropriate thing to display—a word processor marketed as "XWriter" might have an executable with the more convenient name *xw*. The `XtNtitle` resource of the WMShell widget allows you to specify any title you desire for a window. Our XWriter application might put the following line in its resource file, for example:

```
xw.title: X Writer    Copyright \251 1994 Dovetail Systems
```

Note the \251 in this title. Resource files support the same escape sequences that C strings do, so this sequence introduces the character with ASCII code 0251 (in octal). In any font in the ISO8859-1 encoding (as most of the standard X fonts are) 251 octal is the copyright symbol (©). (If you want to use other special characters in a string like this, you can use *xfd* to examine the characters in a font. Click on a character to see its encoding.)

The default title for a main application window is almost always a sensible one—the user generally just typed the name of the executable, so he won't be surprised when a window bearing that name appears. This is not necessarily the case for dialog boxes and other auxiliary windows—they appear, by default, with their widget name as the title, and it is not uncommon to see dialog boxes with names like "pleaseStandBy" that might make sense to a programmer, but are ugly and distracting to a user. Figure 15-2 shows one such dialog box.

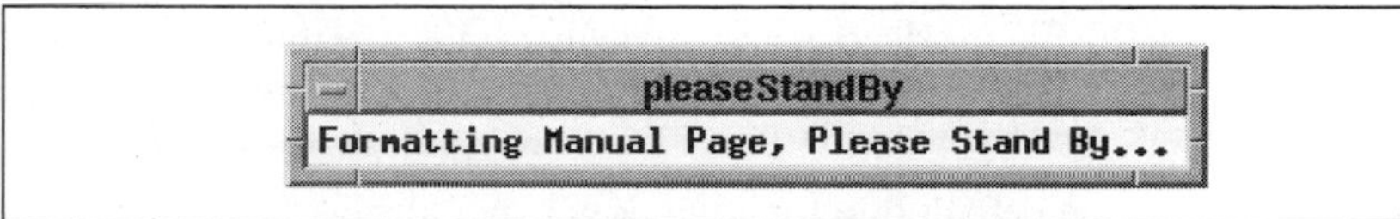

Figure 15-2. A dialog that did not set the XtNtitle resource

The moral is that you should be sure to remember to set the `XtNtitle` resource whenever you create a shell widget for a dialog box.

Most window managers update the title they display whenever the `XtNtitle` resource changes, and you can take advantage of this in some applications. You might use the title bar to display state about an application—a directory browser application might use it to display the name of the directory currently being displayed, as shown in Figure 15-3. Don't rely on this technique for presenting critical information to the user, however, since not all window managers display title bars or update them when the `XtNtitle` resource changes.

```
~/Xmt/book/figures ~/Xmt/book/examples/window_manager ~/Xmt/book ~/Xmt/src/Xmt ~
artemis:16> grep MWM_ /usr/include/Xm/MwmUtil.h | more
 * Contents of the _MWM_HINTS property.
#define MWM_HINTS_FUNCTIONS     (1L << 0)
#define MWM_HINTS_DECORATIONS   (1L << 1)
#define MWM_HINTS_INPUT_MODE    (1L << 2)
#define MWM_HINTS_STATUS        (1L << 3)
#define MWM_FUNC_ALL            (1L << 0)
#define MWM_FUNC_RESIZE         (1L << 1)
#define MWM_FUNC_MOVE           (1L << 2)
#define MWM_FUNC_MINIMIZE       (1L << 3)
#define MWM_FUNC_MAXIMIZE       (1L << 4)
--More--
```

Figure 15-3. A title bar that displays the directory stack of a shell

If you are using the Motif XmBulletinBoard widget, or any subclass of it (such as the XmForm or XmtLayout widgets) as the child of a shell widget, you can also specify the title by setting the XmBulletinBoard `XmNdialogTitle` resource. This resource is somewhat awkward to set, because it requires you to first convert the title to an `XmString`. This resource does support internationalization better, however, so if you want to display a title in some encoding other than ISO8859-1 (a Japanese title, for example) then you might be better off with the `XmNdialogTitle` resource.

15.2 The Icon

Every window manager has some method of "iconifying" client windows—replacing the full-sized window with a small, iconic representation of the window. Iconifying a window is a way for users to temporarily get that window out of the way, and reduce clutter on the desktop. By default, most window managers will just display the application's executable name, or the widget name for dialogs and auxiliary windows (this is the same as the default window title). Some window managers (*mwm*, for example) also display a default bitmap for applications that don't provide their own custom bitmap.

Just as the default title for a window is not always appropriate, the default icon name is not always right either. In an application like *xman* that can create multiple toplevel windows, there should be some way to distinguish between the icons of the multiple windows. One good way to do this would be for each *xman* browser window to use the name of the currently displayed man page as its icon name. Unfortunately, *xman* doesn't do this—see Figure 15-4.

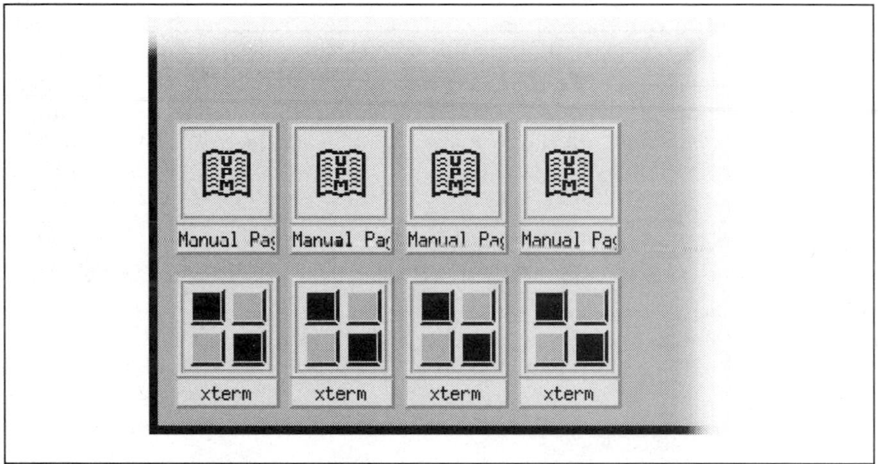

Figure 15-4. A shell game: multiple indistinguishable icons

You can change the name that is displayed with an icon by setting the `XtNiconName` resource of the TopLevelShell widget.* An important point to remember when choosing an icon name is that icons are supposed to be small, and there is not much room for the icon name. In *twm*, a long icon name will result in a really wide icon. In *mwm*, a long icon name will be truncated on both sides, until the icon is selected, at which time the entire name will be displayed. The ideal situation, however, is to keep icon names under 8 or 10 characters.

You can also specify a custom bitmap for the window manager to display in the icon by setting the `XtNiconPixmap` resource of the WMShell widget class. Note that even though the name of this resource contains the word "Pixmap", the `Pixmap` that you specify should be only one-bit deep—i.e., a bitmap. The window manager will use its own foreground and background colors when

*Note that the XmDialogShell widget is not a subclass of TopLevelShell, so you cannot specify an icon name for dialog boxes in this way. This is reasonable, since a properly configured window manager will never allow the user to iconify a dialog box independently of its main window anyway.

displaying this bitmap. The user can usually customize these colors in some sort of WM configuration file; your application does not have any control over them. The `XtNiconMask` resource is designed for use with the `XtNiconPixmap` resource as a way to specify non-rectangular icons. Neither *twm* nor *mwm* honor this resource, however, so it will not often be useful.

Some window managers have a preferred size for their icons, and in particular, they may enforce a maximum size above which your icon bitmap will be truncated. You can call `XGetIconSizes()` to find out what the WM's maximum and preferred icon sizes are. In practice, however, just about any window manager will accept icons between 16x16 and 50x50.

In the same way that you can use the title bar to display useful (but not critical) information to the user, you can use an icon name or icon bitmap to let the user know something about the state of the application. Most window managers (including *twm* and *mwm*) will notice and honor dynamic changes to the `XtNiconName` and `XtNiconPixmap` resources. So, for example, an e-mail reader application might display one icon when the user has no new mail and display a different icon when there is new mail waiting to be read. Or a game application might change its icon bitmap frequently to produce an animation effect. (Since it is the nature of games to distract the user and squander CPU cycles). If you use a technique like this, don't rely on it to provide important information to the user. Some window managers, for example, may not display the icon name when an icon bitmap is specified. Or a user may have configured his window manager to omit the icon bitmaps and display only icon names in a special icon manager window. Or, he might have customized his WM to display a custom icon bitmap for your application. This custom bitmap would then override any changes the application itself made. And remember that the icon names and bitmaps you specify are just hints to the window manager—the WM is free to ignore them if it chooses to.

15.2.1 Color and Non-Rectangular Icons

There are two shortcomings of icons specified with the `XtNiconPixmap` resource. First, they are limited to two-color bitmaps. Second, non-rectangular icons are not really possible, since the `XtNiconMask` resource is ignored by the most common window managers. The workaround to these problems is to use the `XtNiconWindow` resource. This resource specifies a window to be used directly as the icon. Since the application creates this window itself, there is much more freedom about the appearance of the icon. Creating and handling this window is not particularly convenient, however, so Xmt provides three convenience routines:

Xmt/

Icon.c

```
#include <Xmt/Icon.h>
void XmtCreatePixmapIcon(Widget w, Pixmap icon, Pixmap shape);
void XmtDestroyPixmapIcon(Widget w);
void XmtChangePixmapIcon(Widget w, Pixmap icon, Pixmap shape);
```

Use `XmtCreatePixmapIcon()` to create an icon window of this sort. The *`icon`* argument is a multi-plane pixmap, not a monochrome bitmap. It should have the same depth as the root window. Note that one advantage of limiting yourself to a two-color bitmap icon is that since the WM chooses the colors in that case, the icon is guaranteed to match the user's color scheme. If you use a multi-color icon such as the one shown in Figure 15-5, you should probably include some provision in the application to allow the user to customize the colors.

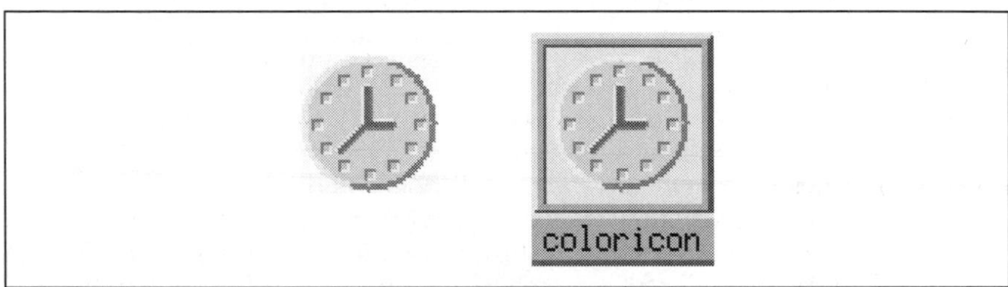

Figure 15-5. A multi-color, non-rectangular icon

The *`shape`* argument is an optional one-bit deep bitmask that specifies the shape of the icon. If it is specified, and if the server supports the SHAPE extension (you can check this by running *xdpyinfo*), the window will be shaped to create a non-rectangular icon. Note, however, that some window managers, notably *mwm*, will reparent this shaped window into a rectangular icon frame, which defeats the purpose of specifying the shape argument. Also, note that some window mangers, notably *twm*, will display only the icon window created by this function, and will not display the icon name along with it. If you feel it is important to display an icon name, you might choose to draw it directly into the Pixmap, either statically when you design the icon, or dynamically with `XDrawString()`.

`XmtDestroyPixmapIcon()` will unset the `XtNiconWindow` resource and destroy the window created by `XmtCreatePixmapIcon()`. This will automatically happen when the shell is destroyed, so you do not usually have to call this function. `XmtChangePixmapIcon()` will change the pixmap displayed in the icon, and optionally change the shape of the icon. As discussed above, you could take advantage of this function to communicate information about the state of the application to the user.

15.3 Controlling Window Resizing

The WMShell widget class has a number of resources which control how windows may be resized. Like the title bar and icon resources, setting these resources on a shell widget sets X Properties on the window of the shell widget. These properties serve as hints to the window manager, which may or may not implement them. ICCCM-compliant window managers, like *twm* and *mwm*, do honor each of the resources described here. Table 15-1 lists the resources, which are detailed in the following subsections.

Table 15-1. WMShell Resources to Control Window Resizing

Resource	Description
Size Limits	***min ≤ window size ≤ max***
`XtNminWidth`	Minimum pixel width of the window
`XtNminHeight`	Minimum pixel height of the window
`XtNmaxWidth`	Maximum pixel width of the window
`XtNmaxHeight`	Maximum pixel height of the window
Aspect Ratio	*Aspect ratio is width ÷ height*
`XtNminAspectX`	Numerator of the minimum aspect ratio
`XtNminAspectY`	Denominator of that ratio
`XtNmaxAspectX`	Numerator of the maximum aspect ratio
`XtNmaxAspectY`	Denominator of that ratio
Resize Units	*Legal sizes are: base + n × increment*
`XtNbaseWidth`	Base width of the window, in pixels
`XtNbaseHeight`	Base height of the window, in pixels
`XtNwidthInc`	Allowed width increment, in pixels
`XtNheightInc`	Allowed height increment, in pixels

15.3.1 Window Size Limits

If you specify a value (in pixels) for `XtNminWidth`, `XtNminHeight`, `Xt-NmaxWidth`, or `XtNmaxHeight`, the window manager will not allow the user to make the window smaller or larger than the specified bounds. It can be useful to specify a minimum size when you know that a given dialog or other window will not be useful at any smaller size. This is the case when buttons or other widgets become truncated at the right or bottom edges, for example, or when the text in buttons becomes truncated by the button.

It is almost always impossible to know in advance what the minimum size of a window should be. Any application that allows the user to customize fonts, margins, and so on will have a variable minimum size. And even when the user is not allowed to make any customizations, fonts can vary from server to server, and you should not assume you will always obtain fonts of the same size. For this reason, you will generally want to set the `XtNminWidth` and `XtNmin-Height` resources of a shell after you have created and managed all of its children, but just before you pop it up. Simply query the width and height of the child of the shell. This is the natural size of the dialog box, and for many dialogs is also a reasonable minimum size.

There are fewer reasons to set the `XtNmaxWidth` and `XtNmaxHeight` resources of a dialog. If you set these maximum size bounds to be the same as the minimum bounds, then you will have effectively turned off resizing for the window. Most main application windows will have some sort of resizeable work area, but dialogs will often have no resizeable components, and in this case you may choose to limit the dialog to its one natural size, not allowing the user to make it smaller or larger.

Some applications may in fact have some natural upper limit to their size—a drawing editor configured for 8.5" x 11" paper, for example, might not allow the user to make the work area larger than the page size. One more possible reason to set a maximum size for a window is for convenience with the maximize function provided by *mwm*. Clicking the maximize button in an *mwm* window border (or invoking the `f.fullzoom` function in *twm*) will zoom the window to its maximum size. By default, this is the full size of the screen, which is rarely a useful size for an application. Instead, it may make sense to pick some fairly large, but still useful, size as a maximum size for your windows, and then the user will have a convenient way to quickly switch back and forth between the regular and large application sizes.

15.3.2 Aspect Ratio Limits

The `XtNminAspectX` and `XtNminAspectY` resources specify the minimum aspect ratio for a shell widget, and `XtNmaxAspectX` and `XtNmaxAspectY` specify the maximum aspect ratio. For the purposes of this discussion, the aspect ratio is defined to be the ratio of window width to window height. These pairs of resources form fractions. To specify a maximum aspect ratio of 3:1 (width three times the height), for example, you would set `XtNmaxAspectX` to 3 and `XtNmaxAspectY` to 1. (or to 6 and 2, 30 and 10, or whatever.) To specify that a window will always be at least as wide as it is high, you could set `XtNminAspectX` and `XtNminAspectY` both to 1.

Some applications do have a natural aspect ratio: a tic-tac-toe game, for example, might want to ask the window manager to keep its window perfectly square, for example, and a program to display pie charts might want the same thing so that its pie charts are circular rather than elliptical. Or, a bitmap editor program editing a 48x64 bitmap might want an aspect ratio of 48:64. The difficulty is that a realistic bitmap editor would have a menubar at the top and a palette of editor tools on the left. These fixed-size components of the interface throw off the aspect ratio calculation—the ideal aspect ratio for the application will be different at different sizes for the application. It is possible to come up with something close to the desired behavior by using minimum and maximum aspect ratios in conjunction with minimum and maximum pixel sizes.

15.3.3 Measuring Windows in Units Other Than Pixels

The resources that specify minimum and maximum size for a window specify that size in pixels. Some applications, however are better measured in other units. *xterm*, for example is measured in rows and columns, using units based on the size of the font. A bitmap editor might be measured in terms of the bitmap size, and a drawing editor might be measured in centimeters.

You may have noticed that when you resize an *xterm* window, the window manager displays the new size in rows and columns, not in pixels, and you may also have noticed that the window will only allow sizes that are full rows and columns. *xterm* has a fixed-size margin all around the window. This is the base size of the window, the size it would have if there were zero rows and zero columns. This size is set on the `XtNbaseWidth` and `XtNbaseHeight` resources. Since *xterm* uses a fixed-width font, every row and column will have a fixed size. These sizes are set on the `XtNwidthInc` and `XtNheightInc` resources. When these resources are set, the window manager will only allow window sizes given by the following formulas:

```
width = XtNbaseWidth + i * XtNwidthInc
height = XtNbaseHeight + j * XtNheightInc
```

and the window manager will display the window size to the user as `(i,j)` rather than in pixels as `(width, height)`.

These resources are only useful for applications that have a main window composed of fixed-size components except for a single resizeable work area, and for which there is some fixed unit size that makes more sense than pixels. The trick, for most applications, is to determine the fixed base size of your window. After creating and managing all widgets in the window, use `XtGetValues()` to query the width and height of the entire window, and the width and height of the resizeable work area widget within the window. Subtracting these two will give you the base size of the window, but note that if the work area has its own set of internal margins you will have to take those into account as well.

15.4 Window Manager Decorations and Functions

The shell widget resources described in the sections above implement protocols for communicating with a window manager that are standardized in the *Inter-Client Communication Conventions Manual*. Since these protocols are standardized, they should work between any client (built with Motif widgets, Xaw widgets, or even just plain Xlib clients that implement their end of the protocol) and any window manager.

The Motif manager window, *mwm*, implements some additional protocols for communicating other information about how windows should be "decorated" (i.e., what controls should be available in the title bar and around the border), what functions should be available in the decorations, what items should appear in the system menu, and so forth. The VendorShell widget supplied by the Motif widget library implements these protocols and supplies resources that you can set to control the appearance of any of your application's windows. Table 15-2 lists these *mwm*-specific resources, which are documented in more detail in the sub-sections below.

It does no harm to set these resources if *mwm* is not running, but if you want to check whether it is, you can use the function `XmIsMotifWMRunning()`.

Table 15-2. Motif Shell Resources Specific to mwm

Resource	Description
`XmNmwmDecorations`	Specifies decorations for title bar and window frame.
`XmNmwmFunctions`	Specifies functions for system menu and window frame.
`XmNmwmInputMode`	Specifies window modality, as an alternative to the XmBulletinBoard `XmNdialogStyle` resource.
`XmNmwmMenu`	Specifies custom items for the mwm system menu.

15.4.1 Mwm Window Decorations

The `XmNmwmDecorations` resource of the Motif VendorShell widget allows you to control which decorations appear in the *mwm* title bar and window border. The possible values are shown in Table 15-3.

Table 15-3. Values for the XmNmwmDecorations Resource

Symbol	Bit	Purpose
MWM_DECOR_ALL	1	Subtract bits from full set
MWM_DECOR_BORDER	2	Window border
MWM_DECOR_RESIZEH	4	Resize handles
MWM_DECOR_TITLE	8	Title bar
MWM_DECOR_SYSTEM	16	System menu
MWM_DECOR_MINIMIZE	32	Iconify button
MWM_DECOR_MAXIMIZE	64	Maximize button

The values in this table are bits to be added together to form a single value. In C code, you should use the symbolic names for each bit. From a resource file, you will have to do the arithmetic yourself and specify a single integer value. The value `MWM_DECOR_ALL` is a special value. If this bit is set in the resource, then the other bits indicate decorations that should be removed from the full set. If this bit is not set, then the other bits indicate the decorations that should appear on the window.

Earlier in this chapter we described how you might use the `XtNminWidth`, `XtNmaxWidth`, `XtNminHeight`, and `XtNmaxHeight` resources to prevent the user from resizing a dialog box or other window when it made no sense to resize that window. This is a case when it would make sense to use the `XmNmwmDecorations` resource to go one step further and remove the resize handles from the dialog box. If you were to do this, you'd probably also want to remove the maximize button from the window as well. Similarly, if you are writing a simple utility application that uses the SHAPE extension to produce a non-rectangular window (*oclock* is an example) you might want to use this resource to remove all of the *mwm* decorations.

Note that this resource only controls the decorations that appear on the window border; it does not affect the list of functions that appear in the system menu. Even if you remove the resize handles from a window, an *mwm* user could still resize the window by selecting **Size** from the system menu or typing **Alt-F8**. The next section explains how you can actually disable these functions.

15.4.2 Mwm Window Functions

The `XmNmwmFunctions` resource is like the `XmNmwmDecorations` resource, but instead of just removing controls from a window's title bar and border, this resource also removes those functions from the system menu, and disables the keyboard shortcuts that invoke them. As with the previous resource, `XmNmwmFunctions` is the sum of individual flags. These flags are shown in Table 15-4.

Table 15-4. Values for the XmNmwmFunctions Resource

Symbol	Bit	Purpose
MWM_FUNC_ALL	1	Subtract bits from full set
MWM_FUNC_RESIZE	2	Resize function
MWM_FUNC_MOVE	4	Move function
MWM_FUNC_MINIMIZE	8	Iconify function
MWM_FUNC_MAXIMIZE	16	Maximize function
MWM_FUNC_CLOSE	32	Close window function

As with the `XmNmwmDecorations` resource, it might make sense to disable the resize and maximize functions for a dialog box that never needs to be resized. You should usually leave the other functions alone. Dialog boxes that are not supposed to be iconified will automatically have the iconify function disabled, and all other windows should allow the user to iconify them. Similarly, no window should disable its move function, or you will only infuriate your users. The "close window" function can be troublesome at times. All windows ought to handle the "close window" message, and we'll describe a fairly easy way to do this in Chapter 16, *Working with the Session Manager*. Don't just remove this function because you don't want to handle it. If a window cannot handle the message, do remove the function, but bear in mind that it will only disable the function for *mwm* users.

15.4.3 Mwm Window Modality

The `XmNmwmInputMode` resource controls the modality of a window. It is similar to the `XmNdialogStyle` resource of the XmBulletinBoard widget, so you only ever need to use this resource when you have created a dialog that does not have an XmBulletinBoard (or a subclass such as XmForm or XmtLayout) as the child of the shell widget. Table 15-5 shows the possible values for this resource. Note that these are actual values, not bits to be added together into a flag value.

Table 15-5. Values for the XmNmwmInputMode Resource

Symbol	**Value**
MWM_INPUT_MODELESS	0
MWM_INPUT_PRIMARY_APPLICATION_MODAL	1
MWM_INPUT_SYSTEM_MODAL	2
MWM_INPUT_FULL_APPLICATION_MODAL	3

The meanings of each of these values are the same as the corresponding values for the XmBulletinBoard `XmNdialogStyle` resource.

15.4.4 Mwm System Menu

The `XmNmwmMenu` resource allows you to add new items to the mwm system menu for a window. This resource is a string that is passed directly to *mwm* and parsed by the window manager. See the *mwm* documentation for full details on the grammar; we'll simply present an example to demonstrate what can be done with this resource.

Example 15-1. Using the XmMmwmMenu Resource

```
*dialog.mwmMenu:  \
        "dummy" f.separator\n\
        "Pass Keys" _K Meta<Key>K f.pass_keys\n\
        "Refresh" _R Meta<Key>R f.refresh_win
```

The first line of this example adds a separator to the menu. The second adds an item labeled **Pass Keys**, with the mnemonic **K** and accelerator **Meta-K**. The function `f.pass_keys` disables *mwm*'s parsing of keyboard accelerators. You would have to use this function if you wanted your application to be able to receive keyboard events like **Alt-F4**, which are usually interpreted by *mwm* and not passed on to the application. The results of this resource setting are shown in Figure 15-6.

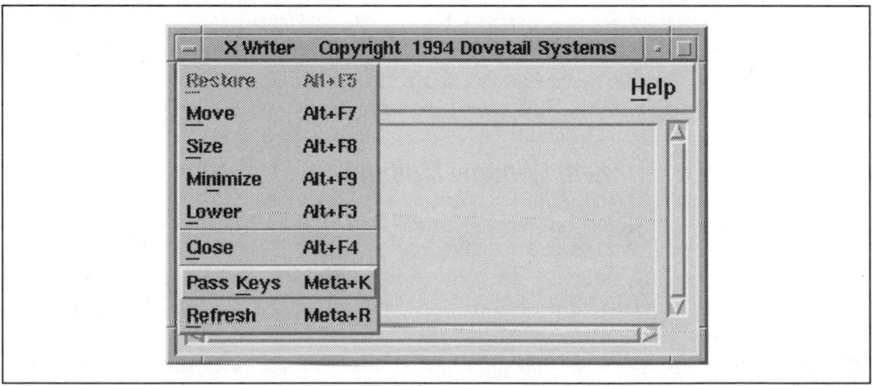

Figure 15-6. An extended mwm system menu

15.5 Manipulating Windows Dynamically

In an application with only one window, you will want to leave the job of iconifying, deiconifying, raising, moving input focus, and so on to the window manager. Your users will be familiar and comfortable with the window manager they use, and there is no need to provide alternate bindings for these basic window manager functions.

In an application with more than one window, and particularly in applications with many windows, however, you may want to consider making some of these window manager features available within your application. In a mail application, for example, you might have one window for reading mail, and another for composing outgoing mail, and you might want to implement a key-binding in each window that would switch the focus to the other window, so that the user could go from reading mail to editing a response without taking her hands from the keyboard. Of course, if you were going to implement a function like this to switch focus, you'd also want to deiconify the window, if necessary, and raise it to the top of the stack.

Another example is a data plotting application. This application might display data sets as scrolled tables in different windows, and then display graphs of selected columns of those tables in other windows. A well-designed application would allow an unlimited number of data sets and an unlimited number of graphs to be displayed at once. In a case like this, the user needs some way to help her keep track of all those windows. Somewhere this application is going to have a main control window that has a **File** menu for loading and saving data, a printer configuration dialog for generating printouts, and so on. It might also be useful to place a **Windows** menu in this main window that lists each of the tables and graphs by name. Or, it might be even better to have two separate menus: **Tables** and **Graphs**. In either case, selecting an item from one of these menus would make the window visible to the user by deiconifying and raising it. If the application has a mechanism like this for quickly bringing a specified window to the user's attention, there should probably also be a mechanism for quickly hiding the window—if it is easy to get rid of the window, they won't clutter up the desktop. You could add a key-binding to each of these windows that would iconify the window. Some window managers, like *mwm*, have default bindings to iconify a window. Others, such as *twm* (tab window manager), do not have default bindings to do this. Adding a special binding to your application will help the *twm* user and will give the *mwm* user a choice. If your bindings is well chosen and integrated with the rest of your keyboard commands, your users may well choose your iconify binding over their native window manager bindings when using your application.

There are a few things to note about this discussion. First, note that I do not suggest here that you add special bindings to iconify the main application window in this case. That window should probably remain exclusively under the control of the window manager. Only in windows that are clearly subordinate to the main application window should the application provide alternatives to window-manager functions.

Second, we are talking about windows that are subordinate to the main application window, but not dialog boxes. Dialogs are not supposed to be iconified at all, and in fact, modal dialogs are not supposed to be raised or lowered—they should remain above the main application window until the user is done interacting with them. You will only want to apply this sort of window management function to windows that are less transient than dialog boxes.

Third, remember that an alternative to iconifying and de-iconifying application windows is to simply pop them down (unmanage them) and pop them back up again (manage them) when needed. There are a lot of applications that behave this way, and this model would work well with the **Windows** menu in the data display and graphing example we described. Simply popping a window down is appropriate for dialog boxes, and is appropriate in many applications, but the advantage to iconifying windows is that they don't just vanish without a trace—an icon is left on the desktop, and the user knows that he can get the window back when he wants; he knows that the application hasn't "lost" the window. A useful rule of thumb is that if a window contains data (text, a picture, a graph of data) that the user has created or requested, never just make the window vanish; instead, iconify it so the user knows that he can bring it back. If a window was generated by the application (a scrolling log of error messages, a pop-up palette of tools) then it is okay to simply pop down the window, without iconifying it, when the user dismisses it.

15.5.1 Initial Window State

The `XtNinitialState` resource of the WMShell widget controls whether a window will be iconic when it first appears on the desktop. Set it to `IconicState` if you wish a window to pop up as an icon. This symbolic value works both in C and from a resource file.

The user can set this resource for the main window of an application with the `-iconic` command-line option, and the choice about the initial state of the main window should remain completely up to the user. If the application creates auxiliary windows, however, there may be times when it will make sense to start them up in an iconic state. If the user specifically requests a window, it should pop up normally, but if the application automatically creates a window in anticipation of a future user need, it might make sense to start it off iconified. An application builder, for example, might open up its main window, and also create a bitmap editor, a color editor, and a widget browser in iconified windows, so that the user knows that those tools are available and ready for use.

Once again, we are not talking about dialog boxes here. The purpose of a dialog is to get information from the user, or to notify the user of some new (and presumably important) condition or error. It would never make sense to create a dialog box and start it in iconic state initially.

15.5.2 Iconifying, Deiconifying, Raising, and Lowering Windows

Both Xlib and Xt provide simple mechanisms for performing simple window manager functions on an application's windows. The task isn't quite simple enough at either level of abstraction, however, so Xmt provides its own set of functions to accomplish these tasks:

Xmt/

ShellUtil.c

```
#include <Xmt/Xmt.h>
void XmtIconifyShell(Widget w);
void XmtDeiconifyShell(Widget w);
void XmtRaiseShell(Widget w);
void XmtLowerShell(Widget w);
```

Each function takes a single widget argument, which may be the shell widget to be operated on, or any descendant of that shell. `XmtRaiseShell()` first calls `XmtDeiconifyShell()` to ensure that the shell will be visible. Some window managers (or some configurations of some window managers) will automatically raise a window when it is de-iconified; others will not. If you want to be sure to bring a window to the user's attention, you should call `XmtRaiseShell()` instead of `XmtDeiconifyShell()`.

You should call these functions only when the user explicitly requests it—an application that raises its windows on its own is uncouth. And an application that deiconifies on its own is simply not following the etiquette of the desktop. Also, you should reserve these functions for the auxiliary windows of an application, and let the user manipulate the main application window through the established window manager functions.

15.5.3 Setting Input Focus

`XmtDeiconifyShell()` will deiconify a window. `XmtRaiseShell()` will deiconify a window, if necessary, and ensure that it is moved to the top of the stack and is visible. Sometimes you will want to do both of these things, and also transfer the input focus to the newly raised window, so that the user can begin to interact with it directly without first moving the pointer.

Unfortunately, the best way to transfer focus to a window depends on the window manager being run, and, to a major extent whether the window manager is operating in *pointer focus* mode, in which input focus follows the pointer directly, or *click-to-type* mode, in which the user must explicitly click on a window to set focus to it. By default, *twm* operates in pointer focus mode, and *mwm* operates in click-to-type mode. Xmt provides three utility functions that can serve to transfer input focus to another window:

Xmt/

ShellUtil.c

```
#include <Xmt/Xmt.h>
void XmtSetFocusToShell(Widget);
void XmtWarpToShell(Widget);
void XmtMoveShellToPointer(Widget);
```

All three functions call `XmtRaiseShell()` to deiconify and raise the shell, if necessary. `XmtSetFocusToShell()` sets the input focus directly by calling `XSetInputFocus()`. This is the "most supported" method for switching focus to another window, and works fine with *mwm* in click-to-type mode. It works with *twm* as well, but there are problems: *twm* doesn't highlight the new window's title bar to indicate that it has focus, and, in pointer focus mode, it leaves the desktop in an inconsistent state—the focus is in one window and the pointer is in another, which could seriously confuse users.

`XmtWarpToShell()` is an alternative that works better with pointer focus mode—it actually moves the mouse pointer into the new window. Warping the pointer is a practice that is quite seriously frowned upon in some circles, because it has potential to confuse the user. Here's what the ICCCM has to say about the matter:

> In general, clients should not warp the pointer. Window managers may do so, for example, to maintain the invariant that the pointer is always in the window with the input focus. Other window managers may wish to preserve the illusion that the user is in sole control of the pointer.

Users who have customized their *twm* configuration to jump between windows with the `f.warpto` function will be quite comfortable with having the pointer move between windows. Other users may not be comfortable with this style. If you do choose to use this function, you should probably provide some mechanism to disable it, and allow the user to switch the focus manually. `XmtWarpToShell()` also calls `XSetInputFocus()`, as `XmtSetFocusToShell()` does, so that it should work even with click-to-type window managers.

`XmtMoveShellToPointer()` is a useful alternative to `XmtWarpToShell()`—instead of moving the pointer it moves the shell so that it is beneath the pointer. There are two major drawbacks to this approach, however. First, a window moved like this will obscure whatever window the user just interacted with; this will probably be the main application window, or some other important window. Second, unless the window is in an iconified state, moving a window like this probably has as much potential to confuse the user as moving the pointer.

In many cases, the best approach to setting focus is not to—let users handle it in whatever manner is comfortable for them. As an application writer, you really cannot know in advance what method is best (unless you are writing for a restricted community of users and know exactly what window manager they use) so the choice is best left to the user. The function XmtFocusShell() does just this, and is the recommended way to set focus to a new window.

Xmt/

ShellUtil.c

```
#include <Xmt/Xmt.h>
void XmtFocusShell(Widget);
```

The first time this function is called, it reads the Xmt focusStyle application resource (class FocusStyle) and uses it to decide how to set focus to the window. If the value is "focus", it calls XmtSetFocusToShell(). If the value is "warp", it calls XmtWarpToShell(). If the value is "move", it calls XmtMoveShellToPointer(). And, if the value is "none", it will deiconify and raise the shell, but will not set focus to it at all. If *mwm* is running, (as reported by XmIsMotifWMRunning()) the default value is "focus"; otherwise the default value is "none", since neither of the other values is entirely satisfactory in this case. Users of *twm* or other window managers who are confident that they won't get confused can set this resource to their liking in order to get your application to automatically set the focus for them.

15.5.4 Preventing User Confusion

The key point to remember when using any of these window management functions, and particularly when changing input focus to new windows, is to only do so in ways that will not become confusing. First keep the user in control: only manipulate windows in direct response to user commands, such as keystrokes or menu selections. Second, be consistent: if you plan to switch focus to one of your windows when you raise it, do so to all of your windows. If you use a keyboard shortcut to iconify one of your auxiliary windows, use the same shortcut to iconify all of them. Third, allow user customization, particularly when switching focus: except in very particular circumstances, you should use XmtFocusShell() and not the lower-level functions it calls internally. Fourth, remember that your application needn't take over all the functions of the window manager. The purpose of the functions described here are simply to allow convenient user shortcuts for a few simple window manager functions.

15.6 Summary

You can request a title to be displayed in the window manager title bar by setting the Shell XtNtitle resource.

You can request that the window manager display a string and a bitmap for an icon by setting the Shell XtNiconName XtNiconPixmap. To request a color or non-rectangular icon for an application, call XmtCreatePixmapIcon().

There are shell resources that allow you to specify a minimum and maximum size, a minimum and maximum aspect ratio, and a discrete resize increment for a window.

15.6

The Motif VendorShell widget provides a number of resources that control the window decorations provided by *mwm*.

When requested by the user, you can perform window-management functions on windows directly with the Xmt functions `XmtIconifyShell()`, `XmtDeiconifyShell()`, `XmtRaiseShell()`, `XmtLowerShell()` and `XmtFocusShell()`.

16

Working with the Session Manager

A *session manager* is a low-level client that runs in the background like a window manager does. It is responsible for starting up a group of clients for the user to form the user's session, and also for ending the session when the user selects some sort of **End Session** or **Logout** button. Generally, session managers will also provide some sort of "snapshot" facility so that sessions can be restarted in the state they were left in.

Note that a session manager is not nearly so important a client as a window manager, and many X users currently run without one. As integrated desktop environments become more and more common, however, so will session managers, and it will become more important for clients to include the session management facilities so that they can interact fully on the desktop.

The *Interclient Communication Conventions Manual* (ICCCM) is a standard of the X Consortium that defines conventions and protocols for communication between clients and session managers. As this book goes to print, Version 1.1 of the ICCCM defines two standard protocols for communications between clients and a session manager, that are in wide use "in the field." These Version 1.1 protocols are really not adequate to the task of full session management, however, and with the release of X11R6, a new version of the ICCCM, Version 2.0, defines a much more elaborate session management protocol.

This chapter begins with a description of the "existing" (Version 1.1) session management protocols, which are well understood, and which will be required for backwards compatibility for some years. These are the protocols used by current versions of the CDE desktop, for example. This chapter also presents an overview of the new X11R6 session management scheme. It is expected that session managers and desktop environments (such as the CDE) will migrate to this new scheme.

16.1 Window Deletion

The ICCCM 1.1 window deletion protocol was designed as a way for a session manager to ask each of the clients in a session to shut down and exit cleanly. In practice, this protocol is used more commonly by window managers as a "Close Window" facility for users—this is the protocol that gets executed when you type **Alt-F4** in an *mwm* window, or execute the `f.delete` command with *twm*. When a client handles this protocol correctly, it provides an easy and consistent way to tell the client to close one of its windows or to exit, without having to hunt up the **Close** or **Quit** button for that particular application.

The workings of this protocol are described in the ICCCM. Briefly, however, a client that participates in the protocol places the `WM_DELETE_WINDOW` Atom in the `WM_PROTOCOLS`* property on each of its participating toplevel windows to indicate that it does participate. When the session manager (or, more often, the user via the window manager) wants to close a window, it sends a ClientMessage event containing the `WM_DELETE_WINDOW` Atom to the window. The client must then respond to this event appropriately.

The Motif VendorShell widget has a built-in handler for this window deletion protocol, and it is appropriate in some circumstances. The response to the protocol depends on the value of the VendorShell resource `XmNdeleteResponse`. If the value is `XmUNMAP`, the shell is simply popped down; this is the default for the XmDialogShell widget. If the resource is `XmDESTROY`, then the shell widget is destroyed, or, if it is the root shell, the ApplicationShell widget for the application, the VendorShell widget calls `exit(0)` to cause the application to exit cleanly.

In some cases, neither of these responses is appropriate, and you can set `XmNdeleteResponse` to `XmDO_NOTHING`. Generally, when you do this, you will want to add your own event handler to catch the `WM_DELETE_WINDOW` message and take the appropriate action. One fairly easy way to do this is with the Motif function `XmAddWMProtocolCallback()`. Xmt provides an even simpler function, however, `XmtAddDeleteCallback()`:

Xmt/

ShellUtil.c

```
#include <Xmt/Xmt.h>
void XmtAddDeleteCallback(Widget shell, int response,
                          XtCallbackProc callback, XtPointer data);
```

This function sets the `XmNdeleteResponse` resource of the shell as specified by *`response`*, and registers the specified callback procedure and client data to be called when the shell receives the "delete window" message.

*The fact that this protocol is implemented using atoms with the WM prefix instead of an SM prefix is a clue that there was some confusion when the conventions were developed as to whether they were window manager or session manager protocols.

There are a number of situations in which the default Motif response is not adequate, and you will want to register your own callback. In dialog boxes, for example, it is often not appropriate to simply pop the dialog down if the user sends a "delete window" message. When the user does this, it ought to be equivalent to clicking on the **Cancel** button, and there may well be a cancel callback that needs to be invoked. If you do not handle this case, it is possible for an application to get into a confused state, in which it thinks that the dialog is popped up when in fact it is not.

In an application with one main window and one or more auxiliary toplevel windows (not just dialog boxes), it is probably inappropriate to destroy those auxiliary windows (the default action) when a "delete window" message is received. The target window should definitely disappear, but the user may well want it back at some later point, and it may make more sense to just unmanage it temporarily instead of destroying it and having to recreate all the widgets later. If you do allow these auxiliary windows to be destroyed, be sure that the application notices that they have been destroyed, and does not attempt to reuse the widget handles. One way to notice this is to register a callback with `XmtAddDeleteCallback()`, and another way is to register a callback on the `XtNdestroyCallback` list of the shell widget.

In an application like *xman* that can pop up any number of browser windows, it probably does make sense to destroy these windows when the user sends a "delete window" message. As noted above, however, you must be sure that your application notices that the window has been destroyed, so it does not attempt to reuse it. This is a special case, however, and you probably do not want to use the `XmDESTROY` value directly. For example, you might choose to always keep one cached browser window around unmanaged so that it can pop up quickly, without the delay of creating widgets. In this case, you might want to unmanage some windows and destroy others. Also, when the user deletes the very last of the existing browser windows, you will probably want to exit the application, unless there is some other main window that allows the user some way to create a new browser window.

If you have an application that creates multiple root shells that behave as separate applications, beware of the default delete response for ApplicationShell widgets—the VendorShell will call `exit()`, making all the root shells created by the process disappear, which is not what the user requested.

Clients need not respond to a "delete window" request instantly; they are allowed to ask for user confirmation, for example. If the user sends a "delete window" request to the main window of an application that has unsaved files, for example, the application should probably ask whether the files should be saved before exiting.

There are a few circumstances when it is reasonable not to respond to the "delete window" request. We said previously that dialog boxes should handle a "delete window" request as if the **Cancel** button had been clicked. If you have a dialog without a **Cancel** button, for example (and are unwilling, for some reason, to add this button), then you may want to disable handling of the "delete window" request. Another example occurs when a "delete window" request causes an application to pop up a confirmation dialog asking if the user wants to "save files and quit," "quit without saving," or "cancel; don't quit." In this case, the meaning of a "delete window" request is ambiguous: treating it as "cancel; don't quit" is counterintuitive, since the confirmation dialog was itself popped up in response to a delete window request, and treating it as either "save files and quit" or "quit without saving" is dangerous, because both of those actions have serious side-effects and neither meaning is at all standard. In this case, it is probably best to disable `WM_DELETE_WINDOW` request handling and force the user to be more explicit by choosing one of the three buttons explicitly. Note, though, that when you do disable the "delete window" response, it is a good idea to register a callback to beep at the user (use `XBell()`) for feedback that the request was actually received, but was ignored.

16.2 Saving Client State

The other ICCCM 1.1 session manager protocol is a method for the session manager to ask clients to save their state, or *checkpoint* themselves, so that the session can be safely terminated and then restarted in the same state at some point in the future. This protocol also provides a method for the client to tell the session manager how to restart it.

16.2.1 The WM_COMMAND Property and the WM_SAVE_YOURSELF Protocol

The first part of this protocol is hardly a protocol at all, just some simple conventions: each client should have exactly one toplevel window with the `WM_COMMAND` and `WM_CLIENT_MACHINE` properties set. This first property is a list of command-line arguments that were used to start the application, or that the session manager can use to restart the application. The second property identifies the host that the client is running on—this won't always be the same as the host that the session manager is running on. If you initialize your application by calling `XtAppInitialize()`, and pass *argv* and *argc* from `main()`, then the ApplicationShell widget that is returned to you will set both of these properties for you. (Run the *xprop* utility, and click on a window to see how Xt automatically sets the value of these properties.)

For simple clients, like *oclock*, simply calling `XtAppInitialize()` is really all that is required for session management—there is no state to save, and the client can be restarted with a simple command line. More complex clients, however, require a more dynamic protocol that gives them the opportunity to save their current state and to update the `WM_COMMAND` property. The ICCCM 1.1 defines the `WM_SAVE_YOURSELF` protocol for this purpose. It works like this:

1. When the session manager wants to save the state of a session so that it can later be restarted, it initiates the save yourself protocol by sending a `WM_SAVE_YOURSELF` message to the client (the message is sent as a Client-Message event, just as the `WM_DELETE_WINDOW` message is).

2. The client responds by taking any action it needs to in order to save its state. The client is not allowed to interact with the user at this point.

3. When the client has saved its state, it signals the session manager that it is done (and may safely be terminated) by updating its `WM_COMMAND` property. As previously, the contents of this property should be a command line that the session manager can use to restart the client in its current state.

16.2.2 Checkpointing an Application

Different clients will have different interpretations of what it means to save their state. A simple text editor, for example, might skip Step 2 in the previous section and just place the name of its current file on the command line, along with a command-line option that specifies the current cursor position within that file. It would place this updated command line on the `WM_COMMAND` property by calling `XSetCommand()`. Then, when the editor was restarted, the same file would be displayed, and the cursor would be placed at its old position.

A more complicated text editor that allowed multiple files to be edited at once might instead use Step 2 to write out a configuration file (a *dot file*) that contained the names of each of the files, cursor positions, selected regions, and so forth. If the editor reads this configuration file automatically at startup, then the `WM_COMMAND` property will probably not need to be changed in Step 3—the original *argv* specified in the call to `XtAppInitialize()` will still be appropriate. Note, though, that `WM_COMMAND` must still be updated somehow—the session manager is waiting for something to happen to the property so that it knows that the client has finished checkpointing itself. To send this signal without disturbing the command line, this client would use `XChangeProperty()` to perform a "zero-length append" to the property.

Note that neither of these editor applications save the file the user is editing in response to this checkpoint request—the user's file is under the user's control alone, and saving it could be a mistake; perhaps the user has decided to discard his changes, for example. The editors probably should update their auto-save files, however, so that the user does not lose data unknowingly, or they should save the file in some private directory so that the file can be restored in its unsaved state when the session resumes. (If there are unsaved files when a session is terminated, the application may also pop up a confirmation dialog, as discussed in the previous section, offering to save the files before exiting. The application should do this in response to `WM_DELETE_WINDOW`, however, not in response to `WM_SAVE_YOURSELF`.)

Most applications contain a tremendous amount of state, and it is not realistic to expect them to be able to restart exactly where they left off. The decision about just what state to save is left to the individual application. The current file or data set or project being worked on is the most obvious state to save. If the user has selected fonts or colors, for example, for use from within the application, then these "preferences" are also fairly important components of the application's state and should be saved. But things like the current selected region in a text widget or the position of a scrollbar in a scrolled list widget are less important (and more difficult) to save.

You usually don't need to save the size or position of your application's main window. This is considered part of the window manager's state, not part of your application's state, and users running a session manager will presumably also be running a window manager that works with the session manager to save this kind of window geometry information.

The window manager will probably also save geometry for your auxiliary toplevel windows, but probably not for any dialog boxes that are popped up. Note that this is the other state that is important to save—if an email application has its **Compose Message** auxiliary window popped up when the `WM_SAVE_YOURSELF` message arrives, it should save this fact as part of its state. When the application restarts itself, the window manager should be able to remember the position of this auxiliary window correctly, but it is up to the application to actually pop the window up. Similarly, if you have online help or other modeless dialogs displayed, you might want to save this fact (and the position of the dialogs) as well. The same applies for the state of tear-off menus (though it is difficult with Motif 1.2 to restore a menu to its torn-off state). Other states you might want to save include the size of each pane in an XmPanedWindow and the state of the toggles in a **View** pulldown menu.

16.2.3 Handling the WM_SAVE_YOURSELF Protocol

Although you can write your own event handler to detect and respond to `WM_SAVE_YOURSELF` requests, an easier technique is to use the Motif functions `XmAddWMProtocols()` and `XmAddWMProtocolCallback()`. Even easier is to use the Xmt convenience routine:

Xmt/

ShellUtil.c

```
#include <Xmt/Xmt.h>
void XmtAddSaveYourselfCallback(Widget shell,
                                XtCallbackProc callback,
                                XtPointer data);
```

The shell you specify must be an ApplicationShell, and if your application creates more than one ApplicationShell widget, only one should have this callback registered. (And only one should have its `XtNargv` resource set.) The callback registered in this way is an ordinary Xt callback procedure. The crucial thing to remember is that this procedure *must* generate a PropertyNotify event for the `WM_COMMAND` property of the application's main window. It can do this by updating the command line stored on the property with `XSetCommand()`, or, if it doesn't need to update that command, by doing a zero-length append to the property with `XChangeProperty()`. Unfortunately, this property cannot be updated by setting the `XtNargv` resource of the root shell—that resource can only be set when the widget is created, and changes with `XtSetValues()` will just be ignored.

16.2.4 Naming Saved Sessions

If you save your application's state in a file (instead of encoding it all into the `WM_COMMAND` command line), then, in order to make session management fully flexible, you'll have to be able to maintain more than one save file. The *xwriter* application couldn't simply save its state in the file *~/.xwriter*, for example, because a user might want to have two instances of the application running in one session. Also, some session managers will allow the user to save multiple named sessions and restore them independently.

Instead, *xwriter* might save its state in a file that contains a unique identifier, based, perhaps, on its process id and the time of day. Suppose that for its initial invocation, *xwriter* decided to save its state in the file *~/.xwriter.11223344*. Then, when it set its `WM_COMMAND` command line, it would include a command like `-session 11223344`. When the session manager restarted it, it could parse this command (perhaps by defining a `session` application resource, and having the `-session` argument automatically parsed into the resource database, as we saw in Chapter 7, *Application Resources and Command-Line Arguments*) and use it to restore the state from the named file. When started up with this `-session` argument, *xwriter* need not create a new unique identifier; it can reuse the session identifier it already has.

This is the approach used by the CDE desktop session manager, which we'll discuss in a little more detail in the following section. The CDE desktop has a client library, however, which provides a convenience routine to automatically generate a session identifier, and also to return a complete filename for the state file (this allows all session save files to be placed in the same directory structure, and prevents the user's home directory from becoming cluttered).

Session management in X11R6 also uses the concept of a "session identifier," except that with the ICCCM 2.0 protocol, it is the session manager that is responsible for assigning this identifier to each client. The identifier provides a good handle for uniquely naming state files, and X11R6 Xt supports a new `-sessionId` resource for saving this identifier across sessions.

16.2.5 Saving State as a Resource File

If you are going to allow checkpointing of your application, the first thing you must do is to decide just what state variables you want to save. The second thing you must do is to decide what format you want to save them in. Given the nature of Xt programming, many of the state variables for your application will be widget resources. And given the resource-file-oriented nature of Xmt programming, it should be clear that saving your application state in resource file format might be a good choice.

Not all of your application's state will be widget resources, of course, so making this approach work may involve defining a number of application resources to contain the other state variables for your application. It may even involve writing custom resource converters to read in non-standard resource types. Still, this effort would be required for any ASCII state file format, so a resource file is as good as anything else, and it has some important advantages. If all your state variables are application or widget resources, then the user has a tremendous amount of flexibility to start up the application in any desired state. And if you define command-line arguments for each of these resources, then you could even save the application's entire state in a single command line on the `WM_COMMAND` property.

A Persistent State Facility

Bill Kayser uses this resource-file approach in his applications, and has written a C++ class to easily let the programmer register the widget and application resources that are to be automatically saved and restored. To do this, he uses `XtGetWidgetResources()` *to figure out the type of a named resource, and then invokes a "reverse converter" to convert the value to a string so that it can be saved in a file. To make this work, he had to write these "reverse converters" for scalar and other common resource types. Saving the resource file is the hard part—reading it in is just a matter of calling* `XmtLoadResourceFile()` *or* `XrmCombineFileDatabase()`*; the widget and application resources will handle all the resource parsing in this case.*

Note that Bill's facility wasn't designed with a session manager specifically in mind—even though his users don't commonly run a session manager now, it is still valuable for them to be able to restart where they left off.

The facility is easy to use for the programmer. Basically all he or she does is to create a PState (persistent state) object after the display is opened but before a widget is created (e.g., after `XtAppInitialize()`, and before `XmtCreateChildren()`):

```
PStateObj = new PState_c(display);
PStateObj->MergeResources();
```

Then for whatever widget/resource name combo the programmer wants to make persistent across invocations of the program, he calls a function like:

```
PStateObj->RegisterWidget(ToggleWidget, XmNset);
```

Before exiting, he calls:

```
PStateObj->SaveResources();
```

to save the current value of all registered widget/resource combos.

The more I thought about this facility, the more areas I could see significant applications for it. Some examples:

A Persistent State Facility (continued)

- User resizes a window with a text area so he can see proportionally more text. The window comes up the same size when he opens the application the next time.
- User likes to make file selection boxes really really long because she typically keeps hundreds of files in directories. After resizing it once, it comes up like that every time.
- User has to fill out a complicated form in the interface, but every time blank form comes up, it contains values from the last time he entered them, even if it was weeks ago.
- User doesn't like the command-line interface area in the main window. After he deselects the toggle button "CLI" in the view menu, the CLI no longer comes up.

—*Bill Kayser*

16.3 Session Management in the CDE

The Common Desktop Environment, or CDE, is a desktop developed by an industry consortium, which is likely to become standard software shipped with most hardware platforms. Current versions of the CDE session manager use the ICCCM 1.1 `WM_SAVE_YOURSELF` protocol, so if you use the techniques discussed above, you will be in a good position to integrate your application with this desktop. Future versions of the CDE will use the X11R6/ICCCM 2.0 session management techniques, but will presumably retain 1.1 compatibility for the sake of older clients.

As discussed above, the one session management extension that the CDE provides is convenience functions for generating a unique session identifier and a name for an application's save file.

16.4 Session Management in X11R6

X11R6 includes new session management conventions in Version 2.0 of the ICCCM, a new standard protocol for communication between clients and a session manager, and a new Xt shell widget, the SessionShell, that is used to provide a high-level interface for the session management protocol. The new facilities are complicated, and a detailed explanation is beyond the scope of this book. This section gives a short summary, however.

The new session management facilities replace the `WM_SAVE_YOURSELF` and `WM_DELETE_WINDOW` protocols with new protocols for application checkpointing and shutdown. In version 2.0 of the ICCCM the `WM_SAVE_YOURSELF` protocol is relegated to the "backwards compatibility" section, and the

WM_DELETE_WINDOW protocol becomes a "close window" protocol to be invoked by users through their window managers (which is what it has always been primarily used for anyway).

The new checkpoint facility is more flexible than WM_SAVE_YOURSELF in a number of ways:

1. It allows clients to interact with the user during the save, and forces clients to do their interactions one at a time. (So when the user clicks the **End Session** button, she doesn't see five confirmation dialogs pop up all at once!)
2. It allows Session termination to be aborted, if the user requests this through a confirmation dialog.
3. It allows transient clients like *xmodmap* to be part of a session—even though these clients run and exit before the session is saved, they will be rerun each time the session is run.
4. It defines a difference between saving local state to be restored and saving global state, such as writing files to a shared filesystem that will be visible to other users.
5. It has facilities for a "fast" shutdown, which could be useful when triggered by battery-backup power system.
6. Because the new session management protocol is defined independently of the X server, non-X clients can participate in sessions.

This new style of session management is a lot more complicated than the old. The new SessionShell widget makes it easier to use, however—instead of manipulating X server Atoms and Properties, and registering event handlers, you need only set resources and add callbacks to your root shell widget. If you want to provide sophisticated confirmation dialogs and allow the user to abort a session shutdown (features that were not available with WM_SAVE_YOURSELF) then you will have to do more work. If you simply want to save your state, then the new scheme is no more difficult than the old.

The basic model of session management is the same in the old and the new protocols—each application must provide a command line that will restart it in its current state. Because this underlying model has not changed, it should be simple to port your WM_SAVE_YOURSELF callbacks to work with the new protocol. For most applications, the bulk of the work involved in session management is not handling the details of the protocol, but actually saving and restoring all their state variables.

16.5 Summary

Session management is still an evolving technology, but one that will become more and more important as desktop environments become more prevalent. The current (May, 1994) state-of-the-art says that applications should handle the WM_DELETE_WINDOW protocol appropriately for all windows, and should at least set the WM_COMMAND property on their toplevel window (this is done automatically by `XtAppInitialize()`). More complicated applications may want to provide a limited checkpoint capability through the `WM_SAVE_YOURSELF` protocol. `XmtAddDeleteCallback()` and `XmtAddSaveYourselfCallback()` make it a little simpler to handle these session management protocols.

17

Communicating with Other Clients

In the same way that computers become more interesting when in a network of communicating computers, applications become more interesting when they have the capability to communicate with other applications. The UNIX shell allows a set of relatively simple commands to be compounded (through pipelines and shell scripts, for example) into more complex commands to address a rich variety of tasks. Communication between applications on the desktop holds the potential for the same sort of thing: the UNIX philosophy of small applications that do one thing well, transformed into a "desktop philosophy," in which the web of possible interactions between applications become more interesting than the features of the individual applications themselves.

This potential hasn't been realized yet, but it does seem clear that interclient communication will become more and more important in coming years, and it is worth your time to think about how your applications could benefit from communication capabilities. The following sections present a survey of some possible interclient communication techniques.

17.1 Cut-and-Paste and Drag-and-Drop

Cut-and-Paste and Drag-and-Drop are two different interfaces or metaphors for the same underlying data transfer mechanism. They are implemented using the X Selection mechanism: when the user "cuts" or "drags" in one client, that client ("the owner") asserts ownership of a Selection (taking ownership away from any client that previously had it). The user then "pastes" or "drops" into another client. This second client, "the requestor," doesn't need to know anything about the first client; it can use the X protocol to request the value of the selection, and the X server will pass this request on to the owner. The request includes the name of a property and the requestor's window ID. The data transfer actually occurs when the owner of the selection places the selected data on this property in the requestor's window. Figure 17-1 diagrams a data transfer through this mechanism.

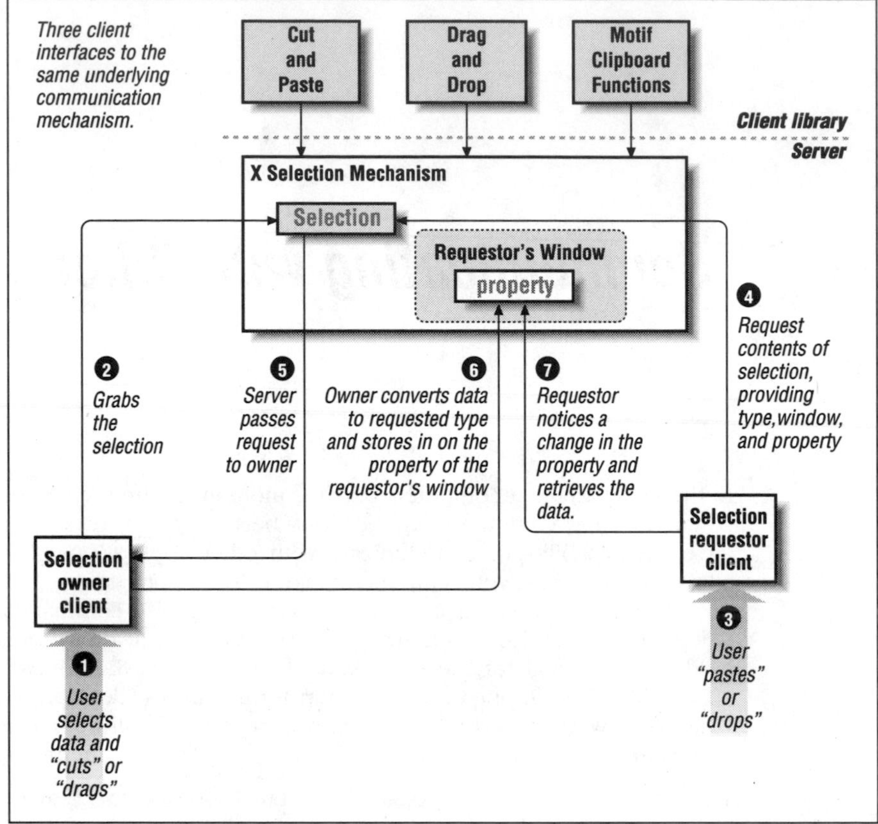

Figure 17-1. Data transfer with X Selections

The salient features of this mechanism are:

- It is user directed, not client directed—the user must "cut" and then "paste" or "drag" and then "drop."
- It is a technique for transferring data between applications, not for sending messages from one application to another (except incidentally as a side-effect of transferring data).
- All data transferred via this mechanism must go through the X server, which can be inefficient, and has the potential to overload the server's limited resources.

The rest of this section describes the practice and potential of cut-and-paste and drag-and-drop in more detail. The following sections discuss other types of interclient communication, suitable in other circumstances.

17.1.1 Transferring Text

Cut-and-paste is used overwhelmingly for the transfer of text—to cut lines out of your news reader and paste them into an e-mail message you are composing, for example. This cut-and-paste ability is built into almost all text widgets, so it is an automatic feature of any Xt program that allows editable text. In Motif 1.2, the ability to drag-and-drop text is also built in.

The ability to transfer text in this way is a crucial feature on any desktop—if you will be writing an application that manipulates or displays text without using one of the standard widgets, you should add a cut-and-paste and/or drag-and-drop ability for that text. Two of the sections below will outline how you can do this. Transfer of text may be a crucial feature, but it is a solved problem, which generally does not require any work by the application programmer, and is not worth dwelling on. The other potential uses of these data transfer techniques are far more interesting.

17.1.2 The Potential for Other Formats

The reason that text transfer is handled well and is so predominant is that there is a standard data format—null-terminated strings of Latin-1 characters—and that there are standard "viewers" for text—text and label widgets. The difficulty with the transfer of other types of data is agreeing on a standard format, and then having the ability to display and make use of the transferred data. Once these problems are solved, however, all sorts of interesting avenues for cooperation between suites of applications open up.

- There are a number of fairly standard graphics formats, and even some utilities for converting between them. It would not be hard to adapt existing applications—bitmap editors, window dumpers, drawing editors, paint programs, and image manipulation programs—to support a few standard formats (GIF, *ppm*, and *xwd*, perhaps) and start communicating through cut-and-paste.
- A potentially quite useful data type is a list of filenames. If the user could select a file or files from a graphical directory browser, then she could drag those files to a lot of interesting places. Dropping on a text editor might cause the editor to read the files in and display them, or dropping them on a drawing editor might cause that editor to read them in (assuming they were of the right file type). Maybe the desktop would have a special drop-target icon that displayed a magnifying glass—dropping the files on this target would pop up a **Search For**: dialog box and run a *grep* over the files.
- In a spreadsheet program, the user might select two columns of numbers. If he pasted them into an xterm or text editor, they might appear simply as two columns of ASCII numbers. If he pasted them into a multi-media word-processor, they might appear instead as a formatted table. And finally, the user might drag those selected columns and drop them into a data-plotting application where they could appear as the X and Y coordinates of a line plot or as two bar charts, placed side-by-side.

The point here is not to enumerate all possible uses of data transfer, but to urge you to think about the possibilities for your applications—what kind of interesting data can your application export? Would the user want to use that data in other applications? Are there other applications that might offer a different "view" of the same data? And on the flip side, what interesting kinds of data could your application import? What views of data can your application provide? One way to think of your application is as a data viewer (and perhaps an editor) that provides a particular service on the desktop. In this desktop model, your application may also be a client of other data viewers or editors.

Text is one of our few "universal" data formats, which is why it is so easy to transfer it between applications. At a higher level of abstraction, the file is probably the most fundamental data type, since it is the basic module of data storage. With the advent of graphical directory browsers, such as that provided by the CDE (Common Desktop Environment) desktop, filenames and lists of filenames may become the second universal (or almost universal) data type to be transferred among applications. The CDE guidelines for integrating applications into the desktop urge strongly that applications should at a minimum allow file icons from the directory browser to be dropped into them.

Data types other than strings and files that are not so universal are of interest in smaller, more specialized domains of related applications. The best way to get a suite of applications to interact well with each other is to design data transfer features into them from the beginning. If your project involves a suite of applications that manipulate a common data type—images, circuit descriptions, financial portfolios, or whatever—then decide on a data transfer format, and design each application to allow free data transfer in and out.

17.1.3 Exporting Multiple Target Types

One of the important features of data transfer via X Selections is that the selection owner can export its data in more than one format. In our previous spreadsheet example, for instance, the spreadsheet application might export its columns of numbers to the *xterm* or text editor as a single ASCII string, and to the data graphing program as arrays of floating point numbers. Or, to take the example even further, if the two columns of numbers were pasted into a color editor application, the data transferred might have nothing to do with the numbers, but instead be the foreground and background colors of the spreadsheet widget.

An application that owns a selection may export its data in any number of formats. Said another way, an application that has a selected region or object or set of objects may export a variety of information about those objects. It is up to the requesting application, when the paste or drop is done, to request the type of information it is interested in. In our spreadsheet example again, the spreadsheet program takes ownership of the selection through the X server when the cut is made or the drag begins. It is saying "I have data available to share." When the user pastes into an *xterm*, that application makes a request for the data, asking, in essence, "show me that data as ASCII text." When the user drops into the graphing program, the application is asking "show me your data as an array of floating point numbers." And if the user drops into the color editor application, that application makes the request, "tell me the color of your data."

When designing the data-transfer facilities for your applications, this is something else to keep in mind—the more data formats you can export, the more your application will be able to inter-communicate.

17.1.4 Implementing Cut and Paste

If you find that you want to allow cut-and-paste of some data type other than text, or from some widget other than a Text widget that allows it automatically, you'll have to implement the functionality yourself. This section does not go into full detail of this implementation; it just points you in the right direction.

When your application has data it would like to make available for pasting, it should call `XtOwnSelection()`, passing a widget and an `Atom` to specify which selection will be used. Usually, you will use `XA_PRIMARY` (defined in *<X11/Xatom.h>*) to specify the PRIMARY selection. (You can use any atom to specify a selection, but will only be able to transfer data to clients that also use that selection. The PRIMARY selection is the standard one for all cut-and-paste.) If this call to `XtOwnSelection()` is successful, then your application is now the sole owner of the PRIMARY selection (or whichever you specified). If another application had owned the selection, it loses it—if there was text highlighted in an *xterm*, for example, available to be pasted, the highlighting will disappear. Because making data available for pasting in this way takes the selection away from other clients, your application should only do so in response to a direct user request, never on its own initiative. Also, the data to be pasted should be highlighted in some way that makes it obvious that it is the current selection.

The third argument to `XtOwnSelection()` is a timestamp. If you have an `XEvent` pointer handy, you can usually extract a suitable timestamp from the event. The easiest thing to do, however, is to call `XtLastTimestampProcessed()` to get a suitable time.

Calling `XtOwnSelection()` simply advertises that your application has data. The actual transfer of data is the work of three callbacks you register with your call to `XtOwnSelection()`. These procedures are of types `XtConvertSelectionProc`, `XtLoseSelectionProc`, and `XtSelectionDoneProc`. The first is called when the data is requested for pasting by some other client. The second is called when another client takes ownership of the selection; your application should respond by unhighlighting the data to indicate that it is no longer available to be pasted. The third callback is called when the data has been successfully transferred—this is an optional callback which you can use to free up any memory or other resources allocated in the `XtConvertSelectionProc`. The `XtConvertSelectionProc` callback is the most important and complicated of the callbacks, but you should read about all three in an Xt reference manual. One good source is *Volume Five: X Toolkit Intrinsics Reference Manual* from O'Reilly & Associates, which contains example procedures for each of these callbacks.

When a user requests that data be pasted, your application should call `XtGetSelectionValue()` to obtain the value of the current selection. (The application has no way of knowing that there is a current selection, or whether it is of an appropriate type of data, but, because the application will only paste in response to a user request, it can generally rely on the user to request pastes only when they make sense.) Since communication between clients is not a synchronous process, `XtGetSelectionValue()` cannot return the selected data directly; instead it registers a callback that is of the type `XtSelectionCallbackProc`, which will be called when the data is ready. You can refer to a reference manual to learn more about these topics; again, *Volume Five* contains example code that you may find useful.

17.1.5 Implementing Drag-and-Drop

Motif Drag-and-Drop is based on the same underlying selection mechanism as cut-and-paste, and once you understand the details of this mechanism (the difference between the selection, target, and type Atoms, for example) you will notice a lot of similarities between the two data transfer methods. Drag-and-Drop in Motif is a huge topic, and this section will only present a very brief overview. *Volume 6A: Motif Programming Manual*, from O'Reilly & Associates, contains a good explanation (a thorough, 55-page one) of Motif Drag-and-Drop. Recall that Drag-and-Drop is not available prior to Motif 1.2.

If an application will allow drags to occur from its window, it must register an event handler or a translation and action procedure that will notice when the user begins a drag with mouse button 2. When a drag begins, the application calls `XmDragStart()`, registering a conversion procedure to be called when the data is dropped. This conversion procedure is very much like the `XtConvertSelectionProc` used for cut-and-paste—in fact, it is an `XtConvertSelectionIncrProc`, a generalized version of the simpler callback mentioned above.

In order for a client to support drops in its windows, it must register its "drop sites." You can do this with `XmDropSiteRegister()`, which specifies a widget as a drop site, and registers a callback to be called when data is dropped on the widget. This callback (a regular `XtCallbackProc`) will then call `XmDropTransferStart()` to actually request the transfer of data. This procedure registers a callback of its own to be invoked when the data is ready. Not surprisingly, this callback is an `XtSelectionCallbackProc`, just like the callback used when pasting into an application.

All of these Motif procedures take a widget-style `ArgList` of named resources and their values. So you specify these various callback procedures with `XtSetArg()`, instead of passing them directly as arguments to the Drag-and-Drop functions. There are a large number of options to control the details (data types, pixmaps, animation, etc.) of the Drag-and-Drop process, so using an `ArgList` in this way allows default values for each of these options and prevents the problem of having procedures with an unwieldy number of arguments. In fact, the Motif Drag-and-Drop implementation even uses some special Xt objects as a way of maintaining a group of related data and information. Calling `XmDragStart()`, for example, returns an XmDragContext object. This is a regular Xt widget, with its own set of resources, and you can set these resources to affect the progress of the drag.

This is just a sketch of the Drag-and-Drop process. If you'll be implementing Drag-and-Drop for a custom data type in your application, you will want to read up on `XmDragStart()`, `XmDropSiteRegister()`, and `XmDropTransferStart()` in a Motif programmer's guide or reference manual. You should also study the XmDragContext, XmDragIcon, XmDropSite and XmDropTransfer objects. *Volume 6B: Motif Reference Manual* has good reference material on these functions and objects. If you are developing an application specifically targeted for the CDE desktop environment, note that the CDE libraries define their own drag-and-drop API on top of the Motif API, and you may want to use this API instead.

17.1.6 The Motif Clipboard

Motif supports another technique for data transfer between clients—the function `XmClipboardCopy()` and the 16 related clipboard functions that go with it. These functions are little more than wrappers around the standard Xt cut-and-paste mechanism. Unfortunately, however, they transfer data via the CLIPBOARD selection instead of the PRIMARY selection. This CLIPBOARD selection was intended for use with a special *clipboard* client, which would automatically grab copies of any "clipped" data and then turn around and export them via the PRIMARY selection. Almost no one actually runs such a client, however, and although Motif clients can intercommunicate using the CLIPBOARD selection using these functions, there are a number of important clients, like *xterm*, that do not use this selection.

The Motif clipboard functions usually more complicated than the underlying Xt selection functions they are based on. Using them will limit the interoperability of your applications (e.g., you won't be able to paste into an *xterm*), so there is really never a reason to use them.

17.2 Communication with Properties

Chapter 15, *Working with the Window Manager*, explained how an application can request that the window manager display a particular title in its titlebar, or a particular bitmap in its icon, for example, and how an application can request that the window manager do things like restrict the application's window size in various ways. There is clearly communication going on between the client and the window manager.

It is a one-way communication, from client to window manager, and it is implemented with Properties on the client's toplevel windows. A Property is a server object associated with a window. It has a name, a type name (for use by clients—the server places no interpretation on property types), and an arbitrary amount of data that may be formatted as an array of 8-bit bytes, 16-bit words, or 32-bit long words.

Communication through properties has the following features:

- It may be user-initiated, but, unlike communication with selections, there is no requirement that the user be involved.
- It is one-way communication. A client (client A) places information on a property of its window so that it can be read by another client (client B). This one-way communication can also go in the other direction, with an external client B setting a property on client A's window, as a way of sending a message and/or data to client A. This is how data is transferred in cut-and-paste, for example.
- It allows a limited kind of broadcast. Communication through properties is not just between two communicating clients. Any client that knows the window ID of client A can read its properties. Both a window manager and a session manager might be interested in some properties on a client A's toplevel window, for example. There is no particular trick to obtaining the window ID for a client—a window manager could do this, for example, by just querying the server for a list of all windows on the screen, and then checking each toplevel window for the desired property.
- The communication can be "passive" or "active." One type of communication through properties requires client B to query ("passive" communication) client A's properties to get their values. But if client B wants to be notified ("active" communication) when a property value changes, it can request PropertyNotify events for Client A's window from the server. Window managers do this, for example, so that they can respond dynamically when a client requests a new string to be displayed in its titlebar.
- It relies on the X server. If a large amount of data is to be communicated, then this technique should be avoided, since server memory should be treated as a scarce resource.

To communicate with the window manager through properties, you just set resources on your shell widgets—these widgets handle setting the appropriate data on the appropriate properties. If you want to do your own communication through properties, you can create a property on a window, or change the value of a property by calling `XChangeProperty()`. You can query the value of a given property for a given window with `XGetWindowProperty()`.

To be notified of property changes for a window, you can ask for PropertyNotify events. Note, though, that before X11R6 it is very difficult to read events that occur on windows that are not widgets in your own application. It is, of course, easy to handle PropertyNotify events for your own widgets, if you want to turn the one-way communication around and have some outside client set properties on your own window.

Sometimes a group of cooperating applications want to share data among themselves. One way to do this is to place that data in a well-known property. But since no client will know what Window ID will be allocated for any of the other clients, the best well-known location is the root window. The *xrdb* client, for example, sets the contents of a resource file on a root window property, and all

Xt applications read this property when they start up. The root window is a shared resource, so if you choose to put a property on it, be sure to use a distinct prefix (like your company name) in order to give the property a unique name.

17.3 Communication with the ClientMessage Event

Chapter 16, *Working with the Session Manager*, explained how a session manager (or a window manager) can send a message to an application with the `WM_DELETE_WINDOW` and the `WM_SAVE_YOURSELF` protocols. This is another type of communication, obviously, and is implemented with `XSendEvent()`—the session manager calls `XSendEvent()` to generate a ClientMessage event and deliver it to the toplevel window of an application. Each client that participates in these protocols has an event handler registered (it may be registered behind the scenes with a convenience function like `XmtAddDeleteCallback()`) to respond to these ClientMessage messages.

The features of this type of communication are:

- It is a message from one client to another, known client, unlike communication through properties, which can be a kind of broadcast, or communication with selections, which is communication between anonymous clients, mediated by the X server and the user. A session manager might use `XSendEvent()` to send a `WM_SAVE_YOURSELF` message to all running clients, but it performs this "broadcast" simply by going through its list of all clients in the session and sending the message multiple times.
- It does not require the user's involvement in the way that communication with selections does. Often, though, a ClientMessage is triggered by some user action, and often the user actually indicates the recipient of the event. (If the user types **Alt-F4** in an *mwm* window, for example, he causes a `WM_DELETE_WINDOW` protocol ClientMessage to be triggered, and indicates the recipient of the message.)
- It can only transfer a limited amount of data. A ClientMessage event has a field to specify the type of the message, and only has room for an additional 20 bytes of data (or 10 words or 5 long words). Thus, while this technique is useful for issuing commands to other applications, it is not useful for transferring data.
- It does involve the X server. While there is no danger of a ClientMessage using up server memory, this still restricts this communication technique to X clients.

The main trick to communication with `XSendEvent()` is figuring out the toplevel Window ID of the client or clients that you want to communicate with. This technique is suited to "manager" clients like window managers and session managers that keep a list of windows around. One brute-force approach to finding a window to communicate with is to query the server for all windows on a display. If you do this, you'll want your "target" clients to set some identifying property on their windows, so you can tell that they are interested in receiving your ClientMessage.

Another approach to finding clients to send messages to is to have those clients append their Window ID into a property on the root window (and to remove it before they exit, of course).

17.4 ICE: The Interclient Exchange Protocol

The ICCCM 2.0 session management protocol implemented in X11R6 does not use `XSendEvent()` and the ClientMessage event as the ICCCM 1.1 version did. In fact, the X11R6 session management protocol can provide session management for clients that are not X clients—the protocol is entirely separate from the X protocol. The new protocol is a complex one, and is similar to the X protocol in many ways. It is implemented on top of the ICE protocol. ICE is a new standard in X11R6. It stands for Interclient Exchange, and is a simple protocol that provides a framework for the definition of more complex protocols. It is described as follows in X Consortium documentation:

> There are numerous possible "interclient" protocols, with many similarities and common needs—authentication, extension, version negotiation, byte order negotiation, etc. The ICE protocol is intended to provide a framework for building such protocols, allowing them to make use of common negotiation mechanisms and to be multiplexed over a single transport mechanism.

The features of interclient communication through a protocol layered over ICE are:

1. It is a client-to-client communication mechanism that does not support broadcasting. Usually, though, one client will act as a server, providing some service to a number of clients that connect to it.
2. The client and server must both know the name of the protocol they want to use. The client must also know an address by which it can connect to the server. This is usually provided to it through something like a `SESSION_MANAGER` environment variable.
3. The X server is not involved. You don't have to worry about over-burdening the X server, but you still get the network transparency, byte-swapping, authentication and other features that the X server provides.

The interclient communication mechanism available with ICE is far more general than any we've discussed above. It is also a lot harder to use. For some forms of interclient communication, the RPC (remote procedure call) model is more natural, and you might want to use this approach instead. But if you want an arbitrarily complex X-style protocol (client sends requests to the server, server sends replies, events, and errors to the client), then you might want to build your protocol on top of ICE.

17.5 Desktop Notification: Broadcasting Messages with ToolTalk

In a fully integrated desktop there are a number of uses for broadcasting messages. An editor application, for example, might want to broadcast "I just created the file */usr/david/foo.c*" so that any graphical directory browsers that are displaying the directory */usr/david* can display an icon for the file. Or, the editor might want to ask, "Is anyone editing */usr/david/foo.c*?" before it allows changes to the file itself, to prevent concurrent changes. Or an email reader might broadcast a message "I've got a message with a PostScript attachment, will someone please display it for me?"

The technical goal here is to be able to efficiently broadcast messages to all the clients on the desktop. This can be accomplished with the ToolTalk service, which was developed by SunSoft, and is not a part of the CDE desktop. ToolTalk messages are broadcast by a ToolTalk server, to which each communicating client connects. ToolTalk predates ICE, but the client-to-ToolTalk connection could certainly be (though it is not) layered over the ICE protocol.

The features of the ToolTalk communication mechanism are:

1. It is client-initiated; while messages may be triggered in response to user actions, the user will not be involved or even aware of the communication.
2. ToolTalk messages are broadcast, and recipients are actively notified of broadcasts.
3. The X server is not involved, though a ToolTalk server is.

The overall communication goal of ToolTalk is to increase the interoperability of "tools" on the desktop. In order to interoperate, they must be able to communicate. ToolTalk ensures this. But communication is not enough—the "tools" must also "speak the same language." To this end, SunSoft and the CDE have also begun to define standard "Message Sets" that define common messages and requests for use in particular problem domains. The "DeskTop Message Set," for example, includes messages like `Iconified` that a client might send when it is iconified and requests like `Get_Iconified` that a client could use to query the iconic state of another. (And this could work even if the clients were not both connected to the same X display.) Similarly, the "Media Exchange Message Set" includes requests like "Display," "Edit," and "Print."

ToolTalk technology is not yet widely available, except to CDE developers, though it is likely to become much more widespread in the future. If used to its full potential, it shows promise to support close integration of clients on the desktop.

17.6 Summary

There are a number of types of interclient communication, of which cut-and-paste and drag-and-drop are the most common. The Motif widgets pretty much guarantee that any application will be able to communicate textual information to another with these mechanisms. However, many applications operate on other, more complex sorts of data as well, and you may want to design your application to allow the import and export of these data types.

If you are writing an application for integration of the CDE or some other desktop, you should plan, at a minimum, to allow file icons to be dragged from a directory browser and dropped on your application.

There are other styles of interclient communication as well, suitable in different situations. Evolving interclient communication technologies, like ICE and ToolTalk, are likely to become important and widely used in the future.

Part Five

Patterns and Tools for the Main Window

Part 4 of this book was about the layout of an application's windows on the desktop. This part narrows the design focus and considers layout and implementation of components that appear within the main window or windows of an application.

This part of the book describes some of the most important and powerful tools in the Xmt library.

18

The Layout Widget: A Tutorial

Before we can discuss the individual components of an application main window (or a dialog box, for that matter) we need some way to arrange those components in the window. The XmtLayout widget is designed for just this task—it is a general-purpose manager widget used for positioning other widgets, and is probably the most important widget in the Xmt library. Like the Motif XmForm widget, the XmtLayout is constraint-based—that is, it arranges its children as specified by constraint resources set on those children. But while the XmForm widget arranges its children according to their "attachments," the XmtLayout widget arranges its children into nested rows and columns, which is a more intuitive scheme, and easier to work with.

A problem with constraint-based manager widgets is that it can become cumbersome to set constraint resources on each child of the widget. For this reason, the Layout widget supports a layout grammar that makes it possible to specify the layout* of an entire window with a single string resource. This layout grammar and the intuitive nested-rows-and-columns scheme make the Layout widget significantly easier to use than the XmForm widget. The Layout also has a number of other important features:

- Layout constraints (and the layout grammar) allow you to specify how children of the Layout should grow and/or reposition themselves when the Layout widget itself is made larger. This means that it is easy to produce self-adjusting layouts that look good at whatever size the window comes up at.
- The Layout widget can draw a caption for any of its children. It does this directly, avoiding the need for any extra XmLabel widgets.

*In this chapter and the next, the word "Layout" refers to the XmtLayout widget, the word "layout" is used as a synonym for "arrangement," and the phrase "lay out" describes what the Layout widget does to its children.

- The Layout widget can draw a shadowed, etched, or solid frame around any of its children, and can also draw a partial frame or separator against any edge of a child. The Layout does this drawing directly, making the XmFrame and XmSeparator widgets unnecessary.
- The Layout widget supports a special type of inexpensive gadget child (which are much more efficient than Motif XmGadgets, for example). There is a gadget that will display a pixmap or bitmap, and another gadget that will display any text that is not a caption.

If the Layout is the most important widget in the Xmt library, it is also the one that requires the most explanation, and the only one to have two chapters devoted to it. This chapter is a tutorial introduction to the features of the widget and to the layout grammar that you will commonly use to lay out your own windows. The next chapter provides more formal documentation of the widget and of the underlying constraint resources that make it work. As usual, detailed reference information about the grammar and the resources is in the reference section.

The tutorial on the following pages progresses from a very trivial layout example using the widget to a layout for a sophisticated dialog box. (This part of the book is about application main windows, but for simplicity in this tutorial, we'll be laying out dialog boxes.) Each section in the tutorial introduces one or two new features, with a listing of example code and a screen dump of the resulting layout.

18.1 Default Layout

When children are added to a Layout widget with no layout information, they are simply arranged in a column. Figure 18-1 shows the result of the following specification. By setting the Layout `XmNorientation` resource to `XmHORIZONTAL`, you can have children laid out in a row instead.

```
tutorial.xmtChildren: XmtLayout layout;
*layout.xmtChildren: XmLabel label;\
                     XmPushButton okay, cancel, help;

*label.labelString: Hello World
```

You can use the Layout widget as a substitute for an XmRowColumn widget in this way, but this layout is otherwise not particularly interesting. Note that here, and elsewhere in this chapter, we've omitted the simple resources that specify labels for the push buttons, specify the font list, and so forth.

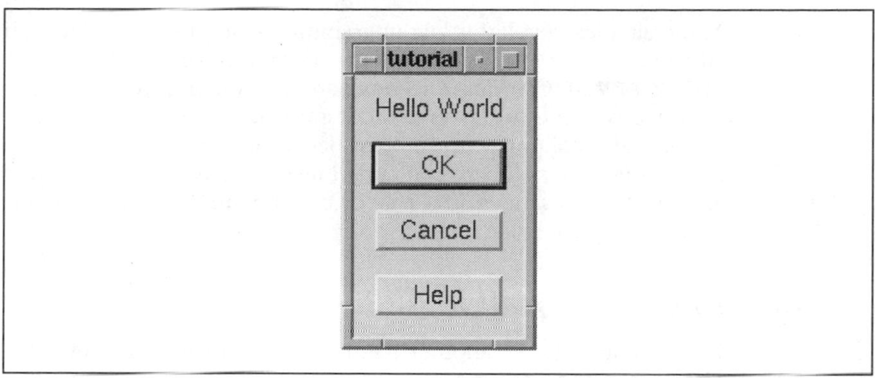

Figure 18-1. The default layout

18.2 A Simple Layout

This example is the same as the one provided in the previous section, except that we've used the XmtNlayout resource of the Layout widget to tell it to arrange its children in a more interesting way, as shown in Figure 18-2.

```
tutorial.xmtChildren: XmtLayout layout;
*layout.xmtChildren: XmLabel label,\
                     XmPushButton okay, cancel, help;

*layout.layout: label\
                Row { okay cancel help }

*label.labelString: Hello World
```

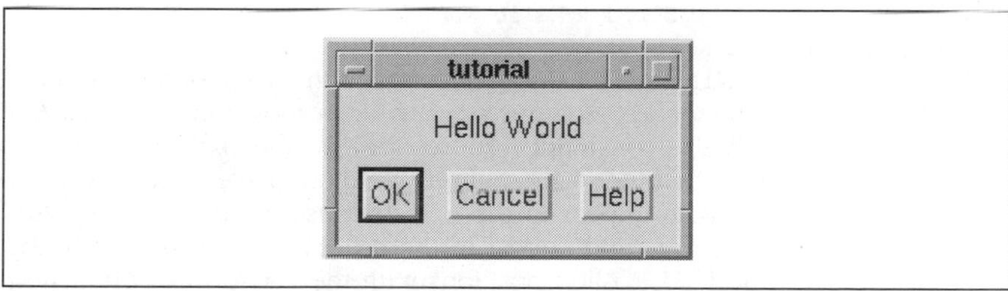

Figure 18-2. A simple layout

The XmtNlayout resource specifies that there are two items in a column: the XmLabel widget named "label", and a row. Within that row are the three buttons, **okay**, **cancel**, and **help**.

At the simplest level, this layout grammar is simply a list of items to be arranged into the outermost column (or row, if XmNorientation is specified as XmHORIZONTAL). Columns and rows are items themselves, however, and can be arranged within other rows and columns. A row is indicated with the Row keyword, and a column with the Col keyword. The contents of a nested row or column are grouped between curly braces just as blocks of C code are. Widgets that are to be arranged in a row or column are specified by name, and are not separated by commas.

18.3 Another Layout Method

This example shows another method you can use to achieve the same layout. The Layout widget is a constraint widget, and provides a number of constraint resources that you can set on any of its children to specify how they should be arranged.

Here we set the XmtNlayoutIn constraint to specify exactly which row or column the buttons should be placed in. This example shows that each row or column in a Layout is actually an object of its own. Here we explicitly create an XmtLayoutBox object named "buttonbox". We set the XmtNorientation resource of that widget to specify that it is a row, not a column. In the previous example, this row was automatically created by the Row keyword in the XmtNlayout resource.

```
tutorial.xmtChildren: XmtLayout layout;
*layout.xmtChildren: XmLabel label;\
                     XmtLayoutBox buttonbox;\
                     XmPushButton okay, cancel, help;

*buttonbox.orientation: XmHORIZONTAL
*okay.layoutIn: buttonbox
*cancel.layoutIn: buttonbox
*help.layoutIn: buttonbox

*label.labelString: Hello World
```

The XmtNlayoutIn resource specifies that each of the buttons should appear in this "buttonbox" row we've created, as shown in Figure 18-3. We don't have to specify this constraint resource for the label, because the default is to place objects in the outermost column. We didn't have to specify where each of the buttons would appear in the row, because, by default, they are placed at the end of the row, and appear in the order in which they are created. We could have specified explicit positions with the XmtNlayoutPos resource, or relative positions with the XmtNlayoutAfter and XmtNlayoutBefore constraints.

Layout constraint resources are the most general way of specifying widget layouts, and are fully explained in Chapter 19, *The Layout Widget: The Details*. For the rest of this tutorial, however, we'll use the XmtNlayout grammar, because it is easier to use and understand.

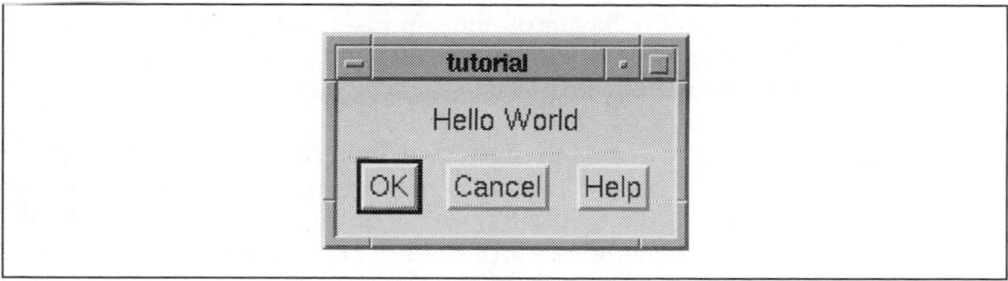

Figure 18-3. A simple layout using constraints

18.4 Stretching the Buttons

In this example, we've reverted to using the `XmtNlayout` resource, and have changed the string displayed by the label in order to make the dialog box wider. Note that the buttons in Figure 18-4 have become wider to take up the available space.

```
tutorial.xmtChildren: XmtLayout layout;
*layout.xmtChildren: XmLabel label;\
                     XmPushButton okay, cancel, help;

*layout.layout: label\
                Row { okay cancel help }

*label.labelString: Hello World.  I know you're out there somewhere...
```

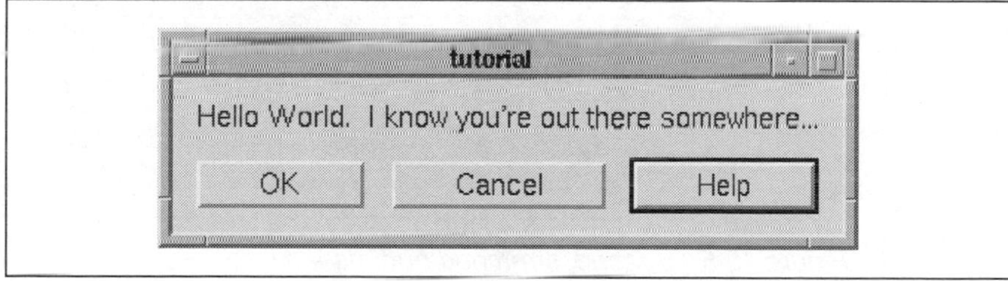

Figure 18-4. Stretched buttons

Two default behaviors of the Layout widget have combined here to produce this effect:

1. By default, items in columns are made as wide as the widest item in the column. So when the label became wider, the row of buttons also became wider to match.

2. The default behavior of items in rows is to stretch horizontally to take up all the available room in the row. So when the row was made wider, the three buttons all became wider as well.

We'll see later that both of these default behaviors can be changed—it is possible to have items in columns that are centered or left or right justified, and thus do not grow to the full width of the column. And it is possible to have items in rows that do not grow wider, or to have items that grow wider at different rates, so some become wider than others.

There is a symmetry between rows and columns, of course: by default all items in a row are made as tall as the tallest item, and by default, items in a column will stretch vertically to take up all the available space in a column.

18.5 Layout Modifiers

The last example showed how the buttons grew to take up all the space in the row. This is generally a nice behavior, but unfortunately, it results in an ugly layout—there needs to be some space between the buttons.

In this example, we use the `Even` keyword as a "modifier" for the row. This keyword indicates that the buttons should be evenly spaced. By default, when the row grows, half of the new extra space will be taken up by increasing the spacing between the buttons, and half will be taken up by increasing the size of the buttons themselves. As you can see in Figure 18-5, the row now looks far less crowded than it did in Figure 18-4.

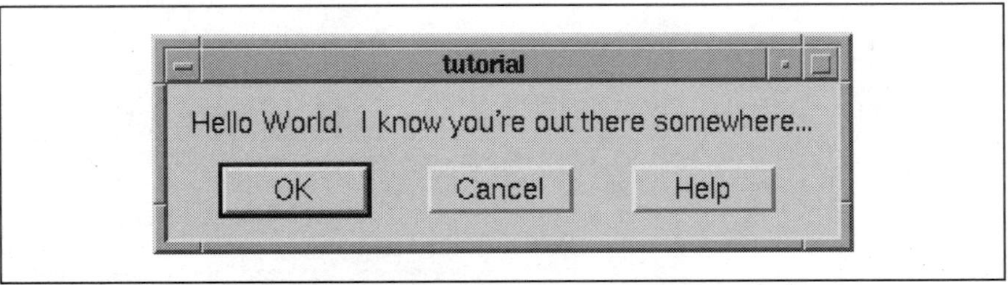

Figure 18-5. Spaced, stretched buttons

We've also used the `Equal` modifier on our row of buttons. This keyword makes all the items in the row the same width (or makes all items in a column the same height). The effect is to make the row look more uniform and less haphazard (compare this layout to the second example in this tutorial). It is particularly useful for rows of buttons like this which have labels of different lengths.

```
tutorial.xmtChildren: XmtLayout layout;
*layout.xmtChildren: XmLabel label;\
                     XmPushButton okay, cancel, help;

*layout.layout: label\
                Even Equal Row { okay cancel help }

*label.labelString: Hello World.  I know you're out there somewhere...
```

There are a number of other modifiers that we'll see. Any item in a layout can have modifiers—generally each modifier corresponds to a constraint resource that you can set on any child. The `Even` and `Equal` modifiers are two that can only be applied to rows or columns—they set resources specific to the row or column, rather than constraint resources applicable to any item.

By now, you may have noticed that the keywords in the layout grammar begin with capital letters. This is to prevent name conflicts with widgets which, by convention, have names that begin with a lowercase letter. If you actually want to name a widget `Even` or `Row`, or any of the other Layout grammar keywords, you will have to lay it out with constraint resources, instead of through the grammar.

18.6 Framing Modifiers

In this example, we add the `Shadowed` modifier to make the Layout widget draw a shadow around the row of buttons, as shown in Figure 18-6

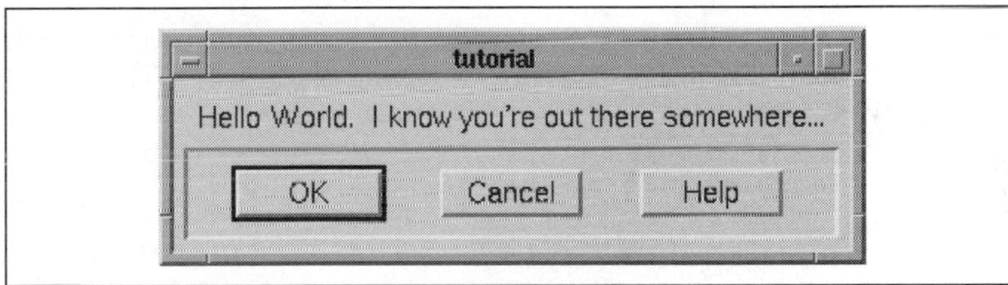

Figure 18-6. A frame

Shadows and other type of frames (shadowed in, as here, shadowed out, etched in, etched out, boxed with a single line and boxed with a double line) are specified through constraint resources, (or through keywords in the layout grammar, of course) and can be drawn around any child of a Layout widget. The Layout widget draws these frames itself, so this is significantly more efficient than using an XmFrame widget.

```
tutorial.xmtChildren: XmtLayout layout;
*layout.xmtChildren: XmLabel label;\
                     XmPushButton okay, cancel, help;

*layout.layout: label\
                Shadowed Equal Even Row { okay cancel help }

*label.labelString: Hello World.  I know you're out there somewhere...
```

The keywords that control the type of frame are `Shadowed`, `Etched`, `Boxed`, and `DoubleBoxed`. `Shadowed` and `Etched` may optionally be followed by `In` or `Out`. The default in both cases is `In`.

18.7 Partial Frames

Drawing a shadow around the row of buttons is not a very appealing look, so we change the shadowed frame to an etched frame, and instead of drawing a box all the way around the row, we draw the etched line only along the top of the row. The result is shown in Figure 18-7.

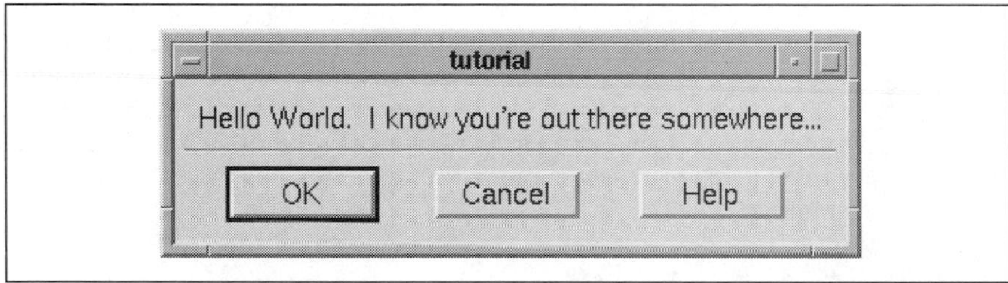

Figure 18-7. A partial frame

The `Etched` keyword specifies the type of frame; the `Top` keyword is a part of the frame specification, and can only appear directly after the frame type.

Just as a full frame is far more efficient than using an XmFrame widget, a partial frame like this is far more efficient than using an XmSeparator or an XmSeparatorGadget.

```
tutorial.xmtChildren: XmtLayout layout;
*layout.xmtChildren: XmLabel label;\
                     XmPushButton okay, cancel, help;

*layout.layout: label\
                Etched Top Equal Even Row {\
                        okay cancel help\
                }

*label.labelString: Hello World.  I know you're out there somewhere...
```

A partial frame can also be drawn on the other sides of a widget using the `Left`, `Right`, and `Bottom` keywords. But note that the frame can only appear on a single side of the widget, not on several. When drawing a partial frame like this, it does not make sense to use the `Shadowed In` and `Shadowed Out` frame types—shadows can only be drawn completely around an object. Also, for partial frames, the keywords `Line` and `DoubleLine` are more sensible synonyms for `Boxed` and `DoubleBoxed`. (i.e., `Line Top` makes more sense than `Boxed Top` does.)

18.8 Adding Some Space

Now that we have a separator between the label and the buttons, our dialog begins to look a little cramped. In Figure 18-8 you can see that we've added a little space between the label and the row of buttons.

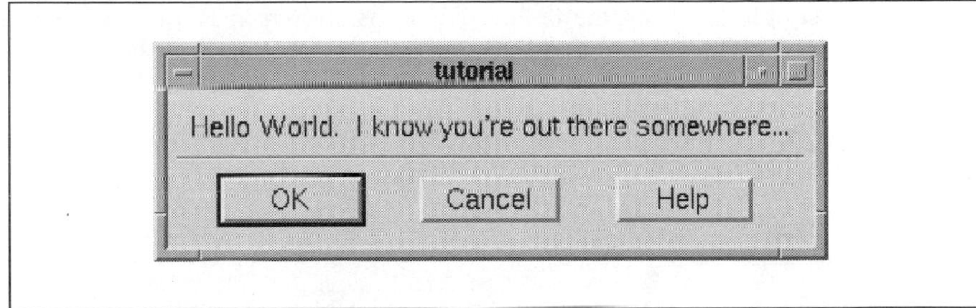

Figure 18-8. Additional space

The # character in the layout is shorthand for a unstretchable space. By default the space takes up 10 pixels in the column, though this amount can be set with the `XmtNdefaultSpacing` Layout resource.

```
tutorial.xmtChildren: XmtLayout layout;
*layout.xmtChildren: XmLabel label;\
                     XmPushButton okay, cancel, help;

*layout.layout: label\
                #\
                Etched Top Equal Even Row { \
                       okay cancel help \
                }

*label.labelString: Hello World.  I know you're out there somewhere...
```

Like other objects in the layout, this space we've added is an object in its own right. When there is an # in the layout grammar, the Layout widget will automatically create an XmtLayoutSpace object, a special, inexpensive gadget type that doesn't draw anything, but simply exists to take up space in a layout.

There are other ways to create spaces as well: ## will create a space twice as large, and ### will create one three times as large. ~ will create a small space that will grow taller (wider) if the column (row) is made taller (wider). <> will create a space that grows larger to the exclusion of all other items in a row or column.

Also, it is possible to impose a uniform sort of spacing on all items in a row or column, as we did with the `Even` keyword for the row of buttons. We'll return to this point later in the tutorial.

18.9 Oops—Checking Layout Syntax

The XmtNlayout grammar doesn't care about spaces, tabs, or newlines. For readability, however, you'll generally want to break a layout string up into a number of indented lines. When you do this, you must always remember to place a \ as the last character on a line. If you forget a backslash, as in this example, part of the layout string will not be read, and some of the items will simply be given the default layout as shown in Figure 18-9. (In this case, the default layout specifies that the widgets are placed in the outermost column in the order that they were created.)

```
tutorial.xmtChildren: XmtLayout layout;
*layout.xmtChildren: XmLabel label;\
                     XmPushButton okay, cancel, help;

*layout.layout: label\
                #\
                Etched Top Equal Even Row {
                        okay cancel help \
                }

*label.labelString: Hello World.  I know you're out there somewhere...
```

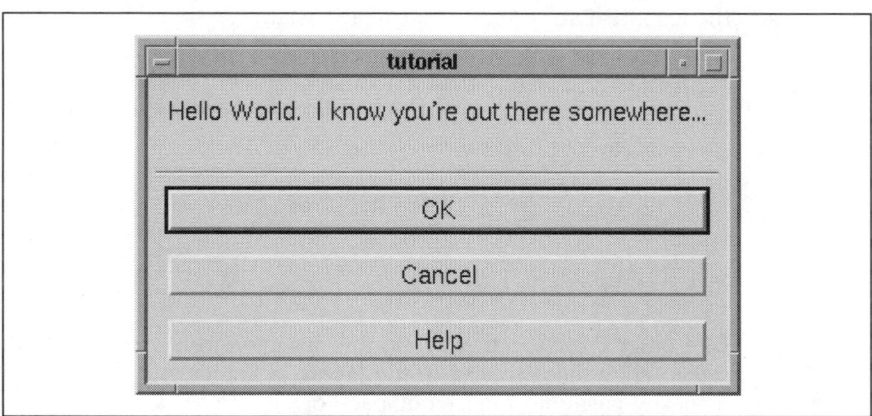

Figure 18-9. An incorrect layout

Backslashes are required as a result of the X resource file syntax—all resources are expected to be a single line, so newlines must be escaped. Forgetting to escape a newline is a very common mistake; it is important to be aware of it. In this example, the layout string is accidentally terminated without a matching } for the { at the beginning of the row, and so the layout widget issues a warning message that will help to track down the error. If the backslash were missing elsewhere, you might see an unexpected layout with no warning message issued.

Also, remember that a backslash will only escape a newline when it is the last character on the line. The *checkres* script described in Chapter 13, *Resource File Utilities: mockup, checkres, and ad2c*, will catch missing and non-terminal backslashes, and help to prevent messed-up layouts like this one.

18.10 The XmtLayoutString Gadget

Just as the Layout widget implements rows and columns with the XmtLayout-Box gadget and spaces with the XmtLayoutSpace gadget, so can it also draw strings with the XmtLayoutString gadget. Figure 18-10 shows an XmtLayout-String gadget. Because this gadget is tailored for use with the Layout widget, it is much more efficient than using an XmLabel or XmLabelGadget.

Using the XmtLayoutString gadget is also much easier than using an XmLabel. When a string appears in double quotes in the layout grammar, the Layout widget will automatically create an XmtLayoutString gadget to display the string. Thus we can simplify our code as follows:

```
tutorial.xmtChildren: XmtLayout layout;
*layout.xmtChildren: XmPushButton okay, cancel, help;

*layout.layout: "@fBHello World!"\
                #\
                Etched Top Equal Even Row { \
                        okay cancel help \
                }
```

Figure 18-10. The XmtLayoutString gadget

The XmtLayoutString gadget displays an XmString, just as an XmLabel does. This means that it can display multi-line and multi-font strings. The Layout widget converts the string you specify to an XmString using `XmtCreateXmString()`, which means you can use the Xmt `@f` syntax for changing fonts in a string. We use that syntax here to display the label in a bold font. (And we assume that the bold font is specified in an `XmFontList` elsewhere.)

18.11 Justification

As mentioned above, items in a column are, by default, made as wide as the column is. In the previous example, the "`Hello World`" label was stretched across the column, but the text itself remained left justified within that space. Compare this to the behavior of the XmLabel in the second example of this tutorial: the XmLabel widget centers its text within the available space; the XmtLayoutString gadget leaves it left-justified.

In this example, we do want the string to be centered, so we use the `Centered` keyword. The result is shown in Figure 18-11.

```
tutorial.xmtChildren: XmtLayout layout;
*layout.xmtChildren: XmPushButton okay, cancel, help;

*layout.layout: Centered "@fBHello World!"\
                #\
                Etched Top Equal Even Row { \
                        okay cancel help \
                }
```

Figure 18-11. A centered label

This modifier can be applied to any item and specifies that it should be centered horizontally in the column that contains it, or vertically centered in the row that contains it. Centered items will not be stretched; they will be left at their natural size.

18.12 More Justification

In this example, we've changed the `Centered` keyword to `FlushRight`, which will position the label flush against the right edge of its column, as shown in Figure 18-12.

```
tutorial.xmtChildren: XmtLayout layout;
*layout.xmtChildren: XmPushButton okay, cancel, help;
```

```
*layout.layout: FlushRight "@fBHello World!"\
                #\
                Etched Top Equal Even Row { \
                        okay cancel help \
                }
```

The keywords that control the justification of items are `FlushLeft` and `FlushRight` for items in columns and `FlushTop` and `FlushBottom` for items in rows. `Centered` will center an item within the width of a column or the height of a row. Also, `Filled`, the default justification, specifies that an item will be stretched to be as wide as its column or as high as its row.

Justification controls the horizontal positioning of items in columns and the vertical positioning of items in rows—that is, in the minor dimension. It may also control the size of an item in this dimension. Justification has no effect on a item's position or size in the other, major, dimension. (This distinction between the "major" and "minor" dimension of rows and columns is an important one, and will come up again.)

Figure 18-12. A right-justified label

To recap: the default justification is `Filled`—it makes an item as wide as the column it is in or as tall as the row it is in. The other kinds of justification, `Centered`, `FlushLeft`, `FlushRight`, `FlushTop`, and `FlushBottom`, do not affect an item's size in this way, but do specify its horizontal position in a column or its vertical position in a row.

18.13 Icons

Just as the XmtLayoutString gadget displays strings in an XmtLayout widget, the XmtLayoutPixmap gadget displays icons. The `Pixmap` keyword automatically creates an XmtLayoutPixmap gadget, and the following string (in double quotes) is taken as the name of the pixmap to display—it will be passed to the String-to-Pixmap converter to convert it to a pixmap. If you have called `XmtRegisterPixmapConverter()`, then the Xmt converter will be used. (See Chapter 5, *Using Icons*, for a discussion of pixmaps and bitmaps in Xmt.)

As shown in Figure 18-13, the "`Hello World`" string is now in a row with the icon, instead of an individual item in a column, its horizontal position is no longer controlled by its justification, so we have removed the `FlushRight` keyword of the last example. The row is filled from left-to-right, so the string is immediately to the right of the icon.

```
tutorial.xmtChildren: XmtLayout layout;
*layout.xmtChildren: XmPushButton okay, cancel, help;

*layout.layout: Row { Pixmap "warning" "@fBHello World!" }\
                #\
                Etched Top Equal Even Row { \
                        okay cancel help \
                }
```

Figure 18-13. The XmtLayoutPixmap gadget

The `Bitmap` keyword also automatically creates an XmtLayoutPixmap gadget. It differs from the `Pixmap` keyword, however, in that it invokes a String-to-Bitmap converter to convert the following name into a bitmap. Unlike the Motif XmLabel widget, the XmtLayoutPixmap gadget can display bitmaps that are 1-bit deep, without first converting them to pixmaps as deep as the screen. For monochrome icons displayed on color screens, using bitmaps results in a substantial savings of server resources.

18.14 Justification in Rows

As mentioned in the previous section, justification no longer controls the horizontal position of the "`Hello World`" string, because it is no longer in a column. Now that the string gadget is contained in a row, its justification controls its vertical position within the row. In this example, we use `FlushBottom` justification to align the string with the bottom of the icon. (The string "Hello World" doesn't have any descenders—if it did, the bottom of the descenders would be exactly lined up with the bottom of the icon.) We've also switched to a bigger font for the title here in Figure 18-14.

```
tutorial.xmtChildren: XmtLayout layout;
*layout.xmtChildren: XmPushButton okay, cancel, help;
```

```
*layout.layout: Row {\
                Pixmap "warning"\
                FlushBottom "@f[BIG]Hello World!"\
        }\
        #\
        Etched Top Equal Even Row { \
                okay cancel help \
        }
```

Figure 18-14. Aligning the pixmap and label vertically

This layout assumes that the icon will always be taller than the font used for the text. If the icon is the tallest item in the row (and if the row is not vertically stretched), then its justification does not matter, because it will always take up all the available vertical space. To be safer, however, we could give the icon `FlushBottom` justification as well.

18.15 Justification of Rows

The justification of the icon and label control their vertical position in the row. The justification of the row itself, however, controls the position of the row within the column. In this example, we try to position the title against the right edge of the dialog by setting the justification of the row. Unfortunately, as you can see in Figure 18-15, this moves the icon as well, which is not the effect we want.

```
tutorial.xmtChildren: XmtLayout layout;
*layout.xmtChildren: XmPushButton okay, cancel, help;

*layout.layout: FlushRight Row { \
                Pixmap "warning"\
                FlushBottom "@f[BIG]Hello World!"\
        }\
        #\
        Etched Top Equal Even Row { \
                okay cancel help \
        }
```

By default, all items, including rows, have `Filled` justification, which means that rows are stretched horizontally to be as wide as the column that contains them. When we set the justification to `FlushRight`, then the row is only as wide as it needs to be to accommodate the items within it.

Figure 18-15. Aligning the Pixmap and Label horizontally

18.16 Spacing

In this example, we use the `LREvenSpaced` keyword to achieve the effect we want: a left-justified icon and a right-justified label. The result is shown in Figure 18-16.

Figure 18-16. Spacing the Pixmap and Label

In an early example in this tutorial, we saw how the `Even` keyword applied to the button box placed an equal amount of space between items in a row, between the leftmost item and the edge of the row, and between the rightmost item and the edge. The `LREvenSpaced` keyword is similar; it places equal amounts of space between every pair of adjacent items, but does not add any space to the left of the leftmost item or the right of the rightmost item. In this case, with only two items, the keyword has the effect of placing the items at opposite ends of the row.

```
tutorial.xmtChildren: XmtLayout layout;
*layout.xmtChildren: XmPushButton okay, cancel, help;

*layout.layout: LREvenSpaced Row { \
                        Pixmap "warning"\
                        FlushBottom "@f[BIG]Hello World!"\
                }\
                #\
                Etched Top Equal Even Row { \
                        okay cancel help \
                }
```

You might want to experiment to see how the `LREvenSpaced` keyword would affect the buttonbox in this dialog when used in place of the `Even` keyword.

Spacing in columns is completely analogous to spacing in rows—it controls the vertical space between items in the column. There are other, more specialized, types of spacing besides `Even` and `LREvenSpaced` available as well; they will be introduced later. By the way, the `Even` keyword is simply a short form of the `EvenSpaced` keyword. Because `Even` spacing is used so frequently, it has this convenient abbreviation.

18.17 Stretching the Dialog

In this example, we've forced the dialog to be wider and taller than its natural size. As you can see in Figure 18-17, several things have happened.

Figure 18-17. A stretched layout

As the dialog got wider, the horizontal space between the icon and the label got larger. This is the `LREvenSpaced` keyword at work—it keeps those items left and right justified. Also, the buttons at the bottom of the dialog have all become wider, and the space between them has also grown. The fact that the buttons became wider is expected; items in a row or column are "stretchable" by default, and grow as needed to fill the row or column. The XmtLayoutString and XmtLayoutPixmap gadgets are an exception to this rule, however; they don't stretch because strings and icons can't be made any wider or taller.

```
tutorial.xmtChildren: XmtLayout layout;
tutorial.width: 275
tutorial.height: 175
*layout.xmtChildren: XmPushButton okay, cancel, help;

*layout.layout: LREvenSpaced Row { \
                        Pixmap "warning"\
                        FlushBottom "@f[BIG]Hello World!"\
                }\
                #\
                Etched Top Equal Even Row { \
                        okay cancel help \
                }
```

The dialog handled its new width nicely. Its new height is more problematical, however. Items in a column, including rows, are also, by default, "stretchable." As the column gets taller, its contents, our two rows, in this case, also become taller. All the buttons have `Filled` justification, so as the button box is made taller, they are stretched vertically to be as tall as the row that contains them. In the top row, the label has `FlushBottom` justification, so it is placed against the bottom of the row. The icon has `Filled` justification, which means that it is made as tall as the row. But since the pixmap image itself cannot be made any taller, the XmtLayoutPixmap displays the image in the upper-left corner of the space available to it.

18.18 Non-stretchable Rows

In the previous example, the buttons were made too tall when the row that contained them was stretched vertically (and it was stretched vertically to occupy the extra space created by making the dialog as a whole larger). One workaround to this problem would be to set the justification of each of the buttons to `FlushBottom`, so that they will remain at their natural height along the bottom of the row. But this wouldn't be quite right—the row would still become taller, and the frame drawn above it as a separator would be far away from the buttons.

Instead, what we want to do is to stop the row from becoming any taller when the dialog is stretched. We can do this with the `Fixed` modifier, which we've applied to both rows in this example. The result is displayed in Figure 18-18.

```
tutorial.xmtChildren: XmtLayout layout;
tutorial.width: 275
tutorial.height: 175
*layout.xmtChildren: XmPushButton okay, cancel, help;

*layout.layout: Fixed LREvenSpaced Row { \
                        Pixmap "warning"\
                        FlushBottom "@f[BIG]Hello World!"\
                }\
                #\
```

```
Fixed Etched Top Equal Even Row { \
        okay cancel help \
}
```

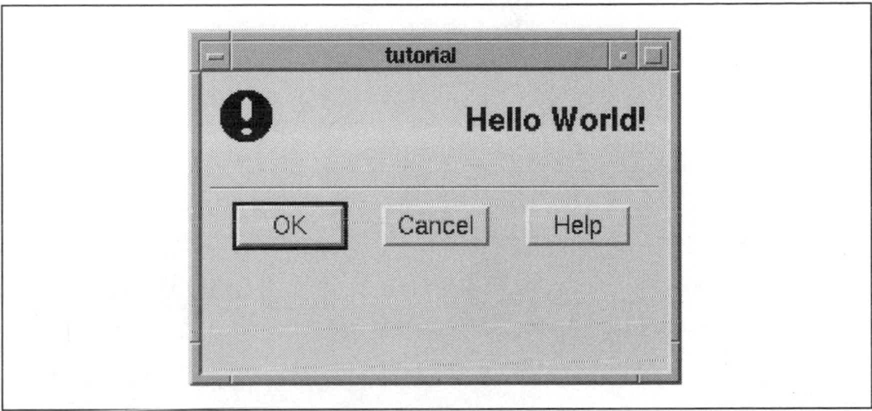

Figure 18-18. Nonstretchable rows

By default, all widgets, rows, and columns have a "stretchability" which controls how they are resized when they are within a row or a column that is larger than its natural width or height. The **Fixed** keyword is a convenient way to set the stretchability of any item to 0—to make it non-stretchable. To see how the **Fixed** keyword applied to items in rows, instead of columns, as shown here, try applying it to the **OK** button. If you do this, though, first remove the **Equal** modifier from the row that contains the buttons.

18.19 Stretchable Space

In the previous example, the outermost column of the layout contained a non-stretchy row, a space, and another non-stretchy row. The space was automatically created with the special # character, which is shorthand for a non-stretchy space. We forced the column to become taller than it needed to be, but since none of the items in this column were stretchable, the extra space was just added at the bottom of the column. The result was not quite what we'd like—rows of buttons are conventionally at the very bottom of dialog boxes, and all that extra space down there looks bad.

In this example, as shown in Figure 18-19, we've converted the space into a stretchy one, so that as the column is made taller, the space will stretch to take up the new pixels. We've made this change by converting the # character into the <> string (it looks something like an arrow).

```
tutorial.xmtChildren: XmtLayout layout;
tutorial.width: 275
tutorial.height: 175
```

```
*layout.xmtChildren: XmPushButton okay, cancel, help;

*layout.layout: Fixed LREvenSpaced Row { \
                        Pixmap "warning"\
                        FlushBottom "@f[BIG]Hello World!"\
                }\
                <>\
                Fixed Etched Top Equal Even Row { \
                        okay cancel help \
                }
```

Figure 18-19. Stretchable space

In this case, there is only one stretchy item in the column, so all the extra space goes to it. When there is more than one stretchy item, the extra space is distributed to them depending on how stretchy they are. The <> keyword actually creates a space with a stretchiness that is effectively infinite, so that all the extra space goes to it, regardless of other stretchy items in the column or row. This means that we could safely remove the `Fixed` keywords from the two rows in the layout. We'd then have three stretchy items, but the space would still do all the stretching. To create a space that is stretchy, but not infinitely stretchy, you can use `~`. If the top and bottom rows were `Fixed`, then this ~ space would be the only stretchy item and would have the same effect as a <> space. On the other hand, if the rows were not `Fixed`, then both rows and the ~ space would be stretchy, and all would grow.

If you remember how we used the `LREvenSpaced` keyword several examples ago, you might have realized that we could use it here to force the top row to always be against the top of the dialog and the bottom row to always be against the bottom. This would work, but unfortunately, the XmtLayout grammar does not provide a way to apply modifiers like `LREvenSpaced` to the outermost column (which is automatically created by the Layout widget), so instead we must arrange the spacing for the column by adding explicit spaces to the layout. (Explicit spaces like these are implemented with the XmtLayoutSpace gadget, by the way—it does nothing other than take up space. Spaces created by the `Even` and `LREvenSpaced` keywords are not objects themselves, so these keywords are more efficient.)

18.20 Captions

In Figure 18-20, we've added a number of new widgets to the dialog. Dialog boxes often serve to get input from the user, and widgets that request input often need some kind of caption to prompt the user for the type of input required. In this example we use the `Caption` keyword to specify such a caption for each of our new XmtInputField widgets. (The XmtInputField widget is a subclass of XmText that will be introduced in Chapter 28, *The Input Field Widget*.)

```
tutorial.xmtChildren: XmtLayou layout;

*layout.xmtChildren:     XmtInputField fname, lname, phone;\
                         XmPushButton okay, cancel, help;

*layout.layout: Fixed LREvenSpaced Row { \
                         Pixmap "warning"\
                         FlushBottom "@f[BIG]Hello World!"\
                 }\
                 Caption "First name:" fname \
                 Caption "Last name:" lname \
                 Caption "Phone number:" phone \
                 <>\
                 Fixed Etched Top Equal Even Row { \
                         okay cancel help \
                 }
```

Figure 18-20. Captioned widgets

The XmtLayout widget can display a caption for any of its children. Like frames, captions are specified entirely through constraint resources, and are not created as separate objects, as XmtLayoutString gadgets are. By default, captions are displayed to the left of an item, but there are other options as well, as we will see in a later example.

18.21 Lining Up Captioned Widgets

When you have a column of XmtInputField or similar widgets, you generally want them to line up with one another. If the widgets are all the same width, then this is easy. When the widgets have captions, as in the last example, however, then lining them up is a little tricky, because the captions will never have exactly the same widths. The trick is to make the widgets right-justified in their column, as shown in Figure 18-21.

The caption is treated as part of the widget, and will be right-justified along with it. The result is a pleasing alignment of widgets and captions, as you see here.

```
tutorial.xmtChildren: XmtLayout layout;

*layout.xmtChildren:     XmtInputField fname, lname, phone;\
                         XmPushButton okay, cancel, help;

*layout.layout: Line Bottom 0 4 Fixed LREvenSpaced Row { \
                         Pixmap "warning"\
                         FlushBottom "@f[BIG]Hello World!"\
                }\
                FlushRight Caption "First name:" fname \
                FlushRight Caption "Last name:" lname \
                FlushRight Caption "Phone number:" phone \
                <>\
                Fixed Etched Top Equal Even Row { \
                         okay cancel help \
                }
```

In this example we've also added a separator between the title and the input fields to keep those parts of the dialog separate. This is done in the same way that we added the separator at the bottom of the dialog—by drawing a partial frame around the row that contains the title and the icon. Instead of using the `Etched Top` keywords to draw an etched line above the row, however, we use the `Line Bottom` keywords to draw a solid line. The following two digits, "`0 4`," are optional and specify the margin between the row and the line, and the width of the line, both in pixels.

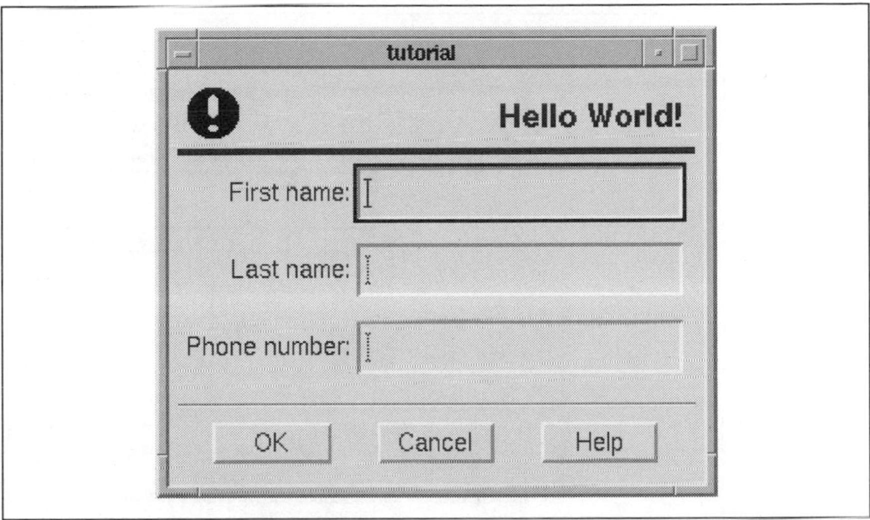

Figure 18-21. Aligning captions

18.22 Caption Fonts and Sensitivity

In this example, we change the captions to an italic typeface, as you can see in Figure 18-22. Captions are displayed using ordinary XmStrings, automatically created with `XmtCreateXmString()` so their typefaces can be set using the standard Xmt `@f` syntax.

```
tutorial.xmtChildren: XmtLayout layout;

*phone.layoutSensitive: False
*phone.sensitive: False

*layout.xmtChildren:    XmtInputField fname, lname, phone;\
                        XmPushButton okay, cancel, help;

*layout.layout: Line Bottom 0 4 Fixed LREvenSpaced Row { \
                        Pixmap "warning"\
                        FlushBottom "@f[BIG]Hello World!"\
                }\
                FlushRight Caption "@fIFirst name:" fname \
                FlushRight Caption "@fILast name:" lname \
                FlushRight Caption "@fIPhone number:" phone \
                <>\
                Fixed Etched Top Equal Even Row { \
                        okay cancel help \
                }
```

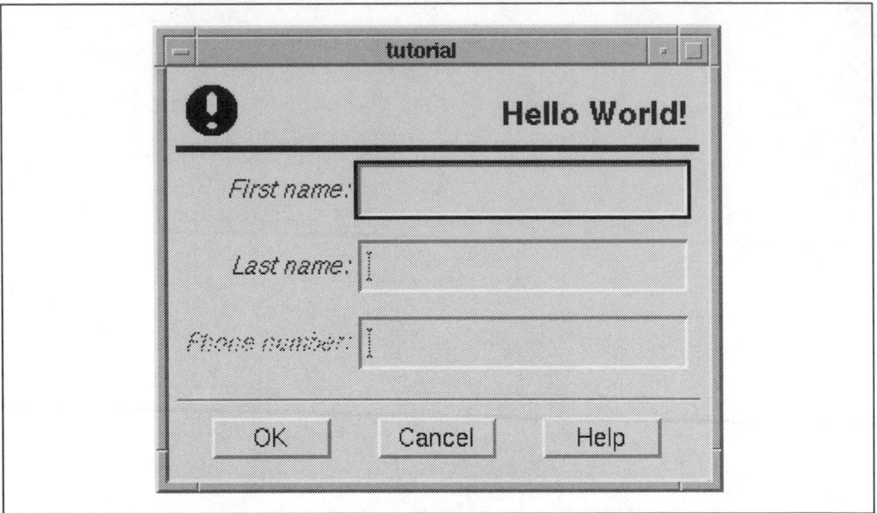

Figure 18-22. Specifying caption fonts and sensitivity

This example also demonstrates that captions can be "grayed out" when the widget they label is insensitive. This cannot be controlled directly through the layout grammar (the grammar specifies a static layout; sensitivity is an attribute that changes dynamically) but we demonstrate it here by setting the `XmtNlayoutSensitive` constraint resource of one of the input fields to `False`. Note that this constraint only controls how the caption is drawn; we also have to set the standard `XtNsensitive` resource (or call `XtSetSensitive()`) to control the sensitivity of the widget itself.

18.23 Combining Frames and Captions

Here we've changed the title and icon at the top of the dialog, and added an XmtChooser widget to the layout—our example is turning into a fairly sophisticated dialog box shown in Figure 18-23. (The XmtChooser widget presents choices of items in a number of formats—it is introduced in Chapter 27, *Presenting Choices*.) One point to note about this layout is that we now have a column inside a row inside the outermost column. Remember that rows and columns can be nested to any depth you need.

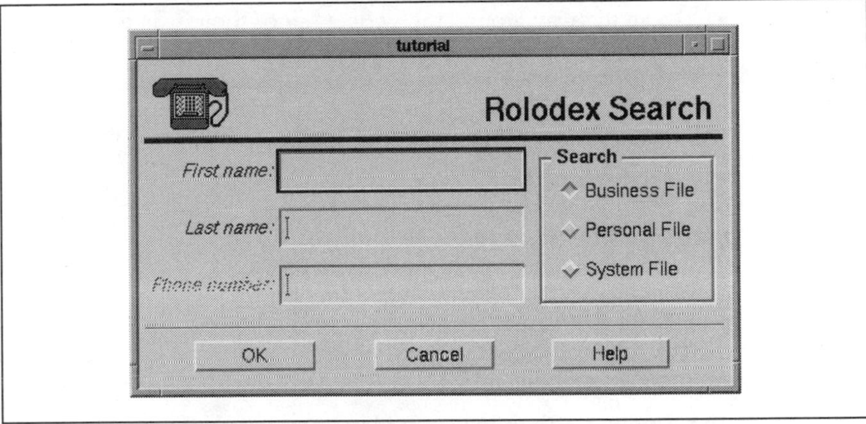

Figure 18-23. Captions and frames

The main point of interest in this example, though, is the interaction between the frame and caption around the new XmtChooser widget.

```
tutorial.xmtChildren: XmtLayout layout;

*phone.layoutSensitive: False
*phone.sensitive: False

*layout.xmtChildren:    XmtInputField fname, lname, phone;\
                        XmtChooser chooser;\
                        XmPushButton okay, cancel, help;

*layout.layout: Line Bottom 0 4 Fixed LREvenSpaced Row { \
                        Bitmap "phone"\
                        FlushBottom "@f[HUGE]Rolodex Search"\
                }\
                Row {\
                        Col {\
                                FlushRight Caption "@fIFirst name:" fname \
                                FlushRight Caption "@fILast name:" lname \
                                FlushRight Caption "@fIPhone number:" phone \
                        }\
                        Etched Through 6 4 Caption tll "@fB Search " chooser\
                }\
                <>\
                Fixed Etched Top Equal Even Row { \
                        okay cancel help \
                }

*chooser.strings: "Business File", "Personal File", "System File"
```

The frame is specified with the string "`Etched Through 6 4`" which means that the frame should:

- Use etched lines

- Go all the way around the widget (since there was no `Bottom`, `Top`, `Left`, or `Right` keyword)
- Pass through the caption
- Have a 6-pixel margin between itself and the item it surrounds
- Be 4 pixels wide

Instead of the `Through` keyword, we could also use `Inside` which would draw the frame inside the caption, or `Outside`, which would draw the frame outside the caption. Overlapping a frame with a caption can produce a pleasing visual effect, and also serves to group and title a set of related widgets. Note that we placed a space at the beginning and end of the caption string in this example, so that the lines of the frame did not abut the text too closely.

The caption for the Chooser widget is on top of the widget, instead of the left, as is the default. We did this by placing the string `tll` after the `Caption` keyword. The `Caption` keyword may be followed by zero to three letters:

- The first letter specifies which edge the caption should appear against: 'l' is the left, 't' is the top, and 'r' and 'b' are the right and bottom. The default edge is the left.
- The second optional letter specifies the justification of that caption along that edge: 'l' is left, 'c' is centered, and 'r' is right. The default justification is centered. For captions along the left and right edges, the justification controls the vertical position of the caption, and you can also use the letters 't' and 'b' for top and bottom justification.
- Finally, the third optional letter specifies the alignment of the caption. The alignment only matters for captions that have more than one line (create a multi-line caption simply by embedding a `\n` in it). Since the lines of a multi-line caption will not be exactly the same length, the alignment specifies how the individual lines should be justified within the bounding box of the entire caption. 'l' specifies left alignment, 'c' specifies center alignment, and 'r' specifies right alignment.

18.24 Debugging a Layout

When a layout gets complicated, as this one is beginning to, it is easy to become confused. Sometimes the layout doesn't look as you expect it to, and you can't figure out why. In this example, we've set the `XmtNdebugLayout` resource of the Layout widget to `True`, in order to help us understand how everything is laid out. What this resource does is to draw a box around every item in the layout, including spaces, rows, and columns (see Figure 18-24). By studying these boxes, it is possible to figure out just which row or column contains each item in the layout.

```
*layout.debugLayout: True
```

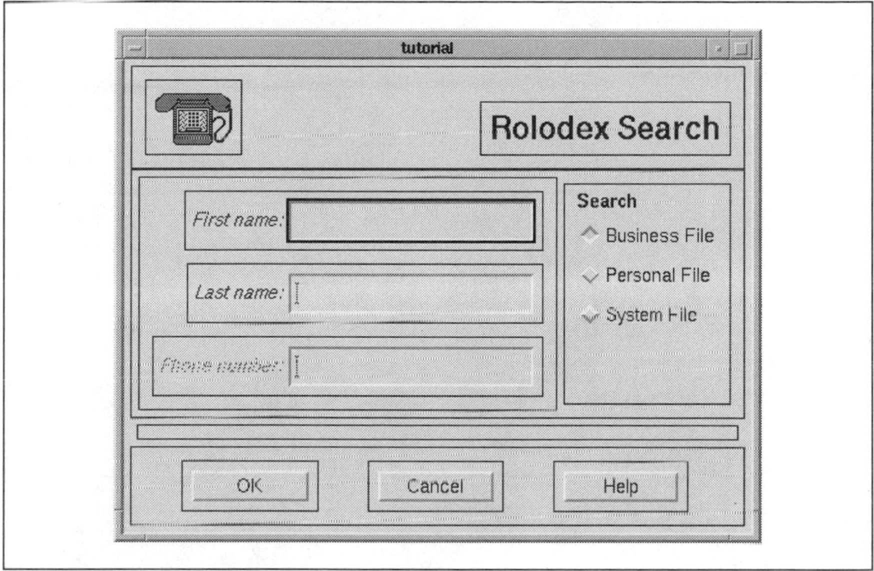

Figure 18-24. Debugging a layout

(Our example code has become quite long. In this and the remaining sections of the tutorial, we'll only show the lines of the resource file that have changed from the previous example.)

Note that the boxes drawn when `XmtNdebugLayout` is `True` take the place of any frames that are ordinarily drawn. So the new frame we added around the Chooser widget, and the two separators that were implemented as partial frames do not appear in this example.

18.25 Automatically Creating Children

This example shows off another trick of the XmtLayout grammar—you can use it to specify the names and types of children to be automatically created. Previously, the **Okay**, **Cancel**, and **Help** push buttons were specified in the `xmtChildren` resource of the layout widget, and were automatically created by a call to `XmtCreateChildren()`, `XmtBuildQueryDialog()`, or some similar function. In this example, we've removed those widgets from the `xmtChildren` resource and now specify their types directly in the layout grammar. These children will now be automatically created by the Layout widget itself when it parses the layout grammar. The result is shown in Figure 18-25.

```
Fixed Etched Top Equal Even Row { \
      XmPushButton okay\
      XmPushButton cancel\
      XmPushButton help\
}
```

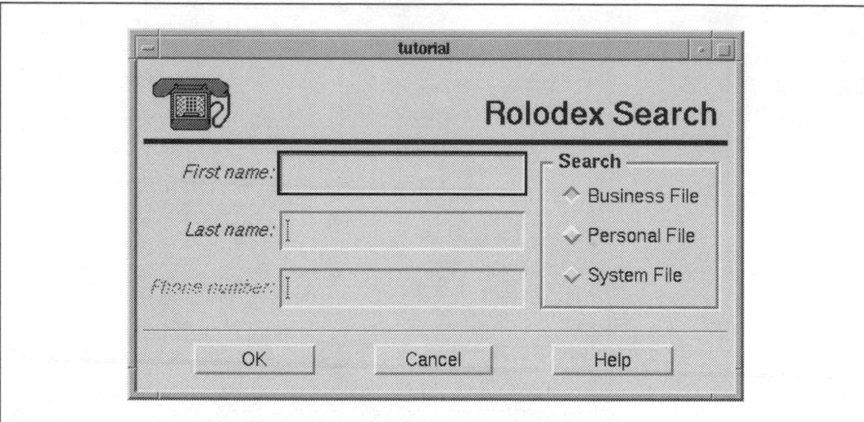

Figure 18-25. Automatically created children

This technique will work in any resource file you use with the *mockup* client. If you want to use it in your own programs, however, you must call the function `XmtRegisterLayoutCreateMethod()`. This automatic creation ability is not automatically built in so that the Layout widget does not automatically link in all the Xmt widget creation functions.

It is also worth noting that the layout grammar will also work with widgets you create from your C code—there is no requirement that the widgets must be specified in the resource file.

18.26 Specifying Sizes and Resolution Independence

The Layout widget has constraints for each child that allow you to specify an explicit width and height for the child, to be used instead of the child's own preferred size. The layout grammar lets you specify sizes for any item (including spaces, rows and columns) and also allows you to specify the sizes using resolution-independent units.

In this example, we've added this string "`1.5 in`" as a modifier to each of the XmtInputField widgets. Note that this only affects the size of the widget, not the combined size of the widget and its caption, as shown in Figure 18-26.

```
Row {\
        Col {\
            1.5 in FlushRight Caption "@fIFirst name:" fname \
            1.5 in FlushRight Caption "@fILast name:" lname \
            1.5 in FlushRight Caption "@fIPhone number:" phone\
        }\
        Etched Through 6 4 Caption tll "@fB Search " chooser\
}\
```

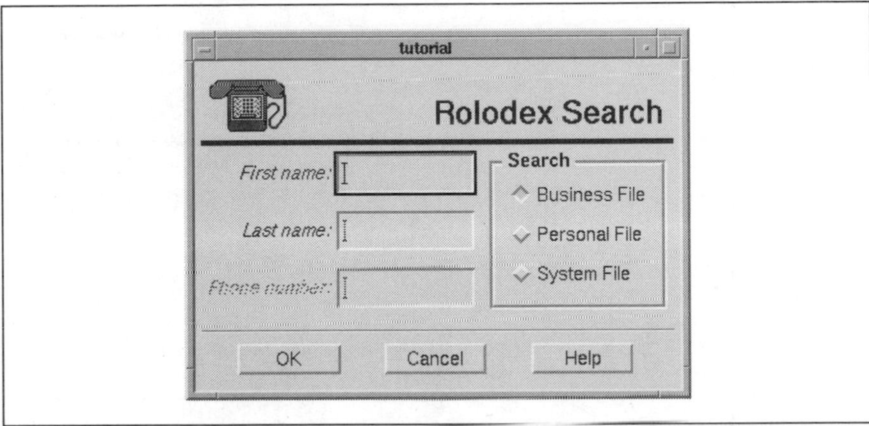

Figure 18-26. Resolution-independent sizes

If just one dimension is specified, as in this example, it is taken to be the width of the item. To explicitly specify the width and/or the height of an item, you can use the `Wide` and `High` keywords: "`25 mm High 1 in Wide`", for example.

The unit specification is optional; if no units are specified, then the numbers are taken to be in pixels. The supported units are inches (`in`), millimeters (`mm`), printer's points (`pt`), ems (`em`) and ens (`en`). A printer's point is 1/72nd of an inch. Ems and ens are units sometimes used in typography—instead of being an absolute unit of measurement, they are relative to the size of a font. An em is the width of the capital letter 'M' in the default font of the Layout widget's `XmtNfontList`, and en is half that width. Note that these unit specification keywords are the only keywords in the layout grammar that do not begin with a capital letter. If you name a child of a Layout widget "`in`", "`mm`", "`pt`", "`em`", or "`en`", then you will have to use constraint resources to lay out that child—the layout parser will think the child name is a unit specification, and will not correctly parse it.

18.27 Color

The XmtLayoutString and XmtLayoutPixmap gadgets both have a `XmtNforeground` resource. The layout grammar lets you specify a value for this resource with the `Color` keyword, as we've done here for the dialog title and icon. The result is shown in Figure 18-27, although it really doesn't look different from the previous dialog, since this book is printed in black and white. You should notice a difference in gray scale, however.

```
*layout.layout: Line Bottom 0 4 Fixed LREvenSpaced Row { \
                        Color "maroon" Bitmap "phone"\
                        Color "maroon" FlushBottom "@f[HUGE]Rolodex Search"\
                }\
```

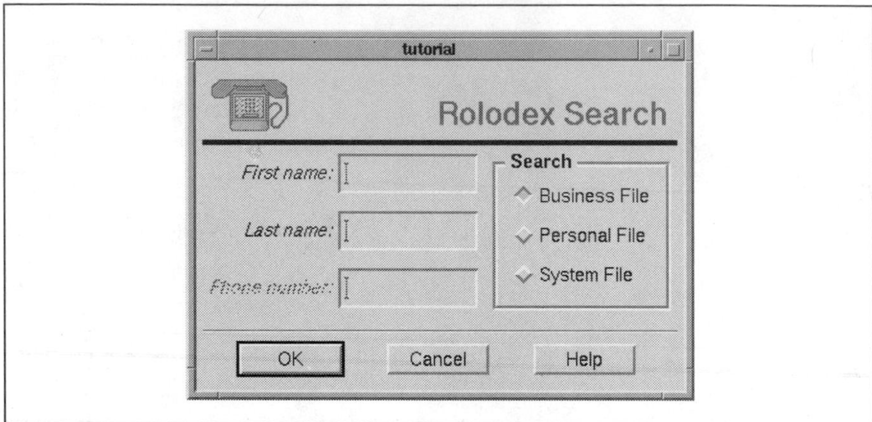

Figure 18-27. Using color

Note that captions are not objects in their own right, and they do not have a foreground color that can be set. Also, note, that the `XmtNforeground` resource of the XmtLayoutPixmap gadget is only used when it is displaying a bitmap. Pixmap data has its colors already coded in, so using the `Color` keyword with the `Pixmap` keyword does not make sense.

19

The Layout Widget: The Details

The previous tutorial chapter showed just how flexible and easy to use the Xmt-Layout widget can be. It explained the basic features of the widget, and showed some cookbook-style examples of how to handle common layout situations. In order to figure out how to handle uncommon layout situations, however, you'll need to understand the Layout widget in more detail. This chapter explains exactly how the Layout widget arranges its children and how it resizes its children when necessary. It also explains captions, frames, gadgets, and the other features of the widget.

While the tutorial focused on explaining features of the layout grammar, this chapter starts by explaining the widget in terms of the underlying constraint resources that define its behavior. Once all the constraints have been documented, a later section of the chapter documents the grammar more formally.

19.1 Creating a Layout Widget

The XmtLayout widget is a subclass of XmBulletinBoard. Its class name is "XmtLayout," and its class structure is `xmtLayoutWidgetClass`.

You can create a Layout widget with the constructor `XmtCreateLayout()`, or create it as a child of an XmDialogShell with XmtCreateLayoutDialog:

Xmt/

Layout.c

```
#include <Xmt/Layout.h>
Widget XmtCreateLayout(Widget parent, String name,
                       ArgList args, Cardinal n)
Widget XmtCreateLayoutDialog(Widget parent, String name,
                             ArgList al, Cardinal ac)
```

Hope for the XmForm Widget?

contrib/

xm_attach/

The XmtLayout widget is almost always more useful than the Motif XmForm widget. If you have to use the XmForm widget for some reason, however, Jonathon Ross has written a utility that makes it much more pleasant to use. His convenience function `xm_attach()` *provides an elegant and compact way to set all of the XmForm constraint attachment resources for any child of the form widget. From his* README *file:*

`xm_attach()` permits specification of XmForm child attachments in a simple and concise manner.

```
xm_attach (Widget w, char *where, ...)
```

w is a child of the XmForm. *where* is a four-character string specifying the top, left, right, and bottom attachments, in that order. Each character determines the attach type and subsequent args read, as follows (all non-widget args are integers):

Character	Attachment Type	Arguments
n	XmATTACH_NONE	None
f	XmATTACH_FORM	Offset
F	XmATTACH_OPPOSITE_FORM	Offset
w	XmATTACH_WIDGET	Widget, Offset
W	XmATTACH_OPPOSITE_WIDGET	Widget, Offset
p	XmATTACH_POSITION	Position
s	XmATTACH_SELF	None
-	Do not attach this side	None

For example:

```
xm_attach(button1, "fnwp", 5, button2, 5, 20);
```

is equivalent to the following mess:

```
XtVaSetValues(button1,
            XmNtopAttachment, XmATTACH_FORM,
            XmNtopOffset, 5,
            XmNleftAttachment, XmATTACH_NONE,
            XmNrightAttachment, XmATTACH_WIDGET,
            XmNrightOffset, 5,
            XmNrightWidget, button2,
            XmNbottomAttachment, XmATTACH_POSITION,
            XmNbottomPosition, 20,
            NULL);
```

—Jonathon Ross

19.2 Positioning Children of the Layout

The Layout widget lays children out in nested rows and columns. Every child of the Layout widget, including the rows and columns themselves, is positioned in a row or a column. The following subsections explain:

- How to specify which row or column a child is positioned in, and how to specify the order of children within a row or column.
- How to specify the spacing of items in a row or column, thereby controlling the horizontal position of children in rows and the vertical position of children in columns.
- How to set the justification of items in rows or columns, thereby controlling the vertical position of children in rows and the horizontal position of children in columns.

19.2.1 Layout in Rows and Columns

Rows and columns in a Layout widget are themselves children of the Layout widget, and are implemented with the XmtLayoutBox gadget. The Layout widget and the LayoutBox gadget work together closely, and much of the important layout functionality of the Layout widget is in fact implemented by the LayoutBox. You can create a LayoutBox with `XmtCreateLayoutBox()`, or with the convenience functions `XmtCreateLayoutRow()` and `XmtCreateLayoutCol()`, which set the `XmtNorientation` resource for you:

```
#include <Xmt/LayoutG.h>
Widget XmtCreateLayoutBox(Widget parent, String name,
                          ArgList args, Cardinal num_args);
Widget XmtCreateLayoutRow(Widget parent, String name,
                          ArgList args, Cardinal num_args);
Widget XmtCreateLayoutCol(Widget parent, String name,
                          ArgList args, Cardinal num_args);
```

We've said that the Layout widget arranges its children into "nested rows and columns," and, in fact, you could achieve similar results using nested XmRowColumn widgets. With this XmRowColumn approach, *nested* means that the widgets in the innermost XmRowColumn would be children and grandchildren of other XmRowColumn widgets in the layout. With the Layout widget, by contrast, all widgets to be laid out, including the rows and columns, are direct children of the Layout widget. So when we talk about nested rows and columns, we mean "nested" in the geometrical sense only—a row (or other object) must fall entirely within the column that contains it, for example. And when we say that a widget is "in" a row or column, we again mean that only in a geometrical sense—the widget is not a child of the row or the column, but it is entirely contained within the bounding box of the row or column.

It is important to understand this distinction between the traditional parent/child widget hierarchy, and the additional container/contained geometrical hierarchy that the Layout widget imposes upon its children. Figure 19-1 illustrates this distinction for a simple layout.

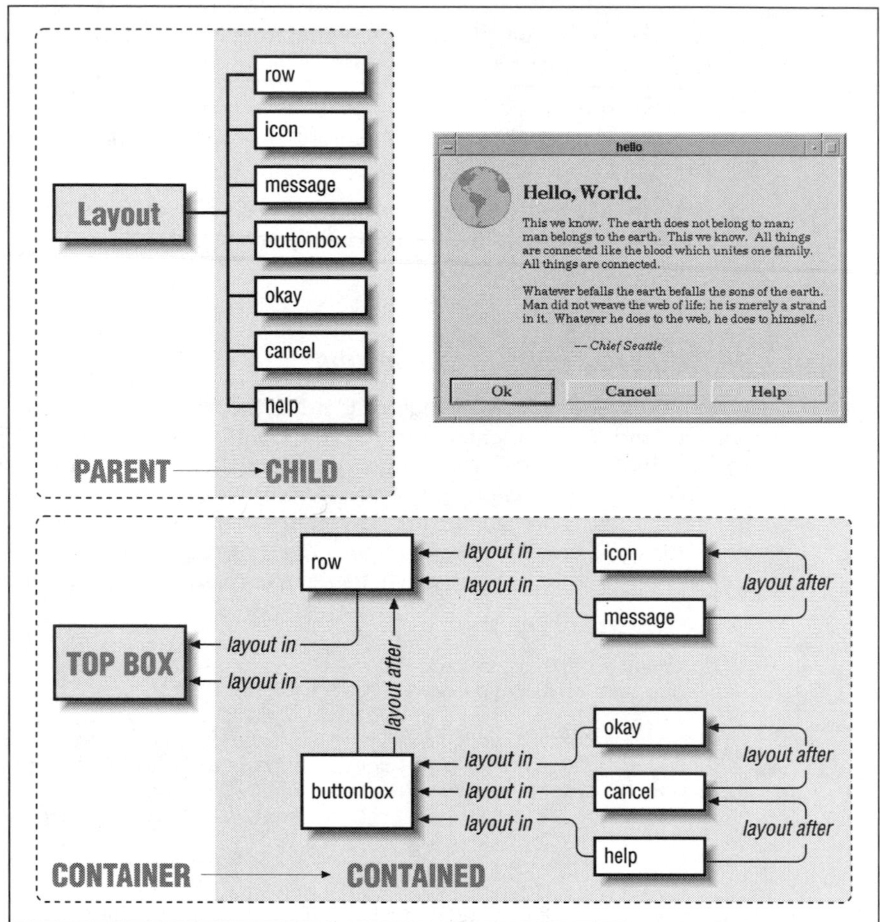

Figure 19-1. The Parent/child and Container/contained hierarchies in the Layout widget

An important point to note about the container/contained hierarchy in the Layout widget is that its root is a row or column (a LayoutBox gadget) automatically created by the Layout widget. This automatically created LayoutBox will be a column if the `XmtNorientation` resource of the Layout widget is `XmHORIZONTAL` (the default), or a row if the resource is set to `XmVERTICAL`.

To specify the row or column that a widget should be placed in, set the `XmtNlayoutIn` constraint resource for the widget to the appropriate LayoutBox gadget. If you leave this constraint unset, or set it to `NULL`, the widget will be placed in the automatically created row or column that is the hierarchy's root.

To specify the position of a widget within a row or column, set the `XmtNlayoutPosition` constraint. This resource specifies only the order of the children within the row or column, *not* their pixel position—if you set `XmtNlayoutPosition` to 0, the child will be the first item in its row or column; if you set it to 2, it will be the third item. The default value for this constraint is -1, a special value that will position the child as the last item in the row or column. Notice that the default values for the `XmtNlayoutIn` and `XmtNlayoutPosition` constraints are such that, if neither is set, the Layout widget will act like an XmRowColumn widget—children will be added at the end of a row or a column, depending on the value of the `XmtNorientation` resource.

You can also specify a container and position for a child by setting the `XmtNlayoutAfter` or `XmtNlayoutBefore` constraint resources. Set the `XmtNlayoutAfter` constraint to any other child of the Layout widget; this will place your widget in the same row or column as that child, at the position immediately following that child. Similarly, you can set `XmtNlayoutBefore` to position your widget before any other child of the Layout. Setting either of these constraints will update the `XmtNlayoutIn` and `XmtNlayoutPosition` constraints appropriately and setting `XmtNlayoutIn` and `XmtNlayoutPosition` will also set `XmtNlayoutAfter` and `XmtNlayoutBefore`. As you can see in Figure 19-1, the `XmtNlayoutAfter` and `XmtNlayoutBefore` constraints form a kind of doubly-linked list. Given a child of a Layout widget, you can obtain a pointer to the widget before or after it in the same row or column by querying these constraints.

Example 19-1 shows a resource file you could use with *mockup* to create the layout shown in Figure 19-1. While this layout could easily be specified with the layout grammar and the `XmtNlayout` resource, this example explicitly creates the necessary LayoutBox gadgets, and then uses `XmtNlayoutIn` and other constraint resources to position children with these boxes. Notice that the order in which the children are created is important—the LayoutBox containers must be created before items can be positioned within them, for example, and a widget must be created before another widget can be positioned after it with the `XmtNlayoutAfter` constraint. Example 19-2 shows a significantly longer resource file you could use to create the same layout with the Motif XmForm widget. Notice how cumbersome the XmForm "attachment" constraints become in this example.

Example 19-1. Placing Widgets in Rows and Columns

examples/

19/hello

```
!!
!! specify the widgets to be created in this example.
!!
hello.xmtChildren: XmtLayout layout;
*layout.xmtChildren: \
        XmtLayoutBox row, buttonbox;\
```

Example 19-1. Placing Widgets in Rows and Columns (continued)

```
        XmtLayoutPixmap icon;\
        XmtLayoutString  message;\
        XmPushButton okay, cancel, help;

!!
!! and put them in the appropriate rows.
!!
*icon.layoutIn: row
*message.layoutIn: row
*okay.layoutIn: buttonbox
*cancel.layoutAfter: okay
*help.layoutAfter: cancel
```

Example 19-2. The Same Layout with an XmForm Widget

examples/

19/form

```
!!
!! specify the widgets to be created in this example.
!!
form.xmtChildren: XmForm layout;
*layout.xmtChildren: \
        XmLabel icon, message;\
        XmPushButton okay, cancel, help;

!!
!! Set default spacing between items
!!
*layout.horizontalSpacing: 10
*layout.verticalSpacing: 10

!!
!! And set form constraints to lay out each item
!!
*icon.topAttachment: XmATTACH_FORM
*icon.leftAttachment: XmATTACH_FORM

*message.topAttachment: XmATTACH_FORM
*message.topOffset: 35
*message.leftAttachment: XmATTACH_WIDGET
*message.leftWidget: icon
*message.rightAttachment: XmATTACH_FORM

*okay.topAttachment: XmATTACH_WIDGET
*okay.topWidget: icon
*okay.bottomAttachment: XmATTACH_FORM
*okay.leftAttachment: XmATTACH_POSITION
*okay.leftPosition: 6
*okay.rightAttachment: XmATTACH_POSITION
*okay.rightPosition: 31

*cancel.topAttachment: XmATTACH_WIDGET
*cancel.topWidget: icon
*cancel.bottomAttachment: XmATTACH_FORM
*cancel.leftAttachment: XmATTACH_POSITION
*cancel.leftPosition: 37
*cancel.rightAttachment: XmATTACH_POSITION
*cancel.rightPosition: 62
```

Example 19-2. The Same Layout with an XmForm Widget (continued)

```
*help.topAttachment: XmATTACH_WIDGET
*help.topWidget: icon
*help.bottomAttachment: XmATTACH_FORM
*help.leftAttachment: XmATTACH_POSITION
*help.leftPosition: 68
*help.rightAttachment: XmATTACH_POSITION
*help.rightPosition: 93
```

19.2.2 Spacing Within a Row or Column

The `XmtNlayoutPosition`, `XmtNlayoutBefore`, and `XmtNlayoutAfter` constraints specify only the order of items within a row or column, not the actual pixel positioning of those items in the box. In fact, the Layout widget does not allow you to explicitly specify pixel positions for its children—layouts using explicit pixel positions are not a good idea, because things like font sizes can vary from server to server. This can throw off the explicit pixel values.

Items in a row are laid out horizontally, in their specified order, from left to right, and items in a column are laid out vertically, from top to bottom. The positions at which they appear on the screen depend on the other items in the row or column, and on the amount of space between those items. The `XmtNspaceType` resource of the row or column specifies how space will be allocated horizontally between the items in a row, or how space will be allocated vertically between the items in a column. There are two important points to notice here. First, the `XmtNspaceType` resource is not a resource to be set on the Layout widget, nor is it a constraint resource to be set on a child of that widget; it is a resource of the LayoutBox gadget, and can only be set on a row or column. And second, the `XmtNspaceType` resource controls the position of items along the *major* dimension of a row or column—horizontally in a row or vertically in a column. The position of items in the other dimension, the *minor* dimension, is controlled by the justification of the individual items, and will be discussed in the next section.

The values of the `XmtNspaceType` resource, and their effects, are described in the following paragraphs. Figure 19-2 shows a row of buttons laid out with each of these types of spacing. For simplicity the descriptions below only explain spacing in rows. Spacing in columns is analogous.

`XmtLayoutSpaceNone`
: This is the default value of the `XmtNspaceType` resource. With this spacing model, no extra space is added between items in a row; items (and their captions and frames, if any) are positioned side by side, separated only by the margins specified with the `XmtNlayoutMarginWidth` resource.

`XmtLayoutSpaceEven`
: This spacing model positions the items in a row evenly by inserting `XmtNspace` pixels of space before the first item, after the last item, and between any two adjacent items. This spacing model is a commonly used one, and is convenient for things like the button boxes that appear at the

bottom of dialogs. Like the `XmtNspaceType` resource, `XmtNspace` is a resource of the LayoutBox gadget, not a resource to be set on the Layout, nor a constraint to be set on children of the Layout.

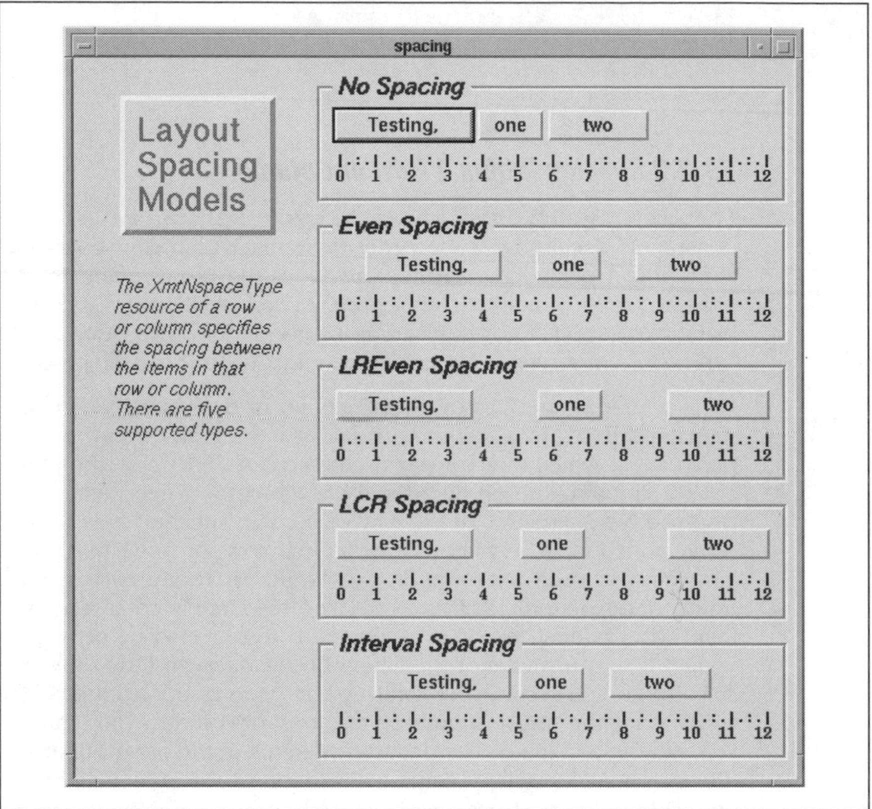

examples/

19/spacing

Figure 19-2. Spacing models of the Layout widget

`XmtLayoutSpaceLREven`
: This model is similar to the `XmtLayoutSpaceEven` model, except that it does not insert space before the first or after the last item in the row—there are `XmtNspace` pixels of space between items, but the first item is flush left in the row, and the last item is flush right in the row. The name `LREven` is a shortened form of "Left/Right/Even."

`XmtLayoutSpaceLCR`
: This spacing model works only for rows with three or fewer items, and it lays those items out flush left, centered, and flush right in the row. (Or flush to the top, centered, and flush to the bottom in a column.) Note that this spacing model is *not* the same as the `LREven` model, except when the three items in a row have the same width. The LCR space model uses the

XmtNspace resource of the row when computing the size of the row, but does not use this resource to actually position the items in the row—items are positioned at the left, center, and right, regardless of the space this leaves between them. This means that this spacing model does not guarantee that items in the row will not overlap. If the three items differ significantly in size, you may have to be careful to ensure that the items do not overlap. (You can ensure this by setting the XmtNspace resource to be sufficiently large.)

XmtLayoutSpaceInterval
: This final model lays items out at equal intervals in the row. If there are three items in the row, for example, they will be centered at the one-quarter point, the two-quarters point, and at the three-quarters point. This provides a similar effect to the Even spacing model, but while that model guarantees equal space between the edges of items, this model guarantees equal space between their centers. Like the LCR model, this Interval spacing model does not guarantee that the items will not overlap, and you will want to make XmtNspace sufficiently large to ensure that they do not overlap.

Figure 19-3 shows a modified version of our "Hello World" dialog box that uses the XmtLayoutSpaceEven spacing model to improve the positioning of the buttons. The only change (besides the inspirational message) is the addition of these two lines:

```
*buttonbox.spaceType: XmtLayoutSpaceEven
*buttonbox.space: 10
```

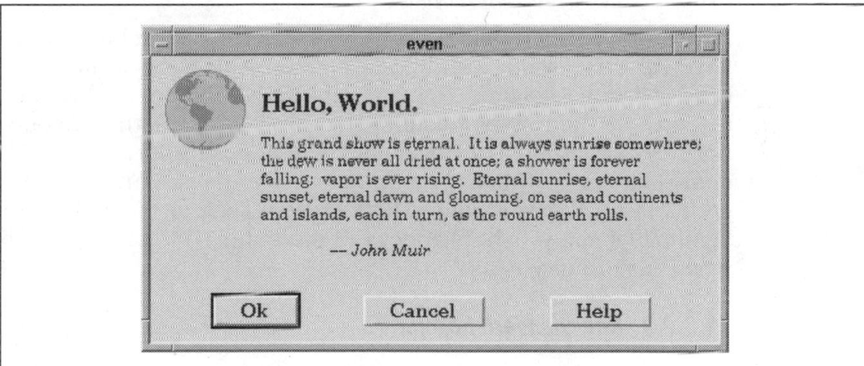

examples/

19/even

Figure 19-3. A row with even spacing

The standard spacing models described are sufficient for most layouts. There are a couple of other factors that can affect the position of items in the major dimension of their row or column, however, and there is also a technique for arranging widgets with non-standard spacings. These are described in the following subsections.

19.2.2.1 Margins

The Layout widget supports three types of margins, each of which serve distinct purposes. First, the Layout inherits the `XmNmarginWidth` and `XmNmarginHeight` resources of its XmBulletinBoard superclass. It changes the default value of these resources to five pixels, and uses these values to provide a margin between each edge of the Layout widget and the nearest child to that edge. This is the only use for those resources; they do not affect the positioning of items with rows or columns.

The second kind of margins the Layout widget provides are the `XmtNlayoutMarginWidth` and `XmtNlayoutMarginHeight` constraint resources, which specify a margin around each child in the layout. The `XmtNlayoutMarginWidth` constraint affects the layout of items in rows, and the `XmtNlayoutMarginHeight` constraint affects the layout of items in columns. The default value for these margin resources is set to half of the `XmtNdefaultSpacing` resource so that two adjacent children (with two adjacent margins) in a row or column (with `XmtLayoutSpaceNone` spacing) will be separated by the default spacing. The margin specified by these resources appears outside of any caption or frame attached to the child.

Finally, the third kind of margins are those that fall inside the caption and inside the frame for each child; they are specified by the `XmtNlayoutCaptionMargin` and `XmtNlayoutFrameMargin` constraints. These margins affect the position items in rows and columns only by affecting the size of those items.

19.2.2.2 Equal-Size Children

In a row, such as a button box, it is sometimes desirable to force all items to have the same width. (And, less commonly, to force all items in a column to have the same height.) You can accomplish this by setting the `XmtNequal` resource on the row or column. (Note that this is another LayoutBox resource, not a Layout resource or constraint.) Setting this resource on a row will force all items in the row, with the exception of LayoutSpace and LayoutSeparator gadgets, which will be introduced later, to be as wide as the widest item in the row. Figure 19-4 shows what happens to the button box of our previous examples when this resource is set.

19.2.2.3 Non-Standard Spacing

The `XmtNspaceType` resource supports the five standard spacing models described before. Sometimes, however, none of these models is appropriate. Figure 19-5, for example, shows a dialog box in which one button in a row is separated from a group of other buttons as a way of giving it added emphasis.

The way to implement a spacing scheme like this is to use the XmtLayoutSpace gadget to explicitly add the desired amount of space in the row. This LayoutSpace gadget has no visual appearance and is designed solely to take up a specified amount of space in a layout. Using a specially created object to simply

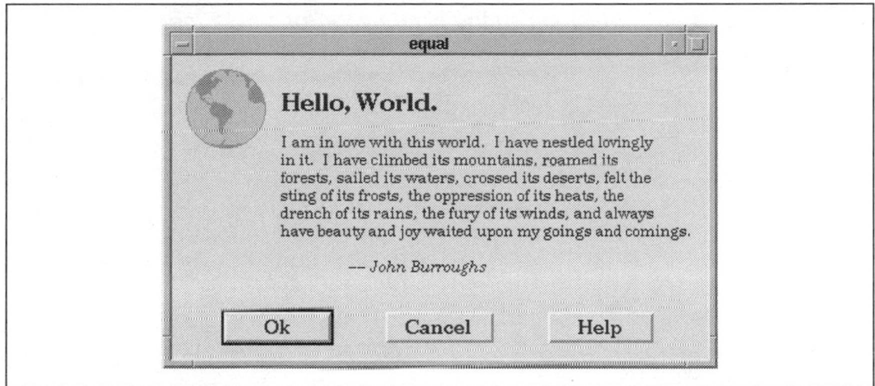

examples/

19/equal

Figure 19-4. Equal-width buttons

examples/

19/extraspace

Figure 19-5. A non-standard spacing

provide a blank area of screen may at first seem awkward and inelegant. What this approach gains us, however, is that the items in a row can be positioned automatically, without the need for an explicit pixel position for each. More importantly, as we will see later in the chapter, using LayoutSpace gadgets like this allows the items in a row to be automatically, and intelligently, repositioned if the row becomes wider.

Example 19-3 shows an excerpt from the resource file that was used to generate the layout shown in Figure 19-5. Note that we explicitly create a LayoutSpace gadget, and place it in the buttonbox exactly as we do with the other buttons. We continue to use the `XmtLayoutSpaceEven` spacing model, which places an equal amount of space between all items. Our LayoutSpace gadget is one of those items, so even if it had no width of its own, it would effectively double the space between the buttons on either side of it. In this example, however, we make the space widget 20 pixels wide.

19.2.2.3

Example 19-3. Using the XmtLayoutSpace Gadget

examples/

19/extraspace

```
!!
!! specify the widgets to be created in this example.
!!
extraspace.xmtChildren: XmtLayout layout;
*layout.xmtChildren: \
        XmtLayoutBox row, buttonbox;\
        XmtLayoutPixmap icon;\
        XmtLayoutString  message;\
        XmPushButton abort, retry, ignore, help;\
        XmtLayoutSpace extra;

!! put the children in the appropriate rows in the appropriate order.
*icon.layoutIn: row
*message.layoutIn: row
*abort.layoutIn: buttonbox
*retry.layoutAfter: abort
*ignore.layoutAfter: retry
*help.layoutAfter: ignore

!! Make the extra space gadget 20 pixels wide, and place it right
!! before the help button.

*extra.layoutWidth: 20
*extra.layoutBefore:help

!! Arrange the buttons Even and Equal in the row

*buttonbox.spaceType: XmtLayoutSpaceEven
*buttonbox.space: 10
*buttonbox.equal: True
```

It should be clear that this is the most flexible spacing option. By setting `XmtNspaceType` to `XmtLayoutSpaceNone`, and using LayoutSpace gadgets between all other items in a row or column, you can produce any spacing that you desire.

19.2.3 Justification in Rows and Columns

We've seen that the position of an item in the major dimension of a row or a column is controlled by that item's `XmtNlayoutPosition` constraint, by the size of the other items in the row or column, and by the `XmtNspaceType` spacing model of the row or the column. An item's position in the minor dimension (vertically in rows and horizontally in columns), on the other hand, is controlled by the `XmtNlayoutJustification` constraint of that item.

A row is normally as high as its highest contained item. If all items have the same height, then all of them will just fit vertically into the row, and no positioning is necessary in that dimension. Sometimes, however, items in a row are of different heights, or a row is forced to become higher than its highest item. Then the items in that row may be positioned flush with the top of the row, centered in the row, or flush with the bottom of the row. Or, instead, the item itself may be stretched to become taller and fill all the vertical space in the row.

The XmtNlayoutJustification constraint specifies what type of justification an item should have in a row or column. Figure 19-6 shows items with each of the legal values for this resource, and their effects on the position of objects.

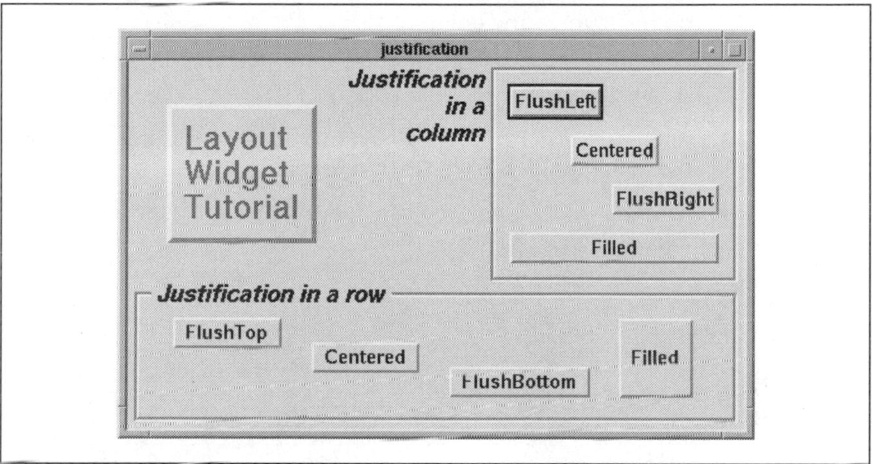

examples/

19/justification

Figure 19-6. XmtNlayoutJustification types and their effects

Justification in columns is analogous to that in rows. (And perhaps more intuitive to understand, because we are used to thinking of justification horizontally rather than vertically.) The justification of an item controls its horizontal position in the column; XmtLayoutFlushLeft replaces XmtLayoutFlushTop, and XmtLayoutFlushRight replaces XmtLayoutFlushBottom, but the other justification types are the same. Again, see Figure 19-6.

The default justification for items in rows or columns is XmtLayoutFilled. Imagine a column of push buttons. A push button is generally as wide as necessary to display its label, but when arranged in a column, buttons look best if they all have the same width. XmtLayoutFilled justification will force them all to be as wide as the widest item in the column. This situation is common enough that XmtLayoutFilled will most often be the correct justification for your widgets.

In the example above, we rely on the default XmtLayoutFilled justification to ensure that the buttons in a column are all as wide as one another. Similarly, this default value will ensure that the buttons in a row are all as high as one another. Notice that this is not the same thing as the LayoutBox XmtNequal resource described above—setting that resource on a row would ensure that all the items in it were as wide as one another, which is a very different thing. The XmtNequal resource is a special case implemented by the LayoutBox gadget; be careful not to confuse it with the more general minor dimension layout possibilities available through the XmtNlayoutJustification constraint.

19.2.4 Summary: Layout Positioning

Table 19-1 summarizes the resources that control the positioning of widgets within a Layout. These resources fall into four categories:

- Layout constraint resources that control this high-level positioning of children into rows and columns
- LayoutBox resources that control the spacing of items in the major dimension within their major dimension
- The justification constraint resource that controls the positioning of items in the minor dimension within the Layout
- Margin resources that influence the position of items in both the major and minor dimensions

Table 19-1. Layout Positioning Constraints and Resources

Row and Column Position	
Constraint	**Purpose**
`XmtNlayoutIn`	The row or column that the widget is to appear in.
`XmtNlayoutPosition`	The ordinal position (*not* pixel position) of the widget within the row or column. The default of -1 means the last position in the row or column.
`XmtNlayoutAfter`	The widget after which this widget should appear. Setting this resource sets both `XmtNlayoutIn` and `XmtNlayout-Position`.
`XmtNlayoutBefore`	The widget before which this widget should appear. Setting this resource sets both `XmtNlayoutIn` and `XmtNlayout-Position`.

Major dimension position. (Note: XmtLayoutBox resources)	
Resource	**Purpose**
`XmtNspaceType`	The spacing model for a row or column.
`XmtLayoutSpaceNone`	No additional space.
`XmtLayoutSpaceEven`	Even spacing around all items.
`XmtLayoutSpaceLREven`	Even spacing between all items, but not at ends.
`XmtLayoutSpaceLCR`	Space three items at the left, center, and right.
`XmtLayoutSpaceInterval`	Position center of children at equal intervals.

Table 19-1. Layout Positioning Constraints and Resources (continued)

Major dimension position. (Note: XmtLayoutBox resources)	
Resource	**Purpose**
XmtNspace	The default amount of space between items in Even and LREven spacing.
XmtNequal	If True, force all items in a row to the same width, or all items in a column to the same height.

Minor dimension position (by constraint resource)	
Constraint	**Purpose**
XmtNlayoutJustification	Specifies the vertical position of an item in a row or the horizontal position of an item in a column.
XmtLayoutFilled	Make widget as tall as row or as wide as column.
XmtLayoutFlushTop	Position against top of row.
XmtLayoutCentered	Center vertically in row or horizontally in column.
XmtLayoutFlushBottom	Position against bottom of row.
XmtLayoutFlushLeft	Position against left of column.
XmtLayoutFlushRight	Position against right of column.

Margin Constraints and Resources	
Resource	**Purpose**
XmtNlayoutMarginWidth	A margin on the left and right of each item; a constraint resource.
XmtNlayoutMarginHeight	A margin on the top and bottom of each item; a constraint resource.
XmtNdefaultSpacing	The default distance between unspaced children. The margin constraints above default to half of this value. A regular Layout resource, not a constraint.
XmNmarginWidth	A margin on the left and right of the Layout; a regular resource.
XmNmarginHeight	A margin on the top and bottom of the Layout; a regular resource.

19.3 Resizing the Layout

The previous sections have explained the fundamental factors that control the position of a child of the Layout widget. They've all assumed, however, that the children were arranged at their natural size. This is only half the story, though. Suppose we have two rows, arranged in a column, and both have the default justification `XmtLayoutFilled`. Both rows will then be made as wide as the column is, or the shorter row will be stretched to become as wide as the longer one. When a row is forced wider like this, it is usually unacceptable to simply add blank pixels at the right-hand side of the row; instead, the position, and perhaps the size, of the items in the row should be adjusted to take up the extra space gracefully. The following subsections explain how the Layout widget accomplishes this.

19.3.1 Natural Size

Before we can explain how items in a Layout are made bigger or smaller, it is important to understand the concept of the natural size of a widget, a row, or a column. Any child of a Layout widget can have a size explicitly specified through the `XmtNlayoutWidth` and `XmtNlayoutHeight` constraint resources. If these constraints are specified, then the Layout widget will treat them as the natural size of the child, and will attempt to lay it out at that specified size.

If these resources are not specified, then the natural size of the child is obtained by calling `XtQueryGeometry()` for the child. This is the size that the child itself thinks it wants to be. For a label widget, for example, the natural size is the size required to display the specified string in the specified font, plus any internal margins. You may request a different size with the `XtNwidth` and `XtNheight` resources, but for something like a label widget, these are simply an "unnatural size" that the Layout widget is not interested in. (This explains why the seeming superfluous `XmtNlayoutWidth` and `XmtNlayoutHeight` constraints are necessary.)

For a text widget, the natural size is the number of pixels required to display the specified number of rows and columns using the specified font. On the other hand, a widget like an XmDrawingArea doesn't contain any text or have any other display semantics that would give it a default natural size, so for a widget like this, the natural size is simply whatever size is requested by the programmer with the core `XtNwidth` and `XtNheight` resources.

The natural size of manager widgets like the XmForm is usually determined by the sizes of their children, and it is the same for row and column LayoutBox gadgets within the Layout widget. The natural width of a row is the sum of the widths of its children (which may include explicit spaces created by the LayoutSpace gadget) plus any width required for the optional frames, captions, and margins of those children, plus any space specified by the combination of the `XmtNspaceType` and `XmtNspace` resources of the row gadget. The natural height of a row is the height of the tallest child, again plus room for optional frame, caption, and margins. The size of a column is computed similarly.

The reason that the Layout widget queries and computes the natural size of its widget children, rows, and columns, is, as we'll see in the following sections, so that it can space, stretch, and shrink those children proportionally to this natural size.

19.3.2 Spacing Children

When a row of buttons, for example, is made wider, one possibility is to leave the buttons at the same size and position, and to leave blank pixels at the end of the row. You can make the Layout widget do this, but it is rarely what you want, and is not the default behavior of the widget. Instead of leaving those extra pixels to just hang at the end of the row, the LayoutBox gadget redistributes them by either making the items in the row wider, by making the spaces between the items larger, or by doing some combination of both.

When the LayoutBox `XmtNspaceType` resource is not `XmtSpaceNone`, the LayoutBox distributes extra pixels to the items and the spaces between them. (When we discuss "spaces" in this section, we are referring exclusively to the automatically generated spaces specified by the LayoutBox `XmtNspaceType` and `XmtNspace` resources. Spaces that are explicitly created with the Layout-Space gadget should be considered "items.") The pixels are divided between items and spaces according to the `XmtNitemStretch` and `XmtNspaceStretch` resources (LayoutBox resources, not constraints) which form a ratio. The default value for both of these resources is 1, so extra pixels are divided 1:1—half are distributed to the items in the row, and half to the spaces between the items. If `XmtNspaceStretch` is set to 2, then the pixels are divided 1:2—one-third go to the items and two-thirds go to the spaces. If `XmtNitemStretch` is set to zero, then all the pixels are divided among the spaces, and if `XmtNspaceStretch` is zero (and `XmtNitemStretch` is not), then all the pixels are divided among the items, while the spaces remain at a constant width.

Figure 19-7 shows a number of rows of buttons, all identical, except for the value of the `XmtNitemStretch` and `XmtNspaceStretch` resources for the rows. The rows use the `XmtLayoutSpaceEven` spacing model and have all been made larger than their natural size. The figure illustrates their resize behavior for different values of these resources.

The `XmtNitemStretch` and `XmtNspaceStretch` resources specify only how extra pixels will be distributed between the items in a row (or column) and the spaces that are automatically placed around those items. These pixels must then be divided again between the individual items and the individual spaces. Extra pixels are always divided evenly among spaces: if there are three items in a row, and four spaces (using the `Even` spacing model), and half of the extra pixels are distributed to the spaces, then each individual space will receive one-eighth of the total number of extra pixels. In the examples shown in Figure 19-6 extra pixels are also distributed evenly among the three buttons in the row, so again, if half of the extra pixels go to the items, then each button ends up with one-sixth of those pixels.

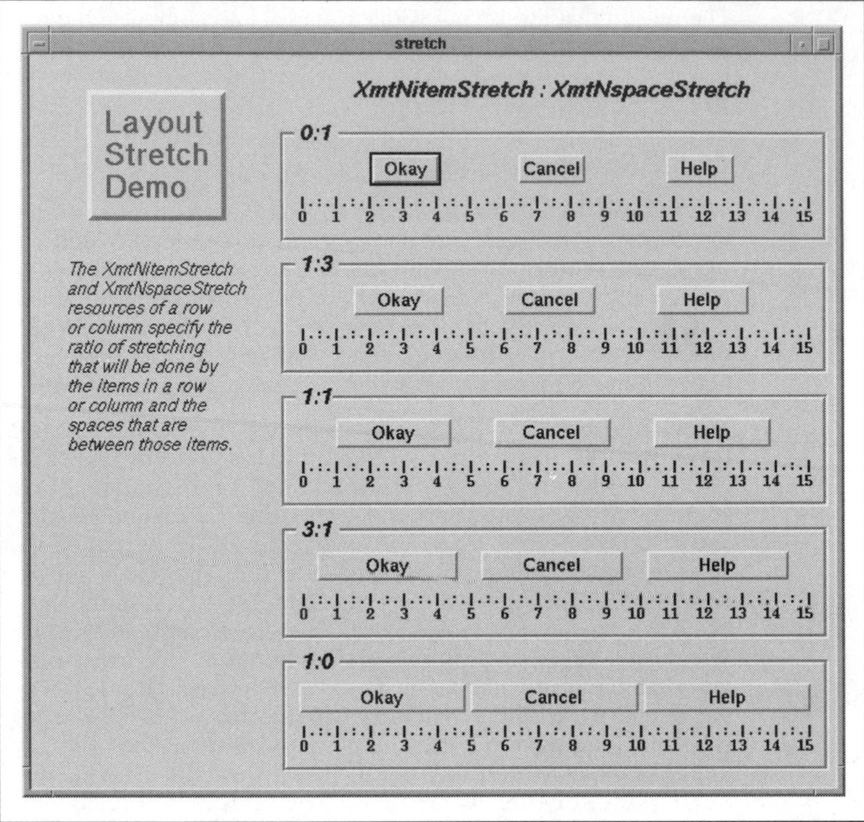

examples/
19/stretch

Figure 19-7. Resizing with various XmtNitemStretch:XmtNspaceStretch ratios

There are two final points to note. First, while the default behavior of the Layout widget is that extra pixels are divided evenly among widget children in a row, as in the pervious examples, we'll see that it is possible to specify that some children should not grow, and to specify that some children should grow in different proportions to others. Also, while extra pixels are by default distributed evenly among *widget* children of a row or column, some of the Layout gadget types do not grow by default.

Second, note that the `XmtNitemStretch` and `XmtNspaceStretch` resources have their most obvious effects when `XmtNspaceType` is `XmtLayoutSpaceEven` or `XmtLayoutSpaceLREven`. For the `XmtLayoutSpaceNone` spacing model, these resources go unused—there is no automatically positioned space, and any extra pixels are divided among the items in the row or column alone. If the spacing model is `XmtLayoutSpaceLCR` or `XmtLayoutSpaceInterval`, then the `XmtNitemStretch` and `XmtNspaceStretch` resources are still used to specify what fraction of extra pixels should be used to make the items in the row bigger, but since neither of these models guarantee that items will be evenly spaced, it doesn't really make sense to think in terms of "dividing" extra pixels among the spaces.

19.3.3 Stretching Children

Let's return to our earlier example of buttons in a column. If the buttons have `XmtLayoutFilled` justification, then the Layout widget will force all the buttons to be as wide as the column, and if the column grows wider, then the buttons will grow wider. If the buttons had some other kind of justification, `XmtLayoutCentered`, for example, then they would be recentered when the column grew wider but would not actually be stretched. Notice that here we are talking about stretching items in the minor dimension of the column, and, as we saw earlier, there are important differences between the way the Layout handles the minor and major dimensions.

In the minor dimension, objects are stretched or not, depending on their `XmtNlayoutJustification` constraint. The more interesting case, however, and the one we were describing in the discussion of spacing above, is stretching children in the major dimension. If we convert our example column of buttons to a column of rows with `Filled` justification, then rows will be stretched so that they are all as wide as the column. So far, this is the same minor dimension case as we saw with the push buttons. When a row is made wider, however, the items within it may also be made wider, and this is the major dimension case.

In the previous section, we saw how the `XmtNitemStretch` and `XmtNspaceStretch` resources specified the fraction of extra pixels that are to go to the items in a row or column and the fraction of them that are to be divided among the spaces automatically placed between those items. In this section we'll consider the distribution of extra pixels among the items. For simplicity, we'll assume a spacing model of `XmtLayoutSpaceNone`, so that all the extra pixels go to the items, but in fact, this discussion applies equally well when there is a spacing model in effect and only some of the extra pixels are to be distributed among the items.

When a row is made wider, the extra pixels are distributed to the children of the row. These extra pixels make them each wider, depending on the "stretchiness" of each child. This stretchiness is controlled by the `XmtNlayoutStretchability` constraint resource. An item with a zero stretchability will never be stretched to become wider. An item with a non-zero stretchability will be stretched according to its proportion of the total stretchability of the row. Thus if a row contains only two stretchable items, and each item has a stretchability of 10, then each item will be stretched by 10/20 or one half of the extra pixels. If one item has a stretchability of 10 and the next a stretchability of 20, then the first would be stretched by one third (10/30) of the available pixels, and the second by two thirds (20/30). If none of the items in the row have any stretchiness, then the extra pixels cannot be redistributed, and remain to the right of the row.

If the `XmtNlayoutStretchability` constraint resource of a child is not set, the default stretchiness depends on the type of the child. Widgets, XmGadgets, and rows, columns, and spaces have a default stretchability of 10. Other XmtLayoutGadget subclasses (strings, pixmaps, and separators) are given a default stretchability of 0, since these gadget types do not draw themselves any differently when forced to be larger than their natural size—they simply add blank space on one or both sides of themselves.

When a column is made higher than its natural height, the items it contains are stretched to become taller in the same way that items in rows are stretched to become wider. Note again that stretching only affects the major dimension—the horizontal dimension of rows and the vertical dimension of columns. Resizing in the minor dimension is controlled exclusively through item justification.

This layout and resizing scheme of the Layout widget is based on the the "boxes and glue" algorithm used by the TeX text formatter, and there are a number of useful layout techniques involving stretchable spaces that can be borrowed from TeX. These techniques rely on explicitly created LayoutSpace gadgets; these layout tricks can often be implemented more efficiently using the `XmtNspaceType` resource to specify an automatic spacing model for the row or column, but they are presented here to give you an idea of the full power of this layout scheme, and because using the LayoutSpace gadget is the most flexible layout scheme.

To arrange buttons equally spaced in a row, place equally stretchable spaces between them. These spaces may be made zero pixels wide by default, and the buttons will initially be separated only by their margins. But if the row is made wider, the spaces will each grow by the same number of pixels because they have the same stretchability. If the buttons are not themselves stretchable, then they will have a fixed width, and only the space gadgets will grow. If the buttons are made stretchable, then they will grow along with the spaces. If all of the spaces have a stretchability of 20 and all the buttons have a stretchability of 10, then two thirds of the extra pixels will be distributed to the space gadgets, and one third will be distributed by making the buttons wider. When spaces all have the same initial size and stretchability like this, you can simply use a spacing model like `XmtLayoutSpaceEven` and set `XmtNitemStretch` and `XmtNspaceStretch` appropriately to get this kind of spacing, saving the overhead of all the space gadgets. Using explicit gadgets is the most general way to do these layouts, however, and allows spaces with different initial sizes and different stretchabilities.

Stretchable spaces are also very useful for centering or positioning items flush left or flush right within a row (or column). Two items in a row may be laid out flush left and flush right in that row by making them non-stretchable and placing a stretchable space between them. If the row is wider than the sum of their widths, then all the extra pixels will be given to the stretchable space in the center of the row, leaving the other two items flush against the left and the right. Items can be centered in a row by positioning equally stretchable spaces at the beginning and the end of the row, so that any extra space is distributed equally on both sides of the row. Note that these schemes rely on spaces that are stretchable and other items that are non-stretchable. By default widget and XmGadget children of a Layout widget are slightly stretchable. It is not necessary to make them strictly non-stretchable for these layout techniques to work; it is only necessary to make the spaces much more stretchable than the items they separate. If a widget of stretchability 10 shares a row with a space of stretchability 1000, then the widget will effectively never be made any wider.

19.3.4 Shrinking Children

When a row or column is made *smaller* than its natural or specified size, then the "shrinkiness" of each of its children comes into play. This is specified with the `XmtNlayoutShrinkability` constraint resource and is analogous to the stretchability of an item—it specifies which items in a row or column should shrink, and in what proportion to one another. If no items in a row or column are shrinkable, and that row or column is made smaller than its natural size, then items or portions of items will disappear off the right edge of the row or the bottom edge of the column. There is one important difference between stretching and shrinking: while there is no limit to how large an item may be stretched to, items will never shrink so much that they have a zero or negative size.

A subtle, but important, point to note about the stretching and shrinking algorithm is that the number of pixels to be distributed among the children is computed as the difference between the new size and the natural size, not the difference between the new size and the current size. Thus, if a column, for example, has a natural height of 100 pixels, and it is resized to be 200 pixels high, the new height of the items it contains is based on the stretchability of those items. If the column is then shrunk by 50 pixels, it is still the stretchability that matters, not the shrinkability: a height of 150 pixels is still greater than the natural height of 100 pixels, so although the column has been shrunk from 200 to 150 pixels, the new size of the items is computed by invoking the stretch algorithm to stretch the column from 100 to 150 pixels. The shrinkability of an item only comes into play when the row or column that contains it is resized to be less than its natural width or height.

The default shrinkiness of an item is handled in the same way as the default stretchability: if `XmtNlayoutShrinkability` is not set, then the default value is 10 for Widgets, XmGadgets, and row, column, and space layout gadgets. The default shrinkability of the other layout gadgets (strings, pixmaps and separators) is 0.

So if a Layout widget is made smaller than its natural size, the shrinkable items in that layout will be made smaller than their natural or specified size. In practice, many widgets do not handle small sizes gracefully (labels in buttons are truncated and become illegible, for example), but this is generally better than the alternative in which items in the layout are simply truncated off the right or bottom edges of the parent Layout widget. If you do want items to be truncated rather than shrunk below their natural size, you can set their `XmtNlayout-Shrinkability` resource to 0. Note that it is possible to request a window manager to enforce a minimum size for a window (see Chapter 15, *Working with the Window Manager*) and not allow the user to shrink it to anything smaller—this is perhaps the best solution to the problem of shrinkability.

Note that there are some cases for which a non-zero shrinkability is necessary. For widgets such as an XmDrawingArea that do not have any concept of a natural size, you will usually assign some reasonable default size through the `XtNwidth` and `XtNheight` resources, or through the `XmtNlayoutWidth` and `XmtNlayoutHeight` constraint resources. Usually, this size is intended as an optimum size, not a minimum size, but the Layout widget will treat it as a natural or specified size, and will never make the child any smaller unless it has a non-zero shrinkability.

A related issue is that some widgets do not keep track of their natural size—when queried for their preferred size, they simply report their current size. If you encounter a child that will grow larger when the Layout widget grows, but will not shrink back to its original ("natural") size when the Layout is restored to its original size, this is probably the problem. One solution is to give the widget a non-zero shrinkability so that it can be made smaller, no matter what it claims its natural size to be. Another solution is to explicitly specify a size with the `XmtNlayoutWidth` and `XmtNlayoutHeight` resources so that the Layout widget uses these as the base size for the widget, rather than relying on the widget to report its preferred size.

19.3.5 The Big Picture

In the above sections, we've been describing the mechanics of stretching and shrinking in great detail. Table 19-2 summarizes the Layout constraints and LayoutBox resources that are involved.

Table 19-2. Layout Resize Resources

Resource	**Purpose**
`XmtNlayoutWidth` `XmtNlayoutHeight`	Constraints that set a base size for the widget. Stretching and shrinking are based on this size. If unspecified, the widget's natural size is used.
`XmtNitemStretch` `XmtNspaceStretch`	XmtLayoutBox resources that specify the relative amount of stretching that the items and spaces in a spaced row or column should perform.
`XmtNlayout-Stretchability` `XmtNlayout-Shrinkability`	The relative amount of stretching or shrinking an item will do. The actual amount depends on these constraints for all items in the row or column.

This stretchability and shrinkability layout scheme can be confusing to get used to, but what it means in practice is that widgets in a Layout widget adapt gracefully to whatever size they are given. To create a button box, for example, that spaces its buttons evenly, you need only place the buttons in a row with the `XmtLayoutSpaceEven` spacing model. Depending on what else appears in the dialog, this row may be stretched beyond its natural size, but when this happens, the row will (by default) handle the resize nicely—the buttons will grow proportionally larger, as will the spaces.

When designing and prototyping a layout with the Layout widget, first make sure it looks right at its natural size. Then try making the window larger and smaller, and see what you think of the default resize behavior. This is when you'll discover that some items in a column need to have their stretchability set to 0 perhaps, or that some items in a row should be centered rather than having filled justification. This is also the appropriate time to fine-tune (by trial and error) the spacing models you use, the size of spaces, and the `XmtNitemStretch` to `XmtNspaceStretch` ratio for your rows and columns.

In the previous subsections, we've been considering what happens when an individual row is stretched to make it as wide as some other row in a column. In practice, rows may contain other columns, and whenever one item is stretched, the stretch may propagate through several nested levels of the layout. In particular, when the Layout widget itself is resized, that size change propagates through all the rows and columns it contains. It is useful to consider this resize process as from the top down.

Figure 19-8 illustrates how the single resize propagates from column to row to column. Suppose that we have a Layout widget as the direct child of a shell widget, and that the user has just interacted with the window manager to make the shell widget wider. The shell widget makes its Layout widget correspondingly wider as well. Now suppose that the Layout widget has an `XmtNorientation` resource of `XmVERTICAL`, meaning that its top-level container is a column. This column is made wider, and each of the items contained in that column have their size and/or position adjusted based on their justification. No stretching or shrinking takes place in this column, because its height has not changed. If one of the items in the column is a row, and if it has a justification of `XmtLayoutFilled`, then it will be resized to be as wide as the new width of the column. Now the stretchable items in this row are stretched to take up the newly available space. If one of the stretch items in the row is a column, then it is made wider, and the items contained in that column are adjusted based on their justification, and so on. Note that if the user had made the shell widget both wider and taller at the beginning of this process, then both the justification adjustments and the stretching would be going on in both rows and columns. It is worth working through this case on your own.

Resizes are not always initiated by the user interacting with a shell widget. Sometimes an application changes the value of a widget resource (such as the string displayed by a label), and in response the widget makes a request to its parent to be made larger or smaller (in order to have enough room to display the new label, for example). By default, the Layout widget will allow resize requests from its children, and will re-compute the layout of all the children and itself request a larger size, if necessary, to accommodate the resized child. The constraint resource `XmtNlayoutAllowResize` makes it possible to tell the Layout widget to not allow resize requests from any of its individual widget or gadget children. This functionality is not often needed, but can be useful to squelch poorly-behaved children that make spurious resize requests.

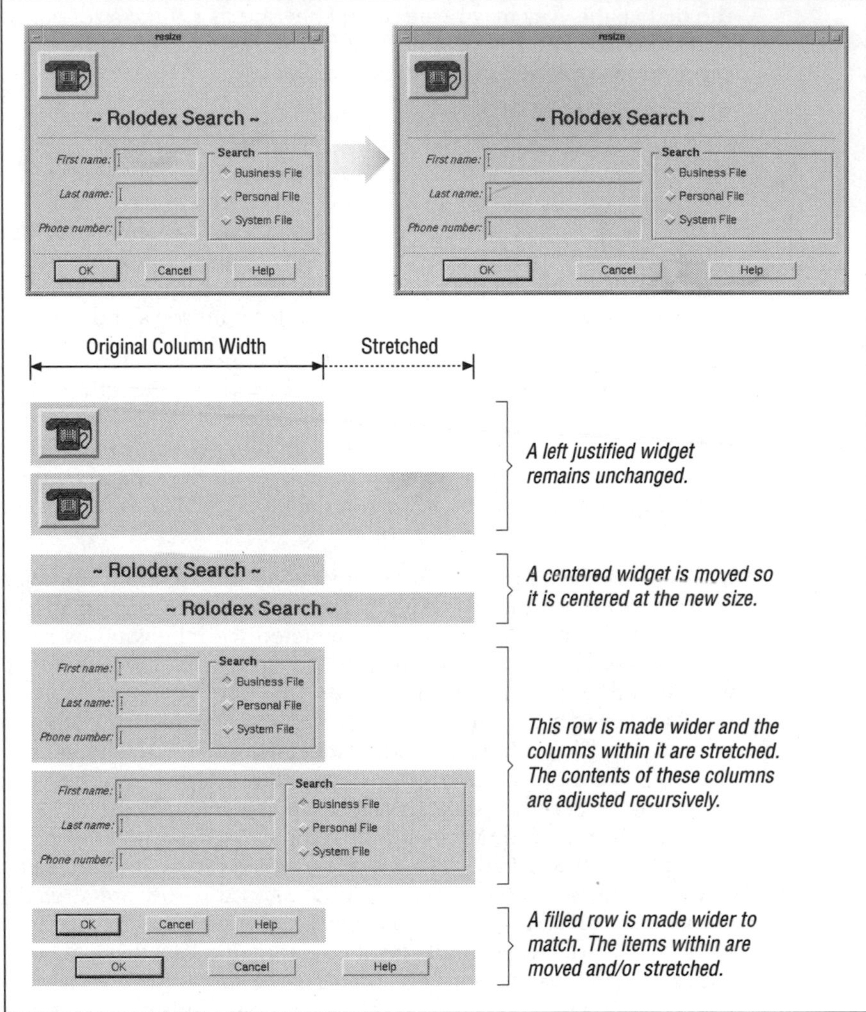

Figure 19-8. Resizing a Layout widget

19.4 Layout Captions, Frames, and Gadgets

Traditional dogma for the X Toolkit says that each widget class should do one thing well, and that you should combine widgets to achieve the results you want. So, for example, if you want a caption on the left of a text input field, you should use a separate label widget to implement the caption, and if you want a frame drawn around a group of widgets, you should place them in a separate manager widget, within something like an XmFrame widgets which exists simply to draw a frame.

While this approach is an elegant one, in practice, however, there are a number of problems. The most obvious is efficiency—if you wanted a lot of frames and captions in your layout, you could easily end up doubling the required number of widgets. Memory and CPU cycles are not yet so cheap that we can afford to totally disregard these concerns. Furthermore, if you use a label widget to caption another widget, then you will have to take special care to arrange that they stay close together in your layout, and don't move apart when the manager widget is resized, for example. And the drawback to using an XmFrame widget is that it takes a single set of widgets in a layout and breaks them into subgroups that must be arranged with independent manager widgets, and it is annoying to program with this hierarchy of manager widgets.

Since captions and frames are common and useful details to include in widget layouts, the Layout widget violates the one-widget-one-task dictum and implements them directly. As we'll see, any child of a Layout widget, including rows and columns, can have a caption or a frame, and a frame can extend all the way around a child, or can be drawn only on one side of a child, effectively serving as a separator widget. Figure 19-9 shows a layout with captions and frames.

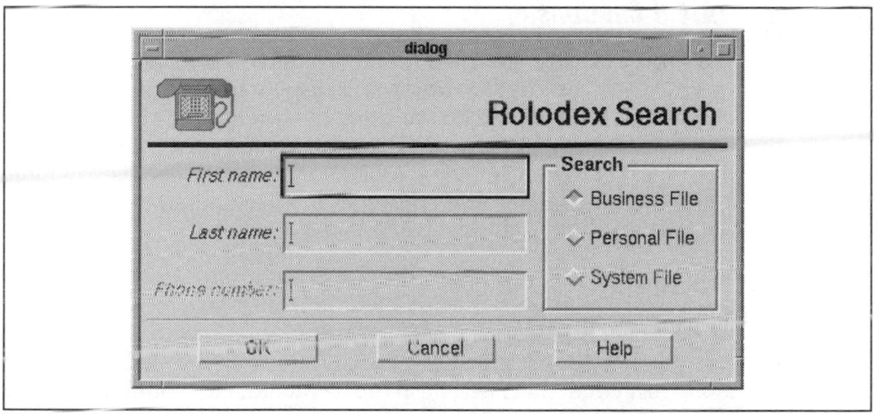

examples/

19/dialog

Figure 19-9. Captions and frames in a layout

Captions and frames are specified for children through constraint resources, and are therefore quite efficient. These constraints will be introduced below.

As we've seen in the previous sections, the LayoutBox and LayoutSpace are special gadgets that are designed to work efficiently with the Layout widget. This same family of gadgets also includes the LayoutString, LayoutPixmap and LayoutSeparator, which draw strings, bitmaps or pixmaps, and etched separators. Since they are specially designed for use with the Layout widget, they are significantly more efficient than the XmLabelGadget and the XmSeparatorGadget. These will also be introduced below.

One Widget, One Task?

Terry Poot argues that the Layout widget does in fact adhere to the "one widget, one task" rule. "It is a matter of perspective," he says. Here's his perspective on the "one task" of the Layout widget:

Xt and Motif manager widgets serve one function: to arrange their children. They do one thing, and do it well. The XmtLayout serves a different function: to create a window of a user interface. This is a higher-level task, and providing frames, captions, pixmaps, strings, etc., is all part of this task. It also does one thing and does it well. Its power is that this "one thing" is the task the UI implementor needs to do.... This is not a matter of creeping featurism, it is a matter of solving the right problem. Sometimes getting the right answer is a matter of asking the right question.

—*Terry Poot*

19.4.1 Captions

If an `XmString` is specified for the `XmtNlayoutCaption` constraint resource of any child, the Layout widget will display that XmString as a caption for the child. The string will be drawn using the foreground color of the Layout widget, and the font list specified on the Layout's `XmtNfontList` resource. Note that if this font list contains multiple fonts, then captions can use multiple fonts. If the `XmtNlayoutSensitive` constraint is `False`, then the caption will be drawn "grayed out" with a stipple.

The position of a caption with respect to the child is controlled by four resources: `XmtNlayoutCaptionPosition` specifies whether the caption is to be drawn against the left, right, top or bottom edges of the child. `XmtNlayoutCaptionJustification` specifies the justification of the caption along that edge: flush left, flush top, centered, etc. For multi-line captions, `XmtNlayoutCaptionAlignment` specifies the justification of each line within the bounding box of the whole string. Finally, `XmtNlayoutCaptionMargin` specifies the distance, in pixels, between the nearest edge of the caption and the child widget, or between the caption and the frame, if there is a frame drawn between the caption and the box. Table 19-3 lists these caption constraints and their possible values, and Figure 19-10 shows captions with various positions, justifications, and alignments.

Table 19-3. Layout Caption Constraint Resources

Resource	Purpose
XmtNlayoutCaption	The caption to draw; an XmString
XmtNlayoutSensitive	If False, caption is stippled
XmtNlayoutCaptionPosition	Which edge the caption is drawn along
XmtLayoutLeft	Caption drawn to the left of child
XmtLayoutRight	Caption drawn to the right of child
XmtLayoutTop	Caption drawn above child
XmtLayoutBottom	Caption drawn below child
XmtNlayoutCaptionJustification	Justification along that edge
XmtLayoutFlushLeft	Left justification along top or bottom
XmtLayoutFlushRight	Right justification along top or bottom
XmtLayoutFlushTop	Top justification along left or right
XmtLayoutFlushBottom	Bottom justification along left or right
XmtLayoutCentered	Centered horizontally or vertically.
XmtNlayoutCaptionAlignment	Alignment of lines within caption
XmALIGNMENT_BEGINNING	Lines are flush left within bounding box
XmALIGNMENT_CENTER	Lines centered within bounding box
XmALIGNMENT_END	Lines are flush right within bounding box
XmtNlayoutCaptionMargin	Pixels between the caption and the child or frame

Figure 19-10 shows a dialog box that uses a number of captions. Note that these captions use different fonts available in the XmFontList, and that one of the captions is stippled out with the `XmtNlayoutSensitive` constraint. Example 19-4 shows an excerpt from the code that was used to produce the captions of Figure 19-10.

Example 19-4. Captions in the Layout Widget

examples/

19/dialog

```
!!
!! Captions for the children
!!
*fname.layoutCaption: @fIFirst name:
*lname.layoutCaption: @fILast name:
*phone.layoutCaption: @fIPhone number:
*phone.layoutSensitive: False

*chooser.layoutCaption: @fB Search
*chooser.layoutCaptionPosition: XmtLayoutTop
*chooser.layoutCaptionJustification: XmtLayoutFlushLeft
```

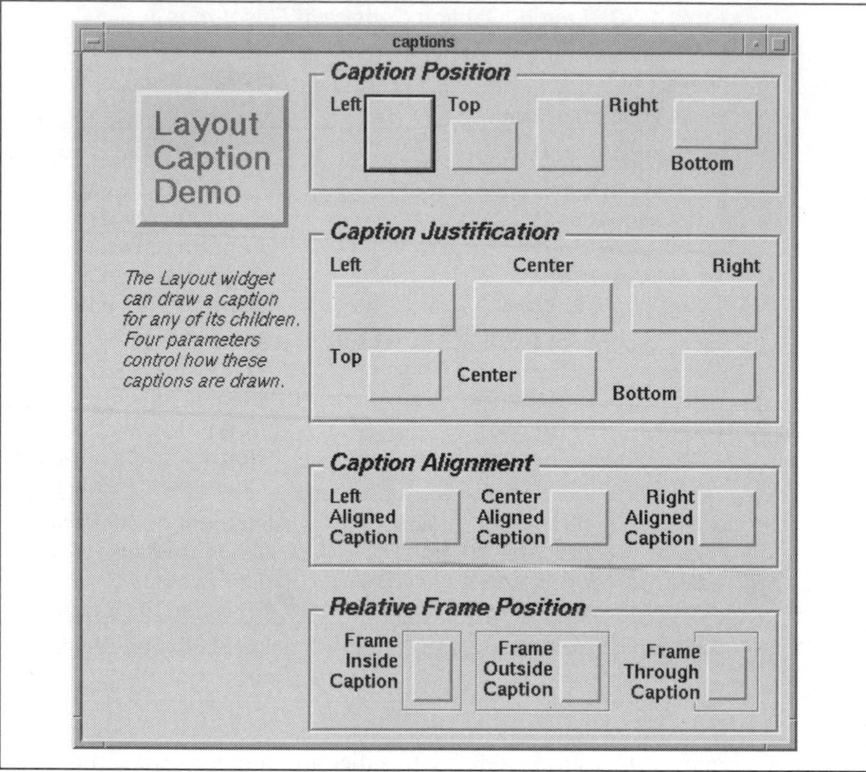

examples/19/captions

Figure 19-10. Caption position, justification, and alignment

19.4.2 Frames

If the `XmtNlayoutFrameType` constraint resource is set to `XmtLayoutFrameBox`, the Layout widget will draw a frame around the child widget, similar to the frames drawn by the Motif XmFrame widget, but without the overhead of an extra widget. If `XmtNlayoutFrameType` is `XmtLayoutFrameLeft`, `XmtLayoutFrameRight`, `XmtLayoutFrameTop`, or `XmtLayoutFrameBottom`, the Layout widget will draw a "frame" along only one edge of the widget. This single-sided frame can serve as a visual separator for the widget layout, much as the Motif XmSeparator widget does, but again, without the overhead of an extra widget.

`XmtNlayoutFrameLineType` controls the style of line drawn for the frame or separator. The Layout widget can draw frames shadowed in or shadowed out, etched in or etched out, and can also draw single thick lines and double thin lines. `XmtNlayoutFramePosition` controls the position of the frame in relation to the caption, if any: the frame can be drawn inside the caption, outside the caption, or it can be drawn so that the caption will fall on top of a portion of it; this often provides a nice visual effect. `XmtNlayoutFrameThickness` controls thickness of the frame, and `XmtNlayoutFrameMargin` specifies the distance from the inside edge of the frame to the nearest edge of the child widget, or to the nearest edge of the caption, if the frame is drawn around the child and its caption. Table 19-4 lists these frame constraint resources and their legal values, and Figure 19-10 illustrates some of permutations of these resources. Frames can be used to provide shadowing for widgets that do not provide it themselves, and therefore do not fit well in a typical Motif interface. More commonly, though, frames are used to provide visual separation and organization for an interface. A set of related option menus in a dialog box, for example, might be placed together in a column and given a frame to indicate their grouping and to keep them separate from other option menus in the dialog. The **OK**, **Cancel**, and **Help** buttons at the bottom of a dialog box are typically placed in a row together. A frame type of `XmtLayoutFrameTop` for this row will provide a visual separator that will emphasize that these buttons are for controlling the dialog, not part of the dialog themselves.

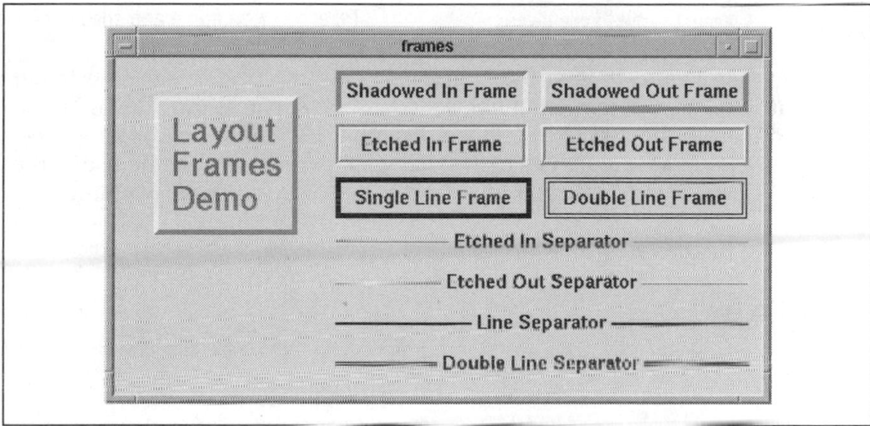

examples/

19/frames

Figure 19-11. Frame types, line types, and positions

Table 19-4. Layout Frame Constraint Resources

Resource	Purpose
`XmtNlayoutFrameType`	Whether to draw a full, partial, or no frame
`XmtLayoutFrameNone`	Child has no frame; the default value
`XmtLayoutFrameBox`	Frame boxes the child
`XmtLayoutFrameLeft`	Frame drawn along left edge of child
`XmtLayoutFrameRight`	Frame drawn along right edge of child
`XmtLayoutFrameTop`	Frame drawn along top edge of child
`XmtLayoutFrameBottom`	Frame drawn along bottom edge of child

Table 19-4. Layout Frame Constraint Resources (continued)

XmtNlayoutFrameLineType	What kind of lines to draw the frame with
XmtLayoutFrameShadowIn	Frame is a shadow into the screen; boxed only
XmtLayoutFrameShadowOut	Frame is a shadow out of the screen; boxed only
XmtLayoutFrameEtchedIn	Frame drawn with lines etched into the screen
XmtLayoutFrameEtchedOut	Frame drawn with lines etched out of screen
XmtLayoutFrameSingleLine	Frame drawn with a single (fat) line
XmtLayoutFrameDoubleLine	Frame drawn with two (thin) lines
XmtNlayoutFramePosition	Relation of frame to caption
XmtLayoutFrameInside	Frame is drawn inside of caption
XmtLayoutFrameOutside	Frame is drawn outside of caption
XmtLayoutFrameThrough	Frame intersects caption
XmtNlayoutFrameThickness	Width, in pixels, of frame lines
XmtNlayoutFrameMargin	Pixel between frame and child or caption

In Figure 19-9, at the beginning of this section, we used a frame to group the column of text input fields, and also to separate the title and the row of buttons from the rest of the dialog. Example 19-5 shows a portion of the code used to generate the frames in this dialog. In particular, note the use of the different line types and of the `XmtLayoutFrameThrough` frame position.

Example 19-5. Frames in the Layout Widget

examples/

19/dialog

```
!!
!! Frames for the children
!! Note: The "XmtLayoutFrame" prefix is optional and may be omitted.
!!
*titlebox.layoutFrameType: XmtLayoutFrameBottom
*titlebox.layoutFrameLineType: XmtLayoutFrameSingleLine
*titlebox.layoutFrameThickness: 4

*chooser.layoutFrameType: XmtLayoutFrameBox
*chooser.layoutFrameLineType: XmtLayoutFrameEtchedIn
*chooser.layoutFramePosition: XmtLayoutFrameThrough
*chooser.layoutFrameThickness: 4
*chooser.layoutFrameMargin: 6

*buttonbox.layoutFrameType: XmtLayoutFrameTop
*buttonbox.layoutFrameLineType: XmtLayoutFrameEtchedIn
```

19.4.3 Layout Gadgets

The Layout widget can manage normal widget children and standard Motif XmGadget children. It also supports children of the special XmtLayoutGadget class. These "layout gadgets" are like XmGadgets in that they do not have their own window, but, because they are used for output only, and because they work only as children of the Layout widget (and not any other manager widgets), they are significantly simpler than XmGadgets, and are implemented a lot more efficiently than those Motif gadgets.

As we've seen, rows and columns in a Layout are implemented with the LayoutBox gadget, and spaces can be explicitly added to a layout with the LayoutSpace gadget. Both of these are special-purpose gadgets used to position other children; neither has any actual appearance on the screen. There are three other gadget types that are useful for drawing strings, icons, and separators.

The XmtLayoutString gadget class takes an XmString label resource, and a foreground color and draws that label using the specified color and the fonts specified on the Layout `XmtNfontList` resource. In many cases, the `XmtNlayoutCaption` constraint resource can be used to draw the necessary text in an interface, but there are times when a text label must stand alone—when used as the title for a dialog box, for example, or in the mode line of a main window. The LayoutString gadget also allows a color to be specified for the label, which is not possible with captions.

The XmtLayoutPixmap gadget is like the LayoutString gadget, but draws a bitmap or pixmap label instead of a textual one. It is useful for cheaply introducing icons into an interface. For example, it is common, and good visual design, to place an identifying icon at the upper left or upper right of dialog boxes. Notice that the LayoutPixmap gadget can display bitmaps (one bitplane) or pixmaps (multiple bitplanes). One of the serious shortcomings of the Motif XmLabel widget is that it requires a pixmap, even for 2-color icons, which can increase server memory usage dramatically.

The XmtLayoutSeparator gadget draws an etched in separator, using colors appropriate to its parent Layout widget. Because the `XmtNlayoutFrameType` constraint resource can be used to draw separators, this gadget is not often needed. Sometimes however, you will find that you want to draw a separator across the entire width of a column, but the items above and below the separator are centered in the column, rather than filled—in this case, a frame below or above these items would not be wide enough. Or, you might choose to use an explicit LayoutSeparator gadget so that it can be laid out as an object of its own—if a column is made taller, for example, you might want the amount of space between the separator and the items on either side of it to grow, which would not be possible with a frame.

The Layout gadgets can be created with the following constructor functions:

Xmt/

Layout*.c

```
#include <Xmt/LayoutG.h>
Widget XmtCreateLayoutPixmap(Widget parent, String name,
                             ArgList args, Cardinal num_args)
Widget XmtCreateLayoutSeparator(Widget parent, String name,
                                ArgList args, Cardinal num_args)
Widget XmtCreateLayoutSpace(Widget parent, String name,
                            ArgList args, Cardinal num_args)
Widget XmtCreateLayoutString(Widget parent, String name,
                             ArgList args, Cardinal num_args)
```

Table 19-5 lists the resources of each of these new gadgets; you can find more detail in the reference section.

Table 19-5. Layout Gadget Resources

Resource	Type	Description
XmtLayoutString Gadget		
`XmtNlabel`	`String`	The string to display if no XmtNlabelString
`XmtNlabelString`	`XmString`	The XmString to display
`XmtNforeground`	`Pixel`	Foreground color of the string
`XmtNbackground`	`Pixel`	Background color of the string
XmtLayoutPixmap Gadget		
`XmtNpixmap`	`Pixmap`	A pixmap to display
`XmtNbitmap`	`Pixmap`	A bitmap to display
`XmtNbitmask`	`Pixmap`	A mask for non-rectangular icons
`XmtNforeground`	`Pixel`	Foreground color for bitmaps
`XmtNbackground`	`Pixel`	Background color for bitmaps
XmtLayoutSeparator Gadget		
`XmtNorientation`	`XmROrientation`	XmHORIZONTAL or XmVERTICAL
`XtNheight`	`Dimension`	Line width for horizontal separators
`XtNwidth`	`Dimension`	Line width for vertical separators

The title string and icon for the dialog box shown in Figure 19-9 were implemented with a LayoutString and a LayoutPixmap gadget. Example 19-6 shows how. Note the use of colors with these gadgets.

Example 19-6. Using LayoutString and LayoutPixmap Gadgets

examples/

19/dialog

```
!!
!! The children of the dialog, including the String and Pixmap gadgets
!!
*layout.xmtChildren:     XmtLayoutBox titlebox, row, col, buttonbox;\
                         XmtLayoutPixmap icon;\
                         XmtLayoutString title;\
                         XmtInputField fname, lname, phone;\
                         XmtChooser chooser;\
                         XmPushButton okay, cancel, help;\

!! Set up the icon and the string
*icon.bitmap: phone
*icon.foreground: maroon
*title.labelString: @f[HUGE]Rolodex Search
```

Example 19-6. Using LayoutString and LayoutPixmap Gadgets (continued)

```
!! Layout the icon and string correctly
*titlebox.spaceType: LREven
*icon.layoutIn: titlebox
*title.layoutIn: titlebox
*title.layoutJustification: FlushBottom
```

19.4.3.1 Layout Gadgets and Color

Three of the Layout gadget classes have color resources, and there are some points you should note when using these resources.

The LayoutString gadget allows you to specify foreground and background colors for its string. There are a number of occasions in which you might want to use a special color with the LayoutString gadget: for a large title at the top of a dialog box, for example, or to highlight important text or instructions in an interface. The captions drawn by the Layout widget can only use the `XmNforeground` resource of that widget, so if you need a caption with a special color, you'll need to use a LayoutString gadget to simulate that caption.

The LayoutPixmap gadget also has `XmtNforeground` and `XmtNbackground` resources. These are the colors that will be used to draw the foreground and background bits of a specified bitmap. Note that these resources are not used with the `XmtNpixmap` resource—pixmaps have multiple planes, and their colors are encoded directly within the pixmap. Many bitmaps are not rectangular do not look good with a background color that does not match the background of the Layout widget, except perhaps when combined with a frame of some sort, or when used with a bitmask. The "Hello World" examples earlier in this chapter use a bitmask like this so that they can use foreground and background colors that are both distinct from the Layout background color.

The LayoutBox gadget also has an `XmtNbackground` resource; if specified, it fills itself with this color before drawing any of the captions, frames, and gadgets that appear in the row or column. When a row or column is surrounded with a shadowed frame, it sometimes looks good to set the background color of the box to something slightly darker than the default background. This color change can be used to call attention to a particular area of the layout. If you use this technique, note that you'll probably also want to set the background color of any widgets or gadgets that appear within the row or column.

19.5 Layout Grammar

The sections above have presented the gadgets and constraint resources that allow you to specify the arrangement of children in the Layout widget. You can create these gadgets and set these resources exactly as you would work with any other widget. The tutorial presented in Chapter 18, *The Layout Widget: A Tutorial*, however, presented an entirely different technique for specifying layouts—the use of the Layout widget's `XmtNlayout` resource.

The `XmtNlayout` resource is a string which specifies the arrangement of the children of the Layout widget, and may also specify XmtLayoutGadget children to be automatically created. The string is a list of items that appear in the toplevel row or column (its orientation is determined by the `XmtNorientation` resource). These items may include nested rows or columns which have a list of their own items within curly braces. Any item may have a list of modifiers which specify size, stretchability, justification, captions, frames, and so on.

Rows, columns, and other layout gadgets can be automatically created as the layout specification is parsed. Widgets and XmGadget items can be specified by name in the layout string. When an item name is encountered without any type, it is assumed to be a widget or gadget that will be created later. The Layout widget remembers the position and modifiers specified for this widget, and applies them when a widget by that name is eventually created.

The Layout widget does not link the parser for this layout grammar by default. If you specify a value for the `XmtNlayout` resource, you should also register the parser by calling `XmtRegisterLayoutParser()`:

Xmt/

LayoutParse.c

```
#include <Xmt/Layout.h>
void XmtRegisterLayoutParser(void);
```

If an application never calls this function, that code will never be linked. This means that statically linked applications that do not use the parser do not pay the overhead of the parser code.

The layout grammar was designed to be easily readable and intuitive. Example 19-7 shows the `XmtNlayout` specification we used in Chapter 18 to lay out a dialog just like the one we used in the previous section.

Example 19-7. Layout with the XmtNlayout Resource

examples/

18/layout22

```
*layout.layout: \
        Line Bottom 0 4 Fixed LREvenSpaced Row { \
                Bitmap "phone"\
                FlushBottom "@f[HUGE]Rolodex Search"\
        }\
        Row {\
                Col {\
                        FlushRight Caption "@fIFirst name:" fname \
                        FlushRight Caption "@fILast name:" lname \
                        FlushRight Caption "@fIPhone number:" phone \
                }\
                Etched Through 6 4 Caption tll "@fB Search " chooser\
        }\
        <>\
        Fixed Etched Top Equal Even Row { \
                okay cancel help \
        }
```

The sections below provide a fairly formal definition of the syntax of the layout grammar, with semantic explanations of each element interspersed. Items in bold are terminal symbols of the grammar—keywords or punctuation that should appear exactly as shown. Items in italics are non-terminals, which are defined elsewhere. Items within curly braces are repeated zero or more times, items within square brackets are optional, and plain roman text is commentary. It is useful to note that the grammar is case-sensitive and that almost all keywords begin with a capital letter. This means that keywords will not conflict with widget names, which, by convention, begin with a lowercase letter.

19.5.1 Items in the Layout

A layout specification consists of a list of items, each of which may be preceded by an optional list of modifiers:

{ { *modifier* } *item* }

The items in the list will be arranged in a row or column; at the topmost level, this is determined by the `XmtNorientation` resource of the Layout widget. Note that the list of items may contain row or column items that will contain nested lists of items. Note that there is no comma or semicolon separator between items.

Items in a layout may be specified in the following ways. The syntax for item modifiers will be described in the next section.

identifier
: An identifier by itself is taken to be the name of a widget that will be created later. The Layout widget remembers this item's position and all of its modifiers, and applies them when the widget is actually created. An identifier is an unquoted string. Legal identifiers follow the same rules that C variable names do; they may not begin with digits or contain punctuation other than the underscore character.

widget-type identifier
: This syntax creates a widget with the specified type and name. It is only handled if you have called `XmtRegisterLayoutCreateMethod()` to link widget type lookup functions and widget creation functions with the Layout widget. *widget-type* is an identifier which has been registered as the name for a widget class or constructor using `XmtRegisterWidgetClass()`, `XmtRegisterWidgetConstructor()`, or a related function. See the section "Automatic Widget Creation" below for more details.

Row [*name*] **{** *layout* **}**
: The **Row** keyword creates a horizontal LayoutBox gadget, using an optionally specified identifier as the name of the gadget. The curly braces here are required tokens in the grammar, and the grammar "recurses" inside them—the open and close brace bind a list of items (with optional modifiers) to appear in the row.

Col [*name*] { *layout* }
The **Col** keyword is just like the **Row** keyword, but creates column instead of a row.

string A quoted string by itself creates a LayoutString gadget to display the string.

String [*name*] *string*
This syntax also creates a LayoutString gadget to display the specified string, but also allows an optional identifier to specify a name for the gadget.

Pixmap [*name*] *pixmap* [, *mask*]
The **Pixmap** keyword creates a LayoutPixmap gadget, with an optionally specified name, to display the specified pixmap and its optional bitmask. Note that *name* is an unquoted identifier, but that *pixmap* and *mask* are quoted icon names. Invokes the String-to-Pixmap converter to obtain the **Pixmap**, and the String-to-Bitmask converter to obtain the bitmask.

Bitmap [*name*] *bitmap* [, *mask*]
The `Bitmap` keyword is much like the `Pixmap` keyword. It also creates a LayoutPixmap gadget, but it invokes the String-to-Bitmap converter to convert the specified *bitmap* string into a **Pixmap**.

VSep This keyword Creates a vertical LayoutSeparator gadget.

| Shorthand for creating a vertical LayoutSeparator gadget.

HSep Creates a horizontal LayoutSeparator gadget.

= Shorthand for creating a horizontal LayoutSeparator gadget.

Space Creates a LayoutSpace gadget

#{#} Creates a non-stretchable LayoutSpace gadget. The space is `XmtNdefaultSpacing` pixels wide or high for each # character that appears.

~{~} Creates a LayoutSpace gadget with a default size of zero. The stretchability of the the space is `XmtNdefaultStretchability` times the number of ~ characters that appear.

<> Creates a LayoutSpace gadget with a default size of zero, and a very large stretchability. This space is intended to act as an infinitely stretchable space, effectively overriding the stretchability of any other items in a row or column.

19.5.2 Modifiers in the Layout

The nested structure of the Layout grammar mirrors the nested layout behavior of the widget. Thus, the `XmtNlayoutIn` and `XmtNlayoutPosition` constraints for each item in the layout are implicitly specified by the position of that item in the `XmtNlayout` string. The other Layout constraints, and even some of the LayoutBox resources, are specified as a list of modifiers that may precede each item in the layout string. Modifier specifications are not separated from one another with commas or any other special punctuation, and may appear in just about any order before the item they modify. Note that there is one ambiguity in the syntax which prevents you from using a frame or spacing modifier directly before a size specification.

The available modifiers, and their syntax, are described in the following sections.

19.5.2.1 Captions and Frames

There are five constraints that specify the caption for an item, and five constraints that specify the frame. This means that the caption and frame modifiers have a more complicated syntax than most:

Caption [*edge*[*just*[*align*]]] [*margin*] *string*

The **Caption** keyword sets the specified *string* on the `XmtNlayoutCaption` constraint. The optional *edge*, *just*, and *align* tokens set the `XmtNlayoutCaptionPosition`, `XmtNlayoutCaptionJustification`, and `XmtNlayoutCaptionAlignment` constraints. Each is a single lowercase letter, and no blank space is allowed between adjacent letters. *edge* can be one of **l**, **r**, **t**, or **b**, which specify the left, right, top, or bottom edges of the child. *just* can be **l**, **r**, **t**, **b**, or **c** which specify that the caption should be flush against one of the edges or that it should be centered. *align* can be **l**, **r**, or **c**, which specify that individual lines in a multi-line caption should be left, right, or center justified. *margin* is an optional integer that sets `XmtNlayoutCaptionMargin`.

Etched [**In**] [*edge*] [*position*] [*margin* [*thickness*]]

Etched Out [*edge*] [*position*] [*margin* [*thickness*]]

Shadowed [**In**] [*edge*] [*position*] [*margin* [*thickness*]]

Shadowed Out [*edge*] [*position*] [*margin* [*thickness*]]

Boxed [*edge*] [*position*] [*margin* [*thickness*]]

Line [*edge*] [*position*] [*margin* [*thickness*]]

DoubleBoxed [*edge*] [*position*] [*margin* [*thickness*]]

DoubleLine [*edge*] [*position*] [*margin* [*thickness*]]

These modifiers specify the constraint resources that define a frame. The first keyword specifies the `XmtNlayoutFrameLineType` constraint. Note that the **Etched** and **Shadowed** keywords may be followed by **In** or **Out**. **In** is the default. Also, **Boxed** and **Line** are synonyms for the `XmtLayoutFrameSingleLine` type and **DoubleBoxed** and **DoubleLine** are synonyms for the `XmtLayoutFrameDoubleLine` type.

edge specifies the `XmtNlayoutFrameType` constraint. It may be one of the keywords **Left**, **Right**, **Top**, and **Bottom**. If set, the frame will be drawn along one edge of the child. If omitted, the frame will box the child.

position specifies the XmtNlayoutFramePosition constraint. It may be **Inside**, **Outside** or **Through**. If omitted, XmtLayoutFrame-Inside will be used.

margin and *thickness* are integers that optionally specify the Xmt-NlayoutFrameMargin and XmtNlayoutFrameThickness constraints. Note that you must specify the margin in order to specify the thickness. Also note that there is an ambiguity in the grammar, and if a size specification directly follows a frame specification, the size will be mistaken for a frame margin or thickness. Therefore, when specifying a size and a frame, you must specify the size first, or must explicitly include the frame margin and thickness in the frame specification.

19.5.2.2 Item Spacing Models

The LayoutBox XmtNspaceType resource is specified with one of the following keywords, and its associated resources with the optional syntax that follows the keyword. Note that it only makes sense to use this modifier with **Row** and **Col** items.

Even [*size*] [+ *space_stretch* [/ *item_stretch*]]

EvenSpaced [*size*] [+ *space_stretch* [/ *item_stretch*]]

LREvenSpaced [*size*] [+ *space_stretch* [/ *item_stretch*]]

LCRSpaced [*size*] [+ *space_stretch* [/ *item_stretch*]]

IntervalSpaced [*size*] [+ *space_stretch* [/ *item_stretch*]]

These keywords specify the spacing model for a row or column. Note that **Even** is simply a shorter synonym for **EvenSpaced**.

The *size* token specifies the value of the XmtNspace resource, which specifies the size of the each of the spaces to be placed between the children of the row or column. This may be a number of pixels, or a resolution independent size specification, explained below.

space_stretch and *item_stretch* are integers that specify the Xmt-NspaceStretch and XmtNitemStretch resources.

To avoid the ambiguity in the grammar, you should specify any width or height for a row or column before you specify the spacing model.

19.5.2.3 Justification

The following keywords set the XmtNlayoutJustification constraint for any item:

Filled Sets XmtNlayoutJustification to XmtLayoutFilled.

FlushLeft Sets XmtNlayoutJustification to XmtLayoutFlush-Left.

FlushTop Sets XmtNlayoutJustification to XmtLayoutFlush-Top.

FlushRight Sets `XmtNlayoutJustification` to `XmtLayoutFlushRight`.

FlushBottom Sets `XmtNlayoutJustification` to `XmtLayoutFlushBottom`.

Centered Sets `XmtNlayoutJustification` to `XmtLayoutCentered`.

19.5.2.4 Item Size, Stretchability, and Margins

The following modifiers allow you to specify the size, stretchability, shrinkability, and margins for an item. Note that for convenience there are alternate forms of most of these modifiers.

size Sets `XmtNlayoutWidth`.

size **Wide** Sets `XmtNlayoutWidth`.

size **High** Sets `XmtNlayoutHeight`.

size % *size* Sets `XmtNlayoutWidth` to the first *size*, and `XmtNlayoutHeight` to the second.

In each of these size specification syntaxes, *size* may be a number of pixels, or a resolution-independent specification, as explained below. Note that if a size specification follows a frame specification, or a spacing model specification, the size may be parsed as frame margin or thickness or as a space size. To avoid this ambiguity in the grammar, specify size constraints before frame constraints and spacing resources.

Equal
This special modifier sets the LayoutBox `XmtNlayoutEqual` resource to True for a row or column. This specifies that all items in a row, except spaces and separators, should be made equally wide, and that items in a column should be made equally high.

Fixed
Specifies that the item should be neither stretchable nor shrinkable—it sets `XmtNlayoutStretchability` and `XmtNlayoutShrinkability` to zero.

Stretchable
Specifies that the item should have a very large stretchability and shrinkability. This effectively makes the item "infinitely" stretchable.

\+ *integer*
Explicitly sets `XmtNlayoutStretchability` constraint.

\- *integer*
Explicitly sets `XmtNlayoutShrinkability` constraint.

Margin *integer*
Sets `XmtNlayoutMarginWidth` and `XmtNlayoutMarginHeight` to the same specified value.

Margin Width *integer*
Sets `XmtNlayoutMarginWidth` as specified.

Margin Height *integer*
Sets `XmtNlayoutMarginHeight` as specified.

19.5.2.5 Other Modifiers

There are three remaining modifiers that do not fall into any of the categories above.

Color *string* — Specifies the `XmtNbackground` resource of a row or column, or the `XmtNforeground` resource of any other XmtLayoutGadget child. The string is converted to a Pixel value by calling the String-to-Pixel converter.

Unresizable — Sets `XmtNlayoutAllowResize` constraint to `False`.

Unmanaged — Specifies that the item should not be managed when created. This only applies to items, such as LayoutString and LayoutPixmap gadgets, that are automatically created by the Layout widget. Note that this modifier does not correspond to any constraint or other resource.

19.5.3 Resolution Independence

The modifiers shown in the section above allow you to set the `XmtNlayoutWidth` and `XmtNlayoutHeight` constraints, and the LayoutBox `XmtNspace` resource to a value specified as a *size*. This value is an integer number of pixels, or a floating-point number, with a resolution-independent unit:

float	A size in pixels; rounded to an integer.
float **in**	A size in inches; converted to pixels and rounded.
float **mm**	A size in millimeters; converted and rounded.
float **pt**	A size in printer's points; converted and rounded.
float **em**	A size in ems; converted and rounded.
float **en**	A size in ens; converted and rounded.

Inches, millimeters, and points are converted to pixels using the resolution of the screen that the widget appears on, as reported by Xlib. A printer's point is converted by treating it as 1/72 of an inch. An em is a font-relative units equal to the width of the capital letter M in the `XmtNfont` or `XmtNfontList` resources. An en is half the width of an em.

Resolution independence can be achieved without the layout parser by calling the unit conversion function `XmtLayoutConvertSizeToPixels()`. It takes a `double` which is the size to convert, an enumerated value which specifies the units for that size, and returns the equivalent size in pixels for the screen and font of the widget.

Note that this resolution independence scheme differs from the standard Motif scheme. The Layout widget does not make use of the XmManager XmNunit-Type resource to automatically convert specified sizes to pixels.

19.5.4 Automatic Widget Creation

The function XmtRegisterLayoutCreateMethod() registers the functions necessary for the layout parser to parse widget type names and automatically create widgets of those types.

Xmt/

LayoutCreate.c

```
#include <Xmt/Layout.h>
void XmtRegisterLayoutCreateMethod(void);
```

The reason this registration function must be called explicitly is the same reason that the layout parser must be explicitly registered: so that applications that do not use this functionality do not pay the overhead of having it automatically linked in.

If this registration function has been called, and the widget types have been registered with XmtRegisterWidgetClass(), XmtRegisterWidget-Constructor() and related functions, then the layout parser will parse widget types and can create the children of the Layout widget while parsing the layout string.

Widget types are registered and parsed, and widgets are created in the same way as is done by XmtCreateChildren() and related functions. See Xmt-LookupWidgetType() for more information about looking up widget types, and XmtCreateWidgetType() for information about creating an instance of a widget given its type.

19.6 Other Layout Features

The sections above have explained the major features of the Layout widget for arranging children. There are a number of minor features that are not so directly related to the layout of children, but which are worth being aware of anyway. They are described in the following subsections.

19.6.1 Dynamic Relayout

One of the features of the Layout widget is the ease with which the layout can be dynamically modified. When a child (a button in a button box, for example) is unmanaged, the layout is recomputed so that the space that the child occupied does not remain blank and unused. Even more powerful (though less commonly useful) is the fact that an object can be moved from one row or column to another by simply changing its XmtNlayoutIn, XmtNlayoutAfter, or XmtNlayoutBefore constraints.

Whenever a child is managed or unmanaged, has its position in the layout changed, or has its size (or caption, frame, or margin size) changed, then the Layout widget must re-calculate the size and position of each of its children. Normally, the Layout widget will automatically perform this relayout whenever it is needed. If you will be making a series of changes that will each trigger this recalculation, however, you can make the process more efficient by disabling the layout calculations before you start and re-enabling them when done. This is done with the functions `XmtLayoutDisableLayout()` and `XmtLayoutEnableLayout()`:

Xmt/

Layout.c

```
#include <Xmt/Layout.h>
void XmtLayoutDisableLayout(Widget layout);
void XmtLayoutEnableLayout(Widget layout);
```

Both of these functions take a Layout widget as their single argument. `XmtLayoutDisableLayout()` instructs the widget to stop recomputing its layout when its children's managed state, size, or position change, but simply to note that a relayout is required. `XmtLayoutEnableLayout()` instructs the Layout widget to relayout its children, if a relayout is necessary, and to begin performing automatic relayouts again. Calls to these two functions are counted and may be nested—layout will not be re-enabled until `XmtLayoutEnableLayout()` has been called as many times as `XmtLayoutDisableLayout()`.

Example 19-8 shows how you might use this pair of functions to manage one child and unmanage another without causing two relayouts. Note that these functions are also available in resource files, if you call `XmtRegisterXmtProcedures()`

Example 19-8. Disabling and Re-enabling Automatic Relayout

```
XmtLayoutDisableLayout(layout);
XtUnmanageChild(text_widget);
XtManageChild(label_widget);
XmtLayoutEnableLayout(layout);
```

19.6.2 Debugging Layouts

Large layouts can become fairly complicated and confusing; it can be difficult to keep track of just what items are contained in which rows and columns. If you find yourself having trouble getting arranging your widgets the way you want them, you can try setting the `XmtNdebugLayout` resource on the Layout widget. (Note that this is not a constraint resource or a LayoutBox resource, but is one of the few actual Layout resources.)

When `XmtNdebugLayout` is set to `True`, the Layout widget will draw a one-pixel box around each of its children, including rows, columns, and spaces. This makes the nested structure of the layout more apparent and can help your debugging. This `XmtNdebugLayout` frame takes precedence over any regular frame you have specified for the widgets, and when this resource is set, the XmtNlayoutFrameType and related frame constraints are ignored.

19.6.3 Default Spacing

Another of the Layout's regular, non-constraint, resources is XmtNdefault-Spacing. This resource is used in two ways. First, when you use the # token in the layout grammar to create a fixed-width LayoutSpace gadget, the width and height of that space is set to the value of XmtNdefaultSpacing. Second, the default value of the XmtNlayoutMarginWidth and XmtNlayout-MarginHeight constraints, for all children other than rows and columns, is set to half of XmtNdefaultSpacing. This means that when two items abut one another in a layout, they will be separated by this default number of pixels.

The default value of XmtNdefaultSpacing is 10 pixels. The Layout widget overrides the defaults for the XmNmarginWidth and XmNmarginHeight resources to both be 5 pixels. What this means is that when an item in the layout is next to an edge of the Layout widget, it will be 10 pixels (5 + 10/2) from the edge, just as it would be separated from another item by 10 pixels.

19.6.4 Fonts and Strings in the Layout

The LayoutString gadget does not have a font resource—it draws its specified string using the font list of it parent Layout widget. This is the same font list that is used to draw captions. You specify this XmFontList with the Layout Xmt-NfontList resource. If you are specifying this resource from C, and if you are using only a single font, rather than a list of fonts, you can alternatively specify an XFontStruct pointer with the XmtNfont resource. A font specified on the XmtNfont resource will be converted internally to an XmFontList by the Layout widget.

In a similar vein, notice that while the XmtNlayoutCaption constraint requires an XmString value, the LayoutString gadget will display an XmString specified on the XmtNlabelString resource, or a regular null-terminated C string specified on the XmtNlabel resource. In C code, it is usually easier to set the XmtNlabel resource, and have the LayoutString gadget automatically convert it (with XmtCreateXmString()) to an XmString for you.

19.6.5 Converting Resolution-Independent Units to Pixels

When specifying a layout with the XmtNlayout string, you can use keywords like **in**, **mm**, and **em** to specify sizes in resolution-independent units. If you want to specify resolution-independent sizes from C code, an extra step is required—you must perform the conversion explicitly with XmtLayout-ConvertSizeToPixels():

Xmt/

Layout.c

```
#include <Xmt/Layout.h>
typedef enum {
    XmtLayoutPoints,          /* 1/72 of an inch */
    XmtLayoutInches,          /* 25.4 millimeters */
    XmtLayoutMillimeters,     /* depends on display resolution */
    XmtLayoutEms,             /* width of 'M' in widget font */
    XmtLayoutEns              /* 1/2 of an em */
} XmtLayoutUnitType;

int XmtLayoutConvertSizeToPixels(Widget layout,
                                 double size,
                                 XmtLayoutUnitType units);
```

This function converts a floating-point size with the specified units to pixels, and returns the pixel size as an integer. The widget argument is necessary because the conversion depends either upon the resolution of the screen of the widget, or upon the size of the font of the widget.

19.6.6 Resource Converters

The Layout widget uses `XmtRegisterEnumConverter()` (see Chapter 8, *Utility Functions*) to register resource converters for all of the enumerated types used in its various constraints: `XmtLayoutJustification`, `XmtLayoutEdge`, `XmtLayoutFrameType`, `XmtLayoutFrameLineType`, `XmtLayoutFramePosition`, and `XmtLayoutSpaceType`.

As is obvious from the examples throughout this chapter, these resource converters allow you to specify resources of these types from resource files using exactly the same string as you would in C. Note that the resource converter is case-sensitive, so you must capitalize values just as you would in C. The converters do allow you to strip leading prefixes off of these values, however, so `XmtLayoutFlushBottom` could be specified as "LayoutFlushBottom", or even just "FlushBottom", for example, and `XmtLayoutFrameEtchedIn` could be specified as "EtchedIn".

20

Easy Menu Creation

A menu bar with its associated pulldown menus is a user interface component common to almost all GUIs. Creating a menu system with the Motif widgets, however, is an annoyingly complex task. First you create the menu bar and add cascade buttons to it. Then you create menu panes as siblings of the cascade buttons, and associate one pane with each button. Finally, you add the push buttons, toggle buttons, labels, and separators that you want to each of the menu panes. To set the labels for the widgets, you must create numerous `XmString`s; if you want mnemonics and accelerators for the buttons, you must

examples/

20/menu.ad

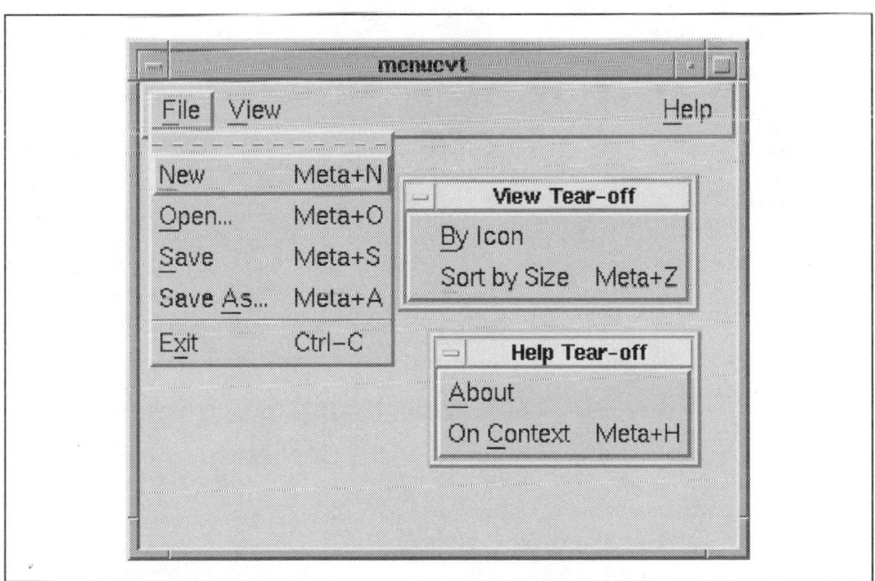

Figure 20-1. A menu bar and its menus

set the appropriate resources, and of course you must register a callback function to be called for each button.

Menus have a repetitive structure, and creating them lends itself well to automation. The Motif SimpleMenu creation routines added in Motif 1.1 go a long way towards making menu creation easier (their greatest weakness is that they only allow one callback to be specified per menu pane). A common approach, and something you may have tried yourself, is to initialize a static array of structures which describe the menus you want, and write a function which reads those structures and creates the menu panes, buttons, labels, and separators they describe. Once this is done, your main application code need only call this one function to create the application's entire menu system.

Instead of a menu-creation function of this sort, Xmt provides a special XmtMenu widget that serves the same purpose. This Menu widget is a subclass of the XmRowColumn widget, which is the widget used to implement menu bar and menu panes in Motif. The new Menu resource `XmtNitems` takes an array of structures that describe the items to appear in a menu bar or menu pane and the widget will automatically create the described items. This chapter describes all the details of the XmtMenu widget.

20.1 Describing a Menu System with Resources

The real innovation of the Xmt menu creation scheme is that it allows menus to be described through resource files, rather than through more awkward C structures. Example 20-1 is an example resource file that, with the functions described in this chapter, was used to create the menu system shown in Figure 20-1.

Example 20-1. Resources that Describe a Typical Menu System

examples/

20/menu.ad

```
*menubar.items: \
Tearoff        "_File" -> file ;\
Tearoff        "_View" -> view ;\
Tearoff Help "_Help" -> help ;

*menubar*file.items: \
        "_New"          [Meta+N]        NewFile();\
        "_Open..."      [Meta+O]        OpenFile();\
        "_Save"         [Meta+S]        SaveFile();\
        "Save _As..."   [Meta+A]        {GetFilename(); SaveFile();}\
        --------- ; \
        "E_xit"         [Ctrl-C]        Quit();

*menubar*view.items: \
        "_By Icon" | "_By Name"         $view_by_name ;\
  Off   "_Sort by Size" [Meta+Z]        $sort_by_size ;

*menubar*help.items: \
        "_About"                        About();\
        "On _Context"   [Meta+H]        ContextHelp();
```

Note that there are only four resources in this example; most lines end with a backslash so that the next actual line is parsed as a continuation of the same logical line. The first resource, `*menubar.items`, specifies that the menu bar will have three cascade buttons, with labels **File**, **View**, and **Help**. The mnemonic characters for these buttons will be `F`, `V`, and `H`, which are preceded by an underscore character in the menu grammar. These characters will appear underlined in the actual menu. Attached to these buttons will be the menu panes named `file`, `view`, and `help`. The description of each menu item is terminated with a semicolon. The **Help** cascade button will appear to the far right of the menu bar because it has the special keyword "Help" in its description, which flags it as the special case help menu. (The Motif style guide specifies that help menus should always appear at the extreme right of the menu bar.)

When the Menu widget `menubar` is created, it will read this `XmtNitems` resource and automatically create the three cascade buttons it describes. Since these cascade buttons have attached panes, however, it will also create new Menu widgets for each of these panes. Thus, creating the single toplevel menu bar widget will cause the entire menu system to be created.

The grammar for describing menus will be explained in detail later in the chapter, but to get an idea of what is possible, take a look at the remaining three resources in Example 20-1. As we saw, a mnemonic is specified with an underscore before the mnemonic character in the item's label. For the buttons in the menu panes themselves, we see that accelerators are specified as modifier plus letter combinations within square brackets. Separators are specified simply as an item consisting of one or more dashes. The items in the **View** menu pane are toggle buttons. The first toggle button in the menu has alternate labels to display in each of its states. The second toggle button has the "Off" keyword, which specifies that it starts in its unselected state. Both toggle buttons have the names of an `XmtSymbol` specified. (The `$` flags the name of a symbol. See Chapter 12, *Symbols*, for more information about Symbols in Xmt.) These `Boolean` Symbols will have their values updated whenever the state of the toggle buttons changes. All of the push buttons in the menu panes are specified with the name of one or more functions that are to be called when that button is selected—these callbacks are parsed by the String-to-Callback converter described in Chapter 10, *Callbacks in Resource Files*.

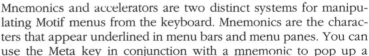

Menu Mnemonics and Accelerators

Mnemonics and accelerators are two distinct systems for manipulating Motif menus from the keyboard. Mnemonics are the characters that appear underlined in menu bars and menu panes. You can use the Meta key in conjunction with a mnemonic to pop up a menu pane from the menu bar. Once the menu pane is popped up, you can simply type the mnemonic of an item within the pane to select it. When building a menu from scratch, you specify the mnemonic for an item with the `XmNmnemonic` resource (a resource of the XmLabel widget).

Menu Mnemonics and Accelerators (continued)

Accelerators are different: an accelerator key sequence is a direct shortcut to invoking a menu item without popping up its menu pane. The XmLabel resource `XmNaccelerator` specifies the key sequence that will invoke the menu item; it is a string using the translation table syntax. The `XmNacceleratorText` resource is an `XmString` that will appear to the right of the item in the menu; it should be a human-readable representation of the accelerator (`Ctrl+A`, for example, instead of the more obscure `Ctrl<Key>A` that would be specified for the `XmNaccelerator` resource).

Note that the XmtMenu widget that is described in this chapter provides much easier ways to specify both mnemonics and accelerators for your menu items. Note also that accelerators are handled quite differently in Motif than in Xt. In Xt, accelerators are a very general mechanism for invoking actions in one widget when certain events occur in another widget. These X Toolkit accelerators are specified with the `XtNaccelerators` resource and installed (bound to another widget in which events will occur) with `XtInstallAccelerators()`.

In Motif, accelerators are used exclusively for invoking menu actions when keyboard events occur in other widgets. Motif uses the Xt accelerator mechanism, but installs accelerators for all menu items automatically on all other widgets in the interface. (All you have to do is specify the `XmNaccelerator` resource—Motif handles the rest.) Since this installation is done automatically, it is difficult to use Xt accelerators in a Motif program without causing conflicts with Motif accelerators.

There's a useful trick you can use with Motif accelerators: sometimes you want to implement a keyboard command for which there is no corresponding menu item. In a drawing editor program, for example, you might want a keypress to select one of the drawing tools displayed in a toolbox or palette. You can implement this kind of keyboard shortcut if you create an unmanaged menu bar, which is never visible but which contains one item (with its `XmNaccelerator` resource set) for each keyboard command you want to implement.

—djf

Consider some of the advantages to a scheme like this for describing menus. The first is the compactness and readability of the format. If we agree that menu labels need to be customizable through the database, then the mnemonics, and probably the accelerators, need to be customizable as well. If we had to specify these all as separate resources for each button, a menu description would be much longer and much harder to figure out.

Describing the menu system through the resource manager not only provides customizability for labels and mnemonics, though; it also allows the users to modify the whole structure of the menu—to add, remove, and rearrange the buttons to suit themselves. Some sophisticated X applications, like *xterm* and the *twm* and *mwm* window managers, for example, provide a number of publicly available action procedures which can be bound to key strokes through a translation table in a user's personal resource file. If your application provides this sort of public function, and if you register those functions as callbacks (instead of or in addition to registering them as actions), then the user or system administrator can customize your application to call them from menu buttons.*

20.2 The XmtMenu widget

Menus in Motif are simply ordinary buttons, labels, and separators placed within XmRowColumn widgets to form menu bars and menu panes. Xmt simplifies menu creation through the XmtMenu widget. This is a simple subclass of XmRowColumn with only a few new resources. The two important new features of this widget, however, are that it will automatically create the widgets needed for the menu items you describe, and that it has a resource converter to parse menu descriptions from a resource file, using an intuitive grammar.

You describe a menu using the `XmtNitems` resource. From C, you specify a null-terminated array of `XmtMenuItem` structures for this resource (you can also specify the `XmtNnumItems` resource if you don't want to null-terminate your array of items.) Each `XmtMenuItem` structure contains the string to appear in the menu, the mnemonic, accelerator, and so on; the fields of this structure are documented in a later section.

When specifying a menu from a resource file, you also use the `XmtNitems` resource, but the Xmt String-to-XmtMenuItemList converter will convert your specification into the requisite null-terminated array of `XmtMenuItem` structures for you. In order to take advantage of this converter, you must register it before creating any menus. You can do this by calling `XmtRegisterMenuItemsConverter()`:

Xmt/

MenuCvt.c

```
#include <Xmt/Converters.h>
void XmtRegisterMenuItemsConverter(void);
```

Many widgets automatically register any resource converters they need. Since this converter is a large, complex one, the Menu widget lets you choose whether or not to register it. Applications that describe their menus exclusively in C need not register it, and will not have to link with this extra code. While on the subject of resource converters, note that the Menu widget uses the Xmt

*There are of course situations in which you do not want the user to be able to override the layout of your menus (or other resources). This does not mean that you have to sacrifice the ease of programming with resources; Chapter 13, *Resource File Utilities: mockup, checkres, and ad2c*, discusses how your application can read a private resource file that the user cannot customize.

String-to-Callback converter to parse the menu item callback specifications shown in the resource file example above. This means that if you want to include callbacks in your menu specification you must also call `XmtRegisterCallbackConverter()`, and must register names for any of the procedures you intend to call with `XmtRegisterProcedures()` or a related function.

Recall that the Menu widget is simply a subclass of XmRowColumn; it acts as a container for a menu bar or a single menu pane. When describing menus, however, you can include pointers to submenus, and the parent Menu widget will automatically create these submenus (themselves Menu widgets) along with any XmMenuShell widgets that are required. Automatic submenu creation enables you to describe an entire menu hierarchy, and then make a single call to create the menu bar, which will automatically create all of the menu panes as well as any subpanes.

You will typically create a Menu widget using one of the four convenience procedures provided:

Xmt/

Menu.c

```
#include <Xmt/Menu.h>
Widget XmtCreateMenubar(Widget parent, String name,
                        ArgList args, Cardinal num_args);
Widget XmtCreateMenuPane(Widget parent, String name,
                         ArgList args, Cardinal num_args);
Widget XmtCreatePopupMenu(Widget parent, String name,
                          ArgList args, Cardinal num_args);
Widget XmtCreateOptionMenu(Widget parent, String name,
                           ArgList args, Cardinal num_args);
```

`XmtCreateMenubar()` is a generic widget constructor function. It is equivalent to creating a Menu widget with `XtCreateWidget()` and the class pointer `xmtMenuWidgetClass`. This is also the function that you will use most often—it will automatically create any submenu of the menu bar.

`XmtCreateMenuPane()` creates a Menu widget for use as a menu pane, and creates each of the items within the pane. It first creates an XmMenuShell widget for the pane, or finds a shell that it can share with a sibling pane. As with `XmtCreateMenubar()`, this function will also automatically create any submenu panes. You can attach the menu pane returned by this function to any cascade button in your interface using the standard `XmNsubMenuId` resource. You might use this function if you wanted to add a new menu pane to the menu bar at runtime.

`XmtCreatePopupMenu()` creates an XmMenuShell widget with a Menu widget as its child. In addition, it will register an event handler on the parent widget you specify that will pop up the menu widget when a specified mouse button/modifier key combination is pressed. This event handler is an extra convenience that is not provided by the standard Motif popup menu creation function.

An option menu is an XmRowColumn widget with an XmLabel and an XmCascadeButton that has a menu pane attached. `XmtCreateOptionMenu()` creates the XmRowColumn, XmLabel, and XmCascadeButton, and a Menu to attach to the cascade button. This constructor is less useful than the others; the XmtChooser widget (see Chapter 27, *Presenting Choices*) is usually an easier way to create and manage option menus.

20.3 Describing Menus with C Structures

For reasons of customizability, it is often a good idea to specify your menus from a resource file. It is also easier to do it this way. If you do want to hardcode them in C, however, you can do so by initializing an array of `XmtMenuItem` structures. This structure is declared in *<Xmt/Menu.h>* and is shown in Example 20-2.

Example 20-2. The XmtMenuItem Structure

```
typedef struct _XmtMenuItem {
    /* public fields: programmer initializes some or all of these */
    unsigned type;
    String label;
    char mnemonic;
    String accelerator;
    String accelerator_label;
    XtCallbackProc callback;
    XtPointer client_data;
    struct _XmtMenuItem *submenu;
    String symbol_name;
    String alt_label;
    char alt_mnemonic;
    String name;

    /* private state: don't initialize these */
    Widget w;               /* the widget or gadget for this menu item */
    Widget submenu_pane;    /* the Menu widget created with cascade buttons */
    String submenu_name;
    short sensitive;
    XmtSymbol symbol;
    XmString label0, label1;
} XmtMenuItem;
```

Note that the `XmtMenuItem` structure has both public fields that may be (or must be) initialized and private fields that are used internally by the Menu widget and should not be set or read by the programmer. The fields in an `XmtMenuItem` structure are arranged in most-commonly-used to least-commonly-used order, so that for most menu items you need only initialize the first few fields you care about, and leave the others uninitialized. (If your array of structures is declared static, then the C language guarantees that uninitialized fields will contain NULL, which is their proper value.) The fields have the following meanings:

`type`
: The type of the item to be created, plus any flags that apply to the item. Set this field to the sum of a legal `XmtMenuItemType` value and any of the flags. The legal types and flags are shown in Example 20-3. Set this field to `XmtMenuItemEnd` only when this is the last element in an array of menu items, and when you will not be specifying the `XmtNnumItems` resource. `XmtMenuItemEnd` is a special value that lets you null-terminate an array of `XmtMenuItem` structures. The meaning of each of the remaining `XmtMenuItemType` values is self-evident; each specifies the type of widget to be created in the menu bar or menu pane. The legal flags and their meanings are as follows:

`XmtMenuItemOn`
: This flag is only meaningful when the item is a toggle button. If set, it specifies that the toggle button should be "on" when the menu is first created. If not set, then the toggle button will start out "off."

`XmtMenuItemHelp`
: This flag only applies to cascade buttons in a menu bar. It specifies that the item is the cascade button for the "Help" menu, and should appear at the far right of the menu bar. Only one item in a menu bar may have this flag set.

`XmtMenuItemTearoff`
: This flag only applies to cascade buttons, and only works in Motif 1.2 and later. It specifies that the menu pane attached to this cascade button should be a tearoff menu that the user can detach and leave posted.

`XmtMenuItemPixmap`
: This flag applies to all items except the separators. It specifies that the `label` field (and the `alt_label` field, if specified) of the `XmtMenuItem` structure contains the name of a Pixmap to be converted with the String-to-Pixmap converter rather than text to display.

`XmtMenuItemCallbackList`
: If this flag is set, it indicates that the `callback` field of the `XmtMenuItem` structure points to a NULL-terminated `XtCallbackList` array, rather than to a function. In this case, the `client_data` field of the `XmtMenuItem` structure is unused. Use this flag when you want to invoke more than one callback procedure for a given menu item.

Example 20-3. Menu Item Types and Flags

```
/* types of menu items */
typedef enum {
    XmtMenuItemEnd,  /* special: used to NULL-terminate the array of items */
    XmtMenuItemPushButton,
    XmtMenuItemToggleButton,
    XmtMenuItemCascadeButton,
    XmtMenuItemSeparator,
```

Example 20-3. Menu Item Types and Flags (continued)

```
    XmtMenuItemDoubleSeparator,
    XmtMenuItemLabel,
} XmtMenuItemType;

/* flags for menu items */
#define XmtMenuItemOn       0x10  /* initial state of toggle button is on */
#define XmtMenuItemHelp     0x20  /* cascade button goes to far right of bar */
#define XmtMenuItemTearoff  0x40  /* this button tears off the menu */
#define XmtMenuItemPixmap   0x80  /* label is a pixmap name, not a string */
#define XmtMenuItemCallbackList 0x100 /* callback is a list, not a func */
```

`label`
: The text or pixmap to appear in the menu item. If the `XmtMenuItemPixmap` flag is not set, then the string will be converted to an `XmString` with `XmtCreateXmString()`. If the flag is set, then this field contains the name of a pixmap which will be converted with the String-to-Pixmap converter. The resulting `XmString` or `Pixmap` will be displayed in the menu item. This field should be set to `NULL` for separators.

`mnemonic`
: The mnemonic character for push buttons, toggle buttons, and cascade buttons. This character will be set on the `XmNmnemonic` resource of the button, and will cause the specified character to be underlined in the item label. This character serves as a shortcut for invoking the menu item when the menu pane has been popped up.

`accelerator`
: The accelerator for a push button or a toggle button. This string will be set on the item's `XmNaccelerator` resource. It specifies a keyboard shortcut for invoking the menu item without ever popping up the menu pane that contains it. The shortcut is specified using translation table syntax.

`accelerator_label`
: The label to appear at the right of a push button or a toggle button to indicate that an accelerator is available. This string will be converted to an `XmString`, using the font tag, if any, that was specified with the Menu `XmtNacceleratorFontTag` resource, and the resulting `XmString` will be set on the `XmNacceleratorText` resource of the item. This field usually contains the same information as the `accelerator` field, but in human-readable form, rather than in the more awkward translation table syntax.

`callback`
: A function to be registered with `XtAddCallback()` on the `XmNactivateCallback` of a push button or on the `XmNvalueChangedCallback` of a toggle button. If the `XmtMenuItemCallbackList` flag is set, then this field specifies an `XtCallbackList` rather than a function (you'll have to use a cast to specify this). In this case, the list of callback procedures will be registered with a call to `XtAddCallbacks()`.

`client_data`
: The untyped data to be registered with and passed to the callback procedure specified on the `callback` field. If the `XmtMenuItemCallbackList` flag is set, then this field is unused.

`submenu`
: For cascade buttons, this field points to an array of `XmtMenuItem` structures which specify the contents of the menu pane that will pop up from the button. This array of `XmtMenuItems` structures must be "null-terminated" with a structure with its `type` set to `XmtMenuItemEnd`. If this `submenu` field is specified, the Menu widget will create another Menu widget for the menu pane, passing this new array of menu items as the `XmtNitems` resource. If you use this field, you generally only need to create the toplevel menu bar—if you've initialized your `XmtMenuItem` structures correctly, all the menu panes for the menu bar will be automatically created. If this field is not set for a cascade button menu item, the Menu widget will issue a warning message.

`symbol_name`
: For toggle buttons, this field optionally specifies the name of a registered `XmtSymbol` of type `Boolean`. This Symbol will be looked up, and the variable it names will be updated every time the user changes the state of this toggle button menu item. Also, the Menu widget will monitor the state of the Symbol, and will update the toggle button state whenever the value of the Symbol changes through a call to `XmtSymbolSetValue()`. Symbols are discussed in Chapter 12, *Symbols*.

`alt_label`
: For toggle buttons, this field specifies a string or the name of a Pixmap to display in the button when the widget is in its selected state. If specified, this string is handled the same way as the `label` field is. If an alternate label is specified, then the toggle button is displayed without its square toggle indicator, since the labels themselves indicate what state the button is in. You could use an alternate label to implement a menu item that read **Show Headers** in one state and **Hide Headers** in the other, for example.

`alt_mnemonic`
: For toggle buttons, this field specifies an alternate mnemonic to use when the button is in its selected state, and the alternate label is being displayed. If the `alt_label` field is not set, then this field is ignored.

`name`
: This field specifies the name of the menu item to be created, for any type of item. By default, items are automatically assigned names by the Menu widget that creates them. In some cases, however, you may want to assign a name explicitly, so that you can look up and manipulate the widget later, for example.

Example 20-4 shows how you could create a simple menu system using an array of `XmtMenuItem` structures.

Example 20-4. Creating Menus from C

examples/

20/menu.c

```
#include <Xmt/Xmt.h>
#include <Xmt/Menu.h>
        .
        .
        .
static XmtMenuItem file_menu_items[] = {
    {XmtMenuItemPushButton, "New", 'N', "Meta<Key>N", "Meta+N", NewFile },
    {XmtMenuItemPushButton, "Open...", 'O', "Meta<Key>O", "Meta+O", OpenFile},
    {XmtMenuItemPushButton, "Save", 'S', "Meta<Key>S", "Meta+S", SaveFile},
    {XmtMenuItemPushButton, "Save As...", 'A', "Meta<Key>A", "Meta+A", SaveAs},
    {XmtMenuItemSeparator},
    {XmtMenuItemPushButton, "Exit", 'x', "Ctrl<Key>C", "Ctrl-C", Quit},
    {XmtMenuItemEnd}
};

static XmtMenuItem view_menu_items[] = {
    {XmtMenuItemToggleButton, "By Icon", 'B', NULL, NULL, NULL, NULL, NULL,
        "view_by_name", "By Name", 'B'},
    {XmtMenuItemToggleButton, "Sort by Size", 'S', "Meta<Key>Z", "Meta+Z",
        NULL, NULL, NULL, "sort_by_size"},
    {XmtMenuItemEnd}
};

static XmtMenuItem help_menu_items[] = {
    {XmtMenuItemPushButton, "About", 'A', NULL, NULL, About},
    {XmtMenuItemPushButton, "On Context", 'C', "Meta<Key>H", "Meta+H",
        ContextHelp},
    {XmtMenuItemEnd}
};

static XmtMenuItem menubar_items[] = {
    {XmtMenuItemCascadeButton + XmtMenuItemTearoff,
        "File", 'F', NULL, NULL, NULL, NULL, file_menu_items},
    {XmtMenuItemCascadeButton + XmtMenuItemTearoff,
        "View", 'V', NULL, NULL, NULL, NULL, view_menu_items},
    {XmtMenuItemCascadeButton+XmtMenuItemHelp+XmtMenuItemTearoff,
        "Help", 'H',  NULL, NULL, NULL, NULL, help_menu_items},
};

void main(int argc, char **argv)
{
    Widget toplevel, layout, menubar;
    Arg args[5];
    int ac;
        .
        .
    ac = 0;
    XtSetArg(args[ac], XmtNitems, menubar_items); ac++;
    XtSetArg(args[ac], XmtNnumItems, XtNumber(menubar_items)); ac++;
    menubar = XmtCreateMenubar(layout, "menubar", args, ac);
    XtManageChild(menubar);
        .
        .
}
```

There are a couple of points to note about this example. First, notice that the items for the menu panes must be declared before the items for the menu bar itself. This is so that each of the cascade button items in the menu bar can point to the array of items in its associated menu pane. Second, notice that we set both the `XmtNitems` and the `XmtNnumItems` resources when we create the menu bar. Thus the array of items for the menu bar does not need to be null-terminated with the special value `XmtMenuItemEnd` in its `type` field. The arrays that describe the menu panes do need to be null-terminated in this way, however, because there is no means of specifying their length in the parent `XmtMenuItem` structure that points to them.

Laying Out a Menu Bar

One of the features of the XmtLayout widget is that it automatically maintains a reasonable margin between adjacent widgets, and between widgets and the edge of the shell widget that contains them. Menu bars happen to be one of the rare cases in Motif of a widget that looks better without a margin. So, when you use the Layout widget to lay out a main window with a menu bar (as opposed to using it for a dialog box) you'll probably want to remove the margins around the menu bar.

There are actually two steps required. First, you must set the margin so that the Layout reserves around its edges to zero:

```
*layout.marginWidth: 0
*layout.marginHeight: 0
```

And then you must set the margin that the Layout provides around the menu bar to zero:

```
*menubar.layoutMarginWidth: 0
*menubar.layoutMarginHeight: 0
```

Resources like these were used to get the menu bar flush against the top, left, and right edges of the window in the first figure of this chapter.

If your menu bar has a lot of items in it, and your main window is otherwise not too large, you might consider using an XmMainWindow widget to lay out the menu bar. The XmMainWindow is not a particularly interesting widget, but it has one useful feature that the XmtLayout and other Motif managers do not have—if the window is not wide enough to accommodate all the items in the menu bar, it will "wrap" the menu bar so that it has two or more rows of cascade buttons. If you use any other manager widget, then cascade buttons that do not fit in the available horizontal space will simply fall off the end of the menu bar and be inaccessible.

—djf

20.4 The Menu Description Grammar

All of the menu description features available with the `XmtMenuItem` structure from C are also available when you describe your menus in a resource file. You can call `XmtRegisterMenuItemsConverter()` to register a String-to-XmtMenuItemList resource converter that will convert your menu description to a null-terminated array of `XmtMenuItem` structures. To the Menu widget it makes no difference whatsoever whether you specify the `XmtNitems` resource from C or from a resource file. Using a resource file makes your application more customizable, however, and is usually easier. This section documents the menu description grammar, using BNF annotated with comments and explanations. In the description below, items in **bold** are terminals of the grammar—that is, they must appear exactly as shown. Items in italics are non-terminals—they will be defined in terms of underlying terminals. Items within square brackets are optional, and items in curly braces are repeated zero or more times.

menu::

{ *item* }

A menu specification is zero or more item specifications.

item::

[*name*] [*type*] { *flags* } [*label*] [*accelerator*] [*submenu*] [*symbol*] **;**

[*name*] [*type*] { *flags* } [*label*] [*accelerator*] [*submenu*] [*symbol*] *callbacks*

A menu item has an optional name, type, label, accelerator, submenu name, symbol name, and callback specifications. It also can have any number of flags set. If no callback or callbacks are specified for the menu item, then the item specification must be followed by a semicolon. When callbacks are specified, the semicolons following the callback calls themselves are sufficient.

[*name*] **-** { **-** } **;**

One or more hyphens, with a name optionally specified, form a special syntax for a single-line separator menu item. The hyphens must be followed by a terminating semicolon.

[*name*] **=** { **=** } **;**

One or more equal signs, with a name optionally specified, form a special syntax for a double-line separator menu item. The equal signs must be followed by a terminating semicolon.

name::

ident **:**

The name of a menu item is specified as an identifier followed by a colon. Any legal C variable name is a legal identifier; identifiers do not appear within quotes.

type::

Title	Item is a label, or a title for the menu
Button	Item is a push button
Toggle	Item is a toggle button
Submenu	Item is a cascade button, with a submenu to be attached
Line	Item is a separator
DoubleLine	Item is a double-line separator

These keywords explicitly specify the type of a menu item. The type of most items can be determined from other parts of the grammar, however, and so these keywords are not often necessary. An item is assumed, by default, to be a push button. If the **On** or **Off** flags appear, then it is assumed to be a toggle button. If a submenu name specification appears, then it is assumed to be a cascade button. There are special syntaxes for specifying separators (see above), and so the **Title** keyword is the only one generally needed. It is used to specify a non-selectable XmLabel item, usually used as the title for a popup menu pane.

flags::

On

Specifies that this item is a toggle button, and that its initial state is on.

Off

Specifies that this item is a toggle button, and that its initial state is off.

Help

Specifies that this item is the special "Help" cascade button that should appear at the far right of the menu bar.

Tearoff

Specifies that this item is a cascade button whose attached menu pane should be a tear-off menu. Note that tearoff menus are not available prior to Motif 1.2.

Pixmap

Specifies that the label specification should be treated as the name of a Pixmap to display rather than a string of text to display.

label::

string-with-mnemonic [| *string-with-mnemonic*]

A *label* is a string in double quotes optionally followed by a vertical bar and another string in quotes. If an underscore character appears in either string, then it precedes the character of the string which is to be the mnemonic for this menu item. This underscore is removed from the string before it is displayed. If the vertical bar and second string are present, then they specify that the item is a toggle button and specify an alternate label and alternate mnemonic to use when the toggle button is in its selected state. If the **Pixmap** flag is set, then the strings are interpreted as names of pixmaps to display, rather than as text to be displayed directly. In this case, underscores are treated as part of the pixmap name, not as mnemonic indicators.

accelerator::

[{ *modifier* + | - } *keysym*]

An accelerator specification is contained within square brackets which are a required part of the grammar. Within the square brackets are any number of modifier key names, each followed by a + or - character, followed by a keysym name. The characters within the square brackets will be set on the `XmNacceleratorText` resource and will appear at the right of the menu item. These characters are also parsed and converted into an accelerator specification in translation table format which will be set on the `XmNaccelerator` resource.

modifier::

Ctrl | **Shift** | **Meta** | **Alt** | **Lock**

Each of the standard modifier keys are legal in accelerator specifications.

keysym::

letter-or-digit

An accelerator keysym can be a single letter or digit, as in the accelerators `[Ctrl-C]` and `[Alt-2]`, for example.

ident

An accelerator keysym can be any of the standard keysym names, such as "Tab," "BackSpace," and "Return," which produce accelerator specifications like `[Shift+Ctrl+Return]`. For a complete list of keysym names see */usr/include/X11/keysymdef.h.*

string

As a special case, an accelerator keysym may be any string of characters within double quotes. In this case, the double quotes are removed from the specification before the accelerator is displayed on the menu item. This type of specification is used for punctuation and for other non-alphabetic characters: `[Meta-IJ.IJ]` or `[Ctrl+Shift-"#IJ]`, for example. Note that Motif may require the **Shift** modifier to be explicitly listed for punctuation characters like `#` that are typed with the **Shift** key.

submenu::

-> *ident*

A submenu is specified for a cascade button with an `->` arrow followed by the name of the submenu that is to pop up. A Menu widget with this name will automatically be created, and it will recursively parse its own `XmtNitems` resource from the resource database in order to create the button, labels, separators, and submenus that it should contain.

symbol::

$ *ident*

A dollar sign followed by an identifier indicates that the menu item is a toggle button, and that it should set its state, whenever that state changes, on the symbol named by the identifier.

callbacks::

callback

{ *callback* { *callback* } }

Callback procedures may be specified for a menu item as a single procedure call, or as a C-style block of one or more procedure calls enclosed within curly braces. The specified procedure or procedures will be registered on the `XmNactivateCallback` callback list of a push button, or on the `XmNvalueChangedCallback` list of a toggle button. Any callbacks you specify must have been registered with `XmtRegisterCallbackProcedure()` or a related function. Also, the Xmt String-to-Callback converter must be registered by calling `XmtRegisterCallbackConverter()`.

callback::
ident ([*arglist*]) ;
A *callback* is a procedure name followed by an open parenthesis; an optional, comma-separated list of arguments; a close parenthesis; and a semicolon. See Chapter 10, *Callbacks in Resource Files*, for more information on the callback grammar.

Example 20-3 shows a menu system described using this grammar, and Example 20-6 in the next section shows a number of popup menus described with the grammar.

20.5 Creating Popup Menus

Creating popup menus with the Menu widget is as straightforward as creating a pulldown menu system. Example 20-5 shows how you might create a popup menu in C, for example.

Example 20-5. A Popup Menu Created from C

examples/

20/menu.c

```
void move(Widget, XtPointer, XtPointer);
void rotate(Widget, XtPointer, XtPointer);
void scale(Widget, XtPointer, XtPointer);
void toggle_grid(Widget, XtPointer, XtPointer);

static XmtMenuItem popup_items[] = {
    {XmtMenuItemLabel, "@fBOperations"},
    {XmtMenuItemSeparator},
    {XmtMenuItemPushButton, "Move", 'M', "Ctrl<Key>M", "Ctrl-M", move},
    {XmtMenuItemPushButton, "Rotate", 'R', "Ctrl<Key>R", "Ctrl-R", rotate},
    {XmtMenuItemPushButton, "Scale", 'S', "Ctrl<Key>S", "Ctrl-S", scale},
    {XmtMenuItemSeparator},
    {XmtMenuItemLabel, "@fBOptions"},
    {XmtMenuItemSeparator},
    {XmtMenuItemToggleButton+XmtMenuItemOn, "Show Grid", 'G',
     "Ctrl<Key>G", "Ctrl-G", toggle_grid, NULL, NULL, NULL, "Hide Grid", 'G'}
};

Widget drawing_area;  /* assume this is created elsewhere */
Widget popup;
Arg args[5];
Cardinal ac;

ac = 0;
XtSetArg(args[ac], XmtNitems, popup_items); ac++;
XtSetArg(args[ac], XmtNnumItems, XtNumber(popup_items)); ac++;
popup = XmtCreatePopupMenu(drawing_area, "popup", args, ac);
```

One of the nice features of `XmtCreatePopupMenu()` is that it automatically registers an event handler to pop up the menu. By default, the menu will pop up when you press mouse button 3 over the parent widget. You can control the required event sequence by setting the `XmNmenuPost` resource of the Menu widget, however. This resource is inherited from the Motif XmRow-

Column widget. If you are creating a popup menu using plain Motif, you must both set this resource and register an event handler to pop up the menu when the appropriate events occur.

As with pulldown menu systems, it is often easier to create popups from a resource file. Example 20-6 shows popup menus created from a resource file, and Figure 20-2 shows the menus the code creates. Take a close look—this example demonstrates a number of useful tricks with popup menus.

examples/

20/popup.ad

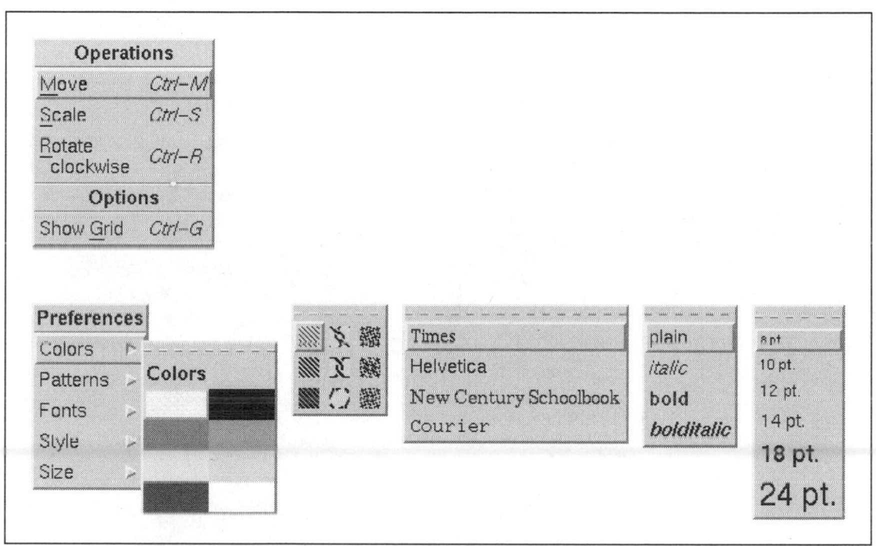

Figure 20-2. Popup menus

Example 20-6. Popup Menus Created from a Resource File

```
popup.xmtChildren: XmDrawingArea drawingarea;

*drawingarea.xmtChildren: unmanaged XmtPopupMenu menu1, menu2;
*drawingarea.width: 200                  The drawing area has 2 popup menu children.
*drawingarea.height: 200                 Note that they are created unmanaged.

*menu1.menuPost: <Btn3Down>              Button 3 pops up one menu
*menu1.menuAccelerator: <Key>F4          and F4 posts it from the keyboard.
*menu2.menuPost: Shift<Btn3Down>         Shift Button 3 pops the other
*menu2.menuAccelerator: Shift<Key>F4     and Shift-F4 posts it from the keyboard.

*drawingarea.background: wheat           We give the popups a slightly darker
*Menu*background: tan                    background; this is a nice visual effect.

*XmtMenu.acceleratorFontTag: I           This specifies the typeface of the accelerators.

*menu1.items: \
Title    "@fBOperations"; \              This label gives the menu a visible title.
         ----;\                          This creates a separator in the menu.
         "_Move" [Ctrl-M] move();\
```

Example 20-6. Popup Menus Created from a Resource File (continued)

```
        "_Scale" [Ctrl-S] scale();\
        "_Rotate\n  clockwise" [Ctrl-R] rotate();\
        ----;\                               Note that the previous item has 2 lines.
Title   "@fBOptions";\
        ----;\                               Note the toggle button with 2 labels
        "Show _Grid" | "Hide _Grid" [Ctrl-G] toggle_grid();

*menu2.items: \
Title   "@fBPreferences"; \
        ----;\                               Popup menus can have "pullright" submenus.
Tearoff "Colors" -> colors;\                 These five submenus are described below.
Tearoff "Patterns" -> patterns;\             They will be automatically created by the
Tearoff "Fonts" -> fonts;\                   parent Menu widget.
Tearoff "Style" -> styles;\
Tearoff "Size" -> sizes;

*colors.items:\
Title "@fBColors";\
yellow: "    " set_color(1); \               Each button in this menu has a name and
red:    "    " set_color(2); \               a blank string. Below, we use the name
green:  "    " set_color(3); \               to set the background color for each button.
blue:   "    " set_color(4); \
Title " "; \                                 The title for the 2nd column (see below).
black:  "    " set_color(5); \
gray1:  "    " set_color(6); \
gray2:  "    " set_color(7); \
white:  "    " set_color(8);

*colors.numColumns: 2                        Menus can have 2 or more columns.
*colors.packing: XmPACK_COLUMN               But you must set the XmNpacking resource too.

*colors.yellow.background: yellow            Here we set the colors using the widget names
*colors.red.background: red                  specified above.
*colors.green.background: green
*colors.blue.background: blue
*colors.black.background: black
*colors.gray1.background: gray50
*colors.gray2.background: gray75
*colors.white.background: white

*patterns.numColumns:3                       These buttons display icons instead of strings.
*patterns.packing: XmPACK_COLUMN             The pixmaps are defined elsewhere.
*patterns.items:\                            We've also omitted callbacks for these items.
        Pixmap "diag1_3";   Pixmap "diag2_2";   Pixmap "diag3_1";\
        Pixmap "fence1";    Pixmap "fence2";    Pixmap "fence3" ;\
        Pixmap "tweed2_2"; Pixmap "tweed4_3"; Pixmap "tweed4_4";

*fonts.items: "@f[times]Times"; \            The remaining 3 menus use a variety of fonts.
        "@f[helvetica]Helvetica"; \          We've omitted the font list and callbacks here.
        "@f[schoolbook]New Century Schoolbook";\
        "@f[courier]Courier";

*sizes.items: "@f[8]8 pt."; "@f[10]10 pt."; "@f[12]12 pt.";\
                 "@f[14]14 pt."; "@f[18]18 pt."; "@f[24]24 pt.";

*styles.items: "plain"; "@fIitalic"; "@fBbold"; "@f(BIbolditalic";
```

There are a number of points worth noting in Example 20-6.

- The `XmtNacceleratorFontTag` resource is used to specify a font from the font list (omitted in this example, for brevity). The specified accelerator strings are formatted into XmStrings using this tag, and will therefore be displayed in the desired font. Doing this can make your menus look more interesting and serve to distinguish the menu item text from the accelerator tag.
- The `XmNmenuPost` resource (which is inherited from the XmRowColumn superclass) is used to specify how the menu should be popped up. It uses translation-table syntax to specify a combination of mouse buttons and modifiers.
- Popup menus can have pullright submenus, just as pulldown menus can. These menus will be automatically created by the parent Menu widget when they are encountered in the menu description.
- Items in a menu need not all have the same color, font, or font size. In this example, we specified fonts simply by using the `@f` font syntax of the Xmt String-to-XmString converter. We specified different colors for the items in the **Colors** menu by giving each item a unique name, and then using those names to explicitly set the `XtNbackground` resource of the buttons.
- Items in a menu can display pixmaps rather than strings. The `Pixmap` keyword in the menu description grammar indicates that the menu item string is the name of a pixmap, rather than a label to display.
- Menus need not have only one column. Since the items in the **Colors** and **Patterns** menus are quite narrow, it makes more sense to arrange them into multiple columns. The XmRowColumn `XmNnumColumns` resource allows this, but you must also set the `XmNpacking` resource to `XmPACK_COLUMN` in order to get it to work.

Posting Popup Menus

The handling of popup menus is one of the more mysterious topics in Motif. The `XmNmenuPost` resource of the menu pane (an XmRowColumn widget) specifies the event sequence that should pop up the menu. This resource is a string in translation table format—in Example 20-6 we use the values `<Btn3Down>` and `Shift <Btn3Down>`. Mouse button 3 is the standard button binding for popup menus. (Note that the example uses Motif 1.2. Prior to that release, it was difficult or impossible to have two popup menus as children of the same widget.)

Specifying this resource is not sufficient to post a Motif popup menu, however—you must register an event handler that will detect an appropriate mouse button event, and then use `XmMenuPosition()` to set the position of the menu and `XtManageChild()` to actually pop it up. But this doesn't mean that the `XmNmenuPost` resource is irrelevant—in some version of Motif, at least,

Posting Popup Menus (continued)

the event that triggers a menu to be posted must match `XmNmenuPost` or Motif will not allow the menu to pop up.

When you create a popup menu with `XmtCreatePopupMenu()`, Xmt automatically registers an event handler on the parent of the menu. This handler looks at all mouse button events, and pops up the menu when it sees one that matches the `XmNmenuPost` specification. Most of the time this will be exactly what you need, and you won't need to worry about writing an event handler to manage your popup menus. This event handler can also handle dynamic changes to the `XmNmenuPost` resource, so you can change button bindings for menus at runtime.

Sometimes you may want direct control over posting menus and won't want Xmt to pop them up automatically for you. A drawing editor, for example, might pop up a different menu depending on what the current selection is—it would decide which menu to pop up within a custom event handler. In a case like this, you'll have to unregister the event handler that Xmt automatically installs for you. The event handler is a public function, `XmtMenuPopupHandler()`, and you can unregister it for a popup menu with code like this:

```
XtRemoveEventHandler(parent, ButtonPressMask, False,
                     XmtMenuPopupHandler, (XtPointer)menu);
```

In this code, *parent* is the widget that you passed to `XmtCreatePopupMenu()`, and *menu* is the menu pane returned by that function.

Popup menus can also be posted with a keyboard command, although this is a little-known feature for most users. The `XmNmenuAccelerator` resource on the menu pane is a string in translation table format that specifies the key/modifier combination that should post the menu. Unlike the `XmNmenuPost` resource, no event handler is required to make this keyboard shortcut work. F4 is the standard keyboard binding for posting a popup menu. In Example 20-6 we use `<Key>F4` and `Shift <Key>F4` for our two menus. (The `XmNmenuAccelerator` resource is also used with menu bars—the default in this case is `F10`, and striking this key in a Motif application should always move the keyboard focus to the menu bar.)

Finally, the XmRowColumn supports a third menu-specific resource. `XmNpopupEnabled` controls whether a popup menu's mnemonics and accelerators will work. Setting this resource to `False` disables keyboard bindings for a popup menu. In at least some versions of Motif, setting this resource to `False` also seems to prevent the menu from popping up.

—*djf*

20.6 Symbols in Menus

Chapter 12, *Symbols*, explains how you can register symbolic names for your application variables through the XmtSymbol mechanism. The Menu is one of the Xmt widgets that provides special handling for Symbols—if you specify the name of a `Boolean` Symbol when creating a toggle button in a menu, that toggle button will get its default value from the named variable, and the named variable will automatically have its value updated any time the user selects the toggle button in the menu.

The first step to accomplishing this is to register symbolic names for your `Boolean` variables:

```
static Boolean name, sort;
XmtVaRegisterSymbols("view_by_name", XtRBoolean, sizeof(Boolean), &name,
                     "sort_by_size", XtRBoolean, sizeof(Boolean), &sort,
                     NULL);
```

Once the Symbols are registered, you can use their symbolic names with your menus by setting the `symbol_name` field of the `XmtMenuItem` structure:

```
static XmtMenuItem view_menu_items[] = {
    {XmtMenuItemToggleButton, "By Icon", 'B', NULL, NULL, NULL,
        NULL, NULL, "view_by_name", "By Name", 'B', },
    {XmtMenuItemToggleButton, "Sort by Size", 'S',
        "Meta<Key>Z", "Meta+Z", NULL, NULL, NULL, "sort_by_size", },
    {XmtMenuItemEnd}
};
```

Or, from a resource file, you can specify a symbol name by preceding it with a $ character. For example, we could specify the same menu of two toggle buttons with this resource:

```
*menubar*view.items: \
        "_By Icon" | "_By Name"          $view_by_name ;\
  Off   "_Sort by Size" [Meta+Z]         $sort_by_size ;
```

The reason that you might want to use Symbols with your menus is that they provide an elegant way to keep your application and your interface separate. The example menus we've shown in this section could be part of a graphical file browser utility, for example. Each time that program scans a new directory, it must decide whether to show the files by icon or by name, and it also must decide whether to sort the files by size or by name. To make these decisions, the application only needs to look at the `name` and `sort` variables that we earlier provided symbolic names for. The Menu widget guarantees that the state of these variables will be in sync with the user's choice in the menu, so the internal, file-sorting parts of the application need know nothing about the user interface. Just checking the state of a variable is obviously much easier than looking up a toggle button widget and checking its state by calling a function like `XmToggleButtonGetState()`.

Another feature of Symbols is that the communication works both ways: not only can the menu update an application variable when the toggle button state changes, the application can notify the menu when the variable has changed under application control, so the menu can update the state of the button. The default state of a toggle button is obtained by querying the button's symbol, if any. Our file browser application, for example, might have command-line options or application resources that specify how files are to be sorted. When the application parses these options or resources, it need only set the `name` `Boolean` we registered—when the menu is created, it will read the value of this variable, and set the initial state of the toggle button correspondingly.

Once the menu has been created, you cannot directly set this `name` variable and expect the Menu widget to notice. What you can do, though, is call the special function `XmtSymbolSetValue()`. This will set the new value into the variable and notify the Menu widget that its value has changed. The Menu widget will then update the state of the button. The only thing to notice about `XmtSymbolSetValue()` is that it takes an argument of type `XmtSymbol` rather than a Symbol name. You can convert a symbol name to an `XmtSymbol` by calling `XmtLookupSymbol()`.

20.7 Manipulating Menus at Runtime

So far in this chapter, we've discussed how to build static pulldown and popup menu systems for your applications. While this will be sufficient for many applications, there are other applications that may want to dynamically set the state of toggle buttons, set the sensitivity of menu items, or change other resources of individual menus and menu panes. Some applications may even want to dynamically add and remove menu panes from a menu bar or add and remove items from a menu pane. This section explains how you can do all these things with the Menu widget.

20.7.1 Specifying and Looking Up Menu Items

Before you can dynamically manipulate menu items, you must have some kind of handle to them. Their `Widget` pointer is one such handle, but since the individual widgets within a Menu are automatically created, you don't know these `Widget` pointers. Most of the menu manipulation functions that we'll describe here take an `XmtMenuItem *` argument to specify which menu item to use. Recall that the `XmtMenuItem` structure is the structure you use to describe a menu item in C. This structure contains both public fields, which you initialize, and private fields, which are filled in by the Menu widget when the menu item is created. So, if you've described your menus with these structures in C, then you can manipulate individual menu items by passing the address of these structures. To operate on the fourth item in your **File** menu, for example, you might use `&file_menu_items[3]`.

Often, however, you will describe your menus from a resource file. In this case, the `XmtMenuItem` structures are automatically created by the String-to-XmtMenuItemList converter, and you don't have direct access to them. To obtain the address of the `XmtMenuItem` structure for a menu item described in a resource file, you must first give that item a name. (Recall that item names are the first thing that appears in the item description, and are followed by a colon.) Then you can look up the `XmtMenuItem` structure for a named item with `XmtMenuGetMenuItem()`:

Xmt/

Menu.c

```
#include <Xmt/Menu.h>
XmtMenuItem *XmtMenuGetMenuItem(Widget menu, String name);
```

The first argument to `XmtMenuGetMenuItem()` is a Menu widget. Generally, this will be your toplevel menu bar, but it can also be any individual menu pane. `XmtMenuGetMenuItem()` performs a recursive search for the named menu item, so you can pass it your menu bar widget and use it to find items in the menu panes of that menu bar or even in submenus of those panes.

A nice feature of looking up menu items in this way is that it provides position independence. As long as you don't change the name of a menu item, you can move it anywhere within a menu pane (or anywhere within the pulldown menu system) without changing any of your code. Position independence is important for customizability when menus are described from resource files, and you may decide to use this naming and lookup approach to increase modularity even when you describe your menus with C structures.

Now that you know how to obtain an `XmtMenuItem` structure for a menu item, the following subsections explain what you can do with it.

20.7.2 Setting Toggle Button State

Given the address of the `XmtMenuItem` structure for a toggle button menu item, you can query and set the state of that button with `XmtMenuItemGetState()` and `XmtMenuItemSetState()`:

Xmt/

Menu.c

```
#include <Xmt/Menu.h>
Boolean XmtMenuItemGetState(XmtMenuItem *toggle);
void XmtMenuItemSetState(XmtMenuItem *toggle,
                         Boolean state, Boolean notify);
```

`XmtMenuItemGetState()` returns `True` if the specified toggle button is selected, and `False` otherwise. `XmtMenuItemSetState()` sets the button state as specified by the *`state`* argument, and if *`notify`* is `True`, it calls any callbacks registered for the toggle button. Both functions will print a warning message if called for a menu item that is not a toggle button.

Note that it is important to set the state of menu toggle buttons with `XmtMenuItemSetState()` rather than with `XmToggleButtonSetState()`, because the former function keeps the Menu widget's internal state in sync with the toggle button state.

Finally, note that when you use Symbols with toggle buttons, as described above, you never really need to query the state of the toggle button, and you can also set the state of the button with `XmtSymbolSetValue()`.

20.7.3 Setting Menu Item Sensitivity

An important type of dynamic behavior found in many menu systems is setting the sensitivity of menu items—"graying out" menu items that currently make no sense to select. It is common, for example, to see grayed out **Cut**, **Copy**, and **Delete** menu items in an **Edit** menu when there is no text or no object selected in the application that these menu items could operate on.

`XmtMenuItemSetSensitivity()` lets you set the sensitivity of a menu item:

Xmt/

Menu.c

```
#include <Xmt/Menu.h>
void XmtMenuItemSetSensitivity(XmtMenuItem *item, Boolean sensitive);
```

As with `XtSetSensitive()`, the second argument to `XmtMenuItemSetSensitivity()` is a `Boolean`. If `True`, the item will be made sensitive; if `False`, the item will be made insensitive, and will be grayed out.

Unlike `XtSetSensitive()`, however, `XmtMenuItemSetSensitivity()` keeps a count of how many times it has been called for an item. If the function is called twice for an item with the `sensitive` argument of `False`, then the item will not become sensitive again until the function is called twice with the argument `True`. This is a useful behavior when there is more than one condition that must be satisfied for a menu item to be selectable—a **Cut** menu item might only make sense, for example, if there is some text selected in the application, and if the application is not displaying a read-only file. In this case, you could start out making the **Cut** item doubly insensitive, and then calling `XmtMenuItemSetSensitivity()` with `True` when each condition is met—the item will not become sensitive until both conditions are true. Finally, note that there is an asymmetry here—while it is possible to make an item extra-insensitive, it is not possible to make it extra-sensitive. So while calling `XmtMenuItemSetSensitivity()` with argument `True` is not guaranteed to make an insensitive item sensitive, calling the function with argument `False` is guaranteed to make a sensitive item insensitive.

The function `XmtMenuItemSetSensitivity()` is at a higher level of abstraction than `XtSetSensitive()` because it abstracts away the item's widget with the `XmtMenuItem` structure. The Xmt library also supports a pair of functions at an even higher level of abstraction for setting the sensitivity of menu items. These functions are `XmtMenuInactivateProcedure()` and `XmtMenuActivateProcedure()`, and the reason for their existence is based on the realization that it is not so much the individual widgets that we want to desensitize, or even the more abstract `XmtMenuItem`, but the procedures invoked when these menu items are selected. If the application does not currently display a selected region, there is no inherent harm in having the user select the **Cut** item in the **Edit** menu, for example. The problem is that it doesn't make sense to invoke the `Cut()` callback that is registered as a callback for that menu item—the reason we make the **Cut** button insensitive is so that the procedure will not be invoked, and so that the user knows that it does not make sense to invoke it.

There are two further insights about menus that prompted the development of the two functions `XmtMenuInactivateProcedure()` and `XmtMenuActivateProcedure()`. First, a well-designed menu and set of menu item callbacks may have procedures that are called from more than one item. The **New** menu item might call `GetNewFilename()`, for example; the **Save** item might call `SaveFile()`, and the **Save As** item might call `GetNewFilename()` and `SaveFile()` in sequence.* So, if there is a circumstance in which it makes no sense to call the `SaveFile()` procedure, then both the **Save** and **Save As** menu items should be made insensitive. The second insight is that some applications will expose the Xmt menu specification grammar to their users, to allow the users to radically customize the menus. In these circumstances, the application cannot know in advance which menu items will invoke which procedures, so it cannot know which items should be made insensitive at which time.

The two functions `XmtMenuInactivateProcedure()` and `XmtMenuActivateProcedure()` were created for these reasons. Given a Menu widget and the address of a procedure, these functions will recursively check every item in the menu and its submenus and desensitize or resensitize any item in the menu that calls the specified procedure.

Xmt/

Menu.c

```
#include <Xmt/Menu.h>
void XmtMenuInactivateProcedure(Widget menu, XtCallbackProc proc);
void XmtMenuActivateProcedure(Widget menu, XtCallbackProc proc);
```

These functions call `XmtMenuItemSetSensitivity()`, so a single procedure can be inactivated multiple times, or a single item can be de-sensitized multiple times, if it calls multiple procedures that have been inactivated.

Some applications, perhaps those with particularly complex or customizable menu systems, will find these two functions quite useful and appropriate. In other cases, they may simply be at too high a level of abstraction, adding no real convenience. In these latter cases, just use `XmtMenuItemSetSensitivity()`.

*The X Toolkit does not guarantee that callback procedures will be invoked in the order that they are registered. The Xmt callback converter, on the other hand, does guarantee that the procedures specified for a single callback list will be invoked in the order specified.

20.7.4 Manipulating Menu Items Directly

When you want to set the state of a toggle button in a Menu or change the sensitivity of a menu item, the functions described above allow you to do this through the abstraction of the `XmtMenuItem` structure. (And, in fact, they require you to do it in this way—if you set toggle button state or item sensitivity directly on the menu item widgets, their state would be out of sync with the state maintained internally by the Menu widget.)

For some purposes, however, you must manipulate the menu widgets directly—you might want to provide emphasis for a menu item by setting its `XmNforeground` resource to a highlight color, for example, or obtain a handle to a submenu pane so that you can add new items to it (as we will do in a section below). The functions `XmtMenuItemGetWidget()` and `XmtMenuItemGetSubmenu()` return the widget pointers you need to make these direct manipulations:

Xmt/

Menu.c

```
#include <Xmt/Menu.h>
Widget XmtMenuItemGetWidget(XmtMenuItem *item);
Widget XmtMenuItemGetSubmenu(XmtMenuItem *item);
```

`XmtMenuItemGetWidget()` returns the widget associated with any menu item. This may be an XmPushButton, an XmToggleButton, an XmCascadeButton, an XmLabel, or an XmSeparator. For menu items that are cascade buttons, `XmtMenuItemGetSubmenu()` returns the Menu widget that forms the menu pane attached to that cascade button. If you call this function for a menu item that is not a cascade button, it will print an error message.

20.7.5 Adding and Removing Menu Items

The XmtMenu widget was designed to automatically create and manage a static menu system—you are not allowed to call `XtSetValues()` on the `XmtNitems` resource to change the displayed resource, for example. A fixed menu system is adequate for many applications. There are times, though, when you may want to add items to a menu dynamically, and since the Menu widget is just a subclass of the Motif XmRowColumn, you can actually do this. Just remember that the Menu widget automatically manages and operates only on menu items that it created itself—if you add items of your own, you'll have to handle them on your own. This section and the next explain what you need to know to do this.

Suppose your application has just created a new toplevel window for some auxiliary purpose, and you want to add a new button to the **Windows** menu pane that will give the user an easy way to raise that window to the top of the stack. If you gavc thc **Windows** cascade button a name when you created it in the Menu menu bar, then you can look up the `XmtMenuItem` structure for that item with `XSXmtMenuGetMenuItem()`, and obtain its submenu pane with `XmtMenuItemGetSubmenu()`. This menu pane is itself a Menu widget, which is a subclass of the XmRowColumn widget, and you can simply add a new item to it. Example 20-7 shows some code that does this.

Example 20-7. Adding a New Item to a Menu Pane

```
XmtMenuItem *windows_menu;
Widget menu_pane;
Widget new_item;

windows_menu = XmtMenuGetMenuItem(menu bar, "windows");
menu_pane = XmtMenuItemGetSubmenu(windows_menu);
new_item = XmCreatePushButton(menu_pane, name, NULL, 0);
XtManageChild(new_item);
```

By default new items added to an XmRowColumn (or a Menu) widget will appear at the bottom of the row. If you are using Motif 1.2, however, you can set the new `XmNpositionIndex` constraint resource on the item to specify any position in the list that you want. In Motif 1.1, you must be satisfied to add new items at the end of the menu.

To remove an item you've added to a menu, you can just destroy it with `XtDestroyWidget()`. Or, if you just want to temporarily make it invisible, you can simply unmanage it XSwith `XtUnmanageChild()`. There are a couple of very important points to note about removing menu items, however. First, remember that the Menu widget keeps track of any of its children that it automatically created from its `XmtNitems` resource. You are not allowed to set the sensitivity of these menu item widgets directly, and, in the same way, you are not allowed to destroy them. If you do so, the Menu widget's internal state will not match the external state of affairs, and it will likely cause a core dump of some sort the next time it attempts to manipulate its already-destroyed child. So, the first important point is that you may only destroy menu items that you have added yourself (although unmanaging other items is okay).

The second point to note is something of a corollary to the first. The Menu widget can only keep track of the menu items that it created itself. If you add a new item, you cannot expect the widget to find that item with a call to `XmtMenuGetMenuItem()`. If you add a menu item that you plan to destroy later, you must either keep a pointer to that widget around, or look up the widget with `XmtNameToWidget()` or some similar function. On the same note, bear in mind that menu items you have added yourself will not be included in the recursive descents of the menu tree performed by `XmtMenuInactivateProcedure()` and `XmtMenuActivateProcedure()`.

20.7.6 Adding and Removing Menu Panes

Adding a new pulldown menu pane to a menu bar or adding a new pullright pane to an existing menu pane is similar to adding a new item to a menu pane. In fact one step is to add a new cascade button to the menu bar or menu pane, which is done exactly as in the previous section. In this case, we must also create the new menu pane itself. Sometimes this may be a menu pane created and managed entirely by yourself with `XmCreatePulldownMenu()` for example. Generally, though, there is no real reason not to take advantage of the Menu widget and create this new menu pane with `XmtCreateMenuPane()`. However you create this new pane, you then set it on the `XmNsubMenuId` resource of the cascade button. Example 20-8 shows code that does this.

Example 20-8. Adding a New Menu Pane to a Menu Bar

```
Arg args[5];
Cardinal ac;

ac=0;
XtSetArg(args[ac], XmtNitems, newitems); ac++;
XtSetArg(args[ac], XmtNnumItems, XtNumber(newitems)); ac++;
pane = XmtCreateMenuPane(menubar, "newpane", args, ac);

ac=0;
XtSetArg(args[ac], XmNsubMenuId, pane); ac++;
XtSetArg(args[ac], XmNpositionIndex, pos); ac++;
cascade = XmCreateCascadeButton(menubar, "New", args, ac);
XtManageChild(cascade);
```

Note that we use the XmRowColumn constraint resource `XmNpositionIndex` in this example. This resource is not available prior to Motif 1.2.

To remove this menu pane, you need only destroy the cascade button and the menu pane you created. Alternatively, you can just unmanage them temporarily. The same caveats mentioned in the previous section apply here—in particular, remember that you may not destroy automatically-created cascade buttons or the menu panes attached to them. You may, however, freely manage and unmanage any automatically-created items.

Also, bear in mind that the Menu widget that controls the menu bar does not know about the new cascade button you have added to it, and so it cannot find that button with `XmtMenuGetMenuItem()`. Since the menu bar does not know about the cascade button, it cannot know about the menu pane attached to that button, even if that menu pane is itself a Menu widget. So be aware that functions like `XmtMenuGetMenuItem()` and `XmtMenuInactivateProcedure()` will not be able to descend into this new menu pane when they recursively search the menu tree. If you have created the new menu pane with `XmtCreateMenuPane()`, however, then you can call these functions directly for that pane, beginning the search at the pane rather than at the menu bar above.

20.8 Style

There are lots of stylistic issues to consider when designing and developing a menu system. The following three subsections list some of them.

20.8.1 Menu Layout and Typography

The *Motif Style Guide* contains some important guidelines for menus, including standard labels and positions in the menu bar, and, for the **File**, **Edit**, and **Help** menus, standard menu items, with standard mnemonics and accelerators. You should follow these guidelines wherever appropriate, unless you have some good reason not to.

When positioning menu items within a pane, put the more frequently used items near the top of the pane so there will be less distance for the user to drag the mouse to invoke the item. Group related items together. If two groups of items are quite distinct, consider placing them in separate menu panes, or at least place a separator between them. A group of toggle buttons should always be separated from a group of push buttons in this way, for example.

Don't place more than about ten items in a menu pane. With more items than that, it becomes difficult for the user to quickly find the one she is looking for. If you think you need more than 10 items to a pane, reconsider your command structure. Perhaps some could go in a separate pane of the menu bar, or could be organized into one or more subpanes. Bear in mind that some selections are just not appropriate for menus: instead of having a **Fonts** menu that contains a listing of 25 available fonts, for example, put a **Fonts**... item in a **Preferences** menu—this item could pop up a font selection dialog box that would let the user choose among hundreds of fonts.

Using pullright menus from a pulldown or popup menu pane is a good way to group a number of related options (like font sizes and styles). Pullright menus are less appropriate for menu items that invoke actions, unless they are very infrequently used commands. Don't nest pullright menus—a pullright menu within a pullright menu is quite awkward and inconvenient to use.

It is a good idea to put a non-selectable title at the top of popup menus to identify the purpose of the menu. This is especially true if there is more than one menu that the user can pop up. Pulldown and pullright menu panes do not need titles, because the cascade buttons they are attached to serve that purpose. Displaying the title in a bold or some other font will set it off from the regular menu items. Centering the title above left-justified menu entries also serves to set it off. This is the default behavior of the XmLabel widget, and so comes automatically to most menus. Placing a separator under a title often looks nice. If a menu contains two or more distinct groups of buttons, you can also use titles in the interior of menus, possibly with a separator widget above and below. If you find yourself wanting an interior title on a pulldown or pullright menu pane, then the items should probably be in two separate menus instead. Since there are a limited number of convenient button bindings for popup menus, it does make sense to combine buttons into a menu like this, even when those buttons require interior titles to explain their disparate purposes.

If selecting a menu item will cause a dialog box to pop up, place the string "`...`" at the end of the menu item. This is a cue that will let the user know what to expect. This is an important point, required by the *Motif Style Guide*, and should not be considered optional. The "`...`" serves a similar function to the arrow icon on the right of cascade buttons (automatically added by the XmCascadeButton widget) that cue the user that the button produces a pullright submenu.

Do not place push buttons or toggle buttons directly into menu bars. The Motif widgets allow you to do this, and many developers find it tempting to put a **Quit** button, for example, directly into their menu bar. Don't do it—this practice is forbidden by the *Motif Style Guide*, it rules out the use of accelerators for those buttons (making them less convenient, instead of more), and it makes your interface design non-portable to other GUI systems that cannot place buttons in menu bars.

Take advantage of Motif font lists to use multiple fonts in your menus. As recommended above, you might use a bold font for menu titles in popup menus. The Menu widget `XmtNacceleratorFontTag` resource provides an easy way to use a different font for your accelerator strings. If you are using a font with serifs (like New Century Schoolbook) for your menu items, a sans-serif font like Helvetica would be a good choice. An italic font is also an option. If you have complex accelerator labels (**Ctrl+Meta-TAB**, e.g.) and want to keep your menus to a reasonable width, you might use a smaller point size for the accelerator labels. To give your application a consistent feel, use the same font for all menu items in all menu bars and menu panes throughout your application—it should usually be the same font that you use in the buttons and similar widgets throughout the app. (The exception would be in a **Fonts** or similar menu that allowed the user to select a font.) The Menu widget allows you to use multiple fonts in a single menu item label, but don't do this—it will just clutter the menu and make it difficult to read.

Give your menu bar and all your menu panes (and popup menus) the same background color. Consider using a color different from the default background color of the application. A different menu bar color will lend some visual interest to your main window, and a different menu pane color will make those menu panes stand out when popped up over the rest of the application.

The Menu widget allows you to use toggle buttons with their traditional square indicator, or to provide two labels to alternate. Instead of a **Grid** item with an indicator, you can have an item that displays **Show Grid** in one state and **Hide Grid** in the other. Both approaches are good ones, and the best choice will vary with context.

Remember that you can use non-standard menu items when you need them: you can use pixmaps instead of strings. You can use different colors for menu items. Menus need not have only a single column. Multiple-column menus are particularly appropriate when the individual menu items are very narrow, as with many pixmaps, and have no accelerators to be displayed. For particularly complex or long menu items, you can use two lines—just place a `\n` in the menu item string. If you do this, indent the second and any subsequent lines with a few spaces so that they are not confused with individual menu items themselves. Don't come to rely on this technique, however—menu items should be short, and easy to read and recognize; if not, the menu will not be easy to use.

Use concise, strong language in your menu entries. Take care that you do not slip into computer jargon—don't say "Dump," for example, when you mean "Write" or "Save." Use active language instead of passive. Start each entry with a verb when possible—menu items describe commands; use the imperative voice and omit articles ("a," "the," etc.) for brevity.

20.8.2 Popups and Tearoffs

Popup menus and tearoff menus can be important components of almost any user interface. Whenever you are designing an application with a work area that displays any kind of object that the user can select and operate on, consider using one or more popup menus as an interface to those operations. If the user selects an object with mouse button 1, for example, it is then quite easy to pop up a menu with button 3 to select an operation on the object. This requires less mousing than it would to move the pointer up to a pulldown menu or over to a palette or button box.

Tearoff menus (not available prior to Motif 1.2) are useful in similar circumstances, and can be even more useful than popups—a tearoff menu stays popped up, and can be moved around as needed. If a user is doing a lot of detailed work in one portion of the work area, for example, she might drag a tearoff menu close to the area she was operating on. In this way, tearoff menus can serve as a convenient, mobile type of palette of operations or tools. They also can serve as a useful type of online help to a user who is trying to learn your application's keyboard shortcuts—by tearing off the menu panes and arranging them around the main application window, she can have all the keyboard accelerators visible at once. Tearoffs are available for free, and are useful enough that there is no reason not to make all of your pulldown menus tearoffs. The only reason that they are not tearoff menus by default is for compatibility with older versions of Motif that did not support them.

Mouse button 3 (**MB3**) is the officially sanctioned button for popup menus. If your application only has one popup over any particular region, **MB3** should pop it up. If you've got more than one, you should probably use keyboard modifiers to distinguish between them—pop up the most commonly used menu with **MB3**, the next most commonly used with **Shift-MB3**, the next with **Ctrl-MB3**, and so forth. Particularly specialized applications may also want to use **MB1** or **MB2** for popup menus, but you should be very careful if you choose to do this—**MB1** is almost always used for selecting objects, and **MB2** (and **MB2** with keyboard modifiers) is reserved for drag-and-drop operations. If you use **MB2** for a popup menu, be *very* sure that your users will never want to drag anything from your application. Also, remember that many users will develop strong habits of using **MB2** for drag-and-drop, and using this button for any other purpose may confuse them.

A shortcoming of popup menus is that they present no cues to the user to indicate that they are available. If your application relies upon popup menus you should try to provide these cues in some way. You could do this by placing an initial message (or a permanent message) in an XmtMsgLine widget in your application: "F1 for Help; MB3 for popup menus," for example. Another approach is to display a diagram of the mouse buttons and their functions somewhere in the application. The amount of cueing that is necessary will depend, of course, upon your audience, their familiarity with your application, and the frequency with which they use it. In some applications it may be sufficient to simply change the pointer cursor to a different shape over the work area.

Another valuable approach to the problem of popup menus without cues is to duplicate all the popup menu items in the main pulldown menu system. Then a novice user has a better chance of finding them.

20.8.3 Mnemonics and Accelerators

Mnemonics and accelerators are a very important part of any menu system. The *Motif Style Guide* defines some standard mnemonics and accelerators to use for standard menu panes and items. Follow these standards unless you have a very good reason to depart from them (for example, if your application is designed to replace an existing system with users accustomed to an existing set of keyboard bindings).

Use mnemonics for all items in the menu bar, at least. Using mnemonics for the individual items in a menu system will make keyboard traversal to those items easier. When choosing mnemonics, use the first letter of the menu item label: the mnemonic for **Edit** would be **E**, for example. When you can't use the first letter of the label, consider the first letter of the second word, or another obvious letter (hard consonants are often good choices): **X** might be a good mnemonic for **Extra**, for example, if **E** was already used. Remember that mnemonics will only conflict with mnemonics used in the same menu pane or menu bar—you can use the same mnemonic for items in different menu panes.

Use accelerators, at least for frequently used items like **Save**, **Load**, **Cut**, and so on. Ideally, you should provide accelerators for all your pulldown and popup menu items. When choosing accelerators, think about the command interface of the application as a whole, and try to integrate your menu accelerator commands into any other command structure you have (editing commands in a multi-line text widget, for example). Think carefully when designing your keyboard command system; don't just throw in random keys as an afterthought. Consider the mnemonic value of the commands you choose, but also consider other factors, like ease of typing. If the user is likely to use a keyboard command while using the mouse (operating on an item that has just been selected, for example) then you should choose a keyboard command that can easily be typed with one hand—only one modifier, and not too much of a stretch. (And you might provide a command set for right-handers and an alternative for left-handers.) If the command will likely be used while the user is touch-typing, then a command that can easily be touch-typed would be a good one. *emacs* is an example of an application that has a complex and well-thought out keyboard command interface. It is the menus, in versions of *emacs* that support them, that were added as an afterthought.

Your choice of accelerator commands is unfortunately somewhat restricted. Accelerators that use the **Meta** or **Alt** modifiers are often your best bet, but if you use these modifiers, be sure you don't conflict with any of the toplevel mnemonics in the menu bar—the **Meta** or **Alt** key is used with mnemonic characters to post menu panes from the menu bar. If your audience is likely to include any *emacs* users, you may want to avoid accelerators like **Ctrl-A** and **Ctrl-E** that are commonly used *emacs* commands, at least if your application has any form of text input widgets. Many fans of this text editor will have specified *emacs*-like keyboard bindings in their *.Xresources* file for the XmText widget. Also, you should be careful with the function keys. These keys are heavily used in PC applications, but they do not have a tradition of heavy use in X applications, and for this reason many of these keys are used for other purposes. The *mwm* window manager uses the function keys with the **Alt** or **Meta** key, for example. It grabs these keys, so applications will never even see these keystrokes. Similarly, many *twm* users may have customized the window manager to grab some of the function keys as keyboard shortcuts—I use **F12** with *twm*, for example, to iconify the current window, and the **F8** key to switch focus to my main *xterm* window. Bear in mind that not all keyboards have all keys, and you cannot always rely on the existence of a **Insert** or **Page Up** key, for example. Finally, remember that in some applications that do not require text input, you can use unmodified alphabetic keys as accelerators—just **A**, instead of **Meta-A**.

The Motif accelerator scheme is convenient, but has some shortcomings. One is that it can only be used for items in menus; there is no easy way to provide shortcuts for other items (except to put them in a hidden, unmanaged menu pane). The second shortcoming is that it is not possible to specify accelerators that require multiple keystrokes. When your set of commands is very rich, this can be required, as with the **Ctrl-X Ctrl-C** command in *emacs*, for example. Don't allow either of these shortcomings to affect the quality of your interface. When necessary, add the required translations to widgets by hand (use `XtOverrideTranslations()`), and do whatever other work is necessary to implement your desired command structure.

20.9 Summary

The Menu widget is a subclass of the XmRowColumn, which is the widget used in Motif to implement menu bars and menu panes. The contents of a Menu widget are described by an array of `XmtMenuItem` structures specified on its `XmtNitems` resource. The Menu widget uses this resource to automati cally create its menu items.

The Xmt library provides a String-to-XmtMenuItemList converter so that menus can be completely described from resource files. In order to take advantage of this converter in your resource files, you must first call the function `XmtRegisterMenuItemsConverter()` in your C code.

The Menu widget can be used to very easily create complete pulldown menu systems—a menu bar with pulldown panes, which may themselves contain pull-right sub menus—and popup menus as well. It is most useful for creating static menus, but it is also possible to dynamically modify the automatically created menus.

The Menu widget API includes functions to set and query the state of automatically-created toggle-button menu items, and to set the sensitivity of any automatically created menu item.

21

Command-Line Input

Until the advent of GUIs, almost all applications ran on text-based terminals and had a command-line style of input. These applications would wait for the user to type a command (`ls`, `get x11r5.tar.Z`, or `plot 'datafile1'`, for example) and then act on that command, or they would prompt the user when they needed particular input ("Enter last name:") and then continue once the user supplied that input. Obviously, there are still a lot of these text-based applications around, and there are a fair number of applications for which a command-line interface is an important component of the whole interface. (Many UNIX hackers would never give up their command-driven shell in favor of a graphical shell, for example.)

So there is a large body of existing code that uses a text-based command-line interface, and even a number of graphical applications that would benefit from the addition of a command-line interface, but unfortunately, Motif (and other widget sets) do not support this style of user interaction well. The XmtCli widget is designed to fill this need. Figure 21-1 shows a screen dump of an XmtCli widget.

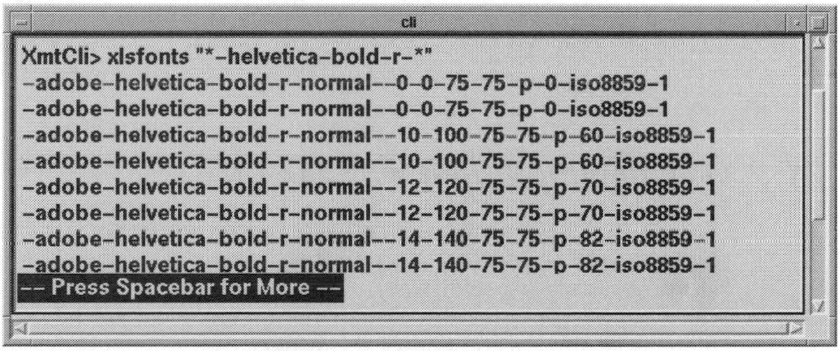

```
cli
XmtCli> xlsfonts "*-helvetica-bold-r-*"
-adobe-helvetica-bold-r-normal--0-0-75-75-p-0-iso8859-1
-adobe-helvetica-bold-r-normal--0-0-75-75-p-0-iso8859-1
-adobe-helvetica-bold-r-normal--10-100-75-75-p-60-iso8859-1
-adobe-helvetica-bold-r-normal--10-100-75-75-p-60-iso8859-1
-adobe-helvetica-bold-r-normal--12-120-75-75-p-70-iso8859-1
-adobe-helvetica-bold-r-normal--12-120-75-75-p-70-iso8859-1
-adobe-helvetica-bold-r-normal--14-140-75-75-p-82-iso8859-1
-adobe-helvetica-bold-r-normal--14-140-75-75-p-82-iso8859-1
-- Press Spacebar for More --
```

Figure 21-1. An XmtCli widget

"CLI" is an acronym for "Command-Line Interface," and the Cli is a nondescript widget that, not surprisingly, looks a lot like an *xterm* might look. The widget is implemented as a subclass of the Motif XmText widget, but designed to behave more like a character-based terminal than a text editor. For example, though the user is allowed to edit the current line freely, she is not allowed to move the cursor to previous lines, to backspace over any prompt text, or to paste text anywhere except at the current cursor position. The Cli widget was designed, in part, to simplify the porting of old terminal-based software to X, and has a number of features that support this. Features include:

- Simple text output with `puts()` and `printf()`-style functions
- Asynchronous input notification through a callback list
- Synchronous input through a `gets()`-style function
- Command history available using arrow keys
- Optional, automatic prompting for each input line
- Optional paging of long output
- Redirection of the standard output and standard error streams to appear in the widget
- Display of asynchronous output from a pipe or socket

21.1 Creating a Cli Widget

The Cli widget is a subclass of XmText. Its class name is "XmtCli," and its class structure is `xmtCliWidgetClass`.

You can create a Cli widget with the constructor `XmtCreateCli()`, or create a Cli widget with a scrollbar with `XmtCreateScrolledCli()`:

Xmt/

Cli.c

```
#include <Xmt/Cli.h>
Widget XmtCreateCli(Widget parent, String name,
                    ArgList args, Cardinal num_args)
Widget XmtCreateScrolledCli(Widget parent, String name,
                            ArgList args, Cardinal num_args)
```

21.2 Displaying Output with the Cli

To display text in an XmText widget, you set the `XmNvalue` resource, or call `XmTextSetString()`. Although the Cli widget is a subclass of XmText, this is not generally a useful way to display text in that widget. When using the Cli, you usually want the text to be appended to whatever else is already there, appearing at the end of the widget, and forcing previous lines to scroll off the top, if necessary.

Since you append text to a Cli, rather than replace all the text in it, the Cli provides special public functions to support this. Since the Cli is designed to provide the same functionality as terminal-based input/output, the Cli output functions are similar to the standard text output functions supported by the C library.

21.2.1 Cli Output Functions

The first of the Cli output functions is `XmtCliPuts()`:

Xmt/

Cli.c

```
#include <Xmt/Cli.h>
void XmtCliPuts(String s, Widget w)
```

This function appends the string *s* to the Cli widget *w*. Note the unusual order of the arguments (customarily the widget is the first argument to any function). The widget is the second argument to this function to mimic `fputs()` which takes a string argument followed by the stream to which it should be output.

If the newly output text would go past the last line of the widget, the Cli widget is automatically scrolled so that all of the output is visible. Text is output after all previous output text, but before any pending user input. If a user is in the middle of typing a command in the Cli widget and the application asynchronously displays output in the same widget, that output will not corrupt the user's input, and he will still be able to see what he is typing.

`XmtCliPrintf()` is a more sophisticated output function:

Xmt/

Cli.c

```
#include <Xmt/Cli.h>
void XmtCliPrintf(Widget w, String format, ...)
```

It is analogous to `fprintf()` and `sprintf()`; it takes the Cli widget as its first argument, followed by a format string, followed by a variable-length list of values to substitute into the format string. `XmtCliPrintf()` and `XmtCliPuts()` use the same underlying output mechanism, so `XmtCliPrintf()` handles scrolling and output before user input in the same way that `XmtCliPuts()` does.

To clear text from a Cli widget, you can use `XmtCliClear()`:

Xmt/

Cli.c

```
#include <Xmt/Cli.h>
void XmtCliClear(Widget w)
```

This function erases all visible text in the Cli widget, and also deletes any text that had scrolled off the top of the widget. After calling `XmtCliClear()`, the widget will be blank, and the user will not be able to scroll up to see previous lines. This function does not affect the command history buffer, however.

21.2.2 Scrolled Lines

When new output is appended at the bottom of a Cli widget, lines scroll off the top of the widget. Unlike traditional hardware terminals (and like the *xterm* terminal emulator), these lines are not immediately lost; the user can scroll up and see them again. If the Cli widget was created with a scrollbar (with `XmtCreateScrolledCli()`), then the user can use this scrollbar to see the scrolled lines. Whether or not there is a scrollbar, the user can scroll with the **PageUp** and **PageDown** keys, or with the other keyboard commands listed in Section 21.6, "Translations and Actions."

The number of lines saved for scrolling is controlled by the `XmtNsaveLines` resource of the Cli widget. (This resource has the same name as the *xterm* resource that performs the same function.) It specifies the total number of lines (the scrolled lines and currently visible lines) that will be remembered by the widget. Any lines beyond this number will be lost, and the user will not be able to review them by scrolling. Since the XmText widget (the superclass of the Cli) does not have a strong line-oriented interface to the text it displays, the operation of purging excess scrolled lines is a relatively expensive one. For this reason, the `XmtNsaveLines` resource is treated as a lower bound on the number of saved lines; lines will be accumulated beyond this point, and will periodically be trimmed back. What it comes down to is that the Cli widget will always save at least the specified number of lines, and while there will be more lines than specified at times, you must never rely on those extra lines to be visible to the user because they may be removed at any time.

21.2.3 Paging Output

When a terminal-based program needs to output more lines of text than there are lines on the terminal, it typically displays that text a page at a time, and asks the user to press the spacebar when he has read one page and is ready to see the next. This is important functionality, and the Cli widget supports automatic paging of output.

Typically, when text is output to the Cli widget, the widget scrolls so that the last line of the output is visible. If the `XmtNpageMode` resource is set to `True`, however, and more than a page of text is output without any intervening user input, then the widget does not scroll to the end of the input, but instead displays a message at the bottom of the widget and enters a special paging mode. In this mode, when the user strikes the **Return** key, the Cli widget will scroll up one line of text, and when the user strikes the spacebar, it will scroll up one page minus one line. All other keys behave as normal in this mode; they scroll to the end and are inserted as user input—a side effect of this is that special paging mode is terminated.

The message *banner* displayed while paging is specified with the `XmtNpageString` resource. The default is "-- Press Spacebar for More --". This banner is implemented with an XmLabel widget. By default, the page banner widget has foreground and background colors reversed so that it contrasts with the Cli widget. If you want it to be displayed with some other color scheme, you can get a pointer to the label widget by querying the Cli `XmtNpageWidget` resource, and then you can set the label's foreground and background colors directly. Note that this label widget is not created until the `XmtNpageMode` resource is set for the first time, so be sure to set `XmtNpageMode` before querying `XmtNpageWidget`.

21.3 Getting Input with the Cli

Traditional terminal-based applications block while waiting for user input. The user's only possible action is to enter a string, so the application can simply sleep until the operating system tells it that the user has typed that string. In a GUI, however, the user is not constrained in this way; she can use the mouse as well as the keyboard, and can usually interact with any part of the application at any time. Because input is not constrained to any one part of the application, GUIs must be "event driven"—they respond to keyboard and mouse events as they occur.

Text-based applications can do *synchronous* input—the programmer calls `gets()`, `scanf()`, or some similar function, and that function blocks until the user types a line, and then returns the user's input which the program can act on. In event driven GUIs, the tables are turned; instead of the application requesting input from the user when it needs it, the user enters input and requests processing from the application when she wants it. To the application, this is *asynchronous* input— instead of calling a function to get the input, the application is notified when input is ready by the arrival of an event, or in the case of the X Toolkit, by the invocation of a callback procedure.

Since it is an X Toolkit widget, the Cli supports asynchronous input notification through a callback list, but because there are a lot of existing applications that rely on synchronous input, it also supports simulated synchronous input with a `gets()`-style function.

21.3.1 The XmtNinputCallback Callback List

Whenever the user types something and strikes the **Return** key, the functions on the Cli `XmtNinputCallback` callback list are invoked. These callback procedures are called with the user's input string as their third argument, the *`call_data`* argument. This is the typical method of obtaining input from a Cli widget. When your `CommandEntered()` (or whatever) callback procedure is called, you take the user's input and operate on it appropriately.

The string passed as *`call_data`* to the `XmtNinputCallback` callback list is owned by the Cli widget and must not be freed by the application. The application may modify the string (by turning whitespace to ' ' characters during token parsing, for example) if desired, though this means that any subsequent callback procedures on the callback list will be passed the modified string. Note that the Cli widget will free the string as soon as all the procedures on the `XmtNinputCallback` list have been invoked. If the application will need to use the string after the callback procedure has returned, then it should make a private copy of that string.

Note that when the Cli is "blocked" in a call to `XmtCliGets()` (as described in later sections), simulating synchronous input, the user's input is returned by that function, and the callback functions are not called.

21.3.2 Command-Line History

When the Cli resource `XmtNsaveHistory` is `True` (the default), then lines of user input are saved in a *command history* buffer. The user can repeat a previous line of input by using the up and down arrow keys to move through this buffer: when the user strikes the up arrow key, the contents of the current input line are replaced with the previously entered command. Similarly, striking the down arrow key replaces the input line with the succeeding line of input from the command history buffer. This feature is very similar to the command-line history features supported by *tcsh*, *bash*, and other modern UNIX command shells.

The `XmtNmaxHistory` resource controls the number of input lines saved in the command history buffer. Unlike the `XmtNsaveLines` resource, the `XmtNmaxHistory` specifies the exact number of lines that will be saved.

It is not uncommon to use asynchronous input notification for command lines, and then to prompt the user synchronously for auxiliary input while processing a command. If you do this and want the command lines to be saved in the command history buffer, but do not want the user's auxiliary input to be saved, you should temporarily disable command history by setting `XmtNsaveHistory` to `False` for the before calling `XmtCliGets()` and restoring it to `True` when the function returns.

Often this automatic interface to command history will be sufficient, but some applications will want to implement commands like the UNIX C-shell's *history*, *!!*, and *!n*. To do this, they need direct access to the command history array, which they can get by querying the `XmtNhistory` resource. This resource is a `char **`, the address of the first element in an array of strings. The first element of this array is the most recently entered command, and later elements are the previously entered commands. The `XmtNmaxHistory` resource specifies the number of elements in this array, and the `XmtNnumHistory` resource specifies the number of elements of this array that contain valid strings. The `XmtNhistory` array and the strings in it belong to the Cli widget and should not be freed by the application.

If you are careful, there are some manipulations you are allowed to do with the history array. The application may rearrange elements in the history array, and may replace elements in the array with other allocated strings. If a history string is replaced, then the old string *should* be freed by the application, and the new string should not be. The application may also delete or insert lines into the history array (to initialize the command history from a save file, for example), as long as it updates the `XmtNnumHistory` resource to match. It may not change the size of the history array directly, but may set the `XmtNmaxHistory` resource which will cause the Cli widget to `realloc()` the array. If the application does this, it must then re-query the `XmtNhistory` resource, because the array may have been moved to a new location.

21.3.3 Escaped Newlines in Input

When the user strikes the **Return** key, the callbacks on the `XmtNinputCallback` are not always called. When doing synchronous input, **Return** ends the input without invoking the callbacks. When paging long output, **Return** causes the Cli to scroll up one line. And when the `XmtNescapeNewlines` resource is `True` (the default), the backslash character (\) can be used to escape the **Return** key. If the user types \ followed by **Return** when `XmtNescapeNewlines` is `True`, the **Return** causes input to continue on the next line, but does not terminate the input. When the user does terminate the input with an unescaped newline, the input string that is reported (synchronously or asynchronously) to the application has each escaped newline sequence replaced with a single space character.

Support for escaped newlines is another standard feature of UNIX shells and many other command-line interfaces. It can be a real convenience to the user when entering long lines of input. It is also possible, of course, to handle escaped newlines at the application level, explicitly removing trailing backslashes, but this does not work automatically with the command history mechanism.

21.3.4 Automatic Prompting

Prompting, like escaping newlines, is something that an application can do explicitly, but is also something that the Cli can handle automatically. If the `XmtNprompt` resource is set to a string, then the Cli widget will automatically display that string after invoking procedures on the `XmtNinputCallback` callback list and displaying any output generated by those procedures.

Note that the prompt is printed after all the input callbacks are dispatched. This means that the prompt does not appear until the widget is ready to begin accepting input again, which is the appropriate behavior. It also means that it is okay for a procedure called by the Cli `XmtNinputCallback` to set the `XmtNprompt` resource; the newly specified prompt will be correctly printed.

The Cli widget does not print a prompt after input that is returned synchronously. If all your input is synchronous, you'll want to handle prompts yourself. If you call synchronous input functions to get extra input in response to the `XmtNinputCallback`, note that the `XmtNprompt` will be displayed when the synchronous input is done, and the callback procedure returns.

21.3.5 Synchronous Input

Text-based applications can use `fgets()` and related functions to read input from the user. If there is no input ready immediately, these functions block and do not return until the user has entered something. This kind of synchronous input is not natural for the X Toolkit, but you can simulate it with the `XmtCliGets()` function.

Xmt/

Cli.c

```
#include <Xmt/Cli.h>
char *XmtCliGets(char *s, int n, Widget w)
```

Since it is an analog of `fgets()`, this function takes the address of a character buffer as its first argument, the length of the buffer as its second argument, and (like `XmtCliPuts()`) a Cli widget as its last argument. The return value of `XmtCliGets()` is always the same as its first argument.

`XmtCliGets()` enters an internal event loop that obtains and dispatches input events until the user strikes the **Return** key. It uses the function `XmtBlock()` to implement this internal event loop and simulate the synchronous behavior of `fgets()`. `XmtCliGets()` also grabs the input focus so that the user's keystrokes go directly to the Cli, and also makes the Cli modal—i.e., it prevents input to any other widgets in the application. The "Implementation Notes" section later in this chapter explains how it does this.

`XmtCliGets()` is a relatively simple function; it behaves analogously to `fgets()` and its actual use doesn't need much explanation. Be aware, though, that this kind of synchronous input does not always fit naturally with the asynchronous, event-driven nature of Xt applications, and you need to be careful not to confuse your users. Calling `XmtCliGets()` is like popping up a modal dialog box—your application enters a special mode in which the user must provide a certain kind of input before she can resume regular use of the application. When a dialog pops up, however, it is very obvious to the user what has happened. This is not always the case with input to the Cli widget, so you should be sure to display a distinct prompt in the widget, and provide whatever other cues are necessary for the user.

`XmtCliGets()` can be a tremendously useful function for doing quick, simple ports of terminal-based applications to a windowed environment. Because of the mismatch between synchronous and event-driven models, however, I recommend getting your input through the `XmtNinputCallback` whenever possible. When you do need to use `XmtCliGets()`, pay attention to the issues of modality described above; make it as clear as possible to the user that input is expected.

21.4 Redirecting Output to a Cli*

When porting a terminal-based application to X, it is simple enough to replace calls to `puts()` and `printf()` with calls to `XmtCliPuts()` and `XmtCliPrintf()`, but there is an even easier way, suitable in some circumstances. If the Cli resources `XmtNdisplayStdout` and `XmtNdisplayStderr` are set, then the Cli widget will intercept any text sent to the standard output and standard error streams, respectively, and display that output itself. If both resources are set, then an application will never display any text in the *xterm* that it was invoked from, which is usually a desirable trait in a windowed application.

`XmtNdisplayStdout` and `XmtNdisplayStderr` may be set independently of one another, and may be turned on and then off again, temporarily redirecting output, and then restoring it to normal. Note that since a process can have only one standard output and one standard error stream, only one Cli widget can redirect these streams at a time. If you attempt to redirect a stream from two different Cli widgets, you will get a warning message from one of the widgets. (And if you've redirected standard error, that warning message will appear in the Cli widget that did successfully redirect the stream.)

While this sort of output redirection is probably most useful for porting text-based applications, there are times it may be useful in other applications as well. If an application allows a user to dynamically set resource values on itself, for example, it is likely that the user will be able to specify invalid resource values that cause the widgets to issue warning messages. In this case, the application could use a Cli widget to redirect the standard error stream and display these warning message in a special part of the window, or even in a popup dialog box. The user is more likely to see the messages this way, and is less likely to get the feeling that the application is "broken" than he would if the messages were being displayed in an *xterm* window.

21.4.1 Monitoring Other Descriptors

The Cli widget can redirect output sent to the standard output and the standard error streams, and it can also perform a related (and perhaps more useful) task: monitoring output from pipes and sockets. If you set the `XmtNfildes`† resource to any open UNIX file descriptor, then the Cli widget will monitor that descriptor, and when any data becomes available on it, it will read and display that data. (The data must be text, obviously, not binary data.)

The most obvious use of this feature is to monitor the output of child processes. Say you were writing a graphical software project management tool with a drag-and-drop interface that integrated some of the features of *RCS* and *make*.

*The material in this section is UNIX-specific. The Cli features described here are not available in VMS.

†Note that this resource name is `XmtNfildes`, not `XmtNfiledes`. If you are not a low-level UNIX hacker, you may be wondering why I picked such a lousy abbreviation for "file descriptor." If you are such a hacker, you know that this is the standard UNIX abbreviation, and your aesthetic sense has probably been so warped that you didn't even think it was strange.

Not infrequently, you'd have to fork child processes to run *make* or *rcsdiff* or *co*, for example, and you'd probably want the user to have a log of the output from these commands—certainly they'd need to see compilation errors, for example. You could arrange for compilation errors to show up in a Cli widget as shown in Example 21-1.

When using the `XmtNfildes` resource to monitor data on a pipe or socket, consider the amount and frequency of data you expect. If you're expecting fairly sparse and asynchronous output, such as console messages or routine status messages about an RPC connection, for example, you probably do not want the Cli to page the output for you. If, on the other hand, you're expecting a larger volume (or higher frequency) of output, or output that it is important that the user not miss, then you will probably want to enable automatic paging of that output by setting the `XmtNpageMode` resource to `True`.

21.4.2 Flushing File Descriptors

The Cli widget uses the standard X Toolkit `XtAppAddInput()` mechanism to monitor the standard output and standard error streams and any other file descriptor specified with the `XmtNfildes` resource. This means that the "input handlers" registered to handle data on any of these streams will only be called from an event loop. If you are performing some sort of time-consuming operation, output to any of these streams will not appear until you return to the application's event loop. If you need to force output to the Cli in the middle of such a computation, use `XmtCliFlush()`:

Xmt/

Cli.c

```
#include <Xmt/Cli.h>
void XmtCliFlush(Widget w)
```

This function is usually only needed when you are using `printf()` or `puts()` to send output (in a roundabout way) to a Cli widget rather than porting the code to call `XmtCliPrintf()` or `XmtCliPuts()`. These Cli output functions display their output immediately; there is no need to return to the event loop.

If you are monitoring the standard output or standard error streams and mix output calls to that stream with direct calls to `XmtCliPuts()` or `XmtCliPrintf()` note that the output may not appear in the order you expect it. Output sent with the Cli functions will appear directly, but output sent to a stream will not appear until the next time `XmtCliFlush()` is called or the application returns to its event loop.

Note that `XmtCliFlush()` is not an analog to the standard C library function `fflush()`. The latter is used to flush a stream's output buffer, and is often used to force output to appear even if that output is not terminated with a newline. If an application uses `fflush()` on a stream to force output to appear on the terminal, it will have to continue to use `fflush()` to force output to appear in a Cli widget that has redirected those streams:

21.4.3 A Caveat: Deadlock

You might think to use the Cli widget to implement a simple shell interface in your application using the following scheme: set the Cli widget to display both standard streams, and then whenever the user inputs a command line, pass that line to the `system()` function to execute it. If you implement this system, it should work for simple commands like *echo* and *date*. If you try something like *ls /dev*, however, you'll likely run into a classic case of deadlock and have to kill your application.

The deadlock arises because the `system()` call does not return until the command it is executing completes. A command like *ls /dev* cannot complete until it has written the names of all the files (generally a lot of them) in the */dev* directory to the standard output stream. The way UNIX handles output to file descriptors is to buffer that output until it is read from the buffer. If the buffer fills up, then the writing process will block until some of the data has been read and there is more room in the buffer. In our scenario, our command *ls /dev* produces a lot of output which fills up the output buffer, and the process blocks, waiting until some of that output is read. Unfortunately, however, the process that contains the Cli widget that would read this data is itself blocked waiting for the `system()` call to return. The Cli widget cannot read any data until the `system()` function returns, and the `system()` call can't return until the Cli widget reads some data. At this point, the only option is to kill the processes.

Deadlock like this is not the fault of the Cli widget; it is just one of the things you must be careful to avoid when using low-level UNIX calls like `system()`. It is possible to work around this deadlock problem if we take a little more effort and use a non-blocking alternative to `system()`. `popen()` works in some cases, or you can do your own `fork()`/`exec()` pair explicitly.

21.5 Implementation Notes

This short section is an aside for readers curious about how the Cli widget implements modality for `XmtCliGets()` and how it monitors file descriptors and output streams. It requires some low-level knowledge of Xt, Motif, and UNIX. You don't need to understand or even read this section in order to make full use of the Cli widget.

21.5.1 Modal Input

As we saw above, `XmtCliGets()` obtains synchronous input from the user, much as the synchronous input dialog functions of Chapter 26, *Simple Input Dialogs*, do. Both `XmtCliGets()` and the Xmt synchronous input dialogs simulate a synchronous function within the asynchronous event-driven X Toolkit architecture by calling `XmtBlock()` to enter an internal event loop.

There is an important difference between synchronous input dialogs and a Cli widget, however. Input dialogs are *modal*, which means that they lock out input from all other parts of the application until the user dismisses them. The input events being handled by the internal event loop in the synchronous input dialog functions can only be events that occur in the dialog. The user cannot ignore the dialog and go on generating events in the application's main window. In particular, the user cannot repeat whatever command it was (a selection from a menu, for example) that made the dialog box pop up. If the user were able to do this, there would then be an internal event loop within an internal event loop within the main event loop.

Though usually only dialogs are made modal, it is possible to do the same to any widget. `XmtCliGets()` calls the Intrinsics function `XtAddGrab()` which locks out user input from any widgets other than the Cli. With this done, the event loop within `XmtCliGets()` will only be passed mouse and keyboard events from the Cli itself; there is no danger of the user ignoring the request for input or starting up a chain of recursive event loops.

Note that `XtAddGrab()`, used by `XmtCliGets()` and by modal dialog boxes, only locks out *user* events (mouse and keyboard events) from the rest of the application. System events like exposes and resizes are dispatched as usual, so an application can still redisplay itself if it is uncovered while a modal dialog is posted, or while within a call to `XmtCliGets()`.

While the technical problem of modal input is solved, there is still a significant difference between a modal dialog and a Cli widget in a call to `XmtCliGets()`. When a modal dialog pops up, that dialog (at least under the Motif window manager, *mwm*) is automatically given the input focus, so the user can begin typing input without moving the mouse pointer. Simply calling `XtAddGrab()` to make the Cli modal is not enough to guarantee that it also has the input focus. Also, when a dialog box pops up, it is a very noticeable event and since the dialog obscures part of the main application window, it serves as an obvious cue that the application is now in a special mode, expecting modal input. The Cli widget cannot provide nearly so obvious a cue.

`XmtCliGets()` addresses the first problem by internally calling `XmProcessTraversal()` to set the input focus to itself, and then calling `XmProcessTraversal()` again after the user's input is complete to restore the keyboard focus to whichever widget previously had it. This also addresses the second problem, because when the Cli widget is given focus, it gets the same sort of highlighting that all Motif widgets do when they have the focus, and its insertion cursor appears (in Motif 1.1) or changes from stippled to solid (in Motif 1.2). These are not really major cues, but in conjunction with whatever prompt the application has printed to solicit input ("Please enter zip code: ", for example) they may be enough to get the user's attention and indicate that the application is now in a special mode expecting keyboard input from the user.

21.5.2 Handling File Descriptors*

If you are familiar with the Xt function `XtAppAddInput()`, then you probably understand how the Cli widget can monitor the file descriptor specified with the `XmtNfildes` resource—the Cli widget registers a handler procedure to be called from `XtDispatchEvent()` whenever there is data available to be read

*This section only applies to UNIX systems.

from that descriptor. This handler procedure reads the data and displays it in the widget.

The Cli widget uses the same basic technique to display text sent to the standard output and standard error streams. The problem here is that these are streams that processes can write to, but not read from. What the Cli does is actually a fairly heavy-handed "redirection" of output to these streams. We'll consider the case of redirecting the standard output stream; redirecting the standard error is very similar. First, the Cli widget creates a pipe with the `pipe()` system call. This call creates two file descriptors; the read end of a pipe and the write end of the pipe. Next, the Cli uses `fcntl()` to put the read end of the pipe into non-blocking mode so that it will not block if it reads from the pipe when there is no data ready for reading. Then it uses `XtAppAddInput()` as mentioned above to monitor the read end of the pipe. At this point, any data written to the other end of the pipe will be detected by Xt and will end up being displayed in the Cli widget.

So far, so good, but we're still monitoring a more or less random file descriptor, not the standard output stream. The real trick goes like this: first the Cli uses the `dup()` system call to make a copy of the standard output file descriptor (which is always file descriptor 1). This copy is saved away for later use. Next the Cli calls the `dup2()` system call passing the write end of the pipe created above and the standard output file descriptor, 1. This call first closes the specified file descriptor 1. Next, `dup2()` makes a copy of the supplied stream and assigns that copy the (now unused) file descriptor 1. That is all there is to it; when the application writes to what it thinks is the standard output stream (file descriptor 1), it is no longer writing to the original file descriptor, but instead to a copy of the write end of the pipe that the Cli created. Since the Cli has set up an input handler to monitor the read end of this pipe, it will detect anything written to the write end.

Since the Cli widget made a copy of the original standard output descriptor with `dup()` before it closed it with the call to `dup2()`, the widget can restore the original descriptor whenever requested to do so by the application. Once this descriptor is restored, output sent to the standard output will be displayed as normal.

21.6 Translations and Actions

The Cli widget handles translations somewhat differently than most widgets do. It inherits an unmodified set of the XmText widget translations. When a Cli widget is created, these default XmText resources are overridden, augmented, or replaced by any resources you (or the end user) specified on the `XtNtranslations` resource (and, in X11R5, also any resources specified with the `baseTranslations` pseudo-resource). This is the same process that all widgets follow to determine their translation table. The Cli widget goes two steps further, however: it overrides this resulting translation table with its own internal set of default Cli-specific translations (shown in Table 21-1) and then, finally, overrides these with any resources you (or the end user) have specified on the `XmtNcliTranslations` resource.

Table 21-1. The Cli-specific Translation Table

Event	Action(s)
`!<Key>osfUp`	previous-command()
`!<Key>osfDown`	next-command()
`Shift<Key>osfUp`	scroll-backward()
`Shift<Key>osfDown`	scroll-forward()
`!<Key>Return`	page-or-end-input()
`!<Key>osfActivate`	page-or-end-input()
`!<Key>space`	page-or-space()
`!Shift<Btn1Down>`	save-cursor-pos() extend-start()
`!<Btn1Down>`	save-cursor-pos() grab-focus()
`~Ctrl ~Meta ~Alt<Btn1Motion>`	extend-adjust()
`~Ctrl ~Meta ~Alt<Btn1Up>`	extend-end() restore-cursor-pos()
`~Ctrl ~Meta ~Alt<Btn2Down>`	copy-primary()
`~Ctrl ~Meta ~Alt<Btn3Down>`	save-cursor-pos() extend-start()
`~Ctrl ~Meta ~Alt<Btn3Motion>`	extend-adjust()
`~Ctrl ~Meta ~Alt<Btn3Up>`	extend-end() restore-cursor-pos()

Many of the translations shown in Table 21-1 are simply bindings for the Cli's new action procedures (described later). Others modify the cut-and-paste bindings to match the standard bindings for *xterm* rather than the standard bindings for the XmText widget: Button3 is used to extend the current selection, for example, and Button2 is used to paste the primary selection (at the insertion cursor position, rather than the mouse pointer position). These bindings also ensure that the user cannot use the mouse to position the cursor within a prompt or other uneditable text.

The Cli widget maintains this separate translation table, merged in as a separate step so that it does not have to duplicate the (lengthy) XmText translation table, and so that it can remain independent of that (unstable) translation table—if the default XmText translations change in a future release of Motif, the Cli widget will not have to be updated to use the new translation table. Therefore, when you want to specify resources for a Cli widget, you should set them on the `XmtNcliTranslations` resource, rather than on the `XtNtranslations` resource, unless you are certain that none of the translations you specify will be overridden by any of the translations shown in Table 21-1. When you set the `XmtNcliTranslations` resource, note that you should not use the `#override` or `#augment` directives in your translations—these directives only work with the `XtNtranslations` resource, which receives special handling by the Intrinsics.

The Cli widget defines ten new action procedures, which are described in the following paragraphs.

`scroll-forward()`
`scroll-backward()`

These actions scroll the Cli widget up or down. By default they scroll by half a page. If passed a number as their first argument, they will scroll by that number of lines, or if passed the string "page" as their first argument, they will scroll by complete pages (where page size depends on the size of the Cli widget).

`previous-command()`
`next-command()`
These actions implement the Cli command history mechanism described above. By default they are bound to the up and down arrow keys. *emacs* users might also want to bind them to **Ctrl-P** and **Ctrl-N**, for example.

`beginning-of-line()`
This action moves the cursor to the beginning of the current input line. It is used to override the XmText action of the same name, because the XmText widget and the XmtCli widget have different notions of where the beginning of the line is. In the Cli widget, the beginning of the line is the position immediately following the prompt, which is generally not the first column of the widget. Furthermore, if the user has typed a lot of input that has wrapped onto more than one line, this action will move to the first input character on first line of that input, not the first character on the current line. Note that this action does not appear in the Cli-specific translation table shown in Table 21-1. Because of the way action procedures are scoped, the `beginning-of-line()` binding in the default XmText translation table will refer to this action procedure, and you can invoke it however you normally invoke the `beginning-of-line()` action on your system.

`save-cursor-pos()`
`restore-cursor-pos()`
These actions are used as a pair at the beginning and end of any sequence of mouse actions that the user is allowed to make. They enforce the rule that the user should not be allowed to move the cursor off the current line of input. Using these actions in conjunction with the standard XmText mouse selection actions allows the user to select text anywhere in the Cli widget by dragging with the mouse, but have the insertion cursor return to its proper place on the current line of input when the selection is complete. These actions do allow the cursor to be moved with the mouse *within* the current line of input, just not off that line.

`page-or-end-input()`
`page-or-space()`
These actions are meant to be bound to the **Return** and **Space** keys. If the Cli widget is currently paging long output, then these actions implement single-line and full-page paging respectively, and if the widget is not currently paging, then `page-or-end-input()` calls the `end-input()` action described below and the `page-or-space()` action calls the XmText `self-insert()` action to insert the space character (or whatever character was used to invoke the action).

`end-input()`
This action tells the Cli widget that the user has entered a line of input. This is the procedure that calls the callbacks on the `XmtNinputCallback` list

or arranges for the `XmtCliGets()` function to stop blocking and return the input to its caller. Note that this action does not appear in the default translation table, because it is instead invoked through the `page-or-end-input()` action.

21.7 Using the Cli Widget

The Cli widget has features that allow you to use it in a number of useful ways. There are at least three important ways it can be used:

- As a straightforward command-line interface
- As a message viewer, serving in an application much the same function that the *xconsole* client server on an X desktop
- As a replacement terminal for porting terminal-based programs to a windowed environment

The next three subsections describe and give examples of each of these general models of use, and the subsection after those discusses things the Cli can *not* do.

21.7.1 As a Command-Line Interface

The Cli widget is so named because its primary purpose is to serve as a command-line interface. Its automatic prompting, handling of escaped newlines, and command history features make it easy to use for this purpose. To use it in your own applications, there is little more to do than create the widget, set a prompt, optionally turn on paging, and add a callback to be invoked when the user types a command. Example 21-1 shows this style of usage.

Example 21-1. Using a Cli Widget as a Command-Line Interface

```
static void input_callback(Widget, XtPointer, XtPointer);

main(int argc, char **argv)
{
    Widget cli;
    Arg args[10];
    Cardinal i;
    .
    .
    .
    i = 0;
    XtSetArg(args[i], XmtNprompt, "command> "); i++;
    XtSetArg(args[i], XmtNpageMode, True); i++
    cli = XmtCreateScrolledCli(layout, "cli", args, i);
    XtAddCallback(cli, XmtNinputCallback, input_callback, NULL);
    XtManageChild(cli);
    .
    .
    .
}
```

Example 21-1. Using a Cli Widget as a Command-Line Interface (continued)

```
static void input_callback(Widget w, XtPointer tag, XtPointer data)
{
    execute_command(parse_command((String)data));
}
```

21.7.2 As a Message Viewer

Another common and convenient way to use the Cli widget is as a message viewer. It is common to display simple messages in dialog boxes, but some applications need to print warnings, status reports, and similar pieces of information that are less ephemeral than text in a dialog box. If these messages are in a scrolled window, then the user can easily scroll backwards to review them when needed.

The Cli widget is ideal for this use because it provides a lot of the necessary functionality automatically:

- Text sent to the Cli is automatically appended to the text already there.
- When new text is added, the Cli automatically scrolls to make that text visible, or enters paging mode to allow the user to view that text a screen at a time.
- The user can review old messages after they have scrolled off the top of the Cli, but the Cli can automatically trim really old messages so that its memory usage does not grow without bounds.
- If the messages are coming through a pipe or socket from some other process, the Cli widget can automatically monitor that file descriptor simply setting the `XmtNfildes` resource.

Example 21-2 shows an example of how the Cli widget might be used like this. Note that since the Cli is not used for input in this model, we don't register a callback, and we even go ahead and make the Cli non-editable. We assume that the messages to be displayed in this widget are short enough and arrive at infrequent enough intervals that we don't want paging on at all times—this would mean that the user would have to page for every message and would simply become an inconvenience.

Example 21-2. Using the Cli Widget as a Message Viewer

```
static Widget message_widget;

static Args message_widget_args[] = {
    {XmtNsaveLines, (XtArgVal)2000}, /* save a lot of lines */
    {XmNeditable, (XtArgVal)False},  /* don't let the user type */
};

void CreateMessageWidget(Widget parent)
{
    Arg args[5];
    int i = 0;
```

Example 21-2. Using the Cli Widget as a Message Viewer (continued)

```
    message_widget = XmtCreateScrolledCli(parent, "messages",
                                          message_widget_args,
                                          XtNumber(message_widget_args);
    XtManageChild(message_widget);
}

/*
 * The app calls this function any time it wants to display a message
 */
void DisplayMessage(String msg)
{
    /* make a permanent record of the message */
    RecordMessageInLog(msg);

    /* display it in the Cli widget */
    XmtCliPuts(msg, message_widget);

    /* and beep to get the user's attention */
    XBell(XtDisplay(message_widget), 0);
}
```

21.7.3 As a Terminal Replacement

The third area in which the Cli widget is generally useful is in doing quick ports of old terminal-based software to a windowed environment. You might port an application that used a terminal for a command-line interface and drew graphs on a pen-plotter device to draw graphs in an X window. One option would be to leave the terminal interface alone, and require the user to run the application in an *xterm*, but a better design might be to have the plotting region and a Cli widget stacked one on top of the other in a main window, and to use the Cli as a simple replacement for the terminal. This approach is not much harder than just using the underlying *xterm* and has a few other advantages:

- Reading input from a terminal with functions like `gets()` that block doesn't mix well with drawing graphics in an X window that may need to have Expose and Resize events serviced asynchronously. The Cli analog to `gets()`, however, appears to block, but because there is an internal event loop, Expose events are still handled.
- Keeping the command-line window and the plotting window attached to one another is a better user interface.
- An application that creates and uses its own windows exclusively is a much more sophisticated X client than those "unfriendly" clients that have to read from and write to the underlying xterm.

Although the Cli widget makes simple ports of terminal-based applications easier, I'd encourage you to consider doing a fuller porting job, to turn the application into a full-blown X client. A command-line interface is appropriate for a lot of applications, but a graphical user interface opens up a host of other possibilities you should consider. Messages that are currently sent to the standard error stream could be placed in an error message dialog box, for example. Simple commands like "save" and "load" that don't have a lot of arguments or sophisticated syntax can be made available in pulldown menus, and even given keyboard shortcuts through menu accelerators. If the application has to query the user for a number of pieces of input, you could design a dialog box to gather the same information. For output, remember that you are no longer limited to text or to a single window. A program that displayed network statistics in histogram form using text characters could be updated to use actual graphics calls to display a much nicer-looking histogram. And while a terminal-based debugger must display program source code, program output, and debugger messages all in the same window, a debugger designed for a graphical environment could display each of these things in a separate window.

There is not time to overhaul every useful terminal-based application like this, however, and there will always be a place for the quick-and-dirty port. Example 21-3 shows how the Cli widget could be used for such a port. In this example, we replace terminal I/O calls with their Cli analogs by using the C preprocessor. Another valid approach, especially when linking with libraries that use terminal I/O directly is to set the `XmtNdisplayStdout` and `XmtNdisplayStderr` resources to intercept output that would otherwise go to the underlying terminal.

Example 21-3. Using the Cli Widget as a Terminal Replacement

```
static Widget toplevel, rowcol;
static Widget terminal_widget;

/*
 * Here we redefine all the output and input commands the app uses.
 * Most apps probably use functions other than these two...
 */
#define puts(s) XmtCliPuts(s, terminal_widget)
#define fgets(buf, n, stream) XmtCliGets(buf, n, terminal_widget)

/* this function is called from the initialization code */
static void create_terminal(void)
{
    terminal_widget = XmtCreateScrolledCli(rowcol, "terminal", NULL, 0);
    XtVaSetValues(terminal_widget,
                  XmtNpageMode, True,
                  XmtNpageString, "--More--",
                  NULL);
}
```

21.7.4 What the Cli Is Not

The Cli widget can do a lot of useful things, but it is important to understand that it is not a terminal emulator widget. It can replace a terminal for applications that use the terminal only to read and write lines of text. It cannot return input character-by-character, does not respond to cursor motion commands, and cannot be used with applications that use the *curses* library.

Many applications have a single "message line" that they use to display simple messages to the user, and sometimes also to get simple synchronous input from him. The Cli widget has these capabilities but is not really appropriate for this role; Xmt library contains a widget specifically designed for this purpose, the XmtMsgLine widget, which is described in Chapter 22, *The Message Line.*

21.8 Style: When to Provide a Command-Line Interface

A lot of applications would benefit from the addition of a command-line interface. Many are probably without them simply because there was no suitable CLI widget available when they were written. When considering whether or not to provide a command-line interface in your applications, here are some points to consider.

Many users, particularly expert users, prefer typing to mousing. The more they can do without taking their hands off the keyboard, the happier they are. This is not to say that you should only provide a command-line interface; novice users may find it much easier to use a good point-and-click interface than to master a command language. (Although some of your novice users may be familiar with command-line interfaces from years of using terminal-based applications, and may be unfamiliar with GUIs.) As with so many other stylistic issues, it is important to know your audience, as this will influence your design decisions.

If you notice that your GUI has a lot of buttons in some sort of "command area" (or in pulldown menus), consider providing a command-line interface for issuing these commands. This is particularly true if your buttons have command-type labels like **Send**, **Goto**, **Open**, **Get File**, **Change Local Directory**, and so on.

A command-line interface can allow more sophisticated commands to be issued than button pushing can. For example, many applications have **Save** and **Save As...** menu items. The **Save As...** button pops up a dialog to request the filename to use. In a command-line interface, a single command "`save`" which accepts an optional filename argument could serve the same function as these two buttons. If you are having to create a lot of buttons that do similar things, or a number of dialogs to query the user for extra information needed to execute commands, your command set is probably complex enough that you'd benefit from a text-based interface in addition to your GUI interface.

If your application has a direct-manipulation interface which allows the user to operate on objects displayed graphically on the screen, consider an interface that allows the user to identify those objects by naming them rather than pointing at them. When moving a file from one directory to another, for example, it might often be easier to type the name of the target directory than it is to point at it, especially if the target directory is several levels away in the directory hierarchy.

Adding a command-line interface to an application opens up a number of new possibilities. The Cli widget allows the user to easily repeat commands using the command history mechanism. It also allows the user to use cut-and-paste to assemble new commands out of pieces from various sources. Having defined a command grammar, it is a simple step to allow command scripts to be read from files.

Don't think of the choice between a CLI and a GUI as an either/or choice. Each style of interaction has its own strengths and weaknesses, and each can be useful to different types of users at different times. An application can (and often should) support both, and in a well-designed application, the command-line interface and the graphical user interface will complement one another.

21.9 Summary

You can send output to a Cli widget with the functions `XmtCliPuts()` and `XmtCliPrintf()`. Additionally, the Cli widget can be configured to display output sent to the standard output and standard error streams (use the `XmtNdisplayStdout` and `XmtNdisplayStderr` resources) or any output sent to a specified file descriptor (use the `XmtNfildes` resource).

The simplest way to get input from a Cli widget is to register a callback on the `XmtNinputCallback` resource; this will provide asynchronous notification when the user has entered a line of input. You can also get input synchronously with the `XmtCliGets()` function, but there are a number of modality and input focus issues to beware of when using this function.

When the `XmtNsaveHistory` resource is `True`, the Cli widget saves each of the user's lines of input. The user can use the up and down arrow keys to view commands in the history buffer; this makes it easy to repeat previously entered commands.

The `XmtNmaxHistory` resource specifies the number of input lines to save in the history buffer. The similar but unrelated resource `XmtNsaveLines` specifies the total number of lines (both input and output) that should be retained by the Cli widget. Lines in excess of this number will be periodically removed.

The `XmtNprompt` resource specifies a string to be automatically displayed as a command-line prompt. The `XmtNescapeNewlines` resource specifies whether or not the user should be allowed to enter multi-line commands by escaping the newline with the backslash character.

When the `XmtNpageMode` resource is `True`, the Cli widget will page (like the *more* program) long pieces of output. The `XmtNpageString` resource specifies the string to appear in the paging banner.

22

The Message Line

Many applications need to display simple messages and prompts to the user, and to obtain simple input from the user. These messages might be instructions ("Select region to invert"), a question ("Do you really want to quit? (y/n):") or a prompt for string input ("Filename:").

The functions described in Chapter 25, *Message Dialogs*, and in Chapter 26, *Simple Input Dialogs*, will allow you to display messages and get simple input with dialog boxes, but popping up a dialog box is "too heavyweight" an operation in some circumstances. If you are an *emacs* user, you are familiar with the extensive use *emacs* makes of its message line, and if you are a *vi* user, you know that typing a colon while in command mode will allow you to enter an extended command on a message line. Imagine using a GUI version of either of these editors in which the message line had been replaced with a dialog box: any time you wanted to do a search and replace operation, read a new file, or issue any sort of extended command, a dialog box would pop up, and you'd probably have to take your hands off the keyboard and use the mouse to interact with the dialog. While dialogs are useful for novice users, and are very good at indicating modality, they can also interrupt the flow of the work the user is trying to accomplish, break his train of thought, and slow him down.

The XmtMsgLine widget is designed to provide a "lightweight" alternative for the display of simple messages and for obtaining simple synchronous input. The MsgLine widget is a simple subclass of the XmText widget. Figure 22-1 shows a screendump of the MsgLine widget requesting input from the user.

The MsgLine widget does not have a particularly interesting on-screen appearance, nor does it have a long list of resources, but it does have a rich set of convenience functions for displaying messages and getting synchronous input. These functions are described in the sections that follow.

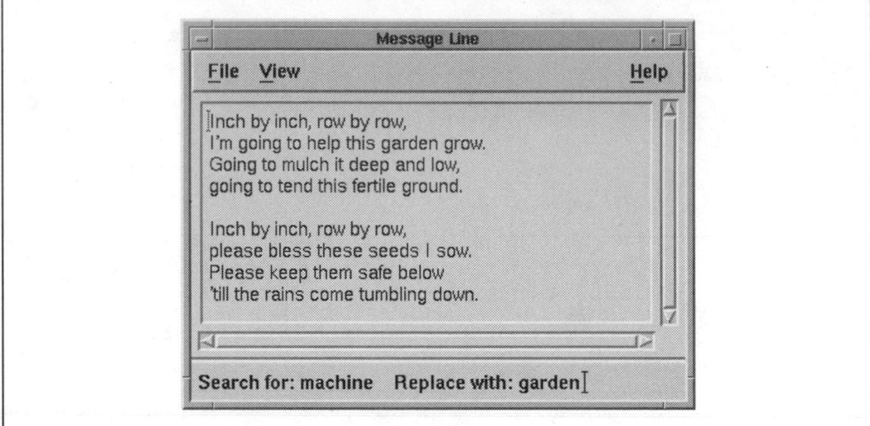

Figure 22-1. A window with a message line

22.1 Creating a Message Line

The MsgLine widget is a subclass of XmText. Its class name is "XmtMsgLine", and its class structure is `xmtMsgLineWidgetClass`.

You can create a MsgLine widget with the `XmtCreateMsgLine()` constructor:

Xmt/

MsgLine.c

```
#include <Xmt/MsgLine.h>
Widget XmtCreateMsgLine(Widget parent, String name,
                        ArgList args, Cardinal num_args)
```

Laying Out a Message Line

In many main windows, the message line and the menubar are laid out in similar ways. The menubar is usually flush with the top of the window and the message line is often flush with the bottom. You may want to give them the same color, and usually neither should have a margin around it.

If you are using an XmtLayout widget to lay out your window, you can remove the margins around a message line with resources like the following:

```
*layout.marginWidth: 0
*layout.marginHeight: 0
*msgline.layoutMarginWidth: 0
*msgline.layoutMarginHeight: 0
```

Laying Out a Message Line (continued)

Since the XmtMsgLine widget is a subclass of the XmText widget, it also has a shadow and a highlight frame that you may want to remove:

```
*msgline.shadowThickness: 0
*msgline.highlightThickness: 0
```

And if you are using the XmtLayout widget, you can keep the message line a fixed size and have the Layout draw a separator above the message line with these resources:

```
*msgline.layoutStretchability: 0
*msgline.layoutFrameType: XmtLayoutFrameTop
*msgline.layoutFrameLineType: XmtLayoutFrameEtched
*msgline.layoutFrameThickness: 4
```

Or, if you are using the `XmtNlayout` resource of the Layout widget, you can instead specify all these layout constraint resources in the layout grammar:

```
Margin 0 Fixed Etched Top 0 4 msgline
```

Finally, if you expect your users to be familiar with the *emacs* text editor editing commands, you might add a few of them to the message line translation table:

```
*msgline.msgLineTranslations:\
Ctrl<Key>a: beginning-of-line()\n\
Ctrl<Key>e: end-of-line()\n\
Ctrl<Key>b: backward-character()\n\
Ctrl<Key>f: forward-character()\n\
Ctrl<Key>d: delete-next-character()\n\
Ctrl<Key>k: kill-to-end-of-line()\n\
Meta<Key>b: backward-word()\n\
Meta<Key>f: forward-word()\n\
Meta<Key>d: kill-next-word()\n\
Meta<Key>osfBackSpace: kill-previous-word()
```

—*djf*

22.2 Displaying Messages with the MsgLine

The MsgLine widget provides a number of public functions that control the text that appears in the widget. These functions allow the programmer to set the displayed message, append to the displayed message, push the displayed message onto a stack of saved messages, and pop this stack of messages.

Another function allows the programmer to clear the message line immediately, or arrange for it to be cleared after some fixed time interval or whenever the next program activity occurs. These functions are described later.

Note that all of the MsgLine functions call `XFlush()` when necessary to force your output to be displayed, even if the application will be busy and not processing events (and therefore not flushing the output buffer) for a while.

22.2.1 Setting the Message

There are three MsgLine functions that display strings in a message line:

Xmt/

MsgLine.c

```
#include <Xmt/MsgLine.h>
void XmtMsgLineSet(Widget w, String s)
void XmtMsgLineAppend(Widget w, String s)
void XmtMsgLinePrintf(Widget w, String fmt, ...)
```

`XmtMsgLineSet()` is the most basic of the MsgLine functions: it takes a MsgLine widget and a string argument and displays the string in the widget, overwriting any message that was there previously. Use this command when you want to display a simple fixed message. In a drawing editor application, you might display a simple instruction message for each drawing mode or item in the palette of "drawing tools." Here's an example: "Draw Rectangle: select a rectangle by dragging. F1 for Help."

`XmtMsgLineAppend()` takes a MsgLine widget and a string argument, and appends the string to the currently displayed message in the widget. Before saving a long file to disk, for example, you could use `XmtMsgLineSet()` to display the message "Saving...", and then when the save was finished, you could use `XmtMsgLineAppend()` to add the string "Done". This kind of feedback is useful to the user, and gives him confidence that the application is working as it is supposed to.

`XmtMsgLinePrintf()` appends to the currently displayed message as `XmtMsgLineAppend()` does, but takes `printf()`-style arguments. The first argument to `XmtMsgLinePrintf()` is a MsgLine widget and the second is a `printf()` format string. These two arguments are followed by a variable-length argument list of values to be substituted into the format string.

`XmtMsgLinePrintf()` is simply a convenient wrapper around `XmtMsgLineAppend()` that saves you the trouble of making a separate call to `sprintf()`. It appends to the currently displayed message, but you can use it to display a separate message if you simply clear the message line of any other messages first, as explained in the next section.

22.2.2 Clearing the Message Line

You can clear the text from a MsgLine with `XmtMsgLineClear()`:

```
#include <Xmt/MsgLine.h>
void XmtMsgLineClear(Widget w, int when)
```

`XmtMsgLineClear()` takes a MsgLine widget as its first argument, and an integer, *when*, as its second argument. If *when* is the constant `XmtMsgLineNow`, then `XmtMsgLineClear()` erases any message in the widget immediately. If *when* is the constant `XmtMsgLineOnAction`, then `XmtMsgLineClear()` arranges for the message in the widget to be erased the next time the user interacts with the application (by typing a key, or clicking on a push button, for example). Finally, if *when* is any positive integer, then `XmtMsgLineClear()` arranges for the message to be erased after *when* milliseconds.

To continue an example started previously, if you had used `XmtMsgLineSet()` to display the message "Saving...", and then called `XmtMsgLineAppend()` to add "Done" to the message, you might next call `XmtMsgLineClear()` to arrange for the message to be automatically erased when the user next interacts with the program. Note that if you clear the message line immediately, then the user will never have the chance to see the extra feedback "Done" that you so considerately provided. On the other hand, if you never clear the message at all, the feedback will remain there until some other message is displayed, which could be quite inappropriate.

To arrange for the message line to be cleared after a fixed interval, `XmtMsgLineClear()` registers a time out with `XtAppAddTimeOut()`. To arrange for it to be cleared on the next user action, `XmtMsgLineClear()` registers an action hook procedure with `XtAppAddActionHook()`. Note that both timeout and action hook procedures are dispatched from the event loop, so if your application is doing some long computation, the message line will not be cleared at least until the application returns to the event loop. Note that it is okay to call `XmtMsgLineClear()` twice, specifying `XmtMsgLineOnAction` once and specifying a time out once. In this case, the message will be cleared when the first user action occurs, or when the time out occurs. Note also that if you arrange for a MsgLine to be cleared at some point in the future and then call some other MsgLine public function (say to append a string to the message) then the pending clear will be done immediately, and the timer and/or action hook procedures will be deregistered.

22.2.3 Saving and Restoring Messages

You can save and restore the contents of a message line with `XmtMsgLinePush()` and `XmtMsgLinePop()`:

Xmt/

MsgLine.c

```
#include <Xmt/MsgLine.h>
void XmtMsgLinePush(Widget w)
void XmtMsgLinePop(Widget w, int when)
```

`XmtMsgLinePush()` saves the contents of a MsgLine widget in a special stack to be later restored with a call to `XmtMsgLinePop()`. It does not clear or modify the contents of the message line in any way, but once a message has been "pushed," a different or temporary message can be displayed (with `XmtMsgLineSet()`, for example), and then the original message can be popped back with `XmtMsgLinePop()`. Any number of messages can be pushed onto the stack, although in practice you will probably rarely need to push more than one or two.

To return to our earlier drawing editor example, say you used a MsgLine to display simple instructions for each of the drawing tools available in a palette—the message line might read "Draw a rectangle by dragging with the mouse." Now if the user types **Ctrl-R**, your accelerator for the **Read New File** command, you might use the MsgLine to prompt the user to enter a filename (we'll see how to use the MsgLine to get user input later in the chapter). To do this, you'll call `XmtMsgLineSet()` to display the prompt "Read File:". If the message line had started out blank, you could display the prompt, read the user's input and then clear the message line again, restoring it to its original state. Since the message line didn't start out blank, you'll need to do something else to restore it to its original state. Using the `XmtMsgLinePush()`/`XmtMsgLinePop()` pair of functions is the easiest way to do this: call `XmtMsgLinePush()` before you display the prompt, and call `XmtMsgLinePop()` after the user has entered her input. These functions work correctly even when the message line does start out blank, so when you are not exactly sure what state the message line may be in, you may want to use the push/pop pair just to be safe.

Since `XmtMsgLinePop()` is, in a sense, a replacement for `XmtMsgLineClear()`, it also takes a *when* argument that specifies when the message is to be popped. If *when* is the constant `XmtMsgLineNow`, then the message is popped immediately. If it is `XmtMsgLineOnAction`, then the message is popped the next time there is a user action, which will give the user time to read the temporary message before it is replaced with the original message. Finally, if *when* is any positive integer, it is taken as the number of milliseconds after which the message should be popped. This interpretation of the *when* argument is the same for `XmtMsgLinePop()` as it is for `XmtMsgLineClear()`. As with delayed clear operations, if an application requests a delayed pop and then calls another MsgLine function before the delay expires or before a user action occurs, the pop will be performed immediately, before the new message line function is executed.

22.3 Getting Input with the XmtMsgLine

Some applications will use a message line for output only. The MsgLine widget can be a very useful tool for these applications, but the full power of the widget is that it also allows input. The MsgLine widget, like the XmtCli widget (see Chapter 21, *Command-Line Input*), supports both synchronous and asynchronous input. The synchronous input functions all contain an internal event loop so that they appear to block when called, and return the user's input on return. Asynchronous input is delivered not when the application requests it through a function call, but when the user enters it, through callback notification.

An important feature of MsgLine input is that the user is not allowed to edit or delete any text that is displayed in the message line as a result of a call to one of the output routines previously described. Only the area after any output (such as a prompt) is editable, and the default translations are such that the user cannot move the cursor out of this editable region, either with the keyboard or with the mouse. Once the user enters some text and strikes the **Return** key, that text itself becomes uneditable, so that subsequent input commands (performed without clearing the message line) do not allow the user to modify previous input values.

22.3.1 Asynchronous Input with the XmtMsgLine

Like the XmtCli widget, the MsgLine widget has an `XmtNinputCallback` callback list, the functions on which are called whenever the user enters input asynchronously on the message line and strikes the **Return** key. Some applications will want to allow this sort of asynchronous input, using the MsgLine as a kind of mini-XmtCli widget. Most, however, will want to keep the MsgLine under the application's control, displaying application messages and getting input from the user only in certain specific circumstances.

The MsgLine widget has a resource, `XmtNallowAsyncInput`, which controls whether or not the message line will accept asynchronous input. The default is `False`. When this resource is set to `False`, the MsgLine widget sets the `XmNcursorPositionVisible`, `XmNeditable`, and `XmNtraversalOn` resources all to `False`, which means that the MsgLine widget will display no input cursor, will not accept input, and will not be part of keyboard navigation—the user will not be able to give it the focus by traversing to it. These resources are temporarily turned on to allow synchronous input when it is requested through one of the synchronous input functions, but remain off at all other times.

If, on the other hand, `XmtNallowAsyncInput` is set to `True`, then `XmNcursorPositionVisible`, `XmNeditable`, and `XmNtraversalOn` are all set to `True`, and the user will be able to traverse to the message line at any time and enter input. When the user enters input and strikes the **Return** key, any functions registered on the `XmtNinputCallback` callback list will be called. The input string will be passed as the third (*`call_data`*) argument to these functions. The callbacks should not free or modify this string, and should make a copy of it if they need to save it for later use.

If you allow asynchronous input, then note that you shouldn't use the MsgLine to display any permanent messages such as instructions—those instructions will probably not be a useful accompaniment for whatever asynchronous input the user will enter. You can still use the MsgLine to display temporary messages such as "Working; please wait . . . ". Presumably while such a message is posted, the application will not be responding to keyboard input and the user would not be able to enter asynchronous input anyway.

22.3.2 Synchronous Input with the XmtMsgLine

Although the MsgLine widget supports asynchronous input like the XmtCli widget does, it was really designed with synchronous input in mind. With asynchronous input, the application is notified when the user's input is ready. For synchronous input, the application stops and waits for the user to complete her input. Synchronous input functions block (like `gets()`) or at least appear to block (like `XmtCliGets()`) while waiting for input—i.e., they do not return to the caller until the user's input is complete.

The MsgLine widget supports a number of these synchronous input functions, which, like the Cli function `XmtCliGets()`, enter an internal event loop, and do not return to the calling function until the user has completed the requested input. The user completes input in a MsgLine widget by striking the **Return** key, or by canceling the input with the **Escape**, **Ctrl-C**, or **Ctrl-G** keys. (These key bindings for entering and canceling input may be changed through the MsgLine translation table, of course.) As with all synchronous input in a GUI, it is important that the user have the option to change her mind and back out of an operation by canceling the input, so all of the MsgLine synchronous input functions return a special value to indicate that the user has canceled the input. Any application that uses these functions should be sure to check for this case, and should back out of whatever operation is in progress if the user requests it. If the user does cancel input, then any partial input the user did enter is erased before any of the synchronous input functions return.

By default, a MsgLine widget does not display an input cursor and is not traversable or editable except when within a call to a synchronous input function. When any of the synchronous input functions are called, they use `XmProcessTraversal()` to set input focus to the MsgLine widget, so that the user does not have to use the mouse or keyboard to traverse there herself. Since synchronous input must always be modal,* the MsgLine input functions call `XtAddGrab()`, the function used to make dialog boxes modal, to tell the Xt Intrinsics that only user events directed at the MsgLine widget should be delivered. Expose and resize events will be handled for the rest of the interface as normal, but mouse and keyboard events for the rest of the interface will be ignored.

*If a synchronous input function weren't modal, the user could repeat the action that invoked the input function, and the application could end up with nested internal event loops—a very messy situation.

There are five MsgLine synchronous input functions, used to input strings, characters, signed and unsigned integers, and floating-point values. They are described in the subsections below.

22.3.2.1 Getting String Input

You can get string input from the user with `XmtMsgLineGetString()`:

Xmt/

MsgLine.c

```
#include <Xmt/MsgLine.h>
String XmtMsgLineGetString(Widget w, String buf, int len)
```

This function takes three arguments: a MsgLine widget, a character buffer, and the length of that buffer. It enters an internal event loop and accepts input until the user either enters or cancels the input. If the user enters the input, it is copied into the supplied buffer (up to the maximum length of the buffer) and the address of the buffer is returned as the function value. If the user cancels the input, the contents of the buffer are not modified, and the function returns NULL.

22.3.2.2 Getting Character Input

You can get a single character of input from the user with `XmtMsgLineGetChar()`:

Xmt/

MsgLine.c

```
#include <Xmt/MsgLine.h>
int XmtMsgLineGetChar(Widget w)
```

This function accepts a single MsgLine widget argument and returns an integer. It enters an internal event loop until the user types a single character or cancels the input. If the user typed a character, it returns the character. Otherwise, if the user canceled the input, it returns the constant `EOF` (which is defined in the header file *stdio.h*). Note that this function only waits for a single character to be typed—the user does not have to strike the **Return** key to enter the input.

22.3.2.3 Getting Numeric Input

The MsgLine widget provides three functions for getting user input of numbers:

Xmt/

MsgLine.c

```
#include <Xmt/MsgLine.h>
Boolean XmtMsgLineGetUnsigned(Widget w, unsigned *u)
Boolean XmtMsgLineGetInt(Widget w, int *i)
Boolean XmtMsgLineGetDouble(Widget w, double *d)
```

XmtMsgLineGetUnsigned(), XmtMsgLineGetInt(), and XmtMsgLine-GetDouble() all accept a MsgLine widget as their first argument, and accept a the address of an unsigned integer, the address of an integer, and the address of a double-precision floating-point value as their second arguments, respectively. They each return a Boolean value: True if the user entered input, and False if the user canceled the input.

These functions accept input of a string, and when the user enters that string, they convert it to an unsigned integer, a signed integer, or a floating-point value and store the result at the specified address. If the user cancels the input, then the value at the specified address is not changed. These functions constrain the user's input to characters that are valid for numeric input. XmtMsgLineGet-Unsigned() accepts only the digits 0 through 9. XmtMsgLineGetInt() accepts only these digits plus the hyphen or "minus sign." XmtMsgLineGet-Double() accepts the digits, the plus and minus signs, the decimal point, and the uppercase and lowercase letter E used in scientific notation.

22.3.3 Setting Default Input Values

When getting user input through dialog boxes, one common feature is the ability to provide a default value for the input. If you can make a reasonable guess at what the user's input will be (the same input she entered previously, for example) then it is often a good idea to display that input as a default and save the user the typing.

One way to do this is to display the default value as part of the prompt (Enter filename: [/home/david/src/MsgLine.c], for example), and then to use the default value if the user simply strikes **Return** and the input function returns an empty input buffer. A shortcoming to this approach is that it does not allow the user to edit the default value—he must accept the default as is, or type a new value from scratch.

So an alternative approach is to display the default value as part of the input string, rather than as part of the prompt string. Recall that the MsgLine output functions XmtMsgLineSet(), XmtMsgLineAppend(), and so on display text (such as prompts) that are not editable by the user. In contrast, the function XmtMsgLineSetInput() adds text to a MsgLine widget that is editable by the user, and is therefore suitable as a default value to be displayed to the user.

Xmt/

MsgLine.c

```
#include <Xmt/MsgLine.h>
void XmtMsgLineSetInput(Widget w, String s)
```

With this function, you could display a prompt with XmtMsgLineSet(), specify a default input value with XmtMsgLineSetInput(), and then ask the user to accept or edit that input value by calling XmtMsgLineGetString(). We'll show an example of this technique later in the chapter. Note that if the shortcoming of the previous technique was that the user couldn't edit the default value, the shortcoming of this technique is that the user must edit the default value—if he wants to enter a new value totally unrelated to the default, he must first delete the default.

`XmtMsgLineSetInput()` has a corresponding query function, `XmtMsgLineGetInput()`, which returns the portion of the text in the MsgLine that is currently editable.

Xmt/

MsgLine.c

```
#include <Xmt/MsgLine.h>
String XmtMsgLineGetInput(Widget w)
```

This function is not normally useful, because synchronous input functions do not return until the user's input is already entered and has become uneditable. It is possible to customize the synchronous input process, however. Because the MsgLine is a subclass of XmText, the XmText `XmNmodifyVerifyCallback` is called for each input character, and you can call `XmtMsgLineGetInput()` from within this callback. Similarly, it is also possible to call this function from within custom action procedures.

If you wanted to support filename completion in the MsgLine widget, for example, you might register a custom action procedure to be invoked when the user typed the **TAB** key. This action procedure would use `XmtMsgLineGetInput()` to obtain the user's current input, would determine if there was a unique completion for that filename, and if so, would use `XmtMsgLineSetInput()` to set the complete filename in the MsgLine widget. When calling `XmtMsgLineSetInput()` from an action procedure like this, note that it does not append to the user's input string; instead, it replaces any current input with the specified string.

There is an example of using these functions to do this kind of dynamic input modification in the "Using the MsgLine Widget" section.

22.3.4 Caveats of Synchronous Input

As with the XmtCli widget, there are issues of keyboard focus and modality to be aware of when using the synchronous input capabilities of the XmtMsgLine. As noted before, the MsgLine uses `XmProcessTraversal()` to set the input focus to itself, and it uses `XtAddGrab()` to ensure that the input is modal—that all user events except those directed at the MsgLine are ignored. The difficulty is not so much with the technical problem of ensuring modality, but with the interface design problem of indicating modality: it should be clear to the user that the application has entered a mode in which only keyboard input to the MsgLine widget will be accepted.

As with the XmtCli widget, the appearance of the highlighting rectangle that goes with keyboard focus, the appearance of a prompt, and of the input cursor are usually enough to indicate this modality to an alert or experienced user. Novice users may experience some confusion when first prompted for input by an XmtMsgLine, but will probably learn quickly. The "Usage" and "Style" sections that follow contain some tips on minimizing this potential for confusion.

22.4 MsgLine Translations and Actions

Like the Cli widget, the MsgLine handles translations somewhat differently than other widgets do. It inherits an unmodified set of the XmText widget translations. When a MsgLine widget is created, these default XmText resources are overridden, augmented, or replaced by any resources you (or the end user) specified on the `XtNtranslations` resource (and, in X11R5, also any resources specified with the `baseTranslations` pseudo-resource). This is the same process that all widgets follow to determine their translation table. The MsgLine widget goes two steps further, however: it overrides this resulting translation table with its own internal set of default MsgLine-specific translations (shown in Table 22-1) and then, finally, overrides these with any resources you (or the end user) have specified on the `XmtNmsgLineTranslations` resource.

Table 22-1. The MsgLine-specific Translation Table

Event	Action(s)
`<Key>Return`	`end-input()`
`<Key>osfCancel`	`cancel-input()`
`Ctrl<Key>C`	`cancel-input()`
`Ctrl<Key>G`	`cancel-input()`
`<Key>Tab`	`self-insert()`
`~Ctrl Shift ~Meta ~Alt<Btn1Down>`	`save-cursor-pos() extend-start()`
`~Ctrl ~Shift ~Meta ~Alt<Btn1Down>`	`save-cursor-pos() grab-focus()`
`~Ctrl ~Meta ~Alt<Btn1Motion>`	`extend-adjust()`
`~Ctrl ~Meta ~Alt<Btn1Up>`	`extend-end() restore-cursor-pos()`
`~Ctrl ~Meta ~Alt<Btn2Down>`	`copy-primary()`
`~Ctrl ~Meta ~Alt<Btn3Down>`	`save-cursor-pos() extend-start()`
`~Ctrl ~Meta ~Alt<Btn3Motion>`	`extend-adjust()`
`~Ctrl ~Meta ~Alt<Btn3Up>`	`extend-end() restore-cursor-pos()`

Some of the translations shown in Table 22-1 are simply bindings for the MsgLine's new action procedures (described in the following list). Others, like the translations of the Cli widget, modify the cut-and-paste bindings to match the standard bindings for *xterm* rather than the standard bindings for the XmText widget: Button3 is used to extend the current selection, for example, and Button2 is used to paste the primary selection (at the insertion cursor position, rather than the mouse pointer position). These bindings also ensure that the user cannot use the mouse to position the cursor within a prompt or other uneditable text. Finally, notice that the MsgLine widget overrides the single-line XmText widget binding for the **TAB** key—since the MsgLine is usually used for synchronous input, it does not make sense to use **TAB** for keyboard traversal.

The MsgLine widget maintains this separate translation table, and merges it in to the widget's final translation table in a separate step so that it does not have to duplicate the (lengthy) XmText translation table, and so that it can remain independent of that (unstable) set of translations—if the default XmText key bindings change in a future release of Motif, the MsgLine widget will not have to be updated to use the new translation table. When you want to specify the resources for a MsgLine widget, you should set them on the `XmtNmsgLineTranslations` resource, rather than on the `XtNtranslations` resource, unless you are certain that none of the translations you specify will be overridden by any of the translations shown in Table 22-1. When you set the `XmtNmsgLineTranslations` resource, note that you should not use the `#override` or `#augment` directives in your translations—these directives only work with the `XtNtranslations` resource that receives special handling by the Intrinsics.

The following paragraphs describe each of the new MsgLine action procedures.

`end-input()`
: When the MsgLine is doing synchronous input, this action causes the synchronous input function to extract the user's input from the widget and return it to the caller. When the MsgLine is doing asynchronous input, this actions causes it to extract the user's input and notify the application by invoking the `XmtNinputCallback` callback list.

`cancel-input()`
: If the MsgLine is doing synchronous input, this action causes the internal event loop to be terminated, the user's input to be erased, and the synchronous input function to return with an indication that the user canceled the input. If the MsgLine is not doing synchronous input, this action has no effect.

`save-cursor-pos()`
`restore-cursor-pos()`
: This pair of actions saves and restores the position of the insertion cursor. They are intended to be used before and after mouse translations so that the insertion cursor can be moved while selecting text anywhere in the widget, but so that the insertion cursor is not left in text that the user is not allowed to edit.

`beginning-of-line()`
: This action has the same name as, and overrides, the XmText `beginning-of-line()` action. Instead of moving the insertion cursor to the actual beginning of the line, however, it moves it to the first editable position; i.e., to the first character after whatever prompt is being displayed. Note that this action does not appear in the MsgLine-specific translation table shown in Table 22-1. Because of the way action procedures are scoped, the `beginning-of-line()` binding in the default XmText translation table will refer to this action procedure, and you can invoke it however you normally invoke the `beginning-of-line()` action on your system.

22.5 Using the MsgLine Widget

The MsgLine widget is simple, but is one of the most versatile widgets in the Xmt library. The subsections below show how you can:

- Display instructions
- Display "working, please wait" messages
- Get string input
- Get character input
- Get numeric input
- Get input with a default value
- Get input with command or filename completion
- Get input with the MsgLine in response to keyboard commands, but get the input with a dialog box when the same command is issued with the mouse

22.5.1 Displaying Instructions

In a drawing-editor application, you might use a MsgLine widget to display instructions for each of the drawing tools available for selection in the palette of tools. Example 22-1 shows a callback that you could register on each button in the palette or toolbox area of your application.

Example 22-1. Using a MsgLine Widget to Display Instructions

```
static Widget MsgLine;

static String instructions[] = {
    "Draw line:  drag to position endpoints of the line.",
    "Erase: drag to select region to be erased",
    "Select: click to select an object; Shift-click for multiple objects",
        .
        .
        .
};

static void InstructionCallback(Widget w, XtPointer tag, XtPointer data)
{
    int tool = (int) tag;

    XmtMsgLineSet(MsgLine, instructions[tool]);
}
```

22.5.2 Displaying Working Messages

Another use of a MsgLine widget is to provide feedback to the user when the application is doing some sort of work in the background that would not otherwise be obvious to the user. Messages of this sort might be things like "Saving file /home/david/drawing1 . . . ". Example 22-2 shows a function that provides this kind of feedback.

Example 22-2. Using a MsgLine Widget to Display Working Messages

```
static Widget msgline;

static void SaveFile(String filename)
{
    /* save any current message */
    XmtMsgLinePush(msgline);

    /* tell the user he'll have to wait a bit */
    XmtDisplayBusyCursor(msgline);

    /* clear any current message; the next function appends */
    XmtMsgLineClear(msgline, XmtMsgLineNow);

    /* and explain what we're doing */
    XmtMsgLinePrintf(msgline, "Saving file %s...", filename);

    /* now actually save the file */
    save_file(filename);

    /* then tell the user we did it successfully */
    XmtMsgLineAppend(msgline, "Done.");

    /* and tell him he can stop waiting now */
    XmtDisplayDefaultCursor(msgline);

    /* arrange to restore the old message when he does anything */
    XmtMsgLinePop(msgline, XmtMsgLineOnAction);
}
```

There are several things to note about this example. First, notice that it calls `XmtMsgLinePush()` and `XmtMsgLinePop()` so that any message previously displayed in the message line (such as an instructional message as described in the previous section) will be restored. Second, notice that the first message says what the application is about to do, then the application does it, and then it appends the message "Done" to tell the user that the operation completed successfully. It uses a delayed pop operation, because otherwise, the appended "Done" message would be popped off the message line right after it was appended, and the user would not have the chance to read it. Remember that `XmtMsgLinePrintf()` and the other MsgLine functions call `XFlush()` to force their output to be displayed immediately—this means that the "Saving file . . . " message is guaranteed to be sent to the X server before the application actually begins to save the file. Finally, note that this function changes the mouse pointer to the "busy" cursor with the `XmtDisplayBusyCursor()` function. (See Chapter 31, *Busy States and Background Work.*) Whenever you display a busy cursor, you should consider displaying an explanation of what the application is busy doing in a message line.

This kind of "Working . . . Done" message is effective when the task being performed (saving a file, for example) takes only a few seconds. For any task that takes longer, it is a good idea to display periodic feedback to the user so she knows that the application has not hung. One way to provide this feedback is to post an XmtWorkingBox dialog. When performing a long task, an application should also take steps to periodically return control to the Intrinsics so that such things as Expose events will be handled. For more information on this issue and on the XmtWorkingBox, see Chapter 31, *Busy States and Background Work*. For now, it is sufficient to note that another good way to provide periodic feedback that the application is still working is to append a `.` to the message line. So an application might start by displaying the string "Working" in the message line, and then append a single period for each chunk of processing it performs.

22.5.3 Getting String Input

The previous sections give examples of using the MsgLine for output-only tasks. MsgLine is also useful for getting input. Example 22-3 shows how a MsgLine widget might be used to get input for a search-and-replace function in a text editor application. Note the way this function checks the return values of its synchronous input functions to see whether the user asked to cancel the operation. As with the previous example, this one uses `XmtMsgLinePush()` and `XmtMsgLinePop()` to ensure that any previous messages are restored.

Example 22-3. Using a MsgLine for String Input

```
static Widget msgline;

static void SearchAndReplace()
{
    char search[100];
    char replace[100];

    /* save old message */
    XmtMsgLinePush(msgline);

    /* prompt for and get string to be replaced */
    XmtMsgLineSet(msgline, "Search for: ");
    if (!XmtMsgLineGetString(msgline, search, sizeof(search))) {
        /* if canceled, restore message immediately and return */
        XmtMsgLinePop(msgline, XmtMsgLineNow);
        return;
    }

    /* prompt for and get replacement */
    XmtMsgLineAppend(msgline, " Replace with: ");
    if (!XmtMsgLineGetString(msgline, replace, sizeof(replace))) {
        XmtMsgLinePop(msgline, XmtMsgLineNow);
        return;
    }

    /*
     * if we get here, the operation wasn't canceled,
     * so say we're doing it, then do it, then say we're done.
```

Example 22-3. Using a MsgLine for String Input (continued)

```
    */
    XmtMsgLineClear(msgline, XmtMsgLineNow);
    XmtMsgLinePrintf("Replacing '%s' with '%s'...", search, replace);
    search_and_replace(search, replace);
    XmtMsgLineAppend(msgline, "Done.");

    /* restore old message next time user does anything */
    XmtMsgLinePop(msgline, XmtMsgLineOnAction);
}
```

22.5.4 Getting Character Input

The MsgLine can also be used to get single-character input instead of string-based input. Example 22-4 is a continuation of Example 22-3 that shows how the function `XmtMsgLineGetChar()` might be used to implement an interactive search-and-replace function that asks the user to confirm each replacement. Note that it allows the user to cancel the operation, and handles invalid input as well.

Example 22-4. Using the MsgLine Widget for Character Input

```
static Widget msgline;
static Widget text;

extern int find(Widget, String);
extern void highlight(Widget, int, int);
extern void replace(Widget, int, int, String);

static void search_and_replace(String search_str, String replace_str)
{
    int search_len = strlen(search_str);
    int pos;
    int reply;

    XmtMsgLinePush(msgline);   /* save original message */

    /* for each occurrence of the search string */
    while((pos = find(text, search_str)) != -1) {
        highlight(text, pos, search_len);/* highlight it */
        XmtMsgLineClear(msgline);           /* and ask whether to replace */
        XmtMsgLinePrintf(msgline, "Replace '%s' with '%s'?: ",
                         search_str, replace_str);
        /* loop until we get a yes, no, or cancel answer */
        for(;;) {
            reply = XmtMsgLineGetChar(msgline);
            if ((reply == 'y') || (reply == 'Y')) {
                /* YES: do the replacement and continue */
                replace(text, pos, search_len, replace_str);
                break;
            }
            else if ((reply == 'n') || (reply == 'N')) {
                /* NO; just continue */
                break;
            }
            else if (reply == EOF) {
                /* CANCELED: stop replacing now */
```

Example 22-4. Using the MsgLine Widget for Character Input (continued)

```
                XmtMsgLinePop(msgline, XmtMsgLineNow);
                return;
            }
            else {
                /* bad input or a request for instructions. */
                /* beep, print instructions, and ask again */
                if (reply != '?') XBell(XtDisplay(msgline), 0);
                XmtMsgLineClear(msgline);
                XmtMsgLinePrintf(msgline,
                 "'Y' to replace; 'N' for next; ESC to cancel. Replace?: ");
            }
        }
    }
    XmtMsgLinePop(msgline, XmtMsgLineNow);/* restore original message */
}
```

22.5.5 Getting Numeric Input

The MsgLine widget also has convenience routines for the synchronous input of numbers. Example 22-5 shows how `XmtMsgLineGetUnsigned()` might be used in an action procedure of a text editor application. `XmtMsgLineGetInt()` and `XmtMsgLineGetDouble()` are analogous.

Example 22-5. Using the MsgLine Widget for Numeric Input

```
static Widget msgline;

/*ARGSUSED*/
static void GotoLine(Widget w, XEvent *e, String *p, Cardinal *np)
{
    unsigned int line;

    XmtMsgLinePush(msgline);                       /* save old message */
    XmtMsgLineSet("Goto Line: ");                  /* prompt */

    if (XmtMsgLineGetUnsigned(msgline, &line)) /* check for cancel */
        goto_line(w, line);

    XmtMsgLinePop(msgline, XmtMsgLineNow);       /* restore message */
}
```

22.5.6 Getting Input with a Default Value

As discussed earlier in this chapter, it sometimes makes sense to provide a default value when you request input from the user. Then the user can enter the default input by simply striking **Return**. One way to enable the user to do this is to make the default part of the fixed prompt. Another technique is to make the default value editable, (with `XmtMsgLineSetInput()`) so that the user can select, edit, or replace it. Example 22-6 and Example 22-7 demonstrate both techniques.

Example 22-6 is an updated version of the `GotoLine()` action procedure of Example 22-5. This action procedure for our hypothetical text editor now displays a default value in its prompt. This provides a simple shortcut on the theory that if the user has jumped to a given line number once, he may want to jump to the same line again—jumping to a line sets a "bookmark" that makes it easy to jump back to the same place. The main change for this example is that we have to use `XmtMsgLineGetString()` instead of `XmtMsgLineGetUnsigned()` and perform the conversion from string to line number explicitly. We do this so that we can detect the case (an empty buffer) in which the user has simply struck the **Return** key to accept the default.

Example 22-6. Displaying a Default Value in the Prompt

```
static Widget msgline;

/*ARGSUSED*/
static void GotoLine(Widget w, XEvent *e, String *p, Cardinal *np)
{
    static int default_line = 1;
    char buf[10];

    /* save old message and prompt */
    XmtMsgLinePush(msgline);
    XmtMsgLineClear(msgline, XmtMsgLineNow);
    XmtMsgLinePrintf(msgline, "Goto Line [%d]: ", default_line);

    if (!XmtMsgLineGetString(msgline, buf, sizeof(buf))) {
        /* return immediately if canceled */
        XmtMsgLinePop(msgline, XmtMsgLineNow);
        return;
    }

    /*
     * if the user actually entered anything, then
     * convert it to a line number.  We should really do
     * some sanity checking on the input.
     */
    if (buf[0]) default_line = atoi(buf);

    /*
     * Now actually go to the line.  If the user just hit Return,
     * then default_line is the same as it was before.
     */
    goto_line(w, default_line);

    /* restore old message */
    XmtMsgLinePop(msgline, XmtMsgLineNow);
}
```

It is appropriate, in Example 22-6, to display the line number as part of the prompt, because the user is likely to either want that exact number, or an entirely different number. She is not likely to want to edit the default line number from 312 to 315, for example, and making the user delete a default value before she could enter a new one would be more trouble than it is worth.

Example 22-7, on the other hand, is a case in which it does make sense to have an editable default value. This is a callback procedure invoked when the user selects the **Save As** menu button. It offers to save the file using whatever name was last used. There is a reasonable chance that the user will want to reuse this filename, or if she doesn't, there is a good chance that she will just want to edit it slightly, to append a version number, perhaps, or change the filename while leaving the directory name unchanged.

There is nothing tricky about the implementation of this procedure—it simply uses `XmtMsgLineSetInput()` to make the default filename the default input value. Unlike the previous example, we do not have to perform any special test to see if the buffer is empty when the input function returns. Notice that this procedure uses a static character buffer to save the last-entered filename between invocations. If the user types a partial filename, and then cancels the operation, `XmtMsgLineGetString()` does not modify the contents of its buffer, so the character buffer in the example is guaranteed to always contain a filename that the user actually entered. Finally, notice that when this function is first invoked, the static character buffer will be empty, and no default value will be displayed.

Example 22-7. Using the MsgLine with a Default Input Value

```
static Widget msgline;
static char filename[200];

/* ARGSUSED */
static void SaveAs(Widget w, XtPointer tag, XtPointer data)
{
    XmtMsgLinePush(msgline);                    /* save old message */
    XmtMsgLineSet(msgline, "Save as: ");        /* prompt */
    XmtMsgLineSetInput(msgline, filename);      /* set default value */

    /* get input, display feedback, save file */
    if (XmtMsgLineGetString(msgline, filename, sizeof(filename))) {
        XmtMsgLineClear(msgline, XmtMsgLineNow);
        XmtMsgLinePrintf(msgline, "Saving %s...", filename);
        save_as(filename);
        XmtMsgLineAppend(msgline, "Done.");
        XmtMsgLinePop(msgline, XmtMsgLineOnAction);
    }
    else /* if canceled, clear and return without saving */
        XmtMsgLinePop(msgline, XmtMsgLineNow);
}
```

22.5.7 Modifying Input Dynamically: Command Completion

An advanced feature of some applications that get synchronous input from an message line is command or filename completion. In the *emacs* text editor, for example, you need only type enough characters of an extended command name to uniquely identify it, and if you strike the spacebar, *emacs* automatically expands your partial input into the full name of the command it matches.

The MsgLine widget does not support this kind of dynamic input modification directly, but it is possible to add it using custom action procedures and the `XmtMsgLineGetInput()` function. Example 22-8 shows how simple command completion might be implemented with MsgLine. Note the call to

`XtAppAddActions()` to register the custom action procedure, and the call to `XtOverrideTranslations()` to bind the **Tab** key to that action procedure. With this new translation in effect, our custom action procedure will be invoked whenever the user strikes the **Tab** key. The action procedure uses `XmtMsgLineGetInput()` to examine the string the user has input so far, and if it is a unique abbreviation for any of the commands it knows about, uses `XmtMsgLineSetInput()` to replace the user's partial input with the full command name.

Example 22-8. Performing Command Completion with the MsgLine Widget

```
static Widget msgline;

/* the list of available commands */
static String commands[] = {
    "account", "append", "ascii", "bell", "binary", "bye",
    "case", "cd", "cdup", "close", "cr", "delete", "debug",
        .
        .
        .
};

/*
 * An action procedure that we'll bind to the TAB key in the MsgLine
 */
static void CompleteCommand(Widget w, XEvent *e, String *p, Cardinal *np)
{
    String input, completion;

    /* get the partial input from the message line */
    input = XmtMsgLineGetInput(msgline);

    /* find a completion for it, if any */
    completion = find_command_completion(input, commands, XtNumber(commands));

    /* replace the partial input with the completion, or beep if none */
    if (completion)
        XmtMsgLineSetInput(msgline, completion);
    else
        XBell(XtDisplay(msgline), 0);

    /* free the returned partial input string */
    XtFree(input);
}

/*
 * Set up a custom action procedure and translation on the MsgLine
 * widget to support command completion.
 */
static void InitializeCommandCompletion(void)
{
    static XtActionsRec completion_actions[] = {
        {"complete-command", CompleteCommand},
    };
    static String completion_translations = "<Key>Tab: complete-command()";
```

Example 22-8. Performing Command Completion with the MsgLine Widget (continued)

```
    XtAppAddActions(XtWidgetToApplicationContext(msgline),
                    completion_actions, XtNumber(completion_actions));
    XtOverrideTranslations(msgline,
                           XtParseTranslationTable(completion_translations));
}
```

22.5.8 Using a MsgLine or a Dialog Box

You'll often find yourself faced with a design choice between using the MsgLine widget for simple messages and simple input and using dialog boxes for the same purpose. As we'll see in Chapter 25, *Message Dialogs*, and Chapter 26, *Simple Input Dialogs*, the Xmt library also provides utilities to simplify message display and simple input with dialogs. Dialog boxes are good at calling attention to themselves; they help prevent beginning users from becoming confused. On the other hand, they are more intrusive than a message line, causing more of an interruption to the user's work. Users will often use the mouse to interact with a dialog box, where they would use the keyboard to interact with the message line. Experienced or "power" users may be happier if they can keep their hands on the keyboard.

Neither the message line nor dialog boxes are the appropriate choice in all circumstances, and rather than making a single choice between the two methods when you design an application, you can write your application to make the choice dynamically, depending on circumstances.

Example 22-9 is an extended example that shows two ways you might do this (and demonstrates many of the features of the MsgLine widget in the process). The first three procedures in this example are support procedures for the last—the `SaveAs()` callback procedure we've seen in previous examples. Here, we've modified this procedure so that it will prompt for the filename using the message line only if the user invoked the callback with a keyboard shortcut. Instead, if the user invoked the callback using the mouse (or using keyboard traversal), then it will prompt for the filename using a dialog box. This solution allows novice users to use easy-to-understand dialogs, and allows advanced users to keep their hands on the keyboards. (The price for this flexibility is the potential for confusion when a user is switching from mousing to using the keyboard shortcuts.)

The other modification to the `SaveAs()` procedure in this example is that it displays an error message if something goes wrong when saving the file. This is an unusual and serious occurrence, and usually this kind of error message should appear in a dialog box. We use a special `DisplayError()` procedure, however, that will display the error message in the message line if the user has set a special application resource—this allows real wizards, or those who really hate dialogs, to see error messages where they want them.

While this example can use a dialog box or the message line to get the filename and to report errors, note that it always uses the message line to provide feedback while the application is busy saving the file. This is a transient state, and it will never last long enough to warrant a dialog box.

This example does its dialog input and output using `XmtAskForString()` and `XmtDisplayError()`, simple Xmt functions that will be explained in later chapters.

Example 22-9. Using the MsgLine Widget and/or Dialog Boxes

examples/

22/dialog.c

```
static Widget msgline, toplevel;
static char filename[200];

/*
 * Get an input string from the message line or a dialog
 * depending on the use_msgline argument.
 */
static Boolean GetString(String prompt, char *buffer, int buffer_len,
                         Boolean use_msgline)
{
    Boolean status;
    if (use_msgline) {
        XmtMsgLinePush(msgline);
        XmtMsgLineSet(msgline, prompt);
        XmtMsgLineSetInput(msgline, buffer);
        if (XmtMsgLineGetString(msgline, buffer, buffer_len))
            status = True;
        else
            status = False;
        XmtMsgLinePop(msgline, XmtMsgLineNow);
    }
    else
        status = XmtAskForString(toplevel, NULL, prompt,
                                 buffer, buffer_len, NULL);
    return status;
}

/*
 * This function returns True if the event e could have triggered
 * the accelerator for the Motif button widget w.
 */
static Boolean IsAcceleratorEvent(Widget w, XEvent *e)
{
    String accelerator;
    char c, lc, uc;
    KeySym key;
    Modifiers mods;

    /* if not a key event, it can't be an accelerator */
    if ((e->type != KeyPress) && (e->type != KeyRelease)) return False;

    /* only subclasses of XmLabel have menu accelerators */
    if (!XmIsLabel(w) && !XmIsLabelGadget(w)) return False;

    /* get the last character of the accelerator string */
    XtVaGetValues(w, XmNaccelerator, &accelerator, NULL);
    c = accelerator[strlen(accelerator)-1];
```

Example 22-9. Using the MsgLine Widget and/or Dialog Boxes (continued)

```
    XtFree(accelerator);
    lc = tolower(c);
    uc = toupper(c);

    /* get the keysym from the event */
    XtTranslateKeycode(e->xany.display, e->xkey.keycode,
                       e->xkey.state, &mods, &key);
    key = key & 0xFF;

    /* X protocol says keysym encoding matches ASCII encoding
     * so we can compare them directly here if we don't care
     * about internationalization.
     */
    if ((key == lc) || (key == uc)) return True;
    else return False;
}

/*
 * Display an error message in a dialog box or the message line
 * depending on the value of the errorInMsgLine app resource.
 */
static void DisplayError(String msg)
{
    static Boolean use_msgline;
    static Boolean got_resource = False;
    static XtResource error_resource[] = {
        {"errorInMsgLine", "ErrorInMsgLine", XtRBoolean,
         sizeof(Boolean), 0, XtRImmediate, (XtPointer) False}
    };

    /* query the app resource first time we are called */
    if (!got_resource) {
        got_resource = True;
        XtGetApplicationResources(toplevel, &use_msgline,
                                  error_resource, 1,
                                  NULL, 0);
    }

    /* display the message depending on the app resource */
    if (use_msgline) {
        XmtMsgLinePush(msgline);
        XmtMsgLineSet(msgline, "ERROR: ");
        XmtMsgLineAppend(msgline, msg);
        XmtMsgLinePop(msgline, XmtMsgLineOnAction);
    }
    else
        XmtDisplayError(toplevel, NULL, msg);
}

/*
 * The SaveAs callback procedure, registered on an menu button and
 * invoked either directly or through an accelerator
 */
static void SaveAs(Widget w, XtPointer tag, XtPointer call_data)
{
    XmPushButtonCallbackStruct *data = (XmPushButtonCallbackStruct *)call_data;
    Boolean status;

    /*
```

Example 22-9. Using the MsgLine Widget and/or Dialog Boxes (continued)

```
     * Get the filename to save as.
     * Use message line if invoked as an accelerator, otherwise a dialog.
     * Check for user cancellation.
     */
    if (!GetString("Save As: ", filename, 200,
                   IsAcceleratorEvent(w, data->event)))
        return;

    /* Provide feedback that we're saving the file using cursor and msgline */
    XmtDisplayBusyCursor(toplevel);
    XmtMsgLinePush(msgline);
    XmtMsgLineClear(msgline, XmtMsgLineNow);
    XmtMsgLinePrintf(msgline, "Saving %s...", filename);

    /* save the file */
    status = save_file(filename);

    /*
     * if successful, give simple feedback in the message line, otherwise
     * display a warning in a dialog box or message line, depending on
     * an application resource.
     */
    if (status) { /* successfully saved */
        XmtMsgLineAppend(msgline, "Done.");
        XmtMsgLinePop(msgline, XmtMsgLineOnAction);
    }
    else {  /* error while saving */
        extern int errno;
        extern char *sys_errlist[];  /* or use strerror() instead */

        XmtMsgLinePop(msgline, XmtMsgLineNow);
        DisplayError(sys_errlist[errno]);
    }

    /* finally, restore the cursor */
    XmtDisplayDefaultCursor(toplevel);
}
```

22.6 Style

The examples in the previous section demonstrate a number of good uses of the MsgLine widget. In this section we'll list and recap some basic stylistic guidelines for using the MsgLine widget.

The bottom of the window is the traditional place for a message line. This tradition comes from UNIX applications like *emacs*, *vi*, and *more*, and is not a hard-and-fast rule. The most important rule about the position of a message line is that it should be near the object about which it is displaying messages (and preferably abutting the bottom edge of it). If you are using a message line only for the display of instructional messages, you have a little more flexibility about positioning it, and may want to consider placing it along the top edge of the object you are giving messages about.

If you are using the MsgLine for output only, you can use multiple message lines to display multiple messages (presumably about different parts of the interface). For synchronous input, however, you should only use a single

MsgLine per shell widget, and if your application has multiple shell widgets, each with its own message line, then the message line should be in approximately the same place in each (running along the bottom, for example). The reason to do all synchronous input through a single message line is so that the user can become accustomed to having the keyboard focus "warped" to that one place when the application needs to do modal input. If there were more than one message line that grabbed the focus, the user could become confused about which message line had it at any one time.

Whenever the application performs an action that is not visible on the screen, it is a good idea to display some feedback that the action has been performed. A message line is often a good place for this feedback. If the action takes more than a half of a second or so, it is a good idea to display a message before starting the action, and then append to that message after completing it. This feedback will be appreciated by your users, and will give them a sense of confidence that the application is behaving in a predictable way.

In general, whenever you change the pointer cursor to a "busy" cursor (with the function `XmtDisplayBusyCursor()`, for example), you should probably display a message (or post a dialog box) explaining what the application is busy doing. Providing this sort of feedback is often reason enough alone to add a MsgLine to your application.

The choice between dialog boxes and a MsgLine widget for displaying messages and for getting simple input will depend heavily on the expected experience of your users, the expected frequency of use of the application, and other similar factors. Message line input is often more convenient for experienced users, but dialog-based input can be less confusing for novices. A good compromise is to support both styles of input and provide an application resource to allow the user to select between the two. Another compromise is to use the message line for input when an action was invoked from the keyboard (through an accelerator, for example) and to use a dialog when the action was invoked with the mouse.

Don't abuse the synchronous input capability of the MsgLine widget. It is legitimate to follow a "Search for:" prompt with a "Replace with:" prompt, but if you need to get more than two pieces of input in a row through the XmtMsgLine, then you should probably use a custom dialog for that purpose. Don't use the MsgLine synchronous input functions as a crutch to help you maintain habits from the old days of terminal-based applications (or if you must use repeated synchronous input calls, use an XmtCli widget instead).

22.7 Summary

The XmtMsgLine widget is a subclass of the XmText. It doesn't have many new resources, but does have a rich API:

- `XmtCreateMsgLine()` creates an XmtMsgLine.
- `XmtMsgLineSet()` displays a message in an XmtMsgLine.
- `XmtMsgLineAppend()` appends text to a message.

- `XmtMsgLinePrintf()` appends text to a message, using `printf()`--style formatting.
- `XmtMsgLineClear()` clears an XmtMsgLine, immediately, after a specified delay, or on the user's next action.
- `XmtMsgLinePush()` saves the current contents of a MsgLine to be restored later.
- `XmtMsgLinePop()` restores the previously "pushed" contents of an XmtMsgLine, immediately, after a specified delay, or on the user's next action.
- `XmtMsgLineGetString()` gets an input string synchronously from the user.
- `XmtMsgLineGetChar()` gets a single input character from the user and returns it synchronously.
- `XmtMsgLineGetUnsigned()`, `XmtMsgLineGetInt()`, and `XmtMsgLineGetDouble()` get numeric input from the user, convert it to the specified type, and return it synchronously.
- `XmtMsgLineSetInput()` sets the text that appears in the editable portion of the MsgLine widget.
- `XmtMsgLineGetInput()` gets the contents of the editable portion of the MsgLine widget. It is only useful when called within an action procedure or callback invoked while the MsgLine is performing synchronous input.

23

The Modeline

A *modeline* or *status line* is a region of an application's window (usually a narrow region that runs the width of the window) in which an application displays text and graphics that indicate its current state. The modeline can be compared to the dashboard of an automobile or the instrument panel of an airplane — it gives the user a single, well-known place to look for information about the state of the application.

The *emacs* text editor has a good example of a modeline; Figure 23-1 shows a particularly busy *emacs* window with three detailed modelines.

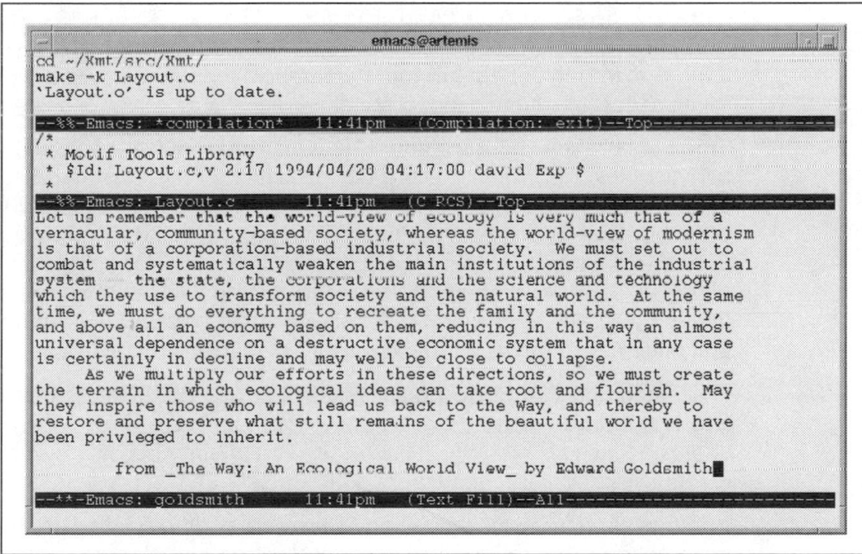

Figure 23-1. An emacs modeline

These modelines show the name of the file or buffer displayed in each region of the window. The two characters at the left of the line indicate a read-only file (%%), or a modified file (**). The items in parentheses indicate the major and minor editing modes that *emacs* is using for each buffer. At the right of the modeline is an indication of how much of the file is currently visible. And, as an bonus, *emacs* also displays the time of day.

emacs allows many files to be edited at the same time, and the new *emacs* user learns quickly to glance down at the modeline when she needs to check whether the current file has been saved, or when she has forgotten the name of the current file. This is just one example of a modeline and how it can be useful. The next section presents other examples, discusses different ways you can use modelines, and describes various kinds of information you can present in them. Other sections present techniques for implementing modelines and offer stylistic advice for integrating your modelines into your application.

23.1 Modeline Design Possibilities

A modeline is not as cut-and-dried an interface component as a message line or a menubar is. There are a great variety of uses you can put a modeline to. The following subsections explore some of the possibilities.

23.1.1 Displaying Application State

The first step, of course, in designing a modeline is to think about the modes or status information the application needs to display to the user. If your application displays data from files, then it should certainly display the filename for the currently displayed data. And if it allows the user to edit that data, it should probably indicate whether the data has been saved since it was last modified. If a file is read-only for any reason, the application might also indicate that, so that the user doesn't attempt to modify it.

Think about the state maintained by your application—go though all your global variables, for instance—and decide which of its parts are interesting to the user. In a text editor, for example, the user might want to know what line the cursor is currently on, and perhaps what column; in a data plotting program, the user might want to know what plot coordinates are under the mouse pointer. Figure 23-2 shows the modeline for the *xfig* drawing editor. It's a large modeline, because the application must display all the graphical attributes (line width and pattern, text justification, and so on) that are currently in effect.

One important feature to notice about this *xfig* modeline is that it uses icons and is not purely text based, as the *emacs* modeline shown above was. Well-chosen icons can be quite valuable in a modeline, because users can learn to recognize and comprehend them quite quickly.

Another point to consider when designing your modeline is that modelines need not be restricted to displaying application-global information. In a graphical directory browser, for example, it might display global information like the name of the current directory, but it could also display specific information about the currently selected file such as its name, permissions, and size.

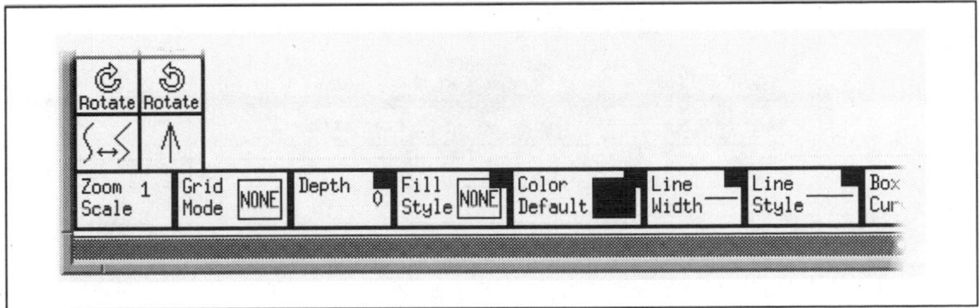

Figure 23-2. The xfig modeline

The status information you choose to display will depend on your audience. In a directory browser application intended for UNIX novices, you would not want to display a string like `-rw-r--r--` in the modeline to indicate file permissions. Instead, you would probably want just a single bit of information—whether the user could write the file or not. On the other hand, if your directory browser was intended for system managers, this compact and conventional representation for UNIX file permissions would be a good one to use.

In part, the items you choose to include in your application's modeline will depend on the scope of your application. In an application like *emacs* which was designed, before the advent of windowing systems, to be a complete user environment, it makes sense to display the time and flag when the user receives new mail on the modeline. In most applications, however, these features would not make sense.

23.1.2 Interactive Modelines

A modeline need not be an output-only interface component. In fact, this area for displaying modes can be a good place to allow the user to set modes as well (see Figure 23-3). Consider the "rulers" often found in WYSIWYG word processors, for example. These graphically display the current line justification and spacing, and also allow the user to change those values by clicking on the desired icon.

When an application is busy doing computation, a database query, or performing any other time-consuming operation, it is important to let the user know that the application will not be responding (or may be responding sluggishly) and also that the application is making progress on the task and has not "hung." One way to provide this feedback is by displaying something special in the modeline. (And Chapter 31, *Busy States and Background Work*, discusses several other good ways as well.) The latest versions of *emacs*, for example, display the string "Compiling" in the modeline when there is a compilation process running in the background. But there is no need to restrict a modeline to text-only—another application might display an hourglass or a wristwatch icon in the modeline when it was busy. And there is no reason to restrict the modeline to static graphics—this application could add additional feedback to indicate that it was making progress by animating the hourglass with falling sand or animating the wristwatch with moving hands.

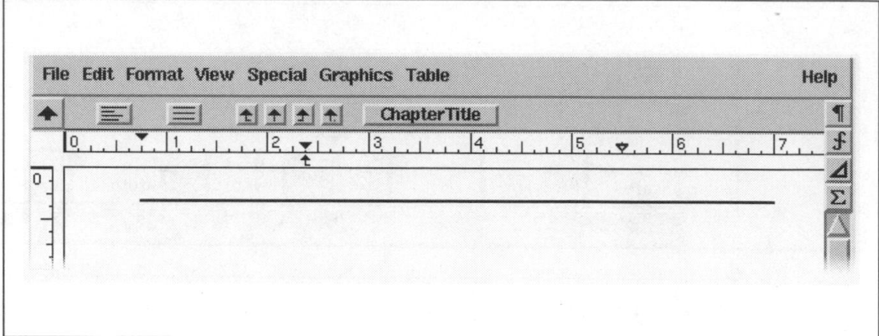

Figure 23-3. A modeline that allows users to set modes

23.1.3 Modelines and Modality

Sometimes an application enters very specific modes in which only a certain kind or subset of input is appropriate (or, as with the busy state described above, in which no input will be accepted). Often an application enters a specific mode when a dialog box pops up, and the presence of the dialog is quite enough to indicate this new mode. Other times, however, the new mode may be more subtle, and it may be important to draw the user's attention to it. If you have keyboard commands that take two keystrokes (like **Ctrl-X Ctrl-C** in *emacs*, for example) then the application will be in a special mode after the user has typed the first keystroke, and you should indicate somehow that the application is waiting for that command to be completed before any new command is issued. Similarly, a drawing editor might allow the user to create a complex type of object by interacting with a dialog box. Once the dialog box is dismissed, the user would then place the object by clicking with the mouse. This is a two-part operation, like a two-keystroke command, and the application is in a special mode when one part has been performed (the dialog filled in and dismissed) and is waiting for the next part to be performed (positioning the new object by clicking.) As with the two-keystroke command, the application should somehow indicate to the user what action is expected next. In this case, the best notification of this mode might use a message line instead of a modeline: "Click to position the object; ESC to cancel."

A more subtle example of different modes in an application involves cut-and-paste. Some applications, like *xterm*, allow you to select text, and automatically make that selected text available for pasting via the PRIMARY selection. Other applications let you select text but require you to explicitly cut or copy that text before it can be pasted into other applications. There are two different modes here: the application can have a highlighted region, or a highlighted, pasteable region, and it is useful to make some distinction between them. (It is particularly important to make the distinction because other applications can take ownership of the PRIMARY selection, making the selected region in the original application non-pasteable again.) Probably the best way to distinguish these two cases is to use two different types of highlighting (different colors, for example). But if the widget in use does not support different highlighting styles, an icon in the modeline (a pair of scissors, for example, to indicate that a cut had been performed) would work almost as well.

23.1.4 Multiple Modelines

While there are usually good reasons for an application to have only a single message line, there is no similar restriction that there be only one modeline. Earlier, we used the example of a directory browser that displayed both application-global information and file-specific information. A modeline need not actually be a single line—our directory browser might display the directory name and path in a line at the top of the window, and the file-specific information in a separate modeline at the bottom of the window. Or, instead, the application might have a double-height modeline that displayed both types of information.

To take this example a step further, imagine that the graphical directory browser allowed the user to open multiple windows, or multiple panes of a single window, to display multiple directories at once. Then each window or pane would need a modeline (or even two) to display its own directory and file information. There is no rule about the number of modelines an application can display. The only requirements are that the modelines be consistently placed for all windows of the application, and that it be obvious to the user what parts of the application a given modeline refers to. The fundamental goal is that the user can easily learn exactly where to look to find the information he wants.

23.2 Modeline Implementation Techniques

The design of modelines is far too variable to come up with a single, general-purpose modeline widget, and so the Xmt library does not provide any explicit modeline support. There are a number of ways you can implement modelines, however, and this section gives examples of several of them.

23.2.1 With a Label or Text Widget

If you will display all your application's status information as text, then one of the easiest ways to implement a modeline is just to display a string in an XmLabel or XmText widget. (If you use an XmText widget, you will want to make the widget non-editable, and probably also set the shadow width to zero. You can also use an XmtMsgLine widget for this purpose, of course.)

To display information in this modeline, you can just use `sprintf()` to format it all into a string, and then set the appropriate resource on the widget. To keep the information from jumping from left to right as it changes, however, you should use a fixed-width font and display each piece of information in a fixed-width field, as Example 23-1 does. (`sprintf()` substitution arguments optionally support a field width specification.)

Example 23-1. Implementing a Modeline with a Text Widget

```
/* some global variables */
char *filename;
int current_line, current_column;

/*
 * The modeline is an XmText widget, so we don't have to use XmStrings.
 * If we used an XmLabel, we would have to use XmStrings, but could have
 * multiple fonts.
 */
Widget modeline;

static void UpdateModeline()
{
    char line[50];

    sprintf(line, "  file: %-20s  line: %-5d col: %-2d",
            filename, current_line, current_column);
    XmTextSetString(modeline, line);
}
```

XmText Versus XmLabel for Rapid Update

Greg Janee prefers an XmText or XmTextField widget to an XmLabel widget when he has to update text rapidly:

If you need to display text that changes dynamically and rapidly (e.g., the coordinates of the mouse as the user moves the mouse within a window), using an XmLabel widget would seem to be the logical choice. But the results will be disappointing because XmLabel is really inefficient at changing its text. The label will be blank a good part of the time and will flash annoyingly.

The results are far superior if you use an XmTextField widget in this kind of situation. I set the following resources to make the text field look just like a label:

```
*coords.cursorPositionVisible:  false
*coords.editable:               false
*coords.highlightThickness:     0
*coords.marginHeight:           2
*coords.marginWidth:            2
*coords.shadowThickness:        0
```

—*Greg Janee*

23.2.2 Text and Icons with an XmtLayout Widget

The disadvantages of implementing a modeline with a Label or Text widget are that they restrict you to a text-only line, that they require a fixed-width font, and attention to field widths to keep information at the same position of the line, and that the whole line must be updated whenever a single item changes. A more sophisticated approach uses a separate widget for each element of the modeline. This way, you can mix text and graphics, you can explicitly control the position of individual items, which means that you need not be restricted to fixed-width fonts, and you can update items independently of each other.

The XmtLayout widget and its XmtLayoutString and XmtLayoutPixmap gadgets provide a convenient way to produce this sort of modeline. Figure 23-4 shows a modeline implemented this way, and Example 23-2 shows the resource file used (with *mockup*) to create the screendump.

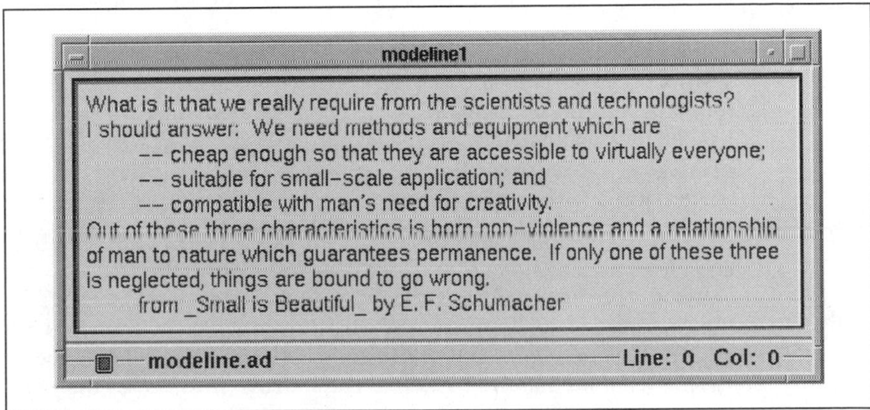

Figure 23-4. A modeline using the XmtLayout widget and its gadgets

Example 23-2. Implementing a Modeline with the XmtLayout Widget

examples/ 23/modeline1.ad

```
*Background: gray
*modeline*background: gray68

*main.marginWidth: 0
*main.marginHeight: 0
*main.layout: 1in High XmText text\
              Fixed Margin 0 Etched Top 0 4 XmtLayout modeline

*modeline.orientation: XmHORIZONTAL
*modeline.layoutJustification: Filled
*modeline*layoutJustification: Centered
*modeline.marginWidth: 0
*modeline.marginHeight: 0
*modeline*layoutMarginWidth: 0
*modeline*layoutMarginHeight: 0
*modeline.layout: \
        .25in =\
        Bitmap saved "toggle_on"\
        .25in =\
        String filename "modeline.ad"\
        Stretchable 1in =\
        String "Line: "\
        String line "0"\
```

Example 23-2. Implementing a Modeline with the XmtLayout Widget (continued)

```
String "  Col: "\
String column "0"\
.25in =
```

This example shows a fairly straightforward use of the XmtLayout widget, but there are a few points to notice. First, note that we assign names to the string and bitmap gadgets automatically created by the layout grammar. This gives us a way to look those gadgets up from C code and change the strings or bitmaps that they display. Also notice that we use the = syntax for creating vertical separators between the various components of the modeline. One of these separators is given the "Stretchable" attribute, and the string and pixmap gadgets are by default unstretchable, so this middle separator will stretch to be as wide as necessary, and also keeps the line and column indicators right justified in the modeline.

Note that this modeline is implemented as a Layout widget within another Layout. It could also be implemented as a row within the main Layout, but using a separate widget makes it easier to use a different background color to highlight the modeline. Finally, note that we set a number of resources in this example to override the default margins of the Layout widget. We set the margins of the Layout itself so that the modeline is a narrow strip across the window, without extra pixels above and below. We also set the constraint resource margins on each of the children of the modeline. This allows our separator gadgets to abut the other components of the modeline, without intervening margins.

Displaying State Graphically with the XmLabel Widget

Greg Ullmann has a convenient way to display a Boolean state variable:

Sometimes I need a label to display one of two different pixmaps, depending on the state of the application. An easy way to switch between two pixmaps on a label is to set one pixmap as the `XmNlabelPixmap` and the other pixmap as the `XmNlabelInsensitivePixmap`. Then to toggle between the two you simply reset the sensitivity with `XtSetSensitive()`. You might end up with a resource file like this:

```
*state.labelType:                pixmap
*state.labelPixmap:              happy.xbm
*state.labelInsensitivePixmap:   sad.xbm
```

—Greg Ullmann

23.2.3 Input with the XmToggleButton and XmtChooser Widgets

As noted previously, the modeline need not be a display-only interface component; it is also a good way to allow the user to select modes. Figure 23-5 shows a modeline that includes an XmToggleButton widget that allows the user to "lock" and "unlock" the file. (This hypothetical application wouldn't let the user accidentally modify a "locked" file.) This example also includes an XmtChooser widget that presents three types of justification. The Chooser widget will be presented in Chapter 27, *Presenting Choices*. Here, the widget is used to display three iconic choices in a palette with "radio box" behavior.

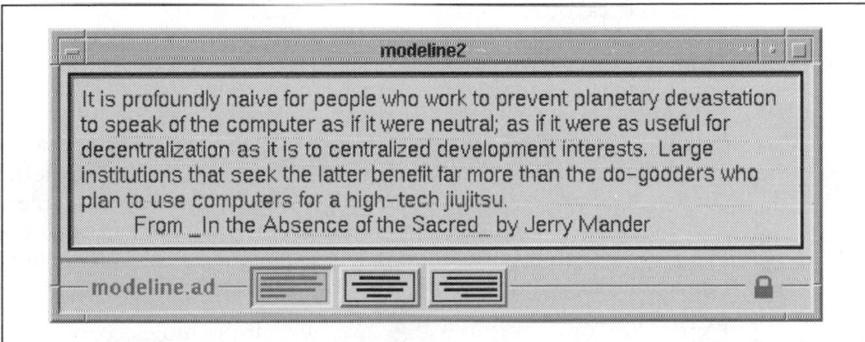

Figure 23-5. A modeline that allows input

Example 23-3 shows the resources used to set up this modeline.

Example 23-3. Modeline Input with the XmtChooser and XmToggleButton

examples/
23/modeline2.ad

```
*main.marginWidth:0
*main.marginHeight:0
*main.layout: 1in High XmText text\
              Fixed Margin 0 Etched Top 0 4 XmtLayout modeline

*modeline.orientation: XmHORIZONTAL
*modeline.marginWidth: 0
*modeline.marginHeight: 0
*modeline*background: gray68
*modeline*layoutMarginWidth: 0
*modeline*layoutMarginHeight: 0
*modeline.layoutJustification: Filled
*modeline*layoutJustification: Centered
*modeline.layout: \
        .25in =\
        Color "maroon" String filename "modeline.ad"\
        .25in =\
        XmtChooser just\
        Stretchable 1in =\
        XmToggleButton lock \
        .25in =
```

Example 23-3. Modeline Input with the XmtChooser and XmToggleButton (continued)

```
*just.chooserType: RadioPalette
*just.orientation: XmHORIZONTAL
*just.labelType: XmPIXMAP
*just.pixmaps: "leftjust", "centerjust", "rightjust"
*just.selectPixmaps: "leftjust", "centerjust", "rightjust" \
                     : foreground = maroon, background = gray64

*lock.labelType: XmPixmap
*lock.labelPixmap: locked:foreground=maroon, background=gray68
*lock.selectPixmap: unlocked:foreground=maroon, background=gray68
*lock.indicatorOn: False
*lock.highlightThickness: 0
*lock.traversalOn: False
```

Example 23-3 is similar in many ways to Example 23-2. The important points to notice are the XmtChooser and XmToggleButton usage. For both the XmToggleButton and the XmtChooser (which creates an XmToggleButton for each choice) we have to explicitly specify colors with the color table syntax of the Xmt String-to-Pixmap converter. (See Chapter 5, *Using Icons*.) This is because Motif widgets only support color Pixmaps, and cannot just take a single-plane bitmap and draw it in the specified foreground and background colors.

For the XmToggleButton widget, we turn off the indicator, because the padlock icon serves as its own indicator. We also set the highlight thickness to zero so that the icon takes up very little room (otherwise, there would be an internal margin, and the icon would look strange with a black box around it). Since this highlight rectangle that we disabled is the only way to tell that the widget has keyboard focus, we also turn off keyboard navigation for this widget, so that the user does not get confused. The application would presumably provide some other keyboard shortcut that allows the file to be locked or unlocked without traversing to this button in the modeline.

Note that the toggle button used in this example works well for displaying status—an application can switch from one state to another simply by calling `XmToggleButtonSetState()`. As used in this example, however, the toggle button provides no cues whatsoever that the user can click on it to switch its state. This lack of cues means that this technique is only appropriate as a shortcut when there is some more obvious way (such as a menu item) to perform the same function. Notice that this is not a problem with the XmtChooser widget—in that case, the shadows around the three choices provide the necessary cue that they may be selected.

23.3 Modeline Style

Modelines work equally well at the top and the bottom of an application window. Some applications may even want mode information displayed at both the top and bottom. A modeline can also serve to separate two regions of an application window such as multiple editing panes within a window (as in *emacs*) or an editing area from a command-line interface or message area, perhaps. The important rule about positioning modelines within a window and positioning components within a modeline is consistency—the user must be able to quickly and consistently find the information she is looking for in an expected position.

A modeline usually needs to be set off from the rest of the application in some way. Using a bold font is one possibility, and using a contrasting color scheme is another. On monochrome systems, it may work to simply reverse the foreground and background colors. If the modeline is at or near the bottom of the window, using the same highlight color that is used for the menu bar will serve to nicely frame the central work area of the window.

The layout of items within the modeline is quite flexible, and will depend largely on how much and what type of information you have to present. If feasible, you might allow users to customize the layout of the modeline—to arrange items in a format that is most familiar and comfortable to them. A modeline might be entirely textual, entirely graphical, or some mixture. It can be several lines high, if there is lots of information to present. Although modelines most commonly extend the full width of the window, this is not strictly necessary—application layout may dictate a "mode rectangle" rather than a modeline.

24

The Work Area

The preceding chapters in this part of the book have introduced user interface components for the main windows of your applications—a menu bar for the top of the window, and a message line for the bottom, for example. A later chapter introduces the XmtChooser widget, which, while primarily intended for dialog boxes, is an ideal way to implement a palette or toolbar at the left or top of a window.

These widgets are all components that go around the periphery of a window. What we have not discussed yet is what goes in the center of your window. This area is sometimes called the "work area" and its contents will vary completely from application to application. The simplest programs that manipulate only textual data may simply have a text widget or a list widget (or both) in this work area. Many other applications, however, will need something more complex. There is a large class of applications that have to do some kind of domain-specific drawing. Programs used by electrical engineers will draw circuits or integrated circuit schematics. Programs used by structural engineers will display structures, load diagrams, and so forth. Chemical engineers need schematic diagrams of chemical processes showing material flows, pressures, and temperatures. Financial analysts use programs that display graphs of market performance and graphically display the results of sophisticated mathematical modeling. Computer system administrators want diagrams of network topologies, and GUI developers may want to see their widget hierarchies displayed in tree form.* See Figure 24-1 for some examples of domain-specific drawings.

*A friend recently pointed out to me that phrases like "graphical interface toolkit" are really bad ways to describe widgets. Most widgets perform a basic user interface function, but do not have any particularly interesting graphical representation. It is the work area of applications where the actual "graphics" (i.e., the visual representation of data) goes on.

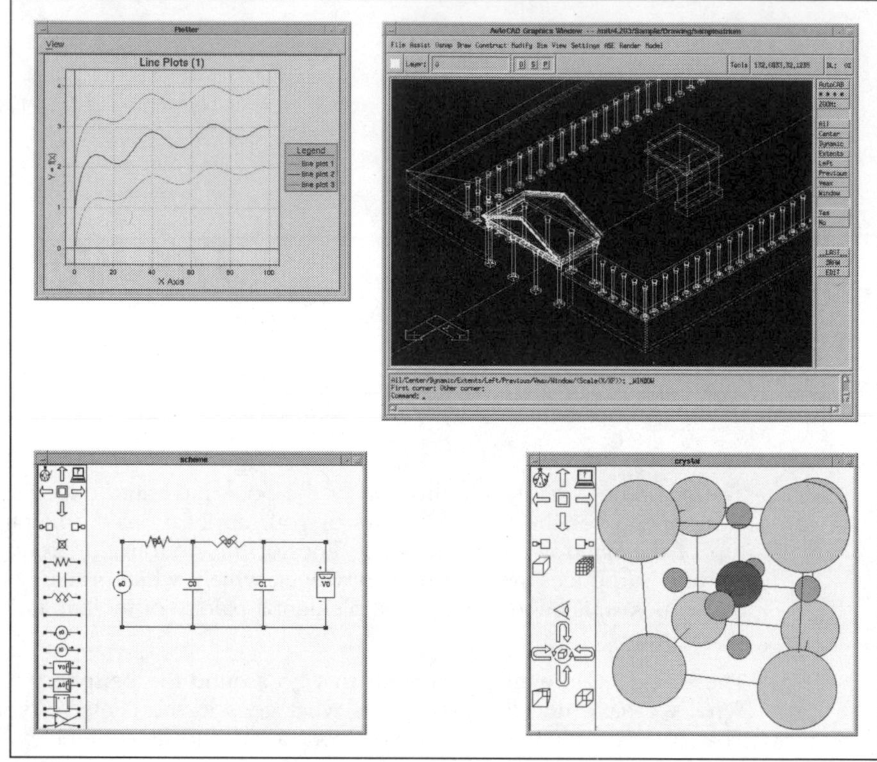

Figure 24-1. Domain-specific drawings

Sometimes, you will be able to obtain widgets or other packages that will handle these domain-specific drawings for you. There are widgets available, for example, that will produce line plots and bar charts, and other widgets that will arrange items into a tree structure. Often, though, you'll find that the cheapest or most efficient way to proceed is to do the drawings yourself.

No one widget or set of convenience functions can come close to handling every application's drawing needs, and the Xmt library doesn't even attempt to provide tools for this purpose. This chapter is about doing your own thing when you don't have a widget that will do it for you. It is about drawing into an widget, getting and processing events with an event handler, and also discusses producing PostScript output from your application. In this age of widgets, these may seem daunting tasks. We forget, though, that it wasn't all that many years ago that we were drawing everything "by hand" like this. This chapter points out a number of techniques that you'll find useful.

24.1 A Window to Draw In

Xlib functions operate on windows, rather than on widgets, so before you can do any drawing you'll need a window to draw in. You can create windows with the Xlib function `XCreateWindow()`, but you don't want to do this, because the X Toolkit architecture only works well with widgets. You can obtain the window associated with any widget by calling `XtWindow()`, and you can just go ahead and draw into this window. Most widgets do their own drawing, however, and you don't want to try to mess with that.

A traditional solution has been to instantiate a Core widget to draw into. Core is a widget meta-class that is not normally instantiated, and therefore does no drawing of its own. It also does no event processing of its own—you can draw and handle events exactly as you please.

With Motif, the XmDrawingArea widget is sometimes a more attractive alternative. This widget is a subclass of XmManager, which means that you can include widgets in your drawings (this can sometimes be a useful technique). It also means that the widget will inherit the default Motif background color from its parent and will participate in keyboard traversal. Another benefit to the XmDrawingArea widget is that it has callbacks to notify your application when the window needs to be redrawn, when the window has been resized, or when the user has pressed a key or clicked a mouse button in the window.

The disadvantage to the XmDrawingArea widget is that it has a fairly complex translation table to support the callback described previously, and to support gadget children and keyboard traversal. This can make it tricky to add your own custom translations for handling user input. If you will not be placing any sub-widgets in your drawing, you may sometimes find it easier to start with the "clean slate" of a Core widget instead of the XmDrawingArea.

Whichever you choose, though, you can get its window ID by calling `XtWindow()`. Note that this is a function, not a macro, so it is most efficient to call it once and store the result in a global variable for use throughout your application (or a static variable for use throughout one module of your application). Remember that widgets don't have windows until they are realized, so you shouldn't call `XtWindow()` until you have called `XtRealizeWidget()` on your toplevel widget. Also, remember that calling `XtRealizeWidget()` won't make your window visible right away—that won't happen until the window manager or the user actually positions your application on the screen. As always with X, you should not draw anything, except in response to an Expose event from the server.

Drawing with Xlib

Drawing with Xlib is actually quite straightforward. Table 24-1 lists the commonly used Xlib drawing commands. *Xlib Programming Manual* and *Xlib Reference Manual* Volumes One and Two, in the X Window System series from O'Reilly & Associates, are useful books to have handy when doing Xlib work.

Drawing with Xlib (continued)

Table 24-1. Common Xlib Drawing Functions

To Draw:	One Item	Many Items	One Filled	Many Filled
Points	XDrawPoint()	XDrawPoints()		
Lines	XDrawLine()	XDrawSegments()		
Polys	XDrawLines()	XFillPolygon()		
Rects	XDrawRectangle()	XDrawRectangles()	XFillRectangle()	XFillRectangles()
Arcs	XDrawArc()	XDrawArcs()	XFillArc()	XFillArcs()
Miscellaneous Functions				
Text	XDrawString()	XDrawImageString()	XDrawText()	
Areas	XCopyArea()	XCopyPlane()	XClearArea()	XClearWindow()

Note that there are functions to draw multiple points, lines, rectangles, and arcs at once. You should use these whenever feasible, because it is a more efficient use of the X protocol and of the X server.

Each Xlib drawing function has the same three first arguments: a `Display` pointer, a `Drawable`, and a `GC`. You can obtain the display pointer with the function `XtDisplay()`. As with `XtWindow()`, it is most efficient to call this function once and save the result in a convenient variable. A `Drawable` is either a window or a pixmap. Usually, you will pass the window ID you obtained by calling `XtWindow()`.

A *GC* is a Graphics Context, and requires some explanation. There are a large number of graphical attributes that control the way even something as simple as a line is drawn. The color, line width, and dash pattern are only a few of the possibilities. Rather than creating drawing functions with an unwieldy number of arguments to specify each of these attributes, and rather than defining a client-server protocol that requires each of the attributes to be specified for each drawing request, X uses Graphics Contexts. A `GC` is an object that exists on the server-side of the connection. You specify a single GC to be used with each drawing request, and this GC defines all of the attributes that are to apply to that request. Table 24-2 shows some commonly used Xlib functions for creating and manipulating GCs. *Xlib Programming Manual* contains an excellent discussion of the various GC drawing attributes and their meanings. *Xlib Reference Manual* explains each of these GC functions and also contains some very useful quick reference tables for GC attributes.

Drawing with Xlib (continued)

Table 24-2. Common Xlib GC Functions

XCreateGC()	XChangeGC()	XCopyGC()	XFreeGC()
XSetForeground()	XSetBackground()	XSetLineAttributes()	XSetDashes()
XSetFillStyle()	XSetStipple()	XSetFunction()	XSetArcMode()
XSetClipMask()	XSetClipOrigin()	XSetClipRectangles()	

One approach to using GCs is to create a single one for your work area, and to explicitly set its graphical attributes as needed before calling each drawing function; another is to create several GCs for each of several distinct types of drawing you must do. You might use one GC for drawing thin lines, one for drawing thick lines, and another for drawing filled rectangles and filled arcs. If you take an object-oriented approach to drawing in your work area, then you might use one GC per object that you draw. In this last case, you should use the X Toolkit GC functions `XtGetGC()`, `XtAllocateGC()`, and `XtReleaseGC()`. These functions cache GCs for reuse, so that if your drawing contains several objects with the same set of graphical attributes they will end up sharing a single GC in the server. This is important because GCs are a limited server resource, and your application should be careful not to create too many.

Once you have the display pointer and the window ID of your drawing widget, and have allocated an appropriate GC or GCs, you can start drawing whatever you please. In order to use some of the drawing functions, of course, you will have to obtain colors, fonts, and pixmaps. You can use Xlib functions to obtain these, but there are easier ways to do so with Xt and Xmt.

—*djf*

24.2 A Coordinate System

Sometimes the natural unit for your drawing will be pixels, but often there will be some more applicable "world coordinate system." In a wind-tunnel simulation program that displays cross-sections of airfoils, for example, the natural units of measurement might be in meters. In this case, you would convert meters to pixels before drawing an airfoil on the screen. An important advantage to this real-world approach is that it is independent of the actual size of the window—the user can stretch or shrink the window, and the airfoil will stretch or shrink to fit.

To perform this kind of transformation, you first need to compute scale factors for the X and Y dimensions. Suppose that the largest airfoil cross-section we want to display is five meters wide by one meter high. We'll set up our coordinate system so that the drawing area is six meters wide by two meters high:

```
double width = 6.0;  /* in meters */
double height = 2.0; /* in meters */
int pixel_width, pixel_height;
double xscale, yscale;

/* find out how big the drawing area is */
XtVaGetValues(drawing_area,
              XtNwidth, &pixel_width,
              XtNheight, &pixel_height,
              NULL);

xscale = pixel_width/width;
yscale = pixel_height/height;
```

With this initial computation done, we can easily convert from an `(x,y)` point in meters to the corresponding `(xpix, ypix)` point in pixels:

```
xpix = x * xscale;
ypix = y * yscale;
```

24.2.1 Scrolling

There are other transformations you can perform as well. Performing a translation is a simple matter of addition. Suppose that our drawing area remains six meters wide, but that we now want to add scrollbars and allow the display of airfoils that are wider than this. Then you might use a transformation like this:

```
xpix = (x - x_scroll_offset) * xscale;
ypix = (y - y_scroll_offset) * yscale;
```

Furthermore, suppose we wanted a margin at the edges of the drawing area, where nothing would be drawn. We could incorporate the margin into our transformation like this:

```
xpix = (x - x_scroll_offset) * xscale + x_pixel_margin;
ypix = (y - y_scroll_offset) * yscale + y_pixel_margin;
```

24.2.2 Zooming

Scaling the coordinate system is another simple type of transformation. To zoom in for more detail and display only three meters in the space that used to display six, for example, we would just modify the scale factors:

```
double zoom_factor = 2.0;  /* zoom in 100% */

xscale = xscale * zoom_factor;
yscale = yscale * zoom_factor;
```

Similarly, we could zoom out by using a zoom factor of less than 1.0.

24.2.3 Rotating

Finally, it is even fairly simple to rotate a figure with a coordinate system transform. It requires a little trigonometry, however. We can rotate by an angle theta measured counterclockwise from the positive X axis like this:

```
/* only compute these once */
static double sintheta = sin(theta);    /* theta is in radians */
static double costheta = cos(theta);

double xrot, yrot;

/* do the rotation in world coordinates */
xrot = x * costheta - y * sintheta;
yrot = y * costheta + x * sintheta;

/* now transform to pixels as before */
xpix = (xrot - x_scroll_offset) * xscale * zoom_factor + x_pixel_margin;
ypix = (yrot - y_scroll_offset) * yscale * zoom_factor + y_pixel_margin;
```

Note that this rotation technique only works if you are drawing points and lines. The X drawing primitives for text and rectangles cannot draw rotated text or rotated rectangles.

24.2.4 Computing Dot Pitch

There is one more transformation technique that is worth noting. In applications such as page-previewers, the transformation we want to perform is not meters-to-pixels but inches or centimeters-to-pixels. Furthermore, in WYSIWYG applications, we want one centimeter of the figure to actually occupy one centimeter of screen space. Assuming that your X server software is correctly configured for your display hardware, you can compute the dots-per-inch, or pixels-per-millimeter figures for the screen like this:

```
Display *dpy = XtDisplay(drawing_area);
int snum = ScreenNumberOfScreen(XtScreen(drawing_area));

/* compute pixels per millimeter */
/* Note: we're careful to do floating point division, not integer division */
double xpitch = ((double)DisplayWidth(dpy, snum))/DisplayWidthMM(dpy, snum);
double ypitch = ((double)DisplayHeight(dpy, snum))/DisplayHeightMM(dpy, snum);

/* convert to dots per inch */
double xdpi = xpitch * 25.4;  /* 25.4 millimeters in an inch */
double ydpi = ypitch * 25.4;
```

With these ratios calculated, it is easy to select a window size to simulate an 8.5 inch by 11 inch piece of paper, for example.

Note that we computed the dot pitch in both the X and the Y dimensions above. Most X displays have square pixels—the same pitch in both dimensions. This is not the case for all displays however. Let's return to our airfoil example, and suppose that we wanted to force a "square" coordinate system so that one meter in the X dimension always appears to the user to be the same distance as one meter in the Y dimension. For our six-meter by two-meter coordinate system, you cannot just assume that a window 600 pixels wide by 200 pixels high will work. You've also got to compare the dot pitch in the X and Y dimensions, and adjust the window size (and therefore the transformation) as necessary.

24.2.5 Handling Resize Events

Recall that the coordinate transforms above were all based on X and Y scale factors that we computed as follows:

```
xscale = pixel_width/width;
yscale = pixel_height/height;
```

Any time the size of the drawing area changes, we will have to recompute these scale factors. If you are using an XmDrawingArea widget, then you can use the `XmNresizeCallback` to detect size changes to your window. Example 24-1 shows one way you might handle it. Later in the chapter we'll see how you can detect window resizes with an event handler or with a translation table.

Example 24-1. Detecting and Handling Resizes with XmNresizeCallback

```
static double real_width, real_height;  /* window size in units */
static double xscale, yscale;

void compute_scales()
{
    int pixel_width, pixel_height;

    /* find out how big the drawing area is */
    XtVaGetValues(drawing_area,
                  XtNwidth, &pixel_width,
                  XtNheight, &pixel_height,
                  NULL);

    xscale = pixel_width/real_width;
    yscale = pixel_height/real_height;
}

void resize_callback(Widget w, XtPointer tag, XtPointer data)
{
    compute_scales();
}

void create_drawing_area()
{
    drawing_area = XmCreateDrawingArea(...);
    XtAddCallback(drawing_area, XmNresizeCallback,
                  resize_callback, NULL);
    XtManageChild(drawing_area);
    /*
     * We won't get the resizeCallback for the widget's initial size.
     * so we've got to set up the initial scale factors here.
     */
    compute_scales();
}
```

24.3 Handling Redraws

The Expose event is a basic fact of life in X programming. This event tells you that your window, or a portion of your window, has been obscured (another window overlapped it, for example) and its contents have been lost. This is something that takes some getting used to when programming with X—you must always be prepared to redraw the contents of a window. Widgets will automatically handle this for you, but when you're doing your own drawing, you must be ready to do the redrawing yourself.

With the XmDrawingArea widget, you can receive notification of the Expose event through the `XmNexposeCallback`. You could also use an event handler or a translation table, as we'll see later. Receiving the event is easy; handling it is the part that can get tricky. The following subsections present a number of techniques you can use.

24.3.1 A Drawing List

You must be prepared to redraw your window whenever an Expose event arrives. What this means is that your application must keep track of everything that it has drawn, so that it can repeat that drawing. This is the idea behind a "drawing list"—you maintain some sort of list of things to be drawn, and you can always go to the beginning of the list and proceed to draw everything over.

There are obviously a number of levels at which you can handle this. An application that displays circuit diagrams will presumably have some internal data structures that represent the circuit—which components go where, and how they are connected. The application knows how to draw the circuit symbols for resistors, transistors, integrated circuits, and so on, and also has heuristics that enable it to draw connections between components in some reasonably intelligent way. When this application needs to redraw itself, it can look through its internal data structures, do some computation to decide where to place each component and where to draw the connections, and then go ahead and draw everything.

This approach obviously requires a lot of computation, but there are ways that redrawing can be made much more efficient. Let's return to our airfoil simulation application, and suppose that the shape of the airfoil cross-section is defined by fitting a smooth spline to some number of control points in the airfoil coordinate system. Now, when this window needs to be redrawn, we could compute the spline, transform the resulting points from world coordinates to pixels, and draw the resulting polygon. But in fact, unless the shape of the airfoil or the size of the window has changed, there is no need to recompute the spline or the transformation. Instead, if we just save the pixel coordinates when we first do the transformation, then we can redraw the airfoil very efficiently. And if we happen to save these pixel coordinates in a convenient array of `XPoint` structures, then we can redraw the entire airfoil with a single call to `XDrawLines()`.

The actual amount of optimization you decide to do will depend on the complexity of your drawing, and how often you expect to have to redraw it. The important thing is that you retain enough information, in some form, that you can do a redraw when you have to.

24.3.2 Other Redraw Techniques

One way you can retain the requisite information for handling redraws is at a high level, as in the case of our abstract circuit-description data structures. A technique at the other end of the spectrum is to keep a copy of the actual pixels that you've drawn. You can do this by creating a `Pixmap` the same size as your window (with `XCreatePixmap()`). You can draw into a pixmap, just as you can draw into a window, but since pixmaps don't appear on the screen, they will never be obscured by other windows and lose their contents—if you draw something into a pixmap, it is guaranteed to stay there.

So this is another approach to handling redraws—do your drawing into a pixmap. Then whenever you get an Expose event on your main window, you can just copy the drawing (use `XCopyArea()`) from the pixmap into the window. This is a useful approach when porting drawing code from systems that did not have to worry about redraws, or when you are drawing a figure so complex that a redraw would take too much time. If you were writing a program to compute and display the Mandlebrot fractal, for example, drawing into a pixmap would be an ideal solution.

The obvious drawback to this approach, of course, is that it is memory intensive. Besides the screen-memory that the server always must allocate, it requires extra off-screen memory to store the pixmap. Most color displays (eight-bit color) require one byte per pixel. So to save a 500-pixel by 500-pixel drawing in a pixmap requires a quarter of a megabyte of memory. This is an issue you have to be particularly careful about when your application will be run from X terminals rather than workstations—X terminals generally do not have virtual memory available, and sometimes will simply not be able to allocate pixmaps as large as you want.

A similar approach is to request "backing store" for your drawing window. A window with backing store has its contents saved where they will not be overwritten by overlapping windows—in effect the drawing is automatically backed up in a pixmap. But not all X servers support backing store, and those that do won't always provide it—if they are low on memory, for example, they might not provide backing store to all windows that request it. Backing store is useful when you have a complex drawing that is difficult and time-consuming to redraw—if the server supports it then you will rarely have to redraw the window. But it is not a guarantee—an application that uses backing store must still be able to redraw its window from scratch.

You can request backing store for a window with code like this:

```
XSetWindowAttributes attr;
attr.backing_store = WhenMapped;
XChangeWindowAttributes(display, window, CWBackingStore, &attr);
```

The constant `WhenMapped` requests backing store for the window only when it is actually mapped onto the display—if the application is iconified, or the drawing window is unmanaged, then the contents of the window will be lost. If you replace this with the constant `Always` then the window contents will be retained even when the window is iconified or unmanaged.

24.3.3 Optimizing Partial Redraws

In the discussion of redrawing above, we've been assuming that you will redraw the entire contents of a window each time you receive an Expose event. In fact, when one window partially overlaps another, the resulting Expose event will only require the redraw of a portion of the window, and performing a full redraw could be wasteful. This section explores various techniques you can use to minimize the amount of redrawing you do. Different techniques will be applicable to different applications.

24.3.3.1 Redrawing Individual Rectangles

The Expose event structure contains the coordinates of the rectangle that needs to be redrawn. The most obvious technique is to simply redraw exactly the specified rectangles. Example 24-2 shows how you might do this.

Example 24-2. Redrawing One Rectangle of a Window

```
static void expose_callback(Widget w, XtPointer tag, XtPointer call_data)
{
    XmDrawingAreaCallbackStruct *data =
        (XmDrawingAreaCallbackStruct *)call_data;

    redraw_rect(w, data->event->xexpose.x, data->event->xexpose.y,
                data->event->xexpose.width, data->event->xexpose.height);
}
```

This rectangle-redraw technique works very well when there is some simple way to redraw any given rectangle. If you are simply copying the rectangle from an off-screen pixmap, for example, then there is no difficulty. In a terminal emulator program like *xterm* it is similarly easy to convert the rectangle in pixel coordinates to a rectangle in character rows and columns, and to only redraw exactly the characters that need it.

24.3.3.2 A Single, Full Redraw

Often, redrawing cannot be done on a simple per-rectangle basis. To return once again to our airfoil example, if we have saved the pixel coordinates of the airfoil into an array and redraw the airfoil with a single call to `XDrawLines()`, then it is not so easy to redraw just a single requested rectangle—in this case the easiest thing to do is to redraw everything.

But things get a little more complicated than this: imagine a window that is partially obscured by two other windows. If this obscured window is raised to the top, then there will be two rectangles that need to be redrawn, and the application will receive two Expose events, one right after the other. If we simply redraw the entire airfoil for each Expose event, then we've done twice as much work as is necessary. Having multiple contiguous Expose events is a common occurrence, and, fortunately, the X server provides a way to optimize this case—the `count` field in the event structure gives the number of Expose events that will follow the current one. When your redraw strategy is to simply redraw the entire window, then you should discard Expose events that have `count` greater than zero. Example 24-3 shows this approach.

Example 24-3. Redrawing the Entire Window, Once Only

```
static void expose_callback(Widget w, XtPointer tag, XtPointer call_data)
{
    XmDrawingAreaCallbackStruct *data =
        (XmDrawingAreaCallbackStruct *)call_data;

    if (data->event->xexpose.count > 0) return;
    redraw_all(w);
}
```

24.3.3.3 Trimming the Drawing List

Neither of the above two approaches is right for every application. Redrawing each exposed rectangle individually only works when the drawing has a very regular structure—a rectangular array of pixels, or a rectangular array of character cells, for example. And always doing a complete redraw isn't appropriate for complex drawings when only one (or a few) subrectangles need redrawing.

Suppose that our application displays a complex circuit diagram, and we don't want to do a full redraw for every Expose event (or even every set of contiguous Expose events). What this diagram does have is a lot of structure—instead of drawing an airfoil cross-section as a single polygon, for example, it will have to draw symbols for lots of circuit components. One way to optimize redrawing in a case like this is to proceed through the drawing list (in whatever form it takes) as if we were going to perform a full redraw, but only actually redraw those parts of the circuit that need it. If, for example, we know that the rectangle that needs redrawing is described by (x1, y1, w1, h1) and we know that the bounding box for a certain transistor symbol is (x2, y2, w2, h2) then we can check whether there is any overlap between these two rectangles. If the transistor falls entirely outside of the exposed region, then we can safely trim it from the drawing list and move on to the next item, without redrawing. In order for this approach to work, of course, you must know a bounding box (it needn't be the smallest possible bounding box) for each item in the display list. You can often compute such a bounding box when transforming from world coordinates to pixel coordinates.

When multiple Expose events are generated, an item in the drawing list may actually intersect more than one of the exposed rectangles, and if we proceed as described for each event in the series of events, then some items might be redrawn more than necessary. What we need is some way of collecting a group of exposed rectangles and then testing whether a given item intersects any of the rectangles in the group. This is possible using the Xlib `Region` facilities—a `Region` is a client-side abstraction that allows operations on lists of rectangles. See `XCreateRegion()` and related functions for details. Example 24-4 shows how you can accumulate exposed rectangles into a single `Region`.

Example 24-4. Merging Exposed Rectangles into a Region

```
static void expose_callback(Widget w, XtPointer tag, XtPointer call_data)
{
    static Region region = NULL;
    XmDrawingAreaCallbackStruct *data =
        (XmDrawingAreaCallbackStruct *)call_data;
    XRectangle rect;

    /* create a region when we receive the first event */
    if (region == NULL) region = XCreateRegion();

    /* save the coordinates of the exposed rectangle */
    rect.x = data->event->xexpose.x;
    rect.y = data->event->xexpose.y;
    rect.width = data->event->xexpose.width;
    rect.height = data->event->xexpose.height;

    /* add the rectangle to the Region */
    XUnionRectWithRegion(&rect, region, region);

    /* if this is not the last Expose in the series do nothing else now */
    if (data->event->xexpose.count > 0) return;

    /* otherwise, do a redraw using the region */
    redraw_all(w, region);

    /* and free the region, and reset for next time */
    XDestroyRegion(region);
    region = NULL;
}
```

With the redraw scheme we've been discussing, you would then use `XRectInRegion()` to determine whether a given item in the drawing list falls within (or partially within) any of the exposed rectangles. The application must still traverse its entire drawing list with this approach, but when the exposed region is only a portion of the window it can dramatically cut down on the number of drawing requests that are actually sent to the server, thus making the redraw much more efficient.

24.3.3.4 Clipping the Drawing

The drawback to the "trimming" approach is that it requires that your drawing list be well organized into separate items that can be individually trimmed, and requires that you know the bounding box of each item. Also, to be efficient, the items themselves must be roughly rectangular. Consider a line that is drawn diagonally from upper left to lower right. The bounding box for this drawing list item is the entire window, so it will be redrawn under this scheme even if it is only the upper-right corner of the window that is exposed.

24.3.3.4

Trimming occurs entirely in the client. An approach you can use instead of (or better, in addition to) trimming is known as *clipping*. The X server automatically clips all drawing requests at the edges of windows, so that a line that goes off the right edge of one window doesn't continue in an adjacent window. By setting attributes in your GC, you can ask the X server to additionally clip to a given `Region`, to a list of rectangles, or to the pixels specified in a bitmask. Given the `Region` we computed in the previous example, we might ask the server to clip our drawing with code like the following:

```
static Display *display;
static GC gc;

static void draw_all(Widget w, Region r)
{
    /* set a clip region for the gc */
    XSetRegion(display, gc, r);

    /* do all the drawing here */

    /* remove the clip region */
    XSetClipMask(display, gc, None);
}
```

Performing trimming, as described, is almost always a good idea, when it is feasible, because it totally throws out some drawing requests. Clipping takes place on the server, so it cannot throw out any drawing requests, and while it may result in less actual drawing, it does require additional computation for each drawing request. Because clipping involves precise boundaries, it can be a relatively expensive operation, particularly when the region involved contains several rectangles. For some drawings, and on some servers, it may actually be quicker to do a redraw without a clipping region than it is to perform the calculations required for clipping.

24.3.3.5 Simplifying the Clipping Region

When you have a `Region` composed of several rectangles, one useful compromise is to clip to the bounding box of the region, rather than to the precise boundaries of the region itself. In this way, you make the clipping region larger, and the server may perform some unnecessary drawing, but you dramatically simplify the clipping computations. Use `XClipBox()` to get the bounding box of a `Region`, and `XSetClipRectangles()` to specify this clipping rectangle:

```
static void draw_all(Widget w, Region r)
{
    XRectangle rect;

    XClipBox(r, &rect);
    XSetClipRectangles(display, gc, 0, 0, &rect, 1, Unsorted);
        .
        .      /* do the drawing here */
        .
    XSetClipMask(display, gc, None);
```

You may want to try this XClipBox() technique when performing trimming in your application. If you will be making many calls to XRectInRegion() (to check many objects in your window), then it will save a lot of time if the region you are checking is a single rectangle rather than a list of rectangles. Again, the computation time will decrease, but the amount of unnecessary drawing will increase.

24.3.3.6 Expose Event Compression

There is one final optimization technique that you might want to consider. As we've described above, the X server will set the count field of the Expose event structure to indicate when there are multiple Expose events that will be arriving as a group. Sometimes several of these groups of Expose events may arrive one after another. When you receive an Expose event, it is possible to scan the event queue, removing all pending Expose events for your window (as long as there are no intervening resize events, or other events that would interfere) and to merge all of these events into a single region or a single rectangle. The Xt Intrinsics can automatically perform this kind of event compression for widgets, when requested to. Neither the Core nor the XmDrawingArea widgets do this, however, so if you want Expose compression for your own work area window, you'll have to do so on your own. See XCheckIfEvent() and related functions.

Using Widgets in Your Drawings

Don't think that everything that appears in the work area of your application must be drawn by hand. There are times when it can be quite useful to integrate widgets with your drawings. Many widgets do some kind of useful drawing that you do not have to duplicate. And all widgets know how to redraw themselves, which makes it easier for you to handle Expose events, when they arrive.

One of the advantages to drawing with the XmDrawingArea widget is that it is a manager widget and accepts children widgets. If you are displaying a network topology, for example, then you might use the XmLabel widget to easily display pixmaps for each of the nodes, and then do your own drawing to connect those nodes with lines. Or, to take the example a step further, you might use XmPushButton widgets instead, so that the user could click on any node in the diagram to pop up a dialog displaying more information about the node.

The XmDrawingArea doesn't try to do any kind of layout on its children (except to enforce its margins, and you can set these margins to 0, if you want) so you can position widgets in your drawing simply by setting their XtNx and XtNy resources. And if you want to move those widgets dynamically, you can do so by changing these resources.

You can use XmGadgets in an XmDrawingArea, but this requires some extra care. Since Gadgets don't have a window of their own, you can draw right over them. If you use regular windowed widgets, then you can be sure that you will not accidentally trash their displays. Also, Gadgets require special translations

Using Widgets in Your Drawings (continued)

on the XmDrawingArea in order to properly handle input events—since you may often want to override the XmDrawingArea translation table, it is easier not to have to worry about them.

One of the useful features of the XmLabel widget is that it allows you to display multi-font strings (in conjunction with `XmtCreateXmString()`) in your drawings much more easily than Xlib does. Actually, it is the Motif XmString module that does the hard work of displaying these strings, and you can use this module directly in your drawings. If you want to display multi-font, multi-line text, take a look at `XmStringDraw()` and `XmStringDrawImage()`; these can be very useful functions.

When you use widgets in your drawings, there are some features you may want to disable. If the drawing does not have a 3D look, then you might want to turn off the 3D shadows of widgets by setting their `XmNshadowThickness` resource to 0. (Or, on the other hand, you might want to leave the shadows on, to emphasize that that the widgets are something special.) If Motif keyboard navigation will not be useful in the drawing, then you might want to set `XmNhighlightThickness` to 0 as well. If you get rid of the highlight rectangle like this, then you should also be sure to set `XmNtraversalOn` to `False` so that the widget never takes the keyboard focus—otherwise, you might end up with confused users who can't figure out which widget has the focus. Once you've turned off a widget's rectangular shadows and highlight border, another technique you can try, if you're feeling adventurous, is to use the SHAPE extension to change a rectangular widget into a non-rectangular one!

—*djf*

24.4 Object-Oriented Drawing

The discussions above of maintaining a drawing list for your drawings, and of trimming items out of that list during partial redraws suggests an object-oriented approach to drawing in your application's work area window. Drawing editor applications are the obvious example of this approach to drawing: when creating a drawing editor using C++, you might implement a `Rectangle` class and an `Ellipse` class, which contain all the code necessary to draw rectangles (including squares) and ellipses (including circles). The fields of these classes would specify the X and Y dimensions and positions of the shapes, as well as things like the line width, color, and pattern to use for the perimeter, and the fill pattern and color to use for the interior of the shapes.

With classes like these defined, the drawing list for the application might simply be a linked list of instances of these classes. To redraw the window, you'd simply traverse the list, calling the `draw()` method of each object. To do a partial redraw of the window, you might first call a `get_bounding_box()` method for each object to determine if it intersected the exposed region of the window.

This kind of object-oriented drawing can be taken a step further to what is sometimes known as *structured graphics*. Structured graphics allow primitive drawing objects like lines, rectangles, and ellipses to be combined into structures or compound objects. These compounded objects can then be moved, redrawn, and so on, as a group. The structured graphics approach is particularly useful when it is possible to store or copy a structure for use as a template—so that a drawing may contain several copies of a compound object, perhaps drawn at different sizes or with different rotations. In a circuit-design application, for example, we might draw all transistor symbols with a `Transistor` structure created with primitive `Circle`, `Line`, and `Arrow` objects.*

An object-oriented approach to drawing makes it easy to maintain a drawing list, and usually makes it easy to optimize redraws by trimming that list. Another advantage is the ease with which drawings of this type may be created and may be modified in your C code. Also, as we'll see later, using objects as drawing primitives makes it easy to do "hit detection" and to dispatch input events.

24.5 Alternatives to Xlib

There is no requirement that you must draw into your work area window at the Xlib level. You may be able to find libraries of higher-level routines that make it easier to do the kind of drawing you want. Libraries exist for drawing graphs and networks, for example. If you are porting an application built around some other graphics library, your first task may well be to port that library to work with the underlying Xlib primitives.

Another alternative to Xlib is offered by extensions to the core X protocol. PEX, the PHIGS Extension to X, was introduced in X11R5, and supports 3D structured graphics. You can use PEX with the PHIGS client library, which is a somewhat cumbersome, high-level interface, or PEXlib, which supports all of the powerful 3D features of the extension, but provides a lower-level, easier-to-use interface to that extension.

Another major extension to X that you may find useful is Display PostScript. Its obvious advantage is that producing WYSIWYG graphics on the screen and in hardcopy is automatic with this extension. The Display PostScript server extension is not available from the X Consortium, and is not supported by all hardware vendors, so if you choose to use it your application may not be portable to all platforms.

The Multi-Buffering Extension, or MBX, isn't really an alternative to Xlib, but can be useful with Xlib or with other X extensions. When you are displaying dynamic data and redrawing your work area window, or portions of it, frequently, this extension allows *double-buffering*, a technique that allows you to perform rapid updates or animation smoothly, without flashing.

*With X11R6, the X Consortium released the Fresco toolkit as a "work in progress." This C++ user interface toolkit has excellent structured graphics capabilities. It is not based on the Xt architecture, however, and so is difficult to integrate with Xt and Motif applications.

Portability is of course the problem when you use any server extension—you can't count on every server to support the extension you need, even when the extension is freely available as PEX is. Portability is particularly a problem with X terminals, which often have their server software in ROM and cannot easily be upgraded. If you are writing an application for a limited audience, and you know that they will all have access to a given extension, then you should certainly use it whenever it is useful.

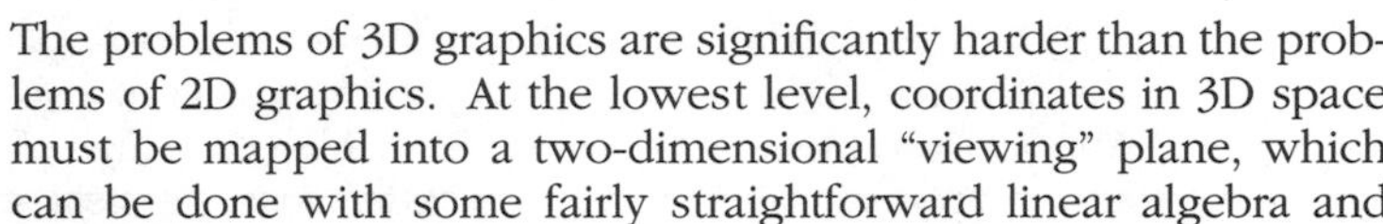

3D Structured Graphics with PEXlib

The problems of 3D graphics are significantly harder than the problems of 2D graphics. At the lowest level, coordinates in 3D space must be mapped into a two-dimensional "viewing" plane, which can be done with some fairly straightforward linear algebra and trigonometry. Beyond this, however, things get much more complicated. Since the transformation to 2D involves floating-point arithmetic, it is common practice in 3D graphics to specify objects in floating-point "world coordinates," and to allow arbitrary transformations on these objects: translations, rotations, and scaling. Also, when the 3D-to-2D transformation is done, it can be done either with or without adjustments for perspective to make further objects appear smaller.

Most applications for 3D graphics are for sophisticated modeling, visualization, or animation tasks, and demand more realistic graphics than are common in 2D. An important step towards realism in 3D graphics is careful handling of color. Any model will be illuminated from one or more sources of light, which may be point or diffuse sources. The apparent color of an object depends on the type and color of the light, on the orientation of the object with respect to the sources of light, the surface properties (shiny, dull, etc.) of the object, and the distance of the object from the viewer. So before a 3D object is drawn into a 2D window, its color must be adjusted by all these factors. Other factors that affect the final outcome of a 3D drawing include such things as the technique to be used for removing hidden surfaces and hidden lines, and the formulas to be used for computing how the color of an object changes with its distance from the observer.

PEXlib is an X Consortium standard library that handles the transformations, the complexities of lighting, and many of the other difficulties of 3D drawing. It is a low-level C programming interface to PEX, an extension to the X server which supports 3D graphics. PEX is an acronym for "PHIGS Extension to X." PHIGS is an international standard for high-level 3D graphics, and PEX was created (and released as part of X11R5) in order to support a client-side PHIGS library on X workstations. PHIGS is an old standard, however, based originally on FORTRAN, and can be fairly cumbersome to use. PEXlib provides an alternative, simple interface to the PEX protocol, and will be useful to graphics programmers who do not want all the overhead of PHIGS.

PEX is implemented as an extension to the X server, and PEXlib can be considered an extension to Xlib. The PEXlib programmer will probably never use any Xlib drawing functions, but PEXlib relies on the Xlib event and error handling

3D Structured Graphics with PEXlib (continued)

mechanisms. What PEXlib provides over Xlib is a whole new set of graphics primitives. While the core X protocol provides requests to draw points, lines, rectangles, and polygons in two dimensions, the PEX protocol provides a number of more complex requests to draw lines and splines in three dimensions, and also requests to draw complete 3D "quadrilateral mesh" surfaces.

One of the most interesting features of PEXlib is that drawing requests need not be executed right away. The PEX protocol also allows the drawing primitives to be sent to a server object known as a Structure, where they are stored to be drawn later. Structures may refer to substructures, which allow a hierarchical definition of 3D objects. A model of a bicycle might be stored in a Structure which contains two references to a structure containing a model of a bicycle wheel, for example.

This sort of structured graphics is different from the immediate mode graphics that is familiar to Xlib programmers. First, note that Structures are reusable. A Structure may be drawn multiple times at different positions on the screen, or can be easily redrawn if the underlying X window receives an Expose event. The drawing attributes of the Renderer can also be changed independently of the Structure, so the same structure may be drawn from different angles, with different sources of lighting, and so on.

Another advantage of Structures is that as server objects they can be efficiently redrawn without sending a number of primitive drawing requests (which can become quite large for complex surfaces) over the wire from client to server. Because of their reusability, Structures can be thought of as analogs to Xlib Pixmaps, but are far more flexible, because they contain a list of drawing commands rather than pure data, because they are hierarchical, because their drawing attributes can be set and changed independently, and because the contents of a Structure can be edited—by adding, removing, or changing the drawing primitives themselves.

—djf
From a column first published in Sun Observer magazine

24.6 Producing PostScript Output

If users want to see data represented graphically in the work area of your application, then it is a safe bet that they'll want to be able to print those pictures out as hardcopy. One trivial way to do this is to simply produce a screendump of the bits that appear in your window. You can do this with code as simple as this:

```
char cmd[200];

sprintf(cmd, "xwd -id %d | xpr > %s",  XtWindow(workarea), filename);
system(cmd);
```

While every application ought to provide this functionality at a minimum, there are a number of problems with this screendump approach. First, and most obviously, the output will be grainy, with resolution no better than that available on the monitor. Since laser printers are capable of such high resolution, it is a shame to use them only for screendumps. Second, since screendumps are done simply by copying the bits in a window, they are large, and slow to print. And finally, this approach requires that the window be totally unobscured—if portions of the window are covered up (by a print dialog box, for example) they will not appear in the output. This is particularly a problem when the work area is a large, scrolled one and can never be totally visible.

The alternative is to use "native PostScript output"—that is, to produce output that consists of the PostScript commands necessary to duplicate your drawing on paper. Instead of just copying the bits from your window, you'll be duplicating the lines, the polygons, the fills, and so forth that originally produced those bits in your window. This approach lets you take full advantage of the higher resolution of PostScript output. It almost always results in smaller and more efficient PostScript files. And it works even when your drawing area widget is totally obscured.

The approach is basically the same you'd take for drawing into your window: just step through your drawing list and draw each item in it. If your world-coordinate to pixel-coordinate transformation routines have been written flexibly, then you will have no problem adapting them to use the PostScript coordinate system instead of pixels. If you've adopted an object-oriented approach, then each of your object classes might have two drawing methods—one method that draws in X and one that draws in PostScript. To do this, of course, you'll have to learn to program with PostScript. It is a stack-based, interpreted language, like Forth, and is very different from C, but once you become familiar with the basic stack model, it is not difficult to work with. The *PostScript Language Reference Manual, Second Edition*, published by Addison-Wesley, is the definitive reference for the language, and also contains an excellent introduction to the PostScript programming and drawing models.

Differences Between X and PostScript

Writing a routine to display a line plot (for example) in PostScript is not intrinsically more difficult than writing a function to display the plot in X. What is a little tricky, however, is that the X and PostScript drawing models differ in some fundamental ways: fonts are named differently in X and PostScript, for example, and there is no general way to translate one name to the other. Also, while Y coordinates increase as they go down the screen in X, they increase as they go up the page in PostScript.

A more difficult difference involves bitmaps. The *bitmap* is a fundamental type in X and is commonly used for things like the glyphs that mark the points in a line plot or the fill patterns used in bar charts. Using bitmaps for these tasks in PostScript is not appropriate because scaling a bitmap can only be done by omitting bits or making the bits larger. So while we can place markers on a

Differences Between X and PostScript (continued)

graph efficiently in X by simply copying the bits from a bitmap, in PostScript each marker must be drawn using the basic PostScript line drawing and filling operators. (Glyphs are supported in Level 2 PostScript, but many printers do not support this enhanced version of the language yet. One way to make glyph drawing more efficient is to define the glyphs as elements of a custom font—some printers will cache the bit patterns and speed up the drawing.)

One of the less obvious, but more fundamental, differences between the two systems is that to draw in X, you dynamically call procedures, but "drawing" in PostScript really just means writing strings to a file. While every Xlib function is passed a `Display *` handle, PostScript drawing functions will need some kind of file handle. The problem is made a little more difficult because the PostScript structuring conventions require special comments at the beginning of the file to list the bounding box, fonts used, and so on. Often, this information is not available until the drawing has already been completed, so creating a PostScript drawing may not be simply a matter of sequentially writing lines to a file.

There are a couple of other differences between X and PostScript that are worth noting. First, PostScript (at least Level 1 PostScript) does not have any equivalent to the X Graphics Context—changes to the graphics state in PostScript are global, though the current state can be saved at any point with the `gsave` operator. This difference is not particularly cumbersome; it is simply a matter of getting used to the stack-oriented nature of PostScript programming.

Another important difference is that PostScript drawings are static, with no equivalent to X Expose events. Because X drawing routines have to be prepared to redraw the window any time, applications will usually have separate resize and expose procedures—the resize procedure does pre-computation to make the expose procedure quicker (converting the floating-point data coordinates to pixel coordinates, for example.) With this done, the expose procedure need only call the various Xlib functions required to display the widget. Since PostScript doesn't have Expose events, and since it is unlikely that the same drawing will be printed twice in a row at the same size, there is no need to keep these resize and expose procedures separate in PostScript—a single drawing procedure can do the coordinate transformation and output the PostScript drawing commands.

—djf

From a paper first published in The X Resource

24.7 Obtaining Input Events

Some applications only need to produce static drawing in their work area, and can rely on other widgets in the user interface for all user interaction. Many interesting applications require some sort of interactivity in the work area, however. In our airfoil design application, for example, perhaps the user is able to alter the shape of the cross-section by interactively dragging the control points of the spline that defines it. Or in an application that draws an electronic circuit, perhaps clicking on a component in the diagram will select that component for editing, and double-clicking on a component will up a dialog box that displays more information about the component. In an application that displays graphs of data, perhaps there will be a modeline that displays the world coordinates under the mouse pointer as the user moves the mouse through the work area.

In order to implement any of these types of interaction you must request notification of user events, and then act on them appropriately when they arrive. The following subsections explain some of the different ways that you can do this.

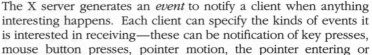

Events in X

The X server generates an *event* to notify a client when anything interesting happens. Each client can specify the kinds of events it is interested in receiving—these can be notification of key presses, mouse button presses, pointer motion, the pointer entering or leaving a window, keyboard focus being given to a window, and so on. In Xlib, each type of event has its own structure type (`XButtonEvent`, for example) that describes the pertinent details. These various event structures are collected together into a single union, the `XEvent`, which is the type that you will most often see when handling events.

When passed an `XEvent *`, you can find out what type of event it is by checking its `type` field:

```
XEvent *event;

switch (event->type) {
    case ButtonPress:       /* user pressed a mouse button */
    case KeyPress:          /* user pressed a key */
    case MotionNotify:      /* user moved the mouse */
    case Expose:            /* window needs to be redrawn */
    case ConfigureNotify:   /* window size or position has changed */
    case FocusIn:           /* window was given keyboard focus */
}
```

Once you know the type of an event, you can access its particular fields either directly through the union, or by casting the union to a more specific type:

```
XEvent *event;
XButtonEvent *button_event;

/* access fields through the union */
```

Events in X (continued)

```
x = event->xbutton.x

/* or by casting */
button_event = (XButtonEvent *)event;
x = button_event->x;
```

In Xlib, you tell the X Server that you are interested in a particular type of event with `XSelectInput()`. When programming with Xt, however, one common way to get events is with `XtAddEventHandler()`. In either case, you describe the kinds of events you are interested in with an *event mask*—a bit-field of values that you can OR together. Note that event masks are not the same as event types. The `ButtonPress` event type is selected with the `ButtonPressMask` mask. There is not a strict one-to-one correspondence between event types and event masks. Both `FocusIn` and `FocusOut` events are selected with the single `FocusChangedMask` bit, since these are events that you would always want to receive in pairs.

There are enough different types of events, with different masks and structures, that a good reference is important to have handy. Appendix C of *X Toolkit Intrinsics Reference Manual* is a complete list of the X event types, their masks, their structures, and the meanings of their fields.

—*djf*

24.7.1 Getting Events with Callbacks

As we've seen, the XmDrawingArea widget will call its `XmNexposeCallback` to notify you when your window needs to be redrawn. Similarly, it will call its `XmNresizeCallback` when the size of the window changes. It will also notify you of button presses, button releases, key presses, and key releases through its `XmNinputCallback`. The *`call_data`* structure passed to this callback is the same structure that is passed to the other two XmDrawingArea callbacks:

```
typedef struct {
    int reason;     /* XmCR_EXPOSE, XmCR_RESIZE, or XmCR_INPUT */
    XEvent *event; /* the event */
    Window window; /* the window.  Same as XtWindow(drawing_area) */
} XmDrawingAreaCallbackStruct;
```

This structure does not provide any special information such as the pointer coordinates of the button press or even which mouse button was pressed—you have to extract this information from the `XEvent` structure yourself.

For simple button and key input, this `XmNinputCallback` may be sufficient. Note, however, that it does not provide mouse motion events, so you can't use it to implement any interactions that involve dragging.

24.7.2 Getting Events with Event Handlers

Probably the most flexible way to obtain events in your programs is to register an *event handler* for your work area widget. An event handler is a procedure of type `XtEventHandler`, usually registered with a call to `XtAddEventHandler()`. Example 24-5 shows the basic structure of an event handler, and how you might register it. See your Xt reference for detailed information about writing and registering event handlers.

Example 24-5. An Event Handler

```
static void drag_handler(Widget w, XtPointer client_data,
                         XEvent *event; Boolean *continue_to_dispatch)
{
    static x1, y1, x2, y2;

    switch(event->type) {
    case ButtonPress:
        if (event->xbutton.button == Button1) {
            /*
             * The user clicked mouse Button 1
             * record the initial click coordinates in (x1, y1)
             * And make a note that a drag has begun.
             */
        }
        else {
            /*
             * If another mouse button is pressed, after a drag has already
             * begun, we treat it as a command to cancel the drag.
             * Otherwise, we just ignore the event.
             */
        }
        break;
    case MotionNotify:
        /*
         * The user has moved the mouse while the Button1 is down.
         * save the new pointer position in x2, y2.  Erase the old
         * rubberband rectangle and draw a new one.
         */
        break;
    case ButtonRelease:
        if (event->xbutton.button != Button1) return;
        /*
         * The user has released the button, so now we have the
         * coordinates of a selected rectangle.  Erase the rubberband
         * and then do whatever we're doing with the selected rectangle.
         * If the user released the mouse outside of the work area, then
         * treat this as a cancel event.
         */
        break;
    }
}

XtAddEventHandler(w,
                  ButtonPressMask | ButtonReleaseMask | Button1MotionMask,
                  False, drag_handler, NULL);
```

There are several possible ways that you can use event handlers. One is to register an event handler for each type of event you are interested in. Then each handler has a single, well-defined task, and knows what kinds of events it will be receiving. On the other hand, events often come in related sequences, like the click-drag-release sequence handled in Example 24-5. Handling sequences of events like this is often easier with shared variables, so handling several related event types with a single handler is often a more useful approach than having a separate handler for each type of event.

Some applications may find it easiest to route all events they are interested in through a single event-handling procedure which processes the events directly, or dispatches them to other procedures.

24.7.3 Getting Events with Translations and Actions

Another way you can be notified of events on your work area's window is with translations and actions. Defining action procedures is something that is usually done by widget writers, but there is nothing to stop application programmers from using this technique as well—you write a procedure of type `XtActionProc` and register it with call to `XtAppAddActions()`. Then you define a translation table that binds your action procedure to an event or sequence of events. You parse this translation table with `XtParseTranslationTable()` and specify it on your work area widget with `XtOverrideTranslations()`.

For some applications, an important advantage of the translations and actions approach is that you can document the names of your actions, and allow your users to customize the translations of the widget used as the work area. If you have any plans to eventually turn your work area implementation into a custom widget, then writing action procedures now will make that process much easier in the future.

If you are using an XmDrawingArea widget, there are a couple of difficulties with translations that you should be aware of. First, if you will be using XmGadget children of the XmDrawingArea, remember that all gadget input is handled by the parent widget, so, for example, if you override the translations for Button1 in the XmDrawingArea, then XmPushButtonGadget children will no longer respond to button clicks. You can overcome this difficulty by looking at the default translation table of the XmDrawingArea, and being sure to include any required actions in your custom translations. Also, since the XmDrawingArea has translations for button-down and button-up events (for gadgets and for the `XmNinputCallback`) it is impossible to add a translation (without overriding the defaults) that will invoke an action on button motion events.

24.8 Processing Events

The preceding section presented three different ways of getting events in your application. They have said very little, however, about what you will do with those events once you receive them. This section presents some common ways that you might want to use them.

24.8.1 User Feedback

One of the most basic kinds of interaction with the user is to provide feedback to the user on her actions. In an application that plots graphs of data in its work area, for example, you might request mouse motion events, and use them to display the current world coordinates of the pointer. These could be displayed in a separate widget—no direct interaction with the drawing in the work area is required but you still must request and process input events.

Or, if your work area displays any kind of insertion cursor, as another example, then you might want to make the cursor visible when the mouse pointer enters the widget or when the widget is given the keyboard focus, and hide the cursor when the pointer leaves the window or when keyboard focus is moved to some other window. This feedback will tell the user when the widget is ready for input. Even if the work area does not have a cursor, you might want to provide a similar kind of feedback by drawing a Motif-style highlight border around the edges of the work area, for example.

These kinds of feedback are fairly simple to implement—they may require some limited drawing in the work area (flashing a cursor, drawing a border), but do not involve direct interaction between the user and the drawing.

24.8.2 Hit Detection

A more difficult kind of user interaction allows the user to perform direct manipulation of the drawing in the work area. In a drawing editor application, this means that the user can use the mouse to select, edit, move, and resize the individual objects in the drawing. In our hypothetical airfoil design application, it might mean that the user can select and reposition the control points that define the curve displayed for the airfoil surface. In a circuit-design application, it might mean that the user can double-click on any component in the circuit diagram to edit the specifications (resistance, capacitance, etc.) of that component.

In order to implement this kind of interaction, you must of course be able to determine when the user has clicked the mouse over a significant part of your drawing. This ability is known as *hit detection.* Hit detection is made easier if your drawing has a well-defined drawing list—then you can scan through your drawing list and determine if a given point is on or within any of the individual components of your drawing. And hit detection is made even easier, of course, with an object-oriented approach to drawing—your `Rectangle` and `Ellipse` objects (or even your `Transistor` and `Resistor` objects) might have a `check_hit` method that will determine whether a given point is within their boundaries.

If you used the "trimming" technique previously described for efficiently handling partial redraws of your window, then you have a bounding box for each item in your drawing list. In some cases, this bounding box will be sufficient—if a mouse click occurs within an item's bounding box, then that item is selected. Note, though, that this only works for items that are more-or-less rectangular—it is no good for detecting hits on diagonal lines, for example.

Sometimes you will want to do hit detection with more accuracy—to require a click on the object, rather than just somewhere within its bounding box. This takes more computation, but can be done. To determine whether a point is within a circle, for example, you might convert its (x,y) coordinates to polar coordinates, and then check the radial distance of the point from the center of the circle. (For efficiency, you might use the square of the circle's radius in your comparisons, to avoid having to compute a square root in your conversion to polar coordinates.) To determine whether a point is within an irregular shape (an airfoil cross-section, for example) you could use `XPolygonRegion()` to define a region for the airfoil polygon, and then use `XPointInRegion()` to determine whether any given point fell within it. Before performing these computationally intensive hit detection checks, of course, it makes sense to first check whether a point falls within a region's bounding box. If it doesn't, you can move on to check the next item in the drawing list with no further computation.

24.8.3 Detecting Double-Clicks

Many common interaction styles use a mouse double-click as a way of selecting an item and of performing some common operation on it. If you are using translations and actions, you can use a special translation syntax to detect double-clicks:

```
<Btn1Up>:    single-click()
<Btn1Up>(2): double-click()
```

This translation table will invoke the `single-click()` action when the user clicks Button 1, and will invoke the `double-click()` action if the user double-clicks the button. The definition of a double-click is two clicks that occur within the multi-click time interval. This value can be set by the user with the `multiClickTime` application resource. The default is 200 milliseconds.

As discussed above, however, you will often want to get events in your window with some technique other than translations and actions. Additionally, a major shortcoming of the translation table mechanism is that it cannot handle both double-clicks and mouse motion. So, for example, you cannot define a translation table that will correctly handle both double-clicks and click-drag-release sequences.

Fortunately, detecting a double click in your own callback or event handler is really not very difficult. You can obtain the multi-click interval requested by the user with `XtGetMultiClickTime()`, and you can look at the `time` field in any ButtonPress or ButtonRelease event. The `time` field is of type `Time`, but this is a typedef for a simple scalar C type, so you can determine the time interval between two button events by simple subtraction. You'll need to use a static variable to save the timestamp of each button event, so that you can compare it to the timestamp of the next event that arrives. You may also want to constrain double-clicks to occur within 10 pixels (for example) of each other, so that if the user clicks twice while moving the mouse quickly it will not be misinterpreted as a double-click on a single item.

Mouse Buttons and Their Meanings

When you want to allow the user to select an item by clicking on it, to perform some default action on an item by double-clicking, or to select some region by dragging, you should use mouse button 1. This is the basic mouse button used for any kind of item selection or command activation. You may also use it in conjunction with modifier keys. For example, a click might select a single item, and a shift-click might allow the selection of multiple items.

Mouse button 2 is reserved for use with drag-and-drop. If your application will not use drag-and-drop, you should probably leave this button unused, unless you have a very complex interface that requires the use of multiple buttons. If you will be allowing drags to be initiated from your work area window, then you will have to detect Button 2 events somehow, and call `XmDragStart()` when they occur.

Mouse button 3 is the traditional button for popup menus. You can bind popups to other mouse buttons as well, but if you have more than one, it is almost always best to bind them to mouse button 3 with various modifier keys. Popup menus can be very convenient with work areas, because they allow the user a quick way to select from a list of operations available on items displayed in the window. Without a popup, the user might have to drag the mouse back and forth between the work area and the main application menubar. If you create your popup menus with `XmtCreatePopupMenu()`, Xmt automatically registers an event handler for you to pop up that menu when the appropriate button plus modifier event occurs. If you are writing other event handlers, you should be careful that none of them handle the same button 3 events, or a single user event could trigger multiple application actions.

—*djf*

24.8.4 Handling Sequences of Events

Previous subsections have mostly discussed handling single events—the user clicks or double-clicks, and the application responds by selecting an item in the work area, popping up a dialog, or whatever. Sometimes, though, you'll have to handle a more complicated sequence of events.

When you want to allow the user to draw a line or select a region of the work area, for example, you'll have to handle a click-drag-release sequence of events. A skeleton event handler for this sequence of events was shown in Example 24-5. Typically, you'll store the coordinates of the initial button press when it occurs, and will not perform the eventual action (zooming in on a selected region, for example) until the user releases the button. In between the button press and the button release, you'll provide some sort of feedback. If the user is drawing a line, you'll draw a line between the initial point and the current point as the user moves the mouse. If the user is selecting a region, then you'll probably draw a "rubberband" box as the user drags the mouse.

Notice that XmPushButton widgets handle a simple sequence of events like this. They highlight themselves when the user presses the mouse button, but don't actually perform any action until the user releases the button. If the user moves the mouse out of the button before releasing, then the button is not activated, which gives the user a way to back out. Most of the time, it is fine to select items in your work area on a button press event, but if you want to perform any more significant actions, it is a good idea to wait for the button release event, and to verify that the button release occurred over the same object that the button press did.

Whenever you are implementing a user interaction that is not atomic (i.e., one that is triggered by a sequence of events rather than a single event) it is important to give the user a way to back out. In the press-drag-release event handler shown before, mouse button 1 was used for the selection. It would have been a good idea to allow the user to cancel the drag by clicking button 2 or button 3 at any time. The **Escape** key is another useful way to allow users to back out of pending input.

Rubberbands and Other Transient Drawing

When the user is selecting a region by dragging with the mouse, you will want to provide feedback by "rubberbanding" a box that shows the selected area as the user drags. In order to do this, you need a technique that allows you to quickly draw and quickly erase the outline of a rectangle without disturbing the underlying graphics that are drawn in the window.

The standard technique for doing this is "drawing with XOR." By setting the `function` member of your GC to the `GXxor`, you tell the X server that drawing should be done by taking the exclusive OR of the foreground pixel value and whatever pixel values are being drawn over. Because of the nature of the exclusive OR operation, you can erase what you have drawn by simply redrawing it—this will restore the original contents of the window.

One further trick is necessary to make this work—a way of choosing what color to draw with. On a monochrome system, you always use the value 1, regardless of whether this happens to represent the color white or the color black. On color systems, however, things are more complicated. Suppose the primary background color of your work area is gray, a color you've allocated as a `Pixel` variable `p1`. And suppose you want your rubberband to appear in bright red. You'd allocated your bright red color in the `Pixel` variable `p2`. Then, when creating the GC you'll use for rubberbanding (since you'll need to use a special XOR function, it is often easiest to use a special GC) you don't actually set `p2` as the foreground color. Instead, you take the exclusive OR of `p1` and `p2` and use that as the foreground color. The result needn't actually be a pixel that has been allocated by your application. The point is that when the value `(p1 xor p2)` is XOR'ed with the background color `p1`, the result will be the desired bright red color `p2`. (If this doesn't make sense to you, try it out—pick arbitrary pixel values, convert them to binary, and then do the Boolean algebra yourself.)

Rubberbands and Other Transient Drawing (continued)

Note that the pixel values we're using in the above Boolean algebra are just `Pixel` variables. On most hardware, these are eight-bit values that represent a color's position in the hardware colormap. Except in specialized cases, these do not correspond to the actual red, green, and blue values of the colors that appear. This fact makes no difference to the end result—the Boolean algebra works anyway.

This XOR approach works well if you know for sure that most of the work area is in fact a single background color. If, in the above example, the user tried to select a region that fell within a green rectangle drawn on the screen, then our carefully chosen color `(p1 xor p2)` would be XOR'ed with some third color `p3`, and we'd end up with a rubberband of some unpredictable color that might or might not be distinguishable from the green rectangle. It can also be difficult to see the rubberband rectangle when it is drawn over regions that contain a lot of text or detailed line drawing or stippled gray patterns. A technique I've found useful is to set the `line_width` member of the GC to 2—the wider lines are much easier to see against a busy background, but are still thin enough to allow accurate region selection.

To summarize, the following lines of code show the basic steps you'd take to create a GC that you could use for drawing with XOR:

```
Pixel background_color, rubberband_color;
XGCValues gcv;

gcv.function = GXxor;
gcv.foreground = rubberband_color ^ background_color;
gcv.line_width = 2;
rubberband_gc = XtGetGC(w, GCForeground | GCLineWidth | GCFunction, &gcv);
```

If your application requires a rubberband (or any other kind of transient highlighting) that is guaranteed to be a single, solid color, then another technique you can use is to allocate an "overlay plane." To do this, you use `XAllocColorCells()` to allocate all the basic colors you'll use for drawing in your work area, and to allocate a special overlay plane that can be used for transient highlighting. This technique uses read-write color cells that can't be shared with other applications, and requires twice as many colors as you would ordinarily use, so it is a more expensive technique than XOR in terms of X server resources.

The `XAllocColorCells()` allocation technique works this way: suppose your drawing requires eight distinct colors, and one special highlight color for rubberbands and the like. Your call to `XAllocColorCells()` would return eight pixels that you could use for your drawing. It would also return a special "plane mask" with a single bit set that can be OR'ed with any of the returned colors to yield a new color cell. These other color cells are also allocated to your application (so you are using 16 colors, rather than the basic eight). What you do is store your eight basic colors in the eight returned color cells. Then you

Rubberbands and Other Transient Drawing (continued)

OR your plane mask with each of these color cell values and store your single highlight color in each of the resulting eight color cells. With this initialization done, you can allocate a special highlighting GC with the `plane_mask` field set to your allocated plane mask. Any drawing done with this special GC will only affect the single bit in each pixel. By setting this bit, you will convert any color in the figure to the highlight color, and by clearing it, the highlight color will revert to its original color. This is admittedly a confusing concept, and you can find a more detailed explanation of it (as well as a description of the basic X color handling model) in Volume One, *Xlib Programming Manual.*

We've used rubberbanding as the basic example of when you might use these transient highlighting techniques, but there are other circumstances where they can be useful as well. When you need to draw a blinking insertion cursor in your window, these are easy ways to draw and erase it, for example. Or perhaps you'll want to draw some special border around items in your drawing when the user has selected them. The difference between rubberbands and other kinds of highlighting is that rubberbands are only drawn while the user has a mouse button down. While the user is busy dragging out a rectangle, she cannot also be moving windows, popping up dialog boxes, or doing anything else that might generate an Expose event over your window.

In other circumstances, it is possible to get Expose events while there is transient drawing visible, and you must handle this case with some care. If you use the XOR technique, and part of your highlighted area receives an Expose event, then erasing the highlighted area by redrawing it will actually end up erasing part of it and redrawing part of it. In this case, you must handle the Expose event before you erase the highlighting. Part of handling the Expose event will be to redisplay the highlighted area. You'll want to either do a full redisplay of the entire window or use a clipping region to be sure that you redraw only the exposed portion of the highlight—otherwise you might end up erasing part of the unexposed highlighted area.

Handling Expose events along with XOR highlighting can get complicated very quickly. For some applications the easiest thing to do in this situation is to clear the entire window and redraw it from scratch. It is also a rare enough occurrence that another technique, suitable for some applications, is to ignore the problem, realizing that the work area may sometimes get into an inconsistent state. If you do this, then you should provide some easy-to-invoke **Redraw Screen** function.

24.8.5 Keyboard Shortcuts and Keyboard Traversal

The user interaction techniques we've discussed up to now have all involved mouse input. The mouse is probably the most useful input device for direct manipulation in your work area, but there are cases when keyboard input can be quite important as well. One obvious case is for implementing keyboard shortcuts. Imagine a drawing editor application with a palette of drawing tools on the left of the work area. For many drawings, the user must frequently switch tools, which can involve repeated mousing across the window. Since the mouse is a one-handed input device, the user has his other hand free, and could easily be using the keyboard to switch from tool to tool.

Another important application for keyboard input is for keyboard traversal. Ideally, a user should be able to run a Motif program without ever having to touch the mouse. The standard Motif widgets all handle this, but if you'll be doing your own drawing and input processing in a work area window, you'll have to implement some kind of keyboard traversal on your own. Our circuit-display application, for example, might draw a box around a component to highlight it, and then allow the operator to use the arrow keys to move it around the diagram. With this scheme, the spacebar could be used to select the currently highlighted item, in the same way that clicking on an item would select it.

Translation tables are particularly convenient for handling keyboard events because their syntax automatically handles modifier keys and the translation between hardware keycodes and portable keysyms. For example:

```
Ctrl<Key>R: set-tool(rectangle)
Ctrl<Key>E: set-tool(ellipse)
Ctrl<Key>P: set-tool(polygon)
```

With these translations specified, **Ctrl-R**, **Ctrl-E**, and **Ctrl-P** would all invoke an action procedure that would implement the keyboard shortcut. Note, though, that the usual caveats of translation tables apply—if you are using the XmDrawingArea, then registering translations like these may interfere with the widget's ability to pass keyboard events on to gadget children, to handle traversal between gadget children, and to invoke the `XmNinputCallback` on key events. If you avoid using XmGadgets, which is a good practice, anyway, then these are probably not serious problems.

A less convenient, but also less roundabout, way of handling keyboard events is through the XmDrawingArea `XmNinputCallback`, or through an event handler. In either case, you will receive a raw KeyPress event, which contains a hardware keycode in the `keycode` field, and a bitmask (in the `state` field) of modifier keys and mouse buttons that are currently pressed. You can use `XtTranslateKeycode()` to translate the keycode into a hardware-independent `KeySym`. All the standard keysyms are defined in the header file *<X11/keysym.h>*—they are symbols that begin with the `XK_` prefix. For the standard alphanumeric and punctuation keys in the Latin-1 character set, keysym numbers have been chosen (and standardized) to correspond to ASCII, so you can compare keysyms to characters. Example 24-6 shows a skeleton event handler that could handle keyboard shortcuts and keyboard traversal.

Example 24-6. An Event Handler for Keyboard Events

```
#include <X11/keysym.h>

static void key_handler(Widget w, XtPointer client_data,
                        XEvent *event; Boolean *continue_to_dispatch)
{
    XKeyEvent keyevent;
    KeySym keysym;
    Modifiers used_modifiers;

    /*
     * this handler is only registered for key events, so we don't
     * have to check the type field of the event.
     */
    keyevent = (XKeyEvent *) event;

    /* translate hardware keycode into a keysym */
    XtTranslateKeycode(XtDisplay(w), keyevent->keycode, keyevent->state,
                       &used_modifiers, &keysym);
    /*
     * If the Ctrl key is down, maybe this is a keyboard shortcut.
     * if it is not down, maybe it is a keyboard traversal.
     */
    if (keyevent->state & ControlMask) {
        /*
         * We know that the Ctrl key is down.  If Shift or Lock were down,
         * they'll produce upper case letters that we'll detect below.
         * We could check for other modifiers, and make those illegal
         * commands, but we don't bother.
         */
        switch(keysym) {
        case XK_r:   /* lower case */
        case XK_R:   /* upper case */
            break;
        case 'e':    /* here's another way to test for ASCII chars */
        case 'E':
            break;
        default:
            /* beep to indicate an unknown command */
            break;
        }
    }
    else {
        switch(keysym) {
        case XK_Up:     /* here we handle keyboard traversal in */
            break;      /* each of the four directions */
        case XK_Down:  break;
        case XK_Left:  break;
        case XK_Right: break;
        default:        /* unknown command; beep */  break;
        }
    }
}
```

24.8.5.1 Synchronous Work Area Input

Sometimes in your application you may find that you want to prompt the user to select a point or drag out a region in the window. If the user selects **Zoom In** from a menu, for example, then you may want to display a message "Drag to select the region to be zoomed, or press Escape to cancel." in the message line and then wait for the user to select the region.* If you have to wait for this kind of input in several places in your application, the easiest thing to do may be to write a synchronous input function. A synchronous input function is one that enters an internal event loop and appears to block until the desired input arrives. Once the user performs the requested input, it returns that input to its caller. We saw synchronous input functions like `XmtMsgLineGetString()` in Chapter 22, *The Message Line*.

You can use `XmtBlock()` to handle the internal event loop. This function takes the address of a `Boolean` variable, and handles events until that variable becomes `False`. So to write a synchronous input function that waited for the user to drag out out a rectangle, you'd modify your event handler to set the appropriate flag to `False` once the user finishes the drag and releases the mouse button. To do this right, you'd also want to register an event handler that would respond to the **Escape** key, or in some other way allow the user to cancel the input. Since synchronous input must also be modal, you'll want to use `XtAddGrab()` and `XtRemoveGrab()` to constrain event processing to your work area window, in the same way that modal dialog boxes constrain input to themselves. If you want to pursue this synchronous input technique in your application, take a look at the implementation of the synchronous functions in the MsgLine widget.

24.9 Style

Because every application will have a different work area, there is not specific stylistic advice that applies here. We can make some useful generalizations, however:

- Many of the style points from Chapter 3, *Displaying Text*, and Chapter 4, *Using Color*, are particularly important in the work area of an application. Similarly, popup menus, as described in Chapter 20, *Easy Menu Creation*, are often a valuable addition to work areas.
- Your basic task, when designing and implementing work areas, is to present data to the user in a useful format. This may mean that you will have to work hard to squeeze a dense amount of information into a relatively small space, or it might mean that your application will have to work hard to filter

*Purists might argue that you shouldn't get into modal situations like this. Alternatives are to make the zoom an atomic operation—zoom in automatically any time the user selects a region, or to make the **Zoom In** menu item insensitive unless the user has just selected a region. In practice, though, prompting for input this way is the most natural input technique.

the raw data to display the pertinent points without clutter. Most technical fields have evolved fairly standard data display formats that you will probably want to emulate, because your users will probably already be familiar with them.

- If your work area handles input events, pay attention to the keystrokes and mouse manipulation that it requires, and how this affects the flow of the human/computer interaction. Every extraneous keystroke or mouse drag you can eliminate will translate, after repeated usage, into a large time savings.

24.10 Summary

This chapter has covered a variety of techniques that are necessary when you need to implement an application's work area and have no suitable widget available:

- Obtaining a window, and drawing with Xlib, or with other libraries
- Defining a coordinate system for your drawing, and performing transformations on that coordinate system
- Handling Expose events and efficiently redrawing your work area
- Transforming your work area graphics into PostScript output
- Getting and handling user input events in your work area

Part Six

Patterns and Tools for Dialogs

Dialog boxes are a fundamentally different part of a user interface than the application main window, which was the subject of Part Five.

The chapters in this part describe Xmt tools and widgets for implementing a variety of different kinds of dialog boxes.

25

Message Dialogs

The Motif widget set includes the XmMessageBox, which is used in dialog boxes that display only a simple message. The Motif convenience functions `XmCreateWarningDialog()`, `XmCreateErrorDialog()`, and `XmCreate-InformationDialog()` all create an XmMessageBox inside of an XmDialog-Shell. These dialogs display a single or multi-line message and have a distinctive icon in the upper left corner which indicates the type (error, warning, or help) of the message. Creating these dialogs is simple enough, but working with them is more difficult:

- The Motif convenience functions create dialogs with **OK**, **Cancel**, and **Help** buttons displayed, even though neither the **Cancel** nor the **Help** button is really appropriate in a dialog that simply displays a message. If you use the convenience functions you must go through the extra, inconvenient step of removing these functionless buttons.
- The Motif convenience functions do not allow you to directly specify the message to be displayed. You must specify it as a resource of the XmMessageBox, and you must specify it as an XmString. These are not difficult, simply inconvenient.
- Applications will often use these simple message dialogs for all their warning and error messages, and for some or all of their online help messages. Because creating widgets is a relatively expensive operation, it is not a good idea to create a message dialog every time the application needs to display a message. Instead, the application should have some sort of caching system that allows the XmDialogShell and the XmMessageBox widgets to be created once and reused as needed.
- From a more philosophical view, perhaps the object-oriented metaphor is inappropriate for an operation as simple as displaying a message. For terminal-based programs, you simply can call `printf()` to display an error message. For graphical applications, you shouldn't have to create an object, set

the message to be displayed by the object, and then display the object. A command-based interface (`DisplayErrorMessage()`) is more convenient here than an object-oriented interface (`CreateErrorMessageObject()`).

The Xmt library contains a number of functions which are not subject to any of the above objections; they are documented in the sections that follow.

25.1 Simple Message Dialogs

The simplest way to display a message to the user in a dialog box is with one of the following three functions:

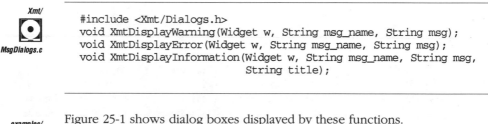

Xmt/

MsgDialogs.c

```
#include <Xmt/Dialogs.h>
void XmtDisplayWarning(Widget w, String msg_name, String msg);
void XmtDisplayError(Widget w, String msg_name, String msg);
void XmtDisplayInformation(Widget w, String msg_name, String msg,
                           String title);
```

examples/

25/msgdialog

Figure 25-1 shows dialog boxes displayed by these functions.

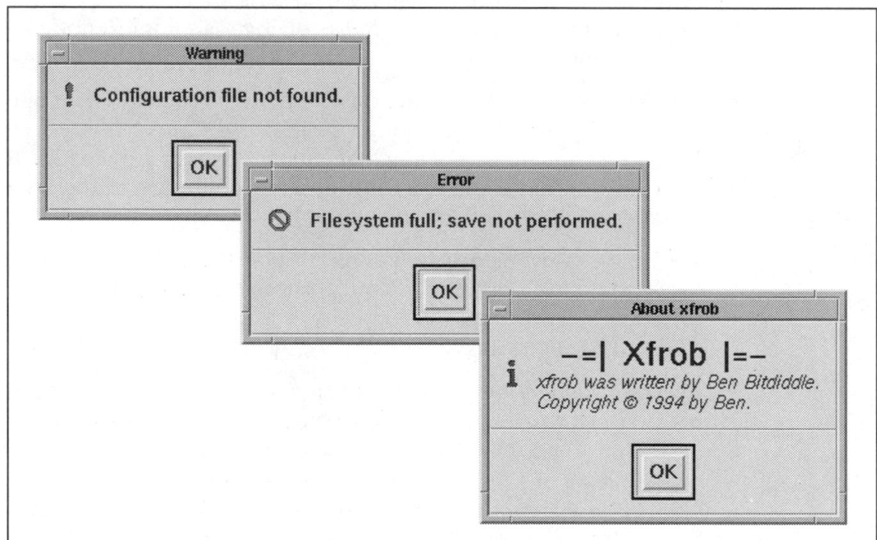

Figure 25-1. Some simple message dialogs

The first argument to each of these functions is a widget. The dialog box will pop up over the shell of this widget. You may pass a shell widget directly, or you may pass any convenient descendant of the desired shell. The second argument to each function is not the message to be displayed; it is a name for the message. This name is used to allow the dialog to be customized. This argument will be explained in more detail later; you may pass NULL. The third argument is the message to be displayed in the dialog. (Actually, it is the default message, since the message can be customized, as explained later.) This is an ordinary NULL-terminated string, which will be converted automatically to an XmString for display with XmtCreateXmString(). This means that you can use the Xmt @f escape sequence in the message to display a message that contains multiple fonts.

Modal and Modeless Dialogs

All dialogs are either *modal* or *modeless*. When a modal dialog is popped up, the application enters a new mode—the user must interact with the dialog and pop it down before he can continue to work in the main application window. When a modal dialog is popped up, the shell underneath the dialog will not respond to keyboard or mouse input. A modal dialog box is used once, and then dismissed by clicking an **OK** button or something similar.

A modeless dialog, on the other hand, does not force the application into a new mode. It is an auxiliary window that the user can use in conjunction with the window he was using; it does not prevent keyboard and mouse input from going to the underlying windows. A modeless dialog might contain online help information that the user can refer to while using the application, for example, or a utility like a color mixer that the user might need now and again while working with the application. The user can interact with a modeless dialog multiple times before it is popped down—modeless dialogs will often have separate **Apply** and **Dismiss** buttons.

The Motif library distinguishes four kinds of modality for a dialog: modeless, primary modal, full modal, and system modal. To specify the modality of a dialog, set the XmBulletinBoard XmNdialogStyle resource of the child of the dialog shell to one ofthe following: XmDIALOG_MODELESS, XmDIALOG_PRIMARY_APPLICATION_MODAL, XmDIALOG_FULL_APPLICATION_MODAL, or XmDIALOG_SYSTEM_MODAL. A dialog that is "primary modal" only blocks out input to its ancestor shells. In an application that has two toplevel shells, a primary modal dialog would only block out input to one of them. A "full modal" dialog blocks out input to all the shells in an application. A "system modal" dialog blocks out input to all applications running on the desktop—this is a very extreme kind of modality, and there are very few situations in which it is appropriate.

Note though, that "primary" and "system" modality require the cooperation of the window manager, and if your users are not running *mwm*, all modal dialogs will probably have "full modal" behavior.

—djf

XmtDisplayWarning() and XmtDisplayError() display their messages in modal dialog boxes, which block out user input to the rest of the application until the user dismisses them. XmtDisplayInformation(), on the other hand, displays its message in a modeless dialog—the user is free to keep the informational or help message around while he continues to use the application. Since it is possible to have several of these modeless dialogs displayed at once, XmtDisplayInformation() takes an additional fourth argument, which specifies the title that should appear in the dialog's title bar. This title can be used to distinguish the purpose of multiple informational dialogs—one might be titled **Help on Help**, for example, and another **Help on Saving Files**.

Figure 25-1 shows some dialogs created by these three functions, and Example 25-1 shows C code that could be used to display these messages. Note that the dialogs are implemented with the XmMessageBox widget, and that the icons displayed in each dialog are the standard Motif warning, error, and information icons. The XmMessageBox widget does not display scrolled text, so you'll probably want to limit your messages to fewer than 20 lines or so.

Example 25-1. Displaying Messages with the Simple Message Dialog Functions

```
XmtDisplayWarning(w, "notfound", "Configuration file not found.");
XmtDisplayError(w, "nomem", "Filesystem full; save not performed.");
XmtDisplayInformation(w, "about", /* Note ANSI string concatenation below */
                      "@f[BIG]   -=|  Xfrob  |=-\n"
                      "@fIxfrob was written by Ben Bitdiddle.\n"
                      "Copyright \251 1994 by Ben.\n",
                      "About xfrob");
```

Example 25-2 shows similar calls specified as callbacks in a resource file. When calling these functions from a resource file, note that no widget argument is required. These functions are registered with the String-to-Callback converter in such a way that the invoking widget is automatically passed as the first argument.

Example 25-2. Displaying Messages from a Resource File

```
*menubar*undo.activateCallback: XmtDisplayWarning(NYI, Not Yet Implemented);
*menubar*about.activateCallback: \
       XmtDisplayInformation(about, \
                                   @f[BIG]   -=|  Xfrob  |=-\n\
@fIxfrob was written by Ben Bitdiddle.\n\
Copyright \251 1994 by Ben.\n,\
                                   About xfrob);
```

25.1.1 Message Names

An important requirement for the message dialogs in Xmt was that they should be customizable from a resource file. This allows internationalization—the ability to run applications in different languages. In order for a dialog to be customized through a resource file, it needs a unique name. Typically, the specified name would be used as the name of the dialog widget, but this conflicts with another design constraint of the message dialog system: for efficiency, the dialogs are created once and then cached for re-use; it is not possible to customize messages using the dialog widget name because the same widget may be used to display many different messages.

The *msg_name* argument to the above functions provides the name that allows customizability. Don't think of this name as a dialog name; think of it as a message name. Later in the chapter, we'll explain just how you'd use this name to customize a message. For now, be aware that you must specify a unique message name for each dialog if you want those messages to be individually customizable. If you are certain that your messages will never need customization, you may specify NULL for the *msg_name* argument.

Similarly, since messages are customizable, you can also specify NULL for the *msg* and *title* arguments to the message dialog functions, and instead specify a message and title from the resource file. I recommend that you use the *msg* and *title* arguments to specify useful default values, but also specify a unique *msg_name* so that you later have the option of overriding these default values.

25.2 Message Dialogs with Substitutions

In the introduction to this chapter, we said that displaying a message in a dialog box should be as easy as calling printf(). The message dialog functions described in the previous section are the simplest available in the Xmt library, and they are as easy to call as printf() is. But the analogy isn't quite a valid one, since those functions don't allow argument substitution into the message in the way that printf() does. This section describes some more complicated Xmt message dialog functions that do allow argument substitution, and have other features as well:

Xmt/

MsgDialogs.c

```
#include <Xmt/Dialogs.h>
void XmtDisplayWarningMsg(Widget w, String msg_name, String msg,
                              String title, String help, ...);
void XmtDisplayErrorMsg(Widget w, String msg_name, String msg,
                            String title, String help, ...);
void XmtDisplayInformationMsg(Widget w, String msg_name, String msg,
                                  String title, String help, ...);
```

These three functions are slightly more complicated versions of the three functions introduced above. They have the same widget, message name, and message arguments as the simpler functions, and all three of these more complicated functions have title arguments (not just the modeless XmtDisplayInformationMsg()). There are two important new features to these functions, however. The first, as promised, is that these functions accept printf()-style substitutions (%s, %d, %f, and so forth) in their message arguments, and take a printf()-style variable-length argument list of values to substitute into the message.

The second major new feature of these functions is that they take an optional help message argument. If this argument is not NULL, then the dialog box will display a **Help** button. If the user clicks on this button, then the contents of the help message will be appended to the displayed message. Figure 25-2 shows a dialog before and after its help message has been displayed. This optional help message may be useful to you when you have additional information that will only be of interest to novice users. It may also be useful for particularly technical information that will only be of interest to very experienced users. Using this information as a help message makes it available, but doesn't distract from the main point of the message aimed at the majority of your users. Note that this help information does not pop up in a dialog of its own, as is traditional, because these message dialogs are too small to warrant subdialogs.

examples/

25/msgdialog

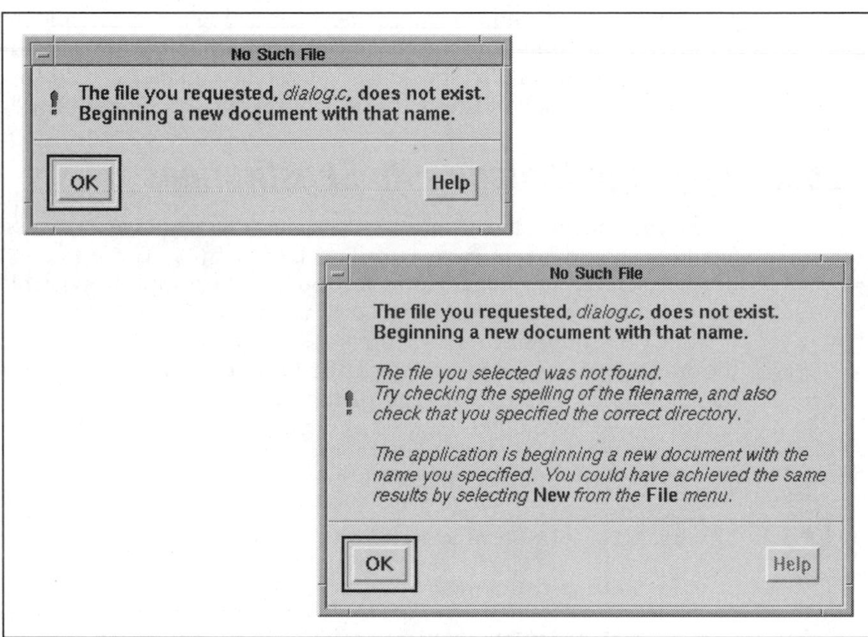

Figure 25-2. A message and its help

As with their simpler counterparts, XmtDisplayWarningMsg() and XmtDisplayErrorMsg() each display modal dialogs, and XmtDisplayInformationMsg() displays a modeless dialog. The dialogs will each display the standard Motif warning, error, and information icons.

25.3 General-Purpose Message Dialogs

All the message dialog functions presented so far in this chapter are simplified versions of a single function, XmtDisplayMessage():

Xmt/

MsgDialogs.c

```
#include <Xmt/Dialogs.h>
void XmtDisplayMessage(Widget w, String msg_name, String msg_class,
                       String message, String title,
                       String help, Pixmap icon,
                       int modality, int type, ...);
```

This function allows substitutions into the message, and lets you explicitly specify both the dialog icon and its modality.

You are already familiar with most of the arguments to this new function. The *msg_class* argument is a new one; it specifies a resource class to be used with *msg_name* for dialog customizations. The *icon* argument specifies a pixmap to display in place of the standard Motif icon. This argument is optional—specify None to omit it.

The *modality* argument specifies whether the dialog should be modal or modeless, and should be one of the four standard Motif values: XmDIALOG_MODELESS, XmDIALOG_PRIMARY_APPLICATION_MODAL, XmDIALOG_FULL_APPLICATION_MODAL, or XmDIALOG_SYSTEM_MODAL.

The *type* argument specifies the default values to use if *msg_class*, *title*, or *icon* are left unspecified. It should be XmDIALOG_WARNING, XmDIALOG_ERROR, or XmDIALOG_INFORMATION if you want one of the standard default icons, or XmDIALOG_MESSAGE if you are supplying your own icon or want no icon displayed at all.

Example 25-3 shows how you might use XmtDisplayMessage() in place of perror() when a system call returns an error status. Figure 25-3 shows a dialog displayed using this function.

Example 25-3. Using XmtDisplayMessage()

```
extern int errno;

void xperror(Widget w, String msg)
{
    char name[10];

    sprintf(name, "osError%d", errno);
    XmtDisplayMessage(w, name, "OSError",          /* widget, name, class */
                      "%s\n    @fI%s@fP",          /* message template default */
                      "Operating System Error",    /* title default */
                      NULL,                        /* help */
                      None,                        /* icon default */
                      XmDIALOG_PRIMARY_APPLICATION_MODAL,    /* modality */
                      XmDIALOG_ERROR,              /* type */
                      msg, strerror(errno));       /* substitution strings */
}
```

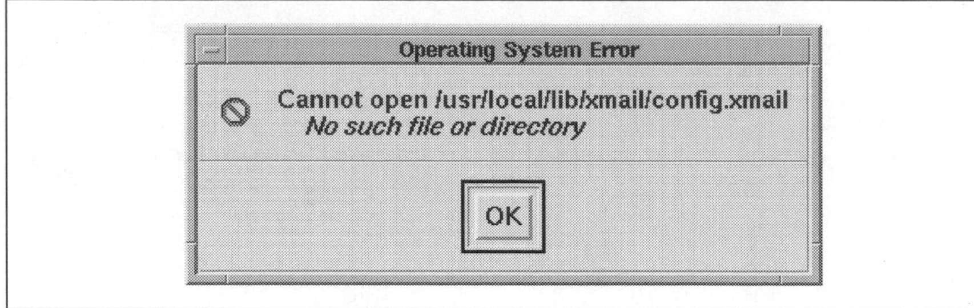

Figure 25-3. A dialog generated with XmtDisplayMessage()

`XmtDisplayMessageVaList()` is a version of `XmtDisplayMessage()` that takes a `va_list` argument instead of a regular `printf()`-style variable-length argument list.

Xmt/

MsgDialogs.c

```
#include <Xmt/Dialogs.h>
void XmtDisplayMessageVaList(Widget w, String msg_name, String msg_class,
                             String message, String title,
                             String help, Pixmap icon,
                             int modality, int type, va_list args)
```

If `XmtDisplayMessage()` is an analog to `printf()`, then `XmtDisplayMessageVaList()` is an analog to `vprintf()`. It is useful when you want to write your own high-level message display functions that take a `printf()`-style argument list, and use the Xmt message dialog functions internally.

25.4 Message Dialogs That Block

The function `printf()` prints its message to stdout and returns immediately to the caller. Similarly, the message dialog functions we have seen so far pop up a dialog box containing their message and immediately return. This is usually, but not always, the desired behavior. There are circumstances when it is more appropriate or more convenient to display the message and then wait until the user responds by clicking the **OK** button to dismiss it. To meet this need, the Xmt library contains blocking versions of three of the message dialog functions we've seen so far:

Xmt/

MsgDialogs.c

```
#include <Xmt/Dialogs.h>
void XmtDisplayWarningMsgAndWait(Widget w, String msg_name, String msg,
                                 String title, String help, ...);
```

```
void XmtDisplayErrorMsgAndWait(Widget w, String msg_name, String msg,
                               String title, String help, ...);
void XmtDisplayMessageAndWait(Widget w, String msg_name, String msg_class,
                              String message, String title,
                              String help, Pixmap icon,
                              int modality, int type, ...);
```

The arguments to these `AndWait` functions are the same as those to their non-blocking relatives. One important difference between blocking and non-blocking versions is that it does not make sense to block for a modeless dialog, since the user can continue to work with the application while the dialog is popped up. This is why there is no function `XmtDisplayInformationMsgAndWait()`. It also means that the *`modality`* argument to `XmtDisplayMessageAndWait()` must not be `XmDIALOG_MODELESS`.

An example of where you might use `XmtDisplayErrorMsgAndWait()` is in a fatal error handler procedure. You could pop up the message "Sorry, a fatal system error has occurred. Click OK to terminate the application.", wait until the user clicks **OK**, and then exit. You may find that when you display an error or a warning message, you may actually want to ask the user for some input, as in the message "Can't save file; file system is full. Abort or Retry?" In this case, you'd use the function `XmtDisplayErrorAndAsk()`. Since it returns input from the user, this is not actually a message dialog. This function is described in Chapter 26, *Simple Input Dialogs.*

25.5 Customizing Message Dialogs

All of the message dialog functions presented in this chapter are customizable through the resource database. If you specify a *`msg_name`* argument to any of these functions, then Xmt will look up resources in the database to override the message, title, help, and icon of the dialog. The resources are looked up as a subpart of the shell over which the dialog is popped up. The name of the subpart is specified by the *`msg_name`* argument. The names of the resources that are looked up are given in Table 25-1.

Table 25-1. Resources for Customizing a Message Dialog

Name	Class	Type	Purpose
message	Message	String	The text of the message to display
helpText	HelpText	String	The help text to display
title	Title	String	The name to appear in the title bar
icon	Icon	Pixmap	The icon to display

Note that these resources allow customization based on the message name passed (the *msg_name* argument) to each of the simple message functions. As we saw before, the XmMessageBox widgets used by these functions are cached, so it is not possible to customize any single message based on an actual widget name. The subsections after this one show how you can customize an entire class of messages (e.g., all warning messages or all error messages) and how you can actually set resources on the message dialog widgets to customize *all* message dialogs, as shown in Figure 25-5.

examples/

25/msgdialog

Figure 25-4. A customized message dialog

Suppose you were going to use `XmtDisplayWarning()` to display a message dialog over your toplevel shell. If the *msg_name* argument were `notfound`, and the name of the shell widget were `xmail` then you could customize the message string for that named message with a resource specification like this:

```
demo.notfound.message: @f[BIG]Warning:\nConfiguration file not found.
```

If you knew that there was only one message named `notfound` in the application (or if you wanted to customize all dialogs with that name), you might use lines like these to customize the title, the icon, and the help:

```
*notfound.title: Configuration Warning
*notfound.icon: newwarning
*notfound.helpText:\
\n@fIThis application may be installed incorrectly.\n\
Consult your system administrator, or see\n\
Chapter 1, Installation, in the manual.
```

Figure 25-4 shows the results of this customization. Compare it to the uncustomized dialog shown at the beginning of the chapter.

You can specify any of these resources for any message dialog, even those produced by the simpler functions that do not have title, help, and icon arguments. Note that a resource specification like these is the only way that you can customize the title of a dialog displayed by `XmtDisplayWarning()` or `XmtDisplayError()`.

25.5.1 Customizing Dialogs by Class

One useful feature of the resource database is that you can specify widgets and resources by class rather than by name, thus affecting a group of widgets or a group of resources with a single specification. The same holds true for message dialogs—each message has a class as well as a name, so you can customize a whole group of related dialogs with a single specification.

If you use `XmtDisplayMessage()` or `XmtDisplayMessageAndWait()`, then you can specify the class directly with the *msg_class* argument. For the remaining functions, or if you specify `NULL` for *msg_class*, then the class depends upon the type of the dialog (as specified implicitly by the function or by the *type* argument), and is one of: `XmtWarningDialog`, `XmtErrorDialog`, `XmtInformationDialog`, or `XmtMessageDialog`.

Example 25-3 showed how you could use `XmtDisplayMessage()` to create a dialog-based analog to the `perror()` function. The dialogs created by that example code all had class `OSError`. To specify an icon for all of these dialogs, you could use a specification like this:

```
*OSError.icon: bomb
```

(This assumes that `bomb` is the name of a bitmap or pixmap that the String-to-Pixmap resource converter can find.)

Similarly, you could set the icon and title of all warning message dialogs with this specification.

```
*XmtWarningMsg.icon: warning_icon
*XmtWarningMsg.title: Achtung
```

Overriding the Standard Motif Icons

The default Motif message dialog icons suffer from several problems: they are too small to be detailed and interesting; they are too small to add much visual impact to the dialogs they decorate; and they are monochrome.

Fortunately, however, these icons are not set in stone. Create a directory named *bitmaps* in your home directory, or in your `XAPPLRESDIR` directory, if you have set that environment variable. Then place XBM bitmap files in this directory with the names *xm_error*, *xm_information*, *xm_question*, *xm_working*, and *xm_warning*. The XmMessageBox widget will read these files when it is first initialized and will use the icons they contain instead of the standard icons, as shown in Figure 25-5.

Overriding the Standard Motif Icons (continued)

examples/

25/{old,new}icons

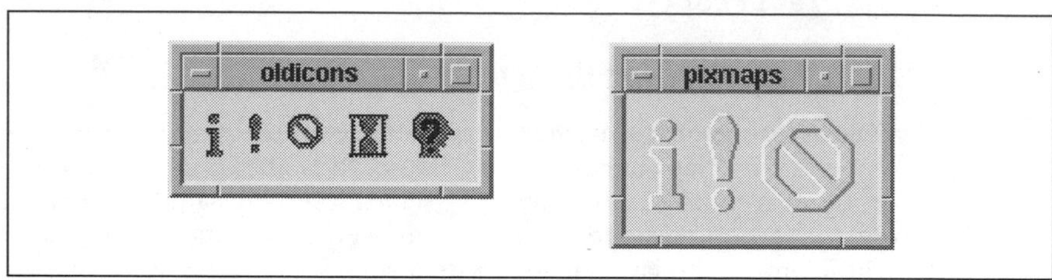

Figure 25-5. The standard Motif icons and some alternatives

Installing the bitmaps like this will affect all Motif applications you run. There are other places you can install these bitmap files, including directories where they will only affect certain applications, and directories under */usr/lib/X11* where they will affect all XmMessageBox widgets for all users on the system. See the documentation for `XmGetPixmap()` for details.

If you want to override the standard icons for an application you are developing, rather than just for applications you run, you can set the `XBMLANGPATH` environment variable in your application to specify a directory in which your application's bitmaps have been installed. Again, see the documentation for `XmGetPixmap()` for more details.

A problem, however, with using bitmap files like this is that it limits you to monochrome icons. Another approach is to use `XmInstallImage()` to register color images with the names `xm_error`, `xm_warning`, and so on. The trick to using this function is that you must obtain your icon in `XImage` format. You can convert an XPM pixmap file to an `XImage` with functions in the native XPM library, or with a combination of `XmtParseXpmFile()` and `XmtCreateXImageFromXmtImage()`. See Chapter 5, *Using Icons*, for more information.

This XPM data to `XImage` conversion is exactly what the function `XmtRegisterImprovedIcons()` does:

Xmt/

Icons.c

```
#include <Xmt/Pixmap.h>
void XmtRegisterImprovedIcons(Widget w, XmtColorTable ctable);
```

If you call this function in your application before you create any XmMessageBox widgets, you'll get the larger "improved" information, warning, and error icons shown in the figure above. Although these are color icons, they are designed to work well on monochrome screens as well.

Overriding the Standard Motif Icons (continued)

You can pass any widget to `XmtRegisterImprovedIcons()`, and can specify `NULL` for the colortable argument—the colors in the default colortable are usually appropriate. You can register the icons from a resource file with a line like the following. Note the use of a dummy colortable:

```
*layout.xmtCreationCallback: XmtRegisterImprovedIcons(self, dummy=black);
```

—*djf*

25.5.2 Customizing Dialog Widgets Directly

The customization examples mentioned previously have shown how to specify per-message resources in the database. These are the resources that are explicitly looked up at each call to `XmtDisplayMessage()` and its relatives. It is also possible to specify resources for the dialog widgets themselves. The XmMessageBox widget created by all of the message dialog functions is named `xmtMessageDialog`, so if you wanted, for example, to change the **OK** button to read "Dismiss" you could use this resource specification:

```
*xmtMessageDialog.okLabelString: Dismiss
```

This resource specification will affect *all* messages displayed by all message dialog functions.

You can also specify widget resources that will affect only messages that appear over a particular shell. (The widgets used by the message dialog functions are cached on a per-shell basis.) For example, an application that had two toplevel shells distinguished by different background colors might want to set the background colors of its message dialogs to some color that complements the main window color:

```
*shell1*background: beige
*shell1*xmtMessageDialog.background: tan

*shell2*background: grey
*shell2*xmtMessageDialog.background: lightblue
```

25.5.3 Argument Substitution and Customized Messages

`printf()`-style functions can be a source of bugs in applications, since most compilers cannot perform type-checking on their variable-length argument list, and because a type mismatch between a substitution character in the format string and the corresponding argument in the argument list can often cause a core-dump.* When the message containing the substitution characters can be

*If you use *gcc*, however, you can use the `-Wformat` command-line argument to have it perform type-checking on `printf()`-style argument lists.

customized through the resource database, however, you have to be especially careful.

If you will be allowing end users or administrators to customize the messages for their own use, then you must document the type of each substitution and the order of the substitutions, so that they can produce customized versions of the message. If the *msg* argument is specified, and an overriding value for the message is found in the resource database, then `XmtDisplayMessage()` (or any of its relatives) will call the special function `XmtCheckPrintfFormat()` to verify that the substitutions in the new message match the types of the old message. If they do match, then the new message will be used. If they do not match, then `XmtDisplayMessage()` will print a warning message to the terminal, and will use the original message. For this reason, it is always a good idea to provide a default message when you call `XmtDisplayMessage()`. If you plan to get the actual message text from the resource database, you can use the *msg* argument to specify a simple template that allows argument type checking. Note that this call to `XmtCheckPrintfFormat()` is intended only to prevent the most common type of error when using customized messages with `printf()`-style functions; it is not a guarantee that the substitutions in a message are entirely well-formed, or that a given message won't trigger a core dump.

Note that many systems now provide an internationalized version of `printf()` which allows substitutions to be made in a different order than that in which they are provided. If your `printf()` allows this, then you can change a format string like `%s %d` to `%2$d %1$s` without changing the order in which the string and integer arguments are specified. Note that `XmtCheckPrintf-Format()` recognizes this syntax as legal, even if your version of `printf()` doesn't.

Finally, don't forget that you must use `%%` if you want the percent character by itself in your message. This is necessary even if the message does not contain any `printf()` substitutions and has an empty variable-length argument list.

25.6 Other Types of Messages and Other Types of Dialogs

The Xmt message dialog functions make it very easy to display messages in simple dialog boxes. But don't fall into the trap of abusing this capability. Sometimes there are other ways to display a message that are more appropriate, and sometimes there are other types of dialogs that are more appropriate.

The message dialog functions are GUI analogs to `printf()`, but there are times when `printf()` itself is the right way to display a message. If the message is an error or debugging message intended for the programmer or system administrator, for example, then it probably does not need to appear in a dialog box. (Ideally, these messages will never appear, anyway, by the time the user sees the application.) Instead of using `printf()` or `fprintf()` to display these messages, you'll probably want to use `XtWarning()`, `XtWarning-Msg()`, or the easier-to-use functions `XmtWarningMsg()` and `Xmt-`

`ErrorMsg()`. All of these functions will send a message to the standard error stream.

Before you decide to display a message in a dialog box, consider that the user will have to go to some effort to dismiss the dialog box and get on with her work. Use message dialogs when the user has specifically requested information, or when an error or warning occurs that is important enough to demand serious attention. Routine messages should be displayed in a less intrusive way. If the user attempts to load a file that doesn't exist, you might decide that this is a routine error, and simply choose to display the message ("File not found.") in the application's message line, instead of popping up a dialog box. (Obviously, if the application were intended for very novice users, you might choose to use a dialog box instead.) A dialog box draws attention to itself very distinctly when it pops up. You could draw sufficient attention to your "File not found" message in a message line, however, by calling `XBell()` to make the computer beep. Message lines are discussed in detail in Chapter 22, *The Message Line.*

Similarly, if you have a multi-line message to display, or perhaps a startup message, you might be better off displaying this (non-critical) information in a text widget or command-line interface (assuming that your application will have such a widget anyway; see Chapter 21, *Command-Line Input*). You could also display a short message, like a copyright or application version number, in a message line widget or in a window's title bar.

Sometimes it is appropriate to display a message in a dialog box, but the message dialog functions are not sufficient for the purpose. We've already mentioned that many error (and some warning) conditions require a response from the user ("Retry or Abort?"). The functions `XmtDisplayWarningAndAsk()` and `XmtDisplayErrorAndAsk()` are useful in these cases, and are described in Chapter 26, *Simple Input Dialogs.* That chapter also describes a number of other functions that prompt the user with a message and return the user's input.

Another common kind of message to display is the "Working; please wait" variety. This kind of message has some special requirements, and functions to handle them are discussed in Chapter 31, *Busy States and Background Work.*

Finally, while `XmtDisplayInformation()` and related functions are suitable for displaying a paragraph of help text, they are not really suitable for anything beyond that, because the text displayed is not scrollable. Displaying larger amounts of help information is a specialized task, and Chapter 30, *Context Help*, presents a widget and convenience functions for displaying scrolled context-help messages.

25.7 Style

The first question to ask about any message dialog is whether it is actually necessary. Consider the points in the previous section, and if you can communicate the information to the user with any other technique, while still conveying the necessary urgency, then do so. Any dialog box that pops up, particularly those that were not specifically requested by the user will interrupt the flow of her work, so it is important to have sufficient reason to create one.

And the second important question to ask is whether your message says what it needs to. Obviously you should check your spelling and grammar, but also check to see that your message is succinct. Avoid jargon; don't use big words or fancy phrases when you don't have to. Don't forget that the user is interested in different things than you, the programmer, are. If an error dialog appears, the user isn't interested in the name of the procedure that generated the error, for example, but he is very interested to know whether his work will be lost as a result of this error. You should phrase your messages in terms that the user cares about: tell him just what he needs to know to go about the task he's working on, and don't confuse him with other details.

If your message is a long one, remember that you can break it into paragraphs: just put two newline characters in a row in the message. When displaying paragraph-length messages using a proportional font, check that the line breaks occur in reasonable places—the XmMessageBox widget will not word-wrap your XmString message for you, so you have to use trial-and-error to verify that each of the lines is approximately the same length.

If your application will be used by novice users, consider providing help information with some of your messages. If you display a "File not found" message, for example, you might add an additional help message that suggests to novice users that they check their spelling of the filename, and check that the directory they specified actually exists. You can also use these help messages as a way to present additional information that is important but won't be of interest to most users.

Consider using custom icons in your dialogs. The default Motif icons are a standard, but not a particularly useful standard, and the icons are unattractive. If you use message dialogs to display several different classes of messages, different icons for each class will serve to distinguish the classes, and give the user a quick initial cue as to what the message will be about.

Finally, remember that you can use the Xmt `@f` escape sequence to change fonts within a message. You can use this feature to provide emphasis for certain words or important parts of the message, or even to provide a title for a message. It can also be useful to display a help message in a different font from the main message—this serves to set it off as additional information.

25.8 Summary

This chapter presented a number of functions for simple message display:

- Use the functions `XmtDisplayWarning()`, `XmtDisplayError()`, and `XmtDisplayInformation()` in order to display simple messages without `printf()`-style substitutions or help text.

- Use `XmtDisplayWarningMsg()`, `XmtDisplayErrorMsg()`, and `XmtDisplayInformationMsg()` to display messages with variable substitutions, a specified title, and optional help text.
- Use the function `XmtDisplayMessage()` when you want to display messages with a custom class and icon.
- Use the functions `XmtDisplayWarningMsgAndWait()`, `XmtDisplayErrorMsgAndWait()`, and `XmtDisplayMessageAndWait()` to display a message in a modal dialog and wait synchronously until the user dismisses it.
- If you specify the *msg_name* argument to these functions, then they will be customizable through the resource database using the specified message name and the `message`, `helpText`, `title`, and `icon` resources. Specify a *msg_name* of NULL to *prevent* customization.

26

Simple Input Dialogs

Chapter 25, *Message Dialogs*, describes a number of reasons why the Motif convenience dialogs are inconvenient for displaying simple messages. Many of the same reasons apply to the Motif simple input dialogs. The Motif library provides functions like `XmCreatePromptDialog()` that create a dialog box which contains a prompt string and a Text widget for the user's reply, but creating the dialog is only the beginning of the process. The programmer must create an XmString, set it as the prompt in the dialog, pop the dialog up, register a callback to be notified when the user clicks **OK**, get the user's string from within that callback, and then, finally, use that string in the program. In a terminal-based application, on the other hand, the programmer can call `printf()` to display a prompt and `scanf()` to get the user's reply as a string, integer, or whatever. In this chapter we present functions that make it easy to get simple user input through dialog boxes.

26.1 Synchronous Input Dialogs

What is so convenient about `scanf()` is that it blocks—the programmer calls it, and when it returns the user's input is ready and the programmer can proceed to process it as necessary. With message dialogs we saw that the object-oriented metaphor was too cumbersome for simple message display. So we developed convenience routines that caused messages to be displayed in dialog boxes without exposing the programmer to the creation or management of the dialog box objects themselves. In the case of dialogs for simple input, it seems that the event-driven programming model is also too cumbersome for real convenience. In this chapter we'll develop routines that display input dialogs (hiding the details of dialog creation and management) and have the same synchronous behavior as `scanf()`—i.e., they return the user's input directly.

It is the nature of event-driven programming that blocking calls, like `scanf()` are not allowed; the application must always be waiting in an event loop, ready to respond to mouse input, keyboard input, exposure events, and so on. The classic event-driven program has only a single event loop from which all events are dispatched, and to which control returns after every event is handled. If we are willing to abandon the purity of this model (purists beware!) we can write functions that appear to block and display the synchronous behavior we desire.

Suppose we want to write a function `XmtAskForString()` which displays a dialog box like that created by `XmCreatePromptDialog()` and returns the user's input in a buffer and a `Boolean` value indicating whether the user clicked on the **OK** or the **Cancel** button. This routine could pop up the dialog, and then enter a private event loop. This private event loop would handle input for the dialog box, handle things like Expose events for the rest of the application, and would exit only when the user had clicked on either the **OK** or the **Cancel** button. When the user selects a button, control returns to the `XmtAskForString()` function, which copies the user's input out of the widget and into the supplied buffer, and then returns either `True` or `False` to the application, depending on which button was selected. The application acts on the response and then presumably returns control to the main application event loop.

It is important to notice that this technique should not be used with modeless dialogs. If it is, flow of control for the application could get nested deeper and deeper in recursive event loops as the user popped up dialogs without responding to them. In fact, we must restrict this technique to dialogs which are modal across the entire application, not just modal for a single window of the application. When a programmer calls a function like `XmtAskForString()`, he makes the assumption that the state of the application will not change between the time he asks for the input and the time he gets it. If, while a dialog is prompting the user for input over one shell, the user goes and changes a parameter global to the application from another shell, then the procedure that popped up the original dialog may not correctly process the user's input. Even with these restrictions, though, simple synchronous input functions are convenient enough to be worthwhile. Figure 26-1 diagrams this sort of synchronous behavior through recursive event loops.

All of the simple input functions described in this chapter have this kind of synchronous behavior. They also have some other features in common, features very much like those of the simple message functions described in Chapter 25. These common features are described in the following subsections.

26.1.1 Dialog Caching, Naming, and Customization

Like the message dialogs, the input dialogs are created once, and then automatically cached for reuse. Since only one synchronous dialog can ever be active in the application at a time, however, these dialogs do not need to be cached on a one-per-shell basis; instead they are cached on a per-screen basis. (Most applications run on a single screen, and will never need more than one of each type of synchronous dialog. Applications that use multiple screens will need one dialog per screen, however, because while shell widgets can be popped up anywhere on a single screen, they cannot be moved between screens.) As with the message dialogs, each of our simple input functions will take a widget as its first argument. This widget specifies, first, the screen for which the cached dialog should be looked up, and second, the shell widget over which the dialog should be popped up.

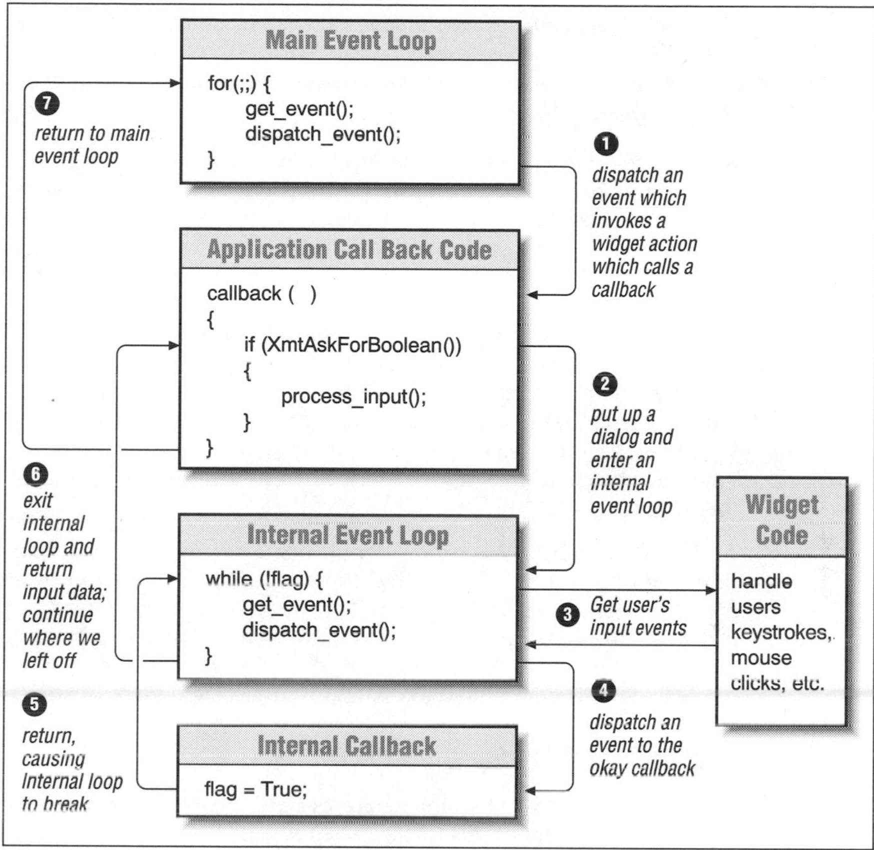

Figure 26-1. Blocking for input with an internal event loop

As with the message dialogs, we want to allow customization of input dialogs through the resource file. But since a single dialog widget is reused each time an input function is called, we cannot specify resources for the dialog widgets directly. Instead, we pass a *query_name* argument to each of the simple input functions—an analog to the *msg_name* argument passed to the simple message functions. This argument provides a unique instance name for each use of the input function, and specifies a location in the resource database under which the dialog's resources can be obtained. An important point to remember about message and query customization in Xmt is that values in the resource database will override values passed directly to the function; this is the opposite of how widget resource values are handled.

Also like the message dialogs, it is possible to directly customize the widgets of the cached simple input dialogs. Any such customization, however, will affect all instances of the dialog on a particular screen. This type of customization can be quite useful for specifying things such as colors and fonts which should affect every instance of the dialog, rather than things such as prompts and button labels, which should only affect individual instances.*

26.1.2 Dialog Help and Titles

Another feature that the simple input functions borrow from the simple message functions is that they all have an optional help string as their last argument. There are a couple of differences, however: while the message dialogs display help by simply appending it to their main message, the more complicated input dialogs display help by popping up a separate message dialog. Also, when there is no help in a message dialog, the **Help** button does not appear. The input dialogs are more complex, and providing online help is more often a requirement. So in this case, when no help is provided, the **Help** button is simply made insensitive, to indicate to users that they can normally find help with that button, but that help is "temporarily" not available for the current dialog. (This feature should also encourage you, the programmer, to at least provide a simple help message, even if it is the same message for all instances of the dialog.)

And finally, each of the simple input functions, like the simple message functions, can have a string specified for the dialog title bar through the resource file. None of the input functions allow the title to be specified as an argument, however, because this is not something that is crucial to be able to customize—since there will never be more than one of these input dialogs active at once, the title is not needed to distinguish the dialog instances from each other.

26.1.3 Cancelling Input

There is one important point where our simple input functions differ from the simple message functions. The message functions simply display a message which the user reads and dismisses. There is no choice involved, and the application is not expecting any input from the user. The simple input functions do expect an interaction with the user, and although we can compare them to `scanf()`, there is an important difference in a graphical interface: with dialog boxes, the user is allowed to abort any operation by clicking the **Cancel** button. All well-designed programs must support the **Cancel** button, and so our simple input functions cannot simply return the user's input, but must also return an indication of whether the user entered the input with the **OK** button or aborted it with the **Cancel** button.

Therefore, our simple input functions (with two special-case exceptions, described later) all have a `Boolean` as their return value. Since the function return value is a status indicator, the user's input will have to be returned indirectly—all the input functions take a character buffer or the address of a variable in which the user's input should be stored. When these functions return

*When you have more than one toplevel shell (i.e., not a dialog shell) on a screen, an interesting point to note is that because the input dialogs are cached on a per-screen basis, rather than a per-shell basis, you cannot know which shell widget the dialog will be created as a child of. Therefore, when specifying resources for these dialogs, you will have to use wildcards.

`True`, it means that the user answered the question that was asked and clicked the **OK** button. In this case, the user's input value will be stored at the specified location. If, on the other hand, these functions return `False`, it means that the user decided not to answer the question and clicked the **Cancel** button. In this case, the input functions guarantee that they will not modify the value stored at the specified address.

When the user clicks **Cancel** when you use a simple input dialog, it means that he wants to abort the entire interaction with the computer; to back out of the operation in progress. If he has selected the **Save As**... item in a menu, and then clicks **Cancel** when you prompt for a filename, for example, it means that he has decided not to save the file after all (or perhaps that his hand slipped, and that he meant to select the **Save** or **Open**... items from the same menu.)

If you use the simple input functions, you must always check and act upon the return value. Example 26-1 shows some common ways that you might structure your code to do this. (The `goto` statement in C is sometimes frowned upon. Note that this example shows one of its legitimate uses.)

Example 26-1. Allowing the User to Cancel Input

```
/*
 * Code structure #1
 */
    char buffer[100];

    /* if user clicked Cancel, return immediately */
    if (!XmtAskForString(..., buffer, ...)) return;

    /* Otherwise, process input normally */

/*
 * Code structure #2; uses XtMalloc() and requires cleanup
 */
    buffer = XtMalloc(100);

    if (XmtAskForString(..., buffer, ...)) {
        /* user clicked "Ok": process the user's input normally */
    }
    else {
        /* user clicked "Cancel", so abort the operation */
        /* first, free any resources already allocated, then return */
        XtFree(buffer)
        return;
    }

/*
 * Code structure #3; multiple calls to input functions
 */
    char *buffer1 = NULL;
    char *buffer2 = NULL;

    buffer1 = XtMalloc(100);
    if (!XmtAskForString(..., buffer1 ...)) goto cleanup;

    buffer2 = XtMalloc(100);
    if (!XmtAskForString(..., buffer2 ...)) goto cleanup;
```

Example 26-1. Allowing the User to Cancel Input (continued)

```
    /*
     * If we get here, then the user answered both questions.
     * So go ahead and process the input normally.
     * and then return.
     */
          .
          .
          .
    return;

cleanup:
    /*
     * If we get here, then the user clicked Cancel at some point.
     * So cleanup and return.
     */
    if (buffer1) XtFree(buffer1);
    if (buffer2) XtFree(buffer2);
    return;
```

These preliminary sections of this chapter have explained a number of the common features of the Xmt simple input functions. With these preliminaries out of the way, the following sections will now explain the details of the individual input functions.

26.2 Getting String Input

You can use the function `XmtAskForString()` to synchronously get string input from the user:

Xmt/

AskForString.c

```
#include <Xmt/Dialogs.h>
Boolean XmtAskForString(Widget w, String query_name,
                        String prompt_default,
                        String buffer, int buffer_length,
                        String help_text_default);
```

Figure 26-2 shows a dialog box created with this function.

As explained above, the first argument *w* is any widget in your interface. The XmPromptDialog used to get the input will be popped up over the shell of this widget. Also, as explained above, *query_name* is the name that is used for customizations to this particular query to the user, and the last argument, *help_text_default*, is a string to appear (unless overridden in the resource database) when the user clicks the **Help** button.

The remaining three arguments are specific to `XmtAskForString()`. Unless overridden in the resource database, *prompt_default* will be converted from a string to an XmString and displayed to prompt the user for input. This string should provide enough information so that the user understands what input is expected of her, and knows what the program will do with it once she enters it.

Figure 26-2. A dialog box displayed by XmtAskForString()

The *buffer* argument is a character buffer. The initial contents of this buffer will be used as the default value to display in the XmTextField of the dialog, and the buffer is also used to return the user's input. Since the initial contents of *buffer* are used by `XmtAskForString()`, you must be sure to initialize it appropriately. If you use a buffer that is an uninitialized automatic variable, for example, you are likely to see a garbage input value in the dialog.

buffer_length specifies the size of the buffer, in bytes—the user will not be allowed to enter more characters than will fit in the buffer. `XmtAskForString()` will always return a NULL-terminated string, so the buffer should in fact be one character longer than the desired maximum input length.

Example 26-2 shows how you might use `XmtAskForString()`. Note, in particular, the use of a static character buffer for input. This buffer automatically starts out empty, and will retain the user's input across invocations of the function. This means that the user's input when first asked the question will become the default value the next time it is asked. Also notice that, for clarity, this example uses the ANSI-C feature of concatenating adjacent strings into a single string.

Example 26-2. Using XmtAskForString()

```
/* ARGSUSED */
static void PrintCallback(Widget w, XtPointer tag, XtPointer data)
{
    static char printer[50];
    Boolean status;

    status = XmtAskForString(w, "printerDialog", "Printer Name:",
                             printer, sizeof(printer),
                             "If you don't know the name of your printer,\n"
                             "then it probably doesn't have one.  Try\n"
                             "clicking @fBOk@fR with no printer name.");
```

Example 26-2. Using XmtAskForString() (continued)

```
    /* If user pressed "Cancel", then abort */
    if (status == False)
        return;

    /* Otherwise go ahead and print.  The printer name is in printer[] */
        .
        .
        .
}
```

26.2.1 Customizing XmtAskForString() Queries

The dialog created by `XmtAskForString()` is an XmSelectionBox named `xmtStringDialog`, and its parent is an XmDialogShell named `xmtStringDialogShell`. You can use these names with wildcards to provide color, font, and similar customizations for these dialog widgets themselves.

In addition, you can provide customizations for individual invocations of the dialog by specifying subpart resources under the name specified by *query_name* or the class `XmtStringDialog`. You should specify these resources under the shell of the specified widget *w*. Table 26-1 lists the resources you can set.

Table 26-1. XmtAskForString() Customization Resources

Resource	Default	Description
`message`	*prompt_default*	Prompt for the dialog
`title`	"Enter a String"	String to appear in the dialog's titlebar
`helpText`	*help_text_default*	Online help for the dialog

Example 26-3 shows how you might use these resources to customize the dialog displayed in the previous example. Note that we use the `@fB` font escape to specify that the prompt should be in bold (assuming that an appropriate font list is defined). You can use font escapes like this in the prompt and the help text, which will be converted to XmStrings before being displayed, but not for the dialog title, which is displayed as an ordinary string by the window manager.

Example 26-3. Customizing an XmtAskForString() Dialog

```
*printerDialog.message: @fBEnter the name of the printer you wish to use:
*printerDialog.title: Enter a Printer Name
*printerDialog.helpText: If you don't know the name of your printer,\n\
ask your system administrator.
```

26.3 Getting Numeric Input

XmtAskForInteger() and XmtAskForDouble() are variations on XmtAskForString() that share the same cached dialog box used by that function, but require that the user's input be a number, optionally within specified bounds.

Xmt/

AskForString.c

```
#include <Xmt/Dialogs.h>
Boolean XmtAskForInteger(Widget w, String query_name,
                         String prompt_default,
                         int *value, int min, int max,
                         String help_text_default);

Boolean XmtAskForDouble(Widget w, String query_name,
                        String prompt_default,
                        double *value, double min, double max,
                        String help_text_default);
```

w, *query_name*, and *help_text_default* are the standard first, second, and last arguments to all of the synchronous input functions; they were explained earlier in the chapter. *prompt_default* is the default prompt to display in the dialog, just as it is for XmtAskForString(). Where these functions differ is in the *value*, *min*, and *max* arguments. *value* is the address of an int or a double that will be used as the default value, and is also the address at which the user's input will be stored. *min* and *max* are lower and upper (inclusive) bounds for the input value.

Figure 26-3 shows dialogs created by these functions.

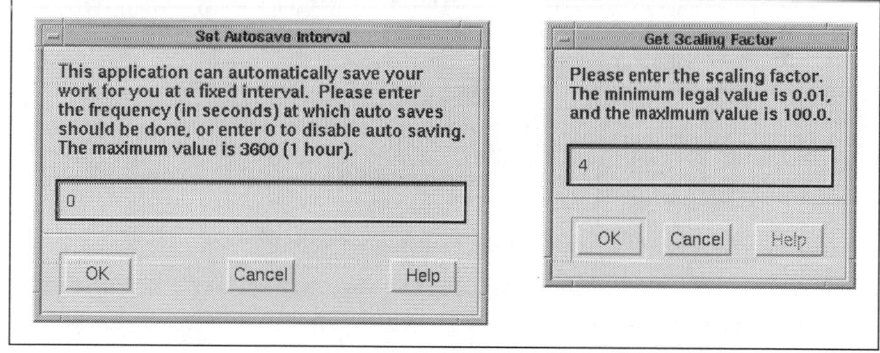

Figure 26-3. Dialogs displayed by XmtAskForInteger() and XmtAskForDouble()

Before XmtAskForInteger() and XmtAskForDouble() return a value, they check that the user's input is a valid int or double value. If the input is valid, then they check that it is greater than or equal to the specified minimum value and less than or equal to the specified maximum value. If any of these tests fail, the function will display an error message (using XmtDisplayError()) and will wait for the user to correct the input and click **OK** again before returning. You can disable the boundary checking on the input value by specifying a *min* and *max* that are equal to each other. 0 or 0.0 is a good choice here. (XmtAskForDouble() takes two double arguments. If you are not using an ANSI-C compiler, remember that the compiler will not automatically promote integers to doubles for you, so be sure that you are using double or float variables, or that you have decimal points in any constant values you use.)

Example 26-4 shows how you might use XmtAskForInteger() and XmtAskForDouble(). Note that both callback procedures shown here check the return value of the input functions they call, and take no action if the user clicks **Cancel**. Also, as with the XmtAskForString() example, both procedures use static variables to retain the input value for use as the default value at the next invocation.

Example 26-4. Using XmtAskForInteger() and XmtAskForDouble()

```
static void AutoSaveCallback(Widget w, XtPointer tag, XtPointer data)
{
    static int auto_save_interval = 300;
    Boolean status =
        XmtAskForInteger(w, "autoSaveIntervalDialog",
                         "This application can automatically save your\n"
                         "work for you at a fixed interval.  Please enter\n"
                         "the frequency (in seconds) at which auto saves\n"
                         "should be done, or enter 0 to disable auto saving.\n"
                         "The maximum value is 3600 (1 hour)."
                         &auto_save_interval, 0, 3600, NULL);
    if (status) SetNewAutoSaveInterval(auto_save_interval);
}

static void ZoomCallback(Widget w, XtPointer tag, XtPointer data)
{
    static double scaling_factor = 2;
    Boolean status;

    status = XmtAskForDouble(w, "zoomFactorDialog",
                             "Enter scaling factor:"
                             &scaling_factor, 0.1, 10.0, NULL);

    /* if the user clicked "Cancel", then abort */
    if (status == False) return;

    /* otherwise go ahead and zoom in or out */
        .
        .
        .
}
```

26.3.1 Customizing Numeric Queries

As mentioned previously, `XmtAskForInteger()` and `XmtAskForDouble()` use the same cached dialog widgets as `XmtAskForString()`. They are an XmSelectionBox widget named `xmtStringDialog` inside of an XmDialogShell named `xmtStringDialogShell`. You can use these names to customize colors, fonts, or similar attributes for the widgets. Because of caching, these customizations will affect all dialogs created by `XmtAskForString()`, `XmtAskForInteger()`, or `XmtAskForDouble()`.

It is also possible to customize the prompt, title, and help text for any individual invocation of these dialogs. `XmtAskForInteger()` and `XmtAskForDouble()` read the same subpart resources as `XmtAskForString()` does; they are shown in Table 26-2. These resources are looked up as a subpart of the shell widget of the argument *w*. The subpart name is specified by *query_name*, and its class is `XmtIntDialog` or `XmtDoubleDialog`.

Table 26-2. XmtAskForInteger() and XmtAskForDouble() Customization Resources

Resource	Default	Description
`message`	*prompt_default*	Prompt for the dialog
`title`	"Enter an Integer" or "Enter a Number"	String to appear in the dialog's titlebar
`helpText`	*help_text_default*	Online help for the dialog

In addition to customizing the input dialogs themselves, you can also customize the error messages they display. `XmtAskForInteger()` and `XmtAskForDouble()` can display four different error dialogs with `XmtDisplayError()`. The names and default messages for these dialogs are shown in Table 26-3. See Chapter 25, *Message Dialogs,* if you need a refresher on how to customize these simple error dialogs. Note, however, that if you customize these error dialogs, the customizations will have effect for all invocations of the input dialog.

Table 26-3. XmtAskForInteger() and XmtAskForDouble() Error Dialogs

Dialog Name	Default Message	When Displayed
`xmtBadIntDialog`	"Please enter an integer."	Invalid integer input
`xmtBadDoubleDialog`	"Please enter a number."	Invalid double input
`xmtTooSmallDialog`	"Please enter a larger number."	input < *min* for either function
`xmtTooBigDialog`	"Please enter a smaller number."	input > *max* for either function

Example 26-5 shows how you might use resources to customize the dialogs created by the previous example, and also to customize the error dialogs displayed by those dialogs.

Example 26-5. Customizing the XmtAskForInteger() and XmtAskForDouble() Dialogs

```
*autoSaveIntervalDialog.title: Set Autosave Interval
*zoomFactorDialog.title: Get Scaling Factor

*zoomFactorDialog.message: \
Please enter the scaling factor.\n\
The minimum legal value is 0.01,\n\
and the maximum value is 100.0.

*zoomFactorDialog.helpText:\
The scaling factor specifies how many times the image should be enlarged.\n\
Numbers greater than 1.0 magnify the image or zoom in.\n\
Numbers between 0.0 and 1.0 shrink the image or zoom out.

*xmtBadIntDialog.message: @fIYour input was not a valid integer.\n\
Please try again.

*xmtTooSmallDialog.message: @fIThe number you entered is too small.\n\
Please enter a larger one.

*xmtTooBigDialog.message: @fIThe number you entered is too large.\n\
Please enter a smaller one.
```

26.4 Getting Yes or No (or Cancel) Input

At first glance it would seem that `XmtAskForBoolean()` would be very similar to `XmtAskForString()`. We would change the XmSelectionBox widget to an XmMessageBox widget and pass a `Boolean *` instead of a character buffer for the returned value. In fact, `XmtAskForBoolean()` turns out to be significantly more complicated than this:

Xmt/

AskForBool.c

```
#include <Xmt/Dialogs.h>
Boolean XmtAskForBoolean(Widget w, String query_name,
                         String prompt_default,
                         String yes_default, String no_default,
                         String cancel_default,
                         XmtButtonType default_button_default,
                         int icon_type_default,
                         Boolean show_cancel_button,
                         Boolean *value_return,
                         String help_text_default)
```

This function does have the standard arguments: *`w`*, *`query_name`*, *`prompt_default`*, and *`help_text_default`*, and it does indeed take the address of a `Boolean` variable as its *`value_return`* argument, in which to return the user's input. There are six other arguments, however, which require some explanation.

First, notice that the expected answers to a yes-or-no question aren't always "Yes" and "No"; they could be "Yes, save and quit" and "No, quit without saving," or even "On" and "Off," so we have to specify labels for the **Yes** and **No** buttons in the dialog with the *`yes_default`* and *`no_default`* arguments. These are `String` arguments which are, as usual, overridden by values from the resource database, and which will be automatically converted to the requisite XmString values.

Second, recall that the Motif function `XmCreateMessageBox()` creates a dialog box with three buttons: **OK**, **Cancel**, and **Help**. If we label the **OK** button with the "yes" response, and the **Cancel** button with the "no" response, and use the **Help** button to display the optional help text, then we are left with no button labeled "Cancel." For some questions, answering "No" is equivalent to selecting **Cancel**: a user who selects the "Save As . . . " menu item in an application might see a dialog that asks "A file by that name already exists. Overwrite it?". In this case, answering "yes" means continue with the save operation, and answering "no" means cancel the operation. There are other questions, however, that admit three possible answers. When asked "There are unsaved files. Save them before quitting?", for example, a user should have three choices: "Yes, save and quit," "No, quit without saving," and "Cancel. Don't quit." Generally, when `XmtAskForBoolean()` is called as a direct result of a user action (instead of an error condition, for example) it should have a cancel button to abort the operation.

What this means is that `XmtAskForBoolean()` will not use an XmMessageBox widget; instead it will create its own custom dialog (implemented with the XmtLayout widget) that displays the message and four buttons. Figure 26-4 shows a dialog created by `XmtAskForBoolean()`.

What this also means is that the function takes a *`cancel_default`* argument to specify the (overridable) label for the **Cancel** button. We could specify that if this *`cancel_default`* argument is `NULL`, and if there is no overriding value in the resource database then the **Cancel** button will not appear in the dialog. This is not a good idea, however, because although the label of the button should be overridable from the resource database, the presence or absence of the button should not be. A programmer who specified that no **Cancel** button will appear in a particular dialog may rely on the fact that `XmtAskForBoolean()` will always return `True` for that dialog. If a user could add a **Cancel** button to the dialog, even when that was not an option supported by the program, then problems could arise. So we will add another, non-overridable, argument, *`show_cancel_button`*, which specifies whether or not a **Cancel** button should be added to the dialog.

Motif dialogs support the concept of a default button—the button that will be activated when the user hits the **Return** key. For consistency with the other simple input functions, we could use the *`value_return`* argument to also specify the default value, which in this case is a button. There are two problems with this approach, however. First, it is bad style to have a default that switches from one button to another, and could even be dangerous in some cases. The default for "Do you really want to reformat your disk?" should always be the **No** button, even if the user clicked on the **Yes** button the last time

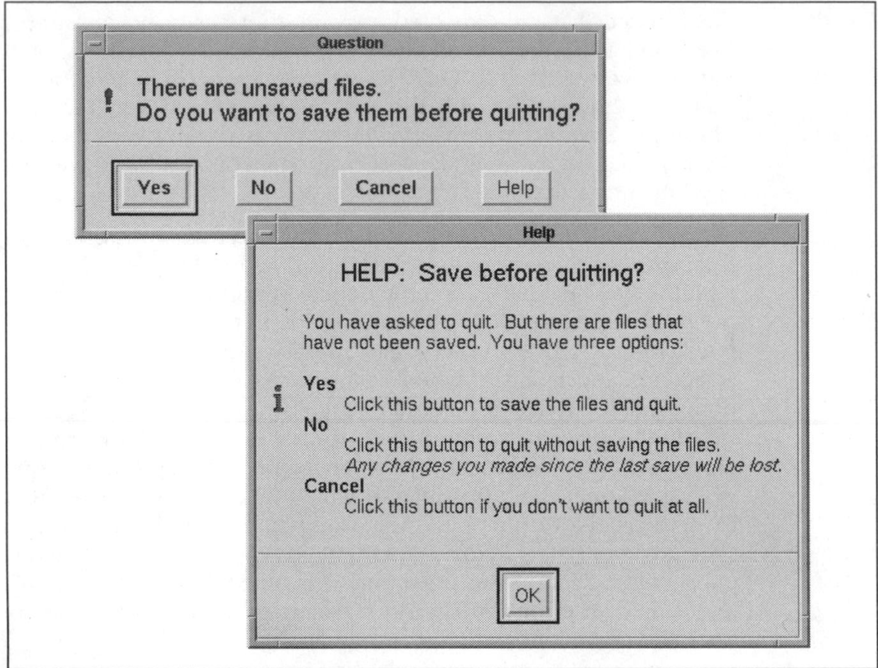

Figure 26-4. A dialog and a help message displayed by XmtAskForBoolean()

the question was asked. Second, there are cases when the default button should be **Cancel** rather than **Yes** or **No**, and a `Boolean` value can't represent all three possibilities. So we have to add another argument to `XmtAskForBoolean()`. *`default_button_default`* is of type `XmtButtonType`, an enumerated type that includes the values `XmtYesButton`, `XmtNoButton`, and `XmtCancelButton`. This argument is overridable from the resource database.

Finally, there is the question of the icon to display in the dialog. When you use `XmCreateQuestionDialog()`, you get a dialog box that displays the standard Motif question mark icon. The custom dialog created by `XmtAskForBoolean()` could use this icon. This is appropriate for many questions, but not all. For the last question, "A file by that name already exists. Overwrite?" for example, a warning icon seems more appropriate. If the question were "Write failed: file system full. Retry?" then an error icon would be best. To allow different dialogs to have different icons, we add another argument to `XmtAskForBoolean()`: *`icon_type_default`*. This argument is an integer which is one of `XmDIALOG_ERROR`, `XmDIALOG_INFORMATION`, `XmDIALOG_MESSAGE`, `XmDIALOG_QUESTION`, `XmDIALOG_WARNING`, or `XmDIALOG_WORKING`. You can use these constants to obtain any of the standard Motif icons—they have the same meaning to `XmtAskForBoolean()` as they do for the Motif XmMessageBox widget. Note that unlike the simple message function `XmtDisplayMessage()`, this icon argument is not itself a Pixmap; it is just an integer that specifies one of a set of default pixmaps.

With all of these arguments explained, Example 26-6 now shows how you might use XmtAskForBoolean(). Pay attention to the distinction between the status and the answer variables in this example.

Example 26-6. Using XmtAskForBoolean()

```
static void QuitCallback(Widget w, XtPointer tag, XtPointer data)
{
    Boolean status, answer;
    if (saved) exit(0);
    status = XmtAskForBoolean(w, "saveAndQuitDialog",
                              "There are unsaved files.  Save before quitting?"
                              "Yes, save and quit",
                              "No, quit without saving",
                              "Cancel, don't quit",
                              XmtYesButton, XmDIALOG_WARNING,
                              True, &answer, NULL);

    if (status == False) /* Abort on Cancel button */
        return;
    if (answer == True) SaveFile();

    exit(0);
}
```

We come out with a grand total of 11 arguments for XmtAskForBoolean(), and because a convenience function with this many arguments is not always convenient, Xmt also provides a couple of simpler variants on XmtAskForBoolean().

As pointed out before, some error and warning messages are not simply messages, but conditions that require a response from the user. In cases like these, the functions XmtDisplayError() and XmtDisplayWarning() introduced in Chapter 25, *Message Dialogs*, are not adequate. By putting simple wrapper functions around XmtAskForBoolean(), however, we can simplify that overly complex function to provide more powerful versions of the overly simple message dialogs:

Xmt/

AskForBool.c

```
#include <Xmt/Dialogs.h>
Boolean XmtDisplayErrorAndAsk(Widget w, String query_name,
                              String message_default,
                              String yes_default, String no_default,
                              int default_button_default,
                              String help_text_default)

Boolean XmtDisplayWarningAndAsk(Widget w, String query_name,
                                String message_default,
                                String yes_default, String no_default,
                                int default_button_default,
                                String help_text_default)
```

XmtDisplayErrorAndAsk() and XmtDisplayWarningAndAsk() will display dialogs without cancel buttons, and with the standard error or warning icons. Because there is no cancel button, these functions return the user's yes-or-no response directly, rather than returning the proceed-or-cancel value that all the other simple input functions return. These simplified forms of XmtAskForBoolean() only have seven arguments, and it is worth noting that the first three arguments are identical to the arguments of XmtDisplayError() and XmtDisplayWarning(). Figure 26-5 shows dialogs created by these two convenience functions, and Example 26-7 shows code that could be used to display them.

Example 26-7. Using XmtDisplayErrorAndAsk() and XmtDisplayWarning-AndAsk()

```
void save_as(char *filename)
{
    if (already_exists(filename)) {
        Boolean overwrite;
        char msg[200];

        /* If the file already exists, ask if it should be overwritten */
        sprintf(msg, "File `%s' already exists.\nOverwrite it?", filename);
        overwrite = XmtDisplayWarningAndAsk(w, "overwriteDialog",
                                            msg, "Overwrite", "Cancel",
                                            XmtNoButton, NULL);
        if (!overwrite) {
            /*
             * If the user asked not to overwrite the file, then we return
             * without saving.  But first, we should probably display some
             * feedback in a message line widget.
             */
            extern Widget msgline;
            XmtMsgLinePush(msgline);
            XmtMsgLineSet(msgline, "Save canceled.");
            XmtMsgLinePop(msgline, XmtMsgLineOnAction);
            return;
        }
    }

    save_file(filename);
}

int open_connection(void)
{
    Boolean connect, retry;

    do {
        connect = OpenDatabaseConnection();
        if (!connect)
            retry = XmtDisplayErrorAndAsk(w, "retryDialog",
                                          "Database server not responding.",
                                          "Retry", "Abort", XmtYesButton,
                                          NULL);
    } while (!connect && retry);
```

Example 26-7. Using XmtDisplayErrorAndAsk() and XmtDisplayWarning-AndAsk() (continued)

```
    if (connect) return connect;
    else return -1;   /* an error code */
}
```

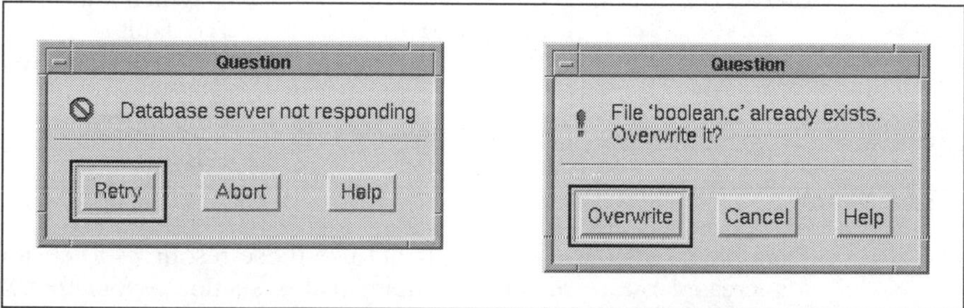

Figure 26-5. Dialogs displayed by XmtDisplayErrorAndAsk() and XmtDisplayWarningAndAsk()

26.4.1 Customizing Boolean Queries

`XmtAskForBoolean()`, `XmtDisplayErrorAndAsk()`, and `XmtDisplay-WarningAndAsk()` all use a single cached dialog box. This dialog is an Xmt-Layout widget named `xmtBooleanDialog` created as a child of an XmDialog-Shell named `xmtBooleanDialogShell`. The Layout widget has four Xm-PushButton children named `yes`, `no`, `cancel`, and `help`, as well as an Xmt-LayoutPixmap child named `icon` and an XmtLayoutString child named `mes-sage`. You can explicitly specify resources for these children to set colors, fonts, and other attributes that you want to affect for all invocations of the dialog.

You can also customize some aspects of the `XmtAskForBoolean()` dialog on a per-invocation basis. Table 26-4 lists the subpart resources read by each invocation of this function. The resources are looked up as a subpart of the shell widget specified by the *w* argument. The name of the subpart is given by *query_name* and its class is `XmtBooleanDialog`.

Table 26-4. XmtAskForBoolean() Customization Resources

Resource	Default	Description
message	*prompt_default*	The prompt for the dialog
title	"Question"	The string in the dialog's titlebar
yesLabel	*yes_default* or "Yes"	The label of Yes button

Table 26-4. XmtAskForBoolean() Customization Resources (continued)

Resource	Default	Description
noLabel	*no_default* or "No"	The label of No button
cancelLabel	*cancel_default* or "Cancel"	The label of Cancel button
defaultButton	*default_button_-default*	Which button is the default
iconType	*icon_type_default*	Which standard icon to display
helpText	*help_text_default*	Online help for the dialog

Example 26-8 shows how you might use these resources to customize the dialog created by a previous example in this section. Note that `XmtAskForBoolean()` registers a resource converter for the `XmtButtonType` type, so that you can specify the `defaultButton` resource, and that Motif registers a resource converter that works with the `iconType` resource.

Example 26-8. Customizing an XmtAskForBoolean() Dialog

```
*saveAndQuitDialog.defaultButton: XmtCancelButton
*saveAndQuitDialog.iconType: XmDIALOG_QUESTION
```

26.5 Getting Filename Input

The `XmFileSelectionBox` is a powerful widget and can be very useful in your applications. We can make it much more convenient, however, by providing automatic dialog caching and synchronous behavior following our by now familiar model:

Xmt/

AskForFile.c

```
#include <Xmt/Dialogs.h>
Boolean XmtAskForFilename(Widget w, String query_name,
                          String prompt_default,
                          String directory_default, String pattern_default,
                          String filename_buffer, int filename_buffer_len,
                          String directory_buffer, int directory_buffer_len,
                          String pattern_buffer, int pattern_buffer_len,
                          String help_text_default)
```

Figure 26-6 shows a dialog using the XmFileSelectionBox widget automatically created and managed with `XmtAskForFilename()`.

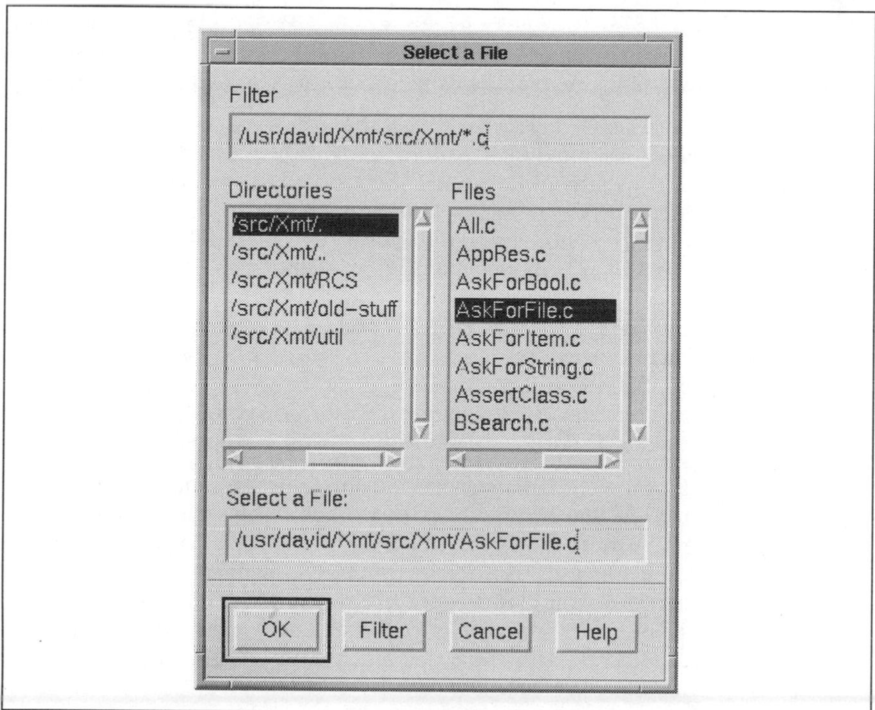

Figure 26-6. A dialog displayed by XmtAskForFilename()

`XmtAskForFilename()` has the standard arguments *w*, *`query_name`*, *`prompt_default`*, and *`help_text_default`*, and returns the user's input in *`filename_buffer`*, a character buffer *`filename_buffer_len`* bytes long supplied by the programmer. The string will be the fully specified path to the file. It will be null-terminated, and its length, including the terminating null, is guaranteed not to exceed the size of the buffer. As in other simple input functions, the initial string in this buffer is used as the default filename in the dialog.

As with `XmtAskForBoolean()`, however, the remaining arguments to `XmtAskForFilename()` require some further explanation. Notice in Figure 26-6 that the XmFileSelectionBox contains two text widgets. The one at the bottom of the dialog contains the filename, and is where the user's input comes from. The one at the top of the dialog contains the name of the directory being displayed and the filter pattern (**.c*, perhaps) that is being used to selectively display files. `XmtAskForFilename()` treats the directory and filter as two separate values, which the XmFileSelectionDialog will concatenate into this single text widget. The remaining six arguments to `XmtAskForFilename()` all have to do with specifying the directory and filter patterns.

The reason six arguments are required is that there are four distinct ways that you may want to handle these arguments. These four scenarios are listed below, along with an explanation of how you can implement them.

1. Sometimes, you want to ask the user for a file using a fixed initial directory and/or a fixed filter pattern, and you want to hard-code this initial directory and pattern in C, so that they are not overridable from the resource database. Every time the file dialog pops up, it will display the same initial directory and pattern—the user can change these, but his change will only have effect for that invocation of the dialog. To implement this scheme, specify the desired directory and pattern as buffers or constant strings on the *directory_buffer* and *pattern_buffer* arguments. Specify *directory_buffer_len* and *pattern_buffer_len* to both be zero, so that the function does not mistake these constant values as actual values that it can write into. In this scenario, *path_default* and *pattern_default* are unused, and you can specify NULL.

2. If you want a dialog that pops up with the same initial directory and/or pattern for each invocation, but which allows the system administrator or the end user to customize that initial directory or pattern through a resource file, then specify NULL for directory_buffer and pattern_buffer (and zero for their lengths), and pass a default initial directory and pattern on the *directory_default* and *pattern_default* arguments. Like other arguments with the *_default* suffix, these can be overridden from the resource database, as we will see soon.

3. Instead of implementing a fixed initial directory or pattern, you will often probably want an "adaptive" directory or pattern—i.e., if the user changes the directory or pattern during one invocation of the dialog, the new value becomes the default for the next invocation. As we've seen with other simple input functions, you can do this with static buffers: pass static buffers as the *directory_buffer* and *pattern_buffer* arguments, and use sizeof to specify the sizes of those buffers. Hard-code the initial directory and pattern into your C code using static initializers. Pass NULL for directory_default and pattern_default, since they will be unused.

4. The previous scenario adapts to user changes to the directory or pattern, but the first time the dialog is displayed, it will use a hard-coded directory-name or pattern. Instead, you may want an adaptive directory or pattern default value that can be customized from the resource database. To achieve this, use static buffers, as described before, but leave them uninitialized, so that they will be empty when XmtAskForFilename() is first invoked.* Then you can pass the default directory or pattern through *directory_default* and *pattern_default*.

*The C language guarantees that static variables without initializers will be filled with NULL bytes—in a character buffer, this results in an empty string. Instead of using a static buffer, you might allocate (and never free) the buffer the first time it is needed. In this case, you'd have to initialize it explicitly to contain the empty string.

Scenario 4 above is the most flexible, and probably what you'll want to use most often. Note, though, that you don't have to use the same model for both the directory and pattern. A data plotting program, for example, might want to follow user's changes to the directory across invocations, but if it can only read a certain type of data file, it might want to reset the pattern to some hard-coded value (**.dat*) at each invocation.

Another way to understand `XmtAskForFilename()` is to think about where it gets the directory name to display. It looks in three places:

1. First, it checks the *`directory_buffer`* argument. If this argument is non-NULL, and has a non-zero length, then it will be updated with any changes the user makes to the directory. If it has a zero length specified, then it is treated as a constant string and never updated.
2. If *`directory_buffer`* is NULL or an empty buffer, then it checks the resource database for a value.
3. If there is no value in the resource database, it uses the *`directory_default`* argument.

`XmtAskForFilename()` obtains the pattern to use in an analogous way.

With that lengthy explanation behind us, Example 26-9 shows how you might use `XmtAskForFilename()`. As with the hypothetical data-plotting application mentioned above, it uses adaptive, customizable model 4 for the directory, and fixed, hard-coded model 1 for the pattern.

Example 26-9. Using XmtAskForFilename()

```
static void OpenFileCallback(Widget w, XtPointer tag, XtPointer data)
{
    static char filename[500];
    static char directory[500];
    Boolean status;

    status = XmtAskForFilename(w, "openFileDialog",
                               "Please type or select a filename:",
                               "~", NULL,
                               filename, sizeof(filename),
                               directory, sizeof(directory),
                               "*.dat", 0,
                               NULL);

    if (status == False) /* abort on Cancel */
        return;

    openfile(filename);
}
```

`XmtAskForFile()` is a simple variation on `XmtAskForFilename()` that performs the extra step of opening the user-specified file with `fopen()`. `XmtAskForFile()` has all the arguments that `XmtAskForFilename()` does, but adds *`value_return`*, the address of a `FILE *` variable at which the opened file will be returned, and *`file_mode`*, a string like "`r`" or "`r+`" to be passed to fopen(). (See your fopen() documentation for details.) Even though XmtAskForFile() returns the user's input as a FILE *, it also returns the filename as a string in the *filename_buffer* argument, and also gets the default filename from this buffer.

Xmt/

AskForFile.c

```
#include <Xmt/Dialogs.h>
Boolean XmtAskForFile(Widget w, String query_name,
                      String prompt_default,
                      String directory_default, String pattern_default,
                      FILE **value_return, String file_mode,
                      String filename_buffer, int filename_buffer_len,
                      String directory_buffer, int directory_buffer_len,
                      String pattern_buffer, int pattern_buffer_len,
                      String help_text_default)
```

26.5.1 Customizing File Queries

XmtAskForFilename() and XmtAskForFile() use the same cached dialog box—an XmFileSelectionBox widget named xmtFileDialog, created as a child of an XmDialogShell named xmtFileDialogShell. You can specify resources using these names to customize fonts, colors, or other widget attributes that you want to affect all uses of the dialog.

You can also customize some of the attributes of the dialog on a per-invocation basis using the subpart resources listed in Table 26-5. The resources are looked up as a subpart of the shell widget specified by the *w* argument. The name of the subpart is given by the *query_name* argument, and the class of the subpart is XmtFileDialog.

Table 26-5. XmtAskForFilename() and XmtAskForFile() Customization Resources

Resource	Default	Description
message	*prompt_default*	The prompt for the dialog
title	"Select a File"	The string in the dialog's titlebar
directory	*directory_default*	The directory to display unless overridden by *directory-_buffer*
pattern	*pattern_default*	The pattern that filenames must match, unless overridden by *pattern_buffer*
helpText	*help_text_default*	Online help for the dialog

If XmtAskForFile() is ever unable to open a selected file, it will display an error message with XmtDisplayError(). You can customize this error dialog using the message name "xmtCantOpenDialog". The default message is the standard system error that would be displayed by perror().

Example 26-10 shows how you might use resources to customize the dialog displayed by `XmtAskForFilename()` in the previous example.

Example 26-10. Customizing the XmtAskForFilename() Dialog

```
!! Here we customize something for one particular instance of
!! XmtAskForFilename().  We make the dialog title match the menu entry.
*openFileDialog.title: Open...

!! Here we specify help text for all dialogs.
!! popped up by XmtAskForFilename()
*XmtFileDialog.helpText:\
To select a file, just double-click on it in the list on the right.\
Or, type its name in the input field near the bottom.

!! Here we customize some of the dialog resources themselves
*xmtFileDialog.background: tan

!! Finally, customize the title of the "Can't Open" error dialog
*xmtCantOpenDialog.title: Can't Open File
```

26.6 Getting Input from a List of Choices

Sometimes you want to ask the user to choose one item from a list of items. You can do this with an XmSelectionBox dialog, or, more conveniently, with the functions `XmtAskForItem()` and `XmtAskForItemNumber()`. Figure 26-7 shows a dialog created by `XmtAskForItem()`.

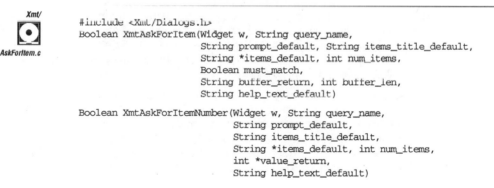

Xmt/

AskForItem.c

```
#include <Xmt/Dialogs.h>
Boolean XmtAskForItem(Widget w, String query_name,
                      String prompt_default, String items_title_default,
                      String *items_default, int num_items,
                      Boolean must_match,
                      String buffer_return, int buffer_len,
                      String help_text_default)

Boolean XmtAskForItemNumber(Widget w, String query_name,
                            String prompt_default,
                            String items_title_default,
                            String *items_default, int num_items,
                            int *value_return,
                            String help_text_default)
```

`XmtAskForItem()` has the standard arguments for a simple input function, and like `XmtAskForString()` it returns the user's input, and gets its default value, from a character buffer, *`buffer_return`*, that is *`buffer_len`* bytes long.

The remaining arguments are straightforward: *`items_title_default`* is a String that will be converted to an XmString and displayed over the XmList widget in the dialog. You can treat this as a title for the List widget, or as an auxiliary prompt that along with *`prompt_default`* tells the user what he is choosing, and why.

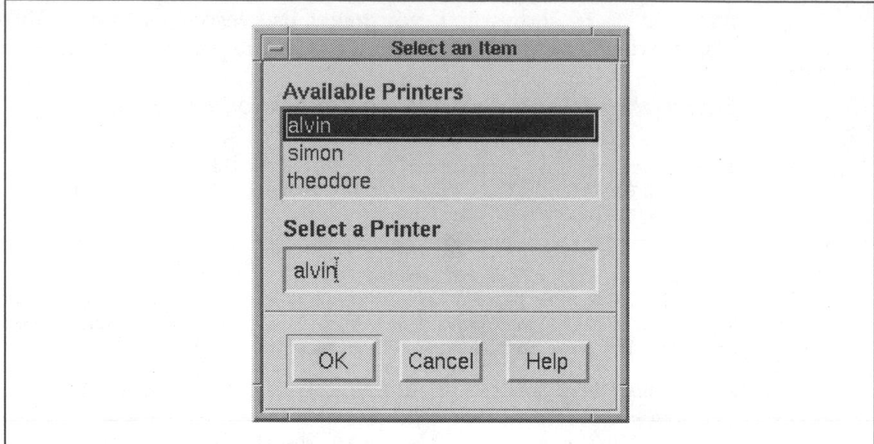

Figure 26-7. A dialog displayed by XmtAskForItem()

items_default is an array of strings that will be converted to XmStrings and displayed in the List widget. This array has *num_items* elements. As we'll see below, these functions register a resource converter so that you can specify a comma-separated list of double-quoted item names from a resource file.

`XmtAskForItem()` uses an XmSelectionBox widget, which allows the user to select an item from the list widget, or to type the name of an item directly into the text widget. If *must_match* is `True`, then any name the user types must match one of the items displayed in the list widget (and an error dialog will be displayed if it doesn't match.) If *must_match* is `False`, then the user can type any value; the items in the list widget become merely suggestions or shortcuts for commonly-used values.

`XmtAskForItemNumber()` is a very similar function, but instead of returning the name of the selected item, it returns that item's position in the list. Therefore, in `XmtAskForItemNumber()`, the *buffer_return* and *buffer_len* arguments have been replaced by a single *value_return* argument—the address of an `int` at which the user's input is stored, and from which the default value is read. Also, the *must_match* argument has been dropped from `XmtAskForItemNumber()` since in this case, the selection must always match.

Example 26-11 shows how you might use `XmtAskForItem()` and `XmtAskForItemNumber()`.

Example 26-11. Using XmtAskForItem() and XmtAskForItemNumber()

```
static void PrintFileCallback(Widget w, XtPointer tag, XtPointer data)
{
    static char printer[100];
    Boolean status;
```

Example 26-11. Using XmtAskForItem() and XmtAskForItemNumber() (continued)

```
    status = XmtAskForItem(w, "getPrinterDialog",
                           "Print to which printer?",
                           "Available Printers",
                           NULL, 0, False,
                           printer, 100, NULL);
    /* abort on Cancel */
    if (status == False)
        return;
    /* Otherwise print! */
    PrintFileTo(printer);
}

/*
 * An excerpt from a hypothetical interface builder application
 */
static String item_names[] = {
    "Warning", "Error", "Information", "Working", "Question"
};

static int item_values[] = {
    XmDIALOG_WARNING, XmDIALOG_ERROR, XmDIALOG_INFORMATION,
    XmDIALOG_WORKING, XmDIALOG_QUESTION;
};

static void CreateDialogCallback(Widget w, XtPointer tag,
                                 XtPointer data)
{
    Boolean status;
    int item, type;

    status = XmtAskForItemNumber(w, "dialogTypeDialog",
                                 "Select the dialog type:"
                                 "Dialog Types",
                                 item_names, XtNumber(item_names),
                                 &value, NULL);
    /* abort on Cancel */
    if (status == False)
        return;

    /* Otherwise convert the item to a dialog type */
    type = item_values[item];

    /* Then go create a dialog of that type. */
        .
        .
        .
}
```

26.6.1 Customizing Item Queries

XmtAskForItem() and XmtAskForItemNumber() use a single cached dialog—an XmSelectionBox widget named xmtItemDialog as a child of an XmDialogShell named xmtItemDialogShell. You can set resources using these names to specify fonts, colors, or other attributes that will affect all dialogs displayed by XmtAskForItem() and XmtAskForItemNumber().

You can also use resources to customize particular invocations of this dialog. Table 26-6 lists the resources you can set. These resources are looked up as a subpart of the shell specified by the *w* argument. The name of the subpart is specified by *query_name*, and the class of the subpart is `XmtItemDialog`.

Table 26-6. XmtAskForItem() and XmtAskForItemNumber() Customization Resources

Resource	Default	Description
`message`	*prompt_default*	The prompt for the dialog
`title`	"Select an Item"	The string in the dialog's titlebar
`listTitle`	*list_title_default*	The title of the List in the dialog
`items`	*items_default*	The list of items to display
`visibleItems`	8	How many items should be visible at once
`helpText`	*help_text_default*	Online help for the dialog

As mentioned above, there is a resource converter for the `items` resource, so you can specify it as a resource. Also, note that the `visibleItems` resource is like the `title` resource in that it has no corresponding argument to `XmtAskForItem()` or `XmtAskForItemNumber()`—this is an attribute that can only be set from a resource file.

In `XmtAskForItem()` when *must_match* is `True`, or in `XmtAskForItemNumber()`, there is a possibility of error if the user types the name of an item that does not exist. When this happens, both functions display an error using `XmtDisplayError()`. The default message is "Please select an item that appears on the list." You can customize this message, and other aspects of the dialog using the name `xmtNoMatchDialog`.

Example 26-12 shows how you might customize the `XmtAskForItem()` dialog created in Example 26-11.

Example 26-12. Customizing XmtAskForItem()

```
*getPrinterDialog.items: "Alvin", "Simon", "Theodore"
*getPrinterDialog.visibleItems: 3
*getPrinterDialog.helpText: If you don't know the name of your printer,\n\
ask your system administrator.
```

26.7 Style

Many of the style tips presented for message dialogs are applicable to input dialogs as well. See Chapter 25, *Message Dialogs*. In particular, pay attention to your use of language, and bear in mind that you can use XmStrings and multiple fonts in your dialogs.

Probably the most important thing to remember about the input dialogs presented in this chapter is that you must always check the return value to see if the user clicked on the **Cancel** button. Because that button is present in the dialogs, you *must* honor it when the user selects it by aborting whatever operation is in progress.

In some circumstances, the user's response to a query should become the default input value the next time the same query is issued. Asking for a printer name is a good example. You can easily handle this kind of default by using a static variable—the simple input functions will use this variable to store the user's input and also to obtain the default input value. Be careful, though; there are other circumstances in which the user is unlikely to repeat previous input, and in this case it is better to have a fixed default input value, or a NULL default. In a spelling-checker dialog box, for example, it is unlikely that the user will want to check the spelling of the same word twice, and it is also unlikely that your application will be able to reliably guess an appropriate default for the user. So in this case, having no default value will save the user the trouble of backspacing over a default that is almost certainly incorrect.

While message dialogs are often self-explanatory, the input dialogs of this chapter are more complex, and can usually benefit from help information. Note that the **Help** button in these dialogs is made insensitive if there is no help information, but it is not unmanaged. For this reason, users will expect most input dialogs to have at least a simple help message. For the particularly complex dialogs, like that displayed by `XmtAskForFilename()`, the help message might explain how to use the dialog. For simpler dialogs, though, help is also important. In an `XmtAskForString()` dialog, the help message might explain what the input string will be used for, and in an `XmtAskForBoolean()` dialog, the help message might explain what the effects of the **Yes**, **No**, and **Cancel** buttons will be.

Popping up a dialog box can disrupt the flow of the human/computer interaction, so it is important not to overuse the functions described in this chapter. One alternative that can work in some cases is to use an XmtMsgLine widget for synchronous input of strings and numbers. Furthermore, it is bad style to pop up two dialogs in a row—if you need to get two integers from the user, don't call `XmtAskForInteger()` twice; instead, create your own custom dialog (or, perhaps, use an XmtMsgLine input function twice.) An exception to this "two dialogs in a row" prohibition is when the types of input requested are very different or are unexpected. For example, you might use `XmtAskForFilename()` and follow it with `XmtDisplayErrorAndAsk()` if there were problems with the requested file.

26.8 Summary

The Xmt library provides the following functions for getting simple, synchronous input from the user:

1. `XmtAskForString()` queries the user for a string.

2. `XmtAskForInteger()` and `XmtAskForDouble()` query the user for integers and floating-point numbers.
3. `XmtAskForBoolean()` gets a response to a yes-or-no question. `XmtDisplayErrorAndAsk()` and `XmtDisplayWarningAndAsk()` are simplified versions of this function.
4. `XmtAskForFilename()` queries the user for a filename; `XmtAskForFile()` does the same, but also automatically opens the file.
5. `XmtAskForItem()` and `XmtAskForItemNumber()` ask the user to select an item from a list.

Each of the dialogs has a **Help** button to display optional help text, and each of these functions returns a status value to indicate whether the user dismissed the dialog with the **Cancel** button.

If you specify a name for your queries with the *query_name* argument, then the resulting dialogs will be customizable through the resource database. Specify a *query_name* of `NULL` to *prevent* customization. Each of the functions supports a different set of resources for customization, but all have the `message`, `title`, and `helpText` resources in common.

27

Presenting Choices

One of the fundamental tasks of a user interface, and particularly of dialog boxes, is to present choices to the user. That this is a common task for an interface is evident from the variety of widgets available:

- Placing XmToggleButtons in `XmONE_OF_MANY` mode (i.e., with diamond-shaped indicators) into a XmRowColumn widget with its `XmNradioBehavior` resource set results in a *radio box*—a list of mutually exclusive options that the user may select.
- If you use square `XmN_OF_MANY` toggle buttons, with `XmNradioBehavior` off, then you'll get a *check box*—a list from which the user can select any number of options.
- If there are more choices than will fit in the available screen space, they can be displayed in an (optionally scrolled) XmList widget. An XmList widget can also be configured in `XmSINGLE_SELECT` or `XmMULTIPLE_SELECT` modes which allow radio box and check box style selection.
- If screen space is at a premium, and the choice is one that the user will only need to make infrequently, then an option menu is an ideal alternative.
- Finally, choices between modes or tools as in direct-manipulation applications are often presented in the form of a palette, and a list of frequently used commands may be presented to the user in a button box instead of a pulldown menu.

The Motif widget set allows a programmer to present choices in all of these forms to the user, but does not provide any uniform or particularly convenient interface for doing so. All the strings to be displayed must first be converted to `XmStrings`, of course. For a list widget, you just need to provide an array of these XmStrings. To present the choice in other forms, you must individually create XmToggleButtons or XmPushButtons to display the XmStrings within an XmRowColumn. For an option menu, the menu pane must be created as a sibling of the XmOptionMenu widget and linked to it through the `XmNsubMenuId` resource. To implement a palette, you must modify your toggle buttons to remove their diamond or square indicators. The `XmCreateSimple()` routines added in Motif 1.1 do simplify the creation of radio boxes, check boxes and option menus, but don't really go far enough.

As we've seen elsewhere, Motif provides the low-level components that are needed, but not at a convenient level of abstraction. When a choice must be presented to the user, it seems natural to consider that choice as a single component of the interface without the distractions of creating, monitoring, and manipulating the lower-level components that comprise it. This chapter presents the XmtChooser widget which allows just this. The XmtChooser widget has the following features:

- A single resource specifies the format (radio box, check box, list widget, palette, option menu, etc.) that the choice should be presented in. The remaining resources and and the Chooser convenience functions can, for the most part, be used regardless of the choice of presentation format.
- The list of choices to be presented in the Chooser widget is provided as a single array of Strings (not XmStrings) or as an array of Pixmaps. The Chooser widget will use the items in these arrays to automatically create the widgets required to display the choices. The Chooser accepts only a fixed list of choices—if your choices will change dynamically, then the Chooser is not an appropriate widget.
- There is a single state variable, the `XmtNstate` resource, that specifies which item or items have been selected. Similarly, there is a single Chooser `XmtNvalueChangedCallback` list that is invoked whenever any of the choices are selected.

27.1 Creating a Chooser Widget

The Chooser widget is a subclass of XmRowColumn. The class name is "XmtChooser," and the class structure is `xmtChooserWidgetClass`.

You can create a Chooser widget with the constructor `XmtCreateChooser()`:

Xmt/

Chooser.c

```
#include <Xmt/Chooser.h>
Widget XmtCreateChooser(Widget parent, StringConst name,
                        ArgList args, Cardinal num_args)
```

You can register the Chooser widget class for use with `XmtCreateChildren()` and other automatic widget creation functions with `XmtRegisterChooser()`:

Xmt/
Chooser.c

```
#include <Xmt/Chooser.h>
void XmtRegisterChooser(void)
```

This function also registers the Chooser for use with the Xmt automatic dialog management facilities, introduced in Chapter 29, *Custom Dialogs and Automatic Dialog Management.*

27.2 Chooser Presentation Formats

The Chooser widget can display the choice of items in eight different formats. The `XmtNchooserType` resource controls which format will be used. Because the value of this resource controls the type of subwidgets that will be created by the Chooser widget, it must be set when the widget is created, and cannot be modified with `XtSetValues()`. The formats and the corresponding `XmtNchooserType` values are described below. Figure 27-1 shows a dialog box with eight Chooser children—one in each of the supported formats.

examples/
27/choosers

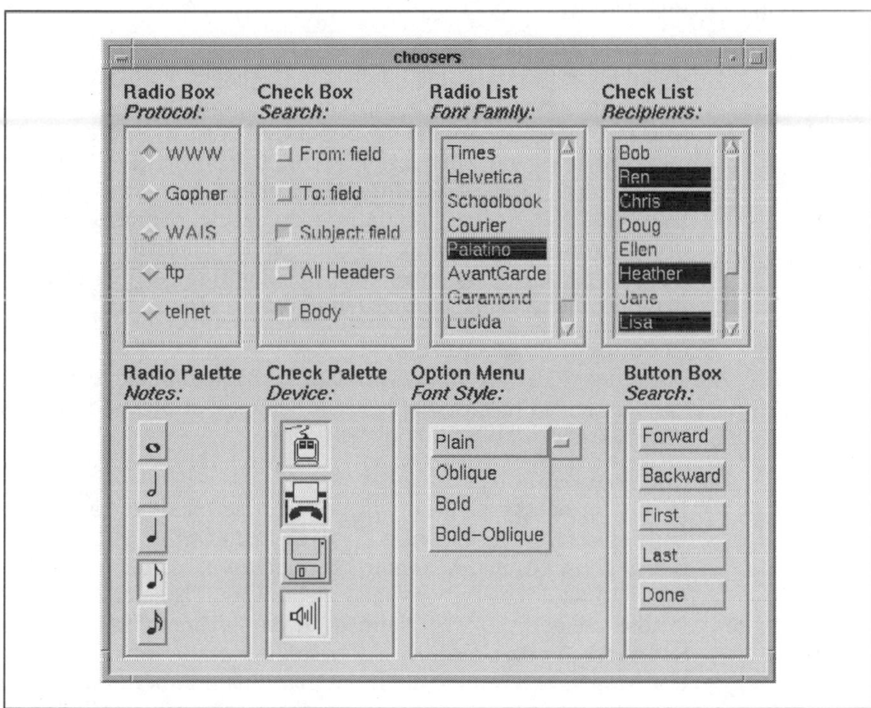

Figure 27-1. The Chooser widget, configured in each of the supported formats

`XmtChooserRadioBox`
In this format (the default), each item is displayed as an XmToggleButton with a diamond ("one-of-many") indicator. The items are laid out in an XmRowColumn widget, and only one item may be selected at a time. A Chooser in this format starts out with a default item selected, and whenever a new item is selected, the previously selected item becomes unselected. This format requires a fair bit of screen space, but makes the available choices very apparent to the user. It is particularly appropriate when the items to choose from are configuration or other options or modes.

`XmtChooserCheckBox`
In this format, each item is displayed as an XmToggleButton with a square ("n-of-many") indicator. The items are laid out in an XmRowColumn widget, and any number of them may be selected and unselected independently of each other. Like the RadioBox format, this format requires screen space, but makes the available choices quite clear. Again, it is particularly appropriate for a list of options or modes. It is possible to use icons instead of text to display the choices in this format and also in the RadioBox format, but this is not particularly appropriate, because icons look awkward next to the square or diamond selection indicators displayed by the toggle buttons.

`XmtChooserRadioPalette`
In the RadioPalette format, items are displayed with XmToggleButton widgets configured to have no special indicator, but instead to indicate their selected state by appearing depressed into the screen. Except for the appearance of the XmToggleButtons, this format is identical to the RadioBox format. It is intended for applications like drawing editors and interface builder tools that allow the user to select some sort of mode, tool, or object from a fixed list. This mode is generally used with the `XmtNpixmaps` and sometimes with the `XmtNselectPixmaps` resources so that the palette displays icons rather than text.

`XmtChooserCheckPalette`
The CheckPalette format is similar to the RadioPalette format, except that the palette can have multiple items selected at once—it displays check box behavior instead of radio box behavior.

`XmtChooserRadioList`
In this format, items are displayed in a scrolled XmList widget configured with an `XmNselectionPolicy` of `XmBROWSE_SELECT`. This selection policy allows only one item to be selected at a time, and as with the RadioBox and RadioPalette formats, a default item is selected when the Chooser is first created, so that there is always something selected. The `XmtNvisibleItems` resource controls the number of visible items in the XmList widget, and if there are more than this number of items, a scrollbar will appear next to the list. This format, because it is scrolled, can take up less screen space than the RadioBox format. Because of the scrollbar, however, this format is a little more difficult for a user to interact with. It is useful when there are more than about eight or ten items to choose from, and is particularly appropriate when those items are things such as available fonts,

hostnames, usernames, and so on. There must be a fixed number of items when a Chooser is created, but if the list of items is determined at runtime (by querying the X server for available fonts, for example) rather than being fixed at compile time, then the List format is a good choice because it takes a constant amount of vertical screen space, regardless of the number of items.

`XmtChooserCheckList`
: The CheckList format is like the RadioList format, except that the XmList widget is configured with an `XmNselectionPolicy` of `XmMULTIPLE_SELECT`. Like the CheckBox format, any number of items (including none) may be selected. This format is appropriate in the same type of situations as the List format, but is less commonly used, because in many lists, (fonts, colors, etc.) it only makes sense to select one item. Note that the XmList widget cannot display icons, and so both the RadioList and CheckList formats must be used with strings rather than pixmaps.

`XmtChooserOption`
: In this format, items are displayed in a standard Motif option menu. As with the RadioBox, RadioPalette, and RadioList formats, there may be only one item selected at any time. The option menu is perhaps the most elegant widget provided with Motif—it takes up very little screen space, looks good, and allows the user to easily and intuitively select an item from a list. The Option Chooser format may be used in place of the RadioBox, RadioPalette, or RadioList format (as long as there aren't too many items in the list) whenever screen space is at a premium. It is particularly useful in dialog boxes where a number of related choices (font family, weight, slant, and size, for example) must be presented to the user.

`XmtChooserButtonBox`
: This format is similar to the RadioBox and RadioPalette formats, except that the XmToggleButtons are replaced with XmPushButtons. It is different from all the other formats in that XmPushButtons do not remain selected after they are clicked on, and so a Chooser in this format does not maintain any currently selected state. This format is useful when you want to present a list of commands to be executed immediately rather than a list of options or objects that will be used or operated on later. Note that the ButtonBox format is not appropriate for the **OK/Cancel/Help** style of button box found at the bottom of dialog boxes—the Chooser widget arranges the buttons in an XmRowColumn that is not able to space the buttons evenly as is done in Motif dialogs. In some applications, however, making a list of commands available with a Chooser in this format may be a useful alternative to commands in pulldown or popup menus.

The Chooser widget registers a resource converter for the `XmtNchooserType` resource—it is case sensitive and allows you to specify Chooser formats exactly as you would specify them in C. It also allows you to strip the `Xmt` and `Chooser` prefixes off of these format names, however, so to specify a chooser configured in `CheckPalette` format, for example, you could use any of the following lines in a resource file:

```
*chooser.chooserType: XmtChooserCheckPalette
*chooser.chooserType: ChooserCheckPalette
*chooser.chooserType: CheckPalette
```

27.3 Specifying Choices

The strings that appear in a Chooser widget are specified as an array of strings on the `XmtNstrings` resource. Note that this array contains regular C strings, not XmStrings. The array may either be NULL-terminated, or may have its number of elements specified in the `XmtNnumItems` resource. If the array is NULL-terminated, then the `XmtNnumItems` resource should be left at its default unspecified value.

That is all there is to specifying a list of choices. There is no need to create XmStrings, and no need to explicitly create individual widgets for each choice. Example 27-1 shows two ways of specifying a list of items for a Chooser from C code.

Example 27-1. Creating Chooser Widgets with Counted and NULL-terminated Arrays

```
static String slant_labels[] = {
    "roman", "italic", "oblique"
};

static String weight_labels[] = {
    "medium", "bold", NULL
};
        .
        .
        .
slants = XtVaCreateWidget("slants", xmtChooserWidgetClass, form,
                          XmtNchooserType, XmtChooserOption,
                          XmtNstrings, slant_labels,
                          XmtNnumItems, XtNumber(slant_labels),
                          NULL);
weights = XtVaCreateWidget("weights", xmtChooserWidgetClass, form,
                           XmtNchooserType, XmtChooserOption,
                           XmtNstrings, weight_labels /* NULL-terminated */,
                           NULL);
```

The reason for supporting two methods of specifying items is that counted arrays (counted at compile time with the `XtNumber()` macro) are often easier to use in C code (because you don't have to remember the NULL), but that NULL-terminated arrays are better when the labels are specified in a resource file—a type converter can be written to convert a string into a NULL-terminated array of strings, and the number of elements in the list need never be hard-coded into the resource file. The Chooser widget provides just such a type converter, so you can specify items as a comma-separated list of quoted strings in a resource file. Example 27-2 shows how this can be done.

Example 27-2. Specifying Chooser Items from a Resource File

```
*slants.chooserType: XmtChooserOption
*slants.strings:     "roman", "italic", "oblique"
```

Note that the items in the `XmtNstrings` resource are delimited by double quotes, and separated from each other by commas.

Note that the `XmtNstrings` array and the `XmtNnumItems` resource must be set when the Chooser widget is created, and cannot be changed once the widget has been created. This is a fundamental part of the Chooser model—the Chooser widget was designed to present a *fixed* list of choices. The choices may be fixed at compile-time, or they may be fixed at runtime by reading it from a configuration file, for example, but they may not change in content or number. Sometimes you will want to present a dynamically changing list of choices to the user; in most cases it will be most appropriate to use a scrolled XmList widget. (And in a few cases, it may be appropriate to use a Chooser widget, and to destroy it and re-create it whenever the list of choices changes.)

27.3.1 Specifying Iconic Choices

By default, as we saw above, the Chooser widget will use the strings specified on the `XmtNstrings` resource as labels for each of the choices it presents. For all of the `XmtNchooserType` formats except `XmtChooserRadioList` and `XmtChooserCheckList`, however, it is also possible to display the choices with iconic labels instead. If the `XmtNlabelType` resource is set to `XmPIXMAP`, then the Chooser widget will use the array of `Pixmap` specified on the `XmtNpixmaps` resource, instead of the strings specified on the `XmtNstrings` resource. As with `XmtNstrings`, the `XmtNpixmaps` array may be `NULL`-terminated, or the number of elements in the array may be specified on the `XmtNnumItems` resource. (Note that the `XmtNlabelType` resource of the Chooser has the same name and the same legal values as the `XmNlabelType` resource of the XmLabel widget.)

Pixmaps are less flexible than textual strings in a couple of ways: it is not possible to change their background color on-the-fly to indicate that an item has been selected, and it is not usually possible to display them "grayed out" when an item is insensitive. For these reasons, there are two other arrays of pixmaps that you may optionally specify for a Chooser. The `XmtNselectPixmaps` resource specifies an array of pixmaps that are to be displayed when the corresponding item in the chooser has been selected, and `XmtNinsensitivePixmaps` specifies an array of pixmaps to be displayed when the corresponding item in the chooser has been made insensitive. Typically, a selected pixmap will have a darker background than the corresponding unselected pixmap, and an insensitive pixmap will be "grayed out" by stippling or by setting the foreground and background colors to shades of gray, or it will have its contrast reduced by setting the foreground color to something close to its background color.

These three pixmap array resources are most useful with the XmtChooser-RadioPalette and XmtChooserCheckPalette formats, which were designed for use with icons. In these formats, the only default indication of the selection state of an item is a relatively small shadow around each item, and so it is valuable to specify the XmtNselectPixmaps array.

The Xmt library contains a String-to-PixmapList converter, but, for the sake of those applications that do not need to use this converter, the Chooser widget does not register it automatically. If you call the function XmtRegister-PixmapListConverter() in your C code, then you can specify the Xmt-Npixmaps and related resources from your resource file. The converter parses a comma-separated list of double-quoted pixmap names (the same format as the StringList converter described above) and passes each name to the Xmt String-to-Pixmap converter for conversion. As with the StringList converter, the PixmapList converter NULL-terminates its array, so there is no need to set the XmtNnumItems resource.

27.4 Chooser State

The Chooser widget keeps track of which of its items are selected in a single consistent location: the XmtNstate resource. For the chooser formats that only allow a single item to be selected (RadioBox, RadioPalette, Radio-List, and Option), the value in XmtNstate is the index (numbered from zero) of the selected item in the XmtNstrings or XmtNpixmaps array. There is no special state value to indicate that no items are selected. In fact, it is a fundamental part of the Chooser widget design that there will always be exactly one item selected in the Chooser—never more and never less. This is appropriate in almost all cases. If you find that you want to present a radio-type choice, and also allow no items to be selected, then either create and manage the widgets of the radio box yourself, or explicitly add this "none of the above" choice to the widget.

For the CheckBox, CheckPalette, and CheckList formats, XmtNstate contains a bitmask of the selected items—if the *n*th item is selected, then the *n*th bit in XmtNstate will be set. You can test whether the *n*th item is set with the following C expression:

```
(state & (1 << n))
```

Note that this limits the number of elements in a CheckBox, CheckPalette, or CheckList Chooser to the number of bits in an integer. This will be at least 32 bits on all systems, and if you've got more than 32 choices, then the Chooser widget isn't really the right interface component to use, anyway. Finally, remember that in the ButtonBox format, the Chooser widget does not maintain any state, because XmPushButton widgets have no state to maintain.

You may query the state of a Chooser with XtGetValues() or XtVaGet-Values(), and you may set it with XtSetValues() or XtVaSetValues(). If you set the state of the Chooser, the state of the subwidgets will be updated to reflect the new state. The default value of the XmtNstate resource is zero. By default, when a Chooser is created, the first item will be selected if it is in one of the radio box formats, or no items will be selected if it is in a format that allows multiple items to be selected. If you want a different initial state than this, set `XmtNstate` when you create the widget.

The Chooser exports two functions which are more efficient than `XtSetValues()` and `XtGetValues()` for setting and querying the Chooser state. They are `XmtChooserGetState()` and `XmtChooserSetState()`, and they have the following prototypes:

Xmt/

Chooser.c

```
#include <Xmt/Chooser.h>
int XmtChooserGetState(Widget w);
void XmtChooserSetState(Widget w, int state, Boolean notify);
```

The only explanation required for these functions is the third argument, *`notify`*, of `XmtChooserSetState()`. If this argument is `True`, then the procedures registered on the `XmtNvalueChangedCallback` list (this callback list is documented in more detail below) will be invoked, just as if the user had selected an item. If this argument is `False`, then the state will be changed, but no callbacks will be invoked. Note that the callbacks will not be invoked when the state is changed through a call to `XtSetValues()`. Example 27-3 shows how `XmtChooserGetState()` might be used to obtain the user's choice of fonts from a font selection dialog.

Example 27-3. Getting the State of a Chooser Widget

```
static Widget font_dialog_style_chooser;    /* a Chooser widget */
static Widget font_dialog_size_chooser;     /* another Chooser widget */
static XFontStruct *font_cache[4][6];       /* A 2-D array of fonts */

/* ARGSUSED */
static void FontDialogOkCallback(Widget w, XtPointer tag, XtPointer call_data)
{
    /*
     * This callback is called when the user clicks "Ok" in the font dialog.
     * It reads the user's choice of font style and font size, looks up
     * the corresponding font, and sets that font.
     */
    int font_style, font_size;

    font_style = XmtChooserGetState(font_dialog_style_chooser);
    font_size = XmtChooserGetState(font_dialog_size_chooser);

    SetNewFont(font_cache[font_style][font_size]);
}
```

27.4.1 Chooser Values

Sometimes, the selection state of the Chooser—the index of the selected item—is not really the value that you are most interested in. In Example 27-3, for instance, we use the index of the selected item in the `font_size` chooser to look up a font in an array of fonts. With a different implementation, we might actually be more interested in the actual font point size associated with each item in the chooser, rather than its index. That is, we are more interested in the values 8, 10, 12, 14, 18, and 24 than in 0, 1, 2, 3, 4, and 5.

You can associate such an array of values with the items in a chooser by setting the `XmtNvalues` resource. This is an array of values, each of which is `XmtNvalueSize` bytes long. The Chooser widget never uses or interprets these values in any way, but maintains them for programmer convenience. There must be as many elements in the array as there are items in the Chooser, of course. Note that the default value for the `XmtNvalueSize` resource is 0, so you must always set this resource when you use `XmtNvalues`. From C code, you should use the `sizeof` operator to compute the size of each element of the array.

Once you have associated values with the items in your chooser, you can use `XmtChooserGetValue()` to obtain the value associated with the currently selected item:

Xmt/

Chooser.c

```
#include <Xmt/Chooser.h>
XtPointer XmtChooserGetValue(Widget chooser);
```

This function serves as an analog to `XmtChooserGetState()`. Note, however, that because the value associated with an item can be of any size specified by `XmtNvalueSize`, this function cannot return the value itself—instead it returns the address within the `XmtNvalues` array at which the value is stored. It returns this address as an `XtPointer`—you will typically have to cast and dereference this return value. Notice that you can only use this function when the Chooser is configured in one of its single-selection `Radio` modes: `RadioBox`, `RadioPalette`, `RadioList`, or `Option`. In other modes there is not a single selected item that can have its value returned.

Since it is possible to specify Chooser items from a resource file, it is also possible to specify Chooser values in that way: if you specify the `XmtNvalueStrings` resource as a comma-separated list of double-quoted strings, and specify a representation type on the `XmtNvalueType` resource, then the Chooser will automatically invoke the appropriate resource converter to convert each of the strings to a value. You must also specify the `XmtNvalueSize` resource in this case, of course, but the Chooser will automatically allocate an array for the `XmtNvalues` resource.*

Example 27-4 shows another way that you might implement font selection through Chooser widgets. The first part of the example is made up of resources that set up the Chooser widgets, and the second part is C code that selects a font based on the values associated with these widgets.

*Note that specifying the `XmtNvalueSize` resource from a resource file is non-portable. It is safer to specify both `XmtNvalueType` and `XmtNvalueSize` from C code, and use `sizeof()` to determine the required size for the type.

Example 27-4. Using Chooser Values

```
!! Two Choosers in a dialog box.
*layout.xmtChildren: XmtChooser size, style;

!! the strings that will be displayed for each item
*size.strings: "8", "10", "12", "14", "18", "24"

!! The values associated with each item.  Here we use 10ths of points.
!! "Int" is the value of the XtRInt representation type; it will be
!! used to convert the valueStrings array to the values array of integers.
!! valueSize hardcodes sizeof(int) to be 4 bytes.
*size.valueStrings:  "80", "100", "120", "140", "180", "240"
*size.valueType: Int
*size.valueSize: 4

!! the style chooser is similar, except that the values are
!! left as Strings, with no conversion required.
*style.strings: "Plain", "@fBBold", "@fIItalic", "@f(BIBold-Italic"
*style.valueStrings: "medium-r", "bold-r", "medium-o", "bold-o"
*style.valueType: String
*style.valueSize: 4

/* The associated C code */
Widget size_chooser, style_chooser;

static void FontDialogOkayCallback(Widget w, XtPointer tag, XtPointer data)
{
    int size;
    String style;
    char fontname[200];

    /*
     * XmtChooserGetValue() is a lot like XmtChooserGetState(),
     * but note how we cast and dereference the returned address.
     */
    style = *(String *)XmtChooserGetValue(style_chooser);
    size = *(int *)XmtChooserGetValue(size_chooser);

    sprintf(fontname, "*-helvetica-%s-*-*-*-%d-*-*-*-*-*-*",
            style, size);
    SetNewFont(fontname);
}
```

27.4.2 The XmtNvalueChangedCallback List

The functions on the `XmtNvalueChangedCallback` list are invoked whenever the user changes the state of the Chooser, or whenever the state is changed through a call to `XmtChooserSetState()` with the *notify* argument `True`. The callbacks are passed a pointer to a structure of type `XmtChooserCallbackStruct` as their *call_data* argument. This structure is defined as follows:

```
typedef struct {
    int state;          /* selected item or OR of items */
    int item;           /* whichever item just was clicked */
    XtPointer valuep; /* address of value from XmtNvalues array */
} XmtChooserCallbackStruct;
```

The fields of this structure are the following:

`state`
: This field is the new state of the Chooser widget. It is identical to the `XmtNstate` resource, and simply saves the step of querying that value in the callback.

`item`
: This field is the index (counting from zero) of the item that was just clicked. For the radio-box formats (`RadioBox`, `RadioPalette`, `RadioList`, and `Option`), this is the same as the state. For the `CheckBox`, `CheckPalette`, and `CheckList` formats, this field indicates which item was most recently selected (or unselected), which is something that cannot be determined from the `state` field alone. In `ButtonBox` format the `item` field indicates which item was clicked, and the `state` field is unused, since the XmPushButtons of a `ButtonBox` never remain selected. Note that when the state of a `CheckBox`-type chooser is changed with `XmtChooserSetState()` the `item` field will be set to -1, since the change in the `state` field may have involved more than one item changing.

`valuep`
: If the `XmtNvalues` or `XmtNvalueStrings` and associated resources are set, then this field is the address of the value associated with the item specified by the `item` field. If `item` is -1, or if there are no values associated with the items in the Chooser, then this field will be `NULL`. As with `XmtChooserGetValue()`, you will generally have to cast and dereference the address in this field.

In most typical uses of the Chooser widget, the `XmtNvalueChangedCallback` is not needed. Usually, an application takes no immediate action when the user changes the state in a Chooser, but allows the user to change that state freely, and then queries the state when it is needed. In Example 27-3 and Example 27-4, for example, we show a `FontDialogOkCallback()`—a procedure registered on the `XmNactivateCallback` list of the **OK** button of our hypothetical dialog box. These procedures are not intended to be registered on the Chooser `XmtNvalueChangedCallback` callback list—instead they are not invoked until the user "locks in" her choice of fonts by clicking the **OK** button. We could enhance this font selection dialog by displaying an example string in the currently selected font size and style. In this case, we *would* need to register callbacks on the Chooser widgets themselves to update the font of the example string.

As another example, imagine a drawing editor application that used Chooser widgets to display option menus of line widths and other drawing attributes. This application wouldn't have to use the Chooser `XmtNvalueChangedCallback` to find out when the user changes attributes. Instead, it could allow the user to change attributes freely, and then always query the attribute Chooser widgets before drawing any new objects. (In fact, if we used XmtSymbols with the Chooser widgets, as described in the next section, this could be done more efficiently without querying the widgets all the time.)

Do notice, though, that the `XmtNvalueChangedCallback` is important for any Chooser configured in `ButtonBox` format—there is no state to query in this case, and each button indicates an immediate action to be taken.

27.4.3 Getting Chooser State Through Symbols

We've seen above that you can obtain the state of the Chooser by explicitly querying it, or through the `XmtNvalueChangedCallback`. You can also obtain this state through Symbols. Chapter 12, *Symbols*, describes how you can use the XmtSymbol abstraction to provide a symbolic name for an application variable. You can use Symbols with the Chooser widget by setting the `XmtNsymbolName` resource to the name of a registered Symbol of type `XtRInt`. If you set this resource, either when the Chooser widget is created, or later with `XtSetValues()`, then the value of the symbol will be used to set the state of the Chooser. Subsequent changes in the Chooser state, whether caused by user interaction or programmatic manipulation, will update the value of the Symbol. Finally, the Chooser will monitor the Symbol for changes in its value, and will update its own widget state if the Symbol value is set with `XmtSymbolSetValue()`. Note that `XmtNsymbolName` works only with the Chooser state; not with the value associated with Chooser items through the `XmtNvalues` resource.

The main reason to use Symbols is that they provide a means of keeping the user interface separate from the back end of the application. In the drawing editor example used in the previous section, for example, the back end of the application (the part that draws the objects, in this case) could register Symbols for its graphical attributes like line width. Then, the front end of the application (the user interface) needs only to know the names of these symbols, not the addresses of the actual attribute variables. By setting the `XmtNsymbolName` resource on its Chooser widgets, the front end can cause these back-end variables to be updated whenever the user selects a new line width, font size, or whatever in the front end. And by corollary, the back end never needs to query the Chooser widget (as it did in the previous example); it need not know anything about them—it can just use its graphical attribute variables directly, knowing that the front end will take care of updating them when the user requests it.

27.4.4 Choosers in Dialogs

The Chooser widget was designed to work well in dialog boxes, and in particular, to work with the Xmt automatic dialog management routines presented in Chapter 29, *Custom Dialogs and Automatic Dialog Management*. We won't describe those automatic dialog functions here, except to note that if you register the Chooser widget with `XmtRegisterChooser()`, the dialog functions will be able to automatically get and set the selection state (or value of the selected item) of your Chooser widgets, and will be able to automatically transfer those state values to and from the fields of your application data structures.

27.5 Chooser Sensitivity

The Chooser widget is often used as a child of the XmtLayout widget, and is often given a caption with the `XmtNlayoutCaption` constraint resource. Because this is a common situation, the Chooser widget will always set its `XmtNlayoutSensitive` resource when its own `XtNsensitive` resource changes. This means that if you make a Chooser insensitive by calling `XtSetSensitive()`, the Chooser's caption, if any, will automatically be grayed out. When you make the Chooser sensitive again, the caption will be made sensitive again as well.

There are times when you do not want to make an entire Chooser insensitive, but do want to temporarily make some of the items in the Chooser unavailable. You can do this with `XmtChooserSetSensitive()`:

Xmt/

Chooser.c

```
#include <Xmt/Chooser.h>
void XmtChooserSetSensitive(Widget chooser, int item,
                            Boolean sensitive);
```

If *`sensitive`* is `False`, this function makes the specified item in the specified Chooser insensitive and unselectable, and if *`sensitive`* is `True`, it makes the item sensitive again. For all formats other than `RadioList` and `CheckList`, insensitive items will be grayed out if they are text items, or displayed with an item from the `XmtNinsensitivePixmaps` array if they are iconic items. The XmList widget does not support grayed-out text or icons, so for the XmList formats, items are displayed as usual, but become unselectable (i.e., if they are selected by the user, the Chooser will immediately deselect them again.)

You can query the sensitivity of an item in a Chooser with `XmtChooserGetSensitivity()`. This function returns `True` if the specified item is sensitive, or returns `False` if it is insensitive.

Xmt/

Chooser.c

```
#include <Xmt/Chooser.h>
Boolean XmtChooserGetSensitivity(Widget chooser, int item)
```

Note that it is possible to obtain pointers to the individual widgets within the Chooser, and to set their sensitivity directly. You should not do this, however, because the Chooser widget itself will not know about the change, and `XmtChooserSetSensitive()` and `XmtChooserGetSensitivity()` will not work correctly.

27.6 Other Chooser Resources and Functions

There are a few Chooser resources and functions that have not been described elsewhere in this chapter. They are described briefly here, and are documented more fully on the Chooser reference page.

The Chooser has its own `XmtNfontList` resource which it uses for the buttons and XmList widgets that it creates. You do not often have to set this resource—it is inherited from the `XmNbuttonFontList` resource of the nearest XmBulletinBoard ancestor (such as an XmtLayout widget).

The remaining Chooser resources depend, in some way, on the value of the `XmtNchooserType` resource, and are documented in the next section.

27.6.1 Format-Specific Resources

There are four resources of the Chooser widget that are only used in certain formats. When a Chooser is configured in `RadioBox`, `CheckBox`, `RadioPalette`, `CheckPalette`, or `ButtonBox` format, then the items are displayed as buttons within an XmRowColumn widget and the XmRowColumn resources (the Chooser is a subclass of XmRowColumn) `XmNorientation` and `XmNnumColumns` control how the buttons are arranged within that XmRowColumn. If `XmNorientation` is `XmVERTICAL` (the default), then the buttons are laid out in columns, with the number of buttons in each column chosen so that there are `XmNnumColumns` columns. If `XmNorientation` is `XmHORIZONTAL`, on the other hand, then the buttons are laid out in rows, with the number of buttons in each row chosen in order to form `XmNnumColumns` rows. Note that the `Option` format also arranges its button children within an XmRowColumn widget but that this is an internal XmRowColumn widget, and is unaffected by setting `XmNnumColumns` and `XmNorientation` on the Chooser.

If a Chooser widget is configured in `RadioList` or `CheckList` format, then the number of items visible in the XmList subwidget at any one time is controlled by the `XmtNvisibleItems` resource. Setting this resource simply sets the corresponding `XmNvisibleItemCount` resource of the XmList widget.

For all formats except `RadioList` and `CheckList`, the `XmtNitemWidgets` resource can be queried to get an array of pointers to the individual widgets that display the choices. Note that this is a read-only resource—setting it has no effect. You can use these individual item widget pointers to do things like set the colors of individual items, or perform other manipulations that are not possible with the Chooser API.* Note, however, that you should not modify the selection state or the sensitivity of the items, or the Chooser widget's internal state will get out of sync with reality.

*You can also use this resource to change the labels displayed the individual widgets in the Chooser. This is a partial workaround to the restriction that the Chooser can display only a fixed list of choices.

These resources break the abstraction that the Chooser widget tries to achieve—complete independence from the format that the choices appear in. They are necessary, however, from a graphic design standpoint. If you hard-code the `XmtNchooserType` resource in C, then there is no problem with using these resources. If you allow `XmtNchooserType` to be set from a resource file, however, you should be sure to also allow `XmNorientation`, `XmNnumColumns`, and `XmtNvisibleItems` to be set from the resource file.

Free-Form Radio Boxes

Not satisfied with the `XmNorientation` *and* `XmNnumColumns` *resources for laying out the choices in your radio boxes? Greg Ullmann has a technique that will enforce radio behavior on the toggle button children of any manager widget—giving you the freedom to arrange the toggles however you choose. This solution does not have the single state variable and the single callback of the XmtChooser widget, but it can be useful nevertheless. And, it is an excellent example of things that you can do with the* `XtNchildren` *resource of the Composite widget class:*

When using toggle buttons, there are times when it would be nice to have the layout flexibility of an XmForm [*or XmtLayout—djf*] widget. However, if you use any manager other than an XmRowColumn, you don't get the `XmNradioBehavior` resource to ensure that one and only one button stays pressed at once. The `EnforceRadioBehaviorCB()` callback shown in the following exmaple is an `XmNvalueChangedCallback` callback that can be placed on every toggle button in the manager. This callback will then enforce the radio style behavior on every toggle button widget or gadget child of the manager.

Note that when the toggle buttons are created with a non-XmRowColumn parent, you must create them with the `XmNindicatorType` set to `XmONE_OF_MANY`. The XmRowColumn usually does this for you automatically.

```
void EnforceRadioBehaviorCB(Widget toggle, XtPointer tag, XtPointer data)
{
    WidgetList  children;
    Cardinal    num_children;
    int         i;

    /*
     *  Always set the calling toggle button to true in case the toggle
     *  was clicked on while already set.  Don't notify, or we will spin
     *  in an infinite loop.
     */
    XmToggleButtonSetState(toggle, True, False);

    /* fetch all of the toggle's siblings */
    XtVaGetValues(XtParent(toggle),
                  XmNchildren, &children,
                  XmNnumChildren, &num_children,
                  NULL);

    /* search the list of children for toggles and turn them off */
    for(i=0; i < num_children; i++)
```

Free-Form Radio Boxes (continued)

```
        if ((children[i] != toggle) &&
            (XmIsToggleButton(children[i]) ||
             XmIsToggleButtonGadget(children[i])))
            XmToggleButtonSetState(children[i], False, False);
}
```

—Greg Ullmann

27.6.2 Getting the Label, Value, and the Index of Chooser Items

On occasion when using a Chooser widget, you may need to obtain the label of a selected (or any) item given the index of that item. This can be done with the function `XmtChooserLookupItemName()`, which requires the index of the item as an argument. On rarer occasions, you may need to go in the other direction, and find the index of an item given its label. This can be done with `XmtChooserLookupItemByName()`. The prototypes for these functions are as follows:

Xmt/

Chooser.c

```
#include <Xmt/Chooser.h>
String XmtChooserLookupItemName(Widget chooser, int item);
int XmtChooserLookupItemByName(Widget chooser, String label);
```

Similarly, you may sometimes want to obtain the value associated with a specified item, or to find out which item a specified value is associated with. You can do this with `XmtChooserLookupItemValue()` and `XmtChooserLookupItemByValue()`:

Xmt/

Chooser.c

```
#include <Xmt/Chooser.h>
XtPointer XmtChooserLookupItemValue(Widget chooser, int item);
int XmtChooserLookupItemByValue(Widget chooser, XtPointer valuep);
```

Finally, you can change the value associated with any item in the Chooser widget with `XmtChooserSetItemValue()`:

Xmt/

Chooser.c

```
#include <Xmt/Chooser.h>
void XmtChooserSetItemValue(Widget chooser, int item, XtPointer valuep);
```

See the reference pages for full documentation on each of these functions.

27.7 Chooser Style

The first decision you'll face when using the Chooser widget is what setting to use for the `XmtNchooserType` resource. Your application design will generally make it clear whether you need a radio-box type (a single choice from a list of mutually-exclusive choices), or a checkbox (any number of choices allowed from a list of independent options). Once this decision is made, however, you still need to decide how the choices will be presented: as a set of toggle buttons, a palette, a list widget, or as an option menu. Each type is appropriate in different circumstances, and there is not always one best choice.

The `XmtChooserRadioBox` and `XmtChooserCheckBox` types use a standard XmToggleButton child for each choice. They take up a lot of space on the screen, but make the list of available choices quite explicit. If vertical space is scarce, consider arranging the choices into two columns using the `XmNnumColumns` resource. Radio boxes and check boxes become cumbersome when there are more than about eight choices. They can also become confusing when there are more than two or three in a dialog box. The `XmtNpixmaps` resource should not be used in these formats, because pixmaps look strange next to the diamond or square indicators displayed by the buttons.

The `XmtChooserRadioPalette` and `XmtChooserCheckPalette` types use XmToggleButton widgets with their diamond or square toggle indicators removed. These formats are generally used with pixmap or very short textual labels, so the items do not take up much space horizontally. These formats are useful for letting the user select a tool, as in many drawing and painting programs which have a palette against the left edge of the main window. They are also good for allowing a choice of modes, as in word processors that allow the user to select line spacing and justification with icons in a region at the top of the main window. The Chooser widget displays the selected items in these formats by drawing the buttons with their shadows in, as if they have been depressed. This shading is often difficult to see; it is better to specify both the `XmtNpixmaps` resource and the `XmtNselectPixmaps` resource when using pixmaps. A useful technique is to make the selected pixmaps look the same as the unselected, except with a darker background color. This can be done by using the same pixmap, but specifying it with a different color table (see Chapter 5, *Using Icons*). Palettes with a number of elements are sometimes arranged into two columns (using the `XmNnumColumns` resource inherited from the XmRowColumn widget), but should generally not be arranged into more than two. A palette can be laid out horizontally by setting the `XmNorientation` resource, also inherited from the XmRowColumn widget.

The `XmtChooserRadioList` and `XmtChooserCheckList` formats display all the items in a single scrolled XmList widget. These formats takes up less vertical space per item, but do not emphasize the individual choices as strongly as individual XmToggleButtons do. These formats are useful when there are a large number of choices, because the Chooser can contain more choices than are visible at once, and the user can view all the choices using the scrollbar. The `XmtNpixmaps` resource is not used in these formats, because the XmList widget can only display textual items.

The `XmtChooserOption` format displays the choices in an XmOptionMenu, and takes up less screen space than any other format. Option menus make it quite clear what the currently selected choice is (they operate in radio mode only, not check mode), and they keep separate choices distinct. They are good in dialog boxes, such as configuration or "preferences" dialogs, that present a number of separate choices to the user, especially when some of the selected values are infrequently changed. The `XmtNpixmaps` resource is sometimes useful with this format, when the choice is between graphical attributes such as colors, line styles, or shading patterns, for example. The `XmtNselect-Pixmaps` resource is not used in this format, since option menus are based on XmPushButton widgets that have only one state, rather than XmToggleButton widgets that have two.

Finally, the `XmtChooserButtonBox` format is quite distinct from the others: it uses XmPushButtons rather than XmToggleButtons, and does not maintain a state at all. It does not present a choice of modes or options, but rather a choice of commands. This format is generally not useful for the **OK**, **Cancel**, **Help** button boxes that appear in dialog boxes, because the buttons it creates are not evenly spaced across the bottom of the dialog. It is sometimes appropriate, however, in main windows of applications that provide a lot of commands to the user, often as an alternative to a command-line interface. A mail reader application might have buttons labeled **Get Mail**, **Next Message**, **Previous Message**, **Send Message**, **Reply to Message**, and **Forward Message**, for example. Be careful not to abuse this format; if there are more than two rows of buttons in a box, finding the desired button can be difficult. If you find that you have a lot of buttons in your main window, consider redesigning the interface to place them in menus, or consider adding a command-line interface to allow the user to type commands.

After considering these options, if you're not sure which Chooser format to use, try several out; one of the convenient things about the Chooser widget is that you can change its appearance without changing the rest of your application.

If you use the Chooser as a child of the XmtLayout widget, it is usually a good idea to give the Chooser a title with the Layout `XmtNlayoutCaption` constraint resource. This title serves as a prompt, and explains to the users what kind of choice they are making. You may also want to use the Layout to provide a frame around the Chooser widget, particularly if you are using the `RadioBox` or `CheckBox` formats, which do not define their own boundaries particularly well. The etched style of frames is generally more appropriate in this case than the shadowed styles are. As shown elsewhere in this chapter and in Chapter 19, *The Layout Widget: The Details*, captions can overlap etched frames to produce a nice visual effect.

Use the same font for all items in a Chooser, unless, perhaps, the choice is between fonts or font attributes (size, family, style). If you provide a title for the Chooser, you may want to display it in a larger font, or in boldface to set it off from the choices.

As always, check your use of language. Check your spelling, avoid jargon that your users won't be familiar with, and make sure that you capture the important information about each choice and express it as concisely as you can. Simple choices should generally just be a list of nouns (10, 12, 14, 18) or adjectives (`Plain`, `Bold`, `Italic`). When the things being chosen among are more complicated, you may have to use phrases or sentence fragments to describe each choice. In this case, make sure that you use the same tense, person, and voice for your verbs and the same number for your nouns throughout the list. Also check for other non-parallelisms. If you find that all your choices begin with the same word or words (`Search for`, for example), you can probably rephrase them to be shorter and move those repeated words to the title caption of the Chooser.

28

The Input Field Widget

The XmtInputField widget is a subclass of XmText designed with a number of features for user input of single-line strings, as found in form-input dialogs, for example. Figure 28-1 shows a dialog box containing XmtInputField widgets.

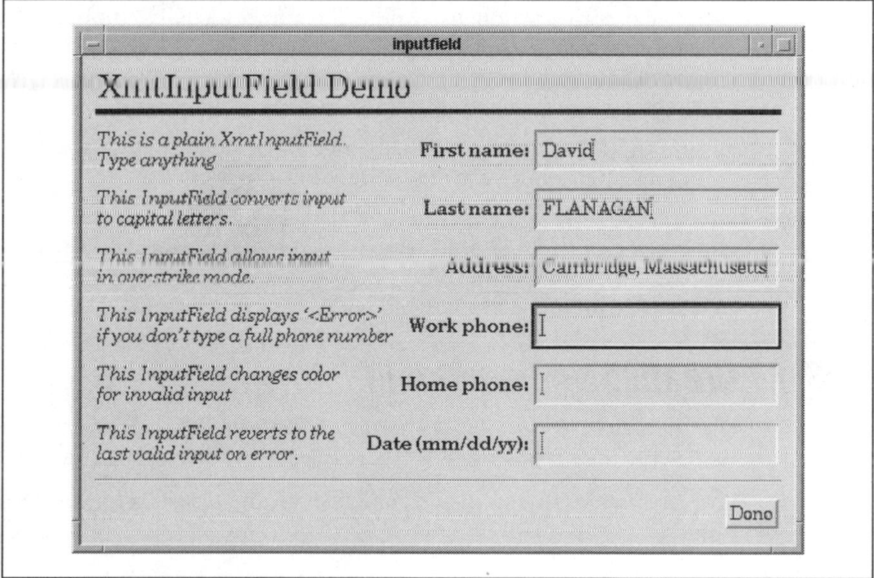

Figure 28-1. InputField widgets

The InputField widget adds the following features to those of the XmText widget:

- The InputField widget stores the user's input in an `XmtNinput` resource which is only updated when the user signals that he is done entering his input by striking **Return** or by traversing out of the widget. This is unlike, and generally more useful than, the `XmNvalue` resource, which the XmText widget updates on every keystroke. Similarly, the `XmtNinputCallback` callback list is only invoked when input is done, unlike the XmText `XmNvalueChangedCallback`.

- When the user enters a string, the InputField widget can automatically store that string into a buffer specified by a named XmtSymbol. It can also convert the string to a specified target type and store the converted value at an address specified by Symbol name.
- The `XmtNpattern` resource can be used to constrain user input to a specified pattern of characters and digits. This is useful for the entry of data with fixed formats, such as zip codes. This resource provides character-by-character validation of input.
- The `XmtNverifyCallback` can be used to accept or reject the user's input. It is invoked when the user enters a string, not on a character-by-character basis as the XmText `XmNmodifyVerifyCallback` is.
- The `XmtNerrorCallback` callback list is invoked when a user's input is rejected by a verify callback, fails to match a specified pattern, or cannot be converted to a specified type. This provides a hook to allow the application to take some action to handle the error. Usually, though, the InputField widget can automatically handle the error by beeping, changing color, displaying a special string (such as `Error`) or by reverting to its last valid input value.
- The InputField widget implements an optional overstrike mode, which is not a feature of the XmText widget prior to Motif 1.2.

While many of these features provide alternatives to XmText features, note that the XmText features are still available. You can use the `XmNmodifyVerifyCallback` with an XmtInputField widget, for example.

28.1 Creating an Input Field

The InputField widget is a subclass of XmText. The class name is "XmtInputField," and the class structure is `xmtInputFieldWidgetClass`.

You can create an InputField widget with the constructor `XmtCreateInputField()`:

Xmt/

InputField.c

```
#include <Xmt/InputField.h>
Widget XmtCreateInputField(Widget parent, StringConst name,
                           ArgList args, Cardinal num_args)
```

You can register the InputField widget class for use with `XmtCreateChildren()` and other automatic widget creation functions with `XmtRegisterInputField()`:

Xmt/

InputField.c

```
#include <Xmt/InputField.h>
void XmtRegisterInputField(void)
```

This function also registers the InputField for use with the Xmt automatic dialog management facilities, introduced in Chapter 29, *Custom Dialogs and Automatic Dialog Management.*

28.2 The Input String

The InputField widget's idea of the user's input is significantly different from the input value maintained by its XmText superclass. The `XmNvalue` resource of the XmText widget is updated every time the user inserts or deletes a character. The InputField's `XmtNinput` value, on the other hand, is only updated when the user has entered a complete value, and signals this by striking the **Return** key or by traversing (by keyboard or by mouse) out of the InputField and moving input focus to another widget. Because this resource is not updated character-by-character, and because the InputField can perform validity checking on input values (described later in the chapter), the `XmtNinput` resource is always guaranteed to contain a complete, valid value. This is a subtle, but crucial distinction between the XmtInputField and the unmodified XmText and XmTextField widgets.

The subsections below explain the different ways that you can obtain the user's input string from the InputField widget. Later sections of the chapter will explain pattern matching, input validation, invalid input handling, and other features of the widget.

28.2.1 Querying and Setting Input

You can query the user's input value, or set the value to be displayed in an InputField widget, by querying and setting the `XmtNinput` resource with `XtGetValues()` and `XtSetValues()`. It is slightly more efficient, and often more convenient, however, to use `XmtInputFieldGetString()` and `XmtInputFieldSetString()`:

Xmt/

InputField.c

```
#include <Xmt/InputField.h>
String XmtInputFieldGetString(Widget inputfield);
void XmtInputFieldSetString(Widget inputfield, String value);
```

Unlike the corresponding XmText resource and convenience function, querying XmtNinput or calling XmtInputFieldGetString() returns a pointer to the InputField's internal value, not a copy of that value. The returned string is owned by the InputField widget, and you must not modify or free it. Also, note that the returned string may change (or be freed) at any time after flow-of-control returns to the event loop, so if you will need to use the string outside of the context of the procedure that queries it, you should make a private copy of the string.

When you set the internal value of the InputField widget with XtSetValues() or XmtInputFieldSetString(), it will affect the string displayed by the widget, and will also set the buffer and target symbols, if any are specified. Setting the input string in this way does not invoke the procedures on the XmtNinputCallback callback list, however. Strings set in this way are also not subject to the normal input validation (the XmtNpattern resource and the XmtNverifyCallback callback list) performed by the InputField widget, so if you do perform input validation, you should be careful never to set illegal values.

Example 28-1 shows how you might use XmtInputFieldGetString() to obtain a user's input values when the user clicks the **OK** button of a dialog box:

Example 28-1. Querying the InputField Value

```
typedef struct {
    char name[50];
    char company[50];
    char phone[20];
} Entry;

/* the InputField widgets in the dialog box */
static Widget name_field, company_field, phone_field;

/*
 * The callback registered on the Ok button of a dialog box
 * in a rolodex program that prompts the user for a name
 * a company and a phone number.
 */
static void NewEntryCallback(Widget w, XtPointer tag, XtPointer data)
{
    Entry *entry = XtNew(Entry);

    /* get the input strings and make copies of them */
    strncpy(entry->name, XmtInputFieldGetString(name_field),
            sizeof(entry->name));
    strncpy(entry->company, XmtInputFieldGetString(company_field),
            sizeof(entry->company));
    strncpy(entry->phone, XmtInputFieldGetString(phone_field),
            sizeof(entry->phone));

    /* now go save this new rolodex entry somewhere */
    insert_entry_in_list(entry);
}
```

28.2.2 Input Notification

A different way to obtain input from the InputField widget is to register a callback procedure on the `XmtNinputCallback` callback list. When the user enters a new value (by striking **Return**, or by traversing to a new widget), that value is first validated (as described later in the chapter), and if it passes the validation tests, all the procedures on the `XmtNinputCallback` list will be invoked with the new input value as their *call_data* arguments.

As with the value returned by `XmtInputFieldGetString()`, this value passed as *call_data* is owned by the widget, and must not be modified or freed by the application. If the application will need to refer to the value after the callback returns, it should make its own private copy of the string. Note that the input callbacks are only invoked if the input string has actually changed. This means that they will not be called when the user is just "passing through" the widget without editing the value.

Don't confuse the `XmtNinputCallback` with the `XmNvalueChanged-Callback`. The XmText callback is invoked whenever a character in the input string changes. The InputField callback is only called when the user is done editing the string. Also, notice that the `XmtNinputCallback` is different from the XmText `XmNactivateCallback`. A text widget is activated when the user strikes **Return**, but not when the user enters input and then uses the **Tab** key (for example) to move on to the next input field.

In Example 28-1 we did not use the `XmtNinputCallback` because we were not interested in the user's input until the user was done with the entire dialog and clicked the **OK** button. In some cases, however, we want to respond immediately to a user's input. Example 28-2 shows how you might use the `XmtNinputCallback` in the same example Rolodex program to display a company name and phone number when the user enters a name into an InputField:

Example 28-2. Using the XmtNinputCallback

```
static void NameCallback(Widget w, XtPointer client_data, XtPointer call_data)
{
    String name = (String) call_data;
    Entry *entry = find_closest_matching_entry(name);

    if (entry) {
        XmtInputFieldSetString(name_field, entry->name);
        XmtInputFieldSetString(phone_field, entry->company);
        XmtInputFieldSetString(phone_field, entry->phone);
    }
    else {
        XBell(XtDisplay(w), 0);
    }
}
```

28.2.3 Input Through Symbols

Yet another way to obtain user input from an InputField widget is through Symbols. (Symbols in Xmt are names for application variables—see Chapter 12, *Symbols*.) If you specify the `XmtNbufferSymbolName` resource, the InputField widget will look up the Symbol you name (which must be of type `XmtRBuffer`) and will store the user's input value into the character array specified by the Symbol. If you specify this resource, the user's input will be constrained to be no longer than the length of the specified buffer. If you specify this Symbol when the InputField widget is first created, and if there is no initial value specified for the `XmtNinput` resource, then the value, if any, of the Symbol will be used as the initial value of the InputField.

One important advantage to using this approach is that the input value is automatically copied into memory owned by the application, which is not the case when you query the input value with `XmtInputFieldGetString()`, for example. Also, using a Symbol to separate the user interface from the application back end allows the back end to get the user's input value without interacting directly with the widget.

The InputField widget also has an `XmtNtargetSymbolName` resource. If specified, this resource names a Symbol which specifies the address, size, and type of an application variable. When the user enters a new value, the InputField will attempt to convert that value (by invoking a resource converter) to the specified type, and, if the conversion succeeds, it stores the converted value at the specified address. If the conversion does not succeed, the user's input is considered invalid, and the widget performs the error handling procedures described later in this chapter.

28.2.4 Input From Dialogs

The InputField was designed with dialog box input particularly in mind, and can be used to good effect with the automatic dialog management functions described in Chapter 29, *Custom Dialogs and Automatic Dialog Management*. Briefly, if you register the InputField widget with the Xmt widget creation routines by calling `XmtRegisterInputField()`, the automatic dialog functions will take care of transferring the user's input value from an InputField to a specified location in an application data structure, and vice versa. The value may be automatically converted to and from a scalar or floating-point type.

28.2.5 Input Size and Widget Width

Don't forget that the InputField widget is a subclass of the XmText widget; there are a number of useful XmText resources that you may want to set. In particular, `XmNcolumns` specifies the width of an XmText or an InputField widget in characters, and `XmNmaxLength` specifies the maximum length of the input string. (In addition, the maximum length of an input string may be specified by the length of the `XmtNpattern` resource and by the size of the Symbol named by `XmtNbufferSymbolName`.

28.3 The Input Pattern

If the `XmtNpattern` resource is set, it controls the number and type of characters that may be entered into the InputField widget, and may also specify certain characters that are to be automatically inserted and deleted as the user types. If the user types a character that does not match the pattern, the InputField will beep and will not insert the character.

The `XmtNpattern` resource is a string containing one character for each character of the desired input string. Several characters have special meaning and when they occur in the pattern, they control the category of characters that the user may enter at that position in the input string. These special characters are shown in Table 28-1.

Table 28-1. Special Characters for the XmtNpattern Resource

Character	Meaning
a	Any; any alphabetic character
b	Both; any alphabetic character or digit
c	Character; any character of any sort
d	Digit; any digit
A	Any alphabetic character; converted to uppercase
B	Both—any alphabetic character or digit; uppercased
C	Any character; converted to uppercase

Any character in the pattern that is not one of these special characters is a literal that must appear at the same position in the input string as it does in the pattern. If the `XmtNautoInsert` and `XmtNautoDelete` resources are `True` (the default), then these constant characters will automatically be inserted and deleted at the appropriate place by the InputField widget as the user types. If the `XmtNmatchAll` resource is `True` (again, the default), then the input string must match every character in the pattern—and must therefore be exactly as long as the pattern string. If this resource is `False`, then the input string is valid even if it only matches a prefix of the pattern. If a pattern is specified, then no input that is longer than the pattern will be allowed. If you specify both a pattern and the XmText `XmNmaxLength` resource, you must be sure that the maximum length is not shorter than the pattern.

The `XmtNpattern` resource is most useful to constrain user input to a fixed size, format, or category of characters. To get a U.S. 5-digit Zip Code as input, for example, you could use this resource setting:

```
zip.pattern: ddddd
zip.matchAll: True
```

This pattern allows only digits as input, and since `XmtNmatchAll` is `True` (the default) the InputField will flag as invalid any input of less than five characters.

To obtain input of any number between 0 and 99999, you could use the same pattern with `XmtNmatchAll` set to `False`. To get input of a U.S.-style phone number, you could use these resources:

```
phone.pattern: (ddd) ddd-dddd
phone.matchAll: True
phone.autoInsert: True
phone.autoDelete: True
```

Since `XmtNautoInsert` is `True` (the default), then the InputField widget will automatically insert the parentheses, the space, and the hyphen if the user omits them. Since `XmtNautoDelete` is `True` (also the default), then the InputField will automatically delete them as the user backspaces. Other sorts of input that can be well handled with the `XmtNpattern` resource are dates, times, identification numbers, and so on.

When the `XmtNpattern` resource is set, insertions and deletions are only allowed at the end of the input string. This is because insertions and deletions shift the position of any following characters and can cause a mismatch against the pattern. Overstrike mode is supported with patterns, however, and works at any position in the input string. Even in overstrike mode, though, forward and backward deletions are only allowed at the end of a line.

Note that the patterns supported by the `XmtNpattern` resource, while often useful, are not particularly general or flexible. Specifying a date pattern of `dd/dd/dd`, for example, requires the user to type two digits for days and months, even when this means typing a leading zero. With a more general pattern syntax, however, it becomes impossible to unambiguously verify each character and insert constant characters that the user omits. If the `XmtNpattern` resource is not flexible enough to perform character-by-character verification of input you need, you can use the `XmtNverifyCallback` callback list (described in the next section) to test the entire string once the user enters it. If your system supports the `regexp()` or `re_exec()` regular expression matching functions, for example, you could use them in a verify callback to check that the input matches a more general pattern.

28.4 Verifying Input

When the user enters a new value into an InputField widget, the new input undergoes several verification steps before it becomes the current value of the widget.

First, if a pattern is specified with the `XmtNpattern` resource, and `XmtNmatchAll` is `True`, then the length of the input string is compared to the length of the pattern. If they do not match, the input is invalid. Note that only the pattern and input length are checked at this point; if a pattern is specified, then all the characters in the input are guaranteed to match the pattern—the InputField widget will not allow the user to enter characters that do not match.

Second, the InputField calls the procedures registered on the `XmtNverifyCallback` callback list, passing each one a pointer to a structure containing the newly entered string and a `Boolean` value. The verify callbacks may replace the input value with a new string, or may reject the input by setting the Boolean to False. If any of the verify callbacks change the value, input verification continues as if the user had typed the new value directly. If any of the callbacks reject the value then the input is invalid.

Finally, if a target type is specified through the XmtNtargetSymbolName resource, then the InputField calls a converter routine to convert the input string to the target type. If this conversion fails for any reason, then the input is invalid.

If the input string passes these three tests, then it is stored at the locations specified by the target and buffer Symbols, if they are specified, and becomes the new value of the XmtNinput resource. Once the value has been stored in these places, the InputField calls the procedures registered on the XmtNinputCallback callback list with the new value passed as *call_data*.

If, on the other hand, the input value fails any of the three verification tests the InputField widget initiates its error-handling procedure to notify the user (and also the application) of the invalid input. The handling of invalid input is described in the next section.

28.4.1 The XmtNverifyCallback

Don't confuse the InputField XmtNverifyCallback list with the XmText XmNmodifyVerifyCallback and XmNmotionVerifyCallback lists. The first is called only when the user enters a new value. The latter two XmText callbacks are called whenever the user inserts or deletes a character and when the user moves the cursor.

The procedures registered on the XmtNverifyCallback callback list are called with a pointer to an XmtInputFieldCallbackStruct as their *call_data*. This structure is the following:

```
typedef struct {
    String value; /* can be replaced, but not modified or freed */
    Boolean okay; /* initially True; set to False if input is bad */
} XmtInputFieldCallbackStruct;
```

The value field of the XmtInputFieldCallbackStruct contains the newly entered string. The string is owned by the InputField widget, and should never be modified or freed by the application. A callback procedure can modify the value field itself, however, so that it points to a different string. If the value field is changed in this way, the InputField widget will make its own private copy of the new value and will proceed as if the user had entered the new string rather than the string it replaced.

The InputField widget invokes the first procedure on this callback list with the okay field of the XmtInputFieldCallbackStruct set to True. Any of the procedures on the list may reject the input value by setting this field to False.

Example 28-3 shows some procedures that you might register on the `XmtNverifyCallback` list of an InputField widget. Note the variety of tasks possible through this callback.

Example 28-3. An InputField Input Verification Callback

```
/*
 * This verify callback expects to be registered with an integer
 * as its client_data on an InputField widget that uses the XmtNpattern
 * resource to insure that only digits are entered.  It uses its
 * client_data as a maximum bound and rejects the input integer
 * if it is larger than the maximum.
 */
void CheckMax(Widget w, XtPointer client_data, XtPointer call_data)
{
    XmtInputFieldCallbackStruct *data =
        (XmtInputFieldCallbackStruct*)call_data;
    int max = (int) client_data;
    int value;

    value = atoi(data->value);
    if (value > max) data->okay = False;
}

/*
 * This verify callback is much like the previous one.  It expects
 * a regular expression as its client_data, and checks that the
 * user's input matches that regular expression using re_comp() and
 * re_exec().
 */
void CheckRegExp(Widget w, XtPointer client_data, XtPointer call_data)
{
    XmtInputFieldCallbackStruct *data =
        (XmtInputFieldCallbackStruct*)call_data;
    String pattern = (String) client_data;

    (void) re_comp(pattern);
    if (re_exec(data->value) != 1) data->okay = False;
}

/*
 * This verify callback doesn't actually perform any checks on the
 * user's input; it just converts that input to upper case.  Note
 * that data->value is replaced, but that the original value is
 * not to be freed by this procedure.  The InputField will make its
 * own private copy of the new value when the callback returns, but
 * will not attempt to free the application's copy of the value.
 * For this reason, a static buffer is the best way to store the value.
 */
void Upcase(Widget w, XtPointer client_data, XtPointer call_data)
{
    XmtInputFieldCallbackStruct *data =
        (XmtInputFieldCallbackStruct*)call_data;
    static char buffer[MAX_INPUT_LEN];
    int i;

    for(i=0; data->value[i]; i++)
```

Example 28-3. An InputField Input Verification Callback (continued)

```
        buffer[i] = toupper(data->value[i]);
    buffer[i] = '\0';
    data->value = buffer;
}
```

The XmText `XmNmodifyVerifyCallback` is good for verifying user input character-by-character, and the InputField `XmtNverifyCallback` is good for verifying input when the user completes a new value, but sometimes neither of these are appropriate verification models for your application. In some dialog boxes, the legal input values for an InputField widget might depend on the user's selection in an adjacent XmtChooser widget. In this case, the best time to perform input verification is when the user clicks the **OK** or **Apply** button. At this point, you have a complete set of input values for the dialog box and can check these values for consistency with each other. In Chapter 29, *Custom Dialogs and Automatic Dialog Management*, we'll present techniques for easily extracting all of the user's input values from a dialog box.

28.5 Handling Invalid Input

When an input value fails any of the input verification tests described above, the InputField widget invokes the procedures registered on the `XmtNerror-Callback` list. This notifies the application that the error has occurred, and provides a hook to the programmer to allow custom error handling. Any procedure in this `XmtNerrorCallback` list can set a field in its *`call_data`* structure (shown below) to specify that the error has been handled by the application, and that the InputField should take no further action to handle it.

If this field in the *`call_data`* structure is not set, then the InputField attempts to call the user's attention to the error. There are a number of ways it can do this: by beeping, by reverting to the last valid input, by displaying a special string (such as "<Error>"), or by highlighting the invalid input. The following resources comprise the InputField's error-handling strategy:

- If the `XmtNbeepOnError` resource is `True` (the default), then the widget will beep when invalid input is entered. This resource can be used in parallel with any of the other error-handling resources described below.
- If `XmtNreplaceOnError` is `True` (the default), then any invalid input entered by the user will be replaced by the last valid input value that was displayed by the widget. By default, this replacement will occur immediately, but if you use the resources described below, then the replacement will not occur until the user begins to enter a new value.
- If the `XmtNerrorString` resource is non-NULL, then the invalid input is temporarily replaced with the string specified by that resource. The next time the user edits or traverses into the widget this special error string will be removed. If `XmtNreplaceOnError` is set, then the error string will be replaced with the last valid input value for the widget. Otherwise, it will be replaced with the current, invalid input value.

- If no error string is set, but `XmtNhighlightOnError` is set, then the invalid input value is highlighted by changing its color or by underlining it. If the `XmtNerrorForeground` or `XmtNerrorBackground` resources are set, and the widget is being displayed on a color screen, then the foreground and/or background colors of the widget are temporarily changed to highlight the bad input. If no colors are specified, or when the widget is on a monochrome screen, the invalid input is displayed with an underline. The next time the user edits the widget or traverses into it, the special colors or underlining will be removed. As with the case above, if the `XmtNreplaceOnError` resource is set, then the invalid input is replaced, at this point, with the last valid input value. If it is not set, then the user is left with the current invalid input displayed.

Figure 28-2 shows InputField widgets signaling invalid input in several different ways.

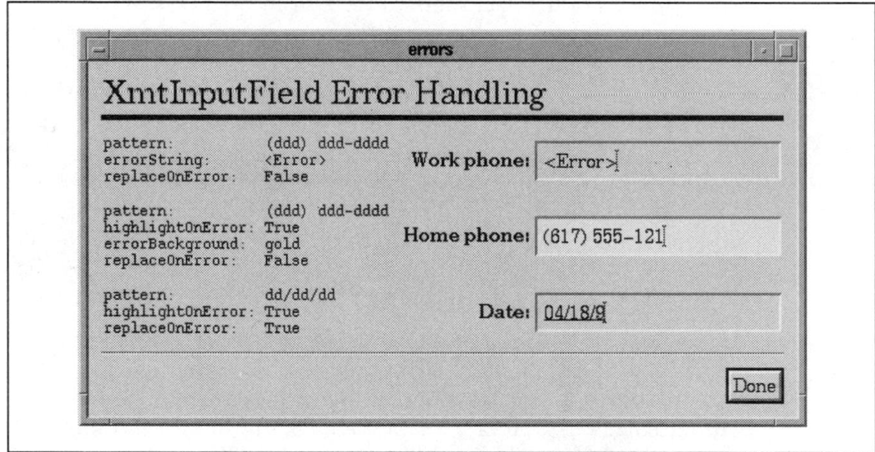

Figure 28-2. Signaling invalid input with an InputField widget

The question of just how to handle invalid input is a difficult one, and there will be different solutions appropriate in different circumstances. The default scheme, beeping and replacing the invalid input immediately, is one of the simplest possible strategies, and is the default. By always replacing bad input with good, it maintains the invariant that after the user has typed **Return** or traversed out of the widget, the `XmtNinput` resource and the displayed value are the same. Note that this invariant doesn't always hold with other error-handling strategies. On the other hand, this scheme offers less feedback than the others, and by switching from invalid input to the last valid input immediately, it tends to take the user "out of the loop." In a similar way, specifying an error string is a good way to make it very clear to the user that the input was bad, but by immediately replacing the invalid input, it doesn't give the user a chance to examine it to determine what was wrong with it.

If you are unsure which error-handling scheme to use, experiment with the feel of each of them. The final choice will depend on just how important it is in the context of the application that the input be valid, and how obvious the notification to the user must be. For any one dialog box, of course, you should always use the same error-handling scheme, and, if practical, you should use the same scheme throughout the application.

Finally, note that dialog boxes can have message lines, and for complex dialog boxes that have sophisticated validity checking or non-obvious constraints on the valid values for input, a message line can be a good way to tell the user just what the problem with his input value is. You can set a message in a message line widget from the error callback, or, often more conveniently, from the verify callback that actually checks the input value. Displaying a message may be sufficient notification in itself, or you might combine it with the `XmtNhighlightOnError` resource, for example, so that it is obvious which InputField the message is referring to. (You could also provide this kind of error feedback with an error dialog box, of course, but this would cause more disruption in the user's work—dialogs within dialogs are rarely justified.)

28.5.1 The XmtNerrorCallback

The procedures registered on this callback list are called when the user enters an invalid value. This callback notifies the application that the error has occurred. Applications that want to notify the user of invalid input themselves can use this callback as a hook to perform the notification, and can also use it to tell the InputField widget not to handle the error. The *call_data* argument for this callback is a pointer to the following structure:

```
typedef struct {
    String value; /* don't modify or free this string or the field */
    Boolean okay; /* set to True to prevent further error handling */
} XmtInputFieldCallbackStruct;
```

Note that this is the same structure that is used by the `XmtNverifyCallback`. Be careful, though; the meaning and usage of the fields is subtly changed for this callback. The `value` field points to the invalid input value that caused the error callbacks to be called. This string is owned by the InputField widget and should not be modified or freed. With the `XmtNerrorCallback`, the `value` field may not itself be changed, as it can with the `XmtNverifyCallback`. The `XmtNerrorCallback` callback is invoked with the `okay` field set to `False`. If a callback procedure sets this field to `True`, then the InputField widget will not perform any subsequent error handling for the invalid value. Note that this is the reverse of how the `XmtNverifyCallback` uses this field.

In practice, you may never have cause to use the `XmtNerrorCallback`. The error-handling responses that the InputField can provide automatically are usually fairly appropriate, so you rarely need to disable them with this callback. The `XmtNerrorCallback` gives your application a way to detect when the user's input has failed verification because of the `XmtNpattern` or `XmtNtargetSymbolName` resources. If the input is invalid because it fails an `XmtNverifyCallback`, however, then the application already knows about the error, and doesn't really need this notification.

Handling the Stippled Cursor

Scott Gregory has found a simple solution to a distracting problem in Motif 1.2—the stippled I-beam cursors that are left in every inactive input field of a dialog box.

Under Motif 1.1, XmText widgets (and TextField) had only one I-beam cursor per application. The cursor tracked focus around the screen, and our users found this good.

Motif 1.2 changed this, so that non-focused Text widgets had a "stippled" I-beam cursor. Our users found this bad. (Therefore so did we, because they pay us to agree with them :-)

So—I implemented a pair of functions to be registered on the `XmNfocusCallback` and `XmNlosingFocusCallback` callback lists of each input field. These functions simply set `XmNcursorPositionVisible` to `True` when an input field gets the input focus, and set it to `False` when the input field loses the focus.

—Scott Gregory

28.6 Overstrike Mode

Prior to Motif 1.2, the XmText widget did not support overstrike mode (in which a typed character replaces the character underneath it, instead of pushing that character to the right). In Motif 1.2, the widget supports overstrike mode, but only through an action available to the user; it is not convenient for the programmer to specify which mode the widget should be in. The InputField widget does support overstrike mode, however, in Motif 1.2 or before.

The `XmtNoverstrike` resource allows the programmer to specify which mode the widget should be in. The choice between the two modes is an intensely personal one, however, and the application programmer really shouldn't set this resource except in response to a user request to set it.

The InputField widget defines a single new action procedure named `overstrike()`. If called with the single argument "on," this action will turn overstrike mode on for the widget by setting the `XmtNoverstrike` resource. If called with the argument "off," it will turn overstrike mode off. If called with no argument, it will toggle the state of overstrike mode.

The InputField widget inherits the translations of the XmText widget, and does not add any new translations of its own. In particular, it does not bind the new `overstrike()` action to any key. If you want to allow the user to be able to switch between insert and overstrike modes in the widget, you must add this translation explicitly.

28.7 Input Field Captions and Sensitivity

An InputField widget almost always needs a caption to prompt the user for the value that is to be entered into it. The easiest way to specify this caption is to use the XmtLayout widget as the parent, and specify the caption with the `XmtNlayoutCaption` constraint resource, or in the `XmtNlayout` string, as explained in Chapter 19, *The Layout Widget: The Details.*

Since the InputField is so often used with captions provided by the XmtLayout widget, the InputField widget takes care to notice when it has been made insensitive (through `XtSetSensitive()`, for example) and will set the `XmtNlayoutSensitive` constraint resource of the XmtLayout widget to gray out its caption in this case as well.

28.8 Style

The InputField is a straightforward widget. There are a few tips, however, that will help you use it better:

- You'll need to provide a caption for each InputField in order to prompt the user for the desired input. This caption should go to the left of the InputField. As with all user-visible text, choose your prompts carefully and use strong, succinct language.
- To help keep captions distinct from input text, you may want to use a font that is bolder than the font used for user input. You can also use different colors. One possible technique is to give the InputField a slightly darker shade of the dialog background—this can work well with the shadowed-in effect provided by the InputField.
- If you will be using the `XmtNverifyCallback`, or the `XmtNpattern`, or `XmtNtargetSymbolName` resources, then it is important that the user understand what has happened if her input is rejected. The InputField widget provides various ways of handling and flagging invalid input, but you may choose to augment them with additional feedback in a dialog box message line, for example.
- It is common to have a group of InputField widgets arranged into a column, and it looks nice when the widgets have the same width and have their left and right edges lined up. When the widgets have captions of different lengths, however, this can be tricky. The solution, when using the XmtLayout widget, is to use flush right justification for each of the InputField widgets. If you use an XmtLayout widget to arrange a column of InputField widgets, you can use that widget to display an etched border around that column—this can provide a nice visual effect to separate the fields from other groups of widgets in the dialog box.
- Don't insist that all your InputFields have the same width, however, if they are designed for input of dramatically different lengths. If an InputField will be used for the input of a three-digit number, for example, then it should not be much wider than three digit widths. Setting an appropriate

width with the `XmNcolumns` resource can be a little tricky when you use a proportionally-spaced font, since the widget will reserve space based on the widest character in the font—this is usually appropriate only if you expect input of digits or capital letters.

29

Custom Dialogs and Automatic Dialog Management

The purpose of dialog boxes in an application is to display information to the user or to get input from the user (or some combination of the two). Chapter 25, *Message Dialogs*, and Chapter 26, *Simple Input Dialogs*, have presented techniques for displaying messages and getting simple input from the user. Most applications, however, will need dialogs that are more complicated than are possible with the convenience functions presented in those chapters. The dialog box shown in Figure 29-1, for example, prompts the user to input a number of values.

The traditional approach to implementng a dialog like this one typically involves at least three custom procedures in your C code. The first procedure creates the widgets required for the dialog box and saves pointers to the important ones (i.e. the output widgets that will display data and the input widgets used for user input) in global variables or in the fields of some custom structure. The second procedure will use these saved widget pointers to initialize the dialog—by setting messages and other data to be displayed in the output widgets, and by setting default input values in the input widgets. And the third procedure reverses the second—it queries the widgets to obtain the user's input values, and then stores those input values somewhere for use by the application.

The first procedure is an easy one to simplify. Chapter 11, *Automatic Widget Creation*, shows how we can use the `xmtChildren` resource to specify the widgets in the dialog and `XmtBuildDialog()` to create those widgets. And Chapter 19, *The Layout Widget: The Details*, shows how we can use the XmtLayout widget's `XmtNlayout` resource to easily describe the arrangement of the widgets in the dialog box.

29.0

examples/

29/net_directory

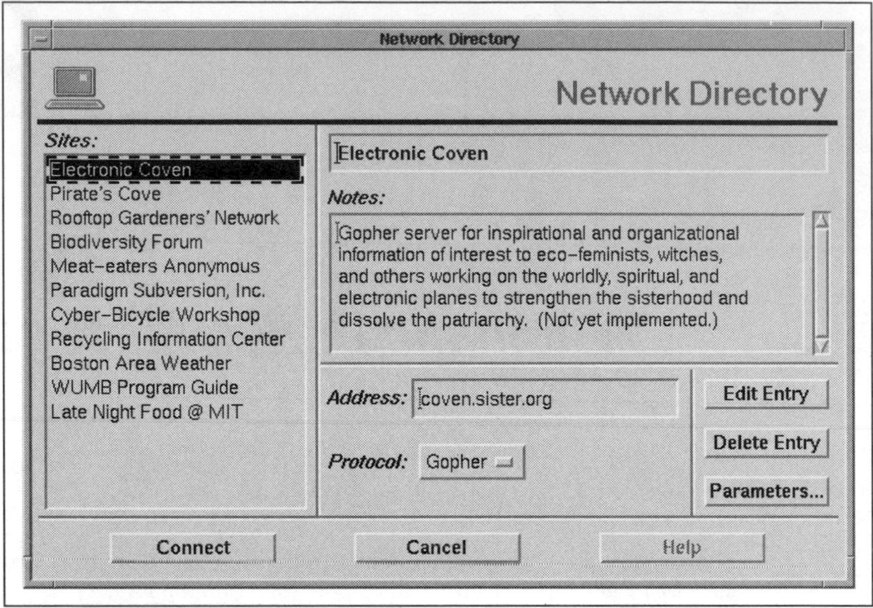

Figure 29-1. A non-trivial dialog box

The task that remains, then, for this sort of non-trivial dialog, is transferring application data to the dialog widgets, and then extracting user input data from the widgets and transferring it to the application. This chapter explains how we can automate this data transfer process, thereby dramatically simplifying the effort required to add new dialogs to an application.

29.1 Overview: Automatic Dialogs

The approach that we'll take to automating dialogs is to develop two procedures, the functions `XmtDialogSetDialogValues()` and `XmtDialogGetDialogValues()`.* The first will copy values from an application data structure and will set those values on the appropriate widgets in a dialog box. The second will extract the user's input from the widgets in a dialog box and will automatically transfer those input values to a data structure. Example 29-1 shows the kind of code you might end up with using these two functions.

*Some programmers remark that these function names are redundant. The first "Dialog" appears in the `XmtDialog` prefix to identify the module of Xmt that they are part of. The second "Dialog" is necessary to clarify the purpose of each function: if a function was named `XmtDialogGetValues()`, it would not be clear whether it "got" values from the dialog and stored them in the application data structures, or "got" them from the application and stored them in the dialog.

Example 29-1. Simplified Dialogs with Xmt

```
/*
 * This is the data structure we'll use in the application.
 * We want to set things up so we can transfer these data values
 * to and from the dialog box.
 */
typedef struct {
    char name[40];
    char street[40];
    char city[20];
    char state[3];
    int zip;
    char phone[30];
} rolodex_entry_t;

/*
 * Here we'd define an XtResourceList that describes the
 * size, offset, and type of each of the fields in the data
 * structure, and gives each field a name.  We've omitted
 * this list for now.
 */
XtResource rolodex_resources[] = {
    .
    .
    .
};

/* the actual instance of the data structure that we'll use */
static rolodex_entry_t entry;

/* the dialog widget we'll be using */
static Widget rolodialog;

static void PopupRolodexDialog(void)
{
    /*
     * The first time this procedure is called, we go and actually
     * create the dialog box.  We're assuming that its widgets are
     * described using the xmtChildren resource, and that the layout
     * of those widgets are also described in the resource file,
     * using the XmtNlayout resource of the XmtLayout widget, for
     * example. After creating the dialog, we register callbacks on
     * its okay and cancel buttons.  (This could also have been done
     * in a resource file, of course.)
     */
    if (!rolodialog) {
        Widget okay_button, cancel_button;
        rolodialog = XmtBuildQueryDialog(toplevel, "rolodex",
                                         rolodex_resources,
                                         XtNumber(rolodex_resources),
                                         "okay", &okay_button,
                                         "cancel", &cancel_button,
                                         NULL);
        XtAddCallback(okay_button, OkayCallback, NULL);
        XtAddCallback(cancel_button, CancelCallback, NULL);
    }
```

Example 29-1. Simplified Dialogs with Xmt (continued)

```
    /*
     * Now we set the current data values on the dialog, and pop it up.
     * That's all we have to do here.  When the user has interacted with
     * the dialog, she'll click Ok or Cancel, and one of the callbacks
     * below will be called.
     */
    XmtDialogSetDialogValues(rolodialog, &entry);
    XtManageChild(rolodialog);
}

static void OkayCallback(Widget w, XtPointer tag, XtPointer data)
{
    /*
     * The user clicked "Okay", so pop down the dialog,
     * get her input values, and do something with them.
     */
    XtUnmanageChild(rolodialog);
    XmtDialogGetDialogValues(rolodialog, &entry);
    add_new_rolodex_entry(&entry);
}

static void CancelCallback(Widget w, XtPointer tag, XtPointer data)
{
    /*
     * The user clicked "Cancel", so just pop down the dialog.
     * ignoring any input.
     */
    XtUnmanageChild(rolodialog);
}
```

Once we've defined the basic functions `XmtDialogSetDialogValues()` and `XmtDialogGetDialogValues()` for transferring data, it is possible to simplify dialog management even further. Later in the chapter we'll see the function `XmtDialogDo()` which performs some basic error checking, calls `XmtDialogSetDialogValues()`, and pops the dialog up.

Even more convenient, in many cases, is the function `XmtDialogDoSync()`, a synchronous version of `XmtDialogDo()`. When you use this function in conjunction with some special, pre-defined callbacks, you can simplify your dialog-handling code even further. Example 29-2 shows a simplified, synchronous version of the code shown in Example 29-1.

Example 29-2. Further Simplified Dialogs

```
static void PopupRolodexDialog(void)
{
    /*
     * In this version, the dialog widget is hidden within this
     * function. Also, we use an automatic structure, here, rather
     * than a static one.
     */
    static Widget rolodialog;
    rolodex_entry_t entry;
```

Example 29-2. Further Simplified Dialogs (continued)

```
    /*
     * As before, create the dialog the first time through.
     * This time, we register two special callbacks,
     * XmtDialogOkayCallback, and XmtDialogCancelCallback on
     * the buttons, but do so in the resource file.
     */
    if (!rolodialog)
        rolodialog = XmtBuildDialog(toplevel, "rolodex",
                                    rolodex_resources,
                                    XtNumber(rolodex_resources));

    /* set default values in the data structure */
    memset((void *)&entry, 0, sizeof(rolodex_entry_t));

    /*
     * Now pop up the dialog and wait for one of the buttons to
     * be clicked. If the user clicks Okay, the data will be
     * transferred to entry, and the function will return True.
     * Otherwise, it will return False.  This function takes care
     * of popping up the dialog and popping it down.
     */
    if (XmtDialogDoSync(rolodialog, &entry))
        add_new_rolodex_entry(&entry);
}
```

In order to make dialog management this simple in your C code, Xmt has to be doing some fairly complex work behind the scenes. The next section explains the mechanics behind the automatic data transfer, and explains what you need to do to set up your dialogs to work with these tools. The sections after that go into detail about `XmtDialogGetDialogValues()`, `XmtDialogDoSync()`, and the other functions for controlling dialogs.

29.2 Background: Automatic Data Transfer

To automatically transfer data between application data structures and dialog boxes, we need a technique for mapping the fields within a data structure to the corresponding widgets within a dialog. We perform this mapping in two stages. First, we use an `XtResourceList` to associate a resource name with the fields in a data structure. (This is a technique that is familiar to widget writers, and to anyone who has worked with application resources. It will also be explained below.) And second, having given names to each of the fields in the data structure, we then associate those names with particular widgets in the dialog, using an extension to the `xmtChildren` widget creation resource. The field-to-name mapping plus the name-to-widget mapping can be combined to map fields to widgets and vice-versa. Figure 29-2 shows a diagram of this mapping.

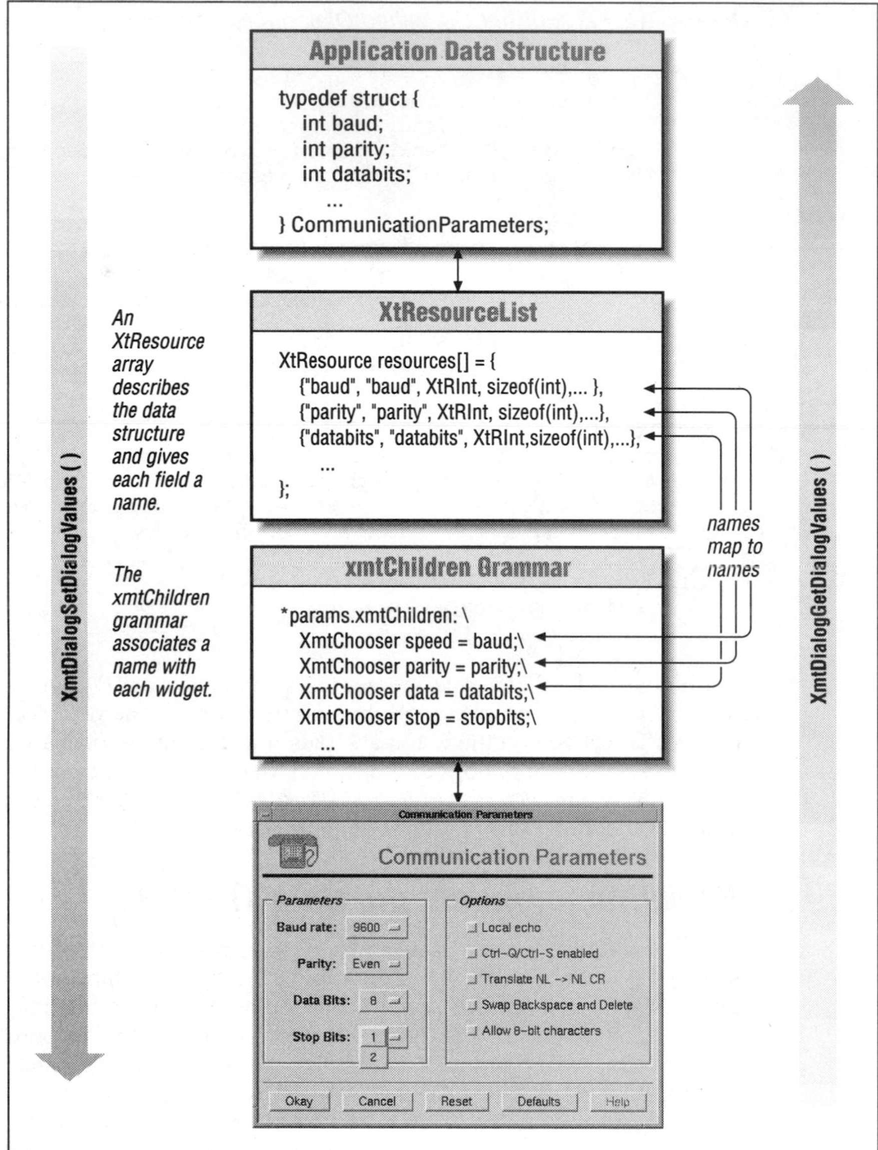

Figure 29-2. Transferring data between application and dialog

With this mapping established there still needs to be a mechanism for performing the actual data transfer. Different widgets store their values in different ways. To set the value of an XmtChooser widget, for example, you might call `XmtChooserSetState()`, but to set the value of an XmText widget you might set the `XmNvalue` resource. Since data transfer techniques vary depending on the type of the widget, we handle the data transfer by registering two procedures for each type of widget—one procedure that knows how to set the value of the widget, and one that knows how to read the value from the widget. These procedures are registered with `XmtRegisterWidgetTypes()`—the same function that is used to register widget types with the automatic creation routines. There are predefined data-transfer procedures for all the Motif and Xmt widgets that accept user input, and convenience routines for registering them. This is explained in more detail below. Figure 29-2 illustrates how these "get value" and "set value" procedures transfer the data.

The following subsections explain in more detail what you need to do in your programs to establish the data-structure to dialog mapping, and how you can specify procedures to actually transfer the data. These subsections do not describe `XmtDialogGetDialogValues()` or the other dialog management functions that we saw in the overview above, but you'll need to read and understand this background material in order to make use of those higher-level functions.

29.2.1 Naming Fields in a Data Structure

The first step in mapping between fields in application data structures and widgets in dialog boxes is to give names to the data structure fields. This is exactly what widget writers do to create named widget resources, and exactly what you do to add application resources to a program. In each of these cases, an `XtResource` is used to specify a name (and a class name) for a field with a specified type, size, position in the structure, and default value. The `XtResource` type is shown in Example 29-3. Note that to describe a number of fields in an application data structure, we use an array of `XtResource`, which is of type `XtResourceList`.

Example 29-3. The XtResource Structure

```
typedef struct _XtResource {
    String      resource_name;  /* Resource name                           */
    String      resource_class; /* Resource class                          */
    String      resource_type;  /* Representation type desired             */
    Cardinal    resource_size;  /* Size in bytes of representation         */
    Cardinal    resource_offset;/* Offset from base to put resource value  */
    String      default_type;   /* Representation type of specified default */
    XtPointer   default_addr;   /* Address of default resource             */
} XtResource, *XtResourceList;
```

See the discussion of application resources in Chapter 7, *Application Resources and Command-Line Arguments*, for a detailed explanation of each of the fields in this structure. An `XtResourceList` is used in the same way for automatic data transfer as it is for application resources. There are a couple of minor differences in the way you initialize an `XtResourceList` in these two cases, however. The dialog data transfer mechanism never makes use of the resource class name, so there is no need to specify a resource class that is different from the resource name. Additionally, while widget and application resources are usually four bytes long (or fewer), with the dialog data transfer mechanism you may often use fixed-size character buffers to store string data, such as that obtained from an XmtInputField widget. In this case, you won't be able to use the `sizeof()` operator to compute the `resource_size` field as you typically would for an application resource.

Example 29-4 shows the application data structure used with one of the dialog boxes pictured at the beginning of this chapter, and shows the statically-initialized resource list that names and describes the fields of this data structure.

Example 29-4. Using an XtResourceList to Describe an Application Data Structure

examples/

29/net_directory.c

```
typedef struct {
    char name[50];
    char address[50];
    char *comments;
    int type;
    CommunicationParameters params;
} DirectoryEntry;

XtResource directory_resources[] = {
{"name", "name", XmtRBuffer,
     XmtSizeOf(DirectoryEntry, name), XtOffsetOf(DirectoryEntry, name),
     XtRImmediate, NULL},
{"address", "address", XmtRBuffer,
     XmtSizeOf(DirectoryEntry, address), XtOffsetOf(DirectoryEntry, address),
     XtRImmediate, NULL},
{"comments", "comments", XtRString,
     sizeof(char *), XtOffsetOf(DirectoryEntry, comments),
     XtRImmediate, NULL},
{"type", "type", XtRInt,
     sizeof(int), XtOffsetOf(DirectoryEntry, type),
     XtRImmediate, (XtPointer)PROTOCOL_MODEM},
};
```

29.2.1.1 Handling String Resources

In Example 29-4 you can see two different ways of handling string data in automatic dialogs. One technique uses a ordinary `char *` field, declared as a resource of type `XtRString`. The other technique instead uses a character buffer—the data structure includes space for the entire string—declared as a resource of type `XmtRBuffer`. Each technique has its advantages and disadvantages, but they handle strings quite differently, and it is important to understand these differences.

`XtRString` is a representation type commonly used for any string resource of a widget; it is a pointer to a string. A resource of this type always has a size of four bytes (or `sizeof(char *)`)—enough space to store the address of the first character in the string. Different widgets handle resources of this type differently. When you query an `XtRString` resource in a Motif widget, the widget will allocate a copy of the resource, and return that copy to you. You are responsible for freeing the allocated memory when you are done with it. This is the case with the XmText and XmTextField widgets, for example.

The XmtInputField widget is different, however. When you query the value of its `XmtNinput` resource, it returns the address of its internal value. This is memory owned by the XmtInputField widget, so you must *not* free it or modify it in any way. Furthermore, the returned value is not guaranteed to remain stable (or even to remain valid) once the application's flow-of-control has returned to the event loop or to the InputField widget. Usually, this is okay—you'll use the value once and then be done with it. If you need a value that will remain valid, you'll have to make a copy of your own.

These different approaches to `XtRString` resources are reflected in the way that data is transferred from a widget to an application data structure. If you specify a four-byte `XtRString` resource in your `XtResourceList`, and then associate that resource with an XmText, XmTextField, or XmScrolledText widget, then the data that will be automatically transferred from the widget to the application data structure will be a pointer to allocated memory that you must remember to free at some point. On the other hand, if you associate your `XtRString` resource with an XmtInputField widget, then the data transferred will be a pointer to memory owned by the InputField, memory that you need not (must not) free, but which may not remain valid once control returns to the InputField widget (which can happen through the event loop, through function calls, or by setting resources.)

Because of the difficulty of handling string data, Xmt supports a special representation type, `XmtRBuffer`. A resource of this type is not the address of the first character in the string, but is the string itself. The size of an `XmtRBuffer` resource is not the size of a `char *`, but the number of characters allocated for the string. With an `XmtRBuffer` resource, the entire string will be copied from the widget into the application data structure, not just its address.

Using an `XmtRBuffer` resource is almost always easier than an `XtRString` resource when dealing with automatic dialogs. Because the string value is copied into a block of memory that you own, you do not have to worry about freeing the string (you may free your whole structure, but don't have to free the string independently of it) or about the potential volatility of the string. The possible drawbacks are that buffers have a fixed size, and that by including string buffers directly in your data structures, you make them larger than they'd otherwise be. For dialog boxes, however, most input values have a fixed maximum size, and this maximum is not so large that you will be using memory extravagantly.

The resource list shown in Example 29-4 contains two `XmtRBuffer` resources, and one `XtRString` resource. The buffers are intended for use with XmtInputField widgets, and the `XtRString` resource is intended for use with a scrolled multi-line text widget. Since the input for this multi-line widget may be quite long, it makes more sense to handle this value as a regular string that must be freed.

Note the use of `XmtSizeOf()` in the declaration of the buffer resources. This is a macro defined in *<Xmt/Xmt.h>*. It takes the same arguments as `XtOffsetOf()` and returns the size, in bytes, of the specified field in the structure of the specified type.

29.2.2 Associating Names with Widgets

The second step in mapping the fields of application data structures to widgets in a dialog box is to associate the resource names we specified above with the individual widgets in the dialog box. This is done with an extension to the widget-creation grammar used with the xmtChildren resource. (See Chapter 11, *Automatic Widget Creation.*) Recall that this resource is used with XmtCreateChildren() and related functions, and allows you to specify the names and types of widgets that will be automatically created. Specifying widgets with xmtChildren is a lot like declaring variables in C. A typical xmtChildren resource might look like this:

```
dialog.xmtChildren: XmLabel message;\
                    XmPushButton okay, cancel, help;
```

To associate a resource name with widgets created in this way, simply follow the widget name with an equal sign, and the name of the resource. This extension to the grammar is similar to a C initializer. Example 29-5 shows how this syntax is used in the definition of the dialog box pictured at the beginning of this chapter. Note that the names following the = character are the resource names declared in Example 29-4, and that they may or may not be the same as the names of the widgets they are associated with.

Example 29-5. Associating Resource Names with Widgets Through xmtChildren

examples/

29/net_directory.ad

```
*net_dialog_shell.xmtChildren: unmanaged XmtLayout net_dialog;

*net_dialog.autoUnmanage: False
*net_dialog.dialogTitle: Network Directory
*net_dialog.xmtChildren: \
        XmScrolledList list;\
        XmtInputField site = name, address = address;\
        XmtChooser protocol = type;\
        XmScrolledText notes = comments;\
        XmPushButton addentry, deleteentry, setparams;\
        XmPushButton connect, cancel, help;
```

29.2.3 Transferring Data

The previous sections have explained how we can use resource names to establish a link between the fields of an application data structure and the widgets in a dialog box. With this link established, we need a mechanism for actually transferring the data from application to dialog and vice versa. As noted above, the mechanics of setting and querying a widget's value vary, so our underlying data-transfer method will depend on the widget type.

Chapter 11, *Automatic Widget Creation*, showed how you can register widget classes and constructors for use with the automatic widget creation routines. The most general-purpose widget type registration function is XmtRegisterWidgetTypes(). This function allows you not only to register a widget class or constructor function, but also to register a set_value procedure and a `get_value` procedure for the widget type. These procedures have the following signatures:

```
#include <Xmt/WidgetType.h>
typedef void (*XmtSetValueProc)(Widget w, XtPointer address,
                                XrmQuark type, Cardinal size);
typedef void (*XmtGetValueProc)(Widget w, XtPointer address,
                                XrmQuark type, Cardinal size);
```

The `XmtSetValueProc` is responsible for setting a value on the widget *w*. The value is stored at *`address`*, and is *`size`* bytes long. *`type`* is a quarkified version of the representation type of the value; the `set_value` procedure should check that this type is one that can legally be set on the widget, and should cast it or convert it as necessary. If the type is not a legal one, the procedure should print a warning message. (Converting strings to quarks converts the process of string comparison to the far simpler process of integer comparison. For a refresher on quarks, see `XrmStringToQuark()`.)

The `XmtGetValueProc` has the same signature, but is responsible for the reverse process—it should query the value of the specified widget, cast or convert the value as necessary for *`type`*, and then store the value in the *`size`* bytes at *`address`*.

Example 29-6 shows the `set_value` and `get_value` procedures Xmt uses for the XmToggleButton widget, and also shows how these procedures are registered with the widget using `XmtRegisterWidgetTypes()`. Xmt provides pre-defined data transfer procedures for all of Motif and Xmt widgets that have values that the user can edit (these widgets are listed below), so you may never have to write these procedures on your own. It is important to understand how they work, however, and later in this chapter we will see an example where it is useful to define your own custom data transfer procedures.

Example 29-6. Automatic Data Transfer Procedures for the XmToggleButton

```
static void setvalue(Widget w, XtPointer address, XrmQuark type, Cardinal size)
{
    int state;

    /*
     * We use some Xmt-defined quarks in these procedures. If you were
     * writing your own procedures, you might register your own type
     * quarks explicitly.
     */
    if ((type != XmtQBoolean) && (type != XmtQBool) && (type != XmtQCardinal)
        && (type != XmtQEnum) && (type != XmtQInt) && (type != XmtQShort)
        && (type != XmtQUnsignedChar)) {
        XmtWarningMsg("XmtDialogSetDialogValues", "toggleb",
                      "Type mismatch: Widget '%s':\n\tCan't set widget value\
from a resource of type '%s'; scalar type expected.",
                      XtName(w), XrmQuarkToString(type));
        return;
```

Example 29-6. Automatic Data Transfer Procedures for the XmToggleButton (continued)

```
    }

    if (size == sizeof(unsigned char)) state = *(unsigned char *)address;
    else if (size == sizeof(unsigned short)) state = *(unsigned short*)address;
    else if (size == sizeof(unsigned int)) state = *(unsigned int *)address;
    else return;

    XmToggleButtonSetState(w, state, False);
}

static void getvalue(Widget w, XtPointer address, XrmQuark type, Cardinal size)
{
    Boolean state;

    if ((type != XmtQBoolean) && (type != XmtQBool) && (type != XmtQCardinal)
        && (type != XmtQEnum) && (type != XmtQInt) && (type != XmtQShort)
        && (type != XmtQUnsignedChar)) {
        XmtWarningMsg("XmtDialogGetDialogValues", "toggleb",
                      "Type mismatch: Widget '%s':\n\tCan't set state on\
resource of type '%s'; scalar type expected.",
                      XtName(w), XrmQuarkToString(type));
        return;
    }

    state = XmToggleButtonGetState(w);

    if (size == sizeof(unsigned char)) *(unsigned char *)address = state;
    else if (size == sizeof(unsigned short)) *(unsigned short*)address = state;
    else if (size == sizeof(unsigned int)) *(unsigned int *)address = state;
}

static XmtWidgetType widget = {
    "XmToggleButton",       /* name */
    NULL,                   /* class */
    XmCreateToggleButton,   /* constructor */
    setvalue,               /* procedure to set a value on widget */
    getvalue,               /* procedure to get a value from widget */
    False                   /* not a popup widget */
};

void XmtRegisterXmToggleButton(void)
{
    _XmtInitQuarks();  /* make sure the Xmt-internal quarks are registered. */
    XmtRegisterWidgetTypes(&widget, 1);
}
```

29.2.3.1 Predefined Data Transfer Procedures

As described in Chapter 11, you can use the functions `XmtRegisterMotifWidgets()` and `XmtRegisterXmtWidgets()` to register all Motif and Xmt widgets. You can also register only the individual widgets that you'll be using with `XmtVaRegisterWidgetConstructors()`, `XmtRegisterWidgetTypes()` and related functions. Xmt also provides special registration functions for the seven Motif and Xmt widgets that have a user editable value. These functions are:

```
#include <Xmt/Chooser.h>
void XmtRegisterChooser(void);

#include <Xmt/InputField.h>
void XmtRegisterInputField(void);

#include <Xmt/WidgetType.h>
void XmtRegisterXmScale(void);
void XmtRegisterXmScrolledText(void);
void XmtRegisterXmText(void);
void XmtRegisterXmTextField(void);
void XmtRegisterXmToggleButton(void);
```

Each of these functions calls `XmtRegisterWidgetTypes()` and provides basic `set_value` and `get_value` procedures for the widgets. Table 29-1 shows the types of data that these pre-defined data transfer procedures can handle. The representation types listed in this table are the types you can use in the `XtResourceList` you define (as described above) for your application's data structure.

Table 29-1. Predefined Data Transfer Procedures for Standard Motif and Xmt widgets

Widget	Supported Representation Types
XmScale	`XtRCardinal`, `XtRDimension`, `XtRPosition`, `XtRInt`, `XtRShort`, `XtRUnsignedChar`
XmScrolledText	`XtRString` (must be freed), `XmtRBuffer`
XmText	`XtRString` (must be freed), `XmtRBuffer`
XmTextField	`XtRString` (must be freed), `XmtRBuffer`
XmToggleButton	`XtRBoolean`, `XtRBool`, `XtRCardinal`, `XtREnum`, `XtRInt`, `XtRShort`, `XtRUnsignedChar`
XmtChooser	Type of XmtNvalueType resource, or any scalar with the same size as int, short, or char
XmtInputField	`XtRString` (must not be freed; volatile), `XmtRBuffer`, or, by conversion: `XtRCardinal`, `XtRDimension`, `XmtRDouble`, `XtRFloat`, `XtRInt`, `XtRPosition`, `XtRShort`

The XmtChooser widget makes a distinction between its *state* (the index of the selected item, or the bitfield of its selected items) and its *value* (an arbitrary value associated with the selected item). If you have specified values for a Chooser widget, then you must also set the `XmtNvalueType` resource. In this case, the Chooser's data transfer procedures will transfer the widget value, but only into a field specified with the same type. If you have not specified any values, then the data transfer procedures will transfer the widget state, copying it into fields with any scalar type. See Chapter 27, *Presenting Choices*, for more information on Chooser state and values.

The XmtInputField widget will generally be used with fields of type `XtRString` or `XmtRBuffer`, but its data transfer procedures can also convert strings into numbers and numbers into strings. If you do use an InputField widget with one of the supported numeric types, you will probably want to set the `XmtNpattern` resource or specify a `XmtNverifyCallback` procedure to ensure that the user enters a legal numeric value. See Chapter 28, *The Input Field Widget*, for more information.

Notice that the XmText, XmTextField, XmScrolledText, and XmtInputField data transfer procedures support both `XtRString` and `XmtRBuffer` representation types. The differences between these types were previously described. Also note that the Motif text widgets handle `XtRString` resources differently than the XmtInputField does.

It is the data transfer procedures for the XmText, XmTextField, XmScrolledText, and XmtInputField widgets that define how `XtRString` and `XmtRBuffer` resources will be handled. If you wanted the InputField to handle `XtRString` resources by making a copy that must be freed, rather than returning a pointer to a volatile internal string, for example, you could write your own `get_value` procedure and register the InputField widget yourself, rather than calling `XmtRegisterInputField()`. The pre-defined data transfer procedures for each of these widgets handle `XmtRBuffer` resources specially—instead of transferring the address of the string, they copy the string itself. They are also careful to check that the length of the input string does not exceed the specified size of the buffer resource, and print a warning message if characters had to be truncated to fit the string into the fixed-size buffer.

29.3 Automatic Dialogs

The background material you just read explained what you have to do to establish a mapping between the fields of your application data structures and the widgets of your dialog boxes, and what you need to do to ensure that data values can be transferred back and forth between the two. We started this chapter with a broad overview of how to create and use dialog boxes with Xmt. With the requisite background material out of the way, we can finally fill in the details of that overview.

29.3.1 Creating Dialogs

Chapter 11, *Automatic Widget Creation*, showed how you can use the `xmtChildren` resource and functions like `XmtCreateChildren()` to automatically create a tree of widgets described in a resource file. The background material above explained how you can use an extension to the `xmtChildren` syntax to associate a resource name with a widget, and also how you can use an `XtResourceList` to associate these resource names with the fields of your data structures. Automatic widget creation and this two-part field-to--name-to-widget mapping come together in the two functions `XmtBuildDialog()` and `XmtBuildQueryDialog()`:

Xmt/

Create.c

```
#include <Xmt/Create.h>
Widget XmtBuildDialog(Widget parent, String name,
                      XtResourceList resources,
                      Cardinal num_resources);
Widget XmtBuildQueryDialog(Widget parent, String name,
                           XtResourceList resources,
                           Cardinal num_resources,
                           ..., NULL);
```

`XmtBuildDialog()` and `XmtBuildQueryDialog()` create an XmDialogShell named *name* as a child of *parent*, and then proceed as if `XmtCreateChildren()` or `XmtCreateQueryChildren()` had been called on this shell widget. Both functions return the child of this shell. Both functions take your `XtResourceList` array and the number of resources in it as arguments—these resources define the half of the mapping that your application back-end needs to know about. The resource file that defines the widgets for the dialog box provides the rest of this mapping.

The background section showed example resource lists and example dialog definitions using the `xmtChildren` resource. Example 29-7 shows how you might use `XmtBuildDialog()` to actually create such a dialog. Note that this example uses the resource list defined in Example 29-4 and relies on the `xmtChildren` resources shown in Example 29-5.

examples/ 29/net_directory.c

Example 29-7. Creating a Dialog Box

```
static Widget directory_dialog;

if (!directory_dialog) {
    directory_dialog = XmtBuildQueryDialog(toplevel, "net_dialog_shell",
                                           directory_resources,
                                           XtNumber(directory_resources),
                                           NULL);
}
```

Notice the use of the static variable for storing the dialog widget pointer. The technique shown here has a couple of important features: first, the dialog box need not be created and destroyed each time it is used, and second, the dialog box is not created until it is actually needed, which decreases initial memory usage and startup time.

On occasion, you may find that you would like to use the Xmt automatic data-transfer mechanism with widgets that are not actually in dialog boxes, or for some other reason are not created with `XmtBuildDialog()` or `XmtBuildQueryDialog()`. You can, in fact, use the dialog data transfer mechanisms with any widgets described with the `xmtChildren` resource, but in order to do so, you must associate an `XtResourceList` with them. If you create the widgets by calling any function other than `XmtBuildDialog()` or `XmtBuildQueryDialog()`, you can associate your resource list with the widgets by calling `XmtDialogBindResourceList()`:

Xmt/

Dialog.c

```
#include <Xmt/Dialog.h>
void XmtDialogBindResourceList(Widget w,
                               XtResourceList resources,
                               Cardinal num_resources)
```

The widget *w* is typically a shell widget. You must call `XmtDialogBindResourceList()` to associate resources with that shell *before* you call `XmtCreateChildren()` (or whatever) to create the children of that shell.

29.3.2 Transferring Data to and from Dialogs

Earlier in the chapter we gave an overview of `XmtDialogSetDialogValues()` and `XmtDialogGetDialogValues()`. Now we can formally introduce these functions:

Xmt/

Dialog.c

```
#include <Xmt/Dialog.h>
void XmtDialogSetDialogValues(Widget dialog, XtPointer address);
void XmtDialogGetDialogValues(Widget dialog, XtPointer address);
```

The *dialog* argument to each of these functions is the widget returned by `XmtBuildDialog()` or `XmtBuildQueryDialog()`. The *address* argument is the address of a data structure of the type described by the `XtResourceList` you passed to the dialog creation function. Example 29-8 shows code fragments that use these functions. While this example is heavily commented, notice how little C code is actually required for the data transfer.

Example 29-8. Using XmtDialogSetDialogValues() and XmtDialogGetDialogValues()

examples/

29/net_directory.c

```
/*
 * This callback is invoked to pop up the dialog
 */
static void do_directory(Widget w, XtPointer tag, XtPointer data)
{
    if (!directory_dialog) {
        /*
         * Use XmtBuildQueryDialog() to create the dialog if
         * this is the first time we've been called.
         */
    }

    /* set current values on the widgets in the dialog */
    XmtDialogSetDialogValues(directory_dialog, &directory[current_entry]);

    /* and pop up the dialog */
    XtManageChild(directory_dialog);
}
```

Example 29-8. Using XmtDialogSetDialogValues() and XmtDialogGetDialogValues() (continued)

```
/*
 * This callback is invoked when the user clicks on the
 * "Edit Entry" button.  It copies data from the dialog widgets
 * into the application data structures, making a permanent
 * copy of any user edits.  In many cases, this would also be
 * the place to pop down the dialog, but in this example, the
 * "Connect" button does that.
 */
static void edit_directory(Widget w, XtPointer tag, XtPointer data)
{
    /*
     * The comments field of our data structure is an allocated string.
     * We've got to free the old value before we overwrite it with a
     * newly allocated value.
     */
    XtFree(directory[current_entry].comments);

    /* Now go get the data from the dialog widgets */
    XmtDialogGetDialogValues(directory_dialog, &directory[current_entry]);
}
```

`XmtDialogSetDialogValues()` and `XmtDialogGetDialogValues()` are the basic dialog data transfer routines—they form the basis for all Xmt automatic dialog handling features. Typically, you'll call `XmtDialogSetDialogValues()` to initialize the values displayed in a dialog right before you pop it up, and then you'll call `XmtDialogGetDialogValues()` from a callback procedure registered on the **OK** button, in order to extract the user's input from the dialog. Using these functions lets you explicitly control how and when data is transferred. In a section below we'll see some convenience procedures that hide the details of data transfer even further—in many cases you'll be able to use these convenience routines, and may not have to call these data transfer functions explicitly.

29.3.3 Automatic Dialog Management

Example 29-8 showed how you can use `XmtDialogSetDialogValues()` to store data in dialog widgets just before you pop up the dialog, and can call `XmtDialogGetDialogValues()` from the callback procedure registered on the **OK** to extract the user's input from the dialog. Xmt provides functions that automate this process still further, however.

`XmtDialogDo()` and `XmtDialogDoSync()` call `XmtDialogSetDialogValues()` to store data values into a specified dialog and then pop that dialog up:

Xmt/

Dialog.c

```
#include <Xmt/Dialog.h>
void XmtDialogDo(Widget w, XtPointer address)
Boolean XmtDialogDoSync(Widget w, XtPointer address)
```

Performing these two steps (setting the dialog data and popping the dialog up) is not so great a convenience in itself. What is convenient is that these functions are designed to be used with special pre-defined callback functions that will pop down the dialog and transfer data in the other direction, from the dialog to the application's data structure. Xmt defines the following callback functions for this purpose:

Xmt/

Dialog.c

```
#include <Xmt/Dialog.h>
void XmtDialogOkayCallback(Widget w, XtPointer tag, XtPointer data)
void XmtDialogCancelCallback(Widget w, XtPointer tag, XtPointer data)
void XmtDialogApplyCallback(Widget w, XtPointer tag, XtPointer data)
void XmtDialogResetCallback(Widget w, XtPointer tag, XtPointer data)
void XmtDialogDoneCallback(Widget w, XtPointer tag, XtPointer data)
```

Using `XmtDialogDo()` and `XmtDialogDoSync()` in conjunction with the pre-defined callbacks means that data transfer is handled entirely behind the scenes—you never need to call `XmtDialogSetDialogValues()` or `XmtDialogGetDialogValues()`. Example 29-9 shows the kind of code that results when you use `XmtDialogDo()` in conjunction with these predefined callbacks.

Example 29-9. Using XmtDialogDo()

```
/*
 * This callback creates the dialog the first time it is called, and
 * uses XmtDialogDo() to pop it up and associate a data structure with
 * it.  The predefined Okay and Cancel callbacks (registered in the
 * resource file) do all the rest.
 */
static void do_parameters(Widget w, XtPointer tag, XtPointer data)
{
    if (!parameters_dialog) {
        parameters_dialog = XmtBuildQueryDialog(toplevel, "params_shell",
                                                parameter_resources,
                                                XtNumber(parameter_resources),
                                                NULL);
    }
    XmtDialogDo(parameters_dialog, &directory[current_entry].params);
}

!!
!! This excerpt from the dialog's resource file definition shows how
!! the predefined callbacks are registered.
!!
```

Example 29-9. Using XmtDialogDo() (continued)

```
*params.okay.activateCallback: XmtDialogOkayCallback();
*params.cancel.activateCallback: XmtDialogCancelCallback();
*params.reset.activateCallback: XmtDialogResetCallback();
```

Example 29-10 shows a variation on the previous example. In Example 29-9, the user's input was simply saved into a data structure for use later. In this example, the data must be operated on immediately. Instead of registering a callback on the **OK** button to perform this operation, we instead use `XmtDialogDoSync()` to use the dialog for a synchronous query (in the same way that functions like `XmtAskForBoolean()` do.) Note that we test the return value of `XmtDialogDoSync()` to see whether the user clicked **OK** or **Cancel**.

Example 29-10. Using XmtDialogDoSync()

```
static void do_parameters(Widget w, XtPointer tag, XtPointer data)
{
    static CommunicationParameters parameters;

    if (!parameters_dialog) {
        /* create the dialog, first time only */
        parameters_dialog = XmtBuildQueryDialog(toplevel, "params_shell",
                                                parameter_resources,
                                                XtNumber(parameter_resources),
                                                NULL);
    }

    /*
     * Pop it up and wait for user to click Ok or Cancel.
     * If the user clicked Ok, go process the input.
     * Otherwise, do nothing with the input.
     */
    if (XmtDialogDo(parameters_dialog, &parameters))
        set_parameters(&parameters);
}
```

Notice, in these two examples, that `XmtDialogDo()`, `XmtDialogDoSync()`, and the pre-defined callbacks provide another subtle but important convenience: they keep track of your data structure for you. In previous examples we've used a static data structure that both the popup routine and the popdown callback know about. `XmtDialogDo()` and `XmtDialogDoSync()`, on the other hand, associate the data structure you specify with the dialog widget, so that the pre-defined callback functions can find it (and store the user's input data in it).

The following subsections document `XmtDialogDo()`, `XmtDialogDoSync()`, and each of the predefined callbacks in more detail.

29.3.3.1 XmtDialogDo()

`XmtDialogDo()` uses `XmtDialogSetDialogValues()` to transfer data from the address you specify to the widgets of the dialog. It also internally associates the address of the data with the dialog, so that the pre-defined call backs can look up the data later. You can use `XmtDialogOkayCallback()`

to pop the dialog down and transfer data from the dialog widgets to the data structure, and you can use XmtDialogCancelCallback() to pop the dialog down without transferring any data.

Once XmtDialogDo() has transferred the data and popped up the dialog, it returns, and control generally returns to the application event loop. This means that if you use XmtDialogOkayCallback() to pop the dialog down, you won't get the chance to do any further processing on the user's input. XmtDialogDo() is most useful when you need to allow the user to specify or edit a set of data values, but will not act on those values right away. In a modem communications application, for example, you might define a dialog to allow the user to specify communications parameters (speed, parity, and so on). XmtDialogDo() would transfer the current settings from a global structure to the dialog, the user would edit them, and then XmtDialogOkayCallback() would transfer the user's edited values back to the global structure. Later, when the user actually started to use the modem, the application would read those data values and act on them. For the dialog box itself, however, no manipulation of the data values is required, other than to simply store them as XmtDialogOkayCallback() does.

29.3.3.2 XmtDialogDoSync()

XmtDialogDo() is most useful in circumstances like those described above when you do not have to do anything with the user's input after she clicks the **Ok** button. Except for configuration dialogs, however, you'll usually have to take some action with the user's data. One way to do this is to register a callback procedure in addition to XmtDialogOkayCallback(). In a resource file, you might specify the callbacks for a dialog like this:

```
*my_dialog.okay.activateCallback:\
        XmtDialogOkayCallback();\
        MyDialogCallback();
*my_dialog.cancel.activateCallback:\
        XmtDialogCancelCallback();
```

A variation on this approach is to call XmtDialogOkayCallback() from within your custom callback, or just to use XmtDialogGetDialogValues() explicitly. None of these approaches are particularly convenient, however, and you'll generally find it easier to use XmtDialogDoSync().

XmtDialogDoSync() is a synchronous version of XmtDialogDo()—it transfers data from the application data structure to the widgets of the dialog, pops up the dialog, associates the data address with the dialog for later use by callbacks, and then enters an internal event loop (just as the XmtAskFor*() synchronous input functions do). This means that XmtDialogDoSync() won't return until something causes this internal event loop to terminate.

When used with XmtDialogDoSync(), the pre-defined callbacks XmtDialogOkayCallback() and XmtDialogCancelCallback() set a special flag that causes the internal event loop to exit and XmtDialogDoSync() to return. When the loop is terminated by XmtDialogOkayCallback(), XmtDialogDoSync() returns True. When the loop is terminated by

XmtDialogCancelCallback(), it returns False. As with any synchronous function, it is important that you check this return value and abort any operation in progress if the user clicks on the **Cancel** button.
Recall that any synchronous dialog you create must be a modal one. Since an application can only be in one event loop at a time, and since synchronous behavior requires an internal event loop, there can only be one synchronous dialog active at any time. Making synchronous dialogs modal is the easiest way to enforce this condition.

XmtDialogDoSync() is not appropriate for all dialogs (sometimes you will want to use the functions XmtDialogSetDialogValues() and XmtDialogGetDialogValues() directly), but in circumstances that you can use it, it dramatically simplifies your code—you might end up with procedures that look like this:

```
/* initialize the default values here, if necessary */
data = default_data;

/* then "do" the dialog, checking for the Cancel button */
if (!XmtDialogDoSync(dialog, &data)) return;

/* then act on the user's input however required */
process_data(&data);
```

29.3.3.3 XmtDialogOkayCallback()

XmtDialogOkayCallback() is a callback procedure designed to be registered on the **Ok** button of an automatic dialog that was popped up with XmtDialogDo() or XmtDialogDoSync(). It performs three tasks:

1. Transfers data from the widgets of the dialog box to the data structure that was passed when the dialog was popped up.
2. Pops the dialog down.
3. If used with XmtDialogDoSync(), it sets an internal flag that causes XmtDialogDoSync() to exit its event loop and return **True** to its caller.

XmtDialogOkayCallback() can be used in both modal and modeless dialogs.

29.3.3.4 XmtDialogCancelCallback()

XmtDialogCancelCallback() is a callback procedure designed to be registered on the **Cancel** button of an automatic dialog that was popped up with XmtDialogDo() or XmtDialogDoSync(). It performs two tasks:

1. Pops the dialog down.
2. If used with XmtDialogDoSync(), it sets an internal flag that causes XmtDialogDoSync() to exit its event loop and return **False** to its caller.

XmtDialogCancelCallback() can be used in both modal and modeless dialogs.

29.3.3.5 XmtDialogApplyCallback()

XmtDialogApplyCallback() is a callback procedure designed to be registered on the **Apply** button of an automatic dialog that was popped up with XmtDialogDo() or XmtDialogDoSync(). Since the **Apply** button is generally used in modeless dialogs, with a separate **Dismiss** or **Done** button, XmtDialogApplyCallback() does not pop the dialog down, nor does it cause XmtDialogDoSync() to exit, as XmtDialogOkayCallback() and XmtDialogCancelCallback() do. Instead, the only thing that XmtDialogApplyCallback() does is to extract the current input values from the widget and store them at the address specified when the dialog was popped up.

Note that XmtDialogApplyCallback() is often not useful by itself—an **Apply** button is used to make the application take some action on the input data, and XmtDialogApplyCallback() simply stores data without taking any further action. From a modeless dialog for which storing the user's input is the only required action, this callback will suffice. In other cases, you can use this callback in conjunction with, or from within a custom callback of your own. And in the "Advanced Dialog Techniques" section below, we'll see techniques that allow you to define custom **Apply** callbacks that are more useful.

An **Apply** button is typically used in modeless dialogs, but you can use XmtDialogApplyCallback() from a modal dialog as well.

29.3.3.6 XmtDialogResetCallback()

XmtDialogResetCallback() is a callback procedure designed to be registered on the **Reset** button of an automatic dialog that was popped up with XmtDialogDo() or XmtDialogDoSync(). It copies data values from the application data structure back into the widgets. This callback is generally used with the XmtDialogApplyCallback(), and has the effect of undoing any user edits since the last time the user clicked the **Apply** button, or since the dialog was popped up.

XmtDialogResetCallback() does not pop down the dialog or cause XmtDialogDoSync() to exit. While typically used in modeless dialogs, it can also be used modally.

29.3.3.7 XmtDialogDoneCallback()

XmtDialogDoneCallback() is a callback procedure designed to be registered on the **Dismiss** or **Done** button of an automatic dialog that was popped up with XmtDialogDo() or XmtDialogDoSync(). It pops down the dialog and sets an internal flag that will cause XmtDialogDoSync() to stop processing events internally and return True.

A **Dismiss** button is generally used in dialogs that also contain an **Apply** button. XmtDialogApplyCallback() followed by XmtDialogDoneCallback() have the same effect as XmtDialogOkayCallback(). While **Dismiss** buttons typically appear in modeless dialogs, you can use XmtDialogDoneCallback() in modal dialogs as well.

29.4 A Complete Example

This chapter begins with a screendump of a "Network Directory" dialog box, and most of the examples so far have been drawn from the implementation of that dialog. Figure 29-3 shows a simpler dialog designed to pop up when you click the **Parameters...** button of that first dialog, and Example 29-11 shows the resource file that defines the dialog, the `XtResourceList` that specifies its data-transfer interface, and and the C code that creates and manages the dialog. This is a fairly typical modal dialog box—it has a simple `XmtDialogDo()` implementation that you may be able to emulate for many of your application dialogs.

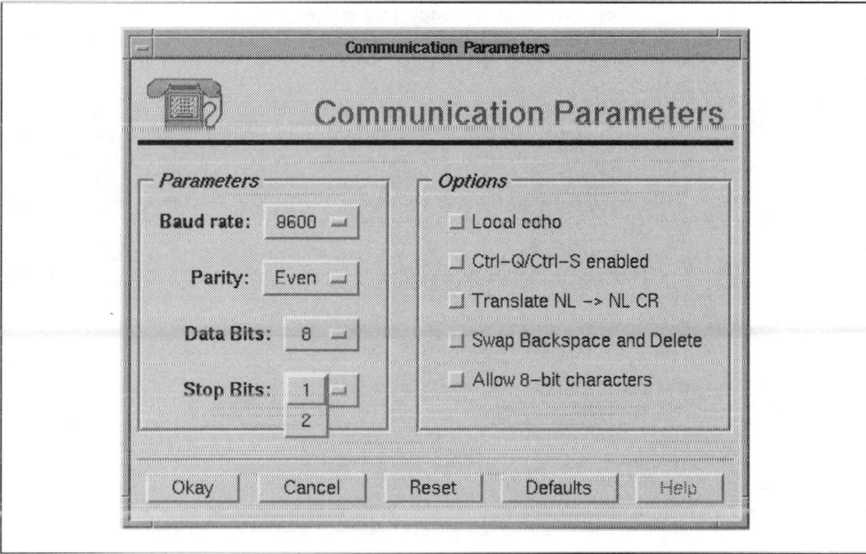

Figure 29-3. A simple dialog box

Example 29-11. Implementing a Simple Dialog Box

examples/29/net_directory.ad

```
!!
!! This resource file contains most of the dialog description.  The
!! xmtChildren resources define the widget hierarchy, and the XmtLayout
!! layout resource defines the arrangement of those widgets.
!! Note the use of the extended xmtChildren `=' syntax to map widgets
!! to data resource names, and note the use of predefined callbacks
!! on the dialog push buttons.
!! The resources that specify the option menus and the button labels
!! have been omitted here.
!!
*params_shell.xmtChildren: unmanaged XmtLayout params;
*params.dialogTitle: Communication Parameters
*params.autoUnmanage: False
```

Example 29-11. Implementing a Simple Dialog Box (continued)

```
*params.dialogStyle: dialog_primary_application_modal
*params.xmtDefaults.baud: 14400
*params.xmtDefaults.flags: 7

*params.xmtChildren: \
        XmtChooser speed = baud;\
        XmtChooser parity = parity;\
        XmtChooser databits = databits;\
        XmtChooser stopbits = stopbits;\
        XmtChooser options = flags;\
        XmPushButton okay, cancel, reset, factory, help;

*params.layout: \
    Line Bottom 0 4 LREvenSpaced Fixed Row { \
        Color "maroon" Bitmap "phone" \
        Color "maroon" FlushBottom "@f[HUGE]Communication Parameters" } \
    # \
    Row {\
        Caption tl " @f(BIParameters " Etched Through 8 4 Col {\
            Margin Height 0 FlushRight Caption "@fBBaud rate:" speed\
            Margin Height 0 FlushRight Caption "@fBParity:" parity\
            Margin Height 0 FlushRight Caption "@fBData Bits:" databits\
            Margin Height 0 FlushRight Caption "@fBStop Bits:" stopbits\
        }\
        # \
        Caption tl " @f(BIOptions " Etched Through 8 4 Col {options}\
    }\
    #\
    Fixed Etched Top Row { okay cancel reset factory help }

*params.options.chooserType: CheckBox
*params.options.strings:\
        "Local echo",\
        "Ctrl-Q/Ctrl-S enabled",\
        "Translate NL -> NL CR",\
        "Swap Backspace and Delete",\
        "Allow 8-bit characters"

*params.okay.activateCallback: XmtDialogOkayCallback();
*params.cancel.activateCallback: XmtDialogCancelCallback();
*params.reset.activateCallback: XmtDialogResetCallback();
==========================================================================
```

examples/ 29/net_directory.c

```
/* Here is the data structure that this dialog will be manipulating,
 * with some #defines for some of the fields.
 */
typedef struct {
    int baud;
    int parity;
    int databits;
    int stopbits;
    int flags;
} CommunicationParameters;

#define PARITY_EVEN   0
#define PARITY_ODD    1
#define PARITY_MARK   2
#define PARITY_SPACE  3
#define PARITY_NONE   4
```

Example 29-11. Implementing a Simple Dialog Box (continued)

```
#define OPTION_ECHO         0x01
#define OPTION_FLOW_CONTROL 0x02
#define OPTION_ADD_CR       0x04
#define OPTION_SWAP         0x08
#define OPTION_8BIT         0x10

/*
 * This is the XtResourceList that gives a name to each of the fields
 * in the data structure, and allows data transfer to and from those
 * fields.
 */
XtResource parameter_resources[] = {
{"baud", "baud", XtRInt,
     sizeof(int), XtOffsetOf(CommunicationParameters, baud),
     XtRImmediate, (XtPointer) 9600},
{"parity", "parity", XtRInt,
     sizeof(int), XtOffsetOf(CommunicationParameters, parity),
     XtRImmediate, (XtPointer) PARITY_EVEN},
{"databits", "databits", XtRInt,
     sizeof(int), XtOffsetOf(CommunicationParameters, databits),
     XtRImmediate, (XtPointer) 8},
{"stopbits", "stopbits", XtRInt,
     sizeof(int), XtOffsetOf(CommunicationParameters, stopbits),
     XtRImmediate, (XtPointer) 1},
{"flags", "flags", XtRInt,
     sizeof(int), XtOffsetOf(CommunicationParameters, flags),
     XtRImmediate, (XtPointer) (OPTION_FLOW_CONTROL | OPTION_8BIT)},
};

/*
 * With the static definitions of the dialog widgets, dialog layout,
 * and dialog data structure, the two function calls in the following
 * procedure is all we need to do to:
 *
 *   1) Create the dialog
 *   2) Transfer initial values to the dialog from the app. data structure.
 *   3) Wait for the user to dismiss the dialog
 *   4) If the Okay button is pressed, transfer the user's input
 *      back to the application data structure.
 */
static void do_parameters(Widget w, XtPointer tag, XtPointer data)
{
    if (!parameters_dialog) {
        parameters_dialog = XmtBuildQueryDialog(toplevel, "params_shell",
                                                parameter_resources,
                                                XtNumber(parameter_resources),
                                                NULL);
    }
    XmtDialogDo(parameters_dialog, &directory[current_entry].params);
}
```

Dynamic Dialog Setup

The last example showed how the widgets and layout of a dialog box can be completely described in a resource file. There are a couple of resources that cannot be set directly, however. The `XmNdefaultButton` resource of the dialog can't be set when the dialog widget is created, for example, because the child that you would set it to has not yet been created. The same is true of the Motif 1.2 `XmNinitialFocus` resource.

It is possible to use the creation callbacks introduced in Chapter 11, *Automatic Widget Creation* to perform dynamic setup of a dialog box after its children have been created, however. The following lines of code are from a simple dialog box with a single input field and some buttons. They set the initial focus to the text field (which would not otherwise be the default) so that the user can just start typing when the dialog pops up. They also set the default button of the dialog box, so that the user can just strike **Return** to dismiss the dialog.

```
*saveas.xmtChildrenCreationCallback: \
        XmtSetValue(self, defaultButton, self.save);\
        XmtSetInitialFocus(self, self.filename);
```

You'll probably find these two callback functions useful for many of the dialog boxes you define.

—*djf*

29.5 Advanced Dialog Techniques

The last example showed a very straightforward use of `XmtDialogDo()` and the related automatic dialog facilities. This section describes some advanced techniques that you may want to use with some of your dialogs.

29.5.1 Getting Dialog Defaults

In Example 29-11 and many of the other examples of this chapter we have set values on the widgets of a dialog box from the fields of a data structure that we assume to have been initialized elsewhere. Commonly, though, you may instead use a single static data structure for the data, as shown in Example 29-10. The important point about this technique is that because the structure is static, the user's input values from one invocation of the dialog box will become the default values for the next invocation of the dialog.

While a static data structure sets appropriate default values for all invocations of the dialog after the first, there is still the matter of the default values for that first invocation. Static structures in C are by default initialized to `NULL` bytes—sometimes this will be a meaningful default value, but in general it is not.

The easiest way to set defaults is to use an initializer when the static data structure is declared. You might use something like this, for example:

```
static CommunicationParameters parameters = {9600,PARITY_EVEN,8,1,0};
```

It will not always be clear what defaults values are best, and sometimes you'll want these initial defaults to be customizable through the resource database, so that users or system administrators can provide default values that are more appropriate. In this case, you can use `XmtDialogGetDefaultValues()`:

Xmt/

Dialog.c

```
#include <Xmt/Dialog.h>
void XmtDialogGetDefaultValues(Widget dialog, XtPointer address,
                               ArgList args, Cardinal num_args);
```

This function has *`dialog`* and *`address`* values just like `XmtDialogSetDialogValues()` and `XmtDialogGetDialogValues()` do. It obtains a default value for each resource associated with the specified dialog and stores them in the fields of the structure at the specified address. It uses `XtGetSubresources()` to look up the default values, which come from one of three possible sources:

1. If the resource name is found in the *`args`* array, the value from that `ArgList` is used. This is another way of hardcoding dialog defaults in your C code.

2. If the resource is not defined in the argument list, then they are looked up in the resource database as a "subpart" of the dialog widget. The name of this subpart is "`xmtDefaults`". (Note that the defaults cannot be looked up directly under the widget itself, because then their names might conflict with actual widget resources.)

3. If no default value is found in the argument list or in the resource database, then the default value from the resource list associated with the dialog is used. This is the value specified on the `default_type` and `default_addr` fields of the `XtResourceList` you define for your dialog. This is usually the appropriate place to specify defaults, because it allows those defaults to be overridden. Note, though, that if you do not plan to use `XmtDialogGetDefaultValues()`, there is no need to initialize those fields of your `XtResourceList`.

Example 29-12 shows how you could use the resource database to override the default values for the dialog defined in Example 29-11.

Example 29-12. Overriding Dialog Defaults

```
*params.xmtDefaults.baud: 14400
*params.xmtDefaults.parity: 1
*params.xmtDefaults.databits: 7
```

Example 29-12. Overriding Dialog Defaults (continued)

```
*params.xmtDefaults.stopbits: 2
*params.xmtDefaults.flags: 25
```

Example 29-13 shows how we could modify Example 29-10 to use these default values

Example 29-13. Using XmtDialogGetDefaultValues()

```
static void do_parameters(Widget w, XtPointer tag, XtPointer data)
{
    static CommunicationParameters parameters;

    if (!parameters_dialog) {
        /*
         * First time we're called, create the dialog, and also
         * look up the default communication parameters
         */
        parameters_dialog = XmtBuildQueryDialog(toplevel, "params_shell",
                                                parameter_resources,
                                                XtNumber(parameter_resources),
                                                NULL);
        XmtDialogGetDefaultValues(parameters_dialog, &parameters, NULL, 0);
    }

    if (XmtDialogDo(parameters_dialog, &parameters))
        set_parameters(&parameters);
}
```

29.5.2 Writing Custom Callbacks

Xmt defines some simple callbacks that are suitable for the buttons of many dialog boxes. But there is no reason that you have to confine yourself to using only these callbacks. When you are using a single global data structure with your dialog, and managing the data transfer yourself, then you can simply use `XmtDialogGetDialogValues()` and `XmtDialogSetDialogValues()` directly in your callbacks, as we saw earlier in the chapter.

When you are managing your dialogs with the simpler functions `XmtDialogDo()` or `XmtDialogDoSync()`, however, you'll need to use another pair of functions to help you write the callbacks:

Xmt/

Dialog.c

```
#include <Xmt/Dialog.h>
XtPointer XmtDialogGetDataAddress(Widget dialog);
void XmtDialogSetReturnValue(Widget dialog, Boolean value);
```

Recall that `XmtDialogDo()` and `XmtDialogDoSync()` will associate your data structure with the dialog for you. `XmtDialogGetDataAddress()` is used to look up that data structure, so that it can be used in the callback.

Also, recall that `XmtDialogDoSync()` blocks until the user selects an appropriate button, and then returns a `Boolean` value to indicate whether the wants to continue with the action (`True`) or abort it (`False`). `XmtDialogSetReturnValue()` can be used in callbacks to stop `XmtDialogDoSync()` from blocking and to specify the value that is to be returned from that function.

29.5.2.1 The Predefined Dialog Callbacks

Before we discuss custom dialog callbacks, you should understand how `XmtDialogGetDataAddress()` and `XmtDialogSetReturnValue()` are used to implement the predefined dialog callbacks. Example 29-14 shows how these two functions are used in `XmtDialogOkayCallback()`.

Example 29-14. The Implementation of `XmtDialogOkayCallback()`

```
void XmtDialogOkayCallback(Widget w, XtPointer tag, XtPointer data)
{
    Widget shell, dialog;
    XtPointer base;

    shell = XmtGetShell(w);  /* get shell widget, and its dialog box child */
    dialog = ((CompositeWidget)shell)->composite.children[0]);
    base = XmtDialogGetDataAddress(shell);      /* look up data structure */
    if (!base) return;
    XmtDialogGetDialogValues(shell, base);      /* transfer input to it */
    XmtDialogSetReturnValue(shell, True);       /* stop blocking; return True */
    XtUnmanageChild(dialog);                    /* and pop down the dialog */
}
```

The `XmtDialogCancelCallback()` is much like `XmtDialogOkayCallback()`, except that it returns `False` through `XmtDialogSetReturnValue()`, and it does not transfer the cancelled user input with `XmtDialogGetDialogValues()`. On the other hand, the predefined `XmtDialogApplyCallback()` does transfer the data values, but does not cause `XmtDialogDoSync()` to stop blocking. You can probably easily imagine the implementation of these procedures.

29.5.2.2 Reset and Defaults Callbacks

The dialog pictured in Figure 29-3 contains **Reset** and **Defaults** buttons. The dialog is implemented using `XmtDialogResetCallback()` for the **Reset** button and a custom procedure for the **Defaults** button. These procedures are shown in Example 29-15. The reset procedure restores the dialog widgets to their state when the dialog was popped up—it acts to undo any user edits during this instantiation of the dialog. The defaults procedure uses `XmtDialogGetDefaultValues()`, which was introduced in the previous section, to set the dialog widgets to a known default state. (Because **Defaults** button uses `XmtDialogGetDialogValues()`, it sets site-specific or user-specific defaults. For some dialogs you might prefer a **Factory Defaults** button that would set the widgets to some well-defined, non-customizable state.)

Example 29-15. Implementing Reset and Defaults Buttons

```
/* The predefined "reset" callback */
void XmtDialogResetCallback(Widget w, XtPointer tag, XtPointer data)
{
    Widget shell = XmtGetShell(w);
    XtPointer base = XmtDialogGetDataAddress(shell):

    if (!base) return;
    XmtDialogSetDialogValues(shell, base);
}

/* The custom Defaults callback. */
static void set_defaults(Widget w, XtPointer tag, XtPointer data)
{
    CommunicationParameters params;

    XmtDialogGetDefaultValues(parameters_dialog, &params, NULL, 0);
    XmtDialogSetDialogValues(parameters_dialog, &params);
}
```

29.5.2.3 Verification Callbacks

Perhaps the most common reason to write a custom callback procedure for use with `XmtDialogDoSync()` is to perform verification on the user's input. Example 29-16 shows how we could modify the **Okay** callback of Example 29-14 to allow verification of the user's input before it is accepted.

Example 29-16. An Okay Callback with Verification

```
void VerifyCallback(Widget w, XtPointer tag, XtPointer data)
{
    Widget shell, dialog;
    XtPointer base;
    CommunicationParameters values;
    char *msg;

    shell = XmtGetShell(w);  /* get shell widget, and its dialog box child */
    dialog = ((CompositeWidget)shell)->composite.children[0]);

    /* First, get the input in a private structure */
    XmtDialogGetDialogValues(shell, &values);

    /*
     * We check the input by calling a hypothetical verification procedure
     * that returns True only if the fields of the structure are all
     * valid.  If it returns False, then the msg parameter will be set
     * to point to an error message that tells the user what is wrong.
     */
    if (!check_params(&values, &msg)) {
        XmtDisplayError(dialog, "verify", msg);  /* display the error msg */
        return;                                  /* and do nothing else */
    }

    /*
     * otherwise, the input values were all okay, so proceed.
     */
    base = XmtDialogGetDataAddress(shell);     /* look up data structure */
    if (!base) return;
```

Example 29-16. An Okay Callback with Verification (continued)

```
    *((CommunicationParameters *)base) = values; /* copy the values into it */
    XmtDialogSetReturnValue(shell, True);      /* stop blocking; return True */
    XtUnmanageChild(dialog);                   /* and pop down the dialog */
}
```

29.5.3 Dialogs with Custom Widget and Data Types

As we saw earlier in the chapter, the actual work of transferring values between fields of a data structure and widgets in a dialog is done by `get_value()` and `set_value()` procedures registered with the widget types. Xmt provides these procedures for each of the standard Motif and Xmt widgets that allow the use to select or edit a value. You are not limited to using only these widget types in your automatic dialogs, however. This section discusses some cases in which you might want to register your own `get_value()` and `set_value()` procedures.

29.5.3.1 New Widget Types

In some cases, you may want to transfer data to a dialog, but not allow it to be edited. In this case, you might want to display it with an XmLabel widget or an XmtLayoutString gadget, for example. Example 29-17 shows how you could register the XmtLayoutString for use in with automatic data transfer in a dialog

Example 29-17. Registering the XmtLayoutString Gadget

```
static void setvalue(Widget w, XtPointer address, XrmQuark type, Cardinal size)
{
    static XrmQuark string_quark, buffer_quark;

    if (!string_quark) { /* first time only */
        string_quark = XrmPermStringToQuark(XtRString);
        buffer_quark = XrmPermStringToQuark(XmtRBuffer);
    }

    if (type == string_quark)
        XtVaSetValues(w, XmtNlabel, *(String *)address, NULL);
    else if (type == buffer_quark)
        XtVaSetValues(w, XmtNlabel, (char *)address, NULL);
    else
        XmtWarningMsg("XmtLayoutString", "type",
                      "Type mismatch:\n"
                      "\tCan't set value from resource of type '%s'.\n"
                      "\tString or Buffer expected.",
                      XrmQuarkToString(type));
}

void RegisterXmtLayoutString(void)
{
    static XmtWidgetType type = {
        "XmtLayoutString",
        NULL,
        XmtCreateLayoutString,
        setvalue,
        NULL
    };
```

Example 29-17. Registering the XmtLayoutString Gadget (continued)

```
    static Boolean registered;

    if (!registered) XmtRegisterWidgetTypes(&type, 1);
    registered = True;
}
```

Tricks with the set_value Procedure

Terry Poot is a fan of custom `set_value()` *procedures:*

It is worth noting that you can use a `set_value()` procedure to set output-only values. I use it to set XmLabels this way, but you could also set button labels, list contents, etc. Many perverse tricks can be done with the right `set_value()` procedure: you could set sensitivity, color, etc. Depends on what you think of as a "value". :-)

—Terry Poot

29.5.3.2 New Data Types

Suppose you want to use an XmtInputField widget in an automatic dialog to display and input dates. You might register the XmtInputField widget with new data transfer procedures just like we did with the XmtLayoutString gadget above. The problem with this approach is that you still probably want to use the XmtInputField for string values as well, and you don't want to have to duplicate all the logic of the standard XmtInputField transfer functions. What you can do is to register the widget with a new name, and new functions for transferring dates only. Then, when you want to create an InputField for use with a date, you can create it using this new name.

Example 29-18 shows how you might do this. (The example shows how you'd register the data transfer functions, but doesn't show the functions themselves.) Note that we use a custom constructor procedure which automatically registers a verification callback on this special "DateField" version of the widget.

Example 29-18. Registering a Widget for Use with New Data Types

```
/* funcs defined elsewhere */
extern void setdate(), getdate(), verifydate();

Widget CreateDateField(Widget parent, String name,
                       ArgList arglist, Cardinal num_args)
{
    Widget w;
    w = XmtCreateInputField(parent, name, arglist, num_args);
    XtAddCallback(w, XmtNverifyCallback, verifydate, NULL);
    return w;
}
```

Example 29-18. Registering a Widget for Use with New Data Types (continued)

```
void RegisterXmtLayoutString(void)
{
    static XmtWidgetType type = {
        "DateField",
        NULL,
        CreateDateField
        setdate,
        getdate
    };
    static Boolean registered;

    if (!registered) XmtRegisterWidgetTypes(&type, 1);
    registered = True;
}
```

29.5.3.3 Derived Widget Types

As noted in Chapter 11, *Automatic Widget Creation*, there are times when it is convenient to define and register a custom widget constructor that does more than any of the exiting widgets. A simple example would be a constructor `CreateMultiLineText()` that creates an XmText widget with its `XmNeditMode` resource set to `XmMULTI_LINE_EDIT`. A more complex example could involve some kind of widget "template". If frequently needed to place an input field side-by-side with a push button widget, for example, you might write a widget constructor that creates a row column widget with the input field and push button as children. Then, by registering this constructor with the name "InputButtonBox", you could easily use it in your `xmtChildren` specifications in a resource file.

When you register these "derived" widget constructors, you need to register data transfer procedures with them, if you ever want to use them in automatic dialog boxes. In both cases, it would be nice if we could make use of the transfer procedures that are already defined. Unfortunately, these data transfer procedures are static, so you have to use a roundabout method to get at them. Example 29-19 shows how this can be done for the MultiLineText by using `XmtLookupWidgetType()` to look up the necessary procedures.

Example 29-19. Registering a Derived Widget Type

```
void RegisterMultiLineText(void)
{
    XmtWidgetType *type;
    static XmtWidgetType newtype = {
        "MultiLineText",
        NULL,
        CreateMultiLineText,
        NULL,   /* we'll look these last two fields up later */
        NULL,
    };
    static Boolean registered;

    /* only do this once */
    if (registered) return;
```

Example 29-19. Registering a Derived Widget Type (continued)

```
    registered = True;

    /* first, make sure the regular text widget is registered */
    XmtRegisterXmText();

    /* Now, look up its type structure */
    type = XmtLookupWidgetType("XmText");
    assert(type != NULL);

    /* Copy its transfer procedures */
    newtype.set_value_proc = type->set_value_proc;
    newtype.get_value_proc = type->get_value_proc;

    /* And register the new type. */
    XmtRegisterWidgetTypes(&newtype, 1);
}
```

Registering procedures for our "InputButtonBox" widget would be trickier than Example 29-19 because if the XmtInputField transfer procedures were used directly, they would be passed the XmRowColumn widget, rather than its input field child. Our registration function would have to look up the InputField procedures, store them in static variables, and then register "wrapper" data transfer procedures that invoke the stored procedures and pass the appropriate widget. (You might store a pointer to the input field widget on the `XmNuserData` resource of the XmRowColumn for easy lookup, for example.)

Registering Derived Widget Constructors

Scott Gregory registers simple "derived constructors" often enough that he wrote a function to do it for him.

contrib/derived/

```
#include <Xmt/Xmt.h>
#include <Xmt/WidgetType.h>

void RegisterDerivedConstructor(String parent_name, String name,
                                XmtWidgetConstructor constructor)
{
    XmtWidgetType *parent_type;
    XmtWidgetType *type;

    parent_type = XmtLookupWidgetType(parent_name);
    if (!parent_type) return;

    type = XtNew(XmtWidgetType); /* never free'd */
    type->name = name;
    type->class = NULL;
    type->constructor = constructor;
    type->set_value_proc = parent_type->set_value_proc;
    type->get_value_proc = parent_type->get_value_proc;
    type->popup = parent_type->popup;

    XmtRegisterWidgetTypes(type, 1);
}
```

—Scott Gregory

Dialogs with Templates

Mike McGary uses the Xmt automatic dialog facilities with the Xmt widget template facilities, and has discovered some mind-bending possibilities. His description contains good examples of how you can use templates for your dialogs.

I made some interesting discoveries about how hard you can push templates that I thought others would be interested in.

I used templates extensively in prototyping the interface of our product. But I foresaw problems when trying to use the dialog resource mappings. Here is the before case:

The following template is a simple combo-widget that is used over and over inside various dialogs. Note that the XmTextField called `value` stores the user's input:

```
_Templates_.ComboEd: \
   .xmtType: XmRowColumn\n\
   .orientation: XmHORIZONTAL\n\
   .xmtChildren: XmPushButton C; \
      XmTextField value; \         <===== this is the item of interest
      XmPushButton i;
```

Here is another template that uses the above template inside itself. Even the type of the template is passed in:

```
!!
!! OneComboBox - dialog with one ComboEd control
!! %0 = type of ComboEd control
!! %1 = name of ComboEd control
!! %2 = Caption of %1
!!
_Templates_.OneComboBox: \
   .xmtType: unmanaged XmtLayout\n\
   .xmtChildren: %0 %1; \   <==== here the above template is used
        XmPushButton OK, Cancel, Help;\n\
   .layout: \
        Caption tll %2 %1 \
        LCRSpaced Equal Row { OK Cancel Help } <>
```

Here is an example of the OneComboBox template being called. Note that the 'ComboEd' specification is passed in:

```
*labelDialog.xmtType:   XmDialogShell
*labelDialog.xmtChildren: \
        OneComboBox(ComboEd, label, "Label") labelDialogMain;
*labelDialog.title: Label
```

Now, if I wanted to use the Dialog mapping, I would need to name the XmTextField above as follows:

```
_Templates_.ComboEd: \
   .xmtType: XmRowColumn\n\
```

Dialogs with Templates (continued)

```
.orientation: XmHORIZONTAL\n\
.xmtChildren: XmPushButton C; \
   XmTextField value=label; \    <== naming occurs here
   XmPushButton i;
```

But, for dialogs that include more than one ComboEd, there would need to be different names for each of the XmTextField's. I attempted something that looked like it was stretching things a bit, but lo and behold.... it worked. I changed the two templates to look like this:

```
_Templates_.ComboEd: \
   .xmtType: XmRowColumn\n\
   .orientation: XmHORIZONTAL\n\
   .xmtChildren: XmPushButton C; \
      XmTextField value=%0; \   <===== the name is passed in
      XmPushButton i;

_Templates_.OneComboBox: \
   .xmtType: unmanaged XmtLayout\n\
   .xmtChildren: %0(%1) %1; \   <== the name is stolen from widget name
        XmPushButton OK, Cancel, Help;\n\
   .layout: \
        Caption tll %2 %1 \
        LCRSpaced Equal Row { OK Cancel Help } <>
```

The section that uses the OneComboBox template doesn't change at all! (Here's a recap.)

```
*labelDialog.xmtType:   XmDialogShell
*labelDialog.xmtChildren: \
        OneComboBox(ComboEd, label, "Label") labelDialogMain;
*labelDialog.title: Label
```

It may not be groundshaking, but the statement '%0(%1)' made my life change. I was about to re-write a whole lot of resource code.

—Mike McGary

29.6 Dialog Style

Many of the general stylistic points described elsewhere in this book apply equally to dialog boxes as to the main window and other parts of your application. This section provides some style hints that are more specific to dialogs.

Probably the most important rule of dialog layout is that the buttons that dismiss the dialog, or otherwise act upon the dialog as a whole—**Ok**, **Cancel**, **Help**, **Apply**, **Reset**, **Done**, etc.—should be arranged along the bottom of the dialog.

In most dialog boxes, you won't need buttons other than this kind. When you do have buttons that affect only portions of the dialog, they should *not* be part of the row of buttons at the bottom.

The widgets in a dialog should be laid out according to the order in which the user will generally want to interact with them, more or less left-to-right and top-to-bottom in the dialog. This gives the user a standard way to figure out how to interact with new dialog boxes.

If your dialog contains a number of widgets with related purposes (a column of XmtInputField widgets, for example) it is useful to group them graphically in some way. With the XmtLayout widget, you can draw a frame around the group. It can also be useful to provide a small title for the group, to identify the purpose they have in common. Similarly, you can use an XmSeparator widget (or an XmtLayoutSeparator gadget with XmtLayout dialogs) to visually separate one group of widgets from the rest of the dialog. It is standard practice, for example to place a separator above the bottom row of buttons in a dialog.

It can be difficult to lay out complex dialogs that display or request a lot of information in a reasonable amount of screen space. Option menus are a very useful way to display choices in limited space. You may also consider reducing the font size for your complex dialogs.

It is often useful to display some sort of identifying icon near the top of each dialog box. This allows the user to quickly identify the purpose of the dialog. (And, if you choose the icons well, can be an effective unifying design theme for your application.) Some dialogs will also benefit by having a title displayed at the top along with the icon. (Most modern window managers will display a title in the titlebar of the dialog, but it may be in a small font, and serves more to identify the window than to identify the purpose of the dialog.)

By default, dialog shells will display their widget name as their title—this is almost never a useful or meaningful string for the user to see. Be sure to set the Shell `XtNtitle` resource, or the XmBulletinBoard `XmNdialogTitle` resource to a more useful string.

One way to add visual interest to dialog boxes is to give them a different background color than your application main window. Be sure to use related colors, however, so that it is clear that your dialogs are related to your main window.

Finally, it is common to put a **Help** button in dialog boxes, and a dialog is a good self-contained portion of your interface which can usually be explained in a single "unit" of help. Online help for a dialog box should explain the overall purpose of the dialog, explain how the requested information will be used, and, if necessary, explain the individual widgets within the dialog. In particular, it is often useful to clearly explain the consequences of clicking **Ok**, **Cancel**, and the other buttons in the dialog.

29.7 Summary

Follow these steps to use the Xmt automatic dialog facilities:

- Register any input widgets you'll use in dialogs with their special Xmt registration functions, e.g., `XmtRegisterInputField()`, `XmtRegisterChooser()`, and `XmtRegisterXmScale()`. You can also use, if you prefer, `XmtRegisterMotifWidgets()` and `XmtRegisterXmtWidgets()`. You can also register widgets explicitly with `XmtRegisterWidgetTypes()`, but if you do this, you must provide your own custom `setvalue()` and `getvalue()` procedures for them.
- Specify the widgets in the dialog with an `xmtChildren` resource, using the *`widget-name = data-name`* syntax to specify the resource name of the fields to be associated each widget.
- Define the data structure you want to use with the dialog, and statically initialize an `XtResourceList` that names and describes (type, size, offset, and default) each of the fields in this structure.
- Create the dialog box, when it is needed, by calling `XmtBuildDialog()` or `XmtBuildQueryDialog()`, passing the `XtResourceList` that describes your data structure. For string data, you may want to use a fixed-size character buffer with the `XmtRBuffer` type rather than a `char *` and the `XtRString` type.
- You can automatically transfer data from an instance of your data structure to a dialog box created in this way by calling `XmtDialogSetDialogValues()`. And you can transfer data in the opposite direction with `XmtDialogGetDialogValues()`. You can also query default values for the fields of the data structure by calling `XmtDialogGetDefaultValues()`.
- You can automate your dialogs still further by using `XmtDialogDo()` or `XmtDialogDoSync()` in conjunction with special callback procedures like `XmtDialogOkayCallback()` and `XmtDialogCancelCallback()`.

30

Context Help

Any non-trivial application should provide the user with online help. The type, quantity, and detail of this online help may vary depending on the complexity of the program, the expected experience level of the users, and on the availability of printed documentation, but there should almost always be at least some help available.

While the largest applications may require some sort of online manual that users can browse, many smaller and medium-sized applications will only need to provide context help. This might be help requested by the user for specific widgets, or it might be help requested by clicking the **Help** button in a dialog box, but in either case, the help is for one particular piece (or context) of the application.

Unfortunately, the closest the Motif widget set comes to an online help facility is the XmInformationDialog. As we've seen, the Xmt simple message dialog and simple input dialogs allow you to specify help messages for those dialogs. This chapter presents the XmtHelpBox widget, which can display scrolled, multi-font help text, with a title, and also Xmt facilities for associating context help text with any widget in your application.

30.1 The XmtHelpBox Widget

Figure 30-1 shows a HelpBox widget. This widget is designed to display a single multi-line, multi-font string in a scrolled window, and is suitable for displaying relatively short help (20 lines or so) on a single topic.

The HelpBox widget is a subclass of the XmtLayout widget. Its class name is "XmtHelpBox," and its class structure is `xmtHelpBoxWidgetClass`. A HelpBox widget can be created with a call to `XmtCreateHelpBox()`. More commonly, you'll call `XmtCreateHelpDialog()` which creates an XmDialogShell with an XmtHelpBox child:

30.1
examples/

30/contexthelp.ad

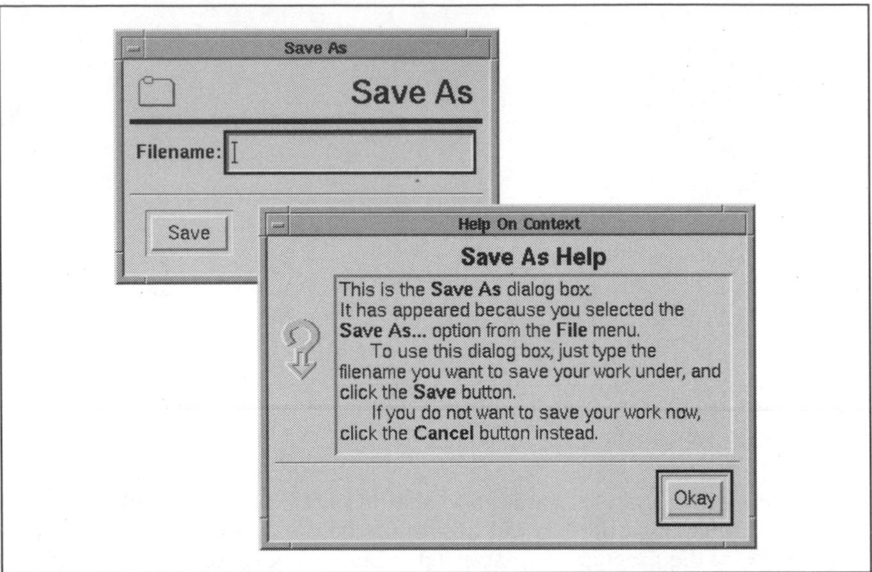

Figure 30-1. The HelpBox widget

Xmt/

HelpBox.c

```
#include <Xmt/HelpBox.h>
Widget XmtCreateHelpBox(Widget parent, String name,
                        ArgList args, Cardinal num_args);
Widget XmtCreateHelpDialog(Widget parent, String name,
                           ArgList args, Cardinal num_args);
```

The HelpBox widget has resources that specify the icon that appears in the upper left, the title that appears in the upper right, the help text that appears in the scrolled area, the number of lines of text that should be visible in that area, and the fonts and colors for the title and the help text. See the reference section for a complete list of the resources for this widget.

The multi-font text that appears in a HelpBox is implemented as an XmString displayed in a scrolled XmLabel widget. The HelpBox widget supports the standard Motif keyboard bindings for scrolling the text up and down, as well as the *emacs* and *more*-style bindings.

The HelpBox widget is suitable for displaying help on a single topic, or displaying a single section of a larger online document. If your application is a small one, and only has a few help topics, you might choose to list each topic explicitly in the **Help** menu and pop up a separate HelpBox dialog for each topic.

Though the widget is named the HelpBox, it need not be limited to displaying online help—it can serve as a general (and more flexible) replacement for the XmMessageBox and its related dialogs, the XmInformationDialog, the XmWarningDialog, and so on. The HelpBox has features that the XmMessageBox does not: it supports scrolled text, it has a separately displayed title string, and allows more control over color.

The HelpBox widget is particularly appropriate for displaying context-sensitive help. Because context help is so important in some applications, the Xmt library contains special context-help routines that use the HelpBox widget. These routines are described in the next section.

30.2 Context-Sensitive Help

Providing context-sensitive help, in the purest sense, means that when the user requests help, the help he sees should be appropriate to whatever he was doing at the time. Obviously, we can't read the user's mind to figure out what he was trying to do and what he needs help on, so no context help system will be perfect. One common and straightforward approach, however, is to provide help for every widget (or every important widget) in an application. Then the widget that has keyboard focus when the user strikes the **Help** key (**F1** on many platforms) becomes the "context" on which to provide help. Alternatively, the user can select **Context Help** from the **Help** menu and then use the mouse to point to the part of the application (i.e., the widget or the "context") that he wants help on.

30.2.1 Specifying Context Help

The trick to implementing context help for an application is associating help information with any (or every) widget in the application. A natural and quite elegant solution to this problem is to use "pseudo-resources" in the resource database: when the user requests help on a widget named `xapp.layout.menubar`, we can simply query the resource database for the value of the `xapp.layout.menubar.xmtHelp` resource, and display any text we find to the user. One of the nice features of this approach is that we can use a single loosely bound resource in the database to specify help for all widgets of a particular class in an application. For example, you could place a line like the following in your resource file:

```
*XmScrollBar.xmtHelp: \
  This is a @fIscrollbar@fP.  To use it, click on the up or down\n\
  arrows at the top and bottom, or drag the inner rectangle with\n\
  mouse button 1.
```

Xmt also reads the `xmtHelpTitle` pseudo-resource, which allows you to specify a title to accompany each piece of context help you provide:

```
*XmScrollBar.xmtHelpTitle: Using the Scrollbar
```

Another useful technique using loosely-bound resource specifications allows you to specify the same context help for a whole subtree of widgets. For example, you might specify context help for a dialog box with a specification like this:

```
*saveas_shell*xmtHelpTitle: Save As Help
*saveas_shell*xmtHelp: \
```

```
This is the @fBSave As@fP dialog box.\n\
It has appeared because you selected the\n\
@fBSave As...@fP option from the @fBFile@fP menu.\n\
\n\
To use this dialog box, just type the filename you want\n\
to save your work under, and click the @fBSave@fP button.
```

With this specification, the user would see this help no matter which widget within the dialog box they requested help on.

Using loose bindings like these does not restrict you to providing only general, vague help. For example, if you wanted to provide specific help for a particularly important scrollbar or for a particular button within a dialog, you only need to specify it with a "tighter" binding:

```
*main_window.scrollbar.xmtHelp:
*saveas_shell*save.xmtHelp:
```

The Xmt library contains function to look up and display context help that has been specified with these pseudo-resources. These function are described in the following subsections.

30.2.2 Looking up Context Help

You can look up the context help text (and title) for a widget with `XmtHelp-GetContextHelp()`:

Xmt/

ContextHelp.c

```
#include <Xmt/Help.h>
void XmtHelpGetContextHelp(Widget helpw,
                           String *help_string, String *help_title)
```

This function is passed a widget and the addresses of two strings. It looks up the context help information for that widget and returns one string which is the help text itself, and one string which is the title string associated with that help text. These strings must be freed with `XtFree()` when they are no longer needed.

Note that this function does not display any help to the user—`XmtHelpGet-ContextHelp()` is a low-level function for those who want to display context help in some special way, such as in a custom widget. Usually, you will use one of the higher-level functions described in the next section to look up *and* display context help.

30.2.3 Displaying Context Help

XmtHelpGetContextHelp() simply obtains the help text for a widget; it does not display it to the user. Having obtained the help text, you can place it in a dialog box, and make it visible, but usually you will want to look up and display the help text in a single step. The function XmtHelpDisplay-ContextHelp() does this for you:

Xmt/

ContextHelp.c

```
#include <Xmt/Help.h>
void XmtHelpDisplayContextHelp(Widget w)
```

XmtHelpDisplayContextHelp() takes a single widget argument, looks up the help text and title for that widget, and displays them in a dialog box containing a HelpBox widget. The dialog shell and HelpBox widget are automatically created as needed by XmtHelpDisplayContextHelp() and are cached for reuse by later calls to the function. If context help is requested for a widget in a main window or a modeless dialog box, then the HelpBox will appear as a modeless dialog. If help is requested for a widget in a modal dialog box, however, the HelpBox will also be modal.

The name of the automatically created HelpBox widget is **xmtHelpDialog**, and the name of its shell is **xmtHelpDialog_shell**. You can use these names in a resource file to specify resources for *all* context help dialogs displayed with this function. Because the context help dialogs are cached, you cannot customize individual dialogs this way. You might use a line like the following to set the color of your context help dialogs, for example:

```
*xmtHelpDialog.background: tan
```

Since XmtHelpDisplayContextHelp() displays help for a specified widget, it is useful in cases when you already know which widget (i.e., which context) the user wants help on. If your application has a command-line interface, and the user has just typed “help save as”, then you might know that the user wants to see help on the **Save As** dialog box, for example. More commonly, though, you might know this because the user has just clicked the **Help** button in that **Save As** dialog box.

Suppose you had specified context help for all descendants of the saveas_shell widget, using a loose binding, as we did above. Then the user could see that help by requesting context help on any widget in that dialog. Logically, clicking the **Help** button should also display this same information. You could implement this with a line like the following in the resource file:

```
saveas_shell*help.activateCallback:
        XmtHelpDisplayContextHelp(*saveas_shell);
```

Or, more generally, for all the dialogs in your application:

```
*XmDialogShell*help.activateCallback: XmtHelpDisplayContextHelp(self);
```

30.2.4 Selecting a Context

XmtHelpDisplayContextHelp() displays the help information for an application-specified widget. More often, however, (when the user selects the **Context Help** menu item, for example) you want display help on a widget selected by the *user*. You can use the function XmtHelpDoContextHelp() to do this:

Xmt/

ContextHelp.c

```
#include <Xmt/Help.h>
void XmtHelpDoContextHelp(Widget w)
```

This function calls XmTrackingLocate(), a standard Motif function designed specifically with context help in mind. XmTrackingLocate() changes the mouse cursor and enters an internal event loop, waiting for the user to press the mouse button. When the user clicks the mouse, XmTrackingLocate() determines which widget the user clicked in and returns that widget to the caller. (And if the user clicks outside of the application, XmTrackingLocate() will just beep and return NULL—the user can use this to cancel the context help request.)

XmtHelpDoContextHelp() takes a single widget argument. This widget can be anywhere in the application; it serves only to identify the application as a whole. It uses XmTrackingLocate() to ask the user which part (or context) of the application she wants help on and then calls XmtHelpDisplayContextHelp() to obtain and display the context help for that widget.

Note that XmtHelpDoContextHelp() puts the application into a special "context help" mode, and does not return until the user has selected a widget. It is a good idea to display a message to the user with instructions ("Click on the item for which you need help") so that she realizes that she has entered a special mode. You can use the XmtMsgLine widget for this purpose.

XmtHelpDoContextHelp() displays a special cursor in order to indicate to the user that it is in a special mode. This cursor is specified by the helpCursor application resource, and its colors are specified by helpCursorForeground and helpCursorBackground. The default cursor is the "question_arrow" cursor from the standard X cursor font. This default cursor is unfortunately a fairly small one, and you may want to replace it in your application with something more noticeable.

Since the widget argument to XmtHelpDoContextHelp() serves only to identify the toplevel shell for your application, any widget will do, and you can call this function from a resource file without specifying any widget (the callback widget is automatically used). Thus, you could provide a context help facility for your application with a line like the following:

```
*context.activateCallback: XmtHelpDoContextHelp();
```

Or, in a menu specification like this:

```
xmail*help.items: \
        "_About xmail"              XmtHelpDisplayContextHelp(xmail);\
        "_Help On Context" [Meta+H] XmtHelpDoContextHelp();\
```

There are two points to beware of when using `XmtHelpDoContextHelp()`. The first is that `XmTrackingLocate()` only recognizes widgets and XmGadgets—it does not understand XmtLayout gadgets, such as XmtLayoutString and XmtLayoutPixmap, and this means that the user will not be able to request context help for these items. This will usually not be a problem; since XmtLayout gadgets are output-only, they generally do not need any explanation.

Also, note that if you make context help available through a pulldown menu in your main window, the user will not be able to operate the menu when a modal dialog is displayed. Thus, you'll need to provide some other means to obtain context help on the widgets of modal dialogs. One good way that we've seen is to make per-dialog help available with a **Help** button. Another technique is to make context help available from the keyboard; the next section shows how this can be done.

30.2.5 Context Help from the Keyboard

When the user selects the **Context Help** button from a menu, she must then identify the widget (the "context") she wants help with by clicking on it. Another model for context help allows the user to strike the **Help** or **F1** keys at any time and receive help on the current context. In this model, since the user is using the keyboard, the current context is probably whichever widget currently has keyboard focus.

All Motif widgets and gadgets have an `XmNhelpCallback` callback list; the procedures registered on this list are invoked when the user strikes the **Help** key (most keyboards don't have a **Help** key, so **F1** is used as the standard help binding instead) while that widget has keyboard focus. Since the **Help** key will invoke the help callback in the current context, it is a simple matter to register a callback that will call `XmtHelpDisplayContextHelp()` to get and display context help for that widget. The Xmt library contains a function suitable for this purpose: `XmtHelpContextHelpCallback()`. If you add this callback to a widget's `XmNhelpCallback` callback list, then the user can obtain context help for that widget (when it has input focus) by striking the **F1** or **Help** keys.

From a resource file, you can register this help callback on all widgets with a line like this:

```
*helpCallback: XmtHelpContextHelpCallback();
```

If you want to register the context help callback like this in C code, however, things are trickier—you've got to set the `XmNhelpCallback` for every widget in your application. To make this easier, the Xmt library contains a convenience function, `XmtHelpInstallContextHelp()`, that will register a callback on the specified widget, and on every descendant of that widget that can take input focus.

```
#include <Xmt/Help.h>
void XmtHelpContextHelpCallback(Widget w, XtPointer tag,
                                XtPointer data)
void XmtHelpInstallContextHelp(Widget w, XtCallbackProc proc,
                               XtPointer data)
```

Calling `XmtHelpInstallContextHelp()` from C is actually more efficient than registering the callback function on every widget from a resource file—this function only registers the callback on widgets that can actually take the input focus. Other widgets, like XmLabels and XmtLayout gadgets, never receive keyboard input and so will never invoke their help callbacks anyway.

`XmtHelpInstallContextHelp()` may be the only function you need to call other than `XmtHelpDoContextHelp()` in order to implement a fully functional context help system. Register `XmtHelpDoContextHelp()` as a callback in your **Help** menu, and call `XmtHelpInstallContextHelp()` on the toplevel shell of your interface once all the widgets are created. Pass `XmtHelpContextHelpCallback()` as the *`proc`* argument, and pass a `NULL` *`data`* argument. If your application creates widgets dynamically while running, (and provides context help for those widgets) you'll probably want to call `XmtHelpInstallContextHelp()` explicitly on those widgets when they are created.

A point to note about the keyboard interface to context help is that it is not always intuitive to users which widget has the input focus. Many users are accustomed to applications based on the Athena widget set and expect keyboard focus to always follow the mouse pointer. These users will sometimes point at a widget with the mouse and attempt to get help on it by pressing the **Help** key; they are confused when the help that appears is on some other widget. There is not much you as an application writer can do to prevent this sort of confusion, other than to be aware of it. You can encourage users who prefer the focus to follow the mouse to set the Motif VendorShell `keyboardFocusPolicy` resource to "pointer" in their *.Xresources* file, or you can provide a careful "Help on Help" dialog that explains how keyboard context help works. You can write a help callback procedure that would get the current position of the mouse, then traverse the widget tree to determine which widget the mouse is over, and then call `XmtHelpDisplayContextHelp()` on that widget, but this scheme would confuse those users who *do* make use of keyboard traversal and who expect the **Help** key to give them help on the widget with the focus, regardless of the pointer position.

30.2.6 The Context Help Database

Context help is an important feature to support for novice users, but is something that experienced users may never need to use. Though you should provide context help for new users, you shouldn't burden experienced users with the overhead (higher memory usage and increased startup time) associated with a large amount of context help information. It is very useful to have context help stored in a resource database, but if it is stored in the application resource database, then all the help information will be read in at application startup, which is something we want to avoid.

Fortunately, we can have the flexibility of a resource file without the overhead if we use a special, separate, resource file for context help. When (and if) the user first requests context help, we can read in this special database, and then query *it* for the context help information. This is in fact what the Xmt library does. The first time `XmtHelpGetContextHelp()` (or `XmtHelpDisplayContextHelp()` or `XmtHelpDoContextHelp()`) is called, the library looks for the resource file named by the `contextHelpFile` application resource. If the file exists, it is read into a resource database. If the resource is not defined, or no such file exists, then the application's regular resource database is used. This means that you can place context help in the app-defaults file while prototyping, or if you only have a little bit of help, but for the finished version of the application, or when the context help begins to get too long, you can move it to a special file, where it will only be read as needed.

30.2.7 Context Help Example

Example 30-1 shows how you might implement some of the context help techniques discussed here in a resource file.

Example 30-1. Implementing Context Help

```
!!
!! This is the general font list used for the program, and also
!! for the context help text.
!!
*FontList: *-helvetica-medium-r-*-*-*-140-*=R,\
        *-helvetica-bold-r-*-*-*-140-*-B,\
        *-helvetica-bold-r-*-*-*-240-*=BIG

!!
!! But we also have to specify an explicit font list for the
!! context help titles.
!!
*XmtHelpBox.titleFontList: *-helvetica-bold-r-*-*-*-180-*

!!
!! This examples shows three different ways of getting context help.
!! #1:  through a special "Context Help..." button.
!!
*context_help.activateCallback: XmtHelpDoContextHelp();

!!
```

Example 30-1. Implementing Context Help (continued)

```
!! #2: by clicking the Help button in the dialog box
!!
*help.activateCallback: XmtHelpDisplayContextHelp(self);

!!
!! #3: by pressing the Help key (usually F1) in any widget with
!! input focus.  (This could be done more efficiently in C with
!! XmtHelpInstallContextHelp().
!!
*helpCallback: XmtHelpContextHelpCallback();

!!
!! And here's the context help itself.  Note the loose binding: This help
!! applies to the entire dialog.  Also note the use of fonts and indents.
!! We could move this context help to a separate resource file, specified
!! by the contextHelpFile application resource.
!!
*saveas_shell*xmtHelpTitle: Save As Help
*saveas_shell*xmtHelp: \
     This is the @fBSave As@fP dialog box.\n\
It has appeared because you selected the\n\
@fBSave As...@fP option from the @fBFile@fP menu.\n\
     To use this dialog box, just type the\n\
filename you want to save your work under, and\n\
click the @fBSave@fP button.\n\
     If you do not want to save your work now,\n\
click the @fBCancel@fP button instead.

!!
!! And here is some more specific, less loosely bound context help.
!!
*saveas_shell*Save.xmtHelp: \
Clicking this button will save your work\n\
with the name you've typed above.
```

30.3 Other Kinds of Online Help

Your application's online help need not be limited to the XmtHelpBox widget and the context help techniques presented thus far. This section explores some alternative approaches you can take.

If your paragraphs of context help are all fairly short, then an XmMessageBox might be a more appropriate widget for displaying that help than the XmtHelpBox widget is. You can write your own version of `XmtHelpDisplayContextHelp()` by calling `XmtHelpGetContextHelp()` to obtain the context help text and title for a widget, and then use `XmtDisplayInformation()` to display that text and title in a cached XmMessageBox dialog. Similarly, you could write your own version of `XmtHelpDoContextHelp()` by calling `XmTrackingLocate()` yourself, and passing the resulting widget to your new context help display function.

On the other hand, if your context help entries become too long to reasonably display with an XmString (as the XmtHelpBox and XmMessageBox do), then you might write a context help display function that displays help text in a scrolled XmText widget. In this case, though, you probably don't want to include all the context help in a single resource database. Instead, you could write a custom version of `XmtHelpGetContextHelp()` that would read a new `xmtHelpFile` pseudo-resource in place of the `xmtHelp` resource, use `XmtFindFile()` to look up the specified file, and then read the contents of the file. This way, each item of context help would be read in when requested.

Some applications don't wait for the user to request context help—they provide it automatically as the user moves the mouse or the keyboard focus through the application. This kind of help is useful in menus and tool palettes, for example, to explain what each button does. It is also useful in complex form input dialogs, to provide more information about what kind of input is requested by each field. This kind of context help will generally be displayed in some kind of message line, and should be limited to a single line of text, without a title.

To implement this kind of automatic context help, you can use `XtAddEventHandler()` to register a procedure to be called on FocusIn or EnterNotify events. Note that you have to register the procedure for each widget in your application. Within the procedure, you could use `XmtHelpGetContextHelp()` to obtain the context help text, and `XmtMsgLineSet()` to display it. Once the context help for a widget is initially looked up, you might use a hash table to associate it with the widget, for more efficient lookup in subsequent calls.

Online help need not be context help in one guise or another. You might also want to provide help on a number of broader topics. For an electronic mail application, for example, you might provide online help "chapters" on reading mail, sending mail, replying and forwarding mail, adding attachments to messages, and so forth. A simple way to provide this help in your interface is simply to make each chapter available as a button in the **Help** menu. In this case, your **Help** menu might contain the items **About xmail...**, **On Context...**, **Reading Mail**, **Sending Mail**, **Attachments**, and so forth.

Generally, you will want to read the help text for these topics from configuration files at run time. For flexibility of installation, you'll want to use `XmtFindFile()` to locate the file, given a base filename. The help text for each of these items could be displayed in an XmMessageBox or XmtHelpBox which allow multiple fonts. Or, if the help is long, a scrolled XmText widget will be more efficient.

Note that you do not necessarily have to read in files and display them in your own application. There are file browser programs in existence; you can also start one of these up (use `fork()` and `exec()`) to allow the user to browse your help file. And, the help files need not be plain text either—you could start up *ghostview*, for example, to allow the user to read help files written in PostScript. Similarly, there are X-based viewers (like *xditview*) for DVI files, for GNU texinfo files, and for other formats.

If you have more than 8 or 10 of these help chapters, then placing them all in the same menu pane is no longer really sufficient. One approach is to divide them up among submenus. Another is to have an **On Topic...** item in your **Help** menu (along with your **On Context...** item) that pops up an

XmSelectionBox that allows the user to scroll through a list of available help topics.

When you have this much online help to provide, however, the best solution is to organize it as a complete online manual and allow the user to read it with a full-featured help browser. Ideally, such a help system will allow the user to read the manual sequentially, section by section, to skip around via cross-references (i.e., have hypertext capability), and to search for topics by keywords. Help browsers of this sort are becoming available commercially, and if you can afford one, this may be your best choice. Failing that, you might consider writing your documentation in the GNU texinfo format, and using one of the browsers for that format.

30.4 Style: Writing Online Help

As with so many things, the most important rule in writing online help is to know your audience and their expected level of expertise. This will help you set an appropriate tone in your writing, and choose an appropriate vocabulary.

Unless you are writing a basic computer-skills tutorial, you can assume in your online help that the user knows how to use the mouse, how to click on buttons, how to pull down menus, and so forth—if you tried to explain all this, you'd find yourself bogged down in details (and your users would find themselves in the same situation).

But while you shouldn't be too simplistic in your help, neither should you be obscure or complicated. In particular, avoid programmer jargon. Since context help is selected on a widget-by-widget basis, be extra careful not to use the word "widget," which is meaningless to anyone who is not a programmer. Instead of writing "Clicking on this widget . . . ", for example, write "Clicking on this button . . . ". Similarly, users are rarely interested in the name of the class of a widget, though they might be interested in the label that appears in or near it. Use words like "icon" or "graphic" instead of "pixmap." Note that it is perfectly reasonable, and may even be useful, to use jargon from the user's own field. If you have written a medical image-processing application, for example, then using the specialized words and acronyms of the medical imaging industry will probably make your help more effective for your expected audience.

Many writers fall into the trap of trying to be too formal, and end up with awkward sentence structures and users who have to read and re-read the help. Don't fall into this trap: just say what you need to say, and remember that your goal is simply to explain your application clearly. An informal tone will probably earn you the confidence and trust of your users more effectively than stilted formal language, but don't go so far that you end up sounding breezy, cocky, or otherwise insincere. Use the active voice—it is almost always more effective than the passive. Whatever you do, though, don't let your language get sloppy—follow the rules of grammar, use strong, precise words and think carefully about what you have written to make sure it is free of ambiguity.

When writing the help for a particular context, try to put yourself in the user's shoes, in the user's context, and try to imagine the kind of information the users need. Explain how the user got to the current context, in case he popped up the dialog, or whatever, by mistake. And always explain how to get out of the context or cancel the operation in progress. In dialog boxes, explain in some detail what all of the buttons do, and what the consequences of clicking on each will be. If a dialog box has input fields, you might also explain what data should be entered into each, and how that data will be used.

You should also provide information about how to get further help—the general help message for a dialog box might tell the user that she can get more detailed help by requesting context help on particular widgets for example. Similarly, the help for one dialog might mention related dialogs—the help for the **Save** As dialog, for example, might mention that you can use **Save** rather than **Save As**... if you don't want to change the filename.

Help needn't only be about how to work the application; it can be about the problem domain as well—an application used by chemical engineers might have a help node containing frequently used (but frequently forgotten) formulas. Or if a dialog asks for input of some parameter in unusual units, the online help might explain what those units are, what the parameter is, how it is related to others, reasonable upper and lower bounds for the input, and so on.

Remember that the XmtHelpBox widget displays help using an XmString, so that you can use multiple fonts in your help. One especially good use for a different font is to distinguish the names of keys, menu items, and button labels from regular text. Write "The **File** menu..." and "Strike the **Return** key...", for example, instead of "The File menu..." and "Strike the Return key...". Similarly, you might use italics for new terms that are being defined, a large font for subheadings within the help topic, and a constant-width font when you need to display tables of items.

The precedence rules in resource files can be tricky (see Chapter 13, *Resource File Utilities: mockup, checkres, and ad2c*, for a discussion of some of the tricks). Be careful when defining context help so that when a user wants help on a dialog box she doesn't get generic help ("This is a push button..." on the **OK** button, for example).

Finally, remember that the **Help** menu is the traditional place for an **About...** button. This menu item should pop up a dialog box that shows copyrights and credits for your application. This is your opportunity to give yourself the credit you're due!

30.5 Summary

- The HelpBox widget displays an icon and a title, and a relatively short amount (20 lines, say) of scrolled, multi-font text. This widget is automatically used by the context help routines.

- You can specify context help text and a context help title for any widget by setting the `xmtHelp` and `xmtHelpTitle` pseudo-resources on that widget. `XmtHelpGetContextHelp()` will look up help specified in this way.
- Use `XmtHelpDisplayContextHelp()` to display context help for a particular widget.
- Use `XmtHelpDoContextHelp()` to display context help on a user-specified context, when the user selects the **Context Help** menu item.
- Register `XmtHelpContextHelpCallback()` on the `XmNhelpCallback` of a widget to allow the user to get context help on that widget by typing the **Help** or **F1** keys. Use `XmtHelpInstallContextHelp()` to install this callback (or another) on all traversable widgets in a widget tree.
- The `contextHelpFile` application resource points to a resource file of context help for the application. This file is read in only when context help is first requested. If no file is specified, then context help is looked up in the application resource database instead.

31

Busy States and Background Work

Almost every application must perform some task now and again that will cause it to temporarily stop responding to user events. These tasks can be as simple as saving a file (which might only cause a quarter-second delay) or as complicated as making a lengthy database query or an RPC call to a network service. During these busy times, your applications should provide feedback to the user to indicate that the application is not responding to events, and perhaps also to explain what it is doing, indicate that it is making progress (i.e., that it is not hung) and, when done, that it has successfully completed. The Xmt library contains tools that allow you to provide these kinds of feedback.

This chapter also discusses ways that you can perform your time-consuming tasks "in the background" and minimize the time your application must spend not responding to events. There are several common approaches to this problem, which is often a source of confusion to application writers. Xmt does not add any new approaches, but this chapter will try to explain the existing methods.

31.1 Feedback with Cursors

Probably the easiest and most common way to indicate that an application is temporarily busy is to change the mouse cursor to an hourglass, a wristwatch, or some other icon that says "please wait." This technique is particularly useful for short busy periods of two seconds or less, because it is unintrusive. If the user isn't paying attention during the busy period, he need not even notice that the application was temporarily unavailable. This technique is also a good one for longer busy periods, but is best used in conjunction with other techniques for these long delays.

Using Cursors

Using cursors with the X Toolkit is a little tricky—none of the Xt widgets, nor any of the Motif widgets have a `XmNcursor` resource that you can set. This means that you must use Xlib functions to set cursors directly on widget's windows, and further means that you cannot set cursors until you have realized your widgets.

Xt provides a very simple String-to-Cursor resource converter by default. You can specify the name of any of the cursors in the standard cursor font in a resource file and this converter will create the appropriate cursor for you. The standard X cursor font contains a full collection of arrow cursors, but except for these and one or two others, the remaining standard cursors are junk, and you may often prefer to use cursors of your own design.

The Xmu library* provides a far more flexible cursor converter that lets you specify cursors from arbitrary fonts or arbitrary bitmaps. To use non-standard cursors, you can rely on this converter, or you can create and manipulate cursors on your own:

- Since cursors are non-rectangular, they require both an image and a mask. You can create a cursor from the standard cursor font with `XCreateFontCursor()`. You can create a cursor using image and mask glyphs from an arbitrary font with `XCreateGlyphCursor()`. You can create a cursor from an arbitrary bitmap and bitmask with `XCreatePixmapCursor()`.
- When done with a cursor, you can free the resource with `XFreeCursor()`.
- Cursors can only have two colors. If you use one of the standard cursors, you will get it in black-and-white. You can specify or change the foreground and background colors of a cursor with `XRecolorCursor()`. Note that cursors also have "transparent" pixels—those parts of the cursor rectangle that are not actually part of the cursor. These pixels are not drawn, and so the background shows through. It is worth looking at the standard cursor font (use `xfd -fn cursor`) to see how these cursors use a mask slightly larger than the cursor image in order to give the cursor an outline in a contrasting color.
- The cursors in the standard X cursor font are all quite small. To get the user's attention with a "please wait" cursor, you might want to use something larger. Note, though, that not all X servers are guaranteed to support cursors larger than 16 pixels square. You can use `XQueryBestCursor()` to see if the server you are using supports a given cursor size.

*The X "Miscellaneous Utilities" library. This library comes with the X distribution from the X Consortium, and contains some useful functions for X and Xt programmers.

Using Cursors (continued)

- You can set a cursor for a window with `XDefineCursor()`, and you can restore the default cursor for a window (its parent's cursor) with `XUndefineCursor()`.

—djf

Xmt provides convenience routines for displaying a busy cursor and for restoring the default cursor for a window:

Xmt/

Cursor.c

```
#include <Xmt/Xmt.h>
void XmtDisplayBusyCursor(Widget w);
void XmtDisplayDefaultCursor(Widget w);
```

These functions look up the shell of the specified widget, verify that the shell has been realized, and then use the Xlib function `XDefineCursor()` on the window of that shell widget. They also call `XFlush()` to force the change to be made immediately.

The cursor used by `XmtDisplayBusyCursor()` is specified by the `busyCursor` application resource. The default value of this resource is the standard "wristwatch" cursor in the X cursor font. `XmtDisplayDefaultCursor()` uses the cursor specified by the `cursor` application resource. The default value for this resource is `None`, which means that the choice of cursor depends on the window manager. You can set these cursor resources from a resource file, with `XmtInitializeApplicationShell()`, or with `XmtSetApplicationValues()`. Or, you can leave it unset, and let your users override the default, if they choose, from their personal resource files. The `cursorForeground`, `cursorBackground`, `busyCursorForeground`, and `busyCursorBackground` resources allow you to specify colors for these cursors.

Example 31-1 shows how you might use `XmtDisplayBusyCursor()` and `XmtDisplayDefaultCursor()`.

Example 31-1. Displaying the Busy Cursor

```
/* ARGSUSED */
void SaveCallback(Widget w, XtPointer tag, XtPointer data)
{
    /*
     * Often this file will be saved very quickly.  But when
     * it is on a networked file system, the save may sometimes
     * take a few seconds.  It is best to be safe and display
     * a busy cursor during the save.
     */
```

Example 31-1. Displaying the Busy Cursor (continued)

```
    XmtDisplayBusyCursor(main_window);
    save_file();
    XmtDisplayDefaultCursor(main_window);
}
```

Note that we don't use the supplied widget *w* in this example. This widget is probably a button in a pulldown menu. As such, it has a menu shell ancestor. We want the busy cursor to appear over the main shell, not a menu shell (which won't be visible at the time, anyway), so we use another widget, which in this example is stored in a global variable. (We could also have called `XmtGetTopLevelShell()` to look up this shell.)

There are some things to beware of when using these Xmt cursor functions. `XmtDisplayBusyCursor()` sets the cursor by calling `XDefineCursor()` on the window of a shell widget. This will set the cursor for any subwindows of that shell window that do not already have cursors of their own defined. Suppose, however, that you have a drawing area that uses special cursors to indicate different modes. In this case, calling `XmtDisplayBusyCursor()` will display the busy cursor for siblings of that drawing area window, but not for it or its children. To display a busy cursor for that window, you'd have to set its cursor yourself. (If you do this, though, be sure to call `XFlush()`, or the change might not be visible until the application starts handling events again—and by that time, it will no longer be busy.) Furthermore, since `XmtDisplayBusyCursor()` calls `XDefineCursor()`, which works on the X window hierarchy, and not on the Xt widget hierarchy, displaying a busy cursor over your main application window will not cause that cursor to be displayed over any dialog boxes that are popped up.

Also, as its name indicates, `XmtDisplayDefaultCursor()` restores the default cursor, which is not necessarily the same as the previous cursor. As with `XmtDisplayBusyCursor()`, `XmtDisplayDefaultCursor()` will have no effect on subwindows that have their own cursors defined. If you've defined a custom cursor on the shell window itself, however, calling `XmtDisplayDefaultCursor()` will not restore that cursor definition.

31.1.1 Initializing the Default Cursor

We've said before that `XmtDisplayDefaultCursor()` restores the default cursor for a shell. In fact, what it does is to set the default cursor for the shell, regardless of what cursor was in use before the busy cursor was displayed. Setting the `cursor` application resource is not in fact sufficient to make the specified cursor appear over a shell. If you specify this resource (or if you document it so that your users can specify it) then you must call `XmtDisplayDefaultCursor()` to actually force the cursor to be displayed. Xmt would do this for you automatically, except for the fact that you cannot specify a cursor for a widget until that widget has been realized. Because Xmt cannot know when you realize your widgets, you must take this step yourself.

In order to set the default cursor when your widgets are initially displayed, you might use code like the following:

```
        .
        .
        .
XmtCreateQueryChildren(toplevel, "dialog_shell", &dialog_shell);
XtRealizeWidget(toplevel);
XmtDisplayDefaultCursor(toplevel);
XmtDisplayDefaultCursor(dialog_shell);
XtAppMainLoop(app_context);
```

31.1.2 Animating the Busy Cursor

One technique for indicating that the application is busy but is making progress is to display a "busy" cursor that is animated.* This indicates to the user that the application is actually doing something, and is not hung. You could define a series of clock cursors, for example, with a second hand in different positions. Then, every quarter second or half second while your application is busy, you could switch cursors; the user will see a clock with a moving hand.

Xmt does not provide any special tools to implement cursor animation, but the task is straightforward: create a series of cursors, and then periodically while the application is busy display a new one. You can do this by calling `XmtSetApplicationValues()` to set the `XmtNbusyCursor` resource, and then calling `XmtDisplayBusyCursor()` to display it, but in this case, since you must create and manage the cursors anyway, it is simpler to use `XmtDisplayCursor()`:

Xmt/

Cursor.c

```
#include <Xmt/Xmt.h>
void XmtDisplayCursor(Widget w, Cursor c)
```

This function works like `XmtDisplayBusyCursor()` except that it displays a cursor that you specify explicitly.

Notice that while animating a cursor is straightforward, scheduling that animation can be difficult. While your application is busy, it usually isn't processing events in the main event loop, so you cannot use `XtAppAddTimeOut()` to call your cursor animation procedure periodically. You'll either have to make cursor animation part of the background task you are performing, or break up your task so that the user interface regains control now and then and can do the animation. This problem is discussed in more detail later in this chapter.

*The image manipulation program *xv* displays a spinning fish cursor when it is busy, for example. Despite the author's questionable taste in cursors, *xv* is an excellent and affordable shareware tool.

Another Busy Cursor Technique

The Frequently Asked Questions list for the comp.windows.x *Usenet newsgroup shows another technique you can use to display a busy cursor. Because this technique uses its own window, it can display a busy cursor without changing the cursors of any of the widgets in your application. This makes it ideal for applications that use custom cursors for some of their widgets. Note, though, that like* `XmtDisplayBusyCursor()`, *this technique only displays a busy cursor for a single shell widget, and will not affect any dialogs displayed above that shell.*

Subject: 113) How do I make a "busy cursor" while my application is computing? Is it necessary to call `XDefineCursor()` for every window in my application?

The easiest thing to do is to create a single InputOnly window that is as large as the largest possible screen; make it a child of your toplevel window and it will be clipped to that window, so it won't affect any other application. (It needs to be as big as the largest possible screen in case the user enlarges the window while it is busy or moves elsewhere within a virtual desktop.) Substitute your topmost widget for "toplevel" here.

```
XSetWindowAttributes attributes;

attributes.do_not_propagate_mask = (KeyPressMask | KeyReleaseMask |
                                    ButtonPressMask | ButtonReleaseMask |
                                    PointerMotionMask);
attributes.cursor = XCreateFontCursor(XtDisplay(toplevel), XC_watch);

XCreateWindow(XtDisplay(toplevel), XtWindow(toplevel), 0, 0,
              32767, 32767, (unsigned int) 0, CopyFromParent, InputOnly,
              CopyFromParent, CWDontPropagate | CWCursor, &attributes);
```

When you want to use this busy cursor, map and raise this window (use `XMapRaised()`); to go back to normal, unmap it (`XUnmapWindow()`). This will automatically keep you from getting extra mouse events; depending on precisely how the window manager works, it may or may not have a similar effect on keystrokes as well.

[Thanks are due to to Andrew Wason (aw@cellar.bae.bellcore.com), Dan Heller (argv@sun.com), and mouse@larry.mcrcim.mcgill.edu; 11/90,5/91]

—*modified from the* comp.windows.x *FAQ list*

31.1.3 Preventing Input During Busy Periods

When the application is busy and cannot process events immediately, the X server does still queue up X events to be processed. If you do nothing to prevent it, these queued events will be processed when your application is no longer busy—the X server automatically supports "type-ahead" and "click-ahead" buffering of events.*

While these features may be useful for advanced users, it is a bad idea to allow them in general. This is especially so when you are displaying a busy cursor—the busy cursor is a sign that input with the mouse is not currently possible, and if you choose to display the cursor, you should be sure to enforce this meaning. If you do allow input while a busy cursor is displayed, you will mislead and/or confuse the user.

You can use the two functions `XmtDiscardButtonEvents()` and `XmtDiscardKeyPressEvents()` to disable click-ahead and type-ahead:

Xmt/

Discard.c

```
#include <Xmt/Xmt.h>
void XmtDiscardButtonEvents(Widget w);
void XmtDiscardKeyPressEvents(Widget w);
```

`XmtDiscardButtonEvents()` throws out all button press, button release, and pointer motion events pending on the display connection of the specified widget. `XmtDiscardKeyPressEvents()` similarly discards all key press events. This function does not discard key release events, because when an action is dispatched because of a key press, the Xt Translation Manager often needs to see the corresponding key release event to keep its internal state consistent. Since it is very rare (and non-portable) to dispatch actions on key release events, any extra, non-discarded release events will be harmlessly ignored.

You'll usually want to call these event-discarding functions right before you restore the default cursor:

```
XmtDiscardButtonEvents(toplevel);
XmtDiscardKeyPressEvents(toplevel);
XmtDisplayDefaultCursor(toplevel);
```

If your application will only be busy for a short while, and you do want to allow click-ahead and type-ahead, then it is probably better not to display a busy cursor at all. This way, the user will never see the "please wait" sign. Instead, they might notice a brief period of unresponsiveness, but this is a fact of life on many computer systems and with much software, and a short unexplained delay in handling input (followed by correct handling of input) might be better in some cases than an interruption during which no input is allowed at all.

Note that type-ahead can be a dangerous feature, unless you can be quite sure which widget will have the keyboard focus during the busy period. If the user clicks on a button, causing a busy period, and then starts trying to type into a

*The X server will not queue events forever, of course, but it will buffer up a significant number of them. You don't need to worry about overflowing the event buffer unless your application will be busy for a long time.

text widget, for example, her key events might in fact be delivered to the button widget. And if she types **Space** or **Return**, then the button might even be activated again! On the other hand, if a busy period is initiated through a keyboard command in a text widget, then it is safer to allow the user to continue typing.

Usually, you should disable type-ahead and click-ahead during busy periods. But if your application has a lot of busy periods, or will be used in a networked environment with unpredictable delays, your advanced users may appreciate the ability to re-enable these features. You can allow this by providing an application resource that they can set. Then you might end up with code like the following:

```
if (!app_resources.allow_type_ahead) {
    XmtDiscardButtonEvents(toplevel);
    XmtDiscardKeyPressEvents(toplevel);
}
XmtDisplayDefaultCursor(toplevel);
```

31.2 Feedback with Messages

Displaying a busy cursor only tells the user that the application is busy; it doesn't tell him what the application is busy doing. When the application cursor is restored, the user only knows that the application is no longer busy; he doesn't know whether the operation that was being performed was successfully completed or not. This extra feedback is often useful, and can be provided by displaying a message to the user. A good way to display this sort of message to the user is with the XmtMsgLine widget, which is described in detail in Chapter 22, *The Message Line*. It is also possible, of course, to display the message in some other widget, such as an XmLabel. Whatever you use, the extra feedback will often let the user feel more comfortable with, and less mystified by, your application.

Consider the following three cases:

- If the user has selected the **Read File** item from a pulldown menu, then if the busy cursor appears, he can assume that the application is busy reading the file. When the file is read in and its contents become visible he will know that the read was successfully completed. There is no need for extra feedback in this case.

- When the same user selects **Save** from the menu, he understands that the application will briefly be busy saving the file, but since saving a file is an important operation, he might like some reassurance that the save was successful—the application will have to make this explicit, since there will be no change in the data displayed by the application. The application could display the message "Saving . . ." while it was busy, and then display "Saving . . . done." when the save was successfully completed. Even more feedback could be provided by displaying the name of the file that is being saved; this lets the user confirm that the program is doing what he thinks it is doing.

- Some applications will periodically do an autosave. In this case, the busy cursor will appear briefly, but since the user has not requested this save explicitly, the application should display a message to the user explaining that an autosave is in progress. Without the message, the user has no way at all of knowing what the application is doing. In this case, a message indicating that the autosave was successful may be less important.

An application that implements auto saving might do so with a procedure like that shown in Example 31-2.

Example 31-2. Providing XmtMsgLine Feedback while the Application Is Busy

```
/* some commonly used widgets */
static Widget toplevel, msgline;

/* ARGSUSED */
static void ActionHook(Widget w, XtPointer data, String name, XEvent *event,
                       String *params, Cardinal *num_params)
{
    static int count;

    /*
     * This is an action hook procedure.  When registered with
     * XtAppAddActionHook(), it will be called before the translation
     * manager dispatches any actions.  Every three hundred key presses
     * or mouse clicks, this action hook will do an autosave, and will
     * provide feedback to the user while the application is busy
     * with the save.
     */

    if ((event->type == KeyPress) || (event->type == ButtonPress)) {
        count++;
        if (count == 300) { /* 300 could be an application resource, instead */
            count = 0;
            XmtDisplayBusyCursor(toplevel);
            XmtMsgLinePush(msgline);
            XmtMsgLineSet(msgline, "Autosaving...");
            autosave();
            XmtMsgLinePop(msgline, XmtMsgLineNow);
            XmtDisplayDefaultCursor(toplevel);
        }
    }
}
```

31.3 Feedback with Dialogs

The techniques described above are suitable feedback when the application will be busy for no more than a few seconds—they are unintrusive techniques; if the user is also busy at the moment, she might not even notice that the application was busy. When the application will be performing a more substantial task (recalculating a large spreadsheet, making a query to a remote database server, etc.) it is often appropriate to provide a more substantial form of notification.

This notification usually takes the form of a dialog box—before the application begins its computation it pops up a dialog explaining that it is busy and what it will be doing, and then pops the dialog down when it is done. Motif provides the XmWorkingDialog for this purpose; it is an XmMessageBox widget in an XmDialogShell, with a special hourglass icon. Xmt provides the XmtWorkingBox widget, which can display the same message, but has several additional features. These dialogs are shown in Figure 31-1.

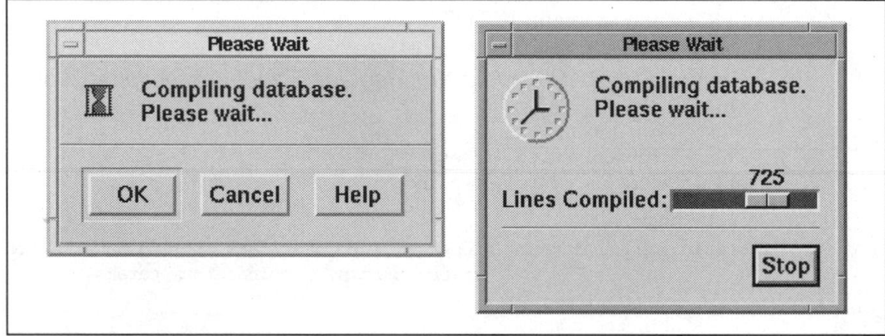

examples/

31/xmt_working_box

Figure 31-1. An XmWorkingDialog and an XmtWorkingBox dialog

31.3.1 The XmtWorkingBox widget

Figure 31-1 shows an XmtWorkingBox widget. As with the XmWorkingDialog, it displays an icon indicating that the application is busy, and a "please wait" message explaining what the application is doing. Unlike the XmWorkingDialog, however, it also optionally displays an XmScale widget, with a caption to show the application's progress, and optionally displays a **Stop** button that the user can use to abort the task being performed.

The `XmtNicon` and `XmtNmessage` resources specify the pixmap and the XmString to be displayed in the widget. The `XmtNscaleLabel` resource specifies a caption for the XmScale widget, and the minimum, maximum, and current values for the XmScale widget are controlled through the `XmtNscaleMin`, `XmtNscaleMax`, and `XmtNscaleValue` resources. `XmtNbuttonLabel` specifies the label (an XmString) for the single push button in the dialog. The default label for this button is **Stop**. The `XmtNshowScale` and `XmtNshowButton` resources are `Boolean` values that specify whether the XmScale and XmPushButton widgets are displayed. Finally, `XmtNscaleWidget` and `XmtNbuttonWidget` are read-only resources that return pointers to the internal XmScale and XmPushButton widgets, which programmers may sometimes want to modify. The WorkingBox widget and its resources are described in more detail on the widget reference page.

The WorkingBox widget is a subclass of the XmtLayout widget. Its class name is "XmtWorkingBox," and its class structure is `xmtWorkingBoxWidgetClass`. You can create a WorkingBox widget with the convenience function `Xmt-`

`CreateWorkingBox()`. You will almost always want to create one of these widgets as a child of an XmDialogShell, however, so Xmt also provides `XmtCreateWorkingDialog()`, which does this for you:

Xmt/

WorkingBox.c

```
#include <Xmt/WorkingBox.h>
Widget XmtCreateWorkingBox(Widget parent, String name,
                           ArgList args, Cardinal num_args)
Widget XmtCreateWorkingDialog(Widget parent, String name,
                              ArgList args, Cardinal num_args)
```

Like the simple message dialogs described in Chapter 25, *Message Dialogs*, a working dialog is the kind of dialog suitable for automatic management and caching. So Xmt provides a simpler interface to using the WorkingBox, which will be described in the next section.

31.3.2 Making Sure the Dialog Is Visible

There is one major obstacle that programmers encounter again and again when using a working dialog (an XmWorkingDialog, a WorkingBox, or any other) to tell the user that the application is busy. Recall that when setting a busy cursor with `XDefineCursor()`, you must call `XFlush()` to force the change to take effect immediately. When you are processing events normally, you rarely need to call `XFlush()`, because the output buffer is always flushed before events are read. If the application will be busy for a while, however, events will not be read, and unless the output buffer is explicitly flushed, the cursor change could remain buffered and not become visible until the application is no longer busy.

A similar problem exists for working dialog boxes. When a widget such as a working dialog is mapped, the window becomes visible on the screen but is initially blank. Widgets do not draw themselves until they receive their first Expose event. So, in order for a working dialog to become visible, the application must wait for and dispatch some events before it begins whatever time-consuming operation it plans to do. The window manager compounds this problem. When a window manager is running, there is an asynchronous delay between the time when the X server reports that it has mapped the window and when the window manager actually makes the window visible.

Because this is a complicated problem that crops up frequently, Xmt provides a solution:

Xmt/

Wait.c

```
#include <Xmt/Xmt.h>
void XmtWaitUntilMapped(Widget w);
```

`XmtWaitUntilMapped()` enters an event loop to wait until the specified widget becomes visible on the screen. Once the dialog has become visible, `XmtWaitUntilMapped()` handles all pending Expose events to ensure that the widget has a chance to draw itself, and then returns. You should use this function whenever you want to be sure that a dialog is visible before your application stops handling events for some period of time.

31.3.3 Automatic Working Dialogs

XmtDisplayWorkingDialog() automatically creates, and caches for reuse, a WorkingBox dialog. Because of the automatic caching and reuse, this function is similar to XmtDisplayMessage() and related routines described in Chapter 25, *Message Dialogs.*

Xmt/

Working.c

```
#include <Xmt/Dialogs.h>
Widget XmtDisplayWorkingDialog(Widget w, String dialog_name,
                              String message_default,
                              String scale_label_default,
                              String button_label_default,
                              int scale_min, int scale_max,
                              Boolean show_scale,
                              Boolean show_button);
```

XmtDisplayWorkingDialog() takes arguments that specify the default values for the dialog title, message, scale widget caption, and button label. It also takes a dialog name argument; if a name is specified, then it will check the resource database for resources to override these title, message, caption, and label defaults. As with the message dialogs, this gives the convenience of not having to set resources and manage the widget yourself, but still provides customizability and internationalization through the resource database.

XmtDisplayWorkingDialog() also takes arguments that specify whether the scale and button should be shown, and what the maximum and minimum values of the scale should be. These arguments cannot be overridden from the database.

XmtDisplayWorkingDialog() calls XmtWaitUntilMapped() internally, so if you use it instead of using a private working dialog, you will not have to call that function. See the XmtDisplayWorkingDialog() reference page for more information on using this function, and on customizing the dialogs it creates.

To pop down a working dialog managed by XmtDisplayWorkingDialog(), you can call XmtHideWorkingDialog(). This function takes a single widget argument, which can be any widget on the same screen as the working dialog. Alternatively, if the working dialog is displayed with its **Stop** button visible, you can wait until the user clicks on it. The WorkingBox has its XmNautoUnmanage resource set, so it will automatically pop down when this button is pressed. If your application completes, and the user has not pressed the **Stop** button to abort it, you may choose to pop down the dialog with XmtHideWorkingDialog(), or instead, you might use the dialog to provide feedback that the operation was successfully completed. You could do this by changing the `XmtNmessage` resource from a "please wait" message to a "operation completed" message, and by changing the button label from **Stop** to **Continue**. Then the user can read the new message, and click on the "Continue" button to go on with the application. (We'll see an example of this technique after a couple more subsections of preliminaries.)

`XmtDisplayWorkingDialog()`, unlike the cached message dialog functions, returns a pointer to the cached widget that it pops up. Message dialogs simply display a message; once popped up, the programmer need not think about them again. Working dialogs, as we will see in the following sections, must often be manipulated by the programmer while they are displayed. The widget pointer returned by `XmtDisplayWorkingDialog()` provides a handle that makes this possible, even though the working dialog is owned, cached and managed by Xmt.

31.3.4 Updating the WorkingBox Scale Value

If you are displaying a WorkingBox dialog (either one you created yourself, or one created by `XmtDisplayWorkingDialog()`) that has its XmScale widget visible, then you will periodically need to update the value displayed in that XmScale widget to let the user know how far to completion the task is. You can do this with `XmtWorkingBoxSetScaleValue()`:

```
#include <Xmt/WorkingBox.h>
void XmtWorkingBoxSetScaleValue(Widget working_box, int value);
```

The first argument to this function is a WorkingBox widget—either the one returned by a call to `XmtDisplayWorkingDialog()`, or one you created yourself. The second argument is the value to be displayed in the XmScale widget. This *`value`* argument is relative to whatever minimum and maximum value you've chosen for the scale—specified by the *`scale_min`* and *`scale_max`* arguments to `XmtDisplayWorkingDialog()`, or the `XmtNscaleMin` and `XmtNscaleMax` resources you set on the widget.

There are some important points about using this technique. First, if you are displaying the progress of the task being performed with an XmScale widget, you must know in advance how long the task will take, or at least be able to place an upper bound on it. This measurement can be in seconds, or in other units, such as the number of files searched, the number of lines compiled, or any other measure appropriate to the task.

Second, you must be able to periodically call `XmtWorkingBoxSetScaleValue()` while the task is being performed. This is not always possible—if it is a blocking database query that is taking up the time, for example, then your user interface code will not regain control in order to update the scale value. A later section in this chapter explains some techniques you can use to avoid this situation, but in general, you will not be able to display values with the scale widget unless your UI code can periodically regain control. If you cannot regain control, then you should not display the XmScale widget in your working dialog, since it will not do anything.

If you are able to call `XmtWorkingBoxSetScaleValue()` periodically, you must determine how often to do so. You should do so often enough that there are not significant pauses between updates to the scale value, even on the slowest platform that you will be running the application on. But you also don't want to call this function so many times that you end up making the task take noticeably longer. In particular, don't call `XmtWorkingBoxSetScaleValue()` with a finer granularity than will be visible on the screen. The XmScale widget in the WorkingBox will generally be 100 to 250 pixels wide. If you are performing an operation in 1000 steps, there is no need to update the scale after each step, because most of those updates wouldn't even result in any motion of the slider. Trial and error may be important here to determine a suitable interval between updates.

Sometimes the task being performed is a series of steps of unequal or unpredictable duration. In this case, you might check the system time (with `time()` or `gettimeofday()`, for example) after each iteration and only call `XmtWorkingBoxSetScaleValue()` if sufficient time has elapsed since the last time you checked.

Example 31-3 shows how you might use `XmtWorkingBoxSetScaleValue()`. In this example, the program busies itself by simply counting; in practice, you'd probably do something a little more meaningful. Note that this example also uses a busy cursor to supplement the busy dialog.

Example 31-3. Using a WorkingBox Dialog

```
void CountCallback(Widget w, XtPointer tag, XtPointer data)
{
    Widget dialog;

    /* display a busy cursor over the main window */
    XmtDisplayBusyCursor(w);

    /* and pop up a working dialog too */
    dialog = XmtDisplayWorkingDialog(w, "waitDialog",
                                     "Counting to 10,000,000\nPlease wait...",
                                     "Iterations (x10,000):", "Abort",
                                     0, 1000, True, True);

    /* get busy:  in this example, we just count to a big number */
    for(j=0; j < 100; j++) {
        /* periodically update the scale */
        XmtWorkingBoxSetScaleValue(dialog, j*10);
        /* also check the button.  if clicked, abort the count */
        if (XmtWorkingBoxHandleEvents(dialog)) break;
        /* count to 100,000.  we do this 100 times */
        for(i=0; i < 100000; i++);
    }
    XmtWorkingBoxSetScaleValue(dialog, j*10);

    /*
     * When we're done, we change the message so the user knows we're done,
     * and change the button so the user knows how to dismiss the dialog.
```

Example 31-3. Using a WorkingBox Dialog (continued)

```
     * Instead, we could just pop the dialog down with XmtHideWorkingDialog()
     */
    XtVaSetValues(dialog,
                  XmtNmessage, "Counting to 10,000,000\nDone.",
                  XmtNbuttonLabel, "Continue",
                  NULL);

    /*
     * Restore the cursor.
     * The dialog is still up, but this is the easiest time to restore it.
     */
    XmtDisplayDefaultCursor(w);
}
```

31.3.5 Handling the WorkingBox Stop Button

If the scale widget is visible in a WorkingBox dialog, you must periodically update the value it displays. Similarly, if the **Stop** button is visible in the dialog, then you must periodically check to see if the user has clicked on it. You can do this by calling `XmtWorkingBoxHandleEvents()`:

```
#include <Xmt/WorkingBox.h>
Boolean XmtWorkingBoxHandleEvents(Widget working_box);
```

`XmtWorkingBoxHandleEvents()` handles any key or mouse button events that have occurred in the specified WorkingBox and returns `True` if the user has clicked on the **Stop** button, and `False` otherwise. If the button is visible, then the application *must* respond to it by aborting the task in progress. If there is some critical point after which the application is still busy, but after which the task can no longer be cleanly aborted, you can make the **Stop** button insensitive once it is no longer effective. In this case you should probably also update the displayed message to indicate to the user that the task has entered this new phase. By default, the `XmNautoUnmanage` resource of the WorkingBox is `True`, which means that the dialog will be automatically popped down when the user clicks the **Stop** button.

As with updating the scale value, you obviously can't call `XmtWorkingBoxHandleEvents()` if you are performing some task that does not return control to your UI code now and then. In this case, you will have to use a working dialog without scale or **Stop** button.

The discussion of timing updates to the scale widget applies equally to checking for button events with `XmtWorkingBoxHandleEvents()`. The more often you call this function, the better the responsiveness of the interface. If you call it too often, however, then your application may end up staying busy for longer than necessary. In practice, you may find that you need to call `XmtWorkingBoxHandleEvents()` more often than `XmtWorkingBoxSetScaleValue()` in order to achieve an acceptably responsive feel. Again, trial and error will help you determine an acceptable interval.

While one of the primary purposes of XmtWorkingBoxHandleEvents() is to check whether the **Stop** button has been pressed, note that it does not only poll for events on that button. XmtWorkingBoxHandleEvents() calls XmUpdateDisplay() internally—this Motif function handles all pending expose events that may have been generated while the application is busy. It also calls XmtDiscardButtonEvents() and XmtDiscardKeyPressEvents() to throw out any other user events that have been generated. You may want to call XmtWorkingBoxHandleEvents() to get these features, even if you don't have a **Stop** button, or you may want to call these Motif and Xmt functions explicitly to duplicate them yourself.

Example 31-3, above, shows how you might use XmtWorkingBoxHandleEvents() with a working dialog.

Note that this example calls XmtWorkingBoxHandleEvents() and XmtWorkingBoxSetScaleValue() directly from the middle of its time-consuming task. When you provide busy feedback of this kind, there usually is an interaction between the application back end that is performing the task and the GUI front end that is displaying the feedback. For modularity, it is a good idea to try to minimize this interaction. Thus, instead of calling XmtWorkingBoxSetScaleValue() and XmtWorkingBoxHandleEvents() directly in your application back end, you might wrap these procedures into a single gui_do_busy_feedback() call defined in your GUI front end module. This will make it easier to port the application back end to other GUI platforms, and provides a centralized place for making changes to the feedback implementation.

Handling Events Yourself

If your application is busy and not responding to events, and you are not using the XmtWorkingBox widget, there may be times that you will want to handle events yourself. At a minimum, you should call XmUpdateDisplay() periodically, to handle any pending Expose events that can occur if the user moves, restacks, iconifies, or deiconifies windows.

In order to handle all pending events, you need to write an event loop that will not block when there are no more events to process. This code will do the trick:

```
while(XtAppPending(app_context))
    XtAppProcessEvent(app_context, XtIMAll);
```

If you want to be more selective about the types of events you process, or the widgets for which you process events, you can use XCheckMaskEvent(), XCheckWindowEvent(), XCheckIfEvent(), or related functions to selectively remove events from the event queue, and XtDispatchEvent() to process them.

—djf

31.3.6 Animating the WorkingBox Icon

Another technique you can use, if you choose to be fancy, is to animate the icon displayed in the WorkingBox widget. If you define a series of similar icons and display them one after another (by setting the `XmtNicon` resource) you can create the illusion of sand falling in an hourglass, of a second hand moving around a clock face, steam rising from a coffee mug, or whatever.*

A Working Dialog as a Separate Process

Joe Kraska points out that sometimes you may want to implement a working dialog as an entirely separate process. Note that in X11R6, you could also use Joe's technique with threads. In either case, your working dialog process or thread could be sophisticated enough to do things like pixmap animation.

`XmtWaitUntilMapped()` assures that a working dialog is mapped on the screen immediately after it is created. This works moderately well, but if the working dialog is overlapped by another window during the waiting period, we are back to square one, because expose events are processed in the main event loop, and the program is stuck because it is not executing its own main event loop. The window can't redraw itself. [*Unless you can periodically call* `XmtWorkingBoxHandleEvents()`, `XmUpdateDisplay()`, *or handle events in some other fashion during the busy period. — djf*]

The bottom line is, if you can live with a working dialog box that doesn't refresh itself once it is drawn, go for the technique using `XmtWaitUntilMapped()`. However, if you are picky enough that you insist on having your working dialogs be refreshable all the time, you'll have to opt for a more advanced technique. Here's one option:

Write a function that creates a pipe to a totally separate X client that gets launched by the function via `fork()` and `exec()`. This slave program, which exists solely to display working dialogs, will be given commands by your function via the pipes that you establish. The slave program will, of course, always be "graphically up to date," because it has its own connection to the X server, and it has its own event loop. Its own windows will always refresh themselves, as that is its primary business—keeping itself refreshed.

—Joe Kraska

---

*An office mate of mine once programmed the audio device of his workstation to play the theme music from the TV show "Jeopardy." His goal was to hack the kernel to play this music when the computer was in disk wait.

31.3.7 Displaying a Working Dialog at Startup

Some applications must do a substantial amount of initialization before their windows pop up and they become usable. If this initialization will take more than a few seconds, then it is a good idea to provide some feedback to the user, so they know that the application has actually been started, and is doing something. One easy way to do this is simply to print a message to the standard output stream. The problem with this approach is that it is not particularly noticeable, and it doesn't work well if the application is started as a background job, or if it is launched from a graphical desktop.

A better technique is to actually display a dialog box. This way the user sees something happen quickly, and you have the opportunity to display a simple title screen or product logo for your application. The *mockup* client displays a dialog like this while it is mocking up the specified resource file.

Figure 31-2. A working dialog during application startup

Example 31-4 shows code you could use to display a dialog like that shown in Figure 31-2. Note that if your application has several time-consuming initialization steps, you might change the message displayed in the dialog to keep the user informed of the application's progress: "Reading configuration files . . . ", "Creating interface . . . ", "Contacting database . . . ".

Example 31-4. Displaying a Working Dialog During Application Startup

```
main(int argc, char **argv)
{
    static char working_font_list[] = "*-helvetica-bold-r-*-*-*-180-*";
        .
        .
        .
    /*
     * First, go create the toplevel shell
     */
    toplevel = XtAppInitialize (&app, appclass, NULL, 0,
                               &argc, argv, fallbacks, NULL, 0);

    /*
     * Then create the "please wait" dialog in a TopLevel shell widget.
     * We rely upon a special case in XmtWaitUntilMapped below that will
     * do the right thing here for TopLevelShell.  A TransientShell
     * or XmDialogShell wouldn't work because the app shell isn't realized
     * yet.
     */
```

Example 31-4. Displaying a Working Dialog During Application Startup (continued)

```
    working_shell = XtVaCreateWidget("working_shell",
                                     topLevelShellWidgetClass,
                                     toplevel,
                                     XtNtitle, "Please Wait",
                                     XtNsaveUnder, True,
                                     NULL);
    /*
     * Create an XmtWorkignBox widget with a mesasge but no button or scale.
     */
    working_box = XtVaCreateManagedWidget("working_box",
                              xmtWorkingBoxWidgetClass,
                              working_shell,
                              XmtNmessage, "Creating interface\nPlease wait...",
                              XtVaTypedArg, XmtNfontList, XtRString,
                                working_font_list, sizeof(working_font_list),
                              XmtNshowScale, False,
                              XmtNshowButton, False,
                              NULL);

    /*
     * Realize the working dialog and pop it up.
     * Then wait to be sure it is visible.
     */
    XtRealizeWidget(working_shell);
    XtPopup(working_shell, XtGrabNone);
    XmtWaitUntilMapped(working_shell);

    /*
     * Now we go do the initialization that takes so long.
     */
    XmtCreateChildren(toplevel);

    /*
     * If we were doing other initialization, we might change
     * the message in the dialog here, before starting the next
     * task.
     */

    /*
     * Now get rid of the working dialog. We pop it down
     * before destroying it because it disappears cleanly that way.
     */
    XtPopdown(working_shell);
    XtDestroyWidget(working_shell);

    /*
     * And finally proceed as normal.
     */
    XtRealizeWidget(toplevel);
    XmtDisplayDefaultCursor(toplevel);
    XtAppMainLoop(app);
}
```

31.4 Performing Tasks in the Background

In the sections above we've assumed that your application will stop processing events (with the exception, perhaps, of calling `XmtWorkingBoxHandleEvents()` periodically) while it performs some time-consuming task. Some tasks, however, can be implemented with Xt work procedures or subprocesses. With these approaches, the task will be performed in the background, and your application need not ever stop processing events. The subsections below will explain how you can do this.*

Note, however that in some cases you may still choose to display "busy feedback" (through a cursor, a message line, or a working dialog) to the user even when you've implemented a task in the background. This could be because the way you've implemented the task requires that the application state remain constant while it is performed. In this case, posting a modal working dialog will effectively block the user from making any changes to that state. Or, it could be that there is really not much else for the user to do until the task completes—most simple applications are "single-tasking"; once the user has composed a database query, for example, she wants to see the results of that query, and probably doesn't want to begin composing a new query. Or you may choose ask the user to wait simply because you expect that most of your users will be novices or PC users who would only be confused by a multi-tasking capability in your application.

31.4.1 Using Work Procedures

The X Toolkit allows you to register a "work procedure" to be called when there are no pending events to process. A work procedure can be registered with an arbitrary `client_data` value through a call to `XtAppAddWorkProc()`. The procedure will be called, with the `client_data` as its only argument, when there are no events pending. A work procedure returns a `Boolean` value; it should return `True` if it has completed the background task and should not be called again, or `False` if it should be called again.

If there are events waiting to be handled, they will be processed, and if there are no events waiting, then the work procedure will be called. In this way, both interface events and work procedure get time. But events will not be processed *while* a work procedure is executing, so in order to perform a background task without giving up the responsiveness of the interface, the task must be implemented so that it can be broken into reasonably sized chunks that can be executed one at a time. If processing a large image, for example, (image processing can involve floating-point math, and a large number of computations) you might process one row of pixels at a time in the work procedure, returning `False` after each row. You would use a static variable, or better, a variable pointed to by the *`client_data`* argument to keep track of which row you had processed last. When the work procedure processed the last row of the image,

*Much of the discussion in this section is specific to UNIX. Some of it makes reference to low-level UNIX calls that may not be portable to all UNIX systems.

then it would return `True` to tell the Intrinsics that it was done and should not be called until explicitly registered again.

If a work procedure takes more than a small fraction of a second to complete its chunk of the background task, the user will notice that the interface is less responsive. If each chunk takes a full second, the change in response time is dramatic enough to make the interface practically unusable. Dragging the mouse through a pulldown menu, or typing quickly into an XmText widget, are examples of where responsiveness is important, and it takes some trial and error to adjust the length of each chunk of computation so that responsiveness is not sacrificed.

If you cannot structure your task so that it can be done in small enough chunks in a work procedure, you may be better off popping up a working dialog and performing the task in the foreground. This way, the user at least knows that the application is busy, and will not be puzzled by periods of decreased responsiveness.

One good use for work procedures is to do pre-computation of values that you anticipate will be needed later. An application might create and quickly display its main window, for example, and then use a work procedure to begin creating its dialog boxes in the background. If a dialog has been created before it is needed, it will be quick to pop up. Since the application will never be sure that the dialogs have already been created by the work procedure, it will have to be prepared to create any needed dialog before using it. Example 31-5 shows how you might implement a work procedure like this. This technique allows you to decrease application startup time by creating only the widgets that will immediately be visible. Since creating widgets can be relatively time consuming, however, the application may be unresponsive for a few seconds after it appears, unless the dialog creation procedure can be broken down into very small chunks.

Example 31-5. Creating Dialogs with Work Procedures

```
Widget toplevel;
Widget file_dialog, help_dialog, search_dialog;
Widget CreateFileDialog(), CreateHelpDialog(), CreateSearchDialog();

/* the work procedure, registered elsewhere */
Boolean BackgroundCreateProc(XtPointer data)
{
    if (file_dialog == NULL) {
        file_dialog = CreateFileDialog();
        return False;
    }
    if (help_dialog == NULL) {
        help_dialog = CreateHelpDialog();
        return False;
    }
    if (search_dialog == NULL) {
        search_dialog = CreateSearchDialog();
        return False;
    }
```

Example 31-5. Creating Dialogs with Work Procedures (continued)

```
    return True;
}

/* a hypothetical function that uses one of the dialogs */
void DoHelp()
{
    /*
     * If the user requests help before the work procedure creates
     * the help dialog, then we must create it ourself.
     */
    if (help_dialog == NULL) help_dialog = CreateHelpDialog();
        .
        .
        .
}
```

Waiting for Idle Time

The X Toolkit does not attempt to do any scheduling of work procedures; it will call a registered work procedure whenever there are no input events pending. This can be a problem when you cannot break your background task into small enough chunks. If each call to the work procedure will take about one second to complete, for example, then there will be a delay of one second between the time that the interface responds to one batch of events and next. This makes the interface respond in jerks, which is very unsettling for the user, particularly when dragging the pointer through a pulldown menu, for example.

One approach to handling this case is to write a work procedure that only performs its one-second chunk of computation when the interface has been idle for a while. With this technique, the work procedure waits until the interface is not busy before spending much time on the background task. If an event occurs while the work procedure is active, then there will be a delay while the work procedure finishes its current chunk of computation. But once the interface has "woken up" and is no longer idle, the work procedure will wait awhile before performing any more large chunks of computation. When the interface has been idle, the user may see a delay in the processing of the first event, but then subsequent events will be handled responsively until the interface becomes idle again.

One way to tell if the interface is idle is to call `XtLastTimestampProcessed()`. The value returned by this function changes each time an event is processed. If you write a timer procedure (registered with `XtAppAddTimeOut()`) that calls `XtLastTimestampProcessed()` every three seconds, say, then you'll be able to tell when the user has not done anything between one invocation of the timer procedure and the next. When you detect an idle period like this, you can try to sneak in some background processing with a work procedure:

Waiting for Idle Time (continued)

```
#define IDLE_PERIOD 3000  /* 3 seconds in milliseconds */

/*
 * This is the timer procedure.  When it finds some idle time,
 * it will register the work procedure to perform background work
 */
static void check_for_idle(XtPointer client_data,
                           XtIntervalId * interval)
{
    static Time last_timestamp;
    Time timestamp;

    timestamp = XtLastTimestampProcessed(XtDisplay(toplevel));

    /* if not idle, just check again later */
    if (timestamp != last_timestamp) {
        last_timestamp = timestamp;
        XtAppAddTimeOut(XtWidgetToApplicationContext(toplevel),
                        IDLE_PERIOD, check_for_idle, NULL);
    }
    else { /* if idle, start the work proc */
        XtAppAddWorkProc(XtWidgetToApplicationContext(toplevel),
                         do_idle_work, NULL);
    }
}

/*
 * This is the work procedure.  It does one chunk of work, and then
 * checks if the interface is still idle.  If not, it reregisters the
 * timer to wait for another idle period.
 */
static Boolean do_idle_work(XtPointer client_data)
{
    Boolean done;

    /* do one chunk of work */
    done = compute_chunk();

    /* if we're all done with the background processing, return True */
    if (done) return True;

    /*
     * Otherwise, there is still work to do.
     * If there are no input events waiting, then return False,
     * so that we'll be called again right away.
     */
    if (XPending(XtDisplay(toplevel)) == 0) return False;

    /*
     * Otherwise, we're no longer idle, so return True, so that
     * the proc won't be called again right away, but re-register
     * the timer, so we'll get some more idle time later
     */
    XtAppAddTimeOut(XtWidgetToApplicationContext(toplevel),
                    IDLE_PERIOD, check_for_idle, NULL);
```

Waiting for Idle Time (continued)

```
    return True;
}
```

Note that the work procedure does not use `XtLastTimestampProcessed()` to check whether the interface is idle—any events that arrived while the work procedure was doing its computation will not have been processed yet, so that approach will not work. Instead, the work procedure simply checks whether any input events are waiting by calling `XPending()`. (Note that this call will sometimes require a round-trip to the server.)

A variation on this scheme is to vary the length of the chunk of computation depending on how long the interface had been idle. That is, the longer the time since a user event, the longer (up to some reasonable maximum value) the work procedure spends computing.

—*djf*

31.4.2 Computing with a Subprocess

Another approach to time-consuming computation is to fork a subprocess to do the computation. This way, the operating system performs task scheduling and gives slices of CPU time to each process. If the user does not interact with the interface during this time, then there will be no input events, and the parent process will sleep, consuming no CPU time while the subprocess computes as fast as it can. If the user continues to interact with the interface while the computation is going on, then she may notice a decreased response time to the interface, but not worse than the decrease that occurs whenever the system load goes up.

The naive approach to forking a process is to use the `system()` function. This call blocks until the child process is done, however, so if you use it, the task is effectively being performed in the foreground, events will not be handled, and you should display a busy cursor and/or a working dialog until the function returns. `popen()` is a more useful function—it does not block, and allows you to read the output of the background process, but it requires that the background process be in a separate executable, to be invoked through */bin/sh*.

A more sophisticated approach, in a UNIX environment, uses `fork()` and `execl()` (or a related function) to establish a child process running in parallel with the parent.

Once the child process is established to perform the computation, the parent and child processes usually must communicate. You'll generally use `pipe()` to create a communications channel, and you may use `dup()` or `dup2()` so that the child can communicate with the parent by reading from the standard input and writing to the standard ouput. If the parent needs to get input from the child, it can register a procedure with `XtAppAddInput()` to be called when there is data available for reading on the pipe. If the output of the child process is to be displayed, you can use an XmtCli widget with its `XmtNfildes` resource set. Another way for parent and child processes to communicate is through the file system. The child might perform a computation on the contents of a file, and write the results into a new file. Then the parent can obtain those results, when needed, by reading the file.

Besides communicating with the child, a parent process often needs to know when the child has exited, so that it can know when the computation is done. One way to determine this is by polling: you might set up an Xt timer procedure to be called every half-second or so which will call `waitpid()` to see if the child is done. Another approach is to set a signal handler for the `SIGCHLD` signal that is generated when a child process exits. It is not safe to do much from within a signal handler, however, so this handler should simply set a flag and return. Then you will need to register a timer procedure or a work procedure to check this flag. Instead, you might enter a private event loop while the child process is running, and then you can check this flag explicitly in your event loop.

A full tutorial on UNIX processes, pipes, and signals is beyond the scope of this book. The tips we've mentioned should be enough to get you started, however.

31.4.3 Using Threads

If you have access to a threads* library for your platform, you can run your user interface code in one thread and your background processing tasks in a separate thread. This can be an ideal technique because threads running in the same process can communicate with each other much more easily than separate processes can. Note, though thread packages aren't yet very standardized, so portability is an issue.

In X11R6, Xlib and the Xt Intrinsics have been made "thread-safe." If your widget set has also been made thread-safe, then you can run multiple threads which make X and Xt calls. Usually, though, you'll only need to have one thread that ever makes X or Xt calls, and in this case, you can use threads even before X11R6.

31.4.4 Handling Signals

When doing background processing or low-level system programming, you may want to handle signals.† You can install a handler procedure for a specified signal with the `signal()` function. Since signals arrive asynchronously, however, and interrupt whatever operation is in progress, it is almost never safe to call any X or Xt functions from within a signal handler. This makes it difficult to handle signals correctly in Xt applications.

---

*A *thread* can be thought of as a "lightweight process"—a separate "thread" of execution, which does not require all the overhead of processes.

†A *signal* is a low-level asynchronous notification from the operating system that some event has occurred.

In X11R6, a signal-handling mechanism has been added to the Intrinsics. When you want a function (the "signal callback") to be invoked in response to a signal, you register that function with the Intrinsics by calling `XtAppAddSignal()`. This function returns an opaque value of type `XtSignalId`. `XtAppAddSignal()` does not itself establish a signal handler to catch the signal of interest; you must still do this with `signal()` or a related function. Another X11R6 function, `XtNoticeSignal()` is defined as the only Xt function that may safely be called from a signal handler. This function is passed the `XtSignalId` that corresponds to the signal callback that should be invoked in response to signal. `XtNoticeSignal()` sets a flag that will make the Intrinsics invoke the signal callback immediately, or when it is done processing any current events.

Example 31-6 shows an example that uses these X11R6 functions to handle the UNIX `SIGINT` signal, which is generated when the user types **Ctrl-C**.

Example 31-6. Handling a Signal in X11R6

```
/*
 * This value identifies the signal callback we registered.
 */
static XtSignalId sigint_id;

/*
 * This is the UNIX signal handler, registered with signal().
 * It uses XtNoticeSignal() to tell the Intrinsics to invoke
 * the signal callback associated with the signal id.
 * It is not allowed to make any other X or Xt calls.
 */
static void sigint_handler(int signal_number)
{
    XtNoticeSignal(sigint_id);
}

/*
 * This is the signal callback; the function we want to be called
 * in response to the signal.  The Intrinsics will invoke this
 * callback when it safe to do so, so unlike the signal handler,
 * the signal callback can freely make X and Xt calls.
 * Since this callback is invoked when the user types Ctrl-C in the
 * controlling terminal, it calls a hypothetical function that pops
 * up a "Really Quit?" dialog box.  This same function could be used
 * from the callback on an "Exit" button.
 */
static void sigint_callback(XtPointer data, XtSignalId *id)
{
    confirm_and_quit();
}

main(int argc, char **argv)
{
        .
        .
        .
```

Example 31-6. Handling a Signal in X11R6 (continued)

```
    /*
     * Here we register the signal callback with Xt, and obtain
     * the signal id for use in the signal handler.
     */
    sigint_id =  XtAppAddSignal(app_context, sigint_callback, NULL);

    /*
     * Here we register the signal handler with the operating system
     */
    signal(SIGINT, sigint_handler);
        .
        .
        .
    XtAppMainLoop(app_context);
}
```

Prior to X11R6, it is more difficult to handle signals. One approach is to simply set a flag in the signal handler, and then write a custom event loop that checks for the flag. The problem with this is that if the event loop is blocked, waiting for an X event, the signal flag will not be noticed until the next X event arrives. Or, if you write an event loop that never blocks, then your application will "busy wait" and will use unnecessary CPU cycles when otherwise idle.

If the signal is not time critical, then one compromise is to use `XtAppAddTimeOut()` to register a procedure to be called every half-second or so. This procedure will check the flag to see if a signal has occurred. Using this workaround, your application will never be completely idle, but at least it will not have to busy-wait.

There is a better workaround to this problem that is based on the following two observations: a UNIX signal handler is allowed to safely call `write()`, and the Xt event loop can be made to stop blocking when it detects activity on a file descriptor or pipe. So, if you need to handle a signal in your application, you first create a pipe with `pipe()`. Then register your signal callback with `XtAppAddInput()` to be invoked when data is written to the pipe. And in your signal handler you write that data into the pipe. When the signal arrives:

1. The OS will invoke the signal handler, which will write data into the pipe.
2. Since data is now available for reading on the pipe, the OS will stop the Intrinsics from blocking in its event loop.
3. The Intrinsics will invoke the signal callback in response to the data. (The signal callback should be sure to remove the data from the pipe, so that it does not get invoked over and over.)

31.4.5 Client/Server Computation

Some Xt applications will be clients to the X server, and also to one or more other servers. Your application might make queries to a database server, or perform RPC calls to some other specialized service on the network, for example. Often, it is not acceptable to simply stop handling X events while communicating with other servers, so some applications will have to be able to handle asynchronous input from two or more separate sources.

Using threads can be an ideal way to handle this situation, but for this discussion, we'll assume that you will not be using threads. So the fundamental problem is that you need to wait for events from two separate sources, in a single thread of execution.

If you are writing the client-side code in your application and are explicitly handling the network connection to the server (the database, for example), then you'll usually use `XtAppAddInput()` to register a special callback to be invoked when there is activity on your specified file descriptor. In this special input procedure you can get and dispatch the input from the server as appropriate. In this model, the connection to the X server is primary, and the other server is secondary—you listen for X events in `XtAppMainLoop()` and handle events from the other server as a special case.

More often, though, you won't be writing your own client-side code, but will instead be using an existing client library. The library may have its own main loop, an analog to `XtAppMainLoop()`, but if it is well designed, there should be some way to obtain a file descriptor to wait for events on, and some other call to retrieve and process events without blocking. If these features are available, then you can just use `XtAppMainLoop()` and `XtAppAddInput()` as described.

If the client library requires you to use its main loop, but has some analog to `XtAppAddInput()`, then you can reverse the model. Make the other server the primary one and use its event loop. Then use the client library's version of `XtAppAddInput()` to listen for events on the file descriptor specified by the X `ConnectionNumber()` macro. Then when X events arrive on that file descriptor, process them from your registered callback with `XtAppProcessEvent()`.

An alternative approach is to write a single combined event loop, using the `select()` system call to wait for events on all of the descriptors you are interested in. This is a low-level approach, but works well if you are communicating with many servers, or if you want to implement a non-trivial scheduling or priority scheme.

Another alternative is to arrange to receive SIGIO signals when there is activity on one or more of your server connections. You cannot safely handle events from a signal handler, but you can set a flag that allows those events to be handled later.

31.5 Style

The most important point to take from this chapter is that you should always provide some kind of feedback to the user when your application will be busy (i.e., not handling user input events) for any noticeable period of time.

The appropriate type of feedback will depend on how long your application will be busy, what it is busy doing, and how much information the user needs about the operation.

- Displaying a special "please wait" cursor is an easy and non-intrusive way to indicate that the application is busy for a short period, performing a routine, safe task.
- Displaying a message in a message line is appropriate feedback for longer periods, or when the action being performed needs explanation or extra feedback of some kind. This technique is usually used in conjunction with a special cursor.
- Popping a dialog box up is appropriate when the application will be busy for more than a few seconds, because it *is* intrusive, and can optionally explain what task is being performed, whether it is progressing, how far it has progressed, and how it can be aborted.

Besides just indicating that the application is busy, you might want to provide feedback for two other purposes:

- To indicate that the application is making progress on its task and is not hung. You can do this by animating a cursor or a pixmap, or by updating a message. If you can know (or reasonably estimate) in advance how long the task will take, you might provide this kind of feedback by indicating how much of the task remains to be completed, with an XmScale widget, for example.
- To indicate whether the operation completed successfully or failed. In some cases this will be apparent from other parts of the interface; in other cases, you'll want to provide this feedback yourself.

If the application becomes busy in response to a user action, then you generally do not need to explain why it is busy. If it becomes busy outside of the user's control (autosaving a file, for example or garbage collecting) then it should display a message or a dialog that explains what is going on. Some operations require feedback that they have successfully completed; others don't. When the integrity of the user's data is at stake (e.g., was the file saved successfully?) it is always a good idea to provide this kind of feedback.

When you display feedback of a busy condition, particularly with a special cursor, you should not allow type-ahead or click-ahead, except perhaps as an option for advanced users.

If your application is busy for more than a couple of seconds, you should try to design the background processing so that you can periodically call `XmtWorkingBoxHandleEvents()`, `XmUpdateDisplay()` or a similar event-processing function. This allows Expose events to be handled by the working dialog and other windows of your application.

If you allow a background task to be aborted with the **Stop** button on the XmtWorkingBox widget, you should call `XmtWorkingBoxHandleEvents()` frequently enough that the button responds soon after being clicked on.

31.6 Summary

You can display a "please wait" cursor (specified by the `busyCursor` application resource) for a shell by calling `XmtDisplayBusyCursor()`. You can display or restore the "default" cursor (specified by the `cursor` application resource) with `XmtDisplayDefaultCursor()`.

You can discard user input events that occurred while a busy cursor was displayed with the functions `XmtDiscardButtonEvents()` and `XmtDiscardKeyPressEvents()`.

Many of the functions described in Chapter 22, *The Message Line*, are also good for displaying feedback while an application is busy.

The XmtWorkingBox widget is useful for "Please Wait" dialog boxes. You can create and manage this widget yourself, or you can display a cached one with `XmtDisplayWorkingDialog()`. In either case you can update the (optional) slider value with `XmtWorkingBoxSetScaleValue()` and you can handle expose events and poll the (optional) **Stop** button with `XmtWorkingBoxHandleEvents()`.

When you display a "Please Wait" dialog, you should make sure it is visible with `XmtWaitUntilMapped()` before your application becomes busy and stops handling events.

Performing a time-consuming task while still allowing some interactivity in the interface can be difficult. If possible, you should implement it so that you can periodically update a message or a working dialog. In some cases, you may want to use a work procedure, a separate process, or a separate thread. Signals may occasionally be useful, but special care is required to handle them.

Part Seven

Reference Manual

All of the preceding chapters are the Programmer's Guide to Xmt. This part of the book is the Reference Manual.

This reference section is in UNIX "man page" format. Because most of the individual reference pages in this section document more than one function, the functions do not appear in strict alphabetical order. If you cannot find the reference page for the Xmt function you are looking for, use the table in the first reference page, "Introduction."

Introduction

Name

Introduction — introduction to the reference pages for Xmt functions and widgets.

Synopsis

The synopsis section of each reference page shows an ANSI-C signature for each function documented on the page. It also shows the header file that must be included to declare the function, and may also show typedefs for structures, enumerated types, or procedure types used by the functions.

These reference pages adopt an unusual convention for describing functions with variable-length argument lists. Each page containing functions that expect a variable-length list of arguments of a specific type or types uses curly braces ({ and }) to indicate the arguments that repeat. If the argument list must be NULL-terminated, the NULL appears at the end of the synopsis. Thus the function `XmtVaRegisterColors()` has the following synopsis:

```
void XmtVaRegisterColors(XmtColorTable table,
                         { String symbolic_name, String color_name, }
                           NULL)
```

Notice how this syntax clearly indicates the arguments that are to be repeated in the variable length portion of the argument list, and also indicates how the list should be terminated.

A number of functions in the Xmt library take a `printf()`-style variable-length argument list. These argument lists don't have any predetermined types, and so the synopses for these functions simply show the standard ANSI-C `...` argument.

Arguments

This section explains each of the function arguments shown in the "Synopsis" section.

Inputs

This subsection describes each of the arguments that pass information in to the function or functions documented on each page.

Outputs

This subsection describes any of the arguments that are used to return information from the function(s). These arguments are always of some pointer type, and you should use the C address-of operator (&) to pass the address of the variable in which the function will store the return value. The names of these arguments are usually suffixed with *_return* to indicate that values are returned in them. Some arguments both supply and return a value; they will be listed in this section and in the "Inputs" section. Finally, note that because the list of function arguments is broken into "Inputs" and "Outputs" sections, they do not always appear in the same order that they are passed to the function(s). See the function signature(s) for the actual calling order.

Returns

This subsection explains the return value, if any, of the function or functions documented on the page. It may also explain how you should free, release, or otherwise deallocate the return value when you no longer need it.

Description

This section of each reference page describes each of the functions and contains any additional information you need in order to use them.

To keep this book a manageable size, many related functions have been documented on the same reference page. This means that the functions do not appear in strict alphabetical order. Until you become familiar with this reference section through repeated use, you may have some trouble locating the reference page that a given function is documented on. To help you find the page you are looking for, the title of each reference page indicates which functions are documented on the page. This is done with a variety of common syntaxes:

- Curly braces indicate a number of alternatives, just as they do for filenames in */bin/csh*. Thus, the reference page titled "XmtCli{Printf,Puts,Clear}()" documents three functions: `XmtCliPrintf()`, `XmtCliPuts()`, and `XmtCliClear()`.
- Square brackets indicate something optional. Thus the reference page titled "XmtDialogDo[Sync]()" documents the functions `XmtDialogDo()` and `XmtDialogDoSync()`.
- Angle brackets and italics indicate an entire category of functions. The reference page titled "XmtCreate<*Widget*>()", for example, documents all of the Xmt widget constructor functions.
- An asterisk serves its usual role as a wildcard. The reference page titled "XmtHashTable*()" documents all of the `XmtHashTable` manipulation functions.
- Note that not all function names can be conveniently fit into a reference page title in this way and some of the more obscure Xmt functions do not appear in the title of their page. If you cannot find the function you are looking for, try the following table—it shows the title of the reference page that each function is documented on.

See Also

The "See Also" section of each reference page refers you to related functions and widgets that you may alwo want to read about.

This section of the book contains "reference pages," not "manual pages"—the rest of this book is the manual for Xmt; this part is just the reference section of that manual. The chapters of this book are the definitive sources of information on most topics, and you'll find that these reference pages will often refer you back to the chapters for a full explanation of functions or of the concepts behind them.

Key to Reference Page Titles

For Function...	*See Page...*
XmtAddDeleteCallback()0	XmtAdd{Delete,SaveYourself}Callback()0
XmtAddSaveYourselfCallback()	XmtAdd{Delete,SaveYourself}Callback()
XmtAllocColor()	Xmt{Alloc,Free,Store}[Widget]Color()
XmtAllocWidgetColor()	Xmt{Alloc,Free,Store}[Widget]Color()
XmtAskForBoolean()	XmtAskForBoolean()
XmtAskForDouble()	XmtAskFor{Double,Integer}()
XmtAskForFile()	XmtAskForFile[name]()
XmtAskForFilename()	XmtAskForFile[name]()
XmtAskForInteger()	XmtAskFor{Double,Integer}()
XmtAskForItem()	XmtAskForItem[Number]()
XmtAskForItemNumber()	XmtAskForItem[Number]()
XmtAskForString()	XmtAskForString()
XmtAssertWidgetClass()	XmtAssertWidgetClass()
XmtBlock()	XmtBlock()
XmtBuildApplication()	XmtBuild[Query]Application()
XmtBuildDialog()	XmtBuild[Query]Dialog()
XmtBuildQueryApplication()	XmtBuild[Query]Application()
XmtBuildQueryDialog()	XmtBuild[Query]Dialog()
XmtBuildQueryToplevel()	XmtBuild[Query]Toplevel()
XmtBuildToplevel()	XmtBuild[Query]Toplevel()
XmtChangePixmapIcon()	Xmt{Create,Change,Destroy}PixmapIcon()
XmtCheckPrintfFormat()	XmtCheckPrintfFormat()
XmtChooserGetSensitivity()	XmtChooserGet{State,Value,Sensitivity}()
XmtChooserGetState()	XmtChooserGet{State,Value,Sensitivity}()
XmtChooserGetValue()	XmtChooserGet{State,Value,Sensitivity}()
XmtChooserLookupItemByName()	XmtChooserLookupItem[By]{Name,Value}()
XmtChooserLookupItemByValue()	XmtChooserLookupItem[By]{Name,Value}()
XmtChooserLookupItemName()	XmtChooserLookupItem[By]{Name,Value}()
XmtChooserLookupItemValue()	XmtChooserLookupItem[By]{Name,Value}()
XmtChooserSetItemValue()	XmtChooserSet{State,Sensitive,ItemValue}()
XmtChooserSetSensitive()	XmtChooserSet{State,Sensitive,ItemValue}()
XmtChooserSetState()	XmtChooserSet{State,Sensitive,ItemValue}()
XmtCliClear()	XmtCli{Printf,Puts,Clear}()
XmtCliFlush()	XmtCliFlush()
XmtCliGets()	XmtCliGets()
XmtCliPrintf()	XmtCli{Printf,Puts,Clear}()
XmtCliPuts()	XmtCli{Printf,Puts,Clear}()
XmtColorTableGetParent()	XmtCreateColorTable()
XmtColorTableSetParent()	XmtCreateColorTable()
XmtConvertStringToBitmap()	XmtConvertStringTo<*Type*>()

For Function...	*See Page...*
XmtConvertStringToBitmask()	XmtConvertStringTo<*Type*>()
XmtConvertStringToCallback()	XmtConvertStringTo<*Type*>()
XmtConvertStringToColorTable()	XmtConvertStringTo<*Type*>()
XmtConvertStringToEnum()	XmtRegisterEnumConverter()
XmtConvertStringToPixel()	XmtConvertStringTo<*Type*>()
XmtConvertStringToPixmap()	XmtConvertStringTo<*Type*>()
XmtConvertStringToPixmapList()	XmtConvertStringTo<*Type*>()
XmtConvertStringToStringList()	XmtConvertStringTo<*Type*>()
XmtConvertStringToWidget()	XmtConvertStringTo<*Type*>()
XmtConvertStringToXmFontList()	XmtConvertStringTo<*Type*>()
XmtConvertStringToXmString()	XmtConvertStringTo<*Type*>()
XmtConvertStringToXmtMenuItems()	XmtConvertStringTo<*Type*>()
XmtCreateChild()	XmtCreate[Query]Child()
XmtCreateChildren()	XmtCreate[Query]Children()
XmtCreateChooser()	XmtCreate<*Widget*>()
XmtCreateCli()	XmtCreate<*Widget*>()
XmtCreateColorTable()	XmtCreateColorTable()
XmtCreateHelpBox()	XmtCreate<*Widget*>()
XmtCreateHelpDialog()	XmtCreate<*Widget*>()
XmtCreateInputField()	XmtCreate<*Widget*>()
XmtCreateLayout()	XmtCreate<*Widget*>()
XmtCreateLayoutBox()	XmtCreate<*Widget*>()
XmtCreateLayoutCol()	XmtCreate<*Widget*>()
XmtCreateLayoutDialog()	XmtCreate<*Widget*>()
XmtCreateLayoutPixmap()	XmtCreate<*Widget*>()
XmtCreateLayoutRow()	XmtCreate<*Widget*>()
XmtCreateLayoutSeparator()	XmtCreate<*Widget*>()
XmtCreateLayoutSpace()	XmtCreate<*Widget*>()
XmtCreateLayoutString()	XmtCreate<*Widget*>()
XmtCreateMenuPane()	XmtCreate<*Widget*>()
XmtCreateMenubar()	XmtCreate<*Widget*>()
XmtCreateMsgLine()	XmtCreate<*Widget*>()
XmtCreateOptionMenu()	XmtCreate<*Widget*>()
XmtCreatePixmapFromXmtImage()	XmtCreate{Pixmap,XImage}FromXmtImage()
XmtCreatePixmapIcon()	Xmt{Create,Change,Destroy}PixmapIcon()
XmtCreatePopupMenu()	XmtCreate<*Widget*>()
XmtCreateQueryChild()	XmtCreate[Query]Child()
XmtCreateQueryChildren()	XmtCreate[Query]Children()
XmtCreateScrolledCli()	XmtCreate<*Widget*>()
XmtCreateWidgetType()	Xmt{Create,Lookup}WidgetType()
XmtCreateWorkingBox()	XmtCreate<*Widget*>()
XmtCreateWorkingDialog()	XmtCreate<*Widget*>()
XmtCreateXImageFromXmtImage()	XmtCreate{Pixmap,XImage}FromXmtImage()
XmtCreateXmString()	XmtCreateXmString()
XmtDeiconifyShell()	Xmt{Iconify,Deiconify,Raise,Lower}Shell()
XmtDestroyColorTable()	XmtCreateColorTable()

For Function...	*See Page...*
XmtMenuPopupHandler()	XmtMenuPopupHandler()
XmtMoveShellToPointer()	XmtFocusShell()
XmtMsgLineAppend()	XmtMsgLine{Set,Append,Printf,Clear}()
XmtMsgLineClear()	XmtMsgLine{Set,Append,Printf,Clear}()
XmtMsgLineGetDouble()	XmtMsgLineGet{String,Double,Int,Unsigned,Char}()
XmtMsgLineGetInput()	XmtMsgLine{Set,Get}Input()
XmtMsgLineGetInt()	XmtMsgLineGet{String,Double,Int,Unsigned,Char}()
XmtMsgLineGetString()	XmtMsgLineGet{String,Double,Int,Unsigned,Char}()
XmtMsgLineGetUnsigned()	XmtMsgLineGet{String,Double,Int,Unsigned,Char}()
XmtMsgLinePop()	XmtMsgLine{Push,Pop}()
XmtMsgLinePrintf()	XmtMsgLine{Set,Append,Printf,Clear}()
XmtMsgLinePush()	XmtMsgLine{Push,Pop}()
XmtMsgLineSet()	XmtMsgLine{Set,Append,Printf,Clear}()
XmtMsgLineSetInput()	XmtMsgLine{Set,Get}Input()
XmtNameToWidget()	XmtNameToWidget()
XmtParseCommandLine()	XmtParseCommandLine()
XmtParseXpmData()	XmtParseXpm{Data,File}()
XmtParseXpmFile()	XmtParseXpm{Data,File}()
XmtPatchVisualInheritance()	XmtPatchVisualInheritance()
XmtRGBToHSL()	XmtHSLToRGB()
XmtRaiseShell()	Xmt{Iconify,Deiconify,Raise,Lower}Shell()
XmtRegisterAll()	XmtRegisterAll()
XmtRegisterBitmapConverter()	XmtRegister<*Type*>Converter()
XmtRegisterBitmaskConverter()	XmtRegister<*Type*>Converter()
XmtRegisterCallbackConverter()	XmtRegister<*Type*>Converter()
XmtRegisterCallbackProcedure()	XmtRegisterProcedures()
XmtRegisterChooser()	XmtRegister<*Widget*>()
XmtRegisterColor()	Xmt[Va]RegisterColor[s]()
XmtRegisterColorTableConverter()	XmtRegister<*Type*>Converter()
XmtRegisterColors()	Xmt[Va]RegisterColor[s]()
XmtRegisterEnumConverter()	XmtRegisterEnumConverter()
XmtRegisterImage()	XmtRegister{Image,XbmData}()
XmtRegisterImprovedIcons()	XmtRegisterImprovedIcons()
XmtRegisterInputField()	XmtRegister<*Widget*>()
XmtRegisterLayoutCreateMethod()	XmtRegisterLayout{Parser,CreateMethod}()
XmtRegisterLayoutParser()	XmtRegisterLayout{Parser,CreateMethod}()
XmtRegisterMenuItemsConverter()	XmtRegister<*Type*>Converter()
XmtRegisterMotifWidgets()	XmtRegister{Motif,Xmt}Widgets()
XmtRegisterPixel()	Xmt[Va]RegisterColor[s]()
XmtRegisterPixelConverter()	XmtRegister<*Type*>Converter()
XmtRegisterPixmapConverter()	XmtRegister<*Type*>Converter()
XmtRegisterPixmapListConverter()	XmtRegister<*Type*>Converter()
XmtRegisterPopupClass()	Xmt[Va]RegisterWidget{Class,Constructor}()
XmtRegisterPopupConstructor()	Xmt[Va]RegisterWidget{Class,Constructor}()
XmtRegisterProcedures()	XmtRegisterProcedures()
XmtRegisterStandardColors()	Xmt[Va]RegisterColor[s]()

For Function...	*See Page...*
XmtRegisterStringListConverter()	XmtRegister<*Type*>Converter()
XmtRegisterStyle()	Xmt{Lookup,Register}{Style,Template}()
XmtRegisterTemplate()	Xmt{Lookup,Register}{Style,Template}()
XmtRegisterUnixProcedures()	XmtRegister{Unix,Xmt,Xt}Procedures()
XmtRegisterWidgetClass()	Xmt[Va]RegisterWidget{Class,Constructor}()
XmtRegisterWidgetConstructor()	Xmt[Va]RegisterWidget{Class,Constructor}()
XmtRegisterWidgetConverter()	XmtRegister<*Type*>Converter()
XmtRegisterWidgetTypes()	XmtRegisterWidgetTypes()
XmtRegisterXbmData()	XmtRegister{Image,XbmData}()
XmtRegisterXmFontListConverter()	XmtRegister<*Type*>Converter()
XmtRegisterXmScale()	XmtRegister<*Widget*>()
XmtRegisterXmScrolledText()	XmtRegister<*Widget*>()
XmtRegisterXmStringConverter()	XmtRegister<*Type*>Converter()
XmtRegisterXmText()	XmtRegister<*Widget*>()
XmtRegisterXmTextField()	XmtRegister<*Widget*>()
XmtRegisterXmToggleButton()	XmtRegister<*Widget*>()
XmtRegisterXmtProcedures()	XmtRegister{Unix,Xmt,Xt}Procedures()
XmtRegisterXmtWidgets()	XmtRegister{Motif,Xmt}Widgets()
XmtRegisterXtProcedures()	XmtRegister{Unix,Xmt,Xt}Procedures()
XmtReleasePixmap()	XmtReleasePixmap()
XmtSetApplicationValues()	Xmt{Get,Set}ApplicationValues()
XmtSetFocusToShell()	XmtFocusShell()
XmtSetInitialFocus()	XmtSetInitialFocus()
XmtSetTypedValue()	XmtSet[Typed]Value()
XmtSetValue()	XmtSet[Typed]Value()
XmtStoreColor()	Xmt{Alloc,Free,Store}[Widget]Color()
XmtStoreWidgetColor()	Xmt{Alloc,Free,Store}[Widget]Color()
XmtSymbolAddCallback()	XmtSymbol{Add,Remove}Callback()
XmtSymbolGetValue()	XmtSymbol{Get,Set}Value()
XmtSymbolRemoveCallback()	XmtSymbol{Add,Remove}Callback()
XmtSymbolSetValue()	XmtSymbol{Get,Set}Value()
XmtTemplateInstantiate()	Xmt{Lookup,Register}{Style,Template}()
XmtVaRegisterCallbackProcedures()	XmtRegisterProcedures()
XmtVaRegisterColors()	Xmt[Va]RegisterColor[s]()
XmtVaRegisterSymbols()	XmtVaRegisterSymbols()
XmtVaRegisterWidgetClasses()	Xmt[Va]RegisterWidget{Class,Constructor}()
XmtVaRegisterWidgetConstructors()	Xmt[Va]RegisterWidget{Class,Constructor}()
XmtWaitUntilMapped()	XmtWaitUntilMapped()
XmtWarningMsg()	Xmt{Error,Warning}Msg()
XmtWarpToShell()	XmtFocusShell()
XmtWorkingBoxHandleEvents()	XmtWorkingBox{HandleEvents,SetScaleValue}()
XmtWorkingBoxSetScaleValue()	XmtWorkingBox{HandleEvents,SetScaleValue}()

Name

XmtAddDeleteCallback(), XmtAddSaveYourselfCallback() — register callbacks for session management protocols.

Synopsis

```
#include <Xmt/Xmt.h>
void XmtAddDeleteCallback(Widget shell,
                          int response,
                          XtCallbackProc proc,
                          XtPointer data)

void XmtAddSaveYourselfCallback(Widget shell,
                                XtCallbackProc proc,
                                XtPointer data)
```

Arguments

Inputs

shell — The shell widget that is to have the callback registered. May be any shell for XmtAddDeleteCallback(). Must be a toplevel ApplicationShell for XmtAddSaveYourselfCallback().

response — A value to be set on the XmNdeleteResponse resource, for XmtAddDeleteCallback() only.

proc — The callback procedure to register. This is a normal Xt callback procedure. When invoked, it will be passed *shell* as its first argument and *data* as its second argument. Its third argument will be unused.

data — An arbitrary untyped value to pass to the callback procedure as its second *client_data* argument.

Description

XmtAddDeleteCallback() sets the Motif VendorShell XmNdelete-Response resource of *shell* to *response*, and calls XmAddWMProtocol-Callback() to specify that the callback *proc* should be invoked when that shell receives a WM_DELETE_WINDOW message from the window manager or the session manager. The value of *response* specifies what actions the shell should perform automatically in response to this message, and the procedure *proc* can perform any other custom actions.

XmtAddSaveYourselfCallback() registers a procedure *proc* to be invoked when the specified *shell* receives a WM_SAVE_YOURSELF message from the session manager. In order to comply with the WM_SAVE_YOURSELF protocol, there must be no more than one callback registered per application, and the callback must set the WM_COMMAND property of the *shell* window before it returns. This function does not have a *response/* argument, since there is no equivalent to a XmNdeleteResponse resource for the

WM_SAVE_YOURSELF session management protocol. Also note that this protocol is replaced with much more sophisticated session management facilities in X11R6.

See Also

Chapter 16, *Working with the Session Manager*
Inter-client Communications Conventions Manual
VendorShell, `XmAddWMProtocolCallback()`

Xmt{Alloc,Free,Store}[Widget]Color()

Name

`XmtAllocColor()`, `XmtAllocWidgetColor()`, `XmtFreeColor()`, `XmtFreeWidgetColor()`, `XmtStoreColor()`, `XmtStoreWidgetColor()` — Xmt color allocation functions.

Synopsis

```
#include <Xmt/Color.h>
int XmtAllocColor(Widget w, Colormap colormap,
                  Visual *visual, XmtColorTable colortable,
                  String colorname, Pixel *color_return)

int XmtAllocWidgetColor(Widget w, String colorname,
                        Pixel *color_return)

void XmtFreeColor(Widget w, Colormap colormap, Pixel color)

void XmtFreeWidgetColor(Widget w, Pixel color)

int XmtStoreColor(Widget w, Colormap colormap,
                  Visual *visual, XmtColorTable colortable,
                  String colorname, Pixel colorcell)

int XmtStoreWidgetColor(Widget w, String colorname,
                        Pixel colorcell)
```

Arguments

Inputs

w — The widget for which the color is to be allocated or freed.

colormap — The colormap in which the color is to be allocated, or `None` to use the colormap of *w*.

visual — The visual of the colormap, used to determine if colors are being allocated for a monochrome display. Pass `NULL` to use the visual of *w*.

colortable — The `XmtColorTable` in which symbolic color names should be looked up, or `NULL` to use the default color table of the application.

colorname — The name of the color to be allocated. This may be a standard X color name, or may use one of the enhanced Xmt color specification schemes.

color — For `XmtFreeColor()` and `XmtFreeWidgetColor()`, specifies a `Pixel` value previously returned by `XmtAllocColor()` or `XmtAllocWidgetColor()`, respectively.

colorcell	For XmtStoreColor() and XmtStoreWidget-Color(), specifies a read/write color cell in *colormap* that the application has previously allocated.

Outputs

color_return	For XmtAllocColor() and XmtAllocWidget-Color(), returns an allocated pixel that contains the specified color.

Returns

XmtAllocColor(), XmtAllocWidgetColor(), XmtStoreColor(), and XmtStoreWidgetColor() return 0 upon successful allocation and non-zero on failure. A return value of 1 means that *colorname* was unrecognized or malformed, and a return value of 2 (for XmtAllocColor() and XmtAlloc-WidgetColor() only) means that the specified *colormap* was full.

Description

These functions allocate and free colors specified with the extended Xmt color name syntax. With these functions, colors may be specified by name, or by RGB components, as usual, but may also be specified by symbolic name, by HSL components, or as HSL deltas relative to a standard background or foreground color. Xmt color names may also provide fallback colors for monochrome systems. See Chapter 4, *Using Color*, for an explanation of the Xmt color syntax.

XmtAllocColor() allocates a shared, read-only color cell in *colormap* and returns it in *color_return*. This returned color cell will contain the color specified by *colorname*. XmtAllocWidgetColor() is a simplified version of the function that uses a default colormap, visual, and colortable—it is equivalent to calling XmtAllocColor() with a NULL colormap, visual, and color table.

XmtFreeColor() frees a color allocated with XmtAllocColor(), and XmtFreeWidgetColor() frees a color allocated with XmtAllocWidget-Color(). Many applications allocate colors when they start up and never need to free them. If your application allocates colors dynamically, however, you may need to free allocated color cells with these functions.

XmtStoreColor() and XmtStoreWidgetColor() are analogs to Xmt-AllocColor() and XmtAllocWidgetColor(), but instead of allocating a shared color cell in a colormap, they store the specified color into the already allocated private read/write color cell, specified by *colorcell*. The application is responsible for allocating this private color cell (with XAllocColor-Cells(), for example) and for freeing it with XFreeColors().

Usage

Many applications can handle all of their color needs through the resource database. Call `XmtRegisterPixelConverter()` to register a resource converter that will allow you to use the extended Xmt color specification syntax in your resource files.

See Also

Chapter 4, *Using Color*
`XmtRegisterPixelConverter()`

XmtAskForBoolean()

Name

`XmtAskForBoolean()` — ask a yes-or-no question with a dialog box and return the user's response.

Synopsis

```
#include <Xmt/Dialogs.h>
Boolean XmtAskForBoolean(Widget w,
                         String query_name,
                         String prompt_default,
                         String yes_default,
                         String no_default,
                         String cancel_default,
                         XmtButtonType default_button_default,
                         int icon_type_default,
                         Boolean show_cancel_button,
                         Boolean *value_return,
                         String help_text_default)
```

Arguments

Inputs

w — The shell widget over which the dialog is to be displayed, or any descendant of that shell.

query_name — The name of this instantiation of the dialog; used to look up resources. `NULL` may be specified, but will result in a dialog that cannot be customized through the resource database.

prompt_default — The prompt message to be displayed in the dialog, unless an overriding value is found in the resource database.

yes_default — The string to be displayed in the **Yes** button, unless an overriding value is found in the resource database. `NULL` may be specified.

no_default — The string to be displayed in the **No** button, unless an overriding value is found in the resource database. `NULL` may be specified.

cancel_default — The string to be displayed in the **Cancel** button, unless an overriding value is found in the resource database. `NULL` may be specified.

default_button_default
The default button (i.e., the button that is activated if the user presses the **Return** key), unless an overriding value is found in the resource database. The legal values for this argument are `XmtYesButton`, `XmtNoButton`, and `XmtCancelButton`.

icon_type_default
: The icon that is to appear in the dialog, unless an overriding value is found in the resource database. The legal values are those supported by the XmNdialogType resource of the Motif MessageBox widget. Note that this argument is not a Pixmap.

show_cancel_button
: Whether the **Cancel** button should appear in the dialog.

help_text_default
: The help text to display when the user clicks the **Help** button, unless an overriding value is found in resource database. NULL may be specified.

Outputs

value_return
: The address of a Boolean owned by the caller. When XmtAskForBoolean() returns True, this Boolean will be set to True if the user clicked the **Yes** button and will be False if the user clicked the **No** button.

Returns

True if the user clicks the **Yes** or **No** buttons to dismiss the dialog, False if the user clicks the **Cancel** button.

Description

XmtAskForBoolean() displays an application modal dialog box similar to the dialog created by XmCreateQuestionDialog(). It processes events in an internal event loop until the user selects the **Yes**, **No**, or **Cancel** button of the dialog, and then returns to the calling procedure. If the user selects **Yes** or **No**, XmtAskForBoolean() stores True or False into the location pointed to by *value_return* and returns True as its value. If the user selects **Cancel**, XmtAskForBoolean() returns False without setting *value_return*.

If help text is found in the resource database for this dialog, or if the *help_text_default* argument is non-NULL, then this text will be displayed (using XmtDisplayInformation()) when the user clicks on the **Help** button. If there is no help available for the dialog, then the **Help** button will be insensitive.

Customization

XmtAskForBoolean() looks up the following subpart resources of the shell specified by *w*. The name of the subpart is given by the *query_name* argument, and the class of the subpart is "XmtBooleanDialog." These subpart resources are looked up every time XmtAskForBoolean() is called, not simply when the widgets are created.

Resource	Default	Description
message	*prompt_default*	The prompt for the dialog
title	"Question"	The string in the dialog's titlebar
yesLabel	*yes_default* or "Yes"	The label of Yes button
noLabel	*no_default* or "No"	The label of No button
cancelLabel	*cancel_default* or "Cancel"	The label of Cancel button
defaultButton	*default_button_default*	Which button is the default
iconType	*icon_type_default*	Which standard icon to display
helpText	*help_text_default*	Online help for the dialog

Widgets

`XmtAskForBoolean()` creates an XmDialogShell widget named `xmtBooleanDialogShell`, and an XmtLayout widget named `xmtBooleanDialog` as a child of the XmDialogShell. It uses XmtLayout gadgets to display the dialog message and icon, and also creates four XmPushButton widgets named `yes`, `no`, `cancel`, and `help`. Once this dialog has been created, it is cached for reuse by subsequent calls, so if you set resources on these widgets, note that they will affect all instances of the dialog.

See Also

Chapter 26, *Simple Input Dialogs*
`XmtAskForDouble()`, `XmtAskForFile()`,
`XmtAskForFilename()`, `XmtAskForInteger()`,
`XmtAskForItem()`, `XmtAskForItemNumber()`,
`XmtAskForString()`, `XmtDisplayErrorAndAsk()`,
`XmtDisplayWarningAndAsk()`

Name

XmtAskForDouble(), XmtAskForInteger() — use a dialog box to prompt for a number and return the user's response.

Synopsis

```
#include <Xmt/Dialogs.h>
Boolean XmtAskForDouble(Widget w, String query_name, String prompt_default,
                        double *value_in_out, double min, double max,
                        String help_text_default)

Boolean XmtAskForInteger(Widget w, String query_name, String prompt_default,
                         int *value_in_out, int min, int max,
                         String help_text_default)
```

Arguments

Inputs

w — The shell widget over which the dialog will be displayed, or any descendant of that shell.

query_name — The name of this instantiation of the dialog; used to look up resources. NULL may be specified, but will result in a dialog that cannot be customized through the resource database.

prompt_default — The prompt message to be displayed in the dialog, unless an overriding value is found in the resource database.

value_in_out — The address of a double or int owned by the caller. On entry to these functions, this variable contains the default value to be presented to the user.

min — The minimum number that the user will be allowed to enter.

max — The maximum number that the user will be allowed to enter.

help_text_default — The help text to display when the user clicks the **Help** button, unless an overriding value is found in resource database. NULL may be specified.

Outputs

value_in_out — The address of a double or int owned by the caller. When these functions return True, the value entered by the user is stored at this address.

Returns

True if the user clicked the **OK** button to dismiss the dialog; False if the user clicked the **Cancel** button.

Description

XmtAskForDouble() and XmtAskForInteger() display an application modal dialog box, of the type created by XmCreatePromptDialog(), to prompt the user to enter a number. They process events in a local event loop until the user selects either the **OK** or **Cancel** button of the dialog, and then return control to the calling procedure. If the user enters a legal number in the correct range, and clicks **OK**, then that number is stored at the location pointed to by the *value_in_out* argument, and the functions return True. If the user clicks the **Cancel** button, the functions immediately return False without checking or storing the input value.

If the user clicks **OK**, and the value entered is not a valid number (e.g., if it contains illegal characters), or if it is not within the minimum and maximum bounds specified for this dialog, then an error message is displayed (using XmtDisplayError()) and control remains within the local event loop so that the user can correct his input. If range checking is not desired with these functions, specify a *min* value that is greater than or equal to *max*.

If help text is found in the resource database for this dialog, or if the *help_text_default* argument is non-NULL, then this text will be displayed (using XmtDisplayInformation()) when the user clicks on the **Help** button. If there is no help available for the dialog, then the **Help** button will be insensitive.

Customization

To allow dialog customization, XmtAskForDouble() and XmtAskForInteger() look up the following subpart resources of the shell specified by *w*. The name of the subpart is given by the *query_name* argument, and the class of the subpart is XmtDoubleDialog or XmtIntDialog. These subpart resources are looked up every time these functions are called, not simply when the widgets are created.

Resource	Default	Description
message	*prompt_default*	The prompt for the dialog
title	"Enter an Integer" or "Enter a Number"	The string to appear in the dialog's titlebar
helpText	*help_text_default*	Online help for the dialog

Widgets

`XmtAskForDouble()` and `XmtAskForInteger()` use the same cached dialog widgets as `XmtAskForString()` does—an XmDialogShell named `xmtStringDialogShell` and its XmSelectionBox child named `xmtStringDialog`.

See Also

Chapter 26, *Simple Input Dialogs*
`XmtAskForBoolean()`, `XmtAskForFile()`,
`XmtAskForFilename()`, `XmtAskForItem()`,
`XmtAskForItemNumber()`, `XmtAskForString()`

XmtAskForFile[name]()

Name

XmtAskForFile(), XmtAskForFilename() — use a file selection dialog box to prompt the user to select a file and return the user's response.

Synopsis

```
Boolean
XmtAskForFile(Widget w, String query_name,
                        String prompt_default,
                        String directory_default,
                        String pattern_default,
                        FILE **value_return, String file_mode,
                        String filename_buffer, int filename_buffer_len,
                        String directory_buffer, int directory_buffer_len,
                        String pattern_buffer, int pattern_buffer_len,
                        String help_text_default)
```

```
Boolean
XmtAskForFilename(Widget w, String query_name,
                            String prompt_default,
                            String directory_default,
                            String pattern_default,
                            String filename_buffer,
                            int filename_buffer_len,
                            String directory_buffer,
                            int directory_buffer_len,
                            String pattern_buffer, int pattern_buffer_len,
                            String help_text_default)
```

Arguments

Inputs

w The shell widget over which the dialog will be displayed, or any descendant of that shell.

query_name
The name of this instantiation of the dialog; used to look up resources. NULL may be specified, but will result in a dialog that cannot be customized through the resource database.

prompt_default
The prompt message to be displayed in the dialog, unless an overriding value is found in the resource database.

directory_default
The initial directory to display in the file selection box, unless an overriding value is found in the resource database or in the *directory_buffer* argument.

pattern_default

The initial pattern to filter filenames against, unless an overriding value is found in the resource database or in the *pattern_buffer* argument.

file_mode

For `XmtAskForFile()` only, a string which specifies how the file should be opened. It will be passed unmodified to `fopen()`.

filename_buffer

A character buffer owned by the caller. On entry to these functions, its contents are used as the default filename to be displayed to the user.

filename_buffer_len

The length in characters of *filename_buffer*.

directory_buffer

A character string owned by the caller, or `NULL`. If it is non-NULL and non-empty on entry, then its contents are used as the initial directory to be displayed, overriding any value in the resource database and the *directory_default* argument.

directory_buffer_len

The length in characters of *directory_buffer*, or 0 if that argument should not be written into.

pattern_buffer

A character string owned by the caller, or `NULL`. If it is non-NULL and non-empty on entry, then its contents are used as the initial pattern to match filenames against, overriding any value in the resource database and the *pattern_default* argument.

pattern_buffer_len

The length in characters of *pattern_buffer*, or 0 if that argument should not be written into.

help_text_default

The help text to display when the user clicks the **Help** button, unless an overriding value is found in the resource database. `NULL` may be specified.

Outputs

value_return

For `XmtAskForFile()` only, the address of a variable of type `FILE *` owned by the caller. If `XmtAskForFile()` returns `True`, the file selected by the user has been opened and stored in this variable.

filename_buffer

A character buffer owned by the caller. When `XmtAskForFile()` returns `True`, this buffer contains the full name (including directory) of the file selected by the user. It is guaranteed to be null-terminated and never to contain more than *filename_buffer_len*-1 characters.

`directory_buffer`

A character string owned by the caller, or NULL. If it is non-NULL, and *`directory_buffer_len`* is not 0, then when `XmtAskForFile()` returns `True` this buffer contains the name of the directory of the user's selected file. It is guaranteed to be null-terminated and never to contain more than *`directory_buffer_len`*-1 characters.

`pattern_buffer`

A character string owned by the caller, or NULL. If it is non-NULL, and *`pattern_buffer_len`* is not 0, then when `XmtAskForFile()` returns `True` this buffer contains the pattern most recently used in the file selection box to match filenames against. It is guaranteed to be null-terminated and never to contain more than *`pattern_buffer_len`*-1 characters.

Returns

`True` if the user clicked the **OK** button or double-clicked on a filename to dismiss the dialog; `False` if the user clicked the **Cancel** button.

Description

`XmtAskForFile()` and `XmtAskForFilename()` display an application modal Motif file selection dialog, of the type created by `XmCreateFileSelectionDialog()`. They process events in a local event loop until the user double-clicks on a filename or selects the **OK** or **Cancel** buttons of the dialog, and then return control to the calling procedure. If the user clicks on the **Cancel** button, these functions return `False` immediately. Otherwise, they store the full name of the selected file into *`filename_buffer`* and return `True`.

In addition to these actions, `XmtAskForFile()` opens the selected file as specified by *`file_mode`*, and stores the opened file at the address specified by *`value_return`*. If the attempt to open the specified file fails, `XmtAskForFile()` displays an error dialog (using `XmtDisplayError()`).

On entry to `XmtAskForFile()` or `XmtAskForFilename()`, the contents of *`filename_buffer`* are used as the default filename to display to the user. In addition, if *`directory_buffer`* and *`pattern_buffer`* are non-NULL and are not empty, then they are used as the initial directory and the initial pattern for the file selection box. If these arguments are NULL, then the initial directory and pattern are looked up in the resource database, and if they are not found there, *`directory_default`* and *`pattern_default`* are used as the defaults.

If *`directory_buffer`* and *`pattern_buffer`* are non-NULL, and *`directory_buffer_len`* and *`pattern_buffer_len`* are not 0, then when these functions return `True`, they store the current directory and pattern of the file selection box into these buffers. You can use these returned values with the next invocation of these functions—see Chapter 26, *Simple Input Dialogs*, for discussion of this point.

If help text is found in the resource database for this instance of the dialog, or if the *help_text_default* argument is non-NULL, then this text will be displayed (using `XmtDisplayInformation()`) when the user clicks on the **Help** button. If there is no help available for the dialog, then the **Help** button will be insensitive.

Customization

To allow customization, `XmtAskForFile()` and `XmtAskForFilename()` look up the following subpart resources of the toplevel shell. The name of the subpart is given by the *query_name* argument, and the class of the subpart is `XmtFileDialog`. These subpart resources are looked up every time the functions are called, not simply when the widgets are created.

Resource	Default	Description
`message`	*prompt_default*	The prompt for the dialog.
`title`	"Select a File"	The string in the dialog's titlebar.
`directory`	*directory_default*	The directory to display unless overridden by *directory_buffer*.
`pattern`	*pattern_default*	The pattern that filenames must match, unless overridden by *pattern_buffer*.
`helpText`	*help_text_default*	Online help for the dialog.

Widgets

`XmtAskForFile()` and `XmtAskForFilename()` create an XmDialogShell widget named `xmtFileDialogShell` and an XmFileSelectionBox widget named `xmtFileDialog` as a child of the XmDialogShell. Once this dialog has been created, it is cached for reuse by subsequent calls.

See Also

Chapter 26, *Simple Input Dialogs*
`XmtAskForBoolean()`, `XmtAskForDouble()`,
`XmtAskForInteger()`, `XmtAskForItem()`,
`XmtAskForItemNumber()`, `XmtAskForString()`

XmtAskForItem[Number]()

Name

XmtAskForItem(), XmtAskForItemNumber() — use a dialog box to prompt the user to select an item from a list and return the selected item.

Synopsis

```
#include <Xmt/Dialogs.h>
Boolean XmtAskForItem(Widget w, String query_name,
                      String prompt_default, String list_title_default,
                      String *items_default, int num_items,
                      Boolean must_match,
                      String buffer_in_out, int buffer_len,
                      String help_text_default)

Boolean XmtAskForItemNumber(Widget w, String query_name,
                            String prompt_default,
                            String list_title_default,
                            String *items_default, int num_items,
                            int *value_in_out,
                            String help_text_default)
```

Arguments

Inputs

w The shell widget over which the dialog will be displayed, or any descendant of that shell.

query_name The name of this invocation of the dialog; used to look up resources. NULL may be specified, but will result in a dialog that cannot be customized through the resource database.

prompt_default The prompt message to be displayed over the XmText widget of the dialog, unless an overriding value is found in the resource database.

list_title_default
The message to be displayed over the XmList widget of the dialog, unless an overriding value is found in the resource database.

items_default An array strings to be displayed in the dialog XmList widget, unless an overriding value is found in the resource database.

num_items The number of elements in the *items_default* array.

must_match For XmtAskForItem() only, a Boolean that indicates whether the user's may type any string, or may only type a string that appears in the list.

buffer_in_out — For `XmtAskForItem()` only, a character buffer owned by the caller. On entry to `XmtAskForItem()` it contains the default item to be selected in the XmList widget and/or displayed in the XmText widget of the dialog.

buffer_len — The length in characters of *buffer_in_out*.

value_in_out — For `XmtAskForItemNumber()` only, the address of an integer owned by the caller. On entry to `XmtAskForItemNumber()`, this variable contains the index in the list of the default item to be displayed to the user.

help_text_default — The help text to display when the user clicks the **Help** button, unless an overriding value is found in the resource database. `NULL` may be specified.

Outputs

buffer_in_out — For `XmtAskForItem()` only, a character buffer owned by the caller. When `XmtAskForItem()` returns `True`, this buffer contains the item selected or the string typed by the user. It is guaranteed to be null-terminated, and to contain no more than *buffer_len*-1 characters.

value_in_out — For `XmtAskForItemNumber()` only, the address of an integer owned by the caller. When `XmtAskForItemNumber()` returns `True`, this integer contains the index of the item selected by the user.

Returns

`True` if the user clicked the **OK** button to dismiss the dialog; `False` if the user clicked the **Cancel** button.

Description

`XmtAskForItem()` and `XmtAskForItemNumber()` display an application modal dialog similar to that created by `XmCreateSelectionDialog()`. They process events in a local event loop until the user double-clicks on an item, types the **Return** key, or selects the **OK** or **Cancel** buttons of the dialog, then they return to the calling procedure.

If the user clicks the **Cancel** button, then these functions immediately return `False`. If the user selects an item by any of the supported methods, then the functions store the user's input as a string or an integer and return `True`.

`XmtAskForItem()` returns the item as a string stored in *buffer_in_out*. If *must_match* is `True` and the user types a string that does not appear in the List widget, then `XmtAskForItem()` will display an error message (with `XmtDisplayError()`) and will not return.

`XmtAskForItemNumber()` returns the user's input differently. It stores the index of the user's selected item at the address specified by *`value_in_out`*. If the user types the name of an item that does not appear in the list, the `XmtAskForItemNumber()` will display an error dialog.

If help text is found in the resource database for this dialog, or if the *`help_text_default`* argument is non-NULL, then this text will be displayed (using `XmtDisplayInformation()`) when the user clicks on the **Help** button. If there is no help available for the dialog, then the **Help** button will be insensitive.

Customization

To allow customization, the functions `XmtAskForItem()` and `XmtAskForItemNumber()` look up the following subpart resources of the toplevel shell. The name of the subpart is given by the *`query_name`* argument, and the class of the subpart is `XmtItemDialog`. These subpart resources are looked up every time the functions are called, not simply when the widgets are created.

Resource	Default	Description
`message`	*`prompt_default`*	The prompt for the dialog
`title`	"Select an Item"	The string in the dialog's titlebar
`listTitle`	*`list_title_default`*	The title of the List in the dialog
`items`	*`items_default`*	The list of items to display
`visibleItems`	8	How many items should be visible at once
`helpText`	*`help_text_default`*	Online help for the dialog

Widgets

These functions create an XmDialogShell named `xmtItemDialogShell` and an XmSelectionBox widget named `xmtItemDialog` as a child of that shell. Once this dialog has been created, it is cached for reuse by subsequent calls.

See Also

Chapter 26, *Simple Input Dialogs*
`XmtAskForBoolean()`, `XmtAskForDouble()`,
`XmtAskForFile()`, `XmtAskForFilename()`,
`XmtAskForInteger()`, `XmtAskForItemNumber()`,
`XmtAskForString()`

Name

`XmtAskForString()` — use a dialog box to prompt the user for a string and return the user's response.

Synopsis

```
#include <Xmt/Dialogs.h>
Boolean XmtAskForString(Widget w,
                        String query_name,
                        String prompt_default,
                        String buffer_in_out,
                        int    buffer_length,
                        String help_text_default)
```

Arguments

Inputs

w — The shell widget over which the dialog will be displayed, or any descendant of that shell.

query_name — The name for this instantiation of the dialog. `NULL` may be specified, but will result in a dialog that cannot be customized through the resource manager.

prompt_default — The prompt message to be displayed in the dialog, unless an overriding value is found in the resource database.

buffer_in_out — A character buffer owned by the caller. On entry to `XmtAskForString()`, this buffer contains the default string to be displayed in the dialog's text widget.

buffer_len — The length in characters of the buffer.

help_text_default — The help text to display when the user clicks the **Help** button, unless an overriding value is found in resource database. `NULL` may be specified.

Outputs

buffer_in_out — A character buffer owned by the caller. When `XmtAskForString()` returns `True`, this buffer contains the string input by the user. The string is guaranteed to be null-terminated and never to contain more than *buffer_len*-1 characters.

Returns

`True` if the user clicked the **Ok** button to dismiss the dialog; `False` if the user clicked the **Cancel** button.

Description

XmtAskForString() displays an application modal dialog box, of the type created by XmCreatePromptDialog(), to prompt the user to input a string. It processes events in a local event loop until the user selects either the **OK** or **Cancel** button of the dialog, and then returns with the user's input, if any, in a programmer-specified buffer.

If help text is found in the resource database for this dialog, or if the *help_text_default* argument is non-NULL, then this text will be displayed (using XmtDisplayInformation()) when the user clicks on the **Help** button. If there is no help for the dialog, then the **Help** button will be made insensitive.

Customization

To allow dialog customization, XmtAskForString() looks up the following subpart resources of the shell specified by *w*. The name of the subpart is given by the argument *query_name*, and the class of the subpart is XmtStringDialog. These subpart resources are looked up every time XmtAskForString() is called, not simply when the widgets are created.

Resource	Default	Description
message	*prompt_default*	The prompt for the dialog
title	"Enter a String"	The string to appear in the dialog's titlebar
helpText	*help_text_default*	Online help for the dialog

Widgets

XmtAskForString() creates a XmDialogShell widget named xmtStringDialogShell, and an XmSelectionBox widget named xmtStringDialog as a child of that shell. Once this dialog has been created, it is cached for reuse by subsequent calls.

See Also

Chapter 26, *Simple Input Dialogs*
XmtAskForInteger(), XmtAskForDouble(),
XmtAskForBoolean(), XmtAskForFile(),
XmtAskForFilename(), XmtAskForItem(),
XmtAskForItemNumber()

XmtAssertWidgetClass()

Name

`XmtAssertWidgetClass()` — verify the type of a widget.

Synopsis

```
#include <Xmt/Xmt.h>
void XmtAssertWidgetClass(Widget w,
                          WidgetClass c,
                          String procname)
```

Arguments

Inputs

w — The widget to be checked.

c — The desired widget class.

procname — An identifying string to be used in the error message displayed if the widget *w* is not of class *c* or a subclass of it. This argument is most useful when it is the name of the procedure that calls `XmtAssertWidgetClass()`.

Description

`XmtAssertWidgetClass()` calls `XtIsSubclass()` to verify that widget *w* is of class *c* or is a subclass of *c*. If so, it returns and takes no action. If *w* is not of class *c* or a subclass, then `XmtAssertWidgetClass()` prints an error message and calls the function `abort()`, which causes the application to dump core and exit.

Usage

`XmtAssertWidgetClass()` is an analog to `assert()`. It is used mainly by widget writers, but also occasionally by application programmers who are writing a function that expects a widget argument of a specific type. Many of the functions in the Xmt library call this function internally.

`XmtAssertWidgetClass()` is useful during the process of application development and debugging because it gives a very clear signal (a message and a core dump with its associated stack trace) of when application code is calling a function with a bad widget argument. Once an application is debugged, you can compile your code (and the Xmt library) with the -DNDEBUG flag, which will cause any calls to `XmtAssertWidgetClass()` to be removed by the C preprocessor.

See Also

Chapter 8, *Utility Functions*
`abort()`, `assert()`, `XtIsSubclass()`

XmtBlock()

Name

XmtBlock() — process events in a recursive event loop.

Synopsis

```
#include <Xmt/Xmt.h>
void XmtBlock(Widget w,
              Boolean *block)
```

Arguments

Inputs

w — Any widget in the application context for which events are to be processed.

block — A pointer to a flag that indicates when this function should return.

Description

XmtBlock() processes events in the application context of *w* by repeatedly calling XtAppProcessEvent() until the Boolean value pointed to by *block* becomes False. Then it performs an XSync() for the display of *w* and calls XmUpdateDisplay() to dispatch any pending expose events.

XmtBlock() is a recursive event loop, and processes events in the same way that XtAppMainLoop() does.

Usage

XmtBlock() is intended for use when you want to write a function that appears to the caller to block and synchronously return a value. The Xmt simple dialog input routines, such as XmtAskForBoolean(), are functions of this sort. True blocking is not possible in X applications because of the asynchronous, event-driven nature of the X programming model.

XmtBlock() should generally only be called when a modal dialog is active, or when the user is in some other way prevented from repeating whatever action caused XmtBlock() to be called. Otherwise it is possible for the application to enter event loops within recursive event loops.

When you use XmtBlock() you should be very sure that you know what causes the flag *block* to be set to False and the loop to exit. This is usually done in a callback or action procedure triggered by some user action. It is equally important that you indicate to the user what action she must take to end the modal, synchronous input.

See Also

Chapter 8, *Utility Functions*
XtAppMainLoop(), XtAppProcessEvent()

Name

XmtBuildApplication(), XmtBuildQueryApplication() — create a root ApplicationShell widget and all of its descendants.

Synopsis

```
#include <Xmt/Create.h>
Widget XmtBuildApplication(String appname, String appclass, Display *display,
                           ArgList args, Cardinal num_args)

Widget XmtBuildQueryApplication(String appname, String appclass, Display *display,
                                ArgList args, Cardinal num_args,
                              { String child_name, Widget *child_address, }
                                NULL)
```

Arguments

Inputs

appname The name of the root application shell to be created.

appclass The resource class name of a root application shell to be created.

display The X Display on which the application shell is to be created.

args An array of name/value pairs of resources to be set on the newly created application shell.

num_args The number of elements in *args*.

child_name The name of a widget to be returned. May be repeated any number of times in a NULL-terminated variable-length argument list.

Outputs

child_address

The address at which the widget specified by *child_name* is to be stored. May be repeated any number of times in a NULL-terminated variable-length argument list.

Returns

The newly created root ApplicationShell widget.

Description

XmtBuildApplication() and XmtBuildQueryApplication() create a root ApplicationShell widget by calling XtAppCreateShell(), with their *appname*, *appclass*, *display*, *args*, and *num_args* arguments. Then they read the xmtChildren resource of the newly created shell and recursively create all the descendants of the shell, in the same way that XmtCreateChildren() and XmtCreateQueryChildren() do. Like XmtCreateQueryChildren(), XmtBuildQueryApplication() can return pointers to some of the widgets it creates.

Usage

Most applications will only have a single root ApplicationShell widget, created by their call to `XtAppInitialize()` or `XmtInitialize()`. Applications that do create additional root widgets may use these functions to create those shells and their descendants.

Use `XmtBuildToplevel()` and `XmtBuildDialog()` to create TopLevel-Shell widgets and dialog boxes in a similar way.

See Also

Chapter 11, *Automatic Widget Creation*
`XmtBuildDialog()`, `XmtBuildToplevel()`,
`XmtCreateChildren()`, `XmtCreateQueryChildren()`,
`XmtInitialize()`, `XtAppCreateShell()`,
`XtAppInitialize()`

Name

XmtBuildDialog(), XmtBuildQueryDialog() — create a dialog shell and its descendants.

Synopsis

```
#include <Xmt/Create.h>
Widget XmtBuildDialog(Widget parent,
                      String dialog_name,
                      XtResourceList resources,
                      Cardinal num_resources)

Widget XmtBuildQueryDialog(Widget parent,
                           String dialog_name,
                           XtResourceList resources,
                           Cardinal num_resources,
                         { String child_name, Widget *child_address, }
                           NULL)
```

Arguments

Inputs

parent — The parent of the dialog shell to be created.

dialog_name — The name of the dialog shell to be created.

resources — An optional resource list that gives names, types, and offsets for each of the data items that will be displayed or input through the dialog box.

num_resources — The number of elements in the *resources* array.

child_name — The name of a widget to be returned. May be repeated any number of times in a NULL-terminated variable-length argument list.

Outputs

child_address — The address at which the widget specified by *child_name* is to be stored. May be repeated any number of times in a NULL-terminated variable-length argument list.

Returns

The child of the newly created dialog shell; a grandchild of *parent*.

Description

XmtBuildDialog() and XmtBuildQueryDialog() create an XmDialogShell widget with the specified name and parent, and then read the xmtChildren resource for that widget database and use it to recursively create all the descendants of the dialog shell, in the same way that `XmtCreateChildren()` and `XmtCreateQueryChildren()` do.

Like `XmtCreateQueryChildren()`, `XmtBuildQueryDialog()` will return pointers to the widgets named in its NULL-terminated variable-length argument list.

`XmtCreateChildren()` and related widget creation functions parse a widget specification grammar described in Chapter 11, *Automatic Widget Creation.* `XmtBuildDialog()` and `XmtBuildQueryDialog()` extend this grammar to allow the name of a data value to be associated with any widget in the dialog. The *`resources`* argument is an array of `XtResource` structures that defines a data type, size, and offset for each of these named data values. These named data values are used by the Xmt automatic dialog management facilities described in Chapter 29, *Custom Dialogs and Automatic Dialog Management.*

Usage

Note that these functions do not return the XmDialogShell widget they create, but rather the child of that widget. (Recall that shell widgets can only have a single child.) You can pop up and pop down the dialog shell by managing and unmanaging its child. If you are using the automatic dialog management facilities of Chapter 29, you can also use convenience functions like `XmtDialogDo()` and `XmtDialogDoSync()`.

See Also

Chapter 11, *Automatic Widget Creation*
Chapter 29, *Custom Dialogs and Automatic Dialog Management*
`XmtBuildToplevel()`, `XmtCreateChildren()`, `XmtDialogDo()`

Name

`XmtBuildToplevel()`, `XmtBuildQueryToplevel()` — create a TopLevelShell widget and all of its descendants.

Synopsis

```
#include <Xmt/Create.h>
Widget XmtBuildToplevel(Widget parent, String name)

Widget XmtBuildQueryToplevel(Widget parent, String name,
                            { String child_name, Widget *child_address, }
                              NULL)
```

Arguments

Inputs

parent — The parent of the shell to be created.

name — The name of the shell to be created.

child_name — The name of a widget to be returned. May be repeated any number of times in a NULL-terminated variable-length argument list.

Outputs

child_address — The address at which the widget specified by *child_name* is to be stored. May be repeated any number of times in a NULL-terminated variable-length argument list.

Returns

The newly created TopLevelShell widget.

Description

`XmtBuildToplevel()` and `XmtBuildQueryToplevel()` call `XtCreatePopupShell()` to create a TopLevelShell with the specified *parent* and *name*. Then they read the `xmtChildren` resource of the newly created shell and recursively create all the descendants of the shell, in the same way that `XmtCreateChildren()` and `XmtCreateQueryChildren()` do.

Like `XmtCreateQueryChildren()`, `XmtBuildQueryToplevel()` can return some of the widgets it creates. If any of the created widgets has a name that appears as a *child_name* argument, then that widget is returned in the corresponding *child_address* argument in the variable-length argument list.

Usage

The TopLevelShell widget is useful for "auxiliary" windows of your application. These windows are unlike dialog boxes in that they can be iconified independently of the application itself. Note that unlike Motif dialogs implemented with the XmDialogShell widget, TopLevelShell widgets must be popped up and down with `XtPopup()` and `XtPopdown()`.

Use `XmtBuildDialog()` to create dialog boxes in a similar way.

See Also

Chapter 11, *Automatic Widget Creation*
`XmtBuildApplication()`, `XmtBuildDialog()`,
`XmtCreateChildren()`, `XmtCreateQueryChildren()`,
`XtCreatePopupShell()`, `XtPopdown()`,
`XtPopup()`

XmtCheckPrintfFormat()

Name

XmtCheckPrintfFormat() — verify that two strings have the same printf() substitutions.

Synopsis

```
#include <Xmt/Xmt.h>
Boolean XmtCheckPrintfFormat(String template,
                             String msg)
```

Arguments

Inputs

template	A string with printf()-style variable substitutions in it.
msg	A string to check against *template*.

Returns

True if *msg* has printf() substitutions that are identical to or compatible with *template*; False otherwise.

Description

XmtCheckPrintfFormat() verifies that the printf() substitutions in *msg* are compatible with the substitutions in *template*. This is useful, for example, with XmtLocalize2(), which allows you to look up a translated verion of a message. If the translated message will be passed to printf(), this function lets you check that it does not contain inappropriate substitutions.

XmtCheckPrintfFormat() supports regular printf() substitutions and also the internationalized style of printf() substitutions that are now supported on many systems. This new substitution syntax allows you to specify the type and the position of the argument to be substituted, and look like %2$d or %1$s.

See Also

Chapter 25, *Message Dialogs*
Chapter 3, *Displaying Text*
XmtLocalize2()

XmtChooser

Name

XmtChooser — a widget that presents a choice to the user.

Synopsis

Include File:	`#include <Xmt/Chooser.h>`
Constructor:	`XmtCreateChooser()`
Class Name:	XmtChooser
Class Pointer:	`xmtChooserWidgetClass`
Class Hierarchy:	Core → Composite → Constraint → XmManager → XmRowColumn → XmtChooser

Description

An XmtChooser is a composite widget which creates and controls the primitive widgets necessary to present a list of selectable items to the user. Depending on the `XmtNchooserType` resource, a Chooser widget will create an XmList widget, an XmOptionMenu, or a number of button children configured to be used as a radio box, a check box, a button box, or a palette. See the section that follows, "Chooser Types," for more information.

The choices to be displayed to the user may be specified in a single array on the `XmtNstrings` or the `XmtNpixmaps` resource. When pixmaps are being used, the resources `XmtNselectPixmaps` and `XmtNinsensitivePixmaps` specify alternate pixmaps to be displayed when an item is selected or insensitive and unselectable.

The Chooser widget keeps track of the choices made by the user in the `XmtNstate` resource. For Chooser types that have radio-style behavior, (i.e., types for which only one item can be selected at a time) the value of this resource is the index of the selected item. For types that allow multiple selected items, this state value is a bit-mask which indicates which items are selected. If the *n*th bit is set in this resource, then the *n*th item displayed by the Chooser is selected. The programmer may query this resource at any time to determine the current selection state. The programmer may also set this resource, and the selection state of the Chooser subwidgets will be changed to reflect the new value. Whenever the state of the Chooser changes, it calls all the procedures registered on its `XmtNvalueChangedCallback` list. See the section "Chooser State" for more information.

The `XmtNvalues` or `XmtNvalueStrings` resources specify an array of values to be associated with the items displayed by the Chooser widget. The Chooser widget does not interpret or use these values in any way, but the value of an item is often more convenient to the programmer than that item's index in the Chooser. See the section "Chooser Values" for more information on specifying values for a Chooser.

The Chooser widget is a subclass of XmRowColumn, and it uses the layout capabilities of and resources of XmRowColumn to arrange its children. Although the Chooser is a composite widget, it creates all of its own children, and should not have additional children added to it.

Resources

Chooser inherits the resources of the XmRowColumn class, and defines the following new resources. In addition, it overrides the default value for two XmRowColumn resources: it sets the default value of `XmNadjustLast` to `False` and of `XmNpacking` to `XmPACK_COLUMN`.

Name	*Class*	*Type*	*Default*	*Access*
XmtNchooserType	XmtCChooserType	XmtRXmtChooserType	RadioBox	CG
XmtNfontList	XmCFontList	XmRFontList	dynamic	CSG
XmtNinsensitive-Pixmaps	XmtCInsensitivePixmaps	XmtRPixmapList	NULL	CG
XmtNitemWidgets	XtCReadOnly	XtRWidgetList	Read-only	G
XmtNlabelType	XmtCLabelType	XmRLabelType	XmSTRING	CG
XmtNnumItems	XmtCNumItems	XtRInt	dynamic	CG
XmtNpixmaps	XmtCPixmaps	XmtRPixmapList	NULL	CG
XmtNselectPixmaps	XmtCSelectPixmaps	XmtRPixmapList	NULL	CG
XmtNstate	XmtCState	XtRInt	0	CSG
XmtNstrings	XmtCStrings	XmtRStringList	NULL	CG
XmtNsymbolName	XmtCSymbolName	XtRString	NULL	CSG
XmtNvalueChanged-Callback	XtCCallback	XtRCallback	NULL	C
XmtNvalueSize	XmtCValueSize	XtRCardinal	0	CSG
XmtNvalueStrings	XmtCValueStrings	XmtRStringList	NULL	CS
XmtNvalueType	XmtCValueType	XtRString	NULL	CSG
XmtNvalues	XmtCValues	XtRPointer	NULL	CSG
XmtNvisibleItems	XmtCVisibleItems	XtRInt	8	CSG

`XmtNchooserType`

The type of the widgets to be created and controlled by the Chooser widget. This is one of the enumerated values of type `XmtChooserType`. The `XmtNchooserType` resource may only be set when the Chooser is created, and may never be changed. There is a type converter for this resource; see the "Converters" section. See the section "Chooser Types" for an explanation of each of the supported types.

`XmtNfontList`

The XmFontList to use to display any strings specified on the `XmtNstrings` resource in the button or list widgets created by the Chooser. If this resource is left unspecified, then the default value is obtained from the `XmNbuttonFontList` resource of the nearest XmBulletinBoard ancestor, or the `XmNdefaultFontList` resource of the nearest VendorShell or XmMenuShell ancestor.

`XmtNinsensitivePixmaps`

An array of `Pixmap` containing `XmtNnumItems` elements. If that resource is unspecified this resource must be `NULL`-terminated. If these pixmaps are specified, and if `XmtNlabelType` is `XmPIXMAP`, then they are used to display choices that are currently unselectable because they have been made insensitive with a call to `XmtChooserSetSensitive()`. This resource must be set when the widget is created, and cannot be changed.

`XmtNitemWidgets`
A read-only resource that can be queried to obtain the array of button children created by the Chooser when the `XmtNchooserType` resource is set to anything other than `XmtChooserRadioList` or `XmtChooserCheckList`. The index of a choice in the Chooser is the same as the index of that choice's widget in this array.

`XmtNlabelType`
Specifies whether the Chooser should display choices using strings or pixmaps. If it is set to the value `XmSTRING`, then the Chooser will display choices using the strings in the `XmtNstrings` array. If set to `XmPIXMAP`, then the Chooser will display choices using the pixmaps in the `XmtNpixmaps` array, and will also use the pixmaps in the `XmtNselectPixmaps` and `XmtNinsensitivePixmaps` arrays to display selected and insensitive choices.

`XmtNnumItems`
Specifies the number of choices to appear in the Chooser. This is the number of elements that must appear in the `XmtNstrings`, `XmtNpixmaps`, and other array resources of the Chooser. If this resource is left unspecified, then the `XmtNstrings`, `XmtNpixmaps`, `XmtNselectPixmaps`, and `XmtNinsensitivePixmaps` arrays must be `NULL`-terminated. Note that any of these resources specified in a resource file will be automatically `NULL`-terminated by the resource converter.

`XmtNpixmaps`
An array of `Pixmap` that contains `XmtNnumItems` elements. If that resource is unspecified, this array must be `NULL`-terminated. When `XmtNlabelType` is `XmPIXMAP`, the Chooser uses these pixmaps to display the choices. Note that pixmaps cannot be used with `XmtChooserRadioList` and `XmtChooserCheckList` types. This resource must be set when the widget is created, and cannot be changed. Call `XmtRegisterPixmapListConverter()` to allow this resource to be specified in a resource file.

`XmtNselectPixmaps`
An array of `Pixmap` that contains `XmtNnumItems` elements. If that resource is unspecified, this array must contain the same number of elements as the `XmtNpixmaps` array and must be `NULL`-terminated. When `XmtNlabelType` is `XmPIXMAP`, these pixmaps are used to display selected choices. This resource can be used to highlight selected items by specifying pixmaps with a darker background color. This resource must be set when the widget is created, and cannot be changed.

`XmtNstate`

The selection state of the Chooser widget—the item or items that are selected. This resource may be queried to obtain the current selection state of the widget, or it may be set, and the Chooser will change its displayed selection state to match the newly specified value. See the section "Chooser State" for an explanation of how this state variable is interpreted.

`XmtNstrings`

An array of strings to be displayed as choices to the user. Note that the strings are of type `String`, not `XmString`. This resource must be set when the Chooser widget is created, and once set, it cannot be changed. If the `XmtNnumItems` resource is set, then this array must have that many elements. If `XmtNnumItems` is not set, then this array must be NULL-terminated. There is a String-to-StringList type converter registered for this resource by the Chooser widget class; see the "Converters" section.

`XmtNsymbolName`

The name of a registered symbol on which the Chooser is to store its state. If a symbol is specified, its initial value is used as the initial value for the Chooser, and any changes made to the symbol value with `XmtSymbolSetValue()` will be reflected in the Chooser widget state. Symbols can be useful for applications that use the state of the Chooser, but do not need to be notified of changes in the state; those applications can register the address of a variable as a symbol, specify the name of that symbol on this resource, and then simply read the state from this variable, without querying the widget. See `XmtRegisterSymbol()` for more information on symbols.

`XmtNvalueChangedCallback`

A list of callback procedures which will be called when the state of the Chooser changes. Each procedure will be called with a *`call_data`* argument of type `XmtChooserCallbackStruct *`, which is documented later in this reference page.

`XmtNvalueSize`

The size, in bytes, of each element in the array of values specified on the `XmtNvalues` resource, or the size, in bytes, of the type specified by the `XmtNvalueType` resource.

`XmtNvalueStrings`

An array of strings, one for each item in the Chooser, which will be converted to the type specified by the `XmtNvalueType` resource and stored in the `XmtNvalues` array. If you specify this resource, you must also specify `XmtNvalueType` and `XmtNvalueSize`. Once the `XmtNvalueStrings` strings have been converted to the `XmtNvalues` values, the Chooser widget resets the `XmtNvalueStrings` resource to NULL, so it never makes sense to query this resource. Since the resource is automatically reset to NULL, however, when a value changes in your array of strings, you can pass the array in another call to `XtSetValues()`. If the resource value had not been reset to NULL, the widget would not notice any change (the array contents have changed, but not the array pointer) and the new values would not be converted.

XmtNvalueType
A representation type string, such as the constants XtRInt and XmRFontList. If the XmtNvalueStrings resource is specified, the strings in that array will be converted to the type specified by this resource, and the converted values stored in the XmtNvalues array.

XmtNvalues
An untyped array containing one element for each item in the Chooser, each element XmtNvalueSize bytes in length. For Chooser types that allow only one selected item at a time, this array specifies a value for each item in the Chooser widget. This value is often more useful to the application programmer than the value on the XmtNstate resource. The contents of the XmtNvalues array are untyped, and are not used in any way by the Chooser widget, but this resource provides a convenient way for an application to associate the values it cares about with each of the elements in the Chooser. If you set this resource, you must also set XmtNvalueSize.

XmtNvisibleItems
If the XmtNchooserType resource is XmtChooserRadioList or XmtChooserCheckList, then this resource sets the XmNvisibleItemCount resource of the list widget, and controls the number of items that are visible at any time. If there are more items in XmtNlabels then XmtNvisibleItems, then the XmList widget will be scrolled.

Chooser Types

The way the Chooser widget presents its choices to the user is specified by the XmtNchooserType resource. This resource is of type XmtChooserType, which has the following enumerated values:

```
typedef enum {
    XmtChooserRadioBox,      /* one-of-many toggle buttons */
    XmtChooserCheckBox,      /* n-of-many toggle buttons */
    XmtChooserRadioPalette,  /* toggle buttons w/o indicators */
    XmtChooserCheckPalette,  /* toggle buttons w/o indicators */
    XmtChooserRadioList,     /* XmList widget in single select mode */
    XmtChooserCheckList,     /* XmList widget in multi-select mode */
    XmtChooserOption,        /* option menu */
    XmtChooserButtonBox,     /* Push buttons in a box */
} XmtChooserType;
```

The enumerated values for this type have the following meanings:

XmtChooserRadioBox
Items are displayed with XmToggleButtons with diamond-shaped ("one-of-many") indicators. Only one item in the list is allowed to be selected at any time.

`XmtChooserCheckBox`
Items are displayed with XmToggleButtons with square ("*n*-of-many") indicators. Any number of the items may be selected.

`XmtChooserRadioPalette`
Items are displayed with XmToggleButtons. The toggle buttons have no indicators, but use shadows to display their selection state instead. Only one item may be selected at a time.

`XmtChooserCheckPalette`
Items are displayed with XmToggleButtons. The toggle buttons have no indicators, but use shadows to display their selection state instead. Any number of items may be selected.

`XmtChooserRadioList`
Items are displayed in an XmList widget in browse-select mode. Only one item may be selected at a time.

`XmtChooserCheckList`
Items are displayed in an XmList widget in multiple-select mode. Any number of items may be selected.

`XmtChooserOption`
Items are displayed in an option menu as created by `XmCreateOptionMenu()`. Only one item may be selected at a time.

`XmtChooserButtonBox`
Items are displayed with XmPushButtons. Since these buttons do not remain selected after they are pushed, the `XmtNstate` resource is unused in Choosers of this type.

For RadioBox, CheckBox, RadioPalette, CheckPalette, and ButtonBox types, the Chooser automatically creates the appropriate button children. The layout of these children is controlled by `XmNnumColumns`, `XmNorientation`, and other inherited XmRowColumn resources. For the Option type, the Chooser widget creates a menu pane and creates the buttons as children of that widget.

For the RadioList and CheckList types, the Chooser automatically creates a scrolled XmList widget to display the choices. The `XmtNvisibleItems` resource controls the number of choices visible at one time in these modes.

Chooser State

The `XmtNstate` resource maintains the selection state of all the items in the Chooser widget. If `XmtNchooserType` is one of the types with radio behavior (such as `XmtChooserRadioBox`, `XmtChooserRadioPalette`, `XmtChooserRadioList`, or `XmtChooserOption`), then the state is simply the index of the currently selected item. Items are numbered beginning at zero, so if this resource is 0, it means that the first item is selected. For these Chooser types with radio-box behavior, there is exactly one item selected at all times, including a default item when the Chooser is created.

If `XmtNchooserType` is a type without radio behavior (`XmtChooserCheckBox`, `XmtChooserCheckPalette`, or `XmtChooserCheckList`), then the state is a bit-mask with one bit indicating the state of each item. In this case, the state of item *n* can be determined with the following C code:

```
(state & (1 << n))
```

Note that there cannot be more items in a Chooser of this type than there are bits in a variable of type `int`. This is at least 32 bits on most systems and should be plenty for most practical applications. Finally, note that if `XmtNchooserType` is `XmtChooserButtonBox` (which uses XmPushButtons rather than XmToggleButtons), then the `XmtNstate` resource is ignored.

Chooser Values

From the `XmtNstate` resource of a Chooser, you can determine the index of the selected item or items within the list of displayed items. Often, however, the application is not interested in the index of the selected item, but instead in some semantic value associated with the item. For a Chooser that lets the user select a font size from a list of five values, for example, the states 0, 1, 2, 3, and 4 are not as interesting as the sizes themselves: 8, 10, 12, 14, and 18.

An application can easily maintain an array of values to map from item number to item value, but as a convenience, the Chooser widget will maintain this array for the application. The `XmtNvalues` resource is an untyped array that contains one element for each item in the Chooser. The length of each element, in bytes, is specified by the `XmtNvalueSize` resource. The Chooser widget never uses or interprets these values, but will pass pointers to them to the application when it invokes the `XmtNvalueChangedCallback`, or when the application calls `XmtChooserGetValue()`.

The Chooser allows values to be specified from resource files with the `XmtNvalueStrings` resource and the `XmtNvalueType` resource. `XmtNvalueStrings` is an array of strings, and `XmtNvalueType` is a string representation type, such as `XtRInt` or `XtRPixel`, for which a resource converter has been registered. (Values beginning with "XtR", "XmR", or "XmtR" are the symbolic names you would use from C. In a resource file, you'd use the strings these symbols stand for—"Int" and "Pixel" in this case.) If `XmtNvalueStrings` is specified, each string in the array will be converted to the specified type. The Chooser widget allocates an array for the `XmtNvalues` resource, with `XmtNvalueSize` bytes for each element, and stores the converted values into this array. Note that if you specify the `XmtNvalues` resource, you must also always specify the `XmtNvalueSize` resource. If you specify the `XmtNvalueStrings` resource, you must always specify both the `XmtNvalueSize` and `XmtNvalueType` resources.

Callbacks

The Chooser widget defines a single callback list, XmtNvalueChangedCallback. The procedures registered on this list are called when the selection state of the widget changes (i.e., when the user chooses on of the displayed items). The *call_data* argument to this callback is a pointer to an XmtChooser-CallbackStruct, which is defined as follows:

```
typedef struct {
    int state;          /* selected item or bitwise OR of items */
    int item;           /* whichever item just was clicked */
    XtPointer valuep; /* address of value from XmtNvalues array */
} XmtChooserCallbackStruct;
```

The state field of this structure is the new value of the XmtNstate resource. The item field is the index of the item that was just selected. For Chooser types with radio behavior, this is the same as the state field. If the Xmt-Nvalues array or the XmtNvalueStrings array is set, then the valuep field is the address of the element of that array that corresponds to the item specified on the item field.

The XmtNvalueChangedCallback is generally called when the user changes the state of the Chooser widget. It is also called when XmtChooser-SetState() is called with its *notify* argument set to True. In this case the item field is always set to -1, because although the state changed, there is not any particular item that the user just selected or deselected. For synthetic state changed like this, if the Chooser is in a radio-box mode, then the valuep field is set to point to the value that corresponds to the single selected item. For check-box modes, the valuep field is set to NULL on synthetic state changes.

For Chooser widgets of type XmtChooserButtonBox, the state field of this callback structure is always set to -1 because the XmPushButtons of a button box do not maintain any state. The item field *will* contain the index of the button just pressed, however, which can be useful to dispatch commands in a switch statement, for example.

Converters

The Chooser class registers converters to convert strings specified in resource files to the types XmtRXmtChooserType and XmtRStringList. The String-to-XmtChooserType converter recognizes strings spelled exactly as its enumerated type is, with the "Xmt" and "Chooser" prefixes optionally removed. Correct capitalization is required by this converter.

The String-to-StringList converter converts a comma-separated list of strings within double quotes into a NULL-terminated array of strings suitable for use on the XmtNstrings and XmtNvalueStrings resources.

The Xmt library also provides a String-to-PixmapList converter that will convert a string to an array of pixmaps suitable for use on the XmtNpixmaps, Xmt-NselectPixmaps, and XmtNinsensitivePixmaps resources. Because many applications will not use the Chooser widget with pixmaps, this converter is not automatically registered by the widget. You can register it explicitly by calling `XmtRegisterPixmapListConverter()`. This converter converts a comma-separated list of pixmap names within quotes, optionally followed by a color table to specify symbolic color substitutions for those pixmaps. See the reference pages for `XmtRegisterPixmapListConverter()`, `XmtRegisterColorTableConverter()`, and `XmtGetPixmap()` for more information.

Translations and Actions

The Chooser widget simply inherits the translations of the XmRowColumn widget class, and does not set translations on any of its automatically created children. It defines no new action procedures.

Sensitivity

Because the Chooser is often used with a caption provided by an XmtLayout parent widget, it takes special care to notice when its own sensitivity state changes, and updates the `XmtNlayoutSensitive` constraint resource as necessary so that any caption will appear greyed out when the Chooser is not sensitive.

The Chooser widget provides a convenience routine, `XmtChooserSetSensitive()`, which sets the sensitivity of individual items within the Chooser. For Chooser types that use buttons, insensitive items are made insensitive with `XtSetSensitive()`, and will be displayed with greyed out textual labels, or with the pixmap, if any, specified in the `XmtNinsensitivePixmaps` array. An insensitive item is not selectable. For Chooser types that use the XmList widget, insensitive items are not displayed in any special way, but are made unselectable.

See Also

Chapter 27, *Presenting Choices*
`XmtChooserGetSensitivity()`, `XmtChooserGetState()`,
`XmtChooserGetValue()`, `XmtChooserLookupItemByName()`,
`XmtChooserLookupItemByValue()`, `XmtChooserLookupItemName()`,
`XmtChooserLookupItemValue()`, `XmtChooserSetItemValue()`,
`XmtChooserSetSensitive()`, `XmtChooserSetState()`,
`XmtCreateChooser()`, `XmtRegisterChooser()`

XmtChooserGet{State,Value,Sensitivity}()

Name

XmtChooserGetState(), XmtChooserGetValue(), XmtChooserGet-Sensitivity() — query an XmtChooser widget about its selected items and item sensitivity.

Synopsis

```
#include <Xmt/Chooser.h>
int XmtChooserGetState(Widget w)

XtPointer XmtChooserGetValue(Widget w)

Boolean XmtChooserGetSensitivity(Widget w, int item)
```

Arguments

Inputs

w An XmtChooser widget.

item The index of an item within *w*.

Returns

See below.

Description

XmtChooserGetState() returns the selection state of the XmtChooser widget *w*. If the XmtNchooserType resource of the widget is XmtChooserRadioBox, XmtChooserRadioPalette, XmtChooserRadioList, or XmtChooserOption, then the returned value is the index of the single selected item. If the XmtNchooserType resource is XmtChooserCheckBox, XmtChooserCheckPalette, or XmtChooserCheckList, then the returned value is a bitfield indicating the selection state of each of the items (up to 32) in the widget. If the XmtNchooserType resource is XmtChooserButtonBox, then the returned value is not meaningful. Calling this function is equivalent to, but more efficient than, querying the XmtNstate resource of *w*.

XmtChooserGetValue() returns the address of the value associated with the selected item in the XmtChooser *w*. The specified widget must have its XmtNchooserType resource set to one of the "single selection" types: XmtChooserRadioBox, XmtChooserRadioPalette, XmtChooserRadioList, or XmtChooserOption. Note that the returned value is an untyped pointer. You must cast and dereference it as appropriate.

XmtChooserGetSensitivity() return True if item *item* in XmtChooser *w* is sensitive, and False otherwise. Use XmtChooserSetSensitive() to set the sensitivity of an item. Insensitive items cannot be selected by the user.

See Also

Chapter 27, *Presenting Choices*
XmtChooser, `XmtChooserSetState()`,
`XmtChooserSetItemValue()`, `XmtChooserSetSensitive()`

XmtChooserLookupItem[By]{Name,Value}()

Name

XmtChooserLookupItemName(), XmtChooserLookupItemValue(), XmtChooserLookupItemByName(), XmtChooserLookupItemByValue() — look up XmtChooser item name and value by index or index by name and value.

Synopsis

```
#include <Xmt/Chooser.h>
String XmtChooserLookupItemName(Widget w, int item)

XtPointer XmtChooserLookupItemValue(Widget w, int item)

int XmtChooserLookupItemByName(Widget w, String name)

int XmtChooserLookupItemByValue(Widget w, XtPointer valuep)
```

Arguments

Inputs

w	An XmtChooser widget.
item	The index of the item in *w* that is to have its name or value looked up.
name	The name of an item in *w* that is to have its index looked up.
valuep	The address of a value associated with an item in *w*.

Returns

See below.

Description

`XmtChooserLookupItemName()` returns the label associated with the specified item in the `XmtNstrings` resource of the XmtChooser widget. If no `XmtNstrings` resource has been specified for the widget then this function returns NULL. The returned string is owned by the widget and must not be modified or freed by the application.

`XmtChooserLookupItemValue()` returns the address of the value associated with the item *`item`* in the XmtChooser *w*. Note that this differs from `XmtChooserGetValue()`, which returns the value associated with the currently selected item.

`XmtChooserLookupItemByName()` looks for an item in the `XmtNstrings` resource of the XmtChooser widget *w* that matches the specified *`label`*. If it finds one, it returns the index of the matching item. If no `XmtNstrings` resource was specified for the widget, or if no match was found, it returns `-1`.

`XmtChooserLookupItemByValue()` compares the value pointed to by `valuep` with each of the values in its `XmtNvalues` resource, and if a match is found, it returns the index of the item that matched. If `w` has a NULL

XmtNvalues resource, or if no match is found, it returns -1. XmtChooser-LookupItemByValue() treats string values as a special case. If the Xmt-NvalueType resource is XtRString, then the contents of the strings are compared, rather than simply comparing the pointers

See Also

Chapter 27, *Presenting Choices*
XmtChooser, XmtChooserGetValue(), XmtChooserSetItemValue()

XmtChooserSet{State,Sensitive,ItemValue}()

Name

`XmtChooserSetState()`, `XmtChooserSetSensitive()`, `XmtChooser-SetItemValue()` — set the current selection in an XmtChooser widget, or the sensitivity or value associated with its items.

Synopsis

```
#include <Xmt/Chooser.h>
void XmtChooserSetState(Widget w, int state, Boolean notify)

void XmtChooserSetSensitive(Widget w, int item, Boolean sensitive)

void XmtChooserSetItemValue(Widget w, int item, XtPointer valuep)
```

Arguments

Inputs

w	An XmtChooser widget.
state	The selection state to be set on the widget.
notify	Whether the widget's `XmtNvalueChangedCallback` should be invoked when the XmtChooser's state is changed. If `True`, the procedures registered on that callback list will be called; if `False`, they will not be called.
item	The index of an item in the XmtChooser that is to have its sensitivity or value set.
sensitive	`True` to make the item *item* in *w* sensitive, `False` to make it insensitive.
valuep	The address of the value to be associated with item *item* in *w*.

Description

`XmtChooserSetState()` sets the selection state *state* on the XmtChooser widget w, and updates the XmtChooser subwidgets to display the new state. If *notify* is `True`, this function will invoke the procedures registered on the XmtChooser `XmtNvalueChangedCallback` list. Calling `XmtChooserSet-State()` with *notify* `False` is equivalent to, but more efficient than, setting the `XmtNstate` resource of the widget.

`XmtChooserSetSensitive()` sets the sensitivity of a specified item, *item*, within the XmtChooser widget *w*. If *sensitive* is `True`, then the specified item will be made sensitive. If *sensitive* is `False`, then the specified item will be made insensitive. Insensitive items may not be selected by the user. In addition, for all XmtChooser types other than `XmtChooserRadioList` and `XmtChooserCheckList`, insensitive items are displayed with stippled ("grayed-out") text, or with the special pixmaps specified in the `Xmt-NinsensitivePixmaps` resource.

`XmtChooserSetItemValue()` copies the value at the address specified by *`valuep`* into an internal array and associates it with item *`item`* of *w*. `valuep` must be the address of a value which has the size specified by the widget's `XmtNvalueSize` resource. It is usually easier to specify values for all items by setting the `XmtNvalues` resource.

See Also

Chapter 27, *Presenting Choices*
XmtChooser, `XmtChooserLookupItemValue()`,
`XmtChooserGetSensitivity()`, `XmtChooserGetState()`,
`XmtChooserGetValue()`

Name

XmtCli — a Command-Line Interface widget.

Synopsis

Include File:	`#include <Xmt/Cli.h>`
Constructor:	`XmtCreateCli()` `XmtCreateScrolledCli()`
Class Name:	XmtCli
Class Pointer:	`xmtCliWidgetClass`
Class Hierarchy:	Core → XmPrimitive → XmText → XmtCli

Description

The XmtCli widget is a simple subclass of the Motif XmText widget that supports command-line (i.e., terminal-style) interaction between the user and an application. As with most terminal-based interfaces, the user is allowed to edit the text on the current line, but may not edit, nor move the cursor to, any previous lines. The Cli widget optionally displays a prompt at the beginning of each new line. The use is not allowed to backspace over this prompt. When the user strikes the **Return** key, the application is notified (via the XmtNinputCallback) of the line just input, and a new line is begun. Lines are retained by the Cli widget after they scroll off the top of the widget, and the user may review them using the (optional) scrollbar. The XmtNsaveLines resource specifies a minimum number of lines that will be retained; when the number of lines exceeds this number, lines at the top of the buffer will be periodically removed to prevent the widget's memory usage from growing without bounds.

The Cli widget supports command history. By default, pressing the up arrow key will cause the widget to display the previously entered command, and pressing the down arrow key will display the next command. The number of commands saved by the Cli widget is controlled by the XmtNhistoryMaxItems resource.

If the XmtNfildes resource is set to a valid file descriptor (generally a pipe or a socket), then the Cli widget will display any text it reads from that socket. Similarly, if the XmtNdisplayStdout or XmtNdisplayStderr resources are True then the Cli widget will reroute the stdout and stderr output streams and capture any text sent to those streams. This can be useful when porting terminal-based programs to X.

Resources

Cli inherits the resources of the XmText class, overrides the default of XmNeditMode to XmMULTI_LINE_EDIT, and defines the following new resources:

Name	*Class*	*Type*	*Default*	*Access*
XmtNcliTranslations	XmtCCliTranslations	XtRTranslation-Table	NULL	CG
XmtNdisplayStderr	XmtCDisplayStderr	XtRBoolean	False	CSG
XmtNdisplayStdout	XmtCDisplayStdout	XtRBoolean	False	CSG
XmtNescapeNewlines	XmtCEscapeNewlines	XtRBoolean	True	CSG
XmtNfildes	XmtCFildes	XtRInt	1	CSG
XmtNhistory	XtCReadOnly	Xmt-RStringList	NULL	G
XmtNhistoryMaxItems	XmtCHistoryMaxItems	XtRShort	50	CSG
XmtNhistoryNumItems	XmtCHistoryNumItems	XtRShort	0	CSG
XmtNinputCallback	XtCCallback	XtRCallback	NULL	C
XmtNpageMode	XmtCPageMode	XtRBoolean	False	CSG
XmtNpageString	XmtCPageString	XtRString	*see below*	CG
XmtNpageWidget	XtCReadOnly	XtRWidget	NULL	G
XmtNprompt	XmtCPrompt	XtRString	NULL	CSG
XmtNsaveHistory	XmtCSaveHistory	XtRBoolean	True	CSG
XmtNsaveLines	XmtCSaveLines	XtRShort	64	CSG

`XmtNcliTranslations`

A translation table that will be used to override the default XmText translations, any translations specified on the `XtNtranslations` resource, and the default Cli-specific translations. See the "Translations" section for more information.

`XmtNdisplayStderr`

Whether this XmtCli widget should display output sent to the standard error stream. If `True`, the stderr stream will be rerouted so that any output sent to it will appear in the XmtCli widget instead of in the *xterm* (or other terminal) that invoked the process. If `False`, the standard error stream will not be rerouted. Because there is only one standard error stream per process, only one XmtCli widget can set this resource `True` at any time.

`XmtNdisplayStdout`

Whether this Cli widget should display output sent to the standard output stream. If `True`, the stdout stream will be rerouted so that any output sent to it will appear in the Cli widget instead of in the *xterm* (or other terminal) that invoked the process. If `False`, the standard output stream will not be rerouted. Because there is only one standard output stream per process, only one Cli widget can set this resource `True` at any time.

`XmtNescapeNewlines`

If `True` (the default), this resource allows the user to continue long lines onto multiple lines. If this resource is `True` and the user types a \ as the last character on the line, then the Cli widget will not call the `XmtNinputCallback` when the user types the **Return** key; instead it will just allow the user to continue input on the next line.

`XmtNfildes`
A UNIX file descriptor. If specified, the Cli widget will display any text that it reads from this descriptor. This file descriptor is usually a pipe established for communication with another process; setting this resource allows a Cli widget to be used to monitor the output of another process.

`XmtNhistory`
A read-only array of strings that contain the command history for the Cli widget. You may not set this resource, but you may query the array and modify the strings it contains.

`XmtNhistoryMaxItems`
The maximum number of lines of user input that will be saved by the command history mechanism. When more command lines than this have been entered, the oldest lines are overwritten. If you set this resource, it will cause the `XmtNhistory` array to be enlarged or shrunk with `realloc()`.

`XmtNhistoryNumItems`
The number of commands that are currently saved by the command history mechanism.

`XmtNinputCallback`
A list of callback procedures that will be invoked when the user enters a command line. They are invoked by the `end-input()` action, which is bound, by default, to the **Return** key. Any text entered by the user since the last invocation of the `end-input()` action will be passed as the third, *`call_data`* argument to the callbacks. This input string does not include a terminating newline character.

`XmtNpageMode`
Whether or not the widget will "page" long blocks of output. If this resource is `True`, then the Cli will simulate a pager like *`more`* when more than one page of output is displayed with intervening input.

`XmtNpageString`
The string to be displayed when the Cli widget is paging long output. The default is "-- Press Spacebar for More --".

`XmtNpageWidget`
A read-only resource that returns the XmLabel widget used to display the `XmtNpageString` message. You might use this resource to set the colors of the page message.

`XmtNprompt`
The string to be automatically displayed whenever the Cli widget is ready to accept input from the user.

`XmtNsaveHistory`
Whether the user's input lines should be saved in the Cli command history buffer. You can set this resource to `False` to disable the saving of lines,

and set it to `True` to re-enable command line saving. Note that setting this resource to `False` does not prevent the user from accessing commands already in the `XmtNhistory` array; it just prevents any new lines from being saved there.

`XmtNsaveLines`
The minimum number of lines of text (input or output) that will be saved by the Cli widget for scrolling. When the number of lines exceeds this number, the widget will periodically trim the number of saved lines so that memory used by the widget does not grow without bounds. Note that this resource specifies the total number of lines saved, not just the number of lines that are saved once they have scrolled out of view.

Callbacks

The Cli widget supports a single callback list, `XmtNinputCallback`. The callbacks on this list are called when the user enters a command line (see the `end-input()` action later in this reference page). The *`call_data`* for this callback is the string entered by the user.

Translations

The Cli widget inherits an unmodified set of the XmText widget translations. When a Cli widget is created, these default XmText resources are overridden, augmented, or replaced by any resources you (or the end user) specified on the `XtNtranslations` resource (and, in X11R5, also any resources specified with the `baseTranslations` pseudo-resource). This is the same process that all widgets follow to determine their translation table. The Cli widget goes two steps further, however: it overrides this resulting translation table with its own internal set of default Cli-specific translations (shown in the table) and then, finally, overrides these with any resources you (or the end-user) have specified on the `XmtNcliTranslations` resource.

The Cli widget's Cli-specific translation table is the following:

```
!<Key>osfUp:                      previous-command()
!<Key>osfDown:                    next-command()
Shift<Key>osfUp:                  scroll-backward()
Shift<Key>osfDown:                scroll-forward()
!Shift<Btn1Down>:                 save-cursor-pos() extend-start()
!<Btn1Down>:                      save-cursor-pos() grab-focus()
~Ctrl ~Meta ~Alt<Btn1Motion>:     extend-adjust()
~Ctrl ~Meta ~Alt<Btn1Up>:         extend-end() restore-cursor-pos()
~Ctrl ~Meta ~Alt<Btn2Down>:       copy-primary()
~Ctrl ~Meta ~Alt<Btn3Down>:       save-cursor-pos() extend-start()
~Ctrl ~Meta ~Alt<Btn3Motion>:     extend-adjust()
~Ctrl ~Meta ~Alt<Btn3Up>:         extend-end() restore-cursor-pos()
!<Key>Return:                     page-or-end-input()
!<Key>osfActivate:                page-or-end-input()
!<Key>space:                      page-or-space()
```

These translations bind the Return key to the `end-input` action, which processes each command line as the user enters it. They bind the up and down arrow keys to the `previous-command` and `next-command` actions, which implement the command history mechanism. The Cli widget does not allow the user to edit anything other than the current line, so these keys are no longer needed for cursor motion. Finally, the translations augment the XmText text selection translations to support *xterm*-style cut-and-paste: mouse button 2 pastes at the cursor location rather than at the mouse pointer location, and mouse button 3 can be used to extend a selection, in the same way that button 1 can be used with the shift key. The `save-cursor-pos` and the `restore-cursor-pos` actions are crucial to allow text to be selected without moving the insertion cursor from its position on the current input line.

Actions

The Cli widget defines ten new action procedures, which are described in the following paragraphs.

`scroll-forward()`
`scroll-backward()`

These actions scroll the Cli widget up or down. By default they scroll by half a page. If passed a number as their first argument, they will scroll by that number of lines, or if passed the string "page" as their first argument, they will scroll by complete pages (where page size depends on the size of the Cli widget.)

`previous-command()`
`next-command()`

These actions implement the Cli command history mechanism. By default they are bound to the up and down arrow keys. *emacs* users might also want to bind them to **Ctrl-P** and **Ctrl-N**, for example.

`beginning-of-line()`

This action moves the cursor to the beginning of the current input line. It is used to override the XmText action of the same name, because the XmText widget and the XmtCli widget have different notions of where the beginning of the line is. In the Cli widget, the beginning of the line is the position immediately following the prompt, which is generally not the first column of the widget. Furthermore, if the user has typed a lot of input that has wrapped onto more than one line, this action will move to the first input character on the first line of that input, not the first character on the current line. Note that this action does not appear in the Cli-specific translation table shown earlier. Because of the way action procedures are scoped, the `beginning-of-line()` binding in the default XmText translation table will refer to this action procedure, and you can invoke it however you normally invoke the `beginning-of-line()` action on your system.

`save-cursor-position()`
`restore-cursor-position()`

These actions are used as a pair at the beginning and end of any sequence of mouse actions that the user is allowed to make. They enforce the rule that the user should not be allowed to move the cursor off the current line of input. Using these actions in conjunction with the standard XmText mouse selection actions allows the user to select text anywhere in the Cli widget by dragging with the mouse, but have the insertion cursor return to its proper place on the current line of input when the selection is complete. These actions do allow the cursor to be moved with the mouse *within* the current line of input; just not off that line.

`page-or-end-input()`
`page-or-space()`

These actions are meant to be bound to the **Return** and **Space** keys. If the Cli widget is currently paging long output, then these actions implement single-line and full-page paging respectively, and if the widget is not currently paging, then `page-or-end-input()` calls the `end-input()` action described below and the `page-or-space()` action calls the XmText `self-insert()` action to insert the space character (or whatever character was used to invoke the action).

`end-input()`

This action tells the Cli widget that the user has entered a line of input. This is the procedure that calls the callbacks on the `XmtNinputCallback` list or arranges for the `XmtCliGets()` function to stop blocking and return the input to its caller. Note that this action does not appear in the default translation table, because it is instead invoked through the `page-or-end-input()` action.

See Also

Chapter 21, *Command-Line Input*
`XmtCliFlush()`, `XmtCliGets()`, `XmtCliPrintf()`,
`XmtCliPuts()`, `XmtCreateCli()`, `XmtCreateScrolledCli()`

Name

XmtCliFlush() — force pending XmtCli output to be displayed.

Synopsis

```
#include <Xmt/Cli.h>
void XmtCliFlush(Widget w)
```

Arguments

Inputs

w The XmtCli widget that is to have its output "flushed."

Description

XmtCliFlush() checks any file descriptors that the specified XmtCli widget is monitoring, and if data is available for reading, causes that data to be displayed in the widget.

If an XmtCli widget is monitoring a pipe or socket with the XmtNfildes resource or has redirected the standard output or standard error streams with XmtNdisplayStdout or XmtNdisplayStderr, then it normally monitors these file descriptors with XtAppAddInput(). Thus the widget detects and displays any output to these sockets only when the application returns to the event loop. If an application needs to force output to be displayed, or will be doing a lot of computation before returning to the event loop, it can use XmtCliFlush() to force any output to be displayed immediately.

Note that any output written to the XmtCli widget with XmtCliPuts() and XmtCliPrintf() is always displayed immediately, and never needs to be flushed with XmtCliFlush(). You will never need to use this function unless you have set one or more of the XmtNfildes, XmtNdisplayStdout, and XmtNdisplayStderr resources.

See Also

Chapter 21, *Command-Line Input*
XmtCli, XmtCliClear(), XmtCliGets(),
XmtCliPrintf(), XmtCliPuts()

XmtCliGets()

Name

XmtCliGets() — get synchronous input from an XmtCli widget.

Synopsis

```
#include <Xmt/Cli.h>
char *XmtCliGets(char *buffer,
                 int buffer_len,
                 Widget w)
```

Arguments

Inputs

buffer_len The number of characters in *buffer*.

w The XmtCli widget from which input is to be read.

Outputs

buffer An array of characters into which user input is stored. No more than *buffer_len*-1 characters will be stored into this buffer, and the input will be null-terminated.

Returns

buffer, the character array into which input is stored.

Description

XmtCliGets() is the XmtCli widget analog to the C library function fgets(). It is a synchronous input function that appears to "block" in an internal event loop, and is designed to be used for simple ports of terminal-based applications to the X toolkit. Note the unusual order of its arguments—the XmtCli widget *w* is last by analogy to the input stream argument to fgets().

XmtCliGets() calls XmProcessTraversal() to give keyboard focus to the XmtCli widget, and calls XtAddGrab() to tell the Intrinsics to ignore user events that occur on any other widgets. Then it enters an internal event loop, processing events until the user has entered a string and typed the **Return** key. When the user completes the input, XmtCliGets() calls XtRemoveGrab() to return event dispatching to normal, and calls XmProcessTraversal() to restore keyboard focus to its previous location. Finally, XmtCliGets() copies the input string (up to a maximum of buffer_len-1 characters) into *buffer*, null-terminates the string, and returns *buffer* as its return value.

See Also

Chapter 21, *Command-Line Input*
XmtCli, XmtCliClear(), XmtCliFlush(),
XmtCliPrintf(), XmtCliPuts()

Name

`XmtCliPrintf()`, `XmtCliPuts()`, `XmtCliClear()` — XmtCli widget output functions.

Synopsis

```
#include <Xmt/Cli.h>
void XmtCliPrintf(Widget w, String format, ...)
```

```
#include <Xmt/Cli.h>
void XmtCliPuts(String s, Widget w)
```

```
#include <Xmt/Cli.h>
void XmtCliClear(Widget w)
```

Arguments

Inputs

w	An XmtCli widget.
format	For `XmtCliPrintf()` only, a `printf()`-style format string.
`...`	For `XmtCliPrintf()` only, a `printf()`-style variable length argument list containing one argument of appropriate type for each `%` substitution that occurs in *format*.
s	For `XmtCliPuts()` only, the string to be displayed. This string may not contain `printf()`-style substitutions.

Description

`XmtCliPrintf()` appends a `printf()`-style formatted string to the text displayed in the specified XmtCli widget.

`XmtCliPuts()` appends the string *s* to the XmtCli widget *w*. Note that this function is unusual in that it does not take the XmtCli widget as its first argument. It takes the widget after the string for analogy to the C library function `fputs()` which takes the output stream as its second argument.

Both `XmtCliPrintf()` and `XmtCliPuts()` will automatically scroll the XmtCli widget, if necessary, so that all of the output text is visible. If there is a partially typed line of input displayed in the widget, then the output string appears after all other output, but before the pending input string—this means that the user's line of input is not disrupted.

`XmtCliClear()` erases all visible text in *w*, and also deletes any text that had scrolled off the top of that widget. After calling `XmtCliClear()`, the widget will be blank, and the user will not be able to scroll up to see previous lines. This function does not affect the command history buffer, however.

See Also

Chapter 21, *Command-Line Input*
XmtCli, `XmtCliFlush()`, `XmtCliGets()`

XmtConvertStringTo<*Type*>()

Name

XmtConvertStringTo<*Type*> — "new style" Xt resource converters for various types.

Synopsis

```
#include <Xmt/Converters.h>
Boolean XmtConvertStringToBitmap(dpy, args, num_args, from, to,
                                  data)

Boolean XmtConvertStringToBitmask(dpy, args, num_args, from, to,
                                   data)

Boolean XmtConvertStringToCallback(dpy, args, num_args, from, to,
                                    data)

Boolean XmtConvertStringToColorTable(dpy, args, num_args, from,
                                      to, data)

Boolean XmtConvertStringToPixel(dpy, args, num_args, from, to, data)

Boolean XmtConvertStringToPixmap(dpy, args, num_args, from, to, data)

Boolean XmtConvertStringToPixmapList(dpy, args, num_args, from, to,
                                      data)

Boolean XmtConvertStringToStringList(dpy, args, num_args, from, to,
                                      data)

Boolean XmtConvertStringToWidget(dpy, args, num_args, from, to, data)

Boolean XmtConvertStringToXmFontList(dpy, args, num_args, from, to,
                                      data)

Boolean XmtConvertStringToXmString(dpy, args, num_args, from, to,
                                    data)

Boolean XmtConvertStringToXmtMenuItems(dpy, args, num_args, from, to,
                                        data)
     Display *dpy;
     XrmValue *args;
     Cardinal *num_args;
     XrmValue  *from, *to;
     XtPointer *data;
```

Arguments

Inputs

dpy	The Display for the conversion.
args	An array of arguments for the converter.
num_args	The number of elements in *args*.
from	The address and size of the value to convert.
to	The address and size of memory in which the converted value is to be stored.

Outputs

to Returns the actual address at which the converted value was stored, and the actual number of bytes it occupies.

data Arbitrary data returned by the converter for use with the resource caching mechanism.

Returns

`True` for successful conversion; `False` otherwise.

Description

These functions are the various resource converters used by the Xmt library. They are all of type `XtTypeConverter`—"new style" Xt resource converters, designed to be registered with `XtSetTypeConverter()`. Note that these functions should never be called directly—they should be registered with the Xt resource manager, and invoked when a resource conversion is requested.

Usage

The easiest way to register these type converters is to use the registration functions that Xmt provides. These functions all have names of the form `XmtRegister`<*Type*>`Converter()`.

See Also

`XmtRegister`<*Type*>`Converter()`, `XtAppSetTypeConverter()`, `XtSetTypeConverter()`, `XtTypeConverter()`

Xmt{Create,Change,Destroy}PixmapIcon()

Name

XmtCreatePixmapIcon(), XmtChangePixmapIcon(), XmtDestroy-PixmapIcon() — handle non-rectangular multi-color window manager icons.

Synopsis

```
#include <Xmt/Icon.h>
void XmtCreatePixmapIcon(Widget w, Pixmap icon, Pixmap shape)

void XmtChangePixmapIcon(Widget w, Pixmap icon, Pixmap shape)

void XmtDestroyPixmapIcon(Widget w)
```

Arguments

Inputs

w — Any child of a toplevel shell (i.e., not a dialog box) that is to have its icon window created, changed, or destroyed.

icon — A multi-color pixmap (i.e., not a monochrome bitmap) to be displayed in the icon window. It should have the same depth as the default depth of the screen.

shape — A bitmask that defines the shape of the icon window, or None for a rectangular icon. This bitmask will be ignored if the X server does not support the SHAPE extension to the X protocol.

Description

Shell widgets allow you to specify icons to be displayed by the window manager with the XtNiconPixmap and XtNiconMask arguments. Unfortunately, XtNiconPixmap only accepts two-color bitmaps, and XtNiconMask is ignored by most window managers. If you want the window manager to display a multi-color or non-rectangular icon for your windows, you must specify the icon window yourself with the XtNiconWindow resource. These functions make this process much easier.

XmtCreatePixmapIcon() creates an icon window for the shell widget of *w*, and displays the pixmap *icon* in it. If the *shape* bitmask is specified and the X server supports the SHAPE extension, XmtCreatePixmapIcon() will make the icon window non-rectangular, giving it the specified shape. Note that some window managers will reparent a non-rectangular icon window into a rectangular frame, defeating the purpose of the *shape* bitmask.

XmtChangePixmapIcon() can be used to change the pixmap displayed in a shell's icon window, to change the shape of that window. Both the *icon* and *shape* arguments are optional to this function—pass None if you do not want to change their current values.

`XmtDestroyPixmapIcon()` destroys the icon window associated with the shell of the widget *w*. The icon window will also be automatically destroyed when the shell is destroyed.

See Also

Chapter 5, *Using Icons*
Chapter 15, *Working with the Window Manager*

XmtCreate[Query]Child()

Name

`XmtCreateChild()`, `XmtCreateQueryChild()` — create a named child and all of its descendants.

Synopsis

```
Widget XmtCreateChild(Widget parent, String name)

Widget XmtCreateQueryChild(Widget parent, String name,
                           { String child_name, Widget *child_address, }
                            NULL)
```

Arguments

Inputs

parent The widget that is to have a named child created.

name The name of the child to be created.

child_name The name of a widget to be returned. May be repeated any number of times in a NULL-terminated variable-length argument list.

Outputs

child_address
The address at which the widget specified by *child_name* is to be stored. May be repeated any number of times in a NULL-terminated variable-length argument list.

Returns

The newly created child of *parent*.

Description

`XmtCreateChild()` and `XmtCreateQueryChild()` are similar to `XmtCreateChildren()` and `XmtCreateQueryChildren()`. While the latter functions read the `xmtChildren` resource of a widget and create *all* of its children, `XmtCreateChild()` and `XmtCreateQueryChild()` create only a single child of the *parent* widget. The name of this child is specified by *name*, and its type is determined by reading its `xmtType` resource, which must specify a registered widget type or template, as described in Chapter 11, *Automatic Widget Creation.*

Once `XmtCreateChild()` and `XmtCreateQueryChild()` have created this first named child, they read the child's `xmtChildren` resource, and proceed to create all of its descendants just as `XmtCreateChildren()` and `XmtCreateQueryChildren()` do. Once all descendants have been created, these functions return the original child widget.

Like XmtCreateQueryChildren(), XmtCreateQueryChild() can return pointers to widgets it creates in the *child_address* arguments in its NULL-terminated variable-length argument list.

Usage

These functions are useful when you want to defer creation of some subtree of your widget hierarchy. XmtBuildDialog() and XmtBuildToplevel() are also useful for this purpose.

See Also

Chapter 11, *Automatic Widget Creation*
XmtBuild[Query]Application(), XmtBuild[Query]Dialog(), XmtBuild[Query]Toplevel(), XmtCreate[Query]Children()

XmtCreate[Query]Children()

Name

XmtCreateChildren(), XmtCreateQueryChildren() — create the descendants of a widget described in the resource file.

Synopsis

```
#include <Xmt/Create.h>
void XmtCreateChildren(Widget parent)
```

```
#include <Xmt/Create.h>
void XmtCreateQueryChildren(Widget parent,
                            { String child_name, Widget *child_address, }
                             NULL)
```

Arguments

Inputs

parent The widget that is to have its descendants created.

child_name The name of a widget to be returned. May be repeated any number of times in a NULL-terminated variable-length argument list.

Outputs

child_address
The address at which the widget specified by *child_name* is to be stored. May be repeated any number of times in a NULL-terminated variable-length argument list.

Description

XmtCreateChildren() and XmtCreateQueryChildren() read the xmtChildren "pseudo-resource" of the specified *parent* widget from the application resource database and create the children specified by that resource. They repeat this process for each newly created child, recursively creating an entire widget tree.

A typical xmtChildren resource in a resource database might look like the following:

```
saveas.xmtChildren: XmLabel prompt;\
                    XmTextField input;\
                    XmSeparator sep;\
                    XmPushButton okay, cancel, help;
```

The formal definition of the xmtChildren grammar is the following:

```
xmtChildren:: { declaration }
declaration:: { modifier } type child {"," child} ";"
modifier::    "managed" | "unmanaged" | registered style name
type::        registered widget type | registered template name
child::       name of child to be created
```

The grammar is explained in detail in Chapter 11, *Automatic Widget Creation*. Note that in order for widgets to be described in a resource file, their types must first be registered in your C code. You can do this with `XmtRegisterWidgetClass()`, `XmtRegisterWidgetConstructor()`, or related functions such as `XmtRegisterMotifWidgets()`. The `xmtChildren` syntax also supports named styles and templates. These are reusable sets of widget resources and predefined widget subtrees. They are explained in Chapter 11.

`XmtCreateQueryChildren()` works like `XmtCreateChildren()`, but it can optionally return pointers to some of the widgets it creates. It takes a `NULL`-terminated, variable-length argument list of pairs of widget names and addresses of widget variables. Each time `XmtCreateQueryChildren()` creates a widget child, it checks the list of *`child_name`* arguments, and if the name of the newly created child matches one of those names, then the pointer to that widget is stored at the corresponding `child_address`.

`XmtCreateChildren()` and `XmtCreateQueryChildren()` also read other pseudo-resources besides `xmtChildren`. The `xmtRequires` resource specifies resource files to be included before widgets are created, and three different creation callback resources specify procedures to be invoked at different points in the widget creation process. These other resources are summarized below, and explained in detail in Chapter 11.

`xmtRequires`
: Specifies one or more files to be looked up and read into the resource database. This resource works like `#include` in C code. It is read and processed for the specified *`parent`* widget and for each child widget, just before the child is created.

`xmtCreationCallback`
: This resource is read for each child that is created, but not for the *`parent`* widget. It specifies a list of procedures to be invoked directly after the child is created.

`xmtChildrenCreationCallback`
: This resource is read for each child that is created, but not for the *`parent`* widget. It specifies a list of procedures to be invoked for the child after that child's own children are created.

`xmtManagedCreationCallback`
: This resource is read for each child that is created, but not for the *`parent`* widget. It specifies a list of procedures to be invoked for the child after it and its descendents have been created and after it has been managed.

Usage

Creating widgets one-by-one by calling widget constructor functions is often one of the most tedious parts of GUI programming. Describing your widget hierarchy in a resource file with the `xmtChildren` resource is easier, especially while prototyping. In most of the Xmt applications, you will call

XmtCreateChildren() or XmtCreateQueryChildren() as part of your initialization code in main(). It is common to pass your root shell widget as *parent*, and to call one of these functions immediately before calling XtRealizeWidget() and XtAppMainLoop().

There are a number of variants on these functions. XmtCreateChild() and XmtCreateQueryChild() create a single named child of a widget, and then proceed to create all the descendants of that child. XmtBuildDialog() and XmtBuildQueryDialog() create an XmDialogShell widget, and then create all the descendants of that dialog. This is useful for deferring the creation of dialog boxes until they are needed. Similar functions exist for creating TopLevelShell and ApplicationShell widgets and their children.

See Also

Chapter 11, *Automatic Widget Creation*
XmtBuild[Query]Application(), XmtBuild[Query]Dialog(), XmtBuild[Query]Toplevel(), XmtCreate[Query]Child(), XmtRegisterMotifWidgets(), XmtRegisterPopupClass(), XmtRegisterPopupConstructor(), Xmt[Va]RegisterWidgetClass(), Xmt[Va]RegisterWidgetConstructor(), XmtRegisterWidgetTypes(), XmtRegisterXmtWidgets()

Name

XmtCreateColorTable(), XmtDestroyColorTable(), XmtColorTableGetParent(), XmtColorTableSetParent() — create and manipulate color tables.

Synopsis

```
#include <Xmt/Color.h>
XmtColorTable XmtCreateColorTable(XmtColorTable parent)

void XmtDestroyColorTable(XmtColorTable table)

XmtColorTable XmtColorTableGetParent(XmtColorTable table)

void XmtColorTableSetParent(XmtColorTable table, XmtColorTable parent)
```

Arguments

Inputs

table — The color table that is to be destroyed, or have its parent queried or set.

parent — The parent color table for the newly created color table or for the specified *table*.

Returns

XmtCreateColorTable() returns a newly created color table. XmtColorTableGetParent() returns the parent of the specified color table.

Description

XmtCreateColorTable() returns a newly created XmtColorTable with no entries. An XmtColorTable maps symbolic color names to actual color names. Symbolic colors can be defined in an XmtColorTable with XmtRegisterColor() and related functions, and can be looked up with XmtLookupColorName().

The *parent* argument specifies another XmtColorTable to which the newly created table is "chained." XmtLookupColorName() looks up symbolic color names by first searching the specified color table, and then by searching its parent, its parent's parent, and so on up the chain, until a color table with a NULL parent is encountered.

XmtDestroyColorTable() frees memory associated with the specified XmtColorTable. Once this function is called, the specified color table should no longer be used.

XmtColorTableGetParent() returns the parent color table of *table*.

XmtColorTableSetParent() sets the parent of *table* to *parent*, thereby chaining the two tables for color lookups with XmtLookupColorName().

See Also

Chapter 4, *Using Color*
`XmtLookupColorName()`, `XmtRegisterColor`,
`XmtRegisterColors`, `XmtRegisterPixel`,
`XmtRegisterStandardColors`, `XmtVaRegisterColors`

Xmt{Create,Lookup}WidgetType()

Name

XmtCreateWidgetType(), XmtLookupWidgetType() — create an instance of a widget type, look up a widget type by name.

Synopsis

```
#include <Xmt/WidgetType.h>
XmtWidgetType *XmtLookupWidgetType(String typename)
Widget XmtCreateWidgetType(String name, XmtWidgetType *type, Widget parent,
                                 ArgList args, Cardinal num_args)
```

Arguments

Inputs

typename	The name of a widget type to be looked up.
name	The name of the widget to be created.
type	The type of the widget to be created.
parent	The parent of the widget to be created.
args	An array of resource name/value pairs to set on the newly created widget.
num_args	The number of elements in *args*.

Returns

XmtLookupWidgetType() returns the XmtWidgetType structure of the named widget type, or NULL if no widget type was registered with that name.

XmtCreateWidgetType() returns a newly created widget with the specified name, type, parent, and resources.

Description

XmtLookupWidgetType() and XmtCreateWidgetType() form the basis for the Xmt automatic widget creation facility. You can use these functions to implement an automatic widget creation scheme based on your own widget hierarchy description.

XmtLookupWidgetType() looks up the XmtWidgetType record for a registered widget type. This structure contains all the information XmtCreateWidgetType() needs to create an instance of the specified type. Note that XmtCreateWidgetType() takes arguments that are much like those of XtCreateWidget().

See Also

Chapter 11, *Automatic Widget Creation*
XmtRegisterMotifWidgets(), XmtRegisterPopupClass(), XmtRegisterPopupConstructor(), XmtRegisterWidgetClass(), XmtRegisterWidgetConstructor(), XmtRegisterXmtWidgets(), XmtVaRegisterWidgetClasses(), XmtVaRegisterWidgetConstructors()

XmtCreate{Pixmap,XImage}FromXmtImage()

Name

XmtCreatePixmapFromXmtImage(), XmtCreateXImageFromXmt-Image() — create a pixmap or XImage from an XmtImage.

Synopsis

```
#include <Xmt/Xpm.h>
Boolean XmtCreatePixmapFromXmtImage(Widget widget, Drawable win,
                                    Visual *visual, Colormap cmap,
                                    unsigned int depth, XmtColorTable colors,
                                    XmtImage *xmtimage,
                                    Pixmap *image_return, Pixmap *mask_return,
                                    Pixel **allocated_pixels_return,
                                    int *num_allocated_pixels_return)
Boolean XmtCreateXImageFromXmtImage(Widget widget,
                                    Visual *visual, Colormap cmap,
                                    unsigned int depth, XmtColorTable colors,
                                    XmtImage *xmtimage,
                                    XImage **image_return, XImage **mask_return,
                                    Pixel **allocated_pixels_return,
                                    int *num_allocated_pixels_return)
```

Arguments

Inputs

widget Any widget in the application. Specifies the display and screen for which the pixmap or XImage is to be created.

win For XmtCreatePixmapFromXmtImage() only, any Window or Pixmap on the same screen that the pixmap is to be created on.

visual The Visual for which the pixmap or XImage is to be displayed. If NULL is specified, the default Visual of the default screen of the display of *widget* will be used.

cmap The colormap in which colors will be allocated for the pixmap or XImage. If None is specified, the default colormap of the default screen of the display of *widget* will be used.

depth The depth of the or XImage to be created. If 0 is specified, the default depth of the default screen of the display of *widget* will be used.

colors An XmtColorTable used to look up any symbolic colors specified in the XmtImage. If NULL is specified, any symbolic colors will be ignored.

xmtimage The XmtImage to be instantiated as a pixmap or XImage.

Outputs

image_return The address at which the pixmap or XImage version of *xmtimage* will be returned.

mask_return The address at which the bitmask, if any, for *xmtimage* will be returned, as a pixmap or XImage. You may specify NULL if you are not interested in mask data for the XmtImage.

allocated_pixels_return
The address of a variable of type `Pixel *` at which an allocated array of the `Pixel` values that were allocated for the pixmap or XImage will be stored. You may specify NULL if you are not interested in this return value. This returned array must be freed with `XtFree()` when it is no longer needed.

num_allocated_pixels_return
The address of an `int` variable in which the number of elements of the *allocated_pixels_return* array will be returned, or NULL if you are not interested in this value.

Returns

`True` if the pixmap or XImage was created successfully, `False` otherwise.

Description

The functions `XmtCreatePixmapFromXmtImage()` and `XmtCreateXImageFromXmtImage()` convert an `XmtImage` to a Pixmap and to an XImage, using the display of the specified widget, and the specified visual, colormap, depth, and table of symbolic colors. If successful, these functions store the converted image at the address specified by *image_return* and return `True`. They may also return a bitmask for the image at the address specified by *mask_return*. If the conversion fails, these functions return `False`.

An `XmtImage` structure is the processed form of an XPM file or XPM data returned by `XmtParseXpmFile()` and `XmtParseXpmData()`. The XPM format allows different color specifications for different visual types, so that when an XmtImage is converted for a color screen it might use a different color scheme than it would when converted for a grayscale screen. The XPM image format and `XmtImage` structure support symbolic colornames which are looked up during the conversion using the `XmtColorTable` *colors*. The XPM image format and the XmtImage structure also support the special "transparent" color named "None". If `mask_return` is non-NULL, and if the image contains any of these "transparent" bits, then this function will also create and return a "bitmask" for the image—a single-plane pixmap or XImage that has bits set for non-transparent pixels and cleared for transparent pixels.

In order to convert an `XmtImage` to a pixmap or to an XImage, this function must allocate colors. If *allocated_pixels_return* and *num_allocated_pixels_return* are not NULL, then they will be filled in with an array of the `Pixel` values that were allocated during the conversion, and a count of the elements in that array. This information can be used to deallocate those pixels when the pixmap is no longer needed. Note that the array of `Pixel` values is allocated memory, and should be freed with `XtFree()` once the Pixel values have been released.

When they are no longer needed, the pixmaps or XImages returned in *image_return* and *mask_return* should be freed with `XFreePixmap()` or `XDestroyImage()`.

See Also

Chapter 5, *Using Icons*
Chapter 4, *Using Color*
`XmtGetPixmap()`, `XmtLookupPixmap()`,
`XmtParseXpmData()`, `XmtParseXpmFile()`

Name

XmtCreate<*Widget*>() — constructor functions for various widget classes.

Synopsis

```
#include <Xmt/Chooser.h>
Widget XmtCreateChooser(parent, name, args, num_args)

#include <Xmt/Cli.h>
Widget XmtCreateCli(parent, name, args, num_args)

#include <Xmt/HelpBox.h>
Widget XmtCreateHelpBox(parent, name, args, num_args)

#include <Xmt/HelpBox.h>
Widget XmtCreateHelpDialog(parent, name, args, num_args)

#include <Xmt/InputField.h>
Widget XmtCreateInputField(parent, name, args, num_args)

#include <Xmt/Layout.h>
Widget XmtCreateLayout(parent, name, args, num_args)

#include <Xmt/LayoutG.h>
Widget XmtCreateLayoutBox(parent, name, args, num_args)

#include <Xmt/LayoutG.h>
Widget XmtCreateLayoutCol(parent, name, args, num_args)

#include <Xmt/Layout.h>
Widget XmtCreateLayoutDialog(parent, name, args, num_args)

#include <Xmt/LayoutG.h>
Widget XmtCreateLayoutPixmap(parent, name, args, num_args)

#include <Xmt/LayoutG.h>
Widget XmtCreateLayoutRow(parent, name, args, num_args)

#include <Xmt/LayoutG.h>
Widget XmtCreateLayoutSeparator(parent, name, args, num_args)

#include <Xmt/LayoutG.h>
Widget XmtCreateLayoutSpace(parent, name, args, num_args)

#include <Xmt/LayoutG.h>
Widget XmtCreateLayoutString(parent, name, args, num_args)

#include <Xmt/Menu.h>
Widget XmtCreateMenuPane(w, name, args, num_args)

#include <Xmt/Menu.h>
Widget XmtCreateMenubar(w, name, args, num_args)

#include <Xmt/MsgLine.h>
Widget XmtCreateMsgLine(parent, name, args, num_args)

#include <Xmt/Menu.h>
Widget XmtCreateOptionMenu(w, name, args, num_args)
```

```
#include <Xmt/Menu.h>
Widget XmtCreatePopupMenu(w, name, args, num_args)

#include <Xmt/Cli.h>
Widget XmtCreateScrolledCli(parent, name, args, num_args)

#include <Xmt/WorkingBox.h>
Widget XmtCreateWorkingBox(parent, name, args, num_args)

#include <Xmt/WorkingBox.h>
Widget XmtCreateWorkingDialog(parent, name, args, num_args)

      Widget   parent;
      String   name;
      ArgList  args;
      Cardinal num_args;
```

Arguments

Inputs

parent The parent of the widget to be created.

name The name of the widget to be created.

args An array of resource name/value pairs to be set on the new widget.

num_args The number of elements in *args*.

Returns

The newly created widget.

Description

These functions are standard Motif-style widget constructors. Some create single widgets and are simply alternatives to calling `XtCreateWidget()`, and others are "convenience constructors" that create more than one widget or have additional behavior. The table explains each constructor's function.

Function	Creates
`XmtCreateChooser()`	XmtChooser widget
`XmtCreateCli()`	XmtCli widget
`XmtCreateHelpBox()`	XmtHelpBox widget
`XmtCreateHelpDialog()`	XmtHelpBox widget in an XmDialogShell
`XmtCreateInputField()`	XmtInputField widget
`XmtCreateLayout()`	XmtLayout widget
`XmtCreateLayoutBox()`	XmtLayoutBox gadget
`XmtCreateLayoutCol()`	XmtLayoutBox gadget with `XmtNorientatation` set to `XmVERTICAL`
`XmtCreateLayoutDialog()`	XmtLayout widget in an XmDialogShell
`XmtCreateLayoutPixmap()`	XmtLayoutPixmap gadget

Function	*Creates*
`XmtCreateLayoutRow()`	XmtLayoutBox gadget with `Xmt-Norientatation` set to `XmHORIZONTAL`
`XmtCreateLayoutSeparator()`	XmtLayoutSeparator gadget
`XmtCreateLayoutSpace()`	XmtLayoutSpace gadget
`XmtCreateLayoutString()`	XmtLayoutString gadget
`XmtCreateMenuPane()`	XmtMenu widget, configured as a menu pane, and an XmMenuShell for that pane if no shared menu pane could be found
`XmtCreateMenubar()`	XmtMenu widget, configured as a menu bar
`XmtCreateMsgLine()`	XmtMsgLine widget
`XmtCreateOptionMenu()`	XmtMenu widget, configured as an option menu
`XmtCreatePopupMenu()`	XmtMenu widget, configured as a popup menu pane, and an XmMenuShell widget for that pane
`XmtCreateScrolledCli()`	An XmtCli widget in an XmScrolledWindow
`XmtCreateWorkingBox()`	XmtWorkingBox widget
`XmtCreateWorkingDialog()`	XmtWorkingBox in an XmDialogShell

See Also

`XtCreateWidget()`

XmtCreateXmString()

Name

`XmtCreateXmString()` — create a multi-line, multi-font XmString.

Synopsis

```
#include <Xmt/Xmt.h>
XmString XmtCreateXmString(String s)
```

Arguments

Inputs

s The string that is to be converted to an XmString.

Returns

An XmString formatted as specified in *s*.

Description

`XmtCreateXmString()` converts the string *s* to an `XmString`. Where the newline character (\n) appears within *s*, the resulting XmString will have a line break. Where the font changing sequence `@f` appears in *s*, the `XmString` will switch fonts to the font specified by the characters following the `@f` sequence.

Three syntaxes for specifying a font are supported, each derived from the *troff* text formatter. If the font name is a single character, such as 'B', that character may be specified immediately following the `f`: `@fB`. If the font name is two characters long, such as "CW", those characters may be specified following an `(`: `@f(CW`. Finally, whatever the length of the font name, it may be specified within open and close square brackets following the `f`: `@f[BOLD]`. Any font names used in the string *s* should be defined in the corresponding `XmFontList` with which the returned XmString will be displayed.

The `XmString` returned by this function should be freed with `XmStringFree()` when it is no longer needed. All Motif widgets that accept `XmString` resources make a copy of that string, so that if an `XmString` is created only so that it may be set on a widget resource, then it may be freed once the widget is created or the resource is set.

See Also

Chapter 3, *Displaying Text*
`XmStringFree()`, `XmtRegisterXmStringConverter()`

Name

`XmtDialogBindResourceList()` — use Xmt automatic dialog data transfer features with widgets that are not dialogs.

Synopsis

```
#include <Xmt/Dialog.h>
void XmtDialogBindResourceList(Widget w,
                               XtResourceList resources,
                               Cardinal num_resources)
```

Arguments

Inputs

w — The root of the widget subtree (usually a shell) that is to be used with the Xmt automatic dialog facilities.

resources — An array of resources that name data values and describe how they are stored in a data structure. This is similar to the list that would be passed to `XmtBuildDialog()`.

num_resources — The number of elements in the *resources* array.

Description

In order for the Xmt automatic dialog data transfer facilities to work, the widgets involved must be described with the `xmtChildren` syntax, and must have a resource list associated with them when they are created. Normally this resource list is supplied in a call to `XmtBuildDialog()` or `XmtBuildQueryDialog()`. On occasion, however, you may want to use the Xmt automatic data-transfer mechanism with widgets that are not actually in dialog boxes, or for some other reason are not created with these special functions.

You can, in fact, use the dialog data transfer mechanisms with any widgets described with the `xmtChildren` resource, but in order to do so, you must associate an `XtResourceList` with them by calling `XmtDialogBindResourceList()`. This function associates the resource list *resources* with the widget (generally a shell widget) *w*. You must call this function *before* you create the children of *w* with `XmtCreateChildren()` or some other function.

See Also

Chapter 29, *Custom Dialogs and Automatic Dialog Management*
`XmtBuildDialog()`, `XmtBuildQueryDialog()`,
`XmtDialogCancelCallback()`, `XmtDialogDo()`,
`XmtDialogDoSync()`, `XmtDialogGetDataAddress()`,
`XmtDialogGetDialogValues()`, `XmtDialogOkayCallback()`,
`XmtDialogSetDialogValues()`, `XmtDialogSetReturnValue()`

XmtDialogDo[Sync]()

Name

XmtDialogDo(), XmtDialogDoSync() — transfer data to an automatic dialog and display it.

Synopsis

```
#include <Xmt/Dialog.h>
void XmtDialogDo(Widget dialog, XtPointer address)

Boolean XmtDialogDoSync(Widget dialog, XtPointer address)
```

Arguments

Inputs

dialog — The child of the dialog shell of an automatic dialog box—i.e., the widget returned by a call to XmtBuildDialog() or XmtBuildQueryDialog().

address — The address of a data structure from which data is to be transferred to the dialog box, and in which the user's input data will later be stored.

Outputs

address — XmtDialogDo() does not modify this field, but when XmtDialogDoSync() returns True, the structure at this address will contain the user's input values.

Returns

XmtDialogDoSync() returns True if the user popped the dialog down normally, and returns False if the user cancelled the dialog with a **Cancel** button.

Description

XmtDialogDo() calls XmtDialogSetDialogValues() to transfer the data pointed to by *address* to the widgets in the dialog box *dialog*. Then it internally associates *address* with *dialog* for later use, pops up the dialog box by calling XtManageChild() on *dialog*, and returns.

XmtDialogDo() is designed to be used with a callback procedure that takes the opposite actions—pops the dialog box down, and transfers the user's input values from the dialog widgets back into the specified data structure. You can write a callback that does this by using XmtDialogGetDataAddress() to look up the stored *address* for a dialog, and then using XmtDialogGetDialogValues() to transfer the dialog data to the structure. Xmt provides predefined callbacks that do just this—XmtDialogOkayCallback(), for example, is designed to be registered on the **OK** button of a dialog box managed with XmtDialogDo().

XmtDialogDoSync() works like XmtDialogDo(), but is usually more convenient. Instead of returning after popping up the dialog box, it enters an internal event loop—so that it appears to block— until the user pops the dialog down.

Like `XmtDialogDo()`, `XmtDialogDoSync()` must be used in conjunction with special callback procedures. If the user clicks the **OK** button or some other button that invokes `XmtDialogOkayCallback()`, then that callback will copy the user's input to the structure at *`address`*, and will pop down the dialog box. It will also cause `XmtDialogDoSync()` to exit its event loop and return `True`. On the other hand, if the user selects the **Cancel** button, or some other button that invokes the `XmtDialogCancelCallback()`, then that callback will pop down the dialog without modifying data at *`address`*, and will cause `XmtDialogDoSync()` to exit its loop and return `False`. If you write your own dialog callback procedures, you can tell `XmtDialogDoSync()` to stop blocking and return a value by calling `XmtDialogSetReturnValue()`.

`XmtDialogDoSync()` performs synchronous input, and to prevent its internal event loops from becoming nested arbitrarily deep, it should only be used with modal dialogs.

See Also

Chapter 29, *Custom Dialogs and Automatic Dialog Management*
`XmtDialogCancelCallback()`, `XmtDialogGetDataAddress()`,
`XmtDialogGetDefaultValues()`, `XmtDialogGetDialogValues()`,
`XmtDialogOkayCallback()`, `XmtDialogSetDialogValues()`,
`XmtDialogSetReturnValue()`

XmtDialogGetDefaultValues()

Name

XmtDialogGetDefaultValues() — read default data values for a dialog from the resource database.

Synopsis

```
#include <Xmt/Dialog.h>
void XmtDialogGetDefaultValues(Widget dialog, XtPointer address,
                               ArgList args, Cardinal num_args)
```

Arguments

Inputs

dialog — The dialog that is to have its default data values looked up. This is a widget returned by a previous call to XmtBuildDialog() or XmtBuildQueryDialog().

args — An optional array of resource name/value pairs which will be used to hardcode some of the default values for the dialog.

num_args — The number of elements in *args*.

Outputs

address — The address of a data structure in which the dialogs default values will be stored.

Description

XmtDialogGetDefaultValues() has *dialog* and *address* arguments just as XmtDialogGetDialogValues() and XmtDialogSetDialogValues() do. Instead of transferring data from or to the widgets of a dialog box, however, this function looks up default values for each of the dialog data items and stores them in a structure. If you call this function before popping up your dialogs, it will allow the user or the system administrator to customize the dialog defaults to their personal or site preferences.

XmtDialogGetDefaultValues() looks up the resource list that was associated with *dialog* when it was created by XmtBuildDialog() or XmtBuildQueryDialog(). It uses this resource list in a call to XtGetSubresources() to obtain default values from the *args* argument list and the resource database and store them in the structure at *address*.

If a resource name appears in the *args* array, then its corresponding value is used as the default. If a hardcoded default does not appear here, then the resource is looked up in the resource database as a subpart of *w*. The name of the subpart is xmtDefaults. (For a resource named orientation of a dialog box named *print, the default would be looked up as *print.xmtDefaults.orientation. If a default value is not found in *args* or in the resource database, then the default comes from the resource list itself—from the default_type and *default_addr* fields of the XtResource structure.

See Also

Chapter 29, *Custom Dialogs and Automatic Dialog Management*
`XmtBuildDialog()`, `XmtBuildQueryDialog()`, `XmtDialogCancelCallback()`, `XmtDialogDo()`, `XmtDialogDoSync()`, `XmtDialogGetDataAddress()`, `XmtDialogGetDialogValues()`, `XmtDialogOkayCallback()`, `XmtDialogSetDialogValues()`, `XmtDialogSetReturnValue()`

XmtDialog{Get,Set}DialogValues()

Name

XmtDialogGetDialogValues(), XmtDialogSetDialogValues() — transfer values between the fields of a data structure and the widgets of a dialog box.

Synopsis

```
#include <Xmt/Dialog.h>
void XmtDialogGetDialogValues(Widget dialog, XtPointer address)

void XmtDialogSetDialogValues(Widget dialog, XtPointer address)
```

Arguments

Inputs

dialog Any widget in a dialog box created with XmtBuildDialog() or XmtBuildQueryDialog()—generally the dialog shell or the child of that shell.

address The address of a data structure from which or to which data is to be transferred.

Description

XmtDialogGetDialogValues() and XmtDialogSetDialogValues() first look up the resource list associated with the dialog box of the widget *dialog*. This is the resource list that was specified in the call to XmtBuildDialog() or XmtBuildQueryDialog() when the dialog was created. (Or it is the resource list specified with XmtDialogBindResourceList() before *dialog* was created.) Each element in this array of resources describes a field in the data structure pointed to by *address*, and each element may also be bound to a widget in the dialog box specified by *dialog* (using a special syntax in the xmtChildren resource.) See Chapter 29, *Custom Dialogs and Automatic Dialog Management*, for details on these mappings between the data structure, the resource list, and the widgets of the dialog box.

For each element of the resource list, XmtDialogGetDialogValues() reads a data value from a widget in the dialog box and stores it into a field in the data structure pointed to by *address*.

XmtDialogSetDialogValues() does the opposite: for each element in the resource list, it copies a value from the data structure and stores it into the corresponding widget in the dialog box.

The actual job of querying and setting values on particular widgets in the dialog is done by "get value" and "set value" procedures registered for widgets of those types. See Chapter 29 and XmtRegisterWidgetTypes() for information.

See Also

Chapter 29, *Custom Dialogs and Automatic Dialog Management*
`XmtBuildDialog()`, `XmtBuildQueryDialog()`,
`XmtDialogBindResourceList()`, `XmtDialogDo()`,
`XmtDialogGetDefaultValues()`

XmtDialog{Okay,Cancel,Apply,Reset,Done}Callback()

Name

XmtDialog{Okay,Cancel,Apply,Reset,Done}Callback(), XmtDialogGetDataAddress(), XmtDialogSetReturnValue() — predefined callbacks for use with automatic dialogs and functions for writing custom dialog callbacks.

Synopsis

```
#include <Xmt/Dialog.h>
void XmtDialogOkayCallback(Widget w, XtPointer client_data,
                           XtPointer data)

void XmtDialogCancelCallback(Widget w, XtPointer client_data,
                             XtPointer data)

void XmtDialogApplyCallback(Widget w, XtPointer client_data,
                            XtPointer data)

void XmtDialogResetCallback(Widget w, XtPointer client_data,
                            XtPointer data)

void XmtDialogDoneCallback(Widget w, XtPointer client_data,
                           XtPointer data)

XtPointer XmtDialogGetDataAddress(Widget dialog)

void XmtDialogSetReturnValue(Widget dialog, Boolean value)
```

Arguments

Inputs

w	The widget on which the callback was registered.
client_data	This argument is unused; register these callbacks with NULL *client_data*.
data	This argument is also unused.
dialog	For XmtDialogGetDataAddress() and XmtDialogSetReturnValue(), any widget in an Xmt automatic dialog.
value	For XmtDialogSetReturnValue(), the Boolean value to be returned by XmtDialogDoSync().

Returns

XmtDialogGetDataAddress() returns the *address* passed in the preceding call to XmtDialogDo() or XmtDialogDoSync() for the dialog specified by *dialog*.

Description

The first five of these functions are predefined callback procedures intended to be registered on buttons in automatic dialog boxes created with `XmtBuildDialog()` or `XmtBuildQueryDialog()` and managed with `XmtDialogDo()` or `XmtDialogDoSync()`. The remaining two are lower-level procedures that you can use to write your own custom callbacks for use with `XmtDialogDo()` and `XmtDialogDoSync()`.

`XmtDialogOkayCallback()` is intended for use on an **OK** button. It performs three tasks: (1) Transfers data from the widgets of the dialog box to the data structure that was passed when the dialog was popped up. (2) Pops the dialog down. (3) If used with `XmtDialogDoSync()`, it sets an internal flag that causes `XmtDialogDoSync()` to exit its event loop and return **True** to its caller.

`XmtDialogCancelCallback()` is intended for use on a **Cancel** button. It does two things: (1) Pops the dialog down. (2) If used with `XmtDialogDoSync()`, it sets an internal flag that causes `XmtDialogDoSync()` to exit its event loop and return **False** to its caller. Note that this callback does not cause any data to be transferred.

`XmtDialogApplyCallback()` is intended for use with an **Apply** button in a modeless dialog. It does not pop down the dialog, but simply transfers data from the dialog widgets into the data structure specified in the preceding call to `XmtDialogDo()`. Usually, it must be used with another callback procedure that notifies the application that its data structure has been updated.

`XmtDialogResetCallback()` is intended for use with a **Reset** button in a modeless dialog. It performs the opposite action to `XmtDialogApplyCallback()`—it transfers data from the application data structure (specified in the call to `XmtDialogDo()`) back into the dialog widgets. This generally has the effect of undoing any user edits since the dialog was popped up or since the **Apply** button was last pressed.

`XmtDialogDoneCallback()` is intended for use with a **Dismiss** or **Done** button in a modeless dialog that has a separate **Apply** button. This callback does not transfer any data to or from the dialog widgets, but simply pops the dialog box down. Although intended for use with `XmtDialogDo()` and a modeless dialog, it may be used with a modal `XmtDialogDoSync()` dialog. In this case it will cause `XmtDialogDoSync()` to stop blocking and return `True`.

`XmtDialogGetDataAddress()` returns the *`address`* that was passed to `XmtDialogDo()` or `XmtDialogDoSync()` when the dialog specified by *`dialog`* was popped up. You can use this address in a call to `XmtDialogGetDialogValues()` or related functions.

If a dialog box specified by *`dialog`* was popped up with `XmtDialogDoSync()`, `XmtDialogSetReturnValue()` will cause that function to exit its internal event loop, and to return the value specified by `value`. It is safe to call `XmtDialogSetReturnValue()` even when a dialog was popped up with `XmtDialogDo()`.

See Also

Chapter 29, *Custom Dialogs and Automatic Dialog Management*
`XmtDialogDo()`, `XmtDialogDoSync()`, `XmtDialogGetDefault-Values()`,
`XmtDialogGetDialogValues()`, `XmtDialogSetDialogValues()`

Name

XmtDialogPosition() — center a dialog box over a widget.

Synopsis

```
#include <Xmt/Dialogs.h>
void XmtDialogPosition(Widget dialog,
                       Widget ref)
```

Arguments

Inputs

dialog The dialog shell widget to be centered.

ref The "reference widget" over which *dialog* is to be centered.

Description

XmtDialogPosition() sets the XtNx and XtNy resources of *dialog* so that when it is popped up it will appear centered over the widget *ref*. If centering *dialog* over *ref* would cause part of that widget to be off the edge of the screen, then the position is adjusted so that all of *dialog* is visible.

Motif dialog boxes are automatically centered over their ancestor shell widget, so you rarely will need to use this function. It is useful when a single dialog box will be popped up over more than one application window.

See Also

XmtDialogDo()

XmtDiscard{Button,KeyPress}Events()

Name

XmtDiscardButtonEvents(), XmtDiscardKeyPressEvents() — discard pending user input events.

Synopsis

```
#include <Xmt/Xmt.h>
void XmtDiscardButtonEvents(Widget w)

void XmtDiscardKeyPressEvents(Widget w)
```

Arguments

Inputs

w Any widget on the display for which events are to be discarded.

Description

XmtDiscardButtonEvents() gets all pending events from the X server, and then removes all ButtonPress, ButtonRelease, ButtonMotion, and PointerMotion events from the Xlib event queue, without processing them. It affects events generated in any window of the application on the same display as *w*.

XmtDiscardKeyPressEvents() removes all pending KeyPress events in the same way. This function does not remove KeyRelease events, because it may be called from callback or action procedures triggered (through a translation table) by KeyPress events, and the Xt Translation Manager expects to see the corresponding KeyRelease events in order to return to its default state. Calling this function may leave a series of KeyRelease events on the queue, but these will generally will not trigger any translations.

XmtDiscardButtonEvents() can be used to prevent "click-ahead" buffering of mouse events while an application is doing any lengthy computation or I/O without servicing events. Similarly, XmtDiscardKeyPressEvents() can be used to prevent "type-ahead". If you will be discarding events, you should be sure to provide feedback to the user that the events will not be processed—display a "please wait" cursor or dialog box. See XmtDisplayBusyCursor() and XmtDisplayWorkingDialog().

See Also

Chapter 31, *Busy States and Background Work*
XmtDisplayBusyCursor(), XmtDisplayWorkingDialog()

XmtDisplay{Busy,Default,}Cursor()

Name

`XmtDisplayBusyCursor()`, `XmtDisplayDefaultCursor()`, `Xmt-DisplayCursor()` — display a cursor over a window.

Synopsis

```
#include <Xmt/Xmt.h>
void XmtDisplayBusyCursor(Widget w)

void XmtDisplayDefaultCursor(Widget w)

void XmtDisplayCursor(Widget w, Cursor c)
```

Arguments

Inputs

w Any widget descendant of the shell that is to have its cursor set.

c For `XmtDisplayCursor()`, the cursor that is to be displayed.

Description

`XmtDisplayBusyCursor()` displays a "please wait" cursor for the window of the immediate shell widget ancestor of the widget *w*. It calls `XFlush()` internally after setting the cursor to guarantee that the cursor will be changed before the function returns. The cursor that is used is specified by the `busyCursor` application resource; the default for this resource is the standard X "wristwatch" cursor.

`XmtDisplayDefaultCursor()` is designed for use with `XmtDisplay-BusyCursor()` and "restores" (or sets for the first time) the cursor specified by the `cursor` application resource. The default value of this resource is None—a cursor of None means that the cursor displayed will depend upon the window manager.

`XmtDisplayCursor()` displays cursor `c` for the shell specified by *w*.

Each of these functions affect the nearest shell ancestor of the supplied widget. Setting the cursor of a shell widget will also set the cursor of any descendant widgets that do not have some other cursor explicitly set. If there are widgets in your hierarchy that do have a cursor explicitly set, this function will have no effect on them.

See Also

Chapter 31, *Busy States and Background Work*

XmtDisplay{Error,Warning}AndAsk()

Name

`XmtDisplayErrorAndAsk()`, `XmtDisplayWarningAndAsk()` — display an error or warning message, ask a yes-or-no question, and return the user's response.

Synopsis

```
#include <Xmt/Dialogs.h>
Boolean XmtDisplayErrorAndAsk(Widget w, String query_name,
                              String message_default,
                              String yes_default, String no_default,
                              XmtButtonType default_button_default,
                              String help_text_default)

Boolean XmtDisplayWarningAndAsk(Widget w, String query_name,
                                String message_default,
                                String yes_default, String no_default,
                                XmtButtonType default_button_default,
                                String help_text_default)
```

Arguments

Inputs

w The shell widget over which the dialog will be displayed, or any descendant of that shell.

query_name The name of this instantiation of the dialog, used to look up resources. NULL may be specified, but will result in a dialog that cannot be customized through the resource database.

prompt_default
The prompt message to be displayed in the dialog, unless an overriding value is found in the resource database.

yes_default The string to be displayed in the **Yes** button, unless an overriding value is found in the resource database. NULL may be specified.

no_default The string to be displayed in the **No** button, unless an overriding value is found in the resource database. NULL may be specified.

default_button_default
The default button (i.e., the button that will be activated if the user presses the **Return** key), unless an overriding value is found in the resource database. Legal values are: `XmtYesButton` and `XmtNoButton`.

help_text_default
The help text to display when the user clicks the **Help** button, unless an overriding value is found in the resource database. NULL may be specified.

Returns

`True` if the user clicked the **Yes** button; `False` if the user clicked the **No** button.

Description

`XmtDisplayErrorAndAsk()` and `XmtDisplayWarningAndAsk()` are simplified interfaces to `XmtAskForBoolean()`. They display a modal dialog box displaying a warning or error message and asking the user for a yes or no response to a question. Then they enter an internal event loop until the user selects either the **Yes** or **No** buttons. They return `True` if the user answers **Yes** and **False** if the user answers with the **No** button. Unlike `XmtAskForBoolean()`, which returns **False** when the user clicks the **Cancel** button, these functions do not display a **Cancel** button, so they directly return the user's response to the question.

If help text is found in the resource database for this dialog, or if the *`help_text_default`* argument is non-NULL, then this text will be displayed (using `XmtDisplayInformation()`) when the user clicks on the **Help** button. If there is no help available for the dialog, then the **Help** button will be insensitive.

If you specify a *`query_name`* argument to these functions, then you can customize a number of attributes of the resulting dialogs through the resource database. See `XmtAskForBoolean()` for more information. Also note that these functions use the same cached dialog widgets that `XmtAskForBoolean()` does, and you can set resources on them as described for that function.

See Also

Chapter 26, *Simple Input Dialogs*
`XmtAskForBoolean()`, `XmtDisplayErrorMsg()`,
`XmtDisplayErrorAndAsk()`, `XmtDisplayWarningMsg()`,
`XmtDisplayWarningAndAsk()`

XmtDisplay{Error,Warning,Information}()

Name

`XmtDisplayError()`, `XmtDisplayWarning()`, `XmtDisplay-Information()` — display a simple message in a dialog box.

Synopsis

```
#include <Xmt/Dialogs.h>
void XmtDisplayError(Widget w, String msg_name, String msg_default)

void XmtDisplayWarning(Widget w, String msg_name, String msg_default)

void XmtDisplayInformation(Widget w, String msg_name,
                           String msg_default, String title_default)
```

Arguments

Inputs

w Any widget; the message dialog will be popped up over the shell of this widget.

msg_name The name of this message, or NULL; used to look up customization resources for the message.

msg_default The text of the message, unless overridden by a value from the resource database.

title_default
For `XmtDisplayInformation()` only, the text to appear in the title bar (if any) of the dialog, unless overridden by a value from the resource database. If you specify NULL, then the default title **Help** will be used, unless it is overridden.

Description

The functions `XmtDisplayError()`, `XmtDisplayWarning()`, and `XmtDisplayInformation()` display a simple message in a XmMessageBox dialog displaying the standard Motif error, warning, or information icons. Once you have called these functions, you need take no further action—the dialog boxes will be managed automatically by Xmt.

The *msg_default* argument specifies the default message to be displayed, but if you have specified a *msg_name* argument, then this default message may be overridden through the resource database. See `XmtDisplayMessage()` and Chapter 25, *Message Dialogs*, for more information on message customization.

`XmtDisplayError()` and `XmtDisplayWarning()` display modal dialog boxes. `XmtDisplayInformation()` displays a modeless dialog box. Because there may be multiple modeless dialogs that are popped up at once, `XmtDisplayInformation()` allows you to specify an optional *title_default* for each message dialog, to help the user distinguish them from one another.

See Also

Chapter 25, *Message Dialogs*
`XmtDisplayErrorMsg()`, `XmtDisplayErrorMsgAndWait()`,
`XmtDisplayInformationMsg()`, `XmtDisplayMessage()`,
`XmtDisplayMessageAndWait()`, `XmtDisplayMessageVaList()`,
`XmtDisplayWarningAndAsk()`, `XmtDisplayWarningMsg()`,
`XmtDisplayWarningMsgAndWait()`

XmtDisplay{Error,Warning,Information}Msg()

Name

XmtDisplayErrorMsg(), XmtDisplayWarningMsg(), XmtDisplayInformationMsg() — display a formatted message in a dialog box.

Synopsis

```
#include <Xmt/Dialogs.h>
void XmtDisplayErrorMsg(Widget w, String msg_name,
                        String msg_default, String title_default,
                        String help_default,
                        ...)

void XmtDisplayWarningMsg(Widget w, String msg_name,
                          String msg_default, String title_default,
                          String help_default,
                          ...)

void XmtDisplayInformationMsg(Widget w, String msg_name,
                              String msg_default, String title_default,
                              String help_default,
                              ...)
```

Arguments

Inputs

w	Any widget; the message dialog will be popped up over the shell of this widget.
msg_name	The name of this message, or NULL; used to look up resources for the message.
msg_default	The text of the message, unless overridden by a value from the resource database. The message may contain printf()-style substitutions.
title_default	The string to appear in the title bar of the dialog box, unless overridden by a value from the resource database.
help_default	Help text for the dialog, unless overridden by a value from the resource database.
...	A printf()-style variable-length argument list of values to be substituted into the message.

Description

The functions XmtDisplayErrorMsg(), XmtDisplayWarningMsg(), and XmtDisplayInformationMsg() perform a printf()-style variable substitution into the specified *msg_default* (or into an overriding message from the resource database) and display the resulting string in a simple dialog box over the shell widget that contains the specified widget *w*.

The dialog is an XmMessageBox dialog displaying the standard Motif error, warning, or information icons. It is automatically created, cached, popped up, and popped down by Xmt. For `XmtDisplayErrorMsg()` and `XmtDisplayWarningMsg()`, the dialog is modal, and for `XmtDisplayInformationMsg()`, it is modeless.

The title bar of the dialog box (if the window manager displays one) will contain the *`title_default`* string, or an overriding value from the resource database. If *`help_default`* is non-NULL, or if there is help specified in the resource database, then the dialog will display a **Help** button. If the user clicks on this button, the help string will be appended to the original message in the dialog.

See `XmtDisplayMessage()` and Chapter 25, *Message Dialogs*, for more information on customizing message dialogs with resources.

See Also

Chapter 25, *Message Dialogs*
`XmtDisplayError()`, `XmtDisplayErrorAndAsk()`,
`XmtDisplayErrorMsgAndWait()`, `XmtDisplayInformation()`,
`XmtDisplayMessage()`, `XmtDisplayMessageAndWait()`,
`XmtDisplayMessageVaList()`, `XmtDisplayWarning()`,
`XmtDisplayWarningMsgAndWait()`

XmtDisplay{Error,Warning}MsgAndWait()

Name

XmtDisplayErrorMsgAndWait(), XmtDisplayWarningMsgAndWait() — display an error or warning message and block until the user pops it down.

Synopsis

```
#include <Xmt/Dialogs.h>
void XmtDisplayErrorMsgAndWait(Widget w, String msg_name,
                               String msg_default,
                               String title_default,
                               String help_default,
                               ...)

void XmtDisplayWarningMsgAndWait(Widget w, String msg_name,
                                 String msg_default,
                                 String title_default,
                                 String help_default,
                                 ...)
```

Arguments

Inputs

w	Any widget; the message dialog will be popped up over the shell of this widget.
msg_name	The name of this message, or NULL; used to look up resources for the message.
msg_default	The text of the message, unless overridden by a value from the resource database. The message may contain printf()-style substitutions.
title_default	The string to appear in the title bar of the dialog box, unless overridden by a value from the resource database.
help_default	Help text for the dialog, unless overridden by a value from the resource database.
...	A printf()-style variable-length argument list of values to be substituted into the message.

Description

XmtDisplayErrorMsgAndWait() and XmtDisplayWarningMsgAndWait() display formatted error and warning messages exactly as XmtDisplayErrorMsg() and XmtDisplayWarningMsg() do. The only difference is that these functions do not return immediately—they enter an internal event loop so that they appear to block until the user dismisses the dialog. See XmtDisplayErrorMsg() and XmtDisplayWarningMsg() for details.

See Also

Chapter 25, *Message Dialogs*
`XmtDisplayError()`, `XmtDisplayErrorMsg()`, `XmtDisplayInformation()`, `XmtDisplayInformationMsg()`, `XmtDisplayMessage()`, `XmtDisplayMessageAndWait()`, `XmtDisplayMessageVaList()`, `XmtDisplayWarning()`, `XmtDisplayWarningMsg()`

Xmt{Display,Hide}WorkingDialog()

Name

XmtDisplayWorkingDialog(), XmtHideWorkingDialog() — display or hide a "please wait" dialog box.

Synopsis

```
#include <Xmt/Dialogs.h>
Widget XmtDisplayWorkingDialog(Widget w,
                               String dialog_name,
                               String message_default,
                               String scale_label_default,
                               String button_label_default,
                               int scale_min,
                               int scale_max,
                               Boolean show_scale,
                               Boolean show_button)

void XmtHideWorkingDialog(Widget w)
```

Arguments

Inputs

w — The shell widget over which the dialog will be popped up or popped down, or any descendant of that shell.

dialog_name — The name for this instantiation of the dialog. This name is used to look up the message and title resources for the dialog. NULL may be specified, but will result in a dialog that cannot be customized through the resource manager.

message_default — The default message to be used if no *dialog_name* is provided, or if no message is found under that name in the resource database.

scale_label_default — The string to display to the left of the XmScale widget if no overriding value is found in the resource database. Specify NULL for the default label.

button_label_default — The string to display in the single XmPushButton widget of the dialog if no overriding value is found in the resource database. Specify NULL for the default label.

scale_min — The minimum value to be displayed by the XmScale widget.

scale_max — The maximum value to be displayed by the XmScale widget.

show_scale — Whether the XmScale widget (and its associated text label) should be displayed in the dialog.

show_button — Whether the XmPushButton widget should be displayed in the dialog.

Returns

A pointer to the XmtWorkingBox widget which was popped up by the function.

Description

The XmtWorkingBox widget is designed to display "Busy; please wait" dialog boxes to the user. `XmtDisplayWorkingDialog()` and `XmtHideWorkingDialog()` provide a simplified interface for handling these dialogs—they automatically create the required dialog widget and cache it for subsequent reuse.

`XmtDisplayWorkingDialog()` displays a modal XmtWorkingBox dialog containing a message and a "working" icon. The dialog is intended to be posted while the application is performing some time-consuming task during which it will not be responding to user input events. It optionally (depending on *`show_scale`*) contains an XmScale widget which can be used to provide feedback to the user about the progress of whatever task is underway. A label, **% Complete:** by default, appears to the left of the XmScale widget. The minimum and maximum bounds for the XmScale slider are specified by *`scale_min`* and *`scale_max`*. The working dialog also contains an optional (depending on *`show_button`*) XmPushButton widget which can be periodically polled to see if the user wants to abort the task. The default label for the button is **Stop**.

`XmtDisplayWorkingDialog()` returns the XmtWorkingBox widget of the dialog. This value can be used in subsequent calls to `XmtWorkingBoxSetScaleValue()` and `XmtWorkingBoxHandleEvents()` to update the XmScale slider value and to poll the XmPushButton widget of the dialog.

`XmtDisplayWorkingDialog()` calls `XmtWaitUntilMapped()` before returning to ensure that the dialog box is visible to the user before returning to the calling function which will generally perform some time-consuming task without handling events.

`XmtHideWorkingDialog()` pops down any XmtWorkingBox dialog that was posted over the shell of *w* by `XmtDisplayWorkingDialog()`. Note that *w* is the same widget passed to `XmtDisplayWorkingDialog()` (or any other descendant of the shell); not the widget returned by `XmtDisplayWorkingDialog()`.

Widgets

`XmtDisplayWorkingDialog()` creates a single XmtWorkingBox dialog for each screen it is called on, and caches that dialog for reuse by subsequent calls to the function. The name of the XmtWorkingBox is `xmtWorkDisplayWorkingDialogingDialog`, and the name of its XmDialogShell parent is `xmtWorkingDialogShell`. If you set resources on these widgets note that, because of the dialog caching, they will affect all instantiations of the working dialog.

Customization

You can also customize individual instantiations of working dialogs by specifying the *dialog_name* argument to XmtDisplayWorkingDialog(). The resources are looked up as a subpart of the shell widget of *w*. The name of the subpart is given by *dialog_name*, and the class of the subpart is XmtWorkingDialog. The table lists the resources that are looked up, their default values, and how they are used.

Name	Default	Purpose
message	*message_default*	Message to be displayed.
scaleLabel	*scale_label_default* or "% Complete:"	Label for the scale widget.
buttonLabel	*button_label_default* or "Stop"	Button label.
title	"Working"	Text for the dialog titlebar.

See Also

Chapter 31, *Busy States and Background Work*
XmtWorkingBox, XmtWaitUntilMapped(),
XmtWorkingBoxHandleEvents(),
XmtWorkingBoxSetScaleValue()

XmtDisplayMessage{,AndWait,VaList}()

Name

`XmtDisplayMessage()`, `XmtDisplayMessageAndWait()`, `Xmt-DisplayMessageVaList()` — display a message in a dialog box.

Synopsis

```
#include <Xmt/Dialogs.h>
void XmtDisplayMessage(Widget w, String msg_name, String msg_class,
                       String msg_default, String title_default,
                       String help_default, Pixmap icon_default,
                       int modality, int type,
                       ...)

void XmtDisplayMessageAndWait(Widget w, String msg_name, String msg_class,
                              String msg_default, String title_default,
                              String help_default, Pixmap icon_default,
                              int modality, int type,
                              ...)

void XmtDisplayMessageVaList(Widget w, String msg_name, String msg_class,
                             String msg_default, String title_default,
                             String help_default, Pixmap icon_default,
                             int modality, int type,
                             va_list args)
```

Arguments

Inputs

w	Any widget; the dialog will be displayed over the shell of this widget.
msg_name	The name of this message; used to look up resources for the message. You may specify NULL.
msg_class	The class of this message; use to look up resources for the message. If you specify `NULL` the class will be based on the value of the *type* argument.
msg_default	The text of the message to display, unless overridden by a value in the resource database. This message may contain `printf()`-style substitutions.
title_default	The title to appear in the dialog's title bar, unless overridden by a value in the resource database. If you specify NULL, the default title will depend on the *type* argument.
help_default	The help text to display, when requested by the user, unless overridden by a value in the resource database.
icon_default	The pixmap to appear in the message dialog, unless overridden by a value in the resource database. If you specify `None`, the default icon will depend on the *type* argument.

modality	The modality of the dialog; one of the values called XmDIALOG_MODELESS, XmDIALOG_PRIMARY_APPLICATION_MODAL, or XmDIALOG_FULL_APPLICATION_MODAL.
type	The type of the dialog; one of the values called XmDIALOG_MESSAGE, XmDIALOG_INFORMATION, XmDIALOG_WARNING, and XmDIALOG_ERROR. This argument controls the title and icon to be used for the dialog, if they are not specified in the resource database or by the *title_default* and *icon_default* arguments.
...	A `printf()`-style variable-length argument list of values to be substituted into the message.
args	A variable-length argument list; it is in `vsprintf()` `va_list` form, and is used by `XmtDisplayMessageVaList()` only.

Description

`XmtDisplayMessage()` displays a message in an automatically created, cached, and managed XmMessageBox dialog. The message to be displayed is formed by performing a `printf()`-style substitution of the arguments in the variable-length argument list into the specified message template. The specified title will appear in the title bar of the dialog (if the user's window manager is configured to display a title bar for these dialog widgets), and the specified icon will be displayed in the upper-left corner of the dialog. If any help text is specified then the dialog box will contain a **Help** button. If the user clicks on this button, the help text will be appended to the displayed message. The *modality* argument lets you specify whether the dialog should be modal or modeless, and the *type* argument lets you display dialogs that display the default Motif information, warning, and error icons.

For customizability and internationalizability, `XmtDisplayMessage()` looks up the message text and other resources for the message dialog in the resource database. Thus, the *message_default*, *title_default*, *icon_default*, and *help_default* arguments are simply default values that can be overridden with resources. The resources are looked up using the message name and class specified by the *msg_name* and *msg_class* arguments. You may specify `NULL` for these arguments, but it will result in a dialog that is not customizable. See the "Customization" section below for more details.

`XmtDisplayMessageAndWait()` behaves similarly to `XmtDisplayMessage()` but enters an internal event loop after displaying the message so that it appears to "block" until the user has seen and responded to the message by clicking the **OK** button.

`XmtDisplayMessageVaList()` is identical to `XmtDisplayMessage()` except that it takes its `printf()` substitution arguments in the form of a `va_list` instead of an actual variable-length argument list. `va_list` is the type initialized by `va_start()` and passed to `vprintf()`. `XmtDisplayMessageVaList()` provides a way for you to write your own `printf()`-style functions that use Xmt message dialogs internally.

Customization

If the *`msg_name`* argument is specified for a dialog, then the message text, title, help text, and icon of the dialog are looked up in the resource database, and any values found there override the values specified by the *`msg_default`*, *`title_default`*, *`help_default`*, and *`icon_default`* arguments.

The resources are looked up as subresources of the shell over which the dialog will be displayed. The name and class of the subpart are given by the *`msg_name`* and *`msg_class`* arguments. The names and classes of the resources that are looked up are the following:

Name	Class	Type	Default	Purpose
`message`	`Message`	`String`	msg_default	The text of the message to display
`helpText`	`HelpText`	`String`	help_default	The help text to display
`title`	`Title`	`String`	title_default	The name to appear in the title bar
`icon`	`Icon`	`Pixmap`	icon_default	The icon to display

Widgets

The first time it is called, `XmtDisplayMessage()` (or any of the related functions based on `XmtDisplayMessage()`) creates an XmMessageBox widget named "xmtMessageDialog" as a child of an XmDialogShell named "xmtMessageDialogShell". The XmDialogShell widget is created as a child of the nearest XmDialogShell, TopLevelShell, or ApplicationShell ancestor of the widget *w*. These message dialog widgets are cached for reuse by subsequent calls to `XmtDisplayMessage()` (or to any related functions).

Dialog Types

The *`type`* argument to `XmtDisplayMessage()` serves mainly to provide default values when the *`msg_class`*, *`title_default`*, or *`icon_default`* arguments are omitted. The legal values for *`type`*, and the defaults it specifies are shown in the following table.

Dialog Type	Default Values		
	Class	Title	Icon
XmDIALOG_MESSAGE	XmtMessageDialog	Message	None
XmDIALOG_INFORMATION	XmtInformationDialog	Help	Standard Motif
XmDIALOG_WARNING	XmtWarningDialog	Warning	Standard Motif
XmDIALOG_ERROR	XmtErrorDialog	Error	Standard Motif

See Also

Chapter 25, *Message Dialogs*
`XmtDisplayError()`, `XmtDisplayErrorMsg()`,
`XmtDisplayErrorMsgAndWait()`, `XmtDisplayInformation()`,
`XmtDisplayInformationMsg()`, `XmtDisplayWarning()`,
`XmtDisplayWarningMsg()`, `XmtDisplayWarningMsgAndWait()`

Name

`XmtErrorMsg()`, `XmtWarningMsg()` — print an error message and exit or print a warning message and return.

Synopsis

```
#include <Xmt/Xmt.h>
void XmtErrorMsg(String name, String type, String msg, ...)
void XmtWarningMsg(String name, String type, String msg, ...)
```

Arguments

Inputs

name — The name of the procedure, widget, or module that is issuing the error message.

type — The type of the error message.

msg — The default text of the message. The message may contain `printf()`-style substitutions to be filled in from the argument list.

`...` — A `printf()`-style variable-length argument list of values to be substituted into the *msg* argument.

Description

`XmtErrorMsg()` and `XmtWarningMsg()` are simplified interfaces to `XtErrorMsg()` and `XtWarningMsg()`, which take a `printf()`-style argument list rather than an awkward array of arguments.

These functions prepend the *name* argument, a colon, and a space to the *msg* argument. Then they convert the argument list into an array of arguments, and call `XtErrorMsg()` or `XtWarningMsg()` to display the message. They passes *name* and *type* as the name and type of the message. `XmtErrorMsg()` passes "XmtError" as the class of the message and `XmtWarningMsg()` passes "XmtWarning" as the message class. The message name, class, and type can be used to provide translated versions of error and warning messages in a special Xt error database.

Note that `XmtErrorMsg()` causes the application to exit, while `XmtWarningMsg()` prints a warning message and returns.

See Also

Chapter 8, *Utility Functions*
`XtErrorMsg()`, `XtWarningMsg()`

XmtFindFile()

Name

`XmtFindFile()` — look for application auxiliary files.

Synopsis

```
String XmtFindFile(Widget w,
                   String type,
                   String objname,
                   String suffix,
                   String rootdir,
                   String path,
                   int where)
```

Arguments

Inputs

w	Any widget in the application; specifies which resource database and application resources to use.
type	The string that describes type of the file; substituted for `%T` in *path*. If you specify NULL, the empty string will be used.
objname	The base name of the file; substituted for `%N` in *path*. If you specify NULL, the application class name will be used.
suffix	The suffix of the file; substituted for `%S` in *path*. If you specify NULL, the empty string will be used.
rootdir	The name of a directory to search under; substituted for `%R` in *path*. If you specify NULL, the `configDir` application resource will be used.
path	A colon-separated list of file specifications to check, or NULL.
where	Flags that specify whether `XmtFindFile()` should also search in standard user, application, and system paths.

Returns

The fully qualified name of a file that exists and is readable, or NULL if no such file could be found. You must free this filename with `XtFree()` when done with it.

Description

`XmtFindFile()` finds a fully qualified filename for an application auxiliary file with a specified base name, type, and suffix. Using `XmtFindFile()` to look up filenames is better than hardcoding those file names in an application because it allows the system administrator flexibility in where she installs the auxiliary files for your application. Also, it allows the flexibility at runtime to read different files depending on the setting of the LANG environment variable, the X11R5 `customization` application resource, and the attributes of the user's display.

`XmtFindFile()` is based on the Intrinsics function `XtResolvePathname()` but extends it in a couple of important ways. It works by performing a standard set of string substitutions (described below) on each of the colon-separated elements of *`path`* in turn. Once the substitution is done, it checks to see if the resulting string names a file that exists and is readable. If so, it returns that filename.

Note that `XmtFindFile()` returns filenames in allocated memory that must be freed with `XtFree()` when you are done with it. Also note that if *`objname`* begins with `/`, `./`, or `../`, then `XmtFindFile()` assumes that it is already a fully qualified (absolute or relative) filename, and simply returns a copy of that name without conducting a search.

The substitutions performed by `XmtFindFile()`, and the paths that it can search are described in the sections below.

Substitutions

`XmtFindFile()` performs the following substitutions on any path it searches. `%R, %H, %a, %A, %v, %z,` and `%d` are added by `XmtFindFile()`; the other substitutions are standard ones supported by `XtResolvePathname()`.

`%R` The "root directory" of the search. This is replaced with the value of the *`rootdir`* argument, or if that is *NULL*, with the value of the `XmtNconfigDir` application resource. When searching the "user path" (as described below), however,`%R` is replaced with the user's home directory, or with the value of the `XAPPLRESDIR` environment variable.

`%H` The user's home directory. This substitution can be useful when looking for configuration files that are always installed in the user's home directory. You could use a path like `%H/.%a`, for example, to find the "dot file" for an application. Note that it generally does not make sense to use both `%R` and `%H` in the same element of a path.

`%a` The application name, as reported by `XtGetApplicationNameAndClass()`.

`%A` The application class name, as reported by `XtGetApplicationNameAndClass()`.

`%v` The visual type of the screen. This substitution is replaced with one of the strings "color" (for color screens) , "gray" (for grayscale screens) and "monochrome" (for monochrome screens).

`%z` The approximate size or resolution of the screen, as determined by its absolute number of pixels, not by screen size in inches or screen resolution in dots-per-inch. This substitution will be replaced by one of the strings "small," "medium," or "large".

`%d` The depth of the screen in bitplanes. Typical values for this substitution are 1 (for monochrome screens), and 8 (for the common variety of 256-color screens).

%T The value of the *type* argument. This is the general category of file, such as "app-defaults," "bitmap," or "help." If *type* is NULL, then the empty string is used.

%N The value of the *objname* argument, or the application's class name if *objname* is NULL.

%S The value of the *suffix* argument. This will generally be some suffix that identifies the type of the file, such as ".xbm" for a bitmap file or ".ad" for an app-defaults file. Note that files are often installed without a suffix when they are in directories (like */usr/lib/X11/app-defaults*) that identify the file type. You should generally supply a *suffix* argument to `XmtFindFile()`, but some paths will never contain the %S substitution. If *suffix* is not specified, then %S will be replaced with the empty string.

%C The value of the `customization` application resource. The user may set this resource to a value such as `-color` to indicate that files (resource files, bitmaps, etc.) appropriate for a color screen should be found, or to `-mono` if they are using a monochrome screen. If this resource is not specified, the empty string is used for the substitution. This substitution is performed only in X11R5 and later releases.

%L The value of the language string associated with the display. This is the value of the `xnlLanguage` resource in Release 4, and in Release 5 and later, it is the value of this resource or the value returned by the language procedure, if any is registered. (See `XtSetLanguageProc()` for more information.) In Release 5, if the `xnlLanguage` resource is not set, the language procedure will usually return the value of the LANG environment variable. The %L substitution in a path allows an application to automatically find internationalized versions of its resources, online help files, pixmaps, and so on.

%l The "language part" of the language string of the display.

%t The "territory part" of the language string of the display.

%c The "codeset part" of the language string of the display.

Other Searches

The *where* argument specifies where `XmtFindFile()` should look for the specified file. It may be one of the following constants, or the bitwise OR of any of them.

`XmtSearchPathOnly`
: This is a symbolic name for the constant 0. When no flags are set in the *where* argument, `XmtFindFile()` searches only the specified *path*, and not in any of the "standard" places. If you do not specify any of the flags below, then you must specify an explicit *path* to be searched.

`XmtSearchUserPath`

This flag specifies that `XmtFindFile()` should search the *standard user path* before it searches anywhere else. Note that this search is performed before even the specified *`path`* is searched. Only specify this flag if you want the user to be able to provide an alternate to whatever file you are looking up.

The standard user path is specified by the `XUSERFILESEARCHPATH` environment variable, or if that variable is not defined, by the `userConfigPath` application resource, or if that resource is not defined, the `XmtFindFile()` default path (which is specified below). When searching the user path, the `%R` substitution is not replaced with the *`rootdir`* argument or the `configDir` application resource. Instead, `%R` is replaced with the `XAPPLRESDIR` environment variable, or with the user's home directory. Searching for user files in this way is consistent with what the Xt Intrinsics do when looking up user app-defaults files for applications.

`XmtSearchAppPath`

This flag specifies that `XmtFindFile()` should search the *standard application path*. The application path is searched after the user path is searched, if `XmtSearchUserPath` is specified, and after the specified *`path`*, if any, is searched.

The standard application path is specified by the `configPath` application resource. If this resource is not specified, a default value (described in the "Default Path" section) that is suitable for most applications is used. For this search, the `%R` substitution is replaced by the value of the *`rootdir`* argument, or if that is not specified, by the value of the `configDir` application resource. The default value for `configDir` is `/usr/lib/X11`, but it will often be set in an app-defaults file to something like */usr/local/lib* or */usr/X11R5/lib*.

This standard application path is usually suitable for almost all auxiliary files that an application must read, so you may often call `XmtFindFile()` with no *`rootdir`* argument, no *`path`* argument, and *`where`* set to `XmtSearchAppPath`.

`XmtSearchSysPath`

This flag specifies that `XmtFindFile()` should search the *standard system path*. This search is only done if any previous searches through the user path, the specified *`path`*, and the application path failed.

The standard application path is defined to be the path that `XtResolvePathname()` searches when no path is specified to it. This is the value of the `XFILESEARCHPATH` environment variable, or if that is not defined, the default `XtResolvePathname()` path. This default path is implementation-dependent, but it is usually under */usr/lib/X11*. This is the path that the Xt Intrinsics use to find an application's app-defaults file. See `XtResolvePathname()` for more information on this default system path.

For the search of the system path, none of the special `XmtFindFile()` substitutions are performed: `%R, %H, %a, %A, %v, %z,` or `%d`. Also, if a *`suffix`* argument was supplied, and the search failed, then the search is performed again, without the suffix. This is done because the default `XtResolvePathname()` path generally includes the %S substitution, but convention seems to be to install files in the system directories without suffixes. (This is at least the case for the app-defaults file in */usr/lib/X11/app-defaults.*)

`XmtSearchEverywhere`
This constant is just the bitwise-OR of each of the other constants; it is shorthand to tell `XmtFindFile()` to search every place it knows how. You can OR together any combination of the `XmtSearchUserPath`, `XmtSearchAppPath`, and `XmtSearchSysPath` for the *`where`* argument.

The Default Path

When searching the user path, `XmtFindFile()` checks the `userConfigPath` application resource, and when searching the application path, it uses the `configPath` application resource. The default value for each of these resources is the following path:

```
%R/%L/%a/%N%C%S:
%R/%L/%a/%N%S:
%R/%l/%a/%N%C%S:
%R/%l/%a/%N%S:
%R/%a/%N%C%S:
%R/%a/%N%S:
%R/%N%C%S:
%R/%N%S
```

Debugging

If you set the `XMTDEBUGFINDFILE` environment variable, then `XmtFindFile()` will print the name of every file it checks for. This can be quite helpful when trying to get your application to correctly look for its configuration files. Compile the Xmt library with the `-NDEBUG` flag to disable this debugging feature.

See Also

Chapter 6, *Managing Auxiliary Files*
Chapter 7, *Application Resources and Command-Line Arguments*
`XtResolvePathname()`, `XtFindFile()`

Name

`XmtFocusShell()`, `XmtMoveShellToPointer()`, `XmtWarpToShell()`, `XmtSetFocusToShell()` — change keyboard focus to a shell widget.

Synopsis

```
#include <Xmt/Xmt.h>
void XmtFocusShell(Widget w)

void XmtSetFocusToShell(Widget w)

void XmtWarpToShell(Widget w)

void XmtMoveShellToPointer(Widget w)
```

Arguments

Inputs

w The shell widget that is to have keyboard focus assigned to it, or any descendant of that widget. The specified shell should be a TopLevelShell, not an XmDialogShell.

Description

The functions `XmtSetFocusToShell()`, `XmtWarpToShell()`, and `XmtMoveShellToPointer()` provide three different techniques for assigning keyboard focus to a given shell widget. Unfortunately, none of these techniques will work appropriately in all circumstances. `XmtFocusShell()` is a wrapper function that lets the user choose, through an application resource, which technique should be used.

`XmtSetFocusToShell()` assigns keyboard focus to the shell by calling `XSetInputFocus()`. This works well with "click-to-type" window managers, such as *mwm*, but doesn't work well with "pointer focus" window managers like *twm*, because it leaves the desktop in an inconsistent state with the pointer in one window and keyboard focus in another.

`XmtWarpToShell()` also calls `XSetInputFocus()`, but first move the mouse pointer to the center of the specified shell widget with `XWarpPointer()`. This works well with window managers like *twm*, but moving the pointer like this can be a very confusing thing to do.

`XmtMoveShellToPointer()` takes another approach—it moves the shell to the pointer, rather than the pointer to the shell. Like `XmtWarpToShell()`, it also calls `XSetInputFocus()`. Moving a shell like this is probably more confusing than moving the pointer is, but can work well if the shell widget was previously iconified.

All of these functions deiconify the specified shell, if necessary, and raise it to the top of the window stack.

Since none of the above three functions will be appropriate for all users or all sites, `XmtFocusShell()` lets the user or the system administrator choose how focus should be assigned by setting the `focusStyle` application resource. The table lists the legal values of `focusStyle` and their meanings. If *mwm* is running (i.e., if `XmIsMotifWMRunning()` returns `True`) then the default value for `focusShell` is `focus`. Otherwise the default value is `none`, since none of the focus methods is always appropriate in this case.

focusStyle	***XmtFocusShell() Action***
`none`	Deiconify and raise only; don't attempt to set focus
`focus`	Call `XmtSetFocusToShell()`
`warp`	Call `XmtWarpToShell()`
`move`	Call `XmtMoveShellToPointer()`

Usage

You should almost always use `XmtFocusShell()` in your applications instead of the more specialized functions that it calls. This will make your applications more customizable and portable.

Remember that the user can also move keyboard focus between windows with the window manager. You should only call these functions in direct response to a user request to move the focus—if you reassign focus unexpectedly you will make the user feel that he has lost control of his desktop. A good time to call `XmtFocusShell()` is when the user has selected a window from a **Windows** menu in your application.

See Also

Chapter 15, *Working with the Window Manager*
`XmtDeiconifyShell()`, `XmtRaiseShell()`

Name

`XmtGetShell()`, `XmtGetApplicationShell()`, `XmtGetTopLevel-Shell()` — return shell ancestors of a widget.

Synopsis

```
#include <Xmt/Xmt.h>
Widget XmtGetShell(Widget w)

Widget XmtGetApplicationShell(Widget w)

Widget XmtGetTopLevelShell(Widget w)
```

Arguments

Inputs

w The widget whose shell ancestor is desired.

Returns

The appropriate shell ancestor of *w*.

Description

`XmtGetShell()` returns the closest widget ancestor of *w* that is a shell widget—i.e., is any subclass of Shell.

`XmtGetTopLevelShell()` returns the closest ancestor of *w* that is a TopLevelShell or a subclass. Thus if *w* is a descendent of a dialog box, this function will skip the dialog shell and return the main window shell that is the ancestor of the dialog box.

`XmtGetApplicationShell()` returns the "root" of the widget hierarchy. This is the ancestor of *w* which has no ancestors of its own. This shell is usually created with `XtAppInitialize()` or `XtAppCreateShell()`, and is usually an ApplicationShell widget.

See Also

Chapter 8, *Utility Functions*
Chapter 14, *Windows on the Desktop*
`XtIsShell()`, `XtIsTopLevelShell()`

XmtGet{Bitmap,Pixmap}()

Name

`XmtGetBitmap()`, `XmtGetPixmap()` — find and return the named bitmap or pixmap.

Synopsis

```
#include <Xmt/Pixmap.h>
Pixmap XmtGetBitmap(Widget w, String name)

Pixmap XmtGetPixmap(Widget w, XmtColorTable table, String name)
```

Arguments

Inputs

`w` A widget or object that specifies the screen, visual, colormap, and depth of the `Pixmap` to be returned.

`table` For `XmtGetPixmap()`, this argument defines symbolic colors to be used in converting XPM data to a pixmap. If you specify NULL, the value of the `colorTable` application resource will be used.

`name` The name of the bitmap or pixmap to be obtained.

Returns

These functions return `None` if no bitmap or pixmap data with the specified name is found. Otherwise, `XmtGetBitmap()` returns a single-plane bitmap, and `XmtGetPixmap()` returns a multi-plane pixmap with the same depth and screen as *w*, containing the image specified by *`name`*, with colors set according to the visual and colormap of *w* and according to *`table`*. The returned bitmap or pixmap should be freed when no longer needed with `XmtReleasePixmap()`.

Description

`XmtGetBitmap()` and `XmtGetPixmap()` look up and return named bitmaps or pixmaps. These functions are very flexible; they form the basis of the Xmt String-to-Bitmap and String-to-Pixmap converters, and look for bitmap and pixmap data in a number of different places:

- The image cache
- The resource database
- The application's auxiliary files

The subsections that follow explain how these functions search each of those places. The descriptions below explain how `XmtGetPixmap()` searches for XPM pixmap data or XBM bitmap data to convert to a pixmap. `XmtGetBitmap()` works in exactly the same way, except that it only performs the searches for bitmap data.

Because `XmtGetPixmap()` forms the basis for the Xmt pixmap resource converter, the *name* argument to that function may also specify a a color table for use in the conversion. This will be explained below.

Note that any bitmap or pixmap returned by these functions will be cached in the Xmt image cache. When they will no longer be needed they should be released with `XmtReleasePixmap()`. This will decrement a reference count, and when that count reaches zero, the bitmap or pixmap will be destroyed.

Searching the Image Cache

The first place `XmtGetPixmap()` looks for the named pixmap is in the Xmt image cache. It calls `XmtLookupPixmap()` (`XmtGetBitmap()` calls `XmtLookupBitmap()`) to check the cache for XPM data registered with `XmtRegisterImage()` or for XBM data registered with `XmtRegisterXbmData()`.

Unless you have registered pixmap or bitmap data with one of these relatively low-level functions, the named pixmap or bitmap will not be found in the image cache. Note however, that whenever `XmtGetPixmap()` or `XmtGetBitmap()` find named image data elsewhere, they register that data in the cache by name so that it will be found quickly by subsequent searches.

Searching the Resource Database

If data is not found in the image cache, then `XmtGetPixmap()` next checks the resource database for a definition of the named pixmap or bitmap. First, it looks for XPM data specified as the value of a resource that matches the following pattern:

`_Pixmaps_.`*`visual.depth.size.language.territory.codeset.name`*

If it does not find pixmap data under `_Pixmaps_` in the resource database, then `XmtGetPixmap()` (as well as `XmtGetBitmap()`) looks for XBM bitmap data under `_Bitmaps_` for a resource that matches the following pattern:

`_Bitmaps_.`*`size.language.territory.codeset.name`*

The components of these searches are the following:

`visual` The default visual type of the screen. This will be one of the strings `color`, `gray`, or `monochrome`.

`depth` The default depth, in bitplanes, of the screen. Typical values are `1` and `8`.

`size` The size or "resolution" of the screen, as determined by the number of pixels. This will be one of the strings `small` (screen is less than 750 pixels wide), `medium`, or `large` (screen is more than 1150 pixels wide).

`language` The "language part" of the language string.

territory The "territory part" of the language string.

codeset The "codeset part" of the language string.

name The *name* argument.

Note that the visual type and depth are not used when searching for bitmap data—bitmaps do not include color data, and so this kind of customization is not required.

If resources matching either of the above patterns are found in the resource database their values are assumed to be XPM or XBM data. This data is parsed, registered by name in the image cache, and then converted to a pixmap or bitmap.

You can convert XPM and XBM files as necessary for inclusion in the resource database with the *xpm2res* and *xbm2res* scripts.

Searching Auxiliary Files

If the searches of the image cache and resource database fail, then *name* is assumed to be the name of a file. The following list explains how `XmtGetPixmap()` looks for the file. Recall that `XmtGetBitmap()` works in the same way, except that it only looks for XBM data; never XPM pixmap data.

The descriptions below assume familiarity with the function `XmtFindFile()`. Note that when `XmtFindFile()` is used to look for pixmap data, it is always passed a *type* of "pixmaps" and a *suffix* of ".xpm". When `XmtFindFile()` is called to look for bitmap data, it is passed a *type* of "bitmaps" and a *suffix* of ".xbm".

1. If the name begins with `/`, `./`, or `../`, then it is assumed to be an absolute or relative filename, and no search is required; it is just read directly.
2. If the `XPMLANGPATH` environment variable is set, then `XmtFindFile()` is used to search this path for an XPM file with the specified name. `XPMLANGPATH` is an Xmt environment variable that is analogous to the `XBMLANGPATH` variable that is searched by the Motif function `XmGetPixmap()`.
3. If the `XBMLANGPATH` environment variable is defined, then `XmtFindFile()` is used to search that path for an XBM file. This is done for compatibility with the search done by `XmGetPixmap()`.
4. Next, `XmtFindFile()` is called again to search for an XPM file in four more places:
   a. The user path specified by the `userConfigPath` resource and the `XUSERFILESEARCHPATH` and `XAPPLRESDIR` resources (see Chapter 6 for details)

   b. The path, if any, specified by the `pixmapFilePath` application resource. The default for this resource is `NULL`, so this search is not usually performed.

   c. The path specified by the `configPath` application resource

   d. The standard system path (see Chapter 6, *Managing Auxiliary Files*, for details)

5. Finally, `XmtFindFile()` is called again, to look for an XBM file in four analogous places:

   a. The user path

   b. The path, if any, specified by the `bitmapFilePath` application resource

   c. The path specified by `configPath`

   d. The system path

If an XPM or XBM file is found in any of these searches, then it is read in, and its data is parsed and stored by name in the image cache. Then the data is used to create a pixmap or bitmap which is returned.

Specifying a Color Table

As mentioned earlier, `XmtGetPixmap()` (but not `XmtGetBitmap()`) can parse a color table specification as part of its supplied *`name`*. If *`name`* contains a `:`, the part before the colon (with whitespace removed) is taken to be the pixmap name, and the part after the colon is taken to be a color table specification, and is parsed by the Xmt color table resource converter. (See Chapter 4, *Using Color*, for the syntax.)

When a color table is specified in this way, it is created with the specified *`table`* as its parent. If no *`table`* argument was specified, then the color table is created with the default application color table as its parent. In either case the resulting "chained" color table is used to look up all symbolic colors for the pixmap.

If `XmtGetPixmap()` finds XPM data, then the color table is used to look up any symbolic colors in the XPM data. If `XmtGetPixmap()` finds bitmap data, then the symbolic colors "foreground" and "background" are looked up and used as the foreground and background colors for the pixmap created from this bitmap data.

See Also

Chapter 5, *Using Icons*
Chapter 4, *Using Color*
Chapter 6, *Managing Auxiliary Files*
`XmtLookupBitmap()`, `XmtLookupBitmask()`,

XmtLookupPixmap(), XmtParseXpmData(),
XmtParseXpmFile(), XmtRegisterImage(),
XmtRegisterXbmData(), XmtReleasePixmap()

Name

`XmtGetHomeDir()` — return the user's home directory.

Synopsis

```
#include <Xmt/Xmt.h>
String XmtGetHomeDir(void)
```

Arguments

Inputs

None.

Returns

The user's home directory. You must not modify or free this value.

Description

For UNIX systems, `XmtGetHomeDir()` figures out where the user's home directory is, and returns it as a fully-qualified directory name. This value is cached so that multiple calls to this function are very efficient. The returned string is owned by Xmt and you must not modify or free it.

See Also

Chapter 8, *Utility Functions*
`XmtFindFile()`

Xmt{Get,Set}ApplicationValues()

Name

XmtGetApplicationValues(), XmtSetApplicationValues() — query and set application resources by name.

Synopsis

```
#include <Xmt/AppRes.h>
void XmtGetApplicationValues(Widget w, ArgList args,
                             Cardinal num_args)

void XmtSetApplicationValues(Widget w, ArgList args,
                             Cardinal num_args)
```

Arguments

Inputs

w — Any descendant of the root shell for which application resource values are to be obtained.

args — An ArgList specifying the names of resources to be queried or set, and the addresses of variables to store their values in (for XmtGetApplicationValues()) or the values to set for those resources (for XmtSetApplicationValues()).

num_args — The number of elements in the args array.

Description

XmtGetApplicationValues() and XmtSetApplicationValues() are analogs to XtGetValues() and XtSetValues(). Instead of querying and setting the resources of a widget, however, they query and set the standard Xmt application resources associated with a root shell widget. See Chapter 7, *Application Resources and Command-Line Arguments*, for a complete list of these application resources. The header file *<Xmt/AppRes.h>* contains symbolic names that you can use to refer to each of these application resources—each name begins with an XmtN prefix, just as Xmt widget resource names do.

Xmt does not make copies of any of its string application resources, so any strings returned by XmtGetApplicationValues() must not be modified or freed. Similarly, Xmt does not make copies of any of its string application resources, so any string values set by this function must be constant strings, or must not be modified or freed for the lifetime of the application.

Not all application resources can be meaningfully set. XmtNforeground and XmtNbackground, for example, are used only within XmtInitialize-ApplicationShell() and are never referenced again; setting them will have no effect.

Calling XmtSetApplicationValues() only sets the specified values; Xmt makes no attempt to update the current application state to reflect the new values. If the "busy cursor" is being displayed by XmtDisplayBusyCursor(), for example, and you set the `XmtNbusyCursor` resource, the cursor that is displayed will not change. The next time you call `XmtDisplayBusyCursor()`, however, the new cursor will be used.

See Also

Chapter 7, *Application Resources and Command-Line Arguments*
`XmtInitializeApplicationShell()`, `XmtParseCommandLine()`

XmtHashTable*()

Name

XmtHashTableCreate(), XmtHashTableDestroy(), XmtHashTable-Store(), XmtHashTableLookup(), XmtHashTableDelete(), XmtHashTableForEach() — hash table functions.

Synopsis

```
#include <Xmt/Hash.h>
XmtHashTable XmtHashTableCreate(int size)

void XmtHashTableDestroy(XmtHashTable table)

void XmtHashTableStore(XmtHashTable table, XtPointer key,
                       XtPointer data)

Boolean XmtHashTableLookup(XmtHashTable table,
                           XtPointer key, XtPointer *data)

void XmtHashTableDelete(XmtHashTable table, XtPointer key)

void XmtHashTableForEach(XmtHashTable table,
                         XmtHashTableForEachProc proc)
typedef void (*XmtHashTableForEachProc)(XmtHashTable table,
                                        XtPointer key,
                                        XtPointer *data);
```

Arguments

Inputs

size For XmtHashTableCreate(), the $\log_2$ of the expected number of entries in the hash table. The hash table will be created with 2^{size} entries pre-allocated.

table The hash table that is to be manipulated.

key An untyped value that identifies the data to be stored in the hash table, looked up in the hash table, or deleted from the hash table.

data For XmtHashTableStore(), an untyped value to be stored in the hash table.

proc For XmtHashTableForEach(), a procedure that will be called for each item in the hash table.

Outputs

data For XmtHashTableLookup(), the address at which the data associated with the specified *key* will be stored.

Returns

`XmtHashTableCreate()` returns the newly created hash table.

`XmtHashTableLookup()` returns `True` if data was found for the specified *`key`*, and `False` if no data was associated with that key.

Description

A *hash table* is a data structure that can efficiently associate arbitrary data with arbitrary keys. It is sometimes known as an associative array. These functions allow you to create and manipulate hash tables.

`XmtHashTableCreate()` creates and returns an `XmtHashTable`. `size` specifies the base 2 logarithm of the number of entries that should be pre-allocated in the table.

`XmtHashTableDestroy()` frees all storage associated with the `XmtHashTable` *`table`*. Once this function is called, *`table`* should never again be referenced. Note that this function does not free storage associated with the individual hash table entries. If pointers to allocated memory have been stored in the hash table, those blocks of memory must be independently freed; you can do this with `XmtHashTableForEach()`.

`XmtHashTableStore()` associates *`data`* with *`key`* in hash table *`table`* for later lookup with `XmtHashTableLookup()`. If there was already data associated with *`key`*, it is overwritten with the new data.

Both *`key`* and *`data`* are untyped values with the same size as the untyped pointer `XtPointer`. The only restriction on values used as keys is that they be unique. Widget pointers are suitable as hash table keys since they are unique within a single process. Windows and other X IDs are not necessarily unique if an application connects to more than one X display. To use a string as a key, first convert it to a quark (a unique identifier for a string) with the Xlib function `XrmStringToQuark()` or `XrmPermStringToQuark()`.

If the data you wish to store in the hash table is the same size or smaller than an `XtPointer`, then you can pass it directly as *`data`*. Otherwise, you should make sure that it is in static or allocated storage and pass a pointer to it as the *`data`* argument. Note that the hash table routines do not distinguish between these cases—*`data`* is simply treated as an untyped value. In particular, when you store pointers in a hash table, the table does not make a copy of the pointed-at storage, nor does it ever free that storage when the table is destroyed.

`XmtHashTableLookup()` looks up the data associated with *`key`* in *`table`* and stores it at the location specified by *`data`*. It returns `True` if data associated with `key` was found in the hash table, or `False` otherwise. Note that `XmtHashTableLookup()` simply looks up an untyped value with the same size as an `XtPointer`. The application may interpret this value as the data itself, or as a pointer to the data.

`XmtHashTableDelete()` removes any entry associated with the key *`key`* from the hash table *`table`*. If no entry associated with *`key`* exists in *`table`*, then `XmtHashTableDelete()` does nothing.

`XmtHashTableForEach()` calls the specified procedure, *`proc`*, once for each key/value pair associated in the hash table *`table`*. *`proc`* is passed three arguments each time it is called: the hash table, the key, and the address of the data associated with the key.

`XmtHashTableForEach()` makes no guarantees about the order in which items will be enumerated. While enumerating the entries in a hash table, you must not take any actions that would change those entries. In particular, the procedure you specify must not delete entries or add new ones by calling `XmtHashTableDelete()` or `XmtHashTableStore()`. Since *`proc`* is passed the address of the *`data`* value associated with each *`key`*, it may safely modify the data value.

See Also

Chapter 8, *Utility Functions*

Name

`XmtHelpBox` — a widget to display scrolled, multi-font help text.

Synopsis

Include File: `#include <Xmt/HelpBox.h>`
Constructor: `XmtCreateHelpBox()`, `XmtCreateHelpDialog()`
Class Name: XmtHelpBox
Class Pointer: `xmtHelpBoxWidgetClass`
Class Hierarchy: Core → XmManager → XmBulletinBoard → XmtLayout → XmtHelpBox

Description

The XmtHelpBox widget displays a multi-line, multi-font message in an XmLabel widget within an XmScrolledWindow widget. It also displays an icon to the left of the scrolled text, and a title centered above the text. The HelpBox is intended to be used as a dialog box, and it positions an **OK** button below the help text so that the user can dismiss the dialog.

Resources

The HelpBox widget inherits the resources of the XmtLayout class, and defines the following new resources:

Name	Class	Type	Default	Access
XmtNhelpBackground	XtCBackground	XtRPixel	*Default background*	CSG
XmtNhelpFontList	XmCFontList	XmRFontList	*NULL*	CS
XmtNhelpForeground	XtCForeground	XtRPixel	*Default foreground*	CSG
XmtNhelpPixmap	XmtCHelpPixmap	XtRPixmap	*None*	CSG
XmtNhelpText	XmtCHelpText	XtRString	*NULL*	CS
XmtNhelpTitle	XmtCHelpTitle	XtRString	*NULL*	CS
XmtNtitleFontList	XmCFontList	XmRFontList	*NULL*	CSG
XmtNtitleForeground	XtCForeground	XtRPixel	*Default foreground*	CSG
XmtNvisibleLines	XmtCVisibleLines	XtRShort	*8*	CSG

`XmtNhelpBackground`
The background color of the help text display area.

`XmtNhelpFontList`
The XmFontList used to display the help text. If multi-font text is to be used, then this font list should contain each of the fonts. Note that this resource may not be queried.

`XmtNhelpForeground`
The foreground color of the help text.

`XmtNhelpPixmap`
A pixmap to be displayed in the upper left corner of the widget.

`XmtNhelpText`
The string to display in the help region of the widget. This string will be converted to an XmString by `XmtCreateXmString()`, and so can use any of the font-changing escape codes supported by that function. Note that this resource may not be queried.

`XmtNhelpTitle`
A string to display as the title of the displayed text. It will be converted to an XmString by `XmtCreateXmString()`, and displayed using the XmFontList specified by the `XmtNtitleFontList` resource. Note that this resource may not be queried.

`XmtNtitleFontList`
The XmFontList used to display the help title. This resource is simply a synonym for the `XmtNfontList` resource of the XmtLayout superclass.

`XmtNtitleForeground`
The color that the title should be drawn in.

`XmtNvisibleLines`
The number of lines of help text that should appear in the widget at one time. Any lines of text beyond this number will be available via a scrollbar.

Translations

The HelpBox widget does not define any translations of its own, because it never takes the keyboard focus itself. It does, however install accelerators for its XmScrolledWindow child onto its XmPushButton child. Because the push button is the only child of the HelpBox that takes the keyboard focus, these accelerators allow the user to scroll the displayed text up and down from the keyboard. Note that these accelerators bind the default Motif scrolling keys, but also allow paging up and down using the standard bindings for the *more* pager and the *emacs* text editor.

```
<Key>space:                  PageDownOrRight(0)
<Key>b:                      PageUpOrLeft(0)
Ctrl<Key>v:                  PageDownOrRight(0)
Meta<Key>v:                  PageUpOrLeft(0)
~Shift ~Ctrl <Key>osfUp:     IncrementUpOrLeft(0)
~Shift ~Ctrl <Key>osfDown:   IncrementDownOrRight(0)
~Shift Ctrl <Key>osfUp:      PageUpOrLeft(0)
~Shift Ctrl <Key>osfDown:    PageDownOrRight(0)
<Key>osfBeginLine:           TopOrBottom()
<Key>osfEndLine:             TopOrBottom()
<Key>osfPageUp:              PageUpOrLeft(0)
<Key>osfPageDown:            PageDownOrRight(0)
```

See the XmScrolledWindow documentation for an explanation of these action procedures.

See Also

Chapter 30, *Context Help*
`XmtCreateHelpBox()`, `XmtCreateHelpDialog()`,
`XmtHelpDisplayContextHelp()`

XmtHelp{Do,Display,Get}ContextHelp()

Name

XmtHelpDoContextHelp(), XmtHelpDisplayContextHelp(), XmtHelpGetContextHelp() — context help functions.

Synopsis

```
#include <Xmt/Help.h>
void XmtHelpDoContextHelp(Widget w)

void XmtHelpDisplayContextHelp(Widget w)

void XmtHelpGetContextHelp(Widget w, String *help_return,
                           String *title_return)
```

Arguments

Inputs

w — For XmtHelpDoContextHelp(), any widget in the application. For XmtHelpDisplayContextHelp() and XmtHelpGetContextHelp(), the widget for which help is to be displayed or obtained.

Outputs

help_return — For XmtHelpGetContextHelp(), returns the context help associated with *w*, or NULL if none is found. The string returned at this address should be freed with XtFree() when no longer needed.

title_return — For XmtHelpGetContextHelp(), returns the title of the context help associated with *w*, or NULL if none is found. The string returned at this address should be freed with XtFree() when no longer needed.

Description

Context help may be associated with any widget in an application by setting the **xmtHelp** and **xmtHelpTitle** pseudo-resources, as described in Chapter 30, *Context Help*. The three functions XmtHelpDoContextHelp(), XmtHelpDisplayContextHelp(), and XmtHelpGetContextHelp() are interfaces to the context help mechanism at three different levels of abstraction.

XmtHelpDoContextHelp() calls the Motif function XmTrackingLocate(), which displays a special cursor, waits until the user clicks the mouse button, and returns the widget that was clicked on. Once a widget is selected, XmtHelpDoContextHelp() calls XmtHelpDisplayContextHelp() to display context help for that specified widget in a dialog box. If no widget was selected, XmtHelpDoContextHelp() sounds the bell to indicate an error.

`XmtHelpDoContextHelp()` prompts the user with a cursor specified by the `helpCursor` application resource. The default value of this resource is the "question_arrow" cursor in the standard X11 cursor font.

`XmtHelpDisplayContextHelp()` calls `XmtHelpGetContextHelp()` to look up the context help for the widget *w*, and then displays the returned help text and title string in an automatically created and cached modeless XmtHelpBox dialog.

If there is no context help text defined for the specified widget, `XmtHelpDisplayContextHelp()` displays the string "There is no help available there." If no help title is defined, it displays the title "Context Help." The pixmap displayed in the XmtHelpBox dialog can be specified with the `XmtNcontextHelpPixmap` application resource. The default pixmap is an enlarged version of the "question_arrow" cursor used as the default context help cursor by `XmtHelpDoContextHelp()`.

The dialog boxes displayed by `XmtHelpDisplayContextHelp()` (and indirectly by `XmtHelpDoContextHelp()`) are not created until they are needed, and are cached for reuse. They are modeless so that the use may keep them displayed for as long as desired and may dismiss them at any time. These dialogs are completely managed by Xmt; you need not, and should not, take any action to destroy or unmanage them.

`XmtHelpGetContextHelp()` looks up and returns context help and a title for that help text for the widget *w*. The returned strings must be freed with `XtFree()` when no longer needed.

`XmtHelpGetContextHelp()` looks these up by reading the `xmtHelp` and `xmtHelpTitle` pseudo-resources for the widget *w*. If the `contextHelpFile` application resource is specified, then the resource file it names will be read in the first time that `XmtHelpGetContextHelp()` is called, and all context help will be looked up in that special help database. If no special `contextHelpFile` is specified, then the context help pseudo-resources are queried from the default database.

See Also

Chapter 30, *Context Help*
XmtHelpBox, `XmtHelpContextHelpCallback()`,
`XmtHelpInstallContextHelp()`

XmtHelpInstallContextHelp()

Name

`XmtHelpInstallContextHelp()`, `XmtHelpContextHelpCallback()` — keyboard bindings for context help.

Synopsis

```
#include <Xmt/Help.h>
void XmtHelpInstallContextHelp(Widget root, XtCallbackProc proc,
                               XtPointer data)

void XmtHelpContextHelpCallback(Widget w, XtPointer unused1,
                                XtPointer unused2)
```

Arguments

Inputs

`root` — The root of the widget tree for which the specified context help callback is to be registered.

`proc` — The callback procedure to register.

`data` — The data to register with the callback procedure.

`w` — For `XmtHelpContextHelpCallback()`, the widget for which context help is to be displayed.

`unused1`, *`unused2`* — These arguments to `XmtHelpContextHelpCallback()` are unused.

Description

`XmtHelpInstallContextHelp()` recursively traverses the widget tree rooted at *`root`* and registers the callback procedure *`proc`* with client data *`data`* on the `XmNhelpCallback` callback list of every widget that is a Motif widget or a subclass and that has its `XmNtraversalOn` resource set to `True`. That is, it calls `XtAddCallback()` for the `XmNhelpCallback` for every widget that can have the keyboard focus. All Motif widgets and their Xmt subclasses have an `XmNhelpCallback` callback list, and invoke the procedures registered on that list whenever they have the keyboard focus and the user strikes the **Help** key (usually bound to **F1**).

`XmtHelpContextHelpCallback()` is a convenience function that calls `XmtHelpDisplayContextHelp()` to display context help on the widget *w*. This function is of type `XtCallbackProc`, so it can be directly registered on the `XmNhelpCallback` callback list supported by all Motif and Xmt widgets. It can also be passed to `XmtHelpInstallContextHelp()` to register it on many widgets at once.

See Also

Chapter 30, *Context Help*
`XmtHelpDisplayContextHelp()`, `XmtHelpDoContextHelp()`, `XmtHelpGetContextHelp()`

XmtHSLToRGB()

Name

`XmtHSLToRGB()`, `XmtRGBToHSL()` — convert between the HSL and RGB color spaces.

Synopsis

```
#include <Xmt/Color.h>
void XmtHSLToRGB(unsigned h, unsigned s, unsigned l,
                 unsigned *r, unsigned *g, unsigned *b)

void XmtRGBToHSL(unsigned r, unsigned g, unsigned b,
                 unsigned *h, unsigned *s, unsigned *l)
```

Arguments

h The Hue of the color. This is an input to `XmtHSLToRGB()` and an output from `XmtRGBToHSL()`.

s The Saturation of the color. This is an input to `XmtHSLToRGB()` and an output from `XmtRGBToHSL()`.

l The Lightness of the color. This is an input to `XmtHSLToRGB()` and an output from `XmtRGBToHSL()`.

r The Red component of the color. This is an input to `XmtRGBToHSL()` and an output from `XmtHSLToRGB()`.

g The Green component of the color. This is an input to `XmtRGBToHSL()` and an output from `XmtHSLToRGB()`.

b The Blue component of the color. This is an input to `XmtRGBToHSL()` and an output from `XmtHSLToRGB()`.

Description

`XmtHSLToRGB()` converts a color specified in the HSL color space to the equivalent color in the RGB color space. `XmtRGBToHSL()` performs the opposite conversion—from the RGB color space to the HSL color space.

In X, the *r*, *g*, and *b* components of an RGB color vary between 0 and 65535. As implemented by Xmt, the Hue of a HSL color is an angle between 0 and 359, and the Saturation and Lightness of a color vary between 0 and 100. Note that the *h*, *s*, and *l* arguments are *unsigned*, not *float* or *double*. See Chapter 4, *Using Color*, for more information on the HSL color space.

See Also

Chapter 4, *Using Color*
`XmtAllocColor()`, `XmtRegisterPixelConverter()`

Xmt{Iconify,Deiconify,Raise,Lower}Shell()

Name

`XmtIconifyShell()`, `XmtDeiconifyShell()`, `XmtRaiseShell()`, `XmtLowerShell()` — perform window manager manipulations on shell widgets.

Synopsis

```
#include <Xmt/Xmt.h>
void XmtIconifyShell(Widget w)

void XmtDeiconifyShell(Widget w)

void XmtRaiseShell(Widget w)

void XmtLowerShell(Widget w)
```

Arguments

Inputs

w — The toplevel shell (i.e., not a dialog shell) that is to be manipulated, or any child of that toplevel shell.

Description

`XmtIconifyShell()` iconifies the specified shell widget.

`XmtDeiconifyShell()` uniconifies the specified shell widget.

`XmtRaiseShell()` uniconifies the specified shell widget, if necessary, and raises the shell window to to the top of the window stack.

`XmtLowerShell()` uniconifies the specified shell widget, if necessary, and lowers the shell window to to the bottom of the window stack.

These functions all work in a way that is compatible with ICCCM-compliant window managers. It is safe to call these functions even for shell widgets that have not been realized yet.

Usage

`XmtFocusShell()` goes a step beyond `XmtRaiseShell()`—it deiconifies and raises a shell, and also sets keyboard focus to it.

Remember that the user can iconify, deiconify, raise, and lower windows through the window manager. You can use these functions to provide shortcuts for window manager actions, but you should call them only in response to an explicit user request to manipulate the window—otherwise you risk confusing the user. You might use `XmtRaiseShell()`, for example when the user selects an item from a **Windows** menu of your application, for example.

See Also

Chapter 15, *Working with the Window Manager*
`XmtFocusShell()`

Name

XmtInitialize() — initialize an Xmt application.

Synopsis

```
#include <Xmt/Xmt.h>
Widget XmtInitialize(XtAppContext *app_context_return,
                     String application_class,
                     XrmOptionDescList options,
                     Cardinal num_options,
                     int *argc_in_out, String *argv_in_out,
                     String *fallback_resources,
                     ArgList args, Cardinal num_args)
```

Arguments

Inputs

application_class
: The application class name

options
: An array that describes arguments to be automatically parsed from the command line

num_options
: The number of elements in *options*

argc_in_out
: The address of the *argc* argument to main()

argv_in_out
: The *argv* command-line argument to main()

fallback_resources
: A NULL-terminated array of resource strings to be used if the application's app-defaults file cannot be located

args
: An array of resource name/value pairs to be set on the returned root ApplicationShell widget

num_args
: The number of elements in *args*

Outputs

app_context_return
: The address at which to return the application's XtAppContext

Returns

A newly created ApplicationShell widget at the root of a widget hierarchy.

Description

XmtInitialize() is a convenience function for initializing Xmt applications. It is a wrapper around XtAppInitialize(), which is the standard Xt initialization function, and has an identical argument list and return value to that function. As part of its initialization sequence, XtAppInitialize()

registers standard Xt resource converters, parses standard Xt command-line arguments, and reads standard Xt application resources. `XmtInitialize()` extends this initialization by registering Xmt resource converters, parsing Xmt-specific command-line arguments, and reading Xmt-specific application resources.

After calling `XtAppInitialize()`, `XmtInitialize()` calls `XmtParseCommandLine()` to read Xmt-specific arguments from the command-line, registers all of the major Xmt resource converters, and then calls `XmtInitializeApplicationShell()` to read the Xmt-specific application resources. See Chapter 7, *Application Resources and Command-Line Arguments*, for a list of application resources, command-line arguments, and resource converters. See `XtAppInitialize()` for more details on the arguments to this function.

See Also

Chapter 7, *Application Resources and Command-Line Arguments*
`XmtInitializeApplicationShell()`, `XmtParseCommandLine()`, `XmtRegisterAll()`, `XtAppInitialize()`

XmtInitializeApplicationShell()

Name

XmtInitializeApplicationShell() — set initial application resource values.

Synopsis

```
#include <Xmt/AppRes.h>
void XmtInitializeApplicationShell(Widget w,
                                   ArgList args,
                                   Cardinal num_args)
```

Arguments

Inputs

w — The root shell widget to be registered and have its application resources read, or any descendant of that widget.

args — An array of resource name/value pairs to override application resource values specified in the resource database or on the command line.

num_args — The number of elements in the *args* array.

Description

XmtInitializeApplicationShell() obtains values for the application resources used by the Xmt library from the resource database and overrides them with any values specified in the *args* array. These values are stored in a private structure associated with the shell widget for later use by the library. This function also initializes some private values that the Xmt library maintains for each root shell in an application. See Chapter 7, *Application Resources and Command-Line Arguments*, for a complete list of the Xmt application resources.

XmtInitializeApplicationShell() does not make copies of any string resources passed to it. This means that any strings passed in the *args* array must be constants or must be in memory that will not be modified or freed.

You need only call XmtInitializeApplicationShell() if you want to explicitly hard-code some application resource values with the args array. If you do not call this function yourself, the Xmt library will call it the first time it needs to look up an application resource.

XmtInitializeApplicationShell() has another purpose—it registers the name of the specified application shell for use by XmtNameToWidget() and the Xmt String-to-Widget converter. This is important only in applications that have more than one root shell widget, and want to be able to refer to widgets by name between the separate widget hierarchies.

See Also

Chapter 7, *Application Resources and Command-Line Arguments*
XmtGetApplicationValues(), XmtInitialize(), XmtNameToWidget(), XmtParseCommandLine(), XmtSetApplicationValues()

XmtInputField

Name

`XmtInputField` — an input field widget.

Synopsis

Include File:	`#include <Xmt/InputField.h>`
Constructor:	`XmtCreateInputField()`
Class Name:	XmtInputField
Class Pointer:	`xmtInputFieldWidgetClass`
Class Hierarchy:	Core → XmPrimitive → XmText → XmtInputField

Description

The XmtInputField widget is a subclass of the Motif XmText widget. It adds features to the XmText to make it easier to get textual input from the user, for example in dialog boxes that require input of various fields of a database record. Input may be performed in insert or overstrike mode, which is not possible with the standard XmText widget prior to Motif 1.2.

The InputField widget maintains the user's input value in the `XmtNinput` resource. This resource does not change (as the `XmNvalue` resource does) as the user types into the field, but only when the user enters a new value by pressing the **Return** key or by moving the keyboard focus on to some other widget. When the user enters a new value and presses **Return** or traverses to another widget, the procedures registered on the `XmtNinputCallback` callback list are called.

The InputField widget also supports two other ways of obtaining the input value. If the `XmtNbufferSymbolName` resource is specified, the InputField will look up the named symbol and store the input string at the specified address. This symbol must be of type `XmtRBuffer`, and must specify the address and the length of a character array allocated by the application.

If the `XmtNtargetSymbolName` resource is specified, the InputField will look up the named symbol, and will attempt to convert the input value to the type specified for that symbol. If the conversion succeeds, it will then store the converted value at the address specified by the symbol. If the conversion fails, then the widget treats the input as an error.

The `XmtNpattern` resource specifies what kind of input the InputField widget will accept. It is helpful when the input, such as a telephone number or a date, requires special formatting and needs to restrict input to digits, for example.

When a new value is entered into an InputField widget, it is passed to the procedures registered on the `XmtNverifyCallback` callback list. Any of these procedures may replace the input with something else, or may reject it. If the input value is rejected, or if a pattern is specified, and the input does not match the pattern, or if a target type is specified, and the input cannot be converted to that type, then the InputField widget calls the procedures registered on the `XmtNerrorCallback` callback list and provides feedback to the user that an error has occurred. This feedback can take a number of forms.

See Chapter 28, *The Input Field Widget*, for more information on all the features of the InputField widget, and in particular for information on InputField patterns, input verification and error handling.

Resources

InputField inherits the resources of the XmText class, and defines the following new resources. In addition, it overrides the default value for the XmPrimitive `XmNnavigationType` resource to be `XmNONE`. This means that traversal is possible between InputField widgets using the up and down arrow keys.

Name	*Class*	*Type*	*Default*	*Access*
XmtNautoDelete	XmtCAutoDelete	XtRBoolean	True	CSG
XmtNautoInsert	XmtCAutoInsert	XtRBoolean	True	CSG
XmtNbeepOnError	XmtCBeepOnError	XtRBoolean	True	CSG
XmtNbufferSymbolName	XmtCBufferSymbolName	XtRString	NULL	CSG
XmtNerrorBackground	XmtCErrorBackground	XtRPixel	*unspecified*	CSG
XmtNerrorCallback	XtCCallback	XtRCallback	NULL	C
XmtNerrorForeground	XmtCErrorForeground	XtRPixel	*unspecified*	CSG
XmtNerrorString	XmtCErrorString	XtRString	NULL	CSG
XmtNhighlightOnError	XmtCHighlightOnError	XtRBoolean	False	CSG
XmtNinput	XmtCInput	XtRString	NULL	CSG
XmtNinputCallback	XtCCallback	XtRCallback	NULL	C
XmtNmatchAll	XmtCMatchAll	XtRBoolean	True	CSG
XmtNoverstrike	XmtCOverstrike	XtRBoolean	False	CSG
XmtNpattern	XmtCPattern	XtRString	NULL	CSG
XmtNreplaceOnError	XmtCReplaceOnError	XtRBoolean	True	CSG
XmtNtargetSymbolName	XmtCTargetSymbolName	XtRString	NULL	CSG
XmtNverifyCallback	XtCCallback	XtRCallback	NULL	C

`XmtNautoDelete`

Whether the InputField should automatically delete constant characters (such as the parentheses around the area code in a telephone number) that appear in the `XmtNpattern` resource. The default is `True`.

`XmtNautoInsert`

Whether the InputField should automatically insert constant characters (such as the parentheses around the area code in a telephone number) that appear in the `XmtNpattern` resource. The default is `True`.

`XmtNbeepOnError`

Whether the InputField should beep when the user enters a bad value. The default is `True`. Note that this is not the same as the XmText `XmNverifyBell` resource, which must be set independently.

`XmtNbufferSymbolName`
The name of an `XmtSymbol` with type `XmtRBuffer` which specifies the address and size of a character array into which the user's input will be stored.

`XmtNerrorBackground`
The background color used to highlight bad input when the `XmtNhighlightOnError` resource is `True`, when the widget is being displayed on a color screen, and when the `XmtNerrorString` resource is unspecified. The default is -1. On some high-end platforms, this may be a valid `Pixel` value, but the InputField widget treats it as a special value indicating that highlighting should not be done by changing background color. If this resource is specified, the widget will be displayed with this background color until the user traverses back to the widget, presses **Return**, or modifies the value in the widget.

`XmtNerrorCallback`
A list of procedures to be invoked when the user attempts to enter a value that does not match the `XmtNpattern` resource, is rejected by a procedure on the `XmtNverifyCallback` callback list, or cannot be converted to the type specified by the `XmtNtargetSymbolName` resource. A procedure on this callback list may provide a new (presumably error-free) string to replace the user's input, and may also set a flag to indicate that the InputField widget should do no further error handling itself.

`XmtNerrorForeground`
The foreground color used to highlight bad input when the `XmtNhighlightOnError` resource is `True`, when the widget is being displayed on a color screen, and when the `XmtNerrorString` resource is unspecified. The default is -1. On some high-end platforms, this may be a valid `Pixel` value, but the InputField widget treats it as a special value indicating that highlighting should not be done by changing foreground color. If this resource is specified, the InputField widget will be displayed with this foreground color until the user traverses back to the widget, presses **Return**, or modifies the value in the widget.

`XmtNerrorString`
A string to display as feedback when the user enters an invalid value. The default is `NULL`. If specified, this string will be displayed until the user traverses back to the widget, presses **Return**, or modifies the value in the widget.

`XmtNhighlightOnError`
Whether an invalid input value should be highlighted to bring it to the user's attention. If either of the resources `XmtNerrorForeground` or `XmtNerrorBackground` are set, and the widget is being displayed on a color screen, then the specified colors will be used for highlighting. Otherwise, the text will be highlighted by underlining. The default is `False`. This resource is only used when `XmtNerrorString` is `NULL`.

`XmtNinput`
: The most recently entered input value. Setting this resource causes the new string to appear in the widget and to be stored in the buffer and target symbols, if they are specified. This resource is not updated as the user edits the value; it only changes when the user types **Return** or traverses out of the widget. Querying this resource returns a string that is owned by the InputField widget and must not be modified or freed. Note that this differs from the `XmNvalue` resource of the widget which changes with every keystroke, and which returns a *copy* of the current value as a string that must be freed. If no initial value is specified for this resource, and `XmtNbufferSymbolName` is specified, the contents of the buffer are used as the initial value.

`XmtNinputCallback`
: A callback list that is invoked when the `XmtNinput` resource changes. The procedures on this list are invoked only when the user edits the value and enters it by typing the **Return** key or by moving the input focus out of the widget. They are not invoked if the user traverses through the widget without changing the value or strikes the **Return** key without making any changes.

`XmtNmatchAll`
: Whether an input string must match the entire pattern, if a pattern is specified with the `XmtNpattern` resource. If `True`, then the input string must match every character in the pattern string. If `False`, then the input string is allowed to match only a prefix of the pattern string. The default is `True`.

`XmtNoverstrike`
: Whether the InputField widget is in overstrike mode. In this mode, characters inserted in the middle of the string overwrite the characters to their right, rather than being inserted before those characters. The default is `False`.

`XmtNpattern`
: The pattern, if any, that the input string must match. If this resource is set, it specifies the characters and types of characters that must appear at each position in the input. It is useful when the user is to enter data with a fixed format, such as a telephone number. See the "Pattern Handling" section for a description of the pattern syntax.

`XmtNreplaceOnError`
: Whether an invalid input value will be automatically replaced with the (valid) current value maintained by the InputField widget. The default is `True`.

`XmtNtargetSymbolName`
: The name of a symbol which specifies the type, address, and size of an application variable. If specified, the InputField will attempt to convert (using a resource converter) any input value to the specified type, and if the conversion is successful, will store the converted value at the specified

address. By default, no target is specified, and the input value will not be converted in this way. This resource provides automatic type conversion, but also allows the application back end to simply read input values from its own variables, without interacting with the widget.

`XmtNverifyCallback`
A callback list that is invoked in order to test the validity of a newly entered input value. The procedures on this list may modify the value, or they may reject it. If the value is rejected, the callbacks on the `XmtNinputCallback` list are not called.

Pattern Handling

If the `XmtNpattern` resource is set, it controls the number and type of characters that may be entered into the InputField widget, and may also specify certain characters that are to be automatically inserted and deleted as the user types. The `XmtNpattern` resource is a string containing one character for each character of the desired input string. Several characters have special meaning and when they occur in the pattern, they control the category of characters that the user may enter at that position in the input string. These special characters are the following:

Character	*Meaning*
`a`	Any; any alphabetic character
`b`	Both; any alphabetic character or digit
`c`	Character; any character of any sort
`d`	Digit; any digit
`A`	Any alphabetic character; converted to uppercase
`B`	Both—any alphabetic character or digit; uppercased
`C`	Any character; converted to uppercase

Any character in the pattern besides these special characters are literals that must appear at the same position in the input string as they do in the pattern.

When the `XmtNpattern` resource is set, insertions and deletions are only allowed at the end of the input string. This is because insertions and deletions shift the position of any following characters and can cause a mismatch against the pattern.

Callbacks

The InputField widget supports the following callback lists:

`XmtNerrorCallback`
The procedures registered on this callback list are called when the user enters an invalid value. The *`call_data`* argument for this callback is a pointer to the following structure:

```
typedef struct {
    String value;  /* don't change this field, modify or free the string */
    Boolean okay;  /* set to True to prevent further error handling */
} XmtInputFieldCallbackStruct;
```

The `value` field points to the invalid input value that caused the error callbacks to be called. This string is owned by the InputField widget and should not be modified or freed. The InputField invokes the `XmtNerrorCallback` callback list with the `okay` field set to `False`. If a callback procedure sets this field to `True`, then the InputField widget will not perform any subsequent error handling for the invalid value.

`XmtNinputCallback`

The procedures registered on this callback list are called whenever the user enters a valid value. A value is entered when the user presses **Return**, or moves the keyboard focus out of the InputField widget, either with the mouse or through keyboard traversal. Note that if the value has not been edited from its previous value, the callbacks are not called. A valid value is one that matches the complete `XmtNpattern` resource, if it is specified and if `XmtNmatchAll` is `True`, that is not rejected by any of the verify callbacks, and that can be converted to the target type, if any is specified. The *`call_data`* argument to the `XmtNinputCallback` is of type `char *`, and is the newly entered value. This string is owned by the InputField widget and must not be modified or freed by the application. The procedures on this callback list are invoked only after the new value has been stored in the buffer and target, if either are specified.

`XmtNverifyCallback`

The procedures on this callback list are called as part of the InputField's error checking procedure. The *`call_data`* argument to these procedures is a pointer to the following structure:

```
typedef struct {
    String value;   /* this string can be replaced, but not modified
                       or freed */
    Boolean okay;   /* initially True; set to False if the string is bad */
} XmtInputFieldCallbackStruct;
```

The `value` field contains the newly entered string. The string is owned by the InputField widget, and should not be modified or freed by the application. A callback procedure can modify the `value` field itself, however, so that it points to a different string. If the `value` field is changed in this way, the InputField widget will make its own private copy of the new value and will proceed as if the user had entered the new string rather than the string it replaced. The InputField widget invokes the procedures on this list with the `okay` field set to `True`. Any of the procedures on the list may reject the input value by setting this field to `False`. Note that the procedures on this list are called before the procedures on the `XmtNinputCallback` callback list.

Translations and Actions

The InputField widget defines a single new action procedure `overstrike()`. If called with the single argument "`on`", it will turn overstrike mode on for the widget by setting the `XmtNoverstrike` resource. If called with the argument "`off`", it will turn overstrike mode off. If called with no argument, it will toggle the state of overstrike mode.

The InputField widget inherits the translations of the XmText widget, and does not add any new translations of its own. In particular, it does not bind the new `overstrike()` action to any key. If you want to allow the user to be able to switch between insert and overstrike modes in the widget, you must add this translation explicitly.

Sensitivity

Because the InputField is often used with a caption provided by an XmtLayout parent widget, it takes special care to notice when its own sensitivity state changes, and updates the `XmtNlayoutSensitive` constraint resource as necessary so that any caption will appear "greyed out" when the InputField is not sensitive.

See Also

Chapter 28, *The Input Field Widget*
`XmtCreateInputField()`, `XmtInputFieldGetString()`,
`XmtInputFieldSetString()`, `XmtRegisterInputField()`

Name

`XmtInputFieldGetString()`, `XmtInputFieldSetString()` — query or set the value of an XmtInputField widget.

Synopsis

```
#include <Xmt/InputField.h>
String XmtInputFieldGetString(Widget w)

void XmtInputFieldSetString(Widget w, String s)
```

Arguments

Inputs

w The XmtInputField widget that is to have its value queried or set.

s For `XmtInputFieldSetString()`, the new string to display in the XmtInputField widget *w*.

Returns

`XmtInputFieldGetString()` returns the input value of the XmtInputField *w*.

Description

`XmtInputFieldGetString()` returns the input value of the specified XmtInputField widget. Calling this function is equivalent to, but somewhat more efficient than, querying the `XmtNinput` resource of the widget. Note that the value returned is a pointer to memory owned by the widget, and should not be modified or freed. The returned string is only guaranteed to be valid until the next time control returns to the XmtInputField widget, so if the value must be used beyond the scope of the current procedure, a copy should be made into memory owned by the application.

`XmtInputFieldSetString()` sets the specified string as the new value to appear in the specified XmtInputField widget. Calling this function is equivalent to, but more efficient than, setting the string on the `XmtNinput` resource of the widget. Note that this function does not subject the specified string to any of the input validation that user strings are subjected to, and it does not cause the `XmtNinputCallback` callback list to be invoked.

See Also

Chapter 28, *The Input Field Widget*
XmtInputField

XmtLayout

Name

`XmtLayout` — a general-purpose manager widget.

Synopsis

Include File: `#include <Xmt/Layout.h>`
Constructor: `XmtCreateLayout()`
Class Name: XmtLayout
Class Pointer: `xmtLayoutWidgetClass`
Class Hierarchy: Core → Composite → Constraint → XmManager → XmBulletinBoard → XmtLayout

Description

The XmtLayout widget is a general-purpose manager widget. It uses constraint resources to provide a dynamic interface for positioning children, and also parses a simple layout grammar which describes the widget layout with a single string resource.

Children of the Layout widget are laid out in nested rows and columns, with specified amounts of blank space between them. All children (including rows and columns), and the space between the children have a "stretchiness" factor that specifies how much each child or space will grow when the widget is resized. This is a fully general layout scheme, derived from the TeX "boxes-and-glue" text layout algorithm. It is as powerful and flexible as the "attachment" scheme used by the XmForm widget, for example, but easier to understand, and through the layout grammar, far easier to specify.

The Layout widget provides some features beyond simple layout of widgets. It will draw a frame around any of its children, will draw a separator running along any edge of any child, and can also display a text caption for each of its children. Since the Layout widget does this drawing itself, the overhead of the XmFrame, XmSeparator, and XmLabel widgets that would otherwise be needed is avoided. The Layout widget also supports special gadget children that display text and pixmap labels. These gadgets are cheaper than widgets, and are even cheaper than the Motif XmGadget types.

Finally, the Layout widget allows the sizes of its children to be specified in resolution-independent units. The static layout grammar allows sizes to be directly specified in inches, millimeters, points, ems or ens, and a public function exists to convert from these units to pixels for dynamic layouts.

Resources

Layout inherits the resources of the XmBulletinBoard class, and defines or overrides the resources, as shown in the following table.

Name	Class	Type	Default	Access
XmtNdebugLayout	XmtCDebugLayout	XtRBoolean	False	CSG
XmtNdefaultSpacing	XmtCDefaultSpacing	XtRDimension	10	CSG

Name	*Class*	*Type*	*Default*	*Access*
XmtNfont	XtCFont	XtRFontStruct	XtDefaultFont	CSG
XmtNfontList	XmCFontList	XmRFontList	NULL	CSG
XmtNlayout	XmtCLayout	XtRString	NULL	C
XmNmarginHeight	XmCMarginHeight	XmRVertical-Dimension	5	CSG
XmNmarginWidth	XmCMarginWidth	XmRHorizontal-Dimension	5	CSG
XmtNorientation	XmCOrientation	XmROrientation	XmVERTICAL	CG

`XmtNdebugLayout`
If `True`, the Layout widget will draw a one-pixel-wide frame around each of its children, including spaces, rows, and columns. This makes it easy to see which nested row or column each child is positioned in, and can help when debugging layouts. When this resource is set, `XmtNlayoutFrameType` and the other frame constraint resources, described below, are ignored.

`XmtNdefaultSpacing`
The width or height, in pixels, of the fixed-size, non-stretchable space specified in the layout grammar with the `#` character. This value is not directly used by the Layout widget or the XmtLayoutSpace gadget.

`XmtNfont`
An `XFontStruct` pointer used to set the `XmtNfontList` resource if it is left unspecified. This resource is provided because it is sometimes more convenient to specify an Xlib `XFontStruct` than a Motif `XmFontList`.

`XmtNfontList`
The `XmFontList` that is be used by all XmtLayoutString gadget children and may also be used other XmtLayoutGadget children that draw text. If this resource is unspecified, the `XmtNfont` resource will be used to create an `XmFontList` instead.

`XmtNlayout`
A string that specifies a static layout for the children of the Layout widget. In order for this resource to work, the application programmer must register the layout grammar parser by calling `XmtRegisterLayoutParser()`. See the "Layout Grammar" section below for more information. This resource should be set when the Layout widget is created, and may never be changed. The Layout widget parses this string once, without modifying it, and never refers to it again. For this reason, the widget does not make a copy of the string, which means that this resource should not be queried.

`XmNmarginHeight`
The height, in pixels of the margin between the top and bottom edges of the widget and the nearest child. This is an XmBulletinBoard resource; the Layout widget overrides the default value to 5 pixels.

`XmNmarginWidth`
The width, in pixels of the margin between the left and right edges of the widget and the nearest child. This is an XmBulletinBoard resource; the Layout widget overrides the default value to 5 pixels.

`XmtNorientation`
The orientation of the topmost (automatically created) row or column of the Layout widget. Children widgets that are not explicitly positioned in a row or column with constraint resources will be placed in this toplevel row or column. Legal values are `XmVERTICAL` and `XmHORIZONTAL`. `XmVERTICAL` is the default, so that the Layout widget arranges its children in a column. This resource may be set when the Layout widget is created, but may never be changed.

Constraint Resources

The Layout widget specifies the layout and decoration of its children through constraint resources. Each of the constraint resource names begins with the prefix "layout" in order to avoid name clashes with the resources of the child widgets to which these constraints are applied.

The Layout constraint resources are the following:

Name	*Class*	*Type*	*Default*	*Access*
XmtNlayoutAfter	XmtCLayoutAfter	XtRWidget	NULL	CSG
XmtNlayoutAllow Resize	XmtCLayoutAllow- Resize	XtRBoolean	True	CSG
XmtNlayoutBefore	XmtCLayoutBefore	XtRWidget	NULL	CSG
XmtNlayoutCaption	XmtCLayoutCaption	XmRXmString	NULL	CSG
XmtNlayoutCaption- Alignment	XmtCLayoutCaption- Alignment	XmRAlignment	XmALIGNMENT_- BEGINNING	CSG
XmtNlayoutCaption- Justification	XmtCLayoutCaption- Justification	XmtRXmtLayout- Justification	XmtLayout- Centered	CSG
XmtNlayoutCaption- Margin	XmtCLayoutCaption- Margin	XtRDimension	2	CSG
XmtNlayoutCaption- Position	XmtCLayoutCaption- Position	XmtRXmtLayout- Edge	XmtLayoutLeft	CSG
XmtNlayoutFrame- LineType	XmtCLayoutFrame- LineType	XmtRXmtLayout- FrameLine- Type	XmtLayoutFrame- EtchedIn	CSG
XmtNlayoutFrame- Margin	XmtCLayoutFrame- Margin	XtRDimension	5	CSG
XmtNlayoutFrame- Position	XmtCLayoutFrame- Position	XmtRXmtLayout- FramePosition	XmtLayoutFrame- Inside	CSG

Name	*Class*	*Type*	*Default*	*Access*
XmtNlayoutFrame-Thickness	XmtCLayoutFrame-Thickness	XtRDimension	2	CSG
XmtNlayoutFrame-Type	XmtCLayoutFrame-Type	XmtRXmtLayout-FrameType	XmtLayoutFrame-None	CSG
XmtNlayout-Height	XmtCLayoutHeight	XtRDimension	0	CSG
XmtNlayoutIn	XmtCLayoutIn	XtRWidget	NULL	CSG
XmtNlayout-Justification	XmtCLayout-Justification	XmtRXmtLayout-Justification	XmtLayout-Filled	CSG
XmtNlayoutMargin-Height	XmtCLayoutMargin-Height	XtRDimension	See below	CSG
XmtNlayoutMargin-Width	XmtCLayoutMargin-Width	XtRDimension	See below	CSG
XmtNlayoutPosition	XmtCLayoutPosition	XtRPosition	-1	CSG
XmtNlayoutSensitive	XmtCLayoutSensitive	XtRBoolean	True	CSG
XmtNlayoutShrink-ability	XmtCLayoutShrink-ability	XtRDimension	See below	CSG
XmtNlayoutStretch-ability	XmtCLayoutStretch-ability	XtRDimension	See below	CSG
XmtNlayoutWidth	XmtCLayoutWidth	XtRDimension	0	CSG

`XmtNlayoutAfter`
The widget directly after which, in the same row or column, this child should be laid out. Setting this resource positions the child in the Layout widget and causes the `XmtNlayoutBefore`, `XmtNlayoutIn`, and `XmtNlayoutPosition` constraint resources to be updated to reflect the new position. If this resource is set, it overrides those other position resources.

`XmtNlayoutAllowResize`
Whether the Layout widget will attempt to grant resize requests from children. If `False`, any geometry request from this child will be refused. The default is True.

`XmtNlayoutBefore`
The widget directly before which, in the same row or column, this child should be laid out. Setting this resource positions the child in the Layout widget and causes the `XmtNlayoutAfter`, `XmtNlayoutIn`, and `XmtNlayoutPosition` constraint resources to be updated to reflect the new position. The `XmtNlayoutAfter` resource overrides this resource, if it is set, and this resource overrides the `XmtNlayoutIn` and `XmtNlayoutPosition` resources.

`XmtNlayoutCaption`
An XmString to be displayed by the Layout widget as a caption for this child. This string is drawn entirely by the Layout widget without the need for an XmLabel or any other widget or gadget.

XmtNlayoutCaptionAlignment

The alignment of lines within a multi-line caption. This resource is of the same type as the XmNalignment resource of the XmLabel widget and has three legal values: XmALIGNMENT_BEGINNING, which draws the lines flush left with the bounding box of the whole string, XmALIGNMENT_CENTER, which centers the individual lines within the box, and XmALIGNMENT_END, which draws the lines flush right. This resource only has an effect when the caption has more than one line; it controls the positioning of individual lines relative to the caption as a whole. Do not confuse it with the XmtNlayoutCaptionJustification resource, which controls the positioning of the entire caption relative to the widget.

XmtNlayoutCaptionJustification

The justification of the caption along the edge specified by the XmtNlayoutCaptionPosition resource. For captions placed along the left or right edges of the widget, this resource controls the vertical justification of the caption, and for captions placed along the top or bottom edges, it controls the horizontal justification. The values XmtLayoutFlushLeft and XmtLayoutFlushTop are equivalent and both produce left or top justification depending upon the XmtNlayoutCaptionPosition resource. The value XmtLayoutCentered centers the caption vertically or horizontally, and the values XmtLayoutFlushRight and XmtLayoutFlushBottom produce right or bottom justification.

XmtNlayoutCaptionMargin

The distance, in pixels, between the closest edge of the caption and the child widget, or between the caption and the frame surrounding the child widget. To save space in the Layout constraint record, this resource is stored in a unsigned character field, and therefore has a maximum value of 255 pixels.

XmtNlayoutCaptionPosition

The edge of the child widget along which the caption should be displayed. Legal values are XmtLayoutLeft, XmtLayoutRight, XmtLayoutTop, and XmtLayoutBottom.

XmtNlayoutFrameLineType

The style of line to be used for the frame. The values XmtLayoutFrameShadowIn, XmtLayoutFrameShadowOut, XmtLayoutFrameEtchedIn, and XmtLayoutFrameEtchedOut draw the standard shadowed and etched frames supported by the XmFrame widget. XmtLayoutFrameSingleLine draws a single line in the foreground color, with its width specified by the XmtNlayoutFrameThickness constraint. XmtLayoutFrameDoubleLine draws two single-pixel wide lines, with a separation determined by the XmtNlayoutFrameThickness constraint. When the XmtNlayoutFrame- Type resource specifies that the frame should be drawn as a separator along only one edge of the widget, the "shadow in" and "shadow out" types are drawn as "etched in" and "etched out."

`XmtNlayoutFrameMargin`
The distance, in pixels, between the inside of the frame and the child widget, or the frame and the caption, if a caption is specified and appears within the frame. For efficiency, this resource is stored in an unsigned character field of the Layout constraint record. Thus the maximum value of this resource is 255.

`XmtNlayoutFramePosition`
How the frame should be positioned with respect to the caption, if any, of the child. The value `XmtLayoutFrameInside` specifies that the frame should be drawn inside of the caption. In this case, the position of the caption may be adjusted, depending on its justification, so that it is flush with an outside edge of the frame rather than an edge of the child widget itself. The value `XmtLayoutFrameOutside` specifies that the frame should surround both the child widget and its caption. The value `XmtLayoutFrameThrough` specifies that the frame and caption should be drawn independently at the distances from the child specified by the `XmtNlayoutFrameMargin` and `XmtNlayoutCaptionMargin` constraints. By default, this will cause the caption to be drawn over a portion of the frame, which produces an appealing visual effect with some line types.

`XmtNlayoutFrameThickness`
The line thickness of the frame to be drawn. This resource is stored in an unsigned character field of the Layout constraint record. Thus the maximum value for this resource is 255.

`XmtNlayoutFrameType`
The type of frame to be drawn. The default value, `XmtLayoutFrameNone`, specifies that no frame is to be drawn. `XmtLayoutFrameBox` specifies that a traditional frame is to be drawn as a box around the child. The remaining legal values for this resource, `XmtLayoutFrameLeft`, `XmtLayoutFrameRight`, `XmtLayoutFrameTop`, and `XmtLayoutFrameBottom`, specify that the frame is to be drawn only along one edge of the widget. In this case, the frame serves as a separator, like those drawn by the Motif XmSeparator widget.

`XmtNlayoutHeight`
The preferred height, in pixels, of this child. If specified, this is the initial height of the child, and is the base height from which the child will stretch or shrink. If set to 0, the child's preferred height will be used. Note that this size does not include any space required for the child's margins, caption, or frame.

`XmtNlayoutIn`
The row or column gadget within which this child should be laid out. Setting this constraint resource, in conjunction with `XmtNlayoutPosition` resource, positions the child in the Layout widget and causes the `XmtNlayoutAfter` and `XmtNlayoutBefore` resources to be set to reflect the position. The `XmtNlayoutAfter` and `XmtNlayoutBefore` resources override this resource, if either is set. If none of these resources are set, then the child will be positioned in the topmost row or column. The orientation of this topmost box is determined by the Layout `XmtNorientation` resource.

`XmtNlayoutJustification`
The justification of this child within the width of its column, or within the height of its row. This resource is of type `XmtLayoutJustification`, which is an enumerated type that has the following legal values: `XmtLayoutFilled`, `XmtLayoutCentered`, `XmtLayoutFlushLeft`, `XmtLayoutFlushTop`, `XmtLayoutFlushRight`, and `XmtLayoutFlushBottom`. The default is `XmtLayoutFilled`, which specifies that the child should be as wide as its containing column or as high as its containing row. The other values indicate that the child should be laid out at its natural size against the left, top, right, or bottom edges of the containing row or column, or centered within its containing row or column. Note that this resource only positions child widgets within the "minor dimension" of a row or column—vertically in a row and horizontally in a column.

`XmtNlayoutMarginHeight`
The height, in pixels, of a margin to be placed above and below the child widget. This margin falls outside of any caption or frame that the child might have. For memory efficiency, this resource is stored in an unsigned character field, and therefore has a maximum value of 255. The default margin for most children is one-half of the space size specified by the `XmtNdefaultSpacing` resource of the Layout widget itself, but the default margin for rows and columns is 0, so that children positioned within nested rows and columns do not become nested within multiple margins.

`XmtNlayoutMarginWidth`
The width, in pixels, of a margin to be placed to the left and to the right of the child widget. This margin falls outside of any caption or frame that the child might have. For memory efficiency, this resource is stored in an unsigned character field, and therefore has a maximum value of 255. The default margin for most children is one-half of the space size specified by the `XmtNdefaultSpacing` resource of the Layout widget itself, but the default margin for rows and columns is 0, so that children positioned within nested rows and columns do not become nested within multiple margins.

`XmtNlayoutPosition`
The numerical position within the containing row or column at which this child should be laid out. Setting this constraint resource, in conjunction with `XmtNlayoutIn` resource, positions the child in the Layout widget

and causes the `XmtNlayoutAfter` and `XmtNlayoutBefore` resources to be set to reflect that position. The `XmtNlayoutAfter` and `XmtNlayoutBefore` resources override this resource, if either is set. The position 0 specifies that the child is to be the first in the row or column, and the special value -1 (the default) specifies that it is to be the last. The defaults for the positioning constraint resources are chosen so that children will be positioned by default at the end of the topmost (automatically created) row or column.

`XmtNlayoutSensitive`
: Specifies whether the child is sensitive or not. If `False`, the child's caption, if any, will be drawn "greyed out" with a stipple. Generally, if a child has a caption, this constraint resource should be set whenever a widget's `XtNsensitive` resource is set either directly or with `XtSetSensitive()`. The XmtChooser and XmtInputField widgets are often used with a caption, and automatically set this resource whenever their `XtNsensitive` resource changes.

`XmtNlayoutShrinkability`
: The "shrinkability factor" for this child, which controls whether, and in what proportion to other children, this child will shrink when the parent Layout widget is made smaller than its default size. The default value is 10 for all widgets, XmGadgets, rows, columns, and XmtLayoutSpace gadgets. For Layout string, pixmap, and separator gadgets, the default is 0.

`XmtNlayoutStretchability`
: The "stretchability factor" for this child, which controls whether, and in what proportion to other children, this child will stretch when the parent Layout widget is made larger than its default size. The default value is 10 for all widgets, XmGadgets, rows, columns, and XmtLayoutSpace gadgets. For Layout string, pixmap, and separator gadgets, the default is 0.

`XmtNlayoutWidth`
: The preferred width, in pixels, of this child. If specified, this is the initial width of the child, and the base width from which the child will stretch or shrink. If unspecified, the child's preferred width will be used. Note that this size does not include any space required for the child's margins, caption, or frame.

Row and Column Resources

The Layout widget arranges its children into nested rows and columns. These rows and columns are themselves children of the Layout widget, implemented as a special gadget type, the XmtLayoutBox. The Layout widget and the XmtLayoutBox gadget work together closely, and much of the important layout functionality of the Layout widget is in fact implemented by the XmtLayoutBox. Because the XmtLayoutBox is so important to the layout process, its resources are summarized here. You can find a more complete listing in the XmtLayoutBox reference page.

Name	*Class*	*Type*	*Default*	*Access*
XmtNbackground	XtCBackground	XtRPixel	*unspecified*	CSG
XmtNequal	XmtCEqual	XtRBoolean	False	CSG
XmtNitemStretch	XmtCItemStretch	XtRDimension	1	CSG
XmtNorientation	XmCOrientation	XmROrientation	XmHORIZONTAL	CSG
XmtNspace	XmtCSpace	XtRDimension	0	CSG
XmtNspaceStretch	XmtCSpaceStretch	XtRDimension	1	CSG
XmtNspaceType	XmtCSpaceType	XmtRXmtLayout-SpaceType	XmtLayoutSpace-None	CSG

Layout Grammar

The `XmtNlayout` resource is a string which specifies the layout of the Widget and XmGadget children of the XmtLayout widget, and may also specify Xmt-LayoutGadget children to be automatically created. The string is a list of items that appear in the toplevel row or column (its orientation is determined by the `XmtNorientation` resource). These items may include nested rows or columns which have a list of their own items within curly braces. Any item may have a list of modifiers which specify size, stretchability, justification, captions, frames, and so on.

Rows, columns, and other layout gadgets are automatically created as the layout specification is parsed. Widgets and XmGadget items can be specified by name in the layout string. When an item name is encountered without any type, it is assumed to be a widget or gadget that will be created later. The XmtLayout widget remembers the position and modifiers specified for this widget, and applies them when a widget by that name is eventually created.

The XmtLayout widget does not link the parser for this layout grammar by default. If you specify a value for the `XmtNlayout` resource, you should also register the parser by calling `XmtRegisterLayoutParser()`. If an application never calls this function, that code will never be linked. This means that statically linked applications that do not use the parser do not pay the overhead of the parser code.

The layout grammar was designed to be easily readable and intuitive. Chapter 18, *The Layout Widget: A Tutorial*, provides an extended tutorial on using the grammar, and Chapter 19, *The Layout Widget: The Details*, contains an annotated definition of the grammar that explains the semantics as well as the syntax.

For reference, the layout grammar is summarized in BNF form below. Items within single quotes are terminal symbols of the grammar—keywords or punctuation that should appear exactly as shown. Items in italics are non-terminals—items that are defined elsewhere in the grammar, or which are implicitly defined. Items within curly braces are repeated zero or more times and items within square brackets are optional. When a non-terminal has more than one possible definition, they are presented on separate lines, or are separated by vertical bars. Note that the grammar is case-sensitive and that almost all keywords begin with a capital letter. This means that keywords will not conflict with widget names which, by convention, begin with a lowercase letter.

layout:: { { *modifier* } *item* }

item:: *widget* | *box* | *label* | *icon* | *separator* | *space*

widget:: *identifier*
registered-widget-type identifier

box:: 'Row' [*name*] '{' *layout* '}'
'Col' [*name*] '{' *layout* '}'

label:: *string*
'String' [*name*] *string*

icon:: 'Pixmap' [*name*] *pixmap-name* [',' *mask-name*]
'Bitmap' [*name*] *bitmap-name* [',' *mask-name*]

separator:: 'VSep' | '|'
'HSep' | '='

space:: 'Space' | '#'{'#'} | '~'{'~'} | '<>'

modifier::
caption | *frame* | *spacing* | *justification* | *size* |b *resize* | *margin* | *misc*

caption:: 'Caption' [*edge*[*just*[*align*]]] [*margin*] 4 flstring

edge:: 'l' | 'r' | 't' | 'b'

just:: 'l' | 'r' | 't' | 'b' | 'c'

align:: 'l' | 'r' | 'c'

margin:: *integer*

frame::
'Etched' ['In'] *[edge] [position] [margin [thickness]]*
'Etched Out' *[edge] [position] [margin [thickness]]*
'Shadowed' ['In'] *[edge] [position] [margin [thickness]]*
'Shadowed Out' *[edge] [position] [margin [thickness]]*
'Boxed' *[edge] [position] [margin [thickness]]*
'Line' *[edge] [position] [margin [thickness]]*
'DoubleBoxed' *[edge] [position] [margin [thickness]]*
'DoubleLine' *[edge] [position] [margin [thickness]]*

edge:: *'Left'* | *'Right'* | *'Top'* | *'Bottom'*

position:: *'Inside'* | *'Outside'* | *'Through'*

margin:: *integer*

thickness:: *integer*

spacing::
'Equal'
'Even' *[space] ['+' space_stretch ['/' item_stretch]]*
'EvenSpaced' *[space] ['+' space_stretch ['/' item_stretch]]*
'LREvenSpaced' *[space] ['+' space_stretch ['/' item_stretch]]*
'LCRSpaced' *[space] ['+' space_stretch ['/' item_stretch]]*
'IntervalSpaced' *[space] ['+' space_stretch ['/' item_stretch]]*

space:: *integer-or-float [units]*

space_stretch::
integer

item_stretch::
integer

justification:: *'Filled'* | *'FlushLeft'* | *'FlushTop'* | *'FlushRight'* | *'FlushBottom'* | *'Centered'*

size:: *integer-or-float [units]*
integer-or-float [units] 'Wide'
integer-or-float [units] 'High'
integer-or-float [units] '%' integer-or-float [units]

resize:: *'Fixed'* | *'Stretchable'*
'+' integer
'-' integer

margin:: *'Margin' integer*
'Margin Width' integer
'Margin Height' integer

misc:: *'Color' string*
'Unresizable'
'Unmanaged'

name:: *identifier*

units:: *'in'* | *'mm'* | *'pt'* | *'em'* | *'en'*

Translations and Actions

The Layout widget inherits the translations of the XmBulletinBoard class, which serve mainly to allow traversal to work for XmGadget children of the widget. The Layout widget does not define any new translations, nor any new actions.

Callbacks

The Layout widget does not define any new callback resources.

Types

A number of the Layout widget and XmtLayoutBox gadget resources and constraint resources use enumerated types. These types are defined as follows in the header file *<Xmt/Layout.h>*.

```
typedef enum {
    XmtLayoutFilled,
    XmtLayoutFlushLeft,
    XmtLayoutFlushTop,
    XmtLayoutFlushRight,
    XmtLayoutFlushBottom,
    XmtLayoutCentered
} XmtLayoutJustification;

typedef enum {
```

```
    XmtLayoutTop,
    XmtLayoutBottom,
    XmtLayoutLeft,
    XmtLayoutRight
} XmtLayoutEdge;

typedef enum {
    XmtLayoutFrameNone,
    XmtLayoutFrameBox,
    XmtLayoutFrameLeft,
    XmtLayoutFrameRight,
    XmtLayoutFrameTop,
    XmtLayoutFrameBottom
} XmtLayoutFrameType;

typedef enum {
    XmtLayoutFrameShadowIn,
    XmtLayoutFrameShadowOut,
    XmtLayoutFrameEtchedIn,
    XmtLayoutFrameEtchedOut,
    XmtLayoutFrameSingleLine,
    XmtLayoutFrameDoubleLine,
} XmtLayoutFrameLineType;

typedef enum {
    XmtLayoutFrameInside,
    XmtLayoutFrameThrough,
    XmtLayoutFrameOutside
} XmtLayoutFramePosition;

typedef enum {
    XmtLayoutSpaceNone,
    XmtLayoutSpaceEven,
    XmtLayoutSpaceLREven,
    XmtLayoutSpaceInterval,
    XmtLayoutSpaceLCR
} XmtLayoutSpaceType;
```

Converters

The Layout widget registers type converters for all of the enumerated types it uses: `XmtLayoutJustification`, `XmtLayoutEdge`, `XmtLayoutFrame-LineType`, `XmtLayoutFrameType`, `XmtLayoutFramePosition`, and `XmtLayoutSpaceType`. The converters are all case-sensitive; the value must appear in a resource file as it would in a C file, except that any of the repeated prefixes may be omitted. Thus the following strings can all be converted to the value `XmtLayoutFrameEtchedIn`: "`XmtLayoutFrameEtchedIn`", "`LayoutFrame- EtchedIn`", "`FrameEtchedIn`", and "`EtchedIn`". See the "Types" section above for a complete list of enumerated types and values used by the Layout widget.

The `XmtNlayout` resource is of type `XtRString`, so the layout grammar specified on this resource does not need a resource converter to convert it into some internal type. Instead, the Layout widget parses this string to create the layout. This "layout parser" is similar to a resource converter, but is not the same thing.

See Also

Chapter 18, *The Layout Widget: A Tutorial*
Chapter 19, *The Layout Widget: The Details*
`XmtCreateLayout()`, `XmtCreateLayoutCol()`, `XmtCreateLayoutRow()`, `XmtLayoutBox`, `XmtLayoutConvertSizeToPixels()`, `XmtLayoutDisableLayout()`, `XmtLayoutEnableLayout()`, `XmtLayoutPixmap`, `XmtLayoutSeparator`, `XmtLayoutSpace`, `XmtLayoutString`, `XmtRegisterLayoutParser()`, `XmtRegisterLayoutCreateMethod()`

Name

`XmtLayoutBox` — the row or column gadget used within the XmtLayout widget.

Synopsis

Include File:	`#include <Xmt/LayoutG.h>`
Constructor:	`XmtCreateLayoutBox()`, `XmtLayoutCol()`, `XmtLayoutRow()`
Class Name:	XmtLayoutBox
Class Pointer:	`xmtLayoutBoxGadgetClass`
Class Hierarchy:	RectObj → XmtLayoutGadget → XmtLayoutBox

Description

The XmtLayoutBox widget is a gadget designed to be used with the XmtLayout widget, which organizes other children of the Layout into rows and columns. The Layout widget organizes its children into nested rows and columns; the LayoutBox acts as a "container" to group items in a row or column together. Note that the LayoutBox is not a composite widget like the XmRowColumn widget. Layout items within a row or column are siblings of the LayoutBox, not children of it. The LayoutBox serves as a placeholder for grouping items—children of an Layout widget can be placed within a particular LayoutBox gadget by setting the `XmtNlayoutIn` constraint resource to point to the LayoutBox. The LayoutBox does not have any visual appearance of its own, but as a child of the Layout widget, it can have a caption or frame automatically provided by the widget. Also, the LayoutBox can specify the way the items it contains will be spaced, and can specify that the items it contains should be made the same width or height.

Resources

XmtLayoutBox inherits the resources of the RectObj and XmtLayoutGadget classes, and defines the following new resources:

Name	Class	Type	Default	Access
XmtNbackground	XtCBackground	XtRPixel	*unspecified*	CSG
XmtNequal	XmtCEqual	XtRBoolean	False	CSG
XmtNitemStretch	XmtCItemStretch	XtRDimension	1	CSG
XmtNorientation	XmCOrientation	XmROrientation	XmHORIZONTAL	CSG
XmtNspace	XmtCSpace	XtRDimension	0	CSG
XmtNspaceStretch	XmtCSpaceStretch	XtRDimension	1	CSG
XmtNspaceType	XmtCSpaceType	XmtRXmtLayoutSpaceType	XmtLayoutSpaceNone	CSG

`XmtNbackground`
The color for the background of the row or column. If specified, the LayoutBox will fill itself with this color before any captions, frames or other decorations are drawn. If no color is specified, the LayoutBox will take no special action, and will have the same background color as its parent Layout widget.

`XmtNequal`
Whether items in a row should have equal widths or items in a column should have equal heights. If this resource is set to `True`, and the LayoutBox is configured as a row, then any items in that widget (except for separator or space gadgets) will have their widths adjusted so that they are all as wide as the widest item. Similarly, items in a column will have their heights adjusted so that they are as high as the highest item. If this resource is `False` (the default), then no special action will be taken to adjust the width or height of items in rows or columns. Setting this resource is often useful for button boxes at the bottom of dialogs in which each button should be as wide as each of the others. Note that this resource adjusts the width of items in a row. The height of items in a row is controlled by the `XmtNlayoutJustification` constraint resource of each item. By default, items in a row are all have a justification of `XmtLayoutFilled`, which means that they will all be forced to be as high as the row is, which implies that they will all have the same height.

`XmtNitemStretch`
If `XmtNspaceType` is not `XmtLayoutSpaceNone`, this resource, with `XmtNspaceStretch`, specifies the relative stretchiness of the items in this row or column to the spaces automatically inserted between those items. If `XmtNitemStretch` is 2, for example, and `XmtNspaceStretch` is 1, then the items of the row will do 2/3rds of the stretching, and the spaces between them will do 1/3 of the stretching. If this resource is zero, then the spaces do all the stretching, and the items stay a fixed width.

`XmtNorientation`
Whether this LayoutBox should be a row or a column. If this resource is `XmHORIZONTAL` (the default), then the LayoutBox will be a row. If it is `XmVERTICAL`, then the LayoutBox will be a column.

`XmtNspace`
If `XmtNspaceType` is not `XmtLayoutSpaceNone`, this resource specifies the amount of space (in pixels) that will be inserted between items in the LayoutBox when computing the natural size of the box.

`XmtNspaceStretch`
If `XmtNspaceType` is not `XmtLayoutSpaceNone`, this resource, with `XmtNitemStretch` specifies the relative stretchiness of the items in this row or column and the spaces that are inserted between those items. If `XmtNspace- Stretch` is 2, for example, and `XmtNitemStretch` is 1, then the spaces are twice as stretchy as the items and will do 2/3rds of the

stretching. If `XmtNspaceStretch` is 0, and `XmtNitemStretch` is not zero, then the spaces will remain a fixed size, and the items will do all the stretching.

`XmtNspaceType`
The model the LayoutBox uses to space its children along its major dimension (i.e., horizontally in rows, and vertically in columns.) The default is `XmtLayoutSpaceNone`, which specifies that items are laid out left-to-right or top-to-bottom with no extra space inserted between them. Other legal values are `XmtLayoutSpaceEven`, `XmtLayoutSpaceLREven`, `XmtLayoutSpaceInterval`, and `XmtLayoutSpaceLCR`. See Chapter 19, *The Layout Widget: The Details*, for an explanation of these spacing models, and of the XmtLayout layout scheme in general.

See Also

Chapter 19, *The Layout Widget: The Details*
`XmtCreateLayoutBox()`, `XmtCreateLayoutCol()`,
`XmtCreateLayoutRow()`, `XmtLayout`,
`XmtLayoutPixmap`, `XmtLayoutSeparator`,
`XmtLayoutSpace`, `XmtLayoutString`

XmtLayoutConvertSizeToPixels()

Name

`XmtLayoutConvertSizeToPixels()` — convert a resolution-independent size to pixels.

Synopsis

```
#include <Xmt/Layout.h>
int XmtLayoutConvertSizeToPixels(Widget w,
                                 double size,
                                 XmtLayoutUnitType units)

typedef enum {
    XmtLayoutPoints,        /* 1/72 of an inch */
    XmtLayoutInches,        /* 25.4 millimeters */
    XmtLayoutMillimeters,   /* depends on display resolution */
    XmtLayoutEms,           /* width of `M' in widget font */
    XmtLayoutEns,           /* 1/2 of an em */
} XmtLayoutUnitType;
```

Arguments

Inputs

w	An XmtLayout widget.
size	The size to be converted.
units	The units that *size* is measured in.

Returns

The pixel equivalent of the *size* measured in *units*.

Description

`XmtLayoutConvertSizeToPixels()` converts a floating-point value measured in millimeters, inches, printer points, ems, or ens to an integral number of pixels and returns that number. Conversion to millimeters, inches, or points depends on the resolution of the screen of *w*. Conversion to ems and ens depends on the `XmtNfont` and `XmtNfontList` resources of *w*. An "em" is the width of the letter "M" in the specified font or in the default font of the font list. An "en" is one half of one em.

See Also

Chapter 19, *The Layout Widget: The Details*
XmtLayout

XmtLayout{Disable,Enable}Layout()

Name

XmtLayoutDisableLayout(), XmtLayoutEnableLayout() — temporarily disable layout computation for an XmtLayout widget.

Synopsis

```
#include <Xmt/Layout.h>
void XmtLayoutDisableLayout(Widget w)

void XmtLayoutEnableLayout(Widget w)
```

Arguments

Inputs

w An XmtLayout widget.

Description

XmtLayoutDisableLayout() stops the XmtLayout widget *w* from recomputing the arrangement of its children when it normally would. XmtLayout-EnableLayout() restores normal layout computation for *w*.

Use these functions if you are making an number of changes to the children of *w* (managing, unmanaging, repositioning, resizing) that would cause *w* to recompute the children's arrangement. By batching all the changes between XmtLayoutDisableLayout() and XmtLayoutEnableLayout() significant unnecessary computation can be avoided.

Calls to these functions are counted and may be nested—layout will not be re-enabled until XmtLayoutEnableLayout() has been called as many times as XmtLayoutDisableLayout().

See Also

Chapter 19, *The Layout Widget: The Details*
XmtLayout

XmtLayoutPixmap

Name

`XmtLayoutPixmap` — an XmtLayout gadget that displays a pixmap or a bitmap.

Synopsis

Include File: `#include <Xmt/LayoutG.h>`
Constructor: `XmtCreateLayoutPixmap()`
Class Name: XmtLayoutPixmap
Class Pointer: `xmtLayoutPixmapGadgetClass`
Class Hierarchy: RectObj → XmtLayoutGadget → XmtLayoutPixmap

Description

The XmtLayoutPixmap widget is a gadget that displays a bitmap or a pixmap within the XmtLayout widget. Because it is specially implemented for this purpose, it is significantly cheaper than using an XmLabel or XmLabelGadget for this purpose. For bitmaps, any foreground and background colors may be specified.

Resources

The LayoutPixmap widget inherits the resources of the RectObj and XmtLayout-Gadget classes, and defines the following new resources:

Name	*Class*	*Type*	*Default*	*Access*
XmtNbackground	XtCBackground	XtRPixel	*unspecified*	CSG
XmtNbitmap	XmtCBitmap	XtRBitmap	*None*	CSG
XmtNbitmask	XmtCBitmask	XmtRBitmask	*None*	CSG
XmtNforeground	XtCForeground	XtRPixel	*unspecified*	CSG
XmtNpixmap	XmtCPixmap	XtRPixmap	*None*	CSG

`XmtNbackground`
The background color to be used to draw `XmtNbitmap`. If unspecified, the background color the parent Layout widget is used.

`XmtNbitmap`
A bitmap to be displayed with the specified `XmtNbackground` and `XmtNbackground` colors. If `XmtNpixmap` is also specified, then `XmtNbitmap` will be ignored.

`XmtNbitmask`
A single-plane bitmask that defines the shape of the bitmap or pixmap to display. If this resource is specified, the LayoutPixmap uses it to display a non-rectangular bitmap or pixmap.

`XmtNforeground`
The foreground color to be used to draw `XmtNbitmap`. If unspecified, the foreground color of the parent Layout widget is used.

`XmtNpixmap`
A multi-plane pixmap with a depth equal to the depth of the Layout widget. If this resource is specified, it overrides any value specified for the `XmtNbitmap` resource. Since pixmaps have colors encoded directly into them, the pixmap specified with this resource is drawn without using `XmtNforeground` or `XmtNbackground`.

See Also

Chapter 19, *The Layout Widget: The Details*
`XmtCreateLayoutPixmap()`, `XmtLayout`,
`XmtLayoutBox`, `XmtLayoutSeparator`,
`XmtLayoutSpace`, `XmtLayoutString`

XmtLayoutSeparator

Name

`XmtLayoutSeparator` — an XmtLayout gadget that draws a line.

Synopsis

Include File:	`#include <Xmt/LayoutG.h>`
Constructor:	`XmtCreateLayoutSeparator()`
Class Name:	XmtLayoutSeparator
Class Pointer:	`xmtLayoutSeparatorGadgetClass`
Class Hierarchy:	RectObj → XmtLayoutGadget → XmtLayoutSeparator

Description

The XmtLayoutSeparator is a gadget that draws an etched line or "separator" horizontally or vertically in an XmtLayout widget. Because it is specially implemented to work with the Layout widget, it is significantly cheaper than using an XmLabel or XmLabelGadget for this purpose.

Resources

The LayoutSeparator inherits the resources of the RectObj and XmtLayout-Gadget classes, and defines the following single new resource:

Name	Class	Type	Default	Access
XmtNorientation	XmCOrientation	XmROrientation	XmHORIZONTAL	CG

`XmtNorientation`

The orientation of the separator. `XmHORIZONTAL` draws a horizontal line, and `XmVERTICAL` draws a vertical line. Note that the value of this resource cannot be changed once the gadget has been created.

See Also

Chapter 19, *The Layout Widget: The Details*
`XmtCreateLayoutSeparator()`, `XmtLayout`,
`XmtLayoutBox`, `XmtLayoutPixmap`,
`XmtLayoutSpace`, `XmtLayoutString`

XmtLayoutSpace

Name

`XmtLayoutSpace` — an XmtLayout gadget that places space between other items in the layout.

Synopsis

Include File:	`#include <Xmt/LayoutG.h>`
Constructor:	`XmtCreateLayoutSpace()`
Class Name:	XmtLayoutSpace
Class Pointer:	`xmtLayoutSpaceGadgetClass`
Class Hierarchy:	RectObj → XmtLayoutGadget → XmtLayoutSpace

Description

The XmtLayoutSpace widget is a gadget that serves to place blank space between items in a row or column of an XmtLayout widget layout. The LayoutSpace gadget has no visual appearance of its own, and defines no resources of its own, but takes up space in a layout, and has all the same constraint resources that any other child of an Layout widget has.

Resources

LayoutSpace inherits the resources of the RectObj and XmtLayoutGadget classes, but defines no new resources of its own.

See Also

Chapter 19, *The Layout Widget: The Details*
`XmtCreateLayoutSpace()`, `XmtLayout`,
`XmtLayoutBox`, `XmtLayoutPixmap`,
`XmtLayoutSeparator`, `XmtLayoutString`

XmtLayoutString

Name

`XmtLayoutString` — an XmtLayout gadget that displays a string.

Synopsis

Include File: `#include <Xmt/LayoutG.h>`
Constructor: `XmtCreateLayoutString()`
Class Name: XmtLayoutString
Class Pointer: `xmtLayoutStringGadgetClass`
Class Hierarchy: RectObj → XmtLayoutGadget → XmtLayoutString

Description

The XmtLayoutString widget is a gadget that displays a Motif XmString within the XmtLayout widget. Because it is specially implemented for this purpose, it is significantly cheaper to use than an XmLabel or an XmLabelGadget. The text is displayed using the Motif `XmStringDraw()` function, which supports strings with multiple lines and multiple fonts.

The LayoutString gadget does not have an `XmFontList` of its own; the string is drawn using the `XmtNfontList` resource of the Layout widget, which can contain whatever fonts are needed for text throughout the Layout widget. When the `XmtNfontList` resource of the Layout widget changes, it notifies all of its LayoutString children so that they can redisplay themselves using the new font list.

Resources

XmtLayoutString inherits the resources of the RectObj and XmtLayoutGadget classes, and defines the following new resources:

Name	*Class*	*Type*	*Default*	*Access*
XmtNbackground	XtCBackground	XtRPixel	*unspecified*	CSG
XmtNforeground	XtCForeground	XtRPixel	*unspecified*	CSG
XmtNlabel	XtCLabel	XtRString	NULL	CS
XmtNlabelString	XmCLabelString	XmRXmString	NULL	CSG

`XmtNbackground`
The background color to use for the displayed text. If unspecified, the LayoutString gadget will use the background color of its Layout parent.

`XmtNforeground`
The foreground color to use for the displayed text. If unspecified, the LayoutString gadget will use the foreground color of its Layout parent.

`XmtNlabel`
The string to display if the `XmtNlabelString` resource is not specified. If no `XmString` is specified for the `XmtNlabelString` resource, then this string (a normal NULL-terminated C string) is converted to an `XmString` using `XmtCreateXmString()` and stored on the

`XmtNlabelString` resource. Note that the value of this string is not copied by the LayoutString gadget. It is converted to an XmString, and then the LayoutString gadget "forgets" it, since it is not stored in memory owned by the gadget. This means that querying this resource will always return an empty string.

`XmtNlabelString`
: An `XmString` to be displayed by the LayoutString gadget. If this resource is not specified, the `XmtNlabel` resource will be used instead. Note that unlike `XmtNlabel`, this resource is copied by the gadget, and can be queried.

See Also

Chapter 19, *The Layout Widget: The Details*
`XmtCreateLayoutString()`, `XmtLayout`,
`XmtLayoutBox`, `XmtLayoutPixmap`,
`XmtLayoutSeparator`, `XmtLayoutSpace`

XmtLoadResourceFile[List]()

Name

XmtLoadResourceFile(), XmtLoadResourceFileList() — find named resource files and read them into the resource database.

Synopsis

```
#include <Xmt/Include.h>
Boolean XmtLoadResourceFile(Widget w, String filename,
                            Boolean user, Boolean override)

void XmtLoadResourceFileList(Widget w, String list)
```

Arguments

Inputs

w	Any widget in the application.
filename	The base name of the resource file to be included.
user	Whether user directories should be searched for the named resource file, in addition to the regular directories.
override	Whether the resources in the named file should override or augment those already in the resource database.
list	For XmtLoadResourceFileList(), a list of files to read in, each filename enclosed in angle brackets or double quotes and separated by whitespace.

Returns

XmtLoadResourceFile() returns True if the named file was successfully loaded, and returns False otherwise.

Description

XmtLoadResourceFile() looks for the named resource file in a number of places and merges it into the application resource database. *filename* specifies the file to read; if it is an absolute filename beginning with /, or a relative name, beginning with ./ or ../, then the file is simply read. Otherwise, XmtLoadResourceFile() uses XmtFindFile() to look for the named resource file in several standard places. If the resourceFilePath application resource is specified, XmtLoadResourceFile() will look in the places it specifies. If that resource is not specified, or if the file is not found there, XmtLoadResourceFile() also looks in the places specified by the configPath application resource, and in the "standard Xt path" (which on many systems is relative to */usr/lib/X11*.) See Chapter 6, *Managing Auxiliary Files*, for details on how the search for named files is performed.

If the *user* argument is True, then the function will also look for a user-specific version of the resource file. If it finds such a file, it reads it in so that resource specifications in the user's file override any conflicting specifications in the application file. If *user* is True, XmtLoadResourceFile() searches for a user file in the places specified by the `userConfigPath` application resource, or as specified by the `XUSERSEARCHPATH` and `XAPPLRESDIR` environment variables. Again, see Chapter 6, *Managing Auxiliary Files*, for details.

If *`override`* argument is `True`, then the resources in the specified file will override resources with the same specification in the database. If `False`, then these new resources will augment those already in the database, but will not override them when conflicts occur. Prior to X11R5, you must specify `True` for this argument, because in X11R4 it is not possible to augment resource files in this way.

`XmtLoadResourceFile()` remembers the full name of each resource file it reads, and will not read any file twice. Note that it does not check whether two different filenames refer to the same actual file (through a symbolic link, for example), nor does it check whether a file has been modified since the last time it was read.

`XmtLoadResourceFileList()` uses `XmtLoadResourceFile()` to read in a list of resource files. The files are specified in the same way that they are on the `xmtRequires` pseudo-resource that is read by `XmtCreateChildren()` and related functions. The *`list`* argument is a whitespace-separated list of filenames each of which is enclosed in angle brackets (< and >) or in quotation marks.

Each filename in this list is passed (with its angle brackets or quotes removed) as the *`filename`* argument in a call to `XmtLoadResourceFile()`. If it was enclosed in angle-brackets, the *`user`* argument will be `False`, and if it was enclosed in quotation marks the *`user`* will be `True`.

The list of filenames may also be interspersed with two special directives: `#override` and `#augment`. By default, `XmtLoadResourceFileList()` calls `XmtLoadResourceFile()` with *`override`* set to `True`. If the `#augment` directive is encountered in the file list, then any subsequent files will be loaded with *`override`* `False`, until an `#override` directive is found.

See Also

Chapter 6, *Managing Auxiliary Files*
Chapter 11, *Automatic Widget Creation*
`XmtCreateChildren()`, `XmtFindFile()`

XmtLocalize()

Name

`XmtLocalize2()`, `XmtLocalize()`, `XmtLocalizeWidget()` — look up a translated version of a string in the resource database.

Synopsis

```
#include <Xmt/Xmt.h>
String XmtLocalize2(Widget w, String default_string,
                    String category, String tag)

String XmtLocalize(Widget w, String default_string, String tag)

String XmtLocalizeWidget(Widget w, String default_string,
                         String tag)
```

Arguments

Inputs

w — Any widget in the application, or, for `XmtLocalizeWidget()`, the widget for which the localization is being performed.

default_string — The untranslated version of the string; used if no translated version is found in the resource database.

category — A "module name" for the string to be looked up.

tag — The name of the string to be looked up.

Returns

A translated version of *default_string*, or *default_string* itself, if no translated version could be found. The returned value should not be modified or freed by the application.

Description

These functions provide a way to internationalize an application—by looking up translations for any strings that would otherwise be hard-coded into the executable. They make it easy for a translator or site administrator or user to provide translations in a resource file.

`XmtLocalize2()` looks in the resource database for a resource specification that matches this template:

Messages.*language.territory.codeset.category.tag*

In this resource specification, *category* and *tag* are the specified arguments to `XmtLocalize2()`, and *language*, *territory*, and *codeset* are the language, territory, and codeset parts of the Xt "language string," usually specified by the `LANG` environment variable. If a resource specification that matches is found, `XmtLocalize2()` returns its value, and if no such resource is found, `XmtLocalize2()` returns *default_string*. The resource specification need not match exactly, of course—the standard resource file wildcards can be used as normal.

`XmtLocalize()` is a simplified version of `XmtLocalize2()` that omits the *`category`* argument in its resource lookup.

`XmtLocalizeWidget()` is another simplified version of `XmtLocalize2()` for use by widget writers. It passes the class name of the specified widget as the *`category`* value.

If the `XMTDEBUGLOOKUP` environment variable is set, these functions will print helpful debugging messages as they look up localized strings. Compile Xmt with the `-NDEBUG` flag to disable this feature.

See Also

Chapter 3, *Displaying Text*

XmtLookupColorName()

Name

`XmtLookupColorName()` — look up the actual color name associated with a symbolic color name in an XmtColorTable.

Synopsis

```
#include <Xmt/Color.h>
String XmtLookupColorName(XmtColorTable table, String symbol)
```

Arguments

Inputs

`table`	The `XmtColorTable` to be searched
`symbol`	The symbolic color name to be looked up

Returns

The actual color name associated with the *`symbol`* in *`table`*, or NULL, if none is found.

Description

`XmtLookupColorName()` returns the name of the color registered with symbolic name *`symbol`* in XmtColorTable *`table`*. If *`symbol`* is not found in *`table`*, then the parent of the specified color table is searched, and then the parent's parent is searched, and so on until a definition of the symbolic color is found, or until a color table with no parent is is encountered. If the symbolic color is not found, `XmtLookupColorName()` returns NULL. This chain of color tables provides a "scoping" mechanism for symbolic color names like that used for variable names in C programming.

The returned value is not guaranteed to be a legal color name; it is simply whatever name was registered with `XmtRegisterColor()` or a related function. Generally, though, the color name returned by `XmtLookupColorName()` is suitable for allocation with `XmtAllocColor()` or a related function.

See Also

Chapter 4, *Using Color*
`XmtAllocColor()`, `XmtColorTableGetParent()`, `XmtColorTableSetParent()`, `XmtCreateColorTable()`, `XmtDestroyColorTable()`, `XmtRegisterColor()`, `XmtRegisterColors()`, `XmtRegisterPixel()`, `XmtRegisterStandardColors()`, `XmtVaRegisterColors()`

Name

XmtLookupPixmap(), XmtLookupSimplePixmap(), XmtLookup-WidgetPixmap(), XmtLookupBitmap(), XmtLookupBitmask() — get a named pixmap or bitmap from the Xmt image cache.

Synopsis

```
#include <Xmt/Pixmap.h>
Pixmap XmtLookupPixmap(Widget w,  Visual *visual,
                       Colormap colormap, unsigned int depth,
                       XmtColorTable colortable, String name)

Pixmap XmtLookupSimplePixmap(Widget w, XmtColorTable colortable,
                             String name)

Pixmap XmtLookupWidgetPixmap(Widget w, String name)

Pixmap XmtLookupBitmap(Widget w, String name)

Pixmap XmtLookupBitmask(Widget w, String name)
```

Arguments

Inputs

w	The widget for which the pixmap or bitmap should be created. This widget specifies the screen on which the pixmap should be created.
visual	The `Visual` for which the pixmap should be created.
colormap	The `Colormap` which should be used for the pixels of the pixmap.
depth	The depth of the created Pixmap.
colortable	The `XmtColorTable` that should be used to look up symbolic color names in `XmtImage` structures.
name	The name of the image to be looked up.

Returns

A multi-plane pixmap or single-plane bitmap created as described below, or `None` if the named data could not be found or converted. When no longer needed, the returned `Pixmap` should be freed with `XmtReleasePixmap()`.

Description

`XmtLookupPixmap()` looks up XBM or `XmtImage` data registered in the image cache with the name *name*. If no data is found, it returns `None`. Otherwise, it looks up and returns a cached `Pixmap` containing that data for the screen of *w* and for the specified depth, visual, colormap, and color table. If no such pixmap is found, it creates one and adds it to the cache.

`XmtLookupSimplePixmap()` is a simplified version of `XmtLookup-Pixmap()`. It uses the visual, colormap and depth of the specified widget *w*.

`XmtLookupWidgetPixmap()` is a further simplified version of `XmtLookup-Pixmap()`. Besides passing the visual, colormap, and depth of *w*, it also passes the default color table of the application, specified by the Xmt `color-Table` application resource.

`XmtLookupBitmap()` looks up the XBM data registered in the image cache with the name *name*. If no data is found, it returns `None`. Otherwise, it looks up and returns a single-plane `Pixmap` for the screen of *w* that contains the data. If no such pixmap already exists, it creates one and adds it to the cache.

`XmtLookupBitmask()` looks up the named image in the Xmt image cache. If that image is XBM data that was registered with a mask, or if it is an `XmtImage` with "transparent" pixels, then this function looks up and returns or creates, caches and returns a single-plane `Pixmap` for the screen of *w* that contains the mask data for the named image.

When the pixmaps returned by these functions will no longer be needed, they can be released from the cache by calling `XmtReleasePixmap()`. This will decrement their reference count and remove them from the cache if that reference count reaches zero.

See Also

Chapter 5, *Using Icons*
`XmtGetBitmap()`, `XmtGetPixmap()`,
`XmtRegisterImage()`, `XmtRegisterXbmData()`,
`XmtReleasePixmap()`

Xmt{Lookup,Register}{Style,Template}()

Name

`XmtRegisterStyle()`, `XmtRegisterTemplate()`, `XmtLookupStyle()`, `XmtLookupTemplate()`, and `XmtTemplateInstantiate()` — handle styles and templates.

Synopsis

```
#include <Xmt/Template.h>
void XmtRegisterStyle(Widget w, String name, String style)

void XmtRegisterTemplate(Widget w, String name, String template)

String XmtLookupStyle(Widget w, String name)

String XmtLookupTemplate(Widget w, String name)

void XmtTemplateInstantiate(Widget parent, String instance,
                            String definition, String *args,
                            Cardinal num_args)
```

Arguments

Inputs

w	Any widget in the application; specifies the resource database in which styles or templates are to be registered, looked up, or instantiated.
name	The name under which the style or template is to be registered or looked up.
style	A string that defines the style to be registered.
template	A string that defines the template to be registered.
parent	For `XmtTemplateInstantiate()`, the parent of the widget for which the style or template is to be instantiated.
instance	For `XmtTemplateInstantiate()`, the name of widget for which the style or template is to be instantiated (this widget will not have been created yet).
definition	The definition of the style or template to instantiate.
args	An array of strings to be substituted for numeric arguments in *template*.
num_args	The number of strings in *args*.

Returns

`XmtLookupStyle()` and `XmtLookupTemplate()` return the definition of the named style or template, or `NULL` if none is found. This string is owned by Xmt and must not be modified or freed.

Description

A *style* is a reusable set of resource definitions that can be copied ("instantiated") into the resource database so that they apply to any individual widget. A *template* is like a style, but may also define a reusable widget subtree. Both styles and templates are used by the Xmt automatic widget creation facilities described in Chapter 11, *Automatic Widget Creation.* See that chapter for more information on defining styles and templates.

Styles and templates are usually defined and used directly in resource files. These functions also allow you to use them in your C code.

`XmtRegisterStyle()` registers *`style`* with name *`name`* in the resource database of *`w`*.

`XmtRegisterTemplate()` registers *`template`* under the name *`name`* in the resource database of *`w`*.

`XmtLookupStyle()` looks for and returns a definition of the style named *`name`* in the resource database of *`w`*. The returned value should not be modified or freed.

`XmtLookupTemplate()` looks for and returns a definition of the template named *`name`* in the resource database of *`w`*. The returned value should not be modified or freed.

`XmtTemplateInstantiate()` *instantiates* a style or template. First it replaces any `%`*`digit`* substitutions in *`definition`* with the corresponding strings in the *`args`* array. Then it copies each of the resource specifications in *`definition`* into the resource database of *`parent`*. The resource are copied into the database so that they appear as resources of the child named *`instance`* of the *`parent`* widget.

See Also

Chapter 11, *Automatic Widget Creation*

XmtMenu

Name

`XmtMenu` — easy-to-create menus.

Synopsis

Include File:	`#include <Xmt/Menu.h>`

Constructor:	`XmtCreateMenubar()`
	`XmtCreateMenuPane()`
	`XmtCreatePopupMenu()`
	`XmtCreateOptionMenu()`

Class Name:	XmtMenu
Class Pointer:	`xmtMenuWidgetClass`
Class Hierarchy:	Core → XmManager → XmRowColumn → XmtMenu

Description

The XmtMenu widget is a subclass of the XmRowColumn widget designed to make it easier to create menus and systems of menus. A Menu widget takes an array of **`XmtMenuItem`** structures on its **`XmtNitems`** resource and automatically creates the items (push buttons, toggle buttons, cascade buttons, labels, and separators) described by those structures. There is a resource converter that parses an intuitive menu description grammar and converts it to an array of these **`XmtMenuItem`** structures. **`XmtMenuItem`** structures, whether statically initialized in C or created by the resource converter, can specify other arrays of menu structures which describe the contents of submenus. The Menu widget will automatically create Menu widget children to display each of these submenus. Thus, it is possible to create an entire pulldown menu system by creating only the menu bar, and letting the Menu widget do the rest.

The Menu widget has four constructor functions, each with somewhat different behavior. **`XmtCreateMenubar()`** creates a Menu widget configured as a menubar. **`XmtCreateMenuPane()`** creates a menu pane in a menu shell widget (it may share the menu shell with other panes). The resulting pane can be attached to any cascade button. **`XmtCreatePopupMenu()`** creates a menu shell and a menu pane to pop up in that shell, and registers an event handler to pop up the menu appropriately. **`XmtCreateOptionMenu()`** creates an XmOptionMenu and a menu pane to pop up in it. This last constructor is less useful than the others; option menus are generally better handled by the XmtChooser widget.

Resources

XmtMenu inherits the resources of the XmRowColumn class, and defines the new resources, shown in the following table.

Name	*Class*	*Type*	*Default*	*Access*
XmtNacceleratorFontTag	XmtCAcceleratorFontTag	XtRString	NULL	CG
XmtNitems	XmtCItems	XmtRXmtMenu-ItemList	NULL	CG
XmtNnumItems	XmtCNumItems	XtRCardinal	-1	CG

`XmtNacceleratorFontTag`
A string that specifies the font that any accelerator labels should be displayed in. If specified, this string should match a "font tag" for one of the fonts an `XmFontList` that will be used by all the buttons in the menu. Note that the Menu widget does not have such a font list resource itself.

`XmtNitems`
An array of `XmtMenuItem` structures, each of which describes one item to appear in the menu. If `XmtNnumItems` is specified, then this array must contain the specified number of elements. If `XmtNnumItems` is left unspecified, then this array must be terminated with a `XmtMenuItem` structure that has the value `XmtMenuItemEnd` in its `type` field. (This is analogous to a NULL-terminated array of strings, for example.)

`XmtNnumItems`
If set to something other than its default of -1, this resource specifies the number of elements in the `XmtNitems` array.

Describing Menus

The Menu widget creates a menu bar or menu pane described by an array of `XmtMenuItem` structures on the `XmtNitems` resource. This array may be specified from a resource file using the resource converter described in the next section, or it may be statically initialized from C code.

The `XmtMenuItems` structure and related types are defined as follows in `<Xmt/Menu.h>`. See Chapter 20, *Easy Menu Creation*, for a complete explanation of how to initialize each of the fields of the structure.

```
/*
 * This structure defines a single menu item.  Initialize an array of
 * them in order to define a menubar or menu pane.
 */
typedef struct _XmtMenuItem {
    unsigned type;                  /* an XmtMenuItemType + any applicable flags*/
    String label;                   /* the item label, or the name of an icon */
    char mnemonic;                  /* the mnemonic character for the item */
    String accelerator;             /* the accelerator; translation table syntax*/
    String accelerator_label;       /* how to display the accelerator */
    XtCallbackProc callback;        /* callback procedure or list for the item */
    XtPointer client_data;          /* data to be registered with the callback */
    struct _XmtMenuItem *submenu;/* the array of items for the submenu */
    String symbol_name;             /* name of a symbol to set for this item */
    String alt_label;               /* an alternate label for a toggle button */
```

```
    char alt_mnemonic;          /* alternate mnemonic for a toggle button */
    String name;                /* item name for later lookup */
    /* the private fields below are omitted here; leave them uninitialized */
} XmtMenuItem;

/* These are the possible types of menu items */
typedef enum {
    XmtMenuItemEnd,             /* used to NULL-terminate the array of items */
    XmtMenuItemPushButton,      /* a push button */
    XmtMenuItemToggleButton,    /* a toggle button */
    XmtMenuItemCascadeButton,   /* a cascade button; has a submenu attached */
    XmtMenuItemSeparator,       /* a single-line etched separator */
    XmtMenuItemDoubleSeparator, /* a double-line etched separator */
    XmtMenuItemLabel            /* a label widget; good for menu titles */
} XmtMenuItemType;

/* These are flags for menu items.  Add these to the type */
#define XmtMenuItemOn       0x10  /* initial state of toggle button is on */
#define XmtMenuItemHelp     0x20  /* cascade button goes to far right of bar */
#define XmtMenuItemTearoff 0x40  /* attached menu pane is a tearoff */
#define XmtMenuItemPixmap   0x80  /* label field is pixmap name, not a string */
#define XmtMenuItemCallbackList 0x100 /* callback field is an XtCallbackList */
```

Note that the `XmtMenuItem` structure has both public fields that may be initialized, and private fields that are used internally by the Menu widget and should set or read by the programmer. The fields in an `XmtMenuItems` structure are arranged in most-commonly-used to least-commonly-used order, so that for most menu items you need only initialize the first few fields you care about, and leave the others uninitialized. If your array of structures is declared static, then uninitialized fields will contain NULL, which is their proper value.

The XmtMenu Grammar

The Xmt library provides a String-to-XmtMenuItems converter for use with the Menu widget. If you register this converter by calling `XmtRegisterMenuItemsConverter()`, then you can specify the contents of a menubar or any of its menu panes with a single string resource in a resource file.

The XmtMenu grammar was designed to be easily readable and intuitive. A BNF definition of the syntax appears below. Items within single quotes are terminal symbols of the grammar—keywords or punctuation that should appear exactly as shown. Items in italics are non-terminals—items that are defined elsewhere in the grammar, or which are implicitly defined. Items within curly braces are repeated zero or more times and items within square brackets are optional. Note that the grammar is case-sensitive and that all keywords begin with a capital letter. This means that keywords will not conflict with item or submenu names, which, by convention, begin with a lowercase letter.

This summary of the grammar is provided here for reference. See Chapter 20, *Easy Menu Creation*, for a semantic explanation of each of the syntactical elements of the grammar, and for examples menu descriptions that use the grammar.

menu::	{ *item* }
item::	[*name*] [*type*] { *flags* } [*label*] [*accelerator*] [*submenu*] [*symbol*] ';' [*name*] [*type*] { *flags* } [*label*] [*accelerator*] [*submenu*] [*symbol*] *callbacks* [*name*] '-' { '-' } ';' [*name*] '=' { '=' } ';'
name::	*identifier* ':'
type::	'Title' | 'Button' | 'Toggle' | 'Submenu' | 'Line' | 'DoubleLine'
flags::	'On' | 'Off' | 'Help' | 'Tearoff' | 'Pixmap'
label::	*string-with-mnemonic* ['|' *string-with-mnemonic*]
accelerator::	'[' { *modifier* '+' | '-' } *keysym* ']'
modifier::	'Ctrl' | 'Shift' | 'Meta' | 'Alt' | 'Lock'
keysym::	*single-letter-or-digit* | *identifier* | *string*
submenu::	'->' *identifier*
symbol::	'$' *identifier*
callbacks::	*callback* '{' *callback* { *callback* } '}'
callback::	*identifier* '(' [*arglist*] ')' ';'

Callbacks

The Menu widget defines no new callback lists of its own. It does allow callback procedures and XtCallbackLists to be specified and registered on the menu item children it automatically creates, however.

Translations

The Menu widget inherits its translations from the XmRowColumn widget class and does not add any new translations of its own.

Actions

The Menu widget defines no new action procedures.

See Also

Chapter 20, *Easy Menu Creation*
`XmtCreateMenuPane()`, `XmtCreateMenubar()`, `XmtCreateOptionMenu()`, `XmtCreatePopupMenu()`, `XmtMenuActivateProcedure()`, `XmtMenuGetMenuItem()`, `XmtMenuInactivateProcedure()`, `XmtMenuItemGetState()`, `XmtMenuItemGetSubmenu()`, `XmtMenuItemGetWidget()`, `XmtMenuItemSetSensitivity()`, `XmtMenuItemSetState()`

XmtMenu{Activate,Inactivate}Procedure()

Name

`XmtMenuActivateProcedure()`, `XmtMenuInactivateProcedure()` — sensitize and desensitize menu items depending on the procedures they call.

Synopsis

```
#include <Xmt/Menu.h>
void XmtMenuActivateProcedure(Widget w, XtCallbackProc proc)

void XmtMenuInactivateProcedure(Widget w, XtCallbackProc proc)
```

Arguments

Inputs

w — An XmtMenu widget whose items are to be made sensitive or insensitive.

proc — A pointer to the procedure that is to be activated or inactivated.

Description

The functions called `XmtMenuActivateProcedure()` and `XmtMenu-Inact- ivateProcedure()` search the XmtMenu widget *w* and any Xmt-Menu pulldown or pullright submenus attached to *w* looking for menu items that invoke the procedure *proc* on their callback lists. `XmtMenu-InactivateProcedure()` makes any such item insensitive and `XmtMenu-ActivateProcedure()` makes any such item sensitive again.

These procedures work by calling `XmtMenuItemSetSensitivity()` which means that the sensitivity state of a menu item is counted—you must call `Xmt-MenuActivateProcedure()` as many times as you have called `XmtMenu-InactivateProcedure()` for a given procedure in order to re-enable menu items that call that procedure.

See Also

Chapter 20, *Easy Menu Creation*
XmtMenu, `XmtMenuGetMenuItem()`, `XmtMenuItemGetSubmenu()`, `XmtMenuItemGetWidget()`, `XmtMenuItemSetSensitivity()`, `XmtMenuItemGetState()`, `XmtMenuItemSetState()`

XmtMenuItem*()

Name

XmtMenuGetMenuItem(), XmtMenuItemGetSubmenu(), XmtMenuItem-GetWidget(), XmtMenuItemSetSensitivity(), XmtMenuItem-GetState(), XmtMenuItemSetState() — look up items in an Xmt-Menu widget by name, and manipulate them.

Synopsis

```
#include <Xmt/Menu.h>
XmtMenuItem *XmtMenuGetMenuItem(Widget w, String name)

Widget XmtMenuItemGetSubmenu(XmtMenuItem *item)

Widget XmtMenuItemGetWidget(XmtMenuItem *item)

void XmtMenuItemSetSensitivity(XmtMenuItem *item,
                               Boolean sensitive)

Boolean XmtMenuItemGetState(XmtMenuItem *item)

void XmtMenuItemSetState(XmtMenuItem *item, Boolean state,
                         Boolean notify)
```

Arguments

Inputs

w	An XmtMenu widget in which an item is to be looked up by name.
name	The name of the item to look up in *w*.
item	The menu item to manipulate.
sensitive	For XmtMenuItemSetSensitivity(), whether the specified item should be made sensitive (True) or insensitive (False).
state	For XmtMenuItemSetState(), the state to set on the specified toggle button item. Specify True to set the button and False to unset it.
notify	For XmtMenuItemSetState(), this argument specifies whether the XmNvalueChangedCallback of the specified toggle button item should be invoked in response to the change.

Returns

XmtMenuGetMenuItem() returns the named menu item, or NULL if it could not be found.

XmtMenuItemGetSubmenu() returns the XmtMenu widget that is associated with the specified cascade button menu item.

`XmtMenuItemGetWidget()` returns the widget associated with the specified menu item.

`XmtMenuItemGetState()` returns `True` if the specified toggle button menu item is selected an `False` if it is unselected.

Description

The items in an XmtMenu widget are described by `XmtMenuItem` structures. If you specify your menu in C code, then you will declare and initialize these structures explicitly. If you specify your menu in a resource file, you can use `XmtMenuGetMenuItem()` to look up the `XmtMenuItem` structure of a named item. The other functions described here perform various manipulations on a specified menu item.

`XmtMenuGetMenuItem()` searches for and returns the menu item named *name* in the XmtMenu widget *w*, and also recursively searches any pulldown and pullright menus attached to *w*. You can specify a name for a menu item created in C code by setting the `name` field of the `XmtMenuItem` structure. You can specify a name for a menu item described in a resource file by specifying the name followed by a colon as the first element in the menu item description. See Chapter 20, *Easy Menu Creation*, for more information.

For menu items that are cascade buttons, `XmtMenuItemGetSubmenu()` returns the XmtMenu widget that forms the menu pane attached to that cascade button. If you call this function for a menu item that is not a cascade button, it will print an error message.

`XmtMenuItemGetWidget()` returns the widget associated with any menu item. This may be an XmPushButton, an XmToggleButton, an XmCascadeButton, an XmLabel, or an XmSeparator.

`XmtMenuItemSetSensitivity()` lets you set the sensitivity of a menu item. Like `XtSetSensitive()`, the second argument to `XmtMenuItemSetSensitivity()` is a `Boolean`. If `True`, the item will be made sensitive; if `False`, the item will be made insensitive, and will be grayed out. Unlike `XtSetSensitive()`, however, `XmtMenuItemSetSensitivity()` keeps a count of how many times it has been called for an item. If the function is called twice for an item with the `sensitive` argument of `False`, then the item will not become sensitive again until the function is called twice with the argument `True`.

`XmtMenuItemGetState()` returns `True` if the specified toggle button is selected, and `False` otherwise. This function will print a warning message if called for a menu item that is not a toggle button.

`XmtMenuItemSetState()` sets the button state as specified by the *`state`* argument, and if *`notify`* is `True`, it calls any callbacks registered for the toggle button. This function will print a warning message if called for a menu item that is not a toggle button.

See Also

Chapter 20, *Easy Menu Creation*
XmtMenu, `XmtMenuActivateProcedure()`,
`XmtMenuInactivateProcedure()`

Name

XmtMenuPopupHandler() — remove the default event handler registered for an XmtMenu popup menu pane.

Synopsis

```
#include <Xmt/Menu.h>
extern void XmtMenuPopupHandler(Widget, XtPointer,  XEvent *,
                                Boolean *);
XtRemoveEventHandler(parent, ButtonPressMask, False,
                     XmtMenuPopupHandler, (XtPointer)menu);
```

Arguments

Inputs

parent — The widget for which the popup event handler is to be removed. This is the parent of the popup menu—the widget that was passed to XmtCreatePopupMenu().

menu — The popup menu pane that you do not want to be automatically popped up. This is the widget returned by a call to XmtCreatePopupMenu().

Description

XmtMenuPopupHandler() is an event handler (of the standard Xt XtEventHandler type) that is automatically registered on all XmtMenu popup menu panes by XmtCreatePopupMenu(). This event handler is appropriate in most circumstances, but there are times when you may want to unregister it so that you can register a custom event handler to pop up the menu under your explicit control.

Since XmtMenuPopupHandler() is never meant to be called directly, its arguments are not described above. Instead, the "Synopsis" section shows a call to XtRemoveEventHandler() that you can use to unregister it.

See Also

Chapter 20, *Easy Menu Creation*
XmtMenu

XmtMsgLine

Name

`XmtMsgLine` — a Message Line widget.

Synopsis

Include File: `#include <Xmt/MsgLine.h>`
Constructor: `XmtCreateMsgLine()`
Class Name: XmtMsgLine
Class Pointer: `xmtMsgLineWidgetClass`
Class Hierarchy: Core → XmPrimitive → XmText → XmtMsgLine

Description

The XmtMsgLine widget is a simple subclass of the Motif XmText widget intended for displaying simple messages and obtaining simple input from the user. There are functions to clear the message line, display text in the message line, append text to the message line, and save and restore the text in the message line.

The MsgLine widget also supports input functions that get input synchronously from the user (i.e., they appear to block like `gets()` and `scanf()` do.) These functions set the keyboard focus to the MsgLine widget, and make the widget "modal" in the same way that dialog boxes can be modal. This means that the user can type into the message line regardless of the pointer position, but cannot interact with any other widgets with mouse or keyboard until a string or a character is entered into the message line, or until the input is canceled with **Ctrl-C** or the **osfCancel** key (see the `cancel-input()` action.) Once input is entered or restored, the application's keyboard focus and modality are restored.

Text may also be entered asynchronously into a MsgLine widget, and the functions on the `XmtNinputCallback` list are invoked when this occurs. This is not a common use of the widget, however, and by default the widget is not editable in this way.

Whether a MsgLine widget is accepting synchronous or asynchronous input, only text typed by the user is editable. Any text output to the widget by the application is uneditable, and once the user enters text with the **Return** key, that text becomes uneditable as well. The insertion cursor is not allowed to leave the editable region of the widget.

Resources

The MsgLine widget inherits the resources of the XmText class, and defines the following new resources.

Name	*Class*	*Type*	*Default*	*Access*
XmtNallowAsyncInput	XmtCAllowAsyncInput	XtRBoolean	False	CSG
XmtNinputCallback	XtCCallback	XtRCallback	NULL	C
XmtNmsgLine-Translations	XmtCMsgLine-Translations	XtRTranslation-Table	NULL	CG

`XmtNallowAsyncInput`
Whether or not the MsgLine widget will allow asynchronous input. If this resource is `False`, then `XmNeditable`, `XmNtraversalOn`, and `XmNcursorPositionVisible` will be set to `False`. This means that the MsgLine will not allow keyboard input, will not be part of keyboard navigation, and will not display a cursor. If `XmtNallowAsyncInput` is `True` then each of those resources will be made `True` and the user will be able to type text in the MsgLine at any time. When asynchronous input input is disabled by setting `XmtNallowAsyncInput` to `False`, the MsgLine synchronous input functions still work—they temporarily set `XmNeditable` and `XmNcursorPositionVisible` to `True`.

`XmtNinputCallback`
A list of callback procedures that will be invoked when the user asynchronously enters text into the MsgLine widget. If `XmtNallowAsyncInput` is `True`, the callbacks on this list are invoked by the `end-input` action, which is bound, by default, to the **Return** key. Any text entered by the user since the last invocation of the ***`end-input`*** action will be passed as the third, *`call_data`* argument to the callbacks. The input string will not include a terminating newline character.

`XmtNmsgLineTranslations`
A translation table that will be used to override the default XmText translations, any translations specified on the `XtNtranslations` resource, and the default MsgLine-specific translations. See the "Translations" section for more information.

Translations

The MsgLine handles translations somewhat differently than other widgets do. It inherits an unmodified set of the XmText widget translations. When a MsgLine widget is created, these default XmText resources are overridden, augmented, or replaced by any resources you (or the end user) specified on the `XtNtranslations` resource (and, in X11R5, also any resources specified with the `baseTranslations` pseudo-resource). This is the same process that all widgets follow to determine their translation table. The MsgLine widget goes two steps further, however: it overrides this resulting translation table with its own internal set of default MsgLine-specific translations and then, finally, overrides these with any resources you (or the end user) have specified on the `XmtNmsgLineTranslations` resource.

These are the default MsgLine translations:

```
<Key>Return:                          end-input()
<Key>osfCancel:                       cancel-input()
Ctrl<Key>C:                           cancel-input()
Ctrl<Key>G:                           cancel-input()
~Ctrl  Shift ~Meta ~Alt<Btn1Down>:    save-cursor-pos() extend-start()
~Ctrl ~Shift ~Meta ~Alt<Btn1Down>:    save-cursor-pos() grab-focus()
~Ctrl ~Meta ~Alt<Btn1Motion>:         extend-adjust()
~Ctrl ~Meta ~Alt<Btn1Up>:             extend-end() restore-cursor-pos()
~Ctrl ~Meta ~Alt<Btn2Down>:           copy-primary()
~Ctrl ~Meta ~Alt<Btn3Down>:           save-cursor-pos() extend-start()
~Ctrl ~Meta ~Alt<Btn3Motion>:         extend-adjust()
~Ctrl ~Meta ~Alt<Btn3Up>:             extend-end() restore-cursor-pos()
<Key>Tab:                             self-insert()
```

Some of the translations shown are simply bindings for the MsgLine's new action procedures. For example, the **Return** key is used to end input, and the **osfCancel**, key or **Ctrl-C** or **Ctrl-G** are used to cancel input. Other translations modify the cut-and-paste bindings to match the standard bindings for *xterm* rather than the standard bindings for the XmText widget: Button3 is used to extend the current selection, for example, and Button2 is used to paste the primary selection (at the insertion cursor position, rather than the mouse pointer position). These bindings also ensure that the user cannot use the mouse to position the cursor within a prompt or other uneditable text. Finally, notice that the MsgLine widget overrides the single-line XmText widget binding for the **TAB** key—since the MsgLine is usually used for synchronous input, it does not make sense to use **TAB** for keyboard traversal.

Actions

The MsgLine widget defines five new actions, used in the translation table shown above. They are the following:

`end-input()`
: When the MsgLine is doing synchronous input, this action causes the synchronous input function to extract the user's input from the widget and return it to the caller. When the MsgLine is doing asynchronous input, this actions causes it to extract the user's input and notify the application by invoking the `XmtNinputCallback` callback list.

`cancel-input()`
: If the MsgLine is doing synchronous input, this action causes the internal event loop to be terminated, the user's input to be erased, and the synchronous input function to return with an indication that the user canceled the input. If the MsgLine is not doing synchronous input, this action has no effect.

`save-cursor-pos()`
`restore-cursor-pos()`

This pair of actions saves and restores the position of the insertion cursor. They are intended to be used before and after mouse translations so that the insertion cursor can be moved while selecting text anywhere in the widget, but so that the insertion cursor is not left in text that the user is not allowed to edit.

`beginning-of-line()`

This action has the same name as, and overrides, the XmText `beginning-of-line()` action. Instead of moving the insertion cursor to the actual beginning of the line, however, it moves it to the first editable position; i.e., to the first character after whatever prompt is being displayed. Note that this action does not appear in the translation table shown above. Because of the way action procedures are scoped, the `beginning-of-line()` binding in the default XmText translation table will refer to this action procedure, and you can invoke it however you normally invoke the `beginning-of-line()` action on your system.

See Also

Chapter 22, *The Message Line*
`XmtCreateMsgLine()`, `XmtMsgLineAppend()`, `XmtMsgLineClear()`, `XmtMsgLineGetChar()`, `XmtMsgLineGetString()`, `XmtMsgLinePrintf()`, `XmtMsgLineSet()`

XmtMsgLineGet{String,Double,Int,Unsigned,Char}()

Name

XmtMsgLineGetString(), XmtMsgLineGetDouble(), XmtMsgLineGetInt(), XmtMsgLineGetUnsigned(), XmtMsgLineGetChar() — use an XmtMsgLine widget to synchronously get input from the user.

Synopsis

```
#include <Xmt/MsgLine.h>
String XmtMsgLineGetString(Widget w, String buf, int len)

Boolean XmtMsgLineGetDouble(Widget w, double *value_return)

Boolean XmtMsgLineGetInt(Widget w, int *value_return)

Boolean XmtMsgLineGetUnsigned(Widget w, unsigned *value_return)

int XmtMsgLineGetChar(Widget w)
```

Arguments

Inputs

w	An XmtMsgLine widget.
len	The size of the character buffer *buf*.

Outputs

buf	For XmtMsgLineGetString(), a character buffer in which the user's input will be returned.
value_return	The address of a double, int, or unsigned variable in which the user's numeric input will be returned.

Returns

XmtMsgLineGetString() returns *buf*, or NULL when cancelled.

The numeric input functions return True for valid input, or False when cancelled.

XmtMsgLineGetChar() returns the input character, or EOF when cancelled.

Description

XmtMsgLineGetString() transfers keyboard focus to the XmtMsgLine widget *w*, disallows events to any other widgets, and enters an internal event loop to wait for the use to enter a string. When the user strikes **Return**, it copies the input string into *buf*, and null-terminates it. Then it resumes normal event handling, restores keyboard focus to its original location, and returns *buf*. The user's input is guaranteed not to be longer than *len -1* characters. The user can also cancel the input, usually by typing **Escape** or **Ctrl-C**. In this case, XmtMsgLineGetString() does not modify the contents of *buf* and returns NULL.

XmtMsgLineGetDouble(), XmtMsgLineGetInt(), and XmtMsgLine-GetUnsigned() are closely related to XmtMsgLineGetString(). They also perform synchronous input, but only accept input characters that are legal in double, int, and unsigned values. When the user strikes **Return**, these functions convert the input to the appropriate numeric type, store it at the address specified by *value_return*, and return True. If the user cancels the input, these functions return False without changing *value_return*.

XmtMsgLineGetChar() also performs synchronous input. It waits for the user to enter a character into the specified XmtMsgLine widget and returns that character, or if the user cancels the input it returns the constant EOF (defined in the header file *<stdio.h>*). This function differs from the other XmtMsgLine synchronous input functions in that it does not require the user to strike the Return key to enter the input—it returns after any single character is typed.

When using any of these functions, you must be sure to check their return values. If they return NULL, False, or EOF then the user has requested that the operation in progress be cancelled.

See Also

Chapter 22, *The Message Line*
XmtMsgLine, XmtMsgLineClear(),
XmtMsgLineGetInput(), XmtMsgLinePop(),
XmtMsgLinePrintf(), XmtMsgLinePush(),
XmtMsgLineSet(), XmtMsgLineSetInput()

XmtMsgLine{Push,Pop}()

Name

`XmtMsgLinePush()`, `XmtMsgLinePop()` — save and restore messages in an XmtMsgLine widget.

Synopsis

```
#include <Xmt/MsgLine.h>
void XmtMsgLinePush(Widget w)

void XmtMsgLinePop(Widget w, int when)
```

Arguments

Inputs

w	An XmtMsgLine widget.
when	For `XmtMsgLinePop()`, specifies when the saved message should be restored.

Description

`XmtMsgLinePush()` "pushes" the currently displayed message onto an internal stack of messages so that it can be later restored with `XmtMsgLinePop()`. The current contents of the message line are not modified by this call. The message stack grows dynamically, as needed, so any number of messages may be saved on it, and restored later in a last-on-first-off fashion.

`XmtMsgLinePop()` restores the message that was most recently saved (with a call to `XmtMsgLinePush()`) in the XmtMsgLine widget *w*. The message is either restored immediately, or at a later time, depending on the value of the *when* argument. If *when* is `XmtMsgLineNow`, then the message is restored immediately. If *when* is `XmtMsgLineOnAction`, then the message is restored the next time a user action (a key press or mouse click, for example) occurs. Otherwise, if `when` is neither of these constants, then it is taken as a time in milliseconds, the message will be restored after the specified time elapses.

If you want a message to be restored either when the user does something, or when a specified time interval elapses, call `XmtMsgLinePop()` twice, once with the constant `XmtMsgLineOnAction`, and once with the time interval. If a message line has a pop pending, and the application calls some other XmtMsgLine function (such as `XmtMsgLinePush()` again) then the pending pop will be performed immediately instead of waiting for a user action or for time to pass.

See Also

Chapter 22, *The Message Line*
XmtMsgLine, `XmtMsgLineAppend()`, `XmtMsgLineClear()`, `XmtMsgLineGetChar()`, `XmtMsgLineGetDouble()`, `XmtMsgLineGetInput()`, `XmtMsgLineGetInt()`, `XmtMsgLineGetString()`, `XmtMsgLineGetUnsigned()`, `XmtMsgLinePrintf()`, `XmtMsgLineSet()`, `XmtMsgLineSetInput()`

XmtMsgLine{Set,Append,Printf,Clear}()

Name

XmtMsgLineSet(), XmtMsgLineAppend(), XmtMsgLinePrintf(), XmtMsgLineClear() — display messages in an XmtMsgLine widget.

Synopsis

```
#include <Xmt/MsgLine.h>
void XmtMsgLineSet(Widget w, String msg)

void XmtMsgLineAppend(Widget w, String msg)

void XmtMsgLinePrintf(Widget w, String fmt, ...)

void XmtMsgLineClear(Widget w, int when)
```

Arguments

Inputs

w	An XmtMsgLine widget.
msg	The message to be displayed in or appended to *w*.
fmt	For `XmtMsgLinePrintf()`, a `printf()`-style format string.
...	For `XmtMsgLinePrintf()`, a `printf()`-style variable-length argument list of values to be substituted into *fmt*.
when	For `XmtMsgLineClear()`, specifies when the XmtMsgLine widget should be cleared. Specify a delay in milliseconds, or one of the constants `XmtMsgLineNow` or `XmtMsgLineOnAction`.

Description

`XmtMsgLineSet()` displays message *msg* in the XmtMsgLine widget *w*, erasing any text previously displayed in that widget.

`XmtMsgLineAppend()` appends *msg* to whatever text is already displayed in *w*.

`XmtMsgLinePrintf()` substitutes the values in its variable-length argument list into *fmt* and appends the resulting message to whatever text is already displayed in *w*.

`XmtMsgLineClear()` clears any text that is displayed in the XmtMsgLine widget *w*, either immediately, or at a later time, depending on the value of the *when* argument. If *when* is `XmtMsgLineNow`, then the message line is cleared immediately. If *when* is `XmtMsgLineOnAction`, then the message line is cleared when the next user action (key press our mouse click, for example) occurs. Otherwise, if when is neither of these constants, then it is taken as a time in milliseconds, and the message line will be cleared after the specified time elapses.

It is legal to call `XmtMsgLineClear()` twice so that the message line will be cleared either when a user action occurs or a specified amount of time elapses. If an XmtMsgLine has a clear "pending," and some other XmtMsgLine procedure is called (e.g., `XmtMsgLineAppend()`), then the clear will be performed immediately before the other procedure takes effect.

See Also

Chapter 22, *The Message Line*
XmtMsgLine, `XmtMsgLineGetChar()`,
`XmtMsgLineGetDouble()`, `XmtMsgLineGetInput()`,
`XmtMsgLineGetInt()`,`XmtMsgLineGetString()`,
`XmtMsgLineGetUnsigned()`, `XmtMsgLinePop()`,
`XmtMsgLinePush()`, `XmtMsgLineSetInput()`

XmtMsgLine{Set,Get}Input()

Name

`XmtMsgLineSetInput()`, `XmtMsgLineGetInput()` — set or query the editable text in an XmtMsgLine widget.

Synopsis

```
#include <Xmt/MsgLine.h>
void XmtMsgLineSetInput(Widget w, String s)

String XmtMsgLineGetInput(Widget w)
```

Arguments

Inputs

w An XmtMsgLine widget.

s For `XmtMsgLineSetInput()`, the input string to be displayed.

Returns

`XmtMsgLineGetInput()` returns the current editable text displayed in the message line. This text must be freed with `XtFree()` when no longer needed.

Description

`XmtMsgLineSetInput()` appends to the text displayed in the XmtMsgLine widget *w*. This function differs from `XmtMsgLineAppend()`, however, in that the appended text may be edited by the user in a subsequent call to one of the synchronous input functions `XmtMsgLineGetString()`, `XmtMsgLineGetInt()`, `XmtMsgLineGetUnsigned()`, or `XmtMsgLineGetDouble()`.

Text inserted into the message line with `XmtMsgLineSet()`, `XmtMsgLineAppend()`, or `XmtMsgLinePrintf()` is never editable by the user. Text inserted with `XmtMsgLineSetInput()` is editable, and becomes the default value for a subsequent call to a synchronous input function. Note that multiple calls to `XmtMsgLineSetInput()` do not append more editable text to previously editable text; each call sets the entire editable text, replacing any editable text previously displayed in the widget.

`XmtMsgLineGetInput()` returns any currently editable text in an XmtMsgLine widget. It returns a copy of the editable text in allocated memory which must be freed by the application, by calling `XtFree()` when it is no longer needed. The only time there is editable text in an XmtMsgLine widget is while one of the synchronous input functions is in progress. At this point, the application is in an internal event loop, and so you must always call `XmtMsgLineGetInput()` from an action procedure or callback invoked by the XmtMsgLine widget.

Note that `XmtMsgLineGetInput()` does not return complete user input, as `XmtMsgLineGetString()` does, but only a snapshot of the current state of the message line. An application might use this partial input to implement "filename completion" with the **Tab** key, for example, but should not treat input as valid until the user has entered it by striking the `Return` key.

See Also

Chapter 22, *The Message Line*
XmtMsgLine, `XmtMsgLineAppend()`, `XmtMsgLineClear()`, `XmtMsgLineGetChar()`, `XmtMsgLineGetDouble()`, `XmtMsgLineGetInt()`, `XmtMsgLineGetString()`, `XmtMsgLineGetUnsigned()`, `XmtMsgLinePop()`, `XmtMsgLinePrintf()`, `XmtMsgLinePush()`, `XmtMsgLineSet()`

XmtNameToWidget()

Name

XmtNameToWidget() — find a descendant or ancestor widget by name.

Synopsis

```
#include <Xmt/Xmt.h>
Widget XmtNameToWidget(Widget ref, String name)
```

Arguments

Inputs

ref The reference widget, relative to which the named widget is looked up.

name The name of the widget to look up. This name may be a hierarchical name, with individual component names separated by periods; it may also contain resource file wildcards, and other special modifiers.

Returns

The named widget, or NULL if no such widget was found.

Description

XmtNameToWidget() is similar to XtNameToWidget(), but is much more flexible than that Xt Intrinsics function. Like XtNameToWidget(), XmtNameToWidget() takes a reference widget as its first argument, and looks up the named widget (the name is the second argument) relative to that reference widget. Hierarchical widget names are specified as they are in resource files; the * and ? wildcards are supported, and widget class names may be used in place of widget instance names.

Explicit Modifiers

XmtNameToWidget() also supports special modifiers at the beginning of a widget name that change the reference widget and start the search from an ancestor widget. Multiple modifiers can be used; they act as unary operators, and are evaluated from right-to-left. The modifiers are the following:

^ This operator changes the reference widget to the parent of the current reference widget.

~ This operator changes the reference widget to the nearest shell ancestor of the reference widget.

^{*name*}
This operator changes the reference widget to the nearest ancestor widget with the instance name name, or if no such ancestor is found, the nearest ancestor with a class or superclass name name.

Implicit Modifiers

If there are modifiers at the beginning of the specified name, those modifiers explicitly specify which widget is to be used as the reference. If there are no explicit modifiers, then the reference widget may be implicitly modified by one of the following rules.

- If the name begins with a `*` wildcard, then the reference widget is not used, and the search is performed relative to the root application shell widget of the specified reference. This provides the same semantics as a name beginning with `*` in a resource file.

If the name does not begin with a modifier or the `*` wildcard, then it must begin with a widget component name. Thus the remaining implicit modification rules all describe ways of finding a widget that matches this name.

- If the first component of the name is the name of a sibling of the reference widget, then the reference widget is implicitly changed to the parent of the reference widget so that the sibling will be found. This is a useful behavior when `XmtNameToWidget()` is invoked through the String-to-Widget converter—when using the XmForm widget, for example, this makes it easy to refer to sibling widgets for form attachments.
- If the first component of the name is the name of a child of the reference widget, then the reference widget is not modified.
- If the first component of the name does not match a sibling or a child of the specified reference widget, then `XmtNameToWidget()` checks to see if it matches the name of any of the root application shells that have been registered with `XmtInitializeApplicationShell()`. If so, it uses that shell as the root of the search. For applications that create multiple root shells, each with an independent widget hierarchy, this provides way to refer to widgets in a separate hierarchy.
- Finally, if there were no modifiers, and if none of the above rules apply, then the widget name is invalid, and `XmtNameToWidget()` returns `NULL`.

Widget Naming

Once the reference widget has been determined by parsing either the modifiers or by examining the first component of the widget name, the search for a matching widget is started with the children of the reference widget, using the remaining components of the name. Widgets are named exactly as they would be in a resource file:

- Each component name may be a widget instance name or a widget class name.
- A `.` between two components is a "tight binding" and indicates that the second component names a direct child of the first.
- A `*` between two components is a "loose binding" and indicates that the second component names any descendant of the first, with zero or more intervening generations of widgets.

- A `?` in place of a component name is a wildcard that matches any single widget, but does not elide any number of generations as the `*` modifier does.

The Search

The search is conducted breadth-first, which means that if several children match the specified name (because of wildcards, for example) then the one with the shortest name (i.e., the closest descendant of the reference widget) will be returned. If there are multiple matching widgets which are the same number of generations removed from the reference widget, the widget returned is arbitrary.

Special Cases

There are also a few special cases in this search:

- If there is no name, or if the name consists only of modifiers, then the reference widget or the modified reference widget is returned. This means that a widget name like `^^` is legal, and returns the grandparent of the specified reference widget. This special case means that it is possible to search up the tree for ancestor widgets (especially using the `^{}` modifier syntax) rather than only searching down the tree for descendants.
- The name "self" is a special case. The name "self" by itself, with no modifiers, will always match the reference widget. This is often useful in resource files with the String-to-Widget converter. Also, you can use "self" (again, only when there are no modifiers) as a way to force `XtNameToWidget()` to start its search at the specified reference widget. If you specify a name "button1", `XtNameToWidget()` will find a sibling with that name in preference to a child with that name. To disambiguate this case you can explicitly use "self.button1" when searching for a child and "^button1" when looking for a sibling.

See Also

Chapter 9, *Looking Up Widgets by Name*
`XmtRegisterWidgetConverter()`, `XtNameToWidget()`

Name

XmtParseCommandLine() — parse the application command line for Xmt-specific arguments.

Synopsis

```
#include <Xmt/AppRes.h>
void XmtParseCommandLine(Widget w, int *argc, char **argv)
```

Arguments

Inputs

w The application shell widget for which application resources are to be set.

argc The address of a variable that contains the number of command-line arguments passed to main().

argv The array of command-line arguments that were passed to main().

Outputs

argc A modified *argc* that specifies the number of arguments now in *argv*.

argv A modified *argv* from which any arguments that were recognized and parsed have been removed.

Description

XmtParseCommandLine() uses XrmParseCommand() to parse command-line arguments the user can use to set Xmt application variables. It is designed to be called immediately after a call to XtAppInitialize() and before the call to XmtInitializeApplicationShell(), if any. XtAppInitialize() parses and removes the standard Xt arguments from the command line, and also any application-specific arguments specified in its *options* array. XmtParseCommandLine() will parse and remove any standard Xmt arguments.

XmtInitialize() is a convenience function suitable for initializing most Xmt applications—it calls XtAppInitialize() and XmtParseCommandLine(), as well as other functions.

The table lists the standard Xmt command-line arguments.

XmtParseCommandLine() *(continued)*

Standard Xmt Command-Line Arguments

-bitmapFilePath	-contextHelpPixmap	-helpCursorBackground
-busyCursor	-cursor	-helpCursorForeground
-busyCursorBackground	-cursorBackground	-helpFilePath
-busyCursorForeground	-cursorForeground	-palette
-colorTable	-focusStyle	-pixmapFilePath
-configDir	-fontFamily	-resourceFilePath
-configPath	-helpCursor	-userConfigPath
-contextHelpFile		

See Also

Chapter 7, *Application Resources and Command-Line Arguments*
`XmtGetApplicationValues()`, `XmtInitialize()`,
`XmtInitializeApplicationShell()`,
`XmtSetApplicationValues()`, `XrmParseCommand()`

Name

XmtParseXpmData(), XmtParseXpmFile(), XmtFreeXmtImage() — parse an XPM pixmap into the intermediate XmtImage format.

Synopsis

```
#include <Xmt/Xpm.h>
XmtImage *XmtParseXpmData(String *data)

XmtImage *XmtParseXpmFile(String filename)

void XmtFreeXmtImage(XmtImage *image)
```

Arguments

Inputs

data	An array of strings defined by an XPM file that has been included into an application.
filename	The name of a file containing pixmap data in XPM format.
image	An XmtImage to be freed.

Returns

XmtParseXpmData() and XmtParseXpmFile() return an XmtImage, or NULL, if the XPM data was invalid or the file could not be found. The returned XmtImage should be freed when no longer need with XmtFreeXmtImage().

Description

XmtParseXpmData() parses the specified array of strings (declared by an #included XPM file) into an XmtImage structure. On success, it returns a pointer to the allocated XmtImage. If the data was invalid, it returns NULL.

XmtParseXpmFile() reads the contents of the specified file, and parses it into an XmtImage structure. It returns a pointer to an allocated XmtImage structure on success, or NULL if the file could not be read, or if the file contained invalid data.

When the XmtImage returned by either of these functions is no longer needed, they may be freed by calling XmtFreeXmtImage().

An XmtImage structure is a parsed representation of an XPM pixmap file. The symbolic color names it contains have not yet been looked up, nor have any pixel values been allocated for a specific display and colormap. An XmtImage may be converted to a Pixmap in an additional step, by calling XmtCreatePixmapFromXmtImage(), or it may be cached for later lookup and conversion in the Xmt image cache by calling XmtRegisterImage().

See Also

Chapter 5, *Using Icons*
XmtCreatePixmapFromXmtImage(), XmtCreateXImageFromXmtImage(), XmtGetPixmap(), XmtLookupPixmap(), XmtRegisterImage()

XmtPatchVisualInheritance()

Name

`XmtPatchVisualInheritance()` — apply a runtime patch to the Shell widget class so that it handles non-default visuals better.

Synopsis

```
#include <Xmt/Xmt.h>
void XmtPatchVisualInheritance(void)
```

Arguments

None.

Description

The Xt Shell widget class inherits the value of its `XtNvisual` resource from the shell's parent window—the root window. Therefore, by default, shell widgets will always use the default visual of the screen. If you are writing an application that uses a non-default visual, then you will probably want all of your application's windows to use the same visual, to minimize color-flashing as the pointer moves from window to window.

Because the Shell widget inherits its `XtNvisual` resource from its parent window rather than its parent widget, you must explicitly set this resource on all shells that you create. This includes dialog box shell widgets, which are often automatically created for you by convenience routines, and which can be difficult to set resources on.

A simpler solution is to call `XmtPatchVisualInheritance()` before you call `XtAppInitialize()` or `XmtInitialize()`. This function applies a patch to the Shell widget class initialize method so that if its `XtNvisual` resource is unset, it will inherit its value from its nearest shell widget ancestor (if it has one) rather than from the screen's root window.

Once you have called this function, you need only set the `XtNvisual` resource for your initial root shell widget; all other shells will inherit this non-default visual.

See Also

Chapter 4, *Using Color*
Shell widget

Name

`XmtRegisterAll()` — register all standard widgets, procedures, and resource converters.

Synopsis

```
#include <Xmt/Xmt.h>
void XmtRegisterAll(void)
```

Arguments

None.

Description

`XmtRegisterAll()` is a convenience procedure that registers all Motif and Xmt widgets for the Xmt automatic widget creation facility, registers all common UNIX, Xt, and Xmt procedures for use with the Xmt callback converter, and registers all of the Xmt-specific resource converters.

`XmtRegisterAll()` is defined as follows:

```
void XmtRegisterAll(void)
{
    XmtRegisterMotifWidgets();
    XmtRegisterXmtWidgets();

    XmtRegisterUnixProcedures();
    XmtRegisterXtProcedures();
    XmtRegisterXmtProcedures();

    /* these are also registered by XmtInitialize() */
    XmtRegisterBitmapConverter();
    XmtRegisterBitmaskConverter();
    XmtRegisterPixmapConverter();
    XmtRegisterColorTableConverter();
    XmtRegisterWidgetConverter();
    XmtRegisterCallbackConverter();
    XmtRegisterXmStringConverter();
    XmtRegisterXmFontListConverter();
    XmtRegisterStringListConverter();
    XmtRegisterMenuItemsConverter();
    XmtRegisterPixmapListConverter();
    XmtRegisterPixelConverter();

    XmtRegisterLayoutParser();
    XmtRegisterLayoutCreateMethod();
}
```

See Also

`XmtRegisterMotifWidgets()`, `XmtRegisterUnixProcedures()`, `XmtRegisterXmtProcedures()`, `XmtRegisterXmtWidgets()`, `XmtRegisterXtProcedures()`

Xmt[Va]RegisterColor[s]()

Name

XmtRegisterColor(), XmtVaRegisterColors(), XmtRegister-Colors(), XmtRegisterPixel(), XmtRegisterStandard-Colors() — define symbolic color names in a color table.

Synopsis

```
#include <Xmt/Color.h>
void XmtRegisterColor(XmtColorTable table,
                      String symbolic_name, String color_name)

void XmtVaRegisterColors(XmtColorTable table,
                       { String symbolic_name,
                         String color_name, }
                         NULL)

void XmtRegisterColors(XmtColorTable table, XmtColorPair *colors,
                       Cardinal num)

void XmtRegisterPixel(XmtColorTable table, String symbolic_name,
                      Display *display, Colormap colormap,
                      Pixel pixel)

void XmtRegisterStandardColors(XmtColorTable table, Widget w,
                               Pixel foreground,
                               Pixel background)

typedef struct {
    String symbolic_name;
    String color_name;
} XmtColorPair;
```

Arguments

Inputs

table The XmtColorTable in which the color or colors are to be registered.

symbolic_name The symbolic name of the color to be registered. For XmtVa-RegisterColors(), this is part of a NULL-terminated variable-length argument list and may be repeated any number of times.

color_name The color name to be associated with the symbolic name. For XmtVaRegisterColors(), this is part of a NULL-terminated variable-length argument list and may be repeated any number of times.

colors For XmtRegisterColors(), an array of XmtColorPair structures that define symbolic names and their associated color names.

num For `XmtRegisterColors()`, the number of elements in the *colors* array.

display For `XmtRegisterPixel()`, the X display on which *pixel* is defined.

colormap For `XmtRegisterPixel()`, the colormap in which *pixel* is defined.

pixel For `XmtRegisterPixel()`, the pixel value that is to be registered with *symbolic_name*.

w For `XmtRegisterStandardColors()`, any widget in the application that specifies a display and colormap for which the *foreground* and *background* pixels are valid.

foreground For `XmtRegisterStandardColors()`, a foreground color to be registered in *table*.

background For `XmtRegisterStandardColors()`, a background color to be used to register the other "standard" colors in *table*.

Description

These functions all provide ways of defining symbolic names for actual color names in an XmtColorTable. `XmtRegisterColor()` is the simplest—it associates *symbolic_name* with *color_name* in *table*.

`XmtVaRegisterColors()` is like `XmtRegisterColor()`, except that it uses a NULL-terminated variable-length argument list to associate any number of *symbolic_name* and *color_name* pairs in *table*.

`XmtRegisterColors()` is a variation on `XmtVaRegisterColors()` that uses a counted array of `XmtColorPair` structures instead of a variable-length argument list of *symbolic_name*/*color_name* pairs.

`XmtRegisterPixel()` defines a symbolic name for an already allocated pixel value. Note that it requires `Display *` and `Colormap` arguments to specify where the *pixel* is valid. The pixel value is registered by querying the RGB components of the color and converting these to a hexadecimal RGB color specification.

`XmtRegisterStandardColors()` registers a number of "standard" symbolic colors based on the specified *foreground* and *background* colors. These "standard" colors are the same ones that appear by default in the `colorTable` application resource. They are listed in the table.

Symbolic Name	*Color Registered*
foreground	The specified *foreground* color
background	The specified *background* color
top_shadow	A lighter shade of the background; for shadows
bottom_shadow	A darker shade of the background; for shadows
select	A slightly darker shade of the background; for armed buttons, etc.

See Also

Chapter 4, *Using Color*
XmtColorTableGetParent(), XmtColorTableSetParent(), XmtCreateColorTable(), XmtDestroyColorTable(), XmtLookupColorName()

XmtRegisterEnumConverter()

Name

XmtRegisterEnumConverter(), XmtConvertStringToEnum() — a resource converter for enumerated types.

Synopsis

```
#include <Xmt/Converters.h>
Boolean XmtConvertStringToEnum(Display *dpy, XrmValue *args,
                               Cardinal *num_args,
                               XrmValue *from, XrmValue *to,
                               XtPointer *data)

void XmtRegisterEnumConverter(String type,
                              String *names, int *values, int num,
                              String *prefixes)
```

Arguments

Inputs

type	The representation type for which the converter is to be registered. This string must be permanently allocated.
names	A sorted array of names for each enumerated value. These names and this array must be permanently allocated.
values	An array of enumerated values that correspond to each of the strings in the *names* array. This array must be permanently allocated.
num_values	The number of elements in the *names* and *values* arrays.
prefixes	A NULL-terminated array of strings which may optionally appear as prefixes of the strings in the *names* array. These strings and this array must be permanently allocated.

Description

XmtConvertStringToEnum() is a "new-style" resource converter of type XtTypeConverter. It is a generalized resource converter appropriate for converting any enumerated type. It is intended to be registered with the Xt resource conversion mechanism rather than being invoked directly, so its arguments are not documented here.

XmtRegisterEnumConverter() registers XmtConvertStringToEnum() for the representation type *type*. The converter is registered so that *type*, *names*, *values*, *num_values*, and *prefixes* are passed to it in its *args* argument.

names is an array of strings that will be recognized by the converter. It must be in alphabetical order so that it can be searched with a binary search algorithm.

`values` is an array of integers that specifies the enumerated value that corresponds to each string in the `names` array. These values are specified as integers, but the converter will work correctly even when conversion is requested to a one-byte or a two-byte value. To save space in widget instance records, enumerated values are often stored in one-byte `unsigned char` fields.

`prefixes` is a `NULL`-terminated array of strings that specify optional prefixes that the converter will recognize in front of any string it converts. Each of these prefixes is optional, but if they do occur, they must appear in the order specified in this array.

All of the strings and arrays passed to this function must be permanent—their values must not change, and if they are in allocated memory, that memory must not be freed for the lifetime of the application. This is generally ensured by using statically initialized arrays.

See Also

Chapter 8, *Utility Functions*

XmtRegister{Image,XbmData}()

Name

XmtRegisterImage(), XmtRegisterXbmData() — register pixmap and bitmap data in the Xmt pixmap cache.

Synopsis

```
#include <Xmt/Pixmap.h>
void XmtRegisterImage(String name, XmtImage *data)

void XmtRegisterXbmData(String name,
                        char *imagedata, char *maskdata,
                        int width, int height,
                        int hotspot_x, int hotspot_y)
```

Arguments

Inputs

name	The name under which the pixmap or bitmap data is to be registered.
data	For XmtRegisterImage(), the parsed XPM data.
imagedata	XBM data to be registered for *name*.
maskdata	An optional bitmask that defines a non-rectangular shape for *imagedata*.
width, *height*	The size, in pixels, of the XBM data.
hotspot_x, *hotspot_y*	Optional (x,y) coordinates of a cursor "hotspot" for the XBM data.

Description

XmtRegisterImage() registers an XmtImage structure by name in the Xmt image cache. The XmtImage structure contains a parsed form of XPM format image data. An XmtImage structure can be obtained by calling XmtParse-XpmFile() or XmtParseXpmData().

Once an XmtImage structure is registered, it can be looked up by name and converted to a Pixmap with XmtLookupPixmap() and related functions. If the image contains "transparent" pixels, a bitmask for the image can be looked up with XmtLookupBitmask().

XmtRegisterXbmData() registers XBM format image data and an optional XBM format image mask by name in the Xmt image cache. The *imagedata* and *maskdata* arguments to this function can be obtained by including an XBM format file into your C code, where it will declare a statically initialized array of characters.

Once this data is registered, it can be looked up and converted to a single-plane `Pixmap` with `XmtLookupBitmap()`, or to a multi-plane `Pixmap` with `XmtLookupPixmap()`. The mask data can be looked up and returned as a single-plane `Pixmap` with `XmtLookupBitmask()`.

See Also

`XmtGetBitmap()`, `XmtGetPixmap()`, `XmtLookupBitmap()`, `XmtLookupBitmask()`, `XmtLookupPixmap()`, `XmtLookupSimplePixmap()`, `XmtLookupWidgetPixmap()`, `XmtParseXpmData()`, `XmtParseXpmFile()`

XmtRegisterImprovedIcons()

Name

`XmtRegisterImprovedIcons()` — replace the standard error, warning, and information icons with larger, "improved" icons.

Synopsis

```
#include <Xmt/Pixmap.h>
void XmtRegisterImprovedIcons(Widget w,
                              XmtColorTable table)
```

Arguments

Inputs

`w` Any widget in the application.

`table` A color table that defines the colors of the icons, or `NULL`.

Description

`XmtRegisterImprovedIcons()` replaces the standard Motif error, warning, and information icons by calling `XmInstallImage()` to register larger, multi-color icons with the names `xm_error`, `xm_warning`, and `xm_information`. Any error, warning, or information dialog created after this function is called will use the new icons.

The improved icons are defined as XPM data and are converted to `XImage` structures using the symbolic color definitions of the color table *`table`*. The new icons use only the standard symbolic color names defined by `XmtRegisterStandardColors()`, so you can usually specify *NULL* for *`table`* and rely on the default application color table.

Note that the improved icons are multi-plane color pixmaps. Since the XmMessageBox widget cannot display non-rectangular icons, these color icons are inappropriate for any XmMessageBox widget that has a background color different than the background color specified in *`table`*.

See Also

Chapter 4, *Using Color*
Chapter 5, *Using Icons*
Chapter 25, *Message Dialogs*
`XmInstallImage()`, `XmtCreateXImageFromXmtImage()`,
`XmtGetPixmap()`, `XmtLookupPixmap()`,
`XmtParseXpmData()`, `XmtRegisterImage()`

XmtRegisterLayout{Parser,CreateMethod}()

Name

XmtRegisterLayoutParser(), XmtRegisterLayoutCreateMethod() — register the parser for the XmtLayout widget layout grammar and allow typed widget creation by the parser.

Synopsis

```
#include <Xmt/Layout.h>
void XmtRegisterLayoutParser(void)

void XmtRegisterLayoutCreateMethod(void)
```

Arguments

None.

Description

The XmtLayout widget is a fairly large widget that can lay out widgets as specified through constraint resources or as specified by a sophisticated layout grammar specified in a resource file. Because the parser for this layout grammar is relatively large, it must be explicitly registered, like a resource converter, before it can be used.

`XmtRegisterLayoutParser()` registers a parser for the XmtLayout widget layout grammar. If you do not call this function, you will not be able to set the `XmtNlayout` resource of your XmtLayout widgets, but your application will have to link with less code. If you will never need the `XmtNlayout` resource, then you shouldn't call this function.

`XmtRegisterLayoutCreateMethod()` is a similar function. If you call it, the Xmt layout parser will be linked with the Xmt automatic widget creation facilities so that you can specify widgets to be automatically created directly in the layout string.

Both `XmtInitialize()` and `XmtRegisterAll()` call both of these registration functions.

See Also

Chapter 19, *The Layout Widget: The Details*
XmtLayout, `XmtInitialize()`, `XmtRegisterAll()`

XmtRegister{Motif,Xmt}Widgets()

Name

XmtRegisterMotifWidgets(), XmtRegisterXmtWidgets() — register the standard Motif and Xmt widget constructors for use with the automatic widget creation facilities.

Synopsis

```
#include <Xmt/WidgetType.h>
void XmtRegisterMotifWidgets(void)

void XmtRegisterXmtWidgets(void)
```

Arguments

None.

Description

XmtRegisterMotifWidgets() registers all of the Motif widget constructors under their common names so that they can be used with XmtCreateChildren and related automatic widget creation routines. It registers the XmToggleButton, XmText, XmScrolledText, XmTextField, and XmScale widgets with special "get value" and "set value" functions for use by the Xmt automatic dialog facilities. See XmtRegister<*Widget*>() for more information.

XmtRegisterXmtWidgets() registers all of the Xmt widget constructors for the same purpose. It registers the XmtChooser and XmtInputField widgets with special "get value" and "set value" functions for use by the Xmt automatic dialog facilities. See XmtRegister<*Widget*>() for more information. This function also registers the Xt shell widget classes.

These functions link in all of the widgets in the Motif and Xmt libraries. Unless you actually use all of them (or are using a shared library) it will unnecessarily increase the size of your application executable.

Note that XmtRegisterAll() calls both XmtRegisterMotifWidgets() and XmtRegisterXmtWidgets().

The tables list the name of the widgets registered by each function.

Widget Types Registered by XmtRegisterMotifWidgets()

XmArrowButton	XmMainWindow	XmScrolledText
XmBulletinBoard	XmMenuBar	XmScrolledWindow
XmBulletinBoardDialog	XmMenuShell	XmSelectionBox
XmCascadeButton	XmMessageBox	XmSelectionDialog
XmCommand	XmMessageDialog	XmSeparator
XmDialogShell	XmOptionMenu	XmSimpleCheckBox
XmDrawingArea	XmPanedWindow	XmSimpleMenuBar
XmDrawnButton	XmPopupMenu	XmSimpleOptionMenu
XmErrorDialog	XmPromptDialog	XmSimplePopupMenu
XmFileSelectionBox	XmPulldownMenu	XmSimplePulldownMenu

XmtRegister{Motif,Xmt}Widgets() *(continued)*

Widget Types Registered by XmtRegisterMotifWidgets() (continued)

XmFileSelectionDialog	XmPushButton	XmSimpleRadioBox
XmForm	XmQuestionDialog	XmText
XmFormDialog	XmRadioBox	XmTextField
XmFrame	XmRowColumn	XmToggleButton
XmInformationDialog	XmScale	XmWarningDialog
XmLabel	XmScrollBar	XmWorkArea
XmList	XmScrolledList	

Widget Types Registered by XmtRegisterXmtWidgets()

ApplicationShell	XmtLayout	XmtMenu
OverrideShell	XmtLayoutBox	XmtMenuPane
TopLevelShell	XmtLayoutCol	XmtMenubar
TransientShell	XmtLayoutDialog	XmtMsgLine
XmtChooser	XmtLayoutPixmap	XmtOptionMenu
XmtCli	XmtLayoutRow	XmtPopupMenu
XmtHelpBox	XmtLayoutSeparator	XmtScrolledCli
XmtHelpDialog	XmtLayoutSpace	XmtWorkingBox
XmtInputField	XmtLayoutString	XmtWorkingDialog

See Also

Chapter 11, *Automatic Widget Creation*
`XmtCreateChildren()`, `XmtRegisterAll()`, `XmtRegister`<*Widget*>

Name

XmtRegisterProcedures(), XmtRegisterCallbackProcedure(), XmtVaRegisterCallbackProcedures() — register procedures for use with the Xmt callback converter.

Synopsis

```
#include <Xmt/Procedures.h>
void XmtRegisterProcedures(XmtProcedureInfo *procedures,
                           Cardinal num_procedures)

void XmtRegisterCallbackProcedure(String name,
                                  XtCallbackProc proc,
                                  String type)

void XmtVaRegisterCallbackProcedures(String name,
                                     XtCallbackProc proc,
                                     String type,
                                   { String name,
                                     XtCallbackProc proc,
                                     String type, }
                                     NULL)

typedef struct {
    String name;
    XmtProcedure function;
    String argument_types[8];
    /* private, internal fields omitted */
} XmtProcedureInfo;
```

Arguments

Inputs

procedures An array of procedure names, pointers, and argument descriptions to be registered.

num_procedures The number of elements in *procedures*.

name The name of an XtCallbackProc to be registered. For XmtVaRegisterCallbackProcedures(), this argument may appear any number of times as part of a NULL-terminated argument list.

proc The XtCallbackProc to be registered for use with the Xmt callback converter. For XmtVaRegisterCallbackProcedures(), this argument may appear any number of times as part of a NULL-terminated argument list.

type This is the representation type of the client_data argument that proc expects. For XmtVaRegisterCallbackProcedures(), this argument may appear any number of times as part of a NULL-terminated argument list.

Description

`XmtRegisterProcedures()` is the general way to register C procedures with the Xmt String-to-Callback converter so that they can be called in resource files.

Each element of the *`procedures`* array is an `XmtProcedureInfo` structure that describes one procedure to be registered. The `function` field of this structure specifies the procedure to be registered. You will have to cast your procedure to the special type `XmtProcedure` to set this field. The `name` field of the structure specifies the name under which the procedure will be registered. The `argument_types` field of the `XmtProcedureInfo` structure is an array of strings that let you specify the representation type of up to eight arguments for the procedure. The Xmt callback converter will parse arguments specified in a resource file and automatically convert them to the appropriate type before calling the procedure. If the procedure being registered expects fewer than eight arguments, leave the unused arguments uninitialized as `NULL`.

You may also specify some special argument types in the `argument_types` array. These special representation types are listed in the table. When a registered procedure takes one of these types, the callback converter will automatically pass a value, and you will not have to specify a value in the resource file.

Type	*Meaning*
XmtRCallbackWidget	Pass the widget that invoked the callback.
XmtRCallbackData	Pass the *`call_data`* argument.
XmtRCallbackAppContext	Pass the application context of the widget.
XmtRCallbackWindow	Pass the window ID of the invoking widget.
XmtRCallbackDisplay	Pass the display of the invoking widget.
XmtRCallbackUnused	Pass `NULL`; good for unused arguments.

See Chapter 10, *Callbacks in Resource Files*, for more information on using the Xmt callback converter, and on registering procedures for it.

`XmtRegisterCallbackProcedure()` is a simplified interface to `Xmt-RegisterProcedures()` that you can use when registering a standard callback procedure of type `XtCallbackProc`. It creates and registers an `Xmt-ProcedureInfo` structure using the specified *`name`* and *`proc`*. It uses the `argument_types` field to specify that the procedure *`proc`* takes three arguments, of types `XmtRCallbackWidget`, *`type`*, and `XmtRCallbackData`. The first and last of these types specify standard callback arguments, as shown in the table. The second argument is the *`type`* that was passed to the function.

`XmtVaRegisterCallbackProcedures()` is like `XmtRegisterCall-backProcedure()`, but it takes a `NULL`-terminated list of (*`name`*, *`proc`*, *`type`*) triples to register.

See Also

Chapter 10, *Callbacks in Resource Files*
`XmtRegisterCallbackConverter()`,
`XmtRegisterUnixProcedures()`,
`XmtRegisterXmtProcedures()`,
`XmtRegisterXtProcedures()`

XmtRegister<*Type*>Converter()

Name

XmtRegister<*Type*>Converter — register resource converters for various types.

Synopsis

```
#include <Xmt/Converters.h>
void XmtRegisterBitmapConverter(void)
void XmtRegisterBitmaskConverter(void)
void XmtRegisterCallbackConverter(void)
void XmtRegisterColorTableConverter(void)
void XmtRegisterMenuItemsConverter(void)
void XmtRegisterPixelConverter(void)
void XmtRegisterPixmapConverter(void)
void XmtRegisterPixmapListConverter(void)
void XmtRegisterStringListConverter(void)
void XmtRegisterWidgetConverter(void)
void XmtRegisterXmFontListConverter(void)
void XmtRegisterXmStringConverter(void)
```

Arguments

None.

Description

These functions call `XtSetTypeConverter()` to register resource converters for various data types. They take no arguments and return no values. It is safe to call these functions multiple times in an application.

Usage

These resource converters are important for the Xmt "programming with resources" approach to application development. If you'll be using callbacks in your resource file, you'll need to register the Callback and the Widget converters. If you'll be using the XmtMenu widget, you want the MenuItems converter. If you use the XmtChooser widget with a resource file, register the StringList and perhaps the PixmapList converters. To take advantage of the Xmt multi-font XmString syntax, register the XmString converter. And to use the Xmt color and icon handling facilities, register the Pixel, ColorTable Pixmap, Bitmap, and Bitmask converters.

You can also register all of these converters by calling `XmtInitialize()` or `XmtRegisterAll()`.

See Also

Chapter 3, *Displaying Text*
Chapter 4, *Using Color*
Chapter 5, *Using Icons*

Chapter 9, *Looking Up Widgets by Name*
Chapter 10, *Callbacks in Resource Files*
Chapter 20, *Easy Menu Creation*
`XmtConvertStringTo<Type>()`, `XmtInitialize()`,
`XmtRegisterAll()`

XmtRegister{Unix,Xmt,Xt}Procedures()

Name

XmtRegisterXtProcedures(), XmtRegisterXmtProcedures(), Xmt-RegisterUnixProcedures() — register commonly used procedures with the Xmt callback converter.

Synopsis

```
#include <Xmt/Procedures.h>
void XmtRegisterXtProcedures(void)
void XmtRegisterXmtProcedures(void)
void XmtRegisterUnixProcedures(void)
```

Arguments

None.

Description

XmtRegisterXtProcedures(), XmtRegisterXmtProcedures(), and XmtRegisterUnixProcedures() register a number of commonly used procedures with the Xmt String-to-Callback converter so that they can be used in resource files.

The listings below show the procedures that are registered by each of these functions and the argument types that each function is registered to expect. Note that not all of these procedures will take the same number arguments when called from a resource file as they do when called from C. See Xmt-RegisterProcedures() and Chapter 10, *Callbacks in Resource Files*, for an explanation of the differences.

XmtRegisterXtProcedures() registers the following procedures:

```
XtAddCallbacks(XtRWidget, XtRString, XtRCallback)
XtAugmentTranslations(XtRWidget, XtRTranslationTable)
XtDestroyWidget(XtRWidget)
XtError(XtRString)
XtInstallAccelerators(XtRWidget, XtRWidget)
XtInstallAllAccelerators(XtRWidget, XtRWidget)
XtManageChild(XtRWidget)
XtOverrideTranslations(XtRWidget, XtRTranslationTable)
XtPopdown(XtRWidget)
XtPopupExclusive(XmtRCallbackWidget, XtRWidget)
XtPopupNone(XmtRCallbackWidget, XtRWidget)
XtPopupNonexclusive(XmtRCallbackWidget, XtRWidget)
XtPopupSpringLoaded(XtRWidget)
XtRealizeWidget(XtRWidget)
XtSetKeyboardFocus(XtRWidget, XtRWidget)
XtSetMappedWhenManaged(XtRWidget, XtRBoolean)
XtSetSensitive(XtRWidget, XtRBoolean)
XtUnmanageChild(XtRWidget)
XtWarning(XtRString)
```

`XmtRegisterXmtProcedures()` registers the following procedures:

```
/* special resource-setting functions */
XmtSetValue(XtRWidget, XtRString, XtRString)
XmtSetTypedValue(XtRWidget, XtRString, XtRString, XtRString)

/* simple message dialog functions */
XmtDisplayError(XmtRCallbackWidget, XtRString, XtRString)
XmtDisplayWarning(XmtRCallbackWidget, XtRString, XtRString)
XmtDisplayInformation(XmtRCallbackWidget, XtRString, XtRString,
                      XtRString)
XmtDisplayWarningMsg(XmtRCallbackWidget, XtRString, XtRString,
                     XtRString, XtRString)
XmtDisplayErrorMsg(XmtRCallbackWidget, XtRString, XtRString,
                   XtRString, XtRString)
XmtDisplayInformationMsg(XmtRCallbackWidget, XtRString, XtRString,
                         XtRString, XtRString)
XmtDisplayWarningMsgAndWait(XmtRCallbackWidget, XtRString, XtRString,
                            XtRString, XtRString)
XmtDisplayErrorMsgAndWait(XmtRCallbackWidget, XtRString, XtRString,
                          XtRString, XtRString)

/* cursor, event, shell and miscellaneous utilities */
XmtAddDeleteCallback(XtRWidget, XmRDeleteResponse, XtRCallback)
XmtAddSaveYourselfCallback(XtRWidget, XtRCallback)
XmtDeiconifyShell(XtRWidget)
XmtDialogPosition(XtRWidget, XtRWidget)
XmtDiscardButtonEvents(XtRWidget)
XmtDiscardKeyPressEvents(XtRWidget)
XmtDisplayBusyCursor(XtRWidget)
XmtDisplayCursor(XtRWidget, XtRCursor)
XmtDisplayDefaultCursor(XtRWidget)
XmtFocusShell(XtRWidget)
XmtIconifyShell(XtRWidget)
XmtLowerShell(XtRWidget)
XmtMoveShellToPointer(XtRWidget)
XmtRaiseShell(XtRWidget)
XmtRegisterImprovedIcons(XtRWidget, XmtRXmtColorTable)
XmtSetFocusToShell(XtRWidget)
XmtSetInitialFocus(XtRWidget,XtRWidget)
XmtWaitUntilMapped(XtRWidget)
XmtWarpToShell(XtRWidget)

/* widget and dialog creation functions */
XmtCreateChildren(XtRWidget)
XmtCreateChild(XtRWidget,XtRString)
XmtBuildDialog(XtRWidget, XtRString, XmtRCallbackUnused,
               XmtRCallbackUnused)
XmtBuildToplevel(XtRWidget, XtRString)
XmtBuildApplication(XtRString, XtRString, XmtRCallbackDisplay,
                    XmtRCallbackUnused, XmtRCallbackUnused)
```

```
/* context help functions */
 XmtHelpDisplayContextHelp(XtRWidget)
 XmtHelpDoContextHelp(XmtRCallbackWidget)
 XmtHelpContextHelpCallback(XmtRCallbackWidget,
                    XmtRCallbackUnused, XmtRCallbackUnused)

 /* XmtMsgLine widget functions */
 XmtMsgLineClear(XtRWidget, XtRInt)
 XmtMsgLineSet(XtRWidget, XtRString)
 XmtMsgLineAppend(XtRWidget, XtRString)
 XmtMsgLinePrintf(XtRWidget, XtRString, XmtRCallbackUnused)
 XmtMsgLinePush(XtRWidget)
 XmtMsgLinePop(XtRWidget, XtRInt)

 /* XmtCli widget functions */
 XmtCliPuts(XtRString, XtRWidget)
 XmtCliPrintf(XtRWidget, XtRString, XmtRCallbackUnused)
 XmtCliClear(XtRWidget)

 /* XmtChooser widget functions */
 XmtChooserSetState(XtRWidget, XtRInt, XtRBoolean)
 XmtChooserSetSensitive(XtRWidget, XtRInt, XtRBoolean)

 /* XmtInputField widget functions */
 XmtInputFieldSetString(XtRWidget, XtRString)

 /* XmtLayout widget functions */
 XmtLayoutDisableLayout(XtRWidget)
 XmtLayoutEnableLayout(XtRWidget)

 /* automatic dialog callback functions */
 XmtDialogOkayCallback(XmtRCallbackWidget)
 XmtDialogCancelCallback(XmtRCallbackWidget)
 XmtDialogApplyCallback(XmtRCallbackWidget)
 XmtDialogDoneCallback(XmtRCallbackWidget)
 XmtDialogResetCallback(XmtRCallbackWidget)
```

Finally, `XmtRegisterUnixProcedures()` registers the following procedures:

```
exit(XtRInt)
puts(XtRString)
system(XtRString)
```

See Also

Chapter 10, *Callbacks in Resource Files*
`XmtRegisterAll()`, `XmtRegisterProcedures()`

Name

XmtRegisterChooser(), XmtRegisterInputField(), XmtRegister-XmScale(), XmtRegisterXmScrolledText(), XmtRegisterXm-Text(), XmtRegisterXmTextField(), XmtRegisterXmToggle-Button() — specially register input widgets for use with Xmt automatic dialog facilities.

Synopsis

```
#include <Xmt/Chooser.h>
void XmtRegisterChooser(void)

#include <Xmt/InputField.h>
void XmtRegisterInputField(void)

#include <Xmt/WidgetType.h>
void XmtRegisterXmScale(void)

void XmtRegisterXmScrolledText(void)

void XmtRegisterXmText(void)

void XmtRegisterXmTextField(void)

void XmtRegisterXmToggleButton(void)
```

Arguments

None.

Description

These functions register certain Xmt and Motif widgets for use with `XmtCreateChildren()` and its related automatic widget creation functions, and also for use with the Xmt automatic dialog facilities. See Chapter 11, *Automatic Widget Creation*, and Chapter 29, *Custom Dialogs and Automatic Dialog Management*, for more information.

These widget classes could trivially be registered with `XmtRegisterWidgetClass()`, for example, but are singled out for custom registration functions because they each accept some form of user input (a text value, a Boolean selection, and so on). Because these widgets can accept user input, they are important in dialog boxes, and these functions register the widgets with `XmtRegisterWidgetTypes()` in order to specify "set value" and "get value" procedures that can be used by the Xmt automatic dialog management facilities to automatically transfer data to and from dialog boxes.

The table lists the data types that are handled by the "get value" and "set value" procedures registered with these functions. See Chapter 29 for details.

Widget	*Supported Representation Types*
XmScale	XtRCardinal, XtRDimension, XtRPosition, XtRInt, XtRShort, XtRUnsignedChar
XmScrolledText	XtRString (must be freed), XmtRBuffer
XmText	XtRString (must be freed), XmtRBuffer
XmTextField	XtRString (must be freed), XmtRBuffer
XmToggleButton	XtRBoolean, XtRBool, XtRCardinal, XtREnum, XtRInt, XtRShort, XtRUnsignedChar
XmtChooser	Type of XmtNvalueType resource, or any scalar with the same size as int, short, or char.
XmtInputField	XtRString (must not be freed; volatile), XmtRBuffer, or, by conversion: XtRCardinal, XtRDimension, XmtRDouble, XtRFloat, XtRInt, XtRPosition, XtRShort

See Also

Chapter 11, *Automatic Widget Creation*
Chapter 29, *Custom Dialogs and Automatic Dialog Management*
XmtRegisterMotifWidgets(), XmtRegisterWidgetTypes(), XmtRegisterXmtWidgets()

Xmt[Va]RegisterWidget{Class,Constructor}()

Name

XmtRegisterWidgetClass(), XmtRegisterWidgetConstructor(), XmtVaRegisterWidgetClasses(), XmtVaRegisterWidget-Constructors(), XmtRegisterPopupClass(), XmtRegister-PopupConstructor() — register names for widget types.

Synopsis

```
#include <Xmt/WidgetType.h>
void XmtRegisterWidgetClass(String name, WidgetClass wclass)

void XmtRegisterWidgetConstructor(String name,
                                  XmtWidgetConstructor constructor)

void XmtVaRegisterWidgetClasses(String name, WidgetClass wclass,
                                { String name,
                                  WidgetClass wclass, }
                                  NULL)

void XmtVaRegisterWidgetConstructors(String name,
                                     XmtWidgetConstructor constructor,
                                     { String name,
                                       XmtWidgetConstructor constructor, }
                                       NULL)

void XmtRegisterPopupClass(String name, WidgetClass wclass)

void XmtRegisterPopupConstructor(String name,
                                 XmtWidgetConstructor constructor)

typedef Widget (*XmtWidgetConstructor)(Widget parent, String name,
                                       ArgList args, Cardinal num_args);
```

Arguments

Inputs

name — The name under which the widget type should be registered. For XmtVaRegisterWidgetClasses() and XmtVaRegister- WidgetConstructors(), this argument must appear at least once, and may appear any additional number of times as part of a NULL-terminated variable-length argument list.

wclass — The widget class to be registered. For XmtVaRegister-WidgetClasses(), this argument must appear at least once, and may appear any additional number of times as part of a NULL-terminated variable-length argument list.

constructor — A Motif-style widget constructor function to be registered. For XmtVaRegisterWidgetConstructors(), this argument must appear at least once, and may appear any additional number of times as part of a NULL-terminated variable-length argument list.

Description

Before `XmtCreateChildren()` and related functions can automatically create widgets described in a resource file, there must be a mapping between the *names* of widget types and the widget types themselves. These functions define that mapping.

`XmtRegisterWidgetClass()` registers a single widget class *`wclass`* with the name *`name`*.

`XmtRegisterWidgetConstructor()` registers a single widget constructor function *`constructor`* with the name *`name`*.

`XmtVaRegisterWidgetClasses()` registers a variable-length list of widget classes.

`XmtVaRegisterWidgetConstructors()` registers a variable-length list of widget constructors.

`XmtRegisterPopupClass()` is like `XmtRegisterWidgetClass()`, but must be used for any widget classes that are subclasses of Shell.

`XmtRegisterPopupConstructor()` is like `XmtRegisterWidgetConstructor()` but must be used for any constructor function that creates a shell widget.

Usage

When prototyping an application, you may find it useful to call `XmtRegisterMotifWidgets()` and `XmtRegisterXmtWidgets()` to register all Xm and Xmt widgets. If you want to register a widget type that will be used with the Xmt automatic dialog management functions, you must use the more general `XmtRegisterWidgetTypes()`.

See Also

Chapter 11, *Automatic Widget Creation*
Chapter 29, *Custom Dialogs and Automatic Dialog Management*
`XmtCreateChildren()`, `XmtRegisterMotifWidgets()`,
`XmtRegisterWidgetTypes()`, `XmtRegisterXmtWidgets()`

Name

XmtRegisterWidgetTypes() — register names for widget types.

Synopsis

```
#include <Xmt/WidgetType.h>
void XmtRegisterWidgetTypes(XmtWidgetType *types,
                            Cardinal num_types)

typedef struct {
    String name;
    WidgetClass class;
    XmtWidgetConstructor constructor;
    XmtSetValueProc set_value_proc;
    XmtGetValueProc get_value_proc;
    int popup;
} XmtWidgetType;

typedef Widget (*XmtWidgetConstructor)(Widget parent,
                String name, ArgList args,
                Cardinal num_args);

typedef void (*XmtSetValueProc)(Widget w, XtPointer address,
                                XrmQuark type, Cardinal size);

typedef void (*XmtGetValueProc)(Widget w, XtPointer address,
                                XrmQuark type, Cardinal size);
```

Arguments

Inputs

types — An array of XmtWidgetType structures describing the widget types and the names to register them under.

num_types — The number of elements in the *types* array.

Description

XmtRegisterWidgetTypes() registers the widgets described in the *types* array. Each element of the array must have a name specified in the name field, and either a widget class pointer or a widget constructor procedure must be specified on the class or constructor fields. Any widget type registered in this way can be used in an xmtChildren or xmtType resource in a resource file, and may be automatically created with XmtCreate-Children() and related functions. Note that the *constructor* field is of type XmtWidgetConstructor. This is a standard Motif-style constructor function.

The last field of the XmtWidgetType structure, popup, should be set to True if the widget is a popup type that can be legally created as a child of a primitive, non-composite widget. If False, then the widget will never be created as a child of a primitive widget. If a widget class is specified, and popup is True, then the widget will be created with `XtCreatePopupShell()`, rather than `XtCreateWidget()`.

The remaining two fields of the `XmtWidgetType` structure, `set_value_proc`, and `get_value_proc`, are optional and are only necessary for widgets, such as the XmtChooser, the XmtInputField, and the XmScale, which maintain a state value and can be used to get input from the user in a dialog box. These fields are procedures that set a value on the widget and get a value from the widget. If you register a procedure with these fields set, you can then use that widget type with `XmtDialogSetDialogValues()`, `XmtDialogGetDialogValues()`, and other automatic dialog creation functions. (See Chapter 29, *Custom Dialogs and Automatic Dialog Management*, for more information.)

The arguments to both procedures are the same: the first is the widget on which the value is to be set, or from which the value is to retrieved. The second argument, ***address***, is the address of the value to be set or the address at which the value is to be stored. ***type*** is a quarkified version of the representation type of the value, and ***size*** is the length in bytes of the value. These ***type*** and ***size*** arguments allow some widgets to handle values of multiple types.

See Also

Chapter 11, *Automatic Widget Creation*
Chapter 29, *Custom Dialogs and Automatic Dialog Management*
`XmtCreateWidgetType()`, `XmtLookupWidgetType()`,
`XmtRegisterMotifWidgets()`, `XmtRegisterPopupClass()`,
`XmtRegisterPopupConstructor()`, `XmtRegisterWidgetClass()`,
`XmtRegisterWidgetConstructor()`, `XmtRegisterXmtWidgets()`,
`XmtVaRegisterWidgetClasses()`, `XmtVaRegisterWidgetConstructors()`

XmtReleasePixmap()

Name

XmtReleasePixmap() — release a pixmap or bitmap from the Xmt image cache.

Synopsis

```
#include <Xmt/Pixmap.h>
void XmtReleasePixmap(Widget widget, Pixmap pixmap)
```

Arguments

Inputs

widget The widget for which the pixmap was obtained.

pixmap The bitmap or pixmap to be released.

Description

XmtReleasePixmap() decrements the cache reference count for a cached pixmap returned by XmtGetPixmap(), XmtGetBitmap(), XmtLookupBitmap(), XmtLookupPixmap(), XmtLookupSimplePixmap(), XmtLookupWidgetPixmap(), or XmtLookupBitmask(). If the reference count reaches zero, it deallocates the pixmap, deallocates any colors allocated for the pixmap, and frees up memory associated with it in the cache.

See Also

Chapter 5, *Using Icons*
XmtGetBitmap(), XmtGetPixmap(),
XmtLookupBitmap(), XmtLookupBitmask(),
XmtLookupPixmap(), XmtLookupSimplePixmap(),
XmtLookupWidgetPixmap(), XmtRegisterImage(),
XmtRegisterXbmData(), XmtReleasePixmap()

XmtSetInitialFocus()

Name

`XmtSetInitialFocus()` — set the widget to receive the initial keyboard focus in a dialog.

Synopsis

```
#include <Xmt/Xmt.h>
void XmtSetInitialFocus(Widget dialog,
                        Widget initial)
```

Arguments

Inputs

dialog — An XmBulletinBoard widget or a subclass; generally the toplevel widget of a dialog box.

initial — The descendant of ***dialog*** that is to receive the keyboard focus when ***dialog*** first pops up or otherwise receives the focus.

Description

`XmtSetInitialFocus()` specifies that the widget ***initial*** should be given keyboard focus when ***dialog*** is next given the focus—generally this means when the dialog is first popped up. Dialog boxes that use the Xm-BulletinBoard widget or a subclass such as the XmForm or XmtLayout widgets will give the initial focus to the default button by default. This is not always desirable, as with the XmPromptDialog where initial focus should be set to the internal text widget.

In Motif 1.2, this function simply sets the **XmNinitialFocus** resource of *dialog*. That resource is new with 1.2, however, so in Motif 1.1, **XmtSetInitialFocus()** must arrange to assign the focus itself. This cannot be done until the dialog widget has received focus itself, and it cannot be done right after popping up the dialog because the window manager imposes an unpredictable delay between the time a window is mapped and the time it actually appears and receives focus. So in Motif 1.1, **XmtSetInitialFocus()** registers a focus callback which registers a timer procedure which sets the focus to the specified ***initial*** widget. **XmtSetInitialFocus()** exists as a utility routine precisely because this process is so complicated.

See Also

Chapter 8, *Utility Functions*

Name

XmtSetValue(), XmtSetTypedValue() — set a named widget resource to a named value.

Synopsis

```
#include <Xmt/SetValue.h>
void XmtSetValue(Widget w, String resource, String value)

void XmtSetTypedValue(Widget w, String resource, String type,
                      String value)
```

Arguments

Inputs

w	The widget that is to have its resource set.
resource	The name of the resource to set.
type	For XmtSetTypedValue() only, the representation type of the resource.
value	The value of the resource, as a string. These functions will automatically convert the string to its appropriate form.

Description

XmtSetValue() and XmtSetTypedValue() are procedures designed for use in resource files with the Xmt String-to-Callback converter. They allow you to set a named widget resource to a value specified as a string. XmtSetValue() takes a widget, the name of a resource, and the value of the resource, expressed as a string. It queries the widget to determine the type of the named resource, converts the specified string value to that type, and then calls XtSetValues() to set the resource on the widget.

XmtSetTypedValue() is a similar function, except that it takes a widget, resource name, resource type, and then the resource value expressed as a string. This version of the function is necessary for those resources, such as the XmNvalue resource of the XmText widget (in Motif 1.1), that are implemented within subparts of the widget, rather than as part of the main resource list for the widget. For these resources, the type must be specified explicitly because Xmt cannot determine the resource type by examining the widget's internal resource list. For XmtSetTypedValue(), the resource type is a *representation type* such as XtRString or XtRInt. The values of these symbolic constants are the strings "String" and "Int". There is no good way to know when you need to use XmtSetTypedValue() instead of XmtSetValue(). Widget documentation might tell you, or you might see a warning message when you call XmtSetValue().

See Also

Chapter 10, *Callbacks in Resource Files*

XmtSymbol{Add,Remove}Callback()

Name

`XmtSymbolAddCallback()`, `XmtSymbolRemoveCallback()` — add and remove a procedure to be called when a symbol's value changes.

Synopsis

```
#include <Xmt/Symbols.h>
void XmtSymbolAddCallback(XmtSymbol s,
                          XmtSymbolCallbackProc proc,
                          XtPointer client_data)

void XmtSymbolRemoveCallback(XmtSymbol s,
                             XmtSymbolCallbackProc proc,
                             XtPointer client_data)

typedef void (*XmtSymbolCallbackProc)(XmtSymbol s,
                                      XtPointer client_data,
                                      XtArgVal value);
```

Arguments

Inputs

s An XmtSymbol for which the callback is to be added or removed.

proc The procedure to be added or removed.

client_data An untyped data value registered (or removed) with *proc*, and which is passed as the second argument to *proc* when it is invoked.

value The untyped value of the symbol. This argument is not passed to `XmtSymbolAddCallback()` or `XmtSymbolRemoveCallback()`, but it is the third argument passed to the registered `XmtSymbolCallbackProc` *proc* when it is invoked.

Description

`XmtSymbolAddCallback()` registers the procedure *proc* to be invoked with the specified *client_data* whenever the value of symbol *s* changes.

`XmtSymbolRemoveCallback()` unregisters the *proc*/*client_data* pair for symbol *s*. This procedure will no longer be called with the specified *client_data* when the value of *s* is updated.

proc is an `XmtSymbolCallbackProc`. It will be invoked with three arguments. The first argument to a symbol callback is the `XmtSymbol` that has had its value changed. The second argument is whatever untyped *client_data* was registered with the callback procedure, and the third argument, *value*, is the new value of the symbol. This is either the value itself, or, if the value is too large to fit in an `XtArgVal` (or if it is of type `XmtRBuffer`), it is a pointer to the value.

See Also

Chapter 12, *Symbols*
`XmtLookupSymbol()`, `XmtSymbolGetValue()`,
`XmtSymbolSetValue()`, `XmtSymbolSetTypedValue()`,
`XmtVaRegisterSymbols()`

XmtSymbol{Get,Set}Value()

Name

XmtSymbolSetValue(), XmtSymbolGetValue() — set or query the value of a symbol.

Synopsis

```
#include <Xmt/Symbols.h>
void XmtSymbolSetValue(XmtSymbol s, XtArgVal value)

void XmtSymbolGetValue(XmtSymbol s, XtArgVal *valuep)
```

Arguments

Inputs

s The XmtSymbol that is to have its value queried or set.

value For XmtSymbolSetValue(), the new value for the symbol.

Outputs

valuep For XmtSymbolGetValue(), the address at which to store the value of the symbol.

Description

XmtSymbolSetValue() sets the value of symbol *s* to *value*. Recall that an XtArgVal is the type used by Xt for untyped values passed to XtSetArg(). As when you are setting resources, you should pass the value itself, if it will fit within an XtArgVal, and otherwise, you should pass the address of the value (you rarely have to do this, however, except when you are using a double value.) Also, notice that XmtRBuffer is a special case here—you always pass the address of the buffer, no matter its size.

XmtSymbolGetValue() stores the current value of the symbol *s* at the address specified by *value*. Note that *valuep* need not actually be the address of an XtArgVal variable, but must be large enough to store the value of the Symbol—you must know the type of the symbol in order to pass an appropriate *valuep*.

Note that the module that registers a symbol can obtain that symbol's value by reading it directly from the address registered with the symbol—there is no need to read it indirectly with XmtSymbolGetValue().

See Also

Chapter 12, *Symbols*
XmtLookupSymbol(), XmtSymbolAddCallback(),
XmtSymbolRemoveCallback(), XmtVaRegisterSymbols()

XmtVaRegisterSymbols()

Name

XmtVaRegisterSymbols(), XmtLookupSymbol() — register a name for application variables, and look up variables by name.

Synopsis

```
#include <Xmt/Symbols.h>
void XmtVaRegisterSymbols(String name, String type, int size,
                          XtPointer address,
                        { String name, String type, int size,
                          XtPointer address, }
                          NULL)

XmtSymbol XmtLookupSymbol(String name)
```

Arguments

Inputs

name The name of a symbol to be registered or looked up. For XmtVaRegisterSymbols() this argument may appear any number of times as part of a NULL-terminated variable-length argument list.

type The representation type of the variable to be registered. This argument may appear any number of times as part of a NULL-terminated variable-length argument list.

size The size, in bytes, of the variable to be registered. This argument may appear any number of times as part of a NULL-terminated variable-length argument list.

address The address of the variable to be registered. This argument may appear any number of times as part of a NULL-terminated variable-length argument list.

Returns

XmtLookupSymbol() returns the opaque XmtSymbol structure created when the named symbol was registered.

Description

XmtVaRegisterSymbols() lets you register symbolic names for application variables. It takes a NULL-terminated list of (*name*, *type*, *size*, *address*) quadruples. For each set of values, it registers *name* as the symbolic name for the variable at *address* with size *size* and representation type *type*.

Both of the String arguments, *name* and *type*, must be constant strings, or at least permanently allocated strings—the symbol registration function does not make copies of these strings, so they must not be in memory that will be freed, nor in memory on the stack. Similarly, of course, you will want the *address* argument to be the address of a static or global variable, or at least the address of memory that has been allocated and will never be freed.

`XmtLookupSymbol()` looks up an `XmtSymbol` structure for a named symbol. The `XmtSymbol` is an internal representation that is created when symbols are registered. It can be used with other symbol manipulation functions.

See Also

Chapter 12, *Symbols*
`XmtSymbolAddCallback()`, `XmtSymbolGetValue()`,
`XmtSymbolRemoveCallback()`, `XmtSymbolSetValue()`

XmtWaitUntilMapped()

Name

`XmtWaitUntilMapped()` — process events until a dialog becomes mapped.

Synopsis

```
#include <Xmt/Xmt.h>
void XmtWaitUntilMapped(Widget w)
```

Arguments

Inputs

w Any descendant of the dialog which is being mapped.

Description

`XmtWaitUntilMapped()` finds the immediate shell ancestor of *w*, and processes events in an internal event loop until that shell widget becomes visible on the screen, or until the shell's TopLevelShell parent becomes non-visible (because if the main window is iconified, the dialog will be iconified too, and will never become visible). It then processes all pending Expose events and returns.

Because window managers must decorate and manage dialog boxes, there is an unpredictable delay between the time that a dialog box is popped up (with `XtManageChild()` or `XtPopup()`) and the time that the dialog actually appears on the screen and has its first Expose event generated. `XmtWaitUntilMapped()` guarantees that the specified dialog box has appeared on the screen and has been drawn (i.e., has had its Expose events handled) before it returns.

This function is most useful when you plan to do some lengthy processing without servicing events, and want to display a "please wait" dialog to the user. If you do not call `XmtWaitUntilMapped()`, the dialog box will appear, but will appear blank (i.e., will not have its Expose events processed) until the lengthy processing is done. Note that the function `XmtDisplayWorkingDialog()` already calls `XmtWaitUntilMapped()`, so you should rarely need to call this function explicitly.

See Also

Chapter 31, *Busy States and Background Work*
XmtWorkingBox, `XmtDisplayWorkingDialog()`

XmtWorkingBox

Name

`XmtWorkingBox` — a widget for "please wait" dialogs.

Synopsis

Include File: `#include <Xmt/WorkingBox.h>`
Constructor: `XmtCreateWorkingBox()`
`XmtCreateWorkingDialog()`
Class Name: XmtWorkingBox
Class Pointer: `xmtWorkingBoxWidgetClass`
Class Hierarchy: Core → XmManager → XmBulletinBoard → XmtWorkingBox

Description

The XmtWorkingBox widget is a compound widget intended to be displayed when the application must perform a lengthy computation or other task which prevents normal processing of events. It provides feedback to the user that the application is busy and that she should not try to interact with it normally. The WorkingBox is designed to provide more sophisticated "working" dialogs than is possible with the Motif `XmCreateWorkingDialog()` function (which simply creates an XmMessageBox widget with an hourglass icon). The WorkingBox widget displays its own "please wait" icon, and a message, just like an XmMessageBox, but it also optionally displays a labeled XmScale widget that can be used to provide feedback on the progress of whatever task the application is performing, and optionally displays an XmPushButton widget that the user can use to abort the task.

Resources

XmtWorkingBox inherits the resources of the XmBulletinBoard class, and defines the following new resources:

Name	*Class*	*Type*	*Default*	*Access*
XmtNbuttonLabel	XmtCButtonLabel	XtRString	"Stop"	CSG
XmtNbuttonWidget	XtCReadOnly	XtRWidget	*N.A.*	G
XmtNicon	XmtCIcon	XtRPixmap	None	CSG
XmtNmessage	XmtCMessage	XtRString	NULL	CSG
XmtNscaleLabel	XmtCScaleLabel	XtRString	"% *Complete:*"	CSG
XmtNscaleMax	XmtCScaleMax	XtRInt	100	CSG
XmtNscaleMin	XmtCScaleMin	XtRInt	0	CSG
XmtNscaleValue	XmtCScaleValue	XtRInt	0	CSG
XmtNscaleWidget	XtCReadOnly	XtRWidget	*N.A.*	G
XmtNshowButton	XmtCShowButton	XtRBoolean	True	CSG
XmtNshowScale	XmtCShowScale	XtRBoolean	True	CSG

`XmtNbuttonLabel`
The label to appear in the XmPushButton widget child of the WorkingBox, if `XmtNshowButton` is `True`.

`XmtNbuttonWidget`
A read-only resource that may be queried to get a handle to the XmPushButton child of the WorkingBox. This widget is created (but left unmanaged) even if `XmtNshowButton` is `False`.

`XmtNicon`
The pixmap to display in the upper left of the widget. If `None` is specified, the WorkingBox will use its default icon—a clock face.

`XmtNmessage`
The message string to appear in the WorkingBox. Note that this resource is a String, not an XmString. It is converted internally to an XmString with the function `XmtCreateXmString()`, and so may include the newline character to begin a new line, and may include the `@f` escape sequence to change fonts. See `XmtCreateXmString()` for more information.

`XmtNscaleLabel`
The label to appear to the left of the XmScale child of the WorkingBox, if `XmtNshowScale` is `True`.

`XmtNscaleMax`
The maximum value to be displayed by the XmScale child of the WorkingBox.

`XmtNscaleMin`
The minimum value to be displayed by the XmScale child of the WorkingBox.

`XmtNscaleValue`
The value to be displayed by the XmScale child of the WorkingBox.

`XmtNscaleWidget`
A read-only resource that can be queried to get a handle to the XmScale child of the WorkingBox. The XmScale child is created (but left unmanaged) even if `XmtNshowScale` is `False`.

`XmtNshowButton`
Specifies whether the XmPushButton child should be visible in the dialog.

`XmtNshowScale`
Specifies whether the XmScale child should be visible in the dialog.

Callbacks

The WorkingBox widget defines no callback list resources.

Translations

The WorkingBox widget defines no new translations or actions.

See Also

Chapter 31, *Busy States and Background Work*
`XmtCreateWorkingBox()`, `XmtCreateWorkingDialog()`,
`XmtDisplayBusyCursor()`, `XmtDisplayDefaultCursor()`,
`XmtDisplayWorkingDialog()`, `XmtHideWorkingDialog()`,
`XmtWaitUntilMapped()`, `XmtWorkingBoxHandleEvents()`,
`XmtWorkingBoxSetScaleValue()`

XmtWorkingBox{HandleEvents,SetScaleValue}()

Name

`XmtWorkingBoxHandleEvents()`, `XmtWorkingBoxSetScaleValue()` — check the push button and update the slider value in an XmtWorkingBox widget.

Synopsis

```
#include <Xmt/WorkingBox.h>
Boolean XmtWorkingBoxHandleEvents(Widget w)

void XmtWorkingBoxSetScaleValue(Widget w, int value)
```

Arguments

Inputs

w	An XmtWorkingBox widget.
value	The value to be displayed by the XmtWorkingBox XmScale widget.

Returns

`XmtWorkingBoxHandleEvents()` returns `True` if the XmPushButton child of the XmtWorkingBox widget has been activated; `False` otherwise.

Description

`XmtWorkingBoxHandleEvents()` calls `XSync()` to flush the X output buffer and enqueue any events not yet delivered from the server. It then makes three passes through the Xlib event queue. On the first pass, it dispatches any events that occurred over the XmtWorkingBox widget or its XmScale and XmPushButton children. On the second pass, it handles any Expose events that occurred anywhere in the application by calling `XmUpdateDisplay()`, and on the third pass, it discards any KeyPress or mouse events that occurred outside of the dialog, thus disabling "type-ahead" and "click-ahead" buffering of events.

If the user has clicked on the XmPushButton child of the XmtWorkingBox, or has otherwise activated that button (by pressing Return, for example), then a flag will be set by a callback invoked during the first pass through the event queue, and `XmtWorkingBoxHandleEvents()` will return `True`. If the button has not been activated, then the function will return `False`.

`XmtWorkingBoxSetScaleValue()` sets the `XmNvalue` resource of the XmScale child of the XmtWorkingBox *w* to *value*. Calling this function is equivalent to, but more efficient than setting the `XmtNscaleValue` resource of the XmtWorkingBox widget. It is safe to call this function even when the `XmtNshowScale` resource of the XmtWorkingBox is `False`.

See Also

Chapter 31, *Busy States and Background Work*
XmtWorkingBox

Part Eight

Appendices

This part contains miscellaneous information that did not fit anywhere else.

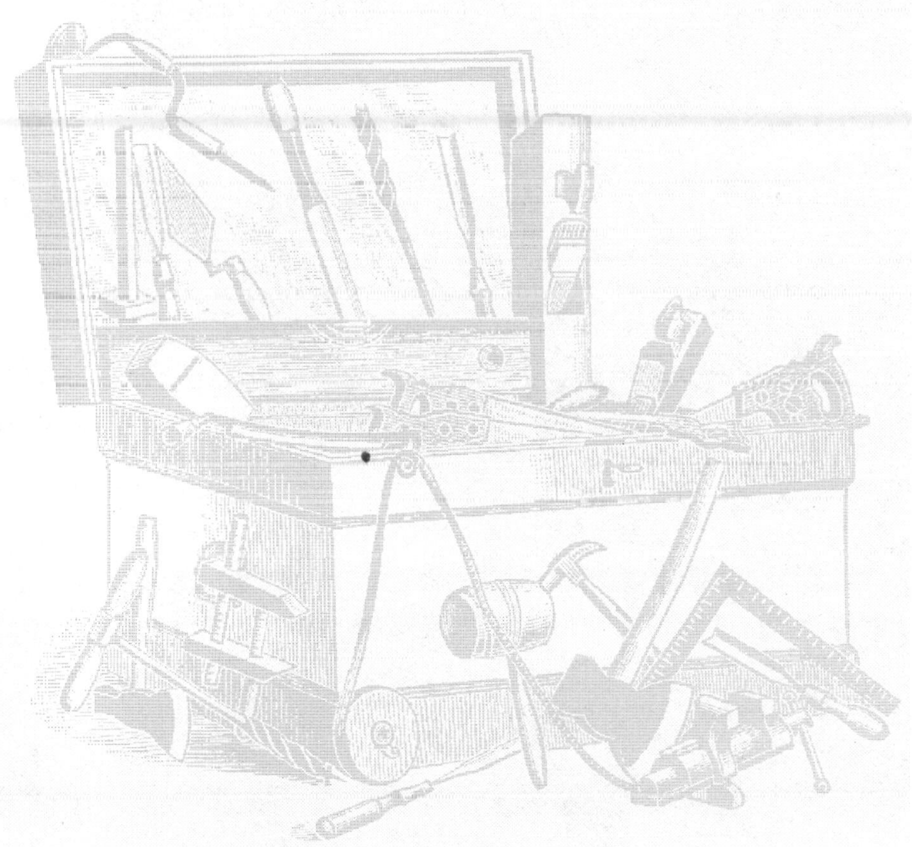

Installing Xmt

This appendix explains how you can get up-and-running with the Xmt library. It explains:

- How to get the Xmt distribution off of the CD-ROM that accompanies the book.
- How to obtain the Xmt distribution by anonymous FTP.
- How to unpack the Xmt distribution, and what files and directories you will find in it.
- How to compile the Xmt library for your platform.
- How to install the Xmt library.
- How to compile and link programs that use the Xmt library.

Be sure to read the *readme* file at the top level of the Xmt distribution. It may contain additional information or list changes that have been made since this book went to press.

A.1 Using the CD-ROM

The CD-ROM that accompanies this book is in the ISO-9660 standard format. This means that you can mount the CD as a read-only filesystem and copy files off of it using the normal *cp* command. On some systems, a CD-ROM is automatically mounted when you place it in the drive, and automatically unmounted when you eject it. If you have one of these systems, you're in luck. Otherwise, you may have to go to a bit more trouble.

If you've mounted CD-ROMs before and copied files off of them, then you probably already know what you are doing, and should just go ahead and mount the CD as usual. If not, the sidebar below should help.

Mounting a CD-ROM

Mounting a CD-ROM can be a tricky process, and on most systems it requires you to know the root password so that you can become the superuser. If you are not using a local CD-ROM drive on a personal workstation, you may need to ask your system administrator for help.

To mount a CD-ROM (or any filesystem), you use the *mount* command, which is generally in */etc* or */usr/etc*. The typical "mount-point" for a CD-ROM is */cdrom*, but you can use any directory you prefer. (But be careful not to mount the CD over an existing, active filesystem like */usr*—that would make everything under */usr* disappear!) Note that you'll need to mount the CD as a read-only filesystem. For many versions of UNIX, you do this with the `-r` option. You'll also have to tell *mount* what kind of filesystem you are mounting—in this case an ISO-9660 filesystem, sometimes also known as a "High Sierra" filesystem. The options for specifying filesystem type vary from system to system.

Table A-1 lists commands for mounting a CD-ROM on some common systems. If you have a different system, or if these commands don't work for you, then consult your system administrator or your system documentation.

Table A-1. Mounting a CD-ROM on Common Systems

Operating System	Mount Command
SunOS	`/etc/mount -r -t hsfs /dev/sr0 /cdrom`
AIX 3.2	`/etc/mount -r -v cdrfs /dev/cd0 /cdrom`
HP-UX	`/etc/mount -r -s cdfs /dev/dsk/c201d2s0 /cdrom`
Ultrix 4.x	`/etc/mount -t cdfs -o noversion /dev/rz3c /cdrom`
SCO UNIX	`/etc/mount -r -fHS,lower,intr,soft,novers \` `/dev/cd0 /cdrom`
IRIX 4.x	`/usr/etc/mount -o ro,notranslate -t iso9660 \` `/dev/scsi/sc0d5l0 /cdrom`
OSF/1 for Alpha AXP	`/etc/mount -t cdfs -o noversion /dev/rz3c /cdrom`

—djf
mount commands researched by Eric Pearce

Once you've mounted the CD-ROM, you can read files from it just as you would read them from any other directory. Assuming you have mounted the CD as */cdrom*, go ahead and look at what is on the CD:

```
ls /cdrom
```

You should see something like this:

```
readme          xmt200.tar
```

The first thing you should do is to read the *readme* file to see if there is any new information not covered in this appendix.

```
more /cdrom/readme
```

Next, you should copy the Xmt distribution to a working directory where you can unpack it and compile it:

```
mkdir /usr/local/source/Xmt-2.0.0
cp /cdrom/xmt200.tar /usr/local/source/Xmt-2.0.0
```

The sections below will describe how you can unpack and compile the Xmt distribution.

Lower-case or Upper-case?

The ISO-9660 filesystem standard is a lot more like MS-DOS or VMS filesystems than like a typical UNIX filesystem. Depending on your system and how you mount your CD-ROM, the files on the CD may appear with lowercase names or with uppercase names. On some systems, they might even appear with a semicolon and a version number attached. Thus, when you type **ls /cdrom**, you might see a listing like this:

```
README;1        XMT200.TAR;1
```

Whatever you see, just use the filenames as they appear in the listing. If there are semicolons in the filenames, you'll have to quote them, so your shell doesn't interpret them as the start of a new command. For example:

```
more '/cdrom/README;1'
```

Another non-UNIX feature of the ISO-9660 filesystem standard is that filenames are limited to eight characters plus a three-character extension. Since many of the filenames in the Xmt distribution are longer than this, Xmt is placed on the CD as a *tar* archive.

—djf

Getting the Latest Version of Xmt

The initial pressing of the *Motif Tools* CD-ROM contains Xmt version 2.0, patchlevel 0. As bugs are reported and fixed, and as features are added to the library, there will be patch releases and new versions of the library. Thus the version of Xmt that you find on the CD-ROM may not be the most up-to-date that is available.

Any new releases of Xmt will be made available for anonymous FTP on the network (and will be included on CD-ROM, of course, when the book and CD are reprinted). To get the most recent version of Xmt, follow the directions in the "Obtaining Xmt by FTP" section below, and look to see whether there are patches that you can apply to your version of Xmt or whether there is a complete release of Xmt with a version number higher than the one you have.

When a new version of Xmt is released, there will be announcements made on network newsgroups, such as *comp.windows.x.motif*.

—*djf*

A.2 Obtaining Xmt by FTP

If you don't have a CD-ROM drive, don't panic. You can also obtain the Xmt distribution by FTP, or even by email. You can get the Xmt distribution from the host *ftp.uu.net* in the directory */published/oreilly/power_tools/motif*.

Example A-1 shows a sample FTP session.

Example A-1. Sample FTP Session

```
% mkdir /usr/local/source/Xmt-2.0.0
% cd /usr/local/source/Xmt-2.0.0
% ftp ftp.uu.net
Connected to ftp.uu.net.
220 FTP server (Version 6.21 Tue Mar 10 22:09:55 EST 1992) ready.
Name (ftp.uu.net:david): anonymous
331 Guest login ok, send domain style email address as password.
Password: david@foobar.com (use your user name and host here)
230 Guest login ok, access restrictions apply.
ftp> cd /published/oreilly/power_tools/motif
250 CWD command successful.
ftp> binary (Very important! You must specify binary transfer for compressed files.)
200 Type set to I.
ftp> get xmt200.tar.Z
200 PORT command successful.
150 Opening BINARY mode data connection for xmt200.tar.Z.
226 Transfer complete.
ftp> quit
221 Goodbye.
%
```

You can also obtain the Xmt distribution from the O'Reilly & Associates FTP server as:

```
ftp.ora.com:/pub/power_tools/motif/xmt200.tar.Z
```

If you get the distribution through FTP, you'll obtain a compressed tar file. You can uncompress it with *uncompress*; we'll explain how to unpack the tar file below.

Getting Xmt Through Email

If your machine is not on the Internet, then you can't use FTP directly. As long as you can send and receive email, however, you can still obtain the Xmt distribution using the FTPMAIL service. This excerpt from O'Reilly & Associates' Unix Power Tools *explains how.*

FTPMAIL is a mail server available to anyone who can send and receive electronic mail to and from Internet sites. This includes most workstations that have an email connection to the outside world, and CompuServe users. You do not need to be directly on the Internet. Here's how to do it.

You send mail to *ftpmail@decwrl.dec.com*. In the message body, give the FTP commands you want to run. The server will run anonymous FTP for you and mail the files back to you. To get a complete help file, send a message with no subject and the single word "help" in the body. The following is a sample mail session that should get you the examples. This command sends you a listing of the files in the selected directory, and the requested examples file. The listing is useful in case there's a later version of the examples you're interested in.

```
% mail ftpmail@decwrl.dec.com
Subject:
reply janetv@foobar.com   (where you want files mailed)
connect ftp.uu.net
chdir /published/oreilly/power_tools/motif
dir
binary
uuencode  (or btoa if you have it)
get xmt200.tar.Z
quit
.              (The dot is a command to send the message, not part of it)
```

A signature at the end of the message is acceptable as long as it appears after "quit."

All retrieved files will be split into 60KB chunks and mailed to you. You then remove the mail headers, concatenate them into one file, and run *uudecode* or *atob* on it. Once you've decoded the file, follow the directions at the top of this section to extract the files from the archive.

—*Tim O'Reilly and Jerry Peek*
From Unix Power Tools

Remember that just because the Xmt source code is freely available on the network, this does not make it free software. Xmt is copyrighted, and you must have a license for it. The easiest way to get a single license is to buy this book, but there are other ways that you can get licenses or get additional licenses if you need them. Appendix B, *Legal Matters*, and Appendix C, *Purchasing Additional Xmt Licenses*, explain these isssues.

And finally, note that sometimes the easiest way to get the Xmt library is to ask a friend or a colleague to make a copy for you. The license allows anyone to make copies of the unmodified Xmt distribution, as long as they don't charge you any money for it.

A.3 Unpacking Xmt

First, you need a directory to unpack and compile Xmt in. Suppose you choose */usr/local/source/Xmt-2.0.0.* If you've obtained Xmt from the CD-ROM, then you should have a tar file in that directory. If you got Xmt through FTP, then you'll probably have a compressed tar file that you'll need to uncompress with *uncompress.* And if got Xmt by FTPMAIL, then you'll have a split, uuencoded, compressed tar file. You'll need to concatenate these split files with *cat*, decode the resulting file with *uudecode*, and then uncompress it with *uncompress.*

You should now have the file *xmt200.tar* in your directory:

```
% cd /usr/local/source/Xmt-2.0.0
% ls
xmt200.tar
```

You can extract the Xmt distribution from this tar archive with a command like the following:

```
% tar xvf xmt200.tar
```

Note that the Xmt distribution "untars" into the current working directory—i.e., it will not create a directory for itself. So be sure to create your own empty directory (such as */usr/local/source/Xmt-2.0.0*) to extract the distribution into.

Table A-2 lists the files and directories that you should see in the distribution.

Table A-2. The Contents of the Xmt Distribution

File or Directory	Contents
README	Important information you should read
Xmt/	A directory containing source code for the Xmt library
clients/	A directory of useful Xmt client applications
examples/	Some examples demonstrating important Xmt features
contrib/	Contributed code that works with the Xmt library

Table A-2. The Contents of the Xmt Distribution (continued)

File or Directory	Contents
man/cat3/	A directory containing ASCII formatted man pages for Xmt.
Imakefile	An *Imakefile* for building the Xmt library and clients
Xmt.tmpl	An Imake template for use with the *Imakefile*
BUGREPORT	A form for submitting bug reports
COPYRIGHT	Copyright information for Xmt
INSTALLATION	Instructions for compiling and installing Xmt
KNOWNBUGS	A list of known Xmt and Motif bugs that you might encounter
LICENSE	The terms and conditions for using Xmt
NO_WARRANTY	An explanation and disclaimer that Xmt has no warranty
SHAREWARE	How to obtain a license for Xmt, and why you should
VERSION	Specifies what version of Xmt you have

A.4 Compiling the Xmt Library

Xmt is distributed in source-code form only. Because it is a library rather than an application, the compiled form of the library will depend on your hardware and operating system, and also on the version of X, Xt, and Motif that you use.

The Xmt distribution comes with an *Imakefile* that you can use with *imake* to build Xmt. The first step in doing this Xmt is to read the file Xmt.tmpl, and set variables in it to customize it for your system. Table A-3 lists the variables that you might want or need to set. Note that some of these variables are C-preprocessor symbols used by *imake*, and others are variables used directly by *make*.

Table A-3. Configuration Variables in Xmt.tmpl

Variable	Purpose
DoNormalLib	Whether to build a normal, non-shared library. YES or NO.
DoSharedLib	Whether to build a shared library. YES or NO.
DoDebugLib	Whether to build a debugging (-g) library. YES or NO.
DoProfileLib	Whether to build a profiled library. YES or NO.
XMTLIBDIR	Where to install the Xmt library.
XMTINCDIR	Where to install the Xmt header files.
XMTXTLIB	Where your X libraries are installed.
XMTXTINC	Where your X header files are installed.
XMTXMLIB	Where your Motif library is installed.
XMTXMINC	Where your Motif header files are installed.
XMTEXTRALIBS	Any extra libraries needed by Motif on your system.

Table A-3. Configuration Variables in Xmt.tmpl (continued)

Variable	Purpose
OLDMOTIFDEFINES	Uncomment this line if you use Motif 1.1.0 or another old version of Motif 1.1
HPDEFINES	Uncomment this line if you use HP's version of Motif 1.1.
DECDEFINES	Uncomment this line, or portions of it, if you are using DECWindows or VMS.
IBMDEFINES	Uncomment this line to work around a bug in IBM's AIX 3.2 version of the X11R4 Xt library.
BSDEFINES	Uncomment this line to work around a backspace bug on some platforms.

Using xmkmf

Once you have edited *Xmt.tmpl* to work on your system, you can build the Xmt distribution with these commands:

```
xmkmf
make World >& makelog &
tail -f makelog
```

This will build the library in the Xmt directory, and the *mockup* client in the clients directory.

Using imake

If you do not have the xmkmf script, installed, you can do the build with these commands:

```
imake -DUseInstalled -I/usr/lib/X11/config
make World >& makelog &
tail -f makelog
```

If your *imake* configuration files are installed somewhere other than */usr/lib/X11/config*, you will have to change the `-I` option above as necessary.

Using Makefile.simple

If you do not have *imake* on your system at all, you'll have to build the distribution by hand. There are simple Makefiles provided to do this:

```
cd Xmt
make -f Makefile.simple
cd ../clients
make -f Makefile.simple
```

You may have to edit these Makefiles to modify the options passed to `cc`, `ar`, and `ranlib` to get it to work correctly on your system.

If even these simple makefiles do not work for you, you can build the distribution by hand. The Xmt library is a very straightforward one—just compile each of the source files, and then combine them into a library with *ar* or its equivalent.

A.5 Installing the Xmt Library and Header Files

Once you have compiled the Xmt library and its clients, you can install the library, the header files, the clients, and the Xmt.tmpl template file by typing:

```
make -k install
```

in the top level directory. If you only want to install the library and the headers, cd to the *Xmt/* directory, and type `make install` there.

The Xmt library and headers will be installed in the locations specified by the `XMTLIBDIR` and `XMTINCDIR` variables you set in the *Xmt.tmpl* file before building Xmt. You can check that these locations are correct by typing

```
make -n install
```

before you do the installation. If you will be installing files in system directories, then you may need to perform the installation as the superuser.

If you type `make -k install` in the toplevel directory, the Xmt clients will be installed wherever the standard X clients are installed on your system (*/usr/bin/X11*, for example). If you want them somewhere else, just put them there by hand. If you don't want them to be installed at all, cd to the *Xmt/* directory and do `make install` there.

Typing `make install` in the toplevel directory will also install the *Xmt.tmpl* template wherever *imake* files go on your system. If you are not running as root, this will probably fail for you. Therefore, you should use `make -k`; the `-k` flag causes *make* to continue even when errors occur.

If you do not have *imake* on your system, then you will have to install the library and headers by hand.

A.6 Compiling and Linking Programs with Xmt

Using the Xmt library is really no different than using any other library. To compile programs that use Xmt, the compiler must be able to find the Xmt header files. If you install them in */usr/include/Xmt*, then the compiler will find them automatically. Otherwise, you'll need to specify a `-I` option to the compiler. Your compilation command lines might look like this:

```
cc -c -I/usr/local/Xmt/include test.c
```

You may also have to specify `-I` options to point to your X and Motif header files as well, of course.

To link a program with the Xmt library, you need to include the `-lXmt` option on the command line, and the linker needs to be able to find the Xmt library. If you install the library in */usr/lib*, then the linker will find it automatically. Otherwise, you'll need to specify the `-L` option. Your linking lines might look like this:

```
cc -o test test.o -L/usr/local/Xmt/lib -lXmt -lXm -lXt -lX11 -lXext
```

Again, you might also have to specify `-L` options to point to your X and Motif libraries.

Note that `-lXext` is included in the above command line. This is the X extensions library, and is required by the Xmt functions `XmtCreatePixmapIcon()` and `XmtChangePixmapIcon()` which use the X SHAPE extension for non-rectangular windows.

B

Legal Matters

This appendix explains some important legal matters about the Xmt library:

- Xmt is copyrighted software. It is not free software, and it is not in the public domain.
- Xmt is provided "as is" with no warranty of any kind.
- The purchase of this book grants you one license to Xmt. This license allows you to use Xmt quite freely, but does not allow you to sell it or to distribute it, except in certain, specific ways.

The sections below explain each of these points in legal detail. Appendix C, *Purchasing Additional Xmt Licenses* explains how you can obtain more licenses for Xmt.

B.1 The Xmt Copyright

The Xmt library and all its supporting programs and documentation are:

Copyright © 1992, 1993, 1994 by Dovetail Systems. All Rights Reserved.

Xmt is not free software. You may use it only under the terms of the Xmt license, which is explained below. Purchase of this book licenses one programmer to use Xmt on one CPU. To license additional developers or additional CPUs, see Appendix C, *Purchasing Additional Xmt Licenses.*

Portions of the Xmt library are derived from other sources, and fall under additional copyrights and restrictions. Where code has been used or modified from other sources, it is noted in the source code at the top of the file, or immediately above the use of that code.

Some code in the Xmt library is derived from the X11R5 distribution, and is copyright MIT and DEC. Some code is derived from the XPM distribution from Groupe Bull. Some is derived from work originally done by the author at MIT Project Athena. The copyright notices on these pieces of the library are given below. Note, however, that the entire Xmt library, including these derivative parts, falls under the more restrictive Dovetail Systems the copyright above, and thus no part of Xmt is freely redistributable, except as provided by the terms of the Xmt license, described below.

This is the MIT and Digital copyright for X11R5 code:

Copyright 1987, 1988 by Digital Equipment Corporation, Maynard, Massachusetts and the Massachusetts Institute of Technology, Cambridge, Massachusetts.

All Rights Reserved

Permission to use, copy, modify, and distribute this software and its documentation for any purpose and without fee is hereby granted, provided that the above copyright notice appear in all copies and that both that copyright notice and this permission notice appear in supporting documentation, and that the names of Digital or MIT not be used in advertising or publicity pertaining to distribution of the software without specific, written prior permission.

DIGITAL DISCLAIMS ALL WARRANTIES WITH REGARD TO THIS SOFTWARE, INCLUDING ALL IMPLIED WARRANTIES OF MERCHANTABILITY AND FITNESS, IN NO EVENT SHALL DIGITAL BE LIABLE FOR ANY SPECIAL, INDIRECT OR CONSEQUENTIAL DAMAGES OR ANY DAMAGES WHATSOEVER RESULTING FROM LOSS OF USE, DATA OR PROFITS, WHETHER IN AN ACTION OF CONTRACT, NEGLIGENCE OR OTHER TORTIOUS ACTION, ARISING OUT OF OR IN CONNECTION WITH THE USE OR PERFORMANCE OF THIS SOFTWARE.

This is the Groupe Bull copyright for the XPM code.

Copyright 1990, 1991 GROUPE BULL

Permission to use, copy, modify, and distribute this software and its documentation for any purpose and without fee is hereby granted, provided that the above copyright notice appear in all copies and that both that copyright notice and this permission notice appear in supporting documentation, and that the name of GROUPE BULL not be used in advertising or publicity pertaining to distribution of the software without specific, written prior permission. GROUPE BULL makes no representations about the suitability of this software for any purpose. It is provided "as is" without express or implied warranty.

GROUPE BULL disclaims all warranties with regard to this software, including all implied warranties of merchantability and fitness, in no event shall GROUPE BULL be liable for any special, indirect or consequential damages or any damages whatsoever resulting from loss of use, data or profits, whether in an action of contract, negligence or other tortious action, arising out of or in connection with the use or performance of this software.

Arnaud LE HORS BULL Research FRANCE — Koala Project

This is the MIT copyright for Project Athena code. Note that none of the software in the Xmt library uses encryption, so the clause pertaining to encryption does not apply.

Copyright © 1990 by the Massachusetts Institute of Technology

Export of software employing encryption from the United States of America is assumed to require a specific license from the United States Government. It is the responsibility of any person or organization contemplating export to obtain such a license before exporting.

WITHIN THAT CONSTRAINT, permission to use, copy, modify, and distribute this software and its documentation for any purpose and without fee is hereby granted, provided that the above copyright notice appear in all copies and that both that copyright notice and this permission notice appear in supporting documentation, and that the name of M.I.T. not be used in advertising or publicity pertaining to distribution of the software without specific, written prior permission. M.I.T. makes no representations about the suitability of this software for any purpose. It is provided "as is" without express or implied warranty.

B.2 Xmt Has No Warranty

The Xmt library comes with no warranty of any kind. We have made our best efforts in preparing the library, this book describing the library, and the disk that accompanies the book. However:

> Dovetail Systems and its principals, the author and contributors to this book, and O'Reilly & Associates make no warranties of any kind, express or implied, with regard to the Xmt library, or any documentation, programs, techniques or data contained in this book or the accompanying disk, and specifically disclaim, without limitation, any implied warranties of merchantability and fitness for a particular purpose with respect to the Xmt library, or any documentation, programs, techniques or data contained in the book or the accompanying disk. In no event shall Dovetail Systems or its principals, or the author or contributors to this book, or O'Reilly & Associates be responsible or liable for any loss of profit or any other commercial damages, including, but not limited to special, incidental, consequential or any other damages in connection with or arising out of furnishing, performance, or use of the Xmt library or any documentation, programs, techniques or data contained in this book or the accompanying disk.

B.3 Single CPU License for the Xmt Library

B.3.1 Preamble

The Xmt library and all its supporting programs and documentation are

Copyright © 1992, 1993, 1994 by Dovetail Systems. All Rights Reserved.

The Xmt library is not free software, and may only be used by under the terms of this license. Purchase of this book gives you a license for one developer to use the Xmt library on one CPU. If Xmt is to be used by more than one developer or on more than one CPU, then you must purchase additional licenses, as described in Appendix C, *Purchasing Additional Xmt Licenses.*

You'll find that this license gives you a lot of flexibility in the ways you use Xmt. It does not allow you, however to sell Xmt or modified versions of Xmt, or to distribute Xmt as part of toolkits of your own.

This license below is a non-standard one, and is longer and more detailed than many. This is because we are trying to give the software developer as much freedom as possible to use Xmt, and at the same time protect some key commercial rights of our own. Paragraphs in **boldface** are the formal definitions, terms, and conditions of this license. Text in *italics* is less formal commentary on those definitions, terms, and conditions.

B.3.2 Definitions

A *licensed user* is anyone who has purchased a copy of the book *Motif Tools,* or who has otherwised purchased a license to the Xmt library.

A *library* means a collection of software functions and/or data prepared so as to be conveniently linked with application programs (which use some of those functions and data) to form executables.

Source code for a work means the preferred form of the work for making modifications to it.

Object code is a compiled, machine-readable form of a work, which has not been linked with libraries or other object code to form an executable.

Linking is the process of combining modules of object code and libraries into a form that can be executed by a computer.

An *executable* is software that has been linked.

Portions of the library mean a subset of the software functions that comprise the library which have been extracted from the library and are distributed directly as part of an application, and not as part of a library or as a library themselves.

B.3.3 Terms and Conditions

1) Permission is granted to copy and distribute unmodified versions of the Xmt library for any non-commercial purpose. This distribution must be under terms identical to those set forth here.

Paragraph 1 of the license covers only distribution of the unmodified library: anyone may give an unmodified copy of this library to anyone who wants it, and anyone may also make the unmodified library available for anonymous FTP, for example. You can't charge money to make copies for people, and you can't distribute modified versions of the library. "Unmodified" means that you have to include all files in the distribution, including those that contain this license. You don't have to be a licensed user to distribute unmodified copies, but note that you aren't allowed to actually use the library unless you are licensed.

2) Permission is granted to licensed users to use and modify the Xmt library, on a single CPU, for any purpose.

Paragraph 2 explains that licensed users can use and modify Xmt however they want. Note, though, that distribution of programs linked with Xmt or modified versions of Xmt is covered separately in the paragraphs below.

3) Permission is granted to licensed users to freely distribute executable programs that have been linked with the Xmt library or with modified versions of the library.

Paragraph 3 says that if licensed users link an application with this library, they can distribute the executable freely; there's no runtime royalty or any other charges.

4) Permission is granted to licensed users to distribute modified or unmodified portions of the Xmt library, in source code or object code form, as part of an application which is itself distributed in source or object code form, provided that the files LICENSE, COPYRIGHT, SHAREWARE, and NO_WARRANTY from the Xmt library are included with the application distribution, and provided that any code derived from Xmt is clearly labeled as such. Documentation for the Xmt library, or for any portion of it, may not be distributed under the terms of this section.

Much useful software is distributed in source-code form. Paragraph 4 allows you to distribute applications that use Xmt in source-code form without requiring all the users of the application to pay a license fee for Xmt: if you write an application that uses only some of the modules from this library, or uses modified modules from the library, and you are distributing the application in source code form, then you can include the source code modules from Xmt or derived from Xmt with the application. You must include the files that explain this license if you do so. Note that you can only distribute portions of the library in this way—not the whole library—and that those portions must be part of an application—they may not form a library themselves. You may not distribute documentation for the portions of the library you distribute under the terms of this section—since your users need only to compile and run your application, there is no need for the Xmt programmer documentation. Distribution of the documentation might encourage modification or reuse of the distributed portions of Xmt, which is forbidden in Paragraph 5.

5) Permission is granted to use, without fee, portions of the Xmt library distributed with an application within that application only.

Paragraph 4 allows application developers to distribute portions of the Xmt library with their applications. Paragraph 5 specifies the terms under which those portions may be used by those who receive the distribution: anyone who receives portions of the Xmt library as part of an application may compile and run that application without becoming a licensed user. But no one may modify those portions, or reuse them in another application, without becoming a licensed user.

6) Any permissions not explicitly granted above are reserved by Dovetail Systems.

Paragraph 6 says that the paragraphs above specify the only ways that you are allowed to use, modify, and distribute the Xmt library. In particular, note that you are not permitted to distribute modified versions of Xmt without the prior written permission of Dovetail Systems; this is to prevent a proliferation of versions and avoid confusion over which version is the "official" one. Also, while you are allowed to distribute portions of the library in or with your applications, you are not allowed to distribute portions of the library in your own libraries or toolkits, or in any way that would allow them to be reused, unless you obtain prior written permission to do so. For example, if you write an interface builder application, you may use the widgets from the Xmt library in your application's executable, but you may not include the source or object code for those widgets in any form that the users of your builder application can use in their applications. Instead, you must require your users to obtain a license for the Xmt library in order to use the Xmt widgets.

C

Purchasing Additional Xmt Licenses

The purchase of this book entitles you to use Xmt on a single CPU. For most readers, this license will be sufficient. But if you want to use Xmt on more than one computer, or if other programmers in your organization want to use Xmt, you'll have to obtain additional licenses. One way to do this is simply to purchase a sufficient number of copies of this book. In many cases, though, it is cheaper (and kills fewer trees!) to purchase additional licenses as described in this appendix.

C.1 How Many Licenses Do I Need?

To figure out how many licenses you'll need, count the number of CPUs that each developer will be working on. For example, if you want to use Xmt on a Sun workstation, a DEC workstation, and an HP workstation, and have bought one copy of the book, then you'll need to buy two more licenses.

Here's another, more complex example. Suppose your company has two programmers, Jill and Jack, and four computers, A, B, C, and D. Jill will be using Xmt on computers A, B, and C, and Jack will be using Xmt on computers C and D. This means that you will need five licenses in all. If Jill and Jack will be sharing a copy of the book (to save paper), then you'll need to purchase four additional licenses.

You can also purchase a site license or a corporate-wide license for Xmt. A site license entitles any number of developers to use Xmt on any number of computers at a single site. A "site" is a single office or working group within the same building. Most small companies constitute a single site. If you need more than twelve licenses, then buying a site license will be the most cost-effective option.

Larger companies or organizations (like universities) may need to purchase multiple site licenses if they have developers located in more than one building, or when they have largely separate groups working independently within the same building. If an organization has more than five sites that will be using Xmt, then it will be cheapest to buy a corporate-wide license. A corporate-wide license entitles anyone affiliated with a company or organization to use Xmt on any number of computers anywhere within the company or organization.

The next section lists the prices for these different kinds of licenses.

C.2 How Much Do Licenses Cost?

Table C-1 lists the prices for single-user/single-CPU licenses, for site licenses, and for corporate-wide licenses for Xmt. All prices are in U.S. dollars. (These prices are current at the time of publication, but are subject to change without notice.) Note that there are discounted prices for universities or other educational institutions, or for anyone affiliated with an educational institution.

Table C-1. Prices for Xmt Licenses

License	Price	Educational Price
Single-user/Single-CPU	\$40	\$25
Site	\$500	\$250
Corporate-wide	\$2500	\$1000

Why Shareware?

You'll notice that there are no license keys required for you to use the Xmt library. It is distributed as unprotected source code, and there is nothing to prevent you from compiling and using it on as many platforms as you like. The Xmt library is shareware—the only thing that will make you pay for it is your own conscience. This is not to say that paying is optional—using Xmt without purchasing the proper licenses is software piracy and is illegal—just that we can't very effectively enforce that you pay.

"Shareware" is a software licensing concept common for PC software, but quite rare in the UNIX world. Much of the best software for UNIX is available off the network free of charge, and this is a large part of what has made UNIX so successful. Philosophically, I'd like to be able to release this library as free software, but pragmatically I have to settle for second best and release it as inexpensive software. Much of the free UNIX software that is available was written by programmers who work for large companies, and who have a regular salary.

Why Shareware? (continued)

I've been working on Xmt for well over two years, and have not been drawing a salary during that time. By purchasing an appropriate number of licenses, you are supporting the work I have done on Xmt, and the work I'll be doing in the future. Thank you.

—djf

C.3 How Do I Pay for Licenses?

You can purchase additional Xmt licenses the same way that you'd order books from O'Reilly & Associates. In the U.S. or Canada, call 1-800-998-9938 between 7am and 5pm PST. Outside of the U.S., call +1-707-829-0515.

D

Reporting Bugs in Xmt

The Xmt library has been in public use since early 1993, and many bugs have been reported and fixed since then. The distribution that accompanies this book is thus fairly stable and robust. Inevitably, as Xmt is used in new and varied ways, new bugs will be uncovered.

If you think that you have found a bug in Xmt, please do the following:

1. Check the *KNOWNBUGS* file to see if this is a bug that has already been reported.
2. Check carefully that it is a bug in Xmt, not in your program, or in your Xt or Motif library.
3. Write a small test program that reproduces the bug. Bugs that are not easily reproducible are very difficult to fix.
4. See if you can find a fix, or at least a workaround for the bug. The beauty of a source-code product like the Xmt library is that you can modify it and debug it yourself! Just as we encourage programmers to customize Xmt for their own purposes, we encourage you attempt to locate any bugs that you find.
5. Fill out a copy of the bug report template in the *BUGREPORT* file, and mail it to *xmt-bugs@ora.com*. Be sure to include the version numbers for your Xt and Motif libraries, and also for your operating system. Also, attach your test program to the bug report, and any workaround or fix you have found.

Bugs sent to *xmt-bugs@ora.com* will be forwared to the author at Dovetail Systems. Please do not call O'Reilly & Associates with Xmt bug reports. They are in the business of writing and selling books and other information technologies, not of supporting software.

We'll try to fix all bugs that are reported. Bear in mind though, that Dovetail Systems is a very small company, and that we are giving away tens of thousands of licenses to our software. There is simply no way that we can afford to give prompt attention to every bug report. If you need rapid service, your best bet will be to do your own debugging. You might also want to look for help and advice on the network, in Usenet newsgroups like *comp.windows.x.motif.*

E

A Sample Xmt Software Project

The best way to learn the techniques and tools described in this book is to use them in one or two medium-sized projects, developed incrementally, and performed either individually or in groups of two or three. A drawing editor is a commonly used, but excellent project:*

You might start with a discussion of Xlib drawing techniques and assign Chapter 24, *The Work Area*, as reading. The project would begin as a simple line-drawing program done with an XmDrawingArea widget.

Study of Chapter 27, *Presenting Choices*, and Chapter 20, *Easy Menu Creation*, will enable students to add a palette of drawing tools and a menubar of commands to the work area. The techniques in Chapter 10, *Callbacks in Resource Files*, and Chapter 11, *Automatic Widget Creation*, will help students to define and implement a clean, modular separation between the "back end" functions that do the drawing, and the "front end" of the application that invokes those back end procedures.

An important reason for choosing a project like a drawing editor is that it is a common application that is well understood, and for which there are a number of models. Once students have a skeletal application up-and-running (which is important to keep their interest), you might assign Chapter 2, *High-Level Application Design*, and put the project in its human context by enouraging a discussion of the application's users and their goals. At this point, different teams might choose to aim their applications at different user communities or tasks—one group might choose to design a drawing editor for children, for example, and other groups might design applications intended for drawing slides and presentation graphics, or for drawing circuits and other highly schematic diagrams. Other groups might even switch from an object-oriented drawing program to a pixel-oriented paint program, and might choose to aim their

*The following project scenario is aimed at course instructors, but it can also serve as a guide for useful self-study.

application at graphic designers or at scientists doing visualization and image processing. It is worth requiring an informal written design document at this stage.

The next step might be to focus on providing user feedback, with some of the techniques described in Chapter 22, *The Message Line*, Chapter 23, *The Modeline*, and Chapter 31, *Busy States and Background Work*.

With the main window of the drawing editor fleshed out at this point, the next step in the development of this application could be the addition of dialog boxes, both the simple ones described in Chapter 25, *Message Dialogs*, and Chapter 26, *Simple Input Dialogs*, and the complex, custom dialogs described in Chapter 29, *Custom Dialogs and Automatic Dialog Management*. Before integrating custom dialogs with the application itself, you might assign Chapter 18, *The Layout Widget: A Tutorial*, and Chapter 13, *Resource File Utilities: mockup, checkres, and ad2c*, and have students spend some time designing, prototyping, and polishing their dialog layouts.

With all the major interface components in place, it is a good time to make another thorough pass over the application, working on "productizing" it. Chapter 3, *Displaying Text*, Chapter 4, *Using Color*, and Chapter 5, *Using Icons*, explain how to make good advantage of fonts, colors, and icons in an application, and Chapter 6, *Managing Auxiliary Files*, Chapter 7, *Application Resources and Command-Line Arguments*, and Chapter 15, *Working with the Window Manager*, describe other important "finishing touches" that are important in a product-quality application.

At the end of the term, if time permits, you might allow students to branch out on their own with this project. Areas for exploration could include PostScript output, the use of the PEX, XIE, or DPS extensions to X, and the use of advanced graphics techniques such as texture and shading models and antialiasing.

Index

C

D

E

F

G

H

I

J

K

L

M

N

O

P

Q

R

S

X

Z

About the Author

David Flanagan is a principal of Dovetail Systems, a company that specializes in custom widget development. He has been programming with X and Xt since their early days at MIT and is an expert on the Motif widgets. David is also the author of *Programmer's Supplement for R5 of the X Window System* and editor of *X Toolkit Intrinsics Reference Manual*, both from O'Reilly & Associates. He holds an S.B. degree in computer science and engineering from the Massachusetts Institute of Technology.

Colophon

Our look is the result of reader comments, our own experimentation, and feedback from distribution channels.

Distinctive covers complement our distinctive approach to technical topics, breathing personality and life into potentially dry subjects.

Shown on the cover of *Motif Tools* is a toolbox stocked with an array of carpentry tools, both basic and more specialized. These tools would enable the skilled carpenter to build almost any piece of furniture. Similarly, the tools in this book will enable the user to build almost any Motif application.

Edie Freedman designed this cover. The cover image is a nineteenth century engraving from *Scan This Book*, a book of copyright-free engravings compiled by John Mendenhall. The cover layout was produced with Quark XPress 3.1 using the ITC Garamond font.

Edie Freedman and Jennifer Niederst designed the page layouts. Text was prepared using the SoftQuad sqtroff text formatter. Lenny Muellner modified and developed the troff macros necessary to implement the book design.

The body text of the book is set in the ITC Garamond typeface; the examples are set in Courier. Headings and captions are set in the Helvetica Condensed Bold Oblique typeface.

The figures were created in Aldus Freehand 4.0 by Chris Reilley and Karla Tolbert.

"For programmers and people who like to understand the full gory detail of how things work, I must recommend the O'Reilly series of X books."

—Peter Collinson, *SunExpert* magazine

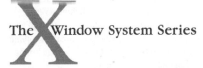

The X Window System Series

When it comes to X, think of these books as the ultimate owner's manuals. Because of its power and flexibility, X is also extremely complex. We help you sort through that complexity with books that show you, step-by-step, how to use, program, and administer the X Window System.

X Protocol Reference Manual

VOLUME 0

Edited by Adrian Nye
3rd Edition February 1992
516 pages, ISBN 1-56592-008-2

Describes the X Network Protocol which underlies all software for Version 11 of the X Window System. Includes protocol clarifications of X11 Release 5, as well as the most recent version of the ICCCM and the Logical Font Conventions Manual. For use with any release of X.

Xlib Programming Manual

VOLUME 1

By Adrian Nye
3rd Edition July 1992
824 pages, ISBN 1-56592-002-3

A complete programming guide to the X library (Xlib), the lowest level of programming interface to X. Updated to cover X11 Release 5. Includes introductions to internationalization, device-independent color, font service, and scalable fonts.

FOR INFORMATION: **800-998-9938**, *707-829-0515;* **NUTS@ORA.COM**

Xlib Reference Manual

By Adrian Nye
3rd Edition June 1992
1138 pages, ISBN 1-56592-006-6

Complete reference guide to the X library (Xlib), the lowest level of programming interface to X. Updated to cover X11 Release 4 and Release 5.

X Window System User's Guide

Standard Edition
By Valerie Quercia & Tim O'Reilly
4th Edition May 1993
836 pages, ISBN 1-56592-014-7

Orients the new user to window system concepts and provides detailed tutorials for many client programs, including the *xterm* terminal emulator and window managers. Uses the *twm* manager in most examples and illustrations. Revised for X11 Release 5.

X Window System User's Guide

Motif Edition
By Valerie Quercia & Tim O'Reilly
2nd Edition January 1993
956 pages, ISBN 1-56592-015-5

Highlights the Motif window manager and graphical interface, including new features such as tear-off menus and drag-and-drop. Revised for Motif 1.2 and X11 Release 5.

X Toolkit Intrinsics Programming Manual

Standard Edition
By Adrian Nye & Tim O'Reilly
3rd Edition April 1993, 567 pages, ISBN 1-56592-003-1

A complete guide to programming with Xt Intrinsics, the library of C language routines that facilitates the design of user interfaces with reusable components called widgets. Available in two editions. The *Standard Edition* uses Athena widgets in examples; the *Motif Edition* uses Motif widgets.

X Toolkit Intrinsics Programming Manual

Motif Edition
By Adrian Nye & Tim O'Reilly
2nd Edition August 1992
674 pages, ISBN 1-56592-013-9

The *Motif Edition* of Volume 4 uses the Motif 1.2 widgets set in examples, and has been updated for X11 Release 5.

X Toolkit Intrinsics Reference Manual

Edited by David Flanagan
3rd Edition April 1992
916 pages, ISBN 1-56592-007-4

Complete programmer's reference for the X Toolkit, providing pages for each of the Xt functions, as well as the widget classes defined by Xt and the Athena widgets. This third edition has been re-edited, reorganized, and expanded for X11 Release 5.

Motif Programming Manual

By Dan Heller, Paula Ferguson & David Brennan
2nd Edition February 1994
1016 pages, ISBN 1-56592-016-3

A source for complete, accurate, and insightful guidance on Motif application programming. In addition to information on Motif, the book is full of tips about programming in general and about user-interface design. It includes material on using UIL, drag-and-drop, tear-off menus, and covers Motif Release 1.2 (while remaining usable with Motif 1.1). Complements Volume 6B, *Motif Reference Manual*.

Motif Reference Manual

By Paula Ferguson & David Brennan
1st Edition June 1993
920 pages, ISBN 1-56592-038-4

A complete programmer's reference for the Motif toolkit. This book provides reference pages for the Motif functions and macros, the Motif and Xt widget classes, the Mrm functions, the Motif clients, and the UIL file format, data types, and functions. The reference material has been expanded from the appendices of the first edition of Volume 6 and covers Motif 1.2. This manual is a companion to Volume 6A, *Motif Programming Manual*.

XView Programming Manual

By Dan Heller, Updated by Thomas Van Raalte
3rd Edition September 1991
(latest update August 1993)
770 pages, ISBN 0-937175-87-0

The *XView Programming Manual* describes both the concepts and the technical approaches behind XView, the poor-man's object-oriented toolkit for building OPEN LOOK applications for X. Along with its companion volume, the *XView Reference Manual*, this book is perfect for the beginner breaking into X programming.

XView Reference Manual

Edited by Thomas Van Raalte
1st Edition September 1991
(latest update August 1993)
311 pages, ISBN 0-937175-88-9

The XView toolkit provides extensive attribute-value pair combinations, convenience routines and object class hierarchies that are too voluminous to memorize without the aid of this comprehensive reference guide. A must-have companion for the *XView Programming Manual*.

X Window System Administrator's Guide

By Linda Mui & Eric Pearce
1st Edition October 1992, CD-ROM Released May 1993
Without CD-ROM: 372 pages, ISBN 0-937175-83-8
With CD-ROM: 388 pages, ISBN 1-56592-052-X

The first and only book devoted to the issues of system administration for X and X-based networks, written not just for UNIX system administrators, but for anyone faced with the job of administering X (including those running X on stand-alone workstations). The *X Window System Administrator's Guide* is available either alone or packaged with the XCD. The CD provides X source code and binaries to complement the book's instructions for installing the software. It contains over 600 megabytes of X11 source code and binaries stored in ISO9660 and RockRidge formats. This will allow several types of UNIX workstations to mount the CD-ROM as a filesystem, browse through the source code, and install pre-built software.

"For those system administrators wanting to set up X11 for the first time, this is the book for you. As an easy-to-use guide covering X administration, it doesn't get bogged down in too much detail.... This is not a book for bedtime reading or to generate an all consuming interest in X windows, but a thoroughly good text to help you over the first hurdle or two."
—*Sun UK User*, August 1993

The X Window System in a Nutshell

Edited by Ellie Cutler, Daniel Gilly & Tim O'Reilly
2nd Edition April 1992
424 pages, ISBN 1-56592-017-1

Indispensable companion to the X Window System Series. Experienced X programmers can use this single-volume desktop companion for most common questions, keeping the full series of manuals for detailed reference. This book has been updated to cover R5 but is still useful for R4.

"If you have a notebook computer and write X code while back-packing the Pennine Way or flying the Atlantic, this is the one for you!"
—*Sun UK User*, Summer 1992

PEXlib Programming Manual

By Tom Gaskins
1st Edition December 1992
1154 pages, ISBN 1-56592-028-7

The *PEXlib Programming Manual* is the definitive programmer's guide to PEXlib, covering both PEX versions 5.0 and 5.1. Containing over 200 illustrations and 19 color plates, it combines a thorough and gentle tutorial approach with valuable reference features. Includes numerous programming examples, as well as a library of helpful utility routines—all of which are available online. You do not need any prior graphics programming experience to use this manual.

PEXlib Reference Manual

Edited by Steve Talbott
1st Edition December 1992
577 pages, ISBN 1-56592-029-5

The *PEXlib Reference Manual* is the definitive programmer's reference resource for PEXlib, containing complete and succinct reference pages for all the callable routines in PEXlib version 5.1. The content of the *PEXlib Reference Manual* stands, with relatively few changes, as it was created by the X Consortium.

PHIGS Programming Manual

By Tom Gaskins
1st Edition February 1992
Softcover: 968 pages, ISBN 0-937175-85-4
Hardcover: 968 pages, ISBN 0-937175-92-7

A complete and authoritative guide to PHIGS and PHIGS PLUS programming. Whether you are starting out in 3D graphics programming or are a seasoned veteran looking for an authoritative work on a fast-rising 3D graphics standard, this book will serve your purposes well.

PHIGS Reference Manual

Edited by Linda Kosko
1st Edition October 1992
1116 pages, ISBN 0-937175-91-9

The definitive and exhaustive reference documentation for the PHIGS and PHIGS PLUS graphical programming language. Contains reference pages for all language functions. Together with the *PHIGS Programming Manual*, this book is the most complete and accessible documentation currently available for the PHIGS and PHIGS PLUS standards.

BOOK INFORMATION AT YOUR FINGERTIPS

*O'Reilly & Associates offers extensive online information through a Gopher server (**gopher.ora.com**). Here you can find detailed information on our entire catalog of books, tapes, and much more.*

The O'Reilly Online Catalog

Gopher is basically a hierarchy of menus and files that can easily lead you to a wealth of information. Gopher is also easy to navigate; helpful instructions appear at the bottom of each screen (notice the three prompts in the sample screen below). Another nice feature is that Gopher files can be downloaded, saved, or printed out for future reference. You can also search Gopher files and even email them.

To give you an idea of our Gopher, here's a look at the top, or root, menu:

```
O'Reilly & Associates (The public Gopher server)

      1.  News Flash! -- New Products and Projects/
      2.  Feature Articles/
      3.  Product Descriptions/
      4.  Ordering Information/
      5.  Complete Listing of Titles
      6.  Errata for "Learning Perl"
      7.  FTP Archive and Email Information/
      8.  Bibliographies/

Press ? for Help, q to Quit, u to go up a menu
```

The heart of the O'Reilly Gopher service is the extensive information provided on all ORA products in menu item three, "Product Descriptions." For most books this usually includes title information, a long description, a short author bio, the table of contents, quotes and reviews, a gif image of the book's cover, and even some interesting information about the animal featured on the cover. (One of the benefits of a Gopher database is the ability to pack a lot of information in an organized, easy-to-find place.)

How to Order

Another important listing is "Ordering Information," where we supply information to those interested in buying our books. Here, you'll find instructions and an application for ordering O'Reilly products online, a listing of distributors (local and international), a listing of bookstores that carry our titles, and much more.

The item that follows, "Complete Listing of Titles," is helpful when it's time to order. This single file, with short one-line listings of all ORA products, quickly provides the essentials for easy ordering: title, ISBN, and price.

And More

One of the most widely read areas of the O'Reilly Gopher is "News Flash!," which focuses on important new products and projects of ORA. Here, you'll find entries on newly published books and audiotapes; announcements of exciting new projects and product lines from ORA; upcoming tradeshows, conferences, and exhibitions of interest; author appearances; contest winners; job openings; and anything else that's timely and topical.

"Feature Articles" contains just that—many of the articles and interviews found here are excerpted from the O'Reilly magazine/catalog *ora.com*.

The "Bibliographies" entries are also very popular with readers, providing critical, objective reviews on the important literature in the field.

"FTP Archive and Email Information" contains helpful ORA email addresses, information about our "ora-news" listproc server, and detailed instructions on how to download ORA book examples via FTP.

Other menu listings are often available. "Errata for 'Learning Perl,'" for example, apprised readers of errata found in the first edition of our book, and responses to this file greatly aided our campaign to ferret out errors and typos for the upcoming corrected edition (a nice example of the mutual benefits of online interactivity).

Come and Explore

Our Gopher is vibrant and constantly in flux. By the time you actually log onto this Gopher, the root menu may well have changed. The goal is to always improve, and to that end we welcome your input (email: **gopher@ora.com**). We invite you to come and explore.

Here are four basic ways to call up our Gopher online.

1) If you have a local Gopher client, type:
   `gopher gopher.ora.com`
2) For Xgopher:
   `xgopher -xrm "xgopher.root\`
   `Server: gopher.ora.com"`
3) To use telnet (for those without a Gopher client):
   `telnet gopher.ora.com`
   login: **gopher** (no password)
4) For a World Wide Web browser, use this URL:
   `http://gopher.ora.com:70/`

COMPLETE LISTING OF TITLES

from O'Reilly & Associates, Inc.

Internet

The Whole Internet User's Guide & Catalog
Connecting to the Internet: An O'Reilly Buyer's Guide
!%@:: A Directory of Electronic Mail Addressing & Networks
Smileys

Using UNIX and X

UNIX Power Tools (with CD-ROM)
UNIX in a Nutshell: System V Edition
UNIX in a Nutshell: Berkeley Edition
SCO UNIX in a Nutshell
Learning the UNIX Operating System
Learning the vi Editor
Learning GNU Emacs
Learning the Korn Shell
Making TeX Work
sed & awk
MH & xmh: E-mail for Users & Programmers
Using UUCP and Usenet
X Window System User's Guide: Volume 3
X Window System User's Guide, Motif Edition: Volume 3M

System Administration

Essential System Administration
sendmail
Computer Security Basics
Practical UNIX Security
System Performance Tuning
TCP/IP Network Administration
Learning Perl
Programming perl
Managing NFS and NIS
Managing UUCP and Usenet
DNS and BIND
termcap & terminfo
X Window System Administrator's Guide: Volume 8
(available with or without CD-ROM)

UNIX and C Programming

ORACLE Performance Tuning
High Performance Computing
lex & yacc
POSIX Programmer's Guide
Power Programming with RPC
Programming with curses
Managing Projects with make
Software Portability with imake
Understanding and Using COFF
Migrating to Fortran 90
UNIX for FORTRAN Programmers
Using C on the UNIX System
Checking C Programs with lint
Practical C Programming
Understanding Japanese Information Processing

DCE (Distributed Computing Environment)

Distributing Applications Across DCE and Windows NT
Guide to Writing DCE Applications
Understanding DCE

Berkeley 4.4 Software Distribution

4.4BSD System Manager's Manual
4.4BSD User's Reference Manual
4.4BSD User's Supplementary Documents
4.4BSD Programmer's Reference Manual
4.4BSD Programmer's Supplementary Documents
4.4BSD-Lite CD Companion

X Programming

The X Window System in a Nutshell
X Protocol Reference Manual: Volume 0
Xlib Programming Manual: Volume 1
Xlib Reference Manual: Volume 2
X Toolkit Intrinsics Programming Manual: Volume 4
X Toolkit Intrinsics Programming Manual, Motif Edition: Volume 4M
X Toolkit Intrinsics Reference Manual: Volume 5
Motif Programming Manual: Volume 6A
Motif Reference Manual: Volume 6B
XView Programming Manual: Volume 7A
XView Reference Manual: Volume 7B
PEXlib Programming Manual
PEXlib Reference Manual
PHIGS Programming Manual (softcover or hardcover)
PHIGS Reference Manual
Programmer's Supplement for R5 of the X Window System

The X Resource

A quarterly working journal for X programmers
The X Resource: Issues 0 through 10

Other

Building a Successful Software Business
Love Your Job!

Travel

Travelers' Tales Thailand

Audiotapes

Internet Talk Radio's "Geek of the Week" Interviews

The Future of the Internet Protocol, 4 hours
Global Network Operations, 2 hours
Mobile IP Networking, 1 hour
Networked Information and Online Libraries, 1 hour
Security and Networks, 1 hour
European Networking, 1 hour

Notable Speeches of the Information Age

John Perry Barlow, 1.5 hours

GREAT GRAPHS!

From the author of Xmt

If you were impressed by the ease-of-use and thoughtful design of the Motif Tools library, then you'll love the Dovetail Plotter Widget library. Designed and developed by the same author, these widgets allow you to easily add technical and business graphs to all your applications.

Flexible and Easy to Use

The Dovetail widgets are elegantly designed and are easier to use than any other plotting widgets on the market. Our Constraint Widget Architecture makes it easy

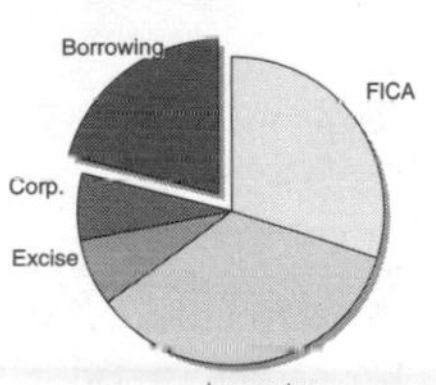

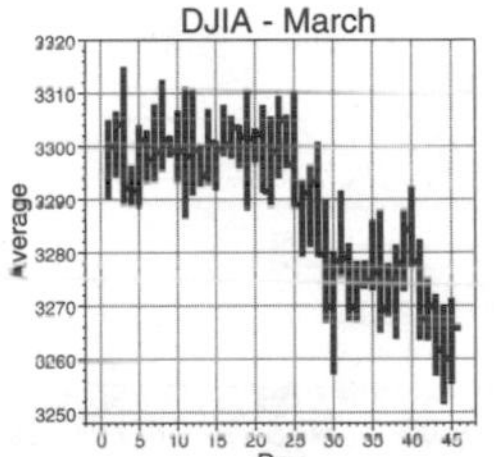

to graph multiple data sets in one window or even to mix different types of graphs in the same window. Our Flexible Data Representation allows the widgets to read your data structures directly—no need to copy your data into some awkward, pre-defined format. The widgets feature over 325 intuitively named resources with sensible default values, so you can control every aspect of a graph's look-and-feel. And not only are the widgets easy to use, the documentation is easy to read! Our 270-page manual was also written by the author of *Motif Tools*.

Clean, Professional Graphics

Our graphic design is second only to our ease-of-use. Our widgets look good, so your applications and data look good—on the screen and as high-resolution WYSIWYG PostScript hardcopy.

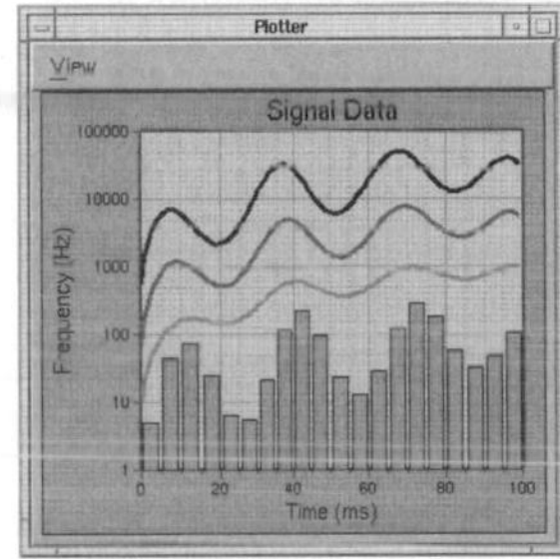

Free Demo Available on CD!

The Dovetail Plotter Widget library is available on the ICS Databook CD-ROM. Try out the demo to see the widgets in action.

Call ICS at 1-800-800-4271

for more information on the Dovetail widgets, or to receive your FREE ICS Widget Databook and CD!

Integrated Computer Solutions Incorporated

201 Broadway, Cambridge, MA 02139 • Phone: 617-621-0060 • Fax: 617-621-9555 • E-mail: info@ics.com

International Distributors

Customers outside North America can now order O'Reilly & Associates' books through the following distributors. They offer our international customers faster order processing, more bookstores, increased representation at tradeshows worldwide, and the high quality, responsive service our customers have come to expect.

EUROPE, MIDDLE EAST, and AFRICA *except Germany, Switzerland, and Austria*

—INQUIRIES—

International Thomson Publishing Europe
Berkshire House
168-173 High Holborn
London WC1V 7AA
United Kingdom
Telephone: 44-71-497-1422
Fax: 44-71-497-1426
E-mail: danni.dolbear@itpuk.co.uk

—ORDERS—

International Thomson Publishing Services, Ltd.
Cheriton House, North Way
Andover, Hampshire SP10 5BE
United Kingdom
Telephone: 44-264-342-832 (UK orders)
Telephone: 44-264-342-806 (outside UK)
Fax: 44-264-364418 (UK orders)
Fax: 44-264-342761 (outside UK)

GERMANY, SWITZERLAND, and AUSTRIA

International Thomson Publishing GmbH
O'Reilly-International Thomson Verlag
Königswinterer Strasse 418
53227 Bonn
Germany
Telephone: 49-228-445171
Fax: 49-228-441342
E-mail (CompuServe): 100272,2422
E-mail (Internet): 100272.2422@compuserve.com

ASIA *except Japan*

—INQUIRIES—

International Thomson Publishing Asia
221 Henderson Road
#05 10 Henderson Building
Singapore 0315
Telephone: 65-272-6496
Fax: 65-272-6498

—ORDERS—

Telephone: 65-268-7867
Fax: 65-268-6727

AUSTRALIA

WoodsLane Pty. Ltd.
Unit 8, 101 Darley Street (P.O. Box 935)
Mona Vale NSW 2103
Australia
Telephone: 61-2-9795944
Fax: 61-2-9973348
E-mail: woods@tmx.mhs.oz.au

NEW ZEALAND

WoodsLane New Zealand Ltd.
7 Purnell Street (P.O. Box 575)
Wanganui, New Zealand
Telephone: 64-6-3476543
Fax: 64-6-3454840
E-mail: woods@tmx.mhs.oz.au

THE AMERICAS, JAPAN, and OCEANIA

O'Reilly & Associates, Inc.
103A Morris Street
Sebastopol, CA 95472 U.S.A.
Telephone: 707-829-0515
Telephone: 800-998-9938 (U.S. & Canada)
Fax: 707-829-0104
E-mail: order@ora.com

How to Order by E-mail

E-mail ordering promises to be quick and easy. Because we don't want you sending credit card information over a non-secure network, we ask that you set up an account with us before ordering by e-mail.

To find out more about setting up an e-mail account, you can either call us at (800) 998-9938 or select `Ordering Information` from the Gopher root menu.

O'Reilly & Associates Inc.

103A Morris Street, Sebastopol, CA 95472

(800) 998-9938 • *(707) 829-0515* • FAX *(707) 829-0104* • order@ora.com

How to get information about O'Reilly books online

- If you have a local gopher client, then you can launch gopher and connect to our server:
`gopher gopher.ora.com`
- If you want to use the Xgopher client, then enter:
`xgopher -xrm "xgopher.rootServer: gopher.ora.com"`
- If you want to use telnet, then enter:
`telnet gopher.ora.com` login: `gopher` [no password]
- If you use a World Wide Web browser, you can access the gopher server by typing the following http address:
`gopher://gopher.ora.com`

WE'D LIKE TO HEAR FROM YOU

Company Name

Name

Address

City/State

Zip/Country

Telephone

FAX

Internet or *Uunet* e-mail address

Which O'Reilly book did this card come from? ____________________

Is your job: ❑ SysAdmin? ❑ Programmer?

❑ Other? What? ____________________

Do you use other computer systems besides UNIX? If so, which one(s)?

____

Please send me the following:

❑ A free catalog of titles

❑ A list of bookstores in my area that carry O'Reilly books

❑ A list of distributors outside of the U.S. and Canada

❑ Information about bundling O'Reilly books with my product

O'Reilly & Associates Inc.

(800) 998-9938 • (707) 829-0515 • FAX (707) 829-0104 • order@ora.com

How to order books by e-mail:

1. Address your e-mail to: `order@ora.com`
2. Include in your message:
   - The title of each book you want to order
     (*an ISBN number is helpful but not necessary*)
   - The quantity of each book
   - Your account number and name
   - Anything special you'd like us to know about your order

____
O'Reilly Online Account Number

Use our online catalog to find out more about our books (see reverse).

NO POSTAGE NECESSARY IF MAILED IN THE UNITED STATES

BUSINESS REPLY MAIL

FIRST CLASS MAIL PERMIT NO. 80 SEBASTOPOL, CA

Postage will be paid by addressee

O'Reilly & Associates, Inc.
103A Morris Street
Sebastopol, CA 95472-9902